THE IRWIN SERIES IN ECONOMICS

CONSULTING EDITOR

LLOYD G. REYNOLDS

YALE UNIVERSITY

BOOKS IN THE IRWIN SERIES IN ECONOMICS

THE PRACTICE OF

COLLECTIVE BARGAINING

THE PRACTICE OF
COLLECTIVE BARGAINING

BY

EDWIN F. BEAL
University of Oregon

AND

EDWARD D. WICKERSHAM
Late of the University of Detroit

THIRD EDITION · 1967
RICHARD D. IRWIN, INC.
HOMEWOOD, ILLINOIS

Third Edition

First Printing, April, 1967

Library of Congress Catalog Card No. 67–14355

PRINTED IN THE UNITED STATES OF AMERICA

To JANET

for E.D.W.

PREFACE

The President of the United States, in his January, 1967 State of the Union message, put forward a proposal to merge the departments of Labor and Commerce under a single Secretary, who would represent both management and labor in the Cabinet. This notion would have been unthinkable a generation ago. Unending—or at least, sporadic—strife between the abstractions called Capital and Labor, over interests conceived to be irreconcilable, was taken for granted even by a public opinion that categorically rejected the ideology of class struggle. Today, while many people were surprised at the President's proposal and many were dubious, few seemed shocked by it, and no one jeered.

If there is indeed any substance to the belief that the interests of managers and workers are basically incompatible, surely putting two government departments under the same administrative roof will not resolve the contradiction; conflict will persist, even as inter-service rivalries (presumably less fundamental) are said to persist in the merged department of Defense. The new proposal has a different rationale. It presumes that managers of enterprises and the unions of their employees have together acquired both the know-how and the will to compose the differences that rise between them and to regulate their mutual relations so that they can be expected to make common cause, and to act jointly on problems facing the nation as a whole, whether in domestic or in international affairs.

This preface is no place to argue the merits of the President's proposal or to speculate on its ultimate fate. The mere fact that he made it testifies to the high degree of public acceptance of collective bargaining, after a generation of experience, as the basis of labor-management relations in America in the 20th century.

Collective bargaining is a growing, changing, dynamic, and intensely important field of activity. In some measure it touches the lives of all, reaches into or affects every community and every station in life. An understanding of its workings has become a necessity not just to direct participants, theoreticians, students, and researchers in the field, but everyone who reads a newspaper or casts a vote.

This is the third edition of a book that has developed with the growth and seasoning of collective bargaining in America. A new arrangement, new material, and extensive updating help the reader keep up with recent changes and perhaps anticipate future trends. The theoretical content of the previous edition has been retained and strengthened. A new chapter extends the field of view to the international scene.

Although much more work needs to be done before the intricacies of collective bargaining can be adequately explained, this book attempts to analyze the practice of collective bargaining in two "model" situations: (1) handicraft industry and craft unionism; (2) mass production industry and industrial unionism. Variants upon these models are noted among professional associations; and in other countries. The viewpoint of this book is set in perspective against developments in the theory of collective bargaining, the ongoing research of behavioral scientists, and the onward march of economic and social progress. The probable effects of recent and anticipated changes in the structure of employment in the United States on collective bargaining are analyzed.

The conclusions set forth in these pages came out of the experience of the authors as teachers, consultants, arbitrators, and representatives in collective bargaining situations in the United States and Europe. Some of this experience dates back as far as the mid-thirties when the CIO was making its first sweep through American industry. Most of the material presented here has been used by the authors in the college classroom and special refresher courses for management and union representatives. Teachers and students who have used this material have been most helpful in suggesting ways of clarifying the issues and improving the presentation of materials.

Some of the explanations and interpretations given by the authors may be found, like other writings in this far-from-settled field, to be controversial. The authors take full responsibility for all such statements of position and for errors or omissions that have eluded them in preparing the material for the press.

The authors are grateful to many people for their constructive criticism and helpful suggestions. Their greatest debt is to Professor Lloyd G. Reynolds of Yale University for reading the first edition manuscript and for his valuable and helpful comments. Professor Dale S. Beach of Rensselaer Polytechnic Institute provided constructive criticism and valuable suggestions that were incorporated in the revised edition. Professor Thomas W. Gavett, West Virginia University, Professor Dalton E. McFarland, Michigan State University, and Professor Thomas H. Patten, Jr., University of Detroit, provided valuable comments that are incorporated in this third edition. Special thanks are due to Mrs. John B. Hanks who gave up a vacation in order to type the manuscript. Both authors are deeply indebted to Wickes Shaw Beal for her endless en-

---

[1] The Bureau of National Affairs, Inc., publisher of *Labor Arbitration Reports*, provided the material used in Cases 6–10 and 138–42. Credit to the arbitrator of these cases is given in the introduction to the cases themselves.

couragement and gentle understanding at critical stages in the preparation of the second and third editions.

Many publishers generously granted permission to reproduce copyrighted material. Special thanks are due to the Bureau of National Affairs, Inc., for the use of cases in Part V[1] of the book. Thanks are also due to: the American Association of University Professors; the American Management Association; the Bureau of National Affairs, Inc.; Commerce Clearing House; the Committee for Economic Development; the Economic Research Department of the Chamber of Commerce of the United States; the Foundation on Employee Health, Medical Care and Welfare, Inc.; *Harvard Business Review;* Division of Research, Graduate School of Business Administration, Harvard University; *Industrial and Labor Relations Review; Industrial Management Review;* Industrial Relations Counselors, Inc.; New York State School of Industrial and Labor Relations at Cornell University; National Industrial Conference Board; Prentice-Hall, Inc.; Public Affairs Press; Professor George Strauss; and John Wiley & Sons, Inc. As in the case of noncopyrighted AFL-CIO and governmental sources, appropriate credit is shown at the places where this material is used.

March, 1967   EDWIN F. BEAL
                                                 EDWARD D. WICKERSHAM

Edward D. Wickersham—A Tribute

Shortly after the manuscript of this third edition went to the publisher, Edward D. Wickersham, co-author, suffered a stroke from which he never recovered. He died on November 24, 1966, at the age of 39. His early death is a great loss to the study and teaching of industrial relations and management in America.

Professor Wickersham's interest in labor relations and collective bargaining began when he was an undergraduate at the University of Illinois, where in 1948 he was graduated with the degree, B.S., Economics, High Honors. He went on to graduate study at Princeton University as a Hicks Fellow in Industrial Relations, and then to Cornell University where he was awarded the Ph.D. degree in 1951 at the age of 24. After two years in the Air Force as an Industrial Manpower Officer, Air Materiel Command, he began teaching at the University of Detroit, where in 1958 he became head of the department of Management. He served as an arbitrator in labor disputes in the Detroit area. He directed research projects on problems of industrial relations, social security, and unemployment, and published monographs on these subjects. Besides co-authoring this book, he wrote many articles, which appeared in the Industrial and Labor Relations Review, Harvard Business Review, Labor Law Journal, *and other scholarly and professional journals, and was a member of several professional and learned societies.*

Besides having a brilliant mind and encyclopedic knowledge, he was a dedicated scholar, a devoted teacher, and above all, a warm and cheerful personality. In all his dealings with others he was honorable, fair, and open; generous to a fault, modest to excess, eager to see good in others, always ready to encourage and to help. He was a gifted administrator and leader of men. He was a true and loyal friend.

In the quarter century of further activity and service that would have been his normal life's expectancy, he would certainly have added great achievements to the career so well begun. This book is an inadequate monument to his unrealized potentialities; these words are an inadequate tribute to his memory. He left no immediate family, but a host of friends who mourn his passing. None feels the loss more keenly than the friend, partner, and co-author whose sad duty it is to write this brief farewell to Ed.

EDWIN F. BEAL

TABLE OF CONTENTS

380 including deductions

PART I. ORGANIZING FOR COLLECTIVE BARGAINING

PART II. COLLECTIVE BARGAINING ACTIVITIES

PART III.   THE ISSUES IN COLLECTIVE BARGAINING

PART V.   CASES IN COLLECTIVE BARGAINING

APPENDIX.   MAJOR STATUTORY LAWS ON COLLECTIVE BARGAINING

INDEXES

PART I

Organizing for Collective Bargaining

Part I of this book explores the nature of the collective bargaining system in the United States and the parties who have a vital interest in the operation of the system. It deals primarily with formal organizations designed to represent the interests of employers, workers, and the general public.

Chapter 1 | THE COLLECTIVE BARGAINING SYSTEM

What is an enterprise?

Collective bargaining centers in the enterprise, where workers and managers meet. From there, it has to look outward and upward, into the International unions and union federations, the employer organizations, the government agencies concerned with labor relations. It also has to look inward and downward to the departments that make up the enterprise, the work groups in the departments, the cliques and factions in the Local union. The point of view remains that of the enterprise, for the enterprise—not the industry, not the state or nation—is the highest autonomous unit of economic activity in capitalist society. The enterprise and the Local union: these are what take up the foreground of the field of view in the study of collective bargaining; and collective bargaining is the only study that takes them both in and concentrates on their relationship.

It is quite true, as later chapters in this book will show, that there is a trend toward carrying the practice of collective bargaining to higher levels, above the individual enterprise. Many of today's labor agreements are reached by unions and associations of employers rather than, in the first instance, between a Local union and its enterprise. That does not take collective bargaining out of the enterprise. The rules laid down in the master agreement reach into the enterprise. They almost always have to leave important questions to be settled specifically and in detail at enterprise level. Local agreements supplement the master agreements and apply their terms to the local situation. Furthermore, administering and enforcing agreement terms is always an enterprise responsibility: management's and the Local union's. One field of enormous present importance deals almost exclusively with enterprise incidents and issues: that is industrial arbitration.

This book makes no apologies for centering the study of collective bargaining in the enterprise, and on the relations between its management and the members and officers of the Local union. It is from this vantage point that the entire system can best be seen in meaningful perspective. But enterprises differ from each other. So do unions; and so, consequently, do the relations between them. No single enterprise is more than a

3

unit—often an inconsiderable one—of the total economy whose markets bind together the whole system of production and exchange of goods and services. In the same way, collective bargaining, which is specific and particular in the enterprise, goes on there as a part and extension of an entire system, the industrial relations system. This is a subsystem of the general social system, and collective bargaining is one of the forms it takes.

The concept of the industrial relations system as a subsystem of the enveloping social system comes from the work of John T. Dunlop, one of the scholars who have attempted to explain collective bargaining in a theoretical setting in the present day.

Dunlop is a prolific writer on economics and on many specific issues of collective bargaining. He brought together some of his ideas on collective bargaining theory, considering the matter as a whole, in a single book, *Industrial Relations Systems,* published in 1958. The introductory first chapter of this book states Dunlop's position in summary form.

It is hard to still further compress ideas already stated in concentrated form, but the main points can be outlined. The writers of this book accept the general framework Dunlop laid down, borrow from it, and acknowledge their debt to him, but do not follow him exactly. What follows is a paraphrase and not a reproduction of Dunlop's thoughts; it rearranges the order of his presentation, but it sticks to the line of argument he laid down and builds upon the base he laid.

THE INDUSTRIAL RELATIONS SYSTEM

Dunlop sees the industrial relations system as a set of relationships between people in society which take place under particular conditions. This can be studied—abstracted—in exactly the way economists study market relations, and political scientists, power relations. The industrial relations system, like the economic system and the political system, is a subsystem of the general social system. All three of these subsystems overlap in part and interact with the others. The industrial relations system, Dunlop says, may be studied in terms of what he calls three contexts. These are the market context, the context of technology at the workplace, and the context of power relations of the enveloping society, as reflected in the workplace.

The Three Contexts

Every enterprise or organization lives and grows (or withers and dies) by satisfying (or failing to satisfy) some human need and effective market demand, whether this be for cigarette lighters or for child welfare services. This is true for the private enterprise, and it is just as true for the governmental agency or nonprofit private organization, where the "market" consists of the budgetary limitations within which the agency must operate. No enterprise can, in the long run, put more into its operation than it gets out of the market. Thus in any given period the market context limits the possibilities open to any given enterprise. The market therefore has a hand in determining the technology of the workplace, which is the second limiting context of the industrial relations system. For example, the mass market for cars at prices buyers are willing to pay practically dictates the technology of mass production and pushes the manufacturers toward automation. Relations between workers and managers in a Detroit factory today take shape in these contexts.

In turn, the technology of the workplace (or work flow, and the kind of jobs created at individual stations along the work flow) determines the kind of people brought into the production process in any given enterprise, and their relations with each other. The sizable remnant of handicraft technology upon which the construction industry still depends brings into that industry the skilled building trades worker who has served a trade apprenticeship and mastered his craft. Mass-production industry, on the other hand, calls mainly for semiskilled workers who get their training on the job. Such jobs consist of simple and usually repetitive tasks, easily learned and leading to no comprehensive mastery of a complex set of skills. In this way both the qualifications of the individual employees and their relations to the work, to those who manage and direct their efforts, and to each other grow out of the technology of the workplace, and work flows.

It may be worthwhile at this point to make clear the concept of workplace technology, as seen by the authors of this book. There are, as they see it, three technologies: handicraft, mass production, and automation.

In *handicraft* production, the goods produced or services rendered and sold by the employer are turned out directly by the labor of skilled craftsmen, working with their hands and with hand tools. These skilled men may have nonskilled helpers, but it is what the skilled men do that transforms the raw materials into the finished product. Thus there may be those who haul bricks and mortar to a construction site, but each brick is placed in the wall, by hand, by a bricklayer who has spent years learning his trade. Neither the contractor nor the construction foreman needs to tell this man *how* to do his job—he knows that; all they need to tell him is *what* they want him to do.

In *mass-production* manufacturing the employer's product is turned out directly by nonskilled operators, working with their hands or with machines, assisted by a few skilled workers. In an automobile assembly plant, for example, the employee working at any station along the line does only a simple, small part of what it takes to put a car together. This employee comes on the job without knowing either what he is to do or how to do it. Management trains him on the job, may even rigidly prescribe the exact bodily motions he has to make to complete his operation cycle. The movement of the conveyor paces the speed at which he works. He is a semiskilled worker. Others more skilled than he may help him, by making the tools and dies, the jigs and fixtures that he uses, or they may set up or repair and maintain his machines; but it is he and his counterparts, the semiskilled, who turn out the product. There is a wide range of semiskills, from almost completely unskilled work to tasks requiring the highest degree of expertise. The difference between expertise and skill in this context is that the expert is a specialist, the skilled worker a generalist in his trade. Later chapters in this book will deal with the question more fully.

Under the technology of *automation,* the product is literally turned out by machines without direct human labor, skilled or nonskilled. Technicians program the work, which the machines perform otherwise unaided. Skilled craftsmen maintain and repair the machines. Semiskilled workers "supervise" the machines; that is, they see that the machines are kept supplied, that nothing occurs that might cause a malfunction, and they turn the machines on and off as necessary or when directed.

These are the three technologies, in their historical order. Mass production displaced handicraft technology in manufacturing wherever there was a mass market. It proved capable of bringing products into common use, like airplanes and refrigerators, that were beyond the practical reach of handicraft technology. It did not exterminate the handicrafts: they flourish today in local and luxury or specialty markets. Automation now seems to be displacing mass production in many areas, but not in all. Automation depends to an even greater degree on mass markets. It cannot completely drive out either mass production or the handicrafts. The three technologies will serve different sectors of the market, different consumer needs.

The three technologies show most clearly in manufacturing, but have their application in the extractive, distributive, and service industries. This will be examined in later chapters. Also, the three general technologies described in principle above take on reality and concrete form in application to various industries, and, within an industry, to an enterprise. Each workplace may be said to have its own technology. This consists of the application of one or more of the three basic technologies, objectified in actual machines and equipment arranged in a specific layout of work stations, designed to carry out the processes of the particular enterprise.

The third of Dunlop's contexts is that of the power relations of the enveloping social system, as reflected in the enterprise. This is probably the hardest to grasp and to explain. It means the influence, authority, prestige, or power managers and workers have outside the shop, that follows them into the shop and affects their relations toward each other. Thus in a country where workers have the right to vote, they stand in a quite different relation to their employer—a fellow citizen—than do workers in a country governed by a feudal or dictatorial regime. The authors of this book consider that collective bargaining is part of the power context in the industrial relations system. When employees organize in an "outside" union, they alter the power context inside the enterprise. The act of organizing is itself a reflection of the power relations of the enveloping social system, which must be such as to tolerate or encourage union organization.

The Contexts Are Dynamic

It should be noted at this point, and never forgotten, that the three contexts are not static elements but dynamic forces. They change; they interact. A context stands as given only for a single period, or point of time, in a particular analysis, not for eternity.

In a given market context, for instance, changes in technology can generate forces that change the market which, in turn, encourages the spread of that technology. Thus at the time of the Industrial Revolution, a growing, but still only potential, mass market welcomed the developing technology of mass production, initially of textiles but subsequently of other factory-made goods. The availability of cheap, high-quality factory products in turn strengthened the market and swept competing handicraft products off the counter.

The United States provides another example drawn from the early years of this century. An existing demand for means of local transportation was met through the local manufacture, by handicraft methods, of horse-drawn buggies and wagons. The earliest automobiles were also custom built by handicraft methods and sold in a luxury market—rich people to whom the mechanical buggies were a new toy and a visible symbol of their wealth. Then Henry Ford adapted the technology of mass production to the new product and began the serialized manufacture of a cheap and practical car, the famous Model T. The Model T welded the scattered local markets of the carriage makers into a national mass market for gas-powered vehicles. Anyone wanting now to serve this market had to compete with Henry Ford and had to adopt mass-production technology.

It ought not to be necessary to multiply examples to underscore the interdependence and interaction of the contexts.

These three contexts make up one of the theoretical concepts Dunlop offers. Another constitutes his identification of what he calls the actors. Who are the actors?

The Actors

Dunlop uses the word "actors" to refer to the participants or parties to industrial relations activity. There seems to be no good reason not to follow his terminology. There are three actors: (1) managers and their hierarchy both within the enterprise and in employer associations at levels above the enterprise; (2) workers and their hierarchy of organized representatives within the enterprise and above it; and (3) agents of government who play specific roles in the industrial relations system, plus nongovernmental agents and agencies (such as, for example, arbitrators) called into being by the other actors.

The actors, as identified by Dunlop, are groups of individuals or organizations. It would be well at the outset to consider what brings individuals into the following groupings: (1) the worker and the enterprise, (2) the worker and the Local union, and (3) the Local union with other union organizations. In a free society, each of these relationships must be based on a degree of mutual consent—a mutually beneficial exchange.

The potential work force of a modern enterprise consists of individuals who are free to contract for their own labor. Of their own free will they may decline a particular offer of employment; but they are driven by individual needs to accept *some* offer, for without a job most people cannot live except on charity. The needs of the individual and the needs of the enterprise are reciprocal. Every individual needs to find a job, and to hold a job or jobs, and to earn a decent living at acceptable levels of effort. The reciprocal needs of the enterprise are to find suitable employees, to hold an appropriate work force, and to get competitive productivity from that work force. The relationship of the worker to the enterprise is explored in greater detail in Chapter 2.

A worker joins and remains a member of a union either because he considers it to be to his advantage or because he believes that the disadvantages of nonmembership outweigh the disadvantages of membership. He may want to belong to a union because he believes that this membership will raise his wages, or give him status, or provide an opportunity for pleasant social contacts, or he may accept union membership only because he feels that this is less onerous than losing his job or enduring social ostracism from his fellow workers.

Union affiliation usually goes beyond simple membership in an autonomous Local union. Union associations beyond the individual and autonomous enterprises or the Local unions are, in part, a rational recognition of market and political forces beyond the enterprise which if not met in a unified way may seriously impede the effectiveness of the autonomous units. Thus it is reasonable to expect that individual and autonomous unions of Chrysler, Ford, and General Motors workers would have certain market interests in common and would form a supralocal union to deal with these problems. On the political scene, a Federation of 15 million members would be a more influential spokesman than 75,000 autonomous but unconnected Locals representing the same membership.

Managers. Managers are the most important actors because they establish the enterprise, set its goals, exercise initiative in choosing the technology to be employed, and ultimately are accountable for the success or failure of the enterprise. Managers create and control the institution which provides employment opportunities. Chapter 2 discusses the problems confronting managers in creating an organization for effective employee relations. The discussion in Chapter 2 will deal with such matters as the relationship between the output of an enterprise, its size, geographic location, and ownership, and the nature of its organizational structure for effective employee relations.

Employee Organizations. This book argues that there are three "model" types of employee representatives: craft unions, industrial unions, and professional associations. Since repeated references to these models will be made throughout the book, it is well to introduce them now. Chapter 3 is devoted to a comparison of the models and to a more conventional discussion of union organizational structure.

The Craft-union Model. Handicraft technology is the technological context in which craft unions appear. The building construction industry is the most prominent example of handicraft technology in modern American industry. Handicraft industry consists of enterprises in which the employer sells a product or service which is turned out directly by the hands of craftsmen. These craftsmen are workers who have served an apprenticeship or have learned by long experience an entire recognized trade, such as plumbing, carpentry, sheet metal work, or electricity.

Skilled labor here is a *direct* factor of production. Without the skilled labor of trained tradesmen, working with hand or power tools, the employer would have no product or service to sell. If he could not find skilled workers, he could not run his business, for it takes time to train skilled workers; often it takes years. If he lost his skilled workers, production would stop, for there is no substitute for their skill.

The construction industry depends upon and uses to this day the handicraft method of production. Its product market is local. Construction work is carried out on the spot by skilled workers, who bring their efforts to bear on the building as it grows in place. Nonskilled workers may haul bricks to a construction site, but the brick is laid in the wall by qualified bricklayers who have served trade apprenticeships and are skilled tradesmen.

Job content in any given area of skill is the same; one carpenter performs the same kind of work as another carpenter; one roofer does the same job as another. Every skilled worker must at various times perform each of a range of tasks associated with the trade. In any given craft the worker qualifications are the same. Each worker must command a certain range of knowledge and of manual skills, common and traditional to the craft. The consequence is that in the handicrafts, for any given craft, labor is homogeneous. It is not entirely surprising, then, to find workers organized according to their particular skills into separate craft unions.

"One craft, one union" might well be the slogan of craft unions. The Local craft union takes in all the craftsmen of its trade in any particular locality, and no others. (This may include, however, helpers and apprentices.) When these skilled men go on the job the employer does not have to tell them or show them *how* to do the work. They know how. He only needs to tell them *what* they are to do. They take it from there.

While it may not be surprising to find craft unions organized along lines of skill, it is still necessary to explain why they do actually so organize. A general contractor employs not only carpenters but masons, bricklayers, plumbers, plasterers—an entire array of skills. Why should not all of these be organized in a single union to bargain for them all with their common employer? Again the context of technology supplies the answer.

Erecting a building calls for the use of skills *in sequence*. At one time the only work performed at a building site is clearing the land and excavation. This is work for pick and shovel men, who are unskilled laborers, or for the semiskilled cat and bulldozer operators who have replaced them. Next, there is the rough carpentry work in the construction of forms for pouring concrete foundations; and work for masons, eventually for bricklayers, perhaps for ironworkers, certainly for carpenters. The plasterers, the painters, the sheet metal workers, the roofers, and many other crafts do not come on the job until later. By the time the electrician has wired the building, for instance, there is usually no further need for masonry workers.

Thus the personnel, the skills involved, and the actual crews employed are seldom the same from one week to the next. There is much overlap; but any given construction project, if surveyed at different points in time, will show a different composition of the work force.

The labor market reflects this technological need of the construction industry. For efficient operation it is necessary to have pools of all the various skills, from which any given construction project may draw at just the time such skills are needed on the job. It is also necessary that those employed when their skills are needed should be released when the need is over, so that they may go on to another project at a different stage of development. The employer needs to have the skills held separate, and administered separately, so that he may get the men he wants when he needs them and let them go when he is through with them. No contractor could afford to keep a crew of painters on his payroll from the time he broke ground just to paint the finished structure, nor to retain the operators of the ground-moving equipment after the foundations had been laid.

The result of these necessary conditions, established by the context of product market and the context of technology, is to bring into being as an actor, opposite the enterpriser, an entire galaxy of local unions organized by skills: craft unions. The fact of unionization introduces a new element in the context of power relations which influence the workplace rules and give rise to craft union practices.

At heart, craft unions are conservative. They guard and hoard an ancient skill and tradition that goes back to the medieval guilds. Though not direct descendants of the guilds, craft unions are their counterparts in today's changed situation and perform for our society the handicraft services the guilds performed for theirs. They are fraternities, entered by initiation and apprenticeship, practicing—as the guilds did—a "mystery," the secrets of the trade.

They make their bargains over wages by a strategy of bidding a restricted supply against what they conceive to be a fixed or relatively fixed demand. The essentially economic nature of their activity gives them a "lump of work" mentality that is hard to alter.

Scarcity of work, scarcity of skills, scarcity of product (always, of course, in relative terms) are the concepts in which craft unions deal in a scarcity sector—the handicraft sector—of the economy. They more often resist than welcome innovation, they more often resist than gladly adopt devices (such as skill-saving machinery) that would change the ways and habits of the craft.

A society moving restlessly and relentlessly forward into the abundance and the potentially limitless production made possible by factory methods puts craft unions on the defensive. The defensive position is a strong one wherever handicraft methods still prevail. Well-entrenched craft unions have even held their own in places where technology has conquered some of the problems of their craft. Craft unions and craft-union bargaining will be with us for a long time.

The Industrial Union Model. Mass-production technology carries even further the *division of labor* by the breakdown of a set of what were formerly skilled operations into a series of simple tasks. No individual is the craftsman of the product turned out by a factory. Instead, the entire factory becomes a composite, or collective, craftsman. Its few skilled workers do not turn out the production; all they do is help the other workers, by preparing work for them, repairing, or setting up their machines. The bulk of the employees are nonskilled. They have come to be called *semiskilled* workers.

Unlike the craftsman, the semiskilled operator has not spent years of apprenticeship or mastered a recognized trade. He learns on the job, while working. He comes to the job without any knowledge of its tasks. The training he gets does not take long. The jobs are easily learned, and each of the workers specializes in a very minor part of the total process. This specialization may in some cases reach the point of a very high degree of *expertise.* It differs from the skill of a craftsman in that it is specialized rather than general, and often not applicable to anything but the particular processes of the workplace where it is exercised.

At this point it would be desirable to draw the distinction carefully between skill and expertise. In common parlance, the word "skill" is very loosely used. For the purposes of this exposition, it needs a tighter definition. What is meant here by _skill_ is the range of knowledge, ability, manual dexterity, and performance capability that is mastered through an apprenticeship in one of the recognized trades.[1]

What is meant by _expertise_ is expertness, deftness, ability, or knowledge of some specialized task or group of tasks, such as can be acquired only through experience at that task, or on the job which groups those tasks. Perhaps an illustration of each of these terms will make them clearer.

Driving an automobile is often loosely called a skill. A person starts out very timidly and clumsily, learns by instruction and experience, and gradually gets better at driving the more hours he spends behind the wheel. Under the definition used in this chapter, that would be expertise. This expertise may become further specialized. The driver of a heavy truck gets to be expert at rolling his big rig uphill and down, swinging it around right-angle corners, and backing it into crowded warehouse docks. The background knowledge of driving and the sensorimotor responses do not much differ from those required for driving a passenger car, but they have become more specialized. The passenger car driver could not take the wheel of the truck, but the truck driver can handle either vehicle.

Even the truck driver does not have skill; what he has is expertise. The skilled work connected with the use of automobiles is that of the auto mechanic. The auto mechanic may be a less competent driver than the owner of the vehicle, but in the shop, if the car breaks down, the auto mechanic can diagnose the trouble and repair the truck. Diagnosing the trouble and repairing the truck are not mere expertise; they are the practice of a skill.

In mass production many jobs are said to call for skill when what they require is a high degree of expertise. Only confusion would result from failure to distinguish between skill and expertise.

Job content, under mass-production technology, consists of a variety of semiskills, up to the highest degree of expertise. Worker qualifications to meet this job content are, initially, simple aptitudes. With training and experience, aptitude turns into ability to perform one particular task or a small group of related semiskills—into expertise.

While there is labor turnover in the factory, and movement in and

---

[1] Some readers may appropriately comment that the authors are putting too great emphasis on a formal apprenticeship and that many journeymen members of craft union locals have not served a formal apprenticeship. Such a criticism is sound and based on solid facts. The authors would respond to this criticism only by arguing that the existence of a formal apprenticeship program does establish the content of a trade and that the apprenticeship program is recognized as the best method of receiving the training necessary to master the trade. Those journeymen who have acquired membership in the union without serving the apprenticeship typically have very long experience working in most if not all of the specialized segments of the trade.

out of the work force, the factory is a stable organization. That is, it replaces individuals from time to time, but there is not much displacement of jobs. The shoe factory must always and simultaneously have people who cut out soles, who stitch uppers, who sew or glue liners, who pack the finished pairs. The automobile assembly plant needs men at every station along the line, all the time, each doing different tasks which are coordinated by the production plans and layout to build the car. The result of this is that the appropriate organization for employees cannot be based on any given skill, for these are not skilled jobs. Organization has to be based on the entire co-ordinated process in the workplace; workplace unionism or industrial unionism.

The slogan of the industrial union might well be "one shop, one union." In the industrial union all the employees working for a given enterprise at a given workplace belong to the same Local union without regard for what they do in the plant. The industrial union Local takes in not only the semiskilled who directly turn out the product but such skilled workers also as may play an auxiliary part in the production process. It takes in, too, the completely unskilled, such as janitors or a yard gang—if there be any in the plant.

In his workplace the factory employee must accept direction, supervision, discipline, that inevitably looks upon him as a "replaceable part." He is a unit in an integrated whole, highly differentiated in its parts, subdivided into specialties and groups of specialties, variable in magnitude up to the factory employing tens of thousands. It is necessary for him, as a worker in this vast complex, to be at his machine or station at the minute when all the others are at theirs, to work while they work, at a set pace, and to quit when they quit work for the day. He moves in crowds as he enters and leaves the gate, and at the noon-hour break.

He never sees the shareholders who own the factory; he rarely sees the man who runs it. Management, to him, is a foreman who is a hired hand like himself, and has a boss who has a boss in an upward chain of command reaching to a shining but far-distant pinnacle. The three simple upward steps in status from apprentice to journeyman to master that stand clear before the craftsman have given way to a dizzy stairway of many steps that leads up out of sight. There is no longer any personal warmth or friendly contact between master and man. Orders come down from on high, to be obeyed; no visible means exists for sending comment and questions back up the line.

The worker who makes his living in a factory has lost the status that skill gives the craftsman. He has lost independence and become dependent. He never learned the craftsman's satisfaction in work as a creative act. What has he gained?

He has gained money wages that outdistance what he could earn elsewhere as an unskilled laborer. He has begun to earn without serving an apprenticeship, and his real wage is such that he has enough to live on. As he gains practice in his specialty he may, under an incentive system, take home pay that compares favorably with the craftsman's earnings.

His union does not fight the technology of the factory, does not object to new machines, new processes. Instead, it seeks to master them. Above all, it strives to secure for its own members, through seniority rights and the right to retraining, the new opportunities technology creates.

Internally, it practices democracy and suffers from ills that beset democratic institutions with a heterogeneous citizenry: the pulling and hauling of special interest groups; the seesaw of ins and outs, and controversy over policy and tactics; membership indifference and inaction when there are no pressing issues in the air. Today, the threat of mass displacement as a result of technological change puts the industrial union under a strain. Fewer and fewer of the overriding issues can be settled in the shop: only a rear-guard action can be fought there against mass displacement. The interests of threatened members can be furthered only by such broad social action as government can take. At the same time, concrete adjustment to the new technology has to be made where it appears: on the shop floor.

Industrial union leadership, with a generation of experience behind it now, is wary, and conscious of the dangers facing it. It is ready to co-operate, but ready still, if necessary, to fight.

Professional Associations. Professional associations fall into two broad categories: (1) associations of the self-employed, e.g., physicians, lawyers, and dentists and (2) associations of professional people who are the employees of enterprises, e.g., teachers, engineers, certified public accountants, and professors. Although the economic and political actions of professional associations of the self-employed are interesting and instructive because of their high effectiveness, the major attention of this book will be focused on the activities of the employed professional. It might be noted in passing, however, that there seems to be an international trend for more members of the medical and legal profession to become employees with the passage of time. If accelerated, this trend would probably cause major policy changes in such venerated professional associations of the self-employed as the American Medical Association and the American Bar Association.

The professions are entered by something that compares with an apprenticeship. It is a long, hard, and expensive one. The number of people willing to make the sacrifice of time and money to become physicians, for example, is somewhat limited, and in times of great national emergency, as in wartime, the government has had to encourage and subsidize people in order to get them to go through this apprenticeship. Occasionally, as in times of depression, there is something approaching an oversupply of such professionals, and at such times reproaches have been voiced that tend to indicate a desire on the part of the practicing professionals to restrict entrance to their professions. Such charges are probably somewhat exaggerated.

Professional associations pay consistent attention to maintaining high standards of qualifications for admission to the profession. The bar exams, the medical internship, the CPA exam, and teacher certification requirements are actual barriers which many fail to pass. Opportunity to practice a profession is restricted to those who pass the qualifications set by licensing boards of various sorts.

The strategies of these two kinds of professional associations will be discussed in Chapter 3.

Government. The third actor in the collective bargaining system is the government. The role of government in American collective bargaining is largely permissive. Nevertheless, the state is the ultimate source of power and order in any economic system. In other countries, the state plays a more important role in setting the conditions of employment than is true in the United States. In some countries the state itself carries out activities which are performed by unions in the United States. The rules for rule making which the United States government establishes are of vital interest to the general public and to the two main actors in the collective bargaining system.

Employer and union organizations designed to influence the formulation of rules for rule making are discussed in Chapters 2 and 3. Chapter 4 is devoted to a discussion of the public interest in collective bargaining and the current status of the rules for rule making in the United States. Other important legislative and judicial matters are dealt with elsewhere in the book.

The result of the interaction of the actors, according to Dunlop, is the establishment in a given industrial relations system of rules, and rules for rule making. The word "rules," in the sense intended here, must be given a very broad interpretation. The rules cover a wide range of regulatory arrangements, from a national labor relations law (a rule for rule making) down to something as detailed and specific as, for example, an agreed vacation schedule in a labor-management agreement. As used in this book "rules for rule making" mean laws, and all lesser manifestations of regulatory power are referred to as "rules."

The Rules

The authors of this book believe that the study of collective bargaining should begin with a study of the rules. It does not end with the rules, but it must rest upon them in the same way that a study of government does not end with laws and constitutions but lacks meaning without reference to them.

The Rules under Nonunion Conditions. Every free employment relationship centers on the wage and effort bargain. It is an exchange of the worker's ability and time for compensation provided by the employer.

This exchange requires a consideration of: (1) pay for time worked, (2) the effort bargain (production standards), (3) premium pay, (4) pay for time not worked, e.g., paid holidays, vacations, and (5) contingent benefits, e.g., Blue Cross and Blue Shield, and pensions. Nonunion employers, regardless of size or industry attachment, must consider these five elements in establishing the conditions of employment. Nonunion workers weigh the value of various employers' "packages" against other employment opportunities or the value of leisure. The wage and effort bargain also provides the base for all collective bargaining agreements.

The larger the scale of an enterprise, the more complex its employee relations problems. Perhaps out of fear of unionization, some medium- and large-scale enterprises have established what will be called individual security measures under collective bargaining. Individual security measures must meet: (1) the individual worker's relative claim to available work and (2) the worker's claim to fair treatment on the job, or the establishment of a system of due process. A relative claim to available work raises such questions as: who gets laid off? who gets recalled from layoff when work becomes available? who gets promoted? and who gets overtime work and overtime pay when it is available? Due process deals with such questions as the fairness of disciplinary rules and the right of an employee to his day in court on disciplinary actions.[2]

Under nonunion conditions, the employer unilaterally establishes the rules on the wage and effort bargain and, perhaps, individual security measures. If he can find workers who will accept these unilaterally established rules, he operates his enterprise without interference, except the veto power always available to a free worker of quitting his employment, or the ability of his employees to force him to change the conditions of employment by restriction of output.

The Rules under Collective Bargaining. Typically the rules under collective bargaining are explicit and written, while under nonunion conditions the rules may be largely implicit. Once a union has won recognition, when the rules must be established bilaterally by negotiation, the substance of the specific rules changes and the coverage of the rules is significantly broadened. The written *labor-management agreement* is the basic rule under a collective bargaining relationship.

The labor agreement performs four functions. It establishes rules for: (1) union security and management rights, (2) the wage and effort

---

[2] The existence of individual security measures in such diverse organizations as the Roman Catholic clergy, the military establishment, and the civil service must be noted as evidence that the need for a system of individual security is more basic than an employer fear of unionization. On the other hand, individual security measures which are unilaterally established and not subject to an impartial outside interpretation can hardly be considered to have the potency of identical measures which have been negotiated by collective bargaining. *Cf.* William G. Scott, *The Management of Conflict: Appeal Systems in Organizations* (Homewood, Ill.: Richard D. Irwin, Inc., and Dorsey Press, 1965).

bargain, (3) individual security, and (4) administration. The two functions of union security and management rights, and administration, are unique to collective bargaining. Union security and management rights may be summarized as four questions to be answered in the agreement: (1) Who speaks for whom? (2) With what authority? (3) For how long? and (4) Except in what conditions? Administration deals with

FIGURE 1–1

THE RULES UNDER COLLECTIVE BARGAINING

Rule	Scope
Union Security and Management Rights	Who speaks for whom? With what authority? For how long? Except in what conditions?
The Wage and Effort Bargain	Pay for time worked The effort bargain (Production standards) Premium pay Pay for time not worked Contingent benefits
Individual Security	Relative claim to available work Absolute claim to fair treatment
Administration	On-the-job representation Arbitration

This presentation is taken from an article by Edwin F. Beal which appeared in the September/October, 1962, issue of *Personnel,* journal of the American Management Association, by permission of the copyright owner. This presentation is expanded upon in Chapter 7 and Figure 7–1.

problems of making the written agreement an operational document in day-to-day activities. It provides a system of on-the-job representation for workers and establishes the procedures by which persons not employed by the enterprise will act if they are called in as neutrals to interpret the collective bargaining agreement. Chapter 8 discusses problems in agreement administration in some detail. The authors of this book would argue that individual security is also unique to the collective bargaining agreement on the assumption that no unilateral system of individual security would be genuinely binding on the employer who created it.

Figure 1–1 provides a preliminary summary of the rules under collective bargaining. Chapter 7 provides a more comprehensive tool for the analysis of labor agreements and contrasts the practices of craft unions, industrial unions, and professional associations in establishing the basic rules of employment. Chapters 9–12 treat the rules in America in some detail. International comparisons and contrasts on the nature of the rules are considered in Chapter 14.

Levels of Application of the Rules. The object of the rules in the long run is to regulate relations at work, in the workplace during the working day, between the two main actors, managers and workers. Every workplace evolves or adopts a body of substantive rules. When the workers are organized in a union, these rules result from collective bargaining; but even without bargaining and without a union, there are always rules, no matter how one-sided. These substantive rules emerge out of procedures, or policies, or customs, or laws that may be called the rules for rule making.

This book distinguishes three levels at which rules and rules for rule making appear. They are the national level, the enterprise level, and various points between, which may be lumped together as an intermediate "level."

National Level. Governmental action through laws, decrees, administrative and judicial decisions normally provides rules for rule making. During a national emergency, as in wartime, the government may intervene directly in the affairs of individual enterprises; but ordinarily it acts in a general and not a specific way. The rules for rule making that are laid down by government cut across industry lines and regional and state boundaries. They affect the entire industrial relations system. Of this nature, for instance, is labor relations law, such as the Taft-Hartley Act.

Enterprise Level. Here is where the substantive rules are made by the actors under rules for rule making that come down from higher levels or that are elaborated on the spot—"ground rules"—by these same direct actors. The substantive rules cover, at a minimum, the wage and effort bargain (money for work) that is the root of the employment relationship. Under collective bargaining conditions they almost always deal with other issues in addition. This book will have a great deal more to say about the substantive rules.

Intermediate Level. Above the level of the enterprise but below the national level, interaction between the actors on industrial relations problems takes many forms designated here as "intermediate." Perhaps the commonest intermediate form in the craft unions is bargaining at regional level and in the industrial unions, at the industry level. A greater proportion of the activity is private and voluntary (rather than government sponsored) at intermediate levels.

Collective bargaining characteristically starts at enterprise level, but the trend seems to be toward progression and expansion, by agreement of the actors, to regional or industry level. A common example of regional bargaining is the building trades union's agreement with an employer association for an entire metropolitan area, or a county, or a whole state. A striking example of the industry trend comes from the steel mills whose managers negotiate an industry agreement with the steelworkers' union.

SUMMARY

This book takes for the center of its field of view the practice of collective bargaining in the enterprise. It looks outward from time to time to the macroeconomic scene, backward into history, forward to the march of technological and social progress, and inward to the psychological and social aspects of the work group in the enterprise and the local union. Chiefly it concerns itself, however, with the enterprise as a whole in its dealings with the union that speaks for the employees there. None of the established disciplines of the social or behavioral sciences has taken, or can take, quite this point of view.

The approach to the practice of collective bargaining will be descriptive, analytical, and theoretical. The main theoretical concept is of collective bargaining as an aspect of the industrial relations system, a subsystem of the social system, linked with and overlapping the economic and political subsystems of the same social system.

The industrial relations system, both at enterprise level and above the level of the enterprise, takes shape in three *contexts*. They are the market context, or budgetary limitations; the technology context, as applied in the workplace; the power relations context of the enveloping social system, as reflected in the workplace.

Within these contexts, the industrial relations system evolves by interaction of the *actors*. They are managers and their hierarchy inside and above the enterprise; workers and their hierarchy of representatives; agents of government, or private agents activated by the other two actors.

The result of the interaction of the actors in the industrial relations sysem is a body of *rules*. They include rules for rule making, and substantive rules.

These rules take force at various *levels*. These may be classified as: national level, enterprise level, intermediate levels.

QUESTIONS FOR DISCUSSION

1. American law does not require nonprofit hospitals to engage in collective bargaining. Why might a hospital administrator find it worthwhile to study collective bargaining?
2. Show how Dunlop's concept of the *Industrial Relations System* requires an interdisciplinary approach to the study of collective bargaining.
3. An hourly wage certainly is an important "rule." Show how this rule might be applied at the national level, the enterprise level, and the intermediate level.
4. How does the prevailing technology of a society influence power relations in that society?
5. Can individual security, as discussed in this chapter, exist without unionism? Besides unionism, what institutions might provide individual security?

Chapter 2 | ENTERPRISE ORGANIZATION FOR EMPLOYEE RELATIONS

This chapter aims to set forth the alternatives available to employers in establishing enterprise organizations for the purpose of achieving effective employee relations. It also seeks to describe some of the major characteristics of the structure of American enterprises. Much of what is said in this chapter will apply equally to unionized and nonunionized enterprises. The next chapter, dealing with worker organizations, emphasizes how the union influences enterprise organization for employee relations.

CHANGING EMPLOYER-EMPLOYEE RELATIONS

The "employer" of antiquity (and the not too distant past) held his "employees" in a bond relation as slaves. Slaves were the personal property of the slaveowner. If he was wise and self-controlled he treated them well and got good work from them by the standards of those days, but he did not have to take their wishes into account and could compel them by force to do his will.

Today's employer cannot compel his workers by any kind of force. He cannot fine them. The most severe disciplinary penalty that he can impose is to dismiss them—terminate the employment contract—so that they cease to be employees. His way of drawing workers to him, keeping them in his service, and motivating them to be productive is to make them want to do the work. Older systems bound one party to the relation and benefited the other. The free labor system binds both parties but binds them only to their mutual benefit. The contract that so binds them lasts only as long as both receive benefit from it. It rests upon consent, and it confers reciprocal advantage.

THE GENERAL OBJECTIVES OF AN ENTERPRISE

Just as a man needs objectives for his life to be meaningful, every enterprise and every human organization needs objectives in order to behave rationally. Management scholars and executives agree that objectives are the starting point of management philosophy and the practice of management.

What should the objectives of an enterprise be? That is, the objectives of the organization as distinct from the aims of those who may happen to own it. Their objectives may stop at profit; but the organization does not make profits in the abstract. It must first produce some good or service that gives satisfaction to the members of the enterprise directly, or to others. This sets its *operating* objectives. The operating objectives of most enterprises are so obvious that they are frequently taken for granted. A few dogmatic statements may serve as a reminder of the importance of operating objectives in several types of enterprise:

> The operating objective of an army *must be* to win a battle or a war.
> The operating objective of a school *must be* to provide educational opportunities.
> The operating objective of a shoe store *must be* to sell shoes.
> The operating objective of a coal mine *must be* to mine coal and to sell it.
> The operating objective of an automobile manufacturer *must be* to make and sell cars.

The operating objective of an enterprise is a very important determinant of the behavior of the enterprise. It takes different kinds of human and material resources to run a school, sell shoes, or mine coal, and the resources that are needed are deployed in different ways to achieve these different objectives. Operating objectives of the sort discussed here transcend such various considerations as the ownership of an enterprise, the personal aspirations of its members, or the very important profit motive.

The profit objective certainly is important in most business enterprises, yet even in the most aggressive business the quest for profit is frequently moderated by self-restraint and a feeling of responsibility to customers, employees, and other individuals or groups associated with the enterprise.

One might suppose that owner-managers would encounter little difficulty in setting objectives for their enterprises, where it would appear impossible for any conflict to develop between personal and enterprise objectives. In practice, however, the operating objectives of owner-managed enterprises are not always subject to control and are frequently set by persons other than the owner alone. This situation creates the possibility of conflict between personal objectives and enterprise objectives.

Possible conflicts of this sort, between ownership and operations, are more strikingly illustrated, however, in the corporate form of business organization. A particular stockholder and true part-owner of a corporation may be solely interested in maximum profit while the officers might run the corporation with the objective of growth or even for their personal gain. It must be emphasized that conflicts between personal objectives and enterprise objectives are not limited to corporate business enterprise; many readers of this book will be able to think of situations where a given college professor's personal objective of supplemental income or professional status conflicted with his college's objective of providing educational service.

The objectives of the enterprise, including the profit motive, are influenced by personal objectives of the members of the enterprise as well as by many external circumstances. The general enterprise objectives which emerge set the framework for the personnel management objectives. These are derivative of the enterprise operating objectives.

PERSONNEL MANAGEMENT OBJECTIVES OF THE ENTERPRISE

The personnel management objectives of any enterprise can be simply stated as: (1) to find suitable employees, (2) to maintain an adequate work force, and (3) to get competitive productivity from that work force. The achievement of these objectives is far from simple and the methods used for their achievement are diverse.

What are *suitable employees* and how can they be found? The answer to this question is provided in part by how management designs jobs. In mass-production industry, management has designed jobs in such a way that the bulk of suitable potential employees need little special prior experience or training, but even in mass-production industry there is a need for some employees possessing substantial experience or training, and these are sometimes in very short supply. In this situation the employer has to search for people possessing the needed skills or take the sometimes more difficult and costly route of training present employees to the skill level needed.

What is an *appropriate work force* and how can it be held? An appropriate work force is the number and kind of employees that management needs at the time that management needs them. Just as management needs enough workers, it also needs to be able to get rid of unneeded workers. Holding an appropriate work force boils down to making employment at a particular enterprise attractive to the kind of employees needed and insuring sufficient management flexibility to escape having unneeded or redundant employees.

The measure of *competitive productivity* is unit labor costs. Low wages give an enterprise a competitive edge only when those low wages are accompanied by output that equals that of higher wage competitors. In the same vein, high wages may mean a competitive advantage over a lower wage competitor if the high-wage firm achieves higher man-hour productivity.

In order to achieve objectives, the work to be done must be assigned to individuals who will perform it. This division of work, with the concomitant delegation of authority and assignment of responsibility, is the task of formal organization.

THE ORGANIZATION OF AN ENTERPRISE

Organization cannot take place without a system of authority. The dictionary defines authority as "legal or rightful power"—which rather unhelpfully turns the question, what is authority? into the question, what is power? The literature of management, and of the social sciences as well, abounds with controversy over the nature and source of power, the meaning of authority. It is tempting—but would be distracting—to join the fray and try to define once and for all these abstract words which stand for a very real and dynamic thing: the thing that seems to make the enterprise go. The authors of this book prefer to sidestep the full philo-sophic implications of the question and instead to say that authority is "something." It is the something that many management writers say flows downward in an enterprise (whether or not the downward flow starts with the owners or with top management); it is a right to make decisions affecting others, to commit resources, to require compliance. It is some-thing that other writers say becomes effective only by acceptance up-ward, from employees at the bottom and at each successively higher level.

To avoid future confusion, the word "authority" in this book may always be understood as something that flows downward through an organization; but the reader must remember that there must always be a corresponding upward flow of acceptance. This upward flow will be noted only when it ceases—that is, when nonacceptance of authority (as, for instance, in a work stoppage or strike) stops the downward flow. Otherwise, the downward flow prevails.

Because authority flows downward, it is more concentrated at the top, and diminishes at successively lower levels as it branches out and divides, by delegation from above. Thus, the higher a person stands in an organization, the greater his authority. The President of the United States possesses greater authority than any other member of the United States federal service. A plant superintendent possesses greater authority than any production worker or foreman in his plant.

For purposes of discussion here, there are four important points to keep in mind about formal authority in the enterprise: (1) organizational authority flows from the top of the hierarchy down, (2) the flow of organizational authority is limited by the willingness of subordinates to accept it, (3) organizational authority is confirmed by employee accept-ance in a free employment relationship, and (4) organizational authority exists even in nonprofit seeking enterprises such as the government, a school, a church, or a union. An individual in the enterprise is a manager if he possesses organizational authority over subordinates. He is not a man-ager if he does not possess organizational authority over subordinates.

One of the major tasks of the man at the top of any organization is designing the formal organization structure. Formal organization structure increases in complexity with the number of employees in the enterprise. The two major components of a complex organizational structure are: the line organization and staff organizations.

The Line Organization

The first step in the development of a complex organization comes when the volume of business done by the enterprise reaches a magnitude that calls for departmentalization. That is, the work increases beyond the power to perform of a single group of workers bossed by a single person. The additional workers hired make up one or more additional gangs or departments.

The principle that the top executive follows in dividing up his labor force by departments depends upon the nature of his operations, but the effect of this division on his relation toward his workers is always the same. One enterprise may simply seek to keep the gangs small enough to be manageable or to divide forces to disperse in space, even though all perform essentially the same work, as a company of infantrymen breaks down into platoons and platoons into squads. Another may form its groups around specialized functions so that each department handles a different process. In either case, creating the new department puts the workers in it under a gang boss or foreman and moves the top man a step away from his employees, with the foreman in between. The foreman now exercises management authority over his work group. He gives the men their orders and assignments and makes, or interprets and applies, enterprise rules or policy that affects them.

Management now consists of two levels, the top executive and his foremen. Ultimate authority still rests in the top manager's hands. His is the last word—and usually the first as well—in general policy decisions, but he delegates to his foremen supervisory authority over the workers, and may also delegate certain policy-making authority. The top manager determines, for instance, what products to manufacture, and in what quantity, for as chief executive he must also be concerned with selling whatever is made. The foreman's job is to see to it that his work group or department turns out its allotted share of production or its expected quota of sales.

Now this is the simplest line organization, a top manager and his foremen. In larger enterprises, the management structure remains a line organization as long as each foreman or subordinate manager has full authority and responsibility for all the activities in his department or group of departments. The line organization is the essential means of getting the work of the enterprise done. It has proved capable of setting large masses of men into motion, directing and controlling them, bringing their combined efforts to bear upon attainment of a common objective determined by or known to the top man or men in the organization. Figure 2–1 illustrates the operation of a pure line organization in a business organization.

FIGURE 2–1
STRAIGHT LINE ORGANIZATIONS

A. Single Plant
  1. President reserves to himself finance and product decisions.
  2. Sales effort organized geographically. Sales personnel decisions delegated to vice-president–sales and district sales managers.
  3. Production organized by process. Production personnel decisions delegated to vice-president–production and department foremen.

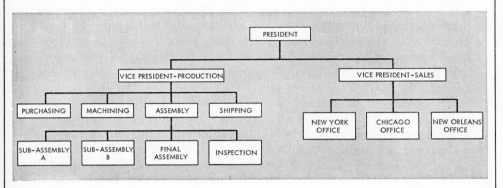

B. Multiplant
  1. President reserves to himself finance and product decisions.
  2. Sales effort organized geographically. Sales personnel decisions delegated to vice-president–sales and district sales managers.
  3. Production organized by location and process. Production personnel decisions delegated to vice-president–production, plant managers, and department foremen.

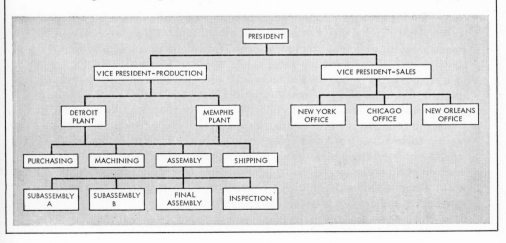

The larger an enterprise grows and the more numerous the levels of management authority, the more apparent become some of the drawbacks and inadequacies of the straight-line form of organization. The man who during the last decade of the nineteenth century and the first decade of the twentieth did most to call attention to the inadequacies of the straight-line organization for manufacturing, and who accomplished the most toward improving it, was Frederick W. Taylor.

Taylor came from a well-to-do Philadelphia family. He made the unusual choice, for a young man of his circumstances, of a career in manufacturing industry and prepared himself by serving an apprenticeship as a machinist. He did this because he intended to work his way up through the ranks and knew that a manufacturing foreman, under the then prevailing line form of organization, had to be proficient in the technology of the work he was to supervise.

Contemporary practice was to hand the department foreman an order for a certain quantity of items to meet stated specifications and expect him to carry on from there. It was up to the foreman to plan the operations necessary to manufacture the part or product, to order materials, to design tools and fixtures, to lay out the sequence of tasks, to train and assign workers and keep them under discipline so that they produced the volume of work required, to inspect their output and maintain quality, to keep the machines in good working order, and at the expected time to deliver the completed order. With all these responsibilities to answer for, the line supervisor had broad authority over the group through which he accomplished the tasks. He had the power to hire and fire, to set hourly rates or piece rates, to grant or withhold pay raises, to punish or reward his workers.

Taylor recognized that so wide a range of duties called for a degree of versatility and ability not often found in any one man. A foreman who was ingenious in solving technical problems might lack understanding in how to get along with his men; while another foreman, effective as a leader, might be weak on the technical side. Taylor's proposed solution was to divide up the foreman's functions between eight specialists, four specialists in the department to boss the workers at their tasks and four in the front office to plan the work. Although the "pure functional" organization form advocated by Taylor is a relic in the history of organization theory, his two basic ideas of assigning several specialists to complex jobs and divorcing planning from operations exerted a mighty influence on most modern-day manufacturing organizations. These two ideas find expression in the development of staff organizations.

Staff Organizations

The purpose of staff organizations is to advise and counsel line management, to serve the line organization, and to carry out management controls over line operations in specified functional areas. Colonel Lyndall

F. Urwick makes a useful distinction between three kinds of staff: personal staff, special staff, and general staff.[1]

Personal staff consists of people who provide personal services which relieve the pressure on a manager's time. The secretary who takes oral dictation and types out letters the manager would otherwise have to write himself is an example of personal staff. Another example is the "Assistant to" the manager. The contribution of these employees is direct personal services to a particular manager, at any level in the organization.

Special staff consists of people who possess special knowledge or other qualifications which the manager whom they serve may be presumed not to have himself. The legal adviser, the engineer, the staff psychologist are special staff people. They give advice, which the manager weighs in making decisions to which the advice is pertinent. Thus, unless he were himself a lawyer, he would not know the legal alternatives available to him in deciding whether to defend, or settle, or make countersuit in a legal process directed against the company. Even though he might be an electrical engineer, he still might need advice on product or process from a chemical engineer or other specialist. The special staff contribution is expert advice and takes the form of *recommendations*, or the analysis of alternatives.

General staff consists of people who do part of the manager's own job but do it in greater detail. The top line manager, for instance, is responsible for the budget, but the controller (a general staff manager) must make sure the figures are correct down to the last decimal point. The line manager's judgment on the components of the budget ought to be as good or better than the controller's. The line manager is quite capable of sizing up the value of the controller's work (as he would not be capable of judging the validity of a chemist's formula) but he needs help in getting detailed proposals in order, coordinating them with all the departments affected, and putting them together in final form.

General staff also provides services, this time not to a specific individual manager but to his entire line organization (example: recruiting personnel for an entire factory, a general staff service of the personnel manager) and counsel to any manager who may ask for it. In addition, general staff carry out routine managerial controls in their various staff fields: i.e., audits by the controller, inspection by the quality control staff, job analysis and evaluation by the personnel staff, and so on. In carrying out services and control, general staff act with organizational authority. They get this, just as any line manager does, by delegation from higher management. They use it on behalf of the whole organization or a division

---

[1] Colonel Lyndall F. Urwick, *Organization in Business: An Address Given at the University of Virginia Graduate School of Business Administration, April 2, 1957* (Occasional Papers on Business Management, No. 2) (Charlottesville: University of Virginia Graduate School of Business Administration, 1958).

thereof under a particular line manager, but strictly within the bounds of their field of responsibility.

In an enterprise employing more than 10,00 persons, the organization of the industrial relations department (a general staff department) may pose a major organizational problem. These large industrial relations departments are important to this discussion because they are found in a relatively few very large corporations and because it is likely that much of the most progressive management thinking on industrial relations problems develops in these large depositories of money and brains.

Figure 2–2, which is a greatly abbreviated sketch of the corporate industrial relations staff of an enterprise employing well over 100,000 persons, provides only a hint of the problems inherent in the organization of the industrial relations department of a giant corporation. Note that this company has three industrial relations specialists bearing the title vice-president and six directors of industrial relations subspecialties. As is the case in many large corporations, Figure 2–2 shows a divorce of functions for hourly and salaried personnel, the vice-president–labor relations having major responsibility in the area of hourly personnel while the vice-president–personnel and organization is primarily concerned with salaried personnel problems. Typically, hourly rated employees are represented by a union while salaried employees frequently are nonunion. The divorce of hourly and salaried personnel activities is significant in at least two respects: (1) the necessity for careful co-ordination of compensation and benefits lest the salaried people feel left out and retaliate by unionization and (2) the rapidly increasing cost of providing tandem adjustments for salaried people as their number increases. Twenty years ago it was not uncommon for the salaried employee head count to represent less than 20 percent of corporate employment. Under these conditions, it was relatively inexpensive to discourage salaried unionism by giving salaried employees a little something extra above and beyond what the union was able to negotiate for hourly rated employees. Today in many large corporations salaried employee head counts equal or surpass hourly employee head counts. Under these present-day conditions it is vastly more expensive to discourage salaried employee unionism by providing extra generous benefits. The problem is further complicated by the fact that any benefits granted to salaried employees this year will certainly be demanded by the union for hourly employees the next time negotiations roll around.[2]

A full discussion of the organization of the industrial relations department in mammoth enterprises is beyond the scope of this chapter. In an investigation of the employee relations function in large-scale enterprises, Professor Dalton E. McFarland has identified four basic structures of employee relations department organization: the integrated depart-

---

[2] Some of the problems of "tandem" adjustments for unionized and nonunion employees in a large corporation are discussed in Case No. 12, pp. 595–99 of this book.

FIGURE 2–2

PARTIAL ORGANIZATION STRUCTURE OF CORPORATE INDUSTRIAL RELATIONS STAFF DEPARTMENT: MULTI-INDUSTRY, MULTINATIONAL, MULTIPLANT CORPORATION

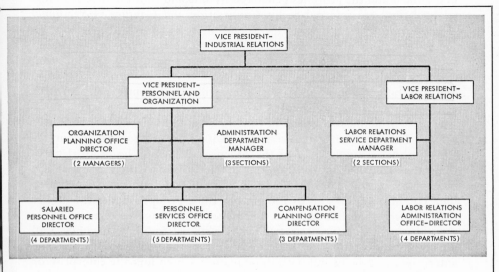

Examples of Advisory Service and Functional Authority Provided by Central Staff Organizations

1. In the personnel administration field, the director, salaried personnel office, provides *advisory service* such as:
   recommending recruitment, selection, and placement policies applicable to salaried personnel,
   recommending training and management development programs applicable to salaried personnel.
   exercises *functional authority* such as
   coordinating company-wide recruitment of college graduate trainees,
   conducting attitude surveys of salaried employees.
2. In the labor relations field, the director, labor relations administration office, provides *advisory service* such as:
   advising on local agreement negotiations,
   advising on content of labor relations training sessions for foremen,
   advising on grievances at steps below umpire appeal level.
   exercises *functional authority* such as:
   negotiating company-wide master agreements with International unions,
   researching present and future issues in collective bargaining,
   presenting grievance cases at the umpire appeal level.

ment, the extended department, the split-function department, and the staff-co-ordinated department. Readers who are concerned with both the structural problems inherent in the organization of the industrial relations department and the attitudes generated by line and staff conflict in industrial relations are referred to his *Cooperation and Conflict in Personnel Administration.*[3]

Formal organization consists of dividing up the work to be done in such ways as to achieve enterprise objectives economically. Organization for personnel administration is the assignment of personnel activities to line and staff organizations so that they will be efficiently performed to achieve enterprise objectives.

The principle of division of functions between line and staff is fairly simple. The line manager is responsible for operations—that is, for results—in the particular unit of the organization which he heads. Everything that concerns the relationship of his people to their tasks, at the workplace, during working hours, is of immediate and vital concern to him. He, in turn, links his own unit with those grouped under the higher manager who is his line superior. The personnel manager is responsible for those matters that have been specifically assigned to him that concern all the employees, at any level, and in any unit, in their relationship with the enterprise as a whole; and with those matters which link the enterprise or any part of it with the body of its employees. An example will make this clear.

A line foreman in a production department has to be the one to say just when a newly trained worker may be put in charge of a delicate or expensive piece of equipment, because the foreman is to blame if an ill-trained worker ruins equipment. Once the foreman has qualified the employee and put him to work on the machine, a staff personnel manager may—if he has been authorized to do so—determine the classification of the newly qualified employee under the rules of a company-wide job evaluation program; and so indirectly designate his pay range. Running the machine is a production department responsibility and working on the machine takes place, in time and space, in the line department. Determining pay ranges under job evaluation may be a company-wide project which has to cut across departmental lines.

The principle of division between line and general staff is clear, but application of the principle is sometimes difficult. It is not more so, however, than inner-organizational relations even between line departments where delegations of authority touch or clash. The production department, under a line manager, may get into a fight with the sales department, also under a line manager, and if the two fail to agree their only recourse is to higher authority. Clear definition of functions helps prevent, but does not eliminate, such clashes.

[3] Dalton E. McFarland, *Cooperation and Conflict in Personnel Administration* (New York: American Foundation for Management Research, 1962).

Assigning Personnel Management Activities within the Enterprise

The general function of manpower management is to insure the efficient procurement, development, and utilization of manpower resources in employment. This general function consists of a host of activities which must be performed in every enterprise, large or small, public or private, profit seeking or nonprofit seeking. These activities are usually performed within the enterprise by line or staff organizations, but some of these activities may be contracted out of the enterprise, either to consultant organizations or to formal employer associations, which may advise the enterprise or act as its agent. In some exceptional cases, to be discussed later, it appears that management has contracted some personnel activities out to the union. The question of who performs these activities is the essence of enterprise organization for personnel management. The methods by which these activities are performed is the reality of personnel management activity and, one might argue, even the essence of management.

One outline of personnel activities[4] lists 110 personnel activities under 14 major classifications—and this list devotes most of its attention to the work of a staff personnel department. Such a comprehensive outline would be most helpful in very large-scale enterprises such as the Big Three automobile producers, the Department of Defense, or the New York City Board of Education. An enterprise must employ more than 500 persons to justify elaborate organizations. It seems unlikely that as many as 10,000 United States enterprises employ as many as 500 people. Nevertheless, such a comprehensive outline does provide an insight on the breadth and complexity of personnel management activities.

A simple outline of personnel management activities is provided in Figure 2–3: Alternative Methods of Performing Personnel Management Activities. With the possible exception of labor law compliance and legislative liaison, the activities listed in Figure 2–3 are closely parallel to the table of contents of most personnel management texts. All of the activities shown in Figure 2–3 could be performed by a pure-line organization. It seems reasonable to say that in most enterprises with less than 100 employees all of the activities shown in Figure 2–3 either are performed by pure-line organization or are neglected or are contracted out. In most cases, an enterprise will not establish a personnel department before its employment reaches or exceeds 100 persons. As will be shown later in the discussion of the structure of American enterprise, it is very important that the reader remember that the problem of sharing personnel management activities between line and staff organizations is a problem of large-scale organizations.

[4] H. H. Carey, "An Outline of Personnel Activities," *Personnel* (May, 1947), pp. 384–87, reproduced in William Grant Ireson and Eugene L. Grant (eds.), *Handbook of Industrial Engineering and Management* (Englewood Cliffs, N.J.: Prentice-Hall, Inc., 1955), pp. 183–85.

FIGURE 2-3

ALTERNATIVE METHODS OF PERFORMING PERSONNEL MANAGEMENT ACTIVITIES

Personnel Activities	In a Large Enterprise, How Activities Might be Shared Between:		In Smaller Enterprises, How Activities Might be "Contracted Out"
	Line Organization	Staff Personnel Department	
Job Description and Analysis	Design of work flows.	Writing job descriptions. Determining transferability of employees between departments of plants.	If contracted out, consultant would perform same functions as assigned to personnel department.
Recruitment	Identify need for new employees.	Develop sources of prospective employees. Conduct search for new employees. Identify candidates for promotion from within.	Search could be contracted out to consultant or employment agency, public or private. Search could be contracted out to union through a hiring hall arrangement.
Selection	Makes final selection from candidates referred by personnel department.	Interview applicants. Aptitude Testing. Psychological testing. Reference checks. Verification of claimed experience. Physical examinations.	Entire process except final selection could be contracted out to consultant.
Training	Identifying training needs.	Run a vestibule school. Provide trainers. Advise on training methods.	Consultant could perform all functions except determining training needs.
Performance Appraisal	Since only line management is in day-to-day contact with employees, it must retain the responsibility for the actual appraisal of individual employees.	Propose a system for performance appraisal. Train supervisors in interviewing techniques. Maintain records on employee performance and development.	Should not be contracted out.
Discipline	Identify needs for rules. Administer the rules.	Advise on rule formulation, drawing on experience from outside the enterprise. Keep records.	Should not be contracted out.

Function			
Wage and Salary Administration	Make final decision on system to be used. Identify changes in job content. Determine wage and salary budget.	Propose alternative systems of job evaluation. Evaluate jobs according to accepted system. Conduct internal and external wage and salary surveys.	Consultant could perform same functions as personnel department.
Employee Benefits and Services	Determine benefits and services to be given, approve system of administration. Identify potentially eligible employees.	Expert advice on sources and costs of benefits. Verify employee eligibility. Keep records.	Consultant could perform same functions as personnel department.
Union Relations	Final decision on contents of agreement. Administering the agreement day by day.	Advise on agreement contents. Negotiating expertise. Surveys of competitive practice. Preparation and presentation of arbitration cases.	Negotiations could be contracted out to attorney or consultant. Negotiations could be contracted out to employers' association. Arbitration cases could be contracted out to attorney or consultant. Liaison could be contracted out, but policy formulation and implementation should not be contracted out.
Labor Law Compliance	Final decision on formulation of company policies, implementing compliance. Application of policy.	Expert advice on interpretation of statutory and administrative law. Education of the line organization on methods of compliance. Expert liaison with enforcement agencies. Record administration needed for compliance.	
Legislative Liaison	Company stand on proposed legislation should be determined by top line officers. Line officers might serve as enterprise representatives at hearings on proposed legislation.	Expert advice to line officers on probable impact of proposed legislation. Employee education on proposed legislation. Expert testimony on enterprise stand. Liaison with industry representative or Chamber of Commerce or National Association of Manufacturers.	Could be contracted out to professional lobbyists. Could be contracted out to industry association. Could be contracted out to organization like Chamber of Commerce or National Association of Manufacturers.

Most large-scale organizations seem to be plagued with conflict between line and staff organizations. This conflict is the subject of much of management literature. The problem appears to be particularly touchy in the personnel management area because the management of men is certainly the very heart of the line manager's job.

The erosion of the old-time authority of the foreman has resulted from the centralization of personnel management activities. The authors of this book believe that five forces are largely responsible for this centralization of personnel management activities: (1) the steadily advancing growth in the size of employing enterprises, (2) recurring acute labor shortages, (3) increasing governmental regulation of the employment relation, (4) collective bargaining, and (5) a movement toward what has been called the professionalization of the personnel administration field. Perhaps there are other equally important forces, but these five merit at least brief discussion.

Between 1945 and 1956, the number of United States firms employing over 100 workers grew from 31,600 to 38,700 while the number of firms employing over 500 workers grew from 6,000 to 6,400.[5] It seems reasonable to assume that as an enterprise grows in size, the complexity of the employment relationship increases and thus accelerates the movement toward centralization of personnel management.

Acute labor shortages, such as those occasioned by World Wars I and II, cause a centralization of personnel management activities within the enterprise. In such periods of labor shortage, millions of new, inexperienced workers must be hired, trained, and introduced to new situations. Such mass activities can be handled only by a central organization. In these times, foremen, too, are hard to find. Thousands of them are newly promoted workers, technically qualified bench and machine hands, but lacking in experience as supervisors. As a class, the quality of foremanship declines in a period of acute labor shortage.

The Wagner Act of 1935 probably was the most smashing single blow to the authority of the American foreman in the twentieth century. Its provisions, which required management to bargain with unions and prohibited discrimination against union members, had the effect of reducing the foreman's authority to hire and fire. Although the provisions of the act did not single out the foreman for regulation, management tended to centralize authority, either to be sure of compliance with the law or to develop the shrewdest methods of evading its letter and intent. The 1964 Civil Rights law's prohibitions on racial discrimination in employment probably will also result in further centralization of personnel management activities.

Collective bargaining greatly reduces the autonomy of the foreman. The grievance procedure and the steward system, which are discussed in

[5] *1962 Statistical Abstract of the United States*, p. 490.

the next chapter, are the mechanisms which check the foreman's freedom of action.

Personnel administration is a growing field of employment, and the practitioners of the function are jealous of their status. There is no question that personnel administration is important and that its practitioners are dedicated to improving the quality of work in the field. However, every step of progress toward the professionalization of personnel administration results in further diminishing the influence of the foreman in the management of his men.

The Foreman's Critical Role in Employee Relations in the Large-Scale Enterprise

It is the foreman who must take the plans of the specialists in the production control department and translate them into units of product by the use of people. In doing so he must exactly conform to the personnel policies and rules laid down in the labor agreement and interpreted by the specialists in the personnel department. His leeway for personal initiative and decision in both the technical and personnel aspects of his job has thus been narrowed; his authority has shrunk with his reduced responsibility, yet he remains management's living link with the human element of production. He is also management's living link with the union in action, for he faces a shop steward not once a year in negotiations, nor once a fortnight in a grievance session, but all day every day. He feels the union's scrutiny and pressure in everything he does. It is not always easy for him to keep his relations with the union entirely impersonal.

The foreman's task and problems indicate the kind of help and training higher management needs to give him. This phase of supervisory training belongs to the personnel department. Two important subjects make up the curriculum: the labor agreement and what may be loosely called human relations.

The Foreman and the Labor Agreement. A foreman ought to know the agreement at least as well as the steward who stands opposite him. In addition, he must be drilled in the company's position on any unclear or controversial provisions. If the personnel department does not give the foreman this understanding, he can only learn by the costly way of trial and error. He will meet with reversals of his actions in grievance cases; and that never adds to a foreman's prestige with his men. Other supervisors above the foreman need to know the agreement, too, but none in such intimate and accurate detail, for none of them is as directly on the firing line as the foreman is in front of his workers. The foreman shares with the personnel department the most vital role in collective bargaining after the actual negotiation of the agreement—that is, living with the agreement.

The Foreman and Leadership by Persuasion: Human Relations. Human relations, the other main subject in the curriculum, aims at teaching the foreman how to get results from his people with the limited resources left to him either of compulsion or reward. In essence, he has to learn to lead by *persuasion*.

Leading by persuasion alone, without the equivalent in hand of either the carrot or the stick, tends to become quite an art. The economist, whose premises giving money wages as the motivator for better and faster work once guided industry, and the psychologist, whose tests of aptitude and measures of mental efficiency were a sensation in their day, have given way of late to teams of social scientists probing the mysteries of interaction and group behavior.

There is no science that has not contributed in some way to industrial progress. No doubt the behavioral sciences are due to have their day in setting the premises of employee relations. Without waiting for detailed findings, it would seem safe at this point to say that in industry the success of leadership by persuasion at the foreman's level depends on two things. One is the pull of the enterprise as a whole on the worker; the other, the foreman's ability to make the worker see, feel, and appreciate this pull.

What economic incentives does the enterprise offer? What is the structure of wages? The level? The method of wage payment? What are the job advancement opportunities? What are the chances of security and what are the fringe benefits? What psychological satisfactions come from, and in, employment with the enterprise? Does the enterprise give outlets that appeal to the individual? Does it absorb him in group efforts toward a common goal?

Answers to questions like these determine the total effect employment with an enterprise has on the employees. Only the central administrative organs of a company can today provide the answers, for the questions all involve matters of policy that belong to top management. To the extent that collective bargaining affects policy, part of the answer comes from the union, acting at top level jointly with management in policy making.

Leadership by persuasion consists, then, first in creating a situation today's generation of workers regards as at least satisfactory and then showing the worker his part in it and how to benefit from it. The whole enterprise thus becomes one great big carrot. The stick is in the threat of banishment from the feast, not by anyone's arbitrary decree, but by the failure to meet the group's standards, to measure up, to "get along with people," in a word—in self-banishment. The foreman, no longer a driver, no longer a keeper of the key to reward, walks alongside the worker as a guide; an older, wiser, successfully integrated fellow employee showing the way.

Not all the results are in from the investigations conducted in the behavioral sciences, but it is still not premature to report that the results to date hint strongly of the importance of leadership by persuasion. The first hint comes from a historic piece of research called the Hawthorne Experiments. These were a series of studies carried out at the Hawthorne Works of the Western Electric Company by the management in co-operation with a team of Harvard University social scientists headed by Elton Mayo, an anthropologist. The experiments were started in the late 1920's and brought to an end by the onset of the depression, but the results remained unpublished until 1938, although Mayo had hinted at some of them in an earlier book. The official report, entitled *Management and the Worker*, by Roethlisberger and Dixon, is the acknowledged landmark and point of departure for the human relations school of thought.

One of the important concepts springing from the findings published in this book is that the face-to-face work group, and not the individual, is the real unit with which management has to deal in the industrial situation. The work group has cohesion, continuity, and control over its members. It can set and enforce standards of individual conduct, including production norms. It has its natural informal leaders. It can enhance or it can retard management objectives and cooperate with or oppose the formal leadership given by line management. This is true with or without the presence of a union; there was, in fact, no union organization at the Western Electric Company when the experiments took place.

The book which brought these facts before the public does not make easy reading. It is formidable in size. It might have had little immediate effect on management thinking if it had not followed as closely as it did the sweep of the CIO unions through manufacturing industry. This union storming of the nonunion fortresses had a shock-wave effect and left factory management bewildered, seeking for an explanation and for guidance in coping with the unfamiliar problem. Some of the popular management journals spread the word about the Hawthorne experiments. The experiments did contain clues to an explanation of what had happened, but they did not give specific guidance on how to deal with the new unions. They also put to work a multitude of laborers in the field across which Hawthorne plowed the first furrow: the field of human relations in industry.

A quarter of a century later, the literature of management, the teaching of management, the practice of management, have all been thoroughly imbued with the lessons of Hawthorne. Management by shared objectives, participative management, democratic management, such are the phrases currently in vogue. As such, they are topics of foreman training.

EMPLOYER ASSOCIATIONS

As noted in Figure 2–3, some important personnel management activities may be contracted to consultants or employer associations or special representational organizations. It is not uncommon for small employers to contract out their collective bargaining negotiations to an employer association.

Management associations, like unions, are membership organizations. The members are the enterprises which pay the expenses and support the activities of the association.

Businessmen organize for many reasons besides collective bargaining. Only a minority of their associations do, in fact, directly engage in it. Others, which do none of it themselves, carry out representational activities (lobbying, public relations, and the like) that may affect the collective bargaining process generally, or they may give aid and advice to member firms involved in specific negotiations, strikes, or other relations with unions. The term "employer association" to designate management groups that directly engage in collective bargaining, will differentiate this type of organization from other management associations.

Conditions for Association Bargaining

No employer association enters in directly when collective bargaining takes place between a single Local union and a single employer, or between a number of Locals and a single employer. Employer association bargaining takes place only in two situations:

The first is when a number of employers each hire workers who are members of the same Local, or group of Locals organized in a Joint Board, or District, of the same International. This occurs, for instance, in the trucking industry; not universally, but in those localities where employers have succeeded in forming an association. It occurs in the garment industry as a normal and regular thing. An untypical but outstanding instance of the same nature shows up in the coal mines. Regional and national employer associations bargain jointly with the United Mine Workers' International.

The unions in this picture are industrial unions, or industrial amalgamations of craft unions, as in the garment trade; and in every case a big union deals with a lot of small companies, all of which are in competition with each other. In all these industries except mining—mining is always an exception—labor costs are a high proportion of total costs. The effect of this industrial union type of multiemployer, or Association, bargaining is to eliminate or reduce competition between companies based on wage differences.

The second situation occurs when a number of employers each hire workers who are members of different Locals of as many different Internationals. This is the characteristic situation in the construction industry. It is the craft-union type of association bargaining, which is not only multiemployer, but multiunion as well. The association negotiates and signs agreements with each of the Locals, and these agreements bind all the members of the association in their dealings with each of the unions. The reason for this is that the employers need and use different kinds of labor at different stages of their construction projects, and so deal with the Local representing that particular craft at the time when its members are on the job; and not before, and not after. Their association gives them the protection of a valid agreement with established rules and terms at the time they have need of that particular trade, or class of employee. It relieves all of the employers from having to negotiate separate agreements with each of the many craft unions.

Not to be confused with true association bargaining is employer *co-operation*. An example of this might be the agreement between New York City newspaper publishers that if any one of their papers is hit by a strike, all the others will suspend publication. This is certainly a strong pledge of support for an enterprise to get from its competitors, but the bargaining, and the agreements signed, are separate.

Problems of Association Bargaining

All bargaining involving more than one employer raises problems of representation. The National Labor Relations Board will, on request, designate by means of an election among workers, the union representation for a given group whether or not all workers in the unit belong to the union. Employers who bargain jointly must, on the other hand, do so by agreement among themselves and on a voluntary basis. A bargain made by the union is binding on all the workers in the bargaining unit, but a bargain struck by the organized employer group is in no way binding on other employers who are not members of the association. In any practically enforceable legal sense, it is not even very binding on Association members.

The employer association has problems that parallel in several curious ways the problems of a union, and are often even more acute. Among the more troublesome are organizing, leadership, and the administration and policing of the labor agreement.

Organization. Employer associations are strictly voluntary since there is no law that compels an enterprise to abide by decisions of a body to which it does not belong. The first hard job in forming an association is to round up members. The next is to keep them in line.

Unions are also, technically, voluntary associations, but through arrangements worked out in collective bargaining (closed shop, union shop) they have found ways of making workers want to join the union—or at least, want not to *refrain from* joining—and to maintain their membership. In any case, a union that has won an election and gained recognition has the legal right to bind the nonunion minority in accordance with the decisions of the prounion majority.

Certain employers, in contrast, may have powerful motives rooted in competition for staying out of the association, or personal inclinations against risking a reduction of accustomed freedom of individual action. In particular, if it is the larger operators who want to play the lone wolf role, the holdouts can cripple the association's effectiveness. Concessions granted to the union by a nonmember can force the hand of the association.

The businessman, more accustomed to competition than co-operation between enterprises—indeed, often dedicated by conviction to that view—is harder to organize than workers who are conditioned to co-operation on the job and accustomed to joint action and discipline.

Leadership. Under a union constitution all employees are equal, but to paraphrase George Orwell's quip, some employers are "more equal" than others: that is, some enterprises are larger, or are under more vigorous management, or make a greater financial contribution to the employer association. Though they may temporarily sink their differences on matters that have to do with the union, they remain in competition with each other. An elected leadership may consequently be subject to distrust or jealousy, and the necessity for consultation over decisions may hamper the speed and decisiveness of action.

As a remedy for these difficulties, many associations turn to the employment of professional labor relations experts to conduct the business of the association. The member firms set general policy and review the results of the neutral hired manager's activities. Assuming an able manager, this seems to be a satisfactory plan.

Administration. It is sometimes easier to negotiate a joint agreement than to make sure of observance of its provisions by those who are party to it. In pursuance of this aim the employer association frequently gets help from the union, which has, perhaps, an even more direct interest than any employer in uniformity of performance and strict adherence to the agreed terms.

Greater difficulty arises when the union, instead of helping, hinders proper enforcement. It may attempt to take advantage of the separation of the enterprises to seek local gains or set precedents that can be used against other signatory employers. This is a variant of the old union game called "whipsawing." It sets the members of the association against each other.

The professional manager proves his worth in this kind of situation. Between negotiations he can devote a great deal of his time to policing the agreement, advising and assisting member firms in the handling of grievance cases, and in many ways assuring uniform application of the agreement terms.

Another device associations also use is the employment, jointly and by agreement with the union, of an impartial umpire, or arbiter. To this man they submit disputes that arise during the life of the agreement, and both sides bind themselves in advance to abide by his decisions. The arbiter's role, which does not differ much whether the agreement is multilateral or bilateral, receives more detailed explanation in Chapter 8.

Essentials of Association Bargaining

Association activity of any sort in the labor relations field always follows the rise of unions and is a reaction against it. It is either a specific response to a need for united employer action to meet an immediate union threat, or a generalized answer to the growth of union influence in the community, state, or nation.

There would seem to be need for united action by employers whenever the union is bigger than the enterprises with which it deals. Now, when is the union "bigger?"

"Big" Unionism. The union is bigger than the employer when the union body with which he deals brings to bear, in the bargaining process, the bargaining power of members who work for all the employers in a given labor or product market. This is true when the union controls the pool from which they all draw their workers, so that labor could be withheld from one employer while his competitors went on unhampered. Obviously, a craft union is in such a position in relation to its employers. An industrial union, ordinarily, is not, for the source of factory labor is open to all, and workers hired in the employment office do not come under union influence until they are part of the factory working force.

The union is also bigger when the union body with which employers make their bargain controls the supply of materials an enterprise needs, or the market to which it sells, or the channels of distribution to the market. A perfect example of this is the Teamsters, an industrial union, which can cut the channels of distribution or supply by refusing deliveries.

Either one of the two situations sketched out above cries out for employer organization. Unless employers facing such situations bargain through an association they are simply inviting exploitation by the union, and may lay the industry open to racketeering. The size of the employer association needs to be exactly proportioned to the size of what was called above the "union body."

This union body may be a Local, as in the building trades. It may be a Joint Board of Locals, as in the garment trades. It may be a District, as in the trucking industry. It may be an entire International, or a major part thereof, as in the coal mining industry.

Without the protection of an association, employers face the prospect of having the union "knock down" the individual enterprises of the industry one by one. The first bargain with the union may consist of seeing an organizer walk in with a printed agreement and say, "Sign here." If the employer signs, knowing that the penalty for not doing so would be a shutdown of his business while competitors continued to operate, the next bargain might be: "Sign here. And slip a C-note into the papers when you hand them back: cash, no checks." Before long an entire industry could get into the hands of racketeers who used the employers to keep the workers in line and beat each of the employers over the head with the threat implied in control of all the others. Once such a condition arrives it is harder than ever for the employers to organize. Association bargaining balances the strength of the opposing forces.

Equality in Bargaining. Some see the union as always bigger than any employer because it organizes all the enterprises in an industry or all the practitioners of a single skilled trade whose craftsmen work for many employers.

The union is not bigger just because it has a million members while the enterprise employs only a thousand workers, if the enterprise bargains only with a Local composed of its own thousand employees. The union's other members in other plants have managements of their own to bargain with; every enterprise in the industry could conceivably be evenly matched with its own segment of the union. That seems, in fact, to be generally the case in mass-production manufacturing. It is undoubtedly one of the reasons why association bargaining is rare in manufacturing outside the garment industries.

Even the "Big Three" auto companies, General Motors, Ford, and Chrysler, only began to approach joint and simultaneous bargaining as a thinkable but potentially dangerous possibility, in their dealings with the challenge of the UAW in 1958, the year the auto agreements expired without renewal and the plants operated without a contract. The Big Three companies would seem, offhand, well suited to engage in association bargaining. Together they produce more than 90 per cent of the nation's cars. They face a common adversary in the big and powerful UAW. They maintain headquarters in the same city of Detroit, where the UAW International also has its offices, and the auto company top managers are personally acquainted and in frequent cordial social contact with each other. Time and again in the past the UAW played off one or another of the three companies against its two competitors to win important gains the others had to match; yet the Big Three held off.

They have held off, in part, perhaps, for fear of antitrust action, always a delicate subject in their circles. Another reason certainly must be competition for the new car market, in which the customer takes performance pretty much for granted and spends his money for style and conveniences. Any one of the companies, convinced that its designers have come up with styling that will catch on with the public, meets an immediate union demand without too much regret, confident that whatever it gives the union, the union will make the other two grant in time. Thus it was, for instance, with the "S.U.B." unemployment benefits plan, first put to General Motors by the union, but first granted by Ford. The UAW is a big union, but the giant corporations of the auto industry are pretty big themselves and are confident and willing to take a chance. Why should they tie their own hands by being timid?

In spite of this, some observers claim to see a trend toward multiemployer bargaining on an industry-wide scale with industrial unions even in the largest enterprises. The logic of events would seem to favor this, but it will probably not come until the big employers are convinced the union really is bigger than they are. Certainly the unions have little to gain by pushing it; they have been doing very well without it. Would Walter Reuther really welcome a united front of the Big Three auto companies against the UAW?

Despite this auto industry exception, the trend is certainly setting in the direction of association bargaining. Besides the industries already mentioned in this chapter, a number of others have engaged in it for years, while some have come to it comparatively recently. The garment unions have been doing it for a long time. The lumber industry, the shipping industry, the canneries on the West Coast, have been at it for two decades or more. In fact, association bargaining is prevalent as a regional phenomenon on the West Coast to an extent unknown as yet in the East or Middle West.

Most notable example of industry-wide bargaining is probably the steel industry negotiations. Technically, this is still only co-operative bargaining, in which the United Steelworkers discusses terms jointly and simultaneously with the huge steel employers; but one product of the 1962 contract was an *industry-wide* seniority pool from which all the firms would draw workers, these workers having gone into the pool as they were displaced from any of the firms by technological improvements.

The standard European practice from the start has favored association bargaining. It would appear that American practice tends in the same direction; but the process still has far to go. The greater portion of the mass-production and mass-distribution industries has not come to it yet.

OTHER MANAGEMENT ASSOCIATIONS

Unions engage not only in collective bargaining but in "representational" activities such as lobbying and public relations, and service activities such as workers' education and research. These kinds of activity, directly or indirectly, frequently supplement collective bargaining. They encourage helpful, or ward off harmful, legislation affecting the process. They promote a favorable climate of public opinion. They provide training for improved union leadership and functioning, and information useful to Locals engaged in negotiations. The bulk of this representational activity goes on at levels above the Local union (which is the primary collective bargaining organization) in any given International, and in the mixed bodies such as City Centrals, State Centrals, and the national union federation.

Similarly, certain management organizations specialize in representational and service activities for employers, and these are likely to be of greater than local scope and mixed in character. Those that unite enterprises of a single industry, unless formed for the express purpose of collective bargaining, are likely to center their attention on technological or marketing problems peculiar to the industry rather than on labor relations.

The National Association of Manufacturers

The employer counterpart of the AFL-CIO, the national union federation, is the National Association of Manufacturers, commonly called the "N.A.M." Of all employer groups engaged principally in representational activity the N.A.M. takes the greatest interest in labor relations. It carries on the most vigorous and massive "pressure-group" activity—similar, but counter to, union pressure tactics—aimed at influencing the legislative and executive branches of government. It conducts the most extensive public relations work and does the most research in the labor relations field. Its network of affiliates throughout the country includes industry groups that contain employer associations for collective bargaining as well as mixed, nonbargaining associations of manufacturers and other industrialists organized on a geographical basis. This heightens the resemblance of the N.A.M. to the organized labor movement opposite which it stands. The N.A.M. structure is much looser than the unions', but the prestige, power, and financial resources of its employer members gives it great influence.

The Chambers of Commerce

Another important network of management associations is the Chamber of Commerce, or "C of C," units of which exist locally and affiliate on a state-wide and national scale. Throughout its structure the C of C is of mixed composition, and so does no bargaining. Local Chambers are largely service and promotional organizations, which are drawn into the representational type of activity that supplements collective bargaining only occasionally, by virtue of the stake and interest many of the member enterprises have in the field. Membership in the C of C, as in other management associations, is voluntary.

In addition to these two nationwide federations of employees, many local and unaffiliated associations, some of a quite informal nature, others well organized and enduring, bring together groups of employers for collective bargaining or representational and service functions. They may be considered analogous to unaffiliated Local unions.

Up to this point, this chapter has discussed some of the alternatives available to employers in establishing enterprise organizations for the purpose of efficient employee relations. It is now appropriate to describe some of the major characteristics of the structure of American enterprise. The material presented in this chapter on the structure of American enterprise runs parallel to the discussion of American unions and professional associations in the next chapter.

THE STRUCTURE OF AMERICAN ENTERPRISE

The organization of an enterprise is influenced by its size, its product or service, its form of ownership, and the prevailing practice of organization followed in its industry. This section seeks to provide some perspectives for understanding the nature of enterprise organization in present-day America.

The Size of American Enterprises

Although there are several valid methods of measuring the size of an enterprise, the number of persons employed is the most relevant to this discussion. The employment of workers in an enterprise is a major determinant of its internal organization and the technology which it employs. In 1962 there were approximately 3,500,000 individual enterprises in the United States. However, only 120,000 of these units employed 50 or more persons.[6] Although the technology used by an enterprise is also conditioned by the particular industry with which the enterprise is associated, it seems fair to assume that most mass-production technology is concentrated in the 120,000 firms employing 50 or more persons each. Formal internal organization also becomes a serious consideration only when an enterprise employs more than a handful of people.

Industrial Composition of American Enterprise

Agricultural employees are excluded from the coverage of American labor relations law and agricultural unionism has never been a significant phenomenon in the United States. Nonagricultural enterprises provided employment for almost 60 million Americans in 1965. Figure 2–4 shows the industrial attachment of nonagricultural employees in 1965. Although manufacturing know-how is an internationally recognized American distinction, trade, government, and service employment make very significant contributions to the national welfare. In the years ahead it seems very likely that nonmanufacturing employment will increase at a more rapid rate than manufacturing employment.

Although precise statistics on the degree of unionization by industrial classification are not available, unions are very significant forces in manufacturing, transportation and public utilities, contract construction, and mining. Union influence is substantially less in trade, government,

---

[6] Figures based on Social Security reporting units, therefore excluding farm workers, domestic workers, self-employed persons, members of the uniformed services of the United States, federal civilian employees, the employees of state and local governments, and railroad workers. (*1965 Statistical Abstract of the United States*, p. 492.)

FIGURE 2–4

NONAGRICULTURAL EMPLOYMENT IN THE UNITED STATES: 1965

(Total in 1965: 58,847,000)

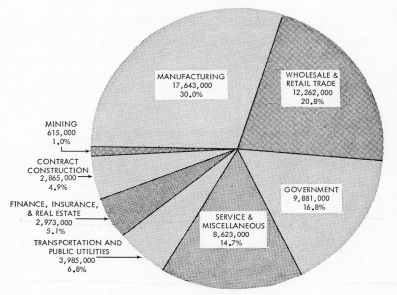

MANUFACTURING
17,643,000
30.0%

WHOLESALE &
RETAIL TRADE
12,262,000
20.8%

MINING
615,000
1.0%

CONTRACT
CONSTRUCTION
2,865,000 →
4.9%

FINANCE, INSURANCE,
& REAL ESTATE
2,973,000
5.1%

TRANSPORTATION AND
PUBLIC UTILITIES
3,985,000
6.8%

GOVERNMENT
9,881,000
16.8%

SERVICE &
MISCELLANEOUS
8,623,000
14.7%

SOURCE: *1965 Statistical Abstract of the United States,* p. 220.

service, and finance. Unions in manufacturing industry provide the basis for this book's model of industrial unionism, while the construction industry unions provide the basis for the model of craft unionism.

Ownership of Business Enterprise

Just as the size and output of an enterprise may be important in influencing its organization structure, the form of ownership may influence organizational structure and enterprise objectives. Although there were over 10 million active sole proprietorships and partnerships in the United States in 1962, their total receipts were only one third of the total receipts generated by 1,268,000 corporations.[7] Sole proprietorships and partnerships typically are small businesses. More importantly most proprietors and partners are owner-managers. Since owner-managers are only accountable to themselves and the law, they can exercise much greater personal discretion in setting organizational objectives than can professional managers in a corporation.

Figure 2–5 reveals the relative importance of various forms of ownership in different broad industrial groups. The complete dominance of the corporate form of ownership in such heavily unionized industries as manufacturing, transportation, and mining should be contrasted with

[7] *1965 Statistical Abstract of the United States,* p. 489.

FIGURE 2–5

PERCENTAGE OF INDUSTRY RECEIPTS GENERATED
BY CORPORATE OWNERSHIP: 1962

Industry Group	Percentage of Receipts Generated by Corporations
Manufacturing....................................	96.8
Transportation, Communication, Electric, Gas and Sanitary Services...............................	93.1
Mining..	86.2
Finance, Insurance, and Real Estate..................	82.0
Wholesale and Retail Trade........................	70.0
Construction.....................................	64.3
Services...	42.2
Agriculture, Forestry, and Fisheries..................	14.5

SOURCE: 1965 Statistical Abstract of the United States, p. 490.

lesser significance of the corporate form of ownership in the heavily unionized construction industry.

Directly comparable data on the structure of various industries are not available. However, the structure of manufacturing industry can be described in some detail and compared to scanty data in other industry classifications.

The Structure of Manufacturing Industry

Figures 2–6 and 2–7 analyze industry employment and enterprise size in manufacturing industry. Several observations are in order:

1. Manufacturing is big business in that it provides almost one third of the nonagricultural job opportunities in the United States.
2. Manufacturing enterprises are big enterprises. For all manufacturing industry, average employment per enterprise exceeds 50 persons.
3. There are nearly 5,000 manufacturing establishments in the United States employing more than 500 persons each.
4. Very large enterprises are particularly evident in transportation equipment, machinery, primary metals, textile mills, paper, petroleum, and tobacco products.
5. Within manufacturing industry, there are very significant differences in enterprise sizes in various Standard Industrial Classifications. Of the ten Standard Industrial Classifications providing the greatest number of job opportunities, five have average enterprise employment levels below the average for all manufacturing industry. Tobacco products, the classification providing the smallest number of job opportunities, has the third highest average employment per enterprise.
6. Some manufacturing industries are typified by relatively small enterprises. Average enterprise employment is below 40 persons in printing and publishing; lumber and wood products; stone, clay, and glass; and furniture and fixtures.

Thus in manufacturing industry as a whole, formal organization and personnel administration within the enterprise tends to be very important. The relatively large size of employing enterprises makes it imperative that policy, systems, and procedures be formalized. Employer association collective bargaining is not imperative in large-scale manufacturing firms

FIGURE 2–6
THE STRUCTURE OF MANUFACTURING EMPLOYMENT IN 1958

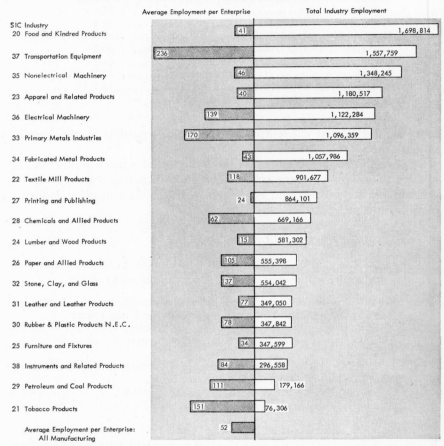

SIC Industry	Average Employment per Enterprise	Total Industry Employment
20 Food and Kindred Products	41	1,698,814
37 Transportation Equipment	236	1,557,759
35 Nonelectrical Machinery	46	1,348,245
23 Apparel and Related Products	40	1,180,517
36 Electrical Machinery	139	1,122,284
33 Primary Metals Industries	170	1,096,359
34 Fabricated Metal Products	43	1,057,986
22 Textile Mill Products	118	901,677
27 Printing and Publishing	24	864,101
28 Chemicals and Allied Products	62	669,166
24 Lumber and Wood Products	15	581,302
26 Paper and Allied Products	105	555,398
32 Stone, Clay, and Glass	37	554,042
31 Leather and Leather Products	77	349,050
30 Rubber & Plastic Products N.E.C.	78	347,842
25 Furniture and Fixtures	34	347,599
38 Instruments and Related Products	84	296,558
29 Petroleum and Coal Products	111	179,166
21 Tobacco Products	151	76,306
Average Employment per Enterprise: All Manufacturing	52	

SOURCE: *1958 Census of Manufactures,* Vol. I—Summary Statistics, pp. 1–25 through 1–27.

because individual enterprises can match the expertise of union negotiators by establishing industrial relations departments. This situation is both paralleled and contrasted in the structure of nonmanufacturing industry.

The Structure of Nonmanufacturing Industry

Figure 2–8 provides some suggestive comparisons and contrasts on the structure of nonmanufacturing industry:

1. Trade, government, and services combined provide more job opportunities than manufacturing industry.
2. Big employing establishments like those in manufacturing industry are prevalent in government, transportation and public utilities, and mining. Direct establishment comparisons are not available, but it seems reasonable to say that the organizational problems confronting a government agency, a transportation enterprise such as a railroad or airline, a public utility, or a mine would be just as complex as the problems confronting a manufacturer of transportation equipment, primary metals, or machinery.
3. Some of the principles of organization and management that are applicable in large manufacturing industry would be equally applicable in the larger scale industry segments of nonmanufacturing industry.
4. Other very important segments of nonmanufacturing industry confront problems similar to those facing small-scale manufacturers. For example, small manufacturing shops in food and kindred products, apparel, printing and publishing, and lumber probably have a good deal in common with much of wholesale and retail trade, services, and contract construction. These smaller enterprises tend to rely on a less

FIGURE 2–7

PREVALENCE OF LARGE-SCALE ESTABLISHMENTS IN
MANUFACTURING INDUSTRIES: 1958

SIC Industry		Industry Employment	Number of Establishments with 500 or More Employees	Number of Establishments with 100 or More Employees
20	Food and kindred products	1,698,814	365	3,764
37	Transportation equipment	1,557,759	458	1,133
35	Nonelectrical machinery	1,348,245	501	2,085
23	Apparel and related products	1,180,517	175	2,658
36	Electrical machinery	1,122,284	486	1,686
33	Primary metal industries	1,096,359	394	1,463
34	Fabricated metal products	1,057,986	319	2,173
22	Textile mill products	901,677	407	2,028
27	Printing and publishing	864,101	220	1,387
28	Chemicals and allied products	669,166	248	1,143
24	Lumber and wood products	581,302	62	967
26	Paper and allied products	555,398	213	1,402
32	Stone, clay, and glass	554,042	141	1,155
31	Leather and leather products	349,050	86	986
30	Rubber and plastic products	347,842	119	559
25	Furniture and fixtures	347,599	72	769
38	Instruments and related products	296,558	109	421
29	Petroleum and coal products	179,166	67	277
21	Tabacco products	76,306	33	138
39	Miscellaneous manufacturing	571,434	143	830
	Total: All Manufacturing Industry	15,393,766	4,618	26,984

SOURCE: 1958 Census of Manufactures, Vol. I–Summary Statistics, pp. 1–25 through 1–27 and 2–3 through 2–5.

sophisticated technology than mass production and have the potentiality for retaining a familylike employment relationship. Workers can readily see the results of their labors. These smaller enterprises are expensive for unions to organize, and when they are organized, their managements would be expected to turn to employer associations for collective bargaining.

In the next chapter, data will be provided on unions which parallels the data provided here on the structure of American enterprise.

FIGURE 2–8

THE STRUCTURE OF NONMANUFACTURING INDUSTRY: 1958–59

Industry	1958–59 Employment	Typical Establishment Size and Exceptions	Comment and Explanation
Retail and whole-sale trade[1]	11,000,000	Small, except for food chains, department stores, and hotels.	Many establishments with no paid employees. Average employment per establishment: wholesale trade 9.8, retail trade 4.4.
Government[2]	8,300,000	Large	Local government provides slightly over half of jobs. About 45 percent of state and local employment in education.
Services[3]	7,000,000	Small, except for hospitals	Average employment per enterprise in "selected" services: 6.5. "Selected" services cover only about one third of service employment.
Transportation and public utilities[4]	4,000,000	Very large, except for local cartage	Average employment per company in selected lines: Class I Railroads—7,930. Class A Telephone Systems—11,832 Scheduled domestic air carriers—3,703. Intercity motor carriers of property —357. Intercity motor carriers of passengers—234.
Finance, insurance, and real estate[5]	2,500,000	Large for banks and insurance carriers, representing half of industry employment.	Little meaningful data available on enterprise size.
Contract construction[6]	2,500,000+	Small	In 1961–62, there were over 700,-000 proprietorships and partnerships in the construction industry as compared to only 84,000 corporations.
Mining[7]	730,000	Medium	No meaningful data on enterprise size. Although heavily capitalized employment per establishment probably approximates small or medium-sized manufacturer.

[1] *1958 Census of Business,* Vol. I, pp. 3–2 through 3–13 and Vol. III, p. 1–5.
[2] *1962 Statistical Abstract of the United States,* pp. 404, 433.
[3] *1958 Census of Business,* Vol. V, pp. 1–5 through 1–7. "Selected" services cover only about one third of employment in the service industries.
[4] *1962 Statistical Abstract of the United States,* pp. 222, 578–83.
[5] *1962 Statistical Abstract of the United States,* p. 222.
[6] *Statistics on Income, U.S. Business Tax Returns,* 1961–62, p. 31.
[7] *1958 Census of Mineral Industries,* Vol. I, p. 3.

SUMMARY AND CONCLUSIONS

Previous systems for the management of labor have shown only two parties in the relationship: the "employer" (slaveowner, lord of the manor) and the "employee" (slave, serf). The present free-labor system shows in addition a third element, the union. The employer may be an individual, or a company of people incorporated as an artificial "person," and acting through agents with delegated authority. The union is always an association of people, acting through representatives. Only the worker is always an individual, full-blooded person. Collectively, he is the flesh-and-blood link between the company and the union.

The "Four Sets of Relations"

Between these three elements there are three sets of relations, and perhaps a fourth that encompasses them all:

1. *The company and the worker.* This is a freewill contract in which the worker exchanges work against wages, under conditions laid down by the employer and accepted by the worker, or agreed upon between them.

2. *The worker and the union.* Here the relationship is a free association between the worker as a member and the union to which he belongs. Technically, at least, it is a voluntary association and the right to enter it comes from the Bill of Rights of the Constitution.

3. *The union and the company.* The relation between the union and the company is usually thought of, and referred to, as a "contract," but it is more nearly analogous to a *treaty* between two sovereign powers. It is an exchange of pledges and promises that have to do with the contract between the company and each of its individual workers.

4. *The "encompassing fourth" relationship.* The company and the union are linked so intimately by the body of the workers, who are at the same time employees of the one and members of the other, that they may be thought of as a three-link chain, or perhaps more appropriately symbolized by overlapping circles.

The "Key" Element

The *key element* that brings the other two into association with it is the company. The *company* organizes the working force around its production processes. The union has to take the workers as it finds them in their relations with each other and with the company, their employer.

But labor-management relations, expressed in bargaining for agreements and in administering the agreements, is a process of interaction. Companies bring unions into existence by creating work groups for the union to organize. Unions act on the company, and the company registers their impact in terms of management organization structure and function.

ing. Internal change is the result, but there are also external effects. Union pressure on separate, independent enterprises forces them into united action and mutual dependence.

Multiemployer bargaining, which long ago reached maturity in the handicraft sector of the economy, spread into mass production and distribution with the growth of industrial unions. Industry-wide bargaining, not yet much developed, seems to be almost in sight, and, some say, sure to come.

Industry-wide bargaining involving the big and decisive mass-production and distribution units of the economy will surely affect management structure and functioning within the enterprise, and the relation of enterprises to the society they sustain with their products and services. The enterprise will no longer be as free and independent as before. The Local union, which is a direct, responsive membership organization, will yield its rights and powers in collective bargaining to the International, which is a delegate organization remote from local control.

While these possibilities unfold, the employer remains the key element. He will hardly remain passive but will act as well as be acted upon. It is to be hoped that in association he will act as effectively as when he stood alone, to help sustain a vigorous economy and provide the material basis for a good society.

QUESTIONS FOR DISCUSSION

1. Foreman training in human relations is a major development of the post-World War II period. Why?
2. What is the influence of the prevailing form of ownership of capital on management organization, objectives, and methods?
3. How do you explain the fact that there frequently is substantial friction between line and staff organizations in the handling of personnel matters in large-scale enterprises?
4. Compare and contrast management objectives and methods in handicraft industry and mass production.
5. In 1947 several proponents of the Taft-Hartley law favored outlawing multiemployer bargaining. Although this proposal continues to crop up occasionally, it is less frequently heard nowadays. What do you think of this proposal and why does it seem to have gone out of style?

CASES: 8, 10, 12.

SELECTED ANNOTATED BIBLIOGRAPHY

AMERICAN TRUCKING ASSOCIATION, EXECUTIVE COMMITTEE. *Collective Bargaining in the Trucking Industry*. Washington, D.C.: The Association, 1956.

Includes 26 recommendations for improving management's position at the bargaining table.

BAKER, HELEN, AND FRANCE, ROBERT R. *Centralization and Decentralization in Industrial Relations*. Princeton, N.J.: Industrial Relations Section, Princeton University, Research Report Series, No. 87, 1954.

Discusses management and union preferences for centralization and decentralization in industrial relations responsibility and authority in multiplant firms and the actual practice of centralization or decentralization in these companies.

BELCHER, A. L. "How Top Management Views the Industrial Relations Function," *Personnel*, Vol. XXXIV (March–April, 1958), pp. 65–70.

Results of a personnel director's survey of some 200 executives and university professors to determine the factors necessary for success as a personnel man.

BROWN, DOUGLASS V., and MYERS, CHARLES A. "The Changing Industrial Relations Philosophy of American Management," *Proceedings of the Ninth Annual Meeting of the Industrial Relations Research Association*, pp. 84–99. Madison, Wis.: The Association, 1957.

Discusses five forces causing changes in the approach of management to industrial relations in the last decade.

DUNLOP, JOHN T., and MYERS, CHARLES A. "The Industrial Relations Function in Management: Some Views on its Organizational Status," *Personnel*, Vol. XXXI (March, 1955), pp. 406–13.

Two leading professors and arbitrators discuss the functions of the industrial relations department, different concepts of its function, and the decision-making process in industrial relations.

HILL, LEE H., and HOOK, CHARLES L., JR. *Management at the Bargaining Table*. New York: McGraw-Hill Book Co., Inc., 1945.

A comprehensive review of the issues and practices of collective bargaining from a management viewpoint. Provides a penetrating insight into management thinking at the end of World War II.

LYNCH, EDITH. "The Personnel Man and His Job: An AMA Survey," *Personnel*, Vol. XXXII (May, 1956), pp. 487–97.

A profile of "the average personnel man" derived from an American Management Association questionnaire survey of 450 participants in a personnel conference.

McCAFFREE, KENNETH M. "A Theory of the Origin and Development of Employer Associations," *Fifteenth Annual Meeting of the Industrial Relations Research Association* (December, 1952), pp. 56–68.

McFARLAND, DALTON E. *Cooperation and Conflict in Personnel Administration*. New York: American Foundation for Management Research, 1962.

Discusses attitudes of co-operation and conflict between line and staff organizations performing the personnel function in large-scale enterprises.

————. "The Labor Relations Consultant as Contract Negotiator," *Personnel*, Vol. XXXIV (May–June, 1958), pp. 44–51.

Discusses the advantages and disadvantages to a company in the use of outside consultant as contract negotiator. Interesting observations on the impact of this practice on internal management organization.

McGREGOR, DOUGLAS. *The Human Side of Enterprise*. New York: McGraw-Hill Book Co., Inc., 1960.

Argues for greater participation in decision making by subordinates in business enterprise.

McMurray, Robert N. "The Case for Benevolent Autocracy," *Harvard Business Review*, Vol. XXXVI (January–February, 1958), pp. 82–90.

A leading management consultant argues against participative management and in favor of his proposed "benevolent autocracy."

————. "War and Peace in Labor Relations," *Harvard Business Review*, Vol. XXXIII (November–December, 1955), pp. 48–60.

A leading management consultant takes issue with the "philosophies" growing out of "causes-of-industrial-peace" type of thinking and advocates a preventive labor relations policy to maintain a balance of power between company and union.

Myers, Charles A., and Turnbull, John G. "Line and Staff in Industrial Relations," *Harvard Business Review*, Vol. XXXIV (July–August, 1956), pp. 113–24.

Professor Myers of M.I.T. and Professor Turnbull of the University of Minnesota survey the organizational placement of the industrial relations in management and propose methods of clarifying the relations between the industrial relations department and line management.

Northrup, Herbert R. "Spatial Relationships in the Collective Bargaining Process," Arnold W. Weber (ed.), *The Structure of Collective Bargaining: Problems and Perspectives*, pp. 77–96. New York: The Free Press of Glencoe, Inc., 1961. Discussion, pp. 97–105.

Discusses the countermovements toward decentralization of authority in labor. Argument that unions are going ahead on their own direction with less ability to adjust inwardly than either employees or management is supported by (*a*) loss of union competitive vigor, (*b*) lack of union growth, (*c*) lack of union appeal to new prospects, (*d*) lack of union appeal to white-collar people, (*e*) lack of union inward adjustment, and (*f*) the trend away from labor-management relations to public and government relations. Discussion deals with contention that management's desire for uniformity in industrial relations practices has facilitated the trend toward consolidation of bargaining structures and a discussion of management attitudes toward democratic, decentralized union decision making in collective bargaining.

Patten, Thomas H., Jr. "Personnel Research: Status Key," *Management of Personnel Quarterly*, Vol. 4 (Fall, 1965), pp. 15–23.

Reviews the personnel research carried out by specific large corporations.

————. "Revitalizing the Role of the Foreman," *Management of Personnel Quarterly*, Vol. 5 (Summer, 1966), pp. 34–43.

Outlines a program for identifying supervisory potential, recognizing supervisory performance, and retaining in the employ of the enterprise employees who have demonstrated proficiency as line supervisors.

Roethlisberger, F. J. "The Foreman: Master and Victim of Double Talk," *Harvard Business Review*, Vol. 43 (September–October, 1965), pp. 22–26.

Reprints the author's 1954 analysis of the foreman's role, with retrospective commentary on the article and its significance.

Scott, William G. *The Management of Conflict: Appeal Systems in Organizations*. Homewood, Ill.: Richard D. Irwin, Inc., and Dorsey Press, 1965.

Examines appeal systems in business and nonbusiness organizations without unions.

Slichter, Sumner H., James J. Healy, and Livernash, E. Robert. *The Impact of Collective Bargaining on Management*. Washington, D.C.: Brookings Institution, 1960.

See Chapter 2, "Issues for Management in Industrial Relations" and Chapter 29, "Line and Staff Cooperation and the Position of Foremen."

Somers, Gerald G. "Pressures on an Employers' Association in Collective Bargaining," *Industrial and Labor Relations Review*, Vol. VI (July, 1953), pp. 557–69.

Compares experience under multiemployer bargaining in the bituminous-coal and flint-glass industries.

Walker, Charles R., Guest, Robert H., and Turner, Arthur N. *The Foremen on the Assembly Line*. Cambridge, Mass.: Harvard University Press, 1956.

Examines the roles and points of view of foremen in an automobile plant.

Whyte, William H., Jr. *The Organization Man*. New York: Simon and Schuster, Inc., 1956.

Examines the ideology, training, neuroses, testing, and behavior of the organization man in business, government, and professional employment.

Wortman, Max S., Jr. "Influences of Employer Bargaining Associations in Manufacturing Firms," *Fifteenth Annual Proceedings of the Industrial Relations Research Association* (December, 1962), pp. 69–82.

Chapter 3

UNIONS AND PROFESSIONAL ASSOCIATIONS

Each worker has a separate employment contract with his employer; but work is social. Any enterprise of moderate size organizes and integrates its tasks so closely that every job is interdependent with all others. The individual cannot bargain for changes in his own job or conditions without affecting others in varying degree so that individual bargaining is ineffective. Changes in individual employment contracts usually depend upon a *general* review of the conditions of employment which can be obtained only by collective pressure on the employer. To exert this pressure, workers form unions. In the factory and other large-scale organizations with a high degree of job specialization, they form industrial unions. In other cases, where skilled craftsmen perform substantially the same work for an employer, or employers, and bring to their work the same qualifications, it seems natural to seek the same employment bargain for all workers possessing the same skills. Again the means of doing this is to form a union, and for skilled men in the handicraft trades, a craft union.

Physicians, attorneys, engineers, and other members of the professions often form professional associations. Although these associations typically do not engage in collective bargaining and shun the label of "unionism," some of their activities tend to parallel the behavior of unions. This chapter will explore some of the comparisons and contrasts between activities of professional associations and unions.

Craft unions, industrial unions, and professional associations seek somewhat different ends and use somewhat different means for accomplishing these ends. In addition to discussing the ends and means of unions and professional associations, this chapter will describe some of the major characteristics of the structure of American labor organizations, a structure which parallels that of American enterprise described in Chapter 2.

THE GENERAL OBJECTIVES OF UNIONS

Unions are *service* organizations; they produce no tangible product. The profit motive which plays such an important role in business enterprise is irrelevant to a discussion of labor organizations.

The general objectives of American unions can best be understood by starting with an assumption deeply imbedded in the tradition of American law and unionism, that is, that unions are *voluntary* and *private* institutions. Under this assumption, it is fairly obvious that the objectives of American unions are two:

1. To raise the living standards *of their members*, that is, to raise wages, shorten the hours of work, and improve working conditions, and
2. To protect *their members* from arbitrary employer actions in the course of employment

The voluntary and private institution assumption is helpful in: (1) providing a rationale for the flow of authority or consent in unions, (2) putting no constraints whatsoever on the nature of union behavior, i.e., leaving unions free to pursue the welfare of their members either by collective bargaining or political activity, and (3) excluding utopian ideological schemes from the realm of union activity. Each of these advantages of the voluntary and private institution assumption merits brief discussion before the assumption itself is modified.

If unions are voluntary and private associations, the members "own" the union and the will of the members must be paramount in all union activities. Thus authority must flow upward in unions from the owner-members to the elected officers. Majority rule and town hall democracy provide the foundation upon which unions must be built. The individual member's inherent right to withdraw from the union provides a constant check on any undemocratic practices of the union leadership. If oligarchy develops, it has been approved through the apathy of the membership. In theory at least, the membership always possesses an absolute veto on any action of the leadership.

The private side of the assumption gives unions great discretion in the means they adopt to achieve their ends. So long as unions do not exceed the freedoms guaranteed to individual citizens, they would be free to engage in all sorts of fraternal and political activities, just as a lodge could endorse a political candidate or contribute to his campaign expenses. Carried to the extreme, as private organizations unions could even become political parties.

Students of the labor movement have argued the relative merits of "bread-and-butter" unionism versus "utopian" unionism for almost a century now. Within the labor movement itself considerable controversy has raged over the obligation of unions to act as the protectors and advocates of the downtrodden in the society. It probably is not an exaggeration to say that the principle which split the labor movement in the formation of the CIO in 1935 was the question of the obligation of the labor movement to bring the benefits of unionism to unorganized workers. If one firmly supports the voluntary and private assumption, the question of organizing the unorganized beyond the immediate jurisdiction of existing unions is largely irrelevant. Certainly the voluntary and private assumption excludes any necessity for action seeking to modify the existing politico-economic structure of society. Today it is fashionable to criticize the failure of American unions to organize the real victims of poverty in the United States, and the authors of this book have frequently joined this lament. However, if the voluntary and private assumption were completely accepted, there would be little justification for this criticism. Under the voluntary and private assumption, union activity in organizing the victims of poverty could be judged a failure only if unorganized poverty-stricken workers posed a threat to the prosperity of the present members of unions.

Although the voluntary and private institution assumption about unions is helpful in explaining union activity and is deeply imbedded in tradition, it must be abandoned today simply because *it is contrary to fact.* Under current law, unions are obligated to represent *all* the workers under an NLRB certification whether they are union members or not. Thus American unions have become instrumentalities of the state at least to some degree. The significance of the quasi-public nature of unionism is discussed in Chapter 4.

Quite apart from the legal obligation to represent some nonmember workers, American unionism has interests which go beyond the simple representation of present members. These interests are dictated by the market context and the broader ideological objectives of *some* unions. Market conditions dictating union activity beyond the representation of present members are fairly noncontroversial. Low-wage, nonunion textile plants pose an obvious threat to the jobs and wages of unionized textile workers; the interests of the members of textile unions can be protected only by organizing the nonunion workers or raising their wages to union levels by law. On the other hand, the obligation of unions to represent the downtrodden in the society is a highly controversial question which ultimately is decided on the ethical standards of the discussants. In the discussion which follows, consideration will be given to the organizational elements best suited for serving these broader representational interests.

Because the voluntary and private institution assumption does not square with present-day facts, this book argues that the *general* objectives of unions are four in number. Individual unions may adopt a mixture of all four of these objectives or they may concentrate all of their energies on only one or two of them. Both the degree of intensity in seeking these objectives and the organizational components established for the purpose of achieving them vary between individual unions, and significant international differences (to be discussed in Chapter 14) exist. The general objectives of unions are:

1. To influence the wage and effort bargain; to take labor out of self-competition.
2. To establish a system of individual security; to obtain justice at the workplace.

3. To influence the rules for rule making; by the process of political representation to obtain legislative, executive, and judicial actions which promote the interests of individual unions, unions in general, and the welfare of the constituency of unions, and

4. To obtain power in the state and over the economy; by political means to create an economic and political environment conducive to the welfare of labor.

Public acceptance of union activity depends, in part, on the objective sought. Although some citizens might argue that union wages are too high or that a particular seniority system was contrary to the general welfare, very few citizens would argue that workers should be denied the right to *influence* the wage and effort bargain or to seek to establish *some* system of individual security. On the other hand, it seems likely that a larger number of citizens would criticize union political activities.

One might suppose that unions would encounter little difficulty in setting their operational objectives; that the goals would be dictated by a democratic vote of the membership and that union officers would be relatively impotent to modify these objectives. This idealistic fiction collapses because of the complexity of union organizational structures and the issues in collective bargaining, the ambition and manipulative skill of union leadership, and the apathy of rank-and-file union members. A few words about the problems of achieving union democracy are in order before discussing the elements of union organizational structure.[1]

Complex union organizational structures and complex issues in collective bargaining tend to frustrate latent union democracy of the town hall variety. Power is where the money is. For reasons to be discussed below, there is a growing tendency in the labor movement for money to be concentrated above the Local union. A natural outgrowth of this is to reduce the autonomy of Local unions and the influence of the members of a union on its policy. One of the factors contributing to the centralization of power in unions at levels above the Local union is the complexity of collective bargaining issues. It probably is fair to say that a majority of union members would like to have pensions; but pension bargaining requires the services of a highly trained expert and this bargaining is beyond the competence of rank-and-file union members. Once an expert enters the bargaining the influence of union members on the final settlement diminishes.

This book argues that the basic determinants of union structure are Dunlop's contexts and that the technology context is the most important single determinant of union structure. Nevertheless, it is obvious that union organizational structures are influenced by the personal characteristics of union leaders. Although the general welfare of the people defines the position of President of the United States, the Presidency itself during

[1] In his classic study of radical *Political Parties* and working-class movements, Robert Michels concludes that every system of leadership is incompatible with the most essential postulate of democracy.

the tenure of Calvin Coolidge was quite different from what it was under Franklin D. Roosevelt. A Teamsters' union under James R. Hoffa would be quite unlike a Teamsters' union under Walter Reuther or George Meany.

Probably the greatest deterrent to town hall democracy in unions is the apathy of rank and file. A good many union members have little interest in union affairs so long as the union is effective in negotiating wage increases and processing their personal grievances. These members pay their dues and expect the union to do a job for them, just as they may hire a neighborhood boy to mow the lawn. As long as the grass gets cut they are satisfied, and they couldn't care less about who cuts it or what methods he uses to do the job.

Union democracy is hard to define. Two dimensions of the meaning of union democracy are suggested by a substantial body of scholarly literature. The legalistic dimension of union democracy is the existence of procedures for fair and regular elections, reasonable trial procedures in applying union discipline, and guarantees that members of the union have a right to express reasoned dissent from union policy.[2] Another, more humanistic, dimension of union democracy deals with the extent to which individual members of unions feel that they are capable of influencing union policy, and their satisfaction with the policies established.[3] It seems fair to say that rank-and-file apathy, the ambition of powerful leaders, and centralization of union decision-making power at levels above the Local tend to dilute union democracy in both the legalistic and humanistic dimensions.

The wage and effort bargain and systems of individual security always originate at the level of the enterprise and the Local union. Political activity more frequently is conducted at higher levels of union organization than the Local.

ELEMENTS OF UNION ORGANIZATIONAL STRUCTURE

The basic elements of union organizational structure in the United States are: (1) the Local union, (2) the International union, and (3) the AFL-CIO. Auxiliary elements of union structure which are directly engaged in the negotiation and administration of collective bargaining agreements include: (1) Districts, (2) Joint Boards, (3) Conference Boards, and (4) Trade Councils. Two auxiliary elements of union structure which are engaged primarily in representational or political activity are: (1) City Centrals and (2) State Centrals. Each of these elements of union structure will be considered separately and then integrated into the overall structure of the American labor movement.

[2] For example, see Philip Taft. *The Structure and Government of Labor Unions* (Cambridge, Mass.: Harvard University Press, 1954).

[3] A classic human relations study is Leonard R. Sayles and George Strauss, *The Local Union* (New York: Harper & Bros., 1953).

THE TWO KINDS OF LOCAL UNIONS

This book argues that there are two basic kinds of Local unions: craft Locals and industrial Locals. Before emphasizing the differences between these types it is well to consider the common characteristics of most Local unions.

The Local union is a voluntary association of workers who, as free citizens with economic interests in common, have banded together for mutual advantage. The members of the Local work for an employer, or for several or many employers, but the union exists as an organization independently of any employer, under the constitutional guarantee of freedom of assembly.

The members "own" the Local and control it by majority vote: one vote per member. They elect officers and an executive board to act for them between meetings. They hold their meetings, ordinarily, at intervals of a month or less, and conduct them by the rules of order of democratic deliberative assemblies.

The membership meeting is the highest authority of the Local union. All members in good standing have voice and vote there. A member maintains good standing by paying dues and assessments and observing the discipline of the union as laid down in the Local constitution and bylaws, and in decisions of the Local at membership meetings. New members gain admission to the union by complying with the conditions and qualifications of the constitution, paying the required initiation fee, and, if the constitution requires it, receiving the affirmative vote of the members.

In structure and the routine conduct of its business a Local union resembles countless other private and independent organizations to which Americans belong: clubs, lodges, church groups, recreational, educational, and service associations. The difference is in the aims the Local union sets itself and the functions it carries out.

The primary aim of the Local union is to represent its members in relation to their employer or employers. Like any other membership association it also carries on social and subsidiary activities, but in pursuit of its primary aim, the most important functions it performs with employers are collective bargaining and grievance handling.

As independent entities, the Local union and the employer of its members negotiate through authorized agents for an agreement defining the terms of the individual work contracts of the employee-members. Negotiation takes place at the policy-making level of the two organizations involved. In the Local union, the membership meeting makes policy and selects agents to negotiate on policy with policy makers in management.

Corollary to the process of negotiating the agreement is grievance-handling, or administration of the agreement. The Local union provides employees with a channel for complaints arising under the agreement and for solving problems not foreseen in the negotiations. An administrative organ of the Local union sees to the application and enforcement of agreement terms.

Both craft Locals and industrial Locals devote their main efforts to influencing the wage and effort bargain and establishing systems of individual security at the workplace. Because their membership base is relatively small, they are capable of exerting only insignificant political influence on either the rules for rule making or power in the state.[4]

The Craft Local. "One craft, one union" is the slogan of the craft union. Craft unions dominate the building construction industry and also play an important role in printing and publishing and in the barbering trade. The "tie that binds" a craft union Local is the mastery by its members of an entire recognized trade, such as plumbing, lithography, or barbering.

A worker typically masters a trade by serving an apprenticeship consisting of classroom instruction and on-the-job training of several years' duration. Approximately 800 detailed trades and occupations or crafts are recognized by government, unions, and employers as eligible to participate in the national and state apprenticeship programs. Figure 3–1 lists some apprenticeable trades in various industries and indicates the normal duration of the apprenticeships.

A craft union Local typically seeks to enroll in its membership all practitioners of its trade in the immediate geographic vicinity regardless of who the employers of its members are. That is, a typical Carpenters' Local would seek to organize all the carpenters in Peoria, Illinois, or in Tompkins County, New York. Journeymen carpenters who had served an apprenticeship or acquired journeyman status by long experience would be joined by apprentices in training and carpenter helpers in a single Local union. One of the major functions of this Local might be joint administration of an apprenticeship program with employers of carpenters in the area. An exception to this general rule might occur when a single employer had a large regular force of tradesmen, for example, a Local of the Electrical Workers' Union composed solely of electrical tradesmen employed by a power and light company.

The key man in a craft union is the Business Agent. A full-time paid employee of the Local union, he plays a critical role in the negotiation of the collective bargaining agreement and in its administration.

Bargaining Activities of Craft Locals. The Business Agent is influential in both the *policy-making* and *policy-enforcement* phases of collective bargaining. Policy making consists of negotiating a collective

---

[4] Although some Local unions are truly massive organizations and politicians eagerly seek their endorsements, single Locals are typically inundated even in city elections. For example, the 40,000 members of Ford Local number 600 of the UAW are lost in a metropolitan Detroit electorate approaching 1 million.

FIGURE 3–1

SOME APPRENTICEABLE TRADES AND THE DURATION OF APPRENTICESHIP

Representative Trades in the Building Construction Industry

Bricklayer	3 years	Painter and Decorator	2–4 years
Carpenter	4 years	Plasterer	3–4 years
Cement Mason	3 years	Plumber-Pipefitter	4–5 years
Electrical Worker	4–5 years	Rigger	2 years
Ironworker	2–4 years	Roofer	2–3 years
Lather	2–3 years	Sheet Metal Worker	3–4 years
Millwright	4 years	Stonemason	3 years
Operating Engineer	3–4 years	Tile Setter	3 years

Representative Trades in Printing and Publishing Industry

Electrotyper	5–6 years	Printer	5–6 years
Engraver	4–5 years	Printing Pressman	5–6 years
Lithographer	4–5 years	Rotogravure Engraver	5–6 years
Mailer	4–5 years	Stereotyper	5–6 years
Photoengraver	5–6 years		

Representative Trades in Service Industries

Arborist	3–4 years	Cosmetician	2 years
Barber	2 years	Photographer	3 years
Cook	3 years	Telephone Worker	4 years

Representative Trades in Manufacturing Industry

Aircraft Fabricator	3–4 years	Machinist	4 years
Brewer	2–3 years	Metal Polisher and Buffer	3–4 years
Butcher-Meat Cutter	3 years	Model Maker	4 years
Candy Maker	3–4 years	Pattern Maker (Foundry)	5 years
Draftsman-Designer	3–5 years	Pottery Worker	3 years
Fabric Cutter	3–4 years	Tool- and Die-Maker	4–5 years
Furrier	3–4 years	Upholsterer	3–4 years

SOURCE: U.S. Department of Labor, Manpower Administration, *The National Apprenticeship Program,* 1965, pp. 9–27.

bargaining agreement with the employers of the Local's members. Policy enforcement consists of checking on employer compliance with the terms of the agreement after it has been negotiated.

The Business Agent typically is the chief negotiator for the craft union Local. He and other officers of the Local meet with the representatives of the Employer Association and hammer out a basic collective bargaining agreement. This agreement is then presented to a general membership meeting of the Local where it is ratified or rejected by a vote of the membership. Once ratified this agreement becomes the policy of the signatory employers and the union.

Labor agreements negotiated by craft unions and internal craft union procedures fulfill the four basic functions of: (1) union security and management rights, (2) the wage and effort bargain, (3) individual security, and (4) administration. Typically, union security is achieved by a clause in the agreement which obligates the business agent to refer tradesmen to signatory employers when they seek to hire additional hands. The wage and effort bargain is settled by establishment of a standard union scale of wages and the tradesmen's traditional control over the tempo of his work. Individual security may be defined by the incorporation into the agreement of rules for employee conduct and by union practices in distributing available work among its members. Administration of the agreement is provided for by a system of on-the-job representation and the arbitration of unresolved grievances. The contents of a typical craft-union agreement are discussed in detail in Chapter 7.

The fact that some carpenter employers in the vicinity may not be members of the Employer Association imposes an additional negotiation responsibility on the Business Agent. After the basic agreement is printed, he then visits nonassociation member employers and insists that they sign a document identical to the basic agreement.

On-the-job Representation in Craft Locals. An agreement setting forth wages, hours, and working conditions has been signed between the Local and all the contractors employing carpenters in a given city. In response to the request of one of these contractors, the business agent of the Local sends union members to work on a construction project. The first man he puts on the job customarily acts as "steward" for the Carpenters' union. The business agent chooses him by sending him out first; or, if the policy of the Local is to refer members to jobs on a strict seniority basis, he is the most senior member of the Local who happens to be looking for work. The craft union job steward is chosen, then, either by the business agent or by chance.

On the job, the steward's duty is to make sure that the contractor lives up to his agreement with the union in the way he pays and treats his carpenters. If the steward observes a violation of the agreement (a copy of which the business agent has given him) he calls it to the attention of the foreman in charge of the carpenters. If the foreman does not correct the violation, the steward reports the matter to the business agent, who takes it up with the contractor. The business agent is often empowered to call the carpenters off the job if the contractor does not adjust the grievance, and keep them off until the dispute is settled.

This system constitutes a simple and effective machinery for enforcing the agreement. It gives the business agent, an administrative official of the union, a live contact with every one of the many jobs on which members of his Local are working. He gets information from them, and can pass out information to the members through them. Several points about this system deserve notice.

Stewards representing different unions on a construction job have no official contact with each other, but only with the business agent of their own Local: carpenters with the Carpenters' union, bricklayers with the Bricklayers, and so on. This need not prevent informal consultation between stewards of different unions, but there is little point in such contact since the members of each union work under a separate agreement. There is no one body of union representatives, or channel of communication, for all the workers employed on the construction project in dealings with their common employer. This will appear as one of the significant differences between craft and industrial unions.

All the stewards representing any one union—again the Carpenters, for instance—on all the projects where members are employed make up a potential "council." That is, they could be called together without calling a meeting of the Local, and provide contact with all the working carpenters in town. Calling them together would have little point, however, because each works for a different employer. The only things they would have in common are matters internal to the union; and for the purpose of considering internal union matters a meeting of the Local would serve the same purpose and would have what the steward body would lack—power to take action affecting policy. This will appear as another of the significant differences between craft and industrial unions.

Craft union stewards, furthermore, do not represent the men on the job. They represent the business agent, who is responsible for enforcing the agreement. The steward personnel is constantly changing as the work on one project comes to an end and the men shift to other jobs in new and random groupings.

The practical consequence of all this is that the craft union stewards, as a group, do not constitute a separate, functioning organization within the structure of the Local union and are not a continuing body. They are simply an extension of the authority of the business agent; an extension, in fact, of his person—his eyes and ears on the jobs where the members are employed. They do not influence the nature of collective bargaining.

Craft-union Locals seldom find it necessary to take unresolved grievances to arbitration. Business Agents and employers in handicraft industry share the tradition of the craft and settle their differences among themselves. The Business Agent, as the sole supplier of the employer's critically needed tradesmen, often holds the ace of trumps in these discussions.

The major activities of both craft and industrial Local unions are influencing the wage and effort bargain and establishing a system of individual security. However, their bargains and systems are quite different from each other, as are their organizational structures for achieving these ends.

The Industrial Local. "One shop, one union" is the slogan of the industrial union. Industrial unions dominate manufacturing industry and also play important roles in trade, transportation, finance, and mining. It seems reasonable to expect that industrial unions will play an increasing role in government employment. The "tie that binds" an industrial Local union is the workplace and the workers' common employer. In the industrial union all the employees working for a given enterprise at a given workplace belong to the same Local union without regard for what they do in the plant.

An industrial Local union typically seeks to enroll in its membership all production and maintenance workers at the place of employment, with the legally imposed exceptions of supervisors and guards. Although many industrial Local unions would very much like to obtain representation rights for white-collar workers employed at their plants, such efforts have been largely unsuccessful to date.

Industrial Local unions typically do not employ full-time Business Agents. Instead the major activities of the union are handled by elected officers who also are working employees at the plant. When a full-time professional union man helps an industrial Local he usually is an International Representative, a full-time employee of the International union, not the Local.

Bargaining Activities of Industrial Locals. Perhaps with the assistance of an International Representative, the officers of the industrial Local and a bargaining committee negotiate an agreement with the management of an enterprise. This agreement is then presented to a general membership meeting of the Local where it is ratified or rejected by a vote of the membership. Once ratified this agreement becomes the policy of the employer and the union.

Industrial union collective bargaining agreements are much more comprehensive and complex than craft union agreements, although they fulfill the same four functions as craft bargains, as will be discussed in detail in Chapter 7. Industrial unions achieve union security by a clause in the agreement requiring the employees of the enterprise to pay union dues. The agreement may also contain a lengthy section describing management rights or managerial prerogatives. Industrial unions find it necessary to negotiate an entire structure of wages, perhaps with as many as 50 different wage rates for a wide variety of jobs in contrast to less than half a dozen wage rates found in the typical craft union agreement. While a craft union agreement may make no reference whatsoever to work tempo, an industrial union agreement may contain several pages of principles and rules by which production standards are established and modified. Industrial union agreements invariably contain long sections on seniority and due process designed to provide the industrial worker with the individual security which a craft unionist receives from the internal operating procedures of his Local union. The industrial union agreement also contains detailed provisions for on-the-job representation and the arbitration of certain unresolved grievances.

For the purpose of enforcing or administering its collective bargaining agreement the industrial Local union makes use of a steward system and a grievance committee. The steward system, sometimes called a shop committee, provides on-the-job representation to the members of the union and sometimes assumes the character of a "union within the union."

On-the-Job Representation in Industrial Locals. Shop stewards in an industrial union are elected by the union members in the departments where they work. The term of office is usually six months or a year, but most unions permit a department to depose its steward by majority vote and elect a new one. (This seldom happens, but the fact that it can is supposed to keep the steward on his toes.) The steward's election may be a very informal affair, done by a show of hands at a department meeting held on the shop floor during noon hour, or it may be by a solemn secret ballot vote at the union headquarters. A steward may be re-elected indefinitely.

(1) The Department Steward. The steward is the eyes and ears of the union in the shop, and its voice as well, and its strong right arm. The stewards as a group provide a two-way flow of communication, information, instructions, sentiment, and advice between the union and the members working in the plant, to its remotest reaches. They enforce not only the union agreement, which is company policy, but union discipline. If there is not yet a "union shop" clause in the agreement, requiring all workers to join the union as a condition of employment, the stewards are the union's organizers, all day and every day in the departments, striving to get nonmembers to join the union or to "make 'em wish they had." If there is no checkoff, the stewards collect dues from the union members and turn the money over to the Local. For their trouble, they usually receive a small percentage of what they collect: five or ten cents on the dollar.

Each steward has a personal constituency. He knows the people who elected him, and they know him. They see each other every working day. They look to him for leadership. In case of strike, they rally around him as their picket captain. There could hardly be more direct or personal contact, or greater confidence, between leader and followers. Unlike the foreman, who works for management, the steward is one of the gang. His fellow workers see him as "on our side."

(2) The Steward Council and the Chief Steward. The Steward Council brings together and co-ordinates the efforts of these natural, elected leaders of the working force. It provides the Local with a "line organization" in the shop that is (or can be) as efficient, and more cohesive, than the company's own management hierarchy. It ties the Local organically to the workers in the shop and to shop operations in a dynamic, reciprocal relationship.

Typically—or at any rate, ideally—the union elects a steward wherever members work under the direction of a first-line supervisor. The stewards then elect a Chief Steward from among their ranks. In a shop where there are several echelons of management, such as, for instance, division superintendents under a Works Manager and over groups of department (first-line) foremen, the stewards of a division may select a "Chief Division Steward." If there is a night shift, the night shift stewards will have a Chief Night Steward. All of these smaller "chiefs" are subordinate to *the* Chief Steward. The union's aim is to place a representative opposite every member of line management—to parallel the line organization of the enterprise. The Chief Steward—and through him, the Local union—thus has "line" channels exactly similar and equivalent to management's, which lead into every part of the enterprise where members of the union work under supervision.

The Chief Steward's election by the department stewards has to be ratified by a majority vote of the members of the Local at a union meeting. That is because he is an *ex officio* member of the Grievance Committee, a highly important committee of the Local which deals centrally with the personnel department (or equivalent authority) on matters of administration of the labor agreement. Ratification of the Chief Steward's election by the membership also asserts the Local's discretion and authority over those who are to represent it in official dealings with management, and is a token of the subordination of the stewards to the Local union.

All of the stewards, including the Chief Steward, are and remain full-time working employees of the company. Their election to the job gives them certain special rights and duties, which the union agreement defines. They get their authority, therefore, from the union's agreement with the company, and exercise it within prescribed limits.

(3) The Steward in Grievance Adjustment. The man who wears the badge of a department steward is entitled to take time off his company job without loss of pay, under most agreements, in order to investigate, discuss, and adjust grievances. His name goes to the top of the seniority list in his department, regardless of his actual length of service, so that he is the last man in the department to be laid off if work gets slack. This is called "superseniority." Elected officers of the union also get superseniority in most agreements. The aim is to keep the union administrative apparatus in the shop intact, despite fluctuations in the level of operations, just as the company keeps intact its management cadres. Of course, an individual loses his superseniority if he ceases to be a steward or is not re-elected to union office.

Grievance adjustment, for which the steward is given paid time off, is the primary function stewards perform in the shop. Most grievances consist of claims that the company has failed to live up to the terms of the agreement in its dealings with an individual or a group of workers. The steward is the union watchdog over contract compliance at the department level. For this purpose—and this purpose only—he is the equal of the company foreman who supervises the group that elected him steward. In all other respects he is merely one of the foreman's subordinates, like any other worker in the department.

It has been shown, but may be repeated here, that the union's agreement with the company has the effect of setting *company* policy in the areas it touches. Foremen and supervisors do not *make* policy for the company. They exercise delegated management authority in directing operations in accordance with company policy. Because they hold this delegated authority, workers under their supervision are bound to carry out their instructions and accept their decisions, but if—through error, ignorance, or other causes—these run counter to policy as set forth in the agreement, the union steward files a grievance.

Filing a grievance means that the steward formally requests the foreman to reverse some action he has taken, or do something he has failed to do, or alter some action or decision affecting workers under his supervision. The foreman, whose challenged action stands until he, or someone in authority over him, alters it, then has to decide whether the steward's demand is justified, and should be granted; or unjustified, and should be rejected. If the foreman says yes, that settles the grievance. If he says no, the steward has the choice of dropping the demand, and thereby accepting the foreman's determination of the issue, or sending the case up to the Grievance Committee (see Figure 3–2).

There may be stages, or grievance-procedure "steps" at intermediate levels between the department steward and the Grievance Committee, but these are relatively unimportant. The number of these intermediate (and often superfluous) steps depends on the size of the enterprise and the extent to which management desires to give its various echelons a chance to "get in on the act," and slow down the process. The two really vital steps are the *first*, in the department where the grievance originated, and the one that puts the issue before the executive responsible for *centralized* administration of personnel policy for the enterprise as a whole, usually the personnel director.

If a grievance remains unsettled after it has been appealed to the central personnel department, it goes to the Local union, and the stewards drop out of the case. They do not have the power to make policy decisions. The Local union, which has the power, must decide whether to accept the company's determination of the issue or carry the case up another step to the policy-making level of management and thereafter—or directly—to arbitration or a strike.

Grievance handling is a duty the steward carries out as much for the benefit of the company as for the employees. Its aim is to ensure compliance with company policy. That is the reason most companies pay the union steward for time spent in grievance activity. The steward has other duties for which the company does not pay; duties the union demands of him as part of his job as steward.

(4) The Steward and the Local Union.   Under the chairmanship of the Chief Steward, the department stewards meet together, either on call, or more commonly at regular intervals, to discuss problems that arise in the course of their grievance activity, and other problems bearing upon the union's relation with the company, and the union's internal affairs.

FIGURE 3–2
AN INDUSTRIAL UNION GRIEVANCE PROCEDURE

This diagram represents a four-step grievance procedure in a manufacturing plant with an industrial union steward system. Grievance procedures may have few or many steps. The only essential requirements are at least one policy *administration* step and at least one policy-*making* step. Almost without exception the first policy *administration* step in a grievance procedure is a conference between the supervisor and a steward. The top and final policy-*making* step is either arbitration or a strike.

The department, at the bottom of the diagram, consists of workers managed by a supervisor, who have elected a steward. The supervisor and the steward are responsible for policy *administration*. If a grievance is not settled at the first step, it proceeds upward in the grievance procedure until it is settled. Grievances may enter the process initially at the second step, when they affect more than one department, or as in the case of a peremptory discharge, when the department supervisor has taken action that puts the case out of range of the department steward.

If a grievance remains unsettled until it involves the top management of the company and the Local (and, sometimes, International) union officers, it becomes a policy-*making* matter because of its company-wide implications. Every grievance ultimately must be settled. Over 90 percent of all American collective bargaining agreements provide for arbitration as the final means of settlement of grievances. However, many of these agreements specify that certain grievances are not arbitrable and, consequently, the strike remains as an alternative final policy-*making* step in the grievance procedure.

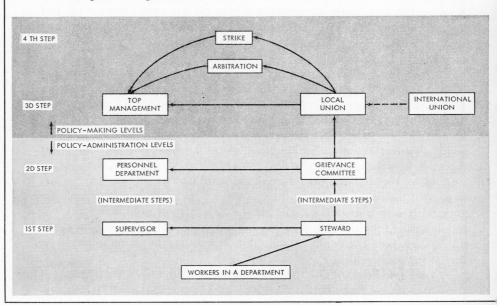

There is often a danger that the Steward Council will encroach upon, or even usurp, the powers of the Local union. Attendance at the Council meetings is sometimes better than at membership meetings of the Local, and the Council is by its nature representative of the whole plant. Whether the Steward Council tail will wag the union dog depends on the strength of leadership of the officers of the Local, who are entitled to attend Steward Council meetings. Most of them are graduates of the Council, and having reached leadership in the chartered Local by way of experience as a steward or Chief Steward, know how to keep the Council in its place.

At Council meetings, members report on events and developments in the shop. A steward whose foreman has rejected a grievance may bring his problem to the Council for advice. The Chief Steward reports on the activities of the Grievance Comittee, and may ask the Council to endorse a recommendation to the Local union on a grievance case unsolved at the last session with the company's personnel department. Officers of the Local explain union policies or outline union programs which the stewards are to support in the shop. As the time for renewing the union agreement rolls around, there is discussion of that. The stewards make suggestions for improving the terms or wording over the old one. After the new agreement is signed, the stewards receive an explanation of its provisions and of the union's interpretation of the way it should be understood. They ask questions about it and plan strategy towards issues that it raises.

The union-linked steward system in industrial relations is unique to the American (U.S. and Canadian) labor movements. Other industrial countries have shop committees operating in the enterprises, but the relation of these committees both to the unions and the workers differs from the steward system. Their existence seems to prove only that some kind of shop committee is a necessity of modern manufacturing and the large enterprise.

The foregoing discussion of craft and industrial Local unions strongly suggests that unaffiliated and totally independent Local unions could influence the wage and effort bargain and negotiate systems of individual security with employers. And, indeed, they can and do. Current membership in such unaffiliated and independent Local unions has been estimated to be as high as 450,000 workers.[5] If unaffiliated, independent Local unions exist and operate, why do most Local unions affiliate with an International union?

The International Union

The typical Local union is a part of an International union. A few present-day Local unions may originally have joined with other Locals in

[5] U.S. Department of Labor, Bureau of Labor Statistics, *Unaffiliated Local and Single-Employer Unions in the United States*, Bulletin No. 1348, 1961.

forming the International union of which they are now a part. Most present-day Locals, however, were themselves organized and established by the International union with which they are affiliated. Even in those instances where a Local took part in the founding of the International, the Local, in so doing, gave up its original identity and took on a new identity by receiving a charter from the International, like any other Local. This charter recognizes, and in a sense *creates*, the Local union.

The International union is a federation of Local unions, usually in the same trade (such as carpentry) or industry (such as steel). The International union stands as "parent" to the Local union, which it creates by issuing a charter. An individual worker does not hold his membership directly in the International union, but in the Local union. The Local union is a "member" of the International. It supports the International financially by contributing a fixed proportion of the dues paid, or "per capita." The amount of per capita is set by the International constitution.

The International union is much like a Local union on a grander scale. Its highest policy-making body is the Convention, called together annually, biennially, or periodically at some other interval according to the provisions of the International constitution. Delegates elected from the Locals, usually with voting rights proportional to the Local membership, take part in the Convention and transact its business. They elect officers and an executive board to act for them between Conventions in accordance with policies and instructions laid down by majority vote in the Convention.

Craft, Industrial, and Mixed International Unions. The fundamental tie between a Local and an International *should* be based on services rendered. An International union composed of craft Locals renders somewhat different services to its constituent Locals than the services rendered by an industrial International to its Locals. Today many International unions have both craft and industrial Locals, a situation which puts considerable stress on their structure or results in the neglect of the needs of the minority group of Locals. In this discussion, International unions composed of significant numbers of both craft and industrial Locals will be referred to as "mixed" Internationals. Internationals composed primarily of craft Locals will be referred to as craft Internationals, while the term industrial International will be applied to Internationals composed primarily of Locals organized on the basis of workplace.

There are approximately 180 International unions in the United States, ranging in size from less than 1,000 affiliated workers to giants claiming over 1 million dues-paying members. Figure 3–3 attempts to classify some of the larger International unions according to the primary organizational units of their constituent Locals: craft, industrial, and mixed. The *sole* criterion for the classification of Internationals shown in Figure 3–3 is the organizational unit of the majority of their constituent Locals. Thus, the United Automobile Workers and the United Steelwork-

FIGURE 3–3
SELECTED INTERNATIONAL UNIONS: NUMBER OF LOCALS, CLAIMED MEMBERSHIP, 1964

Craft Organizations	Locals	Membership
In Manufacturing Industry		
Lithographers and Photoengravers (AFL-CIO)	190	50,000
Printing Pressmen (AFL-CIO)	750	115,589
Typographical Union (AFL-CIO)	756	113,453
In Government		
Fire Fighters (AFL-CIO)	1,058	115,358
Teachers (AFL-CIO)	550	100,000
In Service Industries		
Barbers, Hairdressers, Cosmetologists (AFL-CIO)	850	72,790
Musicians (AFL-CIO)	673	275,254
In Transportation Industries		
Locomotive Engineers (Ind.)	874	40,144
Railroad Trainmen (AFL-CIO)	1,125	185,463
Railway Carmen (AFL-CIO)	898	121,000
In Construction Industry		
Boilermakers, Iron Shipbuilders, Blacksmiths (AFL-CIO)	430	125,000
Bricklayers, Masons, and Plasterers (AFL-CIO)	930	135,168
Carpenters and Joiners (AFL-CIO)	2,800	760,000
Engineers, Operating (AFL-CIO)	335	310,942
Ironworkers, Bridge, Structural and Ornamental (AFL-CIO)	314	142,676
Laborers (AFL-CIO)	899	432,073
Painters, Decorators, and Paperhangers (AFL-CIO)	1,242	199,465
Plumbing and Pipefitting (AFL-CIO)	725	255,765
Sheet Metal Workers (AFL-CIO)	...	100,000
Industrial Organizations		
In Manufacturing Industry		
Automobile Workers (AFL-CIO)	1,264	1,168,067
Clothing Workers (AFL-CIO)	692	377,000
Electrical, Radio, and Machine Workers (AFL-CIO)	552	270,842
Electrical, Radio, and Machine Workers (Ind.)	151	165,000
Garment Workers, Ladies' (AFL-CIO)	463	442,318
Meat Cutters (AFL-CIO)	385	341,366
Mine Workers, District 50 (Ind.)	1,720	210,000
Oil, Chemical, and Atomic Workers (AFL-CIO)	650	162,000
Pulp, Sulphite, and Paper Mill Workers (AFL-CIO)	717	176,048
Rubber, Cork, Linoleum, and Plastic Workers (AFL-CIO)	466	164,661
Steelworkers (AFL-CIO)	3,250	965,000
Textile Workers (AFL-CIO)	643	177,000
In Trade		
Retail Clerks International Association (AFL-CIO)	272	427,555
In Government		
Government Employees (AFL-CIO)	1,105	138,642
Letter Carriers (AFL-CIO)	5,688	167,913
Postal Clerks (AFL-CIO)	6,599	139,000
In Service Industries		
Building Service Employees (AFL-CIO)	371	320,000
Hotel and Restaurant Employees (AFL-CIO)	534	444,581
In Transportation and Public Utilities		
Communications Workers (AFL-CIO)	806	293,000
Maintenance of Way Employees (AFL-CIO)	1,297	121,151
Railway and Steamship Clerks (AFL-CIO)	1,595	270,000
Teamsters (Ind.)	838	1,506,769
Transit Union (AFL-CIO)	387	133,357
Transport Workers (AFL-CIO)	95	135,000
Mixed Organizations		
Electrical Workers, International Brotherhood of (AFL-CIO)	1,719	806,000
Machinists, International Association of (AFL-CIO)	1,934	808,065

SOURCE: U.S. Department of Labor, Bureau of Labor Statistics, *Directory of National and International Labor Unions in the United States, 1965*, Bulletin No. 1493 (April, 1966), pp. 16–33.

ers are classified as *industrial* Internationals, despite the fact that both organizations have Locals in many industries and a few Locals composed of workers who possess an apprenticeable trade. Although the Carpenters' International has a few Locals composed of assembly line workers engaged in the manufacture of furniture, it is classified as a *craft* International because of the predominant role played by its craft affiliates in the building construction industry. The International Brotherhood of Electrical Workers is classified as a "mixed" International because of its extensive apprenticeship orientation in the construction industry paralleled with substantial industrial organization units in the field of public utilities.

Before attempting to differentiate the services provided by craft and industrial Internationals, it is well to discuss the general services which either International might provide to its constituent Locals. To a substantial degree, the difference in services rendered is a matter of the blend of services required by the constituent Locals.

Services Performed by International Unions. The most important service rendered by any International union is organizing the unorganized workers within its jurisdiction. Most Local unions formed in the United States since the 1940's have been organized by the initial expenditure of effort and funds of some parent International union. This means that the International has assigned organizers to the community or place of employment of the potential members, sought to enroll workers in the union, and, frequently, conducted the negotiations with the employers and NLRB prior to obtaining the first collective bargaining agreement. As will be discussed in Chapter 5, this can be a long, difficult, and expensive process. The price that a newly formed Local pays for this service is affiliation with the International union.

Suppose that a Local had been organized by an International in 1942. Why is organizing the unorganized important to that Local in 1967? It really is not very important to the Local or its members *if* the product market served by the employer of the Local's members is fully unionized. On the other hand, any significant number of nonunion competitors poses a vital threat to the conditions of employment that can be established by collective bargaining in unionized enterprises. Even in highly organized industries like automobiles and steel, the International unions spend large sums of money every year for the purpose of maintaining and consolidating a high degree of unionization. If organization is permitted to crumble, Locals will be undercut in their negotiations. Probably the best current example of the impotence of Locals in a partially organized industry is textile manufacturing, where nonunion Southern plants pose a constant threat to the prosperity of unionized textile workers.

Many International unions also provide a variety of expert research, negotiation, and educational services to their constituent Locals. Complex issues such as pensions, health and welfare plans, and the legal intricacies of various hiring hall, strike, and picketing situations require professional research of a variety beyond the competence of the membership of a

Local union. International unions often provide this research and the services of a full-time professional negotiator to their Locals as one of the benefits of affiliation.

One of the initial purposes of unionization in the days before the Wagner Act was the provision of insurance benefits for members at a time when insurance benefits were not readily available in the general market. Some International unions continue to provide these services as supplements to the more recently developed employer-financed insurance and pension arrangements or in the form of retirement homes for members or special union-supported medical centers.

The strike benefits provided by many International unions might be considered to be another form of "insurance." Because of their huge membership base compared to the membership base of any Local union, International unions provide a means of pooling the costs of strikes. A Local union with even 5,000 members has at its disposal relatively insignificant funds for the financing of a strike compared to the taxing power of its parent International with perhaps several hundred thousand potential contributors.

International unions also may perform important political and representational services in behalf of their constituent Locals and their members. Walter Reuther, speaking as the president of a 1-million member UAW, is very likely to get more attention from a congressional committee on social security than a letter written by the president of a 500 member Local union. Among the many political programs important to Local unions and their members are campaigns for minimum wage legislation, social security, workmen's compensation, the income tax, unemployment compensation, and medicare. In many of these fields, the International can provide highly professional representational services at a fraction of the cost of less effective Local efforts.

Services provided by the International are financed from the per capita revenues of the International. The more services provided, the higher the per capita tax must be, and the higher the per capita tax, the less autonomous the Locals and the less influence rank-and-file members of the Locals have on their own fates. Although the members of a Local can properly feel reassured by the promise that the International may pay them substantial strike benefits, the price that must be paid for these benefits is International approval of their proposed strike.

Both craft and industrial Internationals provide bargaining and representational services to their constituent Locals. However, the blend of these services provided, and the degree of autonomy of the two kinds of Locals, differs significantly.

Services Performed by Craft Internationals. Craft union locals tend to have greater autonomy and to receive fewer services from their Internationals than industrial union Locals. This tendency is attributable to the nature of the product market and the history of craft unionism.

As noted above, the Business Agent, a full-time paid employee of the

Local union, plays a key role in craft union bargaining. This role is conditioned by the fact that the product market of craft unions is typically local in nature. Craft unionists earn high hourly rates and pay high union dues which are kept by the Local for the important purposes of negotiating and enforcing the agreement and organizing the unorganized in the community served by the union.

Craft unions have a longer history than industrial unions in the United States. Typically they organized at the Local level first and then affiliated with their International organizations. They have been jealous of their local autonomy and have surrendered very little of it to their Internationals.

Craft Internationals provide important representational services to their Locals by attempting to influence the rules for rule making which have been particularly cumbersome for craft unions since the passage of the Taft-Hartley Act in 1947. Craft Internationals also provide a militant voice for their constituent Locals in the defense of jurisdictional claims within the AFL-CIO. Craft Internationals also play an important role in the national apprenticeship program.

Services Performed by Industrial Internationals.   The typical industrial International provides all the services discussed above for its Local unions in substantial degree. Because of a tradition of "top down" organizing of industrial Locals they typically possess less autonomy than their craft union counterparts.

International unions are completely autonomous bodies usually affiliated with the federation of International unions, the AFL-CIO. Both craft and industrial International unions are members of the AFL-CIO.

The AFL-CIO

The AFL-CIO represents the interests of labor and its constituent International unions at the highest national level. The federation itself engages in no collective bargaining. It serves and advises the Internationals which make it up. Membership by Internationals is voluntary. The federation gets per capita from its member Internationals.

The formation of the merged AFL-CIO in 1955 modified the AFL's traditional policy of noninterference in the internal affairs of constituent Internationals. Under the AFL-CIO constitution International unions can be tried and expelled from the federation if proven corrupt or communist dominated.

The Department of Organization of the AFL-CIO assists affiliated Internationals in the organization of the unorganized. Besides this, various Internationals have co-operated in seeking to organize nonunion areas and enterprises.

In addition to membership in the AFL-CIO itself, most affiliated International unions have elected to pay an additional per capita tax required for affiliation with one or more of the seven trade and industrial departments of the AFL-CIO: (1) Industrial Union Department, (2) Building Trades, (3) Food and Beverage, (4) Maritime Trades, (5) Metal Trades, (6) Railway Employees, and (7) Union Label. Internationals are obligated to pay a department per capita tax which is determined by the number of members coming within the particular department's jurisdiction.

The Industrial Union Department is probably the best financed department in the AFL-CIO and each department is free to manage and finance its own affairs. In some ways, the Industrial Union Department is a "federation within the Federation," since its original membership consisted of unions affiliated with the CIO prior to the AFL-CIO merger in 1955. The Industrial Union Department has been active in co-ordinating the organizing and collective bargaining activities of its constituent Internationals.

Auxiliary Bargaining Elements of Union Structure

Auxiliary elements of union structure which are directly engaged in the negotiation and administration of collective bargaining agreements include: (1) the District, (2) Joint Boards, (3) Conference Boards, and (4) Trade Councils. Although these units appear in only a few industries, they are of great importance in these specific cases.

The District. The District is an administrative division of the International union, usually defined on geographical lines. It has the same structure, on a smaller scale, as the International. Not all Internationals subdivide into Districts, but in some unions the District is a very important and powerful body. The Teamsters' union is an example. Truck hauls on the highway are for the most part more than local but less than nationwide. Certain areas, such as New England, the West Coast, the Chicago area, and the areas around Detroit, Minneapolis, St. Louis, Nashville, and other cities, have well-defined trucking routes that radiate from rail and water terminals of long-distance freight hauling. Effective union control over trucking can best be exercised from the strategic points these terminals create, and must extend over the entire area they serve. Local unions, whose activities cover only a single city, would be impotent beyond their own city limits when trucks took to the road if they did not have the co-operation of other Locals in the area. The District acts as the co-ordinator, and becomes thereby a center of union authority which is much stronger, of course, than any Local; strong enough almost to be independent of the International. District leaders of this union become very powerful figures, as exemplified by Beck, who came to the presidency of the International from the West Coast District, and Hoffa of Detroit, who succeeded him.

Joint Boards. The Joint Board is an affiliation obligatory only in a certain kind of union, the "amalgamated" union. The best examples are the garment workers' unions. In these amalgamations, former separate craft unions have fused into an industrial union International without completely giving up their craft identity. In a given city where there are enterprises of the industry, the Locals elect a Joint Board to carry on collective bargaining for all Locals, since members of each Local are employed in all the firms. The need here is for *joint action* on a common problem.

Joint Boards are seldom formed, and never on an obligatory basis, by Local industrial unions whose members work in separate enterprises with which the separate Locals bargain. They have no need for joint action.

Sometimes Local unions of the same craft form a Joint Board, but this is on a voluntary basis. It occurs in cities which, because of their size or for historical reasons (such as the affiliation of a former independent union in a body with the craft International), support not just one craft Local in a given trade but several. The Joint Board in such cases is a substitute or makeshift for the normal situation of having only one Local union of a craft in a locality and often is a prelude to the actual merger of the Locals that made up the Joint Board.

Conference Boards. Local industrial unions belonging to the *same* International and bargaining with the *same* employer, as in a multiplant manufacturing company, form Conference Boards, under the auspices of the International, to centralize their collective bargaining. Two examples of this would be the General Motors Conference Board of the United Auto Workers and the Westinghouse Conference Board of the International Union of Electrical Workers. The Locals elect delegates who meet before negotiations, draw up a proposed master agreement to cover all the plants of the enterprise, plan strategy, select spokesmen, and then carry out negotiations. After the master agreement has been ratified and signed, each Local negotiates supplements applying the terms of the master agreement to its own separate plant. The Conference Board is not a permanent body, has no constitution or officers, gets no per capita, but usually establishes a permanent "secretariat" at the International headquarters, which is made the responsibility of a specific International officer or representative.

A new variant on the Conference Board organizational element may be emerging in the electrical products industry. Several International industrial unions have collective bargaining relationships with the General Electric Company. In recent years these unions have found bargaining there to be extremely tough and have suspected that the company has played one union off against the others. In order to strengthen their bargaining position these unions, e.g., the International Union of Electrical Workers, the United Autoworkers, and the Machinists, have entered an informal "alliance" that no one union will settle with the company without the concurrence of the other unions.

Trade Councils. Local unions belonging to *different* Internationals in the building construction industry frequently form locality Councils.

The local Building Trades Council groups together the Locals of the construction industry for the purpose of co-ordinating their activities and controlling jurisdictional claims. Facing it, almost inevitably, is to be found an association of building trades employers with a name such as the General Contractors' Association which groups the construction enterprises of the same locality. These two organizations together initiate and oversee the bargaining for the separate trade agreements signed between the Locals and the employer association. Administration of these separate agreements then devolves upon the separate Locals, with the Council (and the Association) standing by to help the Locals and the enterprises keep the wheels turning smoothly.

Districts, Joint Boards, Conference Boards, and Trade Councils are important auxiliary elements of union structure for collective bargaining activity. There are other auxiliary elements of union structure which emerge primarily in political activity.

Auxiliary Political Elements of Union Structure

The City Central and State Central are important political spokesmen for organized labor and engage in a wide variety of welfare activities.

The City Central. The City Central is a federation of Local unions in a given city or county. The AFL City Central traditionally called itself the "Central Trades and Labor Council," and the CIO counterpart the "Industrial Union Council." Now they are merged as AFL-CIO City Councils.

The City Central includes Locals of all the Internationals which have chartered Locals in the area. It does no collective bargaining, but focuses and co-ordinates the activities of organized labor generally in relation to the community. Elected delegates of the various Locals exchange information; engage in programs of mutual aid (such as "Buy Union" campaigns) or they help to organize boycotts of "unfair" firms, give aid to Locals on strike, and carry on other co-operative activities. Elected officers of the City Central represent labor in civic affairs, bring labor influence to bear on local governmental bodies and officials, and advise Local unions on community problems. If a political candidate wants labor's endorsement for his campaign, he tries to get it from the City Central. This in itself wins him few votes, but opens the door for him to the affiliated Locals, the votes of whose members he is courting.

The City Central holds its charter direct from the AFL-CIO and sends a delegate (or delegates) to the AFL-CIO Convention. Through its direct affiliation, it brings news and directives of the federation to the Locals in its community.

It is customary for all AFL-CIO Local unions to join their appropriate City Central. The City Central gets its financial means by a per capita tax on the member Locals.

The State Central. The State Central is a "City Central" on a state-wide scale. It is composed of delegates from Local unions of all Internationals, plus delegates from City Centrals. Some Local unions that maintain affiliation with their City Central do not bother to affiliate with the State Central, which seems more remote for them.

The main activity of the State Central is to bring labor influence to bear on the state legislature and executive. This activity may be very important in connection with such matters as unemployment compensation, workmen's compensation, factory inspection codes, minimum wage legislation, and when the legislature is considering a "right-to-work" law.

THE STRUCTURE OF THE AMERICAN LABOR MOVEMENT

The American labor movement claims about 18 million members in approximately 75,000 local unions. About 85 per cent of this total membership is claimed by the affiliates of the AFL-CIO. Probably somewhere between half and three quarters of all union members belong to industrial Locals as defined in this chapter, with the remainder organized along craft or occupational lines.

Figure 3–4 is a schematic diagram of the structure of the American

FIGURE 3–4

THE STRUCTURE OF THE AMERICAN LABOR MOVEMENT

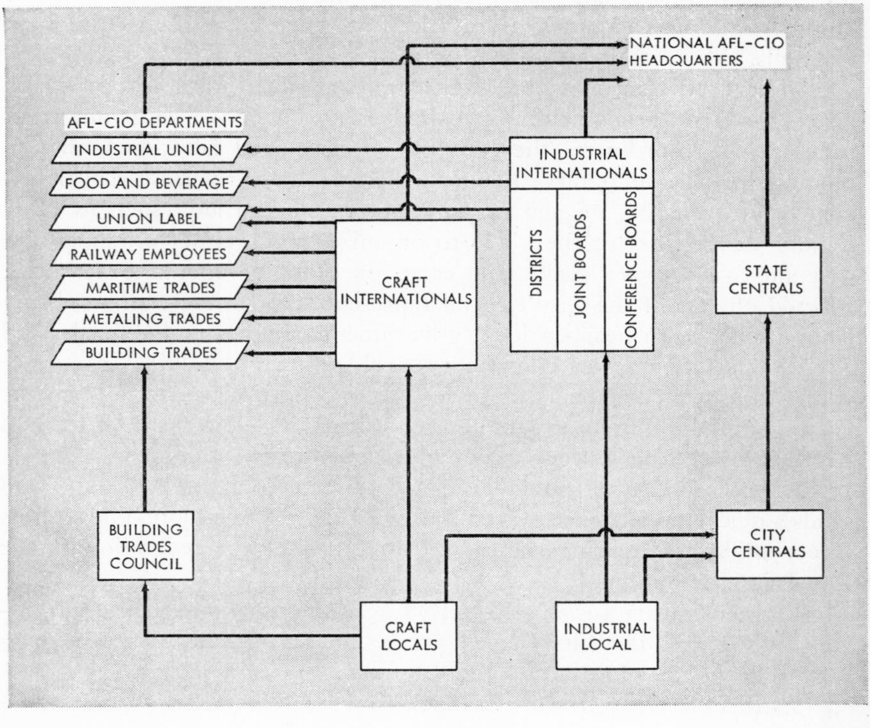

Some Important International Unions Not Affiliated with the American Federation of Labor and Congress of Industrial Organizations

Union	1964 Claimed Membership
Bakery and Confectionery Workers	62,000
Electrical, Radio, and Machine Workers	165,000
Life Insurance Agents	1,900
Rural Letter Carriers	42,300
Locomotive Engineers	40,144
Longshoremen's and Warehousemen's Union	60,000
United Mine Workers' Union	N.A.
United Mine Workers Dist. 50	210,000
Railway Conductors and Brakemen	20,000
Teamsters	1,506,769
Telephone Unions: Alliance of Independent	72,036

labor movement. Organizations shown in the middle and left of this diagram exert most of their efforts in collective bargaining activity, while the organizations shown to the right of the diagram are primarily concerned with representational and political activities.

In Figure 3–4 special attention is called to the membership figures on international and Local unions not affiliated with the AFL-CIO.

Since the beginning, American unions and the American labor movement have concentrated their efforts on the problems of obtaining, keeping, and improving collective bargaining agreements which set the conditions of employment for their members. Representational and political activity has been regarded as a secondary and re-enforcing means of achieving the basic objective of influencing the wage and effort bargain and establishing systems of justice at the workplace. In sharp contrast to the experience in other countries, the present-day AFL-CIO could hardly be called a "movement" dedicated to sweeping economic and political reconstruction of the whole society. The organizational structure which has evolved seems well suited to the achievement of these "bread-and-butter" objectives.

In what sectors of the economy does the labor movement exert direct influence on the conditions of employment and how powerful is the influence exerted? Unfortunately, this very basic question cannot be answered with much statistical authority because of the paucity of data.

Industrial Distribution of Union Membership

Over 40 per cent of all American union members are employed in three major industry groups—metal and machinery, transportation, and construction. Other industry groups with at least 1 million members each are food and tobacco, clothing and leather, transportation equipment, and retail and wholesale trade.

The U.S. Bureau of Labor Statistics is unable to provide detailed data on the extent of union membership by industry, e.g., that 90 percent of employment in over-the-road trucking is unionized. Instead, it only is able to list industry groupings in rank order of unionization as follows:

1. Transportation
2. Contract Construction
3. Transportation Equipment
4. Food, beverages, tobacco
5. Telephone and telegraph
6. Mining and quarrying
7. Electric and gas utilities
8. Furniture, lumber, wood products, and paper
9. Clothing, textiles, and leather products
10. Metals, machinery and equipment, except transportation equipment
11. Stone, clay, and glass
12. Printing and publishing
13. Petroleum, chemicals, and rubber
14. Government
15. Service industries
16. Trade
17. Finance and insurance
18. Agriculture and fishing

The Bureau further estimates that about one half of manufacturing employment is unionized, as compared with one fourth of nonmanufacturing and one seventh of government employment.[6] These estimates tend to understate substantially the significance of union influence because: (1) they are estimates of union membership while the coverage of collective bargaining agreements would be larger (unfortunately, it is impossible to say how much larger), (2) the divisor of each estimate includes employees whom unions do not seek to represent, e.g., managerial and salaried employees who frequently represent as much as 50 per cent of an enterprise's employment,[7] and (3) some enterprises provide employment conditions parallel to unionized enterprises for the purposes of remaining non-union.

Geographical Influence of the Labor Movement

The geographical distribution of union membership is important both as a measure of political influence and as an indication of the significance of organized labor in the economies of the several states. Union officials argue that certain areas, e.g., the South, are particularly hard to organize because of local custom.

Union membership is heavily concentrated in a few states having the largest number of workers in nonagricultural establishments. In 1964, six states, New York, California, Pennsylvania, Illinois, Ohio, and Michigan, accounted for 55 per cent of the nation's total union membership.[8]

[6] U.S. Department of Labor, Bureau of Labor Statistics, *Directory of National and International Labor Unions in the United States, 1965*, Bulletin No. 1493, pp. 55–57.

[7] Unfortunately, no data are available on the extent of "organizable" employment within industries. A *crude* approximation could be made from the ratio of production employees to total employment. Such data are not available for transportation, telephone and telegraph, government, services, finance and insurance, and agriculture and fishing. Of the other industries listed here, the percentages range from a low of 63 percent in printing and publishing to a high of 89 percent in clothing, textiles, and leather products.

[8] *Ibid.*, p. 58.

The top-ranking states in terms of total membership are not necessarily those in which unions have scored their greatest penetration among nonfarm employees. As shown in Figure 3–5, New York ranked third, California ranked thirteenth, and Pennsylvania ranked sixth in terms of degree of union penetration. The highest proportions of unionized workers were recorded in Washington, West Virginia, New York, Michigan,

FIGURE 3–5

UNION MEMBERSHIP AS A PROPORTION OF NONAGRICULTURAL EMPLOYMENT BY STATES, 1964

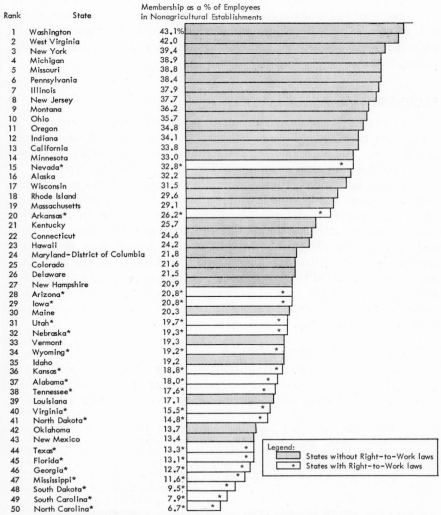

Rank	State	Membership as a % of Employees in Nonagricultural Establishments
1	Washington	43.1%
2	West Virginia	42.0
3	New York	39.4
4	Michigan	38.9
5	Missouri	38.8
6	Pennsylvania	38.4
7	Illinois	37.9
8	New Jersey	37.7
9	Montana	36.2
10	Ohio	35.7
11	Oregon	34.8
12	Indiana	34.1
13	California	33.8
14	Minnesota	33.0
15	Nevada*	32.8*
16	Alaska	32.2
17	Wisconsin	31.5
18	Rhode Island	29.6
19	Massachusetts	29.1
20	Arkansas*	26.2*
21	Kentucky	25.7
22	Connecticut	24.6
23	Hawaii	24.2
24	Maryland–District of Columbia	21.8
25	Colorado	21.6
26	Delaware	21.5
27	New Hampshire	20.9
28	Arizona*	20.8*
29	Iowa*	20.8*
30	Maine	20.3
31	Utah*	19.7*
32	Nebraska*	19.3*
33	Vermont	19.3
34	Wyoming*	19.2*
35	Idaho	19.2
36	Kansas*	18.8*
37	Alabama*	18.0*
38	Tennessee*	17.6*
39	Louisiana	17.1
40	Virginia*	15.5*
41	North Dakota*	14.8*
42	Oklahoma	13.7
43	New Mexico	13.4
44	Texas*	13.3*
45	Florida*	13.1*
46	Georgia*	12.7*
47	Mississippi*	11.6*
48	South Dakota*	9.5*
49	South Carolina*	7.9*
50	North Carolina*	6.7*

Legend:
States without Right-to-Work laws
[*] States with Right-to-Work laws

SOURCE: U.S. Department of Labor, Bureau of Labor Statistics, *Directory of National and International Labor Unions in the United States, 1965,* Bulletin No. 1493, p. 58.

Missouri, Illinois, New Jersey, Montana, and Ohio. Figure 3–5 dramatically reveals the low percentages of union penetration into the economy of the South and, in general, states having right-to-work laws.

Collective bargaining as traditionally defined takes place between employers and employees organized into unions. In the main, unionists are hourly rated employees engaged in blue-collar occupations.[9] Exclusive concentration on traditional collective bargaining overlooks another very important aspect of the world of work—people engaged in white-collar and professional occupations either as self-employed entrepreneurs or as employees. Professional and white-collar occupations are growing more rapidly than the labor force as a whole. Organizations of persons engaged in professional and white-collar occupations are in a state of ferment and it is reasonable to expect that organizational activity in these areas will expand as these occupations continue to increase their significance in the national economy.

PROFESSIONAL ASSOCIATIONS

In 1965 one eighth of all United States workers were engaged in what have been loosely defined as professional, technical, and related occupations. These occupations—employing about 8.9 million people—accounted for more than one quarter of all white-collar employment.[10]

People in administrative and related occupations who run the nation's businesses and manage a wide variety of other organizations, both private and governmental, numbered more than 7,500,000 in 1965. This classification includes corporate officers, supervisors, industrial foremen, and persons who direct the work of others. All of these people are specifically *excluded* from the discussion of professional people here. This exclusion is based on the indefiniteness of educational requirements for entering this field, the lack of licensing requirements, and a belief that economic progress is dependent upon maintaining freedom of enterprise in the form of open entry to managerial positions.

Characteristics of a Profession

Neither white-collar occupations nor professional occupations are easy to define. There are few, if any, white-collar or professional "industries" because industries must be defined in terms of the product produced

[9] The Bureau of Labor Statistics estimates that 14.4 percent of the union members in 1964 were engaged in white-collar occupations. Three quarters of all white-collar members were in 40 International unions where they comprised at least 70 percent of each International's membership. *Ibid.*, p. 54.

[10] U.S. Department of Labor, Bureau of Labor Statistics, *Occupational Outlook Handbook: 1966–67 Edition*, Bulletin No. 1450, p. 23. If the definition of a profession were limited to clergy, physicians, lawyers, teachers, engineers, registered nurses, and certified public accountants, this figure would shrink to about 4 million. See Figure 3–6.

or service rendered. Medical care and education would appear to be identifiable professional industries, but the identification is blurred by the fact that large segments of both industries are government operated. Some professionally qualified persons practice their professions as employees of nonprofessional enterprises, many sole proprietorships are found in the practice of medicine, nonprofit private institutions play a major role in both industries, and both industries employ significant numbers of persons in subprofessional occupations.

An attempt to define professions on the basis of the professional qualifications of the persons engaged in particular occupations is almost as frustrating as the attempt to identify professional industries. Almost everybody wants to be called a professional and almost every occupation or career field has staked out a claim to professional status. Thus, any definition of a profession is arbitrary. It seems best to start with a very restrictive definition. From this base additional occupations can be added, but it should be recognized that each addition dilutes the basic definition.

For purposes of this discussion, a profession is an occupation with *all* of the following characteristics: (1) the requirement of a postgraduate college education, (2) governmental licensing of practitioners of the profession, (3) a primary commitment to the service of humanity by the members of the profession, (4) the acceptance of a code of ethics by the members of the profession, and (5) the existence of a professional association dedicated to the enforcement of the code of ethics. Only a handful of occupations approximate the requirements for professional status enumerated here, i.e., physicians, dentists, lawyers, and clergymen. As the requirements for professional status are relaxed, occupations such as engineering, teaching, certified public accountants, pharmacy, registered nursing, and social work would be included in the professions. From this second wave, the professions flow outward through such categories as chartered life underwriter, certified professional secretary, certified shopping center manager, ultimately to "professional prize fighter."

Professional Occupations and Educational Requirements

Figure 3–6 reveals 1965 employment in the major professional occupations. Employment in the basic professions of religion, medicine, and law totals less than 1 million persons. Elementary, secondary, and college teaching employs over 2 million persons. Engineering and technical employment approaches 2 million. Both accounting (not limited to certified public accountants) and registered nursing are larger occupational callings than any one of the basic professions.

The educational preparation required for entry into the ministry has a wider range than that for most professions. Some religious groups have no formal educational requirements, and others ordain persons who have received varying amounts of training in liberal arts colleges, Bible colleges, or Bible institutes. An increasingly large number of denominations,

FIGURE 3–6

EMPLOYMENT IN SELECTED PROFESSIONAL OCCUPATIONS AND MEMBERSHIP IN RELATED ORGANIZATIONS

Occupation	Employment*	Related Organization(s)†	Membership†
Teachers			
Elementary and Secondary	1,850,000	National Education Association‡	813,000
		American Federation of Teachers§	100,000
College	200,000	American Association of University Professors	62,000
Engineers	1,000,000	American Institute of Electrical and Electronic Engineers‖	156,500
		American Society of Mechanical Engineers‖	59,500
		American Society of Civil Engineers‖	49,000
		American Institute of Aeronautics and Astronautics‖	36,000
		American Institute of Chemical Engineers‖	22,000
Registered Engineers	250,000	National Society of Professional Engineers‖	60,000
Registered Nurses	550,000	American Nursing Association	170,000
Clergymen	300,000	No relevant organization	
Physicians	275,000	American Medical Association	176,000
Lawyers	275,000	American Bar Association	115,000
Dentists	100,000	American Dental Association	100,000
Certified Public Accountants	80,000	American Institute of Certified Public Accountants	48,000

NOTES: * U.S. Department of Labor, Bureau of Labor Statistics, *Occupational Outlook Handbook*, 1966–67 Edition, Bulletin No. 1450, pp. 23, 72.
† Frederick G. Ruffner, Jr., R. C. Thomas, Ann Underwood, and H. C. Young (eds.), *Encyclopedia of Associations*, Vol. 1 (Detroit: Gale Research Company, 1964).
‡ NEA membership includes elementary and secondary schoolteachers, college and university professors, administrators, principals, counselors, and others interested in education. Bulk of membership composed of elementary and secondary teachers and administrators.
§ U.S. Department of Labor, Bureau of Labor Statistics, *Directory of National and International Labor Unions in the United States*, 1965, Bulletin No. 1493, p. 32.
‖ Membership includes students.

however, require a three-year course of professional study in theology following college graduation.

Physicians, attorneys, and dentists face substantial educational requirements. Physicians must complete a four-year course in a medical school after three or four years of premedical college training. In 32 states, physicians must also complete a one-year internship in a hospital before being licensed to practice medicine. Lawyers are admitted to the bar by a written examination which is taken after graduation from an approved four-year law school course which is preceded by three or four years of prelaw college training. Dentists obtain a license by examination after the completion of a four-year approved dental school program. A minimum of two years of predental college work is required for admission to dental school.

Of all the professions, teaching is the largest, and no other profession offers so many employment opportunities for women. Almost 1,500,000 women are teachers, more than twice the number employed in nursing, the second largest field of professional employment for women. Only about one fifth of all college and university teachers are women.[11] The large number of women in elementary and secondary school teaching might have a significant effect on the behavior of teacher organizations. It is frequently said that women are hard to organize into unions because they look on their employment as a short-time experience preparatory to marriage or as a second career after their children are reared. To the extent that women teachers are secondary breadwinners this fact would tend to reduce their militancy. On the other hand, labor force participation rates for women are steadily rising, women now represent a majority of the adult population, and, as a result, steadily increasing numbers of them are undertaking lifetime employment careers.

All states require every teacher in the public elementary and secondary schools to hold a certificate issued by the State Department of Public Instruction. Several states have this same requirement for teachers in parochial and other private elementary and secondary schools. In 1964, 45 states and the District of Columbia issued regular teaching certificates only to persons with at least four years of approved college preparation.[12] Although college teachers are not required to possess teaching certificates, a master's degree is usually required to qualify for beginning positions in college teaching.

Engineering and technical occupations provide employment for approximately 2 million persons.[13] Approximately 1 million persons are considered to be "engineers," more than half of them employed in manufacturing industry. A bachelor's degree in engineering is the generally accepted educational requirement for entrance into engineering occupations. Although some persons without a degree are able to become engineers after long experience in a related occupation, more and more engineering specialties are now requiring postgraduate college training. All 50 states and the District of Columbia have laws providing for the licensing (or registration) of those engineers whose work may affect life, health, or property. In 1964, about 250,000 engineers were registered under these laws in the United States. Generally, registration requirements include graduation from an accredited engineering curriculum, plus at least four years of experience and the passing of a state examination. Examining

[11] *Ibid.*, p. 210.

[12] *Ibid.*, p. 212.

[13] This figure includes approximately 900,000 engineering and science technicians and excludes 400,000 scientists. Jobs as engineering and science technicians usually require post-high school education but less than a college degree. Technicians frequently do work which otherwise would be assigned to engineers. Work as a scientist almost always requires a minimum of a bachelor's degree. Neither scientists nor engineering and science technicians are registered or certified by state agencies.

boards may accept a longer period of experience as a substitute for a college degree.[14]

A license is required to practice professional nursing in all states and in the District of Columbia. To obtain a license, a nurse must have graduated from a school approved by a state board of nursing and pass a state board examination. Approved schools of nursing require a minimum of two years' study beyond high school graduation.

All states require that anyone practicing in the state as a certified public accountant hold a certificate issued by the State Board of Accountancy. Almost half the states have laws that will, by 1970, require CPA candidates to be college graduates.[15]

The professional and managerial occupational groups engaged 8 in every 10 workers with a college education in 1964. Both the numbers of college graduates and their concentration in these occupational groups is steadily increasing. Projections prepared by the United States Office of Education in 1964 indicate an increase from 502,104 bachelor's degrees granted in 1964 to 731,000 in 1970 to 815,000 in 1975. According to the same projections, the number of master's degrees conferred per year may exceed 160,000 and the doctorates may approach 25,000 per year in 1975.[16]

Ethics, Licensing, and the Role of the Professional Association

All of the occupations discussed here are based on a primary commitment of their practitioners to the service of humanity. Unethical conduct by a member of one of these professions will result in his disbarment from practice, usually by revocation of his license. In unlicensed professions like the clergy and college teaching, disbarment procedures may be less formalized but they are operational.

Each of the professional associations shown in Figure 3–6 has a committee or commission on ethical standards and a similar group responsible for advising schools and licensing agencies on educational standards. Members and officers of the appropriate professional association serve as members of examining and licensing boards for their professions and as judges in disbarment proceedings.

Clearly the primary purpose of licensing requirements and ethical standards is to protect the public from incompetent and unscrupulous practice of professions which vitally affect the physical, mental, and spiritual health of humanity. At the same time, the number of persons licensed to practice a particular profession has a profound effect on the price of professional services and the economic welfare of the seller of those services. Each of the professional associations listed in Figure 3–6 has a committee or commission on the economic status of the profession. Are

14 *Ibid.*, p. 72.
15 *Ibid.*, p. 29.
16 *Ibid.*, pp. 24–25.

collective bargaining practices applicable to the maintenance and improvement of the economic status of members of the professions?

The Professions and Collective Bargaining

Professional people would turn to collective bargaining practices only if they felt that their economic status were deteriorating or that, as employees, they needed an individual security system providing job rights and a procedure for due process. Two developments in the economy in the last 20 years suggest that professionals would be well advised to consider what aspects of collective bargaining practices would be useful to them. The first development is the success of unionism in substantially upgrading the status of blue-collar workers. Today union members possess through collective bargaining many of the economic benefits and status symbols which 20 years ago were the sole possession of professionals and white-collar workers, e.g., paid vacations, pensions, severance pay, and hourly wage guarantees which approach the security provided by a salary. Although the conditions of professionals have improved substantially over the last 20 years, the success of unions has narrowed the gap between professionals and union members. In some cases union members have outstripped the incomes of professionals. The second development is the changing structure of markets for the sale of professional services.

The applicability of collective bargaining practices to professionals is dependent upon the market structure for the sale of professional services and the ideology of professionals. Market structures and ideology tend to interact.

The Markets for Professional Services. The markets for professional services are conglomerate. Physicians, lawyers, and certified public accountants typically offer their services on an *ad hoc* basis to anyone needing them; most physicians, lawyers, and CPA's are entrepreneurs and employers rather than employees. In sharp contrast, most teachers, engineers, and nurses practice their professions as employees of a school, business, or hospital. There are many exceptions to both rules, but the professions do seem to divide between entrepreneurs and employees. Within both classifications the structure of markets is dynamic.

The dynamism of markets for professional services is well illustrated in the practice of medicine. Thirty years ago, practically all medical service was sold on an *ad hoc* fee for service basis, the fee being paid directly by the recipients of the service. Today most physicians perform a large portion of their work for Blue Shield and private insurance companies, frequently being paid according to a schedule of fees established by the insuring agency. Under the recent medicare amendments to Social Security, it is reasonable to expect that physicians will be receiving an increasing proportion of their income from sources other than the recipients of services. Prices are influenced by the structure of the market. It hardly seems an exaggeration to say that the market for medical care is undergoing dramatic change from almost atomistic competition between buyers a generation ago toward something approaching monopsony in the foreseeable future. The problems of a seller in a monopsonistic market are not too different from the problems of an employee.

To the extent that physicians, lawyers, and CPA's can learn anything from collective bargaining practice, their "text" would be the program of craft unions. Their economic interests could best be served by maintaining very high standards for admission to the profession, the collective withdrawal of service, and tight control over the methods of "production" in their "industry." Through licensing requirements and a code of professional ethics, they possess the means needed to accomplish their economic ends, as well as to fulfill their basic commitments to the service of humanity.

Teachers, engineers, nurses, and other employed professions have a legitimate interest not only in their salaries but also in a system of individual security which provides job rights and due process. The need for a system of individual security seems to intensify as the size of the employing institution increases and the mobility of its employees declines. Thus the need for a system of individual security seems to loom particularly large in nursing and teaching. One would expect organizations like the National Education Association, the American Federation of Teachers, the American Association of University Professors, the engineering societies, and the American Nursing Association to take an "industrial union" view of their "industries."

At the time that these words are being written, elementary and secondary education are in a national state of ferment with the American Federation of Teachers, an out-and-out union, and the National Education Association, a professional association whose membership includes principals, administrators, and others interested in education as well as teachers, vying with each other in many communities to prove who can bargain best for teachers. In this ferment, the issues are not limited to salaries but include such items as teaching loads, tenure policies, the assignment of teachers to "subprofessional" duties, and the claims to preferential assignment within school districts based on length of service. In a more restrained but nevertheless persistent manner, the American Association of University Professors is pressing for more faculty participation in the government of institutions of higher learning and giving wide publicity to institutional differences in salary levels. The American nurses' association's economic security program authorizes state associations to act as exclusive spokesmen for nurses and encourages them to develop bargaining techniques. In several states, state associations have negotiated formal written agreements with individual hospitals and hospital associations. With the exceptions of the American Association of University Professors and the engineering societies, the basic issues for the employed professionals are almost a carbon copy of the basic industrial union program.

Despite the ferment among professionals, which appears to run deep, there are several strong ideological deterrents to the overnight emergence of a professional (labor) movement. These deterrents are the interpretation of professional ethics by the individual members of the respective professions, the law, and public opinion. Each of these deterrents merits some discussion.

Ethics as a Deterrent to Unionism. All of the professions discussed here are based on a service to humanity, but the severity of human needs for these services varies between the professions and within the professions. The most severe need of humanity is for medical care *at the instant* of serious illness or injury. Some medical needs are less essential and can wait for some time before they are treated. It is a terrifying thought, but nevertheless a genuine possibility, that a community could survive for some time if its physicians chose to provide only "essential" medical services. Although society's need for legal and educational services is basic, these needs are deferrable. The ethics of a profession ultimately must come to grips with the question of propriety of a strike or its equivalent—the mass withholding of the services of the profession for the purpose of improving the economic condition of its practitioners.

The strike issue seems to be central to the question of unionization of professionals. During 1965 and 1966 some physicians and a good many teachers concluded that their personal interpretation of the ethics of their profession justified strike activity. Although teachers' "professional days," mass "sick leaves," and strikes engendered a good deal of bitterness in many communities and certainly created some conflicts for teachers who are also parents, it appears that at least some teachers have decided to take direct action.

The Law as a Deterrent to Unionism. Teachers and nurses employed by government or nonprofit hospitals have no legally protected right to organize under federal law, i.e., their employers have the right to discharge them for union activity. All federal employees and most state employees are specifically denied the right to strike. This means that any union activity by these groups must take the form of lobbying activity or persuasion based on public opinion.

Public Opinion as a Deterrent to Unionism. Present-day methods of communication and the market structure for professional services have a strong impact on public opinion. The government and private foundations have generated a good deal of information on the teacher shortage and vital role played by hospitals in community welfare. The steady stream of public information generated by these sources probably has developed some public sympathy for the plight of teachers and hospital employees. At the same time, fees for medical and hospital services have been undergoing a change from a *personal* fee-for-service experience to an insurance premium (frequently paid by the employer) or governmentally provided services. These concurrent developments probably have a net effect of substantially reducing public resistance to improved compensation and conditions of employment for members of the profession. If present, the reduced resistance tends to relieve professionals from taking the strike route to improved conditions of employment. Public resistance to strikes by professionals who hold the welfare of the community in their hands remains strong.

SUMMARY

This chapter has examined the structure of unions and professional associations as instruments for achieving the goals of employees in collective bargaining. Craft union Locals and industrial union Locals have somewhat different goals in collective bargaining and differ radically in their organizational structures.

At the local level union structure is greatly influenced by the structure of enterprises in particular industries. Industrial union Locals need complex organizational structures to match the generally large employers with whom they bargain. Craft union Locals on the other hand are organized in such a way as to provide service to workers who have intermittent employment with many relatively small employers.

Above the Local level, union structure is conglomerate. In general, industrial International unions provide more service to, and exert more control over, their constituent Locals, which operate in national product markets, than craft International unions do over their constituent Locals, which operate in local product markets.

The political and representational interests of union members are served by the AFL-CIO, the State Federation, and City Central organizations. None of these organizations is homogeneous in terms of either the industrial attachment or of the occupational calling of the workers who form their ultimate constituency.

Some professional associations can be expected to follow the craft union form while other professions will use the structure and techniques of industrial unions.

QUESTIONS FOR DISCUSSION

1. The text argues that the enterprise and the Local union are the most important elements in American collective bargaining. Some American scholars argue that the International is the most important element of the labor movement while others focus on the Local. Discuss the rationale of choosing either the Local or International for study.
2. American unions seem to put somewhat less emphasis on representational activities than do their counterparts in other countries. Why? Do automation, chronic unemployment, and recent developments in social security

suggest that representational activities by American unions will increase in significance?

3. Assume that an independent Local union has been collecting per capita monthly dues of $5 and that this Local has been invited to affiliate with an AFL-CIO International. If it affiliates, its $5 income will be allocated as follows: (1) for the Local union, $2.90; (2) for the International, $2; (3) from the International's $2, 10 cents to the AFL-CIO; (4) to the State Federation, 5 cents; and (5) to the City Central, 5 cents. Carefully show why affiliation would be a "good buy" or a "bad buy" on the basis of benefits received in exchange for payments made.

4. Both the AFL-CIO and International unions perform lobbying activities at the national level. Sometimes congressmen are confronted with *conflicting* labor representation, e.g., the AFL-CIO generally has supported freer trade and lower tariffs while some of its International unions have argued for higher tariffs in their particular industry. As a congressman, how would you react to this conflicting testimony? Why? What kinds of problems does this situation cause for the AFL-CIO president?

CASES: 4, 5, 6.

SELECTED ANNOTATED BIBLIOGRAPHY

BAMBRICK, JAMES J., JR., and HAAS, GEORGE H. *Handbook on Union Government and Procedures.* New York: National Industrial Conference Board Studies in Personnel Policy No. 150, 1955.

    Examination of 194 American union constitutions and the proposed constitution of the then divided AFL-CIO.

————. *Sourcebook of Union Government Structure and Proceedings.* New York: National Industrial Conference Board, 1956.

    A companion volume to the *Handbook,* the *Sourcebook* summarizes the 194 union constitutions and contains verbatim texts of pertinent sections of these constitutions.

BARBASH, JACK. *Labor's Grass Roots: A Study of the Local Union.* New York: Harper & Bros., 1961.

    A description of the organization and functions of the local union, its scope and evolution, its formal constitutional foundations, and its relationships to the international union, other unions, and city and state labor federations. Membership characteristics and attitudes, duties and behavior of business agents, stewards, and other leaders; and internal conflict, controversy, and democracy in the local are studied.

————. *The Practice of Unionism.* New York: Harper & Bros., 1956.

    Examines the reasons why workers join unions and why unions seek to organize; methods by which unions are governed and administered; the nature of collective bargaining; the role of the professional in union affairs; the problem of communism and racketeering; and the challenge to union leadership today.

———— (ed.). *Unions and Union Leadership: Their Human Meaning.* New York: Harper & Bros., 1959.

    A collection of articles representing the views and comments of a wide range of observers. The material covers both such broad concerns as the status of the labor movement today, where it is headed, its impact on society, and also more specific issues as the bargaining relationship, racketeering, communist penetration, the Negro worker in unions, and government intervention.

ESTEY, MARTEN S. "The Strategic Alliance as a Factor in Union Growth," *Industrial and Labor Relations Review*, Vol. IX (October, 1955), pp. 41–53.

A study of interunion alliances in the retail trades. Relates growth of retail union membership to the "strategic alliance" between weaker retail unions and unions having control over strategic positions such as truck drivers, warehousemen, and retail butchers.

GALENSON, WALTER (ed.). *Trade Union Monograph Series*. New York: John Wiley & Sons, 1962.

Each volume in this series describes the government of a major American trade union. The emphasis is on those aspects of government which may be said to further or retard internal democracy. The volumes in this series are:

> HARRINGTON, MICHAEL. *The Retail Clerks.*
>
> HOROWITZ, MORRIS A. *The Structure and Government of the Carpenters' Union.*
>
> KRAMER, LEO. *Labor's Paradox—The American Federation of State, County, and Municipal Employees AFL-CIO.*
>
> PERLMAN, MARK. *Democracy in the International Association of Machinists.*
>
> ROMER, SAM. *The International Brotherhood of Teamsters: Its Government and Structure.*
>
> ROTHBAUM, MELVIN. *The Government of the Oil, Chemical and Atomic Workers Union.*
>
> SEIDMAN, JOEL. *The Brotherhood of Railroad Trainmen: The Internal Political Life of a National Union.*
>
> STIEBER, JACK. *Governing the UAW.*
>
> ULMAN, LLOYD. *The Government of the Steel Workers' Union.*

HARDMAN, J. B. S., and NEUFELD, MAURICE F. (eds.). *The House of Labor.* New York: Prentice-Hall, Inc., 1951.

More than 40 union officials contributed papers on the internal operations of labor unions. Divided into eight parts (American labor movement; unions and political activity; American labor abroad; union publicity and public relations; union research and engineering; welfare, health, and community services; union administration; union education activity; the union staff), this volume is a most comprehensive collection on union organization in the United States.

KENNEDY, VAN DUSEN. *Nonfactory Unionism and Labor Relations.* Berkeley: University of California, West Coast Collective Bargaining Systems Series, 1955.

A study of service-industry unions on the West Coast. Author emphasizes the differences between "factory" and "nonfactory" labor relations. Professor Kennedy's emphasis might be compared with the "industrial union" and "craft union" distinction drawn in this book.

MILLIS, HARRY A., and MONTGOMERY, ROYAL E. *Organized Labor.* New York: McGraw-Hill Book Co., Inc., 1945.

Volume III of the authors' brilliant Economics of Labor series, this book covers labor history through the early 1940's, union government, structure, and policies. Reference to this volume should be one of the early steps in any research undertaking on American unionism.

"Professional and White Collar Unionism: An International Comparison. A Symposium," *Industrial Relations*, Vol. 5 (October, 1965), pp. 37–150.

Contents are as follows:

KASSALOW, EVERETT M. "The Prospects for White Collar Union Growth."

BEN-DAVID, JOSEPH. "Professionals and Unions in Israel."

PRANDY, KEN. Professional Organization in Great Britain."

FIVELSDAL, EGIL. "White-Collar Unions and the Norwegian Labor Movement."

MARTIN, ROSS M. "Australian Professional and White-Collar Unions."

LEVINE, SOLOMON B. "The White-Collar, Blue-Collar Alliance in Japan."

FUHRIG, WOLF D. "A Quasi-Union: West Germany University Association."

STRAUSS, GEORGE. "The AAUP as a Professional Occupational Association."

INGERMAN, SIDNEY. "Employed Graduate Students Organize at Berkeley."

ROBERTS, BENJAMIN C. *Unions in America: A British View*. Research Report Series No. 96, Princeton University Industrial Relations Section, 1959.

A discussion by a leading British authority on labor problems of such contemporary labor issues as corruption in unions, the impact of unions on price inflation, internal union democracy, and the political role of unions.

SAYLES, LEONARD, and STRAUSS, GEORGE. *The Local Union*. New York: Harper & Bros., 1953.

Based on extensive field research, this volume presents a penetrating insight of the place of the local union in the industrial plant.

SEIDMAN, JOEL, and CAIN, GLEN G. "Unionized Engineers and Chemists: A Case Study of a Professional Union," *Journal of Business* (University of Chicago), Vol. 37 (July, 1964), pp. 238–57.

Presents a case study of unionism among professional engineers and chemists in a large oil refinery to learn their view of unionism and to compare it with the concept held by blue-collar workers.

STRAUSS, GEORGE. "Professional or Employee-Oriented; Dilemma for Engineering Unions," *Industrial and Labor Relations Review*, Vol. 17 (July, 1964), pp. 519–33.

Hypothesizes that the tension among engineers between a professional and an employee orientation is reflected in their union organizations and is a principal source of the hardship these have encountered.

————. *Unions in the Building Trades: A Case Study*. Buffalo, N.Y.: University of Buffalo Series No. 24, 1958.

A field study of building trades unions in a community of 400,000 population. Major emphasis is placed on the functions and attitudes of business agents.

TAFT, PHILIP. *The Structure and Government of Labor Unions*. Cambridge, Mass.: Harvard University Press, 1954.

An in-depth study of union elections, dues, discipline, and appeals. Essays on the internal procedures of the unlicensed seafaring unions, the Autoworkers, the Steelworkers, and the Teamsters.

U.S. DEPARTMENT OF LABOR, BUREAU OF LABOR STATISTICS. *Directory of National and International Labor Unions in the United States*. Washington, D.C.: U.S. Government Printing Office.

Issued biennially, this bulletin contains a detailed listing of International unions, officers, location, conventions, publications, and claimed membership of the approximately 200 unions headquartered in the U.S.

WALTON, RICHARD E. *The Impact of the Professional Engineering Union.* Boston: Harvard University, Division of Research, Graduate School of Business Administration, 1961.

Reports on research into the experiences of 11 companies where professionals have organized certified bargaining units. Part I is a historical perspective on collective bargaining by engineers. Part II deals with compensation of engineers. Part III explores other issues in personnel administration. Part IV considers the impact of the union on work assignments, management organization, and employee relations.

WOLMAN, LEO. *Ebb and Flow in Trade Unionism.* New York: National Bureau of Economic Research, 1936.

A study of trends in trade union membership in the United States between 1897 and 1934. Gives considerably more attention to the impact of cyclical factors and government policy on the rise and decline of union membership than does the author's 1924 volume on the same subject.

Chapter	THE GOVERNMENT AND
4	THE PUBLIC INTEREST

This chapter deals with the third actor in the industrial relations system, the government, and its influence on the other two actors, managers and unions. Although laws have indirectly influenced collective bargaining in America ever since colonial times, the first nation-wide labor relations law, the Norris–La Guardia Act, did not come to pass until 1932. The exercise of the judicial and executive powers of government in labor relations has a longer history, but today it appears to follow the guideposts set by the more recent legislation. This chapter examines the current status of legislative, executive, and judicial regulations of the actors and their interaction in collective bargaining.

Government may take many forms, from absolute monarchy to pure democracy. Regardless of its form, a government draws upon the resources of society and organizes the people in it by the exercise of moral authority and the possession of power. In a democracy, the moral authority of government derives from its efforts to represent what is called the public interest. The public interest may be conceived of as a delicate balancing of pluralistic private interests for the common good or as an overpowering, unified popular objective. In either case, a government claiming to promote the public interest cannot be neutral toward the private interests of management and unions, or toward the activity in which they engage their separate, and often opposing, interests: collective bargaining.

In a democratic state, defining and interpreting the public interest is the responsibility of those representatives of the public who wield governmental power: legislators, executives, and judges. Every citizen has a right to his own interpretation of the public interest and the right also to advocate that interpretation, but only the appropriate officials of government have the final say, so long as they retain their position of public trust. Thus at any particular time the public interest is what the legislators say it is when they pass a law, and what the executives say it is when they enforce the provisions of a law, and what the judges say it is when they rule on disputes under the law. The public interest, then, is not something eternal and unchanging. This chapter seeks to show that the public interest has, in fact, changed over the years. It will go on to explain how the present-day public interest, as reflected in present-day law and its enforcement, regulates unions and management. It will point out some areas in which controversy over different interpretations of the public interest has not yet settled down into a determination of law.

CONCEPTS OF THE PUBLIC INTEREST

At various times, different groups of people have viewed labor relations legislation as a vehicle for achieving one or more of the following social goals, which were conceived to be in the public interest: (1) preserving property rights; (2) advancing the civil rights of working people; (3) keeping the government out of economic affairs; (4) lessening or eliminating public inconvenience resulting from labor disputes; (5) controlling monopoly power; (6) controlling the business cycle; (7) equalizing bargaining power between conflicting private interests.

Although several of these goals conflict, each has found some expression in present-day labor relations legislation. A brief statement of each of these concepts will explain the thinking behind them and help evaluate their influence on law.

Preserving Property Rights

The right of an individual to hold property is enshrined in the Constitution; it is not the right that is in question here, but rather various interpretations of what constitutes its proper exercise in management. Some see it as an "inalienable" right not only to set prices, and to determine what goods or services to produce and the way to produce them but also to set wages and employee performance standards, to hire and fire at will and without challenge, to set rules and regulations governing the conduct of employees. So sweeping a view of the management prerogatives derived from property rights would naturally call for the elimination of collective bargaining and for laws prohibiting or severely limiting union activity.

Advancing the Civil Rights of Working People

In contrast to the above, an extreme view of the civil rights of working people would require their participation and consent in every act of management. A more moderate statement of this position would give employees the right to bargain collectively only over the conditions of their employment. Once collective bargaining becomes the method of establishing these conditions, a simple extension of the civil rights concept would insist that workers also have a right to full democratic participation in the affairs of their unions. Further, if racial or religious discrimination violate civil rights, unions themselves must be clean of any taint and must open their membership rolls and activities without racial or religious discrimination.

A twist to this civil rights concept is the "right to work"—the right of an individual to employment, whether or not he elects to join a union.

Keeping the Government Out of Economic Affairs

Classical political economy makes out a very strong case for keeping the government from interfering with labor-management relations in a democratic state with a free enterprise economy. The presumption is that free employers and free unions know what is best for them and have a vital interest, which should not be disturbed, in settling their own affairs.

As a matter of fact, American law on collective bargaining today rather follows this concept and is largely *permissive*, both with regard to the terms and to the methods by which the parties reach agreement. Indeed, if a group of workers and an employer, in total ignorance of the law, were to sit down and bargain out an agreement, it is unlikely that they would agree to anything prohibited by existing laws.

The concept of governmental noninterference must not be confused with neutrality. In terms of the total effect of government policy at any given time, nonintervention in labor-management relations strengthens the hand of either management or the union.

Lessening Public Inconvenience

Most citizens have at one time or another been inconvenienced by a strike. Some strikes go beyond mere inconvenience and may imperil public health or jeopardize the national defense. Public policy, under this concept, looks toward preventing strikes; or if they occur, toward lessening their impact.

It is sometimes forgotten that the Wagner Act (seldom viewed as a strike control measure) virtually eliminated what had been, before its passage, the principal cause of strikes in the United States: the strike for union recognition. The Taft-Hartley law went further and tackled the problem of national emergency strikes. Experience has shown that the attempt was only moderately successful. The legislative quest continues for a solution to the problem of lessening public peril and inconvenience.

Controlling Monopoly Power

This concept has two contradictory aspects. On the one hand there are those who claim that the employer has monopoly—"monopsonistic"—power over job opportunities, so that the individual worker is helpless in bargaining for his labor. Collective bargaining restores the balance. Against this, on the other hand, there are those who see *unions* as the real monopolies and believe they should be broken up under the antitrust laws.

Controlling the Business Cycle

There is little doubt that the idea of increasing purchasing power as a step toward ending the Great Depression won many congressional votes for the passage of the Wagner Act in 1935. It has also been argued that the Taft-Hartley restraints on union power were aimed at controlling inflation in 1947. Both concepts hold that labor relations law is a proper field for countercyclical legislation.

Quite apart from law, government action taking such form as the Presidential "guidelines" of 1965 (withdrawn in 1967), which looked toward wage-price stability, went on the presumption that collective bargaining had a bearing on the health of the economy. The guidelines clearly stated the national objective to be noninflationary full employment, and asked employers and unions to conduct their affairs in harmony with this objective.

Equalizing Bargaining Power

Probably the most venerated concept of the public interest in labor relations is the idea that government should equalize the "bargaining power" of management and unions. This concept implies that labor's interests conflict with management's; that they are bound to fight; and that the stronger will most likely win, to the detriment of broader interests. If, however, government backs up the weaker and thus makes them equal, they may settle their differences without a fight, and if they fail, at least the fight will be fair. Thus the Wagner Act prohibited unfair labor practices by employers, who at the time were felt to be stronger. The Taft-Hartley Act, some 12 years later, turned the same argument around to prohibit unfair labor practices by unions.

Another application of this argument, never enacted in law, holds that some big unions dealing with many employers should be broken into smaller units, just as business combines sometimes are required to divest themselves of their holdings. An example is the United Automobile Workers, which has members working for Chrysler, Ford, and General Motors. Public policy would oppose a merger of the Big Three; why should not the union, it is argued, break down into units that would equalize bargaining power?

These concepts of the public interest have had their partisans, and perhaps all have some validity, though taken together they would be hard to apply to any specific labor-management relationship, or even to any particular piece of legislation. Too frequently an individual's zeal for a particular principle, or his interest in a specific legislative proposal, blinds him to equally valid aspects of the public interest. Somewhere, sometime, the powers that be in government have to make a decision. It is rarely one-sided, but it is never—and it cannot be—completely neutral.

Before discussing the substantive regulation of the parties, it is well to identify the agencies of government currently active in the industrial relations field. In this brief survey of agencies, their major functions and their points of contact with the other actors will be emphasized.

GOVERNMENTAL AGENCIES ACTIVE IN THE INDUSTRIAL RELATIONS FIELD

American government is organized around the legislative, executive, and judicial functions at the federal, state, and local levels. Under the commerce clause of the Constitution, federal authority has emerged as the dominant force in the regulation of collective bargaining.

Legislative Agencies

Since 1932, the U.S. Congress has shown substantial interest in regulating the collective bargaining process. The basic federal law on collective bargaining today is incorporated in three statutes: the Norris–La Guardia Act of 1932, the Taft-Hartley Act of 1947 which amended the Wagner Act of 1935, and the Landrum-Griffin Act of 1959. The Norris–La Guardia Act deals with the use of injunctions in labor disputes. The Taft-Hartley Act provides procedures for establishing union recognition and preventing "unfair labor practices" by managements and unions. The Landrum-Griffin Act regulates the internal affairs of unions and managements.

Beyond the direct regulation of the collective bargaining process, Congress has enacted a substantial body of federal legislation in the social security, wage and hour, taxation and tariff fields which is a legitimate concern of managements and unions. This legislation will be considered in Part Three of this book.

Congress is subjected to consistent pressures from management and labor organizations. Most major corporations maintain legislative liaison departments or offices in Washington and these voices are supplemented by such organizations as the U.S. Chamber of Commerce and the National Association of Manufacturers plus a multitude of associations concerned with the affairs of individual industries. The fact that 55 International unions maintain their headquarters in the city of Washington is some evidence of union interest in legislative affairs. Beyond the individual Internationals, the AFL-CIO and its departments engage in lobbying activity at the federal level.

Under the police power, state legislatures have played a major role in the field of protective labor legislation—child labor, minimum wage, factory inspection, Fair Employment Practices, protective hours limitations, wage payment and collection, time off for voting, and the regulation of private employment agencies. Although much of protective labor legislation is peripheral to the collective bargaining process, unions and managements have a vital interest in state Unemployment Compensation and Workmen's Compensation statutes and, where operative, state labor relations statutes regulating collective bargaining relations which are excluded from the coverage of federal law. Although the federal law is supreme in most collective bargaining areas, the Taft-Hartley law, in ceding jurisdiction to the states for laws restricting union security (so-called right-to-work laws), set the stage for some bitter legislative battles at the state level.

Lobbying at the state level finds Local unions and the State Federation representing organized labor, while enterprises speak for themselves or use the services of state-wide industry associations.

School boards, county road commissions, and city councils almost never regulate the collective bargaining process or the affairs of managements and unions, but they spend a good deal of money on building construction and they employ many civil servants. Enterprises and unions affected by their activities are engaged in attempting to influence their deliberations.

Executive Agencies

As Chief Executive, the President of the United States is concerned with all aspects of American life. His public pronouncements on labor relations have a great weight of authority. Perhaps even more important is the authority which his office carries in behind-the-scenes conversations with the captains of industry and with labor leaders. Most Presidents of the twentieth century have used the power of their office in at least some labor-mangement crises.

Presidents Wilson, Roosevelt, Truman, Eisenhower, Kennedy, and Johnson have all personally intervened in major labor disputes. Although their interventions have taken different forms and their personal philosophies of the desirability of intervention have differed, their actions have demonstrated the significant role which the President himself plays in labor-management relations. It seems that the times in which we live require at least some Presidential participation in labor-management relations. The form that this intervention will take depends upon the personality of the incumbent of that office.

Presidents Wilson, Truman, Kennedy, and Johnson have used the authority of their office in attempts to reconcile the interests of labor organizations and management for the national welfare. President Wilson's first Industrial Conference in 1919 and President Truman's National Labor Management Conference in 1945 failed. It remains to be seen if the President's Advisory Council on Labor-Management Policy, established by President Kennedy and reactivated by President Johnson, will be more successful.

Three independent agencies of the executive branch of the federal government concern themselves directly with labor relations. They are: (1) the National Labor Relations Board, (2) the Federal Mediation and Conciliation Service, and (3) the Department of Labor.

The National Labor Relations Board. First established by the passage of the Wagner Act in 1935, the National Labor Relations Board, its regional offices, and its General Counsel's office are responsible for administering the basic federal law of management-union relations. Many enterprises and unions find it desirable to use the facilities of the NLRB for resolving representation questions even before they negotiate their first collective bargaining agreement. The NLRB also possesses broad authority for investigating charges of noncompliance with the law, and enforcement. Every effort possible to secure voluntary compliance precedes formal action, but in case of controversy NLRB investigators gather evidence and Board lawyers prepare cases for a hearing before a trial examiner appointed by the Board, or the Board itself.

The Federal Mediation and Conciliation Service. Formally established as an independent agency by the Taft-Hartley Act of 1947, the Federal Mediation and Conciliation Service is the successor organization to the Labor Department's Conciliation Service which was established in 1913. The Federal Mediation and Conciliation Service works entirely through the voluntary cooperation of enterprises and unions. It has no power to prosecute anyone or to issue orders; it is even chary of comment and criticism. The function of the Federal Mediation and Conciliation Service is to assist managements and unions in reaching collective bargaining agreements, by the procedures of conciliation and mediation. For many years efforts at conciliation and mediation started only when labor or management were on the point of having a strike or even after a strike was on. Lately mediators have been called in to help much earlier in the game, even in the process of adjusting grievances. The role of mediators is discussed in Chapter 6.

United States Department of Labor. Although the main activity of the U.S. Department of Labor lies in the protective legislation field and in research activities, it is the President's official liaison with organized labor and with employers in their collective bargaining capacity. The Landrum-Griffin Act of 1959 greatly expanded the functions of the Secretary of Labor in the new field of protecting inner-union democracy.

State Executive Agencies. In the 15 states with labor relations statutes, these laws are administered by either the state labor department or a state labor relations board similar to the NLRB. Most states have an executive agency charged with responsibility for assisting in the mediation of labor disputes. Every state has an executive agency responsible for the administration of its Unemployment Compensation and Workmen's Compensation laws and, where applicable, the administration of factory inspection, minimum wage, child labor, and other protective legislation. Particularly serious intrastate strikes, either because of their impact on the state economy or the exceptionally rare violent strikes, often involve the governor of the state.

Local Police. Every strike poses a threat of traffic disruption and possible violence. Although strike violence has practically disappeared from the American scene, the local police force plays a vital role in maintaining order in those exceptional cases where violence does erupt. The role of the police will be discussed in Chapter 6.

The Courts and Collective Bargaining

Judges have at varying times been the villains, and alternately the heroes of the drama of collective bargaining in the eyes of both labor and management. The last word in interpretation of the law comes from the courts.

Before the passage of the Norris–La Guardia Act in 1932, the courts, through the interpretation of the common law, often "legislated" in the collective bargaining field. The subsequent passage of a substantial body of statutory law on collective bargaining has reduced the participation of the courts in labor relations. Today the courts have the very important function of ruling on the constitutionality of labor relations legislation and providing the final say on the interpretation of whatever legislation is enacted by the legislative branch of government and enforced by numerous executive agencies.

Managers and union leaders come in contact with a wide variety of governmental representatives who are responsible for the law of collective bargaining. What is the substance of that law?

FEDERAL LABOR RELATIONS LAW

All American labor relations law that has been written into the federal statutes dates from the twentieth century. That part of it which remains currently valid is embodied in five laws: (1) The Railway Labor Act of 1926, as amended; (2) the Norris–La Guardia Act of 1932; (3) the Wagner Act of 1935; (4) the Taft-Hartley Act of 1947; and (5) the Landrum-Griffin Act of 1959. Some authorities argue that the antitrust laws are labor relations legislation, but their applicability to labor relations has been severely restricted by Supreme Court rulings. Excluding the Railway Labor Act and the antitrust laws, Appendix I contains the full text of current federal labor relations statutes applicable to industry in general.

The discussion of labor relations law in this chapter focuses on several substantive areas of regulation. Figure 4–1 traces the emergence of American legislation on labor relations.

Positive Nonintervention: The Norris–La Guardia Act

The Norris–La Guardia Act was a very modest piece of legislation. It created no new governmental agencies and had the net effect of reducing the work of the courts in labor relations matters. Although

FIGURE 4-1

THE EMERGING SUBSTANCE OF AMERICAN LABOR RELATIONS LAW

Norris–Laguardia Act (1932)	Wagner Act (1935)	Taft–Hartley Act (1947)	Landrum–Griffin Act (1959)
1. "Yellow dog" contract made unenforceable at law	Outlaws "yellow-dog" contract (Sec. 8[B][3])	No change	No change
2. Severely restricts use of injunctions in labor disputes	No change	NLRB empowered to obtain injunctions: (a) in national emergency disputes (Sec. 208–210) and (b) to prevent unfair labor practices (Sec. 10[E]–[M]).	No change
	3. Established NLRB (Sec. 3–6)	Separated General Counsel functions from Board functions (Sec. 3–6)	Representation questions delegated to Regional Directors (Sec. 3)
	4. Empowers NLRB to resolve questions of representation (Sec. 9)*	Special treatment for foremen, guards, and professional employees (Sec. 9[B])* Only one election per year (Sec. 9[C][3])* Decertification elections (Sec. 9[C][1])*	No change
	5. Prohibits management actions aimed at frustrating employee free choice of representatives and organizational efforts (Sec. 8[A][1]–[4])	Employer "free speech" amendment (Sec. 8[C])*	No change
	6. Requires management to bargain with union (Sec. 8[A][5])†	No change	No change
		7. Requires union to bargain (Sec. 8[B][3])†	No change
		8. Prohibits union actions aimed at frustrating employee free choice of representatives (Sec. 8[B][1])	No change
		9. Outlaws closed shop (Sec. 8[B][4])‡	No change
		10. Authorizes State "Right to Work" Laws 14[B])‡	No change
		11. Outlaws secondary boycott (Sec. 8[B][4])*	Outlaws "hot cargo" Agreements except in garment and construction industries.
		12. Requires 60-day notice of contract termination (Sec. 8[D])	No change
		13. Created Federal Mediation and Conciliation Service (Sec. 202–205)†	No change
		14. National Emergency Disputes procedures (Sec. 206–210)†	No change
		15. Makes union subject to suits in federal courts (Sec. 301)	No change
			16. "Bill of Rights" for union members (Title I)
			17. Responsibilities of union officers (Titles II, III, IV)
			18. Safeguards on union funds (Title V)

NOTES:
* Discussed in greater detail in Chapter 5.
† Discussed in greater detail in Chapter 6.
‡ Discussed in greater detail in Chapter 9.

addressed only to restricting the use of injunctions in labor disputes and making the "yellow dog" contract unenforceable in the courts, the Norris–La Guardia Act did state a new policy for the United States on the employment relationship and freedom of contract.

Noting the protection given to property owners in the corporate form of enterprise and other ownership associations, the Norris–La Guardia Act stated:

. . . the individual unorganized worker is commonly helpless to exercise actual liberty of contract and to protect his freedom of labor . . . though he should be free to decline to associate with his fellows, it is necessary that he have full freedom of association, self-organization, and designation of representatives of his own choosing, to negotiate the terms and conditions of his employment and that he shall be free from interference, restraint, or coercion of Employers of labor. . . .

The words "full freedom of association," "representatives of his own choosing," and "free from interference, restraint, and coercion," were to become the cornerstones of American public policy on labor relations.

The Norris–La Guardia Act made the question of representation a private matter between workers, employers, and the unions, not subject to intervention by the courts. It provided no penalties for employer actions seeking to prevent unionization, but it stripped such actions of all legal protection.

The act attacked two abuses that seemed to give management an unfair advantage in fighting unions: the "yellow dog" contract and the unrestricted use of injunctions in labor disputes. Neither of these management abuses had any basis in statutory law, but got their sanction from common law and judicial precedent; they were admittedly not crimes against the unions, only inequities. The act provided positive statute law which deprived these abuses of legal sanction.

The Yellow Dog Contract.   Employers opposed to the unionization of their workers hit upon an ingenious idea, somewhere around the turn of the century, of making workers "take the pledge" against the union. As a condition of employment, each employee had to sign a card in which he affirmed that he was not a union member and would not join a union as long as he went on working for the company. He acknowledged that if he did join or became active on behalf of a union, he would have broken his contract with the company and given cause for terminating his employment. The worker forced to sign the pledge to hold his job, union men said, felt like a dog with his tail between his legs—a yellow dog, at that!

It seemed to many Americans outside the labor movement as well as in it that employers who required the yellow dog contract were forcing men to waive a portion of their inalienable civil rights in order to make a living. This, they argued, deprived a man of freedom. The issue reached the courts and was tested in United States Supreme Court case of *Hitchman Coal and Coke* v. *Mitchell* (1917). The Supreme Court upheld the legality of the yellow dog contract. Since this decision rested on interpretation of the common law, the remedy was a specific statute—the Norris–La Guardia Act of 1932.

Section 3 of the Norris–La Guardia Act declared yellow dog contracts to be contrary to the public policy of the United States. The law simply stated that such contracts "shall not be enforceable in any court of the United States and shall not afford any basis for the granting of legal or equitable relief by any such court."

The Norris–La Guardia Act did *not* outlaw yellow dog contracts, it merely made them unenforceable at law. Under the Norris–La Guardia Act employers were still free to require yellow dog contracts and to fire any worker who joined a union. An official outlawing of the yellow dog contract had to wait until the Wagner Act of 1935 made it an unfair labor practice for an employer to discharge or discriminate against a worker because of his union activity.

Norris–La Guardia Restrictions on the Use of Injunctions. Injunctions are preventative court orders, issued at the discretion of a judge *before* a case has been heard.

A judge issues an injunction to forestall some threatened or contemplated act that is not inherently illegal but that might cause "irreparable" harm. This allows time to examine the case in court by the due processes of law to determine whether the damage that is feared will indeed result if the act is carried out.

The judge may then either withdraw the injunction or make it permanent.

As an example: A man might learn that his neighbor intends to cut down a shade tree on or near the unmarked dividing line between their properties. In discussion with the neighbor it might develop that each contends that the tree is growing on his side of the line. One wants to cut it down because the roots are ruining his garden plot; the other wants to keep it for its shade and beauty. Supposing that they fail to settle the argument in reasonable fashion, and that the tree lover has reason to believe his neighbor intends, perhaps out of spite, to cut the tree down anyway; he could ask for an injunction to prevent it. This would restrain the neighbor (under pain of contempt of court) from using the ax until a resurvey of the boundary established ownership. If in truth it belonged to the neighbor, he would then be free to cut it down; but if he had done so before the survey, and the survey went against him, he would have done irreparable damage which would be hard to measure in money and which he could not replace; for it might take a century to grow a new tree.

Following similar reasoning, an employer threatened with strike action (before the Norris–La Guardia Act) would ask a judge for an injunction against the union, on the ground that the strike would do irreparable damage to his business. Or, with a strike actually in progress, the employer would allege that damage and disorder were imminent if picketing and other strike activity continued, and ask the judge to enjoin the complained-of activities. If the judge agreed—and judges seemed prone to agree on what often seemed very slight grounds—the strike was delayed, frustrated, or brought to a close as soon as police or sheriff's deputies moved to enforce the injunction.

Thus while strikes were not in themselves unlawful, and could not legally be forbidden outright, the terms of an injunction could so hamstring the union's activities as to have the effect of outlawing the strike. It must be remembered that before the passage of the Wagner Act in 1935 a union could not ordinarily win recognition without a strike. In recognition strikes, timing is often a crucial element of failure or success. Even if after a hearing the injunction was withdrawn, the damage to the union's cause might have been done—irreparably—with union members demoralized and intimidated, the union weakened or destroyed.

As with the yellow dog contract, many citizens who were not themselves union members found the abuse of the injunction in labor disputes unfair. It seemed to pervert the law's wise provision for protecting a citizen against threatened harm to his property or person by turning it into a tricky and oppressive device for depriving other citizens, the union members, of rights that were lawfully theirs under the Constitution.

The act did not outlaw the use of the injunction, even in labor disputes when necessary, but made the conditions for getting an injunction so stiff that the effect was almost the same.

Impact of the Norris–La Guardia Act. Professor Charles O. Gregory sees the Norris–La Guardia as the culmination of the philosophy of laissez-faire in union-management relations.[1] Its meaning in the sixties is very different from what it was in the thirties.

The net impact of the Norris–La Guardia Act on the society and on unions and managements depends upon the legal and economic environment of the time in which it is evaluated. At the time of its passage in 1932, the impact of the Norris–La Guardia Act was little more than sweet talk to the unions. Even without a yellow dog contract, the employer's powers of persuasion (the perfectly lawful threat and exercise of discharge for union activity or membership) were indeed effective. In those very rare cases where unions were strong enough to force employers to recognize them, they were free to exert their full power. The Norris–La Guardia Act gave little direct help to unorganized workers and weak unions. In 1932 union membership was at an all-time low. If the Norris–La Guardia Act were to become the sole industrial relations statute in effect in the sixties the net effect of the law would be quite different. Many of the unions in America today could defend themselves quite adequately in a fair fight with management. Under the Norris–La Guardia Act alone, the unions would have full use of the strike, boycott, and picketing. These weapons are very potent indeed when they are supported by a union

[1] Charles O. Gregory, *Labor and the Law* (rev. ed.; New York: W. W. Norton & Co., Inc., 1958), p. 185.

membership in being, and when potential allies are available in the union movement. These weapons were substantially less potent when, as in 1932, the union membership existed only in the hopes of labor leaders.

Positive Protection of the Right to Organize: The Wagner Act of 1935

The Great Depression was three years old, and at its deepest, when Franklin Roosevelt took office in 1933. Almost his first official act was to close all the banks. For reasons fully understandable only to people who lived through those days, this ultimate gesture of economic collapse gave the nation its first breath of confidence. It seemed to wipe the slate clean for a fresh start, or, to use the imagery of those days, it called off all bets and broke out a new deck of cards. In quick succession other measures followed. Preeminent among these was the National Industrial Recovery Act, or NIRA, the predecessor of the Wagner Act of 1935.

The NIRA aimed to build public confidence by halting the decline of prices and encouraging production and jobs. It called upon industry to adopt codes of "fair competition," which were to be drawn up and administered by the participants, promulgated and policed by the government. To this end it authorized the formation of industry associations and suspended the antitrust laws. Minimum prices were part of the plan of fair competition and also minimum wages. As a means toward keeping wage levels up, and hence maintaining purchasing power, the act guaranteed to unions the right of collective bargaining. This was the famous Section 7a.

Worker response to Section 7a was overwhelming. Unions formed spontaneously in plant after plant, and Internationals which mounted a vigorous organizing campaign (like the mine workers and the clothing workers) got an enthusiastic response. The newly formed CIO began its campaign to organize the unorganized in mass-production industry and met with unheard-of success.

In 1935, the Supreme Court declared the NIRA unconstitutional. Immediately, Senator Wagner introduced a bill in Congress that reaffirmed, with amplifications, the substance of 7a.

The Wagner Act passed easily in Congress, but for two years its constitutionality remained in doubt, under challenge of litigation headed for the Supreme Court. This proved no check on the union drive. In 1936, the auto industry sit-down strikes broke out in the Detroit area.

As with the bank closings, one must have lived through this experience to understand fully the impression the sit-downs made on the public mind. American labor relations seemed to be rushing to the brink of violence—and who could be sure?—maybe revolution. In the relative calm of a "cease-fire" between the auto industry and the union, negotiated by the governor of Michigan, the same Supreme Court that had thrown out the NIRA upheld the constitutionality of the Wagner Act. Militant unionism abandoned the sit-down and, for its most pressing aim of recognition, turned to the ballot box in Labor Board elections. Since the

Supreme Court's validation of the Wagner Act, industrial unions have fought their strikes out at the plant gate instead of on the factory floor.

The Wagner Act solved three hard problems that had been plaguing American labor relations for many years: union recognition, company unionism and discrimination against unionists, and company refusals to bargain. Because of the large sector of economic life covered by the Wagner Act and the need for flexibility in administration, the Wagner Act created the National Labor Relations Board to implement its provisions.

The National Labor Relations Board.   The National Labor Relations Board is an independent administrative agency. It is empowered to investigate, to hold hearings, and to issue decisions and orders. The orders and decisions of the Board are subject to court review for their final enforcement, but the courts have shown considerable reluctance in setting aside the orders of the NLRB. The NLRB can impose no penalties for the violation of the laws that it administers. The Board is empowered to prevent unfair labor practices by cease-and-desist orders and to require affirmative action to effectuate the law.

Although the Taft-Hartley law of 1947 and the Landrum-Griffin law of 1959 modified the organization of the Board and its jurisdiction, the present day NLRB is a direct lineal descendent of the organization created by the Wagner Act.

Jurisdiction of the NLRB.   Federal regulation of collective bargaining is based on the commerce clause in the Constitution. As the Supreme Court has interpreted the commerce clause, the federal government has very wide jurisdiction in regulating collective bargaining activities in enterprises of all sorts. This broad constitutional authority is limited by the statutory provisions governing the NLRB and minimum standards which the NLRB has established governing the volume of business that an enterprise must do before the NLRB will exercise its power over an enterprise.

Under Taft-Hartley and the Landrum-Griffin law, the following employers and employees are specifically *excluded* from the jurisdiction of the NLRB:

1. Employers:
   a) The U.S. government and the states or any political subdivision of either.
   b) Federal Reserve bank.
   c) Wholly owned government corporations.
   d) Nonprofit hospitals.
   e) Any employer who is subject to the terms of the Railway Labor Act.
2. Employees:
   a) Agricultural laborers.
   b) Domestic servants.
   c) Any person employed by his parent or spouse.

    d) Any individual employed by an employer who is subject to the Railway Labor Act.

    e) Independent contractors.

    f) Supervisors.

    g) Government employees, federal or state, including government corporations and Federal Reserve banks.

    h) Employees of completely nonprofit hospitals.

Although the Board has legal jurisdiction over enterprises that affect commerce, it has, with the approval of Congress and the courts, limited the exercise of its jurisdiction to enterprises whose affect on commerce, in the opinion of the Board, is substantial. The Board's standards for determining those enterprises over which it will exercise jurisdiction are based on the total annual volume of business done by the corporation, or the total annual volume of sales or of purchases, and these standards are different for different kinds of business. In addition, the Board exercises jurisdiction over all enterprises that affect commerce when their operations have a substantial impact on national defense. The Board, in its discretion, may decline to exercise jurisdiction over any class or category of employees where a labor dispute involving such employees is not sufficiently substantial to warrant the exercise of jurisdiction. The Board has refused to exercise jurisdiction over hospitals operated for profit, racetracks, and real estate brokers.

Section 701 of the Landrum-Griffin Act gives to state labor relations agencies and courts full jurisdiction over any dispute which the NLRB declines to hear, and directs the NLRB to hear every case that was covered by its jurisdictional standards in effect on August 1, 1959. The NLRB is empowered to broaden its jurisdiction up to the full coverage of the law, but is forbidden from reducing its jurisdiction from the coverage in effect on August 1, 1959.

Organization of the NLRB. The Taft-Hartley Act divided the functions of the NLRB into a trial section and an investigative section headed respectively by a Board of five members and by a General Counsel—all appointed by the President. The Board makes decisions on cases which the General Counsel, who is not responsible to the Board, investigates and prepares for hearing. This separates the executive and judicial functions in the enforcement of national labor relations policy.

The work of the National Labor Relations Board consists of two parts: (1) representation cases and (2) unfair labor practices cases. Representation cases deal with the question of union recognition. The Wagner Act prohibited five unfair labor practices by management. Retaining the Wagner Act's unfair labor practices by management, the Taft-Hartley Act added six unfair labor practices by unions and the Landrum-Griffin Act added a seventh.

Union Recognition and Representation Issues. The Wagner Act stated that "Representatives designated or selected . . . by the *majority* of the employees in a *unit appropriate* . . . (for collective bargaining), shall be the *exclusive representatives* for the purpose of collective bargaining." (Emphasis added.) Thus in representation cases, the Board has three problems to solve:

1. What is an appropriate unit?
2. What is the will of the majority of the employees in this unit?
3. How can a change in the will of the majority be accommodated?

These questions and the evolution of Board policies are discussed in some detail in Chapter 5.

The important things to note now about union recognition and representation issues are: (1) *employees* are the sole judges of whether or not they should be represented by a union, (2) a *majority* of the employees can commit what may be a very unhappy minority to representation by a particular union; and (3) it is the job of the NLRB to determine what the majority wants.

The Board may certify a union as the exclusive bargaining agent either by an election or by other means of determining the majority's will. In the early days of the Wagner Act, the Board often placed reliance on union dues books or authorization cards as a means of determining the majority's will. Elections, however, have since the very early days of the act been the principal method of determining the will of the majority. This democratic procedure greatly eased the unions' job of organizing the unorganized. Before the Wagner Act, union members usually had to strike to obtain union recognition. Under the Wagner Act and its successor legislation, all the union had to do was to convince a majority of the employees to vote for it in a secret ballot election conducted by the government. Once the union had won the election and had been certified by the Board, the employer had no choice but to deal with the union.

"Ballot box organizing" initiated by the NLRB under the Wagner Act and continued to this day is unique in the United States. This procedure, which Congress has seen fit to continue and strengthen through 30 years of industrial relations legislation, indicates a strong endorsement of the assumption that collective bargaining is in the public interest.

Unfair Labor Practices by Management. The unfair labor practice section of the Wagner Act specifically protected only employees from interference, restraint, and coercion. The unfair labor practices prohibited by the Wagner Act were all *employer* actions. The Wagner Act sought to balance the position of employees and employers by restricting the activities of employers.

Section 8 of the Wagner Act prohibited five unfair labor practices by management. The prohibited practices were:

1. To interfere with or restrain or coerce employees in the exercise of their right to self-organization.

2. To dominate or interfere in the affairs of the union.
3. To discriminate in regard to hire or tenure or any condition of employment for the purpose of encouraging or discouraging union membership.
4. To discriminate against or discharge an employee because he had filed charges or given testimony under the act.
5. To refuse to bargain with chosen representatives of his employees.

The unfair labor practices section of the Wagner Act was one-sided in that it attacked excesses by management only. At the same time, it is very important to note what the Wagner Act did *not* do. First and foremost, it did *not* make the unfair labor practices a crime; that is, it did not impose any penalties or fines for violation of the act. The "teeth" in the Wagner Act became apparent only when the courts began to uphold NLRB orders instructing employers to reinstate *with back pay* employees who had been discharged in violation of the act. Second, the Wagner Act did *not* require an employer to concede to the demands of a union for higher pay or for anything of substance; but only required acceptance of the act of bargaining. Probably the most difficult problem confronting the NLRB even today is giving practical meaning to the obligation to bargain. This important problem is discussed in Part V.

Redressing the Balance: The Taft-Hartley Act of 1947

Preserved in the Taft-Hartley law, as stated, are all the fundamental principles of the Wagner Act. To these the new law added some things that dismayed union leaders, pleased many management people, and kept the issue simmering just below the boiling point in politics from the day of passage to the present.

During the 12 years following the Wagner Act, unions enormously increased their strength. In advocating his bill to amend the Wagner Act, Senator Taft leaned implicitly on the concept of balancing bargaining power. The employer, he said, had now become the underdog. Union leaders promptly replied that his supposed equalizing measures put the employer on top again. There was probably exaggeration in both views.

The year of reconversion to civilian production following World War II brought on more strikes, and bigger ones, than any year in American history. In contrast to the strike wave following World War I when management shook off the slight hold unions had gained in the factories during the war, this time the unions, for the most part, won their strikes. They won them because they were organized industrially and because, on the crucial recognition issue, the law was on their side. That is, recognition was no longer at stake; the unions could hold concrete, attainable economic issues before the strikers' eyes.

But the American public, newly released from the pressures of war, did not take kindly to the strikes. Many people not hitherto opposed to unions became alarmed by the magnitude and duration of strikes which they saw the big industrial unions were capable of bringing about. In this climate of reaction against the spectacle of union power, the Taft-Hartley bill passed in Congress. President Truman vetoed it, but it passed again over his veto and became law.

What follows is a brief statement of the substance of the new law. Its fuller implications for managements and unions will be discussed in later chapters.

Changes in the Right to Union Representation. Section 7 of the Wagner Act was explicitly amended to give a majority of the workers the protected right to refrain from union organization and collective bargaining. The Taft-Hartley law also contained new election procedures which were designed to permit workers to refrain from collective bargaining. In the case of foremen, plant guards, and professional employees, the Taft-Hartley law defined specific permissible and nonpermissible forms of union recognition. Last but not least, the Taft-Hartley law gave employers a strong voice in influencing workers in their free choice of union representatives.

The Taft-Hartley law provided that the NLRB could hold only one election in any year for a single group of employees. Thus if a union lost an election or employees wanted to rid themselves of a nonrepresentative union, the *status quo* was frozen for one full year. Strikers who had been replaced were not eligible to vote in NLRB representation elections. The Taft-Hartley law created the decertification election by which employees could use the facilities of the NLRB to remove a union which was no longer representative.

Under the Taft-Hartley law, foremen were denied all protection of the law in seeking union recognition. The NLRB was directed to allow plant guards to be represented only by unions composed exclusively of plant guards. Professional employees could be represented by plant unions only if a majority of the professional employees had voted for such representation.

Obviously, employers might very well have preferences about whether or not their employees were represented by a union and which union would represent them. The Wagner Act and NLRB interpretations of that law took the position that employer attempts to influence the outcome of NLRB elections were "interference, restraint, and coercion" of employees in the exercise of their guaranteed right to free choice of representatives. The Taft-Hartley law, Section 8(c), called the "free speech" amendment, stated:

The expressing of any views, argument, or opinion, or the dissemination thereof, whether in written, printed, graphic, or visual form, shall not constitute or be evidence of an unfair labor practice under any of the provisions of this Act, if such expression contains no threat of reprisal or force or promise of benefit.

This free speech amendment substantially increased the influence which employers could exert on the outcome of NLRB elections. We shall discuss the free speech problem in some detail in Chapter 5.

The net effect of the Taft-Hartley law in the area of union recognition was to encourage employees and employers who wanted to avoid collective bargaining. The right to collective bargaining was retained, but the implicit right to refrain from bargaining was made explicit in the words of our national industrial relations policy.

Unfair Labor Practices by Unions.   The Wagner Act defined and prohibited certain unfair labor practices *by management*. That was on the theory that employees and their unions were weaker and needed protection. The Taft-Hartley law extended the concept of unfair labor practices to *unions*, and brought them under the same sanctions and penalties for infractions as were applicable to management. The prohibitions on unfair labor practices by unions were designed to protect employees and employers.

Section 8(b) of the Taft-Hartley law enumerated six unfair labor practices by unions:

1. To restrain or coerce employees in the exercise of their guaranteed rights to engage in, or to refrain from, collective bargaining.
2. To cause an employer to discriminate against an employee who is not a member of a labor union for any reason other than his failure to tender the periodic dues and initiation fees uniformly required as a condition of acquiring or retaining membership.
3. To refuse to bargain with an employer, provided the union is the representative of his employees.
4. To engage in or to induce employees to engage in strikes or concerted refusal to work or boycotts—refusal to use, process, or handle certain goods or materials—when an object of such action is:
   a. forcing or requiring an employer or self-employed person to join any organization or forcing anyone to cease using the products of, or doing business with, any other person,
   b. to force recognition by any other employer of a union unless certified by the NLRB,
   c. to exert pressure against any employer to recognize a particular union when another union has been certified by the NLRB, and
   d. economic pressure in a jurisdictional dispute.
5. To charge an excessive or discriminatory fee as a condition precedent to membership in a union under a union shop clause.
6. To cause or attempt to cause an employer to pay or deliver any money or other thing of value, in the nature of an exaction, for services which are not performed or not to be performed.

The prohibition on unfair labor practices by unions protected employees in several ways. First, employees were protected from union restraint and coercion, just as the Wagner Act had protected them from employer coercion. Employees were also protected from union pressure exerted through their employers—with the sole exception of the obligation to pay union dues under a valid union shop agreement. Section 8(b)(4) protected nonunion workers in nonunion firms from union pressure even if they had obtained business by undercutting the conditions that existed in unionized firms. Under the union shop, employees were also protected from excessive or discriminatory initiation dues and fees.

The protection given to employers by the Taft-Hartley Act was certainly as significant as the protection given to employees. Unions were stripped of their power to induce employers to discharge persons who were antiunion. Section 8(b)(4) gave nonunion employers very substantial new insulation from unions that sought to organize their employees through boycotts. Section 8(b)(3), which required unions to bargain, and Section 8(b)(6) which was aimed at eliminating "featherbedding" were not to prove very significant. The new obligation for unions to bargain was somewhat frivolous since a union's reason for being is to bargain. The prohibition against featherbedding proved to be too vague to be meaningfully interpreted by the NLRB and the courts.

Obligatory Bargaining Procedures. The Taft-Hartley law changed the definition of the obligation to bargain, which the NLRB and courts had formulated, in only one important way—it provided a cooling-off period in the termination of agreements. Section 8(d) requires the party intending to terminate or modify a collective agreement to serve a written notice of such intention on the other party to the agreement 60 days prior to the proposed date of termination or modification. Thirty days after the serving of a termination notice, the Federal Mediation and Conciliation Service and the state mediation agency must be notified of the existence of the dispute. A strike or a lockout before the expiration of this 60-day period or the termination date of the agreement, whichever occurs later, is an unfair labor practice. An employee who strikes in violation of this provision loses all protection of the law and may be discharged for this kind of union activity. We shall discuss the functions of the Federal Mediation and Conciliation Service later.

Regulating the Internal Affairs of Unions. Many of the legislators who supported the Taft-Hartley law were deeply concerned over Communist infiltration of labor unions, the misappropriation of union funds, the monopoly aspects of the closed shop, and undemocratic procedures in unions. These concerns provided a basis for a new legislative departure in regulating the internal affairs of unions.

The Taft-Hartley attack on Communist influence in unions made the services of the NLRB available only to Internationals and Locals whose officers swore out "non-Communist affidavits." This indirectly, for the first time, told unions how to run—or at least how *not* to run—their business. (The Landrum-Griffin law has gone further on this issue by a direct and positive prohibition and added a ban on racketeers.)

Congressional concern over the use of union funds was evidenced by the reporting requirements imposed on labor organizations and the prohibition on political expenditures by unions and corporations. Unions which failed to file annual reports on their finances with the Secretary of Labor were denied all access to the facilities of the NLRB. Violation of the ban on political expenditures was punishable by fines and imprisonment.

The Taft-Hartley ban on the closed shop deprived unions of the time-honored right to *effectively* set their own rules for admission to the union. Although the unions' rights to set their own admission standards were explicitly excepted from the union unfair labor practice of restraint and coercion of employees, the real power to set admission requirements ultimately resides in the ability to force the discharge from employment of the nonmember. In the closed shop ban and the Taft-Hartley's provisions for discharge only for nonpayment of dues, Congress severely restricted the power to set admission requirements. Even the question of "excessive and discriminatory" initiation fees came under the scrutiny of the NLRB. We shall have more to say about the importance of the ban on the closed shop and Section 14(b) which authorized state "right-to-work" laws in Chapter 9.

The Taft-Hartley Act's regulations of the internal affairs of unions were primarily aimed at the disclosure of union rules and procedures to governmental officers and the union membership. The Landrum-Griffin law goes beyond disclosure in prescribing affirmatively how unions shall operate.

National Emergency Strikes.   As defined in the Taft-Hartley Act, a national emergency dispute has two essential features: (1) it affects an entire industry or a substantial part thereof *and* (2) it imperils the national health and safety. In such a dispute, the President is empowered to appoint a board of inquiry to ascertain the causes and circumstances of the disputes. Upon receipt of the report of the board of inquiry, the President may direct the Attorney General to petition any district court for an 80-day injunction against the strike or lockout. The district court will issue the injunction if the dispute has *both* of the features required. The board of inquiry is reconvened when the injunction is issued. If the dispute is not settled in the next 60 days, the board of inquiry reports the positions of the parties and the employer's last offer to the President who in turn makes the report public. The NLRB within the next 15 days conducts a secret ballot of the employees involved to determine if they wish to accept the employer's last offer. If no settlement is reached by the eightieth day, the injunction is discharged. The President then reports to the Congress and *may* recommend legislation to deal with the dispute.

It needs to be emphasized here that after the 80-day injunction the union is free to strike and the management is free to lock out. *Neither* the President *nor* the board of inquiry is empowered to recommend terms of settlement. The procedure consists of an 80-day cooling-off period, extensive publicity to the positions of the parties (but no official judgment of the propriety of those positions), and the permission for Presidential petition of Congress for *ad hoc* legislation if all else fails.

It is neither unfair nor premature to say that the Taft-Hartley provisions did not solve the problem of national emergency strikes. The Landrum-Griffin law did not amend the Taft-Hartley Act on national emergency disputes.

Remedies under the Taft-Hartley Act. Besides substantially increasing the scope of governmental regulation of collective bargaining, the Taft-Hartley law imposed new sanctions in addition to the remedies provided by the Wagner Act, on persons and organizations who violated its provisions. The new sanctions were: criminal penalties of fine and imprisonment, injunctions, and private suits for damages. The criminal penalties applied to violations of the ban on political contributions, false non-Communist affidavits, violations of the rules on checkoff and welfare funds, and willful interference with an agent of the Board. The Board was empowered to obtain injunctions to prevent the occurrence of unfair labor practices. In the case of boycotts, this injunction process was mandatory on the Board. Federal courts were empowered to hear private damage suits against labor unions for violations of collective bargaining agreements.

Just as the substance of the Taft-Hartley law was directed mostly against unions, the new remedies related primarily to union activity. It is important to note that the NLRB (*not* private parties) was empowered to get injunctions against unfair labor practices. The Norris-La Guardia Act was not repealed, it was merely amended, in that a specific governmental agency was empowered to use injunctive relief against specific unlawful acts. As has been indicated above, the injunction is a particularly potent weapon in labor relations. Congress very wisely limited the use of this weapon to a governmental agency.

The Taft-Hartley Act in Perspective. The Taft-Hartley law was passed in a climate of postwar reaction against the upsurge of union power. Time and experience have dissipated much of the emotion that enveloped earlier discussions of the Taft-Hartley Act. What is important about the law today is quite different from what appeared to be most important in the late forties. The law's lasting impression on society and collective bargaining in the enterprise can be briefly summarized.

From the viewpoint of society, the Taft-Hartley Act leaves some unsolved problems as well as some clear failures and some clear progress. Experience with the Taft-Hartley law clearly illustrates the futility of trying to balance the bargaining power of managements and unions exactly in society as a whole. General remedies cannot provide the much sought balance between such diverse relationships as the small union against the giant corporation or the giant union against the tiny employer. Although the Taft-Hartley's legislative recognition of the national emergency disputes probably served the public interest well, the remedies provided by the Taft-Hartley Act leave much to be desired. For better or for worse, the free speech amendment, the ban on secondary boycotts, and the regulation of union security both in the Act and in right-to-work states retarded the spread of unionism in nonunion areas and industries. The seed for the governmental regulation of the internal affairs of unions found in the Taft-Hartley Act sprouted in the Landrum-Griffin Act. It is still too soon to make firm predictions about exactly where the governmental regulation of internal affairs of unions will lead society. Probably the most significant conclusion that can be drawn from the operation of the Taft-Hartley Act is that unions have been recognized as a permanent institution in society.

From the viewpoint of bargaining in the enterprise, the impact of the Taft-Hartley Act was relatively slight. The total fabric of the Taft-Hartley law made organizing more difficult for unions in their formative stages than in earlier years. The Taft-Hartley prohibition on the closed shop in industries with casual and intermittent employment was so unrealistic that it encouraged widespread violation which had to be (at least partially) patched up in the Landrum-Griffin Act. The statutory bargaining procedures provided by the Taft-Hartley Act probably have been helpful to the parties in establishing a better plan for negotiations.

The Landrum-Griffin Act of 1959

When it was first enacted newspaper headline writers called this act the labor reform law. This reflected the hope of some of its sponsors and a large segment of the public that it would bring about inner-union democracy and honest leadership where these might be lacking or in danger. Other observers, not so confident, admitted at least that it put the means for doing this within the grasp of rank-and-file union members. Still others sardonically called it the lawyers' full employment act because of its precedent-shattering provisions, some of which are most obscurely and ambiguously drafted and seem headed for years of test and challenge in the courts.

It will be helpful to look into the events that brought about its passage.

Background of the Act. The issue which split the AFL and called the CIO into being—the issue of industrial unionism—soon ceased to be a difference in practice. Unions of both federations organized industrial locals where that form was appropriate. Reunification of the labor movement thus became thinkable soon after the split, and unfriendly overtones in Taft-Hartley gave unions common cause to heal the breach. Before the merger in 1955, some leaders in both camps opposed reunification. Others who wanted it hesitated, because each side imputed to the other a tolerance of certain evils that were barriers to unity. These were: Communist leadership and influence in some CIO unions; and racketeering in some unions of the AFL.

Reunificaton, therefore, seemed to call for action on both these inner-union problems; and effective action proved difficult. Neither the AFL nor the CIO could step in to straighten out the internal affairs of an autonomous International. Expulsion, the strongest disciplinary measure available, merely drove out the per capita paying members as well as their offending officers, without accomplishing reform. Outside authority was needed.

From 1957 to 1959, a committee headed by Senator McClellan conducted hearings that uncovered evidence of crime, corruption, collusion, malpractices, and dubious dealings in a few old-line AFL unions, notably the Longshoremen (East Coast) and the Teamsters. It was at the height of public excitement over these revelations that the Landrum-Griffin Act became law.

What does it aim to do? How does it propose to do it?

Aims of the Law. The Landrum-Griffin law has two aims: (*a*) to set minimum standards of democratic procedure, responsibility, and honesty in the conduct of the internal affairs of unions and (*b*) to clarify congressional intent on basic labor relations policy as stated in the Taft-Hartley Act. The first six titles of the Landrum-Griffin Act, taken together, lay down a comprehensive program dealing with three problem areas of inner-union democracy: (1) the rights of union members; (2) responsibilities of union officers, and (3) safeguards on the use of union funds. Parenthetically it should be stated that Title II also requires employers to file reports on their financial relationships with union leaders and payments made to persons for the purpose of influencing employees in the exercise of their rights under the law. Title VII amends the Taft-Hartley Act by (1) tightening up the Taft-Hartley regulation of secondary boycotts and hot cargo agreements, (2) liberalizing the Taft-Hartley law on union security and the right of economic strikers to vote in NLRB elections, and (3) imposing additional restrictions on the rights of unions to picket for recognition.

Inner-Union Democracy and Responsibility. Before the passage of the Taft-Hartley Act, no agency except the courts was ever responsible for regulating the internal affairs of unions. It probably is not an exaggeration to say that, in general, unions were viewed as private clubs or fraternal organizations. Like college fraternities, they were free to set their own qualifications for membership and to exclude from membership anyone who violated their rules or incurred the indignation of the officers or the membership. In some unions, particularly the old-line craft unions, racial discrimination played a role in admission to membership. Most unions also took a very dim view of a member who crossed its picket lines. However, racial discrimination in employment was perfectly legal in many states and even churches have been known to crack down on members who violate their rules.

Many persons both sympathetic and hostile to the labor movement were gravely concerned about civil liberties in labor unions. By 1947, many unions were powerful enough to negotiate agreements which made membership in the union a condition precedent to employment. Under a closed shop agreement, the union literally could deny a job to a worker. This concentration of power in the hands of the union could be viewed in three ways. First, it could be argued, as most union leaders did argue, that this power held by unions was no greater than the power held by any employer. This argument, if it carried, would result in no governmental regulation of unions' internal affairs. Second, it could be argued—and this argument carried in the Taft-Hartley Act—that no unions should be permitted to possess this power. The Taft-Hartley Act simply outlawed the closed shop. No matter how distasteful a worker might be to the union, his right to work could be upheld by his employer so long as the worker paid his union dues. Third, it could be said that union members had a legitimate interst in who worked alongside them and that any legislation should be directed at the arbitrary, discriminatory, or antisocial exercise of the power that the closed shop created. Although supported by many public-spirited authorities on labor-management relations and civil liberties, the third argument has not been accepted in legislation. The Taft-Hartley law sought to protect workers from undemocratic unions by depriving all unions of effective control over the act of employment.

The Landrum-Griffin law carries the basic civil liberties rationale of the Taft-Hartley law one step further. It seeks to guarantee union members democratic procedures inside their unions. The Taft-Hartley law's protection of the worker who wants to refrain from membership in a union is unchanged.

a) Rights of Union Members. Title I of the Landrum-Griffin Act sets forth a bill of rights for members of labor organizations. These rights are summarized in Figure 4–2. Members are guaranteed the right to vote on union matters and to engage in political activity within the union. Union dues can be increased only by following a prescribed procedure. Members are given the right to sue the union and its officers in federal courts for deprivation of their guaranteed rights. Title VI makes it a criminal offense punishable by fines and/or imprisonment to use violence or the threat of violence to interfere with a member's exercise of his guaranteed rights.

b) Responsibilities of Union Officers. The Landrum-Griffin Act extended the regulation of union officers started by the Taft-Hartley law and changed the method of applying congressional pressure on the unions. Taft-Hartley denied the use of the NLRB to *unions* whose officers refused to swear out non-Communist affidavits. The Landrum-Griffin Act imposed its penalty on the union *officer* who violated its provisions and repealed the Taft-Hartley's penalty on unions which had noncomplying officers. The Landrum-Griffin Act prohibited former Communists and felons from holding union office for five years after they left the Party or

FIGURE 4–2

THE LANDRUM-GRIFFIN "BILL OF RIGHTS" FOR UNION MEMBERS

Under Title I, every member of a labor organization engaged in an industry affecting interstate commerce is to have the following rights and privileges:

1. *Equal rights* to nominate candidates for union elections, attend membership meetings, and vote on union business.
2. *Freedom of speech and assembly* in and out of union meetings, so long as such conduct does not interfere with the union's performance of its legal or contractual obligations.
3. *Dues and initiation fees* can be increased, and assessments can be levied, only as follows:
    a) by Locals, by secret vote of the membership.
    b) by Internationals,
        (1) by majority vote of the delegates to a convention, or
        (2) by majority vote of the members in good standing voting in a secret ballot referendum, or
        (3) between conventions, if authorized by the union constitution, by the majority of the executive board, but effective only until the next regular convention.
    c) The AFL-CIO and similiar federations of unions are specifically excluded from these regulations.
4. *Members' right to sue.* Unions are prohibited from limiting the right of any member to bring a court action or administrative proceeding against the union. However, union members may be required to exhaust reasonable hearing procedures within the union (but not to exceed a four month lapse of time) before instituting a legal or administrative proceeding against the union or any of its officers.
5. *Procedural safeguards.* No member may be disciplined by a union or any of its officers, except for nonpayment of dues, without being served with written specific charges, given a reasonable time to prepare his defense, and afforded a full and fair hearing.
6. *Retention of existing rights.* Nothing in Title I shall limit the rights of any union member under any state or federal law or before any court or other tribunal, or under any union's constitution or bylaws.
7. *Right to copies of collective bargaining agreements.* Local unions must supply every member who requests it a copy of any agreement made by the Local which directly affects his rights as an employee. International unions are required to supply their constituent units with copies of agreements directly affecting the constituent unit's membership.

Any person whose rights under Title I have been infringed may bring action for appropriate relief including an injunction in a United States District Court.

Section 610 of the law states: "It shall be unlawful for any person through the use of force or violence, or threat of the use of force or violence, to restrain, coerce, or intimidate or attempt to restrain, coerce, or intimidate any member of a labor organization for the purpose of interfering with or preventing the exercise of any right to which he is entitled under the provisions of this Act. Any person who willfully violates this section shall be fined not more than $1,000 or imprisoned for not more than one year, or both."

were convicted of crime, or were released from jail after conviction. Labor organizations and their officers were charged with the responsibility of excluding such persons from union office. Persons who willfully violate this section of the Landrum-Griffin law are subject to fines of up to $10,000 and/or one year in prison.

Title IV of the Landrum-Griffin Act is devoted to the regulation of union elections and internal political campaigns. International unions are required to hold elections for officers at least every five years and more frequently if required by their constitutions. Such elections must be held by secret ballot among the members in good standing or at a convention of delegates chosen by secret ballot. Local unions must elect their officers not less often than once every three years by secret ballot among the members in good standing. If the Secretary of Labor finds that a union constitution does not contain adequate provisions for the removal of officers guilty of misconduct, any officers guilty of such misconduct may be removed, after notice and hearing, by a secret ballot of the membership. A member of the union is authorized to enlist the assistance of the Secretary of Labor and the courts in invalidating improper elections after the member has exhausted the remedies available to him within the union. Title IV also gives candidates for union office an opportunity to examine list of eligible voters and prohibits the expenditure of the union's funds to support candidates for union office.

Many International constitutions permit the executive board or the convention to establish a "trusteeship" or provisional government over a Local union or other subordinate union body. The power to create a trusteeship has been used in the past for such laudatory purposes as preserving a Local's funds from embezzlement or to eliminate Communist or other officers who were undermining the legitimate activities of the Local. The trustee device is also a powerful means of suppressing democracy within the Local, or destroying opposition to the International officers at the grass roots level, or the milking of a Local by the International officers. Title III of the Landrum-Griffin law brings the trustee device under statutory control. Trusteeship may be established only in accordance with the union's constitution for the purposes of: (*a*) correcting corruption or financial malpractice, (*b*) assuring the performance of collective bargaining agreements, (*c*) restoring democratic procedures, or (*d*) "otherwise carrying out the legitimate objects of such labor organization." During a trusteeship the votes of a Local union may be counted in a convention or union election only if the delegates have been chosen by secret ballot in which all members of the Local could vote. The funds of a Local in trusteeship cannot be transferred to the International. The Secretary of Labor must be informed when a trusteeship is imposed and semiannual reports on the operation of the trusteeship must be submitted to him.

c) Safeguards on Union Funds. The officers, agents, shop stewards, and other representatives of a labor organization occupy positions of trust in relation to the union and its members as a group. Title V of the Landrum-Griffin law requires persons holding such positions to hold the union's money and property solely for the benefit of the union and its members. Persons holding offices in unions or employed by unions are prohibited from holding or acquiring any pecuniary or personal interests which conflict with the union's interests. Every union representative who handles union money must be bonded for at least 10 percent of the funds which he normally handles in a fiscal year, but need not be bonded for more than $500,000. Labor organizations may not loan any officer or employee more than $2,000. Unions may not pay the fines of their officers or employees convicted of violating the Landrum-Griffin Act. Theft or embezzlement of union funds is a federal crime subject to a fine of up to $10,000 and/or imprisonment for up to five years.

Before leaving the comprehensive code for the regulation of the internal affairs of unions, a word should be said about new powers and duties of the Secretary of Labor. The Secretary of Labor is not only required to receive a large number of reports on internal union affairs, he also is empowered to conduct investigations on a wide range of union affairs and to assist union members in court cases. Under the Landrum-Griffin Act, the Bureau of Labor-Management Reports of the Department of Labor has become a great depository of all kinds of information on the internal operations of labor unions. The files of the Bureau are a gold mine for persons interested in research on unionism. It is to be hoped that researchers will give us a much better understanding of union operations by taking full advantage of the Bureau's policy of encouraging scholarly research.

In addition to regulating the internal affairs of unions, the Landrum-Griffin Act carried forward the legislative intent of the Taft-Hartley law.

Taft-Hartley Amendments. Secondary boycotts, the rights of economic strikers to vote in NLRB elections, and recognition picketing were regulated by the Taft-Hartley Act. Apparently Congress was dissatisfied with the application of the Taft-Hartley provisions because it substantially amended the previous regulations in all three areas.

a) Secondary Boycotts and Hot Cargo Agreements. Section 8(b)(4)(A) of the Taft-Hartley Act was aimed at "secondary boycotts." Secondary boycotts are not easy to define, but in general they are attempts by a union to induce some other party (union members, consumers, or an employer) to cease doing business with someone. As the NLRB and the courts interpreted Section 8(b)(4)(A) several kinds of activities were not in violation of the Taft-Hartley law, e.g., (1) inducements of a *single* employee to strike or to refuse to handle goods, (2) inducements of employers directly, instead of through a strike of their employees, and (3) inducements of employees excluded from the definition of employees in the Taft-Hartley Act, i.e., railroad workers or municipal employees. The Landrum-Griffin Act amended Section 8(b)(4)(A) of the Taft-Hartley and closed the secondary boycott loopholes tight, by substituting the word "person" for "employees."

A hot cargo clause is an agreement between an employer and a union that the employees covered by the agreement will not be required to handle "unfair" goods, e.g., struck work or nonunion goods. The Landrum-Griffin Act outlawed hot cargo agreements except: (1) in the construction industry agreements relating to "the contracting or subcontracting of work to be done at the site of the construction, alteration, painting or repair of a building, structure or other work," and (2) "persons in the relation of a jobber, manufacturer, contractor or subcontractor working on the goods or premises of the jobber or manufacturer or performing parts of an integrated process of production in the apparel and clothing industry."

The Landrum-Griffin amendments on secondary boycotts and hot cargo severely restrict a union's power to make its strike effective. Under Landrum-Griffin a struck employer is free to transfer work to other plants and to subcontract the work that otherwise would be performed by the people on strike. The hot cargo ban severely restricts the power formerly held by the Teamsters' Union to help strikers by cutting off the flow of goods and services to a struck plant. Although unions have some protected activity in advertising to their members and the general public the presence of unfair goods, they no longer are able to picket an employer who is selling unfair goods or who is performing operations on struck work.

b) Union Security and Economic Strikers.   There was very little in the Landrum-Griffin Act that could be termed prounion. Still, building trades union leaders could be heartened by the new union security provisions, garment union leaders could be encouraged by the exemption of their industry from the hot cargo and secondary boycott bans, and industrial unions could get some comfort from the revised right of economic strikers to vote in NLRB elections.

In 1947, the Taft-Hartley law outlawed the closed shop and thereby threatened to upset long-established ways of doing business in the construction industry. It is not inaccurate to say that the Taft-Hartley law failed to destroy the closed shop practice in many industries. Landrum-Griffin took a step backward toward the realities of life in the construction industry. A new Section 8(f) permits employers and unions primarily engaged in the building and construction industry to enter into agreements before workers are hired and to establish a seven-day union shop. The prehire contract coupled with the seven-day union shop certainly approximates the closed shop *modus operandi* in the construction industry.

Under the Taft-Hartley law strikers not eligible for reinstatement were denied the right to vote in NLRB decertification elections. Under this provision it was possible for an employer to provoke an economic strike, to replace the strikers, and then obtain an NLRB election in which the union members on strike could not vote. Obviously, the assured result of such an election would be the decertification of the striking union. Landrum-Griffin sought to remedy this unfair situation by providing that the NLRB was empowered to permit economic strikers who had been replaced to vote in an NLRB election held within 12 months after the beginning of the strike.

c) Organizational and Recognition Picketing. The Landrum-Griffin Act adds a new Section 8(b)(7) to the National Labor Relations Act. This section makes it an unfair labor practice for a union to picket, or to threaten to picket, where an object is to gain recognition or promote organization of the employees, under three circumstances: (A) where the employer has recognized another labor organization; (B) for 12 months following a valid representation election lost by a union; and (C) where, apart from the foregoing circumstances, "such picketing has been conducted without a petition under section 9(c) being filed within a reasonable period of time, not to exceed 30 days." The circumstances described in (C) are qualified in two respects: (1) the union need not demonstrate "a showing of substantial interest" or claim recognition, and (2) picketing beyond the 30-day period, or other publicity addressed to the public and consumers, is permitted if the effect of the picketing is not to induce a disruption of services at the employer's place of business.

Although the primary aim of Section 8(b)(7) was probably to protect employers from harrassment picketing, this provision does enable a union to obtain a quick NLRB election by the method of picketing.

Section 602 of Landrum-Griffin outlaws extortionate picketing. Any person who carries on picketing for the purpose of personal profit or the enrichment of any other individual (except a bona fide increase in wages or other employee benefits) by taking or obtaining anything of value from an employer against his will is subject to a fine of up to $10,000 and/or imprisonment up to 20 years.

The Significance of the Landrum-Griffin Act. When the Landrum-Griffin Act was passed in 1959, the meaning of many provisions of the Taft-Hartley Act of 1947 was still uncertain because of a lack of full judicial review. It is obviously much too soon to state the impact of the Landrum-Griffin Act except in the most general terms.

The provisions of the Landrum-Griffin Act that strictly belong in the field of labor-management relations are relatively minor. They seek to plug up the loopholes in the Taft-Hartley ban on secondary boycotts; they prohibit hot cargo agreements of the Teamsters and others (but not the garment unions); they restrict organizational and recognition picketing. They potentially extend the jurisdiction of the states in making labor law and improve the speed of case handling by the NLRB. They also meet some long-standing union demands. Economic strikers get the right to vote in NLRB elections. The closed shop, for all practical purposes, is reauthorized in the construction industry.

More important to the future of collective bargaining than these changes in labor relations law is the fact of direct government intervention in the affairs of unions. Unions heretofore were private organizations. Normally they were democratic; sometimes not. In either case, government regulation touched only their relations with other organizations. As long as they kept within the laws of the surrounding democratic society, it was no business of anyone in government whether they were democratic or autocratic, honest or corrupt, run by the members or by self-perpetuating bosses, or, indeed, by thugs. The Taft-Hartley Act provided only minimal regulation of the internal affairs of unions.

The Landrum-Griffin Act changes all that. In the most positive fashion, under the threat of heavy penalties, it *directs*, specifically and in detail over a wide range of issues, that unions shall be democratically administered. Whether it succeeds or fails to reach its aim, there will be repercussions in the years to come not only in the union hall but at the bargaining table.

SUMMARY

The third main actor in the collective bargaining system is the government, personified by many different elected officials and civil servants, each charged with responsibility for protecting the public interest. In some areas, like the obligation to bargain and the right of employees to be represented by representatives of their own choosing, the public interest has been clearly articulated by statutes and administrative rulings. In other areas, like strikes, mediation, and noninflationary wage settlements, the public interest has not been so clearly defined. The public interest changes over time.

Statutory law on labor relations in the United States is largely permissive in nature. The first labor relations law applicable to all interstate commerce, the Norris–La Guardia Act of 1932, restricted the issuance of injunctions in labor disputes and made the yellow dog contract unenforceable at law. The Wagner Act of 1935 created the National Labor Relations Board and gave it broad powers in formulating administrative law. The Wagner Act introduced the ballot box as the basic way of obtaining union recognition and protected employees' right to organize by prohibiting unfair labor practices by management. The Taft-Hartley law of 1947 amended the Wagner Act by protecting the right of workers to refrain from union organization and redressing the balance of power between management and unions by prohibiting unfair labor practices by unions. The Landrum-Griffin Act of 1959 was a major innovation in labor relations legislation in that it provided detailed regulation of the internal affairs of unions.

Part I of this book has introduced the three actors (employers, union, and government) in the collective bargaining system and discussed their goals and methods of operation. Part II is devoted to the interaction of the actors in reconciling their sometimes conflicting goals and establishing a system for living together. Part III is an analysis of the rules which the parties have formulated in different contexts of markets, technology, and power relations. Part IV puts collective bargaining in perspective in time and space: reviews its history, discusses its practice in other countries, and makes some predictions for the future. Part V explores the problems encountered in applying the rules to diverse day-to-day operational conditions.

QUESTIONS FOR DISCUSSION

1. Since American labor relations law is largely permissive, why study it?
2. Show how the Norris–La Guardia Act, the Wagner Act, the Taft-Hartley Act, and Landrum-Griffin Act succeeded or failed in "balancing" the bargaining power of management and unions.
3. Does *protective* labor legislation have any influence on collective bargaining?
4. By reference to specific pertinent provisions of the Wagner Act, Taft-Hartley Act, and Landrum-Griffin Act, trace changes in American public policy on the regulation of the internal affairs of unions. Have American unions become instrumentalities of the state?
5. The Railway Labor Act is noteworthy for the fact that it represented a consensus between management and unions. How might a consensus between managements and unions be developed for future collective bargaining legislation?

CASES: 1, 2, 3.

SELECTED ANNOTATED BIBLIOGRAPHY

AARON, BENJAMIN. "The Labor-Management Reporting and Disclosure Act of 1959," *Harvard Law Review*, Vol. LXXIII (March–April, 1960), pp. 851–907 and 1086–1127.

An authoritative discussion of the Landrum-Griffin Act.

BARNES, STANLEY N., GOLDBERG, ARTHUR J., and MILLER, LAMBERT H. "Unions and the Anti-Trust Laws," *Labor Law Journal*, Vol. VII (March, 1956), pp. 133–36, 178–86, 186–92.

Three papers on unions and the antitrust laws. Mr. Barnes, Assistant Attorney General in charge of the Anti-Trust Division of the Department of Justice, sketches the present statutory pattern and raises problems posed by possible extension of antitrust action to the labor relations area. Mr. Goldberg, special Counsel to the AFL-CIO, examines monopoly charges against individual unions and the AFL-CIO, and boycotts, jurisdictional disputes, and featherbedding as grounds for antitrust action. Mr. Miller, general counsel of the National Association of Manufacturers, compares the structure of modern unionism and modern business and argues that there should be no "double standard" in the application of the antitrust laws.

BROWN, LEO C., S.J. "Consensus in Labor Relations," chap. 8, *Arbitration and Public Policy*, SPENCER D. POLLARD (ed.). Proceedings of the Fourteenth Annual Meeting of the National Academy of Arbitrators, Washington, D.C.: Bureau of National Affairs, 1961, pp. 193–202.

Father Brown argues that industrial relations problems are rapidly increasing in their complexity, that the parties are doing a good job of settling them, and that the purpose of legislation should be to force the parties to face up to the responsibility of settling their own problems.

COHEN, SANFORD. "An Analytical Framework for Labor Relations Law," *Industrial and Labor Relations Review*, Vol. XIV (April, 1961), pp. 350–62.

The author suggests that the timing and character of labor law can be regarded as a variable which is dependent upon the "resultant of the prevailing ideology of property rights and the degree of access to political power enjoyed by private power blocks." This two-variable framework is applied to an analysis of the American legal experience; the concept of "countervailing power" as an alternative explanation is also considered.

COX, ARCHIBALD. "Internal Affairs of Labor Unions Under the Labor Reform Act of 1959," *Michigan Law Review*, Vol. LVIII (April, 1960), pp. 819–54.

Following a summary of the legislative background of the Labor-Management Reporting and Disclosure Act of 1959, the author discusses and evaluates the provisions of the act that deal with the internal affairs of labor organizations.

COX, ARCHIBALD. "The Duty to Bargain in Good Faith," *Harvard Law Review*, Vol. LXXI (June, 1958), pp. 1401–42.

Professor Cox analyzes NLRB decisions having the effect of enlarging the scope of substantive issues in collective bargaining.

CUSHMAN, EDWARD L. "Management Objectives in Collective Bargaining," ARNOLD W. WEBER (ed.), *The Structure of Collective Bargaining: Problems and Perspectives*, pp. 59–75. New York: The Free Press of Glencoe, Inc., 1961.

Mr. Cushman, Vice-President of American Motors Corporation, argues that sound public policy would be (1) dissolution of very large firms under the antitrust laws and (2) limiting the responsibility for collective bargaining with an employer in a basic industry to a union composed solely of the employees of that company. Discusses the decentralization of collective bargaining within American Motors Corporation.

DUNLOP, JOHN T. "The Arbitration of Jurisdictional Disputes in the Building Industry," *Arbitration Today*, JEAN T. McKELVEY (ed.). Proceedings of the Eighth Annual Meeting of the National Academy of Arbitrators, pp. 161–65. Washington, D.C.: Bureau of National Affairs, 1955.

Discusses the early history of the National Joint Board for the Adjustment of Jurisdictional Disputes in the Building and Construction Industry.

EVANS, HYWELL. *Governmental Regulation of Industrial Relations: A Comparative Study of the United States and British Experience*. Ithaca, N.Y.: New York State School of Industrial Relations, 1961.

A critical analysis of the development of public policy in the field of labor-management relations in the United States by a British observer. Attempts to explain the comparative increase in government intervention and control of collective bargaining in the U.S. since the late nineteenth century; comments on the success of mediation, arbitration and emergency-disputes procedures, and appraises the status of unionism since the passage of the Taft-Hartley Act.

GREGORY, CHARLES O. *Labor and the Law*. 2d rev. ed.; New York: W. W. Norton & Co., Inc., 1958.

A scholarly and very readable account of American labor relations law with heavy emphasis on the common-law background.

INDEPENDENT STUDY GROUP, COMMITTEE FOR ECONOMIC DEVELOPMENT. *The Public Interest in National Labor Policy*. New York: CED, 1961.

Clark Kerr, Douglas V. Brown, David L. Cole, John T. Dunlop, William Y. Elliott, Albert Rees, Robert H. Solow, Philip Taft, and George W. Taylor compose the membership of the Study Group. George P. Shultz, Abraham Siegel, and David Burke compose the staff. Discussion of, and recommendations on: the public interest and private responsibilities; function and control of strikes and lockouts; collective bargaining, inflation and effective use of manpower; private power and its control; and individual rights in effective institutions.

MILLIS, HARRY A., and BROWN, EMILY CLARK. *From the Wagner Act to Taft-Hartley: A Study of National Labor Policy and Labor Relations*. Chicago: University of Chicago Press, 1950.

A landmark in labor legislation scholarship. Part I, The Wagner Act, by Professor Brown. Parts II and III, the Taft-Hartley Act, planned and partially written by the late Professor Millis, former Chairman of the National Labor Relations Board. Parts of this book provide a statement of Professor Millis's philosophy of industrial relations. The book includes detailed analyses of a number of the NLRB's major policies and their change over time.

SEIDENBERG, JACOB. *The Labor Injunction in New York City: 1935–1950*. Ithaca, N.Y.: New York State School of Industrial and Labor Relations, 1953.

An exhaustive study of the issuance of labor injunctions by the courts of the state of New York after the passage of the Norris–La Guardia Act.

SHISTER, JOSEPH, AARON, BENJAMIN, and SUMMERS, CLYDE W. (eds.). *Public Policy and Collective Bargaining*. New York: Harper & Row, 1962.

A volume published by the Industrial Relations Research Association. Specialists in industrial relations and law analyze the following: "An Historical Evolution of Public Policy in Labor Relations," by DOUGLASS V. BROWN and CHARLES A. MYERS; "Employer Free Speech," by BENJAMIN AARON; "The Obligation to Bargain in Good Faith," by ROBBEN W. FLEMING; "The Union Security Issue," by PAUL E. SULTAN; "Picketing and Boycotts," by DONALD H. WOLLETT; "Collective Bargaining and the Antitrust Laws," by GEORGE H. HILDEBRAND; "Legal Regulation of Internal Union Affairs," by JOSEPH R. GRODIN; and "A Comparison of U.S. and Canadian Experiences," by HARRY D. WOODS.

SMITH, RUSSELL A. "The Labor-Management Reporting and Disclosure Act of 1959," *Virginia Law Review*, Volume XLVI (March, 1960), pp. 195–251.

An authoritative discussion of the Landrum-Griffin Act.

"The Taft-Hartley Law After Ten Years: A Symposium," *Industrial and Labor Relations Review*, Vol. XI (April, 1958), pp. 327–412.

Seven experts discuss experience under the Taft-Hartley law. Contents: AARON, BENJAMIN. "Amending the Taft-Hartley Act: A Decade of Frustration."

SHISTER, JOSEPH. "The Impact of the Taft-Hartley Act on Union Strength and Collective Bargaining."

TAFT, PHILIP. "Internal Affairs of Unions and the Taft-Hartley Act."

ABELOW, ROBERT. "Management Experience under the Taft-Hartley Act."

KLAUS, IDA. "The Taft-Hartley Experience in Separation of NLRB Functions."

ISAACSON, WILLIAM J. "Federal Preemption under the Taft-Hartley Act."

SUMMERS, CLYDE W. "A Summary Evaluation of the Taft-Hartley Act."

PART II

Collective Bargaining Activities

Part II of this book considers the activities of employers, workers, and government representatives in establishing the collective bargaining relationship and arriving at the collective bargaining agreement; the nature of the collective bargaining agreement; and living with the collective bargaining agreement.

Chapter 5	ESTABLISHING THE COLLECTIVE BARGAINING RELATIONSHIP

The collective bargaining relationship always starts with the recognition of a union by the management of an enterprise. Recognition is preceded by a decision of some of the employees of an enterprise that they will seek union representation, or a union decision that a nonunion enterprise must be organized, or a manager's decision that a unionized operation is the best way to run his newly established business. No matter whether employees, a union, or management takes the initiative in establishing the collective bargaining relationship, an "outside" agent, the union, appears on the scene and solicits members from the employees or prospective employees of the enterprise. What happens in this period *before* the first collective bargaining agreement is negotiated is of great importance to the managers, employees, and union(s) involved. These activities are regulated by law. Prenegotiation activities sometimes generate hostility which leaves a long-lasting scar on the collective bargaining relationship.

THE INITIATIVE IN ESTABLISHING THE COLLECTIVE BARGAINING RELATIONSHIP

Typically management is the initiating force in all employment activities and the preservation of the right of managerial initiative is generally considered to be essential to enterprise efficiency. The major exception to the rule of management initiative is the activity of establishing the collective bargaining relationship. With one small exception, in the contemplation of the law, the initiative in establishing a collective bargaining relationship belongs either to employees or to a union.

Employee Initiative

Every job holds some potential or real dissatisfactions for anyone who might hold it: the pay is too low, the boss is unfair, the pace is too fast, the job itself is insecure or potentially short lived, the hours are too long, the working conditions aren't as good as they should be, or the fellow workers aren't friendly. Each employee has his own "boiling point" and his own evaluation of the qualities of the job, but for some reason a group of employees becomes dissatisfied with the conditions of their employment and conclude that the only way they can get "justice" is to form a union. These employees call a union and an organizing drive begins.

Probably no two union organizing drives are exactly alike, but some general rules do seem to apply. At the early stages of the drive, organization is conducted in secret, the union contacting employees who might join the union through other employees who have shown interest in forming a union. Only after a fair number of employees have shown an active interest will the organization conduct its campaign for members in the open. The secrecy aspect protects the early joiners from management retaliation and gives the union an idea about the prospects of a successful organizing drive before overcommitting itself or its new members. Secrecy also has the advantage of preventing management from killing an incipient union with kindness.

When a group of employees has taken the initiative in calling in a union, the union's organizing job is simplified. The employees who took the initiative can supply the union with information about grievances in the enterprise and the names of employees who most likely would favor a union as well as the names of employees who should be avoided because of their loyalty to the enterprise and the probability that they would inform management that a union organization drive was under way. Employees sympathetic to the union cause also can supply information about the sometimes vital matter of enterprise organizational structure. As a rule, an industrial union seeks membership in all production departments of the enterprise and it is desirable to have union members under the supervision of every foreman in the enterprise. Most important of all, the employees who took the initiative in calling the union serve as union organizers in the shop.

Most union organizing drives are initiated by dissatisfied employees, but some union organizing drives are initiated by unions and managements.

Union Initiative

A union is an institution to some degree independent of both its members and the enterprise which provides jobs for its members. As an independent institution, the union has ambitions for growth and an important defensive strategy of organizing all enterprises which compete with enterprises that it has organized. A pure union initiative in an organizing drive springs from the growth motive or the defensive strategy of organizing the unorganized.

Most International unions keep an eye on developments in their industry. Two examples will suffice: The International Ladies' Garment Workers' Union and the amalgamated Clothing Workers' Union operate in industries where it is very easy to open a small shop. Both unions expend a substantial portion of their resources on finding these new shops and organizing them. A different kind of situation arises when a huge industrial combine like General Motors, General Electric, or United States Steel opens an entirely new facility. The unions which have collective bargaining relationships with the parent organization watch these developments closely and launch organizing drives as soon as they learn of the company's plans.

In all of these cases the motive to unionization is different from when employees take the initiative, but the techniques of organizing are similar. In a union initiated drive, the union looks for, or "manufactures" employee grievances, sells the advantages of union membership, and seeks to start an internal chain reaction among the employees of the enterprise.

Management Initiative

A management initiative in establishing a collective bargaining relationship is extremely rare and poses a serious problem at law. *Only* employers engaged "primarily in the building and construction industry" can take the initiative in establishing a collective bargaining relationship with reasonable immunity from an unfair labor practice charge of interference, restraint, and coercion or company domination of the union.

In the construction industry, new enterprises usually come into being when a unionized tradesman bids successfully for a subcontract. The natural thing for this new entrepreneur to do is to contact a union Business Agent as the source of his potential employees. Under the Landrum-Griffin Act, except in states with general right-to-work laws, employers and unions in the building and construction industry are free to:

1. Make collective bargaining agreements *before* the majority status of the union is established under Section 9 of the law,
2. Require membership in the union as a condition of employment after the *seventh day* following employment or the effective date of the agreement, whichever is later,
3. Require the employer to notify the union of job opportunities or give the union an opportunity to refer qualified applicants for employment, and
4. Specify minimum training or experience qualifications for employment or establish priorities in opportunities for employment.

These provisions of the Landrum-Griffin Act are a substantial step toward reauthorizing long-established methods of doing business in the building trades. The prehire agreement and seven-day union shop are a close approximation of the old-time closed shop. Although the NLRB has ruled that the Landrum-Griffin prehire contract shall not stand as a bar to a petition for an NLRB certification,[1] employers in the building and

---

[1] *Twenty-Sixth Annual Report of the National Labor Relations Board for Year Ended June 30, 1961*, p. 42.

construction industry have very substantial immunity under the law in taking the initiative in establishing a collective bargaining relationship.

Employers not engaged in the building and construction industry are well advised *not* to take the initiative in establishing a collective bargaining relationship. In the early days of the Wagner Act employers frequently sought out "responsible" and "co-operative" unions and entered into "sweetheart" agreements with them. When there is evidence of union and management collusion in the signing of a collective bargaining agreement, the NLRB voids the agreement and brings unfair labor practice charges against the management. Although employer initiatives in establishing collective bargaining relationships are on the outer fringe of lawful employer activity, it is likely that a few employers do take these actions and are able to do so within the bounds of the law or without getting caught. Because union representation is so vitally significant to enterprise welfare and the wide variety of unions which might organize a single employer, it seems fair to expect that many employers are sorely tempted to take the initiative in establishing the collective bargaining relationship even though such action is of questionable legality.

Regardless of whether employees, a union, or the employer takes the initiative in establishing the collective bargaining relationship and whether the union organization drive is conducted openly or in secret, eventually there must be a union and management confrontation on the question of union recognition. Today there are two methods by which union recognition may be established.

THE TWO METHODS OF ESTABLISHING UNION RECOGNITION

Before the passage of the Wagner Act in 1935, a union could obtain recognition only by persuading an employer to grant such recognition voluntarily. Although statistics are not available, it seems quite fair to say that most unions found it necessary to persuade employers through the use of strikes, picketing, and boycotts.

Today there are two methods by which a union may obtain recognition from an employer: (1) *without* governmental intervention and (2) through the processes of the National Labor Relations Board. The law severely restricts the use of picketing by unions as a means of persuading employers to grant recognition. At the same time it provides orderly procedures for obtaining recognition. Governmental intervention is the rule of the day, but the law still protects the rights of the parties to settle their own problems without governmental intervention so long as those private settlements do not violate public policy.

Union Recognition without Governmental Intervention

If a majority of the employees in an enterprise want a certain union to represent them in collective bargaining and that union can satisfy the employer on this point, the employer may voluntarily recognize the union and bargain with it. In such cases, the union usually satisfies the employer by showing authorization cards or petitions signed by a majority of the employees in the unit. This method may be followed in any employee group whether or not the business affects commerce.

In those exceptional cases which are not subject to federal or state labor relations statutes, the union is free to strike, picket, and boycott to obtain recognition. For example, supervisors, agricultural workers, and the employees of completely nonprofit hospitals (none of whom are "employees" under the Landrum-Griffin Act) are free to strike, picket, and boycott for recognition unless prohibited by state law.

Unions of employees who are covered by the Landrum-Griffin law are subject to restrictions on how they may persuade employers to grant recognition. These restrictions on picketing and jurisdictional disputes were designed to curb abuses of the past and to protect employers from conflicting claims for union representation.

Picketing for Recognition.   Under the Landrum-Griffin Act, picketing by a union that is not recognized as bargaining agent and has not been certified by the NLRB, for the purpose of securing recognition or of forcing the employees to select it as bargaining agent, is sharply restricted. Organizational picketing is forbidden altogether where a valid NLRB election has been held within the previous 12 months or the employer lawfully recognizes another union. In such cases, an election petition will not be entertained by the NLRB. In other circumstances, e.g., a nonunion shop with no recent NLRB election, the picketing may not continue for more than 30 days without the filing of a petition for an NLRB election.

Union jurisdiction is a direct concern of the labor movement. Employers can assert only an indirect influence in the resolution of jurisdictional disputes. The old AFL attempted to control interunion competition by issuing mutually exclusive charters to International unions and deciding disputes between unions. When the CIO was born, all restraints on the issuance of overlapping charters lapsed. The high cost of jurisdictional warfare was a major inducement to the merger of the AFL and the CIO in 1955. Because of the high cost of jurisdictional warfare to union treasuries, many unions have entered into "no-raiding" agreements under the auspices of the AFL-CIO. Thus a new form of jurisdictional rights based on established collective bargaining relationships seems to be taking shape from the merger of the AFL and CIO.

The Taft-Hartley law imposes several restrictions on the freedom of unions to fight it out over jurisdictional claims. The law differentiates two types of jurisdictional strikes: (1) strikes for recognition and (2) work assignment disputes. The strike for recognition involves the attempt of a union to establish an initial collective bargaining relationship with the employer. The work assignment dispute is an attempt by a union already having a collective bargaining relationship with the employer to assert its control over certain jobs.

Jurisdictional Strikes for Recognition. The Taft-Hartley law prohibits one union from calling a strike against an employer who is dealing with another union under an NLRB certification. It also prohibits a union from strike action against Employer A for the purpose of forcing Employer B to recognize or bargain with any union which has not been certified by the NLRB as the representative of the employees of Employer B.

The NLRB's interpretation of these provisions may be illustrated by three cases:

1. Employer A deals with Union A under an NLRB certification. Union B violates the law if it calls a strike of A's employees. Union B also violates the law if it pickets A's premises because this is an inducement to strike.
2. Employer A deals with union A and purchases materials from Employer B. Employer B is nonunion or deals with Union B which has been certified by the NLRB. Union A violates the law if it strikes Employer A for the purpose of forcing Employer B to deal with any union other than Union B. Union A also violates the law if it proposes to call off the strike on the condition that Employer A refuses to place further orders with Employer B.
3. The Meat Cutters' Union represents meat buyers in a number of markets. The union wants to organize the meat salesmen of Packer A. The union violates the law if it instructs its meat buyer members not to purchase Packer A's products.

Work-Assignment Disputes. Work-assignment disputes need not involve an employer's original refusal to recognize a union. After recognition has been achieved, two rival unions may both insist on the right of their members to perform a particular task. These disputes most frequently occur in industries like building construction, organized by craft unions. A classic example of this type of dispute is the disagreement between the carpenters and the concrete workers as to who should build the necessary wooden forms. The carpenters claimed the work because the forms were wood and constructed with carpenters' tools. The concrete workers insisted that the forms were incidental to concrete work and, therefore, were within their jurisdiction.

The Taft-Hartley law provides for ultimate NLRB determination of work-assignment disputes if the disputants fail to settle them by themselves. Section 8(b)(4) forbids a labor organization from engaging in or inducing strike action for the purpose of forcing any employer to assign particular work tasks "to employees in a particular labor organization or in a particular trade, craft, or class rather than to employees in another labor organization or in another trade, craft, or class, unless such employer is failing to conform to an order or certification of the Board determining the bargaining representative for employees performing such work."

The Board may not intervene in a work-assignment dispute until certain statutory requirements are fulfilled. Section 10(k) requires that the parties to a jurisdictional dispute be given 10 days, after notice of the filing of charges with the Board, to adjust their dispute. If at the end of that time they are unable to "submit to the Board satisfactory evidence that they have adjusted, or agreed upon methods for the voluntary adjustment of the dispute," the Board is empowered to hear and determine the dispute. Section 10(k) also provides that "upon compliance by the parties to the dispute with decision of the Board or upon such voluntary adjustment of the dispute," the charge shall be dismissed. A complaint issues only if there is a failure to comply with the Board's determination. Also, a complaint may be issued in a case of the failure of the method agreed upon to adjust the dispute.

Before the passage of the Taft-Hartley law, the American Federation of Labor had made several attempts to establish machinery for the adjustment of jurisdictional disputes within the "house of labor." At best, this machinery was able to survive only a short time.

The jurisdictional disputes provisions of the Taft-Hartley law were completely unacceptable to building trades unions. They motivated the formation of a National Joint Board of Adjustment in the Building Construction Industry. This Board is composed of equal numbers of labor and contractor representatives. Its major functions are the arbitration of local jurisdictional disputes and the negotiation of national jurisdictional agreements between unions in the construction industry. The chairman of the Board has a vote to break deadlocks, but has been extremely reluctant to use it. Instead he has used his influence as a mediator of disputes. Because of the reasonably successful operation of the Board, the NLRB has received only a very few construction-industry jurisdictional disputes for arbitration. It seems fair to say that the Taft-Hartley provisions have done a good job in forcing the building trades unions to settle their jurisdictional disputes without resort to extensive strike action.

Union Recognition through the NLRB

If an employer covered by the Landrum-Griffin Act refuses voluntary recognition of a union, and there is a question as to whether the union represents a majority of the employees in the unit, or if there is a dispute over the appropriateness of the unit, the matter can be settled by filing a representation petition with the Regional Office of the NLRB.

Filing a Representation Petition. A petition can be filed by an employee or group of employees or any person or union acting on behalf of a substantial number of employees. An employer who is presented by a union with a claim that it represents a majority of his employees, or with competing claims by two or more unions each seeking recognition, can file a petition to determine the question.

If a union is currently acting as bargaining representative, any employee or group of employees, or any person or union acting on their behalf, can file a petition asking that the current union be thrown out. This is called a "decertification" petition.

A representation petition contains: (1) description of the unit of employees in which an election is sought; (2) the approximate number of employees in the unit; and (3) the names of all unions that claim to represent the employees in the unit.

When a representation petition is filed at the Regional Office, a field examiner is assigned to get answers to determine the following questions of fact:

1. Are the employer's operations within NLRB jurisdictional standards?
2. Is the proposed unit appropriate for collective bargaining?
3. Is there a sufficient showing of employee interest?
4. Is the filing of the petition timely?

In answering these questions the field examiner applies the facts of the particular case to standards that have been established by the NLRB. For a discussion of NLRB jurisdictional standards and the coverage of federal industrial relations legislation see Chapter 4.

The Appropriate Unit for Collective Bargaining. The law requires an employer to bargain with the representatives of his employees. In some instances all of the employees in a plant will want the same union to represent them because their interests are essentially the same. In other cases, different employees in a manufacturing plant may have different interests. For example, the clerical employees in an enterprise may have interests in collective bargaining substantially different from those of production employees in the same plant. In those situations each group of employees, called a "unit" for collective bargaining purposes, is entitled to have a different union represent the unit in bargaining with the employer. Acting through its Regional Director, the NLRB determines which employees should be included in the appropriate unit for collective bargaining.

The Importance of the Unit to Workers, Management, and Unions. The bargaining unit is of considerable importance to employees, management, and the unions seeking representation rights. The wage concessions available to particular groups of employees can be influenced by the bargaining unit established. For example, a small group of skilled employees might be able to negotiate substantially larger wage concessions for themselves (at the expense of the larger less skilled group) in separate bargaining. Such a separate bargaining unit in a factory might be able to impose standard rates prevailing in less regular construction employment. This would not necessarily impose excessive costs on the employer, since he might be able to trim his wage concessions to the larger group of semiskilled (and perhaps nonunion) employees.

The employer may favor small bargaining units in the hope that he can play one unit off against the other and thereby minimize his costs. Or he may favor large units because he thereby avoids the hazards of union "whipsawing" and the costs of multiple agreements and negotiations. The employer may have a particular interest in excluding a few key jobs from the bargaining unit because he feels that such workers should be identified with management, e.g., the chef in a restaurant.

From the union viewpoint, the bargaining unit determination of the NLRB may have a decisive influence in deciding who (if anyone) wins representation rights. A craft union would almost certainly be doomed to failure in an election contest with an industrial union if the NLRB decided that the appropriate unit included all production and maintenance workers. The probable fate of an industrial union in a contest with a craft union over the representation of a small group of employees who had served a traditional apprenticeship is equally certain. Of course, union election units are also potentially subject to the gerrymandering game. The inclusion of groups of employees known to be antiunion in an appropriate unit would have an important influence on the outcome of the election, as for instance the lumping of office staff with manual employees.

Given these diverse interests, what criteria does the NLRB apply in carrying out its statutory obligation to determine the appropriate unit for collective bargaining? The Board is governed by limited statutory guidance and its own long experience in dealing with the unit question.

Statutory Limitations on the Appropriate Unit. The law directs the Board to establish the appropriate unit for collective bargaining "in order to assure to *employees* the fullest freedom in exercising the rights guaranteed by this Act." (Emphasis added.) Beyond this injunction that the *employees'* interest shall prevail over the interests of employers and unions, statutory law on the bargaining unit is sparse, dealing only with: (1) professional employees, (2) plant guards, (3) craft severance, and (4) extent of employee organization.

Section 9(b) of the Taft-Hartley law prohibits the NLRB from including professional employees in a bargaining unit with nonprofessional employees unless a majority of the professional employees vote for inclusion in such unit.

Individuals employed as guards to enforce rules against employees and other persons to protect property of the employer or to protect the safety of persons on the employer's premises may be included only in a unit composed exclusively of guards. No labor organization that admits nonguard employees to membership or is associated with a nonguard organization may be designated as a representative for a guard unit.

Section 9(b)(2) of the Taft-Hartley law governs "craft severance" cases. Aimed at restricting the Board's authority to include craft workers in an industrial unit, this section provides that the Board should not "decide that any craft unit is inappropriate . . . on the ground that a different unit has been established by a prior board determination, unless a majority of the employees in the proposed craft unit vote against separate representation."

The Board is also prohibited from giving controlling weight to the extent to which employees have organized in determining the appropriate unit. If during an organizing drive a union has enrolled in its membership production workers, craft workers, salesworkers, and office workers who have diverse interests, the NLRB is prohibited from ruling that a single unit is appropriate solely because workers in these different groups have all joined the same union.

Before leaving statutory limitations on the Board's authority to establish appropriate units, it should be recalled that certain workers are not "employees" under the law and are therefore excluded from appropriate units and the protection of the law. These excluded persons are supervisors, agricultural workers, and independent contractors.

The Board makes bargaining unit determinations in three types of situations: (1) it establishes new bargaining units when a representation issue arises for the first time, (2) it reconsiders the propriety of established units in "craft severance" cases, and (3) it establishes units for expedited elections in recognition and organizational picketing cases coming under Section 8(b)(7)(C) of the Landrum-Griffin Act. An adequate understanding of the complexity of the Board's problem in determining the appropriate unit can be acquired by a brief consideration of some of the criteria used by the Board in original unit cases and craft severance cases.

NLRB Criteria in Initial Unit Determinations. The Board customarily accepts units agreed to by unions and management, but it does not recognize such stipulations as establishing Board policy. Moveover, union-management agreements to exclude certain individuals from the unit have been set aside by the Board where it believed that the persons involved should properly be included in the unit.

In exercising its power to determine appropriate units, the Board strives to give meaning and practical effect to the actual day-to-day relationships among employees. This aim, the Board has stated, "is best served by giving controlling effect to the community of interest existing among employees." This "community of interest" criterion is certainly basic to any Board determination of the appropriate unit.

Besides the community of interest criterion, the Board has, in different cases, considered such criteria as: union organizational structure, management organizational structure, extent of union representation interest, methods of wage payment, and regularity of employment. Comment on the frequently used criteria of bargaining history, craft or departmental units, and multiemployer units may be helpful.

Bargaining history frequently is a major factor in the Board's considerations. The Board is primarily interested in the bargaining history of the employees directly involved in the petition, but the bargaining history of similar employees in the area or industry may be considered on occasion. In several cases the Board has listed as one factor militating against a single-plant unit the fact that such a unit did not conform in scope to the pattern of relationships for that type of business in the particular area.

The Board will establish craft or departmental units only when the petitioner can show that employees in the proposed unit are functionally distinct *and* that they can be represented effectively as a separate group.

The Board will not establish multiemployer units unless the employers have chosen to bargain jointly and have held themselves bound by the results of these joint negotiations. An employer may withdraw from multiemployer bargaining and thereby re-establish his employees in separate appropriate units. A single-employer unit will be deemed appropriate in such circumstances when the employer manifests an intention to withdraw from group bargaining and to pursue an individual course of action in his labor relations. The Board has found separate single-employer units appropriate where, following a breakdown in association-wide negotiations, individual employers: (1) abandoned group bargaining, (2) did not pay dues or assessments to the association—resulting in automatic termination of membership under the association's bylaws, and (3) indicated their desire to pursue an individual course of action by executing contracts on a single-employer basis.

Craft Severance Cases.   Craft unions use the facilities of the Board in gaining recognition but often prefer the direct approach to the employer. When craft unions use the facilities of the Board, they usually are involved in craft severance cases. In these cases, the craft unions are asking the Board to upset an existing collective bargaining relationship between an employer and an industrial union. The Board's responsibility is to decide the issue in the best interests of the employees. In craft severance cases, the Board's problem is to decide which employees—all the employees or the craft employees—are benefited or hurt most by severance. The authors of the Taft-Hartley law sought to restrict the Board's authority to include craft workers in the industrial unit. Section 9(b)(2) stated that the Board should not "decide that any craft unit is inappropriate . . . on the ground that a different unit has been established by a prior Board determination, unless a majority of the employees in the proposed unit vote against separate representation." In the National Tube Company case,[2] the Board dismissed the petition of a group of steel industry bricklayers for separate representation. The Board reasoned that the only restriction imposed by the law was that a prior determination by the Board "may not be the sole ground upon which the Board may decide that a craft unit is inappropriate without an election."

In passing on petitions for either the establishment of craft units, or the severance of craft or craftlike groups from existing larger units, the Board applies the American Potash rules.[3] Under these rules: (1) a craft unit must be composed of true craft employees having " a kind and degree of skill which is normally acquired only by undergoing a substantial

[2] 76 NLRB 1999.
[3] 107 NLRB 1418 (1954).

period of apprenticeship or comparable training; (2) a noncraft group seeking to be severed must be functionally distinct and must consist of employees who, "though lacking the hallmark of craft skill," are "identified with traditional trades or occupations distinct from that of other employees . . . which have by tradition and practice acquired craftlike characteristics"; and (3) a union which seeks to sever a craft or quasi-craft group from a broader existing unit must have traditionally devoted itself to serving the special interests of the type of employees involved.

Craft severance poses a knotty problem for the Board, for employees, employers, and unions. The Taft-Hartley provisions on craft severance reflected a congressional suspicion that the NLRB has displayed a "pro-CIO" bias in unit determination. There can be little doubt that many skilled workers believed that they could get better terms of employment if they were represented by craft unions instead of being swallowed up in industrial unions. Many employers were seriously concerned about the prospects of craft severance upsetting long-established and effective collective bargaining relationships. Craft severance was a threat to industrial unions, a promise of new hunting ground for craft unions, and a potential trump card for dissident factions within industrial unions.

Experience with craft severance has been significantly less unsettling than expected. American Potash rules restrict the number of severance cases likely to arise. Both industrial unions and employers dealing with them have given more attention to the problems of quasi-craft workers covered by industrial union agreements. Newly formed craft unions drawing their membership from dissident factions in established industrial unions have had tough sledding.[4]

Last but not least, where craft severance has occurred, it has not disrupted stable labor relations to the extent feared; and, generally speaking, it has not seriously harmed the welfare of production workers.[5]

After the NLRB field examiner has decided that the petition is within the jurisdiction of the NLRB and has made a tentative finding on the appropriate unit, he seeks to ascertain if a substantial number of

[4] An example of the problems confronting dissident factions was the 1958 experience in the automobile industry. Newly formed, independent craft unions petitioned for severance of certain skilled employees from individual plants of the General Motors Corporation. Over the years before the petition, the NLRB had established single-plant industrial units at GM. The NLRB dismissed the petition of the new unions on the grounds that individual-plant craft severances would disrupt long-established collective bargaining relationships. In making this decision, the Board disregarded the technicality that it had established plant units and based its decision on the reality of a corporate-wide bargaining unit which had been established by the practice of both the company and union. Simultaneously, the UAW changed its structure to give a greater voice to quasi-craft employees. Although a newly formed union probably could effectively organize on a plant-by-plant basis, such a union would have a hard time in a frontal assault on a corporte-wide unit.

[5] For a careful study of the empirical results of craft severance, see Dallas L. Jones, "Self-Determination vs. Stability in Labor Relations," 58 *Michigan Law Review* (January, 1960), pp. 313–46.

employees want the union to represent them and if the petition is timely.

Sufficient Showing of Interest. This showing of interest is usually made by producing cards signed by employees authorizing the union to represent the signer-employee, or authorizing the petitioner to seek decertification. This evidence must be filed with the petition or submitted to the Regional Office investigator within 48 hours thereafter. Normally the petitioner must establish that at least 30 per cent of the employees in the unit have designated the union as their representative.

If it is the employer who files the petition, the NLRB does not require this sort of a showing of interest. The Regional Director usually proceeds with the matter, provided one or more unions have made a demand on the employer for recognition. Such a demand need not be expressed in words but can be implied from union conduct.

Timeliness of the Petition. The law provides that no election can be conducted in any bargaining unit (or any subdivision of one) in which a valid election has been held during the preceding 12-month period. This provision of the act guarantees to both the employer and employees for this period of time stability in their relations and freedom from disruptions that attend an election.

To further insure stability of industrial relations, the NLRB has established what is called the "contract bar" doctrine. The contract bar doctrine states that a valid collective bargaining agreement between an employer and a union representing his employees will ordinarily prevent the holding of an election among the employees covered by the agreement. In general, the contract bar doctrine rules a petition untimely if it is filed during the term of an existing contract with a three-year maximum in the case of contracts that run for more than three years. Under the rules of the Board, a petition may be filed at least 60 days, but no more than 150 days, before the expiration of a contract. This filing period makes it possible to upset a contractual relationship at an appropriate time.

If the petition meets the Board's requirements on jurisdiction, the appropriate unit, a sufficient showing of interest, and timeliness, the Regional Director either issues a notice of formal hearing or approves a consent agreement made by the parties.

Consent Election Agreements. A consent election agreement between the parties to a representation question includes: (*a*) a description of the appropriate unit; (*b*) the time and place of holding the election; and (*c*) a basis for determining who is eligible to vote. A consent-election agreement, when approved by the Regional Director, eliminates the formal hearing prior to an election.

Formal Hearing on Representation. The representation case hearing is a formal proceeding. It aims to obtain information which the Regional Director needs in order to determine: (1) the appropriateness of the unit; (2) the adequacy of the showing of interest; (3) the timeliness of the petition; (4) the eligibility of employees to vote; and other pertinent matters. All parties who establish their interests are given full opportunity to produce facts to support their positions on the matters to be determined.

Following the hearing, the Regional Director determines the need for an election and the procedures to be followed if an election is directed. In some complex cases the record is furnished to the entire NLRB for consideration before ordering an election.

The Election. Section 9(c)(1) of the Taft-Hartley Act provides that if a question of representation exists, the NLRB must resolve it through an election by secret ballot. The election details are left to the Board. Many observers have cited Board-conducted elections as examples of the best operation of the democratic process. Before discussing the important, and frequently neglected, question of what an employer can do to influence the outcome of an election, it will be well to consider the election mechanics and the election environment.

Election Mechanics. The Board's rules on election mechanics are designed to encourage workers' participation in the election and to assure the integrity of the election process. The arrangements and voting procedure in all elections are the same, whether they are consent elections or elections directed by the Regional Director or the Board.

Under the *Excelsior Underwear* rule,[6] within seven days after the Regional Director has approved or ordered an election, the employer must supply the Board with a list of the names and addresses of all persons in the unit. The Board then gives this list to the union in order that both the union and the employer have equal access to persons eligible to vote in the election.

A Regional Office official will arrange for the posting of notices containing a sample ballot and information about the location of voting places, the timing of the voting, and eligibility rules. The actual voting is always conducted and supervised by Board agents. Secrecy in voting is assured. Either the Board agents or the authorized observers of the parties may challenge for reasonable cause any employee who applies for a ballot. To be entitled to vote, an employee must have worked in the voting unit during the eligibility period and on the date of the election. Challenged employees may mark ballots, but their ballots are not counted until the challenges have been resolved.

Section 702 of the Landrum-Griffin Act states, "Employees engaged in an economic strike who are not entitled to reinstatement shall be eligible to vote under such regulations as the Board shall find are consistent with the purposes and provisions of this Act in any election conducted within twelve months after the commencement of the strike." Generally the Board has ruled that an economic striker forfeits his right to vote under Section 702 when he obtains permanent employment elsewhere before the election.

---

[6] 61 *LRRM* 1217–22.

Ordinarily the Board directs that elections be held within 30 days from the date of direction of the election. However, where an immediate election would occur at a time when there is not a representative number of employees in the voting unit—because of such circumstances as a seasonal fluctuation in employment or a change in operations—a different date will be selected in order to accommodate voting to the peak or normal working force.

Important as the mechanics of an election are, it is obvious that the outcome of an election can be influenced by improper electioneering, threats of violence, or other environmental influences.

The Election Environment. The area of legitimate employer and union conduct during an election campaign is one of the most difficult problems confronting the NLRB. It seems obvious that an employer's opinion on the probable consequences if a union should win an election would not always be free of bias, but would carry great weight with his employees. This would be particularly true if his "opinion" was that widespread layoffs would result, or that he would be forced to close the plant permanently. The NLRB has the delicate task of protecting the employer's freedom of speech and at the same time protecting his employees from undue interference, restraint, or coercion that his speech might exert on them as they express their choice about union representation. Although Section 8(c) of the Taft-Hartley Act, commonly called the "free speech provision," has broadened management's freedom to try to influence the outcome of an NLRB election, management participation in the election process is still limited by law and NLRB rulings.

For more than 30 years, the NLRB has walked this tightrope. An example of two NLRB rules, both now abandoned, may help to illustrate the Board's problem. At one time the NLRB held that a "captive audience" (employees required to listen to the employer's antiunion statements during working hours) was a cause to set aside an NLRB election. At a later time the Board held that a captive audience was legitimate if the employer paid his employees for "equal time" while the union attempted to refute his speech.

Another recurring question is whether foremen or other supervisors exert undue influence on the outcome of an election when they talk about it to individual employees and groups of employees. The Board has consistently set aside elections where the employer resorted to the technique of calling upon all or a majority of the employees in the unit individually, in the employer's office or at their homes, to urge them to vote against a proposed bargaining representative, regardless of whether the employer's remarks to the employees were coercive in character.

Under present rules of the Board, an election will be set aside if it is accompanied by conduct which, in the Board's view, creates an atmosphere of confusion or fear of reprisals and thus interferes with the employees' free choice of a representative guaranteed by the act. In determining whether specific conduct amounts to such interference, the Board does not attempt to assess its actual effect on the employees but concerns itself with whether it is reasonable to conclude that the conduct tended to prevent a free expression of the employees' choice.

Electioneering is vigorously controlled by NLRB rules and the provisions of the law. Under the *Peerless Plywood* rule, the Board prohibits election speeches on company time to massed assemblies of employees within 24 hours before the scheduled time for conducting an election. Electioneering near the polling places during the election is also prohibited. All participants in an election are prohibited from using any document purporting to be a copy of the Board's official ballot, unless the document is completely unaltered in form and content.

The Board will not police and censure the parties' election propaganda except to prevent fraud or coercion. However, in the *Mosler Safe Co.* case, the Board ruled "when one of the parties deliberately misstates material facts which are within its special knowledge, under such circumstances that the other party or parties cannot learn about them in time to point out the misstatements, the Board will find that the bounds of legitimate campaign propaganda have been exceeded and will set aside an election."[7]

Although the Board tolerates intemperate, abusive, and inaccurate statments made by the union during attempts to organize employees, it does not interpret the act as giving either party license to injure the other intentionally by circulating defamatory or insulting material known to be false. In *Linn* v. *Plant Guards Local 114*, the U.S. Supreme Court ruled on February 21, 1966, that a Federal District Court has jurisdiction of a civil action for alleged libel instituted under state law by an official of an employer subject to the Federal Labor-Management Relations Act for defamatory statements published by a union during an organizing drive if the employer's official pleads and proves that the statements were made with malice and injured him.[8]

Many an employer has felt abused in the course of establishing the collective bargaining relationship. Typically the employer finds himself in a surprised, passive, and defensive position when he is first confronted by a union demand for recognition and the processes of the NLRB. Instead of occupying his usual role of planner, decision maker, and allocator of the enterprise's resources, he frequently is swamped by the demands of "ungrateful" employees, the intrusion of "outsiders" who appear to threaten the future of the enterprise, and a governmental proceeding where the "shall nots" outnumber the "shalls" by 1,000 to 1. What can he do?

The Employer in the Rules for Establishing the Collective Bargaining Relationships. Although collective bargaining relationships have

[7] 129 NLRB 747.
[8] 61 *LRRM* 2345–53.

worked amazingly well in vast segments of the American economy, the typical employer undoubtedly would prefer to operate his business on a nonunion basis. Any manager who sought out a collective bargaining relationship would be considered a wild-eyed idealist by the most generous of his colleagues. How does an employer go about staying nonunion, defeating the union in an NLRB election, or getting rid of an unwanted union after it has been certified?

Unions lose about 40 per cent of the NLRB elections held each year. This fact means that some employers *can* and *do* launch effective programs against unionization. There is no easy sure-fire formula to beat the union in an NLRB election, but several possibilities are open to an intelligent and aggressive management. A successful program could be built around the following steps:

1. Long before there is a union organization threat, do a good job of managing personnel. This would include:
   a) Good wages, hours, and working conditions.
   b) A *genuine* "open door" on grievances and perhaps a formal grievance procedure, the latter being particularly important in a large-scale enterprise.
   c) Economic education of employees, not in the abstract, but realistically, in the problems and prospects of the specific enterprise and its industry.
   d) Effective supervision of the labor force with a heavy emphasis on *fair* treatment of employees in disciplinary cases especially.
   e) Effective *upward* communication in the enterprise, with management really listening for employee grievances and suggestions.
2. When the union enters, vigorous campaigning against the union in the election.
   a) This campaigning has to be based on the *substance* of the enterprise being a good place to work, e.g., wages *are* good, the treatment of employees *is* fair, and, in fact, there is little that the employees can gain from unionization. The big hazard of a "hard sell" on how good things are is that if the union wins, the items that management has sold them become the starting point of negotiations. In later negotiations, management cannot claim credit for what the employees had in the preunion period.
   b) Publication of the fact that unionism may mean lost paydays due to strikes and that union membership costs money in terms of dues, assessments, and initiation fees.
   c) Take advantage of any derogatory information about the union which has been revealed in investigations or publicity.
   d) Emphasize the idea that the union is an outsider or third party that comes between the employees and the enterprise management.
   e) Adopt and enforce a uniform rule against all solicitations during working hours and in work areas. Prohibit the distribution of union literature in work areas.
   f) If union organizers can contact employees on public property near the plant, prohibit them from entering the company parking lot or the plant area.
3. Scrupulously *avoid* any actions that are contrary to law and would result in an invalidation of the election. A full list of the "don'ts"

would be very long indeed. The following items are examples only:

a) Don't threaten to close the plant if the union wins.

b) Don't raise wages or benefits prior to the election.

c) Don't promise to increase wages or benefits on condition of the union losing the election.

d) Don't reduce wages or benefits prior to the election.

Probably the most critical matter in the outcome of NLRB elections is timing. An election ordinarily will be held within about 30 days of the union's first filing with the NLRB. If the union's petition comes as a genuine surprise to the employer, and it frequently does, there really isn't much he can do about putting his house in order. In most cases, the employer has to stand or fall on the policies and practices he has used *before* the union makes a formal appearance.

Turning a union out after it has won an NLRB certification election is usually much harder than beating the union in its initial organizing drive. NLRB union decertification procedures will be discussed below.

Certification of Election Results.   Where a valid election has been held, the Regional Director or the Board will issue to the participants a certification of the results. If a union has been chosen by a majority of the employees in the unit, it will receive a certificate showing that it is the official bargaining representative of the employees in the unit. If a majority of the employees have voted that no union be designated as their bargaining representative, the certificate will so state. This certificate protects both the employer and the winning union from a trial by election for 12 months. If an agreement is negotiated, the agreement provides even larger protection under the NLRB's contract bar rules.

The foregoing is an enterprise view of the rules for establishing a collective bargaining relationship in the United States. It is now appropriate to make a few observations about the process from a national and public policy viewpoint.

THE NATIONAL EBB AND FLOW OF UNION RECOGNITION

As discussed above, union recognition may be won either by voluntary action of management or by an NLRB election. Union recognition is lost either through business mortality or an NLRB decertification election. The 30-year trend in industrial relations legislation is a steady upgrading of the importance of an NLRB election as the major method of obtaining union recognition.

Figure 5–1 summarizes the outcome of NLRB elections from 1936 through 1965. Several observations on the experience with NLRB elections are in order:

1. Consistently, workers have shown great interest in NLRB elections. Note that in every year but one over 80 per cent of the workers eligible to vote in NLRB elections have chosen to exercise their right to vote.

FIGURE 5–1

RESULTS OF NLRB REPRESENTATION ELECTIONS, 1936–65

Fiscal Year Ending	Number of Elections Held	Number of Employees Eligible to Vote	Per Cent of Eligible Employees Voting	Valid Votes Cast for Union Representation	Per Cent of Total Vote Cast for Union	Number of Employees in Units Selecting Union as Agent
6/30/36*	31	9,512	79.6%	6,162	59.1%	N.A.
6/30/37*	265	181,424	90.5	142,428	69.1	N.A.
6/30/38*	1,152	394,558	87.1	282,470	82.8	N.A.
6/30/39*	746	207,597	85.4	138,032	77.9	N.A.
6/30/40*	1,192	595,075	89.5	435,842	81.9	N.A.
6/30/41*	2,568	788,111	92.6	589,921	80.9	N.A.
6/30/42*	4,212	1,296,567	82.3	895,091	83.9	N.A.
6/30/43*	4,153	1,402,040	80.3	923,169	81.9	N.A.
6/30/44*	4,712	1,322,225	81.1	828,583	77.2	N.A.
6/30/45*	4,919	1,087,177	82.8	706,569	79.1	N.A.
6/30/46*	5,589	846,431	82.6	529,847	75.8	N.A.
6/30/47*	6,920	934,553	86.2	621,732	77.2	N.A.
6/30/48	3,222	384,565	86.8	256,935	77.0	N.A.
6/30/49	5,514	588,761	87.7	377,360	73.1	N.A.
6/30/50	5,619	890,374	87.8	649,432	83.1	753,598
6/30/51	6,432	666,556	88.2	442,066	75.2	505,322
6/30/52	6,765	771,346	86.6	503,143	75.3	584,030
6/30/53	6,050	737,998	86.7	497,286	77.7	584,450
6/30/54	4,663	511,430	87.9	314,701	70.0	343,092
6/30/55	4,215	515,995	87.9	335,393	74.0	378,962
6/30/56	4,946	462,712	89.6	268,531	64.8	291,292
6/30/57	4,729	458,904	89.5	261,762	63.7	264,920
6/30/58	4,337	351,217	89.8	190,558	60.4	196,334
6/30/59	5,428	430,023	89.7	247,867	64.2	257,028
6/30/60	6,380	483,964	90.2	280,140	64.1	286,048
6/30/61	6,354	450,930	89.4	239,693	59.4	229,283
6/30/62	7,355	536,047	89.8	299,547	62.1	305,976
6/30/63	6,871	489,365	90.3	264,727	59.9	265,747
6/30/64	7,309	538,019	90.4	281,483	57.9	286,897
6/30/65	7,576	531,971	90.3	300,144	62.5	325,698

* During some of the years before 1948, data were presented as a composite of elections and payroll checks or cross checks by the NLRB. After the passage of the Taft-Hartley Act in 1947, the NLRB was empowered to certify a union for collective bargaining only on the basis of an election.

SOURCE: *Annual Reports* of the NLRB.

2. Since 1955, between 350,000 and 550,000 workers have been eligible to vote in NLRB elections each year. NLRB election activity seems to have declined rather steadily since a high-water mark in the early 1940's.

3. Although union success in elections has been slipping since the mid-1950's, unions continue to poll about 60 per cent of the valid votes cast each year. The percentage of votes cast for the unions would be the most accurate measure of the popularity of unions among workers where representation rights were sought. Note the close relationship

between the numbers of votes cast for unions and the number of employees in units selecting a union as representative.

4. The number of employees in units selecting a union as agent is the most important figure for measuring the dynamics of union recognition. This figure shows how many additional workers come under the potential coverage of collective bargaining agreements each year. If a union wins an election by only one vote, it still wins the right to represent all workers in the unit. The number of workers in units selecting the union as a representative is the potential membership base won by the union.

5. Figure 5–1 shows that NLRB elections since 1955 have enabled unions to increase their potential coverage of collective bargaining agreements from less than 200,000 workers in the 1957–58 fiscal year to over 300,000 workers in 1962 and 1965. Although unions could be encouraged by NLRB election trends since 1962, the sixties are a hollow shell of the period before 1955. Of course, any *actual* increase in collective bargaining agreement coverage would equal only this *potential* gain minus any losses due to business mortality, declines in employment in unionized firms, and the employment of firms where unions lost decertification elections.

Union recognition is lost either by business mortality or an NLRB decertification election. Indices of business mortality do not include information on whether or not the business was unionized.

FIGURE 5–2

RESULTS OF NLRB DECERTIFICATION ELECTIONS, 1947–65

Fiscal Year Ending	Number of Elections Held	Number of Employees Eligible to Vote	Per Cent of Eligible Employees Voting	Valid Votes Cast against Unions	Per Cent of Valid Votes Cast against Representation	Number of Employees in Units Choosing Decertification
6/30/48	97	8,836	88.9	3,914	49.8	N.A.
6/30/49	132	18,773	91.0	7,262	42.5	N.A.
6/30/50	112	9,474	89.6	4,164	49.1	4,034
6/30/51	93	6,111	87.5	2,954	55.2	3,429
6/30/52	101	7,378	88.6	3,465	53.0	4,045
6/30/53	141	9,945	90.0	4,389	49.1	5,076
6/30/54	150	10,244	88.7	4,774	52.5	5,935
6/30/55	157	13,002	90.0	5,936	50.2	5,524
6/30/56	129	11,289	91.9	4,761	46.3	5,598
6/30/57	145	11,018	92.9	5,516	54.3	6,888
6/30/58	153	10,124	89.7	4,787	52.7	4,499
6/30/59	216	16,231	90.3	6,984	47.7	7,705
6/30/60	237	17,421	88.1	6,817	44.4	8,695
6/30/61	241	18,364	90.4	6,570	45.6	10,607
6/30/62	285	12,323	86.8	7,365	68.8	6,930
6/30/63	225	13,256	87.9	5,208	53.3	8,033
6/30/64	220	13,732	90.4	5,562	44.8	5,399
6/30/65	200	12,565	88.9	4,618	41.3	4,718

SOURCE: *Annual Reports* of the NLRB.

The authors of the Taft-Hartley Act wanted to provide a means by which employees could rid themselves of unwanted unions. The method provided was the NLRB decertification election. Figure 5–2 summarizes the outcome of NLRB decertification elections since 1947. It should be noted that decertification elections have released fewer than 10,000 workers per year.

Since 1955, American unions have been substantially less successful in extending union recognition than they were in early periods. At least part of this declie can be attributed to the high level of unionization already achieved in many segments of the economy. At the same time, since 1955, unions have usually won the right to represent about 250,000 new employees through NLRB elections each year, while losing the right to represent fewer than 10,000 each year through decertification elections.

A number of important public policy questions on the rules for establishing the collective bargaining relationship are unresolved.

UNRESOLVED PROBLEMS IN PUBLIC POLICY ON UNION RECOGNITION

By now it should be clear that in the United States the government sets the terms of union recognition. It does so by defining the bargaining unit and conducting elections. Although the role of government is firmly established, several unresolved problems remain to plague the Congress, the NLRB, and the courts. The solutions developed to these problems may well have an important long-range effect on the structure of collective bargaining in America. Four major problems deserve attention: (1) employees excluded from NLRB jurisdiction; (2) the peculiar problems of union recognition in industries characterized by casual and intermittent employment; (3) free speech; and (4) the sometimes conflicting objectives of self-determination, stability, and effectiveness in union recognition.

Employees Excluded from the Protection of the Law

In aggregate, a very large number of American workers are excluded from the law's protection of the right to union representation. The largest single group of workers excluded are government workers. Other significant groups of workers excluded are agricultural employees, the employees of small interstate and all intrastate enterprises, hospital employees, and persons in supervisory positions.

It is possible that some of the employees excluded from the protection of the law are the object of deep-seated political pressures which are unlikely to yield. In the case of governmental employment, any system of union recognition would, of necessity, be grafted on established procedures for protecting the employees' interests. In the case of small employers, the administrative costs of extending the protection of the law seem to be greater than the benefits which society would gain.

Government Employees. On January 17, 1962, President Kennedy issued Executive Order 10988, Employee-Management Co-operation in the Federal Service. This order extended to some 2 million employees of the executive branch of the government a unique form of the right to union representation. Executive Order 10988 was a boon to unions representing federal employees, their membership growing to nearly 900,000 in 1964 with 1963 and 1964 membership growing by almost 100,000 per year.[9] The problems of government unions are considered in a case in Part V of this book.

Organizations seeking to represent governmental employees must: (1) disavow the right to strike against the government, (2) not advocate the overthrow of the government, (3) not discriminate with regard to the terms or conditions of membership because of race, color, creed, or national origin, and (4) be free of corrupt or undemocratic influences which are inconsistent with the purposes of the order. When an employee organization has been recognized as the exclusive representative of employees, it shall be entitled to negotiate agreements covering all employees in the unit and shall be responsible for representing the interests of all employees in the unit without discrimination and without regard to employee organization membership.

Union recognition under Executive Order 10988 is required to be consistent with the standards of the Civil Service Commission, the rights of veterans, and the rights available to an individual governmental employee in the absence of union recognition. Heads of agencies are empowered to deny union recognition where they decide that this order cannot be applied in a manner consistent with national security requirements and considerations.

The foregoing brief summary of Executive Order 10988 suggests some of the comparisons and the contrasts in a new experiment of applying national labor policy to public employment. The actual operation of Executive Order 10988 may provide experience applicable to state and local government.

Agriculture, Hospitals, Small Firms. It is probably fair to say that agricultural workers and the employees of hospitals and very small firms usually work under employment conditions less advantageous than those found in most unionized industries. On a humanitarian basis, it might be argued that these employees *need* union representation more than other employees.

It might be argued that hospital employees should be asked to renounce the right to strike, as is required of governmental employees. Obviously, the health and safety of a community depends on the continuous operation of hospitals. On the other hand, hospital employees certainly have interests *as employees* which should be heard.

[9] U.S. Department of Labor, Bureau of Labor Statistics, *Directory of National and International Labor Unions in the United States, 1965*, Bulletin No. 1493, p. 55.

The exclusion of small employers, hospitals, and agricultural employees from the basic law of union recognition usually is justified on the basis of protecting employers who could not remain in business if they had to meet the demands of unions. The authors of this text, nevertheless, wholeheartedly agree with the recommendations of a distinguished independent study group,[10] working under the auspices of the Committee for Economic Development, that the self-determination principle should be extended to cover governmental, hospital, farm, and small firm employees.

One of the problems in drawing up agricultural labor legislation comes from the intermittent and casual nature of employment. This problem also arises in certain other industries.

Casual and Intermittent Employment and Union Recognition. From its very beginning, the NLRB has tried to establish fair rules for getting and keeping union recognition in industries characterized by casual and intermittent employment. The Taft-Hartley ban on union hiring halls and the closed shop aggravated the Board's problems. The Landrum-Griffin law cleared the air a little by permitting prehire contracts in the building construction industry.

As a minimum, the authors of this book believe that the Landrum-Griffin prehire and seven-day union shop permission should be extended to all industries characterized by intermittent and casual employment. Given the extensive protection of the right to membership in unions which is guaranteed by Landrum-Griffin, it is most likely that the best solution to the problem of all industries characterized by casual and intermittent employment would be any hiring hall, closed shop, or other arrangement which employers and unions in those industries worked out together.

Free Speech. The problem of guaranteed free speech at the same time that employees are protected from interference, restraint, and coercion has occupied the NLRB, the Congress, and students of labor relations for almost 30 years.[11] Any policy on free speech influences the outcome of elections and the prevalence of collective bargaining in society. Individual congressmen and members of the NLRB have deep convictions about both free speech and the desirability of extending collective bargaining. Changes in policy probably reflect changes in the composition of Congress and the Board.

[10] Clark Kerr, Chairman; Douglas V. Brown, David L. Cole, John T. Dunlop, William T. Elliott, Albert Rees, Robert M. Solow, Philip Taft, George W. Taylor, Members; George P. Shultz, Staff Director, and Abraham Siegel, Associate Staff Director. See *The Public Interest in National Labor Policy* (New York: Committee for Economic Development, 1961), pp. 74–79, 84–85.

[11] For a definitive statement of the history of this problem and observations on the propriety of various NLRB rulings, see Benjamin Aaron, "Employer Free Speech: The Search for a Policy," chap. 2 of Joseph Shister, Benjamin Aaron, and Clyde W. Summers (eds.), *Public Policy and Collective Bargaining* (New York: Harper & Row, 1962), pp. 28–59.

We believe that most of the argument about free speech can be summarized in the commonplace statement: "It's not only *what* you say, but *how* you say it." Such an interpretation requires that actions be considered in their frequently complex context. The context of election statements varies between regions of the country, the histories of particular enterprises, and the education and attitudes of particular groups of employees.

Free speech is an emotion-laden issue in public policy on labor relations. It probably will remain as an unresolved problem in public policy. This is as much a tribute to the institutions of freedom as it is a source of continued frustration to the parties to collective bargaining and to men of good will who are charged with the responsibility for maintaining an environment consistent with a fair election process.

Most of the remaining unresolved problems in public policy on union recognition have to do with the relative weight to be given to three sometimes conflicting objectives of labor policy: self-determination, stability, and effectiveness of representation.

The Objectives of Self-determination, Stability, and Effectiveness

Probably the cornerstone of American public policy on union recognition is *self-determination* by employees (and, to a lesser degree, by employers) of the method of union recognition. Employees are given the right to vote on what union, if any, will represent them. NLRB unit determination policy on multiemployer bargaining protects the right of individual employers to decide whether they wish to go it alone or be represented by an association. Decertification elections protect the right of employees to "run the rascals out" when they wish to reject a union which they had previously embraced. Craft severance and professional employee elections preserve the right of self-determination for particular groups of employees.

The objective of self-determination sometimes runs afoul of the objective of *stability* in labor relations. NLRB contract bar rules, the statutory 12-month limitation on elections, and NLRB criteria for craft severance are outgrowths of a desire for stability in labor relations. It is obvious that subjecting employees and employers to an election every time a dissident group could muster a following would spell chaos for the employment relationship. At the same time a 12-month ban on elections may deprive employees of the right to representation on a permanent basis. Occasionally unions have lost NLRB elections by a very small margin and have been unable to maintain a semblance of organization for 12 months after the election. The contract bar rules of the NLRB occasionally have enabled an unrepresentative union to maintain its position in a collective bargaining relationship.

The fundamental purpose of national labor policy is to minimize obstructions to the flow of commerce. This would imply an objective of *effectiveness* in labor-management relations. Effectiveness in employee and employer representation might very well dictate a substantial reduction in the freedom of self-determination granted to the parties. For example, one powerful corporate-wide union probably would be most effective in dealing with management, regardless of how poorly it treated the interests of skilled workers or professional employees. It is not altogether certain that management would find such an arrangement distasteful. In a similar vein, in highly competitive industries with many small employers, effectiveness in collective bargaining might be achieved by governmental policing of the membership of an employers' association. There have been numerous cases where both an employer association and the union(s) representing workers in the industry would welcome government support in keeping wayward employers in line. As a final example, few objective observers would argue that archaic lines of jurisdiction over work in the railroads, airlines, and building trades foster efficiency in representation.

The basic problem in union recognition is a delicate balancing of the interests of employees and employers in the pursuit of the objectives of self-determination, stability, and effectiveness in labor relations. Unfortunately, neither society nor the parties can have all their cakes and eat them, too.

QUESTIONS FOR DISCUSSIONS

1. "Ballot box organizing" is unique to the North American continent. Does ballot box organizing fulfill any particular needs of a politically democratic private enterprise society? Does it pose any challenges to free institutions? What might be substituted for ballot box organizing?

2. The Landrum-Griffin Act permitted the NLRB to delegate more authority to its Regional Directors for the handling of representational issues. Do you think it would be a good idea to give the Regional Directors authority to rule on unfair labor practice charges? Justify your position.

3. Since employers have a real interest in the determination of bargaining units, is it fair to make the interests of employees the controlling factor? By the same token, why is the employer's interest considered to be controlling in multiemployer units?

4. "Employers and the general public are always the innocent victims in jurisdictional strikes." Discuss.

5. Attack or defend the proposal that the closed shop be authorized by law.

6. The text recognizes several unresolved problems in public policy on union recognition. What are these problems? How would you resolve them? Why?

Chapter 6

THE PROBLEM OF
REACHING AGREEMENT

Once the collective bargaining relationship is established, the actors must bargain out a collective bargaining agreement and live with it. This chapter deals with the problems and procedures involved in reaching agreement. Chapter 7 explores the nature of the labor agreement, and Chapter 8 discusses the problems of living with whatever agreement the parties reach. Although the end result of negotiations is largely economic in nature, the activities involved in reaching agreement have many political overtones and may be compared to the practice of international diplomacy on a small scale.

Those who own property or legally control it have one-sided authority to dispose of their property as they see fit and to set the conditions under which others may use it. Without collective bargaining, management unilaterally sets the "wages, hours, working conditions, and other conditions of employment" of those who work in and for the enterprise. They may do this without consulting anyone, including those who work for them, so long as they do not violate any specific laws such as, for instance, the minimum wage law.

When a union wins an NLRB election and certification the situation changes significantly. In theory, a manager still possesses unilateral rights to set the conditions of employment. In practice the certification of a union alters power relationships. The manager still determines policy and administers it at his own discretion *unless the union persuades him to do otherwise*.

The law requires an employer to recognize and bargain "in good faith" with a certified union, but it does not force him to agree with the union. He is free to yield to the union's persuasions, but he does not have to be persuaded; providing, always, that he has given the union an opportunity—in good faith—to persuade him.[1]

The union's task is to persuade the employer to accept policies and administrative procedures the union wants. If the union's attempt succeeds and the two parties reach agreement, then the law requires that, at the

---

[1] Case No. 1 deals with some of the legal and policy implications of the obligation to bargain in good faith.

request of either party, they must reduce their agreement to writing. The universal practice is to put the agreement in writing.

This written document, signed by the employer or his agent and by the union representatives, is commonly referred to as a "contract," but in many ways it more closely resembles a treaty between two sovereign powers, the company and the union. It sets the conditions under which the employer offers each individual worker in his employ (that is, within the bargaining unit) a work contract; and it binds him to abide by these conditions. The labor agreement becomes, in effect, company policy, just as a treaty between nations becomes national policy to which the signatory is bound.

Treaties are usually negotiated peacefully by persuasion and diplomacy. The vast majority of collective bargaining agreements are worked out by peaceful labor-management diplomacy with no resort to force. Occasionally, however, an agreement can be reached only by resort to force. To paraphrase von Clausewitz on war, strikes may be considered a continuation of diplomacy (negotiations) *by other means*. Negotiations may temporarily break off during a strike, but a strike cannot be settled without negotiations. Although the threat of strike invariably surrounds negotiations, it is well to consider negotiations first and then the strike.

NEGOTIATIONS: LABOR-MANAGEMENT "DIPLOMACY"

Today most labor-management negotiations are concerned with the revisions of *existing* collective bargaining agreements which regularly expire at intervals usually ranging from one to three years. An *initial* collective bargaining agreement between an employer and a union poses somewhat different substantive problems, but the procedures for either renewing an existing agreement or negotiating the initial agreement are essentially the same.

The People Who Do the Bargaining

Preceding chapters have explored the various combinations of separate, and usually opposing, interests present in negotiations. But negotiating is an activity, carried out by people who meet at a definite point in time and space. These people stand in definite organizational relationships to the interests they represent, and perform definite functions. They come from the ranks of unions, enterprises, and, sometimes, from the government.

The Union Negotiating Committee. There is no set rule about who is to negotiate with the company for the union.

It may be the committee that drew up the demands and saw them through to ratification. It may be a standing committee, such as the union's executive board, or, at the other extreme, a committee elected specially, and at large from the whole membership, expressly for the occasion. It almost always includes, in any case, certain ex officio members such as the President, one or more Vice-Presidents, the Secretary, the Chief Steward. If the Local has a Business Agent, he (or she) will certainly accompany the negotiators.

Also accompanying the negotiators in most cases will be someone who is not a member of the Local union: the International Representative.

The International Representative. On the union side in negotiations sits an "outsider," the International Representative. Of all the participants, often he is the only one who does not make his living by working for the company. He does not work for the Local union either, as a paid officer or Business Agent does, but only in its behalf. He is answerable to the executive board of the International union.

Status of the International Representative. He is there in negotiations by request of the Local union, to guide and counsel; usually, in fact, to act as spokesman, strategist, and tactician for the union side. The company cannot keep him out, despite his outsider status, for the law permits workers to be represented by "agents of their own choosing."

He is a professional, perhaps the only professional in a group whose business, and respective positions, require that they engage in collective bargaining, but only so rarely, and so incidentally to their other concerns, that in comparison they are amateurs. They meet each other to make these solemn agreements no more often than once a year; he engages in like activity, with other groups as well as this, day after day. For everyone else present, the outcome of negotiations will be felt as dollars-and-cents additions to income, or added production costs; he loses not a cent, nor, for that matter, stands to gain a penny by what transpires, though if he is successful it will be a feather in his cap.

He may have entered the negotiations only when he stepped in the door of the conference room, but more likely he had been working with the Local through all the stages or at least the later stages of preparations. The chances are he shared in shaping the demands and putting them in draft-agreement form, and it was through him that the research department of the International channeled information to aid in the negotiations.

Role of the International Representative. This outsider to the group that meets for negotiations is, in a sense, the only full-time "insider" to the collective bargaining process: it is his life and living. He has no authority except the authority to persuade, but he is the key man in negotiations, the professional who really makes collective bargaining work and keeps it going. As will be seen, he is also the key man in strikes. In single-employer bargaining (which accounts for most of industrial unionism) he has no regular counterpart on the employer side. In most negotiations he is the one who calls the signals and sets the tone.

During the discussions with the company he gives tactical leadership to the union committee. His role varies with the circumstances, his own talents and personality. Sometimes he spearheads the attack on the company, perhaps with the aim—and frequently with the effect—of making the Local's committee of company employees look reasonable and moderate to their employer, so that the company will offer them concessions to keep them from following his extremes. Or, with a militant committee, it is he who may seem moderate, receptive to "reasonable" offers of concessions, which he implies he will use his influence to try to "sell" the committee in the recess that he then calls.

He may be a vain and stubborn fellow, or smart or stupid, or sly or sincere—actually; or he may only appear so. Often he has to be an actor, playing a role. Only when he has had a number of encounters with a given management, gotten to know them and be known, can he drop into a consistent natural pattern of behavior with them. He will usually then be found a shrewd and sensible fellow with a good deal of personal integrity, who prides himself—for it is a professional asset—on being a man of his word. Sometimes he becomes almost a mediator between company and union, who soothes ruffled feelings, saves people's faces, and harmlessly grounds dangerous emotional charges that have built up in a labor relations situation. Sometimes he serves the useful function of the scapegoat, who assumes the "sins" of the community—both sides—and carries them away with him, to leave the local people cleansed and reconciled for the next period of the life they have to live together.

There are negotiations in which not one but two or several outside representatives participate, either alternately or together. One may deliberately build up tension, concentrating company hostility on himself so that a colleague, blandly smiling, can walk in and, in the ensuing relief and atmosphere of cordiality, reach the settlement.

The Employer Representatives.   Union agreements set or affect company policy. A line executive responsible for policy—president, vice-president for industrial relations, or at the very least a works manager—sits in directly on this policy-making process, or designates someone with authority to act for him.

Single-Employer Bargaining.   In any single-company negotiations, then, the delegation of authority is a simple matter. The person exercising this authority and speaking for the company is usually a production man and line executive, but he has staff advisers such as the personnel director, and perhaps a public relations expert, and a company lawyer. Of all these, the lawyer has least to contribute, in most cases, to the progress of negotiations.

In contrast to the union representatives, the negotiators for the employer are usually armed with full authority to conclude an agreement, though in some cases the Board of Directors may have to ratify results. There is a simple reason for this: in the company, authority flows downward; in the union, upward. At the policy-making level where negotiations take place, authority is already concentrated on the company side, while in the union there has to be a specific act of delegation, and the delegation is not complete but only provisional and temporary.

Multiemployer Bargaining. Multiemployer bargaining, as has been noted, is more common in the trades, with craft unions, than in manufacturing. There are some notable exceptions—perhaps enough to constitute another rule, and not just exceptions.

In the garment industries, for instance, employer associations bargain as a group both with the Amalgamated Clothing Workers and with the International Ladies' Garment Workers' Union. These two well-known and well-organized industrial unions are the composite modern form of older separate craft unions. Some of these crafts were once truly skilled—cutters, for instance, who are direct descendants of custom tailors—while others formed satellite unions of the unskilled—"floor boys," for example—and of the semiskilled, as new machines created specialities. This is a situation comparable in some ways to the construction unions where skilled men and their unskilled satellites form a complex of closely related unions under the Building Trades Council. The garment workers did not stay separate; they fused; and now they act together just as if they were a single union, though they are still enrolled in Locals based on craft and occupation, not on workplace.

Garment-industry employers, faced with the problem of dealing with the huge, fused union, followed the lead of other similar employers throughout history and organized. The producing units of their industry are small and many; together in an association they are somewhat like a counterpart of the union with which they deal. Member firms promise to abide by bargains the association makes with the union.

The small size of the enterprises seems to be a factor in bringing employers together, but an equally compelling one seems to be competition; competition in both the product market and the labor market. Labor costs are so high a percentage of total costs that once the bulk of the industry was unionized the organized firms found themselves sharing the union's own interest in fighting cutthroat nonunion competition based on lower wages. In this, again, they are like the building trades. They are also like highway transportation, for the pattern already clear in the garment industries appears to be spreading to the trucking industry which is also an area of small firms and a big union.

The Employer Association Representative. This kind of multiemployer bargaining—of "employer unionization"—has brought forth a type of man who may fairly be called the equivalent of the International Representative. That is the labor relations adviser and negotiator on the employer side. He is not universally present in multiemployer bargaining, for many associations speak through respected senior member-firm executives; but the neutral expert is coming to the fore.

His title is likely to be Executive Secretary or Labor Relations Director of the association. His duties are analogous to those of an International Representative, and so is his function in negotiations. He organizes—gets firms to join the association. He helps draw up employer counterproposals to union demands. He directs or arranges for research to back up the proposals. He negotiates. He also inspects the member firms' administration of the agreement, helps take care of grievances and arbitration, and policies the rules of the association. Wherever he is active, he, like the International Representative, is the key man.

(This is a field, incidentally, where the college graduate enamored of the labor relations "game" may find it possible to break in. The unions bring their representatives up from the ranks, while even in a medium-sized corporation it is a long way up from Management Trainee to Industrial Relations Director. But the employer association often has room for a man from the outside who has had experience or training in labor relations work. Being from the outside is, in fact, an advantage. The future may see more professionals, on both sides of collective bargaining, as this trend continues. Even the unions may have to turn to the colleges for representatives as the employers "wise up" and as the union old-timers die off.)

The Government Representative. As long as labor and management obey the law, the government regards collective bargaining between them as a private matter.

But it is not a matter of indifference to the government, nor to the public which government represents, particularly if a strike seems in prospect. In order, therefore, to assist the bargainers reach constructive results that are satisfactory to both, and compatible with the public interest, the government provides—*on a strictly voluntary basis*—the services of its Mediation and Conciliation Service.

The Mediator in Negotiations. The interchangeable terms "conciliator" and "mediator"—not to be confused with *arbiter* or *arbitrator*—apply to anyone who seeks to bring labor and management to agreement in a dispute; but the field is passing to the professional. In some disputes a mayor or other public official, or even on occasion a Presidentially appointed board, may step in with an offer of good offices. More likely, though, it will be an obscure and not overpaid civil servant, a state or federal employee, who makes a career of mediating and conciliating in labor disputes. He comes at the call of either party, or even at his own initiative, but he can do little without the consent of both parties, who must at least agree to talk to him. His job is to help them find a way out of their impasse.

As with negotiation itself, there are no set rules for conciliation and mediation. Much depends on circumstances, and the personalities involved including the personality of the mediator. Wisest procedure usually seems to be for him to meet with each side separately before attempting to get them both together. In that way he hears the uninhibited viewpoint of both sides, and gets a grasp of the problem.

The Mediator's Methods. The mediator listens. He is neutral, and he can sympathize impartially with each disputant in turn as he hears the story of the iniquity and unreasonableness of the other. This allows him to size up the people, who are part of his problem, as well as the facts, and it undoubtedly has cathartic and therapeutic value for the complainants, who are pretty well fed up with each other by the time the mediator arrives. He acts as a lightning rod for charges of mutual hostility between them.

He has more to offer than emotional release, however, for like the "Rep" he has had varied experience, and is a pro. He can suggest ways out of what appear dead ends to the negotiators, because he has seen these ways work in analogous situations before. He had no emotional "blocks" that blind him, as the participants are sometimes blind, to unconsidered possibilities. He talks the language of either side, and both. He can help both "save face" when they have gotten into untenable positions.

Frequently it is he who finds the magic formula that will resolve the dispute. If he is skillful he will bring both sides around, unconsciously, to thinking it was their idea. Successful mediation can avert a strike, or settle a strike when one has broken out, for mediation can occur at any stage. If the strike settlement happens to coincide with the formula the mediator suggested to avert a strike, he never says "I told you so." As smoke comes out of the factory smokestacks again and workers troop through the gates to start drawing paychecks once more, he packs his battered briefcase and smilingly bids goodbye. There is a telegram in his pocket, probably, calling him on to another situation in which a company and Local union are at loggerheads.

Good mediators, like union "Reps" come from all kinds of varied backgrounds. Personal qualities count for more than formal qualifications. Some of the best are former union officials. Mediation is a form of government service open to college-trained men with a consuming interest, as well as background, in active labor relations work; but it is not for the man who has his mind made up in advance about labor's rights, or management's prerogatives. It is not for the show-off or know-it-all.

Skillful, patient mediation can do a lot toward preventing strikes, or settling strikes amicably once they have broken out.

PREPARATION FOR NEGOTIATIONS

The men (and women) who carry on labor-management negotiations shoulder a heavy responsibility. Their work sets policy. Its results are bound to affect the welfare, the earnings, the chances for promotion, the security, the job satisfaction of every member of the union, every employee of the company in the bargaining unit (and some outside it) for the next year, or two years, or even three or five. Equally affected are company profits, productivity, and competitive position, as well as prices and production available to the public.

Negotiating the agreement is the very heart of collective bargaining.

Proper discharge of the responsibilities it lays upon the bargainers calls for preparation.

The Union Initiative

Unions prepare more or less carefully for negotiations. Big national negotiations, such as those between the United Autoworkers and General Motors, have repercussions throughout the national economy and are carefully prepared for a year or more in advance, with full attention to public relations as well as to keeping the members informed. Many smaller Local unions make little or no preparation other than to draw up demands.

Preparation for negotiations involves: (1) drawing up demands, or formulating what the members want; (2) assembling information to support the demands; and (3) publicizing and explaining the demands. This last point usually means merely informing the members, and the workers in the plant, but often requires spreading the information to the public in the community at large.

Drawing up Demands. The union ordinarily initiates negotiations. To the union member the most important thing is what he, personally, will get out of the agreement. Sometimes he knows exactly what he wants. At other times he knows only that he wants "more" than he has, but does not recognize it in concrete form until his union leaders formulate and explain it to him.

If he has had "nothing"—that is, if he has not worked under a union agreement before—then he wants what workers in other shops and unions have already secured: such things as seniority, grievance procedure, a raise in wages, vacations with pay, and the like. If he is already working under a union agreement granting concessions of this sort, he wants more of the same.

"New" Demands. Sometimes union demands appear to be new, but almost invariably they turn out, upon examination, to be merely novel forms and extensions of older ideas. The 1955 demand for a "guaranteed annual wage" worked out in practice, in the "S.U.B." plan of Supplementary Unemployment Benefits, as no more than a strengthening of the existing seniority system with increased pay (from private funds, to supplement public funds) for laid-off workers. The aim of the plan was to satisfy the worker's age-old demand for individual job security. Its proponents also hoped that it would promote steadier employment and cushion the impact of automation. The 1958 demand for profit sharing aimed at least in part to increase worker income by a supplement to wages. This is akin to many bonus schemes that preceded it. Ironically enough, the idea of giving workers a share in profits is one that had often been advanced by management as an antidote to unionism!

A new demand once raised and won by a union in one enterprise, or the enterprises of one industry, gets copied by other unions trying to follow the leader—or outdo him. Thus after the auto workers pioneered the S.U.B. plan the steelworkers took it up and secured even greater concessions based on the same idea. In neither case was the actual program a spontaneous creation that welled up, fully formed, out of the minds of the workers in the shops. In both cases, sophisticated professional labor leaders formulated proposals that appealed to the members' formless and inarticulate yearnings: the human desire to be secure in what one has, and to have a little more.

Spread of a Pattern. The leaders exercise their foresight and inventiveness to devise plans and formulate demands that the members will recognize as corresponding to their needs. Political, and even personal, interunion rivalries spread first worker, and then company, acceptance of those demands that do successfully evoke worker response and support. The most recently organized Local union therefore tends to adopt for its program of demands the schedule of gains registered, step by step, by others organized before it, just as a newly built factory gets the benefit of the latest technological progress.

There is no doubt that some union programs (S.U.B., for example) exert a far-reaching influence on the economy that may affect society in permanent and important ways, for good or ill. If he thinks about this at all, the worker and rank-and-file union member tends to minimize the question. This is only human, and on the order of the well-known fact that a flood in China drowning a whole province is a disaster that does not hit home quite as hard as a leaky pipe that floods a man's own basement. In asking for a raise, the worker undoubtedly likes to have his mind set at ease that he is not sending the national economy into an inflationary spiral—and his union leaders gladly oblige with the necessary assurance—but the question of whether he will get a raise in his next pay envelope is of more immediate interest to the worker. He tends to ignore the possible economic and social effects of an accumulation of separate union demands shaped to the same plan; he pays attention chiefly to the special effects that flow from his own Local's direct action.

Restraints on the Demands. Perhaps, in the back of his mind, he looks to the company to keep the situation from getting out of hand, just as he relies on the company to secure orders, maintain production, and pay wages. He regards the pressing of demands as a test of strength, and a necessary one, for it does not seem likely that he will get what he does not ask for, whereas he feels sure that the company will not give him more than it can truly afford. He is embarked, he feels, with management, on an enterprise making its way upon the vast and sometimes stormy economic sea. He does not want his own ship to sink under him or strike a rock, but he is convinced that the men on the bridge want that no more than he does, and that they will not let it happen. He knows there are profits to be made from the voyage and for his part clamors for what he considers a just return for his work, and a good living. And so he draws up demands, or adapts the demands others like him have drawn up, and presents them; and, if need be, strikes for them.

Some small companies and their unions, and some "sick" industries, have been forced to take a more careful look, and act more co-operatively toward union demands that would raise costs beyond the danger point. Higher wages and other concessions to the union in some situations could depress business and result in unemployment. Wage cuts, instead of wage raises, might even be in order.

Some Problems. This question has many ramifications. Should a union subsidize inefficiency in a small or backward company by permitting low wages and substandard conditions? Or should it force the small-scale, low-pay producer out of business to make way for more progressive enterprises? Can the union help the company increase efficiency by boosting worker productivity? Should the union fight against technological improvements that would throw members out of work?

A consideration of these questions, and others equally pertinent, would lead away from the problem of *drawing up* demands into the *content* of the demands. Such questions might, in a given case, condition the nature of the demands, but the union negotiator is more likely to have to deal with them as they come up during the course of negotiations.

Assembling Information.   A strike threat frequently hangs over negotiations from the start. When this is so, the negotiations are a test of strength, and the end result is likely to register not so much the merits of the case on either side as the relative strength of the parties.

But the parties carry on negotiations by discussion: they talk, they use arguments, they reason and try to convince. In spite of, as well as because of, the strike threat that lurks in the background, in the foreground men sit around a table and try to persuade each other.

They do persuade each other in many things. It is their function to reach an accommodation and reduce it to writing. Even when the general terms of their bargain reflect relative underlying strength rather than abstract objective judgment, these terms must at least be rationalized in wording acceptable to both sides. In order to reach common ground as well as to define their differences, the union and the company negotiators must exchange views and come to a meeting of the minds. Each side must show the logic of its position.

Both sides, therefore, build up information to support their arguments. The union negotiators want, basically, two kinds of information: (*a*) what might be called, by analogy with the military, "intelligence" that will help them gauge the company's strength and intentions and (*b*) facts to back up arguments in favor of the union's specific demands. Under this heading would also come, of course, facts for rebuttal of possible company arguments.

"Intelligence."   The union negotiators stand at a disadvantage unless they can find out something about matters on which the company

already has a good deal of information: the state of the industry and the firm's position in the industry, competition, profits and sales, orders and prospects: in a word, economic and financial data. Some of these factors will indicate the company's ability to pay, others may give an inkling of the company's ability to withstand a strike, or willingness to make concessions. Such data remains confidential with the company, unless the company refuses union demands solely on the grounds of inability to pay. In such cases, the NLRB has ruled the company must open its books and show the union proof of its contention.

The International's research department provides most of the general economic information and financial data on the company. Experts and specialists employed by the International assemble and evaluate the information and make it available to the negotiators as part of the service provided Local unions by the International. Local information along the same lines and word of specific innercompany developments may "leak" to the union from friendly office workers or sources in the community. The reports of shop stewards keep the negotiators abreast on actions taken by management in the various departments. These and other scraps of isolated information, fitted together and evaluated, may give clues to the company's intentions.

Ordinarily the company may be expected to know more about economic and financial prospects than union intelligence can unearth and correctly put together, but unions have steadily gotten better at the game. Through its International, a Local draws on the services of economists, lawyers, and accountants no less expert in their fields than the company's own specialists.

Facts for Argument.   Here again economic and financial data have a bearing, particularly when the costs of specific concessions are at issue, but a great deal of information comes from the shop itself. Experiences gained under the past agreement suggests changes in some of the provisions. The grievance records or other data drawn from practice provide facts for argument. The steward apparatus probably constitutes the main source of information in this category.

On the company side the assembling of information for negotiations shows the same twofold nature: the need to try to gauge the union's strength and determination; and the need for facts and figures to counter union arguments and support the company's position. Sources of information for the company are analogous: employer associations, which correspond to the union International, and the company's own supervisory apparatus and personnel department.

Publicizing and Explaining the Demands.   Both sides have a public to which they appeal for understanding and support, and the most important segment of that public is the working force of the enterprise.

The union keeps its members informed by means of meetings, printed or mimeographed bulletins of various kinds distributed at the plant gate or circulated by union stewards, and, on occasion, mass media such as radio or television. The union also—and most importantly—"talks up" its information through its steward system and circulates it by word of mouth. The department stewards are in daily personal contact with the entire body of employees. They are elected representatives who have the confidence of their constituents. The workers turn to them for facts, advice, and direction as the negotiations proceed.

The wider public which consists of the community does not usually hear much about specific demands under negotiation unless there is a strike. Then both sides take to the newspapers with their versions of the issues and wage a propaganda battle to win, or at least neutralize, public sentiment.

The Employer Defense and Counterinitiative

It stills seems to be the practice of some employers to wait until the union has presented its demands before getting ready for negotiations. This is a purely defensive strategy. There is some justification for it in that decisions go by default to the employer unless the union requests a part in making them, and that most changes that could be made represent concessions by the employer to the union. Why give the union, as it were, things the union does not first ask for? Why not just sit back, see what they want, and say "No"?

Active Preparation for Negotiations. Nonetheless more and more employers are finding it wise to prepare more carefully and to anticipate union demands or deflect them with proposals of their own. Some of these counterproposals may actually be things the union has not asked for! Employer preparation for negotiations gives management an active, instead of a passive, function.

The farsighted employer or employer association calculates in advance the cost and relative desirability of varius alternatives and meets the union with concrete proposals rather than a monotonous "No, no, no" followed, perhaps, by a reluctant "Yes" to an arrangement shaped entirely by union initiative. The General Electric Company has been a leader of this trend. It has come to be known as Boulewareism, after a former G.E. vice-president who initiated it.

This does not mean that the employer gives up the defensive position, which is a strong one despite some disadvantages. It means that he plans his defense and supplements it with counteroffensive strategy that does not leave all the issues, or points of attack, entirely to the union.

The Area to Be Defended. The area of company policy where employees usually desire changes are those defining the employees' individual work-contract with the company. The standard phrase used to designate this area is, "wage, hours, working conditions, and other conditions of employment." It does not normally include, for instance, company sales policy; it does include such policies as layoff order, and practices that have to do with conveyor speeds or the way time studies are taken.

The union's aim is to influence the terms of the individual work-contract the company has with each of its employees. In effect, what the union seeks is to get the employer to *promise* that certain agreed-on conditions affecting wages, hours, working conditions, and other conditions of employment, will become part of this work contract. When the union signs its eventual agreement with the company, that does not make the union itself a party to the individual employee's work contract. The individual still holds that with the company, and holds it directly, delivering work in exchange for wages at certain conditions. The amount of the wages and the nature of the conditions become those the company has promised the union it will pay and perform.

PRESENTING THE DEMANDS

The union starts by drawing up its draft demands and presenting them to the company.

The nature of this process varies between craft and industrial unions, and the demands themselves differ. What follows will describe the process in the typical industrial union situation of the single-union, single-employer pattern.

Procedure in the Local Union

At a meeting of the Local industrial union the members charge a committee, or a group of officers, with the task of drafting proposals for negotiation. In due course this group reports back to the membership with the draft demands they have drawn up. These demands are in the form of a proposed agreement that sets forth the terms the union wants the company to offer and incorporate in the individual work-contracts with each of its employees in the bargaining unit and to adopt as policy in its dealing with all of them. Influences that shape the content of these draft demands have been discussed earlier in this chapter.

The members of the Local discuss the recommendations. They suggest additions, deletions, alterations, and improvements in the terms and wording. Following parliamentary procedure, they go over the document paragraph by paragraph and vote, first on its separate provisions, then on the document as a whole. When they are finished with this procedure they have ratified the demands. Once ratified, the draft agreement becomes the official union program of proposals for the forthcoming negotiations with the company, and the union's instructions to its negotiating committee.

In the case of a new union and an initial agreement, the draft demands usually take for their pattern a standard form recommended by the International union, or copy the model of some similar agreement known to the Local union. The committee fills in specific items, such as wage rates or seniority rules, to make it applicable to local conditions.

In the case of an established union already working under an agreement, the deliberations center on proposed changes and improvements. Perhaps the history of grievance adjustment over the past year points out loopholes that need to be plugged, or too-rigid wording that needs to be relaxed to give the union some leeway. Experience may suggest the addition of new clauses, the deletion of inoperative or undesirable ones. Words may be weighed; punctuation revised. Generally, the agreement grows at least a little every year. Clauses that have stood the test of time remain; new ones, to cover previously unforeseen contingencies, are added. Eventually, the draft demands are ratified and ready for negotiation. The union sends or presents them to the company as a basis for discussion.

THE ACT OF NEGOTIATION

The union presents its demands and asks for a meeting. The employer, ready or not with counterproposals, designates a spokesman and agrees on a date. The two sides meet and start negotiating. They continue to meet until they have achieved some result.

The Context of Negotiations

The union may be newly organized, seeking its first agreement. Negotiations then are new, exceptional to the experience of both management and labor, surrounded with hopes, fears, and uncertainty. They may be charged with tension; there will certainly be a feeling of strangeness. Or, they may be routine renewal talks in an established and stable collective bargaining relationship; expected, understood, and taken very calmly. In any case the workers in the plant or bargaining unit follow them closely, and even the general public may take an interest.

If a strike is in prospect—and this threat lurks somewhere in the background in any negotiations—then union members, other employees of the company, their families, their creditors, and the community in which they live wait anxiously for the outcome. Stockholders of the company may, and the Board of Directors certainly will, be on the alert. The negotiators on both sides are bound to feel the pressure and to realize that what they do will have repercussions. Much is at stake for many, at the bargaining table.

Because of this interest from the outside, the negotiations sometimes attract a good deal of publicity. The sessions themselves almost invariably take place behind closed doors, but the union delegates have to report back to their members, and a union meeting—even a closed one—is no place to tell a secret. Reporters may try to question the participants on either side as they leave the bargaining sessions, or later, and this brings the temptation for the parties to carry their case to the newspapers.

So long as no confidence is violated, the propriety or the wisdom of such a course is a matter of judgment, but it has its dangers. There is, for instance, the danger of being misquoted, or the opposite one of being caught off guard and quoted all too accurately in a rash statement. There is the danger of taking a stand publicly from which it may be necessary later to retreat—publicly. But there are also occasions when a word to the press can become an effective tactical weapon in the bargaining. It all depends. The real negotiating still has to be done in the conference room.

THE CONDUCT OF NEGOTIATIONS

Negotiating is so personal an art, and its practice so dependent upon the mixture of personalities present, as well as the circumstances and issues, that little of a general nature can be said that would be valid in all cases. A few remarks may still be hazarded.

Privacy of the Negotiations. The presence of outsiders seems to inhibit fruitful negotiation, and so does the making of a written or taped record. Real human conflict takes place at the bargaining table, with moments of high suspense and drama. This is part of the process. When an audience is present, participants tend to speak for the effect they hope to make on the audience; that is, instead of making progress with each other, they spout propaganda. Sessions degenerate into ham acting, posing, clowning, or name-calling. Something of the same sort happens when there is a stenographer taking down what people say, or it is known that the proceedings are going on a sound track that may be played back someday. Under such circumstances, only a trial lawyer would feel at ease. Speeches "for the record" take the place of honest bargaining. Spontaneity, and the flexibility of give-and-take disappear; the people "freeze" and act unnaturally.

Informality and an atmosphere of freedom, on the other hand, seem to produce the best effect. People are then not afraid to express themselves; and more important, lest they be made to appear later as ridiculous, or wrong, to reverse themselves if necessary. It is much easier to eat one's words when they have been uttered in private, in the presence of opponents who may also have to eat a few ill-chosen words of their own.

Negotiation Strategies. As for negotiating strategy—that is, the narrow strategy of how to present or defend a case—that depends greatly on the counterstrategy it has to meet, but there are two typical approaches.

The Piecemeal Approach. The first is the piecemeal, or step-by-step approach. This tries to settle the issues one by one in some order such as "easiest" first, or from the beginning to the end of the draft demands. It is the approach that comes naturally to the practical-minded worker, who knows that you do a job by finishing the first task before going on to the second, and so on to completion. Each item arises as a separate issue, is argued out, disposed of, and tucked away, while attention turns to the next.

The Total Approach. The second is the "total" approach, or just the reverse of the piecemeal. This regards nothing as settled until everything is settled. Bargaining "points" are offered and discussed, then laid aside as others are brought forward; every question remains open until suddenly the whole complex is ready to crystallize into a total agreement. This is frequently the company approach. Legal fiction supports this concept of bargaining, for no part of an agreement is valid until the whole has been signed. Management people generally are accustomed to thinking in terms of a complex of interrelated factors, interdependent variables, no one of which can be fixed until its effects on all the others have been calculated.

Combining Strategies. It can readily be seen that there must usually be something of both approaches in any given strategy. The company is understandably reluctant to tie itself down irrevocably on Point A until it sees how great a concession it has to make on Point X. The employees are prone to view with distrust a juggling of issues, as if they are colored balls flying through the air all at once and never coming to rest.

Here is where the easy-to-hard sequence often provides a middle way. The union gets the company fairly well tied down on minor matters, one by one, until there are only a few big issues "up in the air." This provides opportunity for serious efforts at compromise. Offers combining elements of the unsettled issues in different proportions are tried out, considered, rejected, reshuffled, and reworked until finally the mix is right. When that occurs, negotiations are almost over, and successful.

The final formula may be the result of some pretty tall horse trading at the end. Anticipating this, the union's demands and the company's counterproposals usually contain from the start a certain number of built-in bargaining points that are intended to be thrown away, or swapped for something else, at the last moment. Part of the problem for each side is to feel out the other to find out which "vital" demands have been put in just for trading purposes and which are really vital—so much so that they may take a strike to settle. Often these bargaining points are obvious "phonies," but there is enough difference between the oulook and mentality of both sides to lead to occasional serious miscalculations.

Personality in Negotiations

Negotiations are a contest, and like any contest put a strain on the participants. "The union" and "the company" are abstractions, but their representatives at the bargaining table are human beings. Human beings differ in knowledge, skill, attitudes, systems of values, temperament, endurance. It would be hard to overestimate the influence of individual personalities on negotiations.

Different men get their results in different ways. What are the personal characteristics of a good negotiator?

Patience, intelligence, stamina, a level head, an open mind, and integrity; these would seem to be minimal qualities for a good negotiator;

and he must be able to express himself well and convincingly. A sense of humor always helps.

Not all men have these qualities, and even those who have are subject, under strain, to emotional influences. Bargaining sessions coop men up together and pit them against each other. Tempers wear thin. "Bargaining fatigue" resembles the combat hazard of battle fatigue.

Broadly speaking, here is where the International Rep (or in multiemployer bargaining, as pointed out, his management counterpart, the employer association secretary) is at an advantage, like a professional athlete among amateurs. The outcome of the contest is never as deadly personal to him as to the others. It is all part of the day's work, and the stage of frustration and exhaustion may be the very moment he has been waiting for. Gone now is the time when to keep things moving he would crack a joke. Now the negotiations are not moving; they have stalled and show no immediate prospect of getting further. Ugly remarks have passed across the table. Nerves are raw.

At such a moment—always depending on the personalities involved—the Rep may rub the raw nerves of an overstrained company official to the point of provoking anger. In anger many men lose their heads. Or, again depending on personalities, this may be the time when anger drives both sides to greater stubbornness, or exasperation threatens to undo all that has been accomplished. The Rep calls a retreat—a recess or adjournment for a day or two—and takes his men outside to cool off and recuperate.

A CLIMAX IN NEGOTIATIONS

With or without conciliation and mediation, the negotiations have to run a course. Perhaps the parties come to an agreement. They put it down in writing, piecing the text together, perhaps, from parts of the original union draft, the company counterproposals, and notes made during the course of the argument. They initial it, or even sign it.

But sometimes they fail to agree, by contract expiration date or by some other deadline. What then?

Then there may be a strike.

Negotiations now break off, to be resumed under the new conditions and added pressure of strike action. Aside from this added pressure, there is no basic change in the process of negotiation, though the results reflect not just the reason and logic of the parties but the fortunes of the strike. Interest shifts, therefore, to what is going on *outside* the conference room, in the streets, at the plant gate.

THE DECISION TO STRIKE

Although the actual calling of a strike is the union's move, strikes result from decisions made independently by the employer, the union, and the workers involved in the negotiations.[2] Management could always avoid a strike by giving in to the demands of the union and unions could avoid strikes by capitulating to management. In the end, it is the workers who must hit the bricks so their decision is also of great importance. Although some strikes are emotional outbursts, it seems likely that most strikes are the result of at least partially rational decisions made under conditions of uncertainty.

The Management Decision to "Take a Strike"

In negotiations, management seeks "reasonable" labor costs and the flexibility needed to run the enterprise in an efficient manner. If the union's demands represent what management considers to be reasonable labor costs and adequate freedom for unilateral management decisions, management signs up and there is no strike. But union demands are not drawn up for the purpose of being reasonable in management's eyes and they very seldom turn out that way. Methods of determining the costs of a union agreement will be discussed in Chapters 7, 9, 10, 11, and 12.

Typically, then, management is confronted with the difficult choice between accepting "excessive" union demands or incurring the costs of a strike. While the cost of a strike to management depends entirely on the circumstances of the individual enterprise; nevertheless, most strikes at least threaten the loss of anticipated profits, during the strike, continuing fixed costs of operation, shutdown and reopening costs, and permanent loss of customers. These costs can—to some degree—be minimized by building inventories in anticipation of a strike, continued operations during the strike, and profit pooling arrangements between employers when only some of them are struck. In turn, each of these methods of minimizing strike costs involves some additional costs of its own. These include interest and storage costs when building inventories, the costs of obtaining and maintaining replacements for strikers if operations are continued during the strike, and the "premium" on strike insurance or profit pooling arrangements.

The costs of taking a strike also depend on the *duration* of the strike. A stoppage of one week's duration might only be an inconvenience, while a 30-day stoppage might be catastrophic for the enterprise. Once started, neither management nor the union nor the workers can say for sure when the strike will end. To complicate matters further, the union may up the price of an agreement if it has been necessary to strike.

The Union's Decision to Strike

The leadership of the Union is usually confronted with an unhappy choice similar to that confronting management: They can accept an agreement not wholly satisfactory to the membership (and a vociferous

[2] The authors are indebted to Professor Thomas W. Gavett of West Virginia University for suggesting much of the material in this section.

dissatisfied group is almost always present); or they can face the potentially high costs of a strike.

When a union strikes it risks some very heavy costs. The union's greatest risk is that the employer will replace the strikers or go out of business. If the strikers are replaced, the union is dead. Even if the employer makes no attempt to replace the strikers, a strike involves costs for the union in terms of strike benefits, administrative costs, and the possible disaffection of its members if the strike lasts too long or isn't "won big."

The Worker's Decision to Support the Strike

The worker expects the collective bargaining process to provide him with high wages and an opportunity to participate in the decision making of the firm. He is mightily unimpressed by competitive conditions which may depress his wages or any need for flexibility which interferes with his "right" to his job. Although accommodations are imperative, the worker's goal is collective bargaining appears directly contrary to the manager's objectives.

The worker's choice is probably the most difficult decision to be made by any of the decision makers. The decision to strike puts the worker's livelihood on the line, and few things are less willingly undertaken than personal hardship. All the decision makers in negotiations must rely on incomplete information, but the individual worker does not have even the full knowledge of what transpired in negotiations to base his decision on. At very best, his decision must be based on secondhand interpretations of the company's stand and the union's goals and resources. Part of the worker's choice comes when the strike actually begins.

The Strike Vote

At some time during negotiations, and very commonly at the outset, a union is likely to strengthen the hand of its negotiators by taking a strike vote. In many cases this is almost a ritual. Unless it sets a specific date and time, the strike vote taken early in the negotiations is almost always a maneuver: a mere threat, a psychological weapon, a "cold-war tactic." The threat may even be pure bluff.

Any bluff raises the danger of being called, but the strike threat, when it is a bluff, happens to be a fairly safe one just as long as it does not turn into action, because the company has no effective counterbluff. The threat of lockout, potent enough in the craft situation, does not usually fit the factory. All the company can do in the face of a strike threat is to tell the union, in effect, that if the threat turns to action, the company is ready to withstand the strike.

Purpose of the Strike Vote. Taking a strike vote therefore does not inevitably mean that there will be a strike. It conjures up, in visible and dramatic form, the specter that hovers in the background anyway, and pointedly reminds the company (and incidentally, the union) of what may come if negotiations fail. It puts a sense of urgency into the effort to reach agreement.

It is doubtful whether agreements embodying many concessions would ever be reached if the strike threat did not hang over negotiations.

The strike threat does not need to be explicit. The coal miners, for instance, have a slogan that expresses a tradition of their union: "no contract, no work." Neither the mineowner nor union representatives in negotiations ever need doubt that there will be a strike if they do not succeed in coming to agreement before the expiration of the current contract.

Other industrial unions have not developed such a binding tradition. With some exceptions, they bargain not on an industry-wide basis as the miners do, but enterprise by enterprise. The history and experience of a given Local union and the labor relations policy and record of the company with which it deals have much to do with the union's militancy, its willingness to strike. The current level of activity in the enterprise, or highly local and temporary conditions, may affect a union's readiness, its ability to strike.

Effect of the Vote on Union Members.   The threat expressed in a strike vote does not bear solely against the company; it has its psychological effect on the minds of the union members, too. It reminds them of the price they may have to pay to get their demands and sometimes helps keep the demands within reason. A leadership doubtful of membership support in rough going may call for a strike vote early, when conflict seems far away and unlikely, in order to condition the members' minds to the idea, in case it later becomes necessary to mobilize them for strike action.

"Insurance" for the Committee.   Again, an early strike vote is a form of "insurance" for the committee. It puts responsibility back where the authority remains: in the members' hands. Most workers shrink from the perils and inconvenience a strike involves, unless pushed to it, or desperate. Once they have gone on record by a vote, the committee can take the position of urging acceptance of compromises from the original demands, as they develop in negotiations. This is frequently a sounder and more comfortable position than that of having to try to cajole a reluctant membership to strike in support of the committee.

A Form of Referendum.   Besides the initial strike vote, others may be taken at crucial points during the negotiations, according to (but sometimes against) the recommendations of the negotiators. They constitute a sort of referendum of member sentiment, registering the reaction of the workers to the course of negotiations. It can readily be seen that this can have a strong effect upon the negotiations themselves. A committee armed with a fresh and overwhelming vote of confidence returns to the bargaining table for the next session with new strength. There is nothing quite like it on the management side.

Because of the strength that comes from the unique, one-sided value of the strike threat (up to the point where it turns into strike action) union leaders set great store by the strike vote. It would not be to their advantage as negotiators to face the company with poor membership support, so they are careful not to take a strike vote that does not pass. When, on the other hand, they can feel fairly sure of an enthusiastic endorsement by an overwhelming vote, they have nothing to lose and everything to gain by staging a demonstration.

Effect of the Vote on Negotiations. A strike vote strengthens the union negotiators' hand as long as they are careful not to turn the threat into an ultimatum by setting a date when it will certainly turn into a strike. Much of the psychological value of a threat lies in its uncertainty. Once the term is set, the strike-threat pressure ceases to be directed solely against the company, but bears on the union committee too. Then they are under equal compulsion to come to agreement by the time stated—or else! Setting the term too early may unnecessarily harden the company's position so that it gives up nothing, short of actual "war." The strike threat requires flexibility in use and is ordinarily so phrased as to be an authorization to issue a strike call, not itself a call.

Timing. Choosing the time to strike (if strike should come) is a question of high strategic value to the union. Unless negotiations are for an initial agreement, the union of course does not have unrestricted freedom in this choice. The expiration date of the existing agreement is a sort of deadline, but even so the union has some flexibility of action. The old agreement can be extended, by mutual consent, for additional stated periods, or on an indefinite basis. In some cases the union can let the contract expire without an agreement to extend it, and thereby restore the conditions of an initial agreement. This, of course, involves risks for a union, which must go on a "war alert" footing, ready to strike; but the tension puts the company under pressure as well.

Retroactivity. In the past many companies and unions went on bargaining after the expiration date with the understanding that any agreements reached eventually would be retroactive. In more recent years company resistance to this practice has hardened. It relieved the union of all sense of urgency but left the company under pressure—increasing pressure! The trend, therefore, has been toward making the expiration date of the contract the probable date of a strike, *if* there is to be a strike. The strike threat, in negotiations, consists mainly of that "if."

Craft and industrial unions use similar methods in their negotiations with employers, but they seek different kinds of collective bargaining agreements and they strike in different ways to persuade employers to grant these concessions.

UNIONS ON STRIKE

In the conduct of their strikes, craft and industrial unions strike for different aims, follow different strategies, and employ different tactics.

Craft-Union Strikes

The craft union's aim is to get a favorable price for skilled labor and to maintain an acceptable economic supply-demand relation between job openings for workers in the craft and craftsmen seeking jobs. Thus carpenters will strike for a raise in hourly wages, or against a cut. They will also strike against the employment of nonunion workers to do carpenters' jobs, usually on the ground that these nonunion workers are not qualified to do the work. This includes the jurisdictional strike in which some other skilled-worker union claims the right to do work which the carpenters consider "belongs" to them. An example might be the job of installing prefabricated windows. The glaziers claim them because they have glass panes; but so do the carpenters, because the frames are made of wood. In this case a decision either way expands the total demand for one kind of skilled labor and diminishes the demand for another kind. While jurisdictional strikes have fortunately become one of the less common kinds of strike, their incidence most clearly demonstrates the economic orientation of craft-union collective bargaining aims.

Strategy and Tactics.   Strategy in craft-union strikes springs from this supply-demand relation. It aims simply to withdraw a scarce element of production, skill, from the labor market and withhold it until the price is right. It has been pointed out before that craft unions flourish only where handicraft methods still prevail so that the product is directly turned out—as in the building trades—by a skilled craftsman. This craftsman is a man who has passed through an apprenticeship and taken several years to master a trade. When he walks off the job, the employer cannot replace him with any Tom, Dick, or Harry. In the short run he and his fellow craftsmen are irreplaceable. The more completely and the longer they withhold their skilled labor, the stronger grows the demand for it, until an offer of hourly wages is made that seems acceptable as the price of the labor to be supplied.

Tactics under this strategy can be quite simple. Basically, what the union members do is wait. If the strike is against a single employer, or a few out of many, and the others are complying with union terms, the business agent of the Local finds jobs for the striking workers with these other firms. If there are not enough jobs to go around, the union pays individual cash benefits out of its strike fund to the members who are un-

employed because of the strike. That is what the fund was built up for—
to help the members wait it out.

Employer Answer. Employers are not always willing to let the
union pick them off one by one, as just described, but may answer the
union's strike against one member firm of an association with a lockout
by all the firms. That sharpens the struggle, but does not change the
underlying basis of the union's fight. The waiting puts a heavier strain
on the strike fund, but also puts a strain on all the member firms. Sooner
or later the two sides resume negotiations and find a formula acceptable to
both.

Picketing in craft-union strikes is token in nature and may even be
done not by union members but by hired sandwich men. It is to advertise
the fact that a given employer's union workers are on strike, so that a
stranger recruited in another town will not make the mistake of accepting
employment on a struck job. Such a mistake could be very costly to a
craftsman; it could cost him his union card and any future opportunity to
make a livelihood at his trade. And only an out-of-towner would be ignorant of the strike, for the craft-union Local organizes all the craftsmen of
a given skill in one community.

Instances where violence has flared on craft-union picket lines, are,
like jurisdictional strikes today, both rare and illuminating. In most such
cases it will be found that the fight is between local people and members
of the same craft International from another locality. This underlines the
fact that a strike of skilled men can be broken only if other skilled men of
the same craft cross the picket line. This, of course, seldom happens. On
the contrary, craft-union solidarity is generally so strong that members
of one craft will not even cross the picket line of another craft. It takes
no violence to restrain them; respect for picket lines is almost a "religion"
to the craft unionist. He gives it to others when they are on strike, expects
it (and gets it) in return when he is out. It can be said of craft unions:
They win their strikes who only stand and wait.

Industrial-Union Strikes

Very different is the situation in the industrial-union strike. To stand
and wait would be the surest way of losing a strike. The industrial union
goes on strike for economic aims, but gets and holds them by methods
that can only be called, for want of a better term, *political*, in the sense of
power politics.

The Strike Objective. The immediate strike objective of the industrial union in manufacturing is to control physical access to the workplace. This denies the employer the use of his productive plant until he
ransoms it by making a satisfactory settlement. The industrial union in
transportation aims to bring the employer's rolling stock to a standstill.
Industrial unions in other fields have to select their strike objectives in the
light of their particular circumstances, which vary. The underlying strat-

egy in all of them is to prevent the replacement of individual strikers of many varieties and degrees of semiskill, by other individuals who can be taught the strikers' job.

Organization for Strike. The exact date and time of the strike may be set by vote of the members, or authorized by vote and set by call of the union officers or committee. Between Internationals, and even Locals of the same International, practices differ. The range is from a requirement in either the Local or International constitution calling for a secret ballot of all the members, with a two-thirds or three-fourths majority in favor of strike necessary to carry, down to a simple majority of members present and voting at a meeting. The practice is likely to lie somewhere between these extremes, probably nearer the latter, or less rigorous, requirement.

In a factory union, mere prudence on the part of union leaders would indicate the desirability of taking a vote before calling a strike. The members are the union's army in the strike, as well as the union's citizenry. In a democracy, it takes a vote of the citizenry as represented in parliament—the Local meeting—to mobilize the army. The secret-ballot, every-member method of authorizing a strike goes further yet: it submits the question to a referendum.

Opposing Interests within the Union. At the moment of taking the crucial strike vote, the interests of union leaders and union members may not quite coincide. The leaders are out in front, fighting for concessions the members say they want. The leaders are in direct contact with the company. They have presumably reached the conclusion that it will take more than mere arguments to win concessions, and that there are good chances of success through strike action. Conversely they fear the effect on the morale of the union members if they fail to win concessions by failing to strike. The leaders, therefore, want the strike vote to pass. The members (who may be egging their leaders on) want the concessions they have demanded, but hesitate as individuals to pay the price. That price, they know, means paydays missed, picket line duty, maybe a broken head. Even though reason may tell them they can only win by risking the strike, fear holds them back.

It may well be that at the crucial moment only a minority is actively in favor of strike. The rest—as is all too human—have gotten cold feet. But in a crowd situation a militant minority can get its way against a leaderless and wishy-washy majority. As will be shown shortly, it does not necessarily take a majority to close the factory: a militant minority can do it.

Role of the Shop Stewards. The stewards are a key group at a time like this; and indeed their support and activity are vital throughout that test that negotiations and the strike impose. They see the members in the shop from day to day. If properly informed and inspired, they are a flesh-and-blood, word-of-mouth link between the union leaders and the members. They campaign for the strike, and in the strike act as an officer corps to lead the workers.

Thus the strike vote is a critical test. In the typical, democratically organized factory union it cannot be sidestepped, because the citizen army may be mobilized by its own consent but not conscripted by decree; and yet, unless carefully handled, the conduct of the vote may expose the union to danger.

The Union's Forces. The forces at the union's disposal are the union members, a volunteer army usually without experience; they make up the rank and file. Their officers are the shop stewards, who now serve as picket captains, and others who volunteer or are elected by their mates for special strike duties. This group makes up the line organization of the striking union.

The Strike Committee sets up subcommittees for staff and service functions, mostly service. Among the important activities that have to be carried on during a strike are the following: setting up a soup kitchen to feed the picketers (this draws the strikers' wives into active participation); scrounging supplies and soliciting help from friendly sources in the community; publicity; transportation; a welfare center to provide relief in hardship cases; legal defense if trouble breaks out on the picket line; recreation, if the strike is long drawn out; and others.

Strike Headquarters. The union hall is the headquarters where the members meet, and serves as a base for most of the auxiliary activities mentioned in the last paragraph. In addition, the strikers set up a field headquarters near the plant, handy to the picket line. This may be a vacant store hired for the occasion, or a tent that also houses the soup kitchen, or even a public place like a cafe or saloon whose proprietor tolerates the strikers' presence (and gets their business), perhaps even making a back room available for their use. Here the picket captains report, and get encouragement, instructions, and advice from the Rep and the Strike Committee. Pickets drop in between spells of sidewalk duty to drink a cup of coffee, warm their toes, and pick up gossip of the strike. To one who has seen service with front-line troops in combat, it is remarkable how much these other "front-line" headquarters reproduce the atmosphere of selflessness, shared perils, and camaraderie.

Allies. The striking Local's allies are other Locals of the International, and more immediately, other Local unions in the town. The strikers' ambassador to the City Central informs the other delegates of his union's plight, and the support that comes from the labor movement of the home community is almost always warm and often generous. After all, they are neighbors. Most of them can do no more than contribute to the strike fund, send fraternal delegations to the strike meetings, and pass resolutions of support in their own. Sometimes they can give active direct support, as when the Teamsters refuse to cross a strike picket line. But the Teamsters do not always respect picket lines of other unions, and when they do, or others join in a sympathy strike, the situation takes on a new significance beyond that of the situation being examined here, which is the simple strike of factory workers.

The Striking Worker.   The plant gate channels a human stream, regular as the tide, set into motion daily during the week by the onset of the factory shift. The worker bound for his workplace who finds strike pickets at the familiar gate cannot help feeling an initial sense of shock. Not to walk through the open gate runs against habit and impulse. Man is no creature of blind instinct, and when the shop steward meets his people at the gate and diverts them to picket duty, most of them will respond; but the unspent impulse is strong, and tautens nerves.

Emotionalism.   That check to habit is the first of many emotional experiences of the strike. If the picket line keeps the worker from entering the plant the first day of the strike, and starts him on a new routine—the strike routine—the union has accomplished a great deal toward winning the campaign. It cannot always do this at the first try; if not, the task gets harder with each shift that does not see an empty plant. The union cannot always hold the lines after initial success, but that is another problem. The first task is to close down the plant, "shut 'er up tight."

This is not very difficult to do, nor does it necessarily take a majority to do it. A militant and determined minority is usually enough. Probably no more than a good handful assemble anyway, at dawn of the first day of strike, to get instructions and be posted at the gate or gates. They take their stations at all points where workers normally leave public property and step or drive onto the plant premises—parking lot entrances, street gates, and doors. As the first workers come—for habit is strong, and even those who know a strike is on cannot resist the pull of the current setting plantward at the onset of their shift—the strike leaders pass on the union's instructions. It may be to join the pickets and greet later comers with a bigger force. It may be to go to the union hall for a meeting, in cases where the strike leaders deem it desirable to keep the streets clear of crowds.

Those who act bold and confident carry the others along with them. The active ones are under leadership; the passive, leaderless, drift with the new tide. The mere sight from the head of the street of a crowd around the gate is enough to turn timid souls away. Discreetly they retire and go home (which they will find as strange, during working hours, as the deserted shop). From there, after a while, anxiety and curiosity may draw them to the union hall. At the union hall they are caught in the contagion of mass excitement and brought under organized leadership again. The factory worker, a disciplined person, responds to leadership. In a day or two he is taking his turn on the picket line.

The man who walks the picket line is not quite the same man who walked off the job the day before. After the strike, he will never be quite the same man again.

There is no such type of factory worker as the "hardened striker," but one strike will usually "harden" a union. It gives the members a shared experience that changes their attitude toward management—not individually, but as a group, for striking is a social activity. They are like troops that have seen combat.

Lessons of the Strike Experience. For many, it is an illuminating—even exhilarating—experience to learn that they can collectively defy the authority that normally dominates their individual lives and get away with it. This remains true even when they do not clearly win their strike, so long as they regain their places in the factory after it is over. What they have once dared they may do again. They feel a confidence they could not know before. They have learned caution, too, which tempers ther boasts and threats but makes more meaningful, and to the company, ominous, those they do express. One strike is enough to last most factory workers—and factory managers—a long time. The strike transforms them both.

It changes them because, as has been shown above, a strike is a profoundly emotional experience. That does not mean that it is primarily an emotional outburst (strike causes run deeper than that), but it works strongly on the emotions of everyone involved. Most numerous of those involved, and most directly affected, are the workers.

The Picket Line. The aim of the strike is to deprive the company of production and make management sue for terms to get it rolling again.

The first step is to call the workers off their jobs. This is the formal meaning of the strike vote and is easily accomplished since workers leave the plant anyway at the end of the shift.

Shutting down the Plant. The second step is to shut down the plant, and this may be a little harder. Meeting-hall courage has been known to melt away overnight. A man is not counted absent from work until he fails to show up at the start of the next scheduled shift. The strike is not actually on until the shift fails to report. The union therefore must stop the shift from going on. As has been shown, that is not really difficult to do if there is any appreciable amount of strike sentiment and if adequate organizational measures are taken.

The third step, and the one that may be hardest in the long run, is to keep the workers, and strangers who might replace them, from going in to work. This is the aim that animates every move made by the union in the strike, the object of all its vigilance, the reason for any violence that may occur on either side. The way it is carried out is by means of a picket line.

A picket line consists of union members who walk back and forth in front of the plant gate or gates. They warn their fellows, and any others who might seek to enter the factory to work, not to cross the line. They do this by word of mouth and by carrying signs. If words are not enough, they may resort to deeds.

Blockading of the Gate. The picket line at the factory gate is not a siege of the factory. A besieging force is one trying to get into a defended place to which the gates are barred. The factory gate is open during a strike. People walk in and out of it: guards, executives, and supervisors, perhaps the entire office force; even a skeleton crew of maintenance men—union members—who keep the pipes from freezing or preserve other vital installations.

Picketing the plant is not a siege, it is a blockade. It cuts the plant off from a vital element of production: labor. It defends the approaches to the plant against the entrance of people who might provide the labor. Who are these people who might want to go in the open gate? Anybody and everybody, including union members who weaken.

This is an offensive, not a defensive, strategy. The union picketer does not have to wait until someone does something to him; he has to do something to make the potential replacement refrain from entering the gate, as the replacement has every legal right to do. The weapons available to the picketers for carrying out this offensive strategy are of two kinds: moral suasion and force.

Keeping the Line Solid. Moral suasion appeals to some sentiment or belief such as working man's solidarity, or sympathy, or shame. It may be powerful enough to overcome a man's desire to get a job by which he can make a living—at any rate, in that particular plant. It certainly will do so in most cases in a community where the mores contain a tradition of worker solidarity. It may not do so if the replacement is a "stranger," particularly if he comes from a region (as, for instance, the South) where no such sentiments are common. It runs against the traditional belief that ours is a competitive society in which one man has as much right as another to take or refuse any job that is open and offered to him. Moral suasion can suffice, but it is more effective when it is supported by a powerful emotion, fear—fear of the use of force.

The force may be no more than jostling and getting in the way of a strikebreaker trying to enter the gate. No matter which way he turns, he finds somebody standing in front of him and "accidentally" barring the way. This is sometimes called "belly-bumping" and requires a beefy physique. Force may go further than that, to manhandling and beatings.

Or force may be nonviolent with picketers standing in the way of a car headed into the company parking lot. The driver cannot get through the gate without running down the people and making himself liable for their injuries. Again, force may go further than that, to the point of rocking the car and rolling it over with its occupants inside.

The striker knows that the way to his workplace leads through the gate which he is picketing. If he may not go in, he certainly does not want to see others go in, but his attitude toward these others depends upon whether they too have their "own" workplaces inside, or whether they are strangers, not fellow employees. If the person who goes through the gate is a fellow worker who has given in under the pressure, the picketer treats him with scorn for weakening; but if the strikebreaker is a stranger, he shows fury. Any return to work of former employees and union members raises the prospect of having to settle for less than the desired terms, and possible individual victimization, but the advent of new workers threatens permanent displacement.

Where there is danger that many will try to enter the plant, the union's recourse is to the mass picket line. In fact, the mass picket line is the industrial union's natural and characteristic form of strike activity. It keeps the strikers busy and it keep them together, so that they can keep an eye on the company and on each other all the time, and it assembles the force necessary to insure closing the gates.

Under the Taft-Hartley law mass picketing has been held to be illegal—an unfair labor practice—but someone has first to forbid it or disperse it: until then, it simply goes on.

Picket-Line Violence. Mass picketing, the industrial union's most effective way of blockading a plant, is probably the kind of picketing least likely to lead to physical violence unless interfered with. That is because the very size of the picket force discourages entry of strikebreakers. Nonviolent "living wall" tactics, in which the pickets lock arms and stand in the way, can keep out cars as well as people, and any overt violence has to come as an attack on the pickets. Of course, once a fight breaks out in a crowd of people already tense and with their livelihood at stake, there is no telling what may happen. The point is, it is not the strikers in such cases who are likely to start trouble.

But mass picketing, besides being effective, is illegal. A company can get a court order against it. With majestic impartiality (as pointed out earlier) the law prescribes for craft and industrial unions alike the uniform conditions of "peaceful picketing": two (or four, or six) pickets at each gate, spaced 10 (or 20, or 40) yards apart, showing signs to advertise the fact that there is a labor dispute, but not shouting, or calling, or jeering, or threatening any who "in their lawful purposes" may want to enter the plant. With variations, this is the stuff of a court order enjoining mass picketing.

The picketing becomes peaceful by legal definition but, ironically, whatever potential for violence the strike contains may actually build up in proportion to the reduction in the picketers' effectiveness in keeping the plant gate closed. If strikebreakers now feel safe in crossing the picket line, and enough of them do cross it, the union faces the uncomfortable but inescapable dilemma of losing the strike or breaking the law.

How many strikebreakers are "enough"? Only as many as it would take to raise the fear in the minds of the strikers that the company can replace them. If they are strangers that need be only a few, for every striker then feels threatened. If they are employees, perhaps union members, it might be more; but in either case the ones still on strike seek to halt the movement. Breaking the law then becomes one of the risks of battle. It is a risk the union leaders frequently, either out of pure heedless emotion or after due calculation, elect to take.

Financing the Strike.   A strike is financed in two ways.

Basically, of course, the members support it by their self-denial in giving up their potential earnings for the period of the strike, and by the unpaid services they render on the picket line and in such related auxiliary activities as mentioned in the last section. Workers on strike are ineligible for unemployment compensation.

Strike Funds.   The other way is by drawing on strike funds accumulated by the union out of dues and assessments paid in while the members were working. All Internationals have such funds, and most Locals.

To get support from the International, a Local must receive the International's approval before taking strike action. This must not be misunderstood to mean that the Local always has to get permission to strike. As long as the strike does not violate an agreement with the company the Local is usually free to make its own decision, but if it wants International money during the strike (and the help of an International Representative) it has to notify the International beforehand.

Approval by the higher body is usually routine. It would be withheld only in unusual circumstances. Getting this approval is a step the Local can use as part of its psychological war of nerves with the company in negotiations. In cases where a strike has been forced unexpectedly on a Local, approval may still be gotten *ex post facto.*

The craft-union International, with its relatively fixed membership of skilled workers only a small proportion of whom are ever on strike at the same time or for very long, can afford to pay strike benefits to individuals out of a fund accumulated centrally. The industrial union International is in a different situation. Factory strikes often involve tens of thousands of workers, and sometimes last for months.

Strike funds in the industrial union come from a small percentage, rarely more than 10 per cent, of the dues dollar; and dues in turn are a small percentage—perhaps 2 per cent—of a worker's pay. To try to support a striker and his family by paying him directly even a fraction of his normal wage sufficient to live on, and to do this for all the workers who may be on strike, would soon deplete the treasury of the International.

Besides, the aim is not to help the worker wait it out in an industrial union strike; such conflicts are not won by waiting. The aim is to keep alive the striker's militancy; and while an empty stomach makes a man abject, a half-filled belly whets the appetite and keeps the man active. Strike benefits, when paid, are therefore nominal—perhaps $10 to $30 a week—just enough to keep a little change jingling in the striker's pocket for coffee, bus fare or a few gallons of gas, newspapers, cigarettes, and the most pressing personal expenses.

Most of the strike funds go to support general activities and to meet needs that are common to the union as a whole. They pay the rent of the field headquarters and purchase supplies for the soup kitchen where the striker can half-fill his belly. They provide hospital care for any strike casualties and buy bail and legal aid for prisoners arrested for activities on the picket line. Such portion of the strike funds as goes to individuals is given frankly as relief for the emergency. Of course the union's committee will eke out its own resources, if possible, by getting relief for needy cases from public or private welfare agencies, but this resource is not always available. In any case, not to take care of members facing real personal disaster through the strike (rather than mere belt-tightening austerity for a time) would hurt morale; and in a strike, which is a form of combat, morale is vital. A striker threatened with eviction from his home may be provided with rent money to stave off the landlord. A family with small children will get milk and groceries.

Besides the established strike funds of the Local and International, contributions come in from other unions and from individuals in the form of cash and goods, particularly food. "Scrounging committees" solicit groceries from food stores and farmers. (The advent of the supermarket run by a hired manager is closing off this source of supply, but the trend toward part-time farming by industrial workers, and part-time work in industry by farmers, may have opened up another). Every little bit helps: a few sacks of potatoes, a carton of eggs, perhaps a side of beef for the stew pot. In an extremity, the strike army "lives off the country" while it carries on its fight.

Employer Strike Strategy and Tactics

Strike action is by nature drastic in the original sense of the word. The company that permits a strike to occur and the union that calls one both expect to receive some hurt, but hope to win concessions by hurting the other side more. The things they are concerned about during a strike show curious parallels. Neither side wants the plant or equipment to suffer any permanent damage, else they will not be fit to turn out production and provide jobs again. Both hope for a short strike and for the return to work of the entire force. Both envisage, as the worst that could happen, complete replacement of the work force by new employees, but by the logic of their conflict both sides are compelled to act as if that worst were bound to come to pass. That is their main defense against its happening.

Strike Costs.   A strike denies the company the use of its productive equipment, while overhead costs continue. In a sense that is by no means purely figurative, part of that productive equipment consists of the strikers. The most advanced techniques of personnel selection, placement, and training have gone into getting them together and fitting them into management's grand design that makes the factory as a whole a smooth, efficient apparatus of production. They represent the know-how that the company has developed over the years. The cost in money, time, and organizing efforts of replacing all of them at once would be staggering.

Employer Objectives. Obviously, the cheapest and most satisfactory way of getting the factory back in production calls for the return of all the workers—though there might be a few the management would prefer not to recall. This broadly coincides with the union aim of getting all its members—without any exception—back on the job. The only thing that prevents both sides from doing this at once is the thing that led them to take drastic action in the first place: disagreement over the terms at which workers resume their jobs. Until the strike, which hurts them both, hurts one side badly enough to make it give in to the other on these terms, they cannot do what they both fundamentally desire.

A factory in operation, making profits and providing good jobs, is their mutual aim and reason for existence, and even when they are locked in struggle neither side loses sight of this aim. The striking union gives "safe conduct" across the picket line to maintenance men assigned to protect vital plant installations. Strikers in a spiteful mood may commit malicious damage of the petty kind, such as breaking windows, but they will not blow up or set fire to the factory. Their own jobs would go up in the smoke.

If, then, the union wants to get all its people back to work, and the company wants them back, and only the terms of their return prevent this, why should not the company simply close down the plant, as in a craft employer lockout, and wait for the union to give in on terms?

The Lockout and the Factory Strike. In general, the lockout is not the answer to the factory strike or to the demands of the industrial union.

That is not to say that the employer's cause is lost unless he tries from the very start, in a union-declared strike, to break the picket line around his plant. He will certainly want to keep the gate open at least long enough to make sure the union has been able to keep the work force from entering it; but acceptance of the fact that the plant is shut down, while negotiations continue, would be a sensible course in most cases for a time at least. Such action might have a tempering effect on the negotiations, which broke off, presumably, at white heat. It would give the union a chance to reflect on its course. Reopening the gate later, if initial reasonableness has failed of its purpose, might then have greater tactical effect than belligerence right from the start. A decision here depends on circumstances.

But keeping the gate closed indefinitely plays into the union's hands. Overhead costs continue to mount as long as a strike lasts, whether the gate is locked or left open. Locking the gate against an industrial union does not dispel the picket line, it simply makes the picketing job easier. If the employer has initiated the lockout to counter union demands, the workers may even be entitled to draw unemployment compensation while "on strike," which is not the case when the union calls the strike. Unless the terms are settled in negotiations, the pickets will be right back when the gate reopens. Meanwhile, a portion of the work force—and very likely, the best of it—may have dispersed, found other jobs and moved away. Keeping the gate open not only maintains pressure on the union to come to a settlement but concentrates the hopes as well as the fears of the strikers on the plant gate. The implied threat that a man's job will be given to someone else seems to increase his sense of proprietorship toward it. Instead of wandering off, he is more likely to stay and fight for it.

There may be unusual circumstances in which a lockout would be effective. In a one-factory town, for instance, strikers or potential strikers might be intimidated by the threat. A lockout would still be a dangerous move in any community not sufficiently isolated to be beyond an hour's drive from other employment opportunities. Shutting down the plant would almost certainly transfer to the company a share at least of the public opprobrium that would otherwise have been directed at the strikers. The lockout is a negative and passive answer to the union. Its use restricts more active possibilities open to the company.

Tactics. In most factory strikes the gate remains symbolically open all the time, watched from the inside by company guards, patrolled from the outside by union pickets. One of the first concerns of the company is the number of pickets at the gate or gates, and their conduct. If pickets are few and orderly, chances of getting nonstrikers to cross the line and enter the plant are enhanced. The Taft-Hartley law lists mass picketing as an unfair labor practice, but there is always the problem of determining how many pickets constitute mass picketing, and enforcing the ban against it. The responsibility for assuring legal and orderly picketing rests on the public authorities: city police or, outside city limits, the sheriff and his deputies. It is sometimes necessary to apply for a court order enjoining mass picketing and prescribing the number of peaceful pickets.

Picketer Morale. With the number of pickets cut down to no more than a handful at each gate, it is possible to invite workers to return to their jobs. This is often done by mailing circular letters to all employees, sometimes reinforced by newspaper ads or radio announcements. Successful "infiltration" by a few emboldens others who would like to be at work again. Every person who responds "counts double," in the sense that he simultaneously augments the working force and diminishes the ranks of strikers. There may be little of a useful nature for him to do in the plant, but his presence there, with others who trickle in, undermines the morale of those still outside and tempts them back. They weigh the uncertainties of future settlement against present hardships and the invitation of the open gate, and perhaps the trickle turns to a gradually swelling stream. Eventually the balance may shift so far that the union either has to give in or resort to violence.

Violence at the Gate. Violence is double-edged; it may hurt the union, but it also hurts the company by checking the back-to-work flow. It takes effective law enforcement to minimize the likelihood of violent outbreaks and cope with them when they occur. Liaison with law-enforcement agencies, as well as skillful public relations work, has to be an important part of the company's activity during a factory strike.

Nowadays only the exceptional strike erupts into heavy and prolonged violence. For a strike to reach that stage, the issues must be practically insoluble, or else there must be an irreconcilable clash of powerful personalities in the leadership of company and union. The ten-year Kohler strike in Wisconsin seems to be an example of the latter. Both sides in the dispute became so deeply involved that neither could retreat and it developed into a "fight to the death." The strike moved on inexorably to the state that is "the worst that can happen": replacement of a decisive segment of the entire working force by new employees. This brought about the defeat of the Local union and its disappearance as a viable organization in the plant. Had it not been for the massive and sustained intervention of one of the world's richest and most powerful International unions, the Local union and its members would have simply passed from the scene. Although the International union eventually won the largest back-pay settlement in NLRB history ($3 million plus $1,-500,000 for restored pension rights), the lesson of the strike seems to be that a company determined not to give in can beat a Local union in the field by replacing its members on the job; but the fight may be very long and the cost very high indeed.

The "Back-to-Work" Movement. The hope of destroying the union may often be present in the minds of management people during a strike—or indeed, at any time when managers feel the restrictions unions put on freedom of managerial action—yet rarely does a company really aim at unconditional surrender by the union. Rather, the company puts the union through its strike paces in the hope of softening the terms of a proposed agreement. A good healthy back-to-work movement will usually soften up the union, though failure of a move in this direction may have the opposite effect. Just how and when to do it are tactical problems that have to be solved in the circumstances of each specific strike. Several techniques have proved successful in certain cases.

During a strike negotiations continue, mediation efforts increase. The atmosphere in which management and union people meet is even more highly charged than before. Emotional reactions often are transferred from the picket line and plant gate to the conference room. Management people have to hold particularly tight rein on their feelings at such times. A lost temper might prolong the strike, or lose it. The union Rep they deal with is a cold-blooded professional. It is up to the company representatives to stay cool and keep their wits about them.

Military Analogies. To sum it all up: the company's position in a factory strike, by analogy with the military, is defensive, and the defensive position is a strong one. The law is on the company's side in setting the conditions of the battle. The tension and emotionalism that grip the workers during a strike make the morale problem crucial. If the strikers lose their morale, the union loses the strike. Counteroffensive measures open to the company may undermine morale, and the most potent of such measures are those that persuade workers to return to their jobs without waiting for a strike settlement. This forces the union to give in or to resort to violence. Violence as such hurts the company, in most cases, as well as the union, but may be averted, sometimes, by careful co-ordination of efforts with law enforcement agencies.

If active measures fail to bring the strike to an end, and the company can afford it, waiting it out will eventually result in a settlement. Most industrial workers will have run through their savings and reserves in a few weeks, and each additional week subjects them and their families to greater hardship. Unless bitterness deep enough to offset the personal privations has been allowed to creep in, the strikers will eventually surrender.

Assuming that management has not launched a successful back-to-work movement, as the strike continues pressure on both sides mounts for a settlement. The strikers want to go back to work and to start drawing paychecks again. The management's fears of lost business are beginning to become reality as more and more customers look for more reliable sources of supply. The union's funds are running low and the membership is restive.

Negotiations are resumed, perhaps on the urgings of a mediator. Both sides have new facts to consider now and they weigh them with the intelligence of greater maturity that comes from combat. Eventually the negotiators come to an agreement. They initial it, or even sign it.

CONSUMMATION OF THE AGREEMENT

The negotiators' agreement still remains tentative; it lacks vitality until the members of the Local, and perhaps also the International union's Executive Board and the company's Board of Directors have ratified it. The Local does this in a meeting similar to the one at which the members ratified the draft demands. This time they vote on the agreement as a whole. They cannot ratify parts of it and reject other parts. If any part of the agreement is so objectionable to the members that they will not swallow it, the whole agreement fails and the negotiators have to go back and try again. Their job is not complete until the whole of their work has met with membership approval.

The agreement is finally reached and ratified, the outsiders to the dispute (union professionals, mediators, and company consultants) go on about their regular business. The workers go back to work, the company resumes operations, and normal conditions return with no permanent scars from the heat of negotiations and the test of a strike.

SUMMARY AND CONCLUSIONS

The process of reaching a labor agreement can be compared with the relations between two sovereign national powers. Negotiations are analogous to the conduct of international diplomacy. Strikes, like war, are the continuation of diplomacy (negotiations) *by other means.*

In negotiations, the union seeks benefits for its members which pose a serious challenge to management's need for reasonable costs and flexibility in the operation of the enterprise. Both parties arm themselves with whatever facts they have at their disposal, but the negotiations always involve decision making under conditions of uncertainty, and emotions are likely to prevent a purely rational approach to reaching an agreement.

The writers of this book hold that strikes are part of collective bargaining. They are not inevitable, but neither are they abnormal. Still, strikes bring loss to the participants, their dependents, and those who trade with them. They inconvenience, and may even endanger, nonparticipants. When of great magnitude or in a sensitive sector of industry, strikes can imperil the general health and welfare, and even national security. On the other hand, strikes are only one of many causes of economic waste, and by no means the major offender.

There can be no doubt that strikes can be eliminated by governmental action, but only at the expense of personal freedom and civil liberty, and with the danger of eventual violent revolt. To date, the American people have found the price too high, and are unwilling to assume the risks. The inconvenience, loss, and occasional danger incidental to strikes, and the waste they represent, are recognized as part of the price the public has to pay to maintain those free institutions of our society that go far beyond the strike situation and the industrial situation generally.

Unions go on strike when they cannot get an employer to agree with them on terms they feel are right, and are unwilling to accept his terms. The strike thus becomes an additional argument—a direct and powerful one—to back up the stand the union has taken in negotiations. A strike aims to make it expensive and inconvenient for an employer *not* to agree.

Management may occasionally provoke a strike for basically the same reason—to call a union bluff. If the union negotiators fail to get the members to respond to a strike call, or if the vote in favor of a strike is close and unenthusiastic, obviously the argument fails to impress; the strike threat not made good loses its force and softens up, rather than strengthens, the union bargainers.

Craft unions and industrial unions use essentially the same procedures in negotiations, although the agreements they seek are quite different, as will be discussed in Chapter 7. The strike strategy and tactics of craft and industrial unions differ radically.

Craft-union strike strategy consists of withdrawing a scarce skill from the market. Craft unions can win their strikes by merely waiting for supply and demand to come into balance at their desired price.

Industrial union strike strategy depends on closing the plant and keeping it shut *tight*. This is a power strategy, which gets no support from the law and may result in violence at the plant gate. The reason that plant gate violence does not occur more frequently is that most employers do not attempt to operate their plants during an industrial union strike.

Whether invoked by a confident union or provoked by a stubborn management, in either case it is the union that must assume the onus of calling the strike. A strike is the union's move.

Strategically speaking, the union is on the offensive during a strike, the employer on the defensive. The defensive position in a strike (as in classical, pre-H-bomb warfare) is strategically the stronger. An employer defensive, skillfully conducted, may turn into a counteroffensive that puts the union to rout; or the union may prevail, sufficiently (at least) to win an agreement more favorable than had been offered in the preceding negotiations.

The end product of negotiations (diplomacy) and strikes (war) is an agreement (treaty) which management, workers, and the union must try to live with.

QUESTIONS FOR DISCUSSION

1. If you were a plant manager of a firm employing 1,000 persons, would you want a foreman to sit in on negotiations? Why or why not? If you wanted him to sit in, what role should he play?
2. Assume that you are a mediator. How would you go about preparing for your role in a specific set of negotiations?
3. What happens if the Local membership rejects the agreement after it has been negotiated?
4. Compare and contrast the strike strategy and tactics of craft and industrial unions.
5. Although craft and industrial unionists need to behave differently to accomplish their strike objectives, the law does not differentiate between them. Is this sound public policy?
6. An attorney for the UAW has proposed that all picketing be outlawed but that employers be prohibited from hiring new employees while a strike is in progress. Evaluate this proposal.
7. Does a strike deadline help or hinder the negotiation process?
8. Discuss the nonstoppage strike. (See Mangum and Marshall in the bibliography.)

SELECTED ANNOTATED BIBLIOGRAPHY

This bibliography consists of two parts: (1) negotiations and (2) strikes.

1. NEGOTIATIONS

ANON. "How One Company Prepares for Collective Bargaining," *Personnel*, Vol. XXXIII (July, 1956), pp. 58–72.

This article provides a step-by-step guide for management preparations for collective bargaining. Includes examples of well-organized notebook pages and exhibit sheets to organize the facts behind management's position. How to organize the management team and select a chief negotiator are discussed.

CARPENTER, JESSE T. *Employers' Associations and Collective Bargaining in New York City*. Ithaca, N.Y.: Cornell University Press, 1950.

A detailed description of how the collective bargaining process works under employer association bargaining. Discusses development and composition of employer associations, union and employer attitudes, power of employer associations, and their internal organization, patterns of group bargaining and their complexity, and negotiation procedures and strategies.

DOUGLAS, ANN. *Industrial Peacemaking*. New York: Columbia University Press, 1962.

A penetrating psychological analysis of labor-management negotiations under mediation. An intensive study of six sets of negotiations.

FRANCE, ROBERT R. *Union Decisions in Collective Bargaining*. Princeton, N.J.: Industrial Relations Section, Princeton University, Research Report Series No. 90, 1955.

Discusses union preferences for bargaining unit, nature of union decision making under collective bargaining, co-ordination between International and Local unions, and the impact of the level of decision making on the decisions made by 13 International unions and three local independent unions.

INDIK, BERNARD P., GOLDSTEIN, BERNARD, CHERNICK, JACK, and BERKOWITZ, MONROE. *The Mediator: Background, Self-Image and Attitudes*. New Brunswick, N.J.: Research Program, Institute of Management and Labor Relations, Rutgers—The State University, 1966.

Reports on two surveys of the social background, employment conditions, attitudes and opinions of state and federal mediators.

Labor Law Journal, July, 1960. "Proceedings of the 1960 Spring Meeting of the Industrial Relations Research Association."

The following papers all discuss the question of co-operation between employers in an industry in an attempt to meet an industry-wide union: "Mutual Aid in the Airlines," by MARK L. KAHN; "Cooperation Among Auto Managements in Collective Bargaining," by WILLIAM H. McPHERSON; "Company Cooperation in Collective Bargaining in the Basic Steel Industry," by JACK STIEBER; "Cooperation Among Managements in Collective Bargaining," by FRANK C. PIERSON.

LEVINSON, HAROLD M. "Pattern Bargaining: A Case Study of the Automobile Workers," *Quarterly Journal of Economics*, Vol. LXXIV (May, 1960), pp. 296–317.

The essential points brought out by this analysis are that there has been a considerable degree of flexibility in union's approach; the most important variables affecting the union's wage policy were size of firm, relationship to industry, its financial condition, and the desires of unions to obtain "equitable" settlement; and that neither "economic" nor "political" hypothesis above provides an adequate frame of reference for understanding union's policies.

LIVERNASH, E. ROBERT. "Recent Developments in Bargaining Structure," ARNOLD W. WEBER (ed.), *The Structure of Collective Bargaining: Problems and Perspectives*, pp. 33–55. New York: The Free Press of Glencoe, Inc., 1961.

Discusses the postwar growth of centralization in contract negotiation in the local and national product market structures of bargaining. Emphasizes the great diversity of bargaining structures in the U.S.

MARTING, ELIZABETH (ed.). *Understanding Collective Bargaining: The Executive's Guide*. New York: American Management Association, 1958.

Forty-six authors, most of them industrial relations executives, discuss bargaining and the company's future, getting ready to talk contract, bargaining procedures, the contract and its wording, the issues in collective bargaining, the use of mediation, strikes, and explaining management's position.

McCAFFREE, KENNETH M. "Regional Labor Agreements in the Construction Industry," *Industrial and Labor Relations Review*, Vol. IX (July, 1956), pp. 595–609.

Discusses reasons for the changing structure of collective bargaining in the building construction industry.

McKEE, CLINE. Know Your Climate—the Key to Effective Bargaining," *Personnel*, Vol. XXXIV (July–August, 1957), pp. 52–62.

The Industrial Relations Officer of the Canadian Broadcasting Corporation describes management's preparation for collective bargaining as consisting of knowledge of the opposition, the agreement, company objectives and organization. He also describes the formulation and uses of the clause comparison chart which incorporates the existing agreement, union proposals, and management counterproposals.

MEYER, ARTHUR S. "Function of the Mediator in Collective Bargaining," *Industrial and Labor Relations Review*, Vol. XIII (January, 1960), pp. 159–65.

Question of how mediation actually works has long resisted best efforts to find satisfactory answers. In this brief but penetrating distillation of his own experience, the author reveals the method which he employed as mediator and comes close to defining general principles involved in the conduct of mediation.

National Industrial Conference Board. *Preparing for Collective Bargaining*, Studies in Personnel Policy, No. 172. New York: The Board, 1959.

A comprehensive study of management practice in preparation for, and conduct of, negotiations. Two hundred and thirteen companies cooperated. Discusses decision-making process within the management hierarchy, communications with employees and supervisors on collective bargaining, use of bargaining books in negotiations, and negotiations on specific subjects.

NORTHRUP, HERBERT R. "Boulwareism vs. Coalitionism in the 1966 GE Negotiations," *Management of Personnel Quarterly*, Vol. 5 (Summer, 1966), pp. 2–11.

Reviews Boulwareism in light of the attempt at coalition bargaining by a group of unions with G.E. in 1966.

PILLSBURY, WILBUR F. *The Use of Corporate Financial Statements and Re-*

lated Data by Organized Labor. Bloomington: Indiana University, Bureau of Business Research, Report No. 18, 1954.

Discusses sources of corporate financial data for collective bargaining and the use of these data by union research departments. Suggests a series of financial statements which would prove most helpful in achieving factual collective bargaining.

SLICHTER, SUMNER H., HEALY, JAMES J., and LIVERNASH, E. ROBERT. *The Impact of Collective Bargaining on Management.* Washington, D.C.: Brookings Institution, 1960.

See Chapter 30, "Negotiation of Union-Management Contracts."

TAYLOR, GEORGE W. (ed.). *Industry-Wide Bargaining Series.* Philadelphia: University of Pennsylvania.

This series of monographs by experts in industrial relations provides the most comprehensive discussion of multiemployer bargaining available. The monographs in the series include:

KESSLER, SELMA, compiler. *Industry-Wide Bargaining: An Annotated Bibliography.*

TILOVE, ROBERT. *Collective Bargaining in the Steel Industry.*

FRIEDEN, JESSE. *The Taft-Hartley Law and Multi-Employer Bargaining.*

POLLAK, OTTO. *Social Implications of Industry-Wide Bargaining.*

BAHRS, GEORGE O. *The San Francisco Employers' Council.*

KERR, CLARK, and RANDALL, ROGER. *Collective Bargaining in the Pacific Coast Pulp and Paper Industry.*

PIERSON, FRANK C. *Multi-Employer Bargaining: Nature and Scope.*

FISHER, WALDO. *Collective Bargaining in the Bituminous Coal Industry.*

FEINSINGER, NATHAN. *Collective Bargaining in the Trucking Industry.*

KENNEDY, THOMAS. *The Significance of Wage Uniformity.*

GARRETT, SYLVESTER, and TRIPP, L. REED. *Management Problems Inherent in Multi-Employer Bargaining.*

TAYLOR, GEORGE W. (ed.). *Proceedings: Conference on Industry-Wide Collective Bargaining.*

ABERSOLD, JOHN R. *Problems of Hourly Wage Uniformity.*

LEVY, BERT W. *Multi-Employer Bargaining and the Anti-Trust Laws.*

SEYBOLD, JOHN W. *The Philadelphia Printing Industry: A Case Study.*

2. STRIKES

BAMBRICK, JAMES J., JR. "The Strike Manual," *Management Record,* Vol. XIX (July, 1957), pp. 238–39.

Discusses need for, and content of, management strike manuals with plans for evacuating the plant, maintaining essential services, and minimizing strike-inflicted losses.

―――――. "Marquis of Queensbury Rules for Strikes," *Management Record,* Vol. XVIII (March, 1956), pp. 85–87.

A Conference Board Study of 92 disputes shows that experienced managers and unionists tend to adhere to certain rules to be sure that the plant can reopen after a strike. Sometimes these rules appear in the contract, but they are more frequently only spoken agreements, sometimes made after the strike is under way.

BAMBRICK, JAMES J., JR., and DORBANDT, MARIE P. "National Union Strike Benefits," *Management Record,* Vol. XX (July–August, 1958), pp. 242–45, 267–75.

This survey of 78 unions indicates that over half provide strike benefits at the national union level. Detailed tables on source of union strike funds and the amount of individual strike benefits.

BERNSTEIN, IRVING, ENARSON, H. L., and FLEMING, R. W. (eds.). *Emergency Disputes and National Policy.* New York: Harper & Bros., 1955.

BRIGGS, VERNON M., Jr. "The Mutual Aid Pact of the Airline Industry," *Industrial and Labor Relations Review,* Vol. 19 (October, 1965), pp. 3–20.
Describes the establishment, principles, and effectiveness of the mutual assistance scheme adopted by a number of carriers to cope with the problem of whipsawing strikes.

CHAMBERLAIN, NEIL W., and SCHILLING, JANE METZGER. *The Impact of Strikes, Their Economic and Social Costs. New York:* Harper & Bros., 1954.
Discusses the impact of strikes in coal and railroad transportation.

————. *Social Responsibility and Strikes,* New York: Harper & Bros., 1953.
Discusses public opinion on strikes, direct and indirect sanctions in support of public opinion, the reliability of these sanctions, and strikes in a dominant firm and in a public utility.

CULLEN, DONALD E. "The Taft-Hartley Act in National Emergency Disputes," *Industrial and Labor Relations Review,* Vol. VII (October, 1953), pp. 15–30.
A review of experience under the Taft-Hartley national emergency provisions and proposed amendments.

FRANCE, ROBERT R. "Seizure in Emergency Labor Disputes in Virginia," *Industrial and Labor Relations Review,* Vol. VII (April, 1954), pp. 347–66.
A review of experience under the Virginia emergency disputes law.

HAMMETT, RICHARD S., SEIDMAN, JOEL, and LONDON, JACK. "The Slowdown as a Union Tactic," *Journal of Political Economy,* Vol. LXV (April, 1957), pp. 126–34.
Discusses the effectiveness of the slowdown as a union tactic and union members' attitudes toward its use.

KARSH, BERNARD. *Diary of a Strike.* Urbana: University of Illinois Press, 1958.
Story of a strike's effects on individuals directly and indirectly involved, upon the company and entire community. Gives dramatic account or organizing campaign and strike.

KORNHAUSER, ARTHUR, DUBIN, ROBERT, and ROSS, ARTHUR M. (eds.). *Industrial Conflict.* New York: McGraw-Hill Book Co., Inc., 1954.
Experts on sociology, psychology, and economics make an interdisciplinary study of the causes and effects of industrial conflict.

McCALMONT, DAVID B. "The Semi-Strike," *Industrial and Labor Relations Review,* Vol. XV (January, 1962), pp. 191–208.
Briefly notes the nature of, and objections to, several proposed non-stoppage strike plans which provide for uninterrupted production of goods and services while the parties to the dispute incur economic penalties, and develops his own semistrike proposal.

McDERMOTT, THOMAS J. "Ten Years of the National Emergency Procedure," *Labor Law Journal,* Vol. IX (March, 1958), pp. 227–43.
Effectiveness of procedure adopted in Taft-Hartley Act to handle public interest labor disputes examined in light of its application to specific disputes.

MANGUM, GARTH L. "Taming Wildcat Strikes," *Harvard Business Review,* Vol. XXXVIII (May–April, 1960), pp. 88–96.

Argues that "wildcat strikes are management's responsibility—they continue as long as the participants find them profitable; cease when management, through disciplinary action, makes them unrewarding." Experiences with six wildcat strikes are described.

MARSHALL, HOWARD D., and MARSHALL, NATALIE J. "Nonstoppage Strike Proposals—A Critique," *Labor Law Journal*, Vol. VII (May, 1956), pp. 299–304.

A comparative analysis of the various plans for the use of the "statutory strike" as a substitute to reduce public inconvenience resulting from work stoppages in essential industries.

PARNES, HERBERT S. *Union Strike Votes: Current Practices and Proposed Controls*. Princeton, N.J.: Industrial Relations Section, Princeton University, Research Report Series No. 92, 1956.

This study evaluates compulsory strike-vote legislation in terms of experience under such laws and describes the processes whereby strikes are authorized by American unions.

ROSS, ARTHUR M., and IRWIN, DONALD. "Strike Experience in Five Countries, 1927–1947; An Interpretation," *Industrial and Labor Relations Review*, Vol. IV (April, 1951), pp. 323–42.

Suggests reasons for differences in strike incidence in five countries.

ROSS, ARTHUR M., and HARTMAN, PAUL T. *Changing Patterns of Industrial Conflict*. New York: John Wiley & Sons, Inc., 1960, p. 220.

An analysis of national trends and international differences in strike activity in 15 countries of North America, Europe, Asia, Africa, and Australia. An attempt to explain the "withering away" of the strike in most of the countries of Northern Europe. A discussion of the relation between national patterns of industrial conflict and certain features of the industrial relations system.

SCHULTZ, GEORGE P. "The Massachusetts Choice-of-Procedures Approach to Emergency Disputes," *Industrial and Labor Relations Review*, Vol. X (April, 1957), pp. 359–74.

Examines experience under the Slichter choice-of-procedures emergency strike law in Massachusetts.

SLICHTER, SUMNER H., HEALY, JAMES J., and LIVERNASH, E. ROBERT. *The Impact of Collective Bargaining on Management*. Washington, D.C.: Brookings Institution, 1960.

See Chapter 22, "Wildcat Strikes and Union Pressure Tactics."

STAGNER, ROSS. *The Psychology of Industrial Conflict*. New York: John Wiley & Sons, Inc., 1956.

A systematic and comprehensive application of psychological principles and concepts to an understanding of the dynamics of industrial relations.

Chapter 7

THE NATURE OF THE

LABOR AGREEMENT

"CONTRACT?" OR AGREEMENT?

Any company in the regular course of business enters into many contracts, written, verbal, or implied. The "union contract" would seem, at a casual glance, to be merely one of these contracts, much like all the others.

This is far from the case.

When a company purchases materials it enters into a contract with another company, the vendor, under which the vendor supplies the materials and receives money in return. But under the labor agreement the union supplies nothing tangible, receives no money from the company in return. The union does not "supply" labor; the workers supply that, and draw the wages for it. The union does not contract for the labor of its members. It does not own them. It could no more force them to deliver labor promised to the company than the company itself could exact forced labor from them.

When a company sells its products to a customer it makes a contract to deliver goods of specified quality and quantity for a specified price. But the union buys nothing from the company, pays nothing to it.

When a company engages a contractor (again by contract) to erect a building, or to do some hauling, or to manufacture a component part, it pays the contractor who pays the labor used on the job. The union does not pay its members for the work they do for the company, nor does the company pay its workers through the union as an intermediary.

It is because the union "contract" differs so markedly from ordinary business contracts that this text refers to it by preference as the "labor agreement," or "union agreement." Usage has made the other term so common, however, that it would be pedantic to condemn it and hopeless to try to suppress it. There is no harm in using the term "union contract" interchangeably with "labor agreement," so long as the user, or reader, understands how this special kind of agreement differs from other contracts. To do so it is necessary to get a firm understanding of the nature of the labor agreement.

The Contract with the Employee

The company does not contract for labor with the union, but with the company employees. They are the ones who supply something tangible, hours of labor or pieces of finished work, and who receive money wages in return. The company has a contract with each one of them—as many contracts as there are employees. This contract may or may not take form in writing; it may not even be explicitly expressed verbally, but is inherent in the company's offer of a job and the employee's acceptance of the job. This contract—work for wages—is enforceable at law, and so firmly recognized that a "mechanic's lien," or claim for wages due, takes precedence over the claims of all other creditors of an employer. It must be paid in full even though the other creditors get only partial payment.

The union is not a party to this contract, yet shapes it, under collective bargaining, by establishing its terms. The labor agreement negotiated by the union defines the *company's* offer of wages, hours, and working conditions that are to make up the employee's work contract. Any worker is free to accept or reject these terms. If he accepts them he enters into a contract *directly with the company*. He may terminate this contract at will, just by quitting. The company is also theoretically free to terminate it by dismissing him, but part of the terms is usually a promise by the company not to exercise this right except under certain conditions: seniority, "just cause" for discharge, and other restrictions.

The Agreement with the Union

Without altering, therefore, the direct contractual nature of the employer-employee relationship, the labor agreement collectively sets the terms on which the company offers its individual work contracts to each of the employees in the bargaining unit. The labor agreement thus takes the place of company policy—*becomes* company policy—in all areas that it touches.

A great deal of the literature of collective bargaining consists of attempts to define these areas and their boundaries, and to list and classify them. Most factory agreements (in contrast to craft-union contracts) are bulky, complicated documents. Some of them, printed in handbook form in 8-point type, run to more than 100 pages. Attempts to make sense of the many articles and clauses, sections, subsections, paragraphs, and subparagraphs, are often as confusing as the ponderous and pseudolegal phraseology of the documents themselves.

As a working instrument, every labor agreement has to be studied, by those who live under its provisions, as carefully as a code of laws. Every agreement differs in some respect from every other; there is no standard, no pattern, no universal model; and this is particularly true of industrial union agreements, which tend to be long and complicated. What the student needs is a tool of analysis that will unlock the meaning of any agreement.

A Tool for Analysis

This chapter, with the points it makes, constitutes just such a tool. By its aid the bulkiest or most obscurely worded agreement yields its essential purport to analysis. Despite the dissimilarity in organization or topics and presentation of provisions that is found in different labor agreements, all are reducible to certain common denominators.

These are presented in Figure 7–1, and topics in the remaining part of the chapter are arranged to correspond with the chart.[1] Part III, The

FIGURE 7–1

FUNCTIONS OF THE LABOR AGREEMENT

Function	Category	Scope
I. Union Security and Management Rights	a) The bargaining unit b) Form of recognition c) Duration and renewal d) Management rights	*Who speaks for whom* *With what authority* *For how long* *Except in what conditions*
II. The Wage and Effort Bargain	a) Pay for time worked b) The effort bargain c) Premium pay d) Pay for time not worked e) Contingent benefits	*Day rates and base rates; job evaluation* *Standards* *Hours: duration* *Fixed labor costs* *Variable labor costs*
III. Individual Security	a) Job Rights b) Due process	*Relative claim to available work; seniority* *Absolute claim to fair treatment; grievance procedures*
IV. Administration	a) Internal b) External	*On-the-job representation; shop stewards* *Arbitration*

[1] This presentation is taken from an article by one of the authors of this book, which appeared in the September/October, 1962, issue of *Personnel*, journal of the American Management Association, by permission of the copyright owner. Minor changes in terminology have been made in the version given here.

Issues in Collective Bargaining, and Part V, Cases in Collective Bargaining, follow the same format.

FUNCTIONS OF THE LABOR AGREEMENT

The function of a collective agreement as a whole is to set the terms and conditions of employment for the individual employees it covers.

In common usage, this collective agreement is called a contract, but the real contract is between the company and each of the employees in the bargaining unit, so that there are actually as many contracts as there are individuals. They individually do the work and draw the pay; the union agreement merely lays down rules under which each individual contract takes effect. These rules make up two of the four main sections shown on the chart—the Wage and Effort Bargain, and Individual Security. The other two—Union Security and Management Rights, and Administration—define the union's relationship with management, and provide for administration of the terms agreed to.

The four parts further break down into the 13 functional categories listed in Figure 7–1. Following is a detailed explanation of these various categories and what they cover:

I. Union Security and Management Rights

Every labor agreement constitutes recognition by one party of the other, and defines their relationship—who speaks for whom, with what authority, for how long, and except in what conditions. These four categories are shown in the table as:

a) The Bargaining Unit. The bargaining unit is the people for whom the union speaks and for whom the company recognizes the union as spokesman. At any given moment, these people could be listed as names on a payroll, but because people shift jobs, move on and off the payroll, it is customary to describe the unit in terms of jobs. This may be done positively, by listing jobs or job categories, or negatively, by listing exclusions. Or, as is usually the case, it can be done by both methods.

b) Form of Recognition. The statutory form of recognition is sole and exclusive bargaining rights. Other, stronger forms of recognition are also legal, but go beyond the statutory minimum. Some items that will fall in this category are:

1. Union hiring hall.
2. Checkoff of union dues and contributions.
3. Union participation in apprenticeship control.
4. Provisions giving the union power over employment; that is, the individual's right to join and remain in the bargaining unit.

c) Duration and Renewal. The agreement must run some specific term, and usually contains provisions for renewal. Such, for example, are:

1. Notice of termination or negotiation.
2. "Openers" for wage adjustments during the contract period.

d) *Management Rights.* This balances union security. Many agreements do not contain management rights provisions, on the theory that all rights not specifically bargained away belong to management. This assumption is sound enough in theory, but most companies find it more practical to insert reminders that certain specific areas of action and decision remain in management hands. What special rights does management most need to retain? Three stand out:

1. Freedom to select the business objectives of the company.
2. Freedom to determine the uses to which the material assets of the enterprise will be devoted.
3. Power to discipline for cause.

II. The Wage and Effort Bargain

This is the heart of the agreement. It tells the employee how much pay he will get for how much work on a given job. It tells the company how much it will cost—in money—to get desired performance and production. Here we have five categories:

a) *Pay for Time Worked.* This means the hourly, weekly, monthly wage or salary paid for the job, by base rates or day rates. Determining the appropriate rates for the job is part of bargaining, but the technique most commonly used for establishing wage differentials, with or without bargaining, is standard job-evaluation procedure, including such considerations as:

1. Labor grades or classifications and rate ranges.
2. Pay steps within grade.
3. Expected average earnings under piecework systems.

b) *The Effort Bargain.* This part of the basic contract between the company and each of its employees does not always appear explicitly in the agreement, but it is always there, if only by implication. It is as important to management (for it determines costs) as the preceding item is to the employee (since that item determines his income). The effort bargain, in a word, means standards for task performance.

Standards may take very concrete form, as in time studies, or they may be loose and undefined. If management is careless about standards, employees may set them by default. Standards determine the intensity of each hour worked—the miles per hour, rather than distance traveled or hours on the road—the performance expected under the working conditions that surround the task. Incentive plans or piecework may permit variable earnings, but standards are firm. That is, once standards have been properly set, they ought to change only with changes in working conditions, technology, or other alterations in the task itself. The effort bargain makes stipulations such as:

1. Rules for setting standards or making time studies.
2. Crew sizes, manning tables.
3. Quotas.
4. Work rules, including safety rules applying to the task.

c) Premium Pay.   This is what used to be called "penalty pay." Theoretically, it is money that would never be paid if no employee were asked to work outside his regularly scheduled, normal daylight hours. The most common types of premium pay are:

1. Overtime.
2. Call-in pay.
3. Shift differentials.

d) Pay for Time Not Worked.   This item used to be lumped together with the following one, contingent benefits, under the general heading of "fringe benefits." Our outline separates them, putting in category II (*d*) payments that represent fixed labor costs, i.e., costs that are inescapable and predictable—the payments that all employees get such as:

1. Paid Holidays and vacations.
2. Christmas or other bonuses.
3. Minor items, such as paid coffee breaks, washup time, and so forth.

e) Contingent Benefits.   These are usually, though not always, variable labor costs. That is, most companies pay for them on a cents-per-man-hour basis, or as a percentage of payroll. (The other way of paying for them is by a flat sum per head per month, which turns them into fixed costs, or semifixed, at all events.) They differ from the preceding category in that not every employee gets all the benefits they offer; also, employees may contribute to the costs. Actuarial calculations will yield quite an accurate prediction as to the number of employees to whom these benefits will be paid, but the individual claims cannot, of course, be foreseen. Management must judge these items by their cost, whereas employees will judge them by their payoff in individual cases. The main types of contingent benefits are:

1. Death benefits.
2. Pensions.
3. Supplementary unemployment benefits.
4. Severance pay.
5. Health and welfare plans.

III. Individual Security

The wage and effort bargain, outlined above, is the fundamental contract offer the employee accepts when he accepts his job. It obligates the company to pay him according to the terms set down. In turn, it obligates the employee to perform as specified in the agreement, or as directed by management in day-to-day operations. But it contains no guarantee of continuance. An employee who finds the bargain satisfactory wants some guarantee of continuity of employment. Broadly speaking, this attitude coincides with management interests, because the company does not want excessive turnover. Nevertheless, the company has to lay people off when work is slack; at times it needs to transfer people from one job to another; and it should have freedom to select good prospects for promotion. Thus, there has to be an accommodation of company and employee interests. The rules whereby the company, on the one hand, maintains a work force of the optimum quality and numbers, and employees, on the other, are assured of their individual security, fall into two categories:

a) Job Rights. Probably the most common job rights device is seniority. Other common forms are the closed shop or the union hiring hall. In the latter case, union practices or bylaws take care of individual claims to available work; they are then no concern of management. Seniority within the company, on the other hand, is a vast and complicated field of claims and counterclaims by individuals. Seniority is rarely absolute; it gives the individual only a relative claim to available work or other benefits flowing from the enterprise. Three types of seniority can be distinguished—protective, opportunity, and privilege—together with a special concept, the seniority unit, that has a bearing on all three:

To take the special concept first, the seniority unit usually consists of a list of employees' names ranked in order of their seniority. What is important here is the size of the list or lists in relation to the total work force in the bargaining unit. Criteria for compiling the list may range from simple job seniority on up through occupational, departmental, divisional, and plant-wide groupings to company-wide seniority. (The recent steel settlement even extended the concept to a "seniority pool" for the industry, thus cutting across company lines.)

Of the three main types of seniority, the first—protective seniority—applies in the case of layoffs: The most senior employee (within the specified unit) is the last to be let go and the first to be recalled when work picks up.

The second type, opportunity seniority, gives the most senior employee the first chance to get, or qualify for, a better job—or, in case of a cutback, to stay on the payroll. The "bid and bump" system exemplifies this type. Of course, the broader the seniority unit, the closer opportunity seniority comes to being the same thing as protective seniority, and in the plant or company-wide unit they become synonymous.

The third type, privilege seniority, is the employee's right to contingent benefits, such as pensions. This is probably the only completely noncontroversial kind of seniority, as evidenced by the fact that the unit is almost always company-wide, with pensions calculated according to total years of service.

But union agreements rarely make seniority the sole determinant of job rights. The broader the seniority unit, the more it is likely to be affected by such factors as merit or ability to do the job, particularly in cases of opportunity seniority. Hence, in the job-rights category also fall such items as:

1. Superseniority for shop stewards.
2. Breaks in seniority.
3. Criteria other than seniority, such as merit, for individual advancement.

b) Due Process. This category covers the grievance-handling procedure (though not the machinery)—the rules that have been laid down for handling employee complaints of all types, including allegations of simple injustice as well as contract violations. This covers such items as:

1. Steps in the grievance procedure.
2. Time limits for replies to grievances.
3. Procedure for invoking arbitration.
4. No-strike, no-lockout pledges pending arbitration.
5. Warning notices and reprimands.
6. Disciplinary penalties and appeals.

IV. Administration

This section covers the machinery that is set up to put due process into effect, including the delegation of the requisite authority to specific individuals who have been given certain responsibilities in connection with the agreement. Part of this machinery is internal, in that it involves only employees of the company. Part is external, involving outsiders, such as union representatives, government officials, or private arbitrators. This gives us our two final categories:

a) On-the-Job Representation. Though union members may name their representatives, such as shop stewards, the election of those people does not confer authority upon them. They obtain their authority from the agreement, in which the special activities of shop stewards are recognized. Thus, this category covers such arrangements as:

1. Payment for time spent by stewards in handling grievances.
2. Permission for stewards to leave their workplace to confer with employees and with supervisors.

b) Arbitration. This category encompasses those sections of the agreement covering outsiders on whom it confers a certain authority. It includes such items as:

1. Grants of permission to union officials to visit workplaces during working hours, under certain conditions.
2. Composition of a board of arbitrators, or a disciplinary board, if this draws upon people from outside the company.
3. Duties and powers of the arbitrator and any limitations thereon.

DIVERSITY IN LABOR AGREEMENTS

This chapter purports to be a tool for the analysis of labor agreements. To show how this tool works, two labor agreements will be analyzed. This analysis will require consideration of long-established practices of the parties to an agreement as well as the written words. By noting the substantial diversity in the practices of craft and industrial unions, the basic unity of purpose of all collective bargaining agreements becomes apparent.

A Craft Union–Employer Association Agreement

The first agreement to be analyzed is 30 pages long and contains about 9,000 words. It covers the bricklayers in a major metropolitan area. Three Employer Associations and four Local unions of the Bricklayers, Masons and Plasterers' International Union signed the agreement.

Union Security and Management Rights. To understand the union security provisions of this agreement it is necessary to look beyond the written words of the agreement. Such key words as "Union Security" and "Management Rights" appear nowhere in the agreement.

Bargaining Unit. The agreement contains no explicit reference to the "bargaining unit." However, the bargaining unit is defined in three other sections of the agreement: "Article XI: Scope of Work" (which deals with the nature of covered jobs), "Article XIV: Negotiations: Grievances" (which provides for the settlement of jurisdictional disputes), and "Article I" (which defines the relationships of individual employers to the three Associations who are signatories to the agreement).

Article XI: Scope of Work, reads as follows:

> The work covered by this Agreement is described as bricklaying masonry and shall consist of laying bricks, in, under and upon any structure or form of work where bricks are used, whether in the ground or over the surface, or beneath water, in commercial buildings, rolling mills, iron works, blast or smelting furnaces, lime or brick kilns, in mines or fortifications and in all underground work such as sewers, telegraph, electric and telephone conduits; all pointing and cutting of brick walls, fireproofing, block-arching, terra cotta cutting and setting, laying and cutting of all tile, plaster, mineralwool, cork blocks, cement and cinder blocks, glass brick, macotta and metalon, or any substitutes for the above materials where the trowel is used, and setting of all cut stone or artificial stone trimming on brick or stone buildings.

The work defines the jobs covered by the agreement which is the equivalent to the employee side of the bargaining unit question.

Because Article XI might come into conflict with bargaining units defined in other building and construction industry agreements, Article XIV provides for the local settlement of jurisdictional disputes or the ultimate referral of such disputes to the National Joint Board for the Settlement of Jurisdictional Disputes in the Building and Construction Industry.

"Article I" which has no descriptive title provides the answer to the question of what employers are covered by the agreement. The three Associations which signed the agreement represent masonry contractors, general contractors who employ other tradesmen as well as bricklayers, and residential construction contractors. Article I states that the Associations acted only as agents for their members in the negotiation of the contract and that the Associations have an individual, but not joint, obligation to the terms of the contract. Article I also contains a "most favored nation" clause which binds the union not to negotiate more favorable contracts with other employers.

Form of Recognition. The form of recognition or union security provisions of this agreement are contained in "Article VIII: Hiring Employees." The six sections of this article require the employers to notify the union of job vacancies and to give preference in employment to workmen who have previously worked at the trade or to graduates or students in an approved apprenticeship training program. The union agrees to refer qualified workmen to the employer for consideration. Workmen who refuse to join the union within seven days after being hired must be discharged. All this boils down to either a "seven-day union shop" or a "modified closed shop"—neither of which terms can be found anywhere in the words of the agreement.

Duration and Renewal. The provisions for duration and renewal are routine.

Management Rights. The term "Management Rights" is also missing from the written agreement. Article XI, Section 1, states, "There shall be no limits or restrictions as to the amount of work performed by employees," but numerous other paragraphs provide that "No work shall be done which shall destroy the true principles of the trade." All this seems to indicate that management rights are defined by a tradition which places heavy emphasis on judgment of individual tradesmen.

The Wage and Effort Bargain. The wage and effort bargain is the largest single section of the bricklayers' agreement. It covers almost ten of the 30 pages of the agreement. Nevertheless, it is very brief and very simple compared to the typical industrial union agreement.

Pay for Time Worked. The wage scale contained in this agreement provides base wages for only *four* jobs: journeymen, subforemen, foremen, and apprentices. Foremen are paid 50 cents an hour more than journeymen and subformen are paid 25 cents an hour more than journeymen. Apprentices receive a graduated percentage of the journeyman rate depending on how long they have served in the apprenticeship, e.g., 50 per cent during the first six months of apprenticeship up to 80 per cent in the seventh six months.

The Effort Bargain. The bricklayers' contract does not say much about the effort bargain as such. However, it contains quite detailed provisions on the types of scaffolds to be provided, the fact that foremen must be "practical mechanics of the trade," limits on the work activity of foremen, the obligation of workmen to co-operate with one another, and workmanship standards which preserve "the true principles of the trade."

Premium Pay. Work in excess of eight hours per day is prohibited except for a few minutes of work in cases of necessity. Overtime work and work performed on Saturdays, Sundays, and holidays is paid at the rate of double time. Base wages on the second shift and third (or Special) shift are 30 cents and 60 cents per hour higher than on the first shift. The "Special Shift" is any single shift when conditions make it impractical to work a shift wholly between the regular hours of 8 A.M and 4:30 P.M.

Pay for Time Not Worked. Holiday pay is provided by the Bricklayers' Holiday Trust Fund which is supported by a 4 per cent payroll contribution by the employers covered by the agreement. Wash-up time is limited to five minutes before lunch and before quitting time.

Contingent Benefits. The benefits provided by this agreement are described in a separate agreement which has been amended several times since its establishment. The basic agreement, however, provides for employer contributions of 4 per cent of the base wages paid to the Bricklayers' Pension Trust Fund. Insurance is provided by the Construction Workers' Insurance Fund which is financed by employer payments of 15 cents per man-hour worked for all hours worked by his employees. It should be noted that the Holiday Trust Fund, the Pension Fund, and the Insurance Fund are all multiemployer arrangements and that the worker is entitled to his benefits by virtue of employment with any unionized employers in the industry rather than by continuous employment with a single enterprise.

Individual Security. Job rights, or the individual's relative claim to available work, is almost entirely absent from the agreement, since the union refers workers to employment. *Union* rules define the individual's job rights. However, if it becomes necessary to reduce the working force temporarily the foreman is directed to divide the work equally among the crew, and no employee is to receive less than two hours' pay on any day on which the work force is reduced temporarily unless the foreman sends the whole crew home for that day. The workers' absolute claim to fair treatment is described in the sections of the agreement dealing with foremen. The agreement provides that foremen shall be selected by the employer and shall represent the employer on the job. Another paragraph of the agreement states, "It shall be the duty of the foreman to abide by terms of this Agreement and he shall not be required as a condition of employment to violate any part of it." Although the agreement provides a method of wage payment for employees who may be discharged, the agreement lists no grounds for discharge and makes no reference whatsoever to disciplinary procedures.

Administration. Article VI of the agreement provides for a job steward on each job. The steward is a member of the union appointed by the Business Agent to act as steward. The steward and Business Agent may confer with employees during working hours.

If the steward is unable to settle a grievance with the foreman, he refers the grievance to the Business Agent. If the Business Agent is unable to settle the grievance with the employer, the grievance is referred to a Joint Arbitration Board consisting of equal numbers of union and employer representatives. If this Joint Board is unable to render a majority opinion on the grievance, the grievance is then referred to the International union. A representative of the International union and a representative of the Associations then designate an umpire (arbitrator) who is empowered to render a final and binding decision.

The foregoing analysis of a craft union collective bargaining agreement shows: (1) the importance of unwritten practices in industries which have a long history of collective bargaining, (2) the omnipresence of the basic functions of the labor agreement, and (3) when compared to the following industrial union agreement, the great diversity in practice in the provisions of the labor agreement in different circumstances.

An Industrial Union–Single-Plant Agreement

The second agreement to be analyzed is 40 pages long and contains about 16,000 words. By industrial union standards, it is a short (many of them run to several hundred pages) and simple (one plant of a multiplant employer) agreement. Nevertheless, it will be obvious from the discussion that follows that this agreement is much more formal and complete than the typical craft union agreement.

Union Security and Management Rights. The industrial union agreement uses most of the terminology in Figure 7–1 in the form presented there.

Bargaining Unit. Article I—Recognition states that "The Company recognizes the Union as the exclusive bargaining agent with respect to wages, hours of employment or other conditions of employment for all production, maintenance and other factory employees, excepting office employees, office building janitors, time keepers, plant police, administrative employees, foremen, and clerks."

Form of Recognition. The form of recognition granted in this agreement is the agency shop, because the plant is located in a "right-to-work" state. The last paragraph of Article II provides that if the state right-to-work law is repealed the union shop clause will be reinstated in the agreement.

Article III of the agreement provides a voluntary and revocable checkoff of union dues by the employer.

Duration and Renewal. The provisions for duration and renewal are routine.

Management Rights. Article IV of the agreement is entitled "Management of the Plant." Paragraph 4.0 reads as follows:

The management of the plant and the direction of the working force, including the right to hire; discharge for just cause, suspend, discipline, promote, transfer; to decide the machine and tool equipment, the products, methods, schedules of production, processes of manufacturing and assembling together with all designs and engineering, and the control of raw materials, semi-manufactured and finished parts which may be incorporated into the product, shall be vested exclusively in the Company.

Paragraph 4.1 provides that the rights of the company to discharge for just cause, suspend, discipline, to promote and transfer to jobs within the bargaining unit are subject to the provisions of the agreement and the grievance procedure.

The Wage and Effort Bargain.   The wage and effort bargain provisions of this agreement cover approximately fifteen of its 40 pages.

Pay for Time Worked.   Appendix "A" lists the rates of pay for 124 different job descriptions falling into 13 labor grades. The lowest rate of pay is $2.43 per hour and the top rate is $3.22 per hour. New employees start at ten cents per hour below regular rate and receive a five-cent raise after 30 days on the job and another five-cent raise after 90 days on the job.

The Effort Bargain.   The agreement being analyzed here makes no reference to production standards as such, but its grievance procedure is sufficiently broad in coverage to make production standards subject to arbitration.

Premium Pay.   Time and one half is provided for work in excess of eight hours in a day, or forty in a week, or for work on Saturdays. Double-time pay is provided for all work on Sundays and holidays. Fifteen cents per hour of premium pay is provided for workers of the second and third shifts. Four hours of call-in pay are provided.

Pay for Time Not Worked.   Holiday pay is provided for eight holidays. Vacation pay of from one to three weeks is provided for workers having more than one year's seniority. A 10-minute clean-up period is provided for painters before the end of their work shift.

Contingent Benefits.   The company provides Blue Cross and Blue Shield insurance coverage for all members of the bargaining unit. A separate pension agreement provides for company contributions to a pension fund which will permit the payment of a schedule of benefits for workers when they reach the normal retirement age of 65. The pension fund covers only the employees of the company at this one plant.

Individual Security.   Article VIII—Seniority describes the workers' relative claim to available work. The eight pages of Article VIII define the seniority unit, the applications of seniority, superseniority for stewards, and reasons for the revocation of seniority.

The workers' absolute claim to fair treatment is described in Article VIII—Discipline and Discharge. This article provides that all discipline shall be for "just cause." Article XIV provides that violation of company rules will provide a just cause for discipline. Appendix "B" lists 22 "Shop Rules and Regulations" and 10 "Safety Rules." Other provisions of the agreement outline the grievance handling procedure which terminates in arbitration.

Administration. Article V provides for on-the-job representation by stewards to be elected by whatever method the union deems appropriate so long as stewards have at least one year's seniority with the company and the number of stewards is agreed to by the company and union. Stewards are paid by the company when engaged in handling grievances but they must be excused from work by their foremen and the company reserves the right to limit the discussion of a grievance to 15 minutes.

The powers of the arbitrator are very broad under this agreement because he is authorized to "rule on all disputes pertaining to the interpretation or application of this Agreement, provided, however, that he shall have no power to add to, nor subtract from, nor modify any terms of this Agreement." The arbitrator is to be selected by the parties from lists provided by the American Arbitration Association.

SUMMARY

Every employment relationship focuses on a wage and effort bargain. When the employment relationship becomes formalized through collective bargaining, the agreement expands to cover four basic functions: (1) Union Security and Management Rights, (2) The Wage and Effort Bargain, (3) Individual Security, and (4) Administration. These four functions are present in every collective bargaining agreement: sometimes the written agreement is quite explicit in defining these functions and sometimes it is necessary to look carefully at the practice of the parties to identify the functions.

This text has emphasized the diversity of the practice between industrial and craft unions. This diversity remains in the contents of their agreements, but the very diversity in these agreements is proof of the unifying significance of the four basic functions of every collective bargaining agreement.

QUESTIONS FOR DISCUSSION

1. Compare and contrast the union agreement with the "employment relation" entered into between a physician and his patient or a lawyer and his client. Compare both of these relationships with the employment relation in a nonunion enterprise.

2. Would the "functions" discussed in this chapter be helpful in preparing for negotiations? Outline the desirable steps in detail.

Chapter 8 | AGREEMENT ADMINISTRATION

The collective bargaining agreement states the rights and duties of the parties. It is more than a contract; it is a generalized code to govern a myriad of cases which the draftsmen cannot wholly anticipate. . . . It calls into being a new common law—the common law of a particular industry or a particular plant.

The grievance procedure is . . . a part of the continuous collective bargaining process. It, rather than a strike, is the terminal point of a disagreement.

. . . The labor arbitrator is usually chosen because of the parties' confidence in his knowledge of the common law of the shop and their trust in his personal judgment to bring to bear considerations which are not expressed in the contract as criteria for judgment. The parties expect that his judgment of a particular grievance will reflect not only what the contract says but, insofar as the collective bargaining agreement permits, such factors as the effect upon productivity of a particular result, its consequence to the morale of the shop, his judgment whether tensions will be heightened or diminished. For the parties' objective in using the arbitration process is primarily to further their common goal of uninterrupted production under the agreement to make the agreement serve their specialized needs.

—Mr. Justice Douglas
United Steelworkers of America v. *Warrior and Gulf Navigation Company*
June 20, 1960

The above quotation from the majority opinion in the trilogy of arbitration cases decided by the Supreme Court in 1960 is an appropriate introduction to a chapter on agreement administration. Abstracts of the majority and dissenting opinions in these Supreme Court cases are presented in Case No. 2 of this text.

Most collective bargaining agreements have built-in problems. These problems aren't created by the agreement, but no agreement can prevent them from arising. Nor could either of the parties afford to freeze the *status quo* for one year, let alone the longer periods for which agreements are now frequently negotiated. Business enterprise must be dynamic to survive. As a result, in any year, new problems such as the wage rate for new jobs, questions over the interpretation of rules, and changes in products, methods, and personnel are almost certain to arise.

216

Before any grievance can be handled, the management and union must agree to a procedure for processing grievances. As was shown in Chapter 3, grievance procedures take different forms in handicraft and mass-production industry. Regardless of differences in the procedures for handling grievances, the methods of investigating grievances and the methods of settlement available to the parties are the same in handicraft and mass-production industry. In this chapter, we will be discussing general methods of grievance settlement. Our hypothetical grievance is drawn from mass-production industry and is handled through a factory grievance procedure. We shall return to some of the differences in procedural arrangements in Chapter 12, Case No. 39 and Case No. 43.

Given the presence of legitimate and unforseeable problems, what avenues for settlement are available to unions and management during the life of the contract? The possible methods of settlement here are just the same as the possible methods for settlement in negotiating a new contract. The critical difference between day-to-day problem settlement and contract renegotiation settlement is the different emphasis which the parties place on the alternative methods under the two sets of circumstances. Either type of dispute can be settled by: (1) arbitration—submitting the issues to an outside party who has been given authority to issue a binding decision, (2) mediation—asking a "friend of the family" to cool tempers and suggest methods of settlement which the parties may accept or reject, or (3) a strike, a lockout, or other resort to force.[1] Of course, none of these possibilities should be considered before both parties have done their best to settle their disagreement within the privacy of their own home.

It is very important to note that all three of these possibilities may be envisaged in the wording of a collective bargaining agreement. Something in the vicinity of 90 per cent of all collective bargaining agreements provide for arbitration as a final method of settling *some* disputes over the interpretation of their terms. At the same time, some of these *same* contracts clearly provide that certain disputes will *not* be settled by arbitration. For the items *not* subject to arbitration and *not* finally settled by the terms of the contract, the employer reserves the right to institute changes not agreeable to the union and the union reserves the power to veto his changes by the strike. Even in the case of disputes not subject to arbitration because of *planned* loopholes in the arbitration section of the agreement, strikes are infrequent for several reasons. The infrequency of these strikes, the reasons for which will be discussed below, has caused some students to incorrectly assume that *any* strike during the life of an

[1] The use of arbitration as a means of settling contract negotiation disputes is so exceptional that it must be noted lest it be overlooked. Strikes and mediation, instead of arbitration, are so infrequently used in agreement interpretation disputes that they must be noted lest they be overlooked as possibilities.

agreement is an unlawful strike or a strike in breach of the agreement. Many strikes during the life of an agreement are breaches of that agreement, but many are *not* breaches of the agreement because the agreement itself is an agreement to *strike* as the final method of settlement of a very few, but extremely important, kinds of disputes.

DISPUTE SETTLEMENT BETWEEN THE PARTIES BY THE PARTIES THEMSELVES

A grievance is almost always an individual or group human problem. The agreement may define grievances in abstract terms as far as arbitrability goes, but in the day-to-day process of living together the grievances is a human problem. Union stewards' manuals on grievance processing usually contain statements such as the following:

You can usually decide whether a complaint is a genuine grievance by asking yourself two questions:
1. Did the Company violate the contract?
   If the answer is "yes," you've got a grievance for sure.
2. Has the worker been treated unfairly by the Company?
   If the answer is "yes" to this question, you've probably got a grievance even though you're not sure that the contract has been violated. Sometimes this kind of grievance is hard to win, though, because of a loophole in the contract. When this happens, make a note that this clause in the contract should be improved at the next contract negotiations.[2]

The human aspect of grievances is further borne out by company foremen's manuals. The variety of statements is too wide to present a representative quotation, but almost every manual emphasizes the foreman's job of resolving grievances at early stages and *preventing* situations from arising which cause grievances. The company's preventive program is closely akin to the union's fairness program.

A worker *feels* the company has violated the contract or treated him unfairly. This is the beginning of a grievance. Maybe the company hasn't violated the contract or treated the worker unfairly; if he *feels* he has been treated unfairly we have an embryo grievance which can be run through the dispute-settlement process. Sometimes a union representative will "cook up" grievances for the purpose of embarrassing the company. Sometimes a company will work at creating unfair situations in the hope of provoking the union into a strike that the union can ill afford. But wherever the grievance really came from, its first obvious appearance is usually in a worker protest against some actual or alleged management action or inaction.

Assume, for simplicity of discussion, that a worker feels that his foreman is violating the contract when he instructs him to stack his fin-

[2] Department of Education and Research, CIO. *The Shop Steward: Key to a Strong Union* (Washington D.C.: CIO Publication No. 271, 1955), p. 21.

ished pieces in a new and time-consuming way on the cart used to take the pieces to the packing department. The worker claims that this is work "outside of my classification" and is a management speed-up. Since this is a grievance against the individual foreman, the worker will probably take it to his union steward as the first step. The worker tells his story to the steward.

The grievance is now in the lap of the steward. What does he do with it? The first thing the steward should do is get all the facts. Pertinent facts in this case would include such questions as:

1. When did the foreman first give you orders to stack the pieces in a certain way?
2. Did he give similar *new* orders to the other workers in your department?
3. How long has it been your practice to pile the pieces on the cart without stacking them in a certain way? Has the foreman ever told you to stack them this new way before? When? Do the other men stack them this new way?
4. What did you do in the past when you ran off more pieces than you had cart space for? Who picked up and piled this surplus on the next cart that came along?
5. What does the job description for this job say about preparing finished work for transfer? How do other departments with similar jobs handle the stacking problem?
6. Does the production standard or incentive wage rate for this job provide time allowances or money allowances for stacking?
7. What does the contract say about job re-evaluations and changes in production standards?
8. *By actual observation*, what additional fatigue or effort does this new order impose on the worker?
9. What effect would the processing of this grievance have on the overall position of workers in the company? If the grievance were aired and we "lost" would the result be a general speed-up throughout the plant?

In processing the grievance, the steward may consider one other important fact: his own political position within the department and the union. If he is up for re-election, he may show little restraint in processing questionable grievances from his potential political supporters. In a plant without a union-shop agreement, he may show a natural reluctance to energetically process grievances originating with "free riders." When the union is trying to soften up management for impending negotiations, he may even manufacture grievances. Most stewards seldom refuse to process grievances because the individual worker has the right to process his own grievance through exclusively management channels. The steward can ill afford to refuse to process a grievance and have management later grant the individual worker's request for an adjustment. Having noted these possibilities, let us assume that our steward had no political problems and judges this grievance to be fully justified by the facts and the collective bargaining agreement.

The steward's next move is the conference with the foreman. As a general rule, the grievance is not reduced to writing before this conference is held. A steward in preparing for this conference might very well improve his discussion with the foreman by outlining the grievance as it may ultimately be reduced to writing. This process clarifies the grievance in the steward's mind and may suggest further fruitful avenues for discussion. However, both the foreman and the steward frequently prefer to talk it out before the formality of writing out the grievance. This talk before writing gives both sides flexibility in their thinking. If the grievance is clear and justified, both the union and the management profit from better feelings by settling it informally and with dispatch. In the conference with the foreman, the steward requests redress for the alleged injustice.

The foreman listens to the steward's request and asks whatever questions he deems necessary to fully understand the nature of the grievance. Both the foreman and the steward are well advised to control their tempers. The foreman usually postpones his answer to the steward until he has had time to review the agreement and gather his own facts about the situation. One of the critical facts which the foreman usually considers is the opinion of higher management or the personnel department on what disposition should be made of this grievance. It is very important that the foreman do this because any settlement he makes may be used later as a precedent in other departments.[3] After considering these facts, the foreman delivers a decision to the steward. We shall assume that for a good reason he believes this grievance to be invalid and denies the steward's request for an adjustment.

As discussed in Chapter 3, the grievance then moves up through higher echelons of the company and union organizations. We shall assume that our grievance goes through the top echelon of the company and union organizations without a mutually satisfactory adjustment. What happens next?

Although increased interest has recently been shown in grievance mediation, this method of agreement interpretation dispute settlement is still infrequently used. Grievance mediation is closely akin to agreement

[3] In the period 1935–45 many managements, confronted with unionism for the first time, centralized all authority for labor relations matters at a high level. This was a natural, and probably necessary, reaction to militant unionism. Dealing with unions was a radical new departure and a few "experts" monopolized this activity in the management hierarchy. The union itself was a new challenge to the foreman's authority and he was disillusioned when management met this outside challenge by stripping him of his authority in labor relations. Once collective bargaining was established and management became competent in its practice, many managements began training foremen in contract administration and restoring their authority in labor relations. At the present time, the main current of progressive management practice seems to be flowing in the direction of giving foremen increased discretion in labor relations matters. Nevertheless, it is quite likely that consultation with higher management on many grievance settlements will remain a necessity because of their potential precedent-making character.

negotiation mediation. It occurs when the disputants ask for the assistance of an impartial outsider in suggesting possible avenues for agreement. The mediator cools tempers, brings a fresh outlook to the dispute, and may propose perfectly acceptable means of agreement which the disputants overlooked. Grievance mediation seems to be uniquely appropriate when the same mediator has played an influential role in the negotiation of the agreement now in dispute. Although either or both of the disputants might for strategic or tactical reasons oppose resort to this method, when it is acceptable to the parties it is probably the *ideal* means of dispute settlement. In questions of agreement interpretation almost anything that the parties will agree to is preferable to a decision made by an outsider or resort to force. Failure in grievance mediation almost always results in a resort to arbitration or the use of force in achieving a settlement.

The final step, beyond company and union organizations, may be established by the terms of the collective bargaining agreement or improvised at the time of the deadlock. When face-to-face agreement proves impossible, what *others means* for grievance settlement are available to the parties?

GRIEVANCE SETTLEMENT BY MEANS OTHER THAN NEGOTIATION

Depending upon whether management or the union is the grievant, the nature of the grievance itself, and the provisions of the applicable collective bargaining agreement, the dispute may be settled by arbitration or the use of force. We shall discuss the use of force before the much more commonly used method of arbitration. It must be repeated for emphasis that the vast majority of agreement interpretation disputes are settled by resort to peaceful voluntary arbitration.

Use of Force in Agreement Interpretation Disputes

Both unions and managements occasionally use force as a means of settling their disputes over agreement interpretation or matters not specifically covered by the agreement. Sometimes, as in the case of strikes over nonarbitrable issues, they have agreed in advance to fight it out when disagreements arise. Other resorts to force, such as injunctions, law suits, and disciplinary actions against workers violating the terms of an agreement, result from inadequate advanced planning for handling certain particularly tough disagreements. It is an encouraging sign that resort to force seems to be a steadily declining practice because of increased responsibility in agreement observance by both unions and managements.

Five different forms of resort to force may be delineated: (1) strikes over nonarbitrable issues, (2) law suits by either managements, workers, or unions to recover damages suffered as a result of alleged agreement violations, (3) injunctions sought by either managements, workers, or unions to prevent an anticipated breach of the agreement, (4) voiding a contract which has been breached, and (5) disciplinary action against workers who have engaged in strikes, slowdowns, sabotage, or other violations of a collective bargaining agreement. These instruments of force vary in the frequency with which they are used and their utility to each of the disputants.

When an agreement reserves the right to strike for the union over certain nonarbitrable issues during the life of the agreement, management may institute or continue the practice, e.g., higher production standards or a low wage rate on a new job, which the union considers objectionable. The union either "agrees" with the practice by continuing to work under these objectionable conditions or it disagrees by calling a strike. Although the strike power in this situation is a powerful instrument of persuasion, the union is usually extremely reluctant to enforce its claim for "justice." Typically nonarbitrable issues involve only a few workers at a single time. The union leader is frequently confronted with the prospect that hundreds of workers just won't respond to a strike call aimed at obtaining concessions for only a handful of workers. The risks of striking frequently are too great when compared to the possible gains obtainable from winning a strike over contract interpretation.

When workers engage in contract violations such as slowdowns or strikes, management may seek redress through the lockout. Like the strike, this method is seldom used because of the dangers inherent in its use. Although many collective bargaining agreements provide for the right of management to process "grievances against the union," such grievances seldom arise except in the case of slowdowns or strikes in breach of the agreement. The infrequency of "grievances against the union" is due to the fact that management retains the power of initiative in most of the situations unforeseen or not agreed to at the time of negotiations.

Suits for damages and injunctions usually are considered to be the substitute of law for the exercise of force. We have classified them as resorts to force because the initiating party is seeking to enlist the coercive power of government to help it impose its will on the offending party. Enlisting the support of government is perfectly legitimate, but it tends to leave a scar on the collective bargaining relationship just like other resorts to force.

Both unions and managements have the legal right to sue the offending party for breach of contract. From the union viewpoint, there have been a few suits for damages in the case of "runaway" plants, violations of clauses limiting management's right to subcontract or "farm out" work normally performed within the bargaining unit, or for restitution in wage payment cases. From the company viewpoint, suits for damages are possible remedies for such things as boycotts, strikes in violation of the agreement, and slowdowns. Suits for damages are seldom used in present-day collective bargaining because both parties tend to view them as "divorce" actions.[4] Arbitration, strikes, or disciplinary actions against workers are often preferred over suits for damages and injunctions because they leave less severe long-term scars on the company-worker-union relationship.

Injunctions are available, under severely restricted conditions, to either unions or managements as a means of settling disputes over agreement interpretation. The injunction, which stops the threatened misapplication or breach of the agreement, is an *ideal* union remedy against runaway plants. From the management viewpoint, the injunction (if it is obeyed) is the *ideal* remedy for the wildcat strike in violation of a collective bargaining agreement.

When a union or a management misinterprets an agreement to the extent of violating its provisions, the offended party has the legal right to void the entire agreement. There are few recorded cases where this remedy has been used because its application usually results in an immediate strike, suit, or injunction. A hypothetical example may clarify the possible application of this remedy. Assume that a union engages in a strike in violation of the agreement. Management could then reduce wages, discontinue employee benefits, or deny union security on the basis that the whole agreement had been voided by the union's failure to abide by some of its terms.

In wildcat strikes, slowdowns, or sabotage in violation of a collective bargaining agreement, management may discharge or otherwise discipline the workers involved. The value of this remedy depends entirely upon the individual circumstances. When all the workers are on strike, management's *practical* power to discipline even the strike instigators is severely limited if it wants to resume production promptly. In such cases, the union frequently protects the strike leaders by refusing to return to work until an agreement is worked out on disciplinary action. If the strike has solid support and the management strongly wants to resume production, the disciplinary measures against strike leaders may be bargained down to nothing. Mass disciplinary action against very large numbers of strikers or slowdown participants frequently is a practical impossibility since such managerial action would cause even further interruptions to production.

Before leaving these seldom-used methods, it might be well to note again that all of them involve the infliction of injury on one party by the other, sometimes assisted by government. These methods tend, therefore, to leave more or less enduring scars on the collective bargaining relation-

---

[4] It might be noted that many managements insist that the International union be made a signatory party to the collective bargaining agreement. One advantage of this procedure is that the larger financial resources of the International would be available for the satisfaction of any court-awarded financial damages. It seems likely that International unions' urgings of wildcat strikers to return to work are sometimes motivated by a fear of this consequence.

ship. Arbitration is a process which settles the dispute without the unpleasantness of direct combat. Except where the issues are of vital importance to one or both of the parties, they usually prefer to settle their differences over contract interpretation without direct combat. This peaceful adjudication of disputes is our next topic.

Case No. 3 in Part V of this book deals with the remedies available to the parties in event of breach of the agreement.

Voluntary Arbitration: Peaceful Adjudication of Grievance Disputes

Our worker's grievance over stacking finished parts on the cart might very well be a strikeable issue under some collective bargaining agreements. However, we shall assume that like the vast majority of grievances it is not. Under the circumstances, the normal last step is voluntary arbitration. Usually the collective bargaining agreement itself establishes the broad outline of the procedure to be followed for arbitrating disputes over its interpretation.

In arbitration, the disputants ask an impartial person for a determination of the dispute on the basis of evidence and argument presented by them. The disputants agree in advance to accept the decision of the arbitrator as final and binding. Before discussing the preparation for, and conduct of, an arbitration hearing, we shall briefly note the procedural decisions which precede the hearing.

Procedural Arrangements for Arbitration.   The company and the union must create an arbitration tribunal and submit their dispute to that tribunal before the case can be heard and a decision rendered. In writing their collective bargaining agreement or later submitting their dispute to arbitration, they have several choices to make about procedural matters. There are several public and private organizations which will help them in handling these problems.

Creating an Arbitration Tribunal.   Should a different tribunal be established for each dispute (*ad hoc* arbitration) or should a single tribunal be established to decide all disputes between the parties (umpire or permanent chairman system)? *Ad hoc* arbitration is most commonly used in small companies because of the infrequency of arbitration hearings. It has the important advantage of low procedural costs. Even where companies have only a few arbitrations per year, occasionally they establish an umpire system to give continuity to arbitration procedures and decisions. An umpire, like an *ad hoc* arbitrator, serves only so long as he is acceptable to both parties. The powers of the *ad hoc* arbitrator or umpire are detailed and limited by the terms of the collective bargaining agreement or the submission agreement.

Should the arbitration tribunal consist of a single impartial member or should representatives of the disputants also be members of the tribunal? An impartial one-member tribunal offers the advantage of a unanimous decision without compromising the position of either of the disputants or the impartial member. The disputants sometimes favor a tripartite tribunal as an opportunity to educate the impartial member in the full complexities of the dispute and to be certain that he considers all relevant facts and arguments. It may give both disputants a fuller understanding of the award than exists under a one-member tribunal. The tripartite tribunal has the disadvantage of frequently handing down only "majority" decisions. Even here, the impartial member may have to compromise his judgment of the issue in dispute to get a decision from the deadlocked tribunal. A tripartite tribunal may tend to shade off from arbitration into the field of mediation.

How is an impartial person selected as sole arbitrator or as a member of a tripartite tribunal? The disputants are free to select any person as their arbitrator so long as they both agree to his selection. Because labor arbitration is a process requiring complete impartiality, high intelligence, and a knowledge of the issues, unions and managements frequently solicit the assistance of public or private organizations in arranging for an arbitrator's services. The American Arbitration Association, a private nonprofit organization, the Federal Mediation and Conciliation Service, and several state mediation boards maintain rosters of professional arbitrators for selection by the disputants. These organizations supply information about the arbitrator's qualifications to the parties seeking an arbitrator's services.

The collective bargaining agreement itself frequently details the procedures to be followed in selecting an arbitration tribunal. A commonly used method is the standard arbitration clause of the American Arbitration Association:

Any dispute, claim or grievance arising out of or relating to the interpretation or the application of this agreement shall be submitted to arbitration under the Voluntary Labor Arbitration Rules of the American Arbitration Association. The parties further agree to accept the arbitrator's award as final and binding upon them.

This clause is supplemented by a statement providing for an impartial or tripartite tribunal.

When the American Arbitration Association clause is included in an agreement, either party may initiate arbitration proceedings by filing a Demand for Arbitration with the regional AAA office.

When a dispute arises between parties who are not subject to an arbitration clause, they may bring the matter to arbitration by means of a jointly signed statement setting forth the nature of the dispute and affirming their willingness to abide by the arbitrator's award. This statement is called a submission agreement. Submission agreements may also be used when a collective bargaining agreement terminates and the company and the union are unable to agree to new terms.

Selecting an Arbitrator. Selecting an arbitrator is somewhat like selecting a physician. Just as an ill person needs a physician *now*, the parties with an unresolved grievance need an arbitrator *now*. The minimum qualifications of a physician are reasonably easy to establish, but the selection of the *most* able physician is a tough problem for a medical society let alone an ill person. In selecting an arbitrator, the parties may get some help from government and private agencies as well as their trusted neighbors in management or the labor movement.

The use of the procedures of the Federal Mediation and Conciliation Service, the American Arbitration Association, or a State Mediation Board in selecting an arbitrator assures a timely arbitration hearing. Under these procedures, the management and union usually select their own arbitrator from lists submitted by the agency. If none of the arbitrators listed (on a "panel") is acceptable to one of the parties, the agency may designate an arbitrator to hear the case. Although agency designation of arbitrators is unusual, there must be some final power to appoint an arbitrator in order that neither party may void their arbitration agreement by unreasonable delays.

An arbitrator acts in a quasi-judicial capacity. He should possess the judicial qualifications of fairness to both parties so that he may render a faithful, honest, and disinterested opinion. He must lay aside all bias and approach the case with a mind open to conviction and without regard to his previously formed opinions as to the merits of the parties or the case. His conduct must be free from even the inference that either party is the special recipient of his favor. An arbitrator is expected to disqualify himself from any arbitration if he has any financial or personal interest in the result of the arbitration.

Any arbitrator on the panels of the American Arbitration Association, Federal Mediation and Conciliation Service, or State Mediation Board meets certain minimum standards of impartiality, acceptability, and professional competence. These agencies review the arbitrator's education, experience, and general reputation with management and unions. These minimum standards cannot be stated with exact precision. Although most arbitrators possess either law or other postgraduate degrees, some prominent arbitrators did not graduate from college. Arbitration experience cannot be an absolute requirement for membership on an arbitration panel since most arbitrators get their *first* cases by selection from panels. Industrial relations experience as a member of management might make an arbitrator unacceptable to unions, just as industrial relations experience as a union representative might make an arbitrator unacceptable to management. A *perfect* neutral, for example, a college professor or lawyer with no business, union, or arbitration experience, would be of little value as an arbitrator because he would lack the vital knowledge of union-management practice.

Very frequently both the management and the union enter arbitration with the clearcut goal of *winning* the case. If you want to win fairly, you are much more interested in how a specific arbitrator is likely to view your case than you are interested in his general reputation for impartiality. This very natural desire to win results in sometimes extensive investigations of arbitrators' backgrounds and awards. Employers' associations and unions frequently keep extensive records of arbitrators' awards which may be used by members in selecting the arbitrators most likely to be *most* impartial (with a slight leaning to either the management or union side).

The records on arbitrators kept by employers' associations and unions have both desirable and undesirable effects on the arbitration process. It is obviously desirable that both parties have access to detailed information on the qualifications of any arbitrator they might select. The best way to evaluate an arbitrator is by a careful review of his awards. An undesirable effect of using records developed by either an employer's association or a union is that these records may be incomplete or inaccurate. Because not all arbitration awards are published, anyone building a record on an arbitrator is working with incomplete data. An obvious inaccuracy in interpretation would be a record based on a "box score": Arbitrator X is good (or bad) because out of 20 cases he decided 18 for management. Arbitrators can be judged fairly only on an evaluation of the full circumstances of each case.

It seems likely that the desire to *win* will remain as an important criterion for the selection of arbitrators in many collective bargaining relationships. Fortunately for the arbitration process, this attitude is not totally destructive because both parties must accept the arbitrator. Arbitrators who try to play a promanagement or a pro-union game find themselves out of the arbitration business.

Preparing a Case for Arbitration. The American Arbitration Association suggests that companies and unions follow 10 steps in preparing a case for arbitration. These steps are:

1. Study the original statement of the grievance and review its history through every step of the grievance machinery.
2. Examine carefully the initiating papers (Submission or Demand) to determine the authority of the arbitrator. It might be found, for instance, that while the original grievance contains many elements, the arbitrator, under the contract, is restricted to resolving only certain aspects.
3. Review the collective bargaining agreement from beginning to end. Often, clauses which at first glance seem to be unrelated to the grievance will be found to have some bearing on it.
4. Assemble all documents and papers you will need at the hearing. Where feasible, make photostatic copies for the arbitrator and the other party. If some of the documents you need are in the possession of the other party, ask that they be brought to the arbitration. Under some arbitration laws, the arbitrator has authority to subpoena documents and witnesses if they cannot be made available in any other way.

5. If you think it will be necessary for the arbitrator to visit the plant for on-the-spot investigation, make plans in advance. The arbitrator will have to be accompanied by representatives of both parties; it is also preferable that the Tribunal Clerk be present.
6. Interview all witnesses. Make certain they understand the whole case and particularly the importance of their own testimony within it.
7. Make a written summary of what each witness will prove. This will be useful as a checklist at the hearing, to make certain nothing is overlooked.
8. Study the case from the other side's point of view. Be prepared to answer the opposing evidence and arguments.
9. Discuss your outline of the case with others in your organization. A fresh viewpoint will often disclose weak spots or previously overlooked details.
10. Read as many articles and published awards as you can on the general subject matter in dispute. While awards by other arbitrators for other cases have no precedent value, they may help clarify the thinking of parties and arbitrators alike.[5]

If both parties have carefully followed these steps in preparing the case, the arbitration hearing is very likely to run smoothly and provide all the information the arbitrator needs to make a fair decision.

The Hearing. The arbitrator has substantial latitude in establishing the time, place, and conduct of the hearing. His job is to give both sides full opportunity to introduce relevant evidence and argument and to decide the case upon due consideration of that evidence and argument. He may ask whatever questions he deems necessary to the proper consideration of the dispute. All witnesses are subject to cross-examination. Both parties must try to convince the arbitrator of the justice of their positions.

The statements of the American Arbitration Association also provide adequate and concise guidance for the effective presentation of an arbitration case:

Every party approaching arbitration should be prepared with—
1. An opening statement which clearly but briefly describes the controversy and indicates what he will set out to prove. The opening statement lays the groundwork for witnesses and helps the arbitrator understand the relevance of testimony. For this reason it is frequently advisable that the opening statement be in writing, with a copy given to the arbitrator. This opening statement should also discuss the remedy sought.
2. Names of all witnesses in the order in which they will be called, together with a list of the points they are to cover. Questions should be brief and to the point, and witnesses should be instructed to direct their answers to the arbitrators.
3. A list of exhibits in the order in which they are to be introduced and a notation of what each is to establish. It speeds up proceedings considerably and never fails to make a good impression on the arbitrator when copies are available for distribution to all parties.

[5] American Arbitration Association, *Labor Arbitration: Procedures and Techniques* (New York: The Association, 1957), pp. 17–18.

4. A closing statement. This should be a summation of evidence and arguments, and a refutation of what the other side has brought out.

The American Arbitration Association also lists 10 common errors in presenting an arbitration case as follows:

1. Over-emphasis and exaggeration of the grievance.
2. Reliance on a minimum of facts and a maximum of arguments.
3. Using arguments where witnesses or exhibits would better establish the facts.
4. Concealing essential facts; distorting the truth.
5. Holding back books, records and other supporting documents.
6. Tying up proceedings with legal technicalities.
7. Introducing witnesses who have not been properly instructed on demeanor and on the place of their testimony in the entire case.
8. Withholding full cooperation from the arbitrator.
9. Disregarding the ordinary rules of courtesy and decorum.
10. Becoming involved in arguments with the other side. The time to try to convince the other party was before arbitration, during grievance processing. At the arbitration hearing, all efforts should be concentrated on convincing the arbitrator.[6]

Before closing the hearing, the arbitrator determines the wishes of the parties concerning posthearing briefs and arranges for their submission to him through a neutral party. The parties do not communicate directly with him except when both sides are present. The hearing is closed and the arbitrator considers the evidence and issues an award.

The Award. In the case of tripartite tribunals there may be some difficulty in preparing an award. If a deadlock seems likely, the union and management members of the Board of Arbitration may authorize the impartial member to write an award without their concurrence. Failing to achieve this sort of an arrangement, the impartial member may have to compromise his judgment of the dispute in order to achieve a majority opinion. We shall assume that our case is heard by a single impartial arbitrator, thereby avoiding this difficulty.

In writing his award, the arbitrator considers the content of the agreement, the practice of the parties, and the evidence and arguments presented at the hearing in exhibits and briefs. The arbitrator usually defers to the wishes of the parties in the form of the award. A simple statement of his findings and the action required by the decision is an adequate award. In our hypothetical case, an award might read: "Machine operators are required to stack finished work on carts for movement to the packing department in the way presently directed by supervision. The grievance claiming that such work is 'out of classification' is without merit and is denied." However, at the request of the parties, arbitrators usually will summarize the pertinent evidence and arguments, their findings, and the reasoning used to reach a decision. As a rule, the parties want the arbitrator to give them a reasonably detailed award. Such an award, often run-

[6] *Ibid.,* pp. 18–19.

ning to as many as 20 typewritten pages, may be more useful to the parties in their future relationships.

Once the award is delivered the matter is settled. It is no longer a bone of contention between the parties and they can get back to the business of living together. If the award is unsatisfactory, they usually can negotiate a more satisfactory arrangement in their next agreement. The arbitrator has enabled both sides to talk the matter out and he alone is responsible for the results of his award. Either the management or the union or both may be angry about the award, but they should not be angry with each other about it.

Voluntary arbitration deserves much more detailed discussion than it has been given here because it makes a major contribution to harmonious union-management relations.[7] In a few cases, unions and managements have been so satisfied with grievance arbitration that they have adopted voluntary arbitration as a means of settling disputes in contract negotiations. On the other hand, some unions and managements have used arbitration as a means of harassing each other. The act of arbitration may be evidence of good or bad faith. In general, experience with grievance arbitration is a most encouraging sign of increasing trust and mutual respect on the part of American unions and managements. To the authors of this book, an even more encouraging sign is the effort of both parties to avoid arbitration by working hard at settling their disagreements within the grievance procedure. Both of these trends are optimistic signs for the future of collective bargaining.

The Legal Environment of Arbitration.   Although labor arbitration is a quasi-judicial process, it is not governed by a comprehensive code of law. There is no United States Labor Arbitration Act, although such legislation has been advocated by the influential National Academy of Arbitrators. Several states have labor arbitration statutes, but these laws provide only minimal guidance to the conduct of arbitration. In decisions in 1957 and 1960, the U.S. Supreme Court has taken the first steps in fashioning a federal law of labor arbitration from the public policy statements contained in the Labor-Management Relations Act of 1947.

The arbitrator derives his power from the agreement of the parties to submit a dispute (or disputes generally) to him for decision. He operates within the specific or general rules established by the parties in their agreement to utilize his services. In several states, he is given the added legal authority to subpoena witnesses if needed to decide the issues before him. In all cases, the courts will set aside his award if there is evidence

---

[7] Students are urged to read from the bibliography at the end of this chapter. Three books, Copelof's *Management-Union Arbitration*, Elkouri's *How Arbitration Works*, and Stone's *Labor-Management Contracts at Work*, are especially recommended. Frequent references to the proceedings of the annual meetings of the National Academy of Arbitrators are made throughout this book. These proceedings offer an insight on current issues in labor arbitration and recent research findings.

that it was influenced by corruption, fraud, or other undue means. In some cases, the courts will set aside his award if it is clear that it exceeds the authority vested in him by the parties.

The law of arbitration becomes a vital issue when one of the parties refuses to submit an issue to arbitration on the grounds that the issue is not arbitrable under the terms of the agreement to arbitrate. Although such refusals to arbitrate are indeed rare, either party could emasculate an arbitration agreement if it were allowed to be the sole judge of the meaning of the agreement.

The federal law of arbitration which the Supreme Court is fashioning from the public policy statements of the Labor-Management Relations Act deals with the question of arbitrability. Four Supreme Court decisions must be mentioned in a discussion of labor arbitration. In 1957 in the case of *Textile Workers Union of America* v. *Lincoln Mills*, the Supreme Court ruled that federal courts were empowered by Section 301(a) of the Labor-Management Relations Act of 1947 to order specific performance of an agreement to arbitrate grievance disputes. In the cases of *United Steelworkers of America* v. *American Manufacturing Company*, *United Steelworkers of America* v. *Warrior and Gulf Navigation Company*, and *United Steelworkers of America* v. *Enterprise Wheel and Car Corporation*,[8] decided in 1960, the Supreme Court dealt in some detail with questions of arbitrability of grievances in different situations.

In the *Lincoln Mills*[9] case, the employer refused to submit to arbitration grievances involving work assignments and work loads under a collective bargaining agreement which provided for arbitration as the terminal step in the grievance procedure. The Supreme Court ruled that the Norris–La Guardia Act does not withdraw the jurisdiction of federal courts to require specific performance of an agreement to arbitrate grievance disputes. The Court said that the substantive law to be applied suits under Section 301(a) of the Labor-Management Relations Act of 1947 is federal law which the courts must fashion from the policy of national labor laws. Since several sections of the Labor-Management Relations Act of 1947 spoke favorably of labor arbitration as a means of achieving national objectives, the Court reasoned that Section 301(a) authorized federal courts to require specific performance of an agreement to arbitrate. Before the Court ruled in this case, the employer had ceased to do business so the questions of job assignments and work loads were held to be moot. However, the Court ruled that monetary damages to the employees who grieved were not moot.

In *American Manufacturing*, the union sought to force the arbitration of the claim of one Sparks that he was eligible for recall to his job after an absence due to a work injury. Sparks had accepted a settlement

---

[8] Abstracts of the majority and dissenting opinions in these cases are used as cases in Part V of this book (see pp. 526–42).

[9] 353 U.S. 448.

for the work injury based on a permanent partial disability. The District Court held that Sparks, having accepted this settlement on the basis of a disability, was estopped to claim any seniority or employment rights. The Circuit Court of Appeals upheld the District Court on the grounds that Sparks' grievance was "a frivolous, patently baseless one, not subject to arbitration under the collective bargaining agreement." The pertinent provisions of the agreement were: (1) provision for arbitration of all disputes between the parties "as to the meaning, interpretation and application of the provisions of this agreement," (2) managerial authority to suspend or discharge "for cause," and (3) the requirement that the employer employ and promote employees on the principle of seniority "where ability and efficiency are equal." The Supreme Court reversed the lower courts and ordered arbitration of Sparks' grievance. The Supreme Court commented that, "when the judiciary undertakes to determine the merits of a grievance under the guise of interpreting the grievance procedure of collective bargaining agreements, it usurps a function which . . . is entrusted to the arbitration tribunal."

In *Warrior and Gulf Navigation*, the union sought to force the arbitration of a grievance arising from the subcontracting of work. The agreement contained a general arbitration clause and a provision that "matters which are strictly a function of management shall not be subject to arbitration." The employer refused arbitration of the grievance, and the union sued in District Court to require arbitration. The District Court dismissed the union's complaint after hearing evidence that the agreement did not "confide in an arbitrator the right to review the defendant's business judgment in contracting out work." The Circuit Court affirmed, finding that contracting out fell within the exception of "matters which are strictly a function of management." The Supreme Court reversed the lower courts and ordered that the dispute be submitted to arbitration. The Supreme Court found: "whether contracting out in the present case violated the agreement is the question. It is a question for the arbitrator, not for the courts."

In *Enterprise Wheel and Car Corporation*, the union sought judicial enforcement of an arbitrator's award of reinstatement and back pay to employees who had engaged in a wildcat strike. The District Court ordered the employer to comply with the arbitrator's award. On appeal, the Court of Appeals held that the award was unenforceable because it included back pay subsequent to the termination of the agreement and that the expiration of the agreement made the order of reinstatement unenforceable. The Supreme Court agreed with the Court of Appeals that the arbitrator's award of back pay was ambiguous. However, the Supreme Court ruled that an ambiguity in the award did not render the award unenforceable. The Supreme Court remanded the case to the District Court for proceedings "so that the amount due to employees may be definitely determined by arbitration."

The brevity of the foregoing summaries of leading Supreme Court decisions is intentional. The meaning of these cases will be argued in law journals and court proceedings for several years to come. Our single conclusion from these cases is that the Supreme Court has given arbitrators very substantial discretion in deciding the question of arbitrability *within the provisions of the agreement to arbitrate.* If the parties wish to reduce this discretion, it is within their power to agree to arbitration procedures which accomplish their mutual objective.

SUMMARY

In this chapter we have discussed the problems of administering the collective bargaining agreement. Agreement administration is of vital importance to the parties because actions speak louder than words and the word of the agreement frequently must be somewhat imprecise.

The key roles in agreement administration are played by foremen and stewards in their day-to-day activities. When the parties are unable to agree as to the meaning of their agreement or the proper application of their agreement to a particular set of facts and circumstances, they may use either force or voluntary arbitration to resolve their differences. In some disputes, the parties specifically reserve to themselves the right to resort to economic force. Much more commonly today the parties are placing greater reliance on voluntary arbitration to settle agreement interpretation disputes. Recent court decisions have the effect of encouraging the parties to make use of arbitration.

QUESTIONS FOR DISCUSSION

1. What are the functions of an arbitrator?
2. How can the parties to collective bargaining minimize the use of arbitration?
3. What is the legal status of an arbitrator's award?
4. How would you go about selecting an arbitrator from a panel of five provided by the American Arbitration Association?
5. Discuss the importance of preparation for arbitration on the part of both unions and management.

CASES: 39, 40, 41, 42, 43.

SELECTED ANNOTATED BIBLIOGRAPHY

Aaron, Benjamin. "The Uses of the Past in Arbitration," chap. 1, *Arbitration Today,* Jean T. McKelvey (ed.). Proceedings of the Eighth Annual Meeting of the National Academy of Arbitrators. Washington D.C.: Bureau of National Affairs, 1955, pp. 1–12. Discussion by Peerce Davis and Lloyd H. Bailor, pp. 12–23.

Discusses the weight that should be given to an employer's past practice in establishing an arbitration award. AHNER, C. W. "Arbitration: A Management Viewpoint," chap. 2, *The Arbitrator and the Parties*, JEAN T. McKELVEY (ed.). Proceedings of the Eleventh Annual Meeting of the National Academy of Arbitrators. Washington, D.C.: The Bureau of National Affairs, 1958, pp. 76–87. Discussion by Maurice S. Trotta, pp. 87–92.

Ahner urges the more widespread use of tripartite mediation as a substitute for arbitration, the simplification of awards, and arbitrators making themselves available to the parties to explain their awards and to educate foremen and stewards on the agreement and its operation. Trotta disagrees with the proposition that arbitrators should shift from arbitration to mediation as the situation dictates and that "education" on lost awards is almost hopeless.

ALEXANDER, GABRIEL N. "Impartial Umpireships: The General Motors-UAW Experience," chap. 6, *Arbitration and the Law*, JEAN T. McKELVEY (ed.). Proceedings of the Twelfth Annual Meeting of the National Academy of Arbitrators. Washington, D.C.: The Bureau of National Affairs, 1959, pp. 108–51. Discussion by Joseph E. Shister and Sylvester Garrett, pp. 151–60.

Alexander, who served as GM-UAW Umpire from 1948 to 1954, discusses the history of the umpireship, the operation of the system, and appraises its successes and failures. Based on personal experience, previously unavailable information supplied by the parties, and extensive interviews with the umpires, this paper is the first of a series of monographs on umpire systems prepared for the National Academy of Arbitrators. Shister emphasizes the uniqueness of the GM-UAW experience as contrasted with *ad hoc* arrangements. Garrett emphasizes the importance of ideas and personalities in developing a constructive system of arbitration.

————. "Evaluation of Arbitrators: An Arbitrator's Point of View," chap. 4, *The Arbitrator and the Parties*, JEAN T. McKELVEY (ed.). Proceedings of the Eleventh Annual Meeting of the National Academy of Arbitrators. Washington, D.C.: The Bureau of National Affairs, 1958, pp. 93–100. Discussion by James C. Hill, pp. 100–110.

Alexander comments on the failure of labor and management to formulate objective and realistic criteria for the evaluation of arbitrators. Hill discusses the pros and cons of publishing arbitration awards.

BAMBRICK, JAMES J., JR., and SPEED, JOHN J. *Grievance Procedures in Non-unionized Companies.* New York: National Industrial Conference Board Studies in Personnel Policy No. 109, 1950.

Discusses the problem of grievance handling in nonunion companies.

BEAL, EDWIN F. "Origins of Codetermination," *Industrial and Labor Relations Review*, Vol. VIII (July, 1955), pp. 483–98.

Based on several years' field study in Germany, this article traces the relationship between German unions and worker representation in the shop from 1918–55.

BERGER, HARRIET F. "The Grievance Process in the Philadelphia Public Service," *Industrial and Labor Relations Review*, Vol. XIII (July, 1960), pp. 568–80.

A description of the collective bargaining relationship and agreement between the City of Philadelphia and its civil service employees, who are represented by District Council No. 33, AFSCME, AFL-CIO. Principal focus is upon the grievance process within the operation of the collective agreement.

BROOKS, GEORGE W., and GAMM, SARA. "A Union Steward-Training Program," *Industrial and Labor Relations Review,* Vol. IV (January, 1951), pp. 249–56.

A discussion of the subject matter and methods of instruction used in steward training by the International Brotherhood of Pulp, Sulphite, and Paper Mill Workers.

COPELOF, MAXWELL. *Management-Union Arbitration.* New York: Harper & Bros., 1948.

Discusses appropriate questions for arbitration, the selection of an arbitrator, and a wide variety of arbitration cases.

COX, ARCHIBALD. "Rights Under a Labor Agreement," *Harvard Law Review,* Vol. LXIX (February, 1956), pp. 601–57.

Suggests that union and employer should be permitted to specify in their agreement whether the union or individual employees should have the authority to settle claims or sue the employer. When no specific intent is specified in the agreement, Professor Cox would have the courts apply presumptions, based on the nature of the agreement, as to whether the union or individuals have the right to sue.

DAUGHERTY, CARROLL R. "Arbitration by the National Railroad Adjustment Board," chap. 5, *Arbitration Today,* JEAN T. McKELVEY (ed.). Proceedings of the Eighth Annual Meeting of the National Academy of Arbitrators. Washington, D.C.: The Bureau of National Affairs, 1955, pp. 93–120. Discussion by Dudley E. Whiting and Paul N. Guthrie, pp. 120–26.

Discusses the statutory basis for grievance arbitration in the railroad industry, procedures for railroad grievance arbitration, and the nature of a national industry-wide arbitration system. Suggests methods of improving the statutory basis for grievance settlement and reducing the heavy backlog of unarbitrated cases.

DE VYVER, FRANK T. "Labor Arbitration After Twenty-Five Years," *Southern Economic Journal,* Vol. XXVIII (January, 1962), pp. 235–45.

The author's presidential address to the 1961 conference of the Southern Economic Association considers the position of management under the present system of grievance arbitration; how management decision making is affected by arbitration; and suggests alternatives to arbitration.

ELKOURI, FRANK. *How Arbitration Works.* Washington, D.C.: Bureau of National Affairs, 1952.

Discusses scope of labor arbitration, the arbitration tribunal, grievances, standards for determination of contract interpretation and negotiation disputes, evidence and burden of proof, the precedent value of awards, and arbitration and management's rights.

FEINSINGER, NATHAN P., Ross, ARTHUR M., SIMKIN, WILLIAM E., and SMITH, RUSSELL A. "The Role of the Law in Arbitration: A Panel Discussion," chap. 3, *Arbitration and the Law,* JEAN T. McKELVEY (ed.). Proceedings of the Twelfth Annual Meeting of the National Academy of Arbitrators. Washington, D.C.: The Bureau of National Affairs, 1959, pp. 68–89.

Ross views arbitration as a potentially creative instrument in the development of better industrial relations under a system of economic freedom. He proposes steps that the parties and the arbitrators should take to revitalize the process. Simkin outlines 14 points which form an outline for a "Practical Philosophy of Arbitration." Smith discusses the advisability of formulating a "model" arbitration statute and the problems inherent in its formulation.

FLEMING, R. W. "Some Problems of Evidence Before the Labor Arbitrator," *Michigan Law Review,* Vol. LX (December, 1961), pp. 133–68.

Considers the procedures and processes that have evolved for the protection of the parties in arbitration. Based on arbitrators' replies to hypothetical case situations.

FLEMING, ROBBEN W. *Labor Arbitration Process.* Urbana: University of Illinois Press, 1965.
Reviews the growth and development of grievance arbitration and makes recommendations for some of its current problems: costs, time lag, and formality; predictability; individual rights; and problems of evidence and procedural regularity.

GIVENS, RICHARD A. "Responsibility of Individual Employees for Breaches of No-Strike Clauses," *Industrial and Labor Relations Review,* Vol. XIV (July, 1961), pp. 595–600.
Considers the following questions: Is it wise for employers to bring damage actions against individual employee conduct in a wildcat strike? Do such suits for damages conflict with national labor policies? And is legislation to bar individual damage suits desirable when employees peacefully participate in a strike?

JENSEN, VERNON H. "Dispute Settlement in the New York Longshore Industry," *Industrial and Labor Relations Review,* Vol. X (July, 1957), pp. 588–608.
Discusses reasons for recent reduction in wildcat strikes on the New York waterfront and the emerging system for grievance settlement.

KILLINGSWORTH, CHARLES C. "Grievance Adjudication in Public Employment," chap. 6, *The Arbitrator and the Parties,* JEAN T. MCKELVEY (ed.). Proceedings of the Eleventh Annual Meeting of the National Academy of Arbitrators. Washington, D.C.: The Bureau of National Affairs, 1958, pp. 149–63. Discussion by Eli Rock, pp. 163–71.
Distinguishes between the employment relation in government and private business and discusses the methods for adjudication of grievances that have developed in public employment. Argues that a major failing of many governmental grievance procedures is the absence of neutral participation in the final stage of the grievance procedure. Rock argues that employment relations practices in government are in need not only of an adequate grievance system but more sweeping reform.

KUHN, JAMES W. *Bargaining in Grievance Settlement.* New York: Columbia University Press, 1961.
Explores the power relationships inherent in grievance bargaining.

MCPHERSON, WILLIAM H. "Grievance Mediation Under Collective Bargaining," *Industrial and Labor Relations Review,* Vol. IX (January, 1956), pp. 200–212.
Discusses increasing use of grievance mediation in U.S.

MITTENTHAL, RICHARD. "Past Practice and the Administration of Collective Bargaining Agreements," chap. 2, *Arbitration and Public Policy,* SPENCER D. POLLARD (ed.). Proceedings of the Fourteenth Annual Meeting of the National Academy of Arbitrators. Washington, D.C.: The Bureau of National Affairs, 1961, pp. 30–58. Discussion by Alex Elson and John A. Hogan, pp. 58–68.
Discusses characteristics which typify most practices, i.e., clarity and consistency, longevity and repetition, acceptability, and the underlying circumstances. Functions of past practice in clarifying ambiguous language, implementing general contract language, modifying or amending apparently unambiguous language, and as a separate, enforceable condition of employ-

ment are discussed. Mittenthal concludes that in the problem areas of past practice there are so many fine distinctions that the final decision in a case will rest not on any abstract theorizing but rather on the arbitrator's view of the peculiar circumstances of that case. Elson cites examples where past practice may deprive employees of due process. Hogan emphasizes the importance for the parties to try to eliminate inconsistencies between the contract and past practice.

NORTHRUP, HERBERT R., and KAHN, MARK L. "Railroad Grievance Machinery: A Critical Analysis, I and II," *Industrial and Labor Relations Review*, Vol. V (April, July, 1955), pp. 365–82; pp. 540–49.

Discusses and evaluates the unique system of grievance adjustment on U.S. railroads.

SEGAL, ROBERT M. "Arbitration: A Union Viewpoint," chap. 2, *The Arbitrator and the Parties*, JEAN T. MCKELVEY (ed.). Proceedings of the Eleventh Annual Meeting of the National Academy of Arbitrators. Washington, D.C.: The Bureau of National Affairs, 1958, pp. 47–70. Discussion by Lewis M. Gill, pp. 70–75.

Segal discusses a number of criteria used by unions in evaluating arbitrations and the relationship of arbitration of the courts. Gill comments on Segal's list of reasons for "blacklisting" of arbitrators by unions, i.e., mediating when the parties don't want mediation, excessively long and involved opinions, excessive citation of outside decisions, and slowness in the issuance of decisions.

SLICHTER, SUMNER H., HEALY, JAMES J., and LIVERNASH, E. ROBERT. The *Impact of Collective Bargaining on Management*. Washington, D.C.: Brookings Institution, 1960.

Special attention is invited to the following chapters: 23, "The Problem of Grievances"; 24, "Adjustment of Grievance"; 25, "The Grievance Arbitration Process"; and 26, "Arbitration and the Bargaining Relationship."

SMITH, RUSSELL A. "The Question of 'Arbitrability'—The Roles of the Arbitrator, the Court, and the Parties," *Southwestern Law Journal*, Vol. XVI (April, 1962), pp. 1–42.

A penetrating analysis of the 1960 Supreme Court decisions and their impact on the courts, arbitrators, and the parties to arbitration.

SOMERS, GERALD G. *Grievance Settlement in Coal Mining*. Morgantown, W. Va.: West Virginia University, Business and Economic Studies, Vol. IV, No. 4, 1956.

A statistical review of the procedures, subject matter, level of settlement, and disposition of 970 grievance cases heard between 1933 and 1954 in bituminous coal mining.

STONE, MORRIS. *Labor-Management Contracts at Work*. New York: Harper & Bros., 1961.

An analysis of American Arbitration Association awards on reduction in force, seniority and ability, stewards, foremen, call-in pay, holidays, vacations, overtime, and discipline.

U.S. CHAMBER OF COMMERCE. *Model Arbitration Clauses to Protect Management Rights*. Washington, D.C.: The Chamber, 1961.

As a response to Supreme Court decisions on arbitrability, this monograph contains sample clauses on management rights, arbitrator jurisdiction, and no-strike and lockout.

WOLFF, DAVID A., CRANE, LOUIS A., and COLE, HOWARD A. "The Chrysler-UAW Umpire System," chap. 5, *The Arbitrator and the Parties*.

JEAN T. McKELVEY (ed.). Proceedings of the Eleventh Annual Meeting of the National Academy of Arbitrators. Washington, D.C.: Bureau of National Affairs, 1958, pp. 111–41. Discussion by Harry H. Platt and Nathan P. Feinsinger, pp. 141–48.

Wolff has served as the Chrysler-UAW Umpire from the inception of the system in 1943. The UAW-Chrysler system is notable in the few cases that reach the arbitration stage and the formality of Appeal Board Hearings. Platt, Ford-UAW Umpire, contrasts the Chrysler-UAW system with the Ford-UAW system. Feinsinger, GM-UAW Umpire, comments primarily on the exclusion of grievants from Chrysler arbitration hearings. This paper is one of a series on umpire systems prepared for the National Academy of Arbitrators.

WOODCOCK, LEONARD. "Problem Areas in Arbitration," chap. 4, *Arbitration and the Law*. JEAN T. McKELVEY (ed.). Proceedings of the Twelfth Annual Meeting of the National Academy of Arbitrators. Washington, D.C.: Bureau of National Affairs, 1959, pp. 90–97.

A UAW vice-president discusses the need for a more detailed study of arbitrators and arbitrators' awards, more adequate training of the parties in case preparation and presentation, and the rising costs of arbitration.

PART III

The Issues in Collective Bargaining

Part III of this book analyzes the issues in collective bargaining; the areas of disagreement between employers, workers, and unions. The discussion follows the basic format proposed earlier for the analysis of collective bargaining agreements: union security and management rights; the wage and effort bargain; worker insurance and income continuity programs; and individual security. Management and union goals in matters of principle and cost are considered in the two "model" types of collective bargaining relationships.

Chapter 9

UNION SECURITY AND MANAGEMENT RIGHTS

Every collective bargaining agreement constitutes recognition by one party of the other and defines their relationship—who speaks for whom, with what authority, for how long, and except in what conditions. Many, but not all, collective bargaining agreements have sections clearly labeled "union security" and "management rights." As a rule, the full meaning of union security and management rights in a specific enterprise can be determined only by a careful study of the full text of the collective bargaining agreement. Frequently it is necessary to go even beyond the wording of the agreement and study the day-to-day practices of the parties. Union security and management rights provide the framework within which the wage and effort bargain, individual security, and a system of agreement administration are developed.

Without union security there can be no effective, independent employee representation. American law recognizes this fact by providing *minimum* union security. This grants exclusive bargaining rights to a single union through the processes of the National Labor Relations Board.[1] After acquiring bargaining rights, unions negotiate agreements which restrict management's freedom in regard to employee relations. Union security is thus only a "toe in the door" for the union.

Management begins bargaining with extensive control over the operation of the business derived from ownership. Every provision of the collective bargaining agreement tends to dilute this managerial control. Throughout the collective bargaining relationship, management is constantly striving to preserve its right to control the human and material resources of the enterprise.

Since both union security and management rights are hard to measure in a general way, we shall define and discuss them in terms of the needs of unions and managements. Then we shall attempt to analyze general trends and prospects in bargaining on union security and management rights. Finally we shall discuss current bargaining problems on union security and management rights.

[1] See Chapter 5, "Establishing the Collective Bargaining Relationship."

THE UNIONS' NEED FOR UNION SECURITY

From the very beginning, American unions have been preoccupied by the quest for union security. Among the tradesmen of early America, the refusal to work with "strangers" served a dual purpose: (1) protection of the workers' scarce skill and (2) preservation of the union as such. In later days, the drive for union security has benefited the industrial worker only to the extent that it has re-enforced the integrity of the collective bargaining agreement and the union-management relationship. Different forms of union security, legislative proposals, and the unions' apparent preoccupation with union security make sense only when examined in a historical framework. The stories are different for craft unions and industrial unions.

Forms of Union Security

Minimum union security, exclusive bargaining rights, is bestowed upon unions winning NLRB elections. All "stronger" forms of union security can be obtained *only* by the consent of management. Certain of these stronger forms are prohibited or restricted by federal or state law.

The major forms of union security may be defined as follows:

Exclusive Bargaining Rights. The employer recognizes the union as the exclusive bargaining representative for all employees in the appropriate unit for collective bargaining. There is no requirement for union membership by employees or for hiring through the union.

Maintenance of Membership. All employees who are members of the union at a specified time after the agreement is signed and all who later join the union must continue to pay dues to the union for the duration of the agreement. Maintenance of membership agreements are illegal in right-to-work states.

Agency Shop. All employees who do not join the union must pay a fixed sum monthly, usually the equivalent of union dues, as a condition of employment to help defray the union's expenses as bargaining agent for the group. General interest in bargaining for the agency shop is a recent development. In several right-to-work states, it is too early to say whether the language of the laws permits the negotiation of these agreements.

Union Shop. Workers employed under a union-shop agreement need not be union members when hired. However, they must pay initiation fees and union dues to the union within a specified time after hire. They must continue to pay dues as a condition of continued employment. Under the Taft-Hartley Law, the union shop dues obligation cannot begin less than thirty days after the beginning of an individual's employment or the effective date of the agreement. In the building and construction industry, under the Landrum-Griffin Act, union membership may be required after the seventh day following employment or the effective date of the agreement, whichever is later. The union shop is unlawful in right-to-work states.

Closed Shop. Under the closed shop all employees must be members of the union at the time of hiring, and they must remain members in good standing during the period of employment. The closed shop is frequently accompanied by a hiring hall arrangement where the employer requisitions new employees directly from the union business agent. Since the passage of the Taft-Hartley Act in 1947, closed-shop arrangements have been unlawful in the United States.

Checkoff. The checkoff may serve as an auxiliary to any form of union security, ranging from exclusive bargaining rights to the closed shop. It merely provides that the employer withhold union dues from members' paychecks and transmit the money directly to the union. Under the Taft-Hartley Act, the checkoff is lawful only when each individual employee signs a checkoff authorization. These checkoff authorizations may not be irrevocable for more than one year.

Craft unions and industrial unions seek and need different forms of union security.

The Craft Union's Need for the Closed Shop

Craft unions traditionally seek the full closed shop. The rationale of craft unionism is based on the control of a scarce skill. The closed shop is the craft union's most effective method of obtaining and keeping control over the supply of a particular skill.

The closed shop is essential to the craft union for several reasons:

1. Only when union membership is a condition precedent to employment can the craft union be certain that workers in the trade have served their time and are, therefore, fully competent. The presence of green hands might endanger the safety of union members.

2. When only members are employed, the workers can protect their individual and collective job opportunities by working only at a "safe" pace and using only "tried-and-true" methods and tools. Unless the closed shop is enforced, union rules on tempo, methods, and tools become meaningless.

3. The closed shop is helpful in protecting the craft union's jurisdictional claims.

4. Under the collective bargaining agreement, the union is responsible for the conduct of employees on the job. However, without the closed shop, the craft union is without authority to fulfill this responsibility for contract observance by employees.

5. The craft union needs the closed shop to protect itself from treasonable acts by union members. With the closed-shop arrangement in the

industry, workers will think twice before they cross a picket line, reveal union secrets to management, or place the union in disrepute by making slanderous statements about the union's leadership.

6. The closed shop may be used to decasualize employment in certain industries such as longshoring, the building trades, or the maritime trades. The typical employment relationship in these industries is of short duration. A closed shop and a closed union (severe restrictions on the number of new members admitted) could assure decent employment conditions to the union members who were permanently attached to the industry. Some independent authorities favor the closed-shop and closed-union arrangement in industries with casual employment relationships. They argue that nonunionists would be served by the absolute knowledge that no work would be available for them in these industries. Thus the surplus nonunion laborers would actively seek more satisfactory employment in other industries.

7. Finally, the craft union needs the closed shop because it enables the union to continue rendering a service which many employers have grown to expect from the union. Under the closed shop, the craft union is able to keep an adequate supply of competent workmen available to fill the requisitions which employers send to the Business Agent, sometimes on short notice.

The Industrial Union's Need for the Union Shop

Industrial unions have shown little interest in obtaining the traditional closed shop of craft unions. The industrial union's need for union security stems from the fact that the complex of jobs in a typical factory does not require persons possessing clearly defined and scarce skills. Thus the industrial union seeks security by control of the present employees of the firm, rather than by control of the total group of people capable of filling a factory job.

The industrial union considers the union shop to be essential for several reasons:

1. Many industrial union leaders remember the blacklist and the yellow dog contract. Some of them suspect that management is still hostile to unionism. In such a situation, the only way to protect the individual's right to join a union is negotiate a union-shop agreement. If all employees belong to the union, the employer can't play favorites with the individuals who don't belong to the union.

2. In some industries labor turnover is so high that unions need the union shop for the purpose of securing adequate revenues to keep the union out of bankruptcy. Workers who enter the plant for a short period of time receive the benefits of the collective bargaining agreement. Unionists argue that these short-time employees should at least make a financial contribution to the perpetuation of the contractual relationship from which they benefit during their stay in the plant.

3. A union-shop agreement protects a union with contractual relationships against raids by rival unions, dissident political factions, and management-oriented squealers.

4. Like the craft union, the industrial union needs to protect itself from treason.

5. Finally some industrial unions actively seek the closed shop and hiring hall because of the casual nature of employment in their industries. A classic example of this exception is the hiring hall in the longshoring and maritime industries.

In brief, the industrial union is primarily interested in workers *after* they go on the payroll. Thus the typical union security goal of the industrial union is the union shop.

Union security is a condition precedent to effective, independent employee representation. Once union security is established, management's major concern is preserving the right to manage. A union security clause, in itself, does not necessarily interfere with management control. Once union recognition is achieved, almost every act of the union will inevitably curtail the management's exclusive control over the operation of the enterprise.

MANAGEMENT RIGHTS

The job of management frequently is defined as planning, organizing, directing, coordinating, and controlling. In a struggle for survival in the marketplace, managers command the organization's human and material resources.

Management enters its first negotiations with sweeping powers derived from ownership. The only direct responsibility of management which is specifically recognized by law and enforceable at law is the trusteeship of the *owner's* property. With the divorce of ownership and control which typifies modern American business, many managers, at least philosophically, have accepted larger responsibilities which include the interests of such groups as employees, the enterprises' customers, and the community in which the business operates. A fine balancing of these sometimes conflicting responsibilities is a constant philosophical and practical challenge to the men of management.

The general objectives of management may be summarized as: (1) to make a profit (or, in the case of a nonprofit institution, a good record), (2) to produce a saleable product or service, and (3) to do this through the efficient use of the enterprise's human and material resources. The men of management seek these objectives in an ever-changing marketplace with only limited resources at their disposal.

Even without a union to contend with, the management of manpower in a free and affluent society is a ticklish business. Management's general objectives in manpower management may be summarized as:

(1) to find suitable employees, (2) to hold an appropriate work force, and (3) to get competitive productivity from that work force. In accomplishing these objectives, management designs jobs and selects, trains, and motivates an appropriate work force within the contexts of the market, the technology of the workplace, and the power relations of the enveloping society. Industrial and human engineering are called into play in the design of jobs. Worker selection draws on the disciplines of psychology and sociology. Effective training involves methods attuned to a wide variety of human interests, capabilities, and attitudes. Motivation depends on the carrot of economic, social, and personal satisfaction and the stick of banishment from the feast provided by the enterprise. While the social scientist may devote his lifetime to the study of a minute segment of human behavior, the manager must react today to the pressures of the marketplace. Like an army in the field, the life of an enterprise may depend upon the ability of its managers to sacrifice some of the troops to save the army. The manager needs freedom to adjust the size and composition of his work force to fit the needs of his enterprise in the marketplace. How skillfully he uses that freedom may spell prosperity or disaster for his organization. A nonunion firm can fail as certainly as a unionized firm can fail. Unionized firms do not have a monopoly on either inept personnel management or inefficiency. When management fails to perform its functions, it loses its freedom of initiative. Once established, loose standards are hard to change.

Collective bargaining may help or hinder management in achieving its manpower objectives of finding and holding an appropriate work force and getting competitive productivity from it. In a free and affluent society, employers must "sell" jobs to workers. A collective bargaining agreement may help management in obtaining group consent to the conditions of employment. The same collective bargaining agreement may seriously interfere with management's critical freedom to lay off unneeded workers or to obtain competitive productivity from its work force.

What Rights Does Management Need?

Some enterprises need extensive management rights while other managements have found that they want and need a substantially smaller area of sole discretion. For example, most factory managers would insist, quite properly, that they need wide discretion in the design of jobs, while many building contractors are quite satisfied to accept the job territories claimed by the building trades unions in exchange for the implicit assurance that the union will supply competent workmen.

In attempting to analyze what management rights are needed in a specific enterprise, it might be helpful to classify management rights into three groups: (1) rights required for flexibility in operation (generally associated with *jobs* instead of workers), (2) rights required to establish and maintain discipline (always associated with *workers* instead of jobs), and (3) residual rights (not usually directly and immediately related to either workers or jobs). In the discussion that follows, we shall attempt to show how the need for management rights in each of these classifications varies from enterprise to enterprise.

Flexibility in Operation (*Job-Related Rights of Management*). Every organization (profit or nonprofit making) is subject to long-range and short-range variations in the demand for its product or service. Most organizations also experience substantial changes in their technology over time. To operate effectively, management needs the rights to (*a*) lay off workers who are no longer needed and (*b*) to change job content and worker assignments. However, the methods of exerting these rights may be quite different.

The right to lay off unneeded workers is subject to many possible limitations either in the words of the agreement or by the practices of supervision. Today, few managers would argue that seniority should not be a consideration in selecting employees for layoff. In a plant where most jobs were really interchangeable, straight seniority in layoffs over a broad area of occupations would impose little inconvenience on management. Exactly the same layoff procedure would spell total chaos if the jobs covered were significantly different. To negotiate an adequate agreement on seniority, management must carefully determine its real needs *before* negotiating the procedure for layoffs.

The problem of management's need to change job content and to reassign workers requires similar advanced planning. If company policy is to fill new jobs on the basis of seniority between two employees showing equal "merit and ability" for the new job, how are merit and ability to be measured? On exactly what bases may the union challenge management's judgment of merit and ability? To what extent does a commitment to consider present employees for new jobs preclude the management from filling vacancies by new recruitment? Before management can know the probable impact of a union proposal in this area, it must clearly define its own needs for flexibility.

Layoffs and job assignments are only two examples of the job-related needs of management. These needs would be present regardless of the personal characteristics of individual job holders or the work force. The need for discipline arises from individual human differences and general psychological and sociological problems in motivation.

Discipline (*Worker-Related Rights of Management*). Of course the best discipline is self-discipline growing out of an individual's desire and ability to perform at his highest level of effectiveness in a given situation. But effectiveness requires knowledge of what is required or expected in a given situation. The dictionary defines discipline as "to train, to educate, to bring under control, or to establish order." Industrial discipline is essential because of the interdependence of workers and management in the enterprise. Management takes the initiative in establishing discipline by formulating an enforceable set of rules or standards of employee performance. The collective bargaining agreement frequently recognizes management's right to formulate reasonable rules of conduct and to administer them fairly. Occasionally the agreement incorporates a series of rules and graduated penalties for infractions. In this case, the criteria of reasonableness and fairness are partially worked out in the negotiation process. However, most collective bargaining over the application of the rules occurs in the grievance process.

Since most employees readily obey reasonable orders and rules of conduct, disciplinary action is primarily confined to dealing with the individual or the few employees who do not obey. However, failure to correct these exceptional infractions may result in a general disregard for rules. Thus, discipline involves both correcting the individual and maintaining general respect for rules and order.

In discipline, actions speak louder than words. In no other area does supervision have a better opportunity to provide leadership by example and by persuasion. Regardless of company policy, an individual foreman can succeed or fail in developing teamwork, self-discipline, and efficiency. A wise management helps the foreman in this all-important task by providing sound policies on discipline and rewarding the foremen who succeed in this task. Good supervision is the best method of maintaining discipline with or without a union.

Most collective bargaining concerning management rights tends to focus on job-related rights (management's need for flexibility) and discipline. It may extend into other areas less obviously connected with employee relations. We shall refer to these other areas (e.g., product pricing, methods of finance, and plant location) as the residual rights of management.

Residual Rights of Management. On the basis of logic, there really are no aspects of an organization's operations that do not at least indirectly impinge upon the welfare of its employees. Product design influences sales which, in turn, influence employment opportunities and the ability of an enterprise to pay high wages. Such examples could be repeated indefinitely. At the same time, few unions, indeed, have actively sought to bargain about product prices. We are using the term "residual rights" as a catchall for the rights of a specific management which the particular union with which it bargains has not challenged. We shall discuss the possible value of a management rights clause in protecting the residual rights of management below.

The following discussion of the measurements of union penetration of management right should be helpful in understanding the nature of management rights in the individual enterprise.

Measuring Union Penetration of Management Rights

In a study of union participation in decision making in 37 plants, Milton Derber, W. E. Chalmers, and Milton T. Edelman differentiated the *scope* and *depth* of union penetration of management rights.[2] *Scope* of union participation was measured by determining the number of important enterprise activities (e.g., contracting work out, product pricing, job evaluation, etc.) in which the union had a voice either through agreement negotiations or grievance settlement. The *depth* of union penetration was measured in terms of the agreement provision itself or the stage of a decision at which the union became involved. The measurement of *depth* of union penetration may be clarified by comparing two specific measures used by Derber, Chalmers, and Edelman: (1) union security was judged solely on the terms of the agreement provision, i.e., sole bargaining rights, maintenance of membership, union shop, preferential hiring, or closed shop, (2) making major technological change was judged on the stage of a decision at which the union became involved, i.e., decision made without advance notice, advance notice given by management, management consults union, or changes require prior union agreement. Derber, Chalmers, and Edelman used this system of measurement for interfirm comparisons over time. Although individual enterprises might find it desirable to modify the specific measures used by Derber, Chalmers, and Edelman,[3] the measures of *scope* and *depth* certainly are pertinent to the question of management rights. The framework for an analysis of the collective bargaining agreement outlined in Chapter 7 should be helpful in determining the *scope* and *depth* of union penetration of management rights in an enterprise.

The true meaning of the words of a collective bargaining agreement can be determined only by a careful examination of work practices. Work practices take solid form in the grievance procedure, arbitration awards, and the day-to-day actions of supervision. Collective bargaining agreements frequently state that management may discipline and discharge employees "for just cause." But what is just cause? We can find out only by knowing how grievances have been settled at (or before) the arbitration step. Even the disposition of all grievance cases will not tell us for

---

[2] Milton Derber, W. E. Chalmers, and Milton T. Edelman, "Union Participation in Plant Decision-Making," *Industrial and Labor Relations Review*, Vol. XV (October, 1961), pp. 83–101.

[3] The authors of this book, for example, would redefine the *depth* factor in seniority in layoff used by Derber, Chalmers, and Edelman. They use seven categories: (1) seniority given no more weight than other factors, (2) seniority determines if other factors are equal, (3) seniority generally followed but some exceptions, (4) strict seniority, (5) no practice, (6) divided between 2 and 3, (7) divided between 3 and 4. Their seven categories overlook the sometimes critical factor of the area of seniority. "Strict seniority" within a very narrow occupational category might be less costly in terms of efficiency than "seniority given no more weight than other factors" coupled with a plant-wide definition of seniority units.

sure how just cause is defined in a particular union-management relationship, because some supervisors may be so softhearted that they have abdicated the exercise of discipline in their departments. Even within a single firm, arbitration awards must be read carefully, with the clear knowledge that each award refers only to the specific circumstances of that particular case.

Given the great diversity in union and management needs for hard-to-define security or rights, is it possible to appraise the present state and probable future of union security and management rights in the American economy? Probably the best insights on trends and prospects flow from a brief review of history.

TRENDS AND PROSPECTS

Widespread interest in the negotiation of management rights clauses in collective bargaining agreements developed in the post-World War II period. However, the concept of management rights is deeply rooted in ancient history, and the union security issue is as old as unionism.

Under a free labor system, management has *no* rights over the individual worker; if he does not like the conditions of employment, he is free to quit. At the same time, so long as private property is recognized, owners or their representatives will have very substantial rights in establishing the conditions of employment. Within the practice of collective bargaining, the number of serious challenges to the institution of private property in America probably could be counted on a man's fingers. The short-lived Knights of Labor was a mass movement trying to abolish management rights by substituting the institution of producers' co-operation. For a very short time, both the great sit-down strikes of the thirties and the earlier strikes of the IWW posed a very real threat to the essence of management rights. After World War I some of the railroad unions challenged management rights by advocating the nationalization of the railroads under the Plumb Plan. A few more instances could be added to the list, but a totally exhaustive list would be short. The most significant finding of a study of American history is the infrequency and short life of frontal assaults on the institution of management rights by labor organization.

The evolutionary nature of union security and management's rights is clearly illustrated by a brief look at American labor-management history. The two scenes are national labor-management conferences called by the respective Presidents of the United States immediately after the close of World War I and World War II. These conferences provided an opportunity for the public airing of the prevalent views of labor and management spokesmen at turning points in history. The issues discussed and the nature of the agreements to disagree show a dramatic change in the balance of power between labor and management.

President Woodrow Wilson called the first industrial conference in the fall of 1919. The purpose of the conference was to provide for the orderly reconversion of the economy to a peacetime footing. Labor, management, and public representatives were unable to agree on principles to guide postwar labor-management relations. After 17 days of debate, the conference collapsed. Union security was a major stumbling block.

Labor representatives argued that employees should be entitled to representation by unions of their own choosing. The public representatives favored collective bargaining with the proviso that no employee should be denied the right to refrain from joining any organization.

Management representatives steadfastly insisted upon the following principle for employee-employer relations:

There should be no denial of the right of an employer and his workers voluntarily to agree that their relation shall be that of the "closed union shop" or of the "closed nonunion shop." But the right of the employer and his men to continue their relations on the principle of the "open shop" should not be denied or questioned. No employer should be required to deal with men or groups of men who are not his employees or chosen by and from among them.[4]

As a practical matter, the principle advocated by management meant that unions could function only with the *consent* of management. This meant practically *no* union security. The failure of the conference resulted in a continuation of the *status quo* in collective bargaining and labor relations law. This *status quo* was the "closed nonunion shop" in large segments of American industry in 1919. With no legislative protection of the right to organize, employers were successful in extending the "closed nonunion shop" to most segments of American industry by 1930. Shortly after the failure of the conference, most unions lost the "toe in the door" they had gained during World War I. Management rights were protected to the fullest degree possible—*no* union interference.

In 1945 the American people again faced the problem of harmonious reconversion to peacetime production. President Harry S. Truman called a national labor-management conference to tackle the problem. This time management rights were a major issue in the conference. Once again, labor representatives and management representatives were unable to agree to a principle which would guide the reconversion effort.

Management representatives, now on the defensive, stated their case this way:

Labor members of the Committee on Management's Right to Manage have been unwilling to agree to any listing of specific management functions. Management members of the Committee conclude, therefore, that the labor

---

[4] Department of Labor, *Proceedings of the First Industrial Conference (Called by the President) October 6 to 23, 1919* (Washington, D.C.: U.S. Government Printing Office, 1920), p. 82.

members are convinced that the field of collective bargaining will, in all probability, continue to expand into the field of management.

The only possible end of such a philosophy would be joint management of the enterprise. To this the management members naturally cannot agree. Management has functions that must not and cannot be compromised to the public interest. If labor disputes are to be minimized by "the genuine acceptance by organized labor of the functions and responsibilities of management to direct the operation of the enterprise," labor must agree that certain specific functions and responsibilities of management are not subject to collective bargaining.[5]

Labor representatives now spoke with confidence about the desirability of free collective bargaining. The problem of management rights, according to union spokesmen, was fluid and should be handled by unions and managements on a case-by-case basis. Thus the labor representatives insisted:

Because of the complexities of these [diverse union-management] relationships the labor members of the Committee think it unwise to specify and classify the functions and responsibilities of management. Because of the insistence by management for such specification the Committee was unable to agree upon a joint report. To do so might well restrict the flexibility so necessary to efficient operation.

It would be extremely unwise to build a fence around the rights and responsibilities of management on the one hand and the unions on the other. The experience of many years shows that with the growth of mutual understanding the responsibilities of one of the parties today may well become the joint responsibility of both parties tomorrow.[6]

The tide had turned. In 1945, the unions were on the offensive and favored the *status quo*. By refusing to concede to a listing of privileged management rights, the unions kept the door open for possible deeper penetration. It seems unlikely that the unions planned to drive management out of the shops. However, they put management on notice that management rights weren't sacred and must be defended or shared on their merits in a shop-to-shop contest.

A review of the history of management rights and union security in America would be incomplete without some reference to dramatic developments in labor arbitration which occurred in the sixties. On June 20, 1960, the Supreme Court rendered three decisions[7] which made arbitration agreements enforceable at law and gave arbitrators quite wide discretion in determining the arbitrability of a particular issue under an arbitration agreement. Another straw in the wind is the increasing use of arbitration as a means of resolving the knotty problems of major technological change. Although managements and unions still retain the right to settle their own disagreements, there seems to be a trend toward greater participation in the settlement process by arbitrators who owe their primary allegiance neither to management nor unions. It seems likely that

[5] *President's National Labor Management Conference*, Vol. III, Doc. 125 II/13 (November 29, 1945), p. 47.

[6] *Ibid.*, Vol. III, Doc. 120 II/11 (November 28, 1945), p. 45.

[7] These opinions are used as cases in Part V of this book. See pp. 526–42.

this trend will accelerate in the future, but it is quite impossible to foresee its probable long-run impact on either management rights or union security.

Does an understanding of history help managers, union officers, and public representatives when they get down to the hard job of negotiating and administering a collective bargaining agreement? We think it does.

BARGAINING ON UNION SECURITY AND MANAGEMENT RIGHTS

The prevalence of union security provisions in collective bargaining agreements indicates that most managers have accepted union security as a way of doing business. In 1958–59, only 19 per cent of the employees covered by a government survey were employed under agreements granting only the legal minimum of exclusive bargaining rights. The union shop (and closed shop) covered 74 per cent of the surveyed workers while maintenance of membership covered 7 per cent of the workers. Seventy-seven per cent of the workers surveyed were under agreements with checkoff provisions. Of 1,631 agreements examined, only 15 contained agency shop arrangements.[8] Although recent legal developments may encourage the agency shop in some right-to-work states, it seems unlikely that agency shops will play a major role in collective bargaining since three quarters of the organized labor force is already covered by union (and closed) shop arrangements.

Nevertheless, many management people are gravely concerned about union security as a moral question. They argue that employees should not be required to pay tribute to union bosses for the right to work. Associations representing employers, such as the N.A.M., see the union shop as a menace to the free economic society and as a form of labor monopoly. A still more prevalent objection to the union shop is the use of union money for the support of partisan political candidates.

It seems likely that most of the hard bargaining on union security will continue to occur in legislative halls instead of management-union negotiations. Recent history offers little hope either for the repeal of restrictive union security legislation or the enactment of more severe restrictions on the freedom of managements and unions to settle the issue at the bargaining level.[9]

[8] U.S. Bureau of Labor Statistics. *Union Seniority and Checkoff Provisions in Major Union Contracts, 1958–59*, Bulletin No. 1272 (March, 1960), pp. 2, 5, 11. This survey was a study of 1,631 agreements covering 7.5 million workers or almost half of the coverage of collective bargaining agreements outside the railroad and airline industries. The agreements surveyed covered 1,000 or more workers each. It is possible that the prevalence of union security clauses would be different under smaller enterprises or agreements.

[9] Cf. Paul E. Sultan, "The Union Security Issue," chap. 4 of Joseph Shister, Benjamin Aaron, and Clyde W. Summers (eds.), *Public Policy and Collective Bargaining* (New York: Harper & Row, 1962), pp. 88–120.

How are management rights protected in the collective bargaining process? It seems to the authors of this book that management rights are most effectively preserved by effective and decisive management action in the over-all operation of the business, in the negotiation of the whole collective bargaining agreement, and by the religious observance of the terms of the agreement negotiated. If a particular management runs a taut ship in all of its business relations, it will have little difficulty in determining what management rights it needs. With a clear objective in mind, the company's negotiators should be able to sell their position to the union. A good contract *adequately backed up with day-to-day super-visory practices* is within the grasp of any management worthy of its responsibilities.

Many management negotiators and the spokesmen for management organizations advocate the inclusion of management rights clauses in the collective bargaining agreement. These clauses may have an educational effect on the employees and the union over the years when management has had an opportunity to prove that it exercises these rights. When management action is in harmony with the management rights clause, the clause may also be helpful in arbitration hearings. Figure 9–1 contains il-lustrative management rights clauses.

SUMMARY

Specific provisions of the collective bargaining agreement establish the role and status of the union in the employment relationship. Various types of union security clauses protect the integrity of the union as an institution (independent of management and the employees) at the work-place. The forms of union security are as diverse as the products, meth-ods, organizational structure, and attitudes of American management.

Management begins bargaining with extensive control over the op-eration of the enterprise. Every provision of the collective bargaining agreement tends to dilute this managerial control. Throughout the col-lective bargaining relationship, management is constantly striving to preserve its right to control the human and material resources of the en-terprise. In varying degrees, every management needs: (1) flexibility in operation, (2) employee discipline, and (3) residual rights. The suc-cess of a management in obtaining the rights it needs is dependent upon its skill in negotiation and the day-to-day operation of the enterprise.

Union security and management rights establish the framework within which collective bargaining can be conducted and continued. Col-lective bargaining then becomes the process of providing for the needs of employees and management in the wage and effort bargain, personal se-curity, and fair adjustment of disputes.

FIGURE 9–1

ILLUSTRATIVE MANAGEMENT RIGHTS CLAUSES

Some employers prefer a long-form management rights clause like the Company Responsibility clause below. Other employers prefer a short-form clause like the Management Clause below. Employers favoring the short form feel that the enumeration of rights is dangerous, lest some rights be omitted.

Regardless of the form or content of the management rights clause, management functions may be given away, violated, or undermined by *other* clauses in the agreement or in company practices.

COMPANY RESPONSIBILITY

The Company retains the sole right to manage its business, including the rights to decide the number and location of plants, the machine and tool equipment, the products to be manufactured, the method of manufacturing, the schedules of production, the processes of manufacturing or assembling, together with all designing, engineering, and the control of raw materials, semimanufactured and finished parts which may be incorporated into the products manufactured; to maintain order and efficiency in its plants and operations; to hire, lay off, assign, transfer, and promote employees, and to determine the starting and quitting time and the number of hours to be worked; subject only to such regulations and restrictions governing the exercise of these rights as are expressly provided in this agreement.

MANAGEMENT CLAUSE

The management of the business in all its phases and details shall remain vested in the Employer. The rights of the Employer and the employees shall be respected and the provisions of this contract for the orderly settlement of all questions regarding such rights shall be observed.

QUESTIONS FOR DISCUSSION

1. Maintenance of membership was a compromise form of union security suggested by the National War Labor Board during World War II. How do you account for this development at that time and its demise after the end of the war?

2. What are management rights? Why are they important? In a specific situation, how would you go about protecting them from union infringement?

3. Compared to unions in other countries, American unions are preoccupied with union security. Why? Does the law of collective bargaining have anything to do with this? (You may wish to return to this question after Chapter 14.)

CASES: 7, 8, 9, 10.

SELECTED ANNOTATED BIBLIOGRAPHY

CHAMBERLAIN, NEIL W. "Determinants of Collective Bargaining Structures," ARNOLD W. WEBER (ed.), *The Structure of Collective Bargaining: Problems and Perspectives*. New York: The Free Press of Glencoe, Inc., 1961, pp. 3–19. Discussion pp. 21–31.

Chamberlain argues that bargaining units are essentially unstable, due to the pressures exerted by groups of workers within the legally established bargaining units or the bargaining units created by the formal organizational structure of labor organizations. Discusses generally that the power structure within these units is fluid. Suggests that three types of "units" exist concurrently: (*a*) the election districts (frequently established by NLRB order), (*b*) the negotiating area, and (*c*) the area of immediate impact (which accommodates "pattern" bargaining situations).

_____. "The Structure of Bargaining Units in the United States," *Industrial and Labor Relations Review*, Vol. X (October, 1956), pp. 3–25.

An analysis of bargaining units by industries, employers by size of unit, and employee size groups.

_____. *The Union Challenge to Management Control*. New York: Harper & Bros., 1948.

A landmark study of the impact of the union on the authority of management in the large corporation.

DEMPSEY, JOSEPH R., S. J. *The Operation of Right-to-Work Laws*. Milwaukee: Marquette University Press, 1961.

Based on unreported court cases and interviews with jurists, employers, unions, and attorneys, this book compares the statements of state legislators on the meaning of right-to-work laws and the meaning of these laws as developed by the courts.

GOLDBERG, ARTHUR. "Management's Reserved Rights: A Labor View," *Management Rights and the Arbitration Process*, JEAN T. McKELVEY (ed.). Proceedings of the Ninth Annual Meeting of the National Academy of Arbitrators. Washington, D.C.: Bureau of National Affairs, 1957, pp. 118–29.

The then General Counsel of the United Steelworkers of America proposes some standards for the arbitration of management rights controversies.

JUSTIN, JULES J. "How to Preserve Management's Right Under the Labor Contract," *Labor Law Journal*, Vol. XI (March, 1960), pp. 189–215.

Examines the substantive areas where management's rights have been invaded by unions, and presents guideposts to follow in negotiating and administering the labor contract, emphasizing that management must know what its rights are, must understand the political structure of its union, and train its supervision in how to manage within the framework of the contract.

KELLER, LEONARD A. *The Management Function: A Positive Approach to Labor Relations*. Washington, D.C.: Bureau of National Affairs, 1963.

Defines a good labor policy, explores contracts in general, "management rights" clauses in particular, and gives model arbitration clauses which protect management rights. Suggests how to deal with labor attempts to restrict changes in methods, classifications, departments, and work schedules.

MEYERS, FREDERIC. *"Right-To-Work" in Practice*. New York: Fund for the Republic, 1959.

A study of the effects of "right-to-work" legislation on labor and management in Texas over the past several years.

MYERS, A. HOWARD. "Concepts of Industrial Discipline," chap. 5, *Management Rights and the Arbitration Process*, JEAN T. McKELVEY (ed.). Proceedings of the Ninth Annual Meeting of the National Academy of Arbitrators. Washington, D.C.: Bureau of National Affairs, 1956, pp. 59–83.

The author, a professor at Northeastern University and an arbitrator, discusses the meaning of reasonable discipline, the challenge to supervision, the union's responsibility for discipline, and employee conduct off the job. Paper is discussed by Gabriel N. Alexander, Detroit arbitrator and attorney.

PHELPS, JAMES C. "Management's Reserved Rights: An Industry View," *Management Rights and the Arbitration Process*, JEAN T. McKELVEY (ed.). Proceedings of the Ninth Annual Meeting of the National Academy of Arbitrators. Washington, D.C.: Bureau of National Affairs, 1957, pp. 102–17.

An executive of Bethlehem Steel Company proposes some standards for the arbitration of management rights controversies.

SHISTER, JOSEPH, AARON, BENJAMIN, and SUMMERS, CLYDE W. (eds.). *Public Policy and Collective Bargaining*. New York: Harper & Row, 1962.

See "The Union Security Issue" by Paul E. Sultan.

STONE, MORRIS. *Managerial Freedom and Job Security*. New York: Harper & Row, 1964.

A companion volume to the author's earlier *Labor-Management Contracts At Work*, this book addresses itself principally to job security issues, including the subcontracting of work; transfers of work outside the bargaining unit; attempts by the employer to change the content of a job; and out-of-classification assignments to solve special production problems.

Chapter 10 | THE WAGE AND EFFORT BARGAIN

The wage and effort bargain is the heartland of collective bargaining. More clearly than in any other area, the wage and effort bargain represents vital costs to the employer and obvious benefits for the worker. Practically every word in the collective bargaining agreement costs the employer money and establishes some kind of benefit for the workers individually or as a group. In the case of wages the money cost is easily measurable; this is not true in many other segments of the agreement, such as, job rights and due process, shift scheduling, and some of the worker insurance and income-continuity programs.

This chapter examines the wage and effort bargain as it is made at the level of the enterprise. Craft unions and industrial unions approach the wage and effort bargain in different ways with different results. To understand collective bargaining on the wage and effort bargain in large-scale enterprises it is necessary to review job structures and task standards initially established unilaterally by management.

THE WAGE AND EFFORT BARGAIN AS A "PACKAGE"

Wages, hours, and working conditions may be defined as the total benefits package accruing to the worker by virtue of employment on the job. Wage rates, hours schedules, and physical working conditions obviously are the major components of wages, hours, and working conditions. In addition to these, the employer, quite properly preoccupied with cost considerations, is vitally concerned with what are frequently called fringe benefits or "the hidden payroll."

The phenomenal growth of the cost of fringe benefits during the 1947–65 period in companies surveyed biennially by the United States Chamber of Commerce is graphically illustrated in Figure 10–1. The employer's concern over the rising cost of these items is fully justified when it is realized that they frequently exceed 25 per cent of the total payroll or as much as $1,500 per employee per year.

The composition of these costs also merits consideration. It might be argued that legally required payments should be excluded from the cost

258

estimates because they are neither voluntary nor subject to collective bargaining. About half of the remaining cost of fringe benefits goes for pay for time not worked such as vacations, holidays, bereavement pay, and paid sick leave. The other half of nonlegally required payments go for what this book calls worker insurance and income continuity programs.

FIGURE 10–1

COMPARISON OF 1947–65 FRINGE PAYMENTS FOR 84 COMPANIES

Item	1947	1965
All industries (84 companies)		
1. As per cent of payroll, total	16.1	28.1
a) Legally required payments*	2.6	4.2
b) Pensions and other agreed-upon payments*	5.0	9.9
c) Paid rest periods, lunch periods, etc.	1.6	2.4
d) Payments for time not worked	5.6	9.6
e) Profit-sharing payments, bonuses, etc.	1.3	2.0
2. As cents per payroll hour	22.1	88.8
3. As dollars per year per employee	450	1874
All manufacturing (48 companies)		
1. As per cent of payroll, total	14.1	27.6
2. As cents per payroll hour	19.9	87.6
3. As dollars per year per employee	410	1889
All nonmanufacturing (36 companies)		
1. As per cent of payroll, total	18.7	28.5
2. As cents per payroll hour	25.0	87.8
3. As dollars per year per employee	503	1804

*Employer's share only.
SOURCE: Economic Analysis and Study Group, Chamber of Commerce of the United States. *1965 Fringe Benefits.* (Washington, D.C.: Chamber of Commerce of the United States, 1966), p. 27.

Professor George W. Taylor has commented on the changing nature of fringe benefits in recent years as follows:

I am conducting a one-man crusade against the continued use of the word "fringe." I participated in some of the earlier negotiations when the term was first used. The reasoning underlying the use of the term was something like this: An employee works for fifty-one weeks. He gives good value and service. A week off to charge his batteries will make him a better employee. He can, therefore, be given a week off with pay because that doesn't increase costs. Without the vacation, he would be a less efficient employee. It was called a fringe benefit because it was conceived as a supplemental wage payment which did not increase costs.

That concept was modified when vacations were equated with cents-per-hour general wage increases. Vesting in vacations then inevitably developed. Now an employee looks upon vacation pay as a part of his wages. That's the way it was set up. If he quits, he gets his prorated vacation pay because this was provided for "in lieu of a wage increase." The cost impact has changed somewhat.

My one-man crusade is to drop the use of this work "fringe" and call these payments collateral payments supplementary to the basic wage structure.[1]

[1] George W. Taylor, "That Misnomer 'Fringe Benefits,'" *Management Record*, Vol. XIX (August, 1957), p. 281.

Professor Taylor's comments emphasize the *cost* element of collateral payments supplementary to the basic wage structure. We agree with this emphasis but would go one step further.

We believe that wage supplements should be broken into at least two categories: (1) pay for time off the job; that is, pay for time not worked, and (2) contingent benefits, or worker insurance and income-continuity programs.

Pay for time off the job includes such items as paid vacations, paid holidays, paid lunch periods, and wash-up time. We shall discuss these wage supplements later in this chapter.

Although representing important labor costs of doing business, worker insurance and income-continuity programs are quite unique wage supplements. Pensions, health and welfare, and unemployment benefits provide the worker with a degree of insurance or income-continuity protection from certain of the hazards of life. Even the most money-conscious worker frequently has difficulty in equating his pension or health and welfare benefits entitlement to so many cents-per-hour in wages. Receipt of the benefits from these programs is dependent upon some personal calamity befalling the worker. Worker insurance and in-come-continuity programs are frequently integrated with, and always co-ordinated with, governmental social security measures. Because of these unique features and the prospect that worker insurance and in-come-continuity programs will be an ever more important issue in collective bargaining, Chapter 11 is devoted to a discussion of these wage supplements.

BARGAINING ISSUES

Chapter 7 gave among other things a breakdown of the wage and effort segment of the agreement. This major division of the agreement was shown to consist of five parts: (1) pay for time worked, (2) the effort bargain, (3) premium pay, (4) pay for time not worked, (5) contingent benefits, or worker insurance and income-continuity programs. Only the first four will be discussed in this chapter. The fifth of these subdivisions, contingent benefits, seems important enough to merit separate consideration. The worker insurance and income-continuity programs under this heading protect the worker during, before, and after actual employment. Pensions, health and welfare, and unemployment benefit programs are designed to guard the worker against some hazards which are more or less unpredictable in their impact. These programs have assumed and are ever assuming increased importance in collective bargaining negotiations. They will be discussed in detail in Chapter 11.

The rest of this chapter will be devoted to introducing the bargaining issues listed above from (1) through (4). The first of these is pay for time worked.

Pay for Time Worked

The enterprise pays its employees to get something done—to perform work. In return for work performed, the worker receives wages or salary. The amount of pay depends upon the amount and kind of work done, and the wage or salary considered appropriate in the given place at the given time. That raises three issues which have come to be described in the following words: (*a*) the job *structure*, (*b*) the wage or salary *level*, (*c*) the *method* of wage or salary payment.

Job Structure. As just stated, the enterprise pays an employee to perform work. The employee earns his pay on the *job;* the enterprise gets its work by employee performance of *tasks.* The employee who carries out tasks which make up his job must possess qualifications appropriate to the tasks. The tasks, furthermore, may vary in difficulty, in the skill or expertise required, or in the conditions under which they are performed. Two tasks of equal difficulty performed under approximately equal conditions and requiring similar or comparable qualifications on the part of the workers involved ought naturally to entitle the workers who perform them to equal pay. If, on the other hand, the tasks involved are of unequal quality, then it would appear to be just as fair to compensate performance unequally, in proportion to the relative value of the tasks. A job consists of a collection of tasks. Just as one task may be compared with another, a job including many tasks may be compared with other jobs. A job requiring higher qualifications or making greater demands in performance should, under the principle just stated, receive higher compensation. The determination of relative differences between jobs in a given enterprise is called establishing the job structure. The most common way of setting up the job structure is job evaluation.

Job evaluation is a well tested and widely accepted technique of analyzing differences in job worth. It is a means of analyzing jobs and *measuring* the differences between them. It results in ranging them in an order of relative job worth from the least difficult up to the most difficult, or the least valuable to the enterprise up to the most valuable.

The Pay Level. The job structure, or relative position of jobs within the enterprise, is independent of the dollar amount paid for any of the jobs in question. The pay level concept applies money values to the job structure in proportion to the worth of the jobs. Whereas the job structure applies only within the enterprise, the pay level implies comparison with jobs, and the pay for these jobs, in other enterprises, usually in the enterprises which compete in a given labor market. For the kinds of jobs usually covered by collective bargaining agreements this is normally a single urban or metropolitan community.

Unlike the job structure, which always compares jobs in terms of relative worth within the enterprise, wage levels are not necessarily set in terms of comparisons. An enterprise may establish its wage level quite without regard for community rates, but this would be unusual.

If, now, the job structure were to be represented by points on a horizontal line, reading from left to right, so that the low rated jobs were on the left and the higher rated jobs on the right, the relative position of the points representing each job, and their distance from each other, would be the job structure of the enterprise. If, again, pay rates expressed in dollars and cents were ranged on a vertical axis intersecting the horizontal line of the job structure at the point of the lowest rated job, then it would be possible to represent the job level by a line or curve correlating structure with money rates. An illustration of this will be given later. The point here is that structure and level are independent of each other. As long as job content remains unchanged, the structure remains the same. The level, on the other hand, may vary. It may rise with a general increase in wages; it may take a different slope; it may even become distorted by temporary abnormalities of the labor market.

Method of Payment. There are two basic ways of paying wages or salary: (1) time wages, or pay by the hour, day, month, or year, without specifying the amount of work to be done; (2) production wages, or pay related to the amount of work the individual or group performs, more or less disregarding the time involved in its performance. In fact, however, the time element cannot be effectively separated from production, nor production from time. No employer would want to pay his people for an hour of work without having some idea of the amount of work he could expect to get in return. No employee would care to receive production pay, or pay based entirely on output, unless he had some expectation that he would be able to earn an average wage appropriate to the type of work, that is, to the kind of tasks that made up his job. Production wages are often referred to as piecework. The rates paid for piecework depend upon standards which are often set by time study. In setting these rates, however, there must be some presumption about average expected earnings. It can be seen, then, that time and output are really inseparable, but that for purposes of calculating payment two opposite approaches may be made to this problem.

It now becomes possible to define pay for time worked in the sense intended by the category under the wage and effort bargain. Pay for time worked is the *level*, expressed in concrete dollars and cents terms, of the wage or salary paid for a given job within the job structure of an enterprise; or it is the *expected average earnings* for the same job, even though the method of payment may not consist of straight time wage but of piece rates or production wages.

The Effort Bargain

Pay for time worked, or pay for the job, always appears in concrete dollars and cents form. The effort bargain, on the other hand, is not always so easily identified. It consists of the amount of work expected or required during a given period of time. Another way of saying this is, it is the standard or norm expected on a given task. Thus, the effort bargain is always measured in terms of the task. If the entire job consists of a single task endlessly repeated, measuring the time required for that one task in a sense sets the effort bargain on that job. If the job consists of a variety of tasks, then the effort bargain is the sum or composite of the work expected on each and all of the tasks making up the job.

The most obvious and observable way of setting the effort bargain is through time study. At this point only a few important matters need to be noted. The first of these is that the effort bargain implies the working conditions of the phrase quoted at the outset of this chapter: "wages, hours, and *working conditions*." That is, under one set of conditions the output expected may differ from that under an entirely different set of conditions, even though the productive task, and the finished work turned out, may be the same.

Premium Pay

Premium pay consists of rates, or formulas for determining rates, which are to be paid for extra work performed outside the normally scheduled daylight working hours, or at other personal inconvenience to the employee. Under this heading fall such matters as overtime pay (usually calculated at time-and-one-half) after forty hours in any one week or eight hours in any one day; night-shift differentials; call-in pay; travel allowances.

Theoretically, this is money the enterprise would never have to pay if it did not work its employees outside the scheduled daylight hours. It used to be called "penalty pay," because it was intended to punish the employer who made extra demands on his employees and encourage him to schedule his operations more carefully. A foreman ought to know at the end of one shift whether he is going to have work for a man at the beginning of the next shift on the following day. If he does, and fails to tell the man; or if, through poor planning on his part or at levels above him, he does not know, the man may come in to work as usual, find no work waiting for him, and have to be sent home. Without a provision for call in pay, he would have lost not only the day's work but the free time which he might have used for himself—even if only to go fishing. A union agreement requiring that the company either notify him the day before, or give him at least four hours' work or four hours' pay, serves as a powerful reminder to the foreman not to neglect giving appropriate advance notice when he is not going to need one of his regular hourly paid workers.

In practice, overtime pay has come to be regarded as "gravy" which many workers are eager to get. Some companies have even used overtime pay, systematically scheduled, as a means of raising take-home pay for their employees without disturbing the pay rates. Premium pay provisions still remain, basically, a means of regulating not the income to the worker or the cost to the company but the hours worked. This is true whether the maximum (before overtime) is set by law or by union agreement.

Pay for Time Not Worked: Miscellaneous Labor Costs of Doing Business

Pay for time not worked and the miscellaneous labor costs of doing business frequently total between 8 and 10 per cent of payroll costs. Pay for time not worked usually runs to a total of about 8 per cent of payroll costs.

Pay for Time Not Worked. At least four different types of pay for time not worked can be easily identified: (1) vacation pay, (2) holiday pay, (3) paid rest periods, lunch periods, wash-up time, and (4) special bonuses such as Christmas bonuses. The cost of these different items varies tremendously as does the complexity of the collective bargaining agreement which brings them into being or guarantees their continuity.

Vacations. The high potential cost of paid vacations can be seen from a simple example. Assume that all persons on the payroll worked 50 weeks per year and drew 2 weeks' vacation pay. In this case, vacation pay would equal 4 per cent of payroll or 8 cents per hour (assuming an average wage rate of $2 per hour).

An adequate agreement on vacation pay must deal with the following problems:

1. Scheduling vacations: Will the plant shut down for a stated period to allow all workers to take their vacation at the same time or will vacations be staggered over the year? If the plant shuts down for vacations and some workers will be needed during the shutdown, which workers will be required to work and what will be their rate of compensation? If some workers are required to work during the vacation period, will they be given an opportunity for a vacation at another time during the year? If management wishes to operate the plant, due to a backlog of orders, during the vacation period, what compensation will be given in lieu of vacations? If vacations are to be staggered through the year, what method is used in determining when an individual takes his vacation? If vacations are staggered, may a worker use his vacation pay during an illness?

2. Eligibility for vacations: How much seniority must an employee have before he is eligible for a paid vacation? Is a worker on temporary layoff eligible for vacation pay? Are part-time workers eligible for vacation pay? Are paid holidays falling within a vacation period a basis for extra compensation? Does an unauthorized absence immediately before or after the vacation period disqualify a worker for vacation pay?

3. Duration of vacation pay: The length of paid vacation time to which an employee is entitled is frequently related to his length of service, e.g., 1 week for 1 year's seniority; 2 weeks for 3 years' seniority; 3

weeks for 10 years' seniority; 4 weeks for 15 years' seniority. In computing the amount of vacation pay entitlement, what consideration is given to breaks in seniority? Are there any requirements that long vacations must be taken at the convenience of the company or that they must be split so as to minimize interference with production?

4. Computation of vacation pay: Does the vacation pay computation include overtime premium, shift premium, incentive earnings, and personal rates above the base rate for the employee's job? Sometimes vacation pay is computed as a percentage of the previous year's earnings, e.g., 2 per cent of the previous year's earnings would equal one week's vacation pay. This percentage method includes overtime premiums paid, incentive earnings, holiday pay, etc., but tends to reduce the vacation entitlement of workers who have had substantial layoffs or absences in the previous year.

5. Vacation pay for workers temporarily or permanently separated: Is a worker on temporary layoff at the vacation period entitled to vacation pay? If a worker quits or dies does he or his family have a vested right to his "earned" vacation time? Is a worker discharged for cause entitled to his "earned" vacation time at the time of discharge?

The foregoing list of vacation bargaining issues emphasizes the cost element of vacations. This is not an altogether fair emphasis, because some of this cost may be offset by improved employee morale or a saving of unemployment compensation costs. At the same time, it seems logical that the individual employer's gain in employee morale from granting generous vacations has been significantly diluted by almost universal adoption of the practice.

Holidays. Paid holidays vie with vacations as being the most expensive form of pay for time not worked.

Five paid holidays per year would cost about 2 per cent of the annual payroll. One day of holiday pay usually costs the employer more than one day of vacation because holiday pay frequently applies to everyone on the payroll regardless of seniority. Like vacations, paid holidays have become so common that the individual employer only succeeds in avoiding bad morale by granting them.

An adequate agreement on holiday pay must deal with the following problems:

1. Eligibility for holiday pay: How long must an employee be on the payroll before he becomes eligible for holiday pay? Is an employee eligible for holiday pay if he is absent on his scheduled shift immediately before or following the holiday?

2. Work on holidays: Are workers obligated to report to work on holidays if advanced notice is given? What rates of pay will prevail for workers required to work on holidays?

3. Holidays falling on nonwork days: If a paid holiday falls on a nonwork day, is the holiday celebrated on the next or preceding work shift or is holiday pay disregarded in this case?

4. What compensation will be given for holiday pay? Is shift premium,

incentive pay, and normal overtime included in the pay given for holiday?

5. What days will be observed as holidays? The rather striking increase in the number of paid holidays in recent years has pretty well exhausted the list of national holidays available, e.g., Independence Day, New Year's Day, Labor Day, Memorial Day, etc. As a result an increasing number of religious holidays are being added to the list. This poses a serious problem where members of the labor force are adherents of different religious faiths.

Miscellaneous Labor Costs of Doing Business. Depending upon the purpose for which the data are collected, miscellaneous labor costs of doing business are totally insignificant or substantial. Obvious items, such as employer subsidies to cafeterias, supply of special work clothing, and transportation allowances, usually amount to only a very few cents per hour. However, employers frequently wish to impress the total cost of hiring labor on the employees and include such items as unemployment compensation, workmen's compensation, and the employer's share of social security payments and other legally required payments. Although these items are genuine labor costs, it is a matter for discussion whether they should be included in the calculation of the total employment benefits package.

CRAFT-UNION WAGE BARGAINING

When a craft union bargains with an employer, the wage agreement is the essence of simplicity. Worker characteristics and the work to be done are clearly established prior to bargaining by the training of the skilled craftsmen. For example, carpenters perform a variety of operations on wood. The typical agreement with a carpenters' union assigns all wood work to the carpenters' union. Through union rules (written and unwritten) every carpenter knows the content of a "fair day's work" and performs only that amount of work because he controls the tempo of work with his own hands. The only collective bargaining wage problem confronting the skilled craftsman and his employer is what the rate shall be for a known quantity and quality of workmanship. After this problem is handled the auxiliary problems of rates for apprentices and helpers remain. Most employers of craftsmen are specialists employing only one or a few crafts. An employer of several crafts obtains a wage structure which relates the rates of various jobs only after he has carried on several separate negotiations with different unions representing the different crafts. Thus craft-union wage negotiations deal almost exclusively with problems of general wage adjustments.

Collective bargaining in the building trades is an important example of craft-union bargaining. We shall discuss the structure of building-trades bargaining, factors creating a solid community of interest between craft unions and building-trades employers, and the points of disagreement between unions and managements in building-trades wage negotiations.

Structure of Building-Trades Bargaining

Building-trades unions and employers bargain on a local level. Because the product market is local, there is little need for, or benefit to be derived from, bargaining on an area or national basis.[2] Customarily, the collective bargaining agreement covers many employers and the members of a single Local union composed of workers of the same craft, e.g., carpenters, electricians, or plumbers. General contractors have contracts with many unions, while an occasional specialty contractor will have only one contract with one union.

Frequently employers in the same line of business bargain as a group through an employer's association. This employer's association usually includes the largest and most influential firms in the local industry. Very often smaller employers and even a few large employers are not members of the association and, as a result, do not have a direct voice in determining the terms of the master agreement. After negotiations are completed with the employer's association, the nonmember employers usually voluntarily accept the terms of the master agreement or the union forces acceptance of the agreement through strike action. Occasionally, the union permits deviations from the master agreement in the case of nonsignatory employers as an organizational device.

Each craft Local union customarily bargains for itself, but it expects, and usually gets, substantial strike support from the Local unions in other crafts. Craft International unions usually allow their Locals to go their own way on general wage adjustments but may exert powerful influence on working rules and the protection of the union's jurisdictional claims. In those unusual cases where craft International unions have tried to influence wage negotiations, they have met with only very limited success.[3]

---

[2] An important exception to this general rule must be noted in the relations between the Associated General Contractors of Northern California and California Building Trades Unions. Here a master contract covering a broad geographic area has been negotiated. This arrangement seems to be a natural outgrowth of the technology of the California construction industry, where general contractors bid on jobs over a wide area, move heavy equipment from job to job over this area, and recruit labor from the area where the particular job is performed. See Gordon W. Bertram and Sherman J. Maisel, *Industrial Relations in the Construction Industry* (Berkeley: University of California, Institute of Industrial Relations, West Coast Collective Bargaining Systems, 1955).

[3] In the winter of 1957, Mr. Richard Gray, President of the AFL-CIO Building Trades Department proposed a wage freeze in local building-trades bargaining as a countercyclical measure. In many areas, building tradesmen struck for higher wages in the spring of 1958 despite declining construction activity.

Community of Interest between Local Unions and the Construction Industry

In many ways the industry is like one big family. The nature of their work throws construction men into close interaction with each other. Not only are there close social ties among members of a given trade, but the industry as a whole stands apart from the rest of the community.

The class line between employer and employee, supervisor and worker is quite thin. Most contractors and superintendents are former workers. Many still hold union cards. Only a small proportion of the supervisors have had college educations. The social gap which separates management and labor in mass-production industry seems to be lacking. In general they see problems from the same point of view.

As a consequence, relationships are highly personal (in the words of Max Weber, they are particularistic rather than universalistic). Friendships and feuds flourish. To the outsider disputes seem irrational and over-emotional.[4]

The community of interest between building-trades unions and contractors is rooted in both social and economic institutions. The local nature of the product market dictates local day-to-day bargaining. The worker's control of work tempo and the high percentage of labor cost to total cost forces the employers, workers, and union to be cost conscious (at least in those segments of the product market where demand is price elastic). Since a significant part of sales in most markets is to governmental agencies or performed under conditions prescribed by the government, the employer and unions are frequently political allies. Because entry to the industry sometimes involves only a small capital outlay, the unions and present employers share an interest in policing the activities of new firms, be they outsiders trying to invade the local market or individual tradesmen who may undersell the union rate.

Even in the knotty problem of union jurisdiction, there may be a community of interest between employers and the union. Like the tradesmen, many employers are specialists in the use of certain materials and thus share an interest in maintaining a demand for "their" particular type of construction and materials.

Although tradesmen, unions, and employers in the building trades have much in common, they tend to separate on the central issue in craft union bargaining—the "standard rate." Even here, their disagreement is usually over the interpretation of the same facts. Occasionally the union leadership and management are in agreement, with the workers dissenting.

The Wage Dispute

Wages are the central, and frequently the *only*, issue in building-trades bargaining. Union security, production standards, seniority, and other major issues have been settled for so long in most communities that

---

[4] George Strauss, *Unions in the Building Trades: A Case Study* (Buffalo, N.Y.: The University of Buffalo Series, Vol. 24, No. 2, June, 1958), p. 69.

they aren't even discussed in negotiations. Usually these nonwage matters have merely been entrusted to the union's care and negotiations start with the closed shop, union working rules, and jurisdictional claims as settled issues. This normal situation may be upset by new governmental rules or some new union rule or new materials or methods, but such occurrences are exceptional. We turn now to the goals of unions and managements in craft industry wage bargaining.

Craft-Union Wage Goals. Typically, craft unions seek to increase only the standard rate. Recently many craft unions have shown increased interest in the multitude of wage supplements, such as pensions, health and welfare benefits, and insurance which the industrial unions have pioneered, but primary emphasis continues to be placed on the basic wage rate. Because of the irregularity of employment in the building trades, these programs are administered on a market-wide basis with eligibility for benefits based on continuous employment in the industry which usually means continuity of union membership. As a result, when a union seeks a package it really means so many cents for wage increases and so many cents for welfare benefits. Because of the worker's control over tempo, the employer can almost convert this package into a unit labor cost increase. The entire bargain can be stated as income to the worker versus costs to the employer.

How much of an increase will a building-trades Local union demand and strike for in a given year? What factors influence the determination of the union's demands?[5]

Like managers, college professors, and farmers, rank-and-file members of building-trades unions seem to have an insatiable desire for more money. They exert a rather constant pressure on the union leadership to get more. They become particularly insistent when business is good, the cost of living is rising, or other unions have negotiated substantial wage increases. The craft unionist feels that he is entitled to as large a wage increase as other unionists get and frequently he expects his union to get an even larger increase because of his painstakingly acquired skill. On the other hand, the building-trades unionist probably knows more about the general state of business in his trade than the factory worker knows about the state of business in his industry. This greater industry consciousness can be traced to the building-trades unionist's visits to the union hall for work and his employment on different jobs during the course of the year. Because of this industry consciousness, craft unionists as a group may exhibit some concern over the employment effects of their wage demands.

When a building-trades Business Agent enters negotiations with employers, he is representing the interests of a more or less fixed number of

---

[5] Our discussion of some of these factors will be abbreviated in this section. Fuller discussion of some of these factors, especially the cost of living, will be found in the discussion of industrial-union bargaining.

union members. His job is to get the best possible bargain for those members. Most of his members have a substantial investment in an apprenticeship and can earn a return on that investment only through employment in the building trades. When all of his members are working, the Business Agent usually presses for a very substantial wage increase. When many of his members are out of work, he tends to be much more conservative in his wage demands. Several students[6] of building-trades wage bargaining have suggested that Business Agents tend to differentiate "big work" and "small work" in their thinking on wages. For big work such as large buildings and roads, Business Agents tend to believe that cost has little influence on the decision to build or not to build. In this case, the Business Agent would show little regard for the employment effect on his wage demands. In the case of small work, such as residential construction and renovation, Business Agents may believe that cost is a major determinant of the decision to build. Thus, Business Agents might show greater restraint in increasing the wage paid on small work than on big work especially in periods when many unionists were unemployed. If this distinction does enter the thinking of building-trades Business Agents, it is clear that they tend to view the best bargain as consisting of both a wage and an employment component. It should be noted that Strauss indicates that although the Business Agents he studied seemed to be worried about the employment effect he could not discover a single case where they had reduced wage demands because of fear of loss of employment.[7]

Undoubtedly the major consideration in building-trades demand formulation is the Business Agent's perception of the willingness and ability of the employers to meet his demands. If the contract comes up for negotiation at the height of a very busy season with lots of work started and more on the drawing boards, the Business Agent is very likely to make substantial demands. Under these circumstances, even a short strike will hurt the contractors and they will be in a conciliatory frame of mind. If business is slow and no great pickup is expected in the near future, the Business Agent will probably go slow on his wage demands. In this case, a strike threat loses much of its persuasive power. We turn now to the interests of the building contractors in wage bargaining.

Contractor's Wage Goals

The building contractor's wage goals are more intimately associated with the structure and economic health of the industry than are the union's goals. Basically, the individual contractor seeks assurance of *uniform* wages throughout the local industry and a level of wages which will encourage the expansion of business. Large contractors usually have an

[6] William G. Hosking, "Wage Decisions of Building Trades Unions in Central New York," *ILR Research*, Vol. II (December, 1955), pp. 2–5, and Strauss, *op. cit.*

[7] Strauss, *op. cit.*, 76.

influential voice in the decisions of the employer's association. Sometimes smaller employers don't bother to belong to the association because they fear being outvoted by their larger associates or believe that their interests will be represented even if they don't pay their dues.

Typically the union and the employer's association work like hand in glove in policing the industry for compliance with the master agreement. This is a service to the employers in that it protects each employer who abides by the agreement from being underbid by some employer who uses nonunion labor or who shades the prevailing wage scale by other methods. Although each employer probably would like to bid on projects with a personal wage cost advantage, the best interest of all employers is served by eliminating such advantages. The activity of the employer's association and the union, if effective, guarantees an equality of competition in the industry as far as labor costs go.

When building activity is slow, employers naturally start a serious search for methods of generating new business. One means of generating new business is to increase governmental building. Here the employers and unions are complete allies. Another way of stimulating new business that is likely to occur to the contractors is a "bargain sale." Since all building constructon is on a made-to-measure basis, the employers seek ways of reducing their costs. Wages being a major cost of building construction, the employers naturally think of them as a good place to economize, to enable a reduction in prices, to generate more business. Labor costs could be reduced by stepping up the tempo of work and employers will do whatever they can about this, e.g., greater use of precut materials and gentle urging of the craftsman to pay less attention to unimportant details. However, the building contractor can't just speed up the line because the individual worker possesses control over his own tempo of work. As a result, the matter of reducing labor costs quickly becomes a matter of reducing or freezing the standard rate. Here the employer runs up against the combined opposition of all the craftsmen. Usually this opposition is so intense that he gives up or diverts his attention to other areas such as materials where costs may be reduced with less animosity.

On the other hand, when building is booming the contractor is more than likely to be quite generous in wage bargaining. After all, customers are waiting at his door and they only frown when he quotes a price. He and the customer both bemoan the high prices but the customer buys and he adds on the customary profit (which sometimes is figured as a percentage of cost). Like the Business Agent, the employer may worry about the sales effect of high prices, but in periods of good business he is unlikely to do anything about them.

Although the building-trades unions represent the elite of American unionists and compose a substantial portion of the labor movement, the typical building-trades contract is negotiated with little public notice or concern because of the local nature of bargaining. Once the contractors and the unions in a locality have made their peace, the contract goes into operation and exerts practically no influence whatsoever on bargaining in other segments of the economy. Our next topic of discussion is industrial union wage bargaining.

INDUSTRIAL-UNION WAGE BARGAINING

In sharp contrast to craft unions which bargain for a single journeyman rate which includes both questions of job structure and wage levels, industrial unions are confronted with the problems of bargaining on job structures, task standards, wage levels, and the unequal *distribution* of contingent benefits among their constituency. Complex as the industrial union's wage problem is, it is simplified by the fact that the union serves only as a critic of a job structure, task standards, and wage levels originally established by management. To understand the collective bargaining problems involved, it is necessary to review the basic elements of job evaluation.

JOB EVALUATION

What is job evaluation? What are its aims? Its principles?

The principle behind job evaluation, which is acceptable to management and employee alike, could not be better phrased than in the simple slogan: Equal pay for equal work.

But work is not equal; different jobs have different worth. When jobs are unequal, they should not get equal pay. Hence the corollary: Unequal pay for unequal work *in proportion to the inequality*. The problem is to measure the inequality.

The employee gets his income from the *job*, but the enterprise gets its work—its production, or its services—from employee performance of *tasks*. A job may consist of a single task, endlessly repeated, or it may include a variety of different tasks.

The enterprise pays an employee for *doing:* for carrying out a task or a prescribed round or variety of tasks. It is irrelevant in theory whether the tasks call for physical or mental activity, even up to brainwork of the highest intellectual or creative order. The enterprise pays to *get something done*, at some point in time and space, by some person to whom the manager expects to have to pay real money. This person, then, must perform; but he must be capable of performing the kinds of tasks that make up his job—all the tasks, from the simplest to the most difficult.

That means that he must possess certain necessary *qualifications*. He is paid for what he *is* as well as what he *does*—not what he is as a person, but what he is, or has to be, in what he does as a performer on that job. Now, how does job evaluation theory define qualifications? Qualifications for satisfactory performance of a job consist either of: (1) *ability*, or (2) *aptitude*.

Ability—present ability—consists of qualifications that a person already possesses when he starts on a job. They are things he was born with, or acquired by education, training, or experience. A bizarre example of innate qualification for an element of a job came in the airframe industry during World War II. The job of bucking rivets from inside the wing of the plane required workers of small stature. Midgets came to the job with this qualification; persons of normal height and girth could not even acquire it. Examples in abundance of acquired qualifications come from those skilled crafts that can only be learned through a trade apprenticeship. Thus, if the job calls for wiring a circuit from blueprints, only a certified electrician can give acceptable performance. Only a surgeon would be allowed to remove someone's appendix; only a trained accountant assigned to audit a company's books. Present ability for jobs whose tasks require them is a finite and often scarce resource in the labor market.

Aptitude—the other kind of qualification—is the innate capacity to acquire ability, after instruction or experience. Ability is always specific, but aptitude is general. Ability may be inborn, but is generally acquired; aptitude is inborn. It remains undeveloped and plastic until given form and specific direction. Many people have it in a wide range of potentialities. These are almost infinitely present in the population, not rare or scarce in the labor market.

The scarcity factor is negligible, then, for initial hiring on jobs whose tasks require only aptitude plus on-the-job training. Ever since industry broke away from handicraft methods, the trend has been toward designing production jobs to this description. The undeveloped aptitude the worker brings to the job turns, under training and experience, into present ability *for that job*. Developing this ability has cost the enterprise time and money for training, and slow or substandard work during the learning process. It would cost no less to train and develop another worker.

The labor market for potential candidates for that job now consists of a sea of undifferentiated aptitude, plus only that person or those people who have acquired present ability. Present ability on a semiskilled job may be slight as compared with that of the skilled craftsman, the graduate engineer, or the research physicist, but *for that job* it is greater than anyone else's. It sets the possessor off from his competition; gives him comparative scarcity value. His services are worth more than theirs; but not too much more, for the enterprise could always train a replacement—at a cost.

The wage bargain thus consists of three elements: (1) the worker characteristics (e.g., skill, knowledge, strength, etc.) required to perform the assigned task, (2) the amount of work done by the worker, and (3) the amount of compensation exchanged for the type of work and the amount of work performed.

Union Attitudes toward Job Evaluation

Union attitudes on job evaluation vary considerably. Some unions have decided on a job evaluation program jointly with management; they have analyzed jobs and written job descriptions, evaluated jobs, determined labor grades and rate ranges, all on a joint basis. These unions believe that the best way to protect the interests of their members is to know the system "inside-out" and to actively participate in the formulation and administration of the system. An outstanding example of this attitude is the United Steelworkers of America, who co-operated with management in developing a nationwide system of job evaluation for the basic steel industry. Some managements actively seek union participation in the hope of relieving employee distrust of the program. Because union participation in job evaluation may put the union in the embarassing position of arguing against a specific rate increase, some unions have allowed management to unilaterally install job evaluation, but have reserved the right to challenge the results of each step through the grievance procedure. Other unions simply reserve the right to bargain on the results of any management wage determination, regardless of how the determination is made.

The general importance placed on individual job rates by industrial unions is illustrated by the rather common contract provision making the rates on new jobs subject to the grievance procedure but *not* subject to arbitration. This means that the union retains its right to strike over rates on new jobs, even during the life of a collective bargaining agreement.

The over-all union attitude toward job evaluation might be termed healthy skepticism. For example, consider the following advice which the *AFL-CIO Collective Bargaining Report* gives its union readers:

> Development of a wage structure and determination of wage rates for each job is a fundamental area in which unions must protect members' interests through collective bargaining. This responsibility is not eased or changed where formal job evaluation is used.
>
> As long as unions morally and legally have the right to collectively bargain on wages they must subject every aspect of job evaluation to close scrutiny and question. If they are working with job evaluation, voluntarily or otherwise, they must recognize that no part of the evaluation process, either in its development or application, can be removed from the bargaining table.[8]

Before leaving the question of general union attitudes toward job evaluation, let us consider the statement of Dr. William Gomberg, a nationally renowned industrial engineer and former director of the Management Engineering Department of the International Ladies' Garment Workers' Union:

> Trade unionists agree that under no circumstances can the job evaluation plan be used as the sole determinant of the relative wage structure. In addition

[8] "Need for Bargaining on Job Evaluation Plans," *AFL-CIO Collective Bargaining Report* Vol. II (June, 1957), p. 36.

to the relative job content measured by job evaluation techniques, the following elements would have to be considered in determining the final scale:

1. Irregularity of employment.
2. Career prospects of the job—i.e., how high the promotional sequence climbs.
3. Market supply and demand for specific occupations.
4. Traditional wage relationships, as they have evolved in time.[9]

Employers' Legal Obligation to Bargain on Job Evaluation

Section 8(a)(5) of the Taft-Hartley Act makes it an unfair labor practice for an employer to refuse to bargain in good faith with a certified union about wages, hours, and working conditions. Many times the NLRB has been called upon to decide just exactly what information an employer must provide his union to fulfill this obligation. Generally speaking the NLRB and the courts have upheld union demands for access to copies of the job evaluation program itself, job descriptions and specifications, information on individual employee merit increases, and occasionally wage survey data.

Nevertheless, many unions have negotiated contract provisions spelling out their right to complete job evaluation data to avoid later discussions of individual cases where they wanted certain data.

Conditions Precedent to Installation of Job Evaluation

In instituting job evaluation, most employers begin with a policy statement that all jobs evaluated at more than the current rate will be raised to the evaluated rate and all employees receiving a current rate of more than the evaluated rate will continue to receive their current rate as long as they occupy their current jobs. Such personal rates higher than evaluated rates are usually called "red circle" rates. This type of decision is usually essential to employee acceptance of the plan. It necessarily involves an immediate increase in labor costs.

An equally important policy decision is assigning responsibility for the development of the job evaluation program. Should the personnel department be assigned sole responsibility for the program? What use should be made of outside consultants? Should employees whose jobs are being evaluated participate in the evaluation process? What role will the union play in establishing the plan? If management is primarily interested in "scientific precision," the decision will probably be to assign all responsibility to the personnel department or outside consultants. If, on the other hand, management is primarily concerned with employee acceptance of the plan, provision will usually be made for employee and/or union participation in establishing the plan. Under any arrangement, the employees and the union ultimately must be convinced of the desirability of the program.

Gathering Job Facts

In establishing a job evaluation program, the first step is to gather detailed information on what employees are doing. This information may be obtained by three different methods: questionnaires, interviews, and observation of employee performance. In most cases, the best method of obtaining job facts is a combination of interviews with employees and their supervisors and observation of employee performance. Persons assigned to gather job facts receive special training for their assignment. The job analysts attempt to answer the following important questions:

1. *What* does the worker do? What particular skills are required to do it?
2. *How* does the worker do it? With what tools, within what tolerances, on what materials, with what supervision, at what speed?
3. *Where* does the worker do it? Under what working conditions?
4. *Why* does the worker do it? Is it necessary?
5. *When* does the worker do it? Where does the worker fit into the flow of work?

These questions look deceptively easy to answer. Some authorities argue that it takes as long as six months to train a person to reasonable proficiency as a job analyst. Job analysts must be able to recognize small differences in the content of different jobs. Equally important, they must be able to recognize when different titles or rates of pay are concealing the essential identity of two or more jobs. One of the early tasks of the job analyst is combining identical jobs under a single title or identification.

When the analyst has gathered his job facts through questionnaires, interviews, or observation, he prepares a job description. The job description is a detailed and precise statement of the content of the job. Figures 10–2 and 10–3 are job descriptions for a tool maker and a die maker. We shall return to these illustrations later.

Job Pricing for Internal Consistency: Choosing a System of Job Evaluation

A major goal of job evaluation is internal wage consistency. That is, more difficult jobs will receive higher wage rates than less difficult jobs within the employing unit.

After job facts are gathered, the next step is choosing a system of job evaluation. There are four different systems of job evaluation: ranking, job classification, point, and factor comparison. Any specific firm might adopt one of these systems or a hybrid combination of several of them.

Any one of these four systems should give internally consistent wage rates. The accuracy of the results in using any one of these systems

FIGURE 10-2

NO. 1445—TOOL MAKER

Construct and repair all types of tools, dies, jigs, fixtures, and gauges. Lay out the work and determine the sequence of operations and the kind of materials and the tools best suited to the job at hand. May work without benefit of detailed design and specifications and with only limited instruction. Requires the ability to operate all types of tool room machine tools and to perform all types of bench, fitting, and assembly work and to deal with fine tolerances.

This classification applies particularly to tool makers who specialize in bench and assembly work. Tool room machine operators, who specialize in the operation of one or several machines to machine parts required by tool makers, are classified No. 987—Machine Operator—Tool, Die and Maintenance; No. 775—Grinder—Tool Room; or No. 150—Boring Mill.

See also Classification No. 435, Die Maker.

FIGURE 10-3

NO. 435—DIE MAKER

Make, tryout, and rework all types of dies used in the manufacture of sheet metal parts and in metal forming and trimming operations other than forging.

Lay out work and determine sequence of operations and the materials and tools best suited to the job at hand. May work without benefit of detailed design and specifications and with only limited instructions. Requires the ability to operate all types of tool-and-die room machine tools and to perform all types of bench, fitting, and assembly work and to deal with fine tolerances.

This classification applies to die makers who ordinarily specialize in bench and development work including multistation, progressive, and deep drawing dies. Diemaking may be classified under No. 1445, Toolmaker, in small and unspecialized tool-and-die rooms. May be assisted by a Laborer-Tool & Die, Classification No. 938.

See also the following related or specialized classifications:
No. 150 . . . . . Boring Mill
No. 440 . . . . . Die Maker—Trim & Forge
No. 450 . . . . . Die Sinker
No. 775 . . . . . Grinder—Tool Room
No. 930 . . . . . Keller Machine Operator
No. 987 . . . . . Machine Operator—Tool, Die & Maintenance
No. 1203 . . . . Repairman—Die
No. 1445 . . . . Tool Maker
No. 1526 . . . . Welder—Tool & Die

depends upon the care with which it is utilized and the sound judgment that goes into its establishment.

Ranking. Ranking is the simplest method of job evaluation. The person evaluating jobs merely arranges them from most important and difficult to least important and difficult. The ranking system guarantees that wages are higher for more difficult and important jobs. To this extent, it is superior to highly informal systems of paying each job whatever it appears to be worth with no comparison to other jobs. However, ranking does not tell us *how much* more important a tool-and-die maker is than a janitor. The simplicity of the ranking system commends it to situations involving few jobs that are well known to the evaluators.

Job Classification. Job classification consists of grouping jobs of comparable content and difficulty into "classifications." Classifications are then compared and ranked. Rates are assigned to each classification on the basis of the importance and difficulty of the jobs in the classification. The classification system is a refinement of the ranking system. It further rationalizes the rate structure, but is less complex and, therefore, *possibly* less accurate than the point and factor comparison systems.

Point System. The point system is the most widely used formal system of job evaluation. In the point system, a number of "compensable factors" are clearly defined. For example, in the National Metal Trades Association point system there are 11 compensable factors: Education, Experience, Initiative and Ingenuity, Physical Demand, Mental or Visual Demand, Responsibility for Equipment or Process, Responsibility for Safety of Others, Responsibility for Material or Product, Responsibility for Work of Others, Working Conditions, and Unavoidable Hazards. After the factors are selected and defined they are broken down into smaller units called degrees. For example, in the NMTA system, Responsibility for the Work of Others is broken down into five degrees. The low, medium, and highest degrees are defined as follows: First degree—responsible only for own work; Third degree—responsible for instructing, directing, or setting up for a small group of employees usually in the same occupation, up to 10 persons; Fifth degree—responsible for instructing, directing, and maintaining the flow of work in a group of over 25 persons. After degreeing the factors, it is necessary to weight the factors and the degrees. This is a process of assigning a number of points to each factor and degree which represents its relative value to the company. In NMTA, for example, "Experience" is weighted as a maximum of 110 points, while "Education" gets a maximum of 70, and "Unavoidable Hazards" gets a maximum of 25.

The variety of factors, degrees, and weights that can be used in a point system is almost infinite. For this reason, many managements and unions prefer to establish a job evaluation program that is "tailor-made" to the needs of their particular business. For an idea of the variety of point systems, a tailor-made plan which has worked to the satisfaction of one management and union is shown in Figure 10–4. In the basic steel industry, management and the United Steelworkers have co-operated in establishing a form of job evaluation which is used nationally.

Union interest in the factors used in job evaluation programs has been intensified by automation. As new processes dilute "Experience" and

FIGURE 10–4

DIGEST OF A "TAILOR-MADE" JOB EVALUATION SYSTEM

Factor	Minimum Points for First Degree	Maximum Points for Sixth Degree
Work of others............	0	90
Complexity...............	6	90
Physical skill..............	1	30
Experience................	0	30
Education................	0	20
Physical effort............	1	20
Errors...................	0	25
Hazards..................	1	30
Working conditions........	0	15
Outside contacts..........	0	40
Inside contacts............	0	15
Safety of others..........	1	35
Funds or property.........	0	10
Supervision received.......	0	20

'Physical Demand," union leaders have argued that greater weight should be given to such factors as "Responsibility for Equipment," "Responsibility for Material and Product," and "Visual Effort."

The final step in establishing a point system is evaluating jobs. Jobs are evaluated by comparing job descriptions and specifications to the "yardsticks" which have been incorporated in the job evaluation manual. Each job is evaluated at the total of the points it is assigned for each factor.

Relative job worth now appears as points on a scale. This is the *job structure*, graphically represented, after formal evaluation. Once it has been determined with maximum possible accuracy, it is customary to simplify it, for convenience in administration, by grouping the jobs into *labor grades* or classifications. It is now possible to assign a money rate, or *rate range* corresponding to each labor grade. This chapter treats the money rate as an unknown, x; but whatever the actual value of x, a line or curve expressing the relationship between points in the job structure and rates of pay keeps them always in accord with the principle: unequal pay for unequal work in proportion to the inequality. Figure 10–5 shows this in graphic form.

Factor Comparison.   Under the factor comparison system, the first step is the selection of a number of "key" jobs. Key jobs are selected from the complete range of jobs. Each key job must be a job which it is

FIGURE 10–5

JOB STRUCTURE, LABOR GRADES, RATE RANGES

In this diagram, the points on the horizontal axis represent evaluated job worth. The jobs have been classified into Labor Grades (LG). The rate ranges (RR) for each classification appear on the vertical axis. Note that RR I, II, and III overlap. That means that the highest paid (perhaps most senior) individual on a job in LG I, for instance, might receive more pay than a beginner on a LG II job. RR IV, V, and VI are contiguous. RR VII and VIII are discrete. Rarely would an enterprise show a pattern quite like this; it is intended to show all possible variations. Labor Grades never overlap; a job falls in one LG or another—never in between.

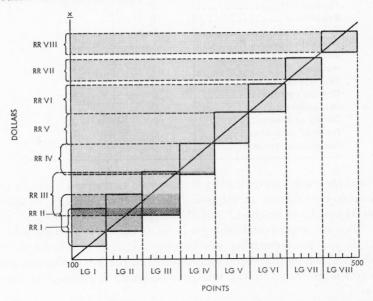

believed is receiving the *right* wage rate now. Each key job is broken down into a number of factors (similar to the factors in a point system) and the money paid for the job is allocated among the various factors. All other jobs are compared to the key jobs on the basis of the factors and rates are imputed to these jobs from the factor comparison with the key jobs.

Paying the Individual Worker

In our discussion so far we have dealt with the question of the worth of the job. However, individual employees may show substantially different results on the same job. These different results present two problems in compensation: (1) in-grade progression and (2) incentive wage rates. Related to these two problems is the problem of promotional opportunities which some employees consider to be part of their wage. Incentive wage rates will be discussed later in this chapter when we discuss the quantity aspect of the wage bargain.

In-grade wage progression is a method of paying different rates to workers performing the same duties under a system of hourly wage payment. It is common practice to recognize differences in individual worker contribution in the form of a rate range on a single job. The rate range should be established so as to reflect the amount of possible variation in worker contribution. This means that a rate range wide enough to compensate for the learning time on the job is desirable on all jobs. A wider range is desirable only to the extent that further variations in employee performance are sought and are measurable. Rate ranges may be expressed in cents-per-hour or as a percentage above and below the structure rate. Logic would dictate that rate ranges on different jobs might be different to compensate for differences in learning time and individual performance. Very wide rate ranges on executive positions are common. Such ranges are merely acknowledgment of the fact that very often the man makes the job.

Industrial unions representing production and maintenance workers frequently negotiate a rate range of from 10 cents to 20 cents per hour. This relatively "narrow" range is due to the short learning time on most factory jobs and reasonably small variations in individual employee performance.

On the other hand, craft unions representing skilled workers negotiate a deeply graduated wage scale for apprentices because of the long training time involved. For example, carpenters usually serve a four-year apprenticeship. During the first eight months of apprenticeship, the learner might receive 60 per cent of the journeyman rate. Not until the forty-fourth through forty-eighth month of apprenticeship would he be entitled to 90 per cent of the journeyman rate. After apprenticeship, all carpenters receive the full journeyman rate. This rate is a *minimum* rate. If the employer wishes to retain the services of a particularly skilled or reliable carpenter, the union imposes no protest against the payment of higher rate to this individual. In periods of labor shortage like 1940–57, many skilled tradesmen were employed at rates higher than the union-negotiated minimum. However, the union does not negotiate any "range" above its standard minimum "journeyman rate." This single minimum journeyman rate probably reflects a certain uniformity in the quantity of output by skilled craftsmen.

Factory in-grade progression can be accomplished by three different methods: (1) automatic, (2) merit, or (3) combinations of merit and automatic.

Automatic Progression. Automatic progression means that a worker moves from the minimum rate to the maximum rate solely on the basis of continued service on a specific job. A twenty-cent per hour range might be allocated as follows: five cents after the 90-day probationary period, five cents after six months, five cents after one year, and the last five cents after two years.

Automatic progression is particularly suited to situations where the individual worker has little control over his contribution to the product. Where a worker has *no* control over his contribution, the only range that could be logically defended is a training rate. Nevertheless, it is not uncommon to provide wider ranges as a means of rewarding continuity of service.

Unions tend to favor automatic progression because it eliminates any opportunity for favoritism on the part of management.

Merit Progression. Merit progression is based on the assumption that the individual employee has substantial control over the contribution of his job to the product. By carefully reviewing the individual's performance on the job, management distributes wage increases to individual workers. The rate range should be wide enough to compensate for variations in individual performance.

Merit progression poses several significant problems for managements and unions which work with it:

1. Exactly what attributes of individual performance should be considered in granting merit increases? Attendance? Quality of production? Quantity of production? Housekeeping? Material wastage? Machine maintenance? Attitude? Longevity?
2. How can these attributes be measured *objectively?* If merit increases in reality are nothing more than plums to be thrown to the foreman's favorites, neither management nor the union benefits from their use.
3. A merit increase once granted becomes permanent, either by the terms of the collective bargaining agreement or as a practical method of doing business. A merit increase can be removed only in the most flagrant cases of unsatisfactory performance.

Combinations of Merit and Automatic Progression. The most common method of in-grade progression is a combination of automatic and merit progression. Thus, it might be decided that progression should be automatic to the mid-point of the rate range and on a merit basis above the mid-point. This compromise method overcomes some of the disadvantages of both types of progression. However, it seems most likely that after a very long time on the job, management would find it virtually impossible to refuse a "merit" increase to most employees regardless of merit.

Our discussion thus far has centered on the differences in job content. Now we direct our attention to the question of how much work is exchanged for a particular wage rate. This problem involves production standards, and incentive wage rates which may be formulated through time study or custom and common sense.

THE QUANTITY OF WORK: TASK STANDARDS

Thus far in our discussion we have assumed that the method of wage payment was time. Pay by the hour, day, week, month, or year is far more common in the United States than production pay (by the piece, value of sales, or time or material saved). Time wages and production wages are each uniquely suited to certain kinds of business operations. However, two managements in the same line of business may have radically different views as to the desirability of production wages. Also unions are split on their attitude toward incentive wages.

Time wages are particularly suited to situations where:

1. The tempo of production is not under the control of the operator.
2. Quality considerations far outweigh quantity considerations in production.
3. Management is unable to schedule production so that the operators receive a steady flow of available work.
4. Operators perform a wide variety of short-cycle operations instead of repetitive uniform tasks.

Aside from these organizational considerations, time wages offer certain advantages. Time wages are easy and inexpensive to compute. The insistence of some unions on time wages can be attributed to a feeling that they are fair because they are equal. In other cases, management has abandoned production wages when the particular incentive system failed to provide the expected reductions in unit labor costs. In the case of white-collar workers, salaries (which are nothing more than long-term time wages) represent important status symbols. The rationale might go something like this: "Because I can be trusted to make my own work, management doesn't need to pay me on the basis of the number of units of work that I finish." Another white-collar argument goes like this: "My work is so varied and complex that it is impossible to accurately measure the true value of my contribution to the company."

Production Standards

It should be noted that time wages are always accompanied by some form of quantity of labor consideration.

Production standards for skilled craftsmen working under a craft union collective bargaining agreement are established during the apprenticeship period and through written and unwritten union rules. These standards plus a uniform hourly rate give employers of union craftsmen roughly equal unit labor costs.

In assembly line production, the speed of the line establishes the rate of production. Workers who don't finish their assigned tasks as the line moves along are subject to disciplinary action. A typical collective bargaining agreement on production standards is a clause like the following:

The right of the Company to establish and enforce production standards is recognized. Such production standards shall be fair and equitable and shall be set on the basis of normal working conditions, the quality of workmanship, and the normal working capacities of normal experienced operators, with due consideration to fatigue and the need for 'personal' time.

Such a clause is usually accompanied by a provision making producton standards subject to the grievance procedure. Because of the importance of production standards, some unions insist that they are not subject to arbitration. Failing to reach a satisfactory settlement with management, the union reserves its right to strike over this critical issue during the life of a contract. Management's vital interest in production standards is illustrated by the great reluctance of management to bargain over them in the past.

There have been a number of instances when unions have made exceptionally good bargains with management on production standards under the threat of a strike at a crucial time such as model changeover time in the automobile industry.

Time Study

Time study is a method of determining the time which should be allowed for a worker to perform a defined task according to a specific method and under prescribed conditions. Time studies are usually made by timing workers with a stop watch while they are doing the task. This time is then adjusted for such factors as delays, fatigue, personal needs, and incentive factors. The task or time standard thus derived may be expressed in terms of units per hour, standard hours per 100 units, or time per unit. If an incentive wage plan is used, the standard may also be expressed in monetary terms, such as one cent per piece produced.

Since most time studies are taken of an individual worker or a small group of workers, disagreements over time studies are usually expressed as grievances on specific task standards at the Local union level.

While International unions can provide expert assistance to their Locals, the investigation and processing of time-study disputes remain primarily a local problem. A recent *AFL-CIO Collective Bargaining Report* outlined various Local union approaches to time study as follows:

1. Some locals prevent the use of time study altogether.
2. Some locals allow management to use any method of setting job standards it desires, but the locals reserve the right to bargain on the results.
3. Some locals participate directly with management in making time studies and in setting standards.
4. A majority of locals allow management to make time studies but insist on bargaining on both the methods and their applications.[10]

[10] "Time Study," *AFL-CIO Collective Bargaining Report*, Vol. II (September, 1957), p. 50.

FIGURE 10–6

UNION HANDLING OF TIME STUDY GRIEVANCES

Time study grievances should be handled the same as any other grievances. The most important factor is that of getting the facts.

While some knowledge of time study is helpful, it is not necessary for the shop steward or other union representative to be a time study man in order to process a time study grievance.

The union representative should:

(1) Secure a copy of the company's record of the operation in dispute.

(2) Make certain that the record of job conditions and the job descriptions is complete. If either is incomplete, it will be impossible to reproduce the job as it was when the time study was made and therefore the company's time study cannot be checked. *This alone is grounds for rejecting the study.*

(3) If the time study sheet does contain sufficient information as to how and under what conditions the job was being performed when the time study was made, then it is necessary to determine whether the job is still being performed in exactly the same way now.

Check to see if there has been any change in machines, materials, tools, equipment, tolerances, job layout, etc. Any change should be checked to see if it affects the ability of the operator to produce at the same rate as that achieved during the time study.

(4) Usually the total operation or job cycle is broken down for timing purposes into parts which are called elements.

Check the elemental breakdown of the job on the time study sheet. See that the beginning and ending point of each element is clearly defined. *If it is not, any attempt to measure elements and give them a time value was pure guesswork.*

(5) Check the descriptions of each element to see if they describe what the operator is presently required to do. *Any change invalidates the original study.*

(6) Make sure that everything the operator is required to do as part of the job has been recorded and timed on the time study sheet. Watch for tasks which are not part of every cycle.

Such things as getting stock, adjusting machines, changing tools, reading blueprints, and waiting for materials are examples of items most frequently missed.

(7) Check for "strike-outs." A time study finding is based on a number of different timings on the same job. The time study man may discard some of his timings as "abnormal."

If the time study man has discarded any of his recorded times he must record his reasons for doing so. This enables the union to intelligently determine if the "strike-out" is valid. The fact that a particular time is larger or smaller than other times for the same element is not sufficient reason for discarding it.

(8) Determine if the time study was long enough to accurately reflect all of the variations and conditions which the operator can be expected to face during the job. Was it a proper sample of the whole job? *If not, the time study should be rejected as its results are meaningless.*

FIGURE 10–6—*Continued*

---

(9) See that only a simple average, and not the median, mode or other arithmetic device was used in calculating the elemental times. The average is the only proper method for time study purposes.

(10) Check the rating factor on the time study sheet. Try to find out if the time study man recorded his rating factor before leaving the job or after he computed the observed times. Ask the operator who was time studied if he feels the rating factor is a proper one.

Watch the worker who was timed work at the pace he considers proper and then at the pace required to produce the company's workload. *The judgment of the worker and the steward are as valid as that of the time study man.*

(11) Make sure that allowances for personal time, fatigue and delays have been provided in proper amounts.

(12) And finally check all the arithmetic for errors.

A final note:

Most union representatives have found it unwise to take additional time studies themselves as a check, except as a last resort. It is more effective to show the errors in management's study than to try to prove a new union time study is a proper one.

A time study taken even by a union is still only the result of judgment. Even when proper methods are used, they tend merely to reduce the inconsistencies of time study, not eliminate them.

SOURCE: "Union Handling of Time Study Grievances," AFL-CIO Collective Bargaining Report, Vol. 2 (September, 1957), pp. 53–54. (Italics added)

Since its introduction in the 1880's, most unions have opposed the use of stop-watch time study. Union opposition probably stems from early abuse of time study in the form of speed-ups. Today union opposition and distrust of time study can be rationalized on the basis of research findings on the scientific limits of the accuracy of time study. Industrial unions have been conspicuously unsuccessful in preventing the introduction of time study because time study is almost essential to the successful operation of a factory. Time study was deeply entrenched as a management technique in factory production long before effective industrial unions had been organized.

In recent years somewhere between one fifth and one quarter of all grievances taken to arbitration by unions have been on time study. When we also consider the number of nonarbitrable grievances on production standards, it is obvious that time study is a major issue in labor-management relations.

The reader can obtain an excellent insight of present-day union thinking on time study by reading Figure 10–6. This figure is a verbatim copy of AFL-CIO advice on the handling of time-study grievances. The entire tone of this advice is to show errors in management's study rather than to try to prove a new union time study is a proper one.

INCENTIVE WAGES

Time-study data may be used to establish incentive wage rates. However, incentive wage rates may be determined without recourse to time study. Incentive wage rates are based on the assumption that workers *can* increase their output substantially and that they *will* increase their output in exchange for higher earnings. The purpose of incentive wage rates is to reduce unit labor costs by allowing workers to earn substantially higher wages in exchange for more production than would be forthcoming under time wages.

The major types of incentive wage plans are:

1. Piecework. Employees are paid a fixed amount for each unit of production completed. (Piecework is frequently accompanied by a minimum guarantee regardless of the number of units produced.)
2. Differential Piecework. These plans follow the famous Taylor Differential Piecework System. They pay a lower piece rate for the first units of production and a higher rate for all units produced beyond a certain standard. Taylor designed this plan to attract top producers and quickly eliminate workers who do not produce at a high rate. The Taylor Differential Piecework System is very rare in present-day practice.
3. Sharing Plans. Under these plans, workers and management share in the gains and losses resulting from varying output. "Normal" production is established for a given wage. When production exceeds or falls short of the "norm," employees and management share the gains or losses on some predetermined basis. *Diminishing* piece rate systems of this type are more common in American industry than the Taylor *increasing* piece rate system.

Time wages are more commonly paid in the United States than are incentive wages. This is primarily due to the organizational, psychological, and engineering difficulties in the effective operation of an incentive system of wage payment. These factors are reinforced by a rather general union opposition to incentive wage plans.

Incentive wage plans are suitable to operations where:

1. Output is controlled by the operator (or group of operators).
2. Output is measurable.
3. Quality considerations are secondary to quantity considerations *or* quality is subject to the direct control of the operator.
4. Production scheduling makes a steady flow of work available to incentive workers.
5. Changes in operations to be performed are relatively infrequent.

In addition to these organizational considerations, it is important that the incentive rates be established in such a way as to win the support of employees. It seems that the major factor in the almost universal practice of restriction of output is a deep-seated fear that rates will be cut when production exceeds a certain level.

For a successful incentive plan to exist under collective bargaining, it must satisfy the needs of the three parties to the agreement: the employer, the employees, and the union.

From the employer's viewpoint the sole requirement for a successful incentive plan is unit labor costs lower than those existing in his competitors' plants or those existing in his plant before the plan was installed.

The employee has more varied requirements for a satisfactory incentive plan. Just earning more money isn't enough. In addition, the plan must be simple enough for the employees to understand it. There must be genuine confidence in management's customary pledge that rates will not be cut because earnings exceed a certain level. The firm's sales picture must be good enough that increased production does not result in substantial layoffs. Most difficult to define, but probably most important, the employees must feel that the plan is "their" plan and that they actively participate in its establishment and operation.

Some unions oppose incentive wages as a matter of International union policy. This position could be traced to several origins. Incentive plans might frustrate a union desire to establish some kind of competitive equality between employers in the industry. Any reduction in actual employment or employment opportunities resulting from higher man-hour production reduces the union's membership base. Incentive plans which cause workers to compete among themselves may weaken union solidarity. The complexity of various incentive plans makes it difficult for Local union negotiating committees to conform to a single "industry practice."

On the other hand, incentive wage rates are used by some unions as a major stabilizing factor in the industry. The International Ladies' Garment Workers' Union, the Amalgamated Clothing Workers of America, and the Textile Workers Union of America each take an active part in the establishment of incentive wage systems in their industries.

Most collective bargaining agreements provide "safeguard" clauses against management abuse of incentive wage systems. The more common of these clauses include: minimum earnings guarantees; guarantees against rate-cutting; negotiation and arbitration or the right to strike on the rates for new jobs; and, occasionally, work-sharing arrangements.

The wage bargain thus consists of three parts: the quality of the labor sold, the quantity of labor sold, and the price of labor sold. Job evaluation is used to compare the quality of labor sold by various operators on diverse jobs. Production standards or incentive wage rates (frequently determined through the technique of time study) determine the quantity of labor delivered by each operator. The price at which labor is sold is a wage rate *plus* a series of wage supplements (e.g., vacations with pay, overtime premiums, pensions, unemployment benefits, etc.). These wage supplements constitute an important part of the wage bargain and impose a heavy cost burden on management. However, we shall consider these elements of the wage bargain (which frequently are not directly related to the quality or quantity of labor sold) in our discussion of worker insurance and income-continuity programs in Chapter 11.

SPECIAL COLLECTIVE BARGAINING PROBLEMS ON WAGE STRUCTURE

Job evaluation, production standards, and, to a lesser degree, incentive wages are integral parts of the operation of a factory. The most militant union cannot realistically expect to turn back the clock by eliminating these basic tools of industrial management. Because of the vitality of these techniques and their impact on employee welfare, issues related to them are a permanent part of the collective bargaining process. Future bargaining on these issues may take any number of possible directions. We shall briefly discuss four illustrations of possible future trends: (1) guaranteeing personal rates against job restudy, (2) wage structures as a cause of internal industrial union stresses, (3) automation and wage structures, and (4) job enlargement.

Job Restudy

The problem of job restudy can be a major problem to a union. The chief union negotiator for a firm confronted with an adverse industry outlook sees the problem like this: "We are opposed to the job evaluation system in principle, but we are living with it. . . . In good times there's no pressure for job re-evaluation because the labor market in our industry is too tight. . . . In a slack period like this, if the company brings its job evaluation system to bear in a plant where technological changes have gone ahead faster than re-evaluation of jobs, wage rates could be cut drastically." The union answer to this problem was to concentrate on the company's job evaluation program instead of pressing wage increase demands in negotiations. The union's demand was that all workers on specific jobs for six months prior to negotiations be "red-circled" and their rates be unchanged even if the job were downgraded after evaluation. The union also sought to protect certain job rates by urging greater emphasis on certain factors in the job evaluation system.[11]

Industrial Union Internal Stresses

The wage structure problem is almost exclusively the problem of the factory-type employer and the industrial union. One of the major problems of job evaluation is fitting the comparatively small number of skilled jobs into a wage structure which is dominated by the many semiskills of the factory. Skilled workers in a factory are usually represented by an industrial union in which they are only a small political minority. Because

[11] "UAW Pratt & Whitney Local Seeks Wage Stability Instead of Boosts," *Wall Street Journal* (Chicago Ed.), Thursday, October 10, 1957, p. 24.

of the need for the militant support of the vast majority of the membership, industrial unions tend to negotiate across-the-board wage increases which reduce the skilled-unskilled wage differential. Many of the wage supplements initiated by industrial union bargaining also tend to reduce or conceal the skilled-unskilled wage differential.

The skilled worker in the factory may have a different type of employment relationship than his counterpart represented by a craft union. Factory employment is not subject to some of the severe seasonal fluctuations in such "craft-union industries" as building construction. The factory employer tends to retain his skilled craftsmen as long as economically feasible in adverse business conditions because of the difficulty of replacing them in periods of business upturn. Many skilled factory workers have acquired their skills at their employer's expense in specialized training programs.

Nevertheless, the wage scales negotiated by craft unions look quite attractive to the skilled factory worker. Also, in periods of booming business activity, most factory skilled workers could find other jobs at higher rates of pay, in job shops or elsewhere. Thus market pressures exert powerful influences on the factory wage structure. Skilled factory workers become restless and begin to believe that they are the "forgotten men" of the industrial unions. They talk about secession from their union and pose a very serious problem for the union leadership.

Wildcat strikes of skilled tradesmen belonging to the UAW plagued the automobile industry for several weeks in 1955 and delayed the ratification of the UAW agreements with General Motors, Ford, and Chrysler. This dissension plus the formation of a dual union, the Society of Skilled Trades, resulted in the UAW giving skilled workers a greater degree of representation in bargaining than they had possessed previously. Exactly how this situation will work out is a matter for speculation only. However, it is quite certain that the problem of compensation for skilled workers will plague both employers and industrial unions for some years to come.

Automation and Job Evaluation

The exact impact of automation on job assignments in different plants is impossible to predict. However, in almost all cases, automation results in very large increases in man-hour productivity, a greater emphasis on rapid machine maintenance, and a reduction of the physical exertion and an improvement in physical working conditions. Such radical changes undoubtedly will change much of our conventional thinking about job evaluation.

Two trends are already discernible. First, unions are advocating greater emphasis on certain "compensable factors" or the introduction of entirely new factors. In an attempt to justify substantially higher rates for automated jobs such factors as "monotony," "visual effort," and a myriad of others are cropping up in negotiation sessions. It seems likely that these or other factors will be recognized by management as a moderate cost for union acceptance of radical new production methods. Second, several cases of negotiation on automated jobs have resulted in a radical reduction in the number of different jobs and job rates. In one case, several hundred different jobs were eliminated for two new jobs: "Automation Tender" and "Automation Equipment Maintenance Technician." This bargain meant very substantial wage increases for all of the workers in the automated plant. From management's viewpoint, such a bargain provided for maximum flexibility in the assignment of workers in the plant.

Job Enlargement

Industrial managers for many years have believed that maximum output could be achieved at minimum cost by breaking jobs down into the smallest possible tasks. Recent experience, expecially during and since World War II, has radically changed this traditional thinking. "Job enlargement," i.e., the combination of several tasks for a single worker, is receiving increasing attention. This new trend is supported by two factors: (1) extreme job simplification actually reduces total output because of monotony and (2) the need for varied skills in certain maintenance jobs. In the case of maintenance work, "down time" on machinery can be extremely costly and waiting for a skilled worker in a particular classification can prevent other maintenance workers from finishing their part of the repair work. Whichever motivating factor is present, job enlargement changes job content (almost always in the direction of increased complexity) and necessitates re-evaluation of the job. When two jobs are combined, should the rate for the new job be equal to the rate of the more complex element? or an average of the two elements? or even higher than the sum of the two elements?

COLLECTIVE BARGAINING ON WAGE LEVELS

Whether confronted by no union, a craft union, or an industrial union, employers always face the problem of establishing a wage level. The wage level is a variable. It fluctuates slowly over time and is not the same in different places or enterprises, whether measured in money or in real wages. Under collective bargaining, the money wage level becomes a major consideration in the negotiation of initial agreements and the renegotiation of agreements in effect.

Job Pricing for External Consistency

Unions and management are pretty much in agreement that wage rates should be externally consistent. The disagreement arises on defining comparable jobs and the area (labor market versus "industry" or product market) of comparability. For management, "consistency" need not mean "equality." A particular firm may decide to pay consistently more, the same, or less than area rates or industry rates. Most profitable firms probably have a policy close to "consistency through equality" or even a bit better than this as a means of attracting and keeping competent employees.

Purpose of External Consistency. Depending upon the particular situation, managements and unions may favor consistency in the labor market or consistency in the product market. In highly competitive industries where labor costs are an important part of total costs, management cannot afford consistency in the labor market if this is more costly than consistency in the product market. A management in the same industry would favor consistency in the labor market if this policy were less costly than consistency in the product market. Labor-market consistency is sound because employers always recruit the bulk of their labor force locally and thus compete locally *for employees*. Product-market or industry consistency is equally sound because the employers' success in product-market competition for sales is at least in part determined by price which may be influenced by labor costs. Like management, unions tend to be opportunistic in their external wage consistency arguments. Unions tend to emphasize "consistency upward" in the product market because one of their major goals is to remove wages from competition. A building-trades union accomplishes this goal when it negotiates a local master agreement with the contractors. In this case, the labor market and the product market are both local. The typical industrial union is confronted with a more complex problem because of the many variations in job content between employers and geographically dispersed product markets.

Does external consistency mean that all jobs will receive a rate consistent with the same jobs elsewhere? It does not. If it did, job evaluation for internal consistency would be meaningless. External consistency in practice means that for certain jobs which are hard to fill, management may give special consideration to market forces in determining the rate of pay. Or it may mean that a management rather frequently compares its rates on several jobs with the going rates for these jobs in the labor market or industry. In discussing the problems of determining what going rates are, we shall see that complete consistency is unattainable. For this reason, external consistency in job evaluation is at best a rather rough approximation for *some* of the jobs in the plant.

Sources of Data for External Wage Consistency. Wage comparisons between employers have a long history. However, the policies of the National War Labor Board in the 1940's probably provided a major impetus to systematic wage comparisons between firms. Since World War II wage data have consistently improved in quantity and quality.

The major sources of wage rate information on individual jobs may be classified as follows:

1. Governmental wage surveys.
2. Employer association wage surveys.
3 Union wage surveys.
4. Individual company wage surveys.

We shall discuss each of these sources before discussing the problems of interpreting what limited data are available.

Governmental Wage Surveys. The Bureau of Labor Statistics gathers wage rates in two important series: Occupational Wage Surveys and the annual Union Wages and Hours surveys. In discussing wage structure problems, we are interested only in wage *rates.* Valuable as detailed *earnings* statistics may be for other purposes, they are irrelevant to questions of wage structure.

Occupational wage surveys are conducted regularly in a number of important industrial centers. In each area, data are obtained by personal visits of BLS field agents to representative firms within six broad industry divisions: manufacturing; transportation (excluding railroads); communication and other utilities; wholesale trade; retail trade; finance, insurance, and real estate; and services. Only firms employing 51 or more workers are surveyed. These surveys are conducted on a sample basis. A greater proportion of large than small establishments is studied. However, all establishments are given their appropriate weight in combining the data.

The occupations selected for study are common to a variety of manufacturing and nonmanufacturing industries. Occupational classification is based on a uniform set of job descriptions designed to take account of interestablishment variation in duties within the same job. A BLS Occupational Wage Survey job description for a tool-and-die maker is presented in Figure 10–7. Factory jobs surveyed are frequently limited to those in maintenance and power plant and custodial and material movement occupations.

Rate data exclude premium pay for overtime and for work on week ends, holidays, and late shifts. Nonproduction bonuses are excluded also, but cost-of-living bonuses and incentive earnings are included. Information is presented also on selected establishment practices and supplementary benefits as they relate to office and plant workers.

Several characteristics of Occupational Wage Surveys limit their usefulness for achieving external wage consistency:

1. They are conducted only in major industrial centers.
2. Surveys are conducted in specific areas only infrequently, e.g., every five years.
3. Frequently the group of jobs studies is small compared to the number of jobs in any particular firm.

We shall discuss the problem of job comparability as it applies to Occupational Wage Surveys later.

FIGURE 10–7
JOB DESCRIPTION FROM BLS OCCUPATIONAL WAGE SURVEY

TOOL-AND-DIE MAKER

(Diemaker; Jig Maker; Toolmaker; Fixture Maker; Gauge Maker)

Constructs and repairs machine-shop tools, gauges, jigs, fixtures or dies for forgings, punching, and other metal-forming work. Work involves *most of the following:* planning and laying out of work from models, blueprints, drawings, or other oral and written specifications; using a variety of tool-and-die maker's handtools and precision measuring instruments; understanding of the working properties of common metals and alloys; setting up and operating of machine tools and related equipment; making necessary shop computations relating to dimensions of work, speeds, feeds, and tooling of machines; heat-treating of metal parts during fabrication as well as of finished tools and dies to achieve required qualities; working to close tolerances; fitting and assembling of parts to prescribed tolerances and allowances; selecting appropriate materials, tools, and processes. In general, the tool-and-die maker's work requires a rounded training in machine-shop and toolroom practice usually acquired through a formal apprenticeship or equivalent training and experience.

For cross-industry wage study purposes, tool-and-die makers in tool-and-die jobbing shops are excluded from this classification.

BLS conducts annual surveys of wage rates and scheduled hours of work for specified crafts or jobs as provided in labor-management agreements in four industries: building construction, printing, local transit, and local trucking. The studies present the wage rates in effect as of July 1 of each year as reported to the Bureau by the appropriate labor organizations in each of the cities.

Union scales are defined as the minimum wage scales or maximum schedules of hours. Rates in excess of the negotiated minimum are not included.

These surveys have the important advantage of frequency. For negotiations in noncovered industries, the rates on particular jobs might give a rough indication of the "going" rate in industries competing for the same skills. These surveys also provide bases for comparison between surveyed cities. The careful selection of a surveyed city might provide a rough guide for wage determination in nonsurveyed communities.

Employers' Associations. Employers' associations collect and distribute to their members vast quantities of wage-rate data. In 1952, Professors N. Arnold Tolles and Robert L. Raimon published the first general guide to nongovernmental wage surveys.[12] Tolles and Raimon present digests of surveys conducted by 120 associations, with 60,000 employer

---

[12] N. Arnold Tolles and Robert L. Raimon, *Sources of Wage Information: Employer Associations,* Cornell Studies in Industrial and Labor Relations, Vol. III (Ithaca, N.Y.: Cornell University, 1952), xvi.

FIGURE 10-8

NUMBERS OF ASSOCIATIONS KNOWN
TO CONDUCT WAGE SURVEYS,
BY INDUSTRY OR BY AREA ORIENTATION

Association	Number
Industry-oriented associations	105
Food and kindred products	7
Textile mill products	6
Lumber, wood, furniture, fixtures	13
Paper and allied products	5
Chemicals and allied products	6
Products of petroleum and coal	2
Leather and leather products	3
Stone, clay, and glass products	7
Primary metal industries	7
Fabricated metal products	8
Machinery, electrical products	13
Miscellaneous manufacturing	2
Transportation	4
Trade: wholesale and retail	7
Finance, insurance, and real estate	3
Medical and health services	4
Miscellaneous nonmanufacturing	3
Area-oriented associations	61
Area employer associations	36
Chambers of commerce	25

SOURCE: N. Arnold Tolles and Robert L. Raimon, *Sources of Wage Information: Employer Associations* (Ithaca, N.Y.: Cornell University, 1952), p. 233.

members, employing 10 million workers, surveying the wages of 4 million employees. Figure 10–8 shows the wage surveying associations that they uncovered in their research. It seems to be a safe guess that the coverage of wage surveys has increased rather than decreased since they made their study.

An area-oriented survey cuts across industry lines within a local labor market. Employers seeking wage consistency in the locality need the data supplied by an area-oriented survey. Employers can conduct their own individual surveys, as some large companies do, or they may utilize the services of an employers' association. A well-managed association survey provides detailed information at minimum cost. However, well-managed association surveys cost money and are most commonly available only in metropolitan centers.

Figure 10–9 is a digest of one well-managed metropolitan wage survey. This survey covers approximately 50 per cent of the employment in the area surveyed. Wage data are collected by job description instead of job title. Rates are reported by four averages and a frequency table. This particular survey does not report on fringe benefits. We shall return to this survey in discussing the use of wage survey data.

FIGURE 10–9

DIGEST OF A METROPOLITAN WAGE SURVEY

Coverage: 129 firms; 50 per cent of local labor force; 30 industries (a cross-section of area industry).

Jobs Surveyed: 81 jobs: Some jobs broken into as many as four difficulty levels.

Pay Period Covered: March 15, 1956.

Specimen Job Data:

Tool-and-Die Maker 1 (most difficult of four levels)

Plan and construct highly intricate tools, dies, fixtures, gauges, to extremely close tolerances. Considerable development work.

Highly skilled fitting, timing, and adjusting. Construct tools where no design is available. Select allowances, devise mechanism details, e.g., multi station progressive and deep forming dies, complex indexing fixtures, subpress dies for parts of delicate outline, optical gauges.

Straight Time		Incentive	
Number firms............	23	Number firms.............	1
Number workers........	1,010	Number workers..........	2
Average rate.............	2.89	Average rate..............	3.00
Weighted average........	2.74	Weighted average........	3.00

Firms Reporting Ranges, 17; Average Minimum Rate, 2.63; Average Maximum Rate, 2.87; Firms Reporting Males Only, 24; Firms Reporting Females Only, 0; Firms Reporting Both, 0.

Frequency Table: Straight Time

Rate	Number Workers	Rate	Number Workers	Rate	Number Workers
2.56..........	30	2.76..........	576	3.00..........	17
2.57..........	18	2.77..........	29	3.03..........	3
2.61..........	42	2.79..........	18	3.06..........	4
2.66..........	67	2.84..........	6	3.11..........	1
2.68..........	1	2.85..........	1	3.15..........	2
2.69..........	2	2.86..........	13	3.18..........	1
2 71..........	142	2.88..........	6	3.21..........	2
2.73..........	7	2.90..........	5	3.47..........	1
2.74..........	4	2.92..........	3	3.80..........	1
2.75..........	8				

As shown in Figure 10–8, the industry-oriented survey is more common than the area-oriented survey. Perhaps the greater number of industry-oriented surveys is a response to the needs of employers dealing with the same union. Although no wage survey can compute comparative unit labor costs, an industry-oriented survey offers a more fruitful opportunity for speculation in this direction than does the area-oriented survey.

Union Wage Surveys. Formal wage surveys conducted by unions are not available to employers. However, unions do have access to wage rates paid in companies having contractual relations with them. These data are sometimes introduced into negotiations in a union attempt to win a particular point. Unions probably would have the most detailed wage information on competitors that would be available from any source. However, these data (like all data for collective bargaining) can be selectively edited. Thus both unions and managements are best advised to regard such data with some caution.

Individual Company Wage Surveys. Many large companies conduct their own wage surveys. Such surveys serve a particularly important function in small communities without other wage data collection agencies. Some companies prefer to conduct their own surveys because they can independently validate the data so collected. Finally a general wage survey is of limited value to a firm requiring highly specialized skills, e.g., certain oil refinery jobs, or the case of women employed by public utilities companies.

Interpreting Wage Survey Data. Wage rate data are *not* generally available. Although we have emphasized the widespread wage survey work done by employers and unions, it is important to remember that these data are always considered at least partially *confidential* and available only to co-operating firms. Only under very exceptional circumstances would an association reveal wage data for a particular firm. The governmental data are available generally, but only with adequate safeguards to the identity of the individual firm.

Job Comparability. Figures 10–2, 10–3, 10–7, and 10–9 should now be considered as a unit in attempting to resolve the problem of job comparability. Figures 10–2 and 10–3 are job descriptions for a tool maker's and a die maker's job in our hypothetical plant. Figure 10–7 is a tool-and-die maker's job description used in a BLS Occupational Wage Survey. Figure 10–9 includes the tool-and-die maker's job description used in a metropolitan wage survey. An employer confronted with this array of current wage rate information would be in an *extremely* fortunate position. He would possess much more "comparative wage data" than is usual. However, he is confronted with a serious problem because of the obvious variations in job content between these four descriptions. If this difficulty seems minor, we need only remember that each of the job descriptions surveyed has been interpreted independently by each of the respondents to the survey. Only in that extremely rare situation when employers actually assign similar duties to workers in a single job is anything approaching real job comparability achieved.

Which Rate? Cheerfully assuming that we have resolved or ignored the problem of job comparability, we proceed now to the selection of a "going rate." Referring to Figure 10–9, which "average rate" do we want to use? The "weighted average" is the rate most nearly approximating the rate received by the "average employee" on the job. However, this rate would be inflated if a majority of the employees surveyed were at the top of the respective ranges for the job. This average is also heavily weighted by the largest employers in the area surveyed. Or we might select the "average rate." In this case a firm employing one tool-and-die maker is considered just as important as a firm employing 500 tool-and-die makers. The "average minimum rate" would be the impression of opportunities that a worker seeking employment would acquire from a careful job hunt. The "modal" rate can be determined by examining the frequency table. Here again, we are giving weight to the position of workers in the rate range.

Despite all the difficulties, management must decide that one of these rates *is* the "going rate." Wage decisions are then based on this choice. To the extent that both unions and management realize the shortcomings of the data available, the ultimate decision is probably improved.

Achieving and Maintaining External Consistency. External consistency and internal consistency may be opposing concepts in some situations. For example, the engineer shortage of the early fifties can be contrasted to the fear of an engineer glut in the immediate postwar period. Has the value of an engineer doing a particular job in a particular company *changed* because of these market pressures? More practically, just what can management do to assure itself of a reasonably contented and adequate supply of workers in a shortage calling? Should internal consistency be completely abandoned?

In his study of "Wage and Salary Administration in a Changing Labor Market," Professor Preston P. LeBreton found that management was gravely concerned with the problem of maintaining both internal and external consistency. Wage and salary administrators referred to the problem as "frustrating" and "plaguing." At least eight alternative approaches ar available to management in solving the problem. As shown in Figure 10–10, management has at least flirted with each of these approaches. In passing it should be noted that several of these approaches vitally effect nonwage clauses in the collective bargaining agreement. For example, subcontracting and use of agency help would undoubtedly be confronted with substantial union opposition.

Union Goals in General Wage Adjustments Bargaining

How does a union decide that it will seek a twenty-cent package in a particular year instead of a ten-cent package or a five-cent package? What standards exist to guide the union in deciding that its *real* goal in a given year will be so much? Having decided on the amount of the package how does the union go about cutting it up into general wage increase demands, wage inequity demands, and wage supplement demands? Or does the union determine the size of the package demand by adding its minimum demands in each of these areas? Is the demand developed through careful application of economic formulas or is it merely some leader's "pipe

FIGURE 10–10

MANAGEMENT APPROACHES TO MAINTAINING AN INTERNALLY CONSISTENT WAGE STRUCTURE WHEN FACED WITH HEAVY LABOR-MARKET PRESSURE

Approach	Number of Companies Using This Approach*
Ignore market conditions and concentrate on maintaining internal consistency. Emphasize fringe benefits and other advantages rather than money rates	18
Bring new workers in at market price regardless of its relationship to company rates	17
Bring new workers in at market price unless it falls out of the established range for the job class	73
Deliberately evaluate the job higher than its objective worth	12
Eliminate the job by contracting out or distributing the work internally	6
Use outside agency help at the required rate (agency workers perform their duties on company premises)	11
Add work to job content thereby increasing its worth to the company	19
Raise the level of all wages in the company	18
Other approaches	23

* NOTE: The total of the right-hand column does not correspond to the total number of participants because some of the correspondents selected several choices.
SOURCE: Preston P. LeBreton, assisted by Thomas R. O'Donovan, *Wage and Salary Administration in a Changing Labor Market* (Detroit, Mich.: University of Detroit, March, 1957), p. 2.

dream"? What role does the rank and file of the union play in evaluating the economic soundness of the union's demand?

A union is confronted with certain economic facts of life when it formulates its demands in any given year. These facts are never simple and almost always contain important uncertainties. Very often these facts can be changed by shrewd business decisions or other developments beyond the control of either the management or the union. However, at any given time, the leadership of a union has some perceptions of the economic condition of the firms with which it bargains and all business in general. These perceptions establish some outside limits on union demands. The economic facts of life are real and certain, but they change, and they are only dimly seen by unions and managements. As bargaining continues, the union's perceptions may be reinforced or radically changed. Within these economic limits, actual demands are a reaction to political factors within the union and the labor movement or the particular preferences of the union leadership.

Economic Facts and Perceptions. The pertinent economic facts take different forms in different industries. Generally, the pertinent facts pertain to the economic position of workers, the situation of the union itself, and the economic position of the firm and/or industry with which the union deals.

Economic Facts about the Workers' Position. The worker is primarily interested in his *real* take-home wages. Real wages are the purchasing power of his money wages. The worker's take-home pay is dependent upon whether he works or is unemployed and how many hours per week he works.

The cost of living has always been a major concern to workers. Historically, money wages have tended to rise in periods of rising prices. "Escalator clauses" which provide for *changes* in wage rates which parallel *changes* in the Consumers' Price Index have been widely adopted in long-term collective bargaining agreements which followed the lead of the General Motors–UAW agreement of 1948. Although escalator clauses cover less than 25 per cent of unionized workers, national publicity is given to escalator wage adjustments. Workers and their wives are more keenly aware of cost-of-living changes now than they were in the past. Where escalators have not been negotiated, general wage adjustments have been negotiated to "catch up" (in the union's terms) or to "anticipate" (in management's terms) increases in the cost of living.

From the worker's viewpoint, his employment status is even more important than his hourly *real* wage. If he doesn't have a job, or only has a part-time job in the form of short workweeks, the family budget may be strained to the breaking point. During the general economic adjustment of 1957–58, a wit defined a "recession" as the situation when your neighbor is unemployed and a "depression" as the situation when you are unemployed. These definitions probably describe worker attitudes between industries and plants quite accurately. However, within a bargaining unit the layoff of many persons has a depressing influence on the workers who are able to keep their jobs. The observable misfortune of others presents a grim prospect of possible personal hardship. Almost any worker confronted with the *personal* and *certain* choice of lower hourly wages or no work would choose the lower hourly wages.

Economic Facts about the Union Itself. The union's ultimate weapon is the strike. The ability of the union to strike successfully depends upon much more than the size of the strike fund, but the union's financial position is certainly a major consideration in formulating its *real* demands. This is clearly indicated by the comments of a delegate to the UAW's Special Convention in January, 1958:

> I work at a GM plant and am ready to hit the bricks for our demands, and I am sure the members of Local 645 are determined to get a much better contract than they have now.
> When we do hit the bricks, we want to have money in the strike fund.

The $16 million that will be raised by this dues increase will not be sufficient to carry on a successful strike this year.

The book prepared by the financial secretary on strike assistance lists 350,000 GM workers and 200,000 auto parts workers who would be involved in a GM strike, thus taking 550,000 off the dues-paying list. This means a balance of only 650,000 dues-paying members not on strike.

The dues from 650,000 workers will not carry the GM workers who are on strike. This book on strike assistance says it will cost $80 million plus to carry on an eleven week strike at GM, and $11,400,000 a week beginning with the twelfth week. If the strike lasts as long as 16 weeks, like the last one did, the cost would be more than $136 million.

I think we should be realistic and have a strike fund that will take care of any trouble that comes up. A $25 million strike fund is too small, and any monies placed in the fund by this dues increase should stay there.

Dues should be found to increase the amount to at least $50 million. I would like to see a fund of $80 million. Then we would have the power to back up our just demands.[13]

The arithmetic would be different for other unions or for the UAW at another time or under different circumstances. For example, if the union found it necessary to strike Chrysler, Ford, and GM at the same time, the delegate's $136 million would only be a drop in the bucket. Nevertheless, this kind of economic arithmetic problem must be worked out by any union as a part of the formulation of its final demands.

Another important economic fact about the union is the question of support by other unions for its strike action. Before striking, most unions have a reasonably good idea what kind of economic support, either in money or direct action, they can expect from the union members who transport the product of the struck firm and other unionists who may be called upon to produce "farmed out" work. These two types of direct support are probably much more important than any amount of loans or gifts that can be expected from other unions in the situation.

Economic Facts about the Company and/or Industry. Economic facts about the firm and/or industry are hard for the union to come by and always subject to diverse interpretations. As a rule, management tries to conceal the significant economic facts not only from the union but also from competitors. Very often business success or failure depends upon the strategic element of surprise. To complicate matters further, the really significant economic facts are usually *expectations* of things in the future, e.g., sales forecasts, anticipated costs, and projected production plans. Even the simplest historical economic facts, such as profits, are the result of *estimates* of depreciation, inventory valuation, and the liquidation value of plants and equipment.

Evasive as these data are, they remain the truly *vital* data for the simple reason that no union can get blood out of a turnip. No matter how rich the union in strike resources or how needy the workers, the eco-

[13] *Proceedings: Special Constitutional Convention, United Automobile, Aircraft and Agricultural Implement Workers of America, January 22–24, 1958*, p. 134.

nomic health of the firm and/or industry sets the ultimate limit on union demands. Where union demands exceed this limit, it is due to union ignorance of the true situation or union misinterpretation of the limited data available. Even so, cases of this sort are hard to identify in concrete terms. A business can encounter very severe economic difficulties for reasons other than labor cost considerations. Business failures usually result from a composite of difficulties, e.g., lack of sales success, poor production planning, high labor costs, financial manipulation, failure to replace obsolete equipment, etc.

Political Factors in Union Demand Formulation. Political factors within the union or labor movement may have a major influence on either the size of the package or the contents of a package of predetermined size. We shall briefly discuss four types of political pressures on union leaders: (1) rival union gains, (2) opposition within the union, (3) the need for uniformity of treatment within the jurisdiction of the union, and (4) the strike temper of the rank and file. It should be noted that some of these factors have already been reflected in part in the leadership's consideration of the economic facts.

Rival Union Gains. Union members look to their leaders to bring home the bacon. They evaluate their leaders on the basis of how well they do this job. What is a good bargain and what is a bad bargain in the eyes of union members? About the only standard to which union members can refer is the gains of other unions in somewhat similar situations. As a result, autoworkers in 1958 expected Mr. Reuther to negotiate a wage increase of at least nine cents per hour because Steelworkers were scheduled to get this much on July 1 under the contract which they had negotiated in 1956. In the minds of many UAW members, Mr. Reuther would have failed had he negotiated no increase or an increase substantially less than nine cents per hour.

The Steelworkers' gains don't pose a threat of secession to the UAW, but they do place the burden of proof on the UAW leader who settles for substantially less. In other years, UAW gains put the burden of proof on the leadership of the Steelworkers, Electrical Workers, and other unions. The union leader who repeatedly fails to meet the expectations of his membership can not expect an indefinite tenure of office.

Rival union gains also strongly influence the contents of the package. In times of business recession, some unions tend to place greater stress on wage supplements than straight wages. In part, this may be attributed to the necessity of matching rival union gains even when wage increases are very hard to come by. For example, a very modest wage increase *plus* "sweeping improvements in pensions, S.U.B., seniority, etc. costing seven cents per hour according to union estimates" might give the impression of a great victory to the rank and file without involving any substantial and immediate increase in labor costs for the company. At some particular times, worker insurance and income-continuity benefits can be substantially liberalized with little or no cost to management. This situation sometimes enables a union leader to accept a moderate increase and to save face with rank and file by selling the great importance of the improved wage supplements. Cents-per-hour can be *easily* compared between unions by members of the rank and file; some forms of wage supplements are not so easily compared.

Opposition within the Union. The less secure the political future of the union negotiator, the more likely he is to insist on excessive wage demands. This situation is illustrated by the preference, frequently expressed by managers, for dealing with International officers rather than Local officers. The typical International officer is quite secure in office through control of appointive jobs and in the frequent practice of electing International officers by convention roll call votes. As a result, he can afford the political luxury of responsibility in dealing with employers. A Local officer who becomes too responsible also tends to become an ex-officer. Even International officers do face occasional opposition at the polls and when they are confronted with this prospect they usually become somewhat less responsible in the eyes of the managements with which they deal.

Need for Uniformity within the Jurisdiction of the Union. A union leader who negotiates substantially different wages for members doing similar work for different employers within the same industry is asking for political trouble. "Equal pay for equal work" has an almost universal political appeal, if we overlook certain regional feelings about racial minorities. The application of this principle may force a union leader to bargain for less than the full amount that could be obtained from the richest employer within the union's jurisdiction. If this absolute maximum victory were attained and the union leader could not follow through with other employers, he might be in a very unfavorable political position.

Strike Temper of the Rank and File. The union leader's ultimate weapon is the strike. The strike is also his most crucial political test. In the strike, the worker plays for the stake of his most valued economic asset, his job. Workers pay union dues with little protest and *vote* to strike almost automatically, but when they strike on a union call they show the absolute maximum of faith in the union leadership. If they return to work before a settlement is negotiated, they are casting the most telling "no-confidence" vote that any union leader can ever receive. True wildcat strikes are also no-confidence votes. If the leader is to survive as a political leader, he must be closely attuned to the willingness (and in some cases, eagerness) of the rank and file to strike. This willingness on the part of the rank and file is undoubtedly the most significant political influence on the union side in the formulation of demands. At the same time that the union leader is the victim of the rank and file willingness to strike, he is also a potentially significant force in determining that willingness. His influence on the rank and file's willingness to strike is part of his job of selling the union demands to members and employers.

The union leader enters negotiations with a set of demands that reflect the economic and political facts of life as he sees them. His job is to sell these demands or modify them on the basis of management's position at the bargaining table.

Management Goals in Wage Bargaining

How does a company's management decide that it will offer a 10-cent package or a 20-cent package in a particular year? What standards exist to guide a management in formulating its offer? Why does a management propose that a given package be distributed between general wage increases, adjustment of wage inequities, and wage supplements in a particular manner?

Customarily the union initiates collective bargaining by announcing and justifying its comprehensive demands. Management usually *appears* to play a passive role of resisting the union's demands or countering them after they are spelled out in detail. Appearances probably bear a substantial relationship to reality in some situations. However, in the case of large companies the employer probably does his own offer-formulating well in advance of the final presentation of the union's demands. Much of this work is based on obtaining and sifting information about the union and its probable demands.

Major employers like the steel industry and automobile industry firms maintain large industrial relations research staffs. These staffs conduct continuing studies on trends in union demands, the nature of problems in the plant, changes in the cost of living, and special studies of labor costs, legal aspects of worker insurance and income-continuity plans, and employee attitudes. Their work may be introduced at bargaining sessions or kept under wraps as factors to be considered only by top management in the final formulation of a company position.

The final decision on the company's position appears usually to be the result of a top-management (president and/or chairman of the board) decision based on the opinions of senior officers of the enterprise, e.g., vice-presidents of industrial relations, finance, production, and sales. Such a decision is usually made when the negotiations have reached a crisis stage and the company negotiators believe that they have a solid knowledge of what the union will really take.

Management people are understandably quite tight-lipped about how they come to their final decision. Some notions about this can be inferred from their occasional public and private utterances. It seems to the authors of this book that what Leland Hazard has labeled "the three P's" is probably the key to understanding these top management decisions. As he puts it:

The factors which move the more influential segments of industrial management to a wage decision are: (a) the compulsion to maintain production, (b) the need to maintain a feasible price, and (c) the *sine qua non*, profit.

My theme is simple: *production, price, profit and the greatest of these is production.*[14]

Obviously production is of great importance to management. It is the stuff out of which sales are made and the enterprise's life is assured. But production takes on different importance at different times and under different conditions. The automobile industry, with bulging dealer inventories, was under no terrible compulsion to produce more cars during June and July, 1958. It was important that the new-model tooling get into place with little interruption during July, August, and September, but actual production was of little significance—most dealers could get along very nicely with a 30-day stoppage of production. This was not so in 1955 when people were buying automobiles like groceries and if Fords weren't available many people would have bought Chevrolets or Plymouths.

Prices must be feasible in two respects: they must be relatively equal between obvious competitors, and even whole industries must be wary of pricing themselves out of the market. The pattern-making employer usually has little to fear from price competition from his obvious competitors in the industry. He is reasonably certain that whatever he agrees to in terms of increased labor costs will be imposed upon his immediate competitors. However, in periods of economic uncertainty, he has little assurance that he can easily pass any cost increase on to the consumer in the form of a price increase. Even in periods of booming business activity, he is haunted by the specter of pricing the industry out of the market.[15]

If the employer is denied the opportunity of increasing prices, he still can maintain a profitable operation, within limits, by cutting costs other than labor costs. Cost cutting is one of his major jobs anyway. In booming times, he probably is less cost conscious than he is in periods of bad business. By the time he becomes really worried about labor costs he

[14] Leland Hazard, "What Economists Don't Know About Wages," *Harvard Business Review*, Vol. 35 (January–February, 1957), p. 49. See also Hazard, "Wage Theory: A Management View," chap. 2 of George W. Taylor and Frank C. Pierson (eds.), *New Concepts in Wage Determination* (New York: McGraw-Hill Book Co., Inc., 1957), pp. 32–50.

[15] In the post-World War II period there was solid tendency for price increases in pattern-making industries like steel and autos to follow hot on the heels of wage increases. Within these industries, there was virtual uniformity of price adjustments between the major producers. This situation was at least temporarily upset in July, 1958, when U.S. Steel and the steel industry did not time price increases to correspond with a wage-cost increase of about 20 cents per hour. The failure of steel to increase prices on July 1 has been attributed to divergent reasons, e.g., fear of antitrust action, foreign competition, or industrial statesmanship aimed at speeding economic recovery. (See "Why Steel Didn't Raise Prices," *Business Week*, July 5, 1958, p. 19.) Whatever the cause, the July, 1958, experience in steel clearly indicates that "a feasible price" is an important management consideration in wage bargaining. Steel prices were increased about August 1, 1958. President Kennedy's action on steel prices in 1962 introduced a new measure of price feasibility.

probably has cut out just about all the fat that he can find. He still holds the hope, which history has almost always justified, that he can find new methods or machines or products which will enable him to make the profit which justifies his existence.

Now about all that we have said is that the manager gives as little as he thinks the union will buy. Sometimes, he even refuses to give that much. When he does, he is willing to take a strike (or he guessed wrong about what the union really wanted). He is willing to take a strike only when he has temporary advantage (peculiarily enough through bad business) or when his perceptions of the future are very dark. Typically, then, the employer is trying to talk the union down on what it is willing to take and he is usually willing to offer something to induce the union to continue production. How does he talk the union down? In formulating his final offer to the union, the employer carefully considers internal economic data about his own company or industry and external economic and political data about the union and the general business climate.

Internal Economic Data about the Company and/or Industry. Probably the most important economic facts about the firm and/or industry for collective bargaining purposes are: (*a*) sales forecasts, (*b*) inventories and orders on hand at the probable strike date, (*c*) alternative methods of meeting customer demands during a strike, and (*d*) break-even points under different wage cost assumptions.

Sales Forecasts. Sales forecasts are critical to sound managerial decision making. The economic concepts of elasticity of demand, expectation of profit yields, and competition in the product market are all reflected in the managerial sales forecast. Most sales forecasts also reflect management's general thinking about the short-run economic future. When management is producing a brand-name product with substantial customer loyalty for what appears to be an expanding market, management may conclude that it can pass any wage increase along to the customer in the form of a price increase. This interpretation of the facts is particularly final in cases where labor costs are a relatively small proportion of total costs of production. When a company has just experienced a record-making sales and profits year, the management often assumes that prosperity is here to stay.

Inventories and Orders on Hand at Probable Strike Date. Large inventories and few orders on hand tend to make management less receptive to union demands. Many unfilled orders and an empty warehouse have the opposite effect.

Sometimes the composition of inventories is as important as the size of inventories. Most manufacturing concerns produce a number of products. An inventory shortage of a reasonably insignificant product from the viewpoint of the company's total production may become the central issue in company thinking on the union's demands. For example, a very small order for an experimental product from a major customer accompanied by the prospect of large "add-on" orders may prove to be the union's strongest bargaining point without the union's even knowing it. Similar situations exist when the company is the sole source of supply to a major customer of some apparently insignificant bit of hardware. These situations take on even more gravity when they are enmeshed with a defense industry contracting and subcontracting structure.[16]

Alternative Methods of Meeting Customer Demands during a Strike. In a variety of situations, a strike imposes only minor inconvenience on the customers of the firm or industry struck. In these cases, management can put up stronger resistance to union demands because it runs a smaller chance of losing its regular customers as a result of failure to deliver during a strike.

In the petroleum industry, the interchange of products between competitors in various markets is a long-established practice aimed at reducing transshipment costs. This same system could be used to satisfy customer demand in the event of a strike against a single firm or refinery. Many firms produce their own brand-name products and have licensing arrangements with other firms. By careful management advanced planning, these licensing arrangements could enable the licensor to continue to supply his brand-name customers almost indefinitely even though his own production facilities were closed down by a strike. Similar potential advantages are available to multiplant, single-product manufacturers who have different unions or contract expiration dates at different plants each one of which is fully integrated. In this case, the employer merely shifts orders from the strike-bound plant to his plants which are operating during the strike.

In each of these situations management can be tough because the employer has insured himself against the *long-range* cost of actually losing his customers to competitors.

Break-even Points under Different Wage Cost Assumptions. Break-even analysis under different wage cost assumptions is primarily important for the economic long run. In the short run, a management may minimize its losses by continuing to produce even though the revenue per unit sold is less than the average total cost of producing that unit. In the short run, management is "stuck" with its fixed costs, e.g., plant and equipment depreciation, property taxes, inventories of materials on hand,

---

[16] Persons familiar with military procurement procedures are fully aware of the importance of inventory composition as a factor in collective bargaining strategy. In 1953, the U.S. Supreme Court ruled that a strike of some steelworkers at the Dunkirk, New York, plant of the American Locomotive Company was a "national-emergency" strike within the meaning of the Taft-Hartley law. This strike was only a part of a national steel strike which was *not* considered to be a national-emergency strike. The court ruled that the strikers in Dunkirk were closing a substantial part of an entire industry (the atomic reactor manufacturing industry) and that their strike imperiled or threatened to imperil the national health and safety. Not even all of the employees of the Dunkirk plant were engaged in work on the A.E.C. order.

etc. As a result, it is good business to incur variable costs, e.g., wages, sales promotion expenses, etc., so long as the product can be sold at a price which exceeds these variable costs. In such a situation, the management may incur substantial losses, but these losses are *less* than the losses that would be incurred if the management chose not to produce. In the economic long run, however, a management will not continue to operate unless it anticipates that sales income from its product will exceed the total (variable plus fixed) costs of production. This is true because in the long run, management has the opportunity of eliminating fixed costs through sale of plant and equipment or simply not replacing plant and equipment as it wears out.

Break-even analysis brings together all business judgment about sales expectations and cost expectations. If it is believed that prices can be raised without adverse effects on the volume of sales, the break-even point is lowered and the promise of profits is enhanced. If it is believed that prices can be raised without adverse effect on the volume of sales, wages can also be increased with a minimum reduction of profits. On the other hand, if prices can't be raised because of the elasticity of demand or competition in the product market or a general business slump, wages can be increased only at the expense of profits. At the same time, there is always the possibility that such wage increases will cause management to discontinue certain lines of production or actually liquidate the business in its entirety. Or management might find it advisable to change the man-machine mix in such a way as to provide substantially less employment. To be sure, as wages rise, the vital *relative* cost of laborsaving machines certainly declines.

This situation is further complicated by the fact that many costs of production are really matters of accounting *judgment*. Two examples, depreciation expense and cost of materials used, will suffice as illustrations. When management purchases a machine for the price of $100,000 it is merely converting cash into another form of asset. The $100,000 becomes a cost only as it is charged against production in the future. If the machine is *judged* to have no scrap value and a life of 10 years or for a total production of 100,000 units, it may be charged off as an expense at the rate of $10,000 per year or $1 per unit produced. In the first year, only 1,000 units are produced because of a general business slump. If the accountant charges the machine off on a straight-line annual depreciation basis, each unit contains $10 of machine cost (as compared to $1 per unit if he uses a unit-produced accounting method). These two possibilities represent only a very small portion of the many variations which give radically different results and are all within the limits of conventional accounting practice. Similar problems arise in *estimating* the cost of materials used in production. No one *really* knows what the cost of materials or machine time is until such time as the business is totally liquidated. Important as it is to know what costs really are, they are impossible to determine with finality as long as the business continues to operate. Obviously the curiosity of managements and unions does not go so far as to recommend this method of finding complete truth. However, accounting methods do become a point of dispute between unions and managements when management pleads inability to pay wage increases.

Most managements contend that unions have no business probing around in the vital area of cost and sales projections. This position is based on two quite sound arguments: (1) that this is the job of management as established by the owners and (2) that unions really don't possess the competency needed to handle this affair properly. On the other hand, unions must probe around in these areas where apparently they have no business because if they don't they must accept at face value anything that management says. If a management is honestly fulfilling its responsibility to the owners, it *must* interpret the facts to the union in such a way as to minimize concessions to the workers. Thus, the union does its own estimating of the situation, much as management does, but with the important disadvantge of less complete knowledge of data for estimating costs and sales prospects.

External Economic and Political Data about the Union and the Economy. Just as the union frequently tries to learn management secrets about production plans, management has an intense interest in union secrets. When a union is weak financially and members have had long periods of unemployment, management tends to be less generous in its offers than when the union appears to be completely capable of supporting a long strike. On rare occasions a particular management will conduct its negotiations in such a way as to support or topple a particularly co-operative or distasteful union representative. The idea here is that long-range management goals can be achieved only by influencing the nature of the incumbent union leadership. Similar considerations about political leaders or the prospect of governmental support may influence management action in particular years.

We turn now to a discussion of the methods used by managements and unions to persuade each other of the propriety of their respective positions.

Negotiations

No matter how economically sound the union's demands, they must be sold to the members and to employers before an agreement can be made. Management, in turn, must sell its position to the employees and the union before an agreement can be made. Most collective bargaining negotiations are private affairs between the union and the management. In pattern-making bargaining, the union and/or management sometimes seek public support for its position. We shall discuss this public bargaining after we have dealt with the semiprivate negotiation process.

The Union's Persuasive Efforts

The typical sales problem of the industrial union is getting its members to back up its high demands. This is accomplished by what the unions call educational activity. Year in and year out, the union leaders emphasize the excessive profits of the industry, the rising cost of living, and the social need for high consumer purchasing power, through speeches to the rank and file and general audiences, the union newspaper, and radio and television programs. This economic education is supplemented with glowing accounts of the great battles where the union *forced* management to give the workers a fair deal. As negotiations draw near, this educational activity is intensified. By the time negotiations reach a crisis, most members of the union believe that the union's demands are morally right and worth fighting for.

Sometimes, however, the union leadership is confronted with the problem of selling moderate demands to the membership. This is a tough job, particularly after the union's consistent arguments that wages can, and should, be increased not only for the benefit of the worker but the whole society. The leader's only possible advantage in this tough spot is that, as a rule, in such situations the members themselves are discouraged or afraid as a result of their personal experience with layoffs and short workweeks. Only the most politically secure industrial union leadership dares to be moderate, lest it be branded for "selling out" to the employer. Even the secure leadership is wary of being too frank in talking about the futility of strike action to the rank and file because the employer is usually listening. Too much talk of moderation to the rank and file may lead the employer to insist on more moderation than the union leader originally intended to show.

More often than not, industrial unions negotiate flat cents-per-hour wage increases. This situation is largely attributable to the fact that in an industrial union the vote of the least skilled member is just as important as the vote of the most highly paid employee in the bargaining unit. As a result, there is a general political pressure on the leadership to get the most possible for everybody on an equal basis. When particular groups seriously threaten to disrupt the union or promise to play a strategic role in convincing the employer, particular attention is paid to obtaining special pay concession for these groups.

At the same time, union leaders can do some skillful gerrymandering in the negotiation of wage supplements. For example, pensions are clearly something extra for high-seniority workers, while unemployment benefits tend to be something special for the newcomers to the firm or industry. Although the union leader's motives may be altruistic, his actions have important political implications in selling the demands to the membership.

Very often, the union leader never really knows how well the membership bought his sales efforts. The union leader always knows how well the management bought his sales efforts; he either gets an agreement to his liking or disliking or has to go through the final painful sales argument of a strike.

In selling a demand to employers, the union has both positive and negative arguments for closing the sale. On the positive side, the union can argue that its proposals are morally right, that the employer can be assured that the same conditions will be imposed on his competitors, and that he may profit from improved employee morale resulting from his willingness to pioneer in recognizing the needs of his employees. On the negative side, the union can point out the adverse effects on the employer for refusing to agree, e.g., a long and bitter strike with the permanent loss of customers or employee bitterness, which may be "spontaneously" demonstrated by slow-downs, costly accidental errors, or general indifference toward the quality of his product. The union can't promise to deliver a more productive, co-operative, or energetic labor force in exchange for higher wages. Rather, it implicitly promises not to interfere with the employer in utilizing his labor force to obtain his goals.

Most employers, especially pattern-making employers, want to do what is *right* by their employees. Instinctively they know that "a good place to work" is important to attracting good employees. They also recognize the benefits to be derived in the sales field from having a reputation as a good employer. At the same time, they do not wish to incur the wrath of customers by overpricing their product or the disrespect of their fellow businessmen by getting a reputation for softness. Very frequently, employers will differ violently with unions over what is *right* for their employees. In general, employers tend to look at their employees as individuals, while the unions tend to be more interested in employees as a group. More important, employers are primarily interested in costs and constantly look for some positive assurance from the union that higher wages will result in greater employee effort.

The union selling point that the same conditions will be imposed on competitors is very persuasive with most employers. In general, employers are confident about their ability to compete successfully with others so long as they are not handicapped by costs exceeding those of their competitors. However, most employers realistically question the ability of the union to impose the same conditions on all of their competitors. Major industrial unions like the Steelworkers, Autoworkers, and the needle-trade unions gan give virtual guarantees of approximate equality within the domestic industry. However, most employers know that their competitors are not all in the domestic industry. The most powerful industrial unions have little control over foreign competition. Equally important, they do not control the total competitive struggle. As the cost of automobiles increases due to wage costs, the ultimate consumer may decide that he would prefer to improve his home, or dress better, or take a vacation than trade the car every two years. In the same way, steel competes with wood, fabric, aluminum, and plastics. As a result, any increase in any cost almost always means a slight worsening of the employer's competitive position, even when he has an absolute assurance that the same costs will be imposed on his most obvious competitors.

Most employers believe that the profits from pioneering in doing *right* by employees are elusive at best and most commonly just do not exist. Most union leaders argue the benefits of pioneering while selling the demand, but forget about them as soon as they are bought and go back to the rank and file with the story of how tough the employer was in volunteering to pioneer. As a result, many of the employer's *initial* gains are diluted. Over the long pull, it is almost a certainty that the pioneering agreement will become commonplace. In some instances, unions have shown special consideration at a later date to employers who earlier had co-operated with the union. However, the employer who pioneers today in hope of special consideration, if needed, at a later date is taking a very long bet. Both employees and union leadership change with the passage of time and many people tend to forget the kindnesses of the past.

Undoubtedly the union's most potent selling arguments are negative. The employer can readily see, at any given time, the immediate losses (or occasionally, gains) accruing to him as a result of a strike. It is more difficult to predict the long-term losses such as breaks in established relations with customer, public disapproval of his stinginess, or union harassment in the future.

The Employer's Persuasive Efforts. Like the union the employer possesses both positive and negative arguments to convince the union to accept his proposal. The positive arguments are to be found in the proposal itself, e.g., a wage increase that keeps the union "in step" with other unions, and the implied promise of continued production and employment. The employer's major negative argument is the same as the union's—a strike, severe privation for union members and ensuing political unrest in the union, the threat that the employees will come back to work after a long strike for terms that the employer is now offering and thoroughly disillusioned about their union leadership, and most devastating of all, that the employer will supply his customers by employing scabs or farming out the work to nonunion plants.

When the union and management sit down to bargain they often have some previously established standards in the terms of a pattern-making bargain. The employer usually enters negotiations with detailed information about the terms of settlements in key national bargains and by his major competitors. This information is available from governmental sources, private reporting agencies (such as the Bureau of National Affairs, Commerce Clearing House, and Prentice-Hall), and many trade associations which maintain staffs for reporting and analyzing this information for their members. Such data are frequently supplemented by information which employers obtain directly from their competitors.

There may be a dispute between union and management at the very outset of negotiations about which bargain is the appropriate pattern maker for their situation. (Of course, in key negotiations like basic steel or the automotive industry there is no appropriate pattern maker. In these situations, both the unions and the managements must bargain for themselves.) For example, food processors in "coal towns" may be confronted with demands which parallel the national coal settlement even though they deal with noncoal unions. Even in those exceptional cases where there is no dispute between the union and the management over what is the appropriate pattern bargain, it is virtually certain that both sides will seek certain modifications of the pattern to fit local conditions. Usually management shows the greatest interest in breaking from the pattern. Naturally management argues for *less than* pattern settlements.

Management quite frequently introduces a wage comparison argument for breaking from the pattern. A comparison of the firm's present rates with prevailing community rates will be introduced by management if such a comparison supports its argument for a less than pattern settlement. A sound logic underlying such a comparison is the fact that the firm recruits its labor locally. Management is likely to introduce a comparison of its present rates with rates for the same type of work in firms producing the same product, wherever located, if such a comparison supports its argument for a less than pattern settlement. This argument is based on the necessity for competitive labor costs. The competitive-labor-cost argument is particularly persuasive when the management supports its contention with specific examples of orders lost due to excessive labor costs.

Management may argue that national changes in the cost of living are inapplicable in the community where the plant is located. Such an argument makes sense in communities where rents are very low or large numbers of employees are also part-time farmers.

In countering union wage increase demands, management frequently introduces data on comparatively excessive coffee breaks, wash-up time, or low production standards. The point of such arguments is that workers in a particular plant are high-cost employees despite what may be comparatively low wage rates.

Management may argue that its competition is winning a larger share of the market through new products and that employment can be maintained only by underselling the competition or improving quality standards without increasing costs.

Management may argue that it is unable to pay higher wages because of financial losses or sharply curtailed profits. This argument really means that the employees are confronted with the choice of working at lower wages or not working at all.

Management may argue that its cost of wage supplements substantially exceeds those existing in competitive firms or the community. Such an argument seeks to establish equality of total labor costs between firms.

Occasionally managements will argue that nonlabor competitive disadvantages necessitate concessions by the union. For example, if continued operation of the plant results in higher transportation costs than in competitive firms, the management may ask the employees to absorb part of these costs in lower wage rates.

The introduction of these arguments poses two serious problems. First, management must be absolutely certain that its facts are right and that these facts in all their implications support its position. If the facts aren't right or have unexpected implications, their introduction may cause a major setback for management. Second, each of these arguments tends to become a long-range commitment. For example, if a company pleads inability to pay in 1959 negotiations and the union makes concessions on this point, the company should expect above pattern demands at a later date when profits are exceptionally good. Similar long-range commitments are inherent in wage rate, fringe benefit, and productivity comparisons.

Management's success in "talking the union down" depends on the logic of management's arguments, the union leader's impression of the sincerity of the management, the union's own strengths and weaknesses, and the rank and file's willingness to accept management's position.

Most large managements carry on employee informational and educational programs. Many of these programs are accompanied by occasional letters to employees informing them about the company's products, plans, and activities. The typical annual report makes reference to employee benefit programs and union-management relations. Some companies have adopted the policy of continuous direct communication to employees about industrial relations matters. Occasionally, these communications take the form of a direct appeal to employees to accept the offer of the company in collective bargaining. When this is done, the company usually argues that its offer is generous, final, and in the best interests of the employees. If this offer is rejected by union leaders, so the sales campaign goes, employees will suffer because of declining employment, or wage inflation which destroys their savings, or the futility of a strike which neither they nor the management wants.

Exactly how far a management goes in making an offer direct to employees seems to be determined by management philosophy and the state of business. Usually, the companies that make their presentations directly to employees on a year-round basis believe that little can be accomplished without going over the heads of the union leaders. At the same time, there seems to be an intensification of appeals to employees in periods of poor business. In these cases, management is probably reasoning that when unemployment is severe employees are more likely to be reasonable than in periods of prosperity. Thus the management's appeal to employees is merely an added argument to the union negotiators. Management believes that its employee appeals will make the union negotiators more certain that it does not intend to grant their excessive demands. These appeals may even suggest that management intends to run the plant if the union calls a strike.

Pattern-making bargaining is frequently accompanied by extensive union and management efforts to gain public approval for their respective positions.

Enlisting Public Support for Management or Union Positions at the Bargaining Table

To the extent that the general public takes any personal interest in union-management negotiations, the public looks on them from the customers' viewpoint. Thus the public starts out solidly on the side of management because management is the advocate of lower costs which should mean lower prices to the general public when they buy. The union's job is to convince the public that its demands need not result in an increase in prices or that the workers' needs are so important that they justify a slight additional cost to the consumer. Needless to say, it is very difficult to convince the public that it should be willing to pay higher prices. As a rule, the unions seek to prove that substantial wage increases are possible *without any increase in prices*. To do this, they frequently outline rather detailed cases for public approval including such items as the cost of living, man-hour productivity, and fair profits.

Many nonunionists tend to be in sympathy with wage increases to catch up with rises in the cost of living. At the same time, many people suspect that union-negotiated wage increases are really the cause for increases in the cost of living for the general public.

Since unions are never satisfied merely to keep even with the cost of living, their public appeals for support in wage bargaining must go beyond the cost of living as a justification for wage increases. The next step in most union arguments is the reference to greatly increasing labor productivity. Historically the man-hour productivity of industrial workers has steadily increased due to technological innovations. Typically the individual worker hasn't increased his effort to cause increased output, but he has profited by new materials, simpler methods, and better mechanical appliances. Today's typical factory job requires more education than a similar job did 50 years ago, but this is more in the nature of historical developments than as a result of individual workers being required to undertake self-improvement programs. Real wages have risen as man-hour productivity increased and the factory worker of today is a rich man compared to his grandfather of 50 years ago.

Difficulties in measuring changes in man-hour productivity are obvious when we list only a few of the factors which affect productivity, e.g., price changes, cost changes, product changes, product mixes within the firm, industry, or economy as a whole, and the *causes* of nonproductive time.

It is certain that man-hour productivity changes unevenly between firms and industries. The barber of 1960 is probably no more productive than his grandfather was in 1900. Employers each use somewhat different "man-machine mixes" and probably the major determinant of differences in man-hour productivity between competing firms is the particular public favor that their products enjoy in a certain year. Similar situations exist between industries and firms. For this reason, most employers are extremely reluctant to commit themselves to guaranteeing an "annual average increase" in wages due to an anticipated increase in man-hour productivity. At the same time, many unions have shied away from the long-term productivity tie-in of wages because they believe that such arrangements emasculate their bargaining power.

When pattern-making unions take their case to the public, they argue implicitly or explicitly that their demands could be granted without increasing prices. They have pretty smooth sailing with the public mind as long as their demands can all be attributed to the cost of living or increases in man-hour productivity. But the usual union package greatly exceeds the percentage increases in cost of living plus 2 or 3 per cent for increased man-hour productivity. This means that the union must find some social justification for the extra amount it is demanding without advocating an increase in prices. This justification is usually found in what the union considers the excessive profits of the business.

In its public arguments for wage increases, the pattern-making union will make the most out of whatever information can be gleaned from corporate financial statements. Usually, this means expressing profits in terms of percentage return on investment (instead of sales) and, if necessary, recalculating profits under more "realistic" accounting procedures for depreciation, etc. If these union interpretations render a rate of return much in excess of 10 per cent on investment, the union will argue that the industry is gouging the consumer and that union demands can easily be financed out of the excessive profits of management.

The union's major selling points with the general public are cost of living, man-hour productivity, and fair profits. In periods of poor business, these are supplemented with the purchasing-power argument. This latter argument is merely that business is poor *because* workers don't have money to spend. Thus, say the unions, the public would benefit from wage increases which would improve business conditions because they would increase spending.

As indicated earlier, management appears to enter negotiations as the representative of the general public's interest. The union is asking for increased wages, which the public has come to associate with increased prices. By keeping costs down, management is helping the general public by keeping prices down. For many years now, major employers have been carrying on major public educational programs to associate higher wages with higher prices and loss to the general public. Management coined the term wage inflation and has consistently impressed it upon the public mind. To what extent does management profit from public support? It is quite obvious that governmental intervention in the form of a wage freeze is not what management is seeking in courting public favor, because a wage-freeze law would probably be accompanied by a price-freeze law. It seems probable that at least part of management's appeals to the general public are really directed at employees.

SUMMARY

Union-management negotiations reach their greatest intensity when wage adjustments are discussed. Although the nature of the wage question differs in the handicraft and manufacturing segments of the economy, it is a major issue in strikes in both segments.

Successful collective bargaining is based on facts. In this chapter we have reviewed the major sources of economic data for collective bargaining. Management possesses most of the vital economic facts that are needed for bargaining. What economic data employers refuse to supply, unions try to obtain by other methods. Economic data for collective bargaining are not cut and dried figures; they are sometimes vague and almost always subject to diverse interpretations.

Unions and managements, as organizations, must cope with certain internal and external pressures on their wage decisions. These economic, political, and social pressures vary from firm to firm, industry to industry, and union to union. The final agreement on general wage adjustments reflects these pressures.

In times of emergency, such as war, the decision-making power in wage controversies may be taken over by the government. Under these conditions, the interest of the consumer receives greater *conscious* consideration than when wages are set through the market pressures of collective bargaining. However, there is little evidence to prove that governmental wage decisions are actually better for the community at large than decisions which emerge from rough-and-tumble collective bargaining.

QUESTIONS FOR DISCUSSION

1. Recently there has been some talk about negotiating a "sabbatical leave" for unionized employees. How would this development fit into the wage and effort bargain?
2. Discuss the role of government in influencing the wage and effort bargain.
3. Develop a set of task standards for a teacher.
4. In compensating teachers, what relative weights would you give to "merit" and "length of service"? Would you encounter any problems in applying these standards?
5. Why do employers frequently follow a policy of external wage consistency? What problems are encountered in following this policy?

6. "Pattern bargaining" was very important in the immediate post-World War II period, but seems to have declined in importance of late. How do you account for this development?

CASES: 11, 12, 13, 14, 15, 16, 17, 18, 19, 20, 21, 22, 23, 24.

SELECTED ANNOTATED BIBLIOGRAPHY

AULEPP, WILLIAM W. "Work Standards and Labor Costs," *Management Record*, Vol. XVIII (July, 1956), pp. 240–42, 254.

Ford Motor Company manager of industrial engineering discusses practical principles for establishing work standards developed at Ford.

BACKMAN, JULES. "The Size of Crews," *Labor Law Journal*, Vol. XII (September, 1961), pp. 805–15.

Reviews the nature and impact of state laws which specify the size of train crews; surveys the evolution and character of contractual arrangements which affect the size of crews on the railroads; examines the experiences of other industries with respect to size of crew and reduction of work force; and estimates the cost of full crew requirements on the railroads.

BACKMAN, JULES. *Wage Determination: An Analysis of Wage Criteria.* Princeton, London, Toronto: D. Van Nostrand Co., Inc., 1959.

Discusses current practices in wage negotiation, including such factors as the structure of wages, cost-of-living changes, worker budget data, ability to pay and nonwage benefits.

BAMBRICK, JAMES J., JR., and BLUM, ALBERT A. "Productivity and Wage Negotiations," *Management Record*, Vol. XIX (October, 1957), pp. 352–59.

Discusses questions such as: who causes productivity and who should get the benefits? The results of a Conference Board survey of major unions and 239 U.S. and Canadian firms.

———. "Comparative Wage Data in Collective Bargaining," *Management Record*, Vol. XIX (February, 1957), pp. 38–41, 69–76.

Discusses gathering and use of area and industry wage rates and wage supplements for employee information and collective bargaining negotiations.

BEHREND, HILDE. "The Effort Bargain," *Industrial and Labor Relations Review*, Vol. X (July, 1957), pp. 503–15.

Through interviews with (British) management and union representatives, the author examines the underlying assumptions of wage incentive systems in the context of labor-management relations.

DANKERT, CLYDE E., MANN, FLOYD C., and NORTHRUP, HERBERT R. (eds.). *Hours of Work.* Industrial Relations Research Association, Vol. 14. New York: Harper & Row, 1965.

Contents include:
NORTHRUP, HERBERT R. "The Reduction in Hours."
MARSHALL, RAY. "The Influence of Legislation on Hours."
DYMOND, W. R., and SAUNDERS, GEORGE. "Hours of Work in Canada."
MOTT, PAUL E. "Hours of Work and Moonlighting."
MEYERS, FREDERICK. "The Economics of Overtime."

Mann, Floyd C. "Shift Work and the Shorter Work Week."
Berry, Dean F. "Automation, Rationalization and Urbanization: Hours of Work in the Office."
Brown, David G. "Hours and Output."
Dankert, Clyde E. "Automation, Unemployment and Shorter Hours."

Dooher, M. Joseph, and Marquis, Viviene (eds.). *The AMA Handbook of Wage and Salary Administration.* New York: American Management Association, 1950.
Provides step-by-step advice on establishing and operating wage and salary administration programs and keeping them current.

Dunlop, John T. *Wage Determination Under Trade Unionism.* Oxford: Basil Blackwell, 1950 ed.
Establishes a model for union behavior which encompasses union wage policies, bargaining power and intermarket relations, and the impact of the business cycle on wages. A landmark in wage theory.

Foley, James J. "How Not to Handle Productivity Disputes," *Harvard Business Review,* Vol. XXXVII (September–October 1959), pp. 68–80.
Four cases where grievances over output standards were submitted to arbitration are used to illustrate the author's belief that all that technical arbitrators can and should do is establish proper output potentials. Suggests that management's responsibility is to motivate workers to realize their potentials.

Haber, William, and Levinson, Harold M. *Labor Relations and Productivity in the Building Trades.* Ann Arbor: Bureau of Industrial Relations, University of Michigan, 1956.
Report of a field survey in 16 cities in 10 states and the District of Columbia. Discusses economic characteristics of the building trades, nature of collective bargaining, the problem of unstable employment, union security, apprentices, new techniques, working rules, wages and hours and jurisdictional disputes. This volume may be considered as a partial updating of Professor Haber's *Industrial Relations in the Building Industry,* published in the 1930's.

Horowitz, Morris A. *Manpower Utilization in the Railroad Industry: An Analysis of Working Rules and Practices.* Boston: Northeastern University, Bureau of Business and Economic Research, 1960.
An analysis of the complex web of working rules that have developed in American railroads over the past four decades. The author presents an objective definition of "featherbedding" and "make-work," and examines working rules to see which have and do not have make-work or featherbed effects. He has selected for close examination the rules and practices that are considered to have the effect of restricting the economic utilization of manpower.

"Inflation: Wages, Productivity, Bargaining Issues," Special Issue, *Management Record,* Vol. XIX (August, 1957).
Papers include:
Garbarino, J. W., "Wages, Prices, and Inflation."
Hagedorn, George E., National Association of Manufacturers. "Are Wages Inflationary? I."
Mullendore, W. C., Southern California Edison Company. "Are Wages Inflationary? II."
Dunlop, John T., Harvard University. "Are Wages Inflationary? III."

Ross, Arthur M., University of California, Berkeley. "New Concept of Compensation?"

Pierson, Frank C., Swarthmore College. "Postwar Structural Wage Strains."

Taylor, George W., University of Pennsylvania. "Wage Incentives and Productivity."

Heineman, Robert K., Aluminum Company of America. "What Happens in Pattern Bargaining."

Zorn, Burton A. "Pattern Bargaining: Why It Developed and What to Do."

Leland Hazard, "Management Action on Wage Inflation."

John Post, Continental Oil. "The Squeeze on Production, Prices, and Profits."

Frederick Harbison, Princeton University. "Summary."

Kahn, Mark L. "Wage Determination for Airline Pilots," *Industrial and Labor Relations Review*, Vol. VI, pp. 317–36.

Discusses the combination of economic and political factors which contributed to the Airline Pilots Association's success in wage bargaining.

Kennedy, Van Dusen. *Union Policy and Incentive Wage Methods.* New York: Columbia University Press, 1945.

A comprehensive survey of union attitudes and policies toward wage incentive methods through the World War II period.

Kilbridge, M. C. "The Effort Bargain in Industrial Society," *Journal of Business,* (January, 1960), pp. 10–20.

Discussion of factors that influence determination of industrial effort. Shows that bargaining enters at both general pace level and level of specific output requirements. Automation and process-paced work are turning discussions of work loads more toward manning assignments, less on output requirements.

Lesieur, Frederick G. (ed.). *The Scanlon Plan: A Frontier in Labor-Management Cooperation.* A publication of the Industrial Relations Section, Massachusetts Institute of Technology. New York: John Wiley & Sons, Inc., 1958.

Presents and evaluates a plan for labor-management co-operation in increasing productivity worked out by a man who had been a steel union official and a member of the Industrial Relations Section at M.I.T. The plan includes a formula for dividing the benefits of increased productivity.

Nunn, Henry L. *Partners in Production: A New Role for Management and Labor.* Englewood Cliffs, N.J.: Prentice-Hall, Inc., 1961.

Outlines the Nunn-Bush Shoe Company's program for labor-management amity and co-operation. Describes the share-of-production plan, how it works, how it compares with the generally accepted plans of compensation, and how it differs from the Rucker and Scanlon plans.

Ross, Arthur M. *Trade Union Wage Policy.* Berkeley, Calif.: University of California Press, 1953 ed.

Major topics include: the trade-union as a wage-fixing institution, the dynamics of wage determination under collective bargaining, responsible union wage policy, union-management relations and wage bargaining, and the influence of unions on earnings. A landmark in wage theory.

Salkever, Louis R. "Toward A Theory of Wage Structure," *Industrial and Labor Relations Review,* Vol. VI (April, 1953), pp. 299–316.

Establishes theoretical concepts which contribute to the understanding of the emergence and change in size of occupational wage rates in America.

SCHULTZ, GEORGE PRATT. *Pressures on Wage Decisions: A Case Study in the Shoe Industry.* New York: Wiley and the Technology Press of M.I.T., 1951.

An attempt to demonstrate how "market forces" and "human decisions" are synthesized in the process of wage determination under collective bargaining.

SLICHTER, SUMNER H., HEALY, JAMES J., and LIVERNASH, E. ROBERT. *The Impact of Collective Bargaining on Management.* Washington, D.C.: Brookings Institution, 1960.

Special attention is invited to the following chapters: 17, "Wage Incentives"; 18, "Measured Day Work"; 19, "Evaluated Rate Structures"; and 20, "Wage Structure Considerations."

TAYLOR, GEORGE W., and PIERSON, FRANK C. (eds.). *New Concepts in Wage Determination.* New York: McGraw-Hill Book Co., Inc., 1957.

Twelve authorities (GEORGE W. TAYLOR, FRANK C. PIERSON, LELAND HAZARD, NATHANIEL GOLDFINGER, EVERETT M. KASSALOW, JOHN T. DUNLOP, E. ROBERT LIVERNASH, ARTHUR M. ROSS, RICHARD A. LESTER, LLOYD G. REYNOLDS, CLARK KERR, and MELVIN ROTHBAUM) discuss recent developments in wage theory and the influences of collective bargaining on wage determination.

WAITE, WILLIAM W. "Problems in the Arbitration of Wage Incentives," chap. 2, *Arbitration Today.* JEAN T. MCKELVEY (ed.). Proceedings of the Eighth Annual Meeting of the National Academy of Arbitrators. Washington, D.C.: Bureau of National Affairs, 1955, pp. 25–34. Discussion by John W. Seybold and S. Herbert Unterberger, pp. 35–44.

Discusses problems of determining the agreement requirements for arbitrating incentive wage rates and the technical problems in establishing a sound incentive rate.

WHYTE, WILLIAM FOOTE. *Money and Motivation.* New York: Harper & Bros., 1955.

A comprehensive analysis of the impact of financial incentives in the factory. The author has drawn on the works of MELVILLE DALTON, DONALD ROY, LEONARD SAYLES, ORVIS COLLINS, FRANK MILLER, GEORGE STRAUSS, FRIEDRICH FUERSTENBERG, and ALEX BAVELAS.

WOLF, WILLIAM B. *Wage Incentives as a Managerial Tool.* New York: Columbia University Press, 1957.

Discusses the nature of wage incentives, impact of wage incentives on manufacturing costs, the theory and logic of wage incentives, and understanding the use of wage incentives.

Chapter 11

WORKER INSURANCE AND INCOME-CONTINUITY PROGRAMS

Worker insurance and income-continuity programs provide benefits designed to protect workers from hazards not necessarily related to the job, e.g., old age, accidents and illness, and unemployment. Collectively bargained protection from these hazards usually supplements governmentally provided protection, e.g., Old Age, Survivors', Disability, and Health Insurance, Workmen's Compensation, and Unemployment Compensation. Collectively bargained supplements to government programs frequently provide benefits for workers' families as well as the worker himself. Under multiemployer bargaining, eligibility for these benefits may be independent of any continuing relationship with a single employer. Some of the hazards involved in these programs are insurable while other programs provide for income continuity against the incidence of uninsurable hazards. For these reasons, the term worker insurance and income-continuity programs seems more appropriate than the commonly used terms of "employee benefit plans" and "fringe benefits."

This chapter briefly examines the hazards of employment and governmental programs aimed at alleviating those hazards. Collective bargaining issues on pensions, medical care, and unemployment are examined in some depth.

The Hazards of Employment

Since we spend between a fourth and a third of our adult lives in the process of making a living, the normal hazards of life are closely related to the work environment. Employment under conditions set by others, the very organization of American economic life, creates additional hazards because we are dependent upon others. Thus, as an employee, the worker is confronted with at least four major hazards: (1) the hazard of being "too young to die and too old to work," (2) disability, (3) untimely death, and (4) the loss of the job or unemployment. Each of these hazards poses somewhat different problems for the worker affected and the agency which seeks to alleviate the hardship which they may cause.

Old age is primarily feared as a cause of economic privation. One way or another people make frequently drastic attempts to avoid spending the later days of life in economic want. After economic means are assured, old age presents serious problems of psychological adjustment. The story of the retired worker who deteriorated physically because of the lack of fruitful outlets for his energy is too commonplace to be overlooked.

Disability and untimely death may impose severe physical suffering, as well as very substantial monetary costs. To an even greater extent than old age, these hazards impose hardship on the loved ones of the victim. The physical and economic marks of a disabling illness or accident frequently continue after the physician has declared the victim to be fully recovered. Indebtedness, worry, or prolonged reductions in physical and mental vigor affect the employer as well as the worker.

Loss of the job is probably the most feared hazard of employment. No matter how much a worker dislikes his job, he usually prefers the job he presently holds to the prospect of no job. Under the best conditions finding a new job usually involves substantial inconvenience, and most workers usually look for new jobs only under adverse conditions. That is, most job hunters are people without jobs and more people are job hunters at the very time when new jobs are scarce. A "short layoff" always contains at least the possibility of becoming a permanent loss of the job. The loss of the present job also means the loss of seniority, medical benefits, pension entitlement, etc. which have been "saved" by the employee during his period of employment.

The fact that many of the hazards of employment are really the hazards of living is worth repeating. However, the incidence of some of these hazards varies between employers, between industries, between geographic areas, and between generations. A few brief illustrations will suffice. Coal miners tend to become too old to work and too young to die at an earlier age than college professors. Lumbering and building construction takes a heavier toll in life and limb than does retail selling. Agricultural workers, coal miners, and building tradesmen tend to expect seasonal unemployment while bank employees expect steady employment for life if they want it. In rural areas and small towns, some kind of job is usually available for the person who looks hard enough for it. In an agricultural economy of large families, the elders of the family could make some contribution to the commonweal and thus avoid forced retirement without pay. With a rapidly aging American population in an industrial age, this problem is changing in both nature and magnitude.

What gains are available by "pooling" the risks within a firm or industry in an insurance system? Again the answer depends upon the nature of the risk and the type of insurance programs available. Cyclical unemployment seems to be an uninsurable risk. Illness, old age, and death are reasonably predictable within a large group. Thus these latter hazards can be insured.

Given the diversity of the hazards, the unpredictability of their incidence, and variations in their "insurability," there is no single *best* way of alleviating them. The complexity of the problem tends to necessitate a combination of methods of alleviation tailored to the unique needs and resources of different individuals and groups of people.

METHODS OF ALLEVIATING THE HAZARDS OF EMPLOYMENT

Any discussion of collective bargaining on worker insurance and income-continuity programs should start with a consideration of the three basic methods of alleviating the hazards of employment or the hazards of life: (1) personal and family responsibility, (2) governmental action, and (3) collective bargaining.

In early America major emphasis was placed on personal and family responsibility supplemented with private charity. Personal thrift was considered to be the best means of providing for personal needs. When an individual couldn't take care of himself the family was expected to fill in to the extent possible. Disasters beyond the means of the immediate family were remedied as well as possible by the neighbors down the road, the local church, or, in later years, by help from the organized charities established through the generosity of the wealthy. In handicraft industry with self-employment the most common way of doing business, this system worked quite well. It is still present in the American society as is clearly shown by Americans' large holdings of private insurance policies, long-established charitable institutions, and a rather general belief that the individual *should* assume first responsibility for his own security.

As our economic society grew more complex and the interdependency of citizens was accentuated by the growth of the corporate form of business and the factory system, we began to place greater emphasis on the government as a means of alleviating some of the personal hazards of employment. Although this trend started with the birth of the federal union, the major landmarks appear in the twentieth century. Factory inspection and workmen's compensation law were followed by the regulation of hours and wages. Federal government participation in the form of Unemployment Compensation, Old Age and Survivors' Insurance, and the Fair Labor Standards Act started in the early days of the New Deal and promises to grow in the coming decades. Government action seems to be based on the principle that the society should do for the worker what he cannot do for himself. There are some indications that this principle is being broadened to include those things which the government can do better or less expensively than the individual. Governmental programs offer two major advantages to workers: (1) risks become more predictable as the size of the covered group increases, thus universal coverage offers a more insurable risk and (2) under governmental programs there is a tendency for the "insurance premium" or tax to be levied on a progressive basis, thus subsidizing low-income wage earners from the taxes levied on more prosperous individuals or business enterprises.

Collective bargaining or union action as a means of alleviating personal hazards has a long history. In the earliest days of the labor movement, unions attempted to help their members solve problems beyond the control of the individual. A classic example of these attempts were the "friendly benefits" (such as the death benefit paid to members' dependents by some unions where private insurance policies were available only at exorbitant premium rates). These programs preceded any kind of governmental action such as workmen's compensation. The later-day industrial unions have devoted much of their energies to developing *supplements* to governmental programs in the form of collectively bargained pensions, health and welfare programs, and even privately financed unemployment compensation or supplemental unemployment benefits.

The long-term trend in worker insurance and income-continuity measures seems to indicate a general downgrading of personal and family responsibility and private charity in the years ahead. This trend is caused by the very complexity of our economic life and taxation policies which severely limit the acquisition of great personal fortunes which form the cornerstone of private charity. At the same time, the welfare aspects of government seem to be on the ascendancy. Future trade-union action will take two forms: (1) lobbying for increased governmental action and (2) the development of supplemental programs designed to the special needs of workers in particular industries. Supplemental programs may take two forms: (1) programs designed to meet exceptional needs, such as the United Mine Workers' Health and Welfare Plan which provides medical care in isolated areas where mines are located, and (2) experimental or pilot programs designed to broaden the scope of coverage. Several experimental programs might be mentioned: the United Automobile Workers' programs on geriatrics, the Machinists' program in preventive medical care, or the long-established cultural programs of the needle-trades unions.

We turn now to a discussion of the views of management, unions, and the government on collective bargaining on worker insurance and income-continuity programs.

MANAGEMENT VIEW OF WORKER INSURANCE AND INCOME-CONTINUITY PROGRAM BARGAINING

Management's view of worker insurance and income-continuity measures through collective bargaining can be best discussed by segregating matters of "principle" and matters of "cost." This classification allows more accurate generalization about frequently contradictory management statements of *the* management position on particular programs.

Management View of "Cost" of Worker Insurance and Income-Continuity Measures

Probably the most important consideration of management is keeping the *total* cost of all programs within reason. "Reasonable" costs are hard to pin down. On the whole, management seems to feel that prevailing practice in the industry and/or area provides a good guidepost to reasonableness. Major breaks with prevailing practice will be traded for union concessions on some other points or after very careful study of the needs of employees. Probably the most common management rationale for the cost of worker insurance and income-continuity measures is that they are granted *in lieu of* equal or greater wage increases.

Long-range cost frequently receives as much management attention as the immediate cost of a particular insurance or income-continuity measure. Accustomed to dealing in complex variables, the management mind seeks to reduce every program to a known *limited* and *predictable* long-term management liability. In the case of pensions, health and welfare programs, and supplemental unemployment benefits, many of the cost-creating factors are not clearly predictable. For example, the long-range cost of pensions depends upon labor turnover, mortality rates, earnings on investment, and the value of the dollar over long periods of time. Since many of these factors cannot be predicted with any accuracy, management insists upon the negotiation of certain protective clauses which places a maximum limit on management's liability no matter how adverse its experience with the program.

Since all cost is relative, management argues that worker insurance and income-continuity measures should be designed to benefit the employer (who usually pays the bill) as well as the employee. Given an almost infinite variety of programs to choose from, management tends to favor those measures which develop better *workers* as contrasted to just better people. Thus, if given a choice between medical care and paid sick leave, management might favor the medical care because it offers greater promise of putting the worker back in working trim.

Management View of "Principles" in Worker Insurance and Income-Continuity Bargaining

Management believes that, to the extent possible, employee benefits should be a reward for individual or group merit. Such a system of benefits furthers the purposes of the business enterprise and reinforces the ideology of a free economy. As a matter of principle, management prefers to relate pension benefits to both earnings in employment and years of faithful service.

The contributory principle also ranks high in management's priority list in worker insurance and income-continuity programs negotiations. This means that the beneficiary (employee) pays part of the cost of the benefits directly. Management feels that this is only fair. At the same time, many managements believe that when the employee knows that he is paying part of the bill because of payroll deductions, he will be less "unrealistic" in incessant demands for the liberalization of the benefits. Practical tax and cost matters have resulted in frequent compromises on this principle, but it still remains high in the thinking of management negotiators.

Management vigorously opposes any worker insurance or income-continuity measures which seriously interfere with the sound operation of the business enterprise. Such an apparently harmless request as extra unemployment benefits is carefully studied to assure that no agreement will limit management's authority to lay off at will, relocate plants, undertake new projects, or create serious morale problems among the workers kept on the payroll. A defense of management rights is partly due to cost considerations, but may also be a matter of principle.

Management is seriously concerned about the possibility that worker insurance and income-continuity benefits may encourage employee malingering. Full pay for sick leave may encourage the exaggeration of minor or nonexistent ills. Complete medical-care programs may result in unneeded surgery, dental care, or hospitalization. Excessively generous unemployment benefits tend to place a premium on idleness.

Finally, as a matter of principle, most managements believe that worker insurance and income-continuity programs should be designed so as to encourage personal thrift and initiative. To the extent that an individual employee can provide for his own security through reasonably priced private insurance, most managements would prefer to limit their participation in the program to informing the employees of the various plans that are available. Under such an arrangement, the employee makes his own decision about whether the plan is worth what it costs. In other cases, such as group medical insurance, where substantial savings are possible through risk pooling, management often favors a plan which will help the individual employee buy more intelligently.

Management usually enters negotiations with considerations of costs and principle in mind. The agreement which concludes negotiations is usually a compromise of union's views and management thinking. We turn now to a brief consideration of the union view of worker insurance and income-continuity programs.

UNION VIEW OF WORKER INSURANCE AND INCOME-CONTINUITY PROGRAMS UNDER COLLECTIVE BARGAINING

Union emphasis on employer commitments to provide extensive insurance and income-continuity benefits coincides with the rise of industrial unions in mass-production industry. To the extent that these programs existed before the rise of the CIO unions, they were provided directly by the union through special funds established from dues money. Industrial union insistence on such measures as pensions, health and welfare programs, and unemployment benefits can be explained merely as an extension of the seniority principle. Since the industrial worker's security is typically dependent upon a single employer, it is natural that industrial unions would do the pioneer work in collective bargaining on worker insurance and income-continuity measures. Craft unions have followed the industrial unions in establishing industry or market-wide employee benefits not dependent upon a single employer.

Unions emphasize matters of principle but temper their demands by a consideration of costs. Frequently unions believe, or hope, that personal security measures are something extra that can be added to the package settlement by skillful negotiations. In the early days of fringe negotiations, this union view was probably sound. Today, however, most managements are keenly aware of the cost of worker insurance and income-continuity programs and grant even the most innocent-appearing union request only after very careful consideration of its probable cost. On the other hand, some of these programs cannot be reduced to any meaningful cents-per-hour cost and thus may be union-desired "something extra."

At the same time, some unions have taken the position that a particular worker insurance or income-continuity program is so important that it should take priority over a more costly management offer in the form of a wage increase.

"Adequate" Benefits

"Adequate" is an evasive term. At least part of the union drive for pensions, unemployment benefits, and health and welfare programs can be directly attributed to what the unions consider to be the inadequacies of governmental programs. In defining what is adequate, unions look to health-and-decency or moderate-income budgets. These budgets change with changes in the cost of living and changes in living standards. Union insistence on adequate benefits takes primacy over any consideration of the cost of providing these benefits.

Noncontributory Programs

Unions advocate noncontributory worker insurance and income-continuity programs for several reasons. A noncontributory program gives the union full credit for the victory at the bargaining table. Under a noncontributory program, benefits appear to be something extra or something for nothing. Noncontributory programs also free the union from the sometimes onerous task of selling the particular program to the membership to the extent of each member approving the program by authorizing a payroll deduction. Universal coverage, which is a natural outgrowth of noncontributory programs, tends to reduce the per capita cost of many worker insurance and income-continuity programs. Finally, noncontributory programs provide very important tax cost savings. Under noncontributory programs, the beneficiary pays income tax on the benefits when they are received. Pension benefits, unemployment benefits, and other wage-loss compensation are subject to a much lower tax bite than wages. For example, under a contributory program, the employee pays, say, $2 per week for his pension. To get this $2, the employee must earn about $2.40 because of withholding tax. Under a noncontributory system, the employer pays $2 directly into the pension fund. The employee pays no income tax on this $2 deposit. When the employee retires he receives, say, $100 per month from the pension fund. This benefit is income for tax purposes and is taxed at the then prevailing rate. However, the employee's total income in retirement will be in the vicinity of $1,200 per year as opposed to $4,500 per year while he is working. The tax on the benefits will be negligible, while the tax on the contributed deposits would be in the range of 20 per cent to 25 per cent.

Actuarially Sound Programs

Many worker insurance and income-continuity programs are designed to provide benefits at times substantially in the future. For example, the major costs of a pension plan relate to persons who are expected to retire at sometime in the future. An actuarially sound program is one which provides for setting aside the cost of all accrued claims in the time period in which these claims are accrued even though the claims are not paid until sometime later.

Union interest in actuarially sound benefit programs is easy to explain. Under actuarially sound funding, the beneficiary is guaranteed that his benefits will be available at the time when he becomes eligible to collect them. Under pay-as-you-go financing, the employer's liability for benefits is limited to the *current* cost of providing the benefits. If the employer goes out of business or encounters grave economic difficulties at some future time, his employees stand a good chance of losing their accrued benefit rights if the program is not actuarially sound.

Joint Administration

Many worker insurance and income-continuity measures involve the accumulation of substantial financial reserves. All of these measures pose problems in the determination of eligibility for benefits. Most unions seek a full voice in the handling of the financial reserves as well as the determinations of eligibility.

The union's demand for participation in the investment of worker insurance and income-continuity funds is based on a belief that the employees own the funds as well as claims against the fund. If this contention is granted, the union can perform two useful functions in participating in the investment of these funds. First, if the union can increase the earnings on the funds, this added income could provide a basis for increased benefits. Second, several unions contend that the investment policy of these funds should be more socially conscious. This means that the funds should be invested in socially desirable (although safe) investments such as low-income housing, co-operative health programs, or employee credit unions. Management frequently resists union participation in the investment of worker insurance and income-continuity funds because it denies that the employees own the funds. Further, management questions the safety of some of the socially desirable investments which some of the unions have advocated. Finally, management insists that it is more skillful in financial matters than unions and that the employees' best interests are served by having the funds managed by the best experts available.

In almost all cases, unions have won an equal voice with management in the settlement of dispute cases over eligibility for benefits.

In summary, unions tend to de-emphasize the cost aspects of worker insurance and income-continuity programs. Instead, they place major emphasis on obtaining generous benefits, guaranteed through sound funding, and augmented by the noncontributory principle and union participation in the administration of the plan.

Industrial unions place greater emphasis on worker insurance and income-continuity benefits than do craft unions. This situation can be partially attributed to the lesser ability of industrial unionists to shift for themselves in periods of widespread unemployment and their general dependence upon their present employer. We believe that another explanation for this phenomenon is to be found in the sympathy of many industrial-union leaders for the welfare state. We know of several cases where industrial-union leaders have privately stated that five cents for pensions or some other worker insurance or income-continuity measure was better than five cents in wages. Exactly what combination of wages and benefits a certain union will negotiate is undoubtedly influenced by the union leadership's view of the need for a particular measure. Where union leaders impose their will on their membership, their actions are analogous to the much condemned management paternalism of the past.

Management and union views should occupy a central position in any discussion of worker insurance and income-continuity programs. At the same time, governmental views provide the framework within which unions and managements must resolve their differences.

GOVERNMENT PROVISION OF RETIREMENT INCOME, MEDICAL CARE, AND UNEMPLOYMENT INCOME

The United States government has encouraged the development of worker insurance and income-continuity programs in two ways. First, there is an extensive governmentally organized and financed program of retirement benefits, medical and hospital care for the elderly, and unemployment compensation. These government programs provide a base upon which collectively bargained supplements are built. Second, rulings of the NLRB, the Internal Revenue Service, and various special governmental boards have the composite effect of encouraging, or compelling, collective bargaining on these issues.

Before discussing collective bargaining issues on pensions, health and welfare plans, and unemployment benefits, the basic characteristics of Old Age, Survivors', and Disability Insurance, the 1965 federal medicare plan, and Unemployment Compensation should be reviewed.

Old Age, Survivors', and Disability Insurance

Old Age, Survivors', and Disability Insurance is a federal program providing cash benefits to retired persons and totally and permanently disabled persons who have worked in covered employment. Beginning in 1955, OASDI covered more than 90 per cent of American citizens who were gainfully employed.

Several characteristics of OASDI financing are important to an understanding of collectively bargained pensions:

1. OASDI is *contributory*. This means that employees pay part of the cost of benefits. In 1967, employers and employees each pay a tax of 4.4 per cent of the first $6,600 of annual wages paid or received.
2. OASDI is *funded*. This means that tax receipts exceed benefit disbursements for the purpose of building an adequate fund to guarantee benefits for young workers when they reach the age of eligibility. Funding of OASDI is not as urgent as funding of collectively bargained pensions because as a practical matter the taxing power of the federal government is the ultimate guarantee of benefits.
3. Under the 1965 amendments to social security, the maximum costs of OASDI are $290.40 per year for *each*—the employer and the employee —in 1967. By 1987 these costs will rise to $372.90 per year for *each* employer and employee. These projected costs are based on the probably unsound assumption that OASDI will not be liberalized in the next 20 years.

OASDI benefits are determined *exclusively* by past earnings and marital status. To be eligible for OASDI benefits, no individual needs to work more than 40 quarters in covered employment. There are lesser eligibility requirements for persons now near retirement age, but the 40 quarters' requirement is most pertinent to young people. A "fully insured" individual will be eligible for retirement benefits as shown below under the 1965 amendments to the Social Security Act:

Average Monthly Earnings*	Single Worker		Worker and Wife (Both Same Ages)†			
	At Age 62	At Age 65	At Age 62	At Age 63	At Age 64	At Age 65
$250	$ 81.40	$101.70	$119.60	$130.70	$141.70	$152.60
$350	99.40	124.20	146.00	159.50	173.00	186.30
$400‡	108.80	135.90	159.80	174.50	189.30	203.90
$550‡	134.40	168.00	197.40	215.60	233.80	252.00

NOTES: *The calculations of average yearly earnings on which benefits are based permit claimants to disregard some years of lowest earnings.
† The assumption that both worker and wife are the same age tends to overestimate OASI benefits since typically the wife is younger than the retiree.
‡ Maximum creditable earnings of $4,800 per year started in 1959 and maximum creditable earnings of $6,600 per year started in 1966. Because of this benefits shown in these two rows will not generally be payable for some years to come.

Assuming retirement at age 65, these figures indicate that most retired persons who had worked under union conditions will be eligible for approximately $100–$135 per month (if single) or $175–$200 per month (if both retiree and wife are 65 at retirement) in OASI benefits.

Three characteristics of OASDI benefits are pertinent to our discussion of collectively bargained pensions:

1. OASDI benefits are *vested*. This means that eligibility for OASI benefits is not contingent upon continuous employment with a single employer or industry. Employees can move from employer to employer without jeopardizing their OASI eligibility.
2. OASDI benefit amounts are related to average earnings rather than duration of continuous employment or seniority.
3. OASDI benefit amounts are related to marital status.

The 1955 amendments to the Social Security Act provided disability wage loss benefits for the first time. A worker who is totally disabled and who meets the work requirements of the law is entitled to receive his full primary OASDI benefit. Benefits are available only to workers who have been totally disabled for six months and whose disability is expected to continue indefinitely. The minor children of disabled workers are also eligible for disability benefits.

Old Age, Survivors', and Disability Insurance provides a firm "floor" program for collectively bargained pensions. This is in sharp contrast to the public medicare plan which has very limited coverage. Because of the unpredictability of the hazard of unemployment, Unemployment Compensation does not provide a "floor" program for collectively bargained supplements.

1965 "Medicare" Amendments to the Social Security Act

Prior to 1965, with the exception of the Armed Forces and veterans, the federal government did not provide any significant health insurance for citizens in the labor force. On the other hand, state workmen's compensation laws, which provide medical care and wage loss benefits to workers injured in the normal course of their employment, are the oldest social insurance scheme in the United States. Federal government action in the area of health insurance began in 1955, with the Social Security Act providing disability pensions to persons totally and permanently disabled and over 50 years of age. The lateness of the federal government's entry into the health insurance field is illustrated by the fact that the major collective bargaining problem posed by the medicare amendments of 1965 was the *withdrawal* of previously provided private care from the new area of public concern.[1]

Under the 1965 medicare amendments, the hospital insurance por-

---

[1] Cf. Emerson H. Beier, "Adopting Group Health Insurance to Medicare," *Monthly Labor Review* (May, 1966), pp. 491–95.

tion (Part A of the amendments) provides for the payment of most of the costs of hospital services, skilled nursing care in extended care facilities (nursing homes) after hospitalization, outpatient diagnostic services, and home health services. Qualification is automatic for this tax-financed coverage for almost all people 65 and older.

The optional medical insurance portion of the act (Part B) covers payments of about 80 per cent of doctor's fees and many other medical items. All people 65 and older may purchase this coverage for $3 per month.

Medicare is landmark legislation of great significance, but it must be emphasized that it applies *only* to persons aged 65 and over. It handles the expensive and troublesome collective bargaining problem of providing health insurance for *retirees*, but it has no immediate impact on the problem of health insurance during the key years of employment or the health of a worker's family. As a part of the Social Security system, medicare is based on the *contributory* principle.

Unemployment Compensation

Unemployment Compensation is a federal-state program providing a degree of income security to unemployed workers. Within a federal framework, each state is free to work out its own eligibility standards, benefit structure, and financing methods. At the present time about 80 per cent of American wage and salary workers and practically all persons working under union conditions are covered by Unemployment Compensation.

Several characteristics of unemployment compensation financing should be noted:

1. Unemployment Compensation is *noncontributory*. This means that U.C. taxes are assessed against the employer. (There is substantial question about who ultimately pays for U.C. benefits. Some authorities argue that the employer passes U.C. costs along to the consumer in the form of price increases. Others argue that the employer must absorb this cost. Still others maintain that employees pay the cost because only so much is available for total labor costs. It seems likely that in competitive industries employers can pass on only the average cost of U.C. in price increases. Employers with very irregular employment probably are forced to absorb their extra U.C. costs under experience rating discussed below.)

2. Unemployment compensation is *funded*. Because future needs for unemployment compensation benefits cannot be predicted with a high degree of accuracy, funding of U.C. is not actuarially sound.

3. Most states use *"experience rating"* in assessing U.C. taxes against the individual enterprise. This means that an employer pays a higher tax rate when he has irregular employment than when he has stable employment.

4. The cost of U.C. fluctuates rather sharply between a minimum tax rate as low as zero in a few states to such relatively high maximum

rates as 7 per cent of the first $3,000 of annual earnings, or 2.7 per cent of the first $7,200 of annual earnings, or 4.6 per cent of the first $3,600 of annual earnings.

Unemployment compensation benefits vary widely between states. *Maximum* benefits tend to be less than $50 per week with a *maximum* duration of about 26 weeks. In 12 states which provide dependents' allowances, *maximum* benefits range up to $75 per week. To be eligible for U.C., a worker must be involuntarily unemployed through no fault of his own and available for suitable work. Obviously, U.C. is primarily helpful in dealing with relatively short-term unemployment.

COLLECTIVE BARGAINING ISSUES ON PENSIONS

Different unions have different goals in pension bargaining. The goals of craft unions differ from the goals of industrial unions. Management goals in pension bargaining may coincide or conflict with union goals. After the basic principles for the establishment of a pension plan have been decided by the compromise of union and management goals, complex problems of real costs, financing methods, and plan administration remain for the union and management pension negotiators. We shall discuss these issues in terms of union goals, management goals, and residual problems.

Union Goals in Pension Bargaining

In bargaining over pensions or in evaluating any existing pension agreement it is wise to consider possible future developments. The industrial unions, as pioneers in the collectively bargained pension field, have been quite articulate in stating their pension goals.[2]

[2] The listing of union pension goals which follows was derived from the statements of union leaders in union conventions, before government boards, and in forums of opinion. The reader's attention is especially directed to the following: Phillip Murray, *The Steelworkers' Case for Wages, Pensions and Social Insurance as Presented to President Truman's Steel Industry Board* (Pittsburgh, Pa.: United Steelworkers of America, 1949), 29 pp. Solomon Barkin, "What Shall We Have: Retirement Benefit or Superannuation Plans?" *Proceedings of the Second Annual Meeting of the Industrial Relations Research Association, New York City, December 29–30, 1949* (Madison, Wis.: Industrial Relations Research Association, 1950), pp. 138–47. Harry Becker, "Labor's Approach to the Retirement Problem," *ibid.*, pp. 116–26. Lane Kirkland, *Pension Plans Under Collective Bargaining: A Reference Guide for Trade Unions* (rev. ed.; Washington, D.C.: American Federation of Labor, December, 1954), vii, 102 pp; "Pensions and the Pensioner," *Proceedings of New York University Ninth Annual Conference on Labor* (Albany, N.Y.: Matthew Bender & Co., Inc., 1956), pp. 147–58; "Problems in the Development of Pension Programs Under Collective Bargaining: Discussion," *Proceedings of the Fifth Annual Meeting of the Industrial Relations Research Association, Chicago, Illinois, December 28–29, 1952* (Madison, Wis.: Industrial Relations Research Association, 1953), pp. 105–8. Leonard Lesser, "Problems in Pension Contributions and Benefits," *ibid.*, pp. 86–92; "Tax Aspects of Collectively Bargained Pension Plans," *Proceedings of New York University Seventh Annual Conference on Labor* (Albany, N.Y.: Matthew Bender & Co., Inc., 1954), pp. 617–26.

The major difficulties in talking about "union goals" are: (1) goals may differ substantially between Locals within the same International union and different International unions may even have conflicting pension goals; (2) union goals frequently are secret or are stated in very general or confusing terms; and (3) as pragmatic organizations, unions abandon or compromise some goals for the satisfaction of other goals. Recognizing these limitations and the ability of management to firmly say "No!" a discussion of union goals on pensions may shed some light on present and future pension bargaining.

Pensions as Part of a Total Collective Bargaining "Package." The Executive Council of the American Federation of Labor established a special committee to study pension trends in 1950. The members of this committee stated the considerations in seeking pensions through collective bargaining as follows:

Whether or not a pension plan is actually a good idea, and the type of plan that ought to be set up, are questions with no single answer that would apply to all groups alike. The right answers can be found only after studying the issue in relation to other economic objectives; in relation to the existing level of wage rates and working conditions; in relation to the effect upon mobility and job tenure of the members; in relation to the characteristics and most pressing needs of the members of the particular group concerned.

A retirement plan should be designed to conform to the needs, characteristics, and resources of the particular group of workers which it is to cover. Its structure, its cost, and its value to the members will depend upon factors which vary from one group to the next. It is therefore a mistake simply to take another union's plan and adopt it, in all its details and without modification, as a model for an entirely different group of workers.[3]

This reasonable advice from the American Federation of Labor has probably been considered at least superficially by unions in the negotiation of pension plans. However, the trend for the extension of coverage of pension plans and their liberalization appears to be firmly set. In a period of reasonably full employment, most unions are convinced that they can get a big enough "package" to include the establishment and/or liberalization of pension plans without excessive sacrifice of wage rates or other working conditions.

Pension Benefits Adequate for a "Modest and Decent" Standard of Living for Retirees. Although unions may dispute the adequacy of the various budgets for an elderly couple, union demands on benefit levels are related to some standard of living for retirees. Usually the BLS elderly couple budget is used by unions as a point of departure in benefit discussions. A frequently advocated supplement to this budget is the cost of full service medical insurance. Further union advocated refinements of this

---

[3] Lane Kirkland, *Pension Plans Under Collective Bargaining: A Reference Guide for Trade Unions* (rev. ed.; Washington, D. C.: American Federation of Labor, December, 1954), pp. v, vi.

budget might include more liberal housing allowances, local variations in the changes in the Consumers' Price Index, and additions of certain items (e.g., automobile maintenance) essential to the maintenance of "an American standard of living."

Collectively Bargained Pensions as a Supplement to Governmentally Provided Retirement Benefits. Many of the initial collectively bargained pension plans provided for a monthly benefit of (say) $100 including whatever Social Security benefits the retiree received. This was direct integration with the Old Age and Survivors' Insurance program provided by the federal government. This benefit base has virtually disappeared in recent pension negotiations due to the liberalization of OASI and the resultant decreases in collectively bargained supplements. However, in determining any adequate pension level, unions will perforce consider the retirees' OASI benefits. In passing, it might be noted that today under most collectively bargained pension plans about two thirds of a retiree's total pension benefit come from OASI and about one third comes from the collectively bargained pension. It seems likely that this ratio will continue for the immediate future.

Pensions Should Be Noncontributory. Unions are in virtually unanimous agreement that the total cost of pensions should be paid by the employer. Ideologically, the unions compare pension costs to management's provision for the depreciation of machines. Another argument against contributory pensions is the administrative difficulties in persuading all employees to come under a contributory system. Finally, the income tax laws provide an incentive to noncontributory pensions. An employer contribution to pensions is not subject to personal income tax at the time of deposit. If the employee contributes to a pension plan, his earnings (from which the contribution is drawn) are taxable at the time of deposit. Employer-financed pension benefits, however, are taxable as income only at the time of withdrawal. A retired worker is in a much lower income bracket than an active employee. Thus employer-financed pensions are subject to a substantially smaller income tax bite than would be the same pensions established under a contributory plan.

Pensions Should Be Funded on an Actuarially Sound Basis. Union insistence on funded pension plans is protection against the possibility of a retired worker's benefits being discontinued because of a lack of funds or business adversity. (An important exception to this general rule is the United Mine Workers of America Welfare Fund which operates on a pay-as-you-go basis.) Business mortality is a constant threat to the worker's security and actuarially sound funding of pension plans tends to minimize this threat. Unions further argue that it is to the advantage of employers to pay a reasonably level cost over time to avoid extremely heavy charges at a later date as a more substantial number of employees become eligible for pension claims.

Actuarially sound funding, however, may be compromised for certain other purposes at least in part. The general nature of this compromise situation was ably stated by Mr. Leonard Lesser of the United Automobile Workers as follows:

The issues have, rather, centered around the determination of basic questions of a choice as to who gets what, when and how much. These basic determinations have raised issues such as whether to allocate the bulk of the limited funds to assure maximum retirement security to older workers at the cost of generally foregoing, for the present, such desirable features as vesting of benefits, transfer of rights and other provisions directed to the special needs of younger workers; whether to tie benefits to earnings and thus divert more of the available funds to higher paid workers, thus leaving less available for the pensions of lower paid workers, or whether, by gearing benefits to service only, to permit the payment of a more adequate benefit to all workers regardless of earnings; whether to provide a benefit for the permanently and totally disabled individual at the expense of a lower benefit for those who retire because of age; whether to give credit for past service and whether such past service should be credited on an equal basis with future service; what conditions of eligibility to require.

It is the answer to questions such as these which are generally involved in the negotiation of the benefit provisions of a pension plan.

The answers will, of course, vary even within a single union depending on differences in the groups of workers who are to be covered by the different plans. . . .[4]

Fixed Employer Payments in Terms of Cents per Hour Rather Than the Guarantee of a Level of Benefits. Employer contributions based on cents per hour provide for a known and limited employer liability. Such contributions provide an equality of competitive costs between employers in the same industry. Equally important, under this system the beneficiaries of the plan accrue all of the benefits derived from profitable investment of the funds and the savings resulting from employee turnover. In most cases where benefit levels have been negotiated the actual employer out-of-pocket costs of the plan have been substantially lower than originally anticipated. These savings have accrued to the employer in the form of lower contribution rates. Had bargaining been on a cents-per-hour basis, these savings would have permitted substantially liberalized benefits.

Benefit Rights Should Be Vested. A nonvested pension deprives a worker of all pension credits he had earned—or thought he had earned—through work performed in the past. Since pensions are deferred compensation, the worker should be able to carry these benefits with him when he quits or loses his job.

Joint Administration of the Pension Plan. Employer payments to a pension plan represent moneys which belong to the workers. It follows logically that the workers should be effectively represented when the

[4] Leonard Lesser, "Problems in Pension Contributions and Benefits," *Proceedings of Fifth Annual Meeting of Industrial Relations Research Association* (Madison, Wis.: Industrial Relations Research Association, 1953), pp. 89, 90.

program is being formulated as well as in the operation of the plan. The total assets of pension funds in the United States run into the billions of dollars. These moneys, which belong to the employees, could be properly invested in a number of *safe* projects which also could be a direct benefit to working people. For example, under joint administration more pension moneys would probably be invested in such worker-benefiting projects as government-insured low-income housing mortgages or for the development of self-liquidating health programs.

Compulsory Retirement Should Be Avoided. If benefits are not sufficient to enable the retiree to live in comfort, workers should not be compelled to retire while they are still able and willing to perform useful and remunerative service. Besides, a plan which permits workers to retire at their own pleasure after reaching retirement age will cost substantially less per unit of benefit than one with compulsory retirement.

Mr. Lane Kirkland, Assistant Director of the AFL Social Security Department, sees the problem of compulsory retirement as follows:

> . . . If benefit levels generally were high enough, this question of compulsory versus voluntary retirement would fade in importance and might even largely solve itself. If they could do so with substantially less financial sacrifice than retirement involves today, most workers would probably elect to retire when the chance comes and the years begin to tell.
>
> . . .
>
> From the standpoint of the trade union, the development of a situation in which there are men at work in the unit who are eligible for retirement at a pension which is in excess of the level of unemployment benefits being received by younger workers who have been laid off following a reduction in force can be expected to have a profound effect on the prevailing view, within the unit, of the relative merits of enforced and voluntary retirement. The problem is then seen as one of choice—not just between enforced and voluntary retirement, but between enforced retirement and the enforced layoff of workers whose family responsibilities may be greater, and whose resources and social insurance benefits may be less, than those of the workers eligible for retirement.
>
> . . .
>
> One approach, worth further exploration, which takes these factors into consideration, would be the application of a *uniform* but *flexible* retirement age policy—subject to variation in the light of economic conditions, manpower needs, and the state of the lay-off rolls. Under such an approach, the joint Board administering the plan might be given the discretion, within certain limits, to invoke and to remove, to raise and to lower, a mandatory retirement age applied uniformly to all workers at the age at which the level might be fixed at any given time.
>
> When a reduction in force occurs, the Board might be empowered to invoke mandatory retirement at, say, age 68, before workers having a certain minimum level of seniority are laid off, where it appears that such action will help to forestall the layoff. Or, as another possible variation, mandatory retirement might be called into play when workers on the lay-off rolls approach the point where U.C. benefits are exhausted.
>
> Subsequently, as employment conditions improve and laid-off workers are recalled, at some point in the process the mandatory requirement policy

may be removed, and workers who had been required to retire might be given the opportunity to return to work if they should choose to do so.

Such an approach would have the merit of enhancing the value of the pension plan to younger members of the work group, who have no immediate prospects of pension benefits.[5]

In summary, it seems that unions are seeking adequate pensions provided by employers on a noncontributory basis with full union participation in the administration of the program. The cents-per-hour goal is a method of maximizing the benefits available to retired workers.

Management Goals in Pension Bargaining

Isolated cases of unilateral management provision of retirement benefits preceded the development of collective bargained pensions. These plans were justified as means of improving employee morale, reducing employee turnover, building the prestige of the employer in the community, and providing for the orderly separation of superannuated employees.

Like union goals, management goals will vary in relationship to the particular firm's work force, profitability, and management philosophy. Nevertheless, some attempt to catalog general management goals should prove useful.

Pension Bargaining Is Inevitable. As collectively bargained pensions have spread, management's morale gains from the institution of pension benefits have been drastically diluted. As Couper and Vaughan state, "To put it rather extremely, very little credit is now given for instituting a pension plan, but vigorous criticism may result from not having such a plan."[6] If unable to avoid pension bargaining, management goals tend to center around minimum cost and maximum management flexibility in administration of the plan.

Adequate Benefits. Management negotiators are likely to be less generous in their definition of adequate benefits than union negotiators. "About all that can be said is that benefits must be large enough to enable a company to retire its superannuated employees without any adverse reaction from other employees or the community. Benefits, in other words, must be large enough to make elderly employees, if not positively willing to retire, at least willing to acquiesce in the termination of their service without any sense of grievance and with some realization that the company has made as generous provision for retirement as could be reasonably expected."[7]

[5] Lane Kirkland, "Problems in the Development of Pension Programs Under Collective Bargaining: Discussion," *Proceedings of Fifth Annual Meeting of Industrial Relations Research Association* (Madison, Wis.: Industrial Relations Research Association, 1953), pp. 105, 106, 107.

[6] Walter James Couper and Roger Vaughan, *Pension Planning: Experience and Trends* (New York: Industrial Relations Counselors, Inc., 1954), p. 172.

[7] *Ibid.*, p. 53.

Collectively Bargained Pensions Should Be Integrated with Government Pensions. The level of Old Age and Survivors' Insurance benefits should be deducted from the needs of retired workers when establishing a collectively bargained pension. If the level of OASI rises rapidly, collectively bargained pension benefits should fade away as the needs of older workers are provided by government. Employers pay half the cost of OASI and should receive full credit for OASI benefits in union negotiations. The employer's retirement costs go up every time OASI is liberalized. The total cost of retirement can be computed only by including the employer's OASI tax payments which currently approximate $290 per year per employee. Money once committed to private pension plans is irretrievable from the employer's viewpoint. Therefore, *anticipated* and current OASI taxes must be considered in current union negotiations.[8]

Ideally, Pension Programs Should Be Based on the Contributory Principle. In a free economy, we should look first to the individual to provide for himself. The contributory principle in pension programs tends to reinforce the employees' self-reliance. Vesting of pensions is probably sound, *if* the employee pays most of the cost of the pension. The contributory principle has been adopted as national policy in the OASI program.

Management Should Be Permitted to Meet Its Accepted Responsibility for Pension Benefits on a Pay-as-You-Go Rather Than a Funded Basis. Many employers believe that pensions could be provided at lower cost on a pay-as-you-go basis rather than by funding. This financing plan is more flexible and would allow management to receive the full benefit of liberalized OASI benefits. Lower costs from pay-as-you-go financing would also result from the frequently true assumption that a profitable enterprise can earn more from the investment of profits in business expansion than low-yield trust company or insurance company investments. Contrariwise, putting off the establishment of a pension plan in almost all organizations increases the outlay required during the initial years of the plan. This is true because the requirement for past service funding increases each year and funding for this has to be done over a period which grows shorter each year.

Management Guarantees a Benefit Level Rather Than a Cents-per-Hour Contribution. A management consultant provided the following rationalization for this position:

> One of my clients came up to negotiations recently for a change in the pension program along the lines of the recent settlement with the Big Three. Up to this time, they had been on a cents-per-hour basis, and the hours had been good because they had some good defense contracts, so they built up a fairly good surplus in the plan over the estimate of five years ago. We added

[8] For a complete development of the employer's interest in OASI as a part of the pension program, see Samuel N. Ain, "OASI—Impact on Private Pension Plans," *Harvard Business Review*, Volume XXXIV (May–June, 1956), pp. 101–8.

most of the recent increases in the General Motors and Ford Pension plans, except for a limitation in years of service, and we got 4½ cents credit in the economic settlement for the pension changes. In one of these cases, the cost to the company over and above the cents-per-hour they were paying into the pension plan, even if they have less than their average employment experience in the future, will be less than one-half cent an hour. They picked up four cents by a shift from cents-per-hour to granting benefits along the lines General Motors and Ford followed.[9]

Pensions Should Not Be Vested. Management resistance to vested pensions is aimed at cost reduction. Vesting of pensions greatly increases the cost of providing any fixed level of benefits. At the same time, most managements feel that pensions are rewards for long and faithful service. Vesting of pensions eliminates their usefulness as a deterrent to voluntary employee separation.

Management Should Retain the Administrative Control over Pension Funds. Management resists union participation in fund administration because union knowledge of costs, investment earnings, etc. could be a wedge for continuing liberalization of benefits and bickering over investment policies. Management pays the bill so it is only reasonable that management should set the investment policies.

Management Should Have Sole Discretion on Retirements after the Date That an Individual Becomes Eligible for a Pension. The pension benefit provided at the cost of management should entitle management to the benefits resulting from the orderly separation of superannuated employees. Enlightened management recognizes the individual differences and desires of older workers. However, selective assignment of older workers with wage adjustments to compensate for reassignment is usually resisted by unions. The kind of stop-and-go retirement-layoff-recall merry-go-round suggested above by Kirkland would destroy management's ability to assemble and direct a reasonably effective labor force. Any employment of workers beyond the regular retirement age should be at the sole discretion of management.

In summary, management's pension goals seem to be moderate retirement costs and a minimum interference with the internal operation of the business.

Problems in Pension Bargaining

The agreement and conflict in the goals of management and unions in pension bargaining take on real meaning only as the parties get down to negotiations. The actual out-of-pocket cost of pensions, a choice of financing methods, and the question of multiemployer pension plans are problems which must be dealt with by negotiators. The resolution of

---

[9] Joseph Daoust, *A Panel Discussion on "The Effect of GAW (or SUB) Settlements on the Foundry Industry at the 57th Annual Meeting of the National Foundry Association on October 7, 1955 at Chicago, Illinois* (mimeo.), p. 19.

these problems are of vital interest to the employer, the employees, and the union involved in the plan.

The Question of Actual Out-of-Pocket Costs. The actual out-of-pocket costs of operating a pension plan in the long run will be determined by:

1. The amount of money paid to each retiring worker per month or other benefit period.
2. The number of workers qualifying for benefits.
3. How long retirees live to receive benefits.
4. The rate of return earned through the investment of the money held in the pension fund (whether held by a trustee or an insurance company).
5. The expenses incurred in administering the pension system.

An employer with a larger number of older workers will incur higher pension costs than another employer with a younger labor force if they both grant the same level of pension benefits. Vesting of pension rights means higher costs than nonvested pensions if the same rate of benefit credit accrual operates in two firms. A pension benefit formula which provides for a fixed maximum consideration to past earnings or years of service is less costly than a formula which allows unlimited personal benefit rights accruals. Should a particular employer's labor force prove to be exceptionally long-lived this employer will incur greater ultimate pension costs than an employer whose labor force proves to have only average longevity. The higher the percentage of women in the work force the higher the probable pension costs because women have a longer life expectancy than men.

These few examples should illustrate the problem of computing the size of reserves needed to provide pensions for any specific work force. Such a problem is usually turned over to an actuary (either an independent consultant or the employee of an insurance company, an employers' association, or a union). The actuary needs detailed information from the employer about the number of employees, their age distribution, their sex distribution, their seniority, their average earnings, and monthly amount of personal pension benefits to be provided, the rate of employee turnover, and a decision of what, if any, vesting is to be provided. From these data he estimates the total fund that would be required to pay these benefits to present employees when they become eligible. He discounts this fund by an assumed number of employee separations without vested rights. Having established the ultimate size of the fund needed, he makes some assumptions about the number of years over which this fund can be accumulated. Obviously, the entire fund need not be established at the time the initial agreement is made. Usually 20 or more years are allowed for the accumulation of the fund. Finally the money in the fund isn't held in cash. Rather it is loaned or invested and earns a return. The actuary assumes that the money will earn a return at, say, 4 per cent per year.

These earnings will reduce the ultimate out-of-pocket expense that must be incurred to pay the benefits. The higher the earnings on the fund, the less the out-of-pocket expense. Under several sets of assumptions, the actuary then tells the parties what he estimates to be the cost of different benefit levels for the particular work force being considered.

When the parties are deciding on benefit levels, management will usually argue that a low rate of investment earnings should be assumed. This more conservative financing can be used by management as an argument for conservative benefits. The union will probably argue for an assumption of higher investment earnings as a justification for higher benefits in the initial stages of the plan. Exactly what the outcome is depends upon the particular work force involved. The question of costs leads to a discussion of financing methods.

Methods of Financing Pension Plans. There are many methods of financing pension plans. The two major methods are (1) insured plans (where certain benefits are purchased from an insurance company) and (2) trusteed plans (where banks or trust companies perform certain administrative and investment services in behalf of the union and/or management under the collective bargaining agreement). Both insured plans and trusteed plans can be divided into almost limitless numbers of variations.

Each system of financing has unique advantages and disadvantages. Costs of administration are different under different financing systems, but it is probably fair to say that the cost variations are reflected in variations of the amount of service received by the parties. The controversy over this comparative cost point is hot, but interestingly enough the dispute is not between labor and management. This dispute is between the trust companies and the insurance companies each arguing that they can serve labor and management better and less expensively than their competitors.[10] Aside from the cost-service dispute various financing methods are more suitable to particular situations.

We shall briefly discuss two insured programs (the group annuity contract and the deposit administration contract) and a self-administered trusteed plan. The best choice between financing alternatives depends upon the desires of a particular management and its union.

The *group annuity contract* is the oldest form of insured pension plan. Under it every year an increment of annuity or retirement income is actually purchased, and immediately guaranteed, for each employee covered by the plan. A group annuity contract can be written for any size firm, with no minimum premium requirement. This plan is pre-eminently

---

[10] For two good examples of these arguments, see: Laurence J. Ackerman, "Financing Pension Benefits," *Harvard Business Review*, Vol. XXXIV (September–October, 1956), pp. 637–4; and William L. Kleitz, "From the Thoughtful Businessman: Re: 'Financing Pension Benefits,'" *Harvard Business Review*, Vol. XXXIV (January–February, 1957), pp. 157–60.

suitable for the employer of less than 50 persons. The insurance company guarantees that the premium paid for each annuity purchased will actually finance the benefits promised. Such a plan is easily vested because the individual retirement benefits are purchased each year. This plan has the disadvantage of the highest original cash outlay and the highest premium over the life of the plan of the three types of plans discussed here. Also, the insurance company does not guarantee the premium rate, which may be adjusted upward or downward after five years of experience under the plan.

The *deposit administration contract* is a recent development in insured plans designed to offer the flexibility in funding which is so attractive in trusteed plans. Under the deposit administration contract the employer makes yearly contributions to the plan, but nothing is purchased for or allocated to individual employees until the time of retirement. Once the pension is purchased, it is guaranteed in the same manner as under a group annuity contract. The advantages of this plan are: (1) flexibility in funding comparable to trusteed plans, (2) the insurance company guarantees benefits for *retirees* (but does not guarantee the adequacy of the fund to purchase benefits for all eligible employees), (3) the investment of the funds is handled by competent investment analysts—the insurance company, (4) the insurance company guarantees the principal of the fund plus a fixed rate of earnings, say 2 1/4 to 2 3/4 per cent per year for the first five years; after the first five years the earnings guarantees are made on a year-to-year basis, and (5) small employers are able to write their own benefit plan while obtaining the pooled investment opportunities available in an insurance company's portfolio. The disadvantages usually accompanying the deposit administration contract are: (1) earnings on investment are limited to the conservative incomes usually earned by insurance companies, (2) insurance companies' retentions are usually higher than the investment management fee charged by a trustee, and (3) this plan sometimes results in higher *original* costs and more modest *original* benefits than a trusteed plan.

Under the *self-administered trusteed plan* the employer deposits with an outside agency, other than an insurance company, the money needed to fund the benefits prescribed in the collective bargaining agreement. The trustee, usually a bank or trust company, does *not* guarantee that the amount of money in the fund will be sufficient to pay the benefits prescribed in the agreement. The trustee's major legal liabilities are for fraud and gross negligence. The advantages of this plan are: (1) possible higher rates of return on investment because trustees are not closely limited by law as to the extent they can invest in corporation stocks, (2) greater flexibility in funding; this plan allows for slower funding of past service credits; it permits heavy funding in good profits years with the resulting tax savings to the employer, (3) lower *initial* cost because insurance plans customarily build up larger reserves for contingencies and rebate the excess in dividends *after* several years of experience, (4) great flexibility in benefits and eligibility bargaining; anything that the parties agree to is automatically reflected in the contribution calculations of the actuary, and (5) this plan *may* avoid certain administrative costs included in the insurance company premium, e.g., commissions, promotional expenses, and state premium taxes. (It is debatable in every case whether insurance company economies of operation offset these additional costs.) Advocates of the trusteed plans usually argue that the insured plans' guarantees are not essential because experience under pension plans is quite stable and spread over a significant time period. Thus, if experience proves to be somewhat less favorable than the actuary assumed, *small* adjustments in contribution rates *over long periods of time* can replenish the fund. The adverse experience (longer life for retirees) is spread out over a number of years and the pension plan in *reality* is a long-term commitment. However adverse the experience may be, it is imposed over a period of several years. The disadvantages of this plan are: (1) possible loss from adverse investment experience, (2) it is not suitable for small groups of employees because investment opportunities are limited and mortality experience may differ radically from actuarial estimates, and (3) less conservative assumptions about mortality, final earnings, expenses, and turnover may result in inadequate funding.

Our discussion of financing methods may be concluded with a few words of caution and some good advice. The foregoing discussion is a very general statement of *some* of the considerations involved in establishing a sound system for pension financing. The great diversity in pension plans and the alternative methods of financing require the attention of a full-time expert. Probably the best way to make these decisions is to employ a pension consultant for advice and obtain competitive bids from several insurance companies and trust companies. Bids should be considered on the basis of long-term cost, the quality of the service rendered by the various bidders, and the flexibility involved in alternative methods of financing the plan.

Multiemployer Pension Plans. As suggested earlier, a fully vested pension is the most expensive way of providing retirement income for superannuated employees. At the same time, unvested pensions tend to reduce *voluntary* employee mobility. The problem of mobility can become a pressing social problem in periods of economic mobilization. Further, many industries such as building construction, clothing manufacturing, and maritime trades provide only short-term employee attachment to a single employer. Such industries pose special problems if retirement income is to be provided through collective bargaining. The solution lies in either full vesting with the extreme disadvantage of very high cost or multiemployer pension plans.

Multiemployer pension plans may be classified as either fully integrated plans providing for equal benefits and uniform employer costs or special arrangements providing for certain financial pooling but allowing for variations in benefits and costs between employers.

Fully integrated plans flow naturally from the logic of multiemployer bargaining and are found almost exclusively as an extension of multiemployer bargaining. Such plans in coal mining, the needle trades, building construction, trucking, and Detroit automotive tool and die making shops offer all the advantages (and disadvantages) inherent in the structure of multiemployer bargaining. Employers are committed to identical pension costs just as they are committed to identical wage rates with the resultant equality of competition in terms of labor. Under these plans, the pension costs of hiring older workers are pooled and thus this economic incentive to discrimination is removed. Each employer avoids any differential costs arising from the age or sex distribution of his labor force or his rate of labor turnover. All employers gain from the reduction in pension costs arising from pooling of investment and the resultant higher rate of return and lower *per capita* administrative costs. Unions like these plans because in some cases they provide the only means by which retirement income can be provided through collective bargaining. In addition, a union would naturally welcome any device which would enable its members to move from job to job within the jurisdiction of the union without the loss of job rights. Single pension negotiations further reduce union overhead costs. The major problems inherent in such plans are the problems of dealing with delinquent employer members and the propriety of a particular charge for new employers joining an established multiemployer pension fund. Multiemployer plans do not provide the same low costs available to large employers. However the small employer's higher costs are inherent in the smallness of his business. Under such circumstances, some of the disadvantages of multiemployer plan may actually be less disadvantageous to the small employer than trying to go it alone.

Large employers engaging in separate bargaining with industrial unions generally have not entered into multiemployer pension plans. The potential advantages of lower costs just don't exist in such situations. For large employers the danger of higher costs is inherent in multiemployer pension plans. For example, employee age and sex distribution and rates of labor turnover are important determinants of long-term pension costs. A pooling of these risks for a group of large corporations at fixed benefits and contribution rates would result in the favorably situated firm subsidizing the pension costs of the less favorably situated firms. Such a program would serve the social purpose of removing the pension costs of hiring older workers and increasing employee voluntary mobility between firms, but the price of these social gains offers no advantage to the typical large employer. At the same time, the multiemployer plan threatens to weaken employer control over investment policies, eligibility standards, and the somewhat nebulous employee loyalty to the firm which provides his pension.

COLLECTIVE BARGAINING ISSUES ON HEALTH AND WELFARE PLANS

Collective bargaining on health and welfare plans flows from the fact that most health and welfare benefits can be provided more cheaply on a group basis than on an individual basis. Group life insurance makes life insurance available to some persons who otherwise would be compelled to pay very high individual premiums. Blue Cross and Blue Shield programs provide lower rates to groups of employees than to single subscribers.

A major function of the early American unions was the provision of health and welfare benefits. Some progressive managements unilaterally introduced comprehensive health and welfare programs in the prosperous 1920's. Unions have pretty much gone out of the business of *directly providing* health and welfare benefits from union funds because of the more recent availability of these benefits from other sources. Many of the health and welfare benefits directly provided by management in the twenties were wiped out by the Great Depression. Collective bargaining on health and welfare benefits is one of the most important postwar developments in labor-management relations. The Bureau of Labor Statistics has estimated that the number of workers covered by collectively bargained health and welfare programs has skyrocketed from 0.5 million in 1945 to 7 million in 1950 to 14.5 million in late 1960.[11] By the end of 1960, health and insurance plan coverage accounted for about 78 per cent of all workers under collective bargaining agreements.[12]

Union Goals in Health and Welfare Bargaining

Union goals in health and welfare bargaining tend to parallel union goals in pension bargaining. However, certain pension goals are not readily adaptable to the *present means* of providing health and welfare benefits. Thus unions have been forced to accept certain types of benefits which they consider "half measures." At the same time, many unions are actively engaged in the work of developing better *means* of providing health and welfare benefits. This community work beyond collective bargaining must be completed before many unions will be satisfied with what they are able to write into collective bargaining agreements.

Benefits Should Prepay the Cost of Comprehensive Medical Care. The AFL-CIO is quite dissatisfied with the types of benefits generally available through health and welfare plans in the United States. Mr. Lane

---

[11] U.S. Department of Labor, *Analysis of Health and Insurance Plans Under Collective Bargaining, Late 1955* (BLS Bulletin No. 1221, 1957) p. iii, and *Health and Insurance, and Pension Plan Coverage in Union Contracts, Late 1960* (BLS Report No. 228), p. 1.

[12] BLS Report No. 228, p. 1.

Kirkland has outlined the following "principles" which the AFL-CIO believes should guide the future development of prepaid medical care plans:

1. *The plan should prepay the cost of comprehensive medical care.* The immediate needs of certain members of any group may be met by emergency surgery, or long-term hospitalization. The needs of others in the group may be met by routine ambulatory care. Nevertheless, for the group as a whole, the need is always for comprehensive service. Anything less will leave some of its members with inadequate protection and care, and every member of the group faces the chance of finding himself among that less fortunate number.

. . .

2. *The program should provide direct medical services, rather than cash payments.* The aim of the trade union movement in negotiating health insurance plans is not simply to put more cash in the hands of its members. The aim is to relieve them of a serious cost burden while providing them with better medical care.

. . .

3. *The program should cover the entire family.* While their number is diminishing, many plans still cover only the wage earner and exclude his wife and children. Even if they were adequate in other respects, the contribution of such plans to the solution of the worker's health needs is small, for the medical expenses of the worker himself are but a small part of the total family medical bill that he has to pay. About 80 per cent of that bill stems from the medical expenses of dependents.

. . .

4. *The benefits of the program should extend beyond the working life of the member.* . . . Some feasible method must be incorporated in these programs, either through advance funding or otherwise, to extend their protection to the retired worker without the curtailment of benefits or the imposition of heavy premium charges upon the reduced incomes of the aged.

. . .

5. *The program should emphasize preventive care,* designed to preserve and improve the health of the individual. Most existing plans which offer in-hospital benefits do not merit the term "health insurance," for they do nothing to promote good health. Only 11 per cent of the services of physicians are performed in hospitals. The 90 per cent of their services that are rendered outside, in their offices, in patients' homes, in health centers or in x-ray and lab facilites is obviously far more important to the promotion and protection of the health of the public as a whole.

. . .

6. *The program should broaden the range of choices available to those it serves.* . . . We believe . . . that our members, and the people of America generally, should have the freedom to choose, not just the services of an individual physician engaged in solo practice of unknown quality, but medical groups offering comprehensive services as a team operation, and staffed by physicians selected in accordance with rigorous standards and governed by effective quality controls.

. . .

7. *The development of better health service programs should be a community-wide,* rather than an isolated, undertaking. We would much prefer to seek the solution of our medical care problems in cooperation with other groups in the community. We believe that those problems require the application of *social insurance* rather than commercial insurance principles. Social

insurance involves the pooling of risks and resources as broadly as possible so as to make possible the full participation of those less favorably situated as well as the preferred risks, and the inclusion of those with little as well as those with much economic or bargaining power.

The device of "experience-rating," in its various forms, militates against this principle, as does the isolation of health service plans and facilities into separate, uncoordinated entities. Lower premium and contribution rates for low-usage groups, with less need for medical services, can only mean higher rates for those whose age, sex, or family size requires more medical care, and prohibitive rates for those who need the protection of insurance the most. The consequences of experience-rating thus provide some of the strongest arguments against those—including many advocates of experience-rating—who argue that the health needs of the nation can be adequately met by voluntary plans and that no governmental action is necessary.[13]

The type of health benefits outlined by Mr. Kirkland generally are not available throughout the United States through ordinary insurance. Two large programs providing approximately the type of benefits to which Mr. Kirkland refers are the Kaiser Foundation Health Plan and the Health Insurance Plan of Greater New York. Figure 11–1 summarizes the major features of these two plans. With a combined coverage of approximately 1,500,000 persons, these plans provide substantial outpatient care as well as hospitalization and physician's services. Considerable attention is given to preventive medicine in the form of health examinations and immunizations. Within the areas they serve (New York City for HIP and San Francisco, Los Angeles, Portland, and Honolulu for the Kaiser Plan) these plans directly provide needed medical service rather than cash reimbursements for services rendered. Until some plan for providing these types of benefits are available, many unions will be very dissatisfied with their health and welfare negotiations. Such benefits could be provided through substantial revision of existing Blue Cross and Blue Shield or other plans or by the formation of new community health plans similar to Kaiser and HIP. In Detroit, the UAW has been a leading sponsor of the Community Health Association which seeks to provide services similar to the Kaiser Plan.

Several unions directly provide medical care to their members financed by employer (and in some cases, employee) contributions. The Amalgamated Clothing Workers of America and the International Ladies' Garment Workers' Union provide extensive medical care through their health centers. The work of the United Mine Workers of America Welfare and Retirement Fund in providing medical care and hospitalization in isolated mining communities is well known. Other unions are in the process of investigating the possibilities of directly providing medical care. However, a major problem in the development of this type of

---

[13] Lane Kirkland, Assistant Director, Department of Social Security, AFL-CIO, *Address before the California State Chamber of Commerce, Insurance Section, San Francisco, California, November 29, 1956: What Kind of Prepaid Medical Care?* (mimeographed, AFL-CIO Social Security Department, 1956), pp. 6–11.

FIGURE 11–1

COMPREHENSIVE, COMMUNITY-WIDE HEALTH PLANS

KAISER FOUNDATION HEALTH PLAN

1. *Eligibility for Participation.* Both group and individual memberships are available. Individuals may continue coverage after dropping out of a group but must pay higher premiums. Spouses and dependent unmarried children under 19 years of age are eligible for coverage.
2. *Benefits.* Benefits provided vary with particular situations or the needs of particular groups of subscribers. *The benefits described below are those provided for employees and dependents covered by the northern California construction industry as provided by the Carpenters Health and Welfare Trust Fund for California.*
   a) All services of physicians, including surgeons and specialists, without charge for in-hospital care. Doctor's care at the office is provided at a fee of $1 per visit. The patient is charged for at least the first home visit. No charges are made for follow-up calls by the doctor or for calls of visiting nurses, when under doctor's orders. Unlimited emergency service is provided in cases of sudden illness or injury.
   b) Hospital care is provided for each illness or injury and its recurrences and complications. Active workers and dependents are provided 80 full days of hospital care per disability and retired workers are provided 60 full days. All charges including anesthetics, medicines, drugs, and needed private-duty nursing care are covered while in the hospital.
   c) No charge for surgical procedures except nominal charges for maternity care and removal of tonsils and adenoids.
   d) X-rays, physiotherapy, laboratory services provided without fee when ordered by the physician.
   e) Patient pays for drugs and medicines when supplied in office or at home. No fee for drugs or medicines during hospitalization.
3. *Coverage.* Almost 900,000 persons in West Coast States and Hawaii. San Francisco, Los Angeles, Portland, and Honolulu are the major areas served by the Kaiser Plan.

HEALTH INSURANCE PLAN OF GREATER NEW YORK

1. *Eligibility for Participation.* Group coverage only. Most members enroll through groups organized by either unions or employers.
2. *Benefits.* The plan provides general medical care, the services of specialists, surgical care, and maternity care at HIP medical centers, in the doctors' offices, in hospitals, and at home. Diagnostic and laboratory services, physical therapy, X-ray treatment, and other special treatments are provided at the health centers. Among other benefits provided are periodic health examinations, visiting nurse service, psychiatric advice, and ambulance service.
3. *Coverage.* Over 600,000 persons in New York City and vicinity.

SOURCE: U.S. Department of Labor, *Digest of One Hundred Selected Health and Insurance Plans Under Collective Bargaining, Winter 1961–62*, BLS Bulletin No. 1330, pp. 211–13.

program is the need for a geographically concentrated union membership or extensive community support for the undertaking.

In the General Absence of Adequate Governmental Programs, Unions Should Attempt Simultaneously to Fill the Gap through Collective Bargaining and Continue to Advocate Needed Governmental Action. Organized labor was a powerful lobbying force in the enactment of the 1965 medicare amendments to Social Security. There is every reason to believe that unions will continue to press for the liberalization of this new program and its extension to persons below retirement age. Simultaneously with the drive for governmentally provided medical care, unions will press for improvements of medical care plans provided under collective bargaining agreements.

Health and Welfare Plans Should Be Noncontributory. Unions advocate noncontributory medical plans because of the tax savings resulting from the employer paying the total cost of the plan. Noncontributory plans also offer the advantage of insuring 100 per cent employee participation without solicitation.

Because of Their Nature, Health and Welfare Plans Are Not Particularly Suitable to Actuarially Sound Funding. Unions should have full participation with management in determining the best method for financing health and welfare plans, be it by purchasing insurance from a commercial carrier, direct provision of service, or self-insurance.

Management contributions to health and welfare programs represent deferred wages for employees. The variety of benefits available from different sources at different prices is almost infinite. As the representative of the best interests of the employees, the union should have a voice in the determination of where the benefits are purchased and an opportunity to pass on the propriety of the fees charged for the benefits rendered. In some cases, Blue Cross and Blue Shield are best and most economical, in other cases commercial indemnity policies are preferable, and in some cases direct provision of service seems most desirable.

Employer's Obligation to Provide Health and Welfare Benefits Should Be Stated in Cents per Hour or Percentage of Payroll Terms Rather than as a Guarantee of Benefits. Unions tend to prefer cost bargaining to benefits bargaining because it makes savings from favorable experience with the plan available to the employees. Such bargaining also gives the union greater choice in the type of benefits to be provided than is available under benefits bargaining.

Union goals in health and welfare bargaining are not as clearly delineated as they are in pension bargaining. This situation is due to a number of factors. First, the types of benefits available from various sources are almost infinite in variety. Second, many unions started their bargaining on health and welfare funds from a program that had been unilaterally established by management (in some cases for many years). Third, there was no "floor" program established by government from which privately established plans could be built. Finally, the newness of the health insurance field and the general unpredictability of the risks involved made for great difficulty in formulating realistic cost estimates.

Management Goals in Health and Welfare Bargaining

A management attempting to formulate goals in health and welfare bargaining is confronted with problems similar to those confronting the union. Management thinking probably focuses on the question of minimum cost consistent with benefits provided and the maintenance of a salutary employee attitude toward the company and the benefit system.

Benefits Should Not Encourage Malingering or Seriously Impair the Employee's Personal Obligation to Budget for Normal Expenses. A major problem in the health insurance field is the question of overutilization of hospitalization and medical benefits. Under some insurance programs, the employee must bear the full, and sometimes substantial, cost of any outpatient medical care. All, or a substantial portion, of these costs are paid as insurance benefits once the employee is admitted to a hospital. Thus, employees seek unneeded hospitalization. Ultimately these uneconomic benefit costs are reflected in the premiums to which the employer contributes.

Health and Welfare Plans Should Be Financed on a Contributory Basis. Employee contributions to health and welfare plans reduce the employer's costs *and* remind employees that health and welfare plans are not something for nothing. Ideologically the insurance forms called deductible and coinsurance are appealing to many managements. As a matter of self-reliance, employees should be able to budget for deductible health insurance benefits just as they budget for deductible automobile collision insurance. Coinsurance which reimburses a fixed percentage of the costs incurred reinforces the employee's proper interest in receiving only needed medical care and paying only a reasonable price for the service received.

Where Possible, Many Managements Prefer to Bargain on Benefits Rather than on Costs. Many large corporations dealing with industrial unions prefer to guarantee benefits rather than bargain directly on costs. By providing benefits, management recovers the gains from favorable experience either directly in the form of dividends or indirectly in the form of reduced costs in future periods. Also by providing benefits management is able to limit its program to the types of benefits generally available from insurance companies and nonprofit service organizations such as Blue Cross and Blue Shield. Of course, in multiemployer bargaining management's commitment is stated in terms of cents-per-hour or as a percentage of payroll. This type of commitment is necessary if benefits are to be provided for employees who move from job to job. The larger the group covered, the lower the cost of providing any medical, hospital, or cash indemnity benefit other than life insurance. However, as the employer enters a larger group, he tends to dilute his personal influence on the amount of benefits ultimately provided.

In General, Management Is Reluctant to Pioneer in the Area of Providing Medical Care and Other Benefits which Are Not Available through Insurance Companies or Other Existing Community Organizations. The risks of medical expense and disability allowances are very unpredictable. The idea of setting up completely new systems of providing medical care is not appealing to many managements because they simply consider it beyond the range of their competence. Other managements fear that once they associate themselves with organizations committed to providing comprehensive medical care, they have no recourse but to ultimately accept the full cost of the plan, no matter how high the cost or how unreasonable the benefits. Finally, many managements believe that they should encourage *private* insurance and *private* medical care as foundation stones in a system of private enterprise.

Special Bargaining Problems on Health and Welfare Plans

Because of the complexity of the types of benefits possible and the diverse means of providing them, we shall limit our discussion of bargaining problems on health and welfare plans to catastrophe insurance and possible means of reducing health and welfare costs. At first glance these programs would appear to be administrative rather than bargaining problems. We consider them as bargaining problems because they vitally affect the ability of management to minimize the cost and the ability of the unions to obtain the benefits they desire for their membership.

Major Medical Expense Insurance. Frequently, major medical policies are written to cover expenses beyond the coverage of basic coverages such as Blue Cross or Blue Shield. Major medical covers all medical expenses whether incurred in outpatient care or in a hospital. The only limits on the reimbursement available to an insured person are: (1) the deductible feature, (2) the coinsurance feature, (3) the total maximum benefits, and (4) a provision that medical charges must be reasonable and necessary.

The deductible feature means that for each incapacity or for each benefit year, the insured must pay a fixed dollar amount of the total medical bill, e.g., $50, $100, or some other such amount. The coinsurance feature means that the insurance company does not pay the total amount of the medical expense beyond the deductible, e.g., the insured person must pay 25 per cent or 20 per cent of the total cost, while the insurance company pays the remaining 75 per cent or 80 per cent of the bill. Total maximum benefits under these plans are established at a high figure such as $5,000 or $10,000 per benefit year. "Reasonable and necessary" medical expenses tend to be broadly interpreted as those prescribed by competent physicians in the area where service is rendered.

Major medical was designed to help meet medical expenses in those cases which too often meant personal catastrophe, those cases where expenses might run as high as an employee's annual earnings. The deductible, coinsurance, and maximum benefit provisions combine to accomplish two essentials for insurance: (*a*) they limit total liability for the insurance company and (*b*) they make the insured cost conscious in contracting for medical services.

Many management people are favorably impressed by major medical expense insurance. The Chamber of Commerce of the United States has praised it as follows:

> The inherent flexibility of Major Medical—the fact that benefits are normally available whether the individual is in or out of the hospital—avoids any inducement for unneeded hospitalizations. For this reason, it appeals strongly to the nation's physicians. Unlike some forms of health insurance, it does not operate to influence the doctor's decision—either directly or indirectly—as to how to furnish the best possible medical care to his patient.
>
> . . .
>
> Major Medical has definitely passed beyond the experimental stage and is now an established and important branch of voluntary health insurance. . . .[14]

The AFL-CIO Executive Council does not share the Chamber's enthusiasm for major medical. It has summed up the objections to major medical as follows:

> The type of "major medical expense" or "catastrophic" insurance policy presently offered by commercial carriers cannot be regarded as a suitable alternative to, or substitute for, a sound basic program of comprehensive insurance protection which provides for diagnosis and treatment in the home or doctor's office as well as in the hospital, and which covers the common as well as the exceptional condition. Where a satisfactory basic program of this type already exists, a "major medical" insurance provision may be useful as a secondary supplement to such a program. The measure of its acceptability, however, should be the extent to which the basic health plan already meets the primary objective—to remove the dollar barrier to comprehensive health services, including preventive care, for the entire family.[15]

Reducing the Costs of Health and Welfare Benefits.   The rapid development of all kinds of health and welfare benefits under collective bargaining has occasionally resulted in poor decisions by unions and managements on what benefits to purchase, where to obtain them, and what they should cost. This problem has been carefully examined in the case of insurance benefits by the Foundation on Employee Health, Medical Care and Welfare, Inc. The Foundation is a joint undertaking of the International Association of Machinists and U.S. Industries, Inc. It plans additional studies for the purpose of educating union and management

[14] "Preface," *Major Medical Expense Insurance* (2d ed.; Washington, D.C.: Chamber of Commerce of the United States, October, 1957).

[15] Raymond Munts, *A Barrier on the Road to Health: Catastrophic Illness Insurance* (Washington, D.C.: American Federation of Labor and Congress of Industrial Organizations, Publication No. 51, May, 1957), pp. 12–13.

representatives in some of the intricacies of health and welfare bargaining.[16]

The *initial* cost of health and welfare benefits is the premium charged by the insuring agency. In determining an initial premium, the insurance carrier considers such factors as:

1. What benefits are to be provided?
2. What are the occupations of the employees? (Certain occupations result in greater claims than others.)
3. Sex distribution of the employees. (Women usually produce more hospitalization and medical claims than men. On the other hand, life insurance premiums for women are lower than for men because they have a longer life expectancy.)
4. Age distribution of the employees. (Group life insurance premiums go up as the labor force ages because the premium is the sum of the monthly premiums charged on behalf of each individual covered. Medical and hospitalization premiums, excluding maternity benefits, also rise with age.)
5. Size of group. (Volume discounts are available on disability, indemnity, and surgical insurance.)
6. Number of employees who have dependents. (In hospitalization and medical programs, a large percentage of the claims paid are for the dependents of covered employees.)

The *long-term* cost of a health and welfare program is determined by the *claim payments plus the insurance company retention*. The insurance company retention includes premium taxes, costs of administering the program, claims handling expenses, commissions and acquisitions expenses, contingency reserves, risk charges, and profit. The amount of benefits will tend to be identical no matter what insurance company carries the program, however the retention may vary substantially between companies. This is due to variations in the service rendered by the carriers, their policies on contingency reserves, and the cost they incur in selling and handling their business, as well as their profit.

The Foundation on Employee Health, Medical Care and Welfare, Inc., suggests the following methods of obtaining the best service for the lowest cost from insurance companies:

1. Obtain competitive bids from several insurance companies using a complete specification letter. These bids should be evaluated on the basis of:
   a) Initial premium cost
   b) Projection of the insurance company's retention estimates
   c) The formula used for establishing reserves for incurred but unpaid claims and the disposition reserves in the event of cancellation of the insurance

---

[16] The discussion of reducing costs which follows is based largely on the Foundation's first report: Foundation on Employee Health, Medical Care and Welfare, Inc., *Problems and Solutions of Health and Welfare Programs: Improving Value and Reducing Costs* (Study No. 1, Part A) (New York: Foundation on Employee Health, Medical Care and Welfare, Inc., May, 1957), 48 pp.

    d) Financial position of the insurance company

    e) Company's experience in health and welfare plans, administrative and claim facilities.

2. Cover as large a group of employees as possible. (Per capita retention declines as the number of covered individuals increases.)

3. Keep commission payment to a minimum by combining policies for commission purposes.

4. Eliminate all unnecessary fees. If the health and welfare fund undertakes to perform services that the insurance company might otherwise perform, the fund should benefit from a reduced retention.

5. Consider using a "self-accounting" system for the health and welfare fund. (Fund prepares its own premium statements to the insurance company. The fund should then receive a reduction in retentions.)

6. Consider using a "draft-book" system for the payment of claims. (When a health and welfare fund is in a position to undertake the clerical work connected with the issuance of benefits, via the "draft-book" system, the result will be a reduction in the insurance company's retention. Frequently the reduction in the retention exceeds the additional clerical expense to the fund for processing the claims.)

7. Changing insurance carriers can be costly. The trustees should carefully evaluate the entire situation before switching from one insurance carrier to another.

8. Conduct an annual review of the fund. A properly conducted review can:

    a) Identify any "leakage" in premiums between the fund and the carrier.

    b) Indicate the propriety of the insurance company's retention.

    c) Indicate the propriety of the insurance company's "reserve for incurred but unpaid claims."

    d) Indicate dividends or "retroactive rate credit" received as the result of more favorable experience than anticipated in the original premium

    e) Compare benefits received by employees against their need for medical and hospitalization service.

There are other methods of both improving benefits and reducing costs. For example, the International Association of Machinists is attempting to fill the gap between existing plans and its long-range goal of comprehensive prepaid medical coverage. The International union is encouraging Local and District unions to undertake a program of multiphasic screening examinations. In co-operation with the underwriting insurance carrier and local physicians, these examinations would make members aware of diseases or abnormalities which might otherwise go unnoticed. Based on the findings of these examinations, preventive measures could be undertaken which might ultimately reduce claims expense for hospitalization and surgery.[17]

Self-insurance offers another possibility for reducing costs. Under such a system, all insurance company retentions would be eliminated.

[17] M. R. Sterns, "Unions, Medical Care, and Health and Welfare Programs," *New York University Ninth Annual Conference on Labor* (Albany, N.Y.: Matthew Bender & Co., Inc., 1956), pp. 197–210.

However, this is not an unmixed blessing. Self-insurance has some inherent dangers. First, the insurance company's retention is a payment for expert service. There is no certainty that a union-management board could bring equal competence to the administration of a health and welfare program at lower cost. Second, employers and unions are under greater *internal political* pressure to allow claims than is a disinterested insurance carrier. (It might be noted that one sometimes advocated argument for self-insurance is that the more liberal approach by the employer and/or union would further the purpose of providing all desirable medical care without undue attention to costs.) Third, the risks of health and welfare guarantees are much greater than the risks of pension guarantees. In both cases, a large group of employees is needed to make the self-insurance approach practical. The greater risk in health and welfare programs results from the fact that health and welfare benefits costs may be incurred in lumps rather than spread over a period of years. Finally, many employers shy away from self-insurance because they consider it to be a union "foot in the door" to greatly liberalized benefits and commensurate cost increases.

COLLECTIVE BARGAINING ISSUES ON UNEMPLOYMENT SCHEMES

The collective bargaining issues on unemployment schemes are not as clearly defined as in the area of pensions and medical care. This confusion is probably attributable to the unpredictability of the hazard and the lack of any experience with a *unified* national program of unemployment compensation, retraining, and relocation. Although unemployment occurs at the enterprise and it should be a cause of deep concern to both management and the union at the level of the enterprise, control over the level of unemployment is probably beyond the competence of the enterprise.[18] Nevertheless, a few managements and unions have developed some highly ingenious schemes for cushioning the impact of unemployment. At this writing, the federal government is engaged in the search for a comprehensive national manpower policy which could cope with such problems as income for unemployed persons, retraining, and relocation of persons in distressed areas. If such a national policy can be formulated and made operational, collective bargaining schemes on unemployment could be integrated with it.

Collective bargaining on unemployment schemes involves "cost" and "principle" considerations similar to bargaining on pensions and medical care. At the propaganda level, unions show little interest in cost; but demands at the bargaining table recognize the limitations of the enter-

---

[18] For historical perspectives on the problem of controlling unemployment at the enterprise level, see Edward D. Wickersham, "Controlling Unemployment at the Company Level," *Industrial and Labor Relations Review*, Vol. 14 (October, 1960), pp. 68–82.

prise's ability to pay. Management's most serious problems in collective bargaining on unemployment schemes are the apparent *unpredictability* of costs, the need for limited liability, and the control of malingering.

The patchwork of various tailor-made schemes for alleviating the hazard of unemployment can be illustrated by severance pay; true guaranteed annual wage plans; work-sharing; retraining, relocation, severance, and early retirement combinations; and Supplemental Unemployment Benefits. This comprehensive array of halfway "solutions" to the unemployment problem gives a management and a union seeking a solution to the unemployment problem a wide choice of alternatives. Nevertheless, each management and union pretty much has to start from scratch in developing their tailor-made plan and any plan that they may develop is severely handicapped by the unpredictability of the hazard and the lack of a comprehensive national manpower policy.

Severance Pay

Severance pay plans are receiving attention because of the threatened or actual impact of technological change. If changes are gradual, dismissal may not occur because of work force attrition or transfers. Severance pay seeks to cushion the dislocation due to the shutdown of a whole plant or department or other large-scale dismissals.

Most severance pay agreements require that an employee have a specified minimum length of service to be eligible for benefits and benefits are graduated upward on the basis of length of service to the company. A fairly common arrangement is to provide one week's severance pay for each year of service. The purpose of severance pay is partially to compensate the worker for the loss of accumulated rights which he has earned over his years of productive service.

Severance pay plans are particularly significant in the enterprises organized by the Steelworkers, Autoworkers, Communications Workers, Ladies' Garment Workers, and International Brotherhood of Electrical Workers. A significant number of enterprises have unilaterally established severance pay plans for their nonunion white-collar workers.

Most commonly severance pay plans are not *funded*, thereby creating for the employer the grim prospect of an *unpredictable* and almost *unlimited* future liability. In view of the widespread adoption of unfunded severance pay schemes, it appears that many employers are sufficiently optimistic about the long-range health of their enterprises to sign an almost "blank check" liability on severance pay. In contrast to unfunded severance pay plans, some severance pay arrangements have been grafted on to Supplemental Unemployment Benefit plans which are funded.

True Guaranteed Annual Wage Plans

A true guaranteed annual wage provides 2,080 hours of work and/or pay for each employee in a 12 month period. Such guarantees are usually limited to high seniority employees, with overtime offsets, and great managerial flexibility in the assignment of workers to whatever jobs may be available. Such plans may involve the establishment of funds or reserves, but generally they are limited in their application to sufficiently stable industries to allow them to operate on a "pay-as-you-go" basis.

True guaranteed annual wage plans are extremely rare. In the Latimer Report of 1947, only 39 plans providing a full 52–40 guarantee were known to be in operation in the United States. The most publicized of these plans, i.e., Nunn-Bush, Proctor & Gamble, and Hormel Meat Packing, do not provide a full 52–40 guarantee because of limitations on eligibility, overtime offsets, etc.

Although the Teamsters' Union has negotiated some true guaranteed annual wage plans, it seems very unlikely that these plans will ever be widely adopted because of the extreme difficulties in accurately predicting employment trends in many industries. However, such plans might be adopted in industries with generally stable employment patterns like the public utilities.

Work-Sharing

Work-sharing is not an unemployment benefit, but it certainly is an important, and frequently used, possible solution to the problem of unemployment. Cynically, it might be termed "sharing the misery." Traditionally, craft unions have used work-sharing as their solution to unemployment. When there isn't enough work to keep all the painters or carpenters working, the Local union merely adopts a 30-hour rule which spreads the work among more unionists. During the Great Depression, management frequently scheduled short workweeks so that as many employees as possible could obtain some income. The emergence of supplemental unemployment benefits has an important impact on the work-sharing problem, as will be discussed later in this chapter.

Work-sharing by industrial unions is less common than in the craft union situation. This is primarily due to the difficulties of job assignments which naturally arise in a factory-type employment relationship. However, factory managers and industrial unions sometimes negotiate limited work-sharing arrangements. For example, industrial union contracts may ban the hiring of new workers, require the dismissal of certain categories of workers such as temporary or probationary employees, or specify limits on contracting-out practices of the employer. If these measures prove inadequate, the contract may provide for some type of work-sharing within departments or occupational groups.[19]

Retraining, Relocation, Severance, Early Retirement Combinations.

Major technological changes, the need to modernize work rules, and a persistently high rate of unemployment in the national economy have

---

[19] Cf. Morton Levine and Theodore Allison, *Collective Bargaining Clauses: Layoff, Recall, and Work-Sharing Procedures* (Washington, D.C.: BLS Bulletin No. 1189, U.S. Government Printing Office, February, 1956), v., 53 pp.

intensified the search for solutions to the problem of unemployment by employers, unions, and the government. The last few years have seen the development of several new approaches to the problem at the bargaining table. We shall briefly discuss developments in West Coast longshoring, the railroad industry, and the meat packing industry.

In the West Coast longshoring industry, employers have obtained wide freedom in the introduction of labor-saving devices in exchange for a $29 million benefit fund to be established over a five and one-half year period. The benefit fund is to be used to finance guaranteed annual wages and generous early retirement benefits for *registered* longshoremen. By excluding a group of nonregistered longshoremen more or less regularly attached to the industry from its benefits, the agreement will reduce the number of persons employed in the industry. Over the long run the net effect of the agreement will be to provide substantial work guarantees to a smaller number of union members who are retained in employment while enabling the employers to take full advantage of technological advancements.[20]

Competition from other modes of transportation has taken a heavy toll in the American railroad industry. The carriers and labor organizations agreed to the creation of a Presidential Railroad Commission in the fall of 1960 for the purpose of recommending solutions to labor relations problems. After intensive study of a wide range of problems, the Commission issued comprehensive recommendations. In recommending that the carriers be allowed to introduce technological change without limitation, the Commission suggested protection for displaced employees in the forms of: (1) displacement allowances or severance pay graduated on years of seniority and employee earnings; (2) employer payment of 75 per cent of the tuition for up to two years of training for another occupation; and (3) a nationwide system of preferential hiring in the industry. The Commission's general recommendations on manpower planning were designed to reduce the number of employees attached to the industry and to distribute employment among those who remain attached. These recommendations included: (1) a nationwide hiring pool giving preference to unemployed operating employees; and (2) compulsory retirement schedules eventually requiring retirement at age 65 or earlier. The Commission's work is a landmark of extensive study of manpower problems as a whole in an industry and an attempt to solve these problems while minimizing their adverse effects on employees.[21]

---

[20] For a discussion of this agreement, the factors leading up to its negotiation, and its probable long-range effects, see Charles C. Killingsworth, "The Modernization of West Coast Longshore Work Rules," *Industrial and Labor Relations Review*, Volume XV (April, 1962), pp. 295–306.

[21] *The Report of the Presidential Railroad Commission* (Washington, D.C.: U.S. Government Printing Office, February, 1962), 327 pp., provides constructive insights to anyone interested in approaching the problems of unemployment from an over-all viewpoint. This volume is supplemented by four Appendix Volumes: I.

In 1959 Armour and Company and two meat packing unions created an Automation Committee to study the problems of technological unemployment in the Company and to recommend methods for alleviating its impact on employees. Financed by a company contribution of up to $500,000 based on one cent per hundredweight of meat shipped from its meat packing houses, the Committee studied relocation allowances, retraining, and the re-employment experience of workers who lost their jobs in plant closings. The published report of the Committee[22] emphasizes the need for governmental action in the areas of employment service assistance, full employment, co-ordination of public and private pension plans, and Unemployment Compensation. The studies of the Committee re-emphasize the well-documented problems of older workers, poorly educated workers, and members of minority groups in finding re-employment when they lose their jobs. A reasonable inference from the work of the Committee is that retraining offers only a very limited promise as a means of alleviating the problems of unemployed workers.

Individually and collectively, the longshoring, railroad, and meat packing experiences offer no pat solutions to the problem of unemployment in any enterprise. Collectively these experiences do provide a worthwhile check list of topics for investigation that could be used in an attempt to meet an enterprise's unique unemployment problems with a collective bargaining program aimed at making the best of a difficult situation.

Supplemental Unemployment Benefits

In 1955–56, the automobile and steel industries negotiated Supplemental Unemployment Benefit plans. By 1967, the coverage of various forms of Supplemental Unemployment Benefits plans approximated two million workers represented primarily by the United Automobile Workers, the United Steelworkers, the National Maritime Union, the United Rubber Workers, and the International Ladies' Garment Workers' Union. Although these plans have proven to be efficient in operation and not prohibitively costly, it appears that their coverage has stabilized.

We shall discuss the major characteristics of S.U.B. plans and their influence on the operation of the individual enterprise.

Characteristics of Major S.U.B. Plans. We shall discuss benefits, financing methods, cost and administrative problems under Supplemental Unemployment Benefits plans.

Benefits. Gross maximum weekly benefits under S.U.B. plans range up to as much as 75 per cent of gross pay for 40 hours of work. These

---

Index-Digest to the Record of the Commission's Hearings; II, Pay Structure Study, Railroad Operating Employees; III, Studies Relating to Railroad Operating Employees; and IV, Studies Relating to Collective Bargaining Agreements and Practices Outside the Railroad Industry.

[22] *Progress Report Automation Committee,* dated June, 1961, 29 pp.

gross benefits include a full offset for any Unemployment Compensation received by the beneficiary. Eligibility for benefits is closely tied to eligibility for Unemployment Compensation. Reduced benefits are available for short workweeks. In the event of total unemployment, some S.U.B. beneficiaries are eligible for unemployment benefits for as long as 52 weeks, despite the fact that Unemployment Compensation eligibility generally expires after 26 weeks of unemployment. Recent amendments to S.U.B plans also provide for lump-sum severance pay settlements. The weekly dollar benefit to which an individual claimant is entitled generally is dependent upon three factors: (1) the claimant's earnings in full-time employment; (2) the claimant's family status; and (3) the Trust Fund Position which reflects the unemployment experience of the contributing employer The duration of benefits is also subject to revision on the basis of the Trust Fund Position. Benefits paid from the Fund are dependent upon the level of Unemployment Compensation benefits paid in the states where the claimants draw U.C.

Financing Methods. Generally S.U.B. is financed exclusively by employer contributions expressed either in cents per man-hour worked or as a percentage of payroll. All benefits are paid from a Trust Fund, and the assets of this fund represent the employer's total liability for benefits. Employers with good unemployment experience are freed of the liability of paying into the Trust Fund so long as a Maximum Trust Fund Position is maintained. Thus the Maximum Trust Fund Position concept follows the principle of *experience rating* in Unemployment Compensation. Employers competing in the same industry may incur substantially different S.U.B. costs depending upon their success or failure is stabilizing employment.

Cost. Employers are primarily interested in the cost of various collective bargaining demands. The initial cost of an S.U.B. plan is the maximum liability which an employer agrees to accept. Actual long-term cost depends on the benefits paid. We can summarize this long-term cost as follows:

1. The number of persons drawing benefits, which is determined by (*a*) the number of persons unemployed and (*b*) the eligibility requirements for benefits.
2. The level of benefits, which is determined by (*a*) wage level of eligible claimants, (*b*) dependency status of eligible claimants, and (*c*) trust fund position *less* (*d*) unemployment compensation offset.
3. The duration of benefits paid, which is determined by (*a*) the success of laid-off employees in finding re-employment (the effort exerted in finding re-employment and the availability of re-employment opportunities), (*b*) the duration of the company's layoff, and (*c*) the seniority of claimants and trust fund position at the time of drawing benefits.

Administrative Problems. Experience with S.U.B. agreements in the auto industry indicates that administrative problems have been relatively minor. Before the plan goes into operation, the company usually trains foremen on the provisions of the plan, prepares instructions for applicants for S.U.B. benefits, makes certain that needed information from the state unemployment compensation agency is available, selects a trustee to hold the funds, and may publicize the plan to all employees. These tasks are substantial, but fit into the routine of most industrial relations, payroll, financial, and legal departments of a corporation. Simplicity of administration is probably due to the auto industry requirement that S.U.B. claimants present their U.C. checks to establish prima facie evidence of eligibility. The fact that the Ford Motor Company was able to establish an entirely new system for S.U.B. for 140,000 employees with the addition of only five extra people[23] is an indication that administrative problems have not been overpowering.

The Influence of S.U.B. on the Individual Enterprise. A central point in management's opposition to the guaranteed annual wage was the fear that it would seriously interfere with the internal operation of the business enterprise. Since the individual business is the focus of collective bargaining and S.U.B. has only a negligible impact on the national economy, the impact of S.U.B. on the firm takes on major importance. S.U.B. has an important influence on the skilled-unskilled differential, technological advance, and work-sharing.

Even more than a cents-per-hour wage increase, S.U.B. tends to narrow the wage and benefits differential between the highly skilled and the semiskilled or unskilled worker. Money contributed to an insured S.U.B. Fund is used to provide benefits for unemployed workers. The worker most likely to become unemployed is the low seniority and less skilled worker. Most employers delay the layoff of their highly skilled men as long as possible because they wish to retain this cadre of key employees for the always expected upturn in business activity. Thus, the skilled employee usually does not expect ever to draw an S.U.B. check. Even if the highly skilled employee becomes eligible for an S.U.B. check, he usually will not receive his full percentage of wage loss because of the maximum limitations on the S.U.B. check.

Does S.U.B. prevent or slow technological change? An important feature of S.U.B. is that it provides an additional economic cushion for workers forced to seek re-employment due to technological change. In periods of widespread unemployment, an employer would consider his increased S.U.B. fund contributions as an integral part of the cost of installing new technological devices. This additional cost might be an influence in the direction of postponing this investment. However, as a rule, rapid technological advance occurs in periods of high employment because the innovator is responding to a high demand for his product. In times of good business expectations, the cost of S.U.B. is so small that it

[23] W. C. Hampton, "Administering an S.U.B. Plan: the Ford Experience," *Personnel,* Vol. XXXIV (July–August, 1957), pp. 76–83.

would not act as a deterrent to further investment. Thus S.U.B. appears to operate in harmony with the major determinants of technological progress.

S.U.B. agreements may have changed union attitudes toward methods of dealing with cyclical unemployment. During the Great Depression many industrial unions advocated work-sharing. The business recession of 1957–58 saw some instances of unions urging employers to lay off workers rather than reduce the workweek.[24] Very probably unions with S.U.B. contracts would accept or urge work-sharing if they were confronted with very severe and long-term unemployment. However, for short-term unemployment it seems likely that unions with S.U.B. contracts may very well continue to urge reductions-in-force rather than reductions in the scheduled workweek.

Before leaving worker insurance and income-continuity programs, future bargaining trends and the social implications of these programs should be briefly considered.

SOCIAL IMPLICATIONS OF WORKER INSURANCE AND INCOME-CONTINUITY PROGRAMS

Undoubtedly the major single problem in pension bargaining is the question of providing adequate pensions for the employees who will retire some 20 to 40 years from now. This problem involves business mortality and skill obsolescence and inflation. How can pension entitlement be provided for workers displaced by technological change and business mortality? Both technological change and business mortality cause very substantial dislocations in employment relationships when we talk about a period as long as 20 years. True protection of earned pension rights can be obtained only by the costly means of full vesting. Partial protection from the hazard of business failure by small employers engaged in stable or expanding industries can be obtained by multiemployer plans covering the whole industry or region. A few figures illustrate the inflationary menace to adequate pensions for workers who are able to maintain the employment relationship prerequisite to pension eligibility. In 1930 the average annual income of workers was $1,400. In 1957, average annual income had risen to $3,900. A pension income of $70 per month would have been 70 per cent of earnings in 1930 but only 22 per cent of income in 1957. Pension agreements in effect in 1960 are pledged to provide retirement

---

[24] A notable example of this was a UAW request to the Caterpillar Tractor Company. The UAW reasons that U.C. plus S.U.B. for laid-off workers plus full-time work for employed members is better than short workweek earnings for all the employees, "U.A.W. Tells Caterpillar It Opposes Reducing Output by Cut in Hours," *Wall Street Journal* (Chicago Ed.), January 8, 1958, p. 26. The UAW made a similar request to the Chrysler Corporation in February, 1958, *Detroit Free Press,* Thursday, February 20, 1958, pp. 1–2.

income for some workers who will not retire before 1990. Under present trends, the pension agreements seem to be liberalized on a rather periodic basis, but there is no systematic method for relating future pensions to the future cost of living. One method that is being considered as a partial hedge against future inflation is the variable annuity which invests part of retirement funds in interest-bearing securities for safety and part of retirement funds in equity securities as a hedge against inflation. Some unions have succeeded in negotiating liberalized pension benefits for *retirees*. In other cases, union attempts to negotiate in behalf of retirees have been strongly resisted by management. If the lengthening of life expectancy continues, it seems likely that management resistance to negotiating increased pensions for persons already in retirement will substantially increase.

Akin to the problem of protecting pension entitlement is the question of compulsory retirement. In the sixties, the American society is confronted with two demographic facts that will have contradictory effects on retirement ages. The demographic facts of life are: (1) the number of old people in the society is increasing rapidly and (2) during the sixties more young people will be seeking their first employment than in any other decade in history. As pensioners, old people represent a drain on the goods and services available to the active participants in the labor force. How long will the young people tolerate this "exploitation" by the retirees? Many older people would prefer to go on working. However, every older worker eligible for a pension who keeps a job by seniority is depriving a younger worker of the opportunity to displace him. In a period when there are more young work seekers than jobs, it can be expected that young job seekers will demand that the old-timers be forced into retirement. All this leads to the obvious conclusion that compulsory retirement will remain a hot issue during the sixties.

The investment problems associated with pensions are just beginning to be considered. With assets running into billions of dollars, pension programs have a significant influence on the capital market. It is to be expected that unions will press for increasing participation in the investment policies of pension programs. Future government regulation of pension funds probably will extend beyond the present area of ethical conduct to such questions as the propriety of certain types of investments.

Health and welfare plans under collective bargaining certainly will undergo change on the basis of experience with medicare. It also seems likely that more comprehensive medical care, perhaps on a group practice basis, is on the way. Insured S.U.B. plans have more notable economic and social implications than other employee benefit plans for several reasons. First, they are designed primarily for persons who remain attached to the labor force. Thus, unlike pensions or disability benefits, they may have a substantial influence on the utilization of the human resource in the society. Second, unemployment is probably the greatest worker hazard in the American economy. Unemployment seems to strike when least expected and may hit far more workers than other hazards. Finally, because of the almost complete unpredictabilty of unemployment, employers and workers are relatively incapable of coping with it. Despite an almost universal agreement that government must act against severe unemployment and that government has the power to minimize its severity, there is widespread disagreement on the best methods of governmental action and some doubt as to the effectiveness of certain as yet untried tools in the government program. The same factors that make insured S.U.B. plans important tend to limit the potency of S.U.B. Because the problem of unemployment is so complex, it seems unlikely that any collective bargaining agreement could solve it.

SUMMARY

The American economic system has created an economic abundance never previously achieved. Nevertheless, the employment relationship contains a number of important hazards for the individual worker. These hazards vary between industries, between employers, between geographic areas, and between generations. American workers have sought to alleviate these hazards through personal thrift, governmental programs, and collective bargaining.

Governmental programs for worker insurance and income continuity include Workmen's Compensation, Unemployment Compensation, and Old Age and Survivors' and Disability Insurance. These governmental programs frequently serve as a floor on which collective bargaining agreements are built.

Management's views of collectively bargained worker insurance and income-continuity measures can be classified as matters of principle and matters of cost. Cost is always of great importance, but the critical point of too much is reached at different times in different industries and firms. On the other hand, there is substantial agreement among managements on matters of principle, e.g., worker insurance and income-continuity benefits should be related to employee merit.

Union interest in worker insurance and income-continuity programs centers on the amount of benefits, financing, and the administration of benefit programs. Bargaining on these programs has received added impetus from the rulings of various governmental agencies.

Collectively bargained worker insurance and income-continuity measures are of great social interest. In part, these private plans influence the need for governmental programs. Collectively bargained programs may have an important impact on individual initiative, economic progress, and the future of "management's prerogatives."

QUESTIONS FOR DISCUSSION

1. The text argues that unions and managements have developed certain principles in bargaining over worker insurance and income-continuity programs. Would you agree that principles exist in this field?
2. Are collectively bargained worker insurance and income-continuity programs compatible with a system of social security?
3. Is it socially desirable to permit the development of worker insurance and income-continuity programs which tie the worker to his employer, or vice versa? Are the ties different in different worker insurance and income-continuity programs?
4. How do you plan to provide for your needs in old age? What will those needs be? What contribution (if any) do you expect your employer to make toward fulfilling those needs?
5. What are the unique advantages and disadvantages of multiemployer pension plans? Multiemployer health insurance plans?
6. Some authorities have advocated governmental reinsurance of private pensions, i.e., freedom to purchase any amount of benefits desired from the social security system. How do you feel about this idea?

CASES: 22, 23, 29.

SELECTED ANNOTATED BIBLIOGRAPHY

This bibliography consists of four parts: (1) General, (2) Pensions, (3) Health and Welfare, and (4) Unemployment Benefits.

GENERAL

BURNS, EVELINE M. *Social Security and Public Policy.* New York: McGraw-Hill Book Co., Inc., 1956.

A penetrating analysis of the major policy questions involved in providing economic security through the instrumentality of government.

BUTLER, ARTHUR. "The Relationship Between Public and Private Economic Security Plans," *Proceedings of the Tenth Annual Meeting of the Industrial Relations Research Association,* pp. 139–45. Madison, Wis.: The Association, 1958.

Discusses possible incompatibility of privately established economic security plans with governmental programs and economic welfare of the society.

LINER, JOHN. "Self-Insurance of Group Welfare Plans," *Harvard Business Review,* Vol. XXXIV (January–February, 1956), pp. 95–100.

Discusses the pros and cons of self-insured welfare plans, privately handled, as opposed to plans administered by insurance companies. The author presents his proposed self-insurance program, and outlines its administrative features, economies, and possible limitations.

MACINTYRE, DUNCAN M. "Regulation of Employee Benefit Programs," *Industrial and Labor Relations Review,* Vol. X (July, 1957), pp. 554–78.

A Cornell professor of industrial and labor relations and occasional staff member of governmental investigating committees on health and welfare programs summarizes the findings of these investigations and proposes some dozen points as guideposts for remedial legislation.

MILLER, GLENN W. "Appraisal of Collectively Bargained and Governmental Programs for Employee Security," in Harold W. Davey, Howard S. Kaltenborn, and Stanley H. Ruttenberg, *New Dimensions in Collective Bargaining.* New York: Harper & Bros., 1959, pp. 117–33.

Analyzes the relationship between public and private employee security programs. Concludes that from the viewpoint of the society as a whole, public programs are preferable to private programs.

MYERS, ROBERT J. "Experience of the UMWA Welfare and Retirement Fund," and "Further Experience of the UMWA Welfare and Retirement Fund," *Industrial and Labor Relations Review,* Vol. X (October, 1956), pp. 93–100, Vol. XIV (July, 1961), pp. 556–62.

Analyzes the experience of Mine Workers program over time. Plan worthy of special consideration because of financing methods, multiemployer form, and pioneering work in medical treatment of most severe occupational injuries.

SLICHTER, SUMNER H., HEALY, JAMES J., and LIVERNASH, E. ROBERT. *The Impact of Collective Bargaining on Management.* Washington, D.C.: Brookings Institution, 1960.

Special attention is invited to the following chapters: 13, "Pension Plans"; 14, "Health and Welfare Plans"; 15, "Employee Benefits"; and 16, "Income Security and Severance Pay Plans."

TURNBULL, JOHN G., WILLIAMS, JR., C. ARTHUR, and CHEIT, EARL F. *Economic and Social Security: Public and Private Measures Against Economic Insecurity.* 2d ed.; New York: The Ronald Press Co., 1962.

A comprehensive discussion of the hazards of ill health, old age, and unemployment and the governmental and private programs for alleviating the distress of these hazards.

WILLCOX, ALLANSON W. "The Contributory Principle and the Integrity of Old Age and Survivors' Insurance: A Functional Evaluation," *Industrial and Labor Relations Review.* Vol. VIII (April, 1955), pp. 331–46.

Discusses the extent to which the method of financing and other elements of OASI are interrelated.

PENSIONS

ACKERMAN, LAURENCE J. "Financing Pension Benefits," *Harvard Business Review,* Vol. XXXIV (September–October, 1956), pp. 63–74.

Outlines the main cost factors involved in pensions and compares the various possibilities under both insured and trusteed funds.

BARTLETT, H. ROBERT, JR. "Patterns of Pensions Fund Investment," *Eighteenth Annual Proceedings of the Industrial Relations Research Association,* pp. 302–11.

Compares fund investment practice of corporate and multiemployer pension funds.

CORSON, JOHN J., and McCONNELL, JOHN W. *Economic Needs of Older People,* New York: Twentieth Century Fund, 1956.

This book deals with the need of older persons for continuing income. Earnings from employment, social insurance and public assistance, private pension plans, and other sources of income are carefully considered. The adequacy of the various income sources to the economic needs of older people, and their impact on the national economy are appraised and assessed.

DEARING, CHARLES LEE. *Industrial Pensions*. Washington, D.C.: Brookings Institution, 1954.

A study of the economics of pension programs, occasioned by the Supreme Court ruling (1950) which made pensions an aspect of "wages" subject to collective bargaining under the Taft-Hartley Act. A good summary of the problem and plans for meeting the various difficulties.

HARBRECHT, PAUL P. *Pension Funds and Economic Power*. New York: Twentieth Century Fund, 1959.

Pensions are charged with being vast aggregations of wealth upon which many have claims but of which none can call himself owner. To remove ambiguity of ownership and to restore line of responsibility, it is proposed that pension funds be treated as deferred wages. This would establish certain rights for the worker and would return to him some of the economic independence the pension system has taken away.

KIRKLAND, LANE. *Pension Plans Under Collective Bargaining: A Reference Guide for Trade Unions*. Rev. ed.; Washington, D.C.: American Federation of Labor, December, 1954.

The basic union source book on collective bargaining on pensions.

LESSER, LEONARD. "Tax Aspects of Collectively Bargained Pension Plans," *New York University Seventh Annual Conference on Labor*, EMMANUEL STEIN (ed.), pp. 617–26. Albany, N.Y.: Matthew Bender & Co., Inc., 1954.

A legal consultant of the UAW Social Security Department discusses tax aspects of different pension contribution bases, termination of pension plans, and pooled pension plans.

McGILL, DAN M. *Fundamentals of Private Pensions*. Homewood, Ill.: Richard D. Irwin, Inc., 1955.

The general approach of this book is to analyze plan provisions, funding media, and funding methods. Emphasis is placed on rationale, concepts, and guiding principles. The book is not intended as a survey of existing plans.

MURRAY, ROGER F. "Management Interests in the Investment of Pension Funds," *Eighteenth Annual Proceedings of the Industrial Relations Research Association*, pp. 312–16.

Defines the primary objective of management in the investment of pension funds as that selection of investment opportunities which will maximize future returns and minimize the costs of retirement benefits within the range of acceptable risks.

OTIS, HENRY W. "Comparing Pension Costs," *Harvard Business Review*, Vol. XXXV (July–August, 1957), pp. 58–66.

Comparison of insured and trusteed type pension plans as to security, flexibility, the makeup of costs, and the different factors which can cause different results in the plans.

TILOVE, ROBERT. "Multi-Employer Pension Plans," *New York University Seventh Annual Conference on Labor*, EMMANUEL STEIN (ed.), pp. 639–58. Albany, N.Y.: Matthew Bender & Co., Inc., 1954.

The Director of the Pension Department of Martin E. Segal & Company outlines the forces which make the establishment of a multiemployer pension plan particularly attractive to small employers and unions whose members have only intermittent employment with a single employer.

————. *Pension Funds and Economic Freedom*. A Report to the Fund for the Republic, New York: Fund, 1959.

Discusses the implications of American private pension plans for the mobility of labor, and for the concentration of economic power through the acquisition of common stock by pension funds.

STEIN, EMANUEL (ed.). *New York University Tenth Annual Conference on Labor.* Albany, N.Y.: Matthew Bender & Co., Inc., 1957.

Most of the volume devoted to pension plans. Partial contents:

HOLLAND, DANIEL M. "The Pension Climate."

COLLINS, ROBERT D. "Economics of Pension Planning."

TILOVE, ROBERT. "The Organization of a Pension Plan."

MEUCHE, A. J. "Past Service Benefits."

MELNIKOFF, MEYER. "Actuarial Bases: The Interest Rate."

WHITE, WILLIAM K. "Actuarial Bases: MortalityTables."

WILLIS, E. S. "Administration of Single Employer Pension Plans."

VLADECK, STEPHEN C. "Public Regulations of Pension Plans."

SHELDON, HORACE E. "Regulation of Pension Plans."

SERGENT, DWIGHT S. "Planning for Retirement."

HINES, JOHN M. "Split-Funding and Insurance Company Plans."

KEARSHES, ANTHONY J. "Method of Funding in Pension Planning: The Trustee Plan."

GOLDSTEIN, MEYER M. "Inflation and Deflation in Pension Planning."

OLMSTEAD, R. G. "The Variable Annuity."

BERNSTEIN, PETER L. "The Financial Aspects of Pension Funds; Problems of Investments."

HOWELL, PAUL L. "Investment Management of Union Pension Funds; Problems of Administration and Sources of Assistance."

O'BRIAN, JAMES J. "Investment Management of Pension Plans: Selection of Investment."

FARNUM, C. WADSWORTH. "Pension Fund Investment Media: Bond Investments.

BUEK, CHARLES W. "The Investment Media: Equity Investments."

JOHNSON, RALPH B. "The Continuing Supervision of Investments."

HEALTH AND WELFARE PLANS

FOUNDATION ON EMPLOYEE HEALTH, MEDICAL CARE AND WELFARE, INC. *Studies* (of Health and Welfare Problems). 477 Madison Avenue, New York 22, New York.

Jointly sponsored by the International Association of Machinists and U.S. Industries, Inc., the Foundation has conducted a number of studies of problems in providing the best medical care benefits at minimum cost. Studies cover financing methods for various plans, types of coverage, e.g., medical, dental, hospitalization, and efficiency of various kinds of carriers. Specific reference to two studies are made in chapter on Health and Welfare. Future studies by the Foundation are in progress.

GARBARINO, JOSEPH W. *Health Plans and Collective Bargaining.* Berkeley, Calif.: University of California Press, 1960.

Study of the provisions of hospital and medical care through collectively bargained health plans, with emphasis upon the attempt by these plans to meet important social problems largely through voluntary, privately administered action.

"Hospital Insurance, Supplemental Medical Insurance, and Old-Age Survivors and Disability Insurance; Financing Basis under the 1965 Amendments," *Social Security Bulletin,* Vol. 28 (October, 1965), pp. 17–28.

Discusses the three systems, financed separately, made possible by the 1965 amendments to the Social Security Act.

SOMERS, HERMAN MILES, and SOMERS, ANNE RAMSAY. *Doctors, Patients and Health Insurance.* Washington, D.C.: Brookings Institution, 1961.

A study of the organization, distribution, and financing of personal medical care. Considers efficiencies of various methods of health insurance and various methods of organizing the distribution of medical care.

UNEMPLOYMENT BENEFITS

BACKMAN, JULES. "High Cost of Liberalizing SUB Plans," *Harvard Business Review,* Vol. XXXIV (November–December, 1956), pp. 69–75.

Outlines a statistical method for estimating the ultimate cost of reducing eligibility standards for S.U.B., lengthening the duration of eligibility, increasing the weekly benefit amounts and other proposed liberalizations of the pioneer S.U.B. plans.

BECKER, JOSEPH M. "Twenty-Five Years of Unemployment Insurance: An Experiment in Competitive Collectivism," *Political Science Quarterly,* Vol. LXXV (December, 1960), pp. 481–99.

A survey and discussion of the U.S. unemployment insurance program as an amalgam of capitalistic and socialistic elements. Discussion concentrates on "two most distinctively competitive aspects of the American program— the existence of separate state systems and the use of that tax technique called experience rating."

FOX, HARLAND, and WORTHY, N. BEATRICE. *Severance Pay Patterns in Manufacturing.* New York: National Industrial Conference Board Studies in Personnel Policy No. 174, 1959.

Study gives broad general picture of severance pay practices in manufacturing. It also outlines patterns in several important industries.

LATIMER, MURRAY W., Research Director. U.S. Office of Temporary Controls. *Guaranteed Wages, Report to the President, by the Advisory Board, Office of War Mobilization and Reconversion.* Washington, D.C.: Government Printing Office, 1947.

An exhaustive study of guaranteed wage proposals, contains estimates of the cost of such plans, and nine case histories of guaranteed wage arrangements.

LESTER, RICHARD A. *The Economics of Unemployment Compensation.* Princeton, N.J.: Princeton University Industrial Relations Section, Research Report No. 101, 1962.

An analysis of state and federal experience during the period 1948–61. Recommendations for improving the system.

McCONNELL, JOHN W. "Supplementary Unemployment Benefits," *Proceedings of the Eighth Annual Meeting of the Industrial Relations Research Association,* L. REED TRIPP (ed.), pp. 167–81. Madison, Wis.: The Association, 1956.

Discusses the impact of S.U.B. on employees, management and the unemployment compensation system.

STIEGLITZ, HAROLD. "Financing the Ford Plan," *Management Record,* Vol. XVII (September, 1955), pp. 350–53, 372–74.

Certainly the most comprehensive, and probably the most authentic, explanation of the thinking of Ford Motor Company executives on the problems of financing a supplemental unemployment benefit plan. Emphasis is placed on statistical tools adapted by Ford for testing the funding of the company's proposal and safety factors built into the plan.

UNTERBERGER, HERBERT S. *Guaranteed Wage & Supplementary Unemployment Pay Plans.* Chicago: Commerce Clearing House, Inc., 1956.

An excellent handbook for the study of G.A.W. and S.U.B. plans. Outlines labor's demand for the G.A.W., management opposition to the G.A.W., and the emergence of S.U.B. Deals with major problems in the operation of a S.U.B. plan: estimating the cost, minimizing the cost, financial problems in operating under a G.A.W. or S.U.B. Plan. Appendix includes full text of Ford, American and Continental Can S.U.B. agreements.

WICKERSHAM, EDWARD D. "Controlling Unemployment at the Company Level," *Industrial and Labor Relations Review*, Vol. XIV (October, 1960), pp. 68–82.

Discusses changes in methods of controlling unemployment at the company level since the Great Depression.

Chapter 12

INDIVIDUAL SECURITY: JOB RIGHTS AND DUE PROCESS

Besides good pay and working conditions, most workers want some kind of a guarantee of continuity of employment and a fair appraisal of their job performance. As we emphasized in Chapter 9, management needs the freedom to lay off workers when business is slack, to transfer workers between jobs, to select good prospects for promotion, and to discipline for just cause. The worker's desire for job rights and fair play roughly coincides with the manager's desire to avoid excessive turnover and to maintain discipline. Workers and unions recognize management's need for flexibility and efficiency. At the same time managers understand the worker's need for security and fair play. These needs of workers and managers are accommodated through the negotiation of rules for job rights and due process under collective bargaining.

Collectively bargained rules protect the types of work usually assigned to union members and establish the individual worker's *relative* claim to available work. Craft unions and industrial unions follow somewhat different methods of establishing job rights.

Collectively bargained rules for due process establish the individual worker's *absolute* claim to fair treatment in the employment relationship. The worker's claim for fair treatment is the *quid pro quo* for his acceptance of the obligation to perform his job as specified in the agreement or as directed by management in day-to-day operations. Rules for due process are similar in the domains of craft and industrial unions.

JOB RIGHTS

It is important to note that union jurisdictional claims and union security arrangements may play an important part in establishing the individual worker's job rights. Union security is a major concern of the union *as an institution*, sometimes totally divorced from its members. At the same time, the effectiveness of the union's claim to all available work sets the outside limits of what job rights are available to its members.

Craft unionists obtain job rights through custom and practice, while industrial unionists obtain job rights through the provisions of their collective bargaining agreements. The cornerstones of the craft union's program of job control are exclusive union jurisdiction, the closed shop, and the hiring hall. The industrial union obtains job rights through agreement clauses restricting the assignment of work to nonrepresented employees and a system of seniority. Both systems aim at protecting work for assignment to union employees and establishing the individual worker's *relative* claim to available work.

Job Rights in Craft Unions

The craft union's claim of jurisdiction becomes a device of job control as soon as an employer signs a collective bargaining agreement. Under the terms of a typical agreement with the Carpenters' union, the employer assigns all of his work "within the jurisdiction of the Carpenters' union" to members of the union. An employer who tries to subcontract carpentry work or to assign it to other craftsmen finds that no carpenters are available to perform duties requiring the skills of a carpenter. Frequently the employer also finds that no plumbers, masons, electricians, or structural steelworkers are available either until he reassigns carpentry work to the carpenter's union.

Craft workers establish their *relative* claim to available work through the union. When the closed shop or the "seven-day union shop" is operative, members of the union have exclusive rights to all available work on unionized jobs. Most craft-union collective bargaining agreements make little or no reference to seniority. This is to be expected because the typical craft unionist has only an intermittent relationship with a single employer. The craft unionist may seek his own job opportunities or use the union hall as his employment office. If he uses the union hall as his base of operations, and craft unionists frequently do, he may find that the Business Agent gives job opportunities first to the unemployed members with the most dues stamps in their union books. If the Business Agent uses this system of allocating job opportunities, the craft unionist carries his seniority in the union. This is a noncontractual seniority system, but it is a seniority system and it works well for workers in industries with intermittent employment relationships. If the Business Agent distributes job opportunities on the basis of how well he knows the members at the union hall, he is following a less formalized seniority system but it probably reflects the relative seniority of unemployed members. Finally, of course it is possible that the Business Agent does not believe in seniority and distributes jobs to his friends regardless of their seniority or to the highest bidder. The only check on this discriminatory action by an unscrupulous Business Agent is the fact that someday he comes up for re-election and an infuriated rank and file can deprive him of his abusive power. When jobs are hard to find, the rank and file probably scrutinize the Business Agent's allocation of jobs with some care.

Job Rights in Industrial Unions

While the craft union's methods of job control are informal, the industrial union obtains job security through a highly formalized contractual arrangement. Industrial unions protect their total claim to available work by collective bargaining clauses which restrict the freedom of management to assign work to nonmembers of the bargaining unit. These clauses take the form of limitations on the amount and type of work that may be performed by foremen and salaried employees, full crew clauses, and restrictions on the freedom of management to subcontract work normally performed in the bargaining unit.[1] In the absence of detailed contractual provisions, industrial unions are sometimes successful in forcing the continuance of management's past practices in the assignment of work through the arbitration process. Almost universally seniority clauses are the method of establishing the individual industrial unionist's *relative* claim to available work.

Seniority Defined. Seniority is a vast and complicated field of claims and counterclaims by individuals. It confers on its possessor only a *relative* claim to available work or other benefits flowing from the enterprise. The collective bargaining agreement tends to be a fine balancing mechanism between the interests of various groups of workers. Seniority grants certain preferential treatment to long-service employees almost at the expense of short-service employees. In times of business distress, the seniority rights of long-service employees may be diluted by work-sharing. For example, instead of 80 per cent of the employees with high seniority working 40 hours per week, all of the employees might be scheduled for 32 hours per week. Another example of the dilution of seniority rights is the rather common procedure of compulsory retirement under a pension plan. In this case, the high seniority employee is forced to convert his seniority rights to pension benefits at the prevailing rate of exchange. Retirement of the high seniority employee, in turn, creates a job opportunity for a lower seniority employee or a new hire.

In the most general terms, seniority is defined as length of service. A worker usually does not acquire seniority until he has served a probationary period. Probationary periods usually range from the first week

[1] A full crew clause specifies the number of persons who must be assigned to a work group. For example, an airliner must have so many crewmen in the cockpit before the plane is permitted to operate. Subcontracting clauses have been very important in the garment industries and building trades for many years. In a 1959 BLS study of subcontracting clauses in agreements covering over 1,000 workers each, less than one in four agreements contained a subcontracting clause. (See *Subcontracting Clauses in Major Collective Bargaining Agreements*, BLS Bulletin No. 1304, 1961, 33 pp.) Some arbitrators have ruled that subcontracting was restricted by other provisions of the agreement even in the absence of a subcontracting clause. Prohibitions on work of nonrepresented employees, full crew rules, and subcontracting clauses are most important to unions in periods of general unemployment.

to the first six months of employment. After the probationary period, the worker is credited with seniority equal to the probationary period. Seniority usually is broken or eliminated by such events as discharge for cause, layoffs of very long duration (say, over one year), retirement, or unauthorized leaves of absence. The definition of seniority is completed by reference to the "area" of seniority. The area of seniority may be as broad as the trade in the case of the craft union, where seniority may be defined as years and months of union membership. Or the area of seniority may be as narrow as the time that an employee has spent on a particular job in a particular plant of the General Electric Company. Between these two extreme areas of seniority is a whole spectrum of "occupational group," "departmental," "plant," "company," "company-community," and other variations. A single worker may possess different "seniorities" (in terms of time of service) in different areas concurrently. Figure 12–1 illustrates various areas of seniority taken from different collective bargaining agreements.

Divergent definitions of the area of seniority take on meaning only when we attempt to apply seniority against the benefits which it bestows on its possessor. We turn now to the problems in the application of seniority.

The Application of Seniority. In Chapter 7 we referred to seniority of protection, opportunity, and privilege. Protective seniority establishes the relative job rights of employees in layoff and recall. Seniority of opportunity involves job promotions and transfers. Seniority of privilege establishes workers' relative claims to wage supplements and worker insurance and income continuity benefits.

Layoff and Recall. Seniority is most frequently used as a criterion in worker layoff and recall. The usual arrangement is that workers with the greatest length of service will be the last to be laid off when business is poor and the first to be recalled when business picks up again. This simple rule poses extremely serious problems for management. The major modifications in the application of the general rule are the area of seniority and "bumping" rights. If length of service were not qualified by a statement of area of application, management might find itself in a position where the high seniority employees still on the job were incapable of performing essential tasks. Because of this potential problem, the areas of seniority described in Figure 12–1 become a critical issue in seniority as applied to layoffs. While areas of seniority determine who is available for layoff, bumping rights are the final determinant of which workers are actually laid off.

Areas of seniority are defined by a union-management compromise within the rather rigid limits established by the work flow of a particular group of employees. From the union point of view, the *ideal* area of seniority would provide the maximum possible security for the senior worker. This would be achieved if the area of seniority were defined as

FIGURE 12–1
ILLUSTRATIVE "AREAS" OF SENIORITY

Occupational Seniority

Noninterchangeable occupational groups will be established on a plant-wide basis. In case of layoff, the Company agrees to give preference to the employee with the greatest seniority in his established noninterchangeable occupational group. Laid-off employees shall be recalled to work within their respective occupational groups in order of their seniority before any new employees are hired by the Company within the same group.

Departmental Seniority

Straight seniority by department for all employees shall be the rule, except as necessarily modified in connection with classification of tasks. If an employee is transferred from one department to another, his seniority shall be determined in the following manner: he shall be considered a new employee in the new department and should a layoff be necessary in the new department before he has worked in the new department a period of time exceeding the amount of time in the previous department, he shall return to the previous department with accumulated time from both departments. However, should an employee have worked in the new department an amount of time exceeding that of the old department, the entire seniority shall be transferred to the new department and they shall have no more seniority in the old department.

Plant-Wide Seniority

Strict plant seniority shall prevail from the original date of hiring on any job the employee is capable of handling. Employees may be retained or recalled on a temporary basis for special jobs out of line with seniority after consultation with the Shop Committee.

Special Variants of above Types:

Plant seniority shall be observed and determined by the last hiring date of each employee. Seniority shall operate as follows: First as to occupation within the department; second on a departmental basis; third on a plant-wide basis.

Seniority lists shall be set up by divisions within the plant. Each intraplant division may include one or more departments. Each employee in the intraplant division shall exercise his seniority in the various occupations within such divisions for which he has been classified by the foreman of the department included in the divisions. The divisions are listed as follows:

(*There follows a detailed listing of company divisions.*)

---

any employment within the jurisdiction of the union regardless of employer, job assignment, or geographic area attachment. For the industrial-union employer, this broad seniority area would pose frequently insurmountable problems. From the employer's viewpoint, the *ideal* area of seniority would be defined so as to minimize interference with efficient operations. The best method of achieving this goal would be to limit the area of seniority to workers doing identical jobs within a single plant. Under such a system, the worker would have little security in a plant employing only a few workers on each of many different jobs. Most seniority agreements are common-sense compromises of the union's desire for worker security and management's desire for efficiency in production. Industrial unions are able to broaden the area of seniority from the single plant and the single job only in cases where many jobs tend to be interchangeable. In general, industrial unions lack the employment-office type of facilities needed to broaden the geographic area of seniority beyond all the plants of a single corporation. Further, the broadening of the area of seniority to cover more than one employer has generally been vigorously opposed by managements dealing with industrial unions. The area of seniority indicates the order in which employees become available for layoff. The question of whether a particular employee is separated from the payroll remains to be settled.

Workers who are available for layoff within their seniority area are not necessarily actually laid off. Whether they are or not depends upon their bumping rights. "Bumping rights" are the contractual privileges of employees available for layoff within their own area of seniority to displace employees with less seniority on jobs in other areas of seniority. For example, if tool-and-die makers and machine-tool operators were separate areas of seniority and a tool-and-die maker with five years' seniority were available for layoff, he might possess the bumping right to displace a machine-tool operator with three years' seniority. The machine-tool operator, in turn, might possess the bumping right to displace a sweeper with two years' seniority. It can readily be seen that unlimited bumping rights might cause a chaotic chain reaction of job reassignments. We are reminded of the case of a two-plant company which granted sweeping seniority rights as an inducement to union co-operation in the first contract after an NLRB election. One plant was located in Brooklyn and the other was located in Garden City, Long Island. At the time of negotiating the first contract, the company had very large government contracts and was expanding employment and production. Three years later the unforeseen cancellation of several government contracts necessitated a 20 per cent reduction in force. Under the seniority arrangements which had been agreed to, it was necessary to reassign some 800 of the 1,000 employees who survived the first layoff. Many workers were reassigned from Garden City to Brooklyn and vice versa. Needless to say, it required several weeks before these reassigned workers could be integrated into an efficient work team. Eventually the seniority provisions of this union contract were renegotiated so as to provide both a degree of security to the workers and needed flexibility to management. However, the management of this company had paid a very dear price for the fair-weather thinking which had dominated in the negotiation of its first union contract. The confusion caused by these transfers may have been partially responsible for further contract cancellations which the company experienced.

If the workers in the Garden City and Brooklyn plants had all been doing *identical* jobs, the bumping experience would have caused no more inconvenience than a longer subway ride or drive for some of the 800 workers who were transferred. But our two-plant company employed its workers on a great variety of different jobs. Most of the jobs were simple, but it required some time for workers to be fitted into a production team. Because of the differences in jobs and the large number of small jobs in most factory situations, bumping rights are usually limited or qualified in the collective bargaining agreement. The exact nature of the restrictions of bumping rights depends upon the individual employment relationship. Usually one or more of the following restrictions on bumping rights are contained in collective bargaining agreements:

1. The area of seniority itself may be narrowly defined. If so, this means that the original impact of reductions-in-force is minimized.
2. Bumping rights may be declared inoperative for short-term (say, less than two-week) layoffs.
3. Before an employee can bump another he may be required to establish proof that he is capable of performing the job into which he wishes to bump.
4. Employees may be permitted to bump only into jobs which they have previously performed satisfactorily.
5. Bumping rights may be conferred only on workers who satisfy a minimum service requirement greater than the probationary period from the date of original hire.
6. Employees may be permitted to bump only into seniority areas in which they have previous experience.
7. Employees wishing to bump may be required to have a specified amount of longer service than the employee they wish to replace.
8. Displaced employees may be placed in a labor pool where they have seniority claims on new jobs which they are capable of performing as created by turnover.

The foregoing list of possible limitations on bumping rights offers several potential problems in administration. For example, should employees claiming ability to perform jobs claimed by bumping rights be given a trial period on the new job? What is a *reasonable* trial period? If an employee fails in the trial period, is he discharged, or laid off, or given another trial period on another job?

Recall rights of seniority workers pose other serious problems in administration. Do recall rights apply only to the specific job from which the worker was separated? or his seniority area? or any new jobs of which he might be capable? How much and what kind of recall notice must be given to a laid-off worker? What reasons for failure to return when a recall notice is received are sufficient to preserve the seniority rights of the worker who fails to report back for work?

Before leaving seniority and its application to layoffs and recall, it is important to note that most industrial unions insist upon "superseniority" for Local union officers and shop stewards or committeemen. A reasonably typical contract clause reads as follows:

The President, 1st and 2nd Vice-President and Financial Secretary shall be given top seniority in their occupational group during their term of office if they have three (3) years' service with the Company and it is agreed that they shall not perform duties of their office during working hours.

The members of the Executive Shop Committee, Chief Stewards and Stewards will have top seniority in the Department or occupational groups which they represent. Such representatives, in order to receive seniority as specified, must have one (1) year's service with the Company. If there is no work in their classification in the departments or occupational groups which they represent, they must, in order to remain employed, be able to qualify for some other job classification within their jurisdiction. Upon such transfer, they will be paid the average hourly rate being paid at the time in the job classification to which they have been transferred.

Such a contract clause preserves union representational rights in the shop even in periods of very high unemployment.

Managements often succeed in trading superseniority for stewards for similar privileges for a group of "key" employees or jobs. Such key employees might include management trainees, setup men, or maintenance experts. A key-employee clause which was obtained in trade for the above superseniority concession for union representatives reads as follows:

Exceptional employees may be retained irrespective of seniority. Exceptional employees are employees whose work in the judgment of the Management and Executive Shop Committee is of exceptional value to the department. The Company agrees to limit the number of such employees to two (2) per cent of the total on the payroll. A list of such exceptional employees is to be furnished to the Executive Shop Committee.

The major application of seniority is in the area of layoffs and recall. Seniority provides *substantial* individual security against the uncertainties caused by business fluctuations. The disciplinary factor has pretty much been removed from layoffs caused by poor business conditions. Whatever jobs are available go to the senior workers capable of performing them. Although seniority is also applicable in promotions and transfers, it is generally of less importance here than in layoffs and recall.

Promotions and Transfers. Seniority also provides a degree of individual opportunity when business is good. It not only protects its possessor in bad times, it gives him some degree of preference when business is improving. Thus seniority may establish certain preferences in the area of job promotions and transfers.

Promotions and transfers are differentiated in many collective bargaining agreements. Generally a "promotion" means a job carrying a higher rate of pay. "Transfer" may be applied to any change in job assignment. In an effort to minimize the interferences to production caused by many shifts in job assignments, management frequently seeks to limit seniority preferences in job assignment to the area of promotions. For the same reasons, management may seek to restrict the application of seniority in such matters as shift preference, leaves of absence for vacations, and overtime allocation.

Seniority is almost universally qualified in its application to promotions. Three examples of promotional arrangements illustrate the variety of possible applications:

1. "When new jobs are created, management shall fill these jobs with the most able and meritorious persons available. Present employees shall be considered before an attempt is made to recruit new employees from outside the plant." (Such an arrangement places a minimum of emphasis on seniority in filling new jobs.)

2. "When new jobs are created, management shall attempt to fill these jobs with the most able and meritorious persons presently in the employ of the company. Notices of new jobs shall be posted and any employee on a lower-graded job may apply for consideration. Such applications shall be carefully considered by management. When two or more employees applying for the new job possess equal merit and ability, management shall award the job to the employee with the greatest seniority. In the event that no person applying for the job possesses the required abilities, the company may seek to fill the job by outside recruitment." (Such an arrangement continues to place primary emphasis on merit and ability, but formalizes the rights to consideration and preference conferred by the possession of seniority.)

3. "When new jobs are created, management shall attempt to fill these jobs with persons presently in the employ of the company. Notices of new jobs shall be posted and any employee on a lower-graded job may apply for consideration. New jobs shall be awarded to the applying employee with the greatest seniority capable of performing the job. Outside recruitment may be used to fill jobs when no capable employee applies." (Such an arrangement places near-maximum emphasis on seniority in filling new jobs. In *very* exceptional cases, even greater emphasis may be placed on seniority by granting the senior applicant preference for whatever training may be necessary for him to learn the new job. Such arrangements are found almost exclusively in situations where outside recruitment of needed skills is impossible.)

The foregoing arrangements introduce two new terms, "merit" and "ability," which must be defined either by custom and usage or in the contract itself. The meaning of these terms determine the actual value of seniority preference in promotions.

"Ability" may mean many things: Able to learn? Able to produce at full efficiency on the day of assignment to the new job? Able to produce at full efficiency after a break-in period?

Perhaps even more important than the meaning of the term "ability" is the question of whose judgment shall be controlling in the case of the individual applicant. If tests of ability are used, is management the sole judge of the reliability and validity of the tests? If tests are not used, may management insist that the only valid proof of ability is previous successful experience on the exact vacancy to be filled?

Many managements feel that a merit consideration alleviates some of the difficulties inherent in the ability criterion and improves the chances of filling jobs with satisfactory persons. "Ability" normally implies a *prediction* of future performance. "Merit" is the evaluation of past performance. By adding a merit consideration, promotions become a reward *earned* by efficient performance in the past. It seems reasonable to expect that an employee who has a record of good performance will work out better on a new job than an employee with a poor record and possessing the same ability to perform the new job.

The more refined the criteria for promotion, the greater the difficulties in finally determining the person eligible for promotion. Merit, like ability, is an evasive concept. In many factory situations, formal merit rating has been abandoned because of difficulties in administration. Without effective merit rating, an attempt to apply merit to promotional situations boils down to disqualifying persons with many disciplinary actions in their personnel records for promotion. Obviously, under these circumstances merit is being measured only in a negative manner.

Many detailed studies have been made of the difficulties inherent in merit-rating systems.[2] We may briefly summarize these difficulties as follows: •

1. Determining and defining the factors to be rated. The major consideration here is that the factors rated should be precisely defined and valid as a measure of efficiency. For example, a vaguely defined "attitude" factor might, in application mean that the employee being rated did or did not have the same political affiliation as the rater. Unless political affiliation were a major determinant of productive efficiency, such interpretation of the factor would grievously thwart the purpose of merit rating.
2. Assuring objectivity in rating. Untrained raters begin the rating process with widely different interpretations of the meaning of the factors and personal standards of excellency. Further, most of us are rather poor observers of human behavior. We tend to put undue emphasis on the *last* thing we have observed or have failed to observe. Finally, we usually fail to analyze people's behavior. We may erroneously attribute observed low production to "poor attitude," or "low intelligence."

To a degree, these difficulties in merit rating may be overcome by improving the definitions of the factor rated and training the raters. The "critical-incident" method of merit rating developed by the General Motors Corporation is an example of an attempt to improve merit ratings.

---

[2] For a discussion of these problems, see M. Joseph Dooher (ed.), *Rating Employee and Supervisory Performance: A Manual of Merit-Rating Techniques* (New York: American Management Association, 1951), 192 pp.; Michael J. Jucius, *Personnel Management* (rev. ed.; Homewood, Ill.: Richard D. Irwin, Inc., 1957), chap. 17, pp. 295–329; Dale Yoder, *Personnel Management and Industrial Relations* (4th ed.; Englewood Cliffs, N.J.: Prentice-Hall, Inc., 1956), chap. 16, pp. 561–97.

Dr. John C. Flanagan of the University of Pittsburgh spent a year with the Corporation in the final development of this new approach to merit rating.

The critical-incident approach to merit rating seeks to make the process more objective and to avoid the problem of lapses of memory between rating periods. Briefly stated, it merely provides for the prompt recording of all incidents which reflect favorably or unfavorably on an employee's performance. Each incident is discussed with the employee at the time of occurrence and becomes a basis for periodic performance review. If a supervisor has misinterpreted an unfavorable incident, the employee is allowed to set the record straight.

Spokesmen for General Motors Corporation state that this system has substantially reduced grievance cases in disciplinary decisions in the Delco-Remy Division. At the same time, they believe that as a result of the system, seniority has been applied as a major criterion in fewer promotional cases than would otherwise be necessary.[3]

The balancing of merit and ability considerations and seniority considerations in promotional decisions poses a delicate problem for managements, unions, and arbitrators called in to decide grievance cases. The delicacy of this problem is clearly illustrated by the summary of a 1956 workshop held by the National Academy of Arbitrators:

There was no attempt to formulate conclusions or to arrive at a consensus of views, and it would belie the nature and purpose of this all-too-brief discussion to summarize it in such terms. The most that might be done is to note certain comments and viewpoints which, to this reporter, seemed to stand out by virtue of their frequency, firmness, or artistic flair with which they were expressed. They are: (1) it all depends on how the contract is written; (2) the arbitrator is concerned, not only with the correctness of the conclusions of the employer or the union, but whether the answers given by either were addressed to the proper questions; (3) the determination of relative skill and ability should be based on evidence and standards which are reasonable, demonstrable, and objective—but with a suggestion here and there, "let's not carry this objectivity too far"; and (4) in determining questions of skill and ability, the judgments of management should not be set aside where they have not been shown by the evidence to be arbitrary, capricious, whimsical, or discriminatory —or different from our own.[4]

Seniority is difficult to apply in the problem of promotional opportunities. At the same time, seniority is the essence of simplicity when applied to the question of eligibility for numerous wage supplements.

Eligibility for Wage Supplements. We have discussed the im-

[3] Algie A. Hendrix and Byron Stewart, "Appraisal of Employee Performance," *Addresses on Industrial Relations, 1957 Series* (Ann Arbor: Bureau of Industrial Relations, University of Michigan, Bulletin No. 25, 1957) Sec. 6, 15 pp.

[4] James C. Hill, "Summary of Workshop on Seniority and Ability," in Jean T. McKelvey (ed.), *Management Rights and the Arbitration Process (Proceedings of the Ninth Annual Meeting of the National Academy of Arbitrators, January 26–28, 1956)* (Washington, D.C.: BNA Incorporated, 1956), p. 49.

portance of seniority in determining eligibility for, and the amount of, such wage supplements as pensions, health and welfare benefits, and supplemental unemployment benefits. In addition, vacation benefits are usually related to seniority. In some cases, overtime is distributed on the basis of seniority as are shift assignments. Severance pay is also graduated to reflect the individual's seniority.

Modified though it may be, seniority is almost universally applied as at least a consideration in layoffs, promotions, and fringe benefits. We turn now to several complex and important seniority problems which are of less general application.

Problems in Seniority.   In this section we will deal with special problems relating to the individual and his seniority status, seniority and automation, and seniority in corporate mergers.

Individual Problems in Seniority.   The accumulation or retention of seniority rights is of great importance to a worker who goes on leave of absence, is called into military service, or who accepts employment outside the bargaining unit with the company.

1. Leaves of Absence.   Most collective bargaining agreements prescribe conditions requiring the company to grant leaves of absence, upon proper application, to persons for official union business. Other leaves of absence and the accumulation of seniority for their duration are frequently left to management's sole discretion.

A common clause on seniority and leaves of absence is: "Seniority shall accumulate during the period of an approved leave of absence." Sometimes such a clause is qualified by limiting the amount of seniority that may accrue during leaves of absence for various causes, e.g., illness, union business, personal business, etc.

2. Military Service.   Since the seniority and re-employment rights of persons in military service are prescribed by law, most collective bargaining agreements contain a clause similar to the following: "Employees now serving in the Armed Forces of the United States or employees who shall hereafter serve in the Armed Forces of the United States shall be entitled to reinstatement upon the completion of such service to the extent and under the circumstances that reinstatement may be required by the applicable laws of the United States." Sometimes such a clause is enlarged with a statement that, "provided that any employee whose discharge from service is other than dishonorable, shall be accorded the same reinstatement rights as such laws provide in the case of persons honorably discharged."

3. Employment outside the Bargaining Unit.   Probably the most troublesome question relating to an individual's seniority rights arises when a worker is promoted to supervision or transferred to a job outside the bargaining unit. The worker is frequently reluctant to risk a new job as supervisor or on other work outside the bargaining unit unless he can retain his security by knowing that he has rights to his old job in the

event of failure on the new one. Some managements seek to preserve the seniority rights of workers promoted to supervision as an inducement to accepting the new job. On the other hand, some managements believe that the new supervisor's break with the union-guaranteed right of seniority should be complete, thereby avoiding any possible conflicts in interest or loyalty on the part of supervision. Many unions oppose long accumulations of seniority by former union members promoted to supervision or outside the bargaining unit because they fear that management might seek to weaken the union by transferring seniority-holding supervisors back into the bargaining unit. Other unions feel that allowing former unionists promoted to supervision to accumulate seniority is conducive to better foreman-worker relationships.

The following provisions from an automobile industry collective bargaining agreement illustrate one method of handling the problem:

A seniority employee in a classification subject to the jurisdiction of the Union, who has been in the past or will be in the future promoted to Assistant Foreman, Foreman, or any other supervisory position, and is thereafter transferred or demoted to a classification subject to the jurisdiction of the Union shall accumulate seniority while working in a supervisory position and when so transferred or demoted shall commence work in a job similar to the one he held at the time of his promotion with the seniority ranking he had at the time of his promotion plus the seniority accumulated while he was working in the supervisory position in conformity with the seniority rules of plants covered by this Agreement.

No temporary demotions in supervisory positions will be made during temporary layoffs.

Seniority and Automation.   Unions argue that automation necessitates a substantial revision of seniority practices. For example, an AFL-CIO publication states:

It may be necessary, for example, substantially to revise seniority provisions in collective bargaining contracts. Unions are giving much thought to the need for the broadening of seniority areas—company-wide or plant-wide seniority, for example—to assure equitable seniority protection for their members and the right to interdepartment and interplant transfer, based on seniority. Preferential hiring provisions are being considered, which will require all plants under contract with the union to give preference to laid-off workers in the same industry and area.

Also seniority systems should assure senior employees a full opportunity to qualify for new higher-skill jobs. Such employees should not be passed over in favor of new or junior employees simply because of age or an employer unwillingness to provide the training to enable qualification for the job.[5]

The exact form of the new seniority clauses which may develop as a result of automation is hard to predict. However, it seems likely that if automation creates any substantial dislocation of the labor force, unions will intensify their efforts for greater security for seniority workers.

[5] AFL-CIO, *Labor Looks at Automation* (Washington, D.C.: AFL-CIO Publication No. 21, May, 1956), p. 23.

A major difficulty in negotiating new types of seniority clauses may be caused by the changes in automated job content. For example, Professor James Bright of the Harvard Business School states that automation creates an entirely new breed of maintenance technicians. Professors Baldwin and Schultz have suggested that "ability to learn" may replace "ability to perform" as the criterion for selecting workers for promotion to automated jobs.

Seniority in Corporate Mergers.[6] The relative employment rights conferred by seniority usually vanish when a business fails. Corporation mergers may cause the transferring of work between plants, changes in the products manufactured, or plant closures. Such developments may reduce the number of available jobs or change the nature of jobs available. Mergers always present new problems in allocating whatever jobs may be available. These problems are particularly acute when the number of jobs

FIGURE 12–2
RANK, RATIO, AND LENGTH OF SERVICE METHODS OF INTEGRATING SENIORITY LISTS

Given: Company A, ten employees, length of service from ten down to one year, respectively.
Company B, five employees, length of service from five down to one year, respectively.

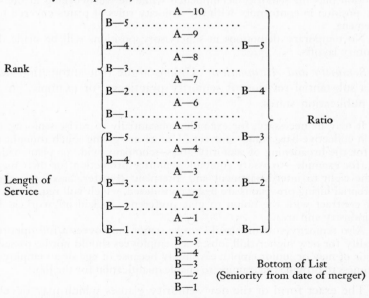

NOTE: In this example, employees of "A" have been given the advantage of any tie in seniority. In a real situation, this problem is not significant since length of service goes back to a particular date, not a particular year.
SOURCE: Mark L. Kahn, "Seniority in Business Mergers," *Industrial and Labor Relations Review,* Vol. VIII (April, 1955), p. 374.

[6] For an excellent discussion of this problem, see Mark L. Kahn, "Seniority Problems in Business Mergers," *Industrial and Labor Relations Review,* Vol. VIII (April, 1955), pp. 361–78.

is substantially reduced, two or more unions are involved, the jobs involve nontransferable skills, the places of employment are geographically remote, and re-employment opportunities elsewhere are scarce. The solution to these problems is never easy and in some instances may do violence to workers' job rights.

Three basic alternative methods of integrating seniority lists have been defined by Professor Mark L. Kahn. They are: by length of service, by ratio, or by rank. Figure 12–2 is an illustration of these three methods. Length of service integration treats service with either company as equivalent to service with the new corporate entity. Ratio integration preserves the proportionate position held by employees on the premerger seniority lists. Rank integration, which is seldom used, places extreme emphasis on the actual distance that each employee stood from the top of the premerger seniority lists. Of course, integration may be rejected by placing all of the employees of one of the groups in a subordinate position.

In merging seniority lists, management's primary concern is assuring the position of employees with hard-to-replace skills. In addition, management seeks to minimize the dislocation caused by bumping. After these two goals are achieved, management may just pass the problem along to the union(s) involved. With the union(s) distributing the seniority rights, the interests of a minority group may be roughly overridden.

DUE PROCESS

A worker's *absolute* claim to fair treatment is analogous to the citizen's constitutional right to due process of law. Under Anglo-Saxon law, the accused is considered innocent until he is proven guilty. The accused is entitled to representation by counsel. His guilt or innocence is determined by a reference to the law by a judge or jury which is free from any personal bias for or against the accused. Ex post facto laws and laws aimed at depriving an individual or group of liberty or property are invalid.

The collective bargaining agreement establishes both the law of employee conduct and the judicial system by which the accused is tried. Unions and managements may negotiate a complex system of rules and penalties. More commonly, the collective bargaining agreement merely states that management has the right to discipline workers for "just cause" or to establish "reasonable" rules of employee conduct. The grievance procedure and arbitration provisions of the agreement create the judicial system of the employment relationship.

The Judicial System under Collective Bargaining

Management is vested with the responsibility for maintaining law and order in the employment relationship under collective bargaining. The initial determination of whether an employee has failed to abide by the rules or his obligation to perform his duties as directed is made by management. If the worker feels that management has treated him unfairly, he calls in the union to act as his defense counsel. In almost all collective bargaining agreements, the worker and the union have final recourse to arbitration in the pursuit of the worker's *absolute* claim to fair treatment.

The Law of Fair Treatment

When the worker's claim finally gets to arbitration, how does the "judge" decide if the worker has been deprived of fair treatment? Like a judge, the arbitrator relies on statutory law (the collective bargaining agreement) or the common law of the employment relationship. If the collective bargaining agreement (statutory law) covers the situation, the arbitrator must weigh the facts and administer justice as defined in the agreement. If the collective bargaining agreement does not cover the situation, the arbitrator must formulate "reasonable and just" laws from the practice of the parties and the mores of the present-day employment relationship. These arbitrator-made rules take on many of the characteristics of a new "common law" of the employment relationship.

The common law of the employment relationship is as difficult to define as the common law of liberty. At the same time, this common law exists and provides very substantial guidance to arbitrators, managers, and unions in providing meaning to the worker's *absolute* claim to fair treatment.

Discharge is frequently called the "capital punishment" of the employment relationship. By examining the common law of just cause for discharge, we obtain an insight on the meaning of due process. Professor J. Fred Holly has analyzed 1,055 discharge arbitration cases. On the basis of his analysis, Professor Holly has formulated eight principles for handling discharge cases which have wide applicability in the arbitration process:

1. Policies must be both known and reasonable.
2. Violation of policies must be proven, and the burden of proof rests on the employer.
3. The application of rules and policies must be consistent:
    a) Employees cannot be singled out for discipline.
    b) Past practice may be a controlling consideration.
4. Where employees are held to a standard, that standard must be reasonable.
5. The training provided employees must be adequate.
6. The job rights of employees must be protected from arbitrary, capricious, or discriminatory action.
7. Actions must be impersonal and based on fact.
8. Where the contract speaks, it speaks with authority.[7]

[7] J. Fred Holly, "The Arbitration of Discharge Cases: A Case Study," in Jean T. McKelvey (ed.), *Critical Issues in Labor Arbitration—Proceedings of the Tenth Annual Meeting National Academy of Arbitrators* (Washington, D.C.: BNA Incorporated, 1957), p. 16.

As Holly states, the application of these principles to the individual case is difficult because of extenuating circumstances which are almost always present. However, the principles do provide a useful guide for unions and management. The principles clearly indicate the need for careful training of supervisors in meting out disciplinary penalties.

SOCIAL IMPLICATIONS OF JOB RIGHTS AND DUE PROCESS

The seniority principle in layoffs probably has worked in the direction of lengthening the average "work life" of employees. Before unionism, discharge for old age was rather common. Seniority means that a worker on the rolls is reasonably free from discrimination because of his age up to retirement age. Of course seniority has no influence at all in preventing discrimination against older workers seeking employment.

The substantial rights granted employees under industrial jurisprudence have emphasized the need for the careful selection and training of new employees. After the short probationary period, the burden of proof in discharges tends to shift to management. To a lesser degree, the employee with the greatest seniority also possesses a claim on whatever higher paying jobs may become available. Although seniority isn't the sole criterion in these areas, and frequently isn't the major criterion, the general significance of seniority is widely recognized and has motivated management to carefully select, appraise, and, when necessary, dismiss new employees before the expiration of the probationary period.

Seniority has probably worked in the direction of reducing voluntary worker mobility. The area of seniority rarely extends beyond the plants of a single corporation. Since seniority provides a degree of job security, many workers are reluctant to leave an employer and forfeit their accrued job rights. Unions have indicated some interest in extending the area of seniority to the entire jurisdiction of the union, but little has been done in this respect in any industry with nonintermittent employment relationships. Substantial employer resistance to this union proposal seems likely to continue as long as each employer insists upon establishing his own qualifications for prospective employees. In the society as a whole, we continue to have substantial worker mobility between employers, especially among the new entrants to the labor market.

Seniority tends to favor present employees over new applicants for employment. It may result in a certain degree of "inbreeding" in a business enterprise.

Of course, the major question about the social implications of seniority is its probable effect on business efficiency. This question is probably impossible to answer. Secure workers are perhaps more efficient than workers constantly worried about their status in the employment relationship. On the other hand, the seniority principle blunts the motivation provided by competitiveness among workers.

Job rights and due process have implications which reach out into the employment relations of nonunion firms. Although workers in nonunion firms do not possess the right to a day in court before an arbitrator, there is little question that many managements have accepted the broad principles of discipline outlined by Professor Holly above. To a lesser degree, many managements also give substantial consideration to an employee's length of service before laying him off or in determining whether he should have a chance at an opportunity for promotion.

SUMMARY

In this chapter we have discussed individual security measures. Individual security measures aim at giving the worker some promise of continuity of employment and fair appraisal of his job performance. Individual security measures are accommodated to the need of management for efficient operations.

The system of establishing a worker's *relative* claim to available work in craft unions may be highly informal. In industrial unions a highly formalized system of seniority establishes the worker's *relative* claim to available work. Both craft and industrial unionists and their unions as institutions are vitally concerned in establishing firm claims to the largest possible number of man-hours of work. In industrial unions, the seniority system establishes the relative claims to available work. In craft unions, the union hiring hall may play a vital role in allocating available work among unionists.

The worker's *absolute* claim to fair play is protected by collectively bargained rules of employment, the grievance procedure, and arbitration. When the collective bargaining agreement provides only general guidelines to fair play, the arbitrator must rely on the common law of the employment relationship.

QUESTIONS FOR DISCUSSION

1. Is it proper to distinguish between an *absolute* right to fair treatment and a *relative* claim to available work?
2. How are job rights distributed in craft unions?
3. Explain the process by which a "common law" of fair treatment has emerged under collective bargaining. Why do few collective bargaining agreements reduce this common law to detailed written "statutory law?"
4. Does a worker have a "property right" to his job? What is the significance of your answer?

CASES: 25, 26, 27, 28, 29, 30, 31, 32, 33, 34, 35, 36, 37, 38.

SELECTED ANNOTATED BIBLIOGRAPHY

BAUMBACK, CLIFFORD M. *Merit and Seniority as Factors in Promotion and In-Grade Progression.* Iowa City: State University of Iowa, Bureau of Labor and Management, Research Series No. 11, 1956.

Discusses bargaining rights and grievance arbitration as related to seniority versus merit in in-grade wage progression and promotion.

BROOKS, GEORGE W., and GAMM, SARA. "The Practice of Seniority in Southern Pulp Mills," *Monthly Labor Review*, Vol. LXXVIII (July, 1955), pp. 757–65.

Two members of the Research and Education Department of the International Brotherhood of Pulp, Sulphite and Paper Mill Workers examine in detail the seniority system as it works in the southern craft or sulphite pulp mill.

BROWN, RICHARD P. "A New Technique in Seniority Administration," *Industrial and Labor Relations Review*, Vol. IX (October, 1955), pp. 32–40.

The director of industrial relations, Mesta Machine Company, Pittsburgh, describes how his company set up a system to provide accurate and current information necessary to administer their seniority policies for layoff, recall, and promotion.

CRAWFORD, DONALD A. "The Arbitration of Disputes Over Subcontracting," chap. 4, *Challenges to Arbitration*. JEAN T. McKELVEY (ed.). Proceedings of the Thirteenth Annual Meeting of the National Academy of Arbitrators. Washington, D.C.: Bureau of National Affairs, 1960, pp. 51–72. Discussion by MARK L. KAHN, pp. 73–77.

Based on an analysis of published arbitration awards, Crawford concludes that "The doctrine seems to be that the company cannot undermine the status of the collective bargaining agent by contracting out work primarily to beat union prices, nor can the company contract out permanent work without compelling reasons other than a seeming desire to reduce the status of the exclusive agent." Kahn discusses the arbitrability of contracting out disputes and emphasizes the bearing of past practice on the contracting out decision.

FLANAGAN, JOHN C., and BURNS, ROBERT K. "Employee Performance Record: A New Appraisal and Development Tool," *Harvard Business Review*, Vol. XXXIII (September–October, 1955), pp. 95–102.

The men who developed the "critical-incident" method of performance review discussed in this chapter tell about its development and operation.

FLEMING, R. W. "Due Process and Fair Procedure in Labor Arbitration," chap. 3, *Arbitration and Public Policy*. SPENCER D. POLLARD (ed.). Proceedings of the Fourteenth Annual Meeting of the National Academy of Arbitrators. Washington, D.C.: Bureau of National Affairs, 1961, pp. 69–91. Discussion by DAVID ZISKIND and IRVIN SOBEL, pp. 91–101.

Discusses the reactions of a broad sampling of members of the National Academy of Arbitrators on how they would handle model situations dealing with (1) notice and appearance, (2) surprise, (3) confrontation, and (4) the agreed case. Ziskind urges that further thought be given to laying down guidelines for weighing the fairness of a hearing. Sobel emphasizes that the worst denials of "due process" take place at other points in the collective bargaining process than arbitration.

HEALY, JAMES J. "The Factor of Ability in Labor Relations," chap. 3, *Arbitration Today*, JEAN T. McKELVEY (ed.). Proceedings of the Eighth Annual Meeting of the National Academy of Arbitrators. Washington, D.C.: Bureau of National Affairs, 1955, pp. 45–61.

A professor at the Harvard Business School and arbitrator discusses the findings of a research study on seniority and merit as factors in promotion. Details the problems in measuring merit and the approach of arbitrators to disputes over merit and seniority in promotions. Paper is discussed by

Professor J. T. McKelvey of Cornell and Gabriel N. Alexander, arbitrator and attorney of Detroit.

Hill, James C. "Summary of the Workshop on Seniority and Ability," *Management Rights and the Arbitration Process*. Jean T. McKelvey (ed.). Proceedings of the Ninth Annual Meeting of the National Academy of Arbitrators. Washington, D.C.: Bureau of National Affairs, 1956, pp. 44–49.
Outlines major contentions of a number of arbitrators on the consideration of merit and ability in disputed cases in labor relations.

Jensen, Vernon H. "Decasualization of Employment on the New York Waterfront," *Industrial and Labor Relations Review*, Vol. XI (July, 1958), pp. 534–50.
Discusses the steps taken by the New York Waterfront Commission to decasualize employment by licensing.

Jones, Dallas L. *Arbitration and Industrial Discipline*. Ann Arbor: University of Michigan, Bureau of Industrial Relations, 1961.
Based on the intensive study of 19 discharge-reinstatement cases, the monograph investigates each phase of the disciplinary process and considers the impact of arbitration upon future policies and worker performance.

Kahn, Mark L. "Seniority Problems in Business Mergers," *Industrial and Labor Relations Review*, Vol. VIII (April, 1955), pp. 361–78.
Discusses the problems of some recent experience in integrating seniority units and evaluates alternative methods of seniority unit integration under the circumstances of a business merger.

Larrowe, Charles P. *Shape-Up and Hiring Hall*. Berkeley, Calif.: University of California Press, 1955.
A study of the International Longshoremen's Association and the International Longshoremen's and Warehousemen's Union in New York and Seattle and their contrasting methods of hiring workers in a casual employment industry.

Meyers, Frederick. "The Analytic Meaning of Seniority," *Eighteenth Annual Proceedings of the Industrial Relations Research Association*, pp. 194–202.
Compares and contrasts seniority and the closed shop as individual security measures.

Phelps, Orme W. *Discipline and Discharge in the Unionized Firm*. Berkeley and Los Angeles: Institute of Industrial Relations, University of California, 1959.
A discussion of the rulings of arbitrators which have produced a definite pattern, consisting of proper grounds for disciplinary action, required procedures, and acceptable penalties and how these factors are qualified by such tests as the burden of proof, firm and industry practices, quality of the evidence, condonation, consistency, extenuating circumstances, and so on.

Ross, Arthur M. "The Arbitration of Discharge Cases: What Happens After Reinstatement," *Critical Issues in Labor Arbitration*. Jean T. McKelvey (ed.). Proceedings of the Tenth Annual Meeting of the National Academy of Arbitrators. Washington, D.C.: Bureau of National Affairs, 1957, pp. 21–60.
Professor Ross, Director of the Institute of Industrial Relations, University of California, Berkeley, reports findings of research study on the success of discharged workers who were reinstated on the job as a result of an arbitrator's award. Comment on the paper by Sidney A. Wolff, New York arbitrator.

SLICHTER, SUMNER H., HEALY, JAMES J., and LIVERNASH, E. ROBERT. *The Impact of Collective Bargaining on Management.* Washington, D.C.: Brookings Institution, 1960.

Special attention is invited to the following chapters: 3, "The Control of Hiring"; 4, "Union Policies on Training and Apprenticeship"; 5, "Basic Concepts of Seniority"; 6, "Work-Sharing and Layoff Systems"; 7, "Promotion Policies and Procedures"; 8, "Work Scheduling"; 9, "Work Assignment and Jurisdiction"; 10, "Subcontracting"; 11, "Make-Work Rules and Practices"; and 21, "Disciplinary Policies and Procedure."

TAYLOR, GEORGE W. "Seniority Concepts," chap. 6, *Arbitration Today.* JEAN T. McKELVEY (ed.). Proceedings of the Eighth Annual Meeting of the National Academy of Arbitrators. Washington, D.C.: Bureau of National Affairs, 1955, pp. 127–47.

Professor Taylor discusses the variations in the use of seniority as a security measure and as an allocator of opportunities between unions and industries. Professor Taylor's long and distinguished experience as an arbitrator and advisor to government results in the formulation of the fundamentals involved in the problem of seniority. The paper is discussed by Professors JOHN A. HOGAN of the University of New Hampshire and CHARLES C. KILLINGSWORTH of Michigan State University.

WIRTZ, W. WILLARD. "Due Process of Arbitration," chap. 1, *The Arbitrator and the Parties.* JEAN T. McKELVEY (ed.). Proceedings of the Eleventh Annual Meeting of the National Academy of Arbitrators. Washington, D.C.: Bureau of National Affairs, 1958, pp. 1–36. Discussion by ABRAM H. STOCKMAN, pp. 37–46.

Drawing on cases and the experiences of several arbitrators, Wirtz discusses problems of maintaining procedural due process in arbitration and the relative weights that should be given to individual interests versus group interests in the grievance process. Stockman generally agrees with Wirtz that arbitration procedures are in the main working well, have no basic flaws, and probably tend to overprotect rather than underprotect individual interests.

PART IV

Collective Bargaining in Perspective

The first 12 chapters of this book have concentrated on the present-day practice of collective bargaining in the United States. Part IV places the subject in perspective in time and space: the past, the future, and other countries. Chapter 13 seeks to answer the question of why collective bargaining has developed as it has in the United States. Chapter 14 compares American practice to developments in collective bargaining in other countries. Chapter 15 attempts to make a short-run forecast of the future of collective bargaining in American society.

AN INTERPRETATION OF AMERICAN UNION HISTORY

This chapter is a departure from the discussion of the contemporary practice of collective bargaining in America. It looks backward into history and documents the historical events which have caused the authors of this book to conclude that there are two model systems of collective bargaining: (1) handicraft industry and craft unionism and (2) mass-production industry and industrial unionism.

QUESTIONS OF IMPORTANCE TO AN INTERPRETATION OF UNION BEHAVIOR

Writing in 1948,[1] John T. Dunlop posed four basic questions which would be of importance to an interpretation of union behavior or the development of a theory which could *predict* union behavior. Here are Dunlop's four questions, somewhat abbreviated, with italics added:

1. How is one to account for the *origin or emergence* of labor organizations?
2. What explains the patterns of *growth and development* of labor organizations?
3. What are the *ultimate goals* of the labor movement?
4. Why do *individual workers join* labor organizations?

Relatively few scholars have given serious thought to the questions raised by Dunlop, or to related questions. The most comprehensive treatment of the subject in America to date, Mark Perlman's *Labor Union Theories in America*, published in 1958, mentions fewer than 20 scholars who dealt with these questions; and Perlman made an exhaustive study.

Before outlining the present authors' interpretation of history, it is desirable to review the work of the most prominent labor union theorists. Here are the names of the important theorists, with the dates of their most significant contributions:

---

[1] John T. Dunlop, in Richard A. Lester and Joseph Shister (eds.), *Insights Into Labor Issues*, "The Development of Labor Organization: A Theoretical Framework," (New York: Macmillan Co., 1948).

In England

Sidney and Beatrice Webb, 1897

In America

Robert Hoxie, 1917
John R. Commons, 1919
Frank Tannenbaum, 1921, 1951
Selig Perlman, 1928

International Schools of Thought

The Marxists, an entire group of writers whose ideas derive from the doctrines first put forth by Karl Marx and Friedrich Engels, beginning in 1847

The Catholics, who expound the social justice doctrines contained in three papal encyclicals, *Rerum Novarum* (Leo XIII, 1891), *Quadragessimo Anno* (Pius XI, 1931), and *Mater et Magistra* (John XXIII, 1961)

An orderly approach would be to see what answers the theorists named in the list have given to these questions, what predictions they have made (if any), and how their answers have stood the test of time.

Origin or Emergence

Sidney and Beatrice Webb regarded unions as the workingman's attempt to regulate and control competition for work opportunities. Unless unionized, every worker faced the competition of every other worker seeking a job. Employers would thus be able to bid down the price of labor, and would, in fact, have to do so in self-defense against the most unscrupulous employer—the one who would drive the meanest bargain—in order to stay in business. The organized worker's answer to this threat took the form, according to the Webbs, of two Devices, which they called the Device of the Common Rule, and the Device of the Restriction of Numbers.

The Common Rule was to standardize wages and conditions of work. This was the defense against that most unscrupulous employer. It also aimed to prevent any one employer from setting his workers in competition with each other to work harder or faster than any of their fellows.

The Restriction of Numbers denied entrance to the trade except to candidates who had passed through an apprenticeship over which the union exercised some control. This had the long-run effect of regulating the total supply of qualified workers to the total demand, so that the bargains made collectively would provide favorable wages and include the Common Rule.

As a background to these two fundamental Devices, the Webbs

identified what they called Doctrines guiding the activities of unions. There were three such Doctrines: Vested Rights, Supply and Demand, and the Living Wage.

Under the Vested Rights doctrine unions opposed innovations and technological changes that would reduce work opportunities for the existing group of qualified workers. Supply and Demand, as the words imply, aimed to restrict the number of qualified workers to the amount of work available. The Living Wage doctrine had to do with the wage level and the amount of work performed for the wage.

The Webb analysis explains craft-union aims and activity. The Webbs saw unions of their day as a regulator of a fundamental economic relationship: the supply of labor of a given quality against the demand for it. Unions were, in short, an economic institution.

Robert Hoxie did not show much interest in the reasons for the origin of unions. He found them on the scene and took them somewhat for granted. To the extent that he gave thought to their emergence, he ascribed it to the psychology of the workingman caught up in an industrial society, without delving very profoundly into the psychological phenomena.

What interested Hoxie was the diversity of unions, their different forms and manifestations. He is the only one of the theorists to stress diversity, rather than to look for similarities. In this he was unique and prophetic even though students who came later have questioned the value of his classifications. Hoxie's awareness of difference takes on significance today because of the emergence of a type of unionism—industrial unionism in mass-production manufacturing—quite different from the craft unions with which his contemporaries were concerned, and beyond which they seem not to have looked.

The work of *John R. Commons* covers a wider time span than the one key date ascribed to him in the list. He was a historian of the labor movement and an active social investigator and reformer as well as a theorist. He saw unions as an economic institution that arose as a result of the separation of the traditional threefold function of the craftsman.

The master craftsman of handicraft industry days had been at one and the same time and in his own person a buyer (of materials), a manufacturer, and a seller (of finished goods). The growth and development of markets divided these functions between the merchant and the manufacturer, and reduced the worker to the status of employee of the manufacturer, who now bought and combined labor and materials and sold finished goods to the wholesale merchant, who resold them. Competition in the market squeezed the manufacturer, who squeezed the worker. Unions were the worker's answer to loss of control over the product market, where he had formerly been able to offer the products of his labor at prices that would bring a fair return. He could counter now only by organizing the labor market, and by raising wage demands seek to assure a fair and sufficient return for his labor. Like the Webbs, therefore, Commons saw the unions as an economic institution, called into being by economic pressure on the workers.

Selig Perlman believed that unionism had its roots in the "scarcity consciousness" of the worker: scarcity of job opportunity. By organizing, the worker could turn these scarce employment opportunities into "job property" through the adoption of rules that gave workers control over the jobs and the conditions of work.

Perlman expressed his views in a somewhat polemic tone. He showed little patience with the programs or the theories of intellectuals (he signaled his scorn for "intellectuals" by always putting the word between quotation marks) but he derived his theory from the actions of the unions themselves. He found these actions sprang from what he called the "job consciousness" of the working man—a kind of practical pragmatism that led the unions, as if by instinct, to do what was necessary to secure and maintain job control: a sort of ownership of the jobs.

Frank Tannenbaum depicted unions as the workingman's answer to the machine and to the role of dependence in which the machine put him. Organized in unions, the worker sought to regain some control over the decisions that affected his living and daily existence.

Tannenbaum published two books on the subject, one in 1921, the other in 1951; but in a sense they are really the same book. The basic analysis is similar; only the conclusions drawn from the analysis differ, and they are poles apart. In 1921 Tannenbaum saw the unions as a revolutionary force, leading toward a reorganization of the industrial system under the control of the workers. In 1951 he saw the unions as a counterrevolutionary force, seeking to give the worker a kind of security reminiscent of the static society of the middle ages, when workers had a fixed, secure status, along with other classes of society.

There is no point here in passing judgment on the conclusions. In either case Tannenbaum's analysis does not picture unions as economic institutions so much as power groups rising out of the worker's psychological response to the insecurity of industrial society.

The Marxists regard unions as only one aspect—and a minor one at that—of the class struggle inherent in the conflict between capital and labor. This struggle, rooted in the contradiction between social production and private ownership of the means of production, is a political struggle to be led by the political party of the working class, whose aim is revolution. Any reform, such as higher wages or better working conditions, can be only temporary and insecure, short of the revolutionary overthrow of the capitalist class: therefore, unions can make no lasting contribution. They do, however, rally the masses for the larger struggle, and so are to be created by the revolutionary party as a training ground and reserve for the political conquest of power.

The Catholic writers regard unions as the workingman's answer to abuses and injustices which are not inherent in the capitalist system, or universally practiced, but which the system makes possible. Unions arise out of the moral need for social justice, and help hold the abuse of power in check.

Patterns of Growth and Development

The fundamental nature of the preceding first question on origins made it desirable to list the explanations of all the theorists in sequence. Needless to say, they have been compressed extremely. The student seriously interested in theory should consult the works themselves, which will be found listed in the bibliography.

Turn now to the second question on growth and development. Here some had nothing to say. Others gave it only minor attention.

The one who had most to say was Hoxie. He found great diversity in the *forms* and in the *functions* (practices) of unions.

Forms. He distinguished the forms by *levels:* local (enterprise), state, and national. He also distinguished by type of industry in which the union occurred, and nature of the attachment: craft, trade (multi-craft), industrial, and labor (multi-industrial). He carried this classification down into even greater detail: compound craft, quasi-industrial, and so on.

Practices. Hoxie observed the ways in which various unions carried out their regular functions, and made an elaborate classification based on this behavior. For a detailed treatment of this and other aspects of his classification, it would be best to consult his own work.

The authors of this book respect Hoxie for recognizing the diversity of forms and functions which unions are capable of assuming. They do not accept his classification system, which to them seems based on fortuitous factors, not rooted in the environment. Use of the Dunlop framework from Chapter 1 of this book, plus application of behavioral science findings, are likely to give results of more lasting value than Hoxie's pioneer classifications; but he is to be honored for seeing the fact and the possibilities.

Hoxie was alone in stressing this point. The others comment upon it, in a sense, only by their silence. That is, they imply that unions are homogeneous organizations and thus deny the prospect of differentiation and change. Comment on the reasons for this, and its significance for use of their theoretical contributions, will appear below after the four questions have been canvassed.

Ultimate Goals

It is on the ultimate goals of organized workers that the Marxists have the most, and all other theorists the least, to say. The Marxists, however, do not see the appropriate organization of workers to be unions, but a revolutionary political party. The unions are the auxiliary troops to be drawn into the revolutionary battles. Industry, by employing them and concentrating them in the workplace, has itself brought about the preliminary organization of workers; on this concentration the revolution is to build its forces around a vanguard of the elite party of the workers.

In the socialist state that is to result from the revolution, again unions are to have a subsidiary role. They are to be the party's auxiliary in maintaining discipline and productivity at the workplace.

Perlman had something to say about ultimate goals, though he was anti-Marxist and condemned all who try to hold ultimate goals before the working man. In the last chapter of his book on theory, Perlman discusses the ideas of a German writer named Carl Zwing, who proposed a plan for the control of industry by joint labor-management councils. This would not actually create a new society, but represents a goal toward which unions might work to insure fair distribution of the fruits of industry. A pale reflection of Zwing's ideas (first put forth in the early 1920's) took shape in German industry after 1946. It is called codetermination—much too complicated to discuss at this point, and not sufficiently significant.

Philip Taft, an associate of Commons and of Perlman, had this to say about the ultimate goals of unions:

American unionism has a philosophy of simple pragmatism. Such a philosophy is not as ostentatious and lacks the architectonic grandeur of philosophical systems such as Marxism. This perhaps makes American trade unionism less attractive to those who enjoy the aesthetic experience of beholding a beautiful intellectual system. However, the absence of these qualities helps to make the American movement more democratic, tolerant, and flexible. Trade unionism in the United States is a means of protecting the individual against arbitrary rule and raising his standard of living. While it may not rank high for philosophy, it deserves high score on the latter count.[2]

Why Individuals Join

This question seems at first glance like a variation on Question 1: Origin and emergence. The individual might be thought of as responding to the forces, or perceiving the rationale, set forth in the analysis of the various theorists.

The cynic may even be heard to say, in answer to that question today, he joins because he is forced to: union shop. Antiunion elements make this the basis of their "right-to-work" laws, on the presumption that if workers did not have to join unions, they wouldn't. If workers join unions purely for individual psychological reasons, or through coercion, this would effectively dispose of all general theory. If not, then one must look for other reasons why unions emerge: economic and political reasons. Theory cannot be disposed of merely by denying that there could be a theory.

[2] Philip Taft, "Theories of the Labor Movement," *Interpreting the Labor Movement* (Industrial Relations Research Association, 1952), p. 38.

But the interaction of the individual with his organization, his enterprise, and his fellow workers is a highly important subject for investigation. It has become the field of the psychologist, the sociologist, the anthropologist, the political scientist, as well as the investigators who originally claimed it, the economists.

In the same book in which Dunlop propounded his four questions, two sociologists also asked some questions. They were Frederick H. Harbison and Robert Dubin. Here are the questions they asked:

There are two categories of extremely pressing, yet for the most part unanswered, questions. First, there are problems relating to the implications of large power concentrations in the hands of private groups. Can large-scale unionization operate within the framework of the present private enterprise system, or must it bring about some modifications in this system? Will the modifications be in the nature of joint economic planning of basic industries? Will concentrations of power in big unions, which parallel similar concentrations of power in big business, inevitably result in some form of bilateral monopoly? Are there automatic or natural limits, inherent in our present economic and political organization, to the exercise of power by large unions and large employers? What social controls through governmental action, if any, should be placed on the accumulation and exercise of such power by either side?

Another set of questions involves the balance of power between individual unions and managements and the resultant kind of union-management relationship which develops. These questions have to do with issues centering in the plant, whose resolution leads to conflict or cooperation, and stability or instability. Under what circumstances do cooperative relationships develop between employers and unions? What changes in human relations accompany the working out of harmonious union-management relations? What social skills are necessary to make such relationships work? What are the limiting factors on union-management collaboration, and, if collaboration is achieved, how stable is it likely to be? Where conflict rather than cooperation prevails, is there an effective basis for mutual survival in labor-management relations?

The questions in this set call for the research methods of the behavioral scientists. Like Dunlop's questions, they are not theory but a call to theoretical work, and a suggested framework for it.

Critique of the Older Theory

The works of the theorists cited represents a sizable body of work by careful observers.

The work they did was adequately descriptive. It took the measure of existing labor organizations, though no one writer covered the entire spectrum. The Webbs dealt almost exclusively with craft unions. So did Perlman, though he devoted some attention to the garment unions, built on the craft pattern but on their way toward developing into industrial unions by amalgamation of the crafts. Hoxie described many types, but based his descriptions on their superficial features without finding the key to their differentiation. Tannenbaum, having himself once been a casual laborer, seems to have been greatly influenced by the plight and mentality of the rootless laborer. This is an unusual kind of worker, and the labor organization he developed—the IWW—was unusual too.

The major phenomenon of our times—industrial unionism—is absent from the descriptions. That is because they were written when industrial unionism was no more than the slogan of the radical left and could be found in practice in only one industry: mining. Mining is not manufacturing. Also, no law required that union agreements be reduced to writing, and in fact a great many were verbal. Craft unions regulate by their own rules many things that are written out between the parties in the industrial union agreement; thus it appeared that the "common rule" of the craft was an essential part of collective bargaining. Writers searching the documentary evidence then available—union constitutions and bylaws, union publications—did not have access to actual labor-management agreements to the extent now possible.

A test of any explanation is to predict behavior and compare what actually happens with the prediction.

One prediction emerges either explicitly or implicitly from all the theories which see unions as an attempt to reduce competition between workers in the face of a scarcity of job opportunities. It is that unions will grow and become strong during periods of prosperity and will decline during periods of depression. Perlman, for one, points out that the AFL was the first national union federation ever to survive a major depression.

The history of craft unionism throughout the nineteenth and early twentieth centuries bore out this analysis. The figures proving this, and therefore the statistical justification of the prediction, were assembled by Leo Wolman in his book, *The Ebb and Flow in Trade Unionism* published in 1936. The facts of industrial unionism in the Great Depression of the 1930's directly contradict the thesis.

The first world war made mass-production industry the major form of production institution and source of national wealth. The 1920's were a period of rising prosperity. During that decade membership in the American Federation of Labor, a federation of craft unions, declined.

The depression brought, as predicted, a still further decline in numbers and bargaining influence of the AFL craft unions; but it also released the greatest organizing drive of all time in America in the mass-production factories.

It might be said of industrial unions that they tend to organize more actively in periods of depression, and to decline—not in absolute numbers or strength, but by deceleration of growth—during periods of prosperity. That has been the history of the CIO and of the industrial-union components of the AFL-CIO since 1935.

Thus the prediction based on past theory that prosperity stimulates union growth and depression destroys it remains true only for one sector—the craft unions, and mainly in their stronghold, the building trades. It fails to account for other sector, the phenomenon of industrial unionism.

Implicit in the older theory, also, is the prediction that doctrines and devices useful to the existing unions would continue to be applied. Any theory based on the premise that unionism is a homogeneous thing implies that future growth will be a quantitative addition to the present, on the same pattern as the past.

As surely as mass-production technology destroyed handicraft production in the national product market, the rise of industrial unionism in mass production broke the pattern.

A general criticism of the older theory may therefore be that the theorists concentrated too closely on unions and failed to take note of the context of technology, which sets the conditions of interaction between the union, one actor, and management and government, the other actors in the system.

The older theory tends to break down when applied to industrial unionism. Various attempts to comprehend the new phenomena of industrial unionism have come to grief by using the older theory without critical re-evaluation. Addition of industrial unionism has also changed the context of power relations, so that older theory may have to be further limited.

This deficiency of older theory is not the result of any failure in observation or scholarship of the theorists. They wrote before industrial unionism came on the scene. Even then at least one of them, Hoxie, foresaw changes which would affect unionism in mass production. They did not have access to a huge body of data that has accumulated since their day, in written form and so available to the scholar. That is the labor agreements themselves.

AN EXCURSION INTO THEORY

The Premises

This excursion into collective bargaining theory starts from the following premises:

1. That collective bargaining, since it is carried on by conscious human beings, is a rational process. This does not imply that emotionalism may not enter into the behavior of the participants. It simply presumes that the parties do have rational ends in view, and that they pursue these ends by means which reason tells them will lead to the desired aim; not in haphazard, random, or irrational fashion.

2. That what unions ask for in collective bargaining indicates what they want.

3. That what unions get from management in labor management agreements represents, on the average and over time, a rational accommodation of what they want with what management in its circumstances and pursuing its

aims can and will give them. That is, union agreements represent limits and boundaries. Each actor has certain ends in view. Each pursues these ends by rational means. Their bargain or agreement represents an accommodation of their separately held aims, whether or not these are antagonistic (requiring compromise), or complementary (requiring only definition).

What this boils down to then is that unionism is a search for security on the part of those dependent on a wage or salary for their living. The industrial relations systems based upon bond labor were long on security, short on individual freedom. The capitalist economic system and democratic political system are long on freedom and short on individual security.

Labor unions emerge when individuals become dependent upon a wage or salary for their living, and are without assurance as individuals of continued employment. Union organization and collective bargaining provide this assurance. It is the rational and effective means of reconciling the needs of employers and of individual workers in an area of reciprocal but not completely identical interests. The employer needs a work force. The employee needs work. The employer's need for workers creates the job opportunities, but it is a matter of indifference to him what individuals occupy these jobs so long as his work gets done. To the worker on the job it is a matter of supreme importance to hold the job. He does not expect work when there is no work available, but as long as he is performing in a satisfactory manner in a given job, he considers it only fair that he be continued in that job. The employer wants "a body." The worker wants to make sure that it is *his* body. They are able to accommodate each other's needs, and do so in the labor agreement.

An individual gets relative security if he possesses characteristics or attributes scarce and desired by society. True skill is a scarce factor of production and gives its possessor relative security compared with the nonskilled worker. Consequently, unions of skilled workers bend their policy to preserve the relative scarcity of their skill. Counterparts of skill in the craft sense, raised to a higher level, may be found in some of the professions. These professions are entered by something that compares with an apprenticeship.

Collective bargaining in the union pattern tends to emerge in answer to felt threats or overt attacks upon individual security, when management fails to provide job rights or observe due process, including effective appeal to impartial review of decisions. It also seeks to influence the terms of the wage and effort bargain.

Union demands on management, and the agreements that result from collective bargaining, reveal that unions are primarily a device for bringing a measure of individual security into the employment relationship and regulating the terms of the work contract—the wage and effort bargain—between the employer and each individual in the bargaining unit. They have no ultimate aims consciously in view. They accept the existing economic system; they accept the existing political system; they seek only to play a regulatory part in the industrial relations system as one actor influencing the rules.

While adjustment by collective bargaining practices will not become universal, it will be the adjustments so arrived at that will set the pattern for the others. The solutions will be, as today and in the past, pragmatic solutions. Because unions will take part in reaching them, they will consider the social welfare. Collective bargaining may somewhat retard the rate of technological progress, or make it more expensive, but it will not obstruct it.

The rest of this chapter offers an interpretation of the history of collective bargaining in America. An interpretation differs from a chronicle in that it tries to point out the significance of events rather than just their sequence. Because this chapter is an interpretation, a chronology of events in collective bargaining history, for reference, follows the chapter. The chronology aims to provide detailed factual support of the narrative; the narrative to give meaning and significance to the sequence of bare facts.

THE TWO HISTORIES OF COLLECTIVE BARGAINING IN AMERICA

Collective bargaining between managers of handicraft enterprises and representatives of craft unions has been going on in the United States almost since the nation won its independence, or for more than a century and a half. It still goes on, for the same ends and in much the same form, in the restricted sector of the economy where handicraft methods prevail. The outstanding example today is the construction industry, with its building-trades unions of skilled craftsmen.

Collective bargaining between industrial unions and the managers of mass-production manufacturing plants, and kindred enterprises mainly employing nonskilled labor, is much newer. It has been going on for barely a third of a century, although factory methods and mass production began to replace handicraft shops at least a century ago.

Not until after the year 1933 did unions succeed in establishing permanent organizations of factory workers, except in the garment trades which were by no means solidly organized. The only sizable industrial union was not in manufacturing but in the coal mines, and seemed then to be struggling against disintegration. The CIO drive to organize the unorganized, which began to gather headway in 1935, built up the weak existing unions to a commanding position in their industries and created new unions where none had been before, as in the automobile and steel industries.

The story of collective bargaining thus becomes, in reality, two stories: a long and consistent, but somewhat discontinuous, tale of craft unions bargaining with handicraft employers in a relatively diminishing sector of the economy; and a brief, spectacular drama of industrial-union bargaining in mass-production industry, whose enterprises make up the vital and decisive elements of the economy today.

Industrial unionism burst on the modern scene suddenly; but nothing as powerful, substantial, and enduring as it has proved to be materializes out of nothing. Three quarters of a century of history lay behind the dramatic appearance.

This chapter aims to outline the developments that led to the CIO sweep through the mass-production manufacturing plants in the late 1930's. The first sign of the emerging pattern comes to light about the time of the Civil War, when craft-union bargaining was an established practice. The craft and industrial strands of the pattern do not lie parallel. They sometimes intertwine, and sometimes spread apart. One of the strands—craft-union bargaining—runs consistently, though intermittently, with very little wavering. The other—industrial unionism, laboring to be born—traces a jagged path.

Three main stages in the quest for industrial unionism preceded the answers found in practical bargaining today. They may be called: (1) industrial unionism *in embryo;* (2) preindustrial unionism *of the left;* and (3) preindustrial unionism *of the right.* Explanations in this chapter will make the three terms clear.

Craft unionism and craft bargaining emerged before the first of the three stages. This chapter starts with the craft-bargaining story and keeps craft-union growth in the field of view as attention focuses on the development of the forces that brought industrial-union bargaining to birth.

At the end of the chapter there is a bibliography containing references that will supplement the brief notes of the chronology and provide a basis of critique and analysis for the interpretation of events.

CRAFT-UNION PREHISTORY IN COLONIAL AMERICA

At the beginning of the colonial period there was no industry; by the end of the period there was still very little. Agriculture, plus a growing trade and commerce, dominated the economy. Manufacturing was in the handicraft stage and largely done at home.

Skilled craftsmen began early to establish a few small shops in the seaboard cities. As their "front room" enterprises grew they took apprentices, and some eventually began to employ wandering journeymen. Their trade was strictly local: village blacksmiths, shoemakers, and menders; tailors; carpenters; printers; tanners.

Not all workers were free laborers; some were slaves, indentured servants, or bound apprentices. Qualifications tended to cluster at the two extremes: a man was either skilled in a trade that had to be learned by serving an apprenticeship, or, whether free or bond, he was an unskilled field hand or common laborer.

There could be no question of union organization of bond laborers. The free laborers worked only singly, or if they were skilled, in small "family" groups, often actually living in the master workman's house and supping at his table.

Wages were high by the standards of those days. From the beginning of settlement in North America there was a chronic shortage of labor, and its price reflected the excess of demand over supply. Attempts to set maximum wages by law all failed, because the need for labor—skilled or unskilled—was so great that the employers themselves broke the law in bidding for labor. Individual, face-to-face bargaining, was the rule.

The Labor Market

Labor is not a commodity in the usual sense, but the price of labor, like commodity prices, may be subject to the fluctuations of supply and demand in the *labor market*. This was particularly true under the conditions that prevailed in the colonies in the early days. Communities were practically isolated from each other, except by water. The main influx of new workers was by ships that came from Europe, and the frontier drained a steady outflow to the west. Thus there would be a certain number of jobs and potential job openings at any given time, and a certain number of workers. A worker on foot could canvass and personally interview all his prospective employers.

The Unskilled Worker. Wages paid for unskilled labor might vary slightly with the physical fitness or the willingness or persuasiveness of the individual, but tended to reach a general level at some point between two extremes: (*a*) In good times, employers seeking labor when it was scarce, bit wages up to the limit of what they could afford to pay and still make a profit. (*b*) In bad times, workers seeking jobs when jobs were scarce bid wages down to the limit of what they could afford to accept and still keep body and soul together—gain their subsistence.

Normally in the colonies there were more jobs or potential jobs than workers, and wages were nearer the upper than the lower limit. As time went on, after the colonial period, steady streams of immigration changed this picture, and the closing of the frontier finally reversed it. There came to be many more people than jobs, and wages dropped to near the lower limit.

Skilled Labor. Just as there was a limit to the number of common laborers available for hire, and free to hire themselves out, there was an absolute limit at a given time to the number who possessed a skill—any particular skill. The same forces that acted on wage levels for common labor in the labor market acted upon wage levels in the smaller labor markets for each skill. Skilled labor was in special demand. A journeyman who had served his time as an apprentice could not "name his own price," but he could bargain within the limits described above, and do it face to face with the man who wanted to employ him. Being free to quit his job, he could get a raise when times were good by further bargaining with his employer.

When individual bargaining worked as well as has been outlined here—and this was the condition in the colonies through a good part of the eighteenth century—there was little need for collective bargaining; and besides, the number of workers employed by one employer was usually small. Many economic and psychological factors also worked against the combination of working men into unions. Land was cheap and easy to get if a man wanted it, and in the growing towns it was easy to make a living and get ahead. Class distinctions, left behind in Europe, had not jelled again too firmly. Society was fluid; most young men expected to rise in the world. So far as the records show, there were no unions, but as time went on there came to be certain kinds of worker organizations.

Worker Organizations

In some of the seaboard cities workers of the same skill or craft founded social clubs, like the clubs of merchants and professional men. Also like the associations of their colonial "betters," these clubs gave status to their members, who were several steps above the immigrant common laborers, bondmen, and slaves. Life insurance was unavailable in those days and there were no workmen's compensation laws, so it is not surprising that some of these clubs turned to establishing mutual funds out of which they paid death benefits to widows and orphans of deceased members, and gave relief to the sick or injured.

Embryo Unions. Members of craftsmen's clubs and mutual benefit societies would not have been human if they had not indulged in "shop talk," and part of shop talk is wages, hours, and working conditions. Members were unwilling to have their wages and conditions undermined by competition from itinerant workers, or "half-baked" craftsmen who would depreciate the standards of workmanship and water down their skill. They found three ways of handling the problem:

The Closed Shop. One method of reducing potential competition was to subsidize itinerant brothers of the craft until they found a job or moved on. This was often done by boarding them around in the homes of members. Another way, more drastic, was to refuse to work with "foreigners," particularly if they had not served their time and mastered the trade. An employer faced with a "turnout" of dependable local workmen would find hiring a floater or an ill-trained man expensive. The result was the informal beginnings of the "closed shop"—the shop that was closed to anyone not a member of the union.

Apprenticeship. In those days youths were bound out for periods of from four to seven years to master workmen, who were the employers. The youngsters learned the tricks of the trade from their employer and other old hands in the shop.

The employers as a group could have relieved the scarcity of skill in the labor market if they had been able to train enough apprentices, but each apprentice during his learning years was a drain on the individual employer, and besides, the already skilled workers did not favor training so many replacements that they would create potential competition for themselves. Since the employers needed the co-operation of the skilled hands to train the replacements, the result was usually a compromise in which the skilled men, as a group, got a voice in setting the number of apprentices. This gave them a large measure of control over the right of access to the trade, and kept their skill scarce in the labor market.

Wages and Output. Finally, there was the question of the speed, or tempo, of the work. Since the craftsman performed this with his own hands, he could control it, but the employer was naturally anxious to encourage the man who worked the fastest, and to hold the others up to his standard. To avoid this, organized members of local groups agreed upon shop rules, either among themselves or with the employers. Once a standard of daily output had been established, it was logical to insist upon a standard daily wage, and this the group negotiated with the employers through spokesmen.

A Craft Union Program. All this adds up to a full-fledged program of craft unionism, valid and practiced (with some additions) to this day. Little of it shows in the records and documents that have come down, for most of it was done by word of mouth, but it can be fairly inferred from what there is in print.

The basic strategy behind it was to control a scarce and vital element of production—skill. Keeping it scarce by limiting the number who possessed it and regulating the terms on which they offered it kept its price up in the labor market.

Any organization with fortunes tied so closely to the labor and product market is bound to suffer with the fluctuations of the economy. Craft unions flourished in a boom, languished when the bust came; appeared, disappeared, reappeared. The story of craft unions up to the Civil War, and after, is one of ebb and flow; it need not be followed in detail. If cats have nine lives, craft unions were like cats. Tied in a sack and drowned during a depression, they came scratching at the employer's door again as soon as times improved. They are still around.

INDUSTRIAL UNIONISM IN EMBRYO: RISE AND DECLINE OF THE KNIGHTS OF LABOR

The independence of the young republic had made possible expansion and activity that colonial status discouraged. Trade with Europe increased, particularly after the Napoleonic wars which ended in 1815. The government encouraged native industry and manufacture, which grew in importance to the economy, though methods of production remained primitive and did not change radically at first. Roads and canals, and, later, railroads linked the cities and connected them with the hinterland. The market for goods ceased to be local and became national. Shoes and guns and yard goods made in New England sold in Michigan and Missouri. The labor market, too, ceased to be narrowly local (though it is never as "national" as the market for wheat or automobiles). Immigration increased greatly. Cities grew in size. Bankers extended their financial operations, and with the increased interdependence of the national economy, national panics and depressions made their periodic appearances.

Rise of the Factory System

England's Industrial Revolution took a generation to cross the Atlantic. American industry felt its influence after about 1840. It brought the factory system. Craft unions continued to grow, because the economy was growing, and handicrafts with it, but factory production began to displace handicraft manufacturing and spread to new areas of enterprise.

The Civil War, 1861–65, gave the factory system an enormous boost. The government, with armies in the field, became an insatiable cash customer for products in quantities such as only mass-production methods could supply. After the war there was a long depression, which brought about the usual eclipse of craft unions and shut down factories; but the factories had come to stay. With the return of prosperity the factories reopened. Craft unions revived in the handicraft shops and occupations that were still active, but the craft unions never succeeded in organizing the factories.

In 1869 a small group of custom tailors in Philadelphia formed a craft union which they called the Knights of Labor. Unlike other organizations of handicraft workers, it did not confine its membership to workers in a single trade, but spread, first as a multicraft federation, then as a general order of working men. By 1878 it had become a national organization. Unknowingly, it contained the embryo of industrial unionism. Though it did not reach the stage of collective bargaining in the factories, it did succeed temporarily on the railways, and it laid the foundations for an industrial union of miners.

What made the factory such a hard nut to crack?

Difficulties of Organizing. The traditional basis of organization was lacking in the factory. Unions could not control entrance to the "trade" because semiskilled work was not a trade and required no apprenticeship. Even apprenticeship for the regular trades slipped from union control in the factory, for factories were big enough to train their own apprentices for replacements. They did not need and did not ask for union help.

Skill itself was no longer vital. Skilled workers made up only a small minority of total factory payroll. The factory easily hired the small number of skilled workers it needed away from union control because it could offer union pay and conditions, or better, plus the inducement of steady work. A 10 per cent raise for the toolmakers or maintenance men might not increase the total wage bill by as much as 1 per cent; thus a factory could pamper its few skilled men. If pampering did not work and the skilled men responded to a union call, the factory could get along without them, for a while at least, because the factory did not depend upon their output as a *direct* element of production. They made tools and dies for the production workers, or repaired machines; they did not turn out the factory's product. That was the job of the majority, the semi-skilled.

The Semiskilled Worker.   The semiskilled worker, trained in a few days or weeks in the factory, was dependent on his job in the factory that trained him. His alternate employment opportunities were at best restricted. Often the work he did was unique to the factory where he worked. If he wanted a job anywhere else, he would have to start as an unskilled trainee. Furthermore, he was easily replaceable—another raw hand could with the same few days or weeks of training that he got easily take his place.

Lack of Union Tradition.   The semiskilled worker ordinarily had had no contact with or experience of unionism. He may have come from the farm, or from a peasant holding in a foreign country. He could hardly feel any solidarity with the skilled man who held himself above the common herd. Semiskilled workers came from every country in Europe, from the country and from the towns, in all ages, shapes and colors, in both sexes. Often they could not, literally, speak the same language.

A Living Wage.   The semiskilled worker did not make as much money as the skilled worker, but he made good money in relation to the learning time invested. The skilled worker must have put in four or more years of practically unpaid labor learning his trade. The semiskilled worker showed up on the job with no training at all, learned it in a matter of days or weeks, and got paid in the process. It was always enough to live on. (Except in certain depressed industries, like textiles, or during times of depression, as in the early 1930's, the factory in America has always paid a living wage). If he came from any European country, he had a higher standard of living at the lowest wage he could earn in America than the majority of his compatriots in the Old Country. What is more, he could sometimes increase his earnings by hard work under a piecework plan, or qualify for higher graded jobs with higher pay. He was not tied, as the skilled worker is, to a single hourly rate for the life of a contract. All these things made it hard to organize him.

Employer Opposition.   Factory employers were more powerful than their handicraft counterparts had been. The factory represents a larger concentration of capital and economic power than the handicraft shop, and the factory employer was richer and more influential, individually and as a group, than the employer of a previous day. He controlled more job openings, exercised greater community leadership, and had more money to spend on lobbying or campaigning for political favors than his predecessors. Many of the early employers smothered potential opposition with kindness, through "paternalism"—providing special benefits and care to their workers. Sometimes, however, this was resented rather than appreciated, but it attracted the loyalty of a part at least of the working force.

The Knights of Labor

The Knights of Labor never squarely met the factory challenge, never fully comprehended it. They did not gain their victories in manufacturing, but they brought factory organization and collective bargaining into the workingman's ken and made them part of his aims. The Knights established the first truly national union movement in America. They wrote a picturesque and honorable page of American labor history.

The Structure of the Knights of Labor. At the height of their development, the Knights showed an organizational structure of three levels, and had three kinds of Local Assemblies.

Levels of Organization. The basic unit of the Knights was the Local Assembly. A dozen or more Local Assemblies, geographically close to each other, made up a District Assembly. All the District Assemblies, taken together, made up the National Assembly, headed by a Grand Master Workman and an executive board.

Kinds of Local Assemblies. The Knights recognized two kinds of Local Assembly. It is possible today to recognize three.

1. Craft Assembly. The first Local Assembly of the Knights was composed exclusively of journeymen tailors, the second, of ship carpenters. In the course of time many other Local Assemblies composed entirely of skilled practitioners of a single craft received charters.

2. Mixed Assembly. The Knights differed from previous labor organizations in accepting for membership any and all who worked for a living, regardless of their skill or lack of it. (In fact, they excluded only tavern keepers, professional gamblers, persons of ill repute, and lawyers. They did not exclude employers, though it does not appear that many big employers joined the Knights). The advance of the factory system produced a category of nonskilled worker called semiskilled. The craft unions had always kept such people out; the Knights took them in. A community with only one Local Assembly of the Knights would have a mixed assembly. After enough craftsmen "swarmed" to found new craft assemblies, those who remained would still constitute a mixed assembly.

3. Industrial Assembly. In any locality where there was only one

employer, what the Knights called a mixed assembly would turn out to be what now may be called an industrial assembly. This condition occurred in such places as textile towns with a single large mill, and in the coal "patches," and by chance in other places here and there. Such assemblies were mixed in the sense that they showed a mixture of various skills and degrees of skill, but they were homogeneous in terms of the industry from which the members came and the identity of their common employer. They were an embryo form of the industrial union Local whose slogan is: One shop, one union.

Activities of Local Assemblies. The craft assemblies of the Knights engaged in collective bargaining exactly as the preceding—and succeeding—craft unions did, and with the same results, depending on the condition of the labor market and the scarcity of skill.

The industrial assemblies provided local and sporadic examples of collective bargaining, notably in railroad strikes in 1885. Local Assemblies of miners also won some battles, but in manufacturing there is no record of success either in conducting strikes or collective bargaining.

The mixed assemblies probably could not do much collective bargaining (the record is blank on this) because it is hard to represent *all* employees in a locality with *all* employers.

Decline of the Knights. The program of the Knights was more ambitious than it lay within their power to attain. They multiplied the number of craft assemblies, but brought nothing new to craft unionism. Eventually they lost their craft assemblies to a rival federation of craft unions willing to concentrate on craft problems and let the semiskilled and unskilled workers go by the board.

Neither did the Knights succeed in working out a consistent program of industrial unionism. For one thing, they did not recognize the problem in their "mixed" assemblies, and for another, change was too rapid and factories were growing too lustily to be unionized.

The very grandeur of the Knights' conception of uniting all labor under a single banner helped seal the doom of the Order. It raised too many hopes, roused too many fears. Quite to its own surprise, the Order found itself fighting too many wars on too many fronts. In the first Wabash strike it won a victory far in advance of the times. This was the first collective bargaining agreement of the industrial-union type. It provided for recognition of local committees and the adjustment of grievances. But when exuberant members tried to repeat and spread the victory, they lost, just one year later, all they had gained, and more. (See the chronology in the appendix to this chapter for details.)

An organization that was content with partial gains, on behalf of only part of the working population, in a part of the economy—and a shrinking part at that—took over where the Knights had nobly failed. That organization was the American Federation of Labor. The AFL fully succeeded, in a humdrum way, in carrying out part of what had been the grandiose total program of the "Noble and Holy Order of the Knights of Labor."

LABOR'S RETREAT, INDUSTRY'S ADVANCE: THE RISE OF THE AMERICAN FEDERATION OF LABOR

The AFL represented what may be called the "production model" of craft unionism, the result of a century of unconscious experimentation in union forms and activities. It discarded the excess weight of the unskilled and semiskilled, and by concentration on the skilled worker, adopted the features of unions that—up to that time—worked. They still work today, but in a steadily declining sector of the national economy.

The craft-union tradition was almost as old as the nation, but the history was broken, discontinuous, and regional. That is, craft unions had sprung up, died, and sprung up again. They were confined before 1860 largely to the eastern seaboard cities. Even though some of them had united in national federations, they had few Locals west of the Alleghenies. It was from one of these craft federations, the Cigar Makers' International Union, that Samuel Gompers came to lead the AFL.

The Knights of Labor gave *craft unionism* a tremendous boost in numbers by organizing *craft assemblies* throughout the land, all the way to the Pacific coast. Still, the older national craft unions retained their identity and held on to their Locals, because craft unionism worked regardless of the label, and there was no room in the structure of the Knights for anything but Local Assemblies. In other words, the Knights did the *new* organizing in the field, the federations held on to the old.

The Craft-Union Strategy

In relation to the Knights, Gompers seems to have had two leading ideas: (1) to keep the already organized craft federations from losing their identity in the vague, mixed structure of the Knights, and (2) to capture the new membership represented in the craft assemblies of the Knights. He and his associates succeeded in both aims. Gompers brought off the coup with two brilliant strokes.

The Strike for the Eight-Hour Day. In 1881 a number of national craft unions came together in the National Federation of Organized Trades and Labor Unions, with Gompers as president. The member unions stuck to winning craft gains while the Knights stood forth as the champions of all labor; yet craft gains attracted the craft assemblies of the Knights.

In 1886 Gompers sent out a call for a nationwide strike on May 1 in favor of a popular demand: the eight-hour day in the building trades. He publicly sought the endorsement of Terence V. Powderly, Grand Master Workman of the Knights, but Powderly declined. He was wary of strikes in general after the spectacular defeat of the "second Wabash" strike earlier in 1886, which had damaged his organization, and he was wary in particular of Samuel Gompers and his craft unions.

But craft assemblies in the Knights wanted the eight-hour day as ardently as any of Gompers' National Federation men, and joined the strike. Then Powderly had a stroke of bad luck.

At a meeting in the Chicago Haymarket called by the Knights to protest violence against strikers, someone (possibly anarchists, possibly police provocateurs) exploded a bomb which killed several people. The Knights of Labor, who had sponsored the meeting, illogically and unjustly got the blame for the bombing, for anarchists charged with the crime were found to have been members of the Knights.

This incident accelerated the disintegration of the Knights. It gave Gompers a further opportunity.

The Breakaway of the Craft Assemblies. The trades and labor Unions federation now proposed that the craft assemblies of the Knights affiliate with their appropriate national craft unions, and that the Federation then affiliate with the Knights in a body. This proposal would have taken the skilled men in the craft assemblies away from their direct affiliation with the Knights and concentrated them, with their brethren of the Organized Trades and Labor Unions, in a virtually independent separate division. To this craft division the Knights might lend their celebrated name, but they could hardly expect to exercise much control over it. Powderly refused, but the craft assemblies proved more receptive to the invitation. It was by now commonly felt that the Knights were on the decline. As one after another of the craft assemblies went over to the Federation's national craft affiliates, the Order began to lose ground. The skilled men had been a cohesive force in the Knights. For them, collective bargaining worked and brought results; without them, the nonskilled industrial workers failed to maintain the Order, and it gradually fell apart.

Gompers picked up the pieces. Not all the pieces; just the pieces he wanted—the craft assemblies. He put them together in a pattern that has lasted to the present day.

Those left out of the new Federation, which reorganized in 1886 as the AFL, found the factory and mass-production industry an even stronger fortress against the assault of unionism, as a result of developments that call for attention at this point.

Scientific Management

The movement that came to be known as "scientific management" dates from the same decade that saw the almost simultaneous dissolution of the Knights of Labor and establishment of the AFL. Scientific management accompanied, and must be regarded as part of, and an adjustment to, a series of technological achievements so advanced that they have been called by some a "new" and essentially "American" industrial revolution.

It was marked by new inventions and the application of new sources of power: the telephone, the electric light, the internal-combustion engine, the electric motor, and many others. It also brought new methods of production. Henry Ford carried to its ultimate, logical development the serialized production of a complex mechanical product, the automobile, built out of interchangeable parts.

Aided by scientific management, the American industrial revolution brought sweeping changes in society and in the work relationship between employer and employee. The factory became the dominant unit of production in the economy, and in the factory the engineers had all but licked the problems of shortage of skill and shortage of unskilled labor. They created instead the place of the semiskilled worker, and in so doing:

a) They cut the ground from under craft unionism in the factory.

b) They nullified, in manufacturing, the labor-market basis of bargaining for skill as a scarce and vital element of production.

c) They increased productivity, built living standards, and made it possible for the untrained worker to come in and earn a living wage, after a few days' factory training.

d) They made the jobs so simple that the worker was just as much an interchangeable and replaceable part as the product he worked on.

All these developments made the factory impregnable to unionism of the old kind. If factories were going to be organized, new ways would have to be found.

It was no use looking to the AFL for the new ways. At the very time when the factory system quickened its advance on a broad technological and managerial front, the AFL beat its historic retreat into the handicrafts, not to move out again for nearly 50 years.

If it could be established that Gompers and his AFL colleagues foresaw, however dimly, what that half century would bring, the retreat might deserve to be called "strategic." The evidence available does not justify using the term in its full conscious implications, but students of the labor movement see in it today at least the strategy of elementary survival: he who simply runs away will live to fight another day.

PREINDUSTRIAL UNIONISM OF THE LEFT

The tangible assets left behind by the Knights of Labor—the craft assemblies—went to the AFL. The spiritual heritage passed to the radicals in and around the labor movement: the political socialists and the nonpolitical syndicalists. The syndicalists, in particular, who in 1905 founded the Industrial Workers of the World, or IWW, built on the grand conception of the Knights, which was a single, all-embracing Order of those who worked for a living. The "Wobblies" (IWW) reached out to organize those working men and women to whom the AFL was closed, because they had no skill—the industrial workers. The Wobblies preached their gospel with a fervor that had not been felt since the great days of the Knights.

The Industrial Workers of the World (IWW)

In 1912 there was a spontaneous walkout of textile workers in some big factories in Lawrence and Lowell, Massachusetts, in protest against wage cuts and unadjusted grievances. The Wobblies, who had members in the mills, assumed the leadership of the strike and led the workers to victory: restoration of the wage cuts, adjustment of grievances. In the face of considerable provocation, they avoided violence, though an attempt was made to blame them for an explosion in the mills that was later discovered to have been set off by one of the factory managers.

This victory was as electrifying for its day as the Knights' victory in the first Wabash strike, but the success was short lived. The following year the IWW lost an equally important strike in the silk mills of Paterson and Passaic, N.J. Taught by the experience of their Massachusetts brethren, the New Jersey mill owners did not wait for a pretext for violent action against the strikers, but turned unremitting violence against them at the plant gate from the very start.

Even if the IWW had won both strikes, there is a question whether they could have built a permanent organization or achieved settled collective bargaining. Their radical ideology opposed the very thought of making "peace with the exploiters." They did not know how to establish a permanent living relationship with management. To be fair, it ought probably to be said that management was no more reconciled than the IWW to the idea of peace and collective bargaining. Industrial workers *had* to strike to get a hearing. The Wobblies showed that such strikes could be won.

Lessons of the IWW Strikes

The IWW experiences in the textile mills showed that the factory was a single, unified, co-ordinated organism. It had to be organized totally, and all at once; it could not be organized piecemeal. The individual was too easy to replace. The entire force had to walk out to stop production.

This called for a *mass movement* of the workers. Mass movements were possible only under unusual conditions, when all the workers were stirred up at once. Spontaneous walkouts against wage cuts or widespread grievances provided the union's best opportunity of organizing.

Once workers were on strike, it became necessary for the union to control *physical access to the plant*. This was for the purpose of keeping not only outside replacements but wavering union members from going to work.

Any strike brings economic pressure to bear on the strikers. Craft unions, which rarely had more than a fraction of their members out on strike at one time, could ease the pressure by paying direct strike benefits. An industrial union that tried to pay benefits to keep strikers from going back would simply go broke, and even if it were possible, that would not keep the employer from hiring outside replacements. Thus the strategy of industrial unionism depended upon control of the plant gate. As long as moral persuasion or appeals to solidarity kept the gate closed, well and good. If these should fail, militants on the picket line had to keep out the timid by threats or violence. Violence on one side evokes it on the other.

Failure of Radical Industrial Unionism

Early industrial unionists had little experience to go on. To many their theories seemed impractical. Industrial unionism had, indeed, existed in the mines since the 1890's, but mining is not manufacturing and has problems that are peculiar to the industry. Radical leadership of industrial unionism failed for several reasons.

It clashed with AFL vested interests. The AFL craft unions claimed jurisdiction over all members of their crafts, including those who worked in factories, even though they were unable to organize the factory craftsmen. They also opposed "dual unionism." Thus they opposed any attempt to organize dual factory unions that would deprive them of their jurisdictional rights.

Radical sponsorship was a liability. The socialists, syndicalists, anarchists, and others who had a program for organizing the factories also had things in their programs that many workers would not swallow. The Wobblies for instance, who were syndicalists, drew a large proportion of their members from itinerant workers—hoboes—whose view of life and mentality differed sharply from that of the stay-at-home factory worker with a roof over his head. The anarchists preached and practiced violence.

The IWW experiment in preindustrial unionism was not the last attempt carried out by leftist elements. After the first world war the newly founded Communist Party led some strikes, all of which were lost. The communists in the AFL formed a "Trade Union Education League" to propagandize for industrial unionism, but were rebuffed and expelled, whereupon they changed the name of their organization to Trade Union Unity League and organized "dual" industrial unions. None of these made any headway toward collective bargaining.

PREINDUSTRIAL UNIONISM OF THE RIGHT

Although there were some further, ineffectual efforts from the left to form industrial unions after the war, the war year, 1917, may be taken as the year of its defeat. The same year marked the start of a new development that evolved into industrial unionism "of the right."

The First World War, 1914–18

Factory production expanded tremendously, mostly in the metal-working industries, under stimulus of the war. For the first time since the appearance of large-scale factory production in America there was an *absolute* shortage of labor in all categories. A foreman could no longer keep a worker in line by pointing to the crowd of job applicants at the gate. There wasn't anybody at the gate any more.

Old ways of doing things had to be discarded. Many supervisors were hastily promoted workmen unaccustomed to the ways of supervision. Foremen who had formerly, for instance, done the hiring of new employees could not spare the time to do it any more. Centralized hiring, centralized training, centralized handling of wages and raises, under newly established personnel departments, became the rule.

Wages skyrocketed as employers bid against each other for the available labor supply. Turnover became a major problem of management as workers shopped around for higher wages. The government had to resort to wage-freeze and job-freeze methods.

The Unions and the War. Gompers and the AFL stoutly supported the war effort. They gave a no-strike pledge for the duration and volunteered their services in war bond drives and other win-the-war activities. As has been seen, they did not have many members in the factories, where the bulk of war production was going on, but now there began to be an AFL influx to the factories.

Boom times are the traditional times of craft-union expansion, for the labor-market situation favors their bargaining power. Union men got jobs in factories, and skilled men in the factories joined unions. Employers had to bargain with the AFL unions in order to keep their men. This did not solve all the employers' problems. He had problems with *all* his men, and dealing with craft unions could, at best, only solve part of his problems. Though an employer might be willing to deal with a craft union on day-to-day problems, as a temporizing measure, he did not relish the idea of permanent *recognition* of an organization—or cluster of organizations—that could not solve his problems.

The National War Labor Board. When in the first world war (as in the second), the government froze wages and jobs it had to provide a substitute for the mechanisms of the market that had been abandoned. Labor relations, and the regulation of labor resources, became emergency problems. The government put these problems in the hands of a National War Labor Board, which had authority to determine questions of wages and representation on a plant-by-plant basis, as trouble developed or threatened.

A device the NWLB tried out to solve labor relations problems in war industry factories was the "works council." This was a plan that permitted employees to select representatives, by departments, and required employers to meet and deal with these representatives on grievances and matters of wages, hours, and working conditions. The program worked so well that it was applied to factory after factory, not only where trouble had broken out, but even in cases where trouble merely threatened. The works councils gave management and employees a way of settling current emergency problems, while side-stepping two issues considered important by management and by the AFL unions, respectively:

Recognition. Management did not have to recognize the unions, but only the elected representatives of their own employees.

Jurisdiction. The works councils, which were not membership organizations, did not challenge the jurisdictional claims of the established unions.

Postwar Industry

The war created larger factories and more of them. The labor shortage vanished when peace returned. This was the result of the loss of war orders, and it was augmented as time went on by reconversion cutbacks and widespread rationalization of plant and equipment.

Experience with Labor Relations. A number of factory managements got their first taste of dealing with employee representatives during wartime. Their experience seems to have taught them that craft unionism provided no constructive answer to the problems involved in running a factory in which craftsmen are a minority, semiskilled workers the majority. The experience with works councils was favorable, or at least neutral. At their best, the works councils helped solve grievances and problems of upward communication, and they gave workers a sense of participation in the effort for production that the entire factory was making.

The Works Councils. When the NWLB disbanded at the end of the war, the legal and official sanctions that had sustained the works councils expired. This left it up to each individual employer to choose whether to continue them under his own sponsorship.

Some employers dissolved their works councils, but a good many continued them. They did so because they had proved to be a good device for grievance adjustment and for securing employee co-operation, and were a hedge against unions, since they performed certain union functions without having either a membership base or outside affiliations.

As time went on, the works-council idea spread in the form of "Employee Representation Plans" or ERP's. This was partly the result of favorable experience of individual employers with the ERP's, and partly on recommendation of employer organizations which made studies of them.

It is noteworthy that the ERP's, while not actually unions, had two important characteristics that go along with industrial unionism. "One shop, one ERP" might be a companion slogan to the industrial union slogan, "One shop, one union." Representation was by department, not by skill or status.

The committees set up by the plans closely correspond to industrial union shop-steward systems.

The Employee Representation Plan Committees. During the years from 1920–30 Employee Representation Plans increased from a total of 196 to 869, and the number of workers covered from 403,765 to 1,547,766.

During the same period AFL membership declined from 4,124,200 to 3,479,800.

The AFL called these plans "company unionism," and condemned them one and all. Looking ahead for a moment to the decade of the 1930's, it might be noted here that several of the CIO unions (steel and autos) got a good part of their start by capturing these company unions. They were, in fact, industrial unionism "of the right," created by management. They needed only to build their management-sponsored representation into a membership base, and gain a union affiliation, to emerge as full-fledged industrial unions.

This brings to an end the prehistory of industrial unionism and industrial-union bargaining in America. Labor gained experience in the ways and workings of the factory; management found that worker consent to factory conditions made for productive operations. The point implicitly at issue between labor and management was not whether there should be factory organizations of workers but whether these organizations should "belong" to management or to the unions.

The answer came in 1933.

THE TRIUMPH OF INDUSTRIAL UNIONISM

The Great Depression of the 1930's was the backdrop for the drama of the rise of industrial unionism. Never before had unions succeeded in establishing themselves in the factories; never since have they been driven out, or lost appreciable ground.

The Great Depression, 1929–40

The tremendous number of persons thrown out of work or into part-time employment by the depression (estimated at up to one third of the working force, with others on reduced pay) had never been equaled, but this is only one measure of the impact of the event. It was a blow to management prestige and confidence. Herbert Hoover had been elected President in 1928 as a "great engineer." With the deepening of the depression, the prestige that had surrounded engineers and managers in the prosperous 1920's disappeared. Not only did the worker lose confidence in the ability of management to solve the problems of depression, but managers lost confidence in themselves. An appreciable number broke with traditional attitudes of independence to ask for help from the government.

The depression brought a growth of radicalism. As has been true whenever economic hardships threatened the worker's subsistence, he turned to radical political solutions. Demonstrations of the unemployed, "bonus marches," "hunger marches," armed skirmishes of farmers against tax sales, and similar instances of direct action took place. The Democratic victory in 1932 was largely a negative anti-Hoover vote. The New Deal program channeled the discontent into positive support for thorough-going measures of reform.

As has been brought out, company unions and Employee Representation Plans (ERP's) followed the wartime works councils into the factories. Management-sponsored and controlled, these organizations performed grievance-handling functions and were a medium of communication with the working force. Raises and benefits that had accompanied prosperity were passed on to employees through the ERP's. When wage cuts took the place of raises, workers lost faith in the efficacy of management-sponsored ERP's.

Effect on the AFL.   The AFL, which had been shrinking in numbers through the preceding decade of prosperity, further lost members and influence as the depression advanced. The industries on which it depended, such as construction, went into stagnation. The AFL leaders turned to political lobbying for public works, and for such measures as the Davis-Bacon Act requiring payment of "prevailing wages" on government work. Prevailing wages, where the unions had any strength at all, meant the union scale.

NRA and the Unions.   The NRA came at a time when the AFL was at its lowest ebb, and did not immediately help it recover. (The NRA, in fact, did not bring actual recovery, though it gave that illusion; genuine recovery came only when the war in Europe began to stimulate American industry with orders.) NRA developments affected the international unions making up the AFL in different ways:

The Craft Unions.   Construction work, the mainstay of the craft unions, was slow to recover. Union men found part-time employment on public works, where they drew (under Bacon-Davis Act provisions) union wages for each hour worked, but shared the hours to spread employment. Craft-union activity waned in the private sector of the economy to concentrate on "pressure-group" tactics with the big employer of the day, the government. Full-scale recovery, when it came, put them back in the business of negotiating with private employers, but this was simply a return to what they had been doing before; depression did not change them.

The Mine Workers.   The only true industrial union in the AFL was John L. Lewis' United Mine Workers. This union came to vigorous life, out of a slump, under the influence of the NRA. It rapidly completed the organization of the independently owned mines, but failed to make headway in the "captive" mines owned by the steel companies. Company unions had employer recognition in the captive mines. These included some of the largest and most productive, and the steel companies were constantly extending their mine holdings. Unless he could sign up the workers in the captive mines, Lewis' hold on the independents was threatened. This constituted pressure—pressure from the right—to organize the steel mills. The Homestead strike of 1892 had taught the lesson that the steel mills could only be organized industrially.

The Garment Unions. Two sizable "quasi-industrial" unions operated in the twin fields of men's and women's clothing: the Amalgamated Clothing Workers (ACW) and the International Ladies' Garment Workers (ILGWU). Each was a collection of craft unions amalgamated or fused into a single top-level organization, with joint boards at membership level to knit the locals together for united action. Under the NRA these garment unions made strides in organizing the many small shops that make up the production units of their industry, the bulk of which was centered in New York. They looked around for other fields to conquer. A special problem for them was the "runaway shops" that moved out of New York to escape the union. In addition, a large proportion of the members were foreign-born, from eastern European and Mediterranean countries. In this group a small but influential core of Communists, surrounded by their sympathizers, strove to take away the leadership of the unions from the conservative Socialists who headed them. Thus for ideological reasons— pressure from the left—the garment unions pressed for industrial organization of the factories throughout the land. This was a long-standing goal of the radical left in the labor movement.

Conflict of Interests and Personalities. It is in the interest of craft unionists to organize all who practice their craft, and no one who does not. To take in others, not qualified, is to water down their greatest asset, skill. Looking at the factories, craft-union leaders saw a minority of skilled workers whom they could accept as members, surrounded by a majority whom they would not. The easiest thing to do—and the most practical—was to let the factories alone, but if someone did organize the factories, the craft unions wanted these skilled men. They wanted them for the job opportunities they represented, and to extend their control over the right to learn the trade. That demand ran counter to a fundamental tenet of industrial unionism: one shop, one union; and only industrial unions could organize the factories.

Tradition also plays a part in any organization, and the tradition of the AFL was to stay out of the factories. Gompers taught them not to dilute their crafts but to concentrate on the skilled trades. They got their fingers burned every time they touched the factories.

Personalities. Human passions and ambition play their part in history. John L. Lewis was an able and ambitious man, with bitter enemies as well as powerful support in the top councils of the labor movement. Hillman was a dedicated man, a "reasonable" and practical labor diplomat and strategist, but nonetheless an old Socialist. Young men were on the way up in the labor movement, too, impatient for power and unwilling to wait for the entrenched old guard labor leaders (who, like old soldiers, never die), to move out and make room for them. No vested interests, no sentimental memories, no hallowed traditions held them to the AFL; they stood to gain more by striking out on their own. Personal factors like this helped bring the CIO into being.

The Factory Workers. Leaders do not entirely determine the direction of events; the "masses"—people, public opinion, in this case, workers—have a share. Most of the new members who flocked spontaneously into the NRA unions were semiskilled workers with no previous experience of unionism. Their working lives had been spent in a factory environment; they thought in terms of "the shop," not any particular skill. They saw no place for their kind in the old-style craft union, and they resented craft-union attempts to split their ranks by taking out the members they prized the most—their own collection of skilled men. (In Akron, for example, after federal Locals were organized in the rubber factories, the AFL tried to put maintenance men from the shops into their corresponding building-trades Locals. The answer was open revolt, and the rubber workers joined the CIO. The skilled factory workers themselves showed that their first loyalty was not to their craft, but with the shop.) Wherever the NRA called new unions into life, the pressure of the rank and file was practically unanimous for the industrial form of organization.

The Rise of the CIO

The moves and countermoves in labor's civil war are listed in the chronology, and the conflicting interests and motives of the contestants have been noted above. Here it is proposed to concentrate on the direction taken by the rebel branch of the labor movement, and the results achieved.

A brief reminder of the lessons taught by the IWW strikes in the textile mills is first in order. That experience showed that there were two essential conditions for success in organizing the mass-production factories (1) organization must be total and simultaneous; and (2) the union must be able to control physical access to the plant.

Ideally, all of the workers of the factory must join the union at the same time. Practically, a good majority (or even, on occasion, a determined minority, provided they had the sympathy of the rest) would be enough, and they would have to join not at the same instant but in a very short time—a few days at most. That was to prevent the factory from hiring replacements, as could easily be done if organization were piecemeal and stretched over time.

Once organized, the union must be able to shut the plant gate by means of a picket line, and keep the plant gate closed. It might not have to do so, but that was the ultimate test of its ability to survive. Again, this was to prevent replacement.

The CIO organizing drive went through three phases, the first of which directly confirms the conditions set forth above. The two later phases do not contradict them, but reflect the modification of the situation that resulted from the Supreme Court's upholding of the Wagner Act.

The Phase of Mass Organization. From the inception of the NRA to the defeat of the bitter strikes in Little Steel, workers literally poured into the new factory unions. It was a mass movement, like water flooding out of a broken dam. It took place during the period when the validity of the Wagner Act was still in doubt and while employer challenges against it were still pending before the Supreme Court which had declared the NRA unconstitutional. Some of the mass movement manifestations were the following:

Spontaneous Organization of "NRA Unions." Some of these unions died as quickly as they were born. Others, as noted, found places in the Internationals such as the mine workers' and the garment workers' unions, that were ready to receive them. Still others, as in autos and rubber, made a nucleus around which new Internationals were formed. Few of these latter unions came into being as the result of any concerted outside organizing drive; they were real instances of "spontaneous generation."

Capture of Company Unions. At least two of today's mightiest industrial unions, the Steelworkers and the Autoworkers, got their start by capturing the councils management had set up in the factories to give employees representation. The members of these ERP councils had been elected by their fellow workers; they were the natural leaders. Depression experiences had shown many of them the futility of trying to get important results for their constituents when they were dependent upon management. Now, by going over in a body to the CIO, a General Motors or United States Steel ERP council could quickly convert its electorate into a *membership*. Membership support made a council independent of management. The issuance of a CIO charter, furthermore, ended the isolation of the individual plants and linked their workers up with others in the industry. The auto Locals had to fight to keep their independence. In big steel, the companies signed up without a fight. In either case, there was a mass shift from company-union status to the CIO.

The Sit-down Strikes. Control of the plant gate is all very well, but when you control physical access to the very machine you work at, only physical violence can get you out to make room for a replacement. There is something hysterical and primitive about this notion, but the sit-downs were not festivals of pure reason: they were direct, emotional reactions to the mass movement of the day. They worked, though even their most ardent advocates knew they would not work forever. Either the emotional outburst that lay behind them would die down, or would develop into the most destructive violence in labor history. To the eternal credit of Governor Murphy of Michigan, the most critical of the sit-down strikes were settled without violence.

The Wagner Act Phase. The Wagner Act modified the situation in several important ways. The issue in the early CIO clashes with industrial management was recognition: recognition always has to be the first issue in labor-management relations. The Wagner Act provided legal ways of getting recognition, and required employers to bargain "in good faith" with the unions that had recognition. It was no longer necessary to shut the shop gate; only to win a majority in a Labor Board election.

Union Jurisdiction and the "Appropriate Unit." The Wagner Act ignored the traditional AFL claim to determine "jurisdiction," with its corollary of "no dual unionism." Regardless of craft claims or industrial ideologies, the Labor Board had the power to determine the appropriate unit. To clinch this even further, the Board gave the union winning recognition an absolute right—a kind of monopoly—to bargain for that unit for a reasonable period of time, without disturbance from rival labor unions. In practice, the Board made the factory the appropriate unit in cases where factory organization was at issue. This was not done just to please the industrial unionists. Management preferred dealing with one union to having the headaches, well known in the building trades, of jurisdictional disputes, rivalry, and strikes between fractional or competing unions.

At first the AFL contested this arrangement, but the Board paid no attention to craft claims unless the contesting craft unions could show a previous history of collective bargaining with the company for the craftsmen in the plant. This, of course, they could not do, for the craft unions had never cracked the factories. Later the Board modified its position (the "Globe doctrine") and permitted small craft units to be carved out of the factories, provided the workers in the smaller unit desired it. This neither harmed the industrial unions very greatly, nor very much benefited the craft unions. The AFL did not succeed in stopping the CIO steam roller until the AFL Internationals decided to reverse their tactics. Old craft unions like the International Association of Machinists and the International Brotherhood of Electrical Workers copied the CIO and started organizing unskilled and semiskilled, as well as skilled men, in the factories. Only when they began to do this was the decline of the AFL checked. A dose of industrial unionism was the medicine that brought recovery.

A Law with Teeth in It. Section 7a of the National Industrial Recovery Act had given workers the right to organize, and warned employers not to interfere with the exercise of that right, but there were no "teeth" in the law. Company unions flourished alongside the affiliated unions under the NRA. The Wagner Act had teeth. It outlawed company unions and effectively prevented employers from discriminating against workers for joining or being active in a union.

This would seem to make the first of the essential conditions mentioned above—simultaneous and total unionization of the factory—no longer essential. Piecemeal organization now seemed possible. The difficulty for the union lay in proving that when a company fired a union man it was on account of his union activity. At first the unions won many cases, because employer habits were strong and methods direct, but as managers refined their tactics it became harder to get the evidence. (At the same time, real management conformity to the law increased.) An unfair labor-practice charge, at best, was not enough to organize a factory, and brought efforts in that direction to a standstill while the case was pending. If the Board's verdict went against the union, previous gains could easily be lost. Workers had never known the kind of protection the act guaranteed. They had to see results before they trusted it.

The company unions also proved harder to deal with than had been expected. Where management gave its support openly, the case was easily proved and the company union disestablished and dissolved. Where the support was secret, or subtly given, it was harder to draw the line between a company union and a genuine independent. It was the experience of most CIO organizers that the company union, except in its most obvious form, was their hardest nut to crack; harder by far than the AFL, until the AFL took up industrial-union tactics.

The Wagner Act phase was by no means a setback for the CIO but it was a period of slower going in organization. The mass movement days were over. A union had to make its way now by winning an election. It had to convince the worker that he ought to vote for the union when he stepped into the polling place and cast his secret ballot.

The Collective Bargaining Phase. The third phase of CIO growth overlapped the second phase in time, but shifted the emphasis from organizing to collective bargaining. Organizing still went on, but it was based on reaching the individual worker by "doorbell-ringing" methods of individual approach, either at home or in his department in the factory. Mass media—handbills, shopgate meetings, loudspeaker appeals—became a supplement to, and not the mainstay of, organizing techniques. Reaching the individual worker, in his tens of thousands, called for inner-union organization. This naturally took the form of departmentalization, after the pattern of the departments in the shop, since it is in his department that the worker meets his fellows and knows them best.

Parallel with this development came grievance handling by the union as a service to its members. Local unions set up grievance machinery in the newly negotiated contracts, and set about gaining experience in settling grievances by contact with their equally inexperienced managements. The departmental organization was a natural for that, too. The inner-union organization that is active in the shop during the working day is the shop-steward system. It would seem that in the steward system, or shop committee, unions in mass-production manufacturing have found the organ that enables them to operate effectively in the factories. In doing so they have solved, quite incidentally, some of management's problems in the field of grievance handling and communications. They have given workers a vital feeling of participation. The stewards make up a complete and flexible on-the-job medium for mutual accommodation and understanding between union and company. How well this medium works for both depends upon their attitudes, their trust in each other, their training and skill in dealing with each other, and the stresses and strains their over-all relationship exposes them to. If stewards were to disappear tomorrow from the factories, management would probably in some form have to call them back.

Subsequent Developments

The situation has not basically changed since the CIO unions reached the third phase of development described above. The process has continued; the parties have matured. It is necessary merely to mention four big incidents in this development:

The Second World War. The demands of national unity in the face of the emergency brought management and labor together for practical co-operation under the sponsorship of government. The two branches of the labor movement also dropped their rivalry for the duration. Both gave a "no-strike" pledge, and in return were given the means of adjusting grievances and disputes with management by representation on the tripartite National War Labor Board. In contrast to the first world war, the labor members now had a membership base, and agreements in the plants whose problems reached the Board. The unions could help with implementing, as well as making, Board decisions. They did much to "sell" the idea of unrestricted output to the war workers in the shops. These workers found that being in a union meant representation on the body that had power over their wages, hours, and working conditions. Union growth, as a consequence, continued and accelerated during the war.

The Strikes of 1946 and the Taft-Hartley Law. Just as the reconversion to peacetime production brought a wave of strikes in 1919, in the course of which management shook off the hold the unions had briefly gotten in the plants, a wave of strikes took place in 1946 after the second world war. This time the unions were industrial unions, and they held their place. While wages, with prices, had been frozen, labor and management had to make their mutual accommodations during wartime mostly at the fringe. After the war, now, pensions and fringe benefits came to the fore along with the traditional issue of wages.

Public reaction against the magnitude of the postwar strike wave created an atmosphere favorable to the passage in 1947 of a law Senator Taft had been pushing for some time. Technically an amendment to the

Wagner Act, the Taft-Hartley law reaffirmed its basic principles, but with some changes. It aimed at restoring balance by weighting the management side of the scale which, Taft contended, had been empty in contrast to the heavy concessions to labor. It is here enough to say that the new law worked out not so badly as labor leaders predicted, nor so well as management people hoped.

The AFL-CIO Merger. It has been shown above that the issue of principle between the craft and industrial unionists, so bitterly contested in labor's civil war, ceased to separate the practice of the parties after the AFL adopted industrial-union forms in addition to its old craft forms. To bring this about it had been necessary to split the labor movement. Once the principle was accepted, there was no reason for the split to continue.

Still, the two labor federations did not come together very quickly. Reasons for their reluctance were various. The left-wing unions in the CIO feared any move that would put them under the domination of the outspokenly anti-Communist AFL. That problem the CIO solved by expelling the left-wing unions and issuing new charters to absorb their former members. Personal rivalries, particularly after the death of Phillip Murray, president of the CIO, also played a part. But logic, and the Taft-Hartley law, inevitably pushed the AFL and the CIO toward a reconciliation.

Why it came exactly when it did, and in the form it did, is a matter for detailed study, but it was bound to come someway, sometime. It finally took place in 1955. The two organizations merged first at the top. The merger worked its way slowly down through state organizations to regional and city councils.

Twelve years later it had not yet brought about much realignment of International union jurisdictions; but interunion rivalry and raiding had been much abated. Strife between former CIO unions and AFL affiliates with industrial Locals had given way, tentatively at least, to co-operation in an Industrial Union Department of the federation, headed by Walter Reuther. Craft unionism, the perennial of American labor, still flourished; and in Landrum-Griffin amendments to the Taft-Hartley law had practically regained the closed shop mainstay of craft strength.

It seems appropriate, therefore, to end this interpretation of the development of collective bargaining in America with the AFL-CIO merger. It marked a turning point; the end of a cycle, the beginning of another. Much has happened since: the expulsion of the Teamsters, the passage of the Landrum-Griffin Act, the accelerated advance of automation. These are all proper subjects for a continuing chronicle; but many events and incidents that today loom large will, in the long view of history, diminish in importance. What matters is that the two main strands of labor and collective bargaining development have come together once again, even if only temporarily; that this time they are both conscious and full-grown; that in uniting, each augments the other's strength. Direction and dynamics, rather than simple chronicle, is what this chapter has tried to trace.

Despite continuing problems and despite defections, the merger has created the most powerful unified labor movement America has ever known. Its member units bargain with the mightiest corporations and employer combinations in American life. The scale on which they do it has depth and breadth and scope that make their interactions part of the experience of this generation. It may well be that the merger will not stand the strain of some internal conflicts that are still unresolved. As this edition went to press, Walter Reuther and the U.A.W. officials had resigned their AFL-CIO posts, but not withdrawn from the federation or given up control of the Industrial Union Department. There is at least a temporary reconciliation in the house of labor; perhaps even a synthesis of contradictory tendencies. Collective bargaining in America has made its way in handicraft and learned to cope with mass production. The actors in the system now stand ready to come to grips with the technology and social problems of automation.

SUMMARY

Collective bargaining in America takes two forms: craft-union bargaining in handicraft industry, and industrial-union bargaining in mass-production industry.

Craft-union bargaining took shape early. It survives today, in the restricted sector of the economy still ruled by handicraft methods, not much changed from its original form.

Industrial-union bargaining did not become a practical reality until long after the rise of the factory system and the development of mass-production methods, which created the conditions for its eventual emergence. The history of the past century is therefore the story of a quest; a search—groping and tentative at first, confident and sure at last—for answers to the social and organizational problems raised by mass-production industry.

It is the story of the industrial worker's fight for something that would give him the kind of say in determining his conditions that craft unions give their members, as he struggled to create organizations that would win him the right to engage in collective bargaining with his employer.

It is also the story of the industrial employer's fight to stay clear of the restraints of collective bargaining in the exercise of his function as enterpriser in a growing economy. Factory methods and machinery freed him from the craft union's control in the first place, and he easily defeated every attempt at forcing him to bargain craft-union style. Industrial unionism in its embryo form posed a stronger challenge, but he defeated that, too, though it sometimes took bloody battles at the plant gate.

But the growth of enterprises, first in mere size, then in the increasing complexity of their internal organization and interdependence in a changing world, created needs—management needs—that in the end only industrial unionism and collective bargaining could answer.

The answers found to date are not final, but as this book has tried to show, they work. They raise new questions, but their study points, perhaps, to solutions that may serve society even better in the future.

APPENDIX: CHRONOLOGY OF EVENTS IN THE HISTORY OF COLLECTIVE BARGAINING IN THE UNITED STATES, 1786–1960.

1786 First recorded strike, called by Philadelphia Journeymen Printers, against a wage cut.

1799 First recorded attempt at collective bargaining by Philadelphia Journeymen Cordwainers (shoemakers) was answered by the employers with a lockout and followed by a negotiated settlement between the union and the employer association.

1806 First criminal conspiracy case against Cordwainers in Philadelphia. Defendants found guilty of a combination to raise wages.

1820 A depression year. Unions died out or became inactive.

1824 With return of prosperity unions became active again. Numerous strikes in the larger cities.

1825 Boston House Carpenters struck for the 10-hour day; lost.

1827 Building-trades workers, striking in Philadelphia for the 10-hour day, formed the first City Central organization of Local unions, the Mechanics' Union of Trade Associations. (This in turn established the first political party of labor, the Working Men's Party, which, like other labor parties of the nineteenth century, suffered defeat but left an imprint on the established political parties by causing them to woo the workingman with planks in the platform such as: free and compulsory public education, abolition of imprisonment for debt, and other reforms demanded by the labor parties.)

1831 New England Association of Farmers, Mechanics and Other Working Men formed in Providence, R.I., spread throughout New England. Seen by some as the first industrial union, but was more a political than a union movement. Agitated for the 10-hour day in textile mills and factories. Died out after 1834.

1833–37 During these years the workingmen's benevolent societies turned into genuine unions of craftsmen. City centrals were established in many cities; there were many strikes for wage demands. Some specific developments during this period were as follows:

1834 First attempt at forming a national organization of Labor: a federation of City Centrals called the National Trades' Union. Disappeared in 1837.

1835 In the Geneva Cordwainers case, and a similar case involving Tailors in 1836, New York courts upheld a law based on the conspiracy doctrine, making concerted activity to get a raise in wages illegal.

1836 Employer Association activity became marked in response to union activity. Fought closed-shop demands by attempting to refuse to employ union members. Turned with greater frequency to court action against unions under the conspiracy doctrine and existing legal precedent.

First national Federation of Local unions of a single craft was organized: the National Cooperative Association of Journeymen Cordwainers. Printers also federated, and other crafts followed in succeeding years.

1837   Depression year. Dropoff of union activity.

1842   In the case of *Commonwealth* v. *Hunt* the very influential Massachusetts Supreme Court overturned the conspiracy doctrine and declared unions not illegal.

1840–60   Gradual (though intermittent) increase in volume of union activity along lines already followed: Local union bargaining with local employer associations, activity of City Centrals, formation and growth of national federations of the various crafts.

Industrial Revolution influence increasingly felt: Bessemer process for steelmaking introduced to U.S.; greater mechanization; intensification of factory methods and invasion of many handicraft fields by the factories. Unions find little success in penetrating factories.

1861–65   The Civil War intensified the trends mentioned above.

1866   National Labor Union, a federation of national craft federations, established under leadership of William H. Sylvis, head of the Iron Moulders' Union. Lasted until 1872.

1869   Knights of Labor founded in Philadelphia by a group of journeymen tailors. Began as a secret society and spread slowly at first among skilled-worker groups; but under the influence of Uriah H. Stephens, a member who had started out to become a Baptist minister, it opened its ranks to all who belonged to the "Brotherhood of Toil."

1873   Financial panic, followed by a long depression.

1877   Strikes against pay cuts on the railways broke out on lines east of the Mississippi, with violent clashes between strikers and federal troops in Baltimore and Pittsburgh. More than 100 killed. Troops finally put down the strikes.

1878   Knights of Labor organized nationally. Stephens, first Grand Master Workman, succeeded by Terence V. Powderly.

Period of recovery from depression began.

1881   Delegates of craft unions met in Pittsburgh to form the Federation of Organized Trades and Labor Unions (the forerunner of the AFL).

1882   After negotiations between Powderly and Cardinal Gibbons of Baltimore, the Knights of Labor renounced secrecy and revised its ritual, and the Roman Catholic church withdrew its ban on membership in the Knights.

Strike of railway workers on the West Coast against wage cuts, led by members of the Knights of Labor, resulted in rescinding of cuts.

1883   Depression year.

1885   Railway workers on the "Southwest System" controlled by Jay Gould, New York financier, struck against wage cuts. Organized into the Knights of Labor after the strike broke out spontaneously, the workers kept the trains from moving until Gould met and signed an agreement in New York with Powderly.

Frederick W. Taylor started experiments at the Midvale and Bethlehem steel plants that led to the discoveries of "scientific management."

1886   A "big year" in labor history.

A strike which started as a "wildcat" on the Gould-controlled MKT line was decisively defeated. The Knights lost prestige and members as a result.

The Federation of Organized Trades and Labor Unions, led by Gompers, called a nationwide strike for the eight-hour day, to start May 1. Powderly refused to give the move the official support of the Knights, but many Local Assemblies of the Knights answered the strike call. Chicago police killed four strikers at the McCormick Reaper works. At a meeting in the Haymarket called to protest these killings, a bomb was thrown that killed several policemen. The Knights of Labor became unjustly associated in the public mind with violence. This caused further loss of prestige and shrinking of membership.

Later in the year the Federation of Organized Trades and Labor Unions (craft unions) proposed a merger with the Knights which would give them control in the affairs of the Craft Assemblies of the Knights. Powderly turned down the merger offer. The Federation then sent out its own call for a convention and met in Columbus, Ohio late that year to form the American Federation of Labor.

The American Federation of Labor elected Samuel Gompers president. As the Knights of Labor began to disintegrate, the AFL picked up most of its Craft Assemblies.

1892   Homestead Steel strike, led by AFL Amalgamated Association of Iron, Steel, and Tin Workers, led to violence between strikers and armed Pinkerton men. The strikers defeated the Pinkertons but were subdued by troops. After the strike only about 800 out of some 4,000 workers were taken back, all others being replaced by nonstrikers from outside.

1894   Pullman strike, put down by federal troops. Eugene V. Debs, Socialist and railway union leader, emerged to national prominence.

Frederick W. Taylor read a paper entitled "A Piece Work System" to the American Society of Mechanical Engineers: his first appearance before them, followed by others which gave him great influence. National Association of Manufacturers organized.

1905   Industrial Workers of the World (IWW) organized in Chicago. "Big Bill" Hayward one of its leaders.

1908   Section 10 of the Erdman Act applying to railroad employees, whereby the "yellow dog" contract was outlawed and an employee was forbidden to discharge a worker for union membership, was declared unconstitutional (*U.S.* v *Adair*).

A boycott by the United Hatters of Danbury, Conn., against D. E. Loewe and Co. was held to be in restraint of trade under the Sherman Anti-Trust Act of 1890. The individual union members were held responsible for the union's acts and assessed damages and costs totaling $252,000.

1911   A congressional committee conducting hearings on legislation for government-operated arsenals and navy yards heard testimony from Taylor and his associates. At these hearings Louis Brandeis, later to become a Supreme Court Justice, coined the term "scientific management," and helped publicize the achievements of the Taylor group, but Congress outlawed the use of the stopwatch and "efficiency" methods in arsenals and navy yards.

1912   Strikes against wage cut and "stretchout" in textile mills in Lawrence and Lowell, Mass., broke out spontaneously and striking workers were quickly organized by the IWW. The industrial form of organization, the well-conducted relief activities, and the nonviolent tactics the IWW employed in this strike resulted in a victory for the strikers, who got wage increases, revision of the stretchout program, and adjustment of grievances.

1913   Strikes in the silk mills of Paterson and Passaic, N.J., led by the IWW, were met by stern police measures, and failed.

1914   Clayton Act approved. It exempted unions from the provisions of the Sherman Act, limited the use of injunctions in labor disputes, and provided that picketing and other union activities were not to be considered unlawful. (Later judicial interpretation reversed the apparent prolabor provisions.)

1914–19   A war-boom period, characterized by labor shortages, rapid expansion of factory production, shifts in the labor force. The AFL under Gompers supported the Allied war effort and pledged co-operation with employers to win the war. AFL membership increased in the factories, but employers were reluctant to recognize unions, while unions were jealous of jurisdictional lines. To resolve these difficulties the National War Labor Board, created by Congress as an emergency measure, ordered the establishment in many factories of "works councils" consisting of elected representatives of workers in the various departments. These councils side-stepped the question of recognition and of jurisdiction, and carried on collective bargaining and grievance-adjusting activities with factory managements.

1917   The Supreme Court upheld the "yellow dog" contract and declared that union efforts to organize workers subject to such contracts were unlawful (*Hitchman Coal and Coke Company v. Mitchell*).

1919   Strike wave in steel and other industries, as industry reconverted and employers withdrew such recognition as they had accorded unions during wartime. Unions of the AFL lost their foothold in the factories.

Legislation creating the National War Labor Board lapsed and works councils created by NWLB lost specific legal sanction, but many companies retained the councils as consultative bodies and for grievance adjustments.

National Industrial Conference Board started a series of studies of the works councils, and Employee Representation Plans that developed from them, and ended by recommending the idea to manufacturing employers.

1920–29   General trends: craft unions were ousted from the factories where they had gained a foothold during the war—"open shop" prevailed in manufacturing with many large companies establishing employee-representation plans; widespread adoption of the lessons of the scientific management movement; mounting prosperity up to the crash of 1929.

1926   Railway Labor Act. Established collective bargaining for the railways to guard against stoppages in vital national transportation system. Outlawed "company unions," provided grievance procedure and arbitration machinery.

1929   Stock-market crash signaled the beginning of depression and large-scale unemployment.

1932   Norris-La Guardia Act. Outlawed the yellow dog contract and made the use of the injunction in labor disputes practically impossible.

1933   A turning-point year for industrial unionism.

Inauguration of Franklin D. Roosevelt as President ushers in the "New Deal" administration.

NRA. Section 7a of the National Industrial Recovery Act gives workers the "right to bargain collectively through representatives of their own choosing without interference, coercion or restraint on the part of the employer."

Unions receive big impetus from Section 7a. This includes company unions as well as the AFL.

AFL Convention votes to hold a Conference to devise ways of organizing industrial workers.

1934   AFL Conference advocates federal Locals for the factories; sidesteps question of craft-union jurisdiction over workers in these Locals.

"Labor's Civil War" begins at AFL San Francisco convention between craft and industrial unionists; first result a compromise.

1935   Supreme Court declares NRA unconstitutional.

Congress re-enacts the substance of Section 7a in the form of the Wagner Act; outlaws company unions; establishes the National Labor Relations Board.

Clash at AFL Atlantic City convention ends with victory of craft unionists. Industrial-union advocates meet in November to form the "Committee for Industrial Organization," CIO.

1936   AFL Executive Council calls on AFL-affiliated unions to sever connection with CIO; few comply.

Sit-down strikes in auto factories in December.

1937   AFL expels unions connected with the CIO.

Auto Workers (UAW-CIO) sign contract with General Motors in February, Chrysler in April; Steelworkers (SWOC) sign with Carnegie-Illinois, U.S. Steel, Jones & Laughlin.

Strikes in "Little Steel" result in union defeats.

Supreme Court upholds constitutionality of Wagner Act.

1938   CIO organizes on permanent basis as "Congress of Industrial Organizations," with John L. Lewis as its first president.

1940   Lewis resigns as president of CIO; Phillip Murray elected in his place.

1941   United States declares war on the Axis powers; gets a "no-strike" pledge from labor; sets up tripartite (labor-management-public) National War Labor Board to deal with wartime disputes.

Ford Motor Co. Signs first contract with UAW-CIO.

1946   Postwar strike wave, most extensive to date in U.S. history. As after World War I, recognition at stake in some of the strikes. Unions succeed in winning new agreements.

1947   Taft-Hartley law.

1955   AFL-CIO merger.

1959   Landrum-Griffin Act.

QUESTIONS FOR DISCUSSION

1. Do organizations have a historical "memory"? Did the craft unions of the AFL profit from the mistakes of the Knights of Labor? Did the industrial unions of the CIO "learn" from the AFL, the Knights, and the Wobblies?

2. "The Knights of Labor was a *class* union; the AFL was a federation of *craft* unions; and the CIO was a federation of *industrial* unions." Carefully show

the accuracy and inaccuracy of this statement. Does this generalization serve any useful purpose?

SELECTED ANNOTATED BIBLIOGRAPHY

This bibliography consists of two parts: (1) the theory of union behavior and (2) history of labor relations.

1. THE THEORY OF UNION BEHAVIOR

BROOKS, GEORGE W., DERBER, MILTON, McCABE, DAVID A., and TAFT, PHILIP (eds.). *Interpreting the Labor Movement*. Madison, Wis.: Industrial Relations Research Association, 1952.

Special attention is invited to: "Theories of the Labor Movement," by PHILIP TAFT; "The Union Role in Industry. Its Extent and Limits," by L. REED TRIPP; "Union Policies As to the Area of Collective Bargaining," by DAVID A. McCABE; and "Union Attitudes Toward Economic and Social Roles of the Modern State," by Rev. GEORGE C. HIGGINS.

CHALMERS, W. ELLISON, CHANDLER, MARGARET K., McQUITTY, LOUIS L., STAGNER, ROSS, WRAY, DONALD E., and DERBER, MILTON. *Labor-Management Relations in Illini City*. Champaign: University of Illinois Institute of Labor and Industrial Relations, 1953. Vol. I: The Case Studies; Vol. II: Explorations in Comparative Analysis.

An interdisciplinary study of labor-management relations. Volume I deals with case studies at the enterprise and the local community. Volume II attempts quantitative analysis.

CHAMBERLAIN, NEIL W. *The Union Challenge to Management Control*. New York: Harper & Bros., 1948.

A study of the impact of the union on the authority of management in the large corporation.

DERBER, MILTON, CHALMERS, W. ELLISON, and STAGNER, ROSS, with the co-operation of MILTON EDELMAN. *The Local Union-Management Relationship*. Urbana: Institute of Labor and Industrial Relations, University of Illinois, 1960.

In 1953–54, the University of Illinois Institute of Labor and Industrial Relations published a two volume report, *Labor-Management Relations in Illini City*, which attempted to lay the foundation for a systematic approach to the study of the process of accommodation between organized labor and organized management at the local establishment level. The *Illini City* project was a study in depth and thereby limited to eight establishments in a single community.

The Local Union-Management Relationship study extends the *Illini City* approach to 41 establishments in three communities. The present study is based on a survey technique involving detailed interviews with only a few top leaders of the management and the union in each establishment. For the most part, data are the *perceptions* of the men and women who were mainly responsible for and best informed about the formulation and general administration of the basic rules by which the day-to-day life of the establishment was guided. As in *Illini City* studies, a further attempt is made at quantitative analysis.

DUNLOP, JOHN THOMAS. *Industrial Relations Systems*. New York: Holt, Rinehart & Winston, Inc., 1958.

Develops an analytical framework for the general study of industrial relations in different countries. Includes a comparative study of work rules in bituminous coal mining in eight nations and in the building industry of nine nations.

———. "Structural Changes in the American Labor Movement and Industrial Relations System," *Proceedings of the Ninth Annual Meeting of the Industrial Relations Research Association*, pp. 12–32. Madison, Wis.: The Association, 1957.

Discusses the impact of the government and the AFL-CIO merger on the structure of the American labor movement.

HOXIE, ROBERT FRANKLIN. *Scientific Management and Labor.* New York: D. Appleton and Co., 1920.

Based on an investigation of scientific management in its relations to labor made for the United States Commission on Industrial Relations. An attempt to compare Taylor's claims for scientific management with the operation of the system in shops.

———. *Trade Unionism in the United States.* New York: D. Appleton and Co., 1917, 1923.

An intensive investigation of the goals and nature of American labor unions. Appendix II, Students' Report on the Trade Union Program, outlines the methods used by Professor Hoxie and his students in their investigations.

LESTER, RICHARD A., and SHISTER, JOSEPH (eds.). *Insights Into Labor Issues.* New York: The Macmillan Co., 1948.

Special attention is directed to: "Toward a Theory of Labor-Management Relations," by FREDERICK H. HARBISON, ROBERT K. BURNS, and ROBERT DUBIN; and "The Development of Labor Organization; a Theoretical Framework" by JOHN T. DUNLOP.

LOZOVSKY, A. *Marx and the Trade Unions.* New York: International Publishers, 1935.

Cited by Philip Taft in his discussion on Marxism in *Interpreting the Labor Movement.*

PERLMAN, MARK. *Labor Union Theories in America: Background and Development.* Evanston, Ill.: Row, Peterson & Co., 1958.

Summarizes and assesses literature on American labor unionism. Classifies theories or "basic interpretations" into five groups: unionism as a moral institution, as a revolutionary institution, as a psychological reaction, as a welfare institution, and as a part of the democratic process.

PERLMAN, SELIG. *A Theory of the Labor Movement.* New York: The Macmillan Co., 1928.

A classic study of the factors responsible for the economic conservatism and limited political involvement of American trade unions. Stresses the job security psychology of the workingman and the adaptation of unions to American conditions. Compares American, British, pre-Nazi German, and Russian experience.

Rerum Novarum, Quadragesimo Anno, and *Mater et Magistra.*

Pope Leo XIII, Pope Pius XI, and Pope John XXIII discuss Roman Catholic views on the conditions of labor and the right of working people to association in encyclical letters in 1891, 1931, and 1961.

TANNENBAUM, FRANK. *The Labor Movement, Its Conservative Functions and Consequences.* New York: Alfred A. Knopf, Inc., 1921.

An analysis of the aims and consequences of labor organization, tinged with the casual worker mentality.

———. *A Philosophy of Labor.* New York: Alfred A. Knopf, Inc., 1951.

Argues that labor unions are a counterrevolutionary force seeking to establish a community of secure relationships analogous to the status system of the Middle Ages.

WEBB, SIDNEY, and WEBB, BEATRICE. *Industrial Democracy*. London: Longmans, Green; First pub. 1897, latest ed., 1920.

A classic study of the internal structure, method of government, regulations, and policies of British trade unions. Part IV presents a theory of the effect of trade unions "on the production and distribution of wealth and the development of personal characters."

2. HISTORY OF LABOR RELATIONS

CHAMBERLAIN, NEIL W., PIERSON, FRANK C., and WOLFSON, THERESA (eds.). *A Decade of Industrial Relations Research, 1946–1956*. New York: Harper & Bros., 1958.

A volume published by the Industrial Relations Research Association. Special attention is invited to: "Collective Bargaining," by JOSEPH SHISTER; "The Economic Effects of Unionism," by GEORGE H. HILDEBRAND; and "Employee Benefit Plans," by ROBERT TILOVE.

COMMONS, JOHN R., and ASSOCIATES. *History of Labour in the United States, 1896–1932*. 4 vols. New York: The Macmillan Co., 6th printing, 1951.

The classic University of Wisconsin study of American labor history, comprising:
Volumes I and II, by JOHN R. COMMONS, DAVID J. SAPOSS, HELEN L. SUMNER, E. B. MITTELMAN, H. E. HOAGLUND, JOHN B. ANDREWS, and SELIG PERLMAN.
Volume III, *Labor Movements*, by SELIG PERLMAN and PHILIP TAFT.
Volume IV, *Working Conditions and Labor Legislation* by DON D. LESCOHIER and ELIZABETH BRANDEIS.

FILIPETTI, GEORGE. *Industrial Management in Transition*. Rev. ed. Homewood, Ill.: Richard D. Irwin, Inc., 1953.

Analyzes the mainstream of management thinking and practice in industrial enterprises. Discusses the emergence of an international scientific management movement.

GALENSON, WALTER. *The CIO Challenge to the AFL: A History of the American Labor Movement, 1935–1941*. Wertheim Publications in Industrial Relations. Cambridge, Mass.: Harvard University Press, 1960.

A descriptive history of labor developments in the steel, auto, coal mining, electrical, rubber, clothing, textile, meat, lumber, petroleum, and maritime industries, as well as those affected by the teamster, machinist, building trades, printing and publishing, and railroad unions. Author relies heavily on hitherto unavailable AFL Executive Council and CIO Executive Board minutes.

HARDMAN, J. B. S. (ed.). *American Labor Dynamics*. New York: Harcourt, Brace & Co., 1928.

Thirty-two labor men, teachers, editors, and technicians discuss the problems of organized labor during the bleak 1920's. Readers will find here a realistic statement of the problems of organizing the unorganized as they existed in the pre-New Deal era.

LANDSBERGER, HENRY A. *Hawthorne Revisited*. Ithaca, N.Y.: Cornell University, 1958.

A critical appraisal of the Hawthorne Experiments and developments in human relations in industry.

MILLIS, HARRY A., Research Director. *How Collective Bargaining Works.* New York: Twentieth Century Fund, 1942.

This volume is a comprehensive statement of collective bargaining processes in 16 industries with notes on 13 more industries up to 1940. The contents are:

TAFT, PHILIP. "Organized Labor and the New Deal."
BURNS, ROBERT K. "Daily Newspapers."
BROWN, EMILY CLARK. "Book and Job Printing."
HABER, WILLIAM. "Building Construction."
FISHER, WALDO E. "Bituminous Coal.
———. "Anthracite."
WOLF, HARRY D. "Railroads."
MYERS, ROBERT J., and BLOCH, JOSEPH W. "Men's Clothing."
TAYLOR, GEORGE W. "Hosiery."
HARBISON, FREDERICK H. "Steel."
McPHERSON, W. H. "Automobiles."
ANTHONY, DONALD. "Rubber Products."
DERBER, MILTON. "Glass."
———. "Electrical Products."
CHRISTENSON, C. LAURENCE. "Chicago Service Trades."
TAFT, PHILIP. "Collective Bargaining Before the New Deal."
———. "Brief Review of Other Industries."

PERLMAN, SELIG. *A History of Trade Unionism in the United States.* New York: The Macmillan Co., 1922.

Part I is a summary of the first two volumes of the *History of Labor in the United States* by J. R. Commons and associates. Part II carries the history down to 1923. In Part III the author begins to develop his own theory of the American labor movement, stressing that the attempt to improve the bargaining position ("job control") of the worker and not the desire for a revolutionary transformation of society "is the key to the conduct of organized labor in America."

SLICHTER, SUMNER H. *Union Policies and Industrial Management, Washington, D.C.: Brookings Institution,* 1941.

The pioneer study of the impact of the union on the management of industrial enterprises and the economic effect of union policies. Most of the research for this volume was completed before the union organization of mass-production industry.

SLICHTER, SUMNER H., HEALY, JAMES J., and LIVERNASH, E. ROBERT. *The Impact of Collective Bargaining on Management,* Washington, D.C.: Brookings Institution, 1960.

A comprehensive treatment of contemporary American collective bargaining practices ranging from such specific topics as control of evaluated rate structures, hiring, and concepts of seniority to such general questions as the importance of line and staff co-operation. Authors resist developing an explicit theory of collective bargaining, but do provide some generalizations regarding the emerging characteristics of collective bargaining. In part, an updating of Slichter's *Union Policies and Industrial Management.*

TAYLOR, FREDERICK WINSLOW. *Scientific Management, Comprising Shop Management, The Principles of Scientific Management, Testimony Before the Special House Committee.* New York: Harper & Bros., 1947.

The father of Scientific Management explains its principles to the American Society of Mechanical Engineers in 1903, the general public, and a special committee of the House of Representatives in the winter of 1911–12.

WEBB, SIDNEY, and WEBB, BEATRICE. *The History of Trade Unionism.* New York: Longmans, Green & Co.; First published, 1894, latest ed., 1920.

A classic history of trade unions in Great Britain. After rejecting the guild theory of the origin of unions and suggesting that unions arose only after "the great bulk of workers ceased to be independent producers," it traces the development of British trade unions from the latter part of the seventeenth century through the first two decades of the twentieth.

WITTE, EDWIN E. *The Evolution of Managerial Ideas in Industrial Relations.* Ithaca, N.Y.: New York State School of Industrial and Labor Relations Bulletin No. 27, 1954.

A leading authority on industrial relations traces the changes in American management's view of industrial relations in the twentieth century.

Chapter 14

COLLECTIVE BARGAINING
IN OTHER COUNTRIES

Every nation has its own industrial relations system, which differs from others just as nations differ. The practice of collective bargaining is widespread in the world, but the forms it takes are never exactly the same in any two industrial relations systems.

To begin with, the contexts vary. The Peruvian market cannot support the local manufacture of automobiles, which have to be imported; this in turn calls for the export of copper, which can be mined locally, to pay for them. Watch-making technology in Switzerland creates a work force of skilled light-industry machinists, whereas the copper mines employ illiterate hand laborers. Power relations generated by the political systems of Portugal or Bulgaria make for different relations between managers and workers than in the Swiss Republic.

The actors also show different attributes. Labor in France is militant, but poorly organized and split between three rival federations; employers are unified and strong; and the government plays little part in bringing them together. Labor in Germany seems to be docile, but highly disciplined and well organized in a central federation; employers too are organized and strong; and the government encourages joint labor-management agreements by extending their terms throughout an industry or area by ministerial decree. In the U.S.S.R. the government is the employer: it plans production, sets quotas, lays down norms, and expects unions to assist managers in enforcing them. It would be pointless to extend the list of examples.

With such diversity in the contexts and actors, the rules, and rules for rule making, inevitably must differ. A book like this one might be written about each of the 115 countries in the United Nations, with additional volumes for those nations not yet affiliated. Is it necessary for an American student of collective bargaining to learn about the practices of all these other countries?

It is not necessary to learn them all, but it may be necessary for some people, during the course of their careers, to learn one or another of them, and it will be helpful for every student of collective bargaining to learn something about a few of them. Many American firms today have foreign subsidiaries, or are founding or acquiring them. Already many Americans working overseas, whether in business, or government, or for labor organizations, have had to learn by trial and error, or what is called the hard way. There are doubtless many ways, but the best way is not to attack the subject country by country but to see whether there may not be certain common characteristics and general principles that apply to all; then, with these as a guide, look at the differences. This chapter offers a key, which may not be perfect, but which does open the door to understanding.

The treatment which follows does not attempt to provide an exhaustive description of any single country's way of doing things, though it will offer examples drawn from representative countries. It will put the student on guard against the kind of selective perception that sometimes tricks a casual observer into reading American meanings into foreign words and ways, but will make use of the knowledge of American ways to illuminate the foreign systems. Just as a person learning a foreign language needs a little grammar and syntax, which he can compare with his own, before he can start thinking in the new vocabulary, a student of comparative labor-management relations needs a bridge from the familiar to the unknown. When he has made the crossing he will find—what he probably suspected all along—that while foreign methods and institutional arrangements take shape and color from diverse cultural conditions and historical developments, the foreign manager and the foreign worker are driving at the same things, under the same motivation, as their American counterparts.

Labor and management in foreign countries, as in the United States, have an interest in the terms of a wage and effort bargain. Workers everywhere seek individual security. Rules at the workplace governing these substantive issues take shape under rules for rule making that define union security and management rights, and provide means of administration. At this point the reader will recognize that the key this book offers for interpreting foreign labor-management relations is the one already outlined in Chapter 7 under the heading, "The Nature of the Agreement." The four main functions listed there, with their subfunctions, will be used as a check list and a guide to the objectives of the actors. This is what all the systems have in common. The way the actors work to achieve their respective objectives, and the resulting rules and arrangements, are what differentiate the systems.

As a first test of the applicability of this key it might be well to survey the activities of an international agency which has taken the lead in making—or at any rate, influencing—the rules for rule making. That is the International Labor Office (ILO), one of the oldest, and probably the most successful, of all the various organizations for international cooperation.

THE INTERNATIONAL LABOR ORGANIZATION

Every two years at Geneva, Switzerland, representatives of the three actors in the industrial relations system of most of the world's independent nations gather to make rules for rule making that have an impact in almost every country and eventually work their way down to influence the substantive rules in the shops. This has been going on since 1919, before many of the member countries were even in existence and before some of the most important developments in labor-management relations (such as industrial unionism's conquest of the factories) had unrolled even in the advanced countries. In June, 1964, 110 countries were members of the ILO.

Between the biennial sessions, called Conferences, which are attended by the full delegations of the countries involved, an executive committee, called the Council, meets as frequently as three or four times a year. Under the Council and subject to its appointment, a Director and permanent staff administer the headquarters, called the Office, and coordinate the far-flung activities of the Organization. Thus the initials ILO refer, in English, both to the general organization in all its aspects and to the office in Geneva, housed in its own ILO building with its permanent staff of international civil servants.

The peace treaty following World War I, in its Article 13, established the ILO, and the United Nations Charter, following World War II, confirmed its role and standing. Members of the ILO are governments. The United States, which declined membership in the League of Nations (created by the same peace treaty that established the ILO) joined the ILO—and, in fact, helped start it. The United States sends delegates to its Conferences, is represented on its Council, and has contributed professional staff, occasional technical experts, and of course funds and support to its activities.

Technically all delegates who attend ILO sessions of any character represent their governments, but the rules of the organization require the governments to nominate an equal number of delegates from the "most representative" labor unions and employer associations. Thus the labor delegates from the United States are in effect nominated by the AFL-CIO, from Britain by the Trades Union Congress, from West Germany by the Deutsche Gewerkshaftsbund. The United States employer delegates, similarly, are the nominees of the N.A.M.; and so on. In addition to these worker and employer delegates, each member nation sends a group of government representatives equal in number to the total of the other two. Thus each national delegation is one-half governmental and one-quarter each, labor and employer. The Council, which is drawn from a number of countries, preserves this ratio and its 48 members comprise 24 from government and 12 each from labor and employer organizations. The same proportion holds throughout the organization whenever representation rather than expertise is the objective; and all policy proceeds from the deliberations and vote of the elected representatives. Policy decisions take the form of what are called Conventions, and of Recommendations; both require a two-thirds affirmative vote.

Recommendations are not simply instructions accompanying and implementing the Conventions. A Convention affirms some principle thought to be important enough to deserve expression as an international engagement, and when ratified has the effect of a treaty binding the member nations. A Recommendation does not create an international engagement, but gives guidance to member governments on internal legislative or administrative action.

Theoretically, if the delegations voted by interest blocs, government plus labor could impose decisions on management, or government plus management, on labor. In practice this simply does not happen. As various issues arise, some governments will side with their labor people, some with their employers; and it is common to find labor (or employer) delegations from different countries voting against their counterparts from other countries. In its long history the ILO has succeeded in keeping its procedures representative and democratic so that, while no policy decision of the ILO takes effect in any country without that country's ratification or consent, every action of the ILO that emanates from these processes carries great weight of influence. In all, the ILO has voted 122 Conventions, which have received from member governments nearly 3,000 ratifications.

The Work of the ILO

Th ILO directs its efforts toward three main objectives: (1) the establishment of norms; (2) research and information; and (3) technical assistance. The main responsibilities fall on different parts of the organization, and results are separate, but all three objectives are interrelated and the activities to which each gives rise reinforce the others. This chapter's analysis focuses on the norms, but first it might be well to glance briefly at the other two.

Research and Information. The day-to-day work of the permanent staff of the ILO consists in gathering information on labor conditions throughout the world, from member governments and other sources, classifying the data, compiling statistics, making analyses, carrying on special studies and research projects, and writing and publishing reports. A number of periodicals emanate from the ILO (notably, the *International Labor Review*) as well as pamphlets, bulletins, monographs, books, and special publications. Internally, in addition, a vast number of memoranda, reports, and draft documents circulate for the use of the policy-making bodies, the Council and the Conference.

Technical Assistance. Since World War II the ILO has cooperated with agencies of the United Nations in providing experts to help developing nations with special problems such as the training of industrial cadres or the operation of labor exchanges or the administration of social security services. The ILO recruits these experts on a temporary basis and sends them out under contract. Project groups of this sort have a great deal of operating autonomy but receive policy direction and co-ordination from the central office.

The Norms: Conventions and Recommendations of the ILO

Only the accredited delegates to the biennial Conferences have authority to establish norms, which become valid as official declarations of policy by a two-thirds majority vote. The Council of 48 may lay down operating policies for the ILO but may not set norms for the organization as a whole or for the member governments, or alter those the delegates have adopted. The norms take the form already mentioned of Conventions or Recommendations. In effect, they define public policy for the world.

They do not have the force of law, though as a rule they express national public policy already accepted and enacted into law in several or many of the member countries. The Convention against forced labor, for example, met no effective opposition when it came to a vote, for it accorded with the principles and practice of most of the member countries. In other instances, however, the ILO has taken the lead by setting a norm most member countries would not dare be the first to enact, even if they wanted to, unless other countries simultaneously promised to do the same. Examples are the norms on hours of work, on child labor, on equal pay for equal work for women. Country-by-country ratification of Conventions, or implementation of recommendations, still poses problems. Here the services of ILO officials by helping to synchronize follow-up action, enable member governments to minimize the risk of putting themselves at a disadvantage toward industrial competitors.

It is time now to see whether the norms so far adopted by the ILO correspond to the functions of the labor agreement; that is, to the issues any labor-management relations system has to face and settle. The first of these functions in the key this chapter uses for testing the hypothesis carries the heading: Union Security and Management Rights.

Union Security and Management Rights. To begin with, the ILO itself is a symbol of labor-management relations. Its structure and rules explicitly recognize the existence and legitimacy of unions and its procedures reinforce the idea of joint decision making. The ILO brings together, literally face to face, representatives of the two main actors in the industrial relations system—labor and management—in equal numbers, with equal vote and authority, in the approving presence of the principal third actor, government. The delegates meet, they argue and dispute, they seek common ground. Eventually, on one important issue after another, they agree. Policy takes shape out of their joint participation.

The policies themselves go beyond mere symbolic representation. There are specific Conventions, having the force of international treaties, that affirm such principles as the legal right of workers to organize in unions and the legitimacy of collective bargaining as a form of activity of unions with employers and employer associations. The legal right to organize surely gives unions their most elemental guarantee of security: without it, there could be no legal bargaining, and no trustworthy agreements. The ILO has on occasion gone beyond merely asserting the right. It has investigated charges of violation, and in cases where the charges proved correct, has made effective representations to the governments of the countries involved.

The conventions cannot go into such detail as to specify the bargaining unit, the form of recognition, the duration and renewal of agreements, or specific management rights. Here each country works out its own rules. What remains in the ILO definition of the norms is a clear encouragement to the parties—and principally to the direct actors, labor and management—to work the problems out themselves, and thus enable, and set in motion, free collective bargaining on the substantive rules.

The Wage and Effort Bargain. Rules for rule making that touch this function, which at shop level gives rise to substantive rules, cannot go beyond defining limits within which the bargainers must stay. Like government, the ILO cannot bargain for the parties, but it can give guidelines. Thus the ILO Convention on a minimum wage cannot fix the peso or dinar or dollar figure, as the law might specify it in a member country, but it does require that a minimum be established and the ILO suggests criteria and procedures for setting the just and proper amount. In any country, only a fraction of the work force receives the bare minimum of pay, but this still provides a base for bargaining for the higher rates. It thus gives guidance under the subfunction of determining *pay for time worked.*

The effort bargain, similarly, has to be specified at the workplace where tasks are performed and standards set, but the law can put limits to the standard-setting. The same task performed on a machine with safety devices and on another without them exacts a different degree or quality of effort. Whether a union demands the safety device or the law requires it, the effort bargain changes when it is put on.

The ILO has always taken the position that workers should not have to carry the whole burden of improving unsafe or unhealthful working conditions, and that the employer who is unscrupulous, or indifferent to the welfare of his workers, should not enjoy a competitive advantage over the employer who is humane. Legislation conforming with the ILO norms on safety and sanitation tend to limit the standards acceptable in the effort bargain.

Other subfunctions provide somewhat broader scope for norms that directly affect the wage and effort bargain. Early in its career the ILO took action aimed at shortening the hours of work. In the key, this is the aim pursued under the subfunction headed *premium pay*. Many countries have adopted legislation setting the maximum permissible working hours even lower than the ILO norm of 48 hours a week, and unions have pushed below this to 40 and even lower, with further restrictions on the length of the working day. The ILO norm stands in the way of going back to sweatshop hours.

Some ILO norms touch on the subfunction of *pay for time not worked*, by calling for rest periods and holidays with pay. Others—indeed, by far the bulk of the ILO contribution—deal with various aspects of social security. These provide the underpinning for the issues in collective bargaining called in the key *contingent benefits*, or worker insurance and income-continuity programs.

The foregoing brief treatment does not exhaust the analysis of ILO actions bearing on the wage and effort bargain, but shows that even where substantive rules are in question, rules for rule making can give impetus and direction to the bargaining.

Individual Security. This is again a function of collective bargaining that produces substantive rules. The individual employee wants a definition of *job rights* that will spell out his relative claim to available work. Of course the ILO cannot set down names on a seniority list or rules for a union hiring hall, but it can take a stand on principle against arbitrary discharge of employees, and has done so; and there is room for other norms that strengthen job rights. One element of a claim to available work is always the qualifications an employee brings to the job, and the ILO has set norms for vocational training, for certificates of competency (as for merchant seamen), and against discrimination in employment. The considerable ILO effort at reducing and combating unemployment, at providing labor exchange services, retraining opportunities, and vocational counseling, indirectly strengthen the job rights of the individual.

The individual's claim to fair treatment, or *due process*, gets support from the ILO norms encouraging joint consultation on personnel decisions and neutral adjudication of disputes, as in a system of labor courts or arbitration. Again, the ILO cannot reach down into any shop, or prescribe the procedures of any country, or act as an international court of appeals to see that individuals get justice, but in all its acts and pronouncements it has made clear the sacredness in which it holds the rights of individuals. Collective measures have their justification in the benefits they bring to the individual; the individual does not exist for the sake of the collectivity. In asserting and championing the dignity and status of the individual the ILO acts as the conscience of humanity.

Administration. As the key brings out, administration is both *internal* and *external*. Internal administration of the substantive rules is, of course, the business of the two main actors. The thrust of ILO action is on external or third-actor participation in administration. Norms dealing with factory inspection help control compliance with the rules for rule making, such as those setting limits on wages or task standards. Norms dealing with conciliation, mediation, or adjudication of disputes between the actors bring control procedures—and people with authority to enforce them—to the administration of the substantive rules.

In Summary

The ILO activity which results in the establishment of international norms centers on the same issues that engage the efforts of the main actors in collective bargaining relations. The procedures the ILO follows in the search for common ground between the nations and the actors are analogous to negotiations between the actors in their search for agreement. Principles expressed in the ILO norms point to the kind of agreements on the various issues that labor wants, that management can live with, and that are acceptable to world public opinion.

This brief survey of ILO activities confirms the applicability of the analytical key to situations beyond the borders of a single country. The aims of the actors remain constant: the issues are universal. The difference between countries consists in the means adopted to achieve the aims. History, tradition, political and social institutions, and the cultural stamp these put on a people, differ from one country to another. They produce corresponding differences in the forms and procedures of collective bargaining.

A TAXONOMY OF LABOR-MANAGEMENT RELATIONS

Taxonomy, in the biological sciences, classes the different species of animals and plants into genera, orders, and phyla. By analogy, each country's labor-management relations system might be considered a species, perhaps with subspecies, and similarities between national systems would permit grouping them into genera. This is of course fanciful; but it is nonetheless possible to distinguish at least five general groupings: (1) the British-American-Canadian, or common-law systems; (2) the Western European, or Napoleonic Code systems; (3) the Eastern European, or Socialist systems; (4) the Iberian peninsula, or Corporative systems; and (5) the systems of the developing nations.

Within each of these systems one country's way of doing things resembles another's more closely than it resembles the ways of a country in a different system, as a mouse resembles a cat more than either resemble a hummingbird. A few exceptions must be noted. One is craft unionism and craft bargaining in construction and printing. These are already familiar to readers of this book, and show a family resemblance throughout the nonsocialist world.

Other exceptions arise in the systems of the developing nations. Closer examination (which will not be attempted in this chapter) would almost certainly break this category down into several new headings. India and China are both developing nations, but mainland China has a socialist economy and a communist political dictatorship, while India permits capitalist enterprise and practices political democracy. And where does one put Japan?—with the developing nations or the advanced? And if the latter, in what category?

Again, some of the developing nations used to be colonies of powers in the common-law group, others were colonies of powers whose law stemmed from the Napoleonic Code. England left its mark on India, Holland on Indonesia. To the extent that unions and collective bargaining got started at all under colonial rule they are bound to reflect European influence.

The bulk of industry, however, and hence of collective bargaining, occurs in the first four listed categories—indeed, mostly in the first three; and for all practical purposes of Western students, in the first two.

The Common-Law Systems

Three English-speaking countries make up this category: Great Britain, Canada, and the United States. Although Canadian practice differs in some respects from that in the United States, the similarities greatly outweigh the differences. Both diverge from British practice which, as might be expected, provides the purest example of a system that evolved under institutions shaped by the Anglo-Saxon common law.

Great Britain: The Actors. Unions started locally at the shop, the pit, the mill. Local people dealt with local owners or their managers on issues arising at the workplace. They grappled with problems in the pragmatic English spirit and they muddled through. From time to time they fought; but employers made no determined drive aimed at destroying the unions. Arrangements the two sides came to tended to stand unless upset in court; resulting judgments set precedents for other arrangements in the future. This is the common-law approach; action precedes the appeal to law. Eventually unions received the sanction of statute law, largely confirming the place they had already made for themselves.

When practical considerations called for common action between union men in one locality and another, they got together. Out of these working alliances grew affiliations of a more permanent character and, eventually, national unions. Employer organization followed. Growth was never even or systematic; many arrangements remained local and special and continue to this day to function quite outside the larger groupings.

The result of this haphazard and seemingly random development appears to an outsider as a confusing tangle of relations that do not make much sense—but which the participants nevertheless make work. Like the British constitution, which is not a single comprehensive document but a collection of precedents, customs, and traditions, labor-management relations seem to have settled down to a system of accepted usage, with elements both formal and informal, often not reduced to writing that either side could appeal to, but which neither side would dream of trying to upset.

Union Organization. British unions divide into the two familiar kinds: craft and industrial. Some of the bigger national unions are really federations of industrial unions—what some call "multi-industrial" unions—or they are mixed federations of craft and industrial unions. Member unions enjoy a great deal of autonomy.

The British workingman belongs to a Branch of his union. The Branch is affiliated with the national union and sometimes with a district or regional intermediate organization. Branches often cover several shops, in which case there are separate and subordinate shop organizations. Each shop elects its own chairman (often called the "Shop Convener") and shop stewards. The steward performs the same function as his counterpart in America. He also carries out a duty American stewards nowadays are seldom called upon to do: he collects dues.

Although there has been a steady trend toward consolidation of unions, the British labor movement entered the decade of the 1960's with a total of more than 700 separate unions. Fewer than 200 of these belong to the Trades Union Congress, or TUC, but those which do comprise about 85 per cent of organized labor. The TUC corresponds to the AFL-CIO. It does no bargaining, but supports and co-ordinates the activities of the autonomous member unions and concentrates their weight and influence in representational activities. Most of this, of course, is political and takes place through the Labor party. The TUC professes to be nonpartisan, but its member unions are active politically. One or two of them—though not the majority, and not the largest or most influential—are under the leadership of avowed Communists.

The Labor Party. The British Labor party, which formed a government with a strong majority in Parliament in 1966, is a creation of the unions and receives much of its financial support from them. This British relationship between the party and the unions reverses what will be found characteristic of continental Europe where the unions were the creation of the parties. It also differentiates Britain from the United States and Canada, although something like an equivalent relationship exists between the AFL-CIO and the liberal wings of the established parties in both North American countries.

Unlike the continental labor parties, the British party has never adopted a specific Marxist orientation, though the activity within it of socialist-minded intellectuals and labor leaders with leftist views gives it a socialist tinge. It did indeed nationalize the steel mills after World War II and threatens to do so again (for the mills did not stay nationalized) but the position the party takes on most issues is no more extreme than many to be found in party platforms in America. It can hardly be supposed that a party which makes peers out of labor leaders and sends them to the House of Lords is intent on overthrowing the established order in Britain.

Employer Organization. The employer counterpart of the TUC is the British Employers' Federation. This is a federation not of individual firms but of employer associations, whose member firms employ about 70 per cent of all British workers outside government service. It assists the member associations in their collective bargaining activities, and like the TUC, carries on general representational work aimed at protecting and advancing employer interests. Politically, it tends to favor the Conservative party, though it is officially nonpartisan.

Government as the Third Actor. Government has played a smaller part in rules for rule making than in North America. The legislation is almost purely permissive. When government does intervene, it in the main encourages collective bargaining. For example, an important bargaining institution consists of the National Joint Industrial Councils, which bring unions and managers together under neutral government chairmanship in government services and utilities. Lately, in addition, the government has begun to take a hand in making substantive rules by statutory wage setting in some industries, such as agriculture, which the unions have found hard to organize. This step was taken, however, largely at labor's insistence. The government also provides statutory appeals machinery for disputes the parties cannot settle by themselves, and conciliation services.

In general, the government keeps its hands off collective bargaining. It has not reserved the right to define the bargaining unit, or to certify worker representatives for collective bargaining, or to lay down a minimum form of union recognition. There is no legal obligation to bargain in good faith. The system implicitly appeals to the participants' sense of fair play.

The Rules. Bargaining takes place at many levels, from the summit of a national industry down to a single workshop, but the bulk of it is between employer associations and national unions. An agreement reached at this level works its way down by supplementary bargaining to apply its terms at successively lower levels, and eventually to work rules on the shop floor. The forms of the agreement vary, but as in North America the content fits a familiar pattern.

Union Security and Management Rights. Recognition—the foundation of union security—has never brought about the sharp conflicts in England that surround the issue in the United States. British unions also have not been as insistent about exerting jurisdictional claims, and do not demand the union shop. Perhaps this is because the British working population, until recent years, was homogeneous. British workers show a natural solidarity that seems to be rooted in consciousness of a fixed class status in a rigidly stratified society.

Union security in England has thus never been challenged at its base, and management rights ("the other side of the coin") never seriously shaken. Nationalization of steel, it should be remembered, did not dilute management rights; it only changed ownership.

Thus the *bargaining unit* can be whatever the parties agree to: a single shop, a group of plants in a multiplant corporation, a department in a shop otherwise represented by a different union—or an entire railway system, or the British merchant fleet and all its vessels. Bargaining on substantive issues may take place at local or at national level, or at whatever level in between the bargainers find appropriate.

The *form of recognition* is in effect sole bargaining rights, but only in the sense that the conditions apply throughout the unit even to employees not members of the union; but these rights are not exclusive, and the agreement may in fact be made with several unions which happen to have members in the unit.

Duration and renewal of the agreement differs from North American forms: it is usually indefinite rather than for a stated length of time. An agreement may therefore be reopened for negotiations when either side desires. The old agreement runs until the new one has been reached. A "no-strike" clause under these conditions would have no meaning.

Management rights may or may not be specified. The tradition in Great Britain seems to accept more authoritarian management practices than in the United States, and British unions do not seem to be as militant in opposition to it. They do seem quicker to "down tools" in solidarity with a discharged fellow worker. This propensity tends to induce management restraint.

The Wage and Effort Bargain. This may cover any unit, from an entire industry down to a department or an occupation in a single enterprise, but the effort part of it almost inevitably is bargained locally. *Pay for time worked*, as always, is the item easiest to express in concrete terms: shilling and pence per hour or pounds per week or month. The *effort bargain* cannot be defined as sharply if the agreement covers more than a single shop. There are exceptions to this. On the railways, nationally applicable work rules set the size of crews and specify task assignments. In the steel industry, on the other hand, each mill bargains its own work rules and task standards, though covered by a national wage agreement. Springing as it does from tasks in a work flow at a particular workplace, the effort bargain tends to be something only those directly affected can determine—or even properly understand.

All other subfunctions of the wage and effort bargain—*premium pay, pay for time worked, contingent benefits*—lend themselves to joint determination at any level and may be defined in national agreements as well as in the rules of a single shop. Contingent benefits in particular rest solidly on a base of legislated social security administered by government, in Britain as in the United States. It is rare, however, for unions to seek to supplement the government programs by means of labor-management agreements. They prefer to bend their efforts toward improving the government programs, and rely on the Labor party to help them.

Individual Security. Practice here resembles that in North America. *Job rights* derive from qualifications and from claims which an agreement can make relative to any criterion the parties think fair. Seniority is a common form, but not so much a fetish as in the United States. *Due process* rests, as in America, on a grievance procedure, whose steps may be set forth in the agreement, or simply a matter of accepted custom. Formal arbitration of the kind familiar in America is seldom resorted to because the law provides statutory machinery for appeal.

Administration. *Internal* administration of agreement terms creates a steward system and gives the stewards authority to present grievances. The steward is a union man, chosen by his fellow workers at the workplace. *External* administration provides for the participation of union officials of the Branch, or district or national organizations, to enter grievance procedures at the appropriate steps. It also takes note of the role of governmental agents in appeals, inspections, and other matters.

In Summary. The British system of labor-management relations reflects British history, temperament, pragmatism—and to a goodly extent, British muddle. It is a system of live-and-let-live, with government standing aside most of the time and not only letting but encouraging the participants to work out their own problems. It is long on freedom, on tolerance, and on the give-and-take of fair play, but perhaps short on efficiency, both for improving the condition of the workers and maintaining the productivity of British industry. Whether it will stand up to the stresses of intensified international competition is a question that is already troubling some of its most ardent admirers.

The Napoleonic Code Systems

The Napoleonic Code Systems include Germany, France, Italy, and most of the countries of western continental Europe.

Historical Perspectives on the Napoleonic Code Systems. A few brief reminders from history will help make the European systems understandable. Four big events associated with famous names have left their mark: (1) the French revolution and Napoleon; (2) Karl Marx and the Socialist International; (3) the Russian revolution; (4) World War II and its aftermath.

The French Revolution and Napoleon. The French Revolution (1789) started a train of events that broke up the feudal pattern in Europe and dethroned the absolute monarchs. The political leaders of France raised armies, first to defend the revolution and, having succeeded in that, later to export it. But armies make the reputations of generals, not politicians, and generals who command troops loyal to them sometimes overthrow the politicians. One such general, Napoleon Bonaparte, seized power.

As Napoleon conquered territories that had been under absolute rule for centuries, he consolidated his hold by passing on the basic reforms of the revolution to people who had not fought for them. He did this by decreeing a set of laws and legal principles known as the Napoleonic Code. So thoroughly did the Code destroy feudal relationships that even after Waterloo, when the old rulers came back, they were not able to govern in the old way.

People accepted reforms by decree as they had formerly accepted rule by decree. They were happy to get them; but there had been no real break in the tradition that rights were granted from above, by the state, not seized from below as the French had done, or the English a century earlier in their "Glorious Revolution." An Englishman who wanted to do something not forbidden by law would just go ahead and do it, and keep on doing it unless forbidden after challenge in a court of law. Not so the continental European. He had to find out first whether it was lawful; otherwise he dared not act. After Napoleon even the French tended to look to the state to tell them their rights and liberties. It made a practical but not theoretical difference that state authority had passed from absolute monarchs to representative assemblies. That is the basic difference between the spirit of the common law and the Napoleonic Code. A point that drives this home most strikingly to Americans is that under common law a person whom the state accuses of a crime is presumed innocent until proved guilty, while under the Napoleonic Code he is presumed guilty until proved innocent.

When people see their rights as flowing only from government permission, they turn naturally to political activity aimed at influencing the government, or capturing it, or overthrowing it.

Karl Marx and the Socialist International.   Marx was in favor of overthrowing the government. Against the bourgeois states which had replaced the feudal regimes he put forth the notion of a dictatorship of the proletariat which would reorganize production and consumption on socialist lines. In the process of destroying all capitalist relationships and stamping out the remnants of bourgeois ideology, this workers' state would create a self-regulating classless society in which eventually the state itself would wither away. The *Communist Manifesto*, published by Marx and Friedrich Engels in 1848, gave trenchant expression to these ideas.

Marx carried his theories into action by founding, in 1864, what subsequently came to be known as the First International. This united a number of revolutionary groups from various countries and led to the formation of Socialist parties. As doctrine, the parties accepted Marx's ultimate aims, but as a tactic on the way to revolution they entered competition with other political parties—"bourgeois" parties—within the framework of the existing states. They offered programs of reforms that might be achieved without first overthrowing the state.

Looked at today, most of these programs seem to be no more than a call for measures of social security that have become a commonplace in every country.

The Socialist parties preached class struggle; they practiced parliamentary politics. Because they expected to get their votes mainly from the working class they organized workingmen in unions, which were auxiliary organs of the party. Organization was from the top down: leaders in each successive descending echelon (national, district, local community) were appointed by and responsible to those who named them. These leaders were party men, and hence doctrinaire. They did not believe the enterprise was the place to look for improvements in the worker's lot, but government. They put their main effort into getting worker support for the party program and election campaigns.

Some unions started direct bargaining anyway: craft unions. As long as economic conditions are favorable, skilled craftsmen in the handicraft sector can always look after themselves. Just before the turn of the century they started a controversy in the German party, largest and most powerful in Europe, when they began signing written contracts with employers. This, to the party leaders, was treason to the cause—dealing with the "class enemy." The doctrinaires seem to have won the argument, but the craft unions kept on signing agreements. Eventually, the practice was accepted.

Factory workers on the other hand faced the same obstacles to bargaining that have been explained elsewhere in this book. They were the proletarian masses of Marxist doctrine; undereducated, working a 12-hour shift for near-subsistence pay, living in slums or cramped and crowded workingmen's quarters. They might well be attracted by the idea of revolution, but they could not wait forever to improve their conditions. Their needs were urgent, here and now. The party programs were addressed to this most numerous body of voters. The way the party pointed out to them was *through political action.*

But the Socialists were not the only party anxious to win the worker's vote, nor for that matter the only party with a strongly held ideology. The Catholic parties of the various countries, in particular, set out to woo the workingman—and incidentally keep him away from atheistic Marxism. The Church already had a hold upon the loyalty of its communicants, and the church parties offered the worker a sinless alternative to Socialism—again through political action. Little wonder that the European unions have consistently taken a political orientation.

Thus the answer to Socialist unions was Christian (Catholic) unions; and eventually, in countries of mixed religion like Holland, Protestant unions. These seem to have arisen not so much to save the Protestant worker from Marx as from the Pope, for in the solidly Protestant Scandinavian countries the Marxist unions had it all their own way.

In addition, then, to the political orientation of the unions—in fact, as a result of it—the labor movement was split. Before World War II Germany had three union federations; France, two; Italy, two; Belgium, two; Holland, three; and so on. All were attached to political parties. Except for a minority of local craft unions, none carried on any real collective bargaining.

The Russian Revolution (1917).   A lasting, and possibly most significant result of the first world war was the overthrow of the tsarist government of Russia and the seizure of power by Lenin and the Bolsheviks. With only the briefest transition Russia went straight from an absolute monarchy of the most backward and brutal sort to a stern Communist dictatorship.

Unions under the tsars were illegal, deemed subversive, and ruthlessly suppressed. Union activity thus became revolutionary activity; and while this did not create much of a climate for collective bargaining, there were some desperate strikes and even a few fleeting victories. The leadership for this illegal activity came from the underground Communist cells, and the scene of action was inevitably the factories.

Again it was from the factories, and from the ranks of the defeated armies, that the Soviets arose to topple the tsar's government. The Worker and Soldier Soviets of 1917 provided Lenin with his base for seizing state power. The Soviet example spread to the Central Powers in the hour of their defeat in 1918: the word for Soviets in German is *Raete*. Socialist-minded workers in the war-weary Allied Powers tried to emulate the example. In Italy worker committees seized the factories and raised the red flag. France was not untouched; or even England, where Shop Steward Councils in 1919 did not attempt to overthrow the government but challenged the leadership of the established unions.

Outside the Soviet Union the worker committees failed to capture state power, or if they did, failed to hold on to it; but they were there in the factories and something had to be done about them. Efforts to dissolve them met with resistance, but eventually they were absorbed in the legal framework of postwar industrial legislation and diverted from political activity toward *collective bargaining at the level of the shop*. They are still at it.

They deal with management in collective bargaining on the work rules. They are not part of the union apparatus, but get their sanction and authority from legislation. Scandinavia is an exception, for neither the war nor the postwar revolutionary wave seriously disturbed the peninsula. While other countries were having their troubles with the shop committees, Sweden and Norway set them up in the shops as union organs, by agreement with the employers.

Where did all this leave the unions?

In its revolutionary phase the factory committee movement so thoroughly frightened both governments and employers that whatever the attitude may have been before, unions began now to look like dear old friends. The unions responded to the overtures made toward them. It may be significant that after 1918, the year the *Raete* seized power briefly in Berlin, the German unions ceased calling the employers their class enemy and called them instead their "social partners." Unions ran slates of candidates in the election for the committee posts, and toned down some of the militancy. Employer associations began bargaining with unions on wages, hours, and such working conditions as can be set at levels above the shop.

The unions remained attached to the political parties. This brought some complications to joint bargaining; and the split between unions, all of which enrolled members in the same shop, often brought dissension that prevented their exerting their full bargaining power. Weakness at the bargaining table turned them back to the familiar ground of parliamentary activity and they continued to press the governments, rather than the enterprises, for concessions. The councils were nonpartisan, were not split, and were not part of the unions, but were present in the shops throughout the working day. They took over the task of representing workers at the workplace.

The upshot in Western Europe has been to create a permanent division of the collective bargaining function. The unions bargain for minimum wages, maximum hours; the shop committees settle with shop management the actual wage—usually above the minimum—and the actual hours, including many items of pay for time not worked. Jointly with management they determine work rules and standards, or the effort bargain. These are what American unionists call the "bread-and-butter" issues—the issues closest to the worker. The committees also establish and enforce job rights and participate in due process, under authority of law. Unions are practically excluded from the shop. They do not seem to mind—they were never really there in the first place. They have instead been taken into the Establishment.

World War II and Its Aftermath. The second world war really changed little in comparison with the first; Hitler's mark on Europe was terrible but fleeting. His most lasting imprint on collective bargaining practices was in Germany. By destroying the three prewar union federations and putting all workers in an auxiliary formation of the Nazi party called the Labor Front, or DAF, he made it possible after the war for the unionists to overcome their former disunity. The result of this unexpected legacy of the DAF is that the German union federation, now known as the DGB, is the largest and strongest in Europe.

The *Raete* survived the war; in fact, they continued, with hardly more than a change of name, throughout the Hitler regime.

Another German development, this time independent of anything Hitler did directly, is codetermination. This is a plan that gives workers representation on the board of directors of their enterprises. It has not spread to any other country.

One further postwar development needs to be mentioned, since it has more widespread significance. That is the capture of the union federations in France and Italy by the Communist party. Large minority segments of the unions in both countries subsequently returned to the Socialists, leaving the federations split. This split between Communist-led and non-Communist unions carried upward into the international union federations which will be dealt with briefly at the end of this chapter. Italy and France both have Catholic unions, which are in a minority.

The Actors in the Napoleonic Code Systems.   On the management side the actors are employer associations, whether the unions they deal with are craft or industrial. Single-plant bargaining is rare in Western Europe.

On the labor side the actors are unions and shop committees. The unions are usually attached to political parties of the left or center. The shop committees are independent both of union and political party affiliation, although their composition often reflects in any given shop the relative strength of these organizations, which run slates of candidates for the committee posts.

Union organization and administration proceeds from the top downward, with authority centralized nationally in the industrial unions. The worker belongs directly to the national union, not a Branch as in England or a Local as in America, but comes under the administrative attention of a local headquarters. The basis of local organization is geographical and covers all the shops in the given industry in the locality. Union leaders carry on little shop-by-shop activity except the quasi-political effort to capture seats on the committees.

The national unions come together in federations at national and regional levels; the regional organizations are often very important. The federations carry on representational activity and mobilize worker support for political programs and party candidates. In almost every country the largest political party of the left wields the decisive influence in the major federation—Socialists in Germany and the Benelux countries, Communists in France and Italy. Smaller Socialist segments have broken off from the Communist-dominated federations. The Catholic union federations usually occupy a strong minority position, with Protestant unions important only in Holland.

The shop committees are unified nonpartisan bodies of elected representatives established by law in enterprises and public services above a given size. Membership on the committees and the right to take part in electing them are reserved to employees of the enterprise. The committees bargain collectively with management on matters which supplement the agreements handed down by the unions and employer organizations, applying their terms to the enterprise, and provide on-the-job representation for workers in the shop. They have no outside affiliations, direct or through the unions, with other committees. Such of their activities as lead outside the shop are with statutory agencies of government.

The third actor in Western European labor-management relations is almost exclusively governmental. The labor laws make government the direct official sponsor and arbiter of the collective bargaining that takes place in the shops. Outside the shops some governments also certify the unions in terms of meeting legal standards of competency to bargain; without this permission they may not conclude agreements. The government may take a further part by extending the agreements reached by certified unions and employer associations to enterprises not directly represented in the negotiations. The power to do this by decree is usually discretionary and vested at the ministerial level.

In summary on the actors; the third actor in the analytical scheme is the first in power and authority in the Napoleonic Code systems, but uses this power to set in motion and orchestrate the activities of the other two. These involve broad-scale and general collective bargaining by unions and employer associations above the shop and specific rule setting at the workplace by shop committees and shop management.

The Rules in the Napoleonic Code Systems. Perhaps the most characteristic rule-making rule in the Western European systems is that which divides the collective bargaining function into the part carried out by unions, and that carried out by shop committees without union participation. This arrangement, like other rules for rule making, is regulated by law.

Union Security and Management Rights. The *bargaining unit* usually covers several or many shops in the same industry in the nation as a whole, or in a region, or sometimes in a city. To give the extreme example: the German metal workers' union signs a single agreement covering over 1 million workers and thousands of shops.

The *form of recognition* does not correspond to American conceptions, since any one shop usually contains members of several or all of the separately affiliated unions active in the industry. Who speaks for whom has to be taken pretty much for granted, and a chair drawn up at the bargaining table for any union which claims it. This naturally opens the door to many problem situations. No way exists in law for designating any one union as the exclusive agent, and majority rule is not accepted as a principle for determining the question.

The agency that has sole and exclusive recognition—though for a restricted aspect of bargaining—is not a union; it is the shop committee.

Provisions for *duration and renewal* of the union agreements, as in America, specify a period of time; always a year or more. *Management rights* are absent from most agreements, since they are implicit in ownership and if elaborated are stated in law.

Individual Security. Several countries have laws protecting an employee from arbitrary discharge, but other aspects of *job rights* are hard to define except at the workplace and in terms of available job opportunities. The shop rules worked out by management jointly with the shop committee serve this function. They also outline the steps in *due process;* or this may simply be part of the unwritten usage of the shop.

The Wage and Effort Bargain. Elements which can be set at levels above the shop include minimum *wages*, maximum hours before *premium pay, pay for time not worked*, as on holidays, and *contingent benefits*, if any, supplementing social security. These are bargained by unions and appear in the printed agreement. Additional concessions may be gained by shop committees bargaining with their managements. The *effort bargain* usually has to be set, and kept in adjustment, at the workplace.

Administration. On-the-job representation is provided by the shop committees—the *Betriebsrat* (German), or the *Comité d'entreprise* (French), or whatever—which participate both in the administration of the union agreement and of statutory requirements arising from *external* sources, and see to their *internal* application.

In Summary. A few historical reasons have been sketched out to help explain the considerable differences between the systems that prevail in the two parts of the Western world with which this chapter has so far dealt. The common-law unions concentrate on the needs of workers at the workplace, but do not neglect political activity as a means to strengthen their efforts. The continental unions concentrate on political activity, neglect the workplace, and look on the members there as a means to strengthen their political influence. Both systems provide the workers with on-the-job representation in the shops, but the committees in the common-law systems link up organically with the unions and through them, with other committees in other shops. They get their sanction from labor-management agreements. The European shop committees do not have this link—and neither do the unions—but get their sanction from government.

This lack of an organic link with the shops frees the European unions from some of the pressure that rank-and-file workers might bring to bear, and relieves them of the task of supervising and co-ordinating a great deal of petty administrative detail, but it seems to the writers of this book a lapse of union leadership and a source of potential union weakness. One ought not to forget that Hitler abolished the powerful prewar German unions in a single day. They died without a champion in the shops to fight for them and without shop roots from which they might spring up again. They had to wait for Hitler's downfall to be restored.

The shop committees in every country are unified by virtue of being at the workplace and by their concern with common problems— even if these seem trivial in comparison to the weighty issues with which unions and parties and parliaments deal. They are in direct contact with workers whose bread-and-butter interests they serve. They appear to be creatures of government enactments but seem to be able to survive, in one form or another, changes in governments even when unions have been swept out of existence. Their universal occurrence and vitality suggest that they are a durable institution which serves the needs both of workers and managers at the workplace. They are perhaps even more essential to modern industry than unions are, or would be without them.

THE SOCIALIST SYSTEMS

Some of the historical background already given will prove helpful here. The Eastern European countries profess Marxism as their official doctrine and insist that they are carrying out the initial stages of Marx's program, which they call Socialism.

Napoleon took Moscow, the tsar's capital, but did not defeat the tsar's armies, and himself had to retreat from Moscow. The reforms embodied in his Code never took root in Russia, which remained a despotism. The Marxist parties consequently never experienced any real freedom to carry on legal political activity. The Bolsheviks in particular organized and led factory workers—Marx's "proletarian masses"—in direct action to redress grievances and for demands which, in any other context, would have looked like modest union proposals. In tsarist Russia they were treated as rebellion—which, in fact, they were. Lenin taught that unions were not to be simply auxiliaries to help legal parties win elections, but training grounds for revolutionaries. Wherever the Bolsheviks could infiltrate, they established factory cells. When, at the decisive moment in 1917, they seized power, they did it with the support of mutinous soldiers of the defeated armies in alliance with—and in the name of—factory committees called, in Russian, Soviets.

It now became the turn of the Soviets to manage the factories. What kind of system have they brought into being under the guidance of the Communist (Bolshevik) party?

The Actors

Industry in the Socialist system countries is nationalized; hence on the *management* side the actor is government.

On the *labor* side, one big union organized by industrial categories enrolls all of the workers. Shop committees, which inevitably consist of union members, are elected by workers in the shops.

The third actor is not so easily identified. Government has already figured on the management side and so lost the theoretical disinterestedness that should characterize the third actor. Perhaps the Communist party comes nearest to filling the role in a one-party state.

Factory managers are government appointees, responsible to higher organs of the state planning bodies that direct industry. A manager's authority at the workplace would seem quite comparable to that of one who reports to the central office of a capitalist corporation. Soviet industry, incidentally, seems to have had just as much trouble as any capitalistic corporation in arriving at the proper degree of autonomy to grant managers of geographically separated operations.

The union is not a mere federation of more or less autonomous national unions but a single monolithic organization departmentalized by industries and directed from the top. A worker belongs to his industrial division of the one big union. The union maintains administrative centers in various regions and in the industrial localities.

The party is everywhere. In the factories it has units which are quite separate from the elected shop committees. At least one member of the factory cell—usually more—will be found on the shop committee; a system of nomination by party-approved slates virtually guarantees this. There are party "fractions" in the union bodies, subject to party discipline from higher echelons. Lenin organized the Communists as a party of the elite—"dedicated revolutionaries"—and whether or not present-day members remain dedicated, party membership is still considered a privilege. It is not something just anybody can attain by signing a card and paying a ruble.

In the rules of the system, to be sketched out below, the party plays no official role, but its pervasive presence, unmistakable influence, and occasional effective intervention make it impossible to leave the party out.

The Rules

The union does not assume an adversary role in bargaining with the government as employer, but collaborates by taking part right at the source in economic and industrial planning. Union officials occupy seats on policy and planning boards at every level. They are expected to make sure that the plan takes care of the social security needs of workers in accordance with legally established standards, for they have operating responsibility in the direct administration of social security services and benefit payments, and a responsibility in general to look after the workers' interests.

The plan for an industry must fit into the larger plan for the nation as a whole, and itself sets the goals and norms for subsidiary plans that carry down eventually to the factories. All these plans try to forecast production costs, including the level of wages and of productivity. At the workplace productivity depends on production standards, or—among other things—the effort bargain.

It can be seen, then, that in the Socialist systems the equivalent of the union agreement is the plan. The "planning table" takes the place of the "bargaining table."

At the factory the manager and the union further plan operations to meet goals set in the industry plan, following that plan's norms. In contrast to the situation in the West, cost estimates and directives tend to dictate *maximum* wages and *minimum* hours, though there are legal minimum wages and maximum hours that are also binding. To the extent that there is any leeway between these limits, a local bargain may be struck.

The manager also discusses the plan with the shop committee, which may raise objections or demands. At this point all the union's weight falls on the side of the manager, for higher bodies of the union are committed to the plan. Collective bargaining of a sort can, indeed, take place on matters about which shop committees in the West as well bargain with operating management, including actual wage levels, as mentioned above; but the scope is restricted.

Interestingly enough, the analytical tool this chapter has applied to the systems of the Western countries applies also to the rules in the Socialist system.

Union Security and Management Rights. The *bargaining (planning) unit* is an entire industry, and, within the industry, a factory. Sole and exclusive bargaining rights with the union shop and the checkoff is, in effect the *form of recognition. Duration* of the agreement (plan) is for a year and *renewal* (replanning) occurs annually, within any current five-year plan. *Management rights,* surprisingly, are like those of a Western manager.

The Wage and Effort Bargain. The plan sets *pay for time worked,* with room for minor adjustments. The *effort bargain* tends to be set at the workplace, jointly between management and the shop committee. Every influence of the union and of party propaganda presses the shop committee to agree—indeed, to insist—on high production standards. *Premium pay* is allowed for in the plan, and also treated in law. *Pay for time not worked* consists mainly of items covered in the law, like paid vacations, but there is room here for local arrangements like wash-up time and short breaks. *Contingent benefits* are almost completely embodied in law, for the state provides a comprehensive system of social security, literally from the cradle to the grave. Some local arrangements not often found in the West, such as child care for working mothers, may supplement the legal programs. The union, and not the government, administers the social security system. Here there may be a germ of the self-regulation that Marx said was to lead to the eventual withering away of the state.

Individual Security. As in some countries of the West, the law protects a Soviet worker from arbitrary discharge; but again, other aspects of *job rights* that govern his relative claim to available work opportunities depend on the situation at the workplace. These can be handled by a shop committee. *Due process* is covered by laws, and includes appeal to the union, or through it, for impartial determination. How well this works is a matter of conjecture.

Administration. *Internal* administration of the plan and of arrangements made locally is the responsibility of management in conjunction with the shop committee. The committee is expected to help enforce production standards and to encourage workers not only to meet but to exceed the norms. The union is mainly responsible for *external* administrative matters.

In Summary

The Socialist and Western systems are far apart in ideology and attitude, but formal differences are not as great as might be expected. This suggests that changes in political institutions and direction do not much alter the tasks of running an industry, and that especially at the level of the shop, managing a workplace is very much the same the world over: the same activities, the same issues, the same *kinds* of solutions. In the factory Marx's utopia begins to look not much different, from the worker's standpoint, from Detroit. It has yet to provide—though, of course, it may in time do so—the Detroit standard of living.

THE CORPORATIVE SYSTEMS

Spain and Portugal are so far from standing in the front rank of the industrial nations that it would be inappropriate to devote a lengthy section just to them. The Corporative system which both follow lost its most important members with the collapse of Mussolini's Italy and the destruction of Hitler's Germany. Spain today seems to be experiencing shocks to its system that may in the course of time leave Portugal alone; the system is on the wane in Europe. A few words about it however, will not be out of place, since the spread of military dictatorships in South America, Africa, and Asia may revive it in transplanted forms.

The Latin peoples can be ruthless, but the Teutonic peoples seem to be more orderly and thorough. The vanished system of Germany during the period of the Third Reich will provide a clearer example than either of the Iberian countries. With variations in practice, the theory is the same. It arises in one-party states ruled by a "strong man" or a clique. It reserves all decisions to the leader and to the state apparatus under his control. It creates advisory bodies in which representation is by "corporations"—agriculture, industry, the professions, the military, sometimes in a one-church state, the Church—which make recommendations to the leader and mobilize support for the regime within their respective corporate segments of the nation. In Germany industry was directed by state decree with the advice of what were called Economic Chambers, and the word for the corporations, in the sense used here, was *Gemeinshaften* (communities). There were industry communities; and each factory was a works community, with its own Fuehrer or leader: the owner, or highest ranking manager.

The Actors

Unions in Nazi Germany were outlawed; thus employer associations for collective bargaining ceased to function. The third actor, government, took complete charge of regulating labor-management relations throughout industry, down to the workplace. Wages were set not in collective bargaining agreements but by decree by a government official called the Trustee of Labor, who exercised all functions that are usually subject to collective bargaining between unions and employer associations. Workers were absorbed by law into a Labor Front that was an auxiliary formation of the Nazi party.

In the factory, the shop committees survived from the pre-Hitler days; the decree that wiped out the unions left them to their functions, though Hitler changed their name and put them under the eye of the Nazi party cell established in each factory.

The Rules

The Trustee of Labor in each district became the personified substitute for collective bargaining, and his decrees took the place of agreements on all matters that could be settled at levels above the shop. He leaned for advice on the Labor Front, or DAF. Since managers as well as workers were members of the DAF, this gave double representation to employers and, except nominally, left labor out.

The Economic Chambers, comprising members of the various communities, planned production at national, regional, and local levels. These plans reached the factory in the form of requisitions and quotas. It was the job of the shop committees to help the management meet these goals. The committee also dealt with issues that could only be handled locally, like the effort bargain and personnel decisions. As with the Soviet shop committees, the Germans were expected to help increase productivity. This tended to take the form of their assenting to longer working hours—up to 14 hours a day in some factories by the end of the second world war—rather than more intense effort per working hour; though that was expected too.

In Summary

Certain obvious resemblances appear between the Corporate system and the Socialist, but they are not identical. The Corporate system preserves private property in the means of production, though it may nationalize some sectors of industry; it preserves the profits of owners, and in fact guarantees them. It destroys freedom of association and freedom to bargain. There is little wonder that it appeals to conservative regimes which rise to dictatorial power.

THE SYSTEM OF THE DEVELOPING COUNTRIES

Nothing will be said in this chapter on this topic other than to point out the category and invite students to elaborate it for themselves by research into the various national systems. A great deal of information needs to reach the developed countries about relations in their less-developed world neighbors. The ILO is performing great services toward this end.

THE INTERNATIONAL UNION FEDERATIONS

Immediately after the second world war the union federations of the nations which had just set up the United Nations joined in forming an international labor federation, the World Federation of Trade Unions or WFTU. The United States was represented by the CIO; the AFL stayed out. Later when it began to appear that the WFTU was falling under Communist influence and serving Communist ends in the cold war that followed the brief honeymoon of good will between the hot war allies, a split occurred in which the Western unions left the WFTU and formed the International Confederation of Free Trade Unions, the ICFTU.

The two international federations are now rivals, and the chief scene of their battles is in the emerging nations of Asia, Africa, and South America. Both the WFTU and ICFTU are recognized by the ILO, though neither can be a member, since membership is by governments. Neither does any collective bargaining. Their existence and activities should be noted, but further treatment of them does not belong in this chapter.

SUMMARY

Collective bargaining in one form or another is a world-wide phenomenon. It accords with what has been called "world public policy" as expressed in the pronouncements of the ILO. It takes forms that vary with the national history and the social and cultural characteristics of the countries where it is practiced. The content of its activities centers on issues that are common to all.

To be able to see the common substance under the variegated forms unlocks its significance in strange situations to those who need to engage in it, as representatives of management, or government, or labor unions; and gives understanding to the student. Its forms will change with time, wth economic development and political upheavals, but the authors of this book believe that it will spread ever more widely as the free society's way of handling industrial relations.

QUESTIONS FOR DISCUSSION

1. Compare the historical development of collective bargaining in America with developments in Great Britain, France, Germany, and the U.S.S.R.
2. Some authorities argue that as American unions and managements mature, we can expect the long-range emergence of a system of management-union co-operation where the union participates in a very broad range of enterprise decisions. Evaluate this prediction on the basis of experience in other countries.

3. In contrast to most of the countries discussed in this chapter, American collective bargaining is highly "legalistic." How do you account for this difference?

SELECTED ANNOTATED BIBLIOGRAPHY

ALEXANDER, ROBERT JACKSON. *Organized Labor in Latin America.* New York: The Free Press of Glencoe, Inc., 1965.

COLE, GEORGE DOUGLAS HOWARD. *An Introduction to Trade Unionism.* London: Allen and Unwin, 1953.

_____. *A Short History of the British Working-Class Movement, 1789–1947.* London: Allen and Unwin, 1948.

_____. *Workshop Organization.* Oxford: The Clarendon Press, 1923.

DERBER, MILTON. "Labor Participation in Management: Some Impressions of Experience in the Metal Working Industries of Britain, Israel, and the United States," *Seventeenth Annual Proceedings of the Industrial Relations Research Association,* pp. 261–69.

EDELMAN, MURRAY, and FLEMING, R. W. *The Politics of Wage-Price Decisions: A Four-Country Analysis.* Urbana: University of Illinois Press, 1965.

GALENSON, WALTER. *Labor in Norway.* Cambridge, Mass.: Harvard University Press, 1949.

_____. *The Danish System of Labor Relations.* Cambridge, Mass.: Harvard University Press, 1952.

HAAS, ERNST B. *Beyond the Nation-State: Functionalism and International Organization,* Stanford: Stanford University Press, 1964.

KNOELLINGER, CARL ERIK. *Labor in Finland.* Cambridge, Mass.: Harvard University Press, 1960.

LORWIN, VAL ROGIN. *The French Labor Movement.* Cambridge, Mass.: Harvard University Press, 1954.

MILLEN, BRUCE H. *The Political Role of Labor in Developing Countries.* Washington, D.C.: Brookings Institution, 1963.

NEUFELD, MAURICE F. *Italy: School for Awakening Countries: The Italian Labor Movement in its Political, Social, and Economic Setting from 1800 to 1960.* Ithaca, N.Y.: New York State School of Industrial and Labor Relations, Cornell University, 1961.

ROBERTS, B. C. (ed.). *Industrial Relations: Contemporary Problems and Perspectives.* London: Methuen & Co., Ltd., 1962.

ROBERTS, BENJAMIN CHARLES. *Labour in the Tropical Territories of the Commonwealth.* Durham, N.C.: Duke University Press, 1964.

STURMTHAL, ADOLPH FOX (ed.). *Contemporary Collective Bargaining in Seven Countries.* Ithaca, N.Y.: Institute of International Industrial and Labor Relations, Cornell University, 1957.

STURMTHAL, ADOLPH FOX. *Workers Councils: A Study of Workplace Organization on Both Sides of the Iron Curtain.* Cambridge, Mass.: Harvard University Press, 1964.

SUFRIN, SIDNEY C. *Unions in Emerging Societies: Frustration and Politics.* Syracuse, N.Y.: Syracuse University Press, 1964.

European Social Security Systems: A Comparative Analysis of Programs in England, Sweden, and the Common Market Countries, together with a description of the U.S. system. Report of the U.S. Joint Economic Committee, 89th Cong., 1st sess. Economic Policies and Practices, Paper No. 9. Washington, D.C.: U.S. Government Printing Office, 1965.

WEBB, SIDNEY, and WEBB, BEATRICE. *Industrial Democracy*. London: Longmans, Green & Co., 1919.

————. *The History of Trade Unionism*. Rev. Ed., extended to 1920. London: Longmans, Green & Co., 1920.

Chapter 15

THE FUTURE OF
COLLECTIVE BARGAINING

The third edition of this book uses Professor John T. Dunlop's concept of *Industrial Relations Systems* as its point of departure and frame of reference. In surveying the future of collective bargaining in America, we return to his three actors and the three contexts. In any society at any time, the actors—workers, managers, and government—are forced to interact in an attempt to cope with the contexts of the market, technology, and societal power relationships. The problems change as do the characters of the actors, but the quest for solutions must continue. A good part of this book has been devoted to a discussion of the rules and rules for rule making which have been developed in the first half of this century in the United States. Now we must grapple with some vital questions for the future:

1. Is collective bargaining a viable process? Will it endure, expand, or wither away in America?
2. Are the present rules and rules for rule making flexible and suitable for the years ahead or are they antiquated and brittle? Will they snap in the changing contexts of the market, technology, and societal power relations?
3. Can we dispense with strikes, haggling over conditions, and legalisms of collective bargaining and replace this perhaps outmoded system with the enlightened human relations approach or the self-disciplined individualism of the professional?

The authors of this book suspect that the answers to these questions will be found at the level of the enterprise *before* aggregate answers for the society as a whole are formulated. Managers and workers have somewhat different perceptions of the operations of the three contexts. Both managers and worker representatives are aware of the power relations of enveloping society. Perhaps they find the assessment of these power relations to be difficult and may misjudge the importance of these forces in their day-to-day activities. Both sides try to influence public opinion, but very few managers or worker representatives devote their full energies to this task. Although considerable effort has been expended in educating workers and their representatives on the pressures of the market, the market remains the home ground of the manager and a distant outpost to the worker. The context of technology is the home ground of both the manager and the worker. A new machine is tangible and the worker knows intuitively what it may mean in terms of his own job security. The questions of lay-offs, rates of pay on new jobs, and the hours of work are the stock in trade of both the union representative and enterprise manager. Our discussion of the future of collective bargaining will proceed from the tangible to the abstract. We start with the adjustment of workers and managers to the changing context of technology in the enterprise and beyond.

MASS PRODUCTION: THREAT TO CRAFT UNIONISM

Craft unions are old hands at dealing with the problem of technological change. Their continued existence is outstanding testimony of their ability to meet the challenge of mass production in some areas. They are reinforced when the consumer demands a unique product. Each year, more prefabricated houses are built and every house contains more prefabricated materials such as dry wall, but consumer demand for unique housing preserves the demand for skilled workmen.

Assuming closed-shop organization and a firmly established jurisdictional claim, minor technological changes pose no serious problems for the craft union. A craftsman does a wide variety of work ranging from the simplest tasks to operations requiring great skill. So long as the employer needs the highly skilled operations, the craft union can insist that the auxiliary simple tasks be accomplished by craftsmen using "tried-and-true" methods. This insistence has the effect of increasing the demand for the craftsmen's services. Frequently this package sale of the craftsmen's services has been called "featherbedding." Although this practice is widely condemned, legislative action to eliminate it presents almost insuperable administrative problems.

How can a craft union react to major technological changes? In his classic study of *Union Policies and Industrial Management*,[1] Professor Sumner H. Slichter analyzed the historical policies of craft unions. The policies of obstruction, competition, and control serve as logical models against which craft union behavior may be evaluated. They are not mutually exclusive in that a union may operate with a combination of these policies. Under the policy of obstruction, the union attempts to prevent the introduction of the technological improvement. Under the policy of competition, the union attempts to prove that the "tried-and-true" methods are better and/or as cheap as the newer methods—at least in some phases of the production process. Under the policy of control, the union allows the new methods to be introduced but seeks to have union members retrained to operate the new machines and to assure that the new

[1] Sumner H. Slichter, *Union Policies and Industrial Management* (Washington, D.C.: Brookings Institution, 1941), pp. 201–81.

methods are introduced gradually to minimize the hardship on unionists. Depending upon the temper of the rank and file, the economic excellence of the particular technological improvement, the economics of the industry, and the strength of the union organization, any one of these policies may be a wise course for unionists and socially desirable. For example, even a policy of obstruction might be desirable if all the craftsmen were elderly and this policy enabled them to finish out their work lives. At the same time, it is obvious that only the policy of control has much chance for success over the long run.

In the building trades, when a local market is solidly organized under closed-shop conditions, the local union possesses the power to effectively control technological progress. If building activity is booming and all the members are fully employed, the local union may adopt a liberal policy toward technological change. However, if many members are unemployed and the union is able to maintain its discipline and closed-shop organization, the local union can be expected to militantly resist the introduction of skill-saving devices. Today nonunion competition in the building trades is pretty well limited to the very small employer, the do-it-yourself fan, or the one-time unionist who has decided to go it alone. Barring very severe and prolonged unemployment, this nonunion competition does not pose a genuine threat to the present-day craft union.

Business depression, prefabricated materials, and governmental policy pose serious threats to craft unions. Craftsmen possess skills which are not easily transferable between industries. When the total demand for carpenters declines sharply, the competition between carpenters for jobs becomes very intense. If the decline in demand is great enough, substantial numbers of carpenters may attempt to follow their trade outside the unionized segments of the industry. When competition for building contracts is intense, contractors are more likely to turn to prefabricated materials as cost-cutting and contract-getting devices. Confronted with the choice of prefabricated work or no work, the craft unions usually accept the work on prefabricated projects.

An effective outlawing of the closed shop could break the resistance of craft unions. Barring this unlikely legislative development, craft unions will continue to flourish in luxury markets requiring a handicraft technology.

We turn now to a discussion of unions and management in an age of automation.

UNIONS AND MANAGEMENT IN AN AGE OF AUTOMATION

Automation poses major challenges for industrial management, unions, and government. It may result in radical changes in the numbers and types of workers in the economy as a whole. It certainly will pose serious problems of adjustment for individual workers and may cause a substantial realignment of business competition. Our major concern here is the impact of automation on collective bargaining. However, the influence of automation on collective bargaining can be understood only in the broader context of business, government, and union policy. Thus we shall consider the impact of automation on management, industrial unions, white-collar workers, and craft unionism.

Automation and Industrial Management

The present degree of automation in manufacturing industry has been popularly exaggerated. In the public mind, any technological change tends to be considered as another evidence of automation. We are now talking about the factory of the future and those few fully automated plants operating today. Progress toward automation seems inevitable in those segments of the economy where very large runs of a standardized product are possible and competition is intense. Automation will not replace mass production over night, just as mass production has not yet totally replaced handicraft methods.

Because automation is still in its infancy, it is very difficult to state its *general* implications for industrial management. However, automation generally means the following to management:

1. The need for longer range advanced planning. Automation equipment is very special-purpose machinery, frequently requiring a long lead-time in its own manufacture and installation. As a result, this machinery must be designed for the products and the materials which will be used several years after the equipment is designed. Further, automation equipment is useful only for large runs of standardized products. Thus, future volumes of demand must be estimated in planning for automation equipment.
2. A willingness to make large outlays of cash for long periods of time without an immediate return on the investment. The most economical automation installations are integrated factories. Although they do not *necessarily* cost more than a gradual plant modernization program, the cost of an automated factory must be absorbed in a short time, while plant modernization can be spread over a longer time period.
3. Much greater thought in product design. Because automation equipment is usually capable of doing only relatively few jobs, changes in product design are much more expensive than in mass production. In mass production, a poor product can be written off at the cost of retooling. Under automation, it is considerably more difficult and expensive to turn around the production process.
4. Greater emphasis on sales efforts. Once committed to automation, management is confronted with heavy fixed costs. Down time, for whatever reason, can be fantastically expensive. Once the automated line is operating successfully, it can be relied upon to turn out a steady stream of high-quality output. Materials and labor, the only remaining variable costs, are reasonably insignificant when compared to the depreciation of the automation equipment. If the business is to survive, the steady stream of output must be sold promptly at a good price.
5. Any breaks in the flow of production must be promptly remedied. In assembly-line operations, bottlenecks are serious and common prob-

lems. However, these bottlenecks occur in an open system and usually can be broken by assigning extra men to the trouble spot. On the other hand, an automated line is more fully integrated and tends to be a closed system. When one phase of an automated operation fails to function, it is seldom possible to fill the gap with extra men. Given the high cost of down time and the difficulty of filling the gaps, preventive maintenance becomes a major concern of management.

Automation reduces unit labor costs and, generally, reduces employment. Labor problems associated with automation tend to take a back seat in management's thinking to such matters as product design, equipment design, financial arrangements, and marketing programs. However, the most highly automated plant will not operate without a few "button-pushers" and some skilled technicians. The chances are that the button-pushers and technicians will have a substantial interest in their conditions of employment and a union will represent them. This means collective bargaining and the grim prospect of the plant being closed by a strike. As a result, management can't ignore the collective bargaining aspects of automation.

Since most automation installations serve as replacements or supplements to mass-production methods, industrial unions will probably play the leading role in collective bargaining at automated plants.

Industrial Unionism and Automation

The traditional policy of most industrial unions is to accept technological advance as such and concentrate union efforts on securing a "fair share" of the fruits of technological progress for their membership. In the typical factory situation, management has fundamental control of the man-machine mix. Given that the original power of decision is in management's hands, the industrial union places dual reliance on governmental programs and collective bargaining to protect the interests of its members.

From the technological viewpoint, Professor James R. Bright of the Harvard Business School has delineated 17 different levels of mechanization.[2] This analysis is helpful in that it places automation in a time perspective and clearly shows the different management, personnel, and production problems in different time periods. Any particular management and union are confronted with different problems at different stages in the development of automated processes.

It seems to us that automation is really a new problem. It is similar in some ways to the development of mass production. However, automation is being introduced in a unique period in American economic life. Never before has management been forced to deal with powerful unions

---

[2] James R. Bright, "Management and Automation," in Edward C. Bursk and Dan H. Fenn, Jr. (eds.), *Planning the Future Strategy of Your Business* (New York: McGraw-Hill Book Co., Inc., 1956), pp. 197–216. See also, James R. Bright, *Automation and Management* (Boston: Division of Research, Graduate School of Business Administration, Harvard University, 1958), 280 pp. xv.

in the major segments of the economy. Governmental full-employment and welfare-state programs were unheard of in the heyday of the assembly line and infant scientific management. Today automation has been introduced in only a few segments of economic life. Grave governmental concern over international tensions is accelerating research in automation systems. Major breakthroughs in research will most certainly result in rapid applications of automation technology to everyday life. This accelerated rate of introduction will further contribute to the newness of the problem.

In our discussion of collective bargaining and automation we shall deal primarily with the very long-range problems. Although such a discussion departs from the realism of day-to-day and year-to-year collective bargaining, it may serve a useful purpose in indicating logical long-term goals for managements and unions. Excessive preoccupation with immediate problems may very well have catastrophic results for unions, managements, and the public at large. At the same time, failure to modify specific agreements to meet immediate problems may have a seriously disruptive effect on the collective bargaining relationship and may thus prevent the realistic solution of long-range problems.

We shall deal first with the industrial unions' political program on automation and then discuss their collective bargaining program.

Industrial Unions, Automation, and the Government. The general outlines of union programs seeking governmental assistance to solve the problems of automation can be inferred from official union statements. Union political goals usually seek to cope with problems which are broader than the unit for collective bargaining. By marshalling governmental assistance, the union strengthens its position at the bargaining table or, more frequently, provides some cushion for workers beyond the area of collective bargaining.

An official publication of the AFL-CIO, *Labor Looks at Automation*, discusses basic problems of national scope relating to automation as follows:

The spreading use of automation equipment poses many problems for the national economy:

Will consumer purchasing power rise sufficiently to provide the rapidly growing consumer markets needed to match the increasingly automated productive capacity of industry and commerce?

Will economic activity expand fast enough during the transition period to provide job opportunities for new workers entering the labor market, as well as for workers who are displaced by automated machines and electronic computers?

Will the costs of introducing automation be so great—and the required output so large—as to produce an increased tendency toward concentration of the control of industry?

What will be the effects of automation on business investment in new plant and equipment?

Will automation speed up the increasing productivity of capital investment (output per unit of capital)? Will private consumption and government expenditures, in combination, grow sufficiently to maintain expanding markets, if the productivity of plant and equipment rises rapidly?

Will automation result in the creation of much secondary investment and new jobs, as did the introduction of the automobile and the ensuing developments in road construction, steel, oil, rubber, and glass?

How will automation affect plant location? Will firms prefer to build automated plants in new areas, rather than renovate existing plants? Will automation encourage abandonment of existing facilities, loss of industry, and economic distress for many communities?

Will power and natural resources be sufficient to gain the potential increased output made possible by automation?

Are the schools training a sufficiently large and adequately skilled labor force to operate and maintain an economy that will be increasingly automated? Is the school system prepared to meet this responsibility?

Will the nation's educational, cultural and recreational facilities be capable of meeting the challenge of increased leisure made possible by automation— longer vacations, reduced work-weeks, two-and-a-half and three-day weekends?[3]

The United Automobile Workers, a most influential industrial union, has long shown an aggressive interest in political action. The automobile industry coined the term "automation" and has long been a leader in technological innovations. What are the general outlines of the UAW's political action program on automation? They were summarized by the union as follows:

The magnitude of the changes which automation will bring should not be underestimated. Some problems will be solved across the bargaining table. Some will require that we join with other likeminded groups in the common fight on the legislative front. The Union will continue to seek the enactment of socially desirable legislation that will give positive direction to technological change. The minimum wage must be raised. National vocational training and retraining facilities must be expanded so that adult members of the labor force will find it easier to acquire the new skills demanded by the changed methods of industrial production. General educational, cultural, and recreational programs must be improved. Drastic improvements in unemployment compensation must be won to cushion the shock of technological displacement for workers not covered by the guaranteed annual wage. The Social Security Act must be amended to provide, if it proves necessary, for earlier retirement for displaced workers who find it impossible to obtain new jobs. Relocation allowances must be provided by law to facilitate the movement to new areas of workers displaced from their home communities by new and more efficient plants located elsewhere.[4]

Industrial unions seem to be mostly concerned about the employment effects of automation. Since the CIO was born in a period of most

[3] American Federation of Labor and Congress of Industrial Organizations, *Labor Looks at Automation* (Washington, D.C.: AFL-CIO, Publication No. 21, May, 1956), pp. 20–21.

[4] UAW-CIO Education Department, *Automation: A Report to the UAW-CIO Economic and Collective Bargaining Conference Held in Detroit, Michigan, the 12th and 13th of November, 1954* (Detroit: UAW-CIO Education Department Publication, Number 331, January, 1955), pp. 27–28.

severe unemployment, it is almost natural that the spectre of mass unemployment seems to haunt the leadership of such unions as the Steelworkers, Autoworkers, Electrical Workers, and the Communications Workers. By far and away the most important plank in the political programs of industrial unions is the achievement and maintenance of full employment in the economy through whatever governmental action may be necessary. Although there may be minor differences between individual unions about emphasis, all industrial unions seem pretty well committed to the idea that government can, and should, maintain full employment by countercyclical fiscal policies. At the same time, industrial unions argue that high wages maintain purchasing power and thus stimulate prosperity.

Secondary factors in the industrial unions' full-employment program include the allocation of governmental contracts to areas of labor surplus and generous unemployment compensation benefits. If unemployment is severe, and governmental action to provide full employment seems impotent, the industrial unions could be expected to advocate the shorter workweek through legislative action. At the state level, several industrial unions have advocated legislation to extend unemployment compensation for workers enrolled in special training courses aimed at enabling them to find useful employment in new fields after the demand for their original training has disappeared.

A number of industrial unions have been plagued with the problems of some members working overtime while other members in the same bargaining unit have experienced long lay-offs. Part of the reason for this phenomenon has been the high cost of wage supplements which the unions has negotiated earlier. Under some of these arrangements it is less costly for an employer to pay workers time and one-half for overtime than to call in other workers for regular wages plus supplements. Several unions have requested that Congress amend the Fair Labor Standards Act to provide for double time for hours in excess of 40 per week. Such a legislative enactment would help to overcome the situation where some union members are working overtime while others are on lay-off.

Important as the legislative program is to the purpose of the industrial unions, it cannot be successful without very considerable assistance from nonunionist voters. Such assistance is pretty hard to muster in periods of rapid technological advance which tend to coincide with prosperity. Thus, the unions place major emphasis on their collective bargaining programs during prosperity.

Collective bargaining promises a better chance of success, but smaller gains in success. That is, collective bargaining is a means of achieving something less than full employment in the whole economy. Before discussing probable future bargaining trends on automation, we shall review recent industrial union bargaining on technological change.

Two Examples of Industrial-Union Bargaining on Technological Change. Every technological change poses its own unique problems in collective bargaining. Unions and managements analyze these problems and work out agreements which are tailor-made to fit the particular situation.

Figures 15–1 and 15–2 are examples of how two managements and two unions solved their particular problems growing out of technological change. The production-worker case involved the gradual modernization of an oil refinery. The office-worker case involved the installation of automatic data-processing equipment in the railroad industry. Neither case involved the total abandonment of old methods or the construction of an entirely new plant. In both cases, the adjustment process was sufficiently satisfactory to unions to be cited as examples by the *AFL-CIO Collective Bargaining Report*.

The ability of unions to negotiate settlements as satisfactory as the ones outlined in Figures 15–1 and 15–2 is severely limited by the economics of the particular industries involved. Labor costs are a relatively insignificant part of total costs in the petroleum industry. The railroad Washington Agreement of 1936 served as the basis for the office workers' settlement. The terms of this agreement make training costs relatively insignificant when compared to the costs of layoffs. As a result, advanced consultation did not impose substantial extra costs on management. In non-railroad offices, technological adjustment is often facilitated by the high turnover rates among female employees.

Although these two cases cannot be directly applied to other situations, they clearly indicate the types of day-to-day collective bargaining problems growing out of technological change.

How will automation affect collective bargaining in the long run? What collective bargaining problems are likely to arise from the construction of new automated plants and the development of entirely new automated industries?

Probable Trends in Industrial Union Bargaining on Automation. The fully automated plant differs from mass production as radically as mass production differs from handicraft industry. However, fully automated plants are replacing mass-production plants gradually. The economy today is a mixture of handicraft, mass production, and automation production techniques. It undoubtedly will remain so for some years to come, but automation techniques will be on the ascendancy while handicraft and mass production techniques will decline in relative importance.

Because of the wide variety of possible technological changes, the collective bargaining agreement in the automated plant should be tailor-made to the particular union-management relationship. Our discussion will take the form of a check list of the major issues involved in a change from mass production to automation in a factory situation.

Bargaining Unit, Union Security, and Management Rights. Undoubtedly automation will cause major changes in the group of jobs and type of people employed in the individual plant. Production jobs in

FIGURE 15–1

INDUSTRIAL-UNION BARGAINING ON TECHNOLOGICAL CHANGE:
PRODUCTION WORKERS

PRODUCTION WORKERS: CHANGE AT A
PETROLEUM REFINERY

The introduction of new automatic equipment and its effects on workers at one petroleum refinery have been studied in detail by the Bureau of Labor Statistics of the U.S. Department of Labor.* The union involved is the Oil, Chemical and Atomic Workers.

The company replaced older refining equipment with new and more automatic equipment in two major steps, introducing catalytic cracking and greater instrumentation in 1949 and a new processing unit in 1954.

Among the major adjustment procedures and results reported by the case study are the following:

(1) *Worker adjustments were negotiated well before the change.* The study states:

"Planning these personnel changes began approximately 15 months before the 1949 technological changes were completed. . . .

(2) *No workers were laid off.*

About 160 workers—a quarter of the work force—were reassigned to new jobs in the first major change, a smaller number in the second change. The study reports:

"Negotiations leading to the 1949 contract helped crystallize two basic principles concerning displacement and reassignment of the plant workers. First, in the matter of layoffs and demotions, seniority status (i.e., length of service) was established as the basis for retention. The objective was to minimize displacement of older men with years of service at the B Oil Refinery. Second, the placement of men in newly created or revised departments and any proposed change in the application of steps in the demotion or promotion practices were made the subject of management and union committee conferences." . . .

(3) *Downgraded workers had former higher wages maintained.* Some 62 percent of the workers in the first change were placed on jobs paying at least the same wage rate they had previously but the remaining 38 percent were downgraded to jobs paying lower rates.

To ease the impact of downgrading, the union negotiated a maintenance-of-job-rate provision under which workers with 5 years' service did not have their wage rank decreased until 6 months after their transfer to the lower-rated jobs.

(4) *Training was provided to prepare for the new jobs.*

"This training was given during working hours and included in plant classroom instruction and direct observation of new equipment. During their training, all workers received their regular wage rates." . . .

* "Studies of Automatic Technology: A Case Study of a Modernized Petroleum Refinery," U.S. Department of Labor, BLS Report No. 120. Available without charge from the Bureau of Labor Statistics, Washington 25, D.C.

SOURCE: *AFL-CIO Collective Bargaining Report,* Vol. III (April–May, 1958), p. 31.

FIGURE 15–2

INDUSTRIAL-UNION BARGAINING ON TECHNOLOGICAL CHANGE:
OFFICE WORKERS

OFFICE WORKERS' PROTECTION NEGOTIATED BY RAILWAY CLERKS

Agreements negotiated by the Brotherhood of Railway Clerks to govern the introduction of large computers and revision of machine accounting practices in the offices of railroad companies illustrate some of the union efforts to cushion the adjustment for the white-collar workers.

A leading example is the agreement negotiated with the Chesapeake & Ohio Railway Company early in 1956 when that company was setting up a new computer center in Cleveland using advanced new office machines to handle much of its accounting load.

The company and union took the following steps in connection with this technological change:

(1) *Nature of new jobs.* An agreement was negotiated on (a) new job classifications (and descriptions) for the new or changed jobs in the new machine operations, (b) the rates of pay for each of these jobs, and (c) in the case of certain pay jobs, the minimum number of employees needed on them.

(2) *Selection of employees.* It was agreed that new jobs would be filled from the existing workforce. The job openings at the new computer installation were announced to all clerical employees covered by the union agreement and opened for bid, with selection made on the basis of seniority. . . .

(3) *Training.* It was agreed that employees entitled to the new jobs would be trained for them at company expense with no loss in pay. . . .

(4) *Protection for displaced workers.* For workers "adversely affected" because their work is turned over to the new machines, the parties agreed to apply the benefit provisions of the "Washington Agreement." The Washington Agreement was negotiated by the nation's railroads and railroad unions back in 1936 to protect workers whose jobs are moved in any consolidation of railroad lines.

Briefly, the Washington Agreement's benefit provisions assure the worker that:

(a) For 5 years he will receive at least the same pay and working conditions he received before his work was moved;

(b) If he is laid off, he will be paid unemployment benefits equal to 60 percent of his normal pay for half a year up to 5 years, the exact duration depending on his length of service;

(c) His hospitalization, pension and other benefits will be maintained for the 5-year protective period;

(d) He may choose in place of unemployment and other benefits a lump-sum severance payment ranging from 3 to 12 months' pay, depending on length of service; and

(e) If he transfers to a new location, he will be reimbursed for all traveling and moving expenses, for any losses on his home because of the move, and for living expenses and wage loss during the period of getting settled in the new location. . . .

SOURCE: AFL-CIO Collective Bargaining Report, Vol. III (April–May, 1958), p. 29.

fully automated plants can be classified as "expert specialist" jobs and "technical maintenance" jobs. A firm's employment is completed by complementary managerial and office jobs. The changes in job requirements—brought about by automation—are sure to have an important and far-reaching influence on bargaining unit, union security, and management rights.

The expert specialist is the operative of automation equipment. Frequently he receives substantial training at his employer's expense. Because of this training, he cannot be considered a replaceable part in the production process. This training distinguishes him from the semiskilled operative in mass-production industry. However, like the semiskilled operative, the know-how that the expert specialist acquires is not necessarily the type which is easily transferable from employer to employer. His expertise is useful primarily to the employer who trained him.

Technical maintenance jobs require an expertise of a different type. The technician's major responsibility is finding and remedying interferences in the *over-all* operation of automation equipment. An automation maintenance job may require substantial knowledge of electronics or mechanical theory. In some cases, the maintenance man acquires this knowledge at his own expense in technical or academic schools. As a result, the technical maintenance man may possess a know-how with greater transferability—and, hence market ability—between employers than the know-how of the expert specialist. The technical maintenance man's transferable know-how and his control over tempo are characteristics which he shares with the craftsman in handicraft industry.

Even in those offices that are not presently automated, the techniques of mass production are becoming increasingly common. As the trend toward automation continues to invade more and more offices a whole new set of job classifications will doubtless emerge. The computer operator's position in the office can be compared to that of the job of the expert specialist in the plant; while the job of programming computer operations may be likened to, and requires a know-how similar to, that possessed by the plant's technical maintenance man.

Individual automated plants will have a smaller number of people on their payrolls than mass-production plants in the same line of work. It also seems likely that the technical maintenance, office, and managerial groups will be proportionately larger in automated plants than in mass-production plants. This absolute and relative change in the number and type of production workers employed may change the general composition of bargaining units within the plant.

The NLRB has traditionally placed major emphasis on the "community of interest" criterion in determining the appropriate unit for collective bargaining. The Board will be called upon to decide whether the interests of the expert specialist and technical maintenance men are compatible or conflicting. Within office groups, similar decisions will have to be made about computer operators and computer programmers. Finally, the Board may be confronted with new conditions concerning the community of interest, or lack of it, between plant workers and office workers. It is too early to predict what the NLRB will decide in particular cases. However, it is possible to outline factors which would promote or mitigate against the severance of technical maintenance and computer programmer employees from production and office bargaining units.

Several factors promoting the severance of technical maintenance workers from the production bargaining unit may be noted. First, the responsibility of technical maintenance workers for minimizing interferences with the production process places them in a semimanagement position. Further impetus to severance of the technical group could come from a management decision to establish special personnel policies for the technical group, e.g., salary instead of hourly rates, special perquisites, etc. Finally, those members of the technical maintenance group who have substantial theoretical training may be considered, and may consider themselves to be, professionals.

On the other hand, there may be a greater community of interest between all plant workers in an automated plant than in a mass-production plant. To the extent that the new technical maintenance men are recruited from the preautomation employees of the company, the old union ties may be strong. Both the technical men and the production men are dependent upon the continued operation of the same equipment. Both employers and unions have shown recent interest in continuing the practice of bargaining on a "one plant—one union" basis. The major present-day craft unions do not seem to offer a happy home to the new breed of technical maintenance men.

Unlike bargaining unit determinations, it seems likely that automation will have little effect on the traditional forms of "union security." The trend toward virtually all union security arrangements being either union shop or closed shop will probably continue. However, automation does pose a serious problem to industrial unions because every *new* shop is always a *nonunion* shop until such time as it is organized. There seems to be a trend toward installing automation equipment in *all-new* plants, frequently far removed from the predecessor plant. This management decision seems to be the result of a careful study of comparative costs of modernizing old plants against building new plants, rather than an attempt to escape from collective bargaining. However, such a decision poses a union security problem in that the union must incur the expense of organizing the employees in the new plant. Organizing new employees in automated plants may be a hard job for the union. A new plant has an attractiveness all its own and new employees may feel a special loyalty to management. Workers in automated plants also have extra personal security in that they feel the new plant will be the last to be shut down by management in a period of economic adversity.

Since automation is the substitution of other factors of production for labor, it would seem that management's rights should be strengthened by the reduced dependence on labor. Automation probably does increase the "bargaining power" of management,[5] but at the same time union leaders' fear of automation increases their insistence upon safeguards which further infringe upon management's rights. In our discussion of wages and personal security, it will be obvious that the collective bargaining agreement has greatly increased the *labor costs* of installing automation equipment. For example, the cost of severance pay or supplemental unemployment benefits is a labor cost which increases the cost of installing automation. These increased *labor costs* act as a deterrent to the installation of automation and thus infringe upon the management right to select methods of production. It seems likely that as automation progresses the industrial unions will become more insistent upon joint consultation with management before new equipment is installed or work is transferred from one plant to another. The net effect of such clauses is to further restrict management's freedom to decide. Finally, most industrial unions have registered a strong condemnation of the long-term (three-, four-, or five-year) collective bargaining agreement. In some cases, e.g., the United Automobile Workers, this condemnation is based on an asserted inability of the union to keep abreast with automation under the long-term contract. Short-term contracts severely restrict management's rights because many technological changes require several years for implementation. If a management is confronted with the prospect of having to bargain over these changes in the process of installation, the advantages of installation may be sharply curtailed.

Wages, Hours, and Working Conditions. Automation poses two separate, but related, wage problems: rates on individual automated jobs and the problem of general wage adjustments. The problem of individual rates is really a *new* problem because the man-requirements of highly automated jobs differ radically even in quality from the factors considered in traditional job evaluation programs.

Professor James R. Bright, in his *Automation and Management,* sees the individual rate problems as follows:

> Traditionally, wages represent compensation for:
> Skill (dexterity, knowledge of the art)
> Experience
> Education and training
> Physical effort

[5] Note, for example, recent telephone strikes where service has been continued with only minor interruptions. Automatic dialing systems, manned by supervisory personnel, apparently can continue to operate almost indefinitely during a strike. Obviously, this situation has a tempering effect on union demands.

Productivity (amount or quality)
Hazards
Job surroundings
Responsibility (measured by many things)
Seniority
Decision making (judgment)
Safety to materials
Safety to others
Safety to equipment

and variations of these and similar factors in countless different proportions. We have seen that, both theoretically and practically, many of these factors are reduced or eliminated as necessary worker contributions by automation. To the extent that this suggested "downgrading" appears, automation creates major job evaluation, wage administration, and contract negotiation problems. They can be summed up simply:

If the operator does not control quantity and quality (and he does less of this as automaticity increases). . . .

If he makes fewer production operation decisions. . . .

If he exerts less physical and mental effort. . . .

If automation reduces the need for skill, education and experience. . . .

If automation removes job hazards and improves working conditions. . . .

Then most of the traditional worker contributions are of lesser or useless economic value. What, therefore, shall be the criteria for wages?

Should the employee be paid less because he contributes less? The same, because of the unfortunate implications of a reduction? Or more? If more, how much more and on what basis?[6]

Professor Bright's statement clearly shows the magnitude of the problem of establishing rates for new automated jobs. The following statement from the United Automobile Workers provides a partial insight into probable union tactics on the matter of rates for automated jobs:

Any efforts by management to extend existing classifications to cover these new automated and semi-automated jobs should be resisted by the Union. It is important, also, that the issue not be left to umpire or arbitrator determination. Umpires and arbitrators should have no role in the determination of new classifications and wage rates because there are no objective criteria which they can apply. Since these new operations will be the basis for the wage and classification structure of the factory of the future, the Union must maintain maximum freedom to exert its full influence in the shaping of that structure.

These new classifications and rates should be established in recognition of the changed nature of jobs in which increased responsibility offsets by far any reduction in physical effort and manual dexterity accompanying automation. This increased responsibility, in most cases, flows from the much larger investment represented by the equipment under the individual worker's control. . . . Even where there is no increase in such investment, the individual worker becomes responsible for a much larger volume of output. Automated equipment is a signpost of changed jobs in the factory requiring the negotiation of new

[6] James R. Bright, *Automation and Management* (Boston: Division of Research, Graduate School of Business Administration, Harvard University, 1958), p. 206.

classifications carrying higher rates reflecting the increased responsibility per worker.[7]

Other industrial unions have followed about the same approach to the problems of rates on automated jobs. Some variations in this approach are to be found in the attempt of a few industrial unions to introduce new factors in existing job evaluation programs. For example, "visual effort," "mental fatigue," and "loneliness pay" have been mentioned. These new factors are in some cases justified by the nature of automated equipment. Studies of the sociological effects of automation show that in some cases workers have been adversely affected by the design of automation equipment. For example, in some plants the operative is more than 100 feet from his nearest fellow worker. For the worker accustomed to the give-and-take of the factory social system, this change may necessitate a rather severe personal adjustment; thus partial justification for the apparently irrational demand for loneliness pay. Another characteristic of work in the highly automated plant that may need to be considered in the establishment of individual pay rates is the forced *inactivity* of some automated jobs. When effort is reduced to almost nil, the worker may be confronted with a serious problem of boredom which may be just as "exhausting" as heavy exertion.

In view of the difficulties of determining the worth of individual jobs, unions and managements may cast aside traditional forms of job evaluation. For example, most plant employees might be given one of two jobs: "automation equipment operator" or "automation maintenance technician."[8] If the number of job classifications were drastically reduced, wage negotiations would center on the issue of general adjustments.

Management's efficiency or productivity is often measured in terms of profits. Some unions have argued that high profits are a clear indication of labor efficiency. If one accepts the argument that profits result from efficiency, it seems possible that more unions will express an interest in profit sharing through collective bargaining. Such a demand would be a logical reflection of the greater interdependence of labor, management, and technology in automated industry.

Organized labor started a drive for the shorter workweek in 1955.

---

[7] UAW-CIO Education Department, *Automation? A Report to the UAW-CIO Economic and Collective Bargaining Conference, Held in Detroit, Michigan, the 12th and 13th of November 1954* (Detroit: UAW-CIO Education Department, Publication Number 331, January, 1955), pp. 16–17.

[8] For an interesting contrast of industrial union views on this subject see, *Automation and Major Technological Change: Collective Bargaining Problems, Papers Presented at a Conference held under the Auspices of the Industrial Union Department, AFL-CIO, April 22, 1958.* Ken Bannon and Nelson Samp of the UAW's Ford Department tell how the UAW has tried to establish the principle of fewer and new jobs in automated plants of the Ford Motor Company (p. 14–17). At the same time Elmer J. Malloy of the United Steelworkers expresses complete satisfaction with the industry-wide job evaluation manual and optimism about revising it should the necessity arise in the future (p. 29–30).

This drive was set back by the recession of 1958. Nevertheless, it seems likely that the motivation to this drive remains and will come to the force again as soon as it becomes economically feasible. The spotlight was on "automation-caused unemployment." This unemployment had not materialized at the time the demand was being voiced, but it was the underlying motivation toward the shorter workweek. Because this union-expected unemployment was to be caused by great increases in man-hour productivity, the unions argued that they should receive the shorter workweek *with no reduction in weekly pay*. These arguments will probably reassert themselves again and again in the next generation.

Automation improves working conditions in that it almost always reduces the physical exertion required to accomplish the job. Very frequently the new technique is also cleaner, safer, less noisy, and not subject to extremes in temperature. Although the net impact of automation is probably in the direction of improved working conditions, some automation equipment has the effect of creating new working conditions problems in the form of personal isolation, increased nervous tension, and a personal feeling of subservience to the machine.[9]

Individual Security. Probably the greatest effect of automation will be found in the individual security aspects of the collective bargaining relationship.

From the viewpoint of the employee, probably the most important question growing out of automation is: "Will I be able to keep a job with my employer?" Most workers would prefer the security of continuing on their present job in the same plant over most other possibilities. Failing that, they want an opportunity to learn a new job with the same employer. If the new job requires them to move their households, they would like to receive financial help with the moving costs, including losses in the sale of real estate. If they don't move or aren't given a new job, they will seek some kind of compensation for the job equities which they surrender when their old job disappears.

Whether or not an employee can keep a job with his employer depends upon the content of automated jobs, the availability of retraining opportunities, the real security which seniority confers under changed job requirements, and the geographic location of the new jobs. These factors are determined in part by the technology of automation and in part by the collective bargaining relationship and the personnel policy of the employer. We shall consider each of these factors separately.

Professor Bright has noted that automation may cause substantial "downgrading" of production jobs in the automatic factory. Nevertheless, it seems certain that even downgraded jobs will require *different* skills than the old jobs. Under usual seniority arrangements preference is given to workers who can do the new jobs and who have good records

[9] Charles R. Walker, "Life in the Automatic Factory," *Harvard Business Review*, Vol. XXXVI (January–February, 1958), pp. 112–14.

of performance of their old jobs. Professors George P. Shultz and George B. Baldwin believe that automation may introduce a new standard for continued employment based on "ability to learn" rather than "ability to do."[10] If such a new standard is introduced, as seems plausible, it will seriously upset the significance of seniority and may very well cause serious problems of personal adjustment. Although *ability* to learn certainly doesn't cease at any particular age, most people become more set in their ways as they grow older. If the job contents of new jobs require greater ability to learn, it is reasonably certain that management will insist upon this as a major criterion for preference in the opportunity for training. Such a criterion would usually give preference to younger workers and might very well give the maximum preference to persons who were new hires. Thus technology might set forces in operation which would place long-service employees in the position of "second-class citizens" or "former employees." Of course, unions would resist such actions to the full limit of their ability. The ability of a union to resist such forces would be severely restricted by a management decision to build new plants away from the site of the old plants. On the brighter side, from the employee viewpoint, is the fact that management often can afford to be generous in its treatment of "blind alley" high-seniority employees. As long as management is dependent upon production from conventional plants and facilities, the union is in a reasonably strong bargaining position. What are unions now doing and trying to do to protect the status of their members in view of possibly radical future changes in job requirements?

Union thinking on seniority and automation is clearly stated by the United Automobile Workers as follows:

> The broader the unit within which seniority applies, the greater is the security provided by that seniority. Local seniority agreements, therefore, should provide for the broadest possible seniority groupings to assure equitable seniority protection for the members of our Union. In addition, these local agreements should also contain simple and direct amendment procedures so that the Union can, through negotiations, meet the impact of sudden unanticipated changes.

> The danger of mass displacement of workers as a result of automation emphasizes in addition the need for extending the protection afforded by seniority beyond the confines of the individual plant and company. This is particularly important for the older workers whose possibilities of finding new employment diminish with advancing years. Our agreements with multi-plant corporations must assure displaced workers of the right to interplant transfers based on seniority. In addition, preferential hiring clauses must be won which require all plants under UAW-CIO contract, when hiring, to give preference to laid-off workers in the same area and industry.[11]

Parallel with union requests for broader seniority units is the request for dislocation allowances for workers who move to assume new jobs

---

[10] George P. Shultz and George B. Baldwin, *Automation: A New Dimension to Old Problems* (Washington, D.C.: Annals of American Economics, Public Affairs Press, 1955), p. 14.

[11] UAW-CIO Education Department, *op. cit.*, Automation, pp. 20–21.

when exercising their seniority claims. Thus, the union's prime goal is security *in employment* without severe economic losses to the worker in following the job wherever it may be.

When industrial unions are unable to secure *employment security* for their members they seek methods of reducing the personal losses incurred by loss of employment. Thus we see a whole array of union demands for the guaranteed annual wage (or its successor, liberalized supplemental unemployment benefits), severance pay, and generous benefits for early retirement under pension plans.

Early retirement provisions in pension agreements ease the financial shock of job loss and *may* provide for more equitable distribution of available jobs and the employees most suited to management's needs. Under such arrangements management gains in that senior employees with lesser ability to learn can be separated without bitterness when their services are no longer required. Of course, the management *pays* for this gain in pension costs, but in some cases it may be a good bargain. The union also gains in that it has fewer *discontented* members. Every retiree produces a job vacancy which can be filled with a younger union member.

Contract Administration.   New issues in collective bargaining tend to produce new problems in contract administration. Our discussion of wage problems on automation indicates a union reluctance to submit rates on new jobs to arbitration. Broader areas of seniority will increase the difficulties in administering the contract. Entirely new standards will need to be formulated for the interpretation of working conditions and joint consultation clauses. Our experience with automation is still too limited to make any reasonable estimates of the probable form of these new standards.

The foregoing discussion of the impact of technology on existing collective bargaining relationships poses some of the problems of the future. Experience to date suggests that in most cases managers and unions, with an occasional boost from government, will be able to solve these problems as they arise. Thus we believe that collective bargaining is a *viable* process that will *endure* in most enterprises where it has been established. Craft unionism will continue to flourish in local and luxury markets served by a handicraft technology. Industrial unionism will maintain its hold in mass-production industry. Whether collective bargaining will exert greater or lesser relative significance in the industrial relations system of the future can be determined only by looking beyond the enterprise. The changing contexts of the market and of power relations will be the center of our field of view.

THE CONTEXTS BEYOND THE ENTERPRISE

The contexts interact. Changes in the market may give rise to a new technology which increases the political power of one segment of the population relative to another segment of the population. Any major change in one of the contexts eventually will have an effect on many enterprises including some not even in existence when the context first changed. In an attempt to discuss the future of collective bargaining in the economy-wide industrial relations system, we must try to estimate the general form of the economic and political structure of the future. About the best that can be done on this very substantial task is to note some trends and to ask some questions.

The Dynamics of Markets and Technology

As never before in history, American public and private enterprise is challenged by competition beyond the territorial borders of the United States. This international competition arises from the arms race, the movement toward freer international trade, the rapid technological progress of the countries of Europe and the emerging economies of Asia and Africa.

Because we have lived for over 20 years under the pressures of war or the threat of war, we tend to forget about the all-pervading influence of the international political situation on our day-to-day lives. Headed toward vaguely defined international objectives, the government rushes forward in a do-or-die race which has no rules. This race, and our standing in it, sets the level of freedom and affluence which individuals, management, and unions may enjoy. The government is the largest domestic buyer of manpower, goods and services, while it provides the people with national security, social security, and welfare measures. As every aircraft worker knows, a change in a government procurement schedule may mean disaster to an entire community. Nor is the level of taxation a matter to be taken lightly.

At the end of World War II, the United States was the undisputed world's champion in technology and production. Our former industrial rivals literally had been *destroyed* by war. We helped them rebuild their plants. Today their all-new plants, and workers who are accustomed to lower wages than American workers, pose a very serious threat to our older plants in most international markets and in even some domestic markets. For compelling political as well as economic reasons, we are encouraging the development of wider areas of freer international trade. This freer trade is certain to have important repercussions in our domestic economy.

Within the remaining domestic private market important changes are taking place. It appears that our ability to produce agricultural goods and perhaps many manufactured products like automobiles and steel has outstripped the world's ability to effectively demand these products. At least one billion human beings are hungry now, but food rots in our storage bins. The want is present, but the effective demand of the market place is absent. Domestically, the market for services such as education is on the upswing while the demand for automobiles, household appliances and foodstuffs is holding steady or increasing at a slower than average rate.

Many of these market changes and technological developments are reflected in long-term trends of the structure of employment in the United States. These changes in the structure of employment contain important clues about the relative significance of collective bargaining in the future industrial relations system. Figure 15–3 highlights some of the major changes in the structure of U.S. employment that have occurred since 1940.

A review of Figure 15–3 gives us a partial insight on probable future trends in the coverage of collective bargaining in American industry. The following trends are especially noteworthy:

1. The boom in white-collar employment. In 1960 white collar workers were the largest single occupational group in the U.S. In 1940 and 1950 manual workers were the largest single occupational group. The prospects of collective bargaining coverage of a few white collar subgroups should be noted:

   a) Technical engineers probably will continue to place primary reliance on their professional associations. However, many technical engineers are employed by the federal government, and Executive Order No. 10988 explicitly gives Government employees the right to collective bargaining. The experience of engineers who engage in collective bargaining with the government might be contagious for technical engineers in private employment. Note that the union organizing potential among technical engineers is almost one million members.

   b) Medical and other health workers are a substantial and rapidly growing occupational group. The 229,000 physicians and surgeons undoubtedly will continue to use their professional association, the American Medical Association, as their economic spokesman. Nurses and medical technicians offer a union organizing potential of over one million members. The ability of the unions to organize this occupational group depends on: (a) the skill of hospital personnel management, (b) the degree to which nurses prefer representation by a professional association, and (c) the problem of worker turnover in these occupations which is related to the high proportion of female employees. During the last decade many hospitals have overhauled their wage structures and instituted general personnel administration programs. These programs undoubtedly have improved the condition of hospital employees and may have squelched latent unrest. Because of the formal training of nurses and the patient-oriented nature of the work, nurses may be more interested in professional organizations than collective bargaining. The great majority of young nurses probably look on their nursing careers as the prelude to marriage. To the extent that workers expect to leave a particular employment they tend to be somewhat indifferent toward the conditions of that employment. A high rate of employee turnover makes the job of the union organizer more difficult. Finally the power relations in enveloping society will have an important influence on the success of union organizing campaigns in hospitals. At present, hospital employees are excluded from the protection of federal law in their attempts to organize. It seems very likely that any militant union activity by hospital employees would be smothered in an outburst of public indignation.

FIGURE 15-3

DISTRIBUTION OF EMPLOYED CIVILIAN WORKERS, BY OCCUPATIONAL GROUPS, UNITED STATES,* 1940, 1950, 1960

	1960		1950		1940		Percent Increase	
	Number†	%	Number†	%	Number†	%	1940–50	1950–60
All employed persons	64,639	...	56,435	...	45,070	...	25.2	14.5
Persons with occupations reported	61,456	100.0	55,692	100.0	44,652	100.0	24.7	10.3
White-collar workers	26,588	43.3	20,819	37.4	14,676	32.9	41.9	27.7
Professional, technical, and kindred workers	7,232	11.8	4,921	8.8	3,580	8.0	37.5	47.0
Engineers, technical	854	1.4	520	0.9	276	0.6	88.6	64.3
Medical and other health workers	1,306	2.1	1,008	1.8	‡	‡	‡	29.6
Nurses, student professional and professional	640	1.0	477	0.9	‡	‡	‡	34.2
Physicians and surgeons	229	0.4	193	0.3	‡	‡	‡	18.9
Technicians, medical and dental	138	0.2	77	0.1	‡	‡	‡	80.2
Teachers, elementary and secondary schools	1,522	2.5	1,043	1.8	‡	‡	‡	45.9
Clerical and kindred workers	9,307	15.1	6,954	12.5	4,382	9.8	58.7	33.8
Secretaries, stenographers, and typists§	2,179	3.5	1,508	2.7	990	2.2	52.3	44.5
Other clerical workers	7,128	11.6	5,447	9.8	3,392	7.6	60.6	30.9
Sales workers	4,639	7.5	3,907	7.0	3,081	6.9	26.8	18.7
Retail trade	2,695	4.4	2,450	4.4	‡	‡	‡	10.0
Manual workers	23,746	38.6	22,437	40.3	16,394	36.7	36.9	5.8
Construction craftsmen‖	2,404	3.9	2,355	4.2	‡	‡	‡	2.1
Locomotive engineers	57	0.1	73	0.1	‡	‡	‡	−22.4
Locomotive firemen	37	0.1	54	0.1	‡	‡	‡	−31.7
Operatives and kindred workers	11,898	19.4	11,180	20.1	8,080	18.1	38.4	6.4
Service workers, including private household	7,171	11.7	5,708	10.2	5,292	11.9	7.9	25.6
Agricultural workers	3,950	6.4	6,728	12.1	8,290	18.5	−18.8	−41.3

SOURCE: Max Rutzick and Sol Swerdloff, "The Occupational Structure of U.S. Employment, 1940–1960," *Monthly Labor Review*, Vol. LXXXV (November, 1962), p. 1211.

Notes:
* 1940 and 1950 adjusted to include Alaska and Hawaii.
† In thousands, rounded to the nearest thousand.
‡ Not available.
§ Female only.
‖ Male only.

c) Teachers are torn between representation by unions or professional associations. The explosion in teacher employment between 1950 and 1960 offers an attractive plum to professional associations and unions. Although most teachers are women, the normal minimum term of teacher employment is one full year. This contractual term of employment gives teachers a somewhat longer-term interest in the conditions of their employment than is true of young nurses. Most teachers are active in their professional associations. The nationwide reaction to the Brooklyn school teachers' strike of 1962 re-emphasizes the context of power relations. The teachers were able to influence their conditions through organization, but they also found that public opinion imposed restraints on their search for self-betterment.

d) Clerical and kindred workers are increasing at a rapid rate and are challenging the manual worker group of operatives and kindred workers as a major occupational group. To the extent that clerical workers are organized in the future they most probably will join enterprise-oriented unions rather than occupation-oriented unions. Because of the wide diversity in the type of enterprises employing clerical workers, it is extremely difficult to estimate the potential union membership which could be derived from this occupational group. The high percentage of female employees in these occupations must be noted.

e) Sales workers as a whole are increasing at a more rapid rate than general employment in the United States. At the same time, consolidations in the retail trade and self-service methods have resulted in a slower than average growth in retail employment. Despite this trend, the Retail Clerks Union has recently increased its membership significantly, and the Teamsters' Union is active in retail organizing. In retailing alone, there is a union membership potential of over 2,000,000.

2. The relative stability and decline of manual worker employment. Manual workers compose the large bulk of American trade union membership. Unless unions can expand their membership in nonmanual occupations, they are doomed to play a less significant role. Within the manual worker classification, several important trends should be noted:

a) Construction craftsmen employment, the home ground of American craft unionism, is playing a declining role in U.S. employment. This declining role is largely attributable to technological changes in construction, particularly the increasing use of off-site prefabrication.

b) For many decades, railroad workers were the aristocrats of American labor. Their organizations were considered the models upon which the unorganized could rise to power and influence. During the decade 1950–60, the locomotive engineers and firemen suffered a decline in employment of almost 25 per cent. The eventual implementation of the 1962 Presidential Railroad Commission's recommendations will undoubtedly take an even higher toll in the decade of the sixties. Technology has humbled the formerly powerful railroad labor organizations.

c) Although mining occupations are not shown in Figure 15–3, technology has taken a heavy toll in mining employment.

d) Employment in service occupations has increased substantially in the fifties. It is extremely difficult to estimate the potential union membership which could be derived from this occupational group because of the wide diversity of types of enterprises employing service workers.

e) Agriculture is the classic example of technological displacement in American enterprise. Agricultural employment has slumped from over 8,000,000 in 1940 to less than 4,000,000 in 1960.

The employment trends shown in Figure 15–3 are the result of the operations of the contexts of the market, technology, and the power relations of the enveloping social system. These employment trends, in turn, shed some light on probable future trends in the power relations of the enveloping society.

The Context of Power Relations

The context of power relations means the influence, authority, prestige, or power managers and workers have outside the shop. The most tangible expression of the power relations context is legislation and governmental administrative regulations. In a democracy governmental favor or disfavor is strongly influenced by the number of votes that a particular cause can rally on election day. The number of votes, in turn, is influenced by the hard core of loyal party members and their ability to project a favorable image to the rest of the electorate.

Unions can find little cause for joy in the present structure of power relations and little cause for optimism in the future. If, as is strongly suggested by the employment trends in Figure 15–3, collective bargaining will occupy a relatively less significant role in the future economy, unions will have relatively fewer hard-core loyal party members to get out the vote. The public image of unionism has been badly tarnished by the McClellan investigations, the Landrum-Griffin Act, and the seemingly endless effort of the government to "get Jimmy Hoffa." Although it seems unlikely that repressive labor relations legislation is in the immediate offing, the unions are definitely on the defensive in political matters.

The defensive political stance of the unions can be illustrated by two events in 1966: (1) the failure to win repeal of Section 14(b) of the Taft-Hartley Act and (2) the "brinkmanship" required to smash the Presidential economic guidelines, first, and most significantly, in the construction industry, most conspicuously in the airlines strike. Section 14(b) of the Taft-Hartley Act, which authorizes states to enact more restrictive legislation on union security than the federal law, had been a thorn in the side of the labor movement for 19 years when a massive attempt to repeal it was defeated by a filibuster of a northern Republican senator. Both the House and Senate had large majorities friendly to labor, but the repeal of 14(b) floundered. The most embarrassing thing to the labor movement about the defeat of repeal legislation must have been that the defeat occurred during a period when labor peace was a fact, corruption was not an issue, and Congress was busily engaged in passing all kinds of "Great Society" legislation. Also in 1966 the labor movement, with the only slightly reluctant co-operation of management, pretty well scrapped the Presidential wage-price guidelines. The fact that the unions could and *did* negotiate wage increases very substantially above the recommended 3.2 per cent level indicates that they possess substantial political power, at least at the bargaining table. But the price of breaking the guidelines *may* prove to be expensive for the unions; they now become the culprits in any argument about who is to blame for inflation and it seems that the general public becomes a little more enamored of compulsory arbitration legislation every time it is inconvenienced by a strike like the 1966 airlines strike.

Unions and their friends have had much more conspicuous success in the protective labor legislation field. Such broadly based legislative endeavors as medicare under Social Security, vocational retraining for technologically displaced workers and depressed areas, massive increases in the federal minimum wage and its coverage, the general "war on poverty" have rolled through Congress with little effective opposition. All of these programs are "labor" programs in that they have long been advocated by unions, but their passage can not be attributed to an upsurge in organized labor's political power.

In some states, unions have substantial political influence, e.g., miners in West Virginia, autoworkers in Michigan, and lumber workers in the Pacific Northwest. When unions are able to effectively exert this influence it pays substantial dividends in such legislative areas as unemployment compensation, workmen's compensation, and freedom from so-called right-to-work laws.

It is still too early to evaluate the long-term significance of a recent upsurge of militancy among civil servants and members of the teaching and nursing professions. It is possible to say, however, that this militancy may be the beginning of a mass movement for the organization of white-collar workers in distinct organizations not unlike the experience in several European countries. The organization of large numbers of salaried employees would strengthen the political and economic influence of the labor movement.

The authors of this book believe that the lesson of the thirties provides the key to prediction for the sixties. If there is no major economic collapse, unionism will endure in a steadily decreasing segment of society. In the unlikely event of a major economic collapse, workers (white collar and blue collar alike) who are able to keep their jobs will rally to the banner of unionism. Workers who lose their jobs may turn to radical political action.

This still leaves us with the problem of the probable future structure of the American industrial relations system beyond the realm of collective bargaining. The broader industrial relations system will draw some of its characteristics from the lessons of collective bargaining. Workers will continue to seek a system of individual security which establishes their relative claim to available work and guarantees their absolute right to fair treatment. Up to the present time in America, collective bargaining has been the major means of establishing job rights. The guarantee of fair treatment has been reinforced by voluntary arbitration of disputes over the interpretation of collective bargaining agreements. In some other industrialized countries job rights and fair treatment have been established by law and enforced by labor courts. It remains to be seen whether enlightened personnel management policies can provide these requirements or whether unorganized workers will turn to government, professional associations, or unions as a means of establishing these rights. For employers and legislators who do not want unionism to spread, the most important single field of study is job security and fair treatment under collective bargaining. These benefits are the cornerstone of enlightened personnel policies in nonunion establishments.

SUMMARY

Collective bargaining is a dynamic process. The actors—managers, workers, and the government—interact in their attempts to control the ever changing contexts of the market, technology, and societal power relationships. Technology most directly impinges on the day-to-day activities of workers and managers.

Traditionally craft unions have dealt with technological change by limiting the application of their members' scarce skill. This strategy will continue to play an important role in local and luxury markets requiring a handicraft technology.

Automation poses a new problem for the industrial unions. Lacking a monopoly of scarce technical skills, the industrial unions must rely on a dual approach of governmental action and collective bargaining. Major technological breakthroughs may result in radical changes in the number and size of employers in particular segments of industry. Governmental action in the areas of retraining, unemployment compensation, full-employment programs, and hours of work will require careful consideration. Collective bargaining agreements will require major overhauling in the age of automation.

The occupational structure of employment in the United States is undergoing major change. Unless unions are able to organize white-collar workers on a broad scale, the *relative* significance of collective bargaining in society will decline. Nevertheless the system of job security and fair treatment which unions and management have forged will leave a lasting impression on the American way of life.

QUESTIONS FOR DISCUSSION

1. What is the influence of collective bargaining on the nonunion enterprise?
2. How would you answer the following questions on the basis of your study of collective bargaining?
   (*a*) How do you account for the origin or emergence of labor organizations?
   (*b*) What explains the patterns of growth and development of labor organizations?
   (*c*) What are the ultimate goals of labor organizations?

(*d*) Why do individual workers join unions?

Are these questions adequate for this day and age? Do you have any proposals for developing more quantitative and less qualitative answers to these questions?

3. Is there a need for an "automation" model in collective bargaining?

4. Discuss the prospects for wide-scale organization of white-collar workers in the United States. How do you account for the fact that white-collar workers in other countries have shown more interest in joining unions than they have in the United States?

SELECTED ANNOTATED BIBLIOGRAPHY

This bibliography consists of two parts: (1) Technological Change and (2) The Future of Collective Bargaining.

TECHNOLOGICAL CHANGE

Automation and Technological Change. Report of the Subcommittee on Economic Stabilization to the Joint Committee on the Economic Report, Congress of the United States, 84th Cong., 1st sess. . . . October 14–28, 1955. Washington, D.C.: U.S. Government Printing Office, 1955.

Findings based on hearings on economic significance and implications for employment, displacement, training, and education.

Report of the Presidential Railroad Commission. Washington, D.C.: U.S. Government Printing Office, February, 1962.

An analysis of railroad labor relations with emphasis on the problems of changing manpower requirements due to technological advancements.

Technology and the American Economy. Report of the National Commission on Technology, Automation, and Economic Progress. Vol. 1, February, 1966. Washington, D.C.: U.S. Government Printing Office.

The Commission offers recommendations including minimum family income guarantees, improved educational opportunities, improved operation of the labor market, and employer actions for the greater humanizing of work.

The Benefits and Problems Incident to Automation and Other Technological Advances. President's Advisory Committee on Labor-Management Policy. January, 1962.

Considers the significance and impact of automation and technological advances, with the purpose of seeking "that course of action which will encourage essential progress in the form of automation and technological change, while meeting at the same time the social consequences such change creates."

BRIGHT, JAMES R. *Automation and Management.* Boston: Division of Research, Harvard Graduate School of Business Administration, 1958.

A penetrating analysis of the nature of automatic manufacturing, experiences with automation, and critical areas of automation based on three years of extensive and intensive field research.

DUNLOP, JOHN T. (ed.). *Automation and Technological Change.* The American Assembly, Columbia University. Englewood Cliffs, N.J.: Prentice-Hall, Inc., 1962.

Contents are:

DUNLOP, JOHN T. "Introduction: Problems and Potentials."

HEILBRONER, ROBERT L. "The Impact of Technology: The Historic Debate."
DUBRIDGE, LEE A. "Educational and Social Consequences."
MANN, FLOYD C. "Psychological and Organizational Impacts."
ANSHEN, MELVIN. "Managerial Decisions."
TAYLOR, GEORGE W. "Collective Bargaining."
WALLIS, W. ALLEN. "Some Economic Considerations."
CLAGUE, EWAN, and GREENBERG, LEON. "Employment."
COOPER, RICHARD N. "International Aspects."
BELLO, FRANCIS. "The Technology Behind Productivity."
WRISTON, HENRY M. "Perspective."
Final Report of the Twenty-first American Assembly

JACOBSON, HOWARD B., and ROUCEK, JOSEPH S. (eds.). *Automation and Society.* New York: Philosophical Library, 1959.
A compendium of articles, papers, testimony, and case studies bringing together in convenient form much of the best available material on the nontechnical aspects of automation. Included are an automation dictionary and annotated bibliographies at end of each article.

PHILIPSON, MORRIS (ed.). *Automation: Implications for the Future.* New York: Vintage Books Division of Random House, 1962.
A collection of readings on automation. Special attention is invited to: "The Challenge of 'Industrial Revolution II,'" by ARTHUR J. GOLDBERG; "The Promise of Automation," by PETER DRUCKER; "Labor Relations and Employment Aspects After Ten Years (1962)," by EVERETT M. KASSALOW.

SHILS, EDWARD B. *Automation and Industrial Relations.* New York: Holt, Rinehart and Winston, 1963.
An appraisal of the problems and pitfalls of adjusting work and labor practices to the accelerated developments in mechanization.

SOMERS, GERALD G., CUSHMAN, EDWARD L., and WEINBERG, NAT (eds.). *Adjusting to Technological Change.* Industrial Relations Research Association Publication No. 29. New York: Harper & Row, 1963.
Contents include:
BUCKINGHAM, WALTER. "Gains and Costs of Technological Change."
TAFT, PHILIP. "Organized Labor and Technical Change: A Backward Look."
BARBASH, JACK. "The Impact of Technology on Labor-Management Relations."
KILLINGSWORTH, CHARLES C. "Cooperative Approaches to Problems of Technological Change."
WEBER, ARNOLD. "The Interplant Transfer of Displaced Persons."
LEVITAN, SAR A., and SHEPPARD, HAROLD L. "Technological Change and the Community."
OLSSON, BERTIL. "Policy Implications of Technological Change in Western Europe."

WALKER, CHARLES R. *Toward the Automatic Factory: A Case Study of Man and Machines.* New Haven, Conn.: Yale University Press, 1957.
A study of the psychological and sociological impact of the transfer of workers from an old steel mill to a highly automated mill.

THE FUTURE OF COLLECTIVE BARGAINING

BAMBRICK, JAMES J., JR., and ZAGAT, HERMINE. "Professional Status—Goal of Engineering Unions," *Management Record,* Vol. XVII (July, 1955), pp. 279–81.

An explanation for typical engineering union demands such as: employer payment of professional society dues, paid time off to attend professional meetings, tuition refunds, educational and professional leaves of absence, and setting of professional standards.

Barkin, Solomon. *The Decline of The Labor Movement, and What Can Be Done About It.* Santa Barbara, Calif.: Center For The Study of Democratic Institutions, 1961.

Begins with an appraisal of the present state of union membership, and then considers the external and internal obstacles and impediments to growth. Summarizes the specific obstacles encountered in trying to form unions among individual work groups, and outlines some new approaches to organization that unions might follow.

Bell, Daniel. "No Boom for the Unions," *Fortune,* Vol. LIII (June, 1956) pp. 136–37.

The Labor Editor of *Fortune* surveys the organizing potential of the American labor movement.

Bruner, Dick. "Has Success Spoiled the Unions?" *Harvard Business Review,* Vol. XXXVIII (May–June, 1960), pp. 73–78.

American labor movement has not only lost the fervor of the 1930's but has undergone psychological revolution and is developing character of middle-class special interest group. Much of economic history which has brought automation, decentralization of industry, prosperity, complacency on part of satisfied workers, and creeping conservatism to union leaders themselves is primary force militating against unions.

Collective Bargaining in the Basic Steel Industry. A Study of the Public Interest and the Role of Government. Washington, D.C.: U.S. Department of Labor, 1961.

Prepared by E. R. Livernash and others. A comprehensive study of the way in which the collective bargaining process has worked in the basic steel industry. Reports on the impact of steel strikes, the character of collective bargaining in steel, the public policy problems, effects upon the economy and on wages and prices; and it evaluates government intervention. Appendices: A. Profiles of Negotiations in Basic Steel, 1937–59. B. Strikes and Industrial Relations in the Steel Industries of Selected Countries, by Abraham J. Siegel.

Dankert, Clyde E. "Shorter Hours—in Theory and Practice," *Industrial and Labor Relations Review,* Vol. XV (April, 1962), pp. 307–22.

Analytical discussion of the relationship between shorter hours, total output, worker satisfaction, and employer profits.

Free and Responsible Collective Bargaining and Industrial Peace. President's Advisory Committee on Labor Management Policy. Washington, D.C.: May, 1962.

Recommendations for reconciling the parties' interests with those of the larger community, reducing interruptions to work, improving mediation, and handling critical and national emergency disputes.

Garbarino, J. W. "The Economic Significance of Automatic Wage Adjustments," in Harold W. Davey, Howard S. Kaltenborn, and Stanley H. Ruttenberg, *New Dimensions in Collective Bargaining.* New York: Harper & Bros., 1959.

Concludes that automatic wage adjustment systems probably add to the inflationary potential of wage policy.

Healy, James J. (ed.). *Creative Collective Bargaining: Meeting Today's*

Challenges to Labor-Management Relations. Englewood Cliffs, N.J.: Prentice-Hall, Inc., 1965.

Detailed studies of the Human Relations Committee, the Kaiser Long-Range Sharing Plan, the Armour Automation Committee, the West Coast Longshore Mechanization and Modernization Agreement, and other examples of institutional inventiveness.

HILDEBRAND, GEORGE H. "The Use of Neutrals in Collective Bargaining." chap. 5, *Arbitration and Public Policy,* SPENCER D. POLLARD (ed.). Proceedings of the Fourteenth Annual Meeting of the National Academy of Arbitrators. Washington, D.C.: The Bureau of National Affairs, 1961, pp. 135–55. Discussion by FREDERICK R. LIVINGSTON and BEN FISCHER, pp. 155–67.

Considers the Kaiser steel, basic steel, railroad Presidential Study Committee, the ILNW and Pacific Maritime Association, Armour, and Pittsburgh Plate Glass and United Glass and Ceramic Workers cases as illustrations of four ways in which neutrals have been introduced, i.e., (1) ex post mediation, (2) the study committee, (3) consultants, and (4) contract arbitration. Hildebrand argues that the informed neutrals have a new contribution to make to the great objective of developing a consensus between management and labor. Livingston supports Hildebrand's argument by discussing the Armour experience in greater detail, but re-emphasizes the urgent need for absolute voluntarism in the use of neutrals. Fischer argues that neutrals can do little to facilitate agreement that the parties themselves cannot do.

KASSALOW, EVERETT M. "New Union Frontier: White-Collar Workers," *Harvard Business Review,* Vol. XXX (January-February, 1962), pp. 41–52.

Discusses the significance of the changing occupational structure of the American labor force from the viewpoint of union membership and organization. Outlines structural changes in the AFL-CIO necessary for a successful appeal to nonmanual workers; and explores the possible forms of white-collar and professional unions.

MAGRATH, PETER C. "Democracy in Overalls: The Futile Quest for Union Democracy," *Industrial and Labor Relations Review,* Vol. XII (July, 1959), pp. 503–25.

A critical study of major literature on problem of union democracy concludes that it is a mistake to equate problem of union democracy with that of relationship of individual member to the union and its officers. While union members should be protected from abuse of their rights as members, democracy in union government is probably an unattainable ideal.

NATIONAL PLANNING ASSOCIATION. *Causes of Industrial Peace Under Collective Bargaining.*

The NPA series of monographs on industrial peace consists of studies listed below:

1. KERR, CLARK, and RANDALL, ROGER. *Crown Zellerbach and the Pacific Coast Pulp and Paper Industry,* 1948.
2. HARBISON, FREDERICK H., and CARR, KING. *The Libbey-Owens-Ford Glass Company and the Federation of Glass, Ceramic and Silica Sand Workers of America,* 1948.
3. McGREGOR, DOUGLAS, and SCANLON, JOSEPH N. *The Dewey and Almy Chemical Company and the International Chemical Workers Union,* 1948.
4. STRAUS, DONALD B. *Hickey-Freeman Company and Amalgamated Clothing Workers of America,* 1949.
5. MILLER, J. WADE, JR. *Sharon Steel Corporation and the United Steelworkers of America,* 1949.

6. KERR, CLARK, and HALVERSON, GEORGE. *Lockheed Aircraft Corporation and International Association of Machinists,* 1949.
7. MYERS, CHARLES A., and SHULTZ, GEORGE P. *Nashua Gummed and Coated Paper Company and Seven AFL Unions,* 1950.
8. FLEMING, R. W., and WITTE, E. E. *Marathon Corporation and Seven Labor Unions,* 1950.
9. ZINKE, GEORGE W. *Minnequa Plant of Colorado Fuel and Iron Corporation and Two Locals of the United Steelworkers of America,* 1951.
10. SHULTZ, GEORGE P., and CRISARA, ROBERT P. *The Lapointe Machine Tool Company and the United Steel Workers of America,* 1952.
11. PAUL, GEORGE S. *American Velvet Company and Textile Workers Union of America,* 1953.
12. GILMAN, GLENN W., and SWEENEY, JAMES W. *Atlantic Steel Company and United Steel Workers of America,* 1953.
13. HARBISON, FREDERICK W., and COLEMAN, JOHN R. *Working Harmony: A Summary of the Collective Bargaining Relationship in 18 Companies,* 1953.
14. COMMITTEE ON THE CAUSE OF INDUSTRIAL PEACE OF THE NATIONAL PLANNING ASSOCIATION. *Fundamentals of Labor Peace: A Final Report,* 1954.

SAYLES, LEONARD R. *Behavior of Industrial Work Groups. Prediction and Control.* New York: John Wiley & Sons, Inc., 1958.

An extensive series of case studies describing work group behavior. Portrays important differences in the type and structure of work groups in industry. A realistic picture of life in the plant with respect to the source and nature of grievances and grievance handling.

SHERMAN, HERBERT L. *Arbitration of the Steel Wage Structure.* Pittsburgh: University of Pittsburgh Press, 1961.

Full texts of decision of the Board of Arbitration for U.S. Steel Corporation and U.S.A. on job description and classification disputes and related wage problems involving production maintenance, and nonconfidential clerical issues.

STIEBER, JACK W. "Evaluation of Long-Term Contracts," in HAROLD DAVEY, HOWARD S. KALTENBORN, and STANLEY H. RUTTENBERG (eds.). *New Dimensions in Collective Bargaining.* New York: Harper & Bros., 1959, pp. 137–53.

Argues that long-term agreements are socially desirable and that it is likely that they will remain a prevalent feature of American collective bargaining.

STIEBER, JACK W. *The Steel Industry Wage Structure: A Study of the Joint Union-Management Job Evaluation Program in the Basic Steel Industry.* Cambridge, Mass.: Harvard University Press, 1959.

WHYTE, WILLIAM FOOTE. *Pattern for Industrial Peace.* New York: Harper & Bros., 1951.

A very readable account of the transition from open conflict to co-operation in labor-management relations at the Chicago plant of the Inland Steel Container Company.

PART V

Cases in Collective Bargaining

CASES

INTRODUCTION

Part V of this book contains 46 cases, all of them true, but with the names of individuals, companies, and unions disguised in a few instances. Questions about the issues the cases raise or illustrate accompany the presentation of the facts. Many of the cases come from arbitration records, and appear here by courtesy of the Bureau of National Affairs, which first published them, and has kindly permitted their reproduction for student use. Other cases are drawn from the opinions of the courts on important matters.

Now, why study cases?

Arbitration and legal proceedings account for no more than a small part of the sum total of collective bargaining activities, yet for several reasons the study of arbitration and law cases is unusually rewarding.

To begin with, the arbitration and legal processes leave a written record. This is not true of all aspects of collective bargaining. Where such a record is not kept, cases have to be written up in narrative form (like a few of those in this section) and lack the authority of official record. The decision of an arbitrator or court usually concentrates on a single, seemingly narrow point, but the record of the hearing often preserves for scrutiny a range of facts and testimony that illuminates a much broader field of view. Furthermore, an issue that has gone all the way to arbitration or to court usually embodies some aspect of the relationship between the contending parties that is unique, with important implications that touch on fundamental principles.

The cases in this book present concrete issues that have arisen between bargaining partners in spite of their best efforts to settle differences in advance by written agreement. Practical problems rising out of the living process of collective bargaining appear here in all the confusion and fragmentation of the forms in which they confront actual participants.

It will be the student's task to analyze the problems as they come before him in raw form, applying the principles he may have learned from the text, from collateral reading opened up by the text, and from classroom instruction and discussion. The cases, therefore, help the student develop his powers of reasoning, his ability to move from the general to the particular, and, perhaps, back from the particular to strengthen his grasp of the general. They demand logical organization of ideas and clarity of oral and written expression. (This they demand all the more because in their raw state they are themselves not models of clarity or logic.)

Finally, cases permit the student to express and test value judgments based on his own moral and ethical code. So far as possible, value judgments have been kept out of the text, because the aim there was to present only the facts. Where any value judgments have been made, the authors have taken care to label them as only their personal opinion and have not tried to pass them off as gospel. Here, in handling cases, the student can —and should—give thought to what he thinks is right and wrong, what should and should not be. He will undoubtedly find some who disagree with him; he may sway them, or be swayed. Collective bargaining surely cannot stand exempt from ethics and morality, any more than from economic law or any other influence at work in society, and it is only by free exchange of views and values that understanding (if not full agreement) can be reached.

Like almost everything in this book, the cases here presented do not pretend to be exhaustive, but suggestive. There is no limit to the number of true-life cases students could collect and subject to the process of analysis these cases demonstrate. Having started with these cases, let students bring in their own experiences and observations, either in oral or written form, for presentation to the class and for class discussion.

HOW TO USE THE CASES

Chapter 8 contains the valuable advice of the American Arbitration Association on how to prepare for arbitration. This is worth reviewing before tackling a case problem. After that, two ways of using the cases stand open to the instructor and the class.

One way is to take the case as the starting point for a written exercise. The student writes what he considers should be the arbitrator's award, or in the cases not drawn from arbitration records, directly answers the questions. In either event, he should justify his solution.

Another way, and probably better, is the role-playing method. A team of two or three students can take the union side, a similar team the management side, with a student (or the instructor) to sit as arbitrator and act as chairman. The two sides then act out their roles before the class.

Oral presentation in this manner should not neglect the value—perhaps it might be said, the necessity—of written support in the form of a brief of the argument, and perhaps also "exhibits" in lieu of testimony where "evidence" consists of facts drawn from the printed case. After the class has heard the arguments, each member may then write an "award" as if he were the arbitrator. Other variations will undoubtedly suggest themselves.

A word about briefs and a hint on their preparation.

Most college students will have last encountered brief-writing in their freshman English course, or perhaps in high school. Here is a chance to review an important subject and develop a useful skill.

The hint is this: study the *questions* that follow the cases for clues that will lead to the most logically developed argument, along lines indicated by the interest to be defended, or the value judgment to be upheld. Merely to summarize the arguments already put forward in the "union position," or "management position" of the printed case will fail to develop the full strength of either side's position.

This cases section of the book calls for active student participation, and brings the practice of collective bargaining into play in a form as realistic as it is possible to get in the classroom. A mock arbitration hearing or role-playing session should not be allowed to degenerate into clowning or farce, but need not exclude humor and good spirits. This part of the course can be, and ought to be, good fun as well as good instruction.

TABLE OF CASES

Case 1

THE OBLIGATION TO BARGAIN UNDER FEDERAL LAW

This case consists of three parts: (1) a brief discussion of the obligation to bargain under federal law; (2) opinions of the United States Supreme Court in three leading cases; and (3) two scholarly comments on sound public policy in this area.

PART I. THE LEGAL OBLIGATION TO BARGAIN

One of the most difficult problems confronting the NLRB and the courts in interpreting the Taft-Hartley Act is defining the obligation to bargain in good faith. Sections 8(a)(5) and 8(b)(3) impose the obligation to bargain on employers and unions respectively. Section 8(d) states that collective bargaining

. . . is the performance of the mutual obligation of the employer and the representative of his employees to meet at reasonable times and confer in good faith with respect to wages, hours, and other conditions of employment, or the negotiation of an agreement, or any question arising thereunder, and the execution of a written contract incorporating any agreement reached if re-quested by either party, but such obligation does not compel either party to agree to a proposal or require the making of a concession: . . .

The words of the statute provide only sketchy guidelines to the definition of the obligation to bargain. The NLRB and the courts have interpreted the statute as applying to both the conduct of the parties in the act of bargaining and the substantive issues in bargaining. Thus the NLRB requires that both parties meet and discuss their proposals, and it determines whether a party may refuse to discuss certain specific proposals.

Substantative issues in collective bargaining are divided into three legal categories: (1) unlawful issues; (2) mandatory issues; and (3) non-mandatory issues. The parties are forbidden to agree on unlawful issues, e.g., the closed shop. Either party is within the law when it demands a mandatory issue and refuses to sign an agreement unless its demand is satisfied. Both parties are required to bargain about any mandatory subject proposed by the other party. Neither party is obligated to agree to any specific mandatory subject. Unions and managements may agree to bar-gain about nonmandatory subjects, and any agreement they voluntarily reach on nonmandatory subjects is lawful. However, neither party is obligated to bargain on nonmandatory subjects, nor is either party permit-ted to insist upon a demand for a nonmandatory subject. A few illustrations of mandatory and nonmandatory subjects may help to clarify the significance of these categories.

The following are examples of mandatory subjects for collective bargaining:

1. Employee stock purchase plans.
2. Profit-sharing retirement plans.
3. Group insurance.
4. Pensions.
5. Christmas bonuses.
6. No-strike clauses.

Suppose that the union and management had agreed on wages, hours, seniority provisions, grievance procedures, and all other matters usually in an agreement. The union would not be guilty of refusal to bargain if it demanded, and struck for, an extra bonus to be distributed at Christmas. Nor would the employer be guilty of refusal to bargain if he refused to sign an agreement incorporating these understandings unless the union agreed to include a no-strike clause in the agreement.

The following are examples of nonmandatory subjects for collective bargaining:

1. Demands that a union post a performance bond.
2. Demands that an employer post a performance bond.
3. Demands that a union withdraw an unfair labor practice charge.
4. Demands that a union forego certain appropriate bargaining subjects for all time.
5. Demand that a supervisor be discharged.

An employer may agree with the union that a supervisor will be discharged as a means of improving the labor relations climate, or a union may withdraw its pending unfair labor practice charge against the employer for the same reason. However, the union is guilty of refusal to bargain if it strikes for the purpose of causing a supervisor's discharge; and the employer is innocent of refusal to bargain if he steadfastly refuses to listen to the union's protestations about the supervisor. The employer is guilty of refusal to bargain if he insists that he will not sign an agreement until the union withdraws its unfair labor practice charges.

The real significance of the division between mandatory and nonmandatory subjects is difficult to assess. Nevertheless, it seems reasonable to conclude that an NLRB and Supreme Court labeling of, say, pensions as a mandatory subject for collective bargaining is a tacit governmental approval of a union drive to negotiate such plans. Also, an NLRB and supreme Court ruling that a union may not strike to force an employer to post a performance bond as a condition precedent to a collective bargaining agreement tends to reduce the prevalence of such provisions in collective bargaining agreements.

In general, statutory law specifically prohibits relatively few collective bargaining clauses, e.g., closed shops and, under the 1959 law, "hot cargo" clauses.

The complexity of the problems confronting the NLRB and the courts in determining mandatory and nonmandatory subjects is illustrated by the following three abstracted Supreme Court rulings.

PART II. THREE SUPREME COURT DECISIONS

The Truitt Manufacturing Company case, decided in 1956, deals with the obligation of an employer to substantiate his claim of inability to pay a wage increase demanded by the union. This case deals with the process of negotiations rather than a new substantive issue like profit sharing or displacement allowances for workers who lose their jobs in a plant closure.

The Borg-Warner case, decided in 1958, deals with the demand of an employer for a "ballot clause" in a collective bargaining agreement. This case requires a decision on whether a new substantive issue is a mandatory subject for collective bargaining.

The Insurance Agents case, decided in 1960, deals with a union slowdown and other harassment of an employer during the progress of negotiations. Do pressures exerted outside the bargaining sessions provide evidence of a refusal to bargain in good faith?

The reports of the cases presented below have been abstracted. Readers are encouraged to read the full opinions available in U.S. Reports. *Dissenting opinions have been included in the abstracts because of the richness of their insight.*

Supreme Court of the United States
National Labor Relations Board v. Truitt Manufacturing Company
May 7, 1956, 351 U.S. 149

Mr. Justice Black delivered the opinion of the Court.

The National Labor Relations Act makes it an unfair labor practice for an employer to refuse to bargain in good faith with the representative of his employees. The question presented by this case is whether the National Labor Relations Board may find that an employer has not bargained in good faith where the employer claims it cannot afford to pay higher wages but refuses requests to produce information substantiating its claim.

The dispute here arose when a union representing certain of respondent's employees asked for a wage increase of 10 cents per hour. The company answered that it could not afford to pay such an increase, it was undercapitalized, had never paid dividends, and that an increase of more than 2½ cents per hour would put it out of business. The union asked the company to produce some evidence substantiating these statements, requesting permission to have a certified public accountant examine the company's books, financial data, etc. This request being denied, the union asked that the company submit "full and complete information with respect to its financial standing and profits," insisting that such information was pertinent and essential for the employees to determine whether or not they should continue to press their demand for a wage increase. A union official testified before the trial examiner that "(W)e were wanting anything relating to the Company's position, any record or what have you, books, accounting sheets, cost expenditures, what not, anything to back the Company's position that they were unable to give any more money." The company refused all the requests, relying solely on the statement that "the information . . . is not pertinent to this discussion and the company declines to give you such information; you have no legal right to such."

On the basis of these facts the National Labor Relations Board found that the company had "failed to bargain in good faith with respect to wages in violation of Section 8(a)(5) of the Act." The Board ordered the company to supply the union with such information as would "substantiate the Respondent's position of its economic inability to pay the requested wage increase." The Court of Appeals refused to enforce the Board's order, agreeing with respondent that it could not be held guilty of an unfair labor practice because of its refusal to furnish the information requested by the union. In *Labor Board* v. *Jacobs Mfg. Co.*, the Second Circuit upheld a Board finding of bad-faith bargaining based on an employer's refusal to supply financial information under circumstances similar to those here. Because of the conflict and the importance of the question we granted certiorari.

The company raised no objection to the Board's order on the ground that the scope of information required was too broad or that disclosure would put an undue burden on the company. Its major argument throughout has been that the information requested was irrelevant to the bargaining process and related to matters exclusively within the province of management. Thus we lay to one side the suggestion by the company here that the Board's order might be unduly burdensome or injurious to its business. In any event, the Board has heretofore taken the position in cases such as this that "It is sufficient if the information is made available in a manner not so burdensome or time-consuming as to impede the process of bargaining." And in this case the Board has held substantiation of the company's position requires no more than "reasonable proof."

We think that in determining whether the obligation of good-faith bargaining has been met the Board has a right to consider an employer's refusal to give information about its financial status. While Congress did not compel agreement between employers and bargaining representatives, it did require collective bargaining in the hope that agreements would result. Section 204(a)(1) of the Act admonishes both employers and employees to "exert every reasonable effort to make and maintain agreements concerning rates of pay, hours, and working conditions. . . ." In their effort to reach an agreement here both the union and the company treated the company's ability to pay increased wages as highly relevant. The ability of an employer to increase wages without injury to his business is a commonly considered factor in wage negotiations. Claims for increased wages have sometimes been abandoned because of an employer's unsatisfactory business condition; employees have even voted to accept wage decreases because of such conditions.

Good-faith bargaining necessarily requires that claims made by either bargainer should be honest claims. This is true about an asserted inability to pay an increase in wages. If such an argument is important enough to present in the give and take of bargaining, it is important enough to require some sort of proof of its accuracy. And it would certainly not be farfetched for a trier of fact to reach the conclusion that bargaining lacks good faith when an employer mechanically repeats a claim of inability to pay without making the slightest effort to substantiate the claim. Such has been the holding of the Labor Board since shortly after the passage of the Wagner Act. . . . We agree with the Board that a refusal to attempt to substantiate a claim of inability to pay increased wages may support a finding of a failure to bargain in good faith.

The Board concluded that under the facts and circumstances of this case the respondent was guilty of an unfair labor practice in failing to bargain in good faith. We see no reason to disturb the findings of the Board. We do not hold, however, that in every case in which economic inability is raised as an argument against increased wages it automatically follows that the employees are entitled to substantiating evidence. Each case must turn upon its particular facts. The inquiry must always be whether or not under the circumstances of the particular case the statutory obligation to bargain in good faith has been met. Since we conclude that there is support in the record for the conclusion of the Board here that respondents did not bargain in good faith, it was error for the Court of Appeals to set aside the Board's order and deny enforcement.

Reversed.

Truitt Manufacturing Company
Concurring and Dissenting Opinion

Mr. Justice Frankfurter, whom Mr. Justice Clark and Mr. Justice Harlan join, concurring in part and dissenting in part.

This case involves the nature of the duty to bargain which the National Labor Relations Act imposes upon employers and unions. Section 8(a)(5) of the Act makes it "an unfair labor practice for an employer . . . to refuse to bargain collectively with the representatives of his employees," and Section 8(b)(3) places a like duty upon the union *vis-à-vis* the employer. Section 8(d) provides that "to bargain collectively is the performance of the mutual obligation of the employer and the representative of the employees to meet at reasonable times and confer in good faith with respect to wages, hours, and other terms and conditions of employment, or the negotiation of an agreement, or any question arising thereunder, and the execution of a written contract incorporating any agreement reached if requested by either party, but such obligation does not compel either party to agree to a proposal or require the making of a concession. . . ."

These sections obligate the parties to make an honest effort to come to terms; they are required to try to reach an agreement in good faith. "Good faith" means more than merely going through the motions of negotiating; it is inconsistent with a predetermined resolve not to budge from an initial position. But it is not necessarily incompatible with stubbornness or even with what to an outsider may seem unreasonableness. A determination of good faith or of want of good faith normally can rest only on an inference based upon more or less persuasive manifestations of another's state of mind. The previous relations of the parties, antecedent events explaining behavior at the bargaining table, and the course of negotiatons constitute the raw facts for reaching such a determination. The appropriate inferences to be drawn from what is often confused and tangled testimony about all this makes a finding of absence of good faith one for the judgment of the Labor Board, unless the record as a whole leaves such judgment without reasonable foundation.

An examination of the Board's opinion and the position taken by its counsel here disclose that the Board did not so conceive the issue of good-faith bargaining in this case. The totality of the conduct of the negotiation was apparently deemed irrelevant to the question; one fact alone disposed of the case. "(I)t is settled law (the Board concluded), that when an employer seeks to justify the refusal of a wage increase upon an economic basis, as did the Respondent herein, good-faith bargaining under the Act requires that upon request the employer attempt to substantiate its economic position by reasonable proof."

This is to make a rule of law out of one item—even if a weighty item—of the evidence. There is no warrant for this. The Board found authority in *Labor Board* v. *Jacobs Mfg. Co.* That case presented a very different situation. The Jacobs Company had engaged in a course of conduct which the Board held to be a violation of Section 8(a)(5). The Court of Appeals agreed that in light of the whole record the Board was entitled to find that the employer had not bargained in good faith. Its refusal to open its "books and sales records" for union perusal was only part of the recalcitrant conduct and only one consideration in establishing want of good faith. The unfair labor practice was not founded on this refusal, and the Court's principal concern about the disclosure of financial information was whether the Board's order should be enforced in this respect. The court sustained the Board's requirement for disclosure which "will be met if the respondent produces whatever relevant information it has to indicate whether it can or cannot afford to comply with the union's demands." This a very far cry indeed from a ruling of law that failure to open a company's books establishes lack of good faith. Once good faith is found wanting, the scope of relief to be given by the Board is largely a question of administrative discretion. Neither Jacobs nor any other Court of Appeals' decision which has been called to our attention supports the rule of law which the Board has fashioned out of one thread drawn from the whole fabric of the evidence in this case.

The Labor Board itself has not always approached "good faith" and the disclosure question in such a mechanical fashion. In Southern Saddlery Co., the Board also found that Section 8(a)(5) had been violated. But how differently the Board there considered its function.

Bargaining in good faith is a duty on both sides to enter into discussions with an open and fair mind and a sincere purpose to find a basis for agreement touching wages and hours and conditions of labor. In applying this definition of good faith bargaining to any situation, the Board examines the Respondent's conduct as a whole for a clear indication as to whether the latter has refused to bargain in good faith, and the Board usually does not rely upon any one factor as conclusive evidence that the Respondent did not genuinely try to reach an agreement.

The Board found other factors in the Southern Saddlery case. The employer had made no counterproposals or efforts to "compromise the controversy." Compare, McLean-Arkansas Lumber Co., Inc. Such specific evidence is not indispensable, for a study of all the evidence in a record may disclose a mood indicative of a determination not to bargain. That is for the Board to decide. It is a process of inference-drawing, however, very different from the *ultra vires* law-making of the Board in this case.

Since the Board applied the wrong standard here, by ruling that Truitt's failure to supply financial information to the union constituted *per se* a refusal to bargain in good faith, the case should be returned to the Board. There is substantial evidence in the record which indicates that Truitt tried to reach an agreement. It offered a 2½-cent wage increase, it expressed willingness to discuss with the union "at any time how our wages compare with those of our competition," and it continued throughout to meet and discuss the controversy with the union.

Because the record is not conclusive as a matter of law, one way or the other, I cannot join in the Court's disposition of the case. To reverse the Court of Appeals without remanding the case to the Board for further proceedings implies that the Board would have reached the same conclusion in applying the right rule of law that it did in applying a wrong one. I cannot make such a forecast. I would return the case to the Board so that it may apply the relevant standard for determining "good faith."

Supreme Court of the United States
National Labor Relations Board v. Wooster Division of Borg-Warner Corporation
May 5, 1958, 356 U.S. 342

[This case involved the management's insistence on the inclusion in a collective bargaining agreement of a "ballot" clause and a "recognition" clause. The abstract presented here deals only with the "ballot" clause.]

Mr. Justice Burton delivered the opinion of the Court.

. . . The issue turns on whether . . . the "ballot clause" comes within the scope of mandatory collective bargaining as defined in Section 8(d) of the Act. For the reasons hereafter stated, we agree with the Board . . . [this clause does not come] within that definition. Therefore, we sustain the Board's order directing the employer to cease insisting upon . . . [this clause] as a condition precedent to accepting any collective bargaining contract.

The "ballot" clause . . . provides that, as to all nonarbitrable issues (which eventually included modification, amendment or termination of the contract), there would be a 30-day negotiation period after which, before the union could strike, there would have to be a secret ballot taken among all employees in the unit (union and nonunion) on the company's last offer. In the event a majority of the employees rejected the company's last offer, the company would have an opportunity, within 72 hours, of making a new proposal and having a vote on it prior to any strike. The unions' negotiators announced they would not accept this clause "under any conditions."

. . .

The company's good faith has met the requirements of the statute as to the subjects of mandatory bargaining. But that good faith does not license the employer to refuse to enter into agreements on the ground that they do not include some proposal which is not a mandatory subject of bargaining. We agree with the Board that such conduct is, in substance, a refusal to bargain about the subjects that are within the scope of mandatory bargaining. . . .

Since it is lawful to insist upon matters within the scope of mandatory bargaining and unlawful to insist upon matters without, the issue here is whether the "ballot" . . . clause is a subject within the phrase "wages, hours, and other terms or conditions of employment" which defines mandatory bargaining. The "ballot" clause is not within that definition. It relates to the procedure to be followed by the employees among themselves before their representative may call a strike or refuse a final offer. It settles no term or condition of employment—it merely calls for an advisory vote of the employees. It is not a partial "no-strike" clause. A "no-strike" clause prohibits the employees from striking during the life of the contract. It regulates the relations between the employer and the employees. . . . The "ballot" clause, on the other hand, deals only with relations between the employees and their unions. It substantially modifies the collective bargaining system provided for in the statute by weakening the independence of the "representative" chosen by the employees. It enables the employer, in effect, to deal with its employees rather than their statutory representative. . . .

. . .

Accordingly, the judgment of the Court of Appeals in No. 53 is reversed and the cause remanded for disposition consistent with this opinion.

Wooster Division of Borg-Warner Corp.
Dissenting Opinion

Mr. Justice Harlan, whom Mr. Justice Clark, Mr. Justice Whittaker, and Mr. Justice Frankfurter join, dissenting.

. . .

The legislative history behind the Wagner and Taft-Hartley Acts persuasively indicates that the Board was never intended to have power to prevent good faith bargaining as to any subject not violative of the provisions or policies of those Acts. . . .

It must not be forgotten that the Act requires bargaining, *not* agreement, for the obligation to bargain ". . . does not compel either party to agree to a proposal or require the making of a concession" 8(d). Here the employer concededly bargained but simply refused to *agree* until the union would accept what the Court holds would have been a lawful contract provision. It may be that an employer or union, by adamant insistence in good faith upon a provision which is not a statutory subject under Section 8(d), does in fact require the other party to bargain over it. But this effect is traceable to the economic power of the employer or union in the circumstances of a given situation and should not affect our construction of the Act. If one thing is clear, it is that the Board was not viewed by Congress as an agency which should exercise its powers to aid a party to collective bargaining which was in an economically disadvantageous position.

The most cursory view of decisions of the Board and the circuit courts under the National Labor Relations Act reveals the unsettled and evolving character of collective bargaining agreements. Provisions which two decades ago might have been thought to be the exclusive concern of labor or management are today commonplace in such agreements. The bargaining process should be left fluid, free from intervention of the Board leading to premature crystallization of labor agreements into any one pattern of contract provisions, so that these agreements can be adapted through collective bargaining to the changing needs of our society and to the changing concepts of the responsibilities of labor and management. What the Court does today may impede this evolutionary process. . . .

As unqualifiedly stated [by this Court in American National Life Insurance, 343 US 409] it is through the "good faith" requirement of Section 8(d) that the Board is to enforce the bargaining provisions of Section 8. A determination that a party bargained as to statutory or nonstatutory subjects in good or bad faith must depend upon an evaluation of the total circumstances surrounding any given situation. I do not deny that there may be instances where unyielding insistence on a particular item may be a relevant consideration in the overall picture in determining "good faith," for the demands of a party might in the context of a particular industry be so extreme as to constitute some evidence of unwillingness to bargain. But no such situation is presented in this instance by the "ballot" clause. . . .

. . . here the Court recognizes, as it must, that the clause is lawful under the Act, and I think it clear that the Company's insistence upon it violated no statutory duty to which it was subject. . . .

Supreme Court of the United States
NLRB v. Insurance Agents; International Union, AFL-CIO
February 23, 1960, 361 U.S. 477

Mr. Justice Brennan delivered the opinion of the Court.

. . . The precise question is whether the Board may find that a union, which confers with an employer with the desire of reaching agreement on contract terms, has nevertheless refused to bargain collectively, thus violating this provision solely and simply because during the negotiations it seeks to put economic pressure on the employer to yield to its bargaining demands by sponsoring on-the-job conduct designed to interfere with the carrying on of the employer's business.

. . .

In January, 1956, Prudential and the union began the negotiation of a new contract to replace an agreement expiring in the following March. Bargaining was carried on continuously for six months before the terms of the new contract were agreed upon on July 17, 1956. It is not questioned that, if it stood alone, the record of negotiations would establish that the union conferred in good faith for the purpose and with the desire of reaching agreement with Prudential on a contract.

However, in April, 1956, Prudential filed an 8(b)(3) charge of refusal to bargain collectively against the union. The charge was based upon actions of the union and its members outside the conference room, occurring after the old contract expired in March. . . .

A complaint of violation of 8(b)(3) issued on the charge and hearings began before the bargaining was concluded. It was developed in the evidence that the union's harassing tactics involved activities by the member agents such as these: refusal for a time to solicit new business, and refusal (after the writing of new business was resumed) to comply with the company's reporting procedures; refusal to participate in the company's "May Policyholders' Month Campaign"; reporting late at district offices the days the agents were scheduled to attend them, and refusing to perform customary duties at the offices, instead engaging there in "sit-in-mornings," "doing what comes naturally" and leaving at noon as a group; absenting themselves from special business conferences arranged by the company; picketing and distributing leaflets outside the various offices of the company on specified days and hours as directed by the unions; distributing leaflets each day to policyholders and others and soliciting policyholders' signatures on petitions directed to the company; and presenting the signed policyholders' petitions to the company at its home office while simultaneously engaging in mass demonstrations there.

. . .

. . . the Board . . . entered a cease and desist order. . . . The Court of Appeals for the District of Columbia Circuit . . . set aside the Board's order. . . .

. . . Obviously there is a tension between the principle that the parties need not contract on any specific terms and a practical enforcement of the principle that they are bound to deal with each other in a serious attempt to resolve differences and reach a common ground. And in fact criticism of the Board's application of the "good-faith" test arose from the belief that it was forcing employers to yield to union demands if they were to avoid a successful charge of unfair labor practice. Thus, in 1947, in Congress the fear was expressed that the Board had "gone very far, in the guise of determining whether or not employers had bargained in good faith, in setting itself up as the judge of what concessions an employer must make and of the proposals and counterproposals that he may or may not make.". . . Since the Board was not viewed by Congress as an agency which should exercise its powers to arbitrate the parties' substantive solutions of the issues in their bargaining, a check on this apprehended trend was provided by writing the good-faith test of bargaining into 8(d) of the Taft-Hartley Act. . . .

. . .

. . . It is apparent from the legislative history of the whole Act that the policy of Congress is to impose a mutual duty upon the parties to confer in good faith with a desire to reach agreement, in the belief that such an approach from both sides of the table promotes the over-all design of achieving industrial peace.

. . .

. . . It must be realized that collective bargaining, under a system where the government does not attempt to control the results of negotiations, cannot be equated with an academic collective search for truth—or even with what might be thought to be the ideal of one. The parties—even granting the modification of views that may come from a realization of economic interdependence—still proceed from contrary, and to an extent antagonistic, viewpoints and concepts of self-interest. The system

has not reached the ideal of the philosophic notion that perfect understanding among people would lead to perfect agreement among them on
values. The presence of economic weapons in reserve, and their actual
exercise on occasion by the parties, is part and parcel of the system that
the Wagner and Taft-Hartley Acts have recognized. . . .

. . . we think the Board's approach involves an intrusion into the
substantive aspects of the bargaining process—again, unless there is some
specific warrant for its condemnation of the precise tactics involved here.
The scope of 8(b)(3) and the limitation on Board power which were the
design of 8(d) are exceeded, we hold, by inferring a lack of good faith
not from any deficiencies of the union's performance at the bargaining
table by reason of its attempted use of economic pressure, but solely and
simply because tactics designed to exert economic pressure were employed
during the course of the good-faith negotiations. Thus the Board in the
guise of determining good or bad faith in negotiations could regulate what
economic weapons a party might summon to its aid. And if the Board
could regulate the choice of economic weapons that may be used as part
of collective bargaining, it would be in a position to exercise considerable
influence upon the substantive terms on which the parties contract. As the
parties' own devices became more limited, the government might have to
enter even more directly into the negotiation of collective agreements.
Our labor policy is not presently erected on a foundation of government
control of the results of negotiations. . . .

. . . The Board contends that because an orthodox "total" strike is
"traditional," its use must be taken as being consistent with 9(b)(3); but
since the tactics here are not "traditional" or "normal," they need not be
so viewed. Further, the Board cites what it conceives to be the public's
moral condemnation of the sort of employee tactics involved here. But
again we cannot see how these distinctions can be made under a statute
which simply enjoins a duty to bargain in good faith. Again these relevant
arguments when the question is the scope of the concerted activities given
affirmative protections by the Act. But as we have developed, the use of
economic pressure by the parties to a labor dispute is not a grudging
exception to some policy of completely academic discussion enjoined by
the Act; it is part and parcel of the process of collective bargaining. On
this basis, we fail to see the relevance of whether the practice in question
is time-honored or whether its exercise is generally supported by public
opinion. It may be that the tactics used here deserve condemnation, but
this would not justify attempting to pour that condemnation into a vessel
not designed to hold it. . . .

. . . These distinctions essayed by the Board here, and the lack of
relationship to the statutory standard inherent in them, confirm us in our
conclusion that the judgment of the Court of Appeals, setting aside the

order of the Board, must be affirmed. For they make clear to us that when the Board moves in this area, with only 8(b)(3) for support, it is functioning as an arbiter of the sort of economic weapons the parties can use in seeking to gain acceptance of their bargaining demands. It has sought to introduce some standard of properly "balanced" bargaining power, or some new distinction of justifiable and unjustifiable, proper and "abusive" economic weapons into the collective bargaining duty imposed by the Act. The Board's assertion of power under 8(b)(3) allows it to sit in judgment upon every economic weapon the parties to a labor contract negotiation employ, judging it on the very general standard of that section, not drafted with reference to specific forms of economic pressure. We have expressed our belief that this amounts to the Board's entrance into the substantive aspects of the bargaining process to an extent Congress has not countenanced.

It is one thing to say that the Board has been afforded flexibility to determine, for example, whether an employer's disciplinary action taken against specific workers is permissable or not, or whether a party's conduct at the bargaining table evidences a real desire to come into agreement. The statute in such areas clearly poses the problem to the Board for its solution. . . . It is quite another matter, however, to say that the Board has been afforded flexibility in picking and choosing which economic devices of labor and management shall be branded as unlawful. Congress has been rather specific when it has come to outlaw particular economic weapons on the part of unions. . . . But the activities here involved have never been specifically outlawed by Congress. To be sure, the express prohibitions of the Act are not exclusive—if there were any questions of a strategem or device to evade the policies of the Act, the Board hardly would be powerless. . . . But it is clear to us that the Board needs a more specific charter than 8(b)(3) before it can add to the Act's prohibitions here.

· · ·

It is suggested here that the time has come for a reevaluation of the basic content of collective bargaining as contemplated by the federal legislation. But that is for Congress. Congress has demonstrated its capacity to adjust the nation's labor legislation to what, in its legislative judgment, constitutes the statutory pattern appropriate to the developing state of labor relations in the country. Major revisions of the basic statute were enacted in 1947 and 1959. To be sure, then, Congress might be of opinion that greater stress should be put on the role of "pure" negotiation in settling labor disputes, to the extent of eliminating more and more economic weapons from the parties' grasp, and perhaps it might start with the ones involved here; or in consideration of the alternatives, it might shrink from such an undertaking. But Congress' policy has not yet moved to this point, and with only 8(b)(3) to lean on, we do not see how the Board can do so on its own.

Affirmed.

Insurance Agents Separate Opinion

Separate opinion of Mr. Justice Frankfurter, which Mr. Justice
Harlan and Mr. Justice Whittaker join.

. . .

I agree that the position taken by the Board here is not tenable. In
enforcing the duty to bargain the Board must find the ultimate fact
whether, in the case before it and in the context of all its circumstances,
the respondent has engaged in bargaining without the sincere desire to
reach agreement which the Act commands. I further agree that the
Board's action in this case is not sustainable as resting upon a determination that respondent's apparent bargaining was in fact a sham, because the
evidence is insufficient to justify that conclusion even giving the Board, as
we must, every benefit of its right to draw on its experience in interpreting the industrial significance of the facts of a record. . . . What the
Board has in fact done is lay down a rule of law that such conduct as was
involved in carrying out the "Work Without a Contract" program necessarily betokens bad faith in the negotiations.

The Court's opinion rests its conclusion on the generalization that
"The ordinary economic strike is not evidence of a failure to bargain in
good faith . . . (because) there is simply no inconsistency between the
application of economic pressure and good faith collective bargaining."
This large statement is justified solely by reference to 8(b)(3) and to the
proposition that inherent in bargaining is room for the play of forces
which reveal the strength of one party, or the weakness of the other, in
the economic context in which they seek agreement. But in determining
the state of mind of a party to collective bargaining negotiations the
Board does not deal in terms of abstract "economic pressure." It must
proceed in terms of specific conduct which it weighs as a more or less
reliable manifestation of the state of mind with which bargaining is
conducted. No conduct in the complex context of bargaining for a labor
agreement can profitably be reduced to such an abstraction as "economic
pressure." An exertion of "economic pressure" may at the same time be
part of a concerted effort to evade or disrupt a normal course of negotiations. Vital differences in conduct, varying in character and effect from
mild persuasion to destructive, albeit "economic," violence are obscured
under cover of a single abstract phrase.

While 8(b)(3) of course contemplates some play of "economic
pressure," it does not follow that the purpose in engaging in tactics
designed to exert it is to reach agreement through the bargaining process
in the manner which the statute commands, so that the Board is precluded
from considering such conduct, in the totality of circumstances as evidence of the actual state of mind of the actor. Surely to deny this scope
for allowable judgment to the Board is to deny to it the special function
with which it has been entrusted. . . .

. . . One need not romanticize the community of interest between employers and employees, or be unmindful of the conflict between them, to recognize that utilization of what in one set of circumstances may only signify resort to the traditional weapons of labor may in another and relevant context offend the attitude toward bargaining commanded by the statute. . . .

. . . . .

. . . The broadly phrased terms of the Taft-Hartley Law should be applied to carry out the broadly conceived policies of the Act. At the core of the promotion of collection bargaining which was the chief means by which the great social purposes of the National Labor Relations Act were sought to be furthered, is a purpose to discourage, more and more, industrial combatants from pressing their demands by all available means to the limits of the justification of self-interest. This calls for appropriate judicial construction of existing legislation. The statute lays its emphasis upon reason and a willingness to employ it as the dominant force in bargaining. That emphasis is respected by declining to take as a postulate of the duty to bargain that the legally impermissable exertions of so-called economic pressure must be restricted to the crudities of brute force. . . .

. . . . .

The Board urges that this Court has approved its enforcement of 8(b)(3) by the outlawing of conduct *per se,* and without regard to ascertainment of a state of mind. It relies upon four cases: . . . These cases do not sustain its position. . . . To the extent that in any of these cases language referred to a *per se* proscription of conduct, it was in relation to facts strongly indicating a lack of a sincere desire to reach agreement.

. . . . .

. . . Viewed as a determination upon all the evidence that the respondent was bargaining without the sincere desire to compose differences and reach agreement which the statute commands, the Board's conclusion must fall for want of support in the evidence as a whole. . . . From the conduct of its counsel before the Trial Examiner, and from its opinion, it is apparent that the Board proceeded upon the belief that respondent's tactics were, without more, sufficient evidence of a lack of a sincere desire to reach agreement to make other consideration of its conduct unnecessary. For that reason the case should be remanded to the Board for further opportunity to introduce pertinent evidence, if any there be, of respondent's lack of good faith.

Viewed as a determination by the Board that it could, quite apart from respondent's state of mind, proscribe its tactics because they were not "traditional," or were thought to be subject to public disapproval, or because employees who engaged in them may have been subject to discharge, the Board's conclusion proceeds from the application of an erroneous rule of law.

The decision of the Court of Appeals should be vacated, and the case remanded to the Board for further proceedings consistent with these views.

PART III. COMMENTS ON PUBLIC POLICY

The first following comment was prepared by a distinguished Independent Study Group of nine members under the chairmanship of Clark Kerr, President of the University of California.

The second following comment is by Stanley M. Jacks, Associate Professor of Industrial Management, Massachusetts Institute of Technology.

"The Duty to Bargain in Good Faith"*

The present national policy also calls on both employers and unions to bargain in good faith over wages, hours, and working conditions. The original intent of this provision was to ensure a minimal degree of recognition so that efforts to decide the question of representation by an orderly process would not be frustrated. Senator David I. Walsh, then Chairman of the Senate Committee on Education and Labor, in arguing for this provision in 1935, said:

When the employees have chosen their organization, when they have selected their representatives, all the bill proposes to do is to escort them to the door of the employer and say, "Here they are, the legal representatives of your employees." What happens behind those doors is not inquired into, and the bill does not seek to inquire into it.

Senator Walsh's objective was a sensible one, and an appealingly simple one, too. Unfortunately, as time has passed, the simplicity has been lost. It has been succeeded by a flood of litigation and an increasingly complex set of regulations stemming from amendments of the original provisions and from interpretations by the NLRB and the courts. The efficacy of the process is achieving a more ambitious objective—to compel the parties to bargain in good faith—is at best doubtful.

Parties have been told that they must bargain in good faith, and elaborate tests have been devised in an attempt to determine "objectively" whether the proper subjective attitude prevails. The limitations and artificiality of such tests are apparent, and the possibilities of evasion are almost limitless. In the light of the realities of the bargaining situation, distinctions between matters that are subject to "mandatory bargaining" and those that are not have a hollow ring. Basically, it is unrealistic to expect that, by legislation, "good faith" can be brought to the bargaining table. Indeed, the provisions designed to bring "good faith" have become a tactical weapon used in many situations as a means of harassment.

* Excerpts from *The Public Interests in National Labor Policy* by an Independent Study Group, Committee for Economic Development, 1960, pp. 81–82.

Delays in processing duty-to-bargain cases and in getting final court orders have undoubtedly contributed to the ineffectiveness of the efforts in this area and to the use of economic force *in lieu* of resort to the legal machinery. But, too much cannot be expected in the way of reducing delay, since the area is one in which delays can easily be provoked if one party so desires.

The subjects to be covered by bargaining, the procedures to be followed, the nuances of strategy involving the timing of a "best offer," the question of whether to reopen a contract during its term—such matters as these are best left to the parties themselves. Indeed, the work load of the National Labor Relations Board and of the parties could be substantially reduced by returning these issues to the door of the employer or union, where Senator Walsh wisely left them.

"National Labor Policy and the Duty to Bargain Collectively"*

Converting the obligation to bargain collectively toward more limited goals, however, poses problems which the CED Report does not consider and, in fact, tends to obscure. The duty to bargain collectively in good faith serves more than one purpose. It compels acceptance of the principle of collective bargaining as well as good faith at the bargaining table. The principle of collective bargaining excludes unilateral action by the employer or the negotiation of terms and conditions with individual employees. It requires that the employer treat union demands as something more than suggestions to which he can respond or not at his pleasure. If the recommendation in the CED Report that "the effort to legislate bargaining in good faith should be abandoned" is to be implemented, a question arises whether the requirement of good faith acceptance of the principle of collective bargaining is to be retained. Assuming that it is desired to retain this requirement, a point on which the CED Report is not clear, it follows that the good faith concept cannot be entirely extirpated from the law. The problem becomes one of delimiting the concept so as to leave the parties free to negotiate after their own fashion.

.   .   .

It is not clear, however, whether the authors of the CED Report seek to contain the law of bargaining or whether they would abolish it. If the Report is read to recommend a policy aimed only at orderly selection of employee representatives (a policy which the Report erroneously attributes to the framers of the Wagner Act) the foundation for the current law of bargaining would be removed. Such a proposal would raise profound questions for the future of labor relations in the unorganized sector of the economy and for parts of the organized sector as well. If the law were now to withdraw the obligation of the employer to deal in any

* Excerpts from an article by Stanley M. Jacks appearing in *Industrial Management Review*, Vol. III (Spring, 1962), pp. 46–59.

meaningful sense with the representative selected by the employees and impose no constraints upon employer conduct other than the requirement that he not deal with a minority union, the mode of establishing collective bargaining relationships would be drastically altered. While strategically situated employees, particularly those backed by powerful unions, would not feel the full impact of the change, other employees, such as the Southern textile workers, those engaged in agriculture, workers in service trades, etc., would feel keenly the absence of the legal leverage in effectuating collective bargaining which labor has enjoyed for the past quarter century. Even in organized companies the employer would find himself related very differently to the union. While the impact would vary depending on the power of the union and the quality of the relationship between the parties, aggressive managements might be encouraged to force a test of strength.

. . . The following statutory definition of bargaining, however, would appear to achieve the principal objectives of the CED proposals. The phrase "to bargain collectively" would then be defined as:

The performance of the mutual obligation of the employer and the representative of the employees to meet at reasonable times and confer with respect to wages, hours, and other terms and conditions of employment, or the negotiation of an agreement, or any question arising thereunder, and the execution of a written contract incorporating any agreement reached if requested by either party, but such obligation does not compel either party to agree to a proposal or make a counterproposal or require the making of a concession. Nor shall such obligation limit the right of either party to insist upon the inclusion of any lawful provision as a condition of agreement.

QUESTIONS

1. What is the obligation to bargain in good faith?
2. Following the line of thought presented in the dissents and separate opinions in Truitt, Wooster Division of Borg-Warner, and Insurance Agents, how would the Board put proper emphasis on particular subjects for bargaining when considered in a context of bargaining tactics?
3. In creating "nonmandatory" subjects has the Board usurped the power of Congress to create "unlawful" subjects? What alternative was available to the Board?
4. Although Professor Jacks has drafted a clause to implement the Independent Study Group's recommendation, he has serious misgivings about enacting the clause into law. Are his misgivings well founded?

Case 2

LABOR ARBITRATION AND THE COURTS

Voluntary labor arbitration is widely used in the United States. It has been estimated that over 90 per cent of all American labor agreements provide for voluntary arbitration as the terminal point in the handling of some grievances. In some parts of the world, governmentally established labor courts perform the functions assigned to private arbitrators in the United States.

The Supreme Court decisions which make up most of this case deal with the question of the legal enforceability of an agreement to arbitrate and judicial review of arbitrators' awards. In addition to dealing with an important legal question, the opinions in these cases contain interesting comments on the arbitration process and its function in the broader process of collective bargaining.

Supreme Court of the United States
United Steelworkers of America v. American Manufacturing
Company
June 20, 1960, 363 U.S. 564

Mr. Justice Douglas delivered the opinion of the Court.

The suit was brought by petitioner union in the District Court to compel arbitration of a "grievance" that petitioner, acting for one Sparks, a union member, had filed with the respondent, Sparks's employer. The employer defended on the ground (1) that Sparks is estopped from making his claim because he had a few days previously settled a workmen's compensation claim against the company on the basis that he was permanently partially disabled; (2) that Sparks is not physically able to do the work; and (3) that this type of dispute is not arbitrable under the collective bargaining agreement in question.

The agreement provided that during its term there would be "no strike" unless the employer refused to abide by a decision of the arbitrator. The agreement sets out a detailed grievance procedure with a provision for arbitration (regarded as the standard form) of all disputes between the parties "as to the meaning, interpretation and application of the provisions of this agreement."

The agreement also reserves to the management power to suspend or discharge any employee "for cause."

It also contains a provision that the employer will employ and promote employees on the principle of seniority "where ability and efficiency are equal." Sparks left his work due to an injury and while off work brought an action for compensation benefits. The case was settled, Sparks's physician expressing the opinion that the injury had made him 25 percent permanently partially disabled. That was on September 9. Two weeks later the union filed a grievance which charged that Sparks was entitled to return to his job by virtue of the seniority provision of the collective bargaining agreement. Respondent refused to arbitrate and this acton was brought. The District Court held that Sparks, having accepted the settlement on the basis of permanent partial disability was estopped to claim any seniority or employment rights and granted the motion for summary judgment. The Court of Appeals affirmed for different reasons. After reviewing the evidence it held that the grievance is "a frivolous, patently baseless one, not subject to arbitration under the collective bargaining agreement." The case is here on a writ of certiorari.

Section 203(d) of the Labor Management Relations Act, 1947, states "Final adjustment by a method agreed upon by the parties is hereby declared to be the desirable method for settlement of grievance disputes arising over the application or interpretation of an existing collective-bargaining agreement***." That policy can be effectuated only if the means chosen by the parties for settlement of their differences under a collective bargaining agreement is given full play.

. . . The collective agreement required arbitration of claims that courts might be unwilling to entertain. Yet in the context of the plant or industry, the grievance may assume proportions of which judges are ignorant. Moreover, the agreement is to submit all grievances to arbitration, not merely those that a court may deem to be meritorious. There is no exception in the "no-strike" clause and none therefore should be read into the grievance clause since one is the *quid pro quo* for the other. The question is not whether in the mind of a court there is equity in the claim. Arbitration is a stabilizing influence only as it serves as a vehicle for handling every and all disputes that arise under the agreement.

The collective agreement calls for the submission of grievances in the categories which it describes irrespective of whether a court may deem them to be meritorious. . . . The function of the court is very limited when the parties have agreed to submit all questions of contract interpretation to the arbitrator. It is then confined to ascertaining whether the party seeking arbitration is making a claim which on its face is governed by the contract. Whether the moving party is right or wrong is a question of contract interpretation for the arbitrator. In these circumstances the moving party should not be deprived of the arbitrator's judgment, when it was his judgment and all that it connotes that was bargained for.

The courts therefore have no business weighing the merits of the grievance, considering whether there is equity in a particular claim, or determining whether there is particular language in the written instrument which will support the claim. The agreement is to submit all grievances to arbitration, not merely those the court will deem meritorious. The processing of even frivolous claims may have therapeutic values which those who are not a part of the plant environment may be quite unaware.

The union claimed in this case that the company had violated a specific provision of the contract. The company took the position that it had not violated that clause. There was, therefore, a dispute between the parties as to "the meaning, interpretation and application" of the collective bargaining agreement. Arbitration should have been ordered. When the judiciary undertakes to determine the merits of a grievance under the guise of interpreting the grievance procedure of collective bargaining agreements, it usurps a function which under that regime is entrusted to the arbitration tribunal.

Reversed.

Mr. Justice Frankfurter concurs in the result.

Mr. Justice Whittaker, believing that the District Court lacked jurisdiction to determine the merits of the claim which the parties had validly agreed to submit to the exclusive jurisdiction of a Board of Arbitrators, concurs in the result of this opinion.

Mr. Justice Black took no part in the consideration or decision of this case.

Supreme Court of the United States
United Steelworkers of America v. Warrior and Gulf Navigation Company
June 20, 1960, 363 U.S. 574

Mr. Justice Douglas delivered the opinion of the Court.

Respondent transports steel and steel products by barge and maintains a terminal at Chicasaw, Alabama, where it performs maintenance and repair work on its barges. The employees at that terminal constitute a bargaining unit covered by a collective bargaining agreement negotiated by petitioner union. Respondent between 1956 and 1958 laid off some employees, reducing the bargaining unit from 42 to 23 men. This reduction was due in part to respondent contracting maintenance work, previously done by its employees, to other companies. The latter used respondent's supervisors to lay out the work and hired some of the laid-off employees of respondent (at reduced wages). Some were in fact assigned to work on respondent's barges. A number of employees signed a grievance which petitioner presented to respondent, the grievance reading:

We are hereby protesting the Company's actions, of arbitrarily and unreasonably contracting out work to other concerns, that could and previously has been performed by Company employees.

This practice became unreasonable, unjust and discriminatory in view of the fact that at present there are a number of employees that have been laid off for about 1 and ½ years or more for allegedly lack of work.

Confronted with these facts we charge that the Company is in violation of the contract by inducing a partial lockout, of a number of the employees who would otherwise be working were it not for this unfair practice.

The collective agreement had both a "no-strike" and a "no-lockout" provision. It also had a grievance procedure which provided in relevant part as follows:

Issues which conflict with any Federal statute in its application as established by Court procedure or matters which are strictly a function of management shall not be subject to arbitration under this section.

Should differences arise between the Company and the Union or its members employed by the Company as to the meaning and application of the provisions of this Agreement, or should any local trouble of any kind arise, there shall be no suspension of work on account of such differences but an earnest effort shall be made to settle such differences immediately in the following manner:

A. For Maintenance Employees:

First, between the aggrieved employees, and the Foreman involved; Second, between a member or members of the Grievance Committee designated by the Union, and the Foreman and Master Mechanics.***

Fifth, if agreement has not been reached, the matter shall be referred to an impartial umpire for decision. The parties shall meet to decide on an umpire acceptable to both. If no agreement on selection of an umpire is reached, the parties shall jointly petition the United States Conciliation Service for suggestion of a list of umpires from which selection will be made. The decision of the umpire shall be final.

Settlement of this grievance was not had and respondent refused arbitration. This suit was then commenced by the union to compel it. . . . The District Court granted respondent's motion to dismiss the complaint. It held after hearing evidence, much of which went to the merits of the grievances, that the agreement did not "confide in an arbitrator the right to review the defendant's business judgment in contracting out work." It further held that "the contracting out of repair and maintenance work, as well as construction work, is strictly a function of management not limited in any respect by the labor agreement involved here." The Court of Appeals affirmed by a divided vote, the majority holding that the collective agreement had withdrawn from the grievance procedure "matters which are strictly a function of management" and that contracting-out fell in that exception. The case is here on a writ of certiorari.

We held in *Textile Workers* v. *Lincoln Mills* that a grievance arbitration provision in a collective agreement could be enforced by reason of paragraph 301(a) of the Labor Management Relations Act and that the policy to be applied in enforcing this type of arbitration was that reflected in our national labor laws. The present federal policy is to promote industrial stabilization through the collective bargaining agreement. A major factor in achieving industrial peace is the inclusion of a provision for arbitration of grievances in the collective bargaining agreement.[4]

Thus the run of arbitration cases become irrelevant to our problem. There the choice is between the adjudication of cases or controversies in courts with established procedures or even special statutory safeguards on the one hand and the settlement of them in the more informal arbitration tribunal on the other. In the commercial case, arbitration is the substitute for litigation. Here arbitration is the substitute for industrial strife. Since arbitration of labor disputes has quite different functions from arbitration under an ordinary commercial agreement, the hostility evinced by courts toward arbitration of commercial agreements has no place here. For arbitration of labor disputes under collective bargaining agreements is part and parcel of the collective bargaining process itself.

The collective bargaining agreement states the rights and duties of the parties. It is more than a contract; it is a generalized code to govern a myriad of cases which the draftsmen cannot wholly anticipate. . . . It calls into being a new common law—the common law of a particular industry or of a particular plant.

. . .

A collective bargaining agreement is an effort to erect a system of industrial self-government. When most parties enter into contractual relationship, they do so voluntarily. In the sense that there is no real compulsion to deal with one another, as opposed to dealing with other parties. This is not true of the labor agreement. The choice is generally not between entering or refusing to enter into a relationship, for that in all probability pre-exists the negotiations. Rather it is between having that relationship governed by an agreed upon rule of law or leaving each and every matter subject to a temporary resolution dependent solely upon the relative strength, at any given moment, of the contending forces. The mature labor agreement may attempt to regulate all aspects of the complicated relationship, from the most crucial to the most minute over an extended period of time. Because of the compulsion to reach agreement and breadth of the matters covered, as well as the need for a fairly concise and readable instrument, the product of negotiations (the written document) is, in the words of the late Dean Shulman, "a compilation of diverse provisions; some provide objective criteria almost automatically applicable; some provide more or less specific standards which require reason and judgment in their application; and some do little more than leave problems to future consideration with an expression of hope and good faith." Gaps may be left to be filled in by reference to the practices of the particular industry and of the various shops covered by the agreement. Many of the

[4] Complete effectuation of the federal policy is achieved when the agreement contains both an arbitration provision for all unresolved grievances and an absolute prohibition of strikes, the arbitration agreement being the *quid pro quo* for the agreement to strike.

specific practices which underlie the agreement may be unknown except in hazy form, even to the negotiators. Courts and arbitration in the context of most commercial contracts are resorted to because there has been a breakdown in the working relationship of the parties; such resort is the unwanted exception. But the grievance machinery under a collective bargaining agreement is at the very heart of the system of industrial self-government. Arbitration is the means of solving the unforeseeable by molding a system of private law for all the problems which may arise and to provide for their solution in a way which will generally accord with the variant needs and desires of the parties. The processing of disputes through the grievance machinery is actually a vehicle by which meaning and content is given to the collective bargaining agreement.

Apart from matters that the parties specifically exclude, all of the questions on which the parties disagree must therefore come within the scope of the grievance and arbitration provisions of the collective agreement. The grievance procedure is, in other words, a part of the continuous collective bargaining process. It, rather than a strike, is the terminal point of a disagreement.

. . .

The labor arbitrator performs functions which are not normal to the courts; the considerations which help him fashion judgments may indeed be foreign to the competence of courts. The labor arbitrator's source of law is not confined to the express provisions of the contract, as the industrial common law—the practices of the industry and the shop—is equally a part of the collective bargaining agreement although not expressed in it. The labor arbitrator is usually chosen because of the parties' confidence in his knowledge of the common law of the shop and their trust in his personal judgment to bring to bear considerations which are not expressed in the contract as criteria for judgment. The parties expect that his judgment of a particular grievance will reflect not only what the contract says but, insofar as the collective bargaining agreement permits, such factors as the effect upon productivity of a particular result, its consequence to the morale of the shop, his judgment whether tensions will be heightened or diminished. For the parties' objective in using the arbitration process is primarily to further their common goal of uninterrupted production under the agreement to make the agreement serve their specialized needs. The ablest judge cannot be expected to bring the same experience and competence to bear upon the determination of a grievance, because he cannot be similarly informed.

The Congress, however, has by para. 301 of the Labor Management Relations Act, assigned the courts the duty of determining whether the reluctant party has breached his promise to arbitrate. For arbitration is a matter of contract and a party cannot be required to submit to arbitration any dispute which he has not agreed so to submit. Yet, to be consistent with congressional policy in favor of settlement of disputes by the parties through the machinery of arbitration, the judicial inquiry under para. 301 must be strictly confined to question whether the reluctant party did agree to arbitrate the grievance or agreed to give the arbitrator power to make the award he made. An order to arbitrate the particular grievance should not be denied unless it may be said with positive assurance that the arbitration clause is not susceptible to an interpretation that covers the asserted dispute. Doubts should be resolved in favor of coverage.[7]

We do not agree with the lower courts that contracting-out grievances were necessarily excepted from the grievance procedure of this agreement. To be sure the agreement provides that "matters which are strictly a function of management shall not be subject to arbitration." But it goes on to say that if "differences" arise or if "any local trouble of any kind" arises, the grievance procedure shall be applicable.

Collective bargaining agreements regulate or restrict the exercise of management functions; they do not oust management from the performance of them. Management hires and fires, pays and promotes, supervises and plans. All these are part of its function, and absent a collective bargaining agreement, it may be exercised freely except as limited by public law and by the willingness of employees to work under the particular, unilaterally imposed conditions. A collective bargaining agreement may treat only with certain specific practices, leaving the rest to management but subject to the possibility of work stoppages. When, however, an absolute no-strike clause is included in the agreement, then in a very real sense everything that management does is subject to the agreement, for either management is prohibited or limited in the action it takes, or if not, it is protected from interference by strikes. This comprehensive reach of the collective bargaining agreement does not mean, however, that the language, "strictly a function of management" has no meaning.

"Strictly a function of management" might be thought to refer to any practice of management in which, under particular circumstances prescribed by the agreement, it is permitted to indulge. But if courts . . . determine what is permitted and what is not, the arbitration clause would be swallowed up by the exception. Every grievance in a sense involves a claim that management has violated some provision of the agreement.

Accordingly, "strictly a function of management" must be interpreted as referring only to that over which the contract gives management complete control and unfettered discretion. Respondent claims that the contracting out of work falls within this category. Contracting out

---

[7] It is clear that under both the agreement in this case and that involved in American Manufacturing Co., the question of arbitrability is for the courts to decide. Where the assertion by the claimant is that the parties excluded from court determination not merely the decision of the merits of the grievance but also the question of its arbitrability, vesting power to make both decisions in the arbitrator, the claimant must bear the burden of a clear demonstration of that purpose.

work is the basis of many grievances; and that type of claim is grist in the mills of the arbitrators. A specific collective bargaining agreement may exclude contracting-out from the grievance procedure. Or a written collateral agreement may make clear that contracting out was not a matter for arbitration. In such a case a grievance based solely on contracting out would not be arbitrable. Here, however, there is no such provision. Nor is there any showing that the parties designed the phrase "strictly a function of management" to encompass any and all forms of contracting out. In the absence of any express provision excluding a particular grievance from arbitration, we think only the most forceful evidence of a purpose to exclude the claim from arbitration can prevail, particularly where, as here, the exclusion clause is vague and the arbitration clause quite broad. Since any attempt by a court to infer such a purpose necessarily comprehends the merits, the court should view with suspicion an attempt to persuade it to become entangled in the construction of the substantive provisions of a labor agreement, even through the back door of interpreting the arbitration clause, when the alternative is to utilize the services of an arbitrator.

The grievance alleged that the contracting out was a violation of the collective bargaining agreement. There was, therefore, a dispute "as to the meaning and application of the provisions of this Agreement" which the parties had agreed would be determined by arbitration.

The judiciary sits in these cases to bring into operation an arbitral process which substitutes a regime of peaceful settlement for the older regime of industrial conflict. Whether contracting out in the present case violated the agreement is the question. It is a question for the arbiter, not for the courts. Reversed.

Mr. Justice Frankfurter concurs in the result.

Mr. Justice Black took no part in the consideration or decision of this case.

Warrior and Gulf Dissenting Opinion

Mr. Justice Whittaker, dissenting.

Until today, I have understood it to be the unquestioned law, as this Court has consistently held, that arbitrators are private judges chosen by the parties to decide particular matters specifically submitted; that the contract under which matters are submitted to arbitrators is at once the source and limit of their authority and powers; and that their power to decide issues with finality, thus ousting the normal functions of the courts, must rest upon a clear, definitive agreement of the parties, as such power can never be implied. . . . I believe that the Court today departs the established principles announced in these decisions.

Here, the employer operates a shop for the normal maintenance of its barges, but it is not equipped to make major repairs, and accordingly the employer has, from the beginning of its operations more than 19 years ago, contracted out its major work. During most, if not all, of this time the union has represented the employees in that unit. The District Court found that "(t)hroughout the successive labor agreements between these parties, including the present one, ******* (the Union) has unsuccessfully sought to negotiate changes in the labor contract, and particularly during the negotiation of the present labor agreement, ******* which would have limited the right of the (employer) to continue the practice of contracting out such work."

The labor agreement involved here provides for arbitration of disputes respecting the interpretation and application of the agreement and, arguably, also some other things. But the first says: "(M)atters which are strictly a function of management shall not be subject to arbitration under this section." Although acquiescing for 19 years in the employer's interpretation that contracting out work was "strictly a function of management," and having repeatedly tried—particularly in the negotiation of the agreement involved here—but unsuccessfully, to induce the employer to agree to a covenant that would prohibit it from contracting out work, the union, after having agreed to and signed the contract involved, presented a "grievance" on the ground that the employer's contracting out work at a time when some employees in the unit were laid off for lack of work, constituted a partial "lockout" of employees in violation of the antilockout provision of the agreement.

Being unable to persuade the employer to agree to cease contracting out work or to agree to arbitrate the "grievance," the union brought this action in the District Court, under para. 301 of the Labor Management Relations Act for a decree compelling the employer to submit the "grievance" to arbitration. The District Court, holding that the contracting out of work was, and over a long course of dealings had been interpreted and understood by the parties to be "strictly a function of management," and was therefore specifically excluded from arbitration by the terms of the contract, denied the relief prayed. The Court of Appeals affirmed, and we granted certiorari.

The Court now reverses the judgment of the Court of Appeals. It holds that the arbitrator's source of law is "not confined to the express provisions of the contract," that arbitration should be ordered "unless it may be said with positive assurance that the arbitration clause is not susceptible to an interpretation that covers the asserted dispute," that "(d)oubts (of arbitrability) should be resolved in favor of coverage," and that when as here, "a no-strike clause is included in the agreement, then ******* everything that management does is subject to (arbitration)." I understand the Court thus to hold that the arbitrators are not confined to the express provisions of the contract, that arbitration is to be ordered unless it may be said with positive assurance that arbitration of a particular dispute is excluded by the contract, that doubts of arbitrability are to be resolved in favor of arbitration, and that when as here the contract contains a no-strike clause, everything that management does is subject to arbitration.

This is an entirely new and strange doctrine to me. I suggest, with deference, that it departs both the contract of the parties and the controlling decisions of this Court. I find nothing in the contract that purports to confer upon arbitrators any such general breadth of private judicial power. The Court cites no legislative or judicial authority that creates for or gives to arbitrators such broad general powers. . . .

With respect, I submit that there is nothing in the contract here to indicate that the employer "signified (its) willingness" to submit to arbitrators whether it must cease contracting our work. Certainly no such intention is "made manifest by plain language," as the law "requires," because such consent "is not to be implied." To the contrary, the parties by their conduct over many years interpreted the contracting out of major repair work to be "strictly a function of management," and if, as the concurring opinion suggests, the words of the contract can "be understood only by reference to the background which gave rise to their inclusion," then the interpretation given by the parties over 19 years to the phrase "matters which are strictly a function of management" should logically have some significance here. By their contract, the parties agreed that "matters which are strictly a function of management shall not be subject to arbitration." The union over the course of many years repeatedly tried to induce the employer to agree to a covenant prohibiting the contracting out of work, but was never successful. The union again made such an effort in negotiating the very contract involved here, and, failing of success, signed the contract, knowing, of course, that it did not contain any such covenant, but that, to the contrary, it contained, just as had the former contracts, a covenant that "matters which are strictly a function of management shall not be subject to arbitration." Does not this show that instead of signifying a willingness to submit to arbitration the matter of whether the employer might continue to contract out work, the parties fairly agreed to exclude at least that matter from arbitration? Surely it cannot be said that the parties agreed to such a submission by any "plain language." Does not then the Court's opinion compel the employer "to submit to arbitration (a) question which (it) has not agreed so to submit"?

. . .

I agree with the Court that courts have no proper concern with the "merits" of claims which by contract the parties have agreed to submit to the exclusive jurisdiction of arbitrators. But the question is one of jurisdiction. Neither may entrench upon the jurisdiction of the other. The test is: Did the parties in their contract "manifest by plain language" their willingness to submit the issue in controversy to arbitrators? If they did, then the arbitrators have exclusive jurisdiction of it, and the courts, absent fraud or the like, must respect that exclusive jurisdiction and cannot interfere. But if they did not, then the courts must exercise their jurisdiction, when properly invoked, to protect the citizen against the attempted use by arbitrators of pretended powers actually never conferred. That question always is, and from its very nature must be, a judicial one. Such was the question presented to the District Court and the Court of Appeals here. They found the jurisdictional facts, properly applied the settled law to those facts, and correctly decided the case. I would therefore affirm the judgment.

Supreme Court of the United States
United Steelworkers of America v. Enterprise Wheel and Car Corporation
June 20, 1960, 363 U.S. 593

Mr. Justice Douglas delivered the opinion of the Court.

Petitioner union and respondent during the period relevant here had a collective bargaining agreement which provided that any differences "as to the meaning and application" of the agreement should be submitted to arbitration and that the arbitrator's decision "shall be final and binding on the parties." Special provisions were included concerning the suspension and discharge of employees. The agreement stated:

Should it be determined by the Company or by an arbitrator in accordance with the grievance procedure that the employee has been suspended unjustly or discharged in violation of the provisions of this Agreement, the Company shall reinstate the employee and pay full compensation at the employee's regular rate of pay for the time lost.

The agreement also provided:

* * * It is understood and agreed that neither party will institute *civil suits or legal proceedings* against the other for alleged violation of any of the provisions of this labor contract; instead all disputes will be settled in the manner outlined in this Article III—Adjustment of Grievance.

A group of employees left their jobs in protest against the discharge of one employee. A union official advised them at once to return to work. An official of respondent at their request gave them permission and then rescinded it. The next day they were told they did not have a job any more "until this thing was settled one way or the other."

A grievance was filed; and when respondent finally refused to arbitrate, this suit was brought for specific enforcement of the arbitration provisions of the agreement. The District Court ordered arbitration. The arbitrator found that the discharge of the men was not justified, though their conduct, he said, was improper. In his view the facts warranted at most a suspension of the men for 10 days each. After their discharge and before the arbitration award, the collective bargaining agreement had expired. The union, however, continued to represent the workers at the plant. The arbitrator rejected the contention that expiration of the agreement barred reinstatement of the employees. He held that the provision of the agreement above quoted imposed an unconditional obligation on the employer. He awarded reinstatement with back pay, minus pay for a 10-day suspension and such sums as these employees received from other employment.

Respondent refused to comply with the award. Petitioner moved the District Court for enforcement. The District Court directed respondent to comply. The Court of Appeals, while agreeing that the District Court had jurisdiction to enforce an arbitration award under a collective bargaining agreement, held that the failure of the award to specify the amounts to be deducted from the back pay rendered the award unenforceable. That defect, it agreed, could be remedied by requiring the parties to complete the arbitration. It went on to hold, however, that an award for back pay subsequent to the date of termination of the collective bargaining agreement could not been enforced. It also held that the requirement for reinstatement of the discharged employees was likewise unenforceable because the collective agreement had expired.

The refusal of courts to review the merits of an arbitration award is the proper approach to arbitration under collective bargaining agreements. The federal policy of settling labor disputes by arbitration would be undermined if courts had the final say on the merits of the awards. . . .

When an arbitrator is commissioned to interpret and apply the collective bargaining agreement, he is to bring his informed judgment to bear in order to reach a fair solution of a problem. This is especially true when it comes to formulating remedies. There the need is for flexibility in meeting a wide variety of situations. The draftsmen may never have thought of what specific remedy should be awarded to meet a particular contingency. Nevertheless, an arbitrator is confined to interpretation and application of the collective bargaining agreement; he does not sit to dispense his own brand of industrial justice. He may of course look for guidance from many sources, yet his award is legitimate only so long as it draws its essence from the collective bargaining agreement. When the arbitrator's words manifest an infidelity to this obligation, courts have no choice but to refuse enforcement of the award.

. . . A mere ambiguity in the opinion accompanying an award, which permits the inference that the arbitrator may have exceeded his authority, is not a reason for refusing to enforce the award. Arbitrators have no obligation to the court to give their reasons for an award. To require opinions free of ambiguity may lead arbitrators to play it safe by writing no supporting opinions. This would be undesirable for a well-reasoned opinion tends to engender confidence in the integrity of the process and aids in clarifying the underlying agreement. Moreover, we see no reason to assume that this arbitrator has abused the trust the parties confided in him and has not stayed within the areas marked out for his consideration. It is not apparent that he went beyond the submission. The Court of Appeals' opinion refusing to enforce the reinstatement and partial back pay portions of the award was not based upon any finding that the arbitrator did not premise his award on his construction of the contract. It merely disagreed with the arbitrator's construction of it.

The collective bargaining agreement could have provided that if any of the employees were wrongfully discharged, the remedy would be reinstatement and back pay up to the date they were returned to work. Respondent's major argument seems to be that by applying correct principles of law to the interpretation of the collective bargaining agreement it can be determined that the agreement did not so provide, and that therefore the arbitrator's decision was not based upon the contract. This plenary review by a court of the merits would make meaningless the provisions that the arbitrator's decision is final, for in reality it would almost never be final. . . . . [As we emphasized in American Manufacturing Company] the question of interpretation of the collective bargaining agreement is a question for the arbitrator. It is the arbitrator's construction which was bargained for; and so far as the arbitrator's decision concerns construction of the contract, the courts have no business overruling him because their interpretation of the contract is different from his.

We agree with the Court of Appeals that the judgment of the District Court should be modified so that the amounts due the employees may be definitely determined by arbitration. In all other respects we think the judgment of the District Court should be affirmed. Accordingly, we reverse the judgment of the Court of Appeals except for that modification and remand the case to the District Court for proceedings in conformity with this opinion.

It is so ordered.

Mr. Justice Frankfurter concurs in the result.

Mr. Justice Black took no part in the consideration or decision of this case.

Enterprise Wheel and Car Dissenting Opinion

Mr. Justice Whittaker, dissenting.

Claiming that the employer's discharge on January 18, 1957, of 11 employees violated the provisions of its collective bargaining contract with the employer—covering the period beginning April 5, 1956, and ending April 5, 1957—the union sought and obtained arbitration, under the provisions of the contract, of the issues whether these employees had been discharged in violation of the agreement and, if so, should be ordered reinstated and awarded wages from the time of their wrongful discharge. In August, 1957, more than four months after the collective agreement had expired, these issues were tried before and submitted to a Board of Arbitrators. On April 10, 1958, the arbitrators made their award, finding that the 11 employees had been discharged in violation of the agreement and ordering their reinstatement with back pay at their regular rates from a time 10 days after their discharge to the time of reinstatement. Over the employer's objection that the collective agreement and the submission under it did not authorize nor empower the arbitrators to award reinstatement or wages for any period after the date of expiration of the contract (April 5, 1957), the District Court ordered enforcement of the award. The Court of Appeals modified the judgment by eliminating the requirement that the employer reinstate the employees and pay them wages for the period *after* expiration of the collective agreement, and affirmed it in all other respects, and we granted certiorari.

That the propriety of the discharges, under the collective agreement, was arbitrable under the provisions of that agreement, even after its expiration, is not in issue. Nor is there any issue here as to the power of the arbitrators to award reinstatement status and back pay to the discharged employees to the date of expiration of the collective agreement. It is conceded, too, that the collective agreement expired by its terms on April 5, 1957, and was never extended or renewed.

The sole question here is whether the arbitrators exceeded the submission and their power in awarding reinstatement and back pay for any period after expiration of the collective agreements. Like the Court of Appeals, I think they did. I find nothing in the collective agreement that purports to so authorize. Nor does the Court point to anything in the agreement that purports to do so. Indeed, the union does not contend that there is any such covenant in the contract. Doubtless all rights that accrued to the employees under the collective agreement during its terms, and that were made arbitrable by its provisions, could be awarded to them by the arbitrators, even though the period of the agreement had ended. But surely no rights *accrued* to the employees under the agreement after it had expired. Save for the provisions of the collective agreement, and in the absence, as here, of any applicable rule of law or contrary covenant between the employer and the employees, the employer had the legal right to discharge the employees at will. The collective agreement, however, protected them against discharge, for specified reasons, during its continuation. But when that agreement expired, it did not continue to afford rights *in futuro* to the employees—as though still effective and governing. After the agreement expired the employment status of these 11 employees was terminable at the will of the employer, as the Court of Appeals quite properly held . . . and the announced discharge of these 11 employees then became lawfully effective.

Once the contract expired, no rights continued to accrue under it to the employees. Thereafter they had no contractual right to demand that the employer continue to employ them, and *a fortiori* the arbitrators did not have power to order the employer to do so; nor did the arbitrators have power to order the employer to pay wages to them after the date of termination of the contract, which was also the effective date of their discharge.

The judgment of the Court of Appeals, affirming so much of the award as required reinstatement of the 11 employees to employment status and payment of their wages until expiration of the contract, but not thereafter, seems to me to be indubitably correct, and I would affirm it.

Concurring Opinion to Decisions in:
American Mfg. Co. (360)
Warrior and Gulf Navigation Co. (443)
Enterprise Wheel and Car Corp. (538)

Mr. Justice Brennan, with whom Mr. Justice Harlan joins, concurring.

While I join the Court's opinions in Nos. 443, 360, and 538, I add a word in Nos. 443 and 360.

In each of these cases the issue concerns the enforcement of but one promise—the promise to arbitrate in the context of an agreement dealing with a particular subject matter, the industrial relations between employers and employees. Other promises contained in the collective bargaining agreements are beside the point unless, by the very terms of the arbitration promise, they are made relevant to its interpretation. And I emphasize this, for the arbitration promise is itself a contract. The parties are free to make that promise as broad or as narrow as they wish for there is no compulsion in law requiring them to include any such promise in their agreement. The meaning of the arbitration promise is not to be found simply by reference to the dictionary definitions of the words the parties use, or by reference to the interpretation of commercial arbitration clauses. Words in a collective bargaining agreement, rightly viewed by the Court to be the charter instrument of a system of industrial self-government, like words in a statute, are to be understood only by reference to the background which gave rise to their inclusion. The Court therefore avoids the prescription of inflexible rules for the enforcement of arbitration promises. Guidance is given by identifying the various considerations which a court should take into account when construing a particular clause—considerations of the milieu in which the clause is negotiated and particularly underscored that the arbitral process in collective bargaining presupposes that the parties wanted the informed judgment of an arbitrator, precisely for the reason that judges cannot provide it. Therefore, a court asked to enforce a promise to arbitrate should ordinarily refrain from involving itself in the interpretation of the substantive provisions of the contract.

To be sure, since arbitration is a creature of contract, a court must always inquire, when a party seeks to invoke its aid to force a reluctant party to the arbitration table, whether the parties have agreed to arbitrate the particular dispute. In this sense, the question of whether a dispute is "arbitrable" is inescapably for the court.

On examining the arbitration clause, the court may conclude that it commits to arbitration any "dispute, difference, disagreement, or controversy of any nature or character." With that finding the court will have exhausted its function, except to order the reluctant party to arbitration. Similarly, although the arbitrator may be empowered only to interpret and apply the contract, the parties may have provided that any dispute as to whether a particular claim is within the arbitration clause is itself for the arbitrator. Again the court, without more, must send any dispute to the arbitrator, for the parties have agreed that the construction of the arbitration promise itself is for the arbitrator; and the reluctant party has breached his promise by refusing to submit the dispute to arbitration.

In American, the Court deals with a request to enforce the "standard" form of arbitration clause, one that provides for the arbitration of "any disputes, misunderstandings, differences or grievances, arising between the parties as to the meaning, interpretation and application of this agreement***." Since the arbitration clause itself is part of the agreement, it might be argued that a dispute as to the meaning of that clause is for the arbitrator. But the Court rejects this position, saying that the threshold question, the meaning of the arbitration clause itself, is for the judge unless the parties clearly state to the contrary. However, the Court finds that the meaning of that "standard" clause is simply that the parties have agreed to arbitrate any dispute which the moving party asserts to involve construction of the substantive provisions of the contract, because such a dispute necessarily does involve such a construction.

The issue in the Warrior case is essentially no different from that in American, that is, it is whether the company agreed to arbitrate a particular grievance. In contrast to American, however, the arbitration promise here excludes a particular area from arbitration—"matters which are strictly a function of management." Because the arbitration promise is different, the scope of the court's inquiry may be broader. Here a court may be required to examine the substantive provisions of the contract to ascertain whether the parties have provided that contracting out shall be a "function of management." If a court may delve into the merits to the extent of inquiring whether the parties have expressly agreed whether or not contracting out was a "function of management," why was it error for the lower court here to evaluate the evidence of bargaining history for the same purpose? Neat logical distinctions do not provide the answer. The Court rightly concludes that appropriate regard for the national labor policy and the special factors relevant to the labor arbitral process, admonish that judicial inquiry into the merits of this grievance should be limited to the search for an explicit provision which brings the grievance under the cover of the exclusion clause since "the exclusion clause is vague and arbitration clause quite broad." The hazard of going further into the merits is amply demonstrated by what the courts below did. On the basis of inconclusive evidence, those courts found that Warrior was in no way limited by any implied covenants of good faith and fair dealing from contracting out as it pleased—which would necessarily mean that Warrior was free completely to destroy the collective bargaining agreement by contracting out all the work.

The very ambiguity of the Warrior exclusion clause suggests that the parties were generally more concerned with having an arbitrator render decisions as to the meaning of the contract than they were in restricting the arbitrator's jurisdiction. The case might of course be otherwise were the arbitration clause very narrow, or the exclusion clause quite specific, for the inference might then be permissible that the parties had manifested a greater interest in confining the arbitrator; the presumption of arbitrability would then not have the same force and the Court would be somewhat freer to examine into the merits.

The Court makes reference to an arbitration clause being the *quid pro quo* for a no-strike clause. I do not understand the Court to mean that the application of the principles announced today depends upon the presence of a no-strike clause in the agreements.

Mr. Justice Frankfurter joins these observations.

QUESTIONS

1. Law journals and industrial relations periodicals have published many commentaries on the significance of these court decisions. Special attention is called to the incisive analysis, "The Question of 'Arbitrability'—the Roles of the Arbitrator, the Court and the Parties," by Russell A. Smith, *Southwestern Law Journal*, Vol. XVI (April, 1962), pp. 1–42, and the pamphlet *Model Arbitration Clauses to Protect Management Rights*, by the Labor Relations and Legal Department, Chamber of Commerce of the United States, 1961. In view of the decisions, what phraseology would you suggest for an arbitration clause in an agreement? Would you want to limit the power of the arbitrator and exclude cases from his jurisdiction? What might be the practical labor relations consequences of severely restricting the jurisdiction of the arbitrator?

2. What is the probable effect of the court's comments on the nature of arbitration on arbitrators and the lower courts? As an arbitrator would you interpret the decisions as a new "Bill of Rights" for your profession?

3. Given these decisions, what are the benefits and dangers to unions and management in a loosely drawn collective bargaining agreement? Apart from the arbitration clause, do you think that these decisions will motivate the parties to tighten up the wording of their agreements on such matters as just cause for discipline, definition of the bargaining unit, duration of the agreement, and so on? How would you go about reviewing your agreement for loopholes?

4. "The grievance procedure is . . . a part of the continuous collective bargaining process." Discuss.

5. Contrast and evaluate Justice Whittaker's view, "arbitrators are private

judges by the parties to decide particular matters specifically submitted," with Justice Douglas's view that "doubts should be resolved in favor of coverage."

6. Note the differences in the specific issues posed for the Court in these cases: Enterprise involves the enforceability of a faulty award after the fact, while Warrior and Gulf and American involve the coverage of the agreement to arbitrate. What questions about arbitrability and the enforcement of awards do these cases leave unanswered?

Case 3

REMEDIES FOR BREACH OF CONTRACT

This case consists of abstracts of two Supreme Court decisions dealing with the question of remedies for breach of the collective bargaining agreement.

Supreme Court of the United States
Atkinson et al. v. Sinclair Refining Company
June 18, 1962, 370 U.S. 238

Mr. Justice White delivered the opinion of the Court.

The respondent company employs at its refinery in East Chicago, Illinois, approximately 1,700 men, for whom the petitioning international union and its local are bargaining agents, and 24 of whom are also petitioners here. In early February, 1959, the respondent company docked three of its employees at the East Chicago refinery a total of $2.19. On February 13 and 14, 999 of the 1,700 employees participated in a strike or work stoppage, or so the complaint alleges. On March 12, the company filed this suit for damages and an injunction, naming the international and its local as defendants, together with 24 individual union member-employees.

Count I of the complaint, which was in three counts, stated a cause of action under Section 301 of the Taft-Hartley Act against the international and its local. It alleged an existing collective bargaining agreement between the international and the company containing, among other matters, a promise by the union not to strike over any cause which could be the subject of a grievance under other provisions of the contract. It was alleged that the international and the local caused the strike or work stoppage occurring on February 13 and 14 and that the strike was over the pay claims of three employees in the amount of $2.19, which claims were properly subject to the grievance procedure provided by the contract. The complaint asked for damages in the amount of $12,500 from the international and the local.

Count II of the complaint purported to invoke the diversity jurisdiction of the District Court. It asked judgment in the same amount against 24 individual employees, each of whom was alleged to be a committeeman of the local union and an agent of the international, and responsible for representing the international, the local, and their members. The complaint asserted that on February 13 and 14, the individuals, "contrary to their duty to plaintiff to abide by such contract, and maliciously confederating and conspiring together to cause the plaintiff expense and damage, and to induce breaches of said contract, and to interfere with performance thereof by the said labor organizations, and the affected employees, and to cause breaches thereof, individually and as officers, committeemen and agents of said labor organizations, fomented, assisted and participated in a strike or work stoppage* * *."

Count III of the complaint asked for an injunction but that matter need not concern us here since it is disposed of in *Sinclair Refining Co.* v. *Atkinson*, decided this day.

The defendants filed a motion to dismiss the complaint on various grounds and a motion to stay the action for the reasons (1) that all of the issues in the suit were referrable to arbitration under the collective bargaining contract and (2) that important issues in the suit were also involved in certain grievances filed by employees and said to be in arbitration under the contract. The District Court denied the motion to dismiss Count I, dismissed Count II, and denied the motion to stay. The Court of Appeals upheld the refusal to dismiss or stay Count I, but reversed the dismissal of Count II, and this Court granted certiorari. . . .

I. We have concluded that Count I should not be dismissed or stayed. Count I properly states a cause of action under Section 301 and is to be governed by federal law. Under our decisions, whether or not the company was bound to arbitrate, as well as what issues it must arbitrate, is a matter to be determined by the Court on the basis of the contract entered into by the parties. "The Congress * * * has by Section 301 of the Labor Management Relations Act, assigned the courts the duty of determining whether the reluctant party has breached his promise to arbitrate. For arbitration is a matter of contract and a party cannot be required to submit to arbitration any dispute which he has not agreed so to submit." We think it unquestionably clear that the contract here involved is not susceptible to a construction that the company was bound to arbitrate its claim for damages against the union for breach of the undertaking not to strike.

While it is quite obvious from other provisions of the contract that the parties did not intend to commit all of their possible disputes and the whole scope of their relationship to the grievance and arbitration procedures established in Article 26, that article itself is determinative of the issue in this case since it precludes arbitration boards from considering any matters other than employee grievances. . . .

Article 26 then imposes the critical limitation. It is provided that local arbitration boards "shall consider only individual or local employee or local committee grievances arising under the application of the currently existing agreement." There is not a word in the grievance and arbitration article providing for the submission of grievances by the company. Instead, there is the express, flat limitation that arbitration boards should consider only employee grievances. Furthermore, the article expressly provides that arbitration may be invoked only at the option of the union. At no place in the contract does the union agree to arbitrate at the behest of the company. The company is to take its claims elsewhere, which it has now done.

The union makes a further argument for a stay. Following the strike, and both before and after the company filed its suit, 14 of the 24 individual defendants filed grievances claiming reimbursement for pay withheld by the employer. The union argues that even though the company need not arbitrate its claim for damages, it is bound to arbitrate these grievances; and the arbitrator, in the process of determining the grievants' right to reimbursement, will consider and determine issues which also underlie the company's claim for damages. Therefore, it is said that a stay of the court action is appropriate.

We are not satisfied from the record now before us, however, that any significant issue in the damage suit will be presented to and decided by an arbitrator. The grievances filed simply claimed reimbursement for pay due employees for time spent at regular work or processing grievances. Although the record is a good deal less than clear and although no answer had been filed in this case, it would appear from the affidavits of the parties presented in connection with the motion to stay that the grievants claimed to have been disciplined as a result of the work stoppage and that they were challenging this disciplinary action. The company sharply denies in its brief in this Court that any employee was disciplined. In any event, precisely what discipline was imposed, upon what grounds it is being attacked by the grievants, and the circumstances surrounding the withholding of pay from the employees are unexplained in the record. The union's brief here states that the important issue underlying the arbitration and the suit for damages is whether the grievants instigated or participated in a work stoppage contrary to the collective bargaining contract. This the company denies and it asserts that no issue in the damage suit will be settled by arbitrating the grievances.

The District Court must decide whether the company is entitled to damages from the union for breach of contract. The arbitrator, if arbitration occurs, must award or deny reimbursement in whole or in part to all or some of the 14 employees. His award, standing alone, obviously would determine no issue in the damage suit. If he awarded reimbursement to the employees and if it could be ascertained with any assurance that one of his subsidiary findings was that the 14 men had not participated in a forbidden work stoppage—the critical issue according to the union's brief—the company would nevertheless not be foreclosed in court since, even if it were bound by such a subsidiary finding made by the arbitrator, it would be free to prove its case in court through the conduct of other agents of the union. In this state of the record, the union has not made out its case for a stay.

For the foregoing reasons, the lower courts properly denied the union's motion to dismiss Count I or stay it pending arbitration of the empoyer's damage claim.

II. We turn now to Count II of the complaint, which charged 24 individual officers and agents of the union with breach of the collective bargaining contract and tortious interference with contractual relations. The District Court held that under Section 301 union officers or members cannot be held personally liable for union actions, and that therefore "suits of the nature alleged in Count II are no longer cognizable in state or federal courts." The Court of Appeals reversed, however, ruling that "Count II stated a cause of action cognizable in the courts of Indiana and, by diversity, maintainable in the District Court."

We are unable to agree with the Court of Appeals, for we are convinced that Count II is controlled by federal law and that it must be dismissed on the merits for failure to state a claim upon which relief can be granted.

Under Section 301 a suit for violation of the collective bargaining contract in either a federal or state court is governed by federal law and Count II on its face charges the individual defendants with a violation of the no-strike clause. After quoting verbatim the no-strike clause, Count II alleges that the 24 individual defendants "contrary to their duty to plaintiff to abide by" the contract fomented and participated in a work stoppage in violation of the no-strike clause. The union itself does not quarrel with the proposition that the relationship of the members of the bargaining unit to the employer is "governed by" the bargaining agreement entered into on their behalf by the union. It is universally accepted that the no-strike clause in a collective agreement at the very least establishes a rule of conduct or condition of employment the violation of which by employees justifies discipline or discharge. The conduct charged in Count II is therefore within the scope of a "violation" of the collective agreement.

As well as charging a violation of the no-strike clause by the individual defendants, Count II necessarily charges a violation of the clause by the union itself. The work stoppage alleged is the identical work stoppage for which the union is sued under Count I and the same damage is alleged as is alleged in Count I. Count II states that the individual defendants acted "as officers, committeemen and agents of said labor organizations" in breaching and inducing others to breach the collective bargaining contract. Count I charges the principal, and Count II charges the agents for acting on behalf of the principal. Whatever individual liability Count II alleges for the 24 individual defendants, it necessarily restates the liability of the union which is charged under Count I, since under Section 301(b) the union is liable for the acts of its agents, under familiar principles of the law of agency (see also Section 301(e)). Proof the allegations of Count II in its present form would inevitably prove a violation of the no-strike clause by the union itself. Count II, like Count I, is thus a suit based on the union's breach of its collective bargaining contract with the employer, and therefore comes within Section 301(a). When a union breach of contract is alleged, that the plaintiff seeks to hold the agents liable instead of the principal does not bring the action outside the scope of Section 301.

Under any theory, therefore, the company's action is governed by the national labor relations law which Congress commanded this Court to fashion under Section 301(a). We hold that this law requires the dismissal of Count II for failure to state a claim for which relief can be granted—whether the contract violation charged is that of the union or that of the union plus the union officers and agents.

When Congress passed Section 301, it declared its view that only the union was to be made to respond for union wrongs, and that the union members were not to be subject to levy. . . . In the debates, Senator Ball, one of the Act's sponsors, declared that Section 301, "by providing that the union may sue and be sued as a legal entity, for a violation of contract, and that liability for damages will lie against union assets only, will prevent a repetition of the Danbury Hatters case, in which many members lost their homes."

Consequently, in discharging the duty Congress imposed on us to formulate the federal law to govern Section 301(a) suits, we are strongly guided by and do not give a niggardly reading to Section 301(b). We would undercut the Act and defeat its policy if we read Section 301 narrowly. We have already said in another context that Section 301(b) at least evidences "a congressional intention that the union as an entity, like a corporation, should in the absence of agreement be the sole source of recovery for injury inflicted by it." This policy cannot be evaded or truncated by the simple device of suing union agents or members, whether in contract or tort, or both, in a separate count or in a separate action for damages for violation of a collective bargaining contract for which damages the union itself is liable. The national labor policy requires and we hold that when a union is liable for damages for violation of the no-strike clause, its officers and members are not liable for these damages. Here, Count II, as we have said, necessarily alleges union liability but prays for damages from the union agents. Where the union has inflicted the injury, it alone must pay. Count II must be dismissed.

The case is remanded to the District Court for further proceedings not inconsistent with this opinion.

It is so ordered.

Mr. Justice Frankfurter took no part in the consideration or decision of this case.

Supreme Court of the United States
Sinclair Refining Company v. Atkinson et al.
June 18, 1962, 370 U.S. 195

Mr. Justice Black delivered the opinion of the Court.

The question this case presents is whether Section 301 of the Taft-Hartley Act, in giving federal courts jurisdiction of suits between employers and unions for breach of collective bargaining agreements, impliedly repealed Section 4 of the pre-existing Norris–La Guardia Act, which, with certain exceptions not here material, barred federal courts from issuing injunctions "in any case involving or growing out of any labor dispute."

The complaint here was filed by the petitioner Sinclair Refining Company against the Oil, Chemical and Atomic Workers International Union and Local 7–210 of that union and alleged: that the International Union, acting by and with the authority of the Local Union and its members, signed a written collective bargaining contract with Sinclair which provided for compulsory, final, and binding arbitration of "any difference regarding wages, hours or working conditions between the parties hereto or between the Employer and an employee covered by this working agreement which might arise within any plant or within any region of operations"; that this contract also included express provisions by which the unions agreed that "there shall be no slowdowns for any reason whatsoever" and "no strikes or work stoppages * * * (f)or any cause which is or may be the subject of a grievance;" and that notwithstanding these promises in the collective bargaining contract the members of Local 7–210 had, over a period of some 19 months, engaged in work stoppages and strikes on nine separate occasions. . . . In this situation Sinclair claimed there was no adequate remedy at law which would protect its contractual rights and the court should therefore enter orders enjoining the unions and their agents "preliminary at first, and thereafter permanently, from aiding, abetting, fomenting, advising, participating in, ratifying, or condoning any strike, stoppage of work, slowdown or any other disruption of, or interference with normal employment or normal operation or production by any employee within the bargaining unit at plaintiff's East Chicago, Indiana, refinery covered by the contract between the parties dated August 8, 1957, in support of, or because of, any matter or thing which is, or could be, the subject of a grievance under the grievance procedure of the said contract, or any extension thereof, or any other contract between the parties which shall contain like or similar provisions."

. . .

We agree with the courts below that this case does involve a "labor dispute" within the meaning of the Norris–La Guardia Act. Section 13 of that Act expressly defines a labor dispute as including "any controversy concerning terms or conditions of employment, or concerning the association or representation of persons in negotiating, fixing, maintaining, changing, or seeking to arrange terms or conditions of employment, regardless of whether or not the disputants stand in the proximate relation of employer and employee." Sinclair's own complaint shows quite plainly that each of the alleged nine work stoppages and strikes arose out of a controversy which was unquestionably well within this definition.

Nor does the circumstance that the alleged work stoppages and strikes may have constituted a breach of a collective bargaining agreement alter the plain fact that a "labor dispute" within the meaning of the Norris–La Guardia Act is involved. Arguments to the contrary proceed from the premise that Section 2 of that Act, which expresses the public policy upon which the specific anti-injunction provisions of the Act were based, contains language indicating that one primary concern of Congress was to insure workers the right "to exercise actual liberty of contract" and to protect "concerted activities for the purpose of collective bargaining." From that premise, Sinclair argues that an interpretation of the term "labor dispute" so as to include a dispute arising out of a union's refusal to abide by the terms of a collective agreement to which it freely acceded is to apply the Norris–La Guardia Act in a way that defeats one of the purposes for which it was enacted. But this argument, though forcefully urged both here and in much current commentary on this question, rests more upon considerations of what many commentators think would be the more desirable industrial and labor policy in view of their understanding as to the prevailing circumstances of contemporary labor-management relations than upon what is a correct judicial interpretation of the language of the Act as it was written by Congress.

In the first place, even the general policy declarations of Section 2 of the Norris–La Guardia Act, which are the foundation of this whole argument, do not support the conclusion urged. That section does not purport to limit the Act to the protection of collective bargaining but, instead, expressly recognizes the need of the anti-injunction provisions to insure the right of workers to engage in "concerted activities for the purpose of collective bargaining *or other mutual aid or protection.*" Moreover, the language of the specific provisions of the Act is so broad and inclusive that it leaves not the slightest opening for reading in any exceptions beyond those clearly written into it by Congress itself. . . .

Since we hold that the present case does grow out of a "labor dispute," the injunction sought here runs squarely counter to the proscription of injunctions against strikes contained in Section 4(a) of the Norris–La Guardia Act, to the proscription of injunctions against peaceful picketing contained in Section 4(e) and to the proscription of injunctions prohibiting the advising of such activites contained in Section 4(i). For these reasons, the Norris–La Guardia Act deprives the courts of the United States of jurisdiction to enter that injunction unless, as is contended here, the scope of that Act has been so narrowed by the subsequent enactment of Section 301 of the Taft-Hartley Act that it no longer prohibits even the injunctions specifically described in Section 4 where such injunctions are sought as a remedy for breach of a collective bargaining agreement. Upon consideration, we cannot agree with that view. . . .

The language of Section 301 itself seems to us almost if not entirely conclusive of this question. It is especially significant that the section contains no language that could by any stretch of the imagination be interpreted to constitute an explicit repeal of the anti-injunction provisions of the Norris– La Guardia Act in view of the fact that the section does expressly repeal another provision of the Norris–La Guardia Act dealing with union responsibility for the acts of agents. If Congress had intended that Section 301 suits should also not be subject to the anti-injunction provisions of the Norris–La Guardia Act, it certainly seems likely that it would have made its intent known in this same express manner. That is indeed precisely what Congress did do in Sections 101(h) and 208(b) of the Taft-Hartley Act, by permitting injunctions to be obtained, not by private litigants, but only at the instance of the National Labor Relations Board and the Attorney General, and in Section 302(e), by permitting private litigants to obtain injunctions in order to protect the integrity of employees' collective bargaining representatives in carrying out their responsibilities. . . .

When the inquiry is carried beyond the language of Section 301 into its legislative history, whatever small doubts as to the congressional purpose could have survived consideration of the bare language of the section should be wholly dissipated . . . at the conference the provision of the House bill expressly repealing the anti-injunction provisions of the Norris–La Guardia Act, as well as the provision of the bill passed by the Senate declaring the breach of a collective agreement to be an unfair labor practice, was dropped and never became law. . . .

. . .

We cannot accept the startling argument made here that even though Congress did not itself want to repeal the Norris–La Guardia Act, it was willing to confer a power upon the courts to "accommodate" that Act out of existence whenever they might find it expedient to do so in furtherance of some policy they had fashioned under Section 301. . . .

. . . The question of whether existing statutes should be continued in force or repealed is, under our system of government, one which is wholly within the domain of Congress. . . .

Nor have we found anything else in the previous decisions of this Court that would indicate that we should disregard all this overwhelming evidence of a congressional intent to retain completely intact the anti-injunction prohibitions of the Norris–La Guardia Act in suits brought under Section 301. *Brotherhood of Railroad Trainmen* v. *Chicago River & Indiana R. Co.*, upon which Sinclair places its primary reliance, is distinguishable on several grounds. There we were dealing with a strike called by the union in defiance of an affirmative duty, imposed upon the union by the Railway Labor Act itself, compelling unions to settle disputes as to the interpretation of an existing collective bargaining agreement, not by collective union pressures on the railroad, but by submitting them to the Railroad Adjustment Board as the exclusive means of final determination of such "minor" disputes. Here, on the other hand, we are dealing with a suit under a quite different law which does not itself compel a particular, exclusive method for settling disputes nor impose any requirement, either upon unions or employers, or upon the courts, that is in any way inconsistent with a continuation of the Norris–La Guardia Act's proscription of federal labor injunctions against strikes and peaceful picketing. . . .

Textile Workers Union v. *Lincoln Mills*, upon which some lesser reliance is placed, is equally distinguishable. There the Court held merely that it did not violate the anti-injunction provisions of the Norris–La Guardia Act to compel the parties to a collective bargaining agreement to submit a dispute which had arisen under that agreement to arbitration where the agreement itself required arbitration of the dispute. In upholding the jurisdiction of the federal courts to issue such an order against a challenge based upon the Norris–La Guardia Act, the Court pointed out that the equitable relief granted in that case—a mandatory injunction to carry out an agreement to arbitrate—did not enjoin any one of the kinds of conduct which the specific prohibitions of the Norris–La Guardia Act withdrew from the injunctive powers of United States courts. An injunction against work stoppages, peaceful picketing, or the nonfraudulent encouraging of those activities would, however, prohibit the precise kinds of conduct which subsections (a), (e), and (i) of Section 4 of the Norris–La Guardia Act unequivocally say cannot be prohibited.

Nor can we agree with the argument made in this Court that the decision in Lincoln Mills, as implemented by the subsequent decisions in *United Steelworkers* v. *American Manufacturing Co.*, *United Steelworkers* v. *Warrior & Gulf Navigation Co.*, and *United Steelworkers* v. *Enterprise Wheel & Car Corp.*, requires us to reconsider and overrule the action of Congress in refusing to repeal or modify the controlling commands of the Norris–La Guardia Act. To the extent that those cases relied upon the proposition that the arbitration process is "a kingpin of federal labor policy," we think that proposition was founded not upon the policy predelictions of this Court but upon what Congress said and did when it enacted Section 301. Certainly we cannot accept any suggestion which would undermine those cases by implying that the Court went beyond its proper power and itself "forged * * * a kingpin of federal labor policy" inconsistent with that section and its purpose. Consequently, we do not see how cases implementing the purpose of Section 301 can be said to have freed this Court from its duty to give effect to the plainly expressed congressional purpose with regard to the continued application of the anti-injunction provisions of the Norris–La Guardia Act. The argument to the contrary seems to rest upon the notion that injunctions against peaceful strikes are necessary to make the arbitration process effective. But whatever might be said about the merits of this argument, Congress itself has rejected it. In doing so, it set the limit to which it was willing to go in permitting courts to effectuate the congressional policy favoring arbitration and it is not this Court's business to review the wisdom of that decision.

The plain fact is that Section 301, as passed by Congress, presents no conflict at all with the anti-injunction provisions of the Norris–La Guardia Act. Obedience to the congressional commands of the Norris–La Guardia Act does not directly affect the "congressional policy in favor of the enforcement of agreements to arbitrate grievance disputes" at all for it does not impair the right of an employer to obtain an order compelling arbitration of any dispute that may have been made arbitrable by the provisions of an effective collective bargaining agreement. At the most, what is involved is the question of whether the employer is to be allowed to enjoy the benefits of an injunction along with the right which Congress gave him in Section 301 to sue for breach of a collective agreement. . . .

It is doubtless true, as argued, that the right to sue which Section 301 gives employers would be worth more to them if they could also get a federal court injunction to bar a breach of their collective bargaining agreements. Strong arguments are made to us that it is highly desirable that the Norris–La Guardia Act be changed in the public interest. If that is so, Congress itself might see fit to change that law and repeal the anti-injunction provisions of the Act insofar as suits for violation of collective bargaining agreements are concerned, as the House bill under consideration originally provided. It might, on the other hand, decide that if injunctions are necessary, the whole idea of enforcement of these agreements by private suits should be discarded in favor of enforcement through the administration machinery of the Labor Board, as Senator Taft provided in his Senate bill. Or it might decide that neither of these methods is entirely satisfactory and turn instead to a completely new approach. The question of what change, if any, should be made in the existing law is one of legislative policy properly within the exclusive domain of Congress—it is a question for law-makers, not law-interpreters. . . .

The District Court was correct in dismissing Count 3 of petitioner's complaint for lack of jurisdiction under the Norris–La Guardia Act. The judgment of the Court of Appeals affirming that order is therefore
Affirmed.

Mr. Justice Frankfurter took no part in the consideration or decision of this case.

Sinclair Refining Dissenting Opinion

Mr. Justice Brennan, with whom Mr. Justice Douglas and Mr. Justice Harlan join, dissenting:

I believe that the Court has reached the wrong result because it has answered only the first of the questions which must be answered to decide this case. Of course Section 301 of the Taft-Hartley Act did not, for purposes of actions brought under it, "repeal" Section 4 of the Norris–La Guardia Act. But two provisions do co-exist, and it is clear beyond dispute that they apply to the case before us in apparently conflicting senses. Our duty, therefore, is to seek out that accommodation of the two which will give the fullest possible effect to the central purposes of both. Since such accommodation is possible, the Court's failure to follow that path leads it to a result—not justified by either the language or history of Section 301—which is wholly at odds with our earlier handling of directly analogous situations and which cannot be woven intelligibly into the broader fabric of related decisions.

I. Section 301 of the Taft-Hartley Act, enacted in 1947, authorized Federal District Courts to entertain "(s)uits for violation of contracts between an employer and labor organization * * * ." It does not in terms address itself to the question of remedies. As we have construed Section 301, it casts upon the District Courts a special responsibility to carry out contractual schemes for arbitration, by holding parties to that favored process for settlement when it has been contracted for, and, by then regarding its result as conclusive. At the same time, Section 4 of the Norris–La Guardia Act, enacted in 1932, proscribes the issuance by federal courts of injunctions against various concerted activities "in any case involving or growing out of any labor dispute." But the enjoining of a strike over an arbitrable grievance may be indispensable to the effective enforcement of an arbitration scheme in a collective agreement; thus the power to grant that injunctive remedy may be essential to the uncrippled performance of the Court's function under Section 301. Therefore, to hold that Section 301 did not repeal Section 4 is only a beginning. Having so held, the Court should—but does not—go on to consider how it is to deal with the surface conflict between the two statutory commands.

The Court has long acted upon the premise that the Norris–La Guardia Act does not stand in isolation. It is one of several statutes which, taken together, shape the national labor policy. Accordingly, the Court has recognized that Norris–La Guardia does not invariably bar injunctive relief when necessary to achieve an important objective of some other statute in the pattern of labor laws. . . . In Chicago River we insisted that there "must be an accommodation of (the Norris–La Guardia Act) and the Railway Labor Act so that the obvious purpose in the enactment of each is preserved." . . . I think that there is nothing in either the language of Section 301 or its history to prevent Section 4's here being accommodated with it, just as Section 4 was accommodated with the Railway Labor Act.

II. It cannot be denied that the availability of the injunctive remedy in this setting is far more necessary to the accomplishment of the purposes of Section 301 than it would be detrimental to those of Norris–La Guardia. Chicago River makes this plain. We there held that the federal courts, notwithstanding Norris–La Guardia, may enjoin strikes over disputes as to the interpretation of an existing collective agreement, since such strikes flout the duty imposed on the union by the Railway Labor Act to settle such "minor disputes" by submission to the National Railroad Adjustment Board rather than by concerted economic pressures. We so held, even though the Railway Labor Act contains no express prohibition of strikes over "minor disputes," because we found it essential to the meaningful enforcement of that Act—and because the existence of mandatory arbitration eliminated one of the problems to which Norris–La Guardia was chiefly addressed, namely, that "the injunction strips labor of its primary weapon without substituting any reasonable alternative."

That reasoning is applicable with equal force to an injunction under Section 301 to enforce a union's contractual duty, also binding on the employer, to submit certain disputes to terminal arbitration and to refrain from striking over them. The federal law embodied in Section 301 stresses the effective enforcement of such arbitration agreements. When one of them is about to be sabotaged by a strike, Section 301 has as strong a claim upon an accommodating interpretation of Section 4 as does the compulsory arbitration law of the Railway Labor Act. . . .

In any event, I should have thought that the question was settled by *Textile Workers* v. *Lincoln Mills*. In that case, the Court held that the procedural requirements of Norris–La Guardia's Section 7, although in terms fully applicable, would not apply so as to frustrate a federal court's effective enforcement under Section 301 of an employer's obligation to arbitrate. It is strange, I think, that Section 7 of the Norris–La Guardia Act need not be read, in the face of Section 301, to impose inapt procedural restrictions upon the specific enforcement of an employer's contractual duty to arbitrate; but that Section 4 must be read, despite Section 301, to preclude absolutely the issuance of an injunction against a strike which ignores a union's identical duty.

III. The legislative history of Section 301 affords the Court no refuge from the compelling effect of our prior decisions. That history shows that Congress considered and rejected "the advisability of repealing the Norris–La Guardia Act insofar as suits based upon breach of collective bargaining agreements are concerned* * * ." But congressional rejection of outright repeal certainly does not imply hostility to an attempt by the courts to accommodate all statutes pertinent to the decision of cases before them. Again, the Court's conclusion stems from putting the wrong question. When it is appreciated that there is no question here of "repeal," but rather one of how the Court is to apply the whole statutory complex to the case before it, it becomes more clear that the legislative history does not support the Court's conclusion. First, however, it seems appropriate to discuss, as the Court has done, the language of Section 301 considered in light of other provisions of the statute.

There is nothing in the words of Section 301 which so much as intimates any limitation to damage remedies when the asserted breach of contract consists of concerted activity. The section simply authorizes the District Courts to entertain and decide suits for violation of collective contract. Taking the language alone, the irresistible implication would be that the District Courts were to employ their regular arsenal of remedies appropriately to the situation. That would mean, of course, that injunctive relief could be afforded when damages would not be an adequate remedy. . . .

Sound reasons explain why repeal of Norris–La Guardia provisions, acceptable in other settings, might have been found ill-suited for the purpose of Section 301. And those reasons fall far short of a design to preclude absolutely the issuance under Section 301 of any injunction against any activity included in Section 4 of Norris–La Guardia. . . .

. . . The Congress understandably may not have felt able to predict what provisions would crop up in collective bargaining agreements, to foresee the settings in which those would become subjects of litigation, or to forecast the rules of law which the courts would apply. The consequences of repealing the anti-injunction provisions in this context would have been completely unknowable, and outright repeal, therefore, might well have seemed unthinkable. Congress, clearly, had no intention of abandoning wholesale the Norris–La Guardia policies in contract suits; but it does not follow that Section 301 is not the equal of Section 4 in cases which implicate both provisions.

. . .

The statutory language thus fails to support the Court's position. The inference is at least as strong that Congress was content to rely upon the courts to resolve any seeming conflicts between Section 301 and Section 4 as they arose in the relatively manageable setting of particular cases, as that Congress intended to limit to damages the remedies courts could afford against concerted activities under Section 301. The Court then should so exercise its judgment as best to effect the most important purposes of each statute. It should not be bound by inscrutable congressional silence to a wooden preference for one statute over the other.

Nor does the legislative history of Section 301 suggest any different conclusion. . . .

I emphasize that the question in this case is not whether the basic policy embodied in Norris–La Guardia against the injunction of activities of labor unions has been abandoned in actions under Section 301; the question is simply whether injunctions are barred against strikes over grievances which have been routed to arbitration by a contract specifically enforceable against both the union and the employer. Enforced adherence to such arbitration commitments has emerged as a dominant motif in the developing federal law of collective bargaining agreements. But there is no general federal antistrike policy; and although a suit may be brought under Section 301 against strikes which, while they are breaches of private contracts, do not threaten an additional public policy, in such cases the anti-injunction policy of Norris–La Guardia should prevail. Insistence upon strict application of Norris–La Guardia to a strike over a dispute which both parties are bound by contract to arbitrate threatens a leading policy of our labor relations law. But there may be no such threat if the union has made no binding agreement to arbitrate; and if the employer cannot be compelled to arbitrate, restraining the strike would cut deep into the core of Norris–La Guardia. Therefore, unless both parties are so bound, limiting an employer's remedy to damages might well be appropriate. The susceptibility of particular concrete situtions to this sort of analysis shows that rejection of an outright repeal of Section 4 was wholly consistent with acceptance of a technique of accommodation which would lead, in some cases, to the granting of injunctions against concerted activity. Accommodation requires only that the anti-injunction policy of Norris–La Guardia not intrude into areas, not vital to its ends, where injunctive relief is vital to a purpose of Section 301; it does not require unconditional surrender.

IV. Today's decision cannot be fitted harmoniously into the pattern of prior decisions on analogous and related matters. Considered in their light, the decision leads inescapably to results consistent neither with any imaginable legislative purpose nor with sound judicial administration.

. . .

The question arises whether today's prohibition of injunctive relief is to be carried over to state courts as a part of the federal law governing collective agreements. If so, Section 301, a provision plainly designed to enhance the responsibility of unions to their contracts, will have had opposite effect of depriving employers of a state remedy they enjoyed prior to its enactment.

On the other hand, if, as today's literal reading suggests and as a leading state decision holds, states remain free to apply their injunctive remedies against concerted activities in breach of contract, the development of a uniform body of federal contract law is in for hard times. So long as state courts remain free to grant the injunctions unavailable in federal courts, suits seeking relief against concerted activities in breach of contract will be channeled to the states whenever possible. Ironically, state rather than federal courts will be the preferred instruments to protect the integrity of the arbitration process, which Lincoln Mills and the Steelworkers decisions forced into a kingpin of federal labor policy. Enunciation of uniform doctrines applicable in such cases will be severely impeded. Moreover, the type of relief available in a particular instance will turn on fortuities of locale and susceptibility to process—depending upon which States have anti-injunction statutes and how they construe them.

· · ·

V. The decision deals a crippling blow to the cause of grievance arbitration itself. Arbitration is so highly regarded as a proved technique for industrial peace that even the Norris–La Guardia Act fosters its use. But since unions cannot be enjoined by a federal court from striking in open defiance of their undertakings to arbitrate, employers will pause long before committing themselves to obligations enforceable against them but not against their unions. The Court does not deny the desirability, indeed, necessity, for injunctive relief against a strike over an arbitrable grievance. The Court says only that federal courts may not grant such relief, that Congress must amend Section 4 if those courts are to give substance to the congressional plan of encouraging peaceful settlements of grievances through arbitration.

· · ·

In the case before us, the union enjoys the contractual right to make the employer submit to final and binding arbitration of any employee grievance. At the same time, the union agrees that "There shall be no strikes * * * for any cause which is or may be the subject of a grievance." The complaint alleged that the union had, over the past several months, repeatedly engaged in "quickie" strikes over arbitrable grievances. Under the contract and the complaint, then the District Court might conclude that there have occurred and will continue to occur breaches of contract of a type to which the principle of accommodation applies. It follows that rather than dismissing the complaint's request for an injunction, the Court should remand the case to the District Court with directions to consider whether to grant the relief sought—an injunction against future repetitions. This would entail a weighing of the employer's need for such an injunction against the harm that might be inflicted upon legitimate employee activity. It would call into question the feasibility of setting up *in futuro* contempt sanctions against the union (for striking and against the employer (for refusing to arbitrate) in regard to prospective disputes which might fall more or less clearly into the adjudicated category of arbitrable grievances. In short, the District Court will have to consider with great care whether it is possible to draft a decree which would deal equitably with all the interests at stake.

I would reverse the Court of Appeals and remand to the District Court for further proceedings consistent with this dissenting opinion.

QUESTIONS

1. The majority opinion suggests that Congress might (a) repeal the anti-injunction provisions of the Norris–La Guardia Act insofar as violations of collective bargaining agreements are concerned, or (b) give the NLRB power to enforce collective bargaining agreements, or (c) take an entirely new approach in regard to agreement enforcement. Discuss the desirability of each of these alternatives.
2. "This decision deals a crippling blow to the cause of grievance arbitration." Discuss.
3. Discuss the relationship between the Sinclair, Lincoln Mills, Warrior and Gulf Navigation, American Manufacturing, and Enterprise Wheel and Car cases.
4. Before the Sinclair cases, texts on collective bargaining usually said that an employer confronted with a wildcat strike in breach of an agreement had the following remedies available to him: (a) cancellation of the whole agreement, (b) discharge or other discipline for the strikers, (c) suits for damages, and (d) injunction against the strike or picketing. How do the Sinclair cases change these remedies? If you were an employer confronted with a wildcat strike over a grievance subject to arbitration how would you go about getting the strikers back to work? Justify your proposed course of action.

Case 4

REPRESENTATION OF THE ECONOMIC INTERESTS OF THE COLLEGE TEACHING PROFESSION

On May 1, 1966, the Council of the American Association of University Professors adopted a policy opposing the extension of the principle of exclusive representation to faculty members in institutions of higher learning. However, under this policy, where an AAUP chapter is threatened with the prospect that another organization may win exclusive representation rights, that chapter may request the approval of the AAUP's General Secretary to seek to become an exclusive representative of the faculty.

This policy of the AAUP was formulated in response to recently enacted state statutes providing for collective bargaining by public employees including faculty members in tax-supported colleges and universities. Both the National Education Association and the American Federation of Teachers were engaged in organizing teachers particularly in junior and community colleges.

The text of this case is part of a dissent from the AAUP policy by

Professor Robert Bierstedt of New York University and Professor Fritz Machlup of Princeton University. This statement provides an insight into the operations of one professional association and contrasting views on how the economic interests of a profession can be most effectively represented.

Dissenting Statement
by Professors Robert Bierstedt and Fritz Machlup.*

. . . Our objection is one of basic principle. The notion of collective bargaining, supported by most of us in the industrial context, is wholly inappropriate in the academic situation. A university is not a corporation in which the interests of labor and management are opposed, a zero-sum arrangement in which one group gains only at the expense of the other. On the contrary, trustees, regents, and board members have nothing to gain by depressing our salaries. They have no personal financial interests in the matter and they win prestige only as they provide stipends high enough to attract the most capable scholars and scientists among us to their institutions. Their prestige in fact is wholly dependent upon the prestige of the faculties they manage to recruit and to retain.

The differences between the union approach and our own is fundamental. We could not possibly support union tactics in negotiation because they denigrate and ultimately deny our professional status. We do not consider ourselves employees. Whatever the legal definition may be, there is a genuine sense in which we can assert that we *are* the university. We can conceive of a university without students—The Institute for Advanced Study at Princeton, the Center for Advanced Study in the Behavioral Sciences at Palo Alto, and All Souls College, Oxford—and we can conceive of a university with only a minimal administration (the same examples can serve again), but we cannot conceive of a university without professors.

As teacher-scholars we own an ancient tradition and it is one not lightly to be surrendered. It is the tradition of the scholar whose services are sought by his society because he is the man who knows. He knows something that no one else does, and for this reason students congregate around him, as they surrounded Peter Abelard in the streets of Paris long ago, and as they press now for admission into our laboratories and lecture halls. We subscribe to contracts with certain persons, members of boards of trustees, to disseminate our knowledge to others and ask, in addition to a monetary return, for a place in which to indulge in the study and research that will increase this knowledge. Why then should we surrender this status, this status as independent scholars, for the quite different status of employees? To do so would be to sacrifice our historic role.

* *AAUP Bulletin*, Vol. 52, No. 2 (June, 1966), p. 233.

To do so would also subvert our own endeavors as members of the AAUP. Two of our important committees operate on principles that have nothing to do with collective bargaining. One of these is Committee Z, on the Economic Status of the Profession. Since 1959, to the benefit of us all, this Committee has made annual surveys of faculty salaries throughout the country and its grading system is a public challenge to those institutions whose governing boards have permitted them to fall behind. This program carried on with astonishing efficiency by the Association, is clearly more impressive and influential than any local bargaining could be. It is a process that has been called one of "persuasive exposition" and it is, above all, a professional process. To substitute for this process, with its national publicity, a series of local negotiations would surely retard our cause.

Even more serious, however, is the situation with respect to Committee T on College and University Government. Any concession to the principle of representation by an outside organization—even if the organization were a chapter of the AAUP itself—would render vain and trivial the work of this Committee. For it is the policy of the Association that the only appropriate body to represent the faculty of a university is the faculty itself, or its elected representatives sitting in council or senate. The direct thrust of Committee T in recent years has been to win recognition for this principle and to increase the number of colleges and universities that conform to it. The Committee, furthermore, is currently engaged in preparing a tripartite statement with the American Council on Education and the Association of Governing Boards, which will set out guidelines for the respective roles that each of three components of the university—the board, the president, and the faculty—should be expected to play.

The AAUP, in short, has always maintained that the operation of a university is one of shared responsibility. Once an exception is made, no matter how extraordinary the circumstances, the situation is radically transformed into one of antagonistic and even hostile opposition. Once this happens—even once—we become employees of an administration and of a governing board. Once this happens the administration is no longer working for us, but we are working for it. And this, we submit, is too high a price to pay. The authors of the Report recognize this, of course, but only as a matter of preference. We, on the contrary, regard it as a matter of principle, a principle so important that we cannot conceive of circumstances that would compensate for its surrender.

We conclude therefore that collective bargaining by any agent outside the faculty of a university itself not only contravenes the principles and policies of the AAUP but would fundamentally alter the nature of the Association. It would transform it from a professional association into something else. It would do more. It woud alter irrevocably the character of the academic profession and do violence to the very idea of a university.

QUESTIONS

1. Under what conditions would a process of "persuasive exposition" be effective in raising the compensation of faculty members? What does the process of "persuasive exposition" assume about the geographic mobility of college professors? What different strategies would be needed for private institutions, tax-supported institutions, junior colleges, undergraduate colleges, universities, and different geographic regions?
2. How widely held is the view that "professors *are* the university"?
3. Under the doctrine of "shared responsibility," who *manages* a college or university?

Case 5

COLLECTIVE BARGAINING BY FEDERAL EMPLOYEES

Federal, state, and local governments are major employers in the United States. Nuclear physicists, physicians, teachers, stenographers, millwrights, and porters are employed by the government. As an employer, government possesses the businessman's interest in efficiency. Civil servants, like their counterparts in private business, have interests as employees.

This case consists of the text of Executive Order 10988 signed by President Kennedy on January 17, 1962, and some comments on experience under it through the summer of 1964. This order is the framework for a unique kind of collective bargaining by government employees of the executive branch of the federal government.

EXECUTIVE ORDER 10988: EMPLOYEE-MANAGEMENT COOPERATION IN THE FEDERAL SERVICE*

WHEREAS participation of employees in the formulation and implementation of personnel policies affecting them contributes to effective conduct of public business; and

WHEREAS the efficient administration of the Government and the well-being of employees require that orderly and constructive relationships be maintained between employee organizations and management officials; and

WHEREAS subject to law and the paramount requirements of the public service, employee-management relations within the Federal service should be improved by providing employees an opportunity for greater participation in the formulation and implementation of policies and procedures affecting the conditions of their employment; and

WHEREAS effective employee-management cooperation in the public service requires a clear statement of the respective rights and obligations of employee organizations and agency management:

NOW, THEREFORE, by virtue of the authority vested in me by the

* *Federal Register*, Friday, January 19, 1962, pp. 551–56.

Constitution of the United States, by section 1753 of the Revised Statutes (5 U.S.C. 631), and as President of the United States, I hereby direct that the following policies shall govern officers and agencies of the executive branch of the Government in all dealings with Federal employees and organizations representing such employees.

Section 1. (a) Employees of the Federal Government shall have, and shall be protected in the exercise of, the right, freely and without fear of penalty or reprisal, to form, join and assist any employee organization or to refrain from any such activity. Except as hereinafter expressly provided, the freedom of such employees to assist any employee organization shall be recognized as extending to participation in the management of the organization and acting for the organization in the capacity of an organization representative, including presentation of its views to officials of the executive branch, the Congress or other appropriate authority. The head of each executive department and agency (hereinafter referred to as "agency") shall take such action, consistent with law, as may be required in order to assure that employees in the agency are apprised of the rights described in this section, and that no interference, restraint, coercion or discrimination is practiced within such agency to encourage or discourage membership in any employee organization.

(b) The rights described in this section do not extend to participation in the management of an employee organization, or acting as a representative of any such organization, where such participation or activity would result in a conflict of interest or otherwise be incompatible with law or with the official duties of an employee.

Sec. 2. When used in this order, the term "employee organization" means any lawful association, labor organization, federation, council, or brotherhood having as a primary purpose the improvement of working conditions among Federal employees, or any craft, trade or industrial union whose membership includes both Federal employees and employees of private organizations; but such term shall not include any organization (1) which asserts the right to strike against the Government of the United States or any agency thereof, or to assist or participate in any such strike, or which imposes a duty or obligation to conduct, assist or participate in any such strike, or (2) which advocates the overthrow of the constitutional form of Government in the United States, or (3) which discriminates with regard to the terms or conditions of membership because of race, color, creed or national origin.

Sec. 3. (a) Agencies shall accord informal, formal or exclusive recognition to employee organizations which request such recognition in conformity with the requirements specified in sections 4, 5 and 6 of this order, except that no recognition shall be accorded to any employee organization which the head of the agency considers to be so subject to corrupt influences or influences opposed to basic democratic principles that recognition would be inconsistent with the objectives of this order.

(b) Recognition of an employee organization shall continue so long as such organization satisfies the criteria of this order applicable to such recognition; but nothing in this section shall require any agency to determine whether an organization should become or continue to be recognized as exclusive representative of the employees in any unit within 12 months after a prior determination of exclusive status with respect to such unit has been made pursuant to the provisions of this order.

(c) Recognition, in whatever form accorded, shall not—

(1) preclude any employee, regardless of employee organization membership, from bringing matters of personal concern to the attention of appropriate officials in accordance with applicable law, rule, regulation, or es-

tablished agency policy, or from choosing his own representative in a grievance or appellate action; or

(2) preclude or restrict consultations and dealings between an agency and any veterans organization with respect to matters of particular interest to employees with veterans preference; or

(3) preclude an agency from consulting or dealing with any religious, social, fraternal or other lawful association, not qualified as an employee organization, with respect to matters or policies which involve individual members of the association or are of particular applicability to it or its members, when such consultations or dealings are duly limited so as not to assume the character of formal consultation on matters of general employee-management policy or to extend to areas where recognition of the interests of one employee group may result in discrimination against or injury to the interests of other employees.

Sec. 4. (a) An agency shall accord an employee organization, which does not qualify for exclusive or formal recognition, informal recognition as representative of its member employees without regard to whether any other employee organization has been accorded formal or exclusive recognition as representative of some or all employees in any unit.

(b) When an employee organization has been informally recognized, it shall, to the extent consistent with the efficient and orderly conduct of the public business, be permitted to present to appropriate officials its views on matters of concern to its members. The agency need not, however, consult with an employee organization so recognized in the formulation of personnel or other policies with respect to such matters.

Sec. 5. (a) An agency shall accord an employee organization formal recognition as the representative of its members in a unit as defined by the agency when (1) no other employee organization is qualified for exclusive recognition as representative of employees in the unit, (2) it is determined by the agency that the employee organization has a substantial and stable membership of no less than 10 per centum of the employees in the unit, and (3) the employee organization has submitted to the agency a roster of its officers and representatives, a copy of its constitution and by-laws, and a statement of objectives. When, in the opinion of the head of an agency, an employee organization has a sufficient number of local organizations or a sufficient total membership within such agency, such organization may be accorded formal recognition at the national level, but such recognition shall not preclude the agency from dealing at the national level with any other employee organization on matters affecting its members.

(b) When an employee organization has been formally recognized, the agency, through appropriate officials, shall consult with such organization from time to time in the formulation and implementation of personnel policies and practices, and matters affecting working conditions that are of concern to its members. Any such organization shall be entitled from time to time to raise such matters for discussion with appropriate officials and at all times to present its views thereon in writing. In no case, however, shall an agency be required to consult with an employee organization which has been formally recognized with respect to any matter which, if the employee organization were one entitled to exclusive recognition, would not be included within the obligation to meet and confer, as described in section 6(b) of this order.

Sec. 6. (a) An agency shall recognize an employee organization as the exclusive representative of the employees, in an appropriate unit when such organization is eligible for formal recognition pursuant to section 5 of this order, and has been designated or selected by a majority of the employees of such unit as the representative of such employees in such unit. Units may be established on any plant or installation, craft, functional or other basis which will ensure a clear and identifiable community of interest among the employees concerned, but no unit shall be established solely on the basis of the extent to which employees in the proposed unit have organized. Except where otherwise required by established practice, prior agreement, or special circumstances, no unit shall be established for purposes of exclusive recognition which includes (1) any managerial executive, (2) any employee engaged in Federal personnel work in other than a purely clerical capacity, (3) both supervisors who officially evaluate the performance of employees and the employees whom they supervise, or (4) both professional employees and nonprofessional employees unless a majority of such professional employees vote for inclusion in such unit.

(b) When an employee organization has been recognized as the exclusive representative of employees of an appropriate unit it shall be entitled to act for and to negotiate agreements covering all employees in the unit and shall be responsible for representing the interests of all such employees without discrimination and without regard to employee organization membership. Such employee organization shall be given the opportunity to be represented at discussions between management and employees or employee representatives concerning grievances, personnel policies and practices, or other matters affecting general working conditions of employees in the unit. The agency and such employee organization, through appropriate officials and representatives, shall meet at reasonable times and confer with respect to personnel policy and practices and matters affecting working conditions, so far as may be appropriate subject to law and policy requirements. This extends to the negotiation of an agreement, or any question arising thereunder; the determination of appropriate techniques, consistent with the terms and purposes of this order, to assist in such negotiation, and the execution of a written memorandum of agreement or understanding incorporating any agreement reached by the parties. In exercising authority to make rules and regulations relating to personnel policies and practices and working conditions, agencies shall have due regard for the obligation imposed by this section, but such obligation shall not be construed to extend to such areas of discretion and policy as the mission of an agency, its budget, its organization and the assignment of its personnel, or the techology of performing its work.

Sec. 7. Any basic or initial agreement entered into with an employee organization as the exclusive representative of employees in a unit must be approved by the head of the agency or an official designated by him. All agreements with such employee organizations shall also be subject to the following requirements, which shall be expressly stated in the initial or basic agreement and shall be applicable to all supplemental, implementing, subsidiary or informal agreements between the agency and the organization:

(1) In the administration of all matters covered by the agreement officials and employees are governed by the provisions of any existing or future laws and regulations, including policies set forth in the Federal Personnel Manual and agency regulations, which may be applicable, and the agreement shall at all times be applied subject to such laws, regulations and policies;

(2) Management officials of the agency retain the right, in accordance with applicable laws and regulations, (a) to direct employees of the agency, (b) to hire, promote, transfer, assign, and retain employees in positions within the agency, and to suspend, demote, discharge, or take other disciplinary action against employees, (c) to relieve employees from duties because of lack of work or for other legitimate reasons, (d) to maintain the efficiency of the

Government operations entrusted to them, (e) to determine the methods, means and personnel by which such operations are to be conducted; and (f) to take whatever actions may be necessary to carry out the mission of the agency in situations of emergency.

Sec. 8. (a) Agreements entered into or negotiated in accordance with this order with an employee organization which is the exclusive representative of employees in an appropriate unit may contain provisions, applicable only to employees in the unit, concerning procedures for consideration of grievances. Such procedures (1) shall conform to standards issued by the Civil Service Commission, and (2) may not in any manner diminish or impair any rights which would otherwise be available to any employee in the absence of an agreement providing for such procedures.

(b) Procedures established by an agreement which are otherwise in conformity with this section may include provisions for the arbitration of grievances. Such arbitration (1) shall be advisory in nature with any decisions or recommendations subject to the approval of the agency head; (2) shall extend only to the interpretation or application of agreements or agency policy and not to changes in or proposed changes in agreements or agency policy; and (3) shall be invoked only with the approval of the individual employee or employees concerned.

Sec. 9. Solicitation of memberships, dues, or other internal employee organization business shall be conducted during the non-duty hours of the employees concerned. Officially requested or approved consultations and meetings between management officials and representatives of recognized employee organizations shall, whenever practicable, be conducted on official time, but any agency may require that negotiations with an employee' organization which has been accorded exclusive recognition be conducted during the non-duty hours of the employee organization representatives involved in such negotiations.

Sec. 10. No later than July 1, 1962, the head of each agency shall issue appropriate policies, rules and regulations for the implementation of this order, including: A clear statement of the rights of its employees under the order; policies and procedures with respect to recognition of employee organizations; procedures for determining appropriate employee units; policies and practices regarding consultation with representatives of employee organizations, other organizations and individual employees; and policies with respect to the use of agency facilities by employee organizations. Insofar as may be practicable and appropriate, agencies shall consult with representatives of employee organizations in the formulation of these policies, rules and regulations.

Sec. 11. Each agency shall be responsible for determining in accordance with this order whether a unit is appropriate for purposes of exclusive recognition and, by an election or other appropriate means, whether an employee organization represents a majority of the employees in such a unit so as to be entitled to such recognition. Upon the request of any agency, or of any employee organization which is seeking exclusive recognition and which qualifies for or has been accorded formal recognition, the Secretary of Labor, subject to such necessary rules as he may prescribe, shall nominate from the National Panel of Arbitrators maintained by the Federal Mediation and Conciliation Service one or more qualified arbitrators who will be available for employment by the agency concerned for either or both of the following purposes, as may be required: (1) to investigate the facts and issue an advisory decision as to the appropriateness of a unit for purposes of exclusive recognition and as to related issues submitted for consideration; (2) to conduct or supervise an election or otherwise determine by such means as may be appropriate, and on an advisory basis, whether an employee organization represents the majority of the employees in a unit. Consonant with law, the Secretary of Labor shall render such assistance as may be appropriate in connection with advisory decisions or determinations under this section, but the necessary costs of such assistance shall be paid by the agency to which it relates. In the event questions as to the appropriateness of a unit or the majority status of an employee organization shall arise in the Department of Labor, the duties described in this section which would otherwise be the responsibility of the Secretary of Labor shall be performed by the Civil Service Commission.

Sec. 12.   The Civil Service Commission shall establish and maintain a program to assist in carrying out the objectives of this order. The Commission shall develop a program for the guidance of agencies in employee-management relations in the Federal service; provide technical advice to the agencies on employee-management programs; assist in the development of programs for training agency personnel in the principles and procedures of consultation, negotiation and the settlement of disputes in the Federal service, and for the training of management officials in the discharge of their employee-management relations responsibilities in the public interest; provide for continuous study and review of the Federal employee-management relations program and, from time to time, make recommendations to the President for its improvement.

Sec. 13.   (a) The Civil Service Commission and the Department of Labor shall jointly prepare (1) proposed standards of conduct for employee organizations and (2) a proposed code of fair labor practices in employee-management relations in the Federal service appropriate to assist in securing the uniform and effective implementation of the policies, rights and responsibilities described in this order.

(b) There is hereby established the President's Temporary Committee on the Implementation of the Federal Employee-Management Relations Program. The Committee shall consist of the Secretary of Labor, who shall be chairman of the Committee, the Secretary of Defense, the Postmaster General, and the Chairman of the Civil Service Commission. In addition to such other matters relating to the implementation of this order as may be referred to it by the President, the Committee shall advise the President with respect to any problems arising out of completion of agreements pursuant to sections 6 and 7, and shall receive the proposed standards of conduct for employee organizations and proposed code of fair labor practices in the Federal service, as described in this section, and report thereon to the President with such recommendations or amendments as it may deem appropriate. Consonant with law, the departments and agencies represented on the Committee shall, as may be necessary for the effectuation of this section, furnish assistance to the Committee in accordance with section 214 of the Act of May 3, 1945, 59 Stat. 134 (31 U.S.C. 691). Unless otherwise directed by the President, the Committee shall cease to exist 30 days after the date on which it submits its report to the President pursuant to this section.

Sec. 14.   The head of each agency, in accordance with the provisions of this order and regulations prescribed by the Civil Service Commission, shall extend to all employees in the competitive civil service rights identical in adverse action cases to those provided perference eligibles under section 14 of the Veterans' Preference Act of 1944, as amended. Each employee in the competitive service shall have the right to appeal to the Civil Service Commission from an adverse decision of the administrative officer so acting, such appeal to be processed in an identical manner to that provided for appeals under section 14 of the Veterans' Preference Act. Any recommendation by the Civil Service Commission submitted to the head of an agency on the basis of an appeal by an employee in the competitive service shall be complied with by the head of the agency. This section shall become effective as to all adverse actions commenced by issuance of a notification of proposed action on or after July 1, 1962.

Sec. 15. Nothing in this order shall be construed to annul or modify, or to preclude the renewal or continuation of, any lawful agreement heretofore entered into between any agency and any representative of its employees. Nor shall this order preclude any agency from continuing to consult or deal with any representative of its employees or other organization prior to the time that the status and representation rights of such representative or organization are determined in conformity with this order.

Sec. 16. This order (except section 14) shall not apply to the Federal Bureau of Investigation, the Central Intelligence Agency, or any other agency, or to any office, bureau or entity within an agency, primarily performing intelligence, investigative, or security functions if the head of the agency determines that the provisions of this order cannot be applied in a manner consistent with national security requirements and considerations. When he deems it necessary in the national interest, and subject to such conditions as he may prescribe, the head of any agency may suspend any provision of this order (except section 14) with respect to any agency installation or activity which is located outside of the United States.

Approved—January 17th, 1962.

JOHN F. KENNEDY

The White House
January 17, 1962.
(F.R. Doc. 62–700; filed, Jan. 18, 1962; 10:18 A.M.)

EXPERIENCE UNDER EXECUTIVE ORDER 10988[1]

By late summer of 1964, about two and one-half years after the issuance of the President's Executive Order establishing a uniform labor relations policy for the executive departments of the federal government, 209 formal collective bargaining agreements, covering about 600,000 federal employees, had been negotiated under the terms of the order. For most of the agencies and several of the unions, collective bargaining was a new experience, and some of the first agreements simply recast the Executive Order. Since the major terms of compensation and supplementary benefits for federal workers are established by the Congress, the scope of bargaining with individual agencies can never be as wide as in private industry.

Coverage of Agreements

Figure I summarizes the coverage of federal collective bargaining agreements in the late summer of 1964. Nearly 90 per cent of the agree-

[1] The discussion which follows is based on U.S. Department of Labor, Bureau of Labor Statistics, *Collective Bargaining Agreements in the Federal Service, Late Summer, 1964*, Bulletin No. 1451 (August, 1965).

ments were negotiated by unions affiliated with the AFL-CIO, representing 87 per cent of all covered workers. By far the largest number of workers, more than 471,000, were accounted for by a national agreement between the Post Office Department and six unions. Outside the Post Office, the largest agreement and worker coverage was in the Department of Defense agencies—109 agreements for 88,507 employees.

FIGURE 1

COVERAGE OF FEDERAL COLLECTIVE BARGAINING AGREEMENTS
BY AGENCY AND UNION AFFILIATION, LATE SUMMER, 1964

Agency	Number		Union affiliation			
			AFL–CIO		Unaffiliated	
	Agreements	Employees covered	Agreements	Employees covered	Agreements	Employees covered
Total............	209	599,542	*183	525,274	*27	74,268
Agriculture..........	3	2,983	2	2,558	1	425
Commerce..........	3	230	3	230	–	–
Defense............	1	264	1	264	–	–
Air Force..........	9	7,210	7	4,910	2	2,300
Army..............	34	14,337	30	10,445	4	3,892
Navy..............	65	66,696	58	64,568	7	2,128
Health, Education, and Welfare......	10	12,259	9	12,207	1	52
Interior............	14	724	12	609	2	115
Labor..............	3	4,079	3	4,079	–	–
Post Office........	1	471,414	¹1	408,333	¹1	63,081
Treasury...........	5	732	5	732	–	–
Atomic Energy Commission..........	1	22	1	22	–	–
Civil Aeronautics Board...........	1	11	1	11	–	–
Federal Aviation Agency..........	4	839	4	839	–	–
General Services Administration.....	21	1,772	16	1,221	5	551
Interstate Commerce Commission.......	1	20	1	20	–	–
National Labor Relations Board.......	1	42	–	–	1	42
Railroad Retirement Board...........	1	1,800	1	1,800	–	–
Smithsonian Institution.	1	30	1	30	–	–
Tariff Commission....	1	7	1	7	–	–
Veterans Administration.............	29	14,071	26	12,389	3	1,682

* National Post Office Agreement covers four unions affiliated with the AFL-CIO and two unaffiliated unions. Agreement coverage, however, is allocated by affiliation.

SOURCE: U.S. Department of Labor, Bureau of Labor Statistics, Collective Bargaining Agreements in the Federal Service, Late Summer, 1964, Bulletin No. 1451 (August, 1965), p. 5.

The National Postal Agreement

The postal agreement is noteworthy for the extent of its worker coverage, but also, when compared to other federal agreements, for the scope and detail of its provisions. Its 25 articles and 5 supplements (for particular crafts) cover 87 printed pages. Since this agreement is national in scope, it covers, in addition to labor-management relations at the national and regional level, procedures which govern local negotiations and alleged violations of the national agreement at local installations. Local post offices and various unions were expected to negotiate over 20,000 supplementary local agreements.

The Unions Involved. Six unions were granted exclusive recognition in 1962. Their employment coverage and their total membership for 1964 were as follows:

	Employment Coverage	1964 Membership
Union Federation of Postal Clerks (AFL-CIO)	228,740	139,000
National Association of Letter Carriers of the U.S.A. (AFL-CIO)	171,351	167,913
National Rural Letter Carriers' Association (Ind.)	43,276	42,300
National Association of Post Office and General Services Maintenance Employees (Ind.)	19,805	8,424
National Federation of Post Office Motor Vehicle Employees	4,224	6,200
The National Association of Special Delivery Messengers	4,018	1,500

The Post Office Department also deals with six other organizations, including three associations of supervisors, which had secured formal recognition by late summer, 1964.

Some Key Provisions of the National Agreement. Two related topic, discipline and actions arising therefrom, are treated at length in separate sections. Article VIII, Policy on Discipline, emphasizes that "the action taken shall be corrective rather than punitive and that it must be influenced by impartial considerations of the dignity of the individual, justice, and equality." Two types of disciplinary actions are described— informal, to consist of discussions, counseling, and a letter of warning; and formal, leading to reprimand, suspension, and finally, removal. An elaborate appeals procedure is available to employees faced with an "adverse action" (suspension, discharge, furlough without pay, and reduction in rank or compensation).

The negotiated grievance procedure applies to any employee's "dissatisfaction" arising out of his job and where the remedy sought "is within the authority of the Postmaster General. . . ." and can also be invoked in promotion disputes and alleged violations of local agreements.

Advisory arbitration can be resorted to in adverse actions and grievances after the first and second level of appeal, respectively, but, by mutual consent, can also be used to resolve differences regarding the meaning and application of agreement provisions, including violations of the national agreement at local installations. Before arbitration can be invoked, the union must agree to pay one half of the cost.

QUESTIONS

1. What is the difference between informal and formal recognition? Why is informal recognition created in government employment and specifically denied in private employment covered by the Labor-Management Relations Act?
2. Compare and contrast the methods of determining the appropriate unit for collective bargaining in government and in private employment covered by the Labor-Management Relations Act.
3. In terms of managerial discretion or rights, would you rather be a government employer or a private employer? Why?
4. What will be the substantive issues that government managers and government employee organizations will bargain over?
5. What role will arbitration play in the emerging industrial relations system for government employees?
6. In Chapter 6 of the text the authors suggest that strikes are a vital part of the collective bargaining process. Can there be real collective bargaining on behalf of government employees who are denied the right to strike? What nonstrike pressures might be applied by government employee associations?

Case 6

WHO SPEAKS FOR THE UNION?

COMPANY: Midwest Manufacturing Corporation
Galesburg, Illinois

UNION: International Association of Machinists
Midwest Lodge No. 2063

ARBITRATOR: Charles N. Anrod

This case involves the authority of representatives and the procedures for amending an agreement during its term.

The following discussion of the issue and the facts in this case was prepared by Charles W. Anrod, the arbitrator.

The Corporation, a wholly owned subsidiary of Admiral Corporation, is engaged in the manufacture of refrigerators, freezers, air conditioners, and electric ranges at Galesburg, Illinois. It employs about 1,750 persons of whom approximately 1,400 are in the bargaining unit represented by the Union.

For many years, the employees in said bargaining unit were represented by Federal Labor Union No. 22,278 which entered into successive collective bargaining agreements with the Corporation. In February, 1956, the employees decided, however, to affiliate with the International Association of Machinists (AFL-CIO) and received a charter therefrom for the Union. Since the transfer occurred during the period of the 1955–56 collective bargaining agreement between the Federal Labor Union and the Corporation, the Union became a party to that agreement in lieu of the Federal Labor Union until it expired at about the end of October, 1956. Thereafter, the Union negotiated with the Corporation a collective bargaining agreement which was signed on November 26, 1956, and which became effective for the period from November, 1956, to November, 1957 (hereinafter referred to as the "1956–57 Agreement"). It was signed on behalf of the Corporation by L. H. Moos, vice-president and general manager, and on behalf of the Union by the members of a committee consisting of five Union representatives, among them William E. Boen, its president. The signature of William Hammond, special representative of the International Association of Machinists, AFL-CIO, was also affixed to it.

The grievances of three employees in the press room, namely, Virgil F. Odean, Ira D. Luallen, and Howard Hook, which are the subject of this arbitration arose out of the following facts:

The 1955–56 collective bargaining agreement provided initially for strict departmental seniority in the event of temporary layoffs. The application of that rule had, however, caused some dissatisfaction among the employees. As a result, the Federal Labor Union and the Corporation entered into a written agreement, dated June 16, 1955, which modified the pertinent provision of the 1955–56 collective bargaining agreement as follows:

> It is agreed between the Company and the Union that when it is necessary to reduce the working force the least senior employee in the classification in the department and on the shift in which the reduction is necessary shall be laid off (Company Exh. No. 4).

This agreement was signed by Harley Morss, then president of the Federal Labor Union, and by Don E. Johnson, director of personnel of the Corporation.

During the negotiations preceding the 1956–57 Agreement, the matter of a satisfactory seniority rule in case of temporary layoff was again discussed between the parties. The Corporation pointed out that, if strict departmental seniority should be applied (as was originally provided in the 1955–56 collective bargaining agreement), it could happen that the youngest employees in a department who had to be laid off temporarily were on the night shift and that their positions had then to be filled by employees from the day shift. This, the Corporation stated, had, in the past, created certain difficulties because some employees so transferred had contended they had been on specific shifts by their choice and felt that they should stay there. Accordingly, the Corporation proposed the following provision for the 1956–57 Agreement:

In applying departmental seniority in temporary layoffs, the least senior employees in the classification and on the shift in which the surplus occurs shall be the first to be laid off . . . (Company Exh. No. 5).

The Union rejected, however, the Corporation's proposal. Its spokesman asserted that, if classification and shift were determining in applying departmental seniority, employees with greater seniority could conceivably be laid off while employees with less seniority remained at work.

The parties finally agreed to restore strict departmental seniority in case of temporary layoffs (as was originally provided in the 1955–56 collective bargaining agreement) and, thereby, rescinded the agreement, dated June 16, 1955 (quoted above).

Their understanding was incorporated into Article VI, Section 6, of the 1956–57 Agreement which provides, so far as pertinent, the following:

In case of a temporary layoff departmental seniority shall prevail (joint Exh. No. 1, P. 8).

Yet, the matter did not come to rest. Shortly after the signing of the 1956–57 Agreement, a temporary layoff occurred. In accordance with the departmental seniority rule as stipulated in said Article VI, Section 6, some employees who happened to be on the night shift were laid off and other employees were then transferred from the day shift to the night shift. This procedure caused unrest among the transferees. They did not want to go on the night shift and also raised the question of overtime premium contending they were working outside their regularly scheduled shifts.

In an effort to find a satisfactory solution, the parties again discussed the question as to which seniority rule should be applied in case of temporary layoffs. They reached a tentative agreement under which seniority in the department and on the shift should govern in such instances. This understanding was submitted to a regular meeting of the Union by William Boen, its president, and approved in said meeting. The parties then entered into the following written agreement:

It is agreed by the parties hereto that the provisions of Article VI Section 6 shall be amended as follows: In case of a temporary layoff the least senior employee in the department and on the shift where such surplus exist shall be first laid off.

(*signed*) Don E. Johnson
　　　　　 Director of Personnel
(*signed*) William Boen, President
　　　　　 Midwest Lodge #2063

January 31st, 1957 (Union Exh. No. 1)

Thereafter, the Corporation followed the seniority rule as agreed upon in the above agreement of January 31, 1957. About three months later, the membership of the Union voted, however, to rescind said agreement and sent the following letter dated April 23, 1957, to the Company:

> Re: Agreement signed 1–31–57
> This will inform you that the membership of Lodge 2063, at their last regular meeting, voted to return to the provisions of the current contract, and to declare the agreement made and signed by the Management and the Union Representatives on the 31 day of the first month in 1957 void. This agreement will have to do with Article VI, Section 6, . . . on the subject of Seniority.
> > (*signed*) Roy E. Routt, Rec. Sec'y.
> > Midwest Lodge #2063

The Corporation took the position that the Union could not unilaterally rescind the written agreement of January 31, 1957. It disregarded, therefore, the Union's letter of April 23, 1957, and continued to make temporary layoffs in accordance with the January 31, 1957, agreement.

On May 16 or 17, 1957, the three grievants were temporarily laid off in conformity with the seniority rule stipulated in said agreement. They then filed the instant grievances (Union Exh. Nos. 3, 4 and 5). The Corporation denied the grievances which are now before the Board of Arbitration for decision.

At the same time these layoffs occurred, John R. Healey, an employee in the inspection department, was also temporarily laid off. His foreman made that layoff in accordance with the original wording of Article VI, Section 6, of the 1956–57 Agreement, i.e., on the basis of strict departmental seniority. Healey filed a grievance which was submitted to the Corporation by John J. Cox, a Union steward. On or about June 4 1957, the Corporation paid an amount equal to 16 hours' straight time to Healey in settlement of his grievance.

UNION'S POSITION

The Union does not dispute the above-related facts. But it contends that the agreement of January 31, 1957, which amended Article VI, Section 6, of the 1956–57 Agreement regarding the seniority rule in case of temporary layoffs was void.

In support of such contention, the Union asserts the correct procedures as prescribed by the constitution and bylaws of the International Association of Machinists (I.A.M.) were not followed. It particularly states that the agreement of January 31, 1957, was not signed by an international representative of the I.A.M. and, therefore, did not become effective.

It also states that, while said agreement was approved in a regular union meeting, the subject was not posted in advance on the bulletin board as required under the rules of the I.A.M.

The Union concedes that the letter of April 23, 1957, was afflicted with the same defects and, therefore, regards it void, too.

As a result, the Union concludes that the strict departmental seniority rule as originally contained in Article VI, Section 6, of the 1956–57 Agreement was still in effect when the three grievants were laid off. Since the Corporation followed the terms of the agreement of January 31, 1957, the Union argues that the Corporation violated said Article VI, Section 6.

With respect to the grievance filed by John R. Healey, the Union claims that the Corporation made the payment to Healey for the sole reason that it (the Corporation) was in default of the time limits prescribed for the handling of grievances in the 1956–57 Agreement but not in recognition of the substantive merits of that grievance.

For the above mentioned reasons, the Union seeks an award which would require the Corporation to reimburse the three grievants for the time lost on May 16 and/or 17, 1957.

CORPORATION'S POSITION

The Corporation points out that, while the immediate issue before the Board of Arbitration is whether or not the grievants were properly laid off, there is implicitly a broader question of considerable interest to it involved in this case, namely, whether the Union must live up to and be bound by an agreement made by its duly authorized officers.

The Corporation submits that it had in the past entered into a number of supplementary agreements with the president of the Federal Labor Union during the period of a collective bargaining agreement and that such supplementary agreements had always been carried out by both parties.

Moreover, the Corporation states that, prior to the grievances under consideration, it had no knowledge or notice of any restrictions on the authority of the Union's president to enter into such a supplementary agreement. It specifically emphasizes that it was not aware of any rules or regulations of the I.A.M. requiring the signature of an international representative or the posting of a subject on the bulletin board prior to its discussion in a Union meeting.

The Corporation argues that it acted in good faith when it entered into the January 31, 1957, agreement with the Union and is of the opinion that both parties were bound thereby.

It asserts that, when it was informed of the proper steps as outlined in the rules and regulations of the I.A.M. after the instant grievances had arisen, it readily agreed to respect the requirement of a signature or approval of an international representative in the future and also to adhere no longer to the January 31, 1957, agreement. At the same time, the

Corporation contends, it was, however, made clear to the representative of the Union that its (the Corporation's) concessions would not apply retroactively to actions taken in accordance with said agreement in the past.

As to the grievance of John R. Healey, the Corporation contends that it immediately recognized the foreman had made a mistake and informed the Union's representative over the telephone on or about the day of the filing of the grievance that payment would be made.

For the above-mentioned reasons, the Corporation asks that the three grievances here involved be denied.

QUESTIONS

1. Precisely state the issue to be decided by the Board of Arbitration.
2. What "lessons" does this kind of a situation contain for both union and management about (a) the nature of the agreement, (b) the credentials and authority of representatives, and (c) seniority provisions.

Case 7

UNION SECURITY AND THE BARGAINING UNIT

COMPANY: Kimball Tire Company, Inc.
              San Luis Obispo, California

UNION: International Brotherhood of Teamsters
          Truck Drivers and Helpers Local Union No. 381

ARBITRATOR: Grady L. Mullenix

This case involves the obligation of two employees to join the union under a union shop agreement. Although this case is not an NLRB dispute over the appropriate unit for collective bargaining, it illustrates some of the criteria which the NLRB often considers.

The following discussion of the issue and facts in this case was prepared by Grady L. Mullenix, the arbitrator.

The question submitted for arbitration, as set forth in the "Agreement to Arbitrate," is as follows:

"Shall William Wall and Ree Anderson become members of Teamsters Union Local 381?"

FACTS

The Kimball Tire Company is a corporation owned and controlled by two men.

The Company is engaged in the retail and wholesale tire business which includes sales and service of new and used tires and tubes and retreading. It also handles batteries. There are 13 employees, including 2 owners, who work at the one place of business at 252 Higuera Street, San Luis Obispo. However, two of the employees travel throughout a designated area contacting customers and potential customers doing sales and customer relations work.

On August 5, 1960, the Company filed a Petition with the National Labor Relations Board requesting a representation election to determine whether or not its employees wished to be represented by the Union. The NLRB conducted the election on August 19, 1960, and the Union was officially certified on August 29, 1960, as the exclusive bargaining agent for the employees in the appropriate bargaining unit agreed upon in the Consent Agreement which was the same as that petitioned for by the Company, as follows:

Included: Production and maintenance employees, including vulcanizers, tire changers and salesmen.
Excluding: Office clericals and supervisors within the meaning of the Act.

A collective bargaining agreement was eventually reached and was signed on March 6, 1961. Section 2 of that agreement is especially pertinent to this arbitration. It reads as follows:

Membership in good standing in the Union (as provided by law) on or after the 30th day following the beginning of employment or the effective date of this agreement, whichever is later, shall be a condition of employment.
The employer shall discharge an employee within seven (7) days after receipt of written notice from the Union that said employee has not become or remained a member in good standing.

In a letter dated April 7, 1961, addressed to Mr. Robenstine of the Company and signed by Mr. Earing for the Union, the following message was delivered:

This is to inform you that William Wall and Ree Anderson, having been in your employ in excess of 30 days, have not become members in good standing with Truck Drivers and Helpers Union, Local No. 381 as provided in Section 2 of our agreement. We therefore request they be discharged.

Anderson was an employee of the Company at the time of the NLRB election and voted in the election. Wall was employed later but was on the payroll prior to the date of the collective bargaining agreement.

CONTENTIONS OF THE PARTIES

The Union contends that Section 2 of the agreement requires that Wall and Anderson, as well as other employees, become members of the

Union as a condition of employment. They have not done so, and the Company has refused to discharge them as required by the agreement. The Union does not seek their discharge if it can be avoided, but instead requests that the two men be required to join the Union and that dues be paid by or for them retroactively to 30 days following the date of the agreement.

The Company's position is that Wall and Anderson are not in the bargaining unit and therefore are not required to join the Union. It is contended that Wall was hired as the service manager and that Anderson is now the commercial sales manager. Both are paid on a monthly salary basis, while the union members are all on hourly rates. The Company also argues that both Wall and Anderson intend to buy into the business and will be owners as well as managers in the near future.

The Union challenges the Company's position and denies that either of the subjects is a supervisor or managerial employee. In the case of Anderson, the Union offers testimony that he actually voted in the NLRB election and therefore was recognized by all concerned as properly within the bargaining unit. It is further stated that Anderson's ballot was at first challenged by the Union on the basis that he was an owner of the Company, but in a conference between the parties and the NLRB agent Mr. Robenstine assured them that Anderson did not own stock in the Company but was merely planning to buy in. The Company argued that he was in the bargaining unit and should be permitted to vote. On the basis of this information, the Union withdrew it challenge and Anderson's ballot was counted along with the others.

During negotiations, a question arose about four employees who were receiving salaries above the scale agreed upon for their classifications and the parties agreed that those employees would not suffer a reduction as a result of the contract. Section 10 of the agreement was adopted to cover this situation. The Union makes the point that Anderson was one of the four men involved and that he was discussed along with the others and that the Company did not at that time contend that he was excluded from the bargaining unit.

According to the Union, after the agreement was signed and approximately 30 days had elapsed, Mr. Earing, business representative, called Mr. Robenstine, president of the Company, and pointed out that Anderson and Wall had not applied for membership in the Union as required by Section 2. Mr. Robenstine replied that he was in the process of selling the business to Anderson, Wall, and one other person but that the sale had not reached the final stages. The Union then sent the letter of April 7 requesting the discharge of the two employees. A few days later a meeting was held between the parties and at that time Mr. Robenstine argued that Wall and Anderson were not in the bargaining unit because Wall was the service manager and Anderson was to be made the commercial sales manager.

The Union contends that Anderson is doing exactly the same work now as at the time of the NLRB election and that another employee, Mr. King, also does sales work identical to that performed by Anderson. King is in the Union; Anderson is not.

Likewise, it is contended that Wall performs the same tasks in the service area as other floormen and is not in fact a supervisor.

The Company asserts that changes have been made in the organizational structure of the business since the NLRB election which have changed the classification of Anderson and resulted in the creation of a new classification and position now occupied by Wall. Prior to the signing of the agreement, the Company did not feel that it was necessary to discuss the details of its plans and activities with the Union, thus the Union's lack of information about the changes. According to Mr. Robenstine the business has grown beyond the scope of his ability to manage it alone, so he has planned for some time to make some changes. In fact, at one time in the past he did hire a service manager who resigned after a short time. Since, no one had been found who was competent to fill the job until Wall came along.

Both Robenstine and Wall testified that Wall was hired with the understanding that he would buy a controlling interest in the business eventually and that in the meantime he would be the service manager. However, in order for him to learn all aspects of the business, it was agreed that he would spend about six months working in all phases of the operation. This, it is argued, accounts for the fact that he has worked along with other men rather than strictly in supervision. On this point it is also emphasized that the erratic nature of the tire business makes it necessary at times for all managerial employees, including the president, to work on the floor.

A few weeks prior to the arbitration hearing Wall was actually put on duty in the role of service manager and worked as such for about two weeks, according to the Company. However, because of an emergency resulting from a breakdown of the boiler, he has since been working on that problem.

The Company's description of the primary job of Wall is:

Meets customers as they come in; determines their needs; assigns the work to the proper employee; makes decisions on pricing, discounting, etc.; responsible for billing, making up invoices for customers and seeing that proper records of all transactions are made and kept; also, plans layout and work procedures.

The Union challenges this description of Wall's duties, contending that this may be his future duties but that in the past he has been doing the same work as others. The Company admits that he has done the other work for purposes of learning the business and contends that if he were in the Union he would have to be in one of the designated classifications and could not be shifted from job to job.

Anderson, according to the Company, calls on wholesalers, ranchers, and commercial customers; picks up and delivers tires; takes orders for sales and service; maintains contact with customers; when not traveling, works on the floor in sales and service.

Anderson does not supervise other employees and does substantially the same work as King, but the Company contends that Anderson is the top salesman and is responsible for the commercial area and, further, that a person can be a manager without supervising anyone.

Anderson is paid a salary of $570 per month; King receives $2.37 per hour as provided by the contract. King was also on a salary basis prior to the collective bargaining agreement.

QUESTIONS

1. How would you rule in this case?
2. What criteria for determining the appropriate unit for collective bargaining are illustrated by the arguments in this case?
3. If Wall and Anderson were ordered to join the Union in this case and later became stockholders in the Corporation or were appointed officers of the Corporation, would they still be required to pay Union dues?
4. Why did this case go to arbitration instead of the National Labor Relations Board or the courts?

Case 8

SENIORITY STATUS OF A DEMOTED FOREMAN

COMPANY: Boardman Co.

UNION: United Steelworkers of America, AFL-CIO Local 2561

ARBITRATOR: A. T. Singletary

When a foreman is demoted what seniority rights does he have to bid on a job in the bargaining unit? What problems are likely to occur in the exercise of these rights?

The following discussion of this case was prepared by A. T. Singletary, the arbitrator.

BIDDING BY SUPERVISOR

These two grievances arise out of the same set of facts, involve closely related issues, and for all practical purposes may be considered as one grievance.

The first grievance raises the issue as to whether M—— N—— was entitled to bid on a posted vacancy, and the second grievance raises the issue: If he was entitled to bid on the vacancy, from what date was he entitled to measure his seniority?

BACKGROUND

M—— N—— was hired by the Boardman company as a welder on December 5, 1944. In February of 1957 he was promoted from welder to foreman, a supervisory position carrying a monthly salary.

The Union became the bargaining agent for employees of the Company in the summer of 1960. Following certification of the election results by the National Labor Relations Board, the Company and the Union negotiated an agreement which became effective October 3, 1960, and expired one year later. The present agreement is for a term of three years beginning October 3, 1961.

On April 8, 1963, the Company notified N—— that he was being demoted from the position of foreman, effective the end of the day, April 15, 1963.

In conformity with the contract, on April 8, 1963, the Company posted notice of vacancy of one opening in Machine Operator, Third Grade. Three men bid on this vacancy, they were:

M—— N——, who was hired December 5, 1944.
Wayland E. Weeks, who was hired March 11, 1963.
R. L. Bender, who was hired March 18, 1963.

The Company found N—— to be qualified for the vacancy and awarded him the job on the basis of his qualifications and seniority. The Company used the hiring date of December 5, 1944, as the date from which N——'s seniority should be calculated.

APPLICABLE CONTRACT PROVISIONS

Article XIII, Section 5:

When a vacancy in any classification other than that of helper occurs, a bulletin advising of that vacancy shall be posted.

Employees interested in such vacancy may bid on any such vacancy by completing a job bid form in duplicate obtained from the Personnel Office.

The vacancy shall remain posted for a period of three (3) normal working days, after which said bulletin shall be withdrawn, and the vacancy awarded in accordance with Section 3 of this Article.

Section 3 provides:

It is understood that in all cases of promotion within the bargaining unit and in all cases of demotion through a decrease in the working forces, the following factors shall govern:

(A) Ability to perform the work skillfully and efficiently, according to Appendix A, Job Descriptions.

(B) Physical Fitness, and

(C) Length of continuous service (seniority).

Factor (C) shall be applicable only where Factors (A) and (B) are relatively equal.

Article XIII, Section 1:

Seniority shall be accumulated in days, months and years starting from the official last hiring date of the employee, and shall at all times be subject to the provisions of Section 11 of this article. Departmental seniority will apply in promotion and demotion. Plant wide seniority will apply in layoff and recall.

Article I, Section 1:

The Company recognizes the Union as the sole and exclusive bargaining representative for all production and maintenance employees at the Company's Oklahoma City, Oklahoma plant, including shipping and receiving employees and leadmen, but excluding plant clerical employees (including engineers and draftsmen), project draftsmen, watchmen, guards, and all supervisors as defined in the National Labor Relations Act as amended.

The term 'employee' or 'employees' when used in this Agreement shall refer to those employees of the Company working in the above classifications.

Mr. Weeks has been a member of the bargaining unit since the date of his original hire, March 11, 1963, and Mr. Bender has likewise been a member of the bargaining unit since the date of his original hire, March 18, 1963.

The issue raised by the grievances is not broad enough to determine whether Weeks or Bender, or either of them, should be awarded the job in the event N—— is determined ineligible for the job. The sole and only issue raised here concerns M—— N——. No testimony was offered from which the arbitrator could determine whether Weeks and/or Bender were qualified, and no such determination is herein made.

The issue raised here is whether or not N——'s seniority can be computed from his original date of hire, that is, December 5, 1944, when it is admitted by all parties that he has never been a member of the bargaining unit, for the bargaining unit was not established until some three years after N—— was promoted to a supervisory position. It is further admitted that N—— held that supervisory job until April 15, 1963, and was in fact a member of supervision at the time he bid on the job and at the time the job was awarded to him.

THE COMPANY'S POSITION

The Company takes the position that Section 1 of Article I defines an "employee" as an employee of the Company working in *any* and *all* of the classifications set forth in Section 1, regardless of whether or not the Union is the bargaining representative for that particular classification.

Following this reasoning, the Company contends that N—— was an employee as contemplated by the contract, with the right to bid on job vacancies, and whose seniority shall start from his hiring date, that is, December 5, 1944.

The Company contends that it makes no material difference that N—— was not a member of the bargaining unit at the time he bid on the job, was not a member of the bargaining unit at the time the job was awarded to him, and did not become a member until after he had been awarded the job. Since he admittedly was qualified for the job on which he bid, and since he had, according to the Company's computation, some 19 years' accumulated seniority, the Company contends that he was the proper person to be awarded the job.

The Company calls attention to the fact that at the time the Union and the Company were engaged in negotiations for their original contract in 1960, the Union proposed the following definition of "employee":

The term 'Employee' or 'Employees' when or wherever used in this Agreement shall mean those engaged in production and/or maintenance work including shipping and receiving employees, leadmen, plant clerical employees and project draftsmen, but excluding all office clerical employees, professional and technical employees, (including engineers and draftsmen), watchmen, guards, or salaried employees or any supervisory employees that are identifiable as such under the provisions of the Labor-Management Act of 1947, as amended.

This proposal of the Union is substantially the same as the language to be found in the contract existing between this Union and the George E. Failing Company, and which contractual provision was construed by this arbitrator in 1959. In the Failing case, this arbitrator found that persons in a position similar to that of N—— in the instant case had no accumulated seniority in the bargaining unit, and that they began to accumulate seniority from the date they became members of the bargaining unit.

The Company takes the position that they were aware of the language of the Failing agreement at the time the present agreement was negotiated, and to avoid a similar construction of this provision having to do with the definition of "employee," the Company rejected the Union's proposal as set forth above, and the present Section 1 of Article I was accepted by the parties in lieu of that Union proposal.

The last paragraph of Section 1, Article I, is: "the term 'employee' or 'employees' when used in this agreement shall refer to those employees of the Company working in the above classifications." The Company argues in its brief that thus the definition of employees embraces *all* of the "above classifications," and since the list includes classifications both within and without the bargaining unit, the Company has successfully avoided any possibility of having the present contract construed in the same manner as the Failing contract has been construed.

THE UNION'S POSITION

The Union takes the position that there is no substantial difference between the language in the Failing contract and the language in the instant contract, and that the instant contract should be construed in the same manner as was the Failing contract, to the end that no employee of the Company outside the bargaining unit, and who had never been a member of the bargaining unit, could acquire any seniority in the bargaining unit until he became a member of the bargaining unit, and he would accumulate seniority only from that date.

The Union takes the further position that since N—— had never been a member of the bargaining unit, and was not an employee within the meaning of the contract at the time he bid on the job vacancy, he was ineligible to bid on a posted job vacancy.

Under the Union's reasoning, since N—— was ineligible to bid, it follows that the Company violated the provisions of the agreement in awarding the job to him.

QUESTIONS

1. In unionized shops, management frequently encounters difficulties in recruiting bargaining unit members for supervisory positions because of fear of later demotion. M—— N—— was recruited before unionization and demoted after unionization. The Company apparently tried to protect supervisors in the wording of the agreement in the event of future demotion. Why would the Company be concerned about people like M—— N——?
2. Why is the Union giving M—— N—— a bad time? When would the Union's position on this case be a matter of principle and a matter of personalities?
3. If the arbitrator ruled for the Company, what problems would be created for the Union?
4. If the arbitrator ruled for the Union, what problems would he create for the Company?
5. If the arbitrator ruled for the union, what would be the fate of M—— N——?
6. How would you rule in this case? Why?

Case 9

PREFABRICATION OF MATERIALS

COMPANY: Safeway Stores, Incorporated
San Diego, California

UNION: Amalgamated Meat Cutters and Butcher Workmen of North America Local No. 229

ARBITRATOR: Thomas T. Roberts

Does an employer undermine the union when he introduces prefabricated materials which change the customary work of union members in a retail store?

Thomas T. Roberts, arbitrator in this case, prepared the following discussion of the issues and facts involved.

ISSUE

The stipulated issues are:

a) Did the employer breach the contract by introducing packaged ground beef in one- and two-pound packages in visking casings for direct sale to consumers in the San Diego markets covered by the Contract?

b) If so, what shall the remedy be?

STATEMENT OF FACTS

This grievance arose under, and is controlled by, the agreement between the parties entered into on November 5, 1962, and by its terms in full force and effect until the first Monday of November, 1964.

The Company operates a national chain of food supermarkets. The Union is the exclusive collective bargaining representative for employees working in the meat departments of the Company's markets located in San Diego, California, and surrounding communities. A collective bargaining relationship has existed between the parties since 1937.

This dispute involves the introduction by the Company, in September of 1963, of prepackaged ground beef sold directly to customers in the San Diego area in one- and two-pound quantities encased within visking wrapping. For many years prior to that time, it was the practice of the Company to prepackage ground beef in visking casings of 15- or 20-pound sizes (known as "catch weights") at a central cutting plant located in Los Angeles, California. Two types of ground beef prepackaged in this manner were then supplied to the retail stores in the San Diego area. The first was a coarse ground product which had to be reground before being offered for sale in the markets. The second was a fine grind which did not have to be reground at the store level, except that if it had been placed on display it was sometimes necessary that it be reground prior to being offered for sale on the succeeding day.

The coarse grind ground beef, after its receipt at the market, was removed from its visking casing, reground, packaged, priced, and displayed for sale. The fine grind ground beef, with the exception noted above, required no regrinding at the store. It was simply sliced, packaged, priced, and then displayed for sale. As to both the coarse and find grinds, all of the above operations conducted at the store level were performed by employees within the jurisdiction of the Union.

In September of 1963, the Company discontinued the shipment to the San Diego area of fine grind beef in the larger catch-weight quantities. In its stead, one- and two-pound "chubs" of prepackaged ground beef in visking casings were introduced. Upon their receipt at the markets, the chubs are simply priced and then displayed for sale in their original package. As was formerly the case with catch-weight quantities, the grinding and packaging of the chubs is accomplished in Los Angeles.

The Union learned of the pending introduction of these chubs and on August 30, 1963, sent the Company two telegrams and a letter protesting that the use of chubs would be a violation of that portion of the collective bargaining agreement which is set forth hereinafter. The Company has nevertheless continued the sale of chubs in the San Diego area and the parties, being unable to resolve their differences, have submitted the matter to arbitration.

CONTROLLING CONTRACT PROVISIONS

SECTION III
JURISDICTION OF MERCHANDISE
DISPLAYED AND SOLD

a) All fish, poultry, rabbits, meat and/or kindred products, fresh or frozen, cooked or uncooked except as hereinafter provided shall be displayed, handled, and sold under the jurisdiction of Local #229 by journeymen meat cutters under the terms and conditions contained in this Agreement. Wherever any of the above described products and merchandise is being offered for sale at least one (1) employee classified as a head meat cutter or journeyman meat cutter, an employee covered by this Contract, shall be on duty, except during the lunch hour in markets manned by one employee. All sales of products enumerated immediately above shall be credited to the meat department and/or division of the undersigned Employer. All meat products enumerated immediately above shall be cut, prepared, and fabricated on the Employer's premises or immediately adjacent thereto so as to enable said Employer to effectively supervise such operation and conduct the same under sanitary conditions. With regard to beef, veal, lamb and/or pork in carcass form, it is agreed that an exception will be made and the same may be broken down into primal cuts such as rounds, ribs, chucks, plates and loins off the premises, but said primal cuts shall be fabricated on the premises by employees covered by this Contract, and all sales shall be credited to the meat department and/or division of the undersigned Employer. With regard to luncheon meats, pre-sliced bacon, dissected and pre-fabricated fowls, ground beef and pork sausage in visking casings, Fish, Rabbits and/or frozen packaged meat, which pursuant to current custom and practices are presently pre-fabricated, pre-dissected and pre-cut, said products not be cut on the premises, but all of the above products will likewise be handled and sold by employees covered by this Contract, and the sales thereof shall likewise be credited to the meat department and/or the division of the undersigned Employer.

POSITION OF THE UNION

It is the position of the Union that the introduction of chubs to the San Diego area was a violation of Section III of the agreement between the parties. It asks that the sale of such chubs be prohibited in those markets within the jurisdiction.

The Union argues that Section III prohibits the handling, displaying, and selling of ground beef by its members unless such meat is cut, prepared, and fabricated at the markets. It is contended that the new chubs do not qualify as an exception to this mandate because the merchandising of such items is not pursuant to the custom and practice existing at the time the present Agreement was executed in November, 1962.

The Union points out that prior to the introduction of the chubs, the sole use of visking casing as a method of packaging ground beef was the transportation of catchweight quantities from Los Angeles to the San Diego markets. Ground beef was never sold directly to the customer in its original visking casing.

At the hearing, the Union introduced an interoffice memo directed to the Company's store managers in San Diego and announcing the pending introduction of the chubs. It is argued that the statements contained therein acknowledge that the new product dispenses with the cutting, packaging, and weighing of fine grind ground beef, all of which were formerly done in the markets.

The alleged failure of the Company to respond to the letter and telegrams from the Union protesting the chubs is cited as an admission on the part of management that the introduction of the new items did in fact involve a violation of the agreement.

The Union draws the attention of the arbitrator to the fact that the agreement does not contain a so-called Management Prerogatives clause and states that the unilateral introduction of the chubs by the Company amounts to "contracting out" bargaining unit work to the derogation of the rights of members of the Union. It is contended that the reduction of work operations here involved constitutes a threat to job security of affected employees and has resulted in layoffs within the meat departments.

POSITION OF THE COMPANY

It is the position of the Company that the introduction of chubs to the San Diego area was not a violation of Section III of the agreement because that provision expressly recites that ground beef in visking casings need not be fabricated in the markets.

The Company contends that in any event Section III restricts the fabrication of meat products only to the "employer's premises" and asserts that the preparation of chubs at its Los Angeles facility falls within the purview of that language. In this regard, it is noted that the employees in the Los Angeles central cutting plant of the Company are represented by the Amalgamated Meat Cutters and Butcher Workmen of North America.

Finally, the Company states that the "existing practice and custom" referred to in the agreement means the packaging of prefabricated ground beef in visking casings of whatever form or weight and the chubs are therefore in conformance with the language of Section III.

QUESTIONS

1. Is the Los Angeles cutting plant part of "the employer's premises" as contemplated by Section III of the agreement?
2. To what does the "current custom and practices" phrase of Section III refer? cutting? grinding? visking casings? or the quantities encased in visking casings?
3. Why is the union grieving in this case?

Case 10

ASSIGNMENT OF AN EMPLOYEE TO WORK OUTSIDE HIS JOB CLASSIFICATION

COMPANY: Phillips Petroleum Company
Kansas City, Missouri

UNION: Oil Chemical and Atomic Workers International Union
Local 5–64

ARBITRATOR: Marion Beatty

This case involves the performance of work outside of an employee's job description.

The following discussion of the issue and facts in this case was prepared by Marion Beatty, the arbitrator.

The issue is "whether or not the work assignment given to S. Hachinsky on December 25, 1956, pertaining to lineups to tanks on vacuum flasher stream and lube asphalt stream was a violation of the working agreement, particularly Exhibit A thereof."

The Union seeks an award ordering the Company to cease such assignments and allowing the low man in the "asphalt blender loader/senior loader group" on December 25, 1956, to work four hours at overtime rate to correct the alleged violation.

The Company denies that the work assignment in question violated any part of the contract and takes the further position that the arbitrator has no authority to issue any injunctive type of relief applying to the future conduct of the Company.

CONTRACT PROVISIONS

Contract provisions cited by the parties as relevant to the issues in dispute include the Management Prerogatives clause, the Arbitration clause defining the authority and jurisdiction of the arbitrator, a provision for four hours' call-in pay, Article VII, Section 6, entitled "Procedure for Filling Temporary Shift Vacancies," and an Appendix A to the contract which is a chart entitled "Employment, Progression, Regression and Classification Chart." This chart shows three job classifications in the asphalt and loading section and they are, from high to low, "Asphalt blender loader/senior loader," "Loader A," and "Loader-operating helper." It also shows three pumper classifications in a separate section known as the transfer section or pumper section. They are from high to low, "senior pumper," "special pumper," and "pumper."

All of these were considered.

STATEMENT OF FACTS

On December 25, 1956, when many employees in the refinery were off with a paid holiday, S. Hachinsky was employed as a pumper on the 8 A.M. to 4 P.M. shift. His job is in the transfer section. Ordinarily he does not work in the asphalt plant. The asphalt plant was down for the holiday, but several valves had to be turned to make changes in lineups and tanks on the vacuum flasher stream and lube asphalt stream. A supervisor requested Hachinsky to come a short distance from his regular station in the pumping section to the asphalt plant to turn the necessary valves as directed by the supervisor. The turning of such valves is a type of work regularly performed by Hachinsky, but he does not work at the asphalt plant. The work involved required approximately 10 minutes. Hachinsky had ample leisure time to perform the work and did perform the work promptly as directed, but under protest.

These duties ordinarily are performed and are the responsibility of the "asphalt blender loader/senior loader," the title given to the employee who is stationed at the asphalt plant and whose duties embrace, among other things, the turning of such valves for making lineups of charge and yield streams to and from the vacuum flasher and lineups for loading of trucks and tank cars with asphalt.

The Company knew in advance of December 25 that these valves would have to be turned. It could have called in a regular employee in the asphalt plant and paid him four hours at premium rate. It chose to use Hachinsky, a pumper who ordinarily did the same kind of valve turning at a nearby section.

POSITION OF THE UNION

The Union contends that the above-described assignment to Hachinsky violated the working agreement and particularly Article VII, Section 6c and Appendices A and B. The Union states that this work was the duty and responsibility of an "asphalt blender loader/senior loader" and that in his absence it should have been assigned to another employee in the asphalt and loading section in accordance with Article VII, Section 6c of Appendix A, the "Employment Progression, Regression and Classification Chart." It maintained that Hachinsky was regularly employed in the pumper section, not a part of the asphalt and loading section, and that even though he might have known how to turn valves under supervision, he was not familiar with these valves in the asphalt loading section and should not have been called to do any work in another section either permanent or temporary and that an employee in the asphalt section was entitled to the work.

The Union maintains that one of the purposes of the "Progression, Regression and Classification Chart" is to give "organizational status" to the many job classifications shown thereon, not only for the purpose of progression and regression, but also for the filling of vacancies, both temporary and permanent, and for the assignment of work in each basic classification, and that the Company could not cross the definite classification, and for the assignment of work from one to another.

It maintains that the Company violated the contract for the purpose of saving four hours of premium pay which otherwise would have gone to an employee in the asphalt loader section.

POSITION OF THE COMPANY

The Company states that the turning of these valves in making these lineups is the sort of work normally done by pumpers, that all Hachinsky had to do was to turn several valves as directed by the supervisor, the same kind of work which he did normally and regularly, and that it was no violation of any part of the contract, and was proper and reasonable under the circumstances. It states that the work in question is identical in job content and skill required to that work which is performed by him and other pumpers every day.

The Company admits that if it had called in an employee especially for this assignment it would have called someone regularly employed within the asphalt and loading section, but points out that it was not necessary to call one for 10 minutes on a Christmas holiday, and that therefore Article VII, Section 6c, and Appendix A do not apply for they provide a procedure for filling temporary shift vacancy and that no shift vacancy was involved.

The Company contends that there is nothing in the contract which prohibits it from assigning the work in question to pumper Hackinsky who was on duty, qualified and available, doing the same kind of work elsewhere, and in the absence of restriction has the right to exercise its managerial prerogatives.

The Company further contends that the Union is attempting to read jurisdictional lines into the contract where none are provided, and that the contract as well as the progression chart attached thereto is not an outline of job jurisdiction and that jurisdictional lines were never discussed in negotiation.

Lastly the Company points out that it has on 14 previous occasions made similar assignments of pumpers to perform jobs in the asphalt plant when the regular staff was off on holidays.

QUESTIONS

1. The contract and exhibits do not clearly prohibit the Company from assigning Hachinsky to this fill-in job. What sorts of inferential material could be introduced by the Union to support its claim?
2. If the arbitrator upheld this grievance, what effect would his ruling have on plant operations?
3. This dispute appears to be over a very minor issue: "ten minutes" versus "four hours' pay." What are its deeper implications for workers, the Company, and the Union?

Case 11

REOPENERS, DEFERRED WAGE INCREASE, AND ESCALATOR CLAUSES

During the 1930's and early 1940's, collective bargaining agreements typically were of one year's duration or of an indefinite duration. Under these short-term agreements both managements and unions protected themselves from drastic changes in business conditions. The obvious disadvantage of short-term agreements was the possibility of conflict over annual or more frequent wage negotiations. Frequent wage negotiations complicate problems of long-range planning and pricing and tax the energies of both parties.

At different times in recent history a long-term agreement posed a serious hazard for either management or the union. In the thirties when industrial unions were making their original collective bargaining agreements, there were grave uncertainties about the return of prosperity. Under these conditions, management assumed a substantial risk when it undertook such a modest promise as no wage cuts for 12 months. In more recent times, general prosperity, changes in the cost of living, and interunion rivalry often made it hazardous for union leaders to commit their membership to any wage agreement of long duration lest they be left behind by other workers not so committed.

This case, which is based on a Bureau of Labor Statistics[1] analysis of major collective bargaining agreements, illustrates some basic general wage adjustment clauses in long-term agreements and raises some questions about their operation and the feasibility of applying them to diverse enterprises. These clauses also provide an insight on the problem of management and unions in committing themselves to "principles" or "criteria" for general wage adjustments such as: the cost of living, productivity, ability of the enterprise to pay, and comparable wages in the industry or community.

THE GENERAL MOTORS–UAW AGREEMENT OF 1948–67

A major development in the history of long-term agreements occurred in 1948 when General Motors and the United Automobile Workers concluded an agreement which incorporated an "escalator" clause providing for wage adjustments based on changes in the Consumers' Price Index and an "annual improvement factor" providing wage increases related to general technological increases in productivity. The 1948 GM–UAW agreement provided for a flat annual improvement factor increase of three cents per hour, which was subsequently raised to four and then to five cents. The 1955 agreement shifted the increase to a percentage of wages with a minimum cents-per-hour provision. Although the formulas have been adjusted several times since 1948, the basic system of escalation plus an "annual improvement factor" remained unchanged from 1948 at least until September, 1967—a very long time in labor relations.

(*a*). The Annual Improvement Factor in the 1964–67 GM–UAW Agreement

From the agreement between:

General Motors Corporation and
International Union, United Automobile,
Aerospace and Agricultural
Implement Workers of America
(expiration date: September, 1967)

(101)(a)   The annual improvement factor provided herein recognizes that a continuing improvement in the standard of living of employees depends upon technological progress, better tools, methods, processes and equipment, and a co-operative attitude on the part of all parties in such progress. It further recognizes the principle that to produce more with the same amount of human effort is a sound economic and social objective. Accordingly, effective as of September 6, 1965, each employee covered by this agreement shall receive an annual improvement factor increase of 2½ per cent of his straight-time hourly wage rate (exclusive of cost-of-living allowance and shift premium), or 6 cents per hour, whichever is the greater in accordance with table 1:

[1] U.S. Department of Labor, Bureau of Labor Statistics, *Deferred Wage Increase and Escalator Clauses*, Bulletin 1425–4 (January, 1966).

TABLE I

Straight-time hourly wage rate*	Annual improvement factor increase (cents per hour)
Less than $2.60..............	6
$2.60–$2.99...............	7
$3.00–$3.39...............	8
$3.40–$3.79...............	9
$3.80–$4.19...............	10
$4.20–$4.59...............	11
$4.60–$4.99...............	12
$5.00–$5.39...............	13

Effective as of September 5, 1966, each employee covered by this agreement shall receive an annual improvement factor increase of 2.8 percent of his straight-time hourly wage rate (exclusive of cost-of-living allowance and shift premium), or 7 cents per hour, whichever is the greater, in accordance with table II:

TABLE II

Straight-time hourly wage rate*	Annual improvement factor increase (cents per hour)
Less than $2.68..............	7
$2.68–$3.03...............	8
$3.04–$3.39...............	9
$3.40–$3.74...............	10
$3.75–$4.10...............	11
$4.11–$4.46...............	12
$4.47–$4.82...............	13
$4.83–$5.17...............	14
$5.18–$5.53...............	15

NOTE: In the case of a classification, the rate for which is determined by a wage rule in the local wage agreement relating the rate for classification to the rate for another classification or classifications, the above tables will determine the rate for the classification where there is a conflict with such wage rule
* The "straight-time hourly wage rate" for an employee paid under an incentive method of pay is defined in appendix E.

(b) In addition, effective September 5, 1966, each employee covered by this agreement shall receive a wage increase of 2 cents per hour. This 2 cents per hour shall be added to the "wage rate" or "base rate" as provided in paragraphs (101)(d) or (101)(e)(1) whichever is applicable after such "wage rates" or "base rate" have been adjusted to include the September 5, 1966, annual improvement factor increase provided for in paragraph (101)(a).

(c) In addition, each employee covered by this agreement shall receive a cost-of-living allowance in accordance with the provisions of paragraphs (101)(g) and (101)(h).

It is agreed that only the cost-of-living allowance will be subject to reduction so that, if a sufficient decline in the cost of living occurs, employees will immediately enjoy a better standard of living. Such an improvement will be an addition to the annual improvement factor increase provided for in paragraph (101)(a).

(*d*) The improvement factor increases in base rates provided for in paragraph (101)(a) and the 2 cents-per-hour increase provided for in paragraph (101)(b) shall be added to the wage rates (minimum, intermediary, and maximum) for each daywork classification.

(*e*)(1) The amount of the improvement factor increase shown in the tables in paragraph (101)(a) for the "straight-time hourly wage rate" of an incentive job classification and the 2 cents-per-hour increase provided in paragraph (101)(b) shall be added to the base rate of that job classification, except as the parties to this agreement may provide otherwise in writing.

THE ESCALATOR CLAUSE IN THE 1964–67 GM–UAW AGREEMENT

From the agreement between:

General Motors Corporation and
International Union, United Automobile,
Aerospace and Agricultural Implement
Workers of America
(expiration date: September, 1967)

BLS Consumer Price Index	Cost-of-living allowance, in addition to wage scale by job classification (cents per hour)
106.4 or less..............	None
106.5–106.8..............	1
106.9–107.2..............	2
107.3–107.6..............	3
107.7–108.0..............	4
108.1–108.4..............	5
108.5–108.8..............	6
108.9–109.2..............	7
109.3–109.6..............	8
109.7–110.0..............	9
110.1–110.4..............	10
110.5–110.8..............	11
110.9–111.2..............	12
111.3–111.6..............	13
111.7–112.0..............	14
112.1–112.4..............	15
112.5–112.8..............	16
112.9–113.2..............	17
113.3–113.6..............	18
113.7–114.0..............	19
114.1–114.4..............	10

And so forth with 1 cent adjustment for each 0.4 change in the index.

(*i*) The amount of the cost-of-living allowance which shall be effective for the period September 1, 1964, through September 30, 1964, shall be 14 cents per hour.

(*j*) The amount of any cost-of-living allowance in effect at the time shall be included in computing overtime premium, night-shift premium, vacation payments; holiday payments, call-in pay, bereavement pay, and paid absence allowance.

(*k*) In the event the Bureau of Labor Statistics does not issue the Consumer Price Index on or before the beginning of the pay period referred to in paragraph (101)(g), any adjustments required will be made at the beginning of the first pay period after receipt of the index.

(*l*) No adjustments, retroactive or otherwise, shall be made due to any revision which may later be made in the published figures for the BLS Consumer Price Index for any base month.

(*m*) The parties to this agreement agree that the continuance of the cost-of-living allowance is dependent upon the availability of the monthly BLS Consumer Price Index in its present form and calculated on the same basis as the index for July 1964, unless otherwise agreed upon by the parties. If the Bureau of Labor Statistics changes the form or the basis of calculating the BLS Consumer Price Index, the parties agree to request the Bureau to make available, for the life of this agreement, a monthly Consumer Price Index in its present form and calculated on the same basis as the index for July 1964.

(*n*) Effective October 1, 1964, 9 cents shall be added to the base wage rates (minimum, intermediary, and maximum) for each daywork classification in effect on that date, except that said 9 cents shall not be taken into account for incentive pay calculation purposes. In the case of employes on an incentive basis of pay, the 9 cents shall be added to the earned rate of such employes. Simultaneously, 9 cents shall be deducted from the cost-of-living allowance in effect on September 30, 1964, and thereafter the cost-of-living allowance shall be computed in accordance with paragraphs (101)(g) and (101)(h) above.

C. The Consumer Price Index: Selected Periods, 1964–1966

October 1964	108.5
January 1965	108.9
April 1965	109.3
July 1965	110.2
October 1965	110.4
January 1966	111.0

GENERAL WAGE ADJUSTMENTS INDEPENDENT OF FORMULAS

Frequently long-term agreements simply provide for fixed wage increases at specified dates as follows:

(*a*) Effective September 7, 1964, all wage rates in effect immediately prior to the effective date of this agreement shall be increased 3 per cent, but not less than six cents per hour,

(*b*) Effective September 7, 1965, all wage rates shall be increased 3.1 per cent, but not less than seven cents per hour, and

(*c*) Effective September 7, 1966, all wage rates shall be increased 3.2 per cent, but not less than seven cents per hour."

QUESTIONS

1. Assume that you were a UAW member employed by General Motors on September 3, 1964, at a "straight-time hourly rate" (exclusive of cost-of-living allowance and shift premium) of $3.00. What would your gross

hourly rate be on: (a) December 9, 1964, (b) September 29, 1965, (c) April 15, 1966? As of April 15, 1966, what is the lowest level to which your gross hourly rate may fall before the expiration of the agreement in 1967?

2. Over the total duration of the GM agreement, what will happen to your real wages?

3. What should be an escalator "equivalent" to GM for a firm paying wages ranging from $1.25 to $2.00 per hour in September, 1964? What would be an "equivalent" annual improvement factor for the same firm? Justify your answer.

4. Some union leaders have been highly critical of the UAW for "selling out" to the automobile companies on long-term agreements with annual improve-ment factor and escalator clauses. Some management people have been equally critical of GM for initiating these kinds of agreements. Comment on these criticisms.

5. Assume that you were a union member under "general wage adjustment independent of formulas" clause quoted above. Assume further that your hourly rate on September 1, 1964, was $1.70. What percentage and cents per hour wage increases would you have accrued by September 10, 1966? How would you compare your experience to the experience of the GM employe referred to in questions 1–4?

Case 12

"TANDEM" COMPENSATION ADJUSTMENTS FOR NONUNION PERSONNEL

Names and places in this case are fictitious. The case involves the determination of a policy on salary adjustments for both nonunion and unionized employees. "Mr. Allen" employed one of the authors of this book as a consultant on this problem.

BACKGROUND

The Ralta Company is engaged in the manufacture and distribution of products in an expanding industry. At the present time, it is about midway in a 15-year program of product and process diversification. Profits of both Ralta and its principal competitors reflect the general prosperity and expansion of the industry. In this industry labor costs equal between 15 per cent and 20 per cent of total costs of production. Ralta sells its products in a somewhat restricted geographic area and could be seriously hurt by geographic price wars which sometimes plague the industry.

In his 1957 report to stockholders, the president of Ralta said, "With regard to the outlook for 1957, we anticipate that demand for our prod-ucts will average 4 per cent to 5 per cent higher than 1956. Ordinarily we would expect such an increase to result in moderate gain in profits. While management seeks this result, it cannot now be assumed with any assurance because our industry faces more than the usual number of uncertainties." Over the past five years, industry estimates of increased volume have leveled off at the 4 per cent to 5 per cent figure from a higher estimate of progress in the previous decade. Actual progress in the industry has fallen somewhat short of these estimates. However, Ralta has expanded each year approximately at the 4 per cent to 5 per cent industry estimated rate.

The Ralta Company employs 12,000 wage and salary workers. They are engaged in diverse operations geographically spread over the eastern seaboard and southeastern states. Five thousand hourly employees are concentrated in two plants: one in Pennsylvania employing 4,500 and one in Texas employing 500. Hourly employees are represented by one union in Pennsylvania and by a rival union in Texas. Another 5,000 employees work for a commission or in isolated locations and are not related to the present problem. The direct concern of this case is with 2,310 salaried employees, about 700 of whom are represented by the Pennsylvania union.

The salaried employees of the Ralta Company can be classified into three groups:

A) Earning between $25,000 and $100,000 per year—55 employees—not represented by a union.
B) Earning between $15,000 and $25,000 per year—155 employees—not represented by a union.
C) Earning less than $15,000 per year—2,100 employees—this group includes middle-management people, production supervisors, engineers, and staff personnel (about 1,400 people) earning more than the top rate paid to union represented workers and about 700 employees earning less than the top rate paid to union represented workers. The latter 700 employees include secretarial, clerical, and custodial personnel, some of whom are represented by the union.

Union-negotiated wage increases over the last 15 years have been substantial and frequent (almost annually). The Company and Union have never agreed on basic principles which should be uniformly applied in wage determination. However, changes in the cost of living, Company profitability, wage increases and wage levels paid by the Company's competitors, and changes in productivity have been discussed in negotiations and probably exerted an influence on what was finally agreed to.

For the last 15 years, the Ralta Company has followed the practice of granting salary increases approximately equal to the negotiated wage increases immediately upon the conclusion of negotiations with the union. On several occasions the Company bypassed the A Group positions or gave a fixed dollar increase which was less than the full percentage increase to Group A positions. All employees in Groups A, B, and C may receive annual *merit* increases until they reach the maximum of their salary classification. These merit increases have been awarded apart from and *in addition to* the general "tandem" adjustments for salaried employees.

THE PROBLEM

Members of the top management of the Ralta Company became concerned over the prospect that salaried employees might feel that the unions were negotiating for the salaried people. Management did not want the salaried people to have this sympathetic interest in the success of the unions. When this matter was discussed in the operating executives' meeting, the president of Ralta directed Mr. Allen, the industrial relations director, to look into the situation and recommend a solution.

GATHERING THE FACTS

Mr. Allen started his analysis by stating the following Company objectives:

1. To provide fair and equitable compensation for salaried employees.
2. To retain and attract competent salaried employees at all salary levels.
3. To build management morale and loyalty to the company.
4. To pay salaries which have an incentive value.
5. To provide flexibility in salary administration.
6. Not to prejudice the company's position in collective bargaining.
7. To minimize the belief among salaried employees that their pay is determined by union negotiations.

This listing of objectives by Mr. Allen represented his beliefs concerning the relative priority of each goal. He realized that the goals were not mutually exclusive. He recognized that salary increases had closely paralleled wage increases negotiated with the unions. However, he insisted that this is "natural" since the same economic forces which generated wage increases are responsible for salary increases. Announcement of general salary increases before reaching agreements with rival unions would seriously prejudice the company's position in collective bargaining.

In wage negotiations, Ralta had openly accepted only two criteria for wage increases: (*a*) practice of industry competitors—"meeting the average" and (*b*) rapid and substantial increases in the cost of living. However, it was obvious that competitors' concessions and Ralta's willingness to "meet the average" were strongly influenced by the high profits in the industry and the firm. This in turn could be related to rapid technological progress and increasing man-hour productivity.

Mr. Allen wrote to other companies in his industry about how they handled this problem. The responses indicated that every major company in the industry followed Ralta's practice and that they were equally disturbed about its bad psychological effect. No one in the industry proposed a more satisfactory way of handling the problem.

Not satisfied with these responses, Mr. Allen broadened his inquiry to other industries. Some dozen industrial relations directors responded to Allen's inquiry. They added the following possibilities as methods for handling the salary problem:

1. Grant a percentage increase equal to the union-negotiated increase but announce it at times so that it will not be associated with collective bargaining negotiations. "When adjustments were made considerably after union negotiations, it usually became a question in management personnel's minds whether the adjustments granted were related to the last increase given to the union or were a forecast of the next increase to be negotiated. We are not sure that all of the confusion so generated has been to the advantage of the Company."

2. Award all salary increases exclusively on a "merit" basis. Prepare an annual forecast of total salary adjustments and budget funds to each department on the basis of this forecast. Allow each department head to award salary increases to approximately one twelfth of his employees each month. Each meritorious employee receives his salary increase on a strictly personal and confidential basis. "We have encountered two problems with this system. First, if we overestimate or underestimate the forecast in one year, we try to compensate for this error the next year. Although we have been generally successful in providing equity *over a number of years,* inequities have arisen in some individual years. The other problem is the timing of the increases. An employee receiving his increase in January may receive a greater annual increase than a more meritorious employee who receives his increase in November."

3. Announce general adjustments at a predetermined annual date. The amount of the annual adjustment will be determined by an analysis of economic conditions at the time of the announcement.

4. Adopt a fixed formula for general adjustments to be made at a predetermined annual date. One such formula might consider changes in the Consumers' Price Index plus a fixed percentage increase to reflect increases in general "productivity."

5. Provide for salaried employees to participate in a stock-purchase or profit-sharing plan.

RECOMMENDATIONS

You are Mr. Allen. Next week you must present your recommendations to the operating executives' committee.

Prepare your recommendations on the basis of the alternatives developed in your research. Weigh each of the alternatives against the objectives outlined above.

Precisely state the problems surrounding the application of your recommendations.

To what extent is this problem an "economic" problem? an "ideo-logical" problem?

Case 13A

ARBITRATION OF A GENERAL WAGE ADJUSTMENT

This case represents a rare and unusual situation in arbitration: the submission of a general wage adjustment under a wage reopener clause to an arbitrator after the parties have failed to reach agreement. The case is also somewhat unusual in that the parties gave the arbitrator no guidelines to consider in reaching his decision.

BACKGROUND

The Company is located in a rural area and is engaged in the winter time manufacture of a novelty item which has a very short retail market life of March through August. Employing a peak labor force of 250 people, the Company dominates the market (in excess of 60 per cent of national sales) for its product. The Company has been in operation as a tightly held family organization for over 100 years. The present officers are the direct lineal descendants of the founder of the Company. Although wages have always been low, the Company took a paternalistic attitude toward its employees prior to their union organization in late 1962. When the first union agreement was signed in December, 1962, the Company discontinued its paternalistic practices and became, in the words of its president, a "hard-nosed employer." Although the Company is profitable, the market for its products involves great risks and there is no evidence that profits are excessive or that the family is "milking" the Company.

THE AGREEMENT

The first collective bargaining agreement between the Company and the Union was signed on December 10, 1962, scheduled to expire on December 10, 1964. This agreement froze all the personal wage rates that the Company had been paying prior to collective bargaining and granted wage increases to individuals ranging from 15 cents to 60 cents per hour which resulted in a wage structure based on jobs performed and seniority with the Company. The agreement provided for a reopening on wages only on December 1, 1963, 30 days of negotiation, and then a right to strike if no new wage agreement could be reached. The agreement did not provide for arbitration of the unresolved wage issue.

Negotiations during December, 1963, did not provide a wage agreement. The parties submitted the wage dispute to an arbitrator with full authority to decide the issue.

WAGE FACTS

Prior to the arbitration, the prevailing wages of employees of the Company were as follows:

Group I employees: Minimum $1 per hour, Maximum $1.15 per hour
Group II employees: Minimum $1.05 per hour, Maximum $1.25 per hour
Group III employees: Minimum $1.05 per hour, Maximum $1.25 per hour
Group IV employees: Minimum $1.15 per hour, Maximum $1.50 per hour

All of the jobs were light work, the difference in jobs in each group consisting of personally acquired manual dexterity and experience in working with the wide variety of items which the Company produced. Employees in Groups I, II, and III did highly routinized jobs while Group IV workers frequently had to improvise methods on special jobs. At peak employment, Groups I, II, and III would occupy 225 people, while about 25 people held Group IV jobs. From five to ten years of employment with the Company was a usual prerequisite to assignment to a Group IV job.

UNION'S FINAL WAGE DEMAND

Groups I, II, III employees   10 cents per hour across the board

Group IV
with 90 or more days seniority on Jan 1, 1964   10 cents per hour
with over 2 years' seniority on Jan 1, 1964   20 cents per hour
with over 4 years' seniority on Jan 1, 1964   30 cents per hour
with over 5 years' seniority on Jan 1, 1964   40 cents per hour

If the Union's demands were met, 3 Group IV employees would be eligible for 20 cents per hour, 4 Group IV employees would be eligible for 30 cents per hour, and 18 employees would be eligible for 40 cents per hour. The top rate for Group IV employees would be $1.90 per hour.

THE COMPANY'S FINAL WAGE OFFER

The Company's final wage offer was tied exclusively to seniority. It provided:

Employees with 3 months to 6 months seniority   5 cents per hour
Employees with 6 months to 3 years seniority   7½ cents per hour
Employees with 3 years to 5 years seniority   10 cents per hour

Employees with 5 to 10 years seniority	15 cents per hour
Employees with 10 years to 15 years seniority	20 cents per hour
Employees with over 15 years seniority	25 cents per hour

If the Company's wage offer were to be applied, 10 employees (including Group IV employees) would receive 7½ cents per hour, 200 employees (including 5 Group IV employees) would receive 10 cents per hour, 29 employees (including 8 Group IV employees) would receive 15 cents per hour, 6 employees (including 5 Group IV employees) would receive 20 cents per hour, and 5 employees (5 Group IV employees) would receive 25 cents per hour.

QUESTIONS

1. Do the Union demands and Company offer reflect different "philosophies" of wage payment?
2. Compare the cost of the Union's demand and the company offer.
3. Write an award in this case justifying whatever criteria you elect to apply to your decision.

Case 13B

ARBITRATION OF A GENERAL WAGE ADJUSTMENT

COMPANY: Remco Industries

UNION: International Brotherhood of Teamsters
       Teamsters Industrial and Allied Workers, Local No. 97

ARBITRATOR: Daniel House

Cases of this type are rarities. Only in very exceptional cases will a management and a union entrust to an arbitrator the question of general wage adjustments which is vital to both management and the union.

What criteria should an arbitrator use in making or refusing to make a general wage adjustment?

The following discussion of the issue and facts in this case was prepared by Daniel House, the arbitrator.

ISSUE

"Should an increase be granted under Article XXI, Section 2, of the Agreement between the parties; if the answer is in the affirmative, how much shall the increase be?"

The parties agreed that if an increase was granted, it was to be made retroactive to December 23, 1963, and paid to all employees with seniority on that date.

CONTRACT PROVISIONS

Article XXI, Section 2, of the agreement is as follows:

Effective thirty (30) days before December 23, 1963, the Company and the Union shall negotiate wages; failure to agree, the matter shall be submitted to arbitration in accordance with Article VIII, Section 1(d) of this Agreement.

Article VII, Section 1(d), provides for the selection of an arbitrator by the New Jersey State Board of Mediation.

THE CONTROVERSY

Following a strike by the Union, the parties entered into a three-year agreement, effective December 23, 1962, providing, among other things, a general increase of seven cents per hour effective December 23, 1962, and wage negotiations in each of the following two years, subject to arbitration in the event of failure to come to agreement. The parties failed to agree on the wage question in the December, 1963, negotiations. The Union requested a general wage increase of fifteen cents per hour; the Company refused to concede any wage increase.

THE COMPANY'S ARGUMENT

The Company is engaged in the manufacture and sale of toys. The industry is a highly competitive and volatile one, differences of a fraction of a cent an item often making the difference between a sale and no sale, a "fad item" catching on (but with an indeterminate life) suddenly lifting employment in the manufacturing end and, as suddenly, dropping it. Employment in this Company ranges from 200 to 2,000 employees in production during a year.

The Company argues that its business has been off since 1961; that from an annual net profit ranging, for all the years up to 1961, from 7 to 9 per cent, it has reduced each year since, and for the calendar year 1963 was just over 4 per cent; that its stock, as a result, is now reduced to about one-half its 1959 value; that it entered into the agreement with the Union in 1962 with misgivings about the wisdom of the seven-cent general increase provided therein but agreed to it as "a token of confidence," hoping that a new item it was about to introduce would go well; that the new item was a disappointment and 1963 a worse year even than 1962; that the Company had ceased to pay cash dividends in 1962 as a result of the declining profit picture; that the financial problems of the successive poor seasons had been compounded by the costs of financing of the new plant they had built to try to keep competitive in manufacturing operations; and that the wage rates paid were in line with those of the major competitors in the area.

The Company stated that the average base rate (before piecework earnings) is about $1.40 per hour. A Union witness thought that the average would be closer to $1.30 per hour. By agreement of the parties, the arbitrator examined payrolls at the Company plant; the data was duplicated and copies submitted to the arbitrator and to the Union by mail. The arbitrator's examination of the records showed that the average base hourly rate for the "basic crew" is $1.38 per hour. The parties agreed that the "basic crew" consisted of about 400 employees who were laid off for only brief periods between seasons; they further agreed that the crew employed at the time of the hearing would be representative of the "basic crew."

In summary, the Company took the position that since its pay rates were not out of line with the competition in the area, since its profit picture was poor, and since the seven-cent wage increase in 1962 had been unwarranted, and the anticipated good season to justify it had not materialized, the 1962 error should not be repeated; the Company urged, therefore, that no wage increase be awarded.

THE UNION'S ARGUMENT

The Union did not contest that the industry is highly competitive and volatile, nor that the Company's wage rates were in line with the area competition. However, the Union argued that the Company was not losing money; that the reduction in profits for the last few years had been more than offset by the continued adequate rate of profits for all the many years prior to 1962; that the Company should have had the foresight to set aside from the profits of the fat years enough to take care of the employees' legitimate desires for improvements in the lean years; further, the Union claimed that the effect of the seven-cent increase in 1962 was in part negated by the operation of the federal law establishing $1.25 minimum wage rate in 1963. For these reasons the Union requested an award of 15 cents per hour general increase.

QUESTIONS

1. What criteria for general wage adjustments are argued by the parties in this case? Do the criteria argued by the parties exhaust a list of conceivably valid criteria? As an arbitrator would you feel obligated to consider only the criteria argued by the parties?
2. As representative of the union, how would you justify your demand for a 15 cents per hour general wage increase?
3. Why did the parties in this case sign a reasonably common three-year agreement with annual reopeners? Why did the parties sign an agreement with the *very unusual* provision for arbitration of the general wage adjustment disputes arising at reopening dates?

Case 14

DISCONTINUANCE OF FREE MEALS

COMPANY: Lutheran Medical Center
UNION: Retail, Wholesale and Department Store Union, Drug
            and Hospital Employees Union
            Local 1199
ARBITRATOR: Benjamin H. Wolf

Can an employer practice of providing free meals be discontinued without bargaining with the union? Does the fact that the employer "bought back" the free meals from the union in previous negotiations justify the discontinuance of the meals a long time after the employer bargained the meals away?

The following discussion of the issues and facts in this case was prepared by Benjamin H. Wolf, the arbitrator.

BACKGROUND

This arbitration is concerned with a protest made by the Union against the decision by the Employer to discontinue the practice of supplying meals to its employees in the dietary department.

The parties are in substantial agreement on the facts. Prior to 1951, the employees ate their meals family style at a big table and received their meals without charge. That year a change was made. A cafeteria was established and the hospital announced that employees eating in the cafeteria would be required to pay for whatever food they ate. To compensate for the loss of three meals a day, the employees were given wage increases ranging from $10 to $20 per month.

In 1953 Mrs. Fevang became personnel director of the hospital. At that time all the employees were paying for their meals. Some time between 1953 and 1956 the employees of the dietary department stopped paying for their food. No one seems to know when and how this happened but there is no denial that some of the lower echelon supervisory employees knew about it. When the administrator learned of it, he issued a memorandum directing that dietary employees should no longer receive their meals free and again, in order to compensate them, he announced that they would be paid $10 a month in addition to their regular wage. Sometime between July, 1956, when the memorandum was issued and June, 1963, when the Union agreement was signed, the dietary employees again began eating their meals without paying for them.

Mr. Johnson, the present administrator, came to the hospital in August, 1962. It is conceded by the Employer that Mr. Johnson, who headed the management team in the negotiation of the Union agreement, was aware that the employees in the dietary department were eating meals in the cafeteria and not paying for them. He was not aware, however, of the history of this problem, and that on two occasions the Employer had "brought back" the practice of furnishing free meals to the employees for substantial wage increases.

In November, 1963, the hospital engaged an independent contractor to manage the dietary department. He informed Mr. Johnson that the dietary employees were not paying for their meals. On July 1, 1964, the Hospital notified the dietary employees that from July 15, 1964, on they would have to pay for their meals.

It was stipulated that Marshall Dubin telephoned Mrs. Fevang shortly after July 1, 1964, and told her that the employees were dissatisfied with the notice. He requested a meeting, which was held on July 22.

POSITIONS OF THE PARTIES

On the merits of the controversy, the Union argued that a practice which had existed for a long period of time and which had not been changed by the contract should be left undisturbed by the parties until they jointly agreed to alter it. The Union urged that the granting of a meal to an employee is not only a condition of employment but a method of compensation and that by taking the meal away the Employer reduced the wages of these employees. Thus, it was a basic change not only in the working conditions which existed at the time the bargain was entered into but also in the compensation they had received for more than a year since the contract was signed.

Although there is no provision in the contract which covers the granting of free meals to these employees, the Union urged that the myriad of conditions which exist outside of the contract are part of the collective bargaining relationship and hence, part of the agreement between the parties.

The position of the Employer is that the free meals were not an existing benefit or a past practice in the conventional sense of the word. It urged that the Employer, having already twice bought itself out of this practice, should not be required to negotiate itself out a third time. It stated that the hospital never deemed the free meals as compensation to the employees and, therefore, never reported them on the W-2 tax forms. Under the Internal Revenue Code, therefore, the meals were deemed to have been furnished as a convenience to the hospital, not as compensation to the employees.

The Employer argued that the problem was analogous to the discontinuance of a Christmas bonus when parties made no reference to the bonus and cited two New York Supreme Court cases in support of its position.

QUESTIONS

1. Were the meals for dietary employees "wages" or a "bonus"?
2. What weight should be given to a practice that apparently arose by mistake?
3. How many times must the hospital "buy back" the meals?
4. How would you rule in this case?

Case 15

ELIMINATION OF A JOB BY THE COMPANY

COMPANY: Potter and Brumfield, Inc.
             Princeton, Indiana

UNION: International Association of Machinists
             Local Lodge No. 1459

ARBITRATOR: Carl A. Warns, Jr.

The case involves the right of the Company to eliminate a job.

The following discussion of the issue and the facts in this case was prepared by Carl A. Warns, Jr., the arbitrator.

The question before the arbitrator is whether or not the Company has violated the contract by eliminating the job of group leader in Department 41.

The Company manufactures electrical relays. Actual production takes place on production lines of varying sizes dependent upon the type of work of each line. Prior to the strike, Line 41, in addition to the usual complement of employees actually servicing the line, contained a "group leader" whose duties are set forth in a job description and whose job title and rate are listed in Appendix A ("a part" of the contract). The group leader on Line 41 did not return to the employ of the Company after the strike and the Company did not replace him. The Union asserts in this grievance that this failure to assign another group leader to the line violates the collective agreement between the parties. The Company explains that time did not justify the training of a new group leader since the line would be moved to another plant within a short time. The group leader's supervisory duties were assigned to the foreman and the remainder of his work to a material handler. The Company states in their post-hearing brief that subsequent to the hearing on this case the line has been in fact moved and that the relays previously produced on Line 41 are manufactured elsewhere. Regardless of this factor, however, it is the position of the Company that they retain the right under the current agreement to eliminate jobs and that there is no contractual basis for this grievance challenging the failure to fill the job of group leader on Line 41 after the strike.

CONTRACT PROVISIONS INVOLVED

ARTICLE X—Wages

Section 1: Effective the first pay period after this contract is signed, the Company will grant a general wage increase of five (5) cents per hour and include such increase in Exhibit "A" attached hereto and made a part hereof. On February 4, 1957 all employees shall receive a wage increase of five (5) cents per hour which increase shall be added to the then present rates as shown in Exhibit "A" attached.

. . .

Section 3: Production rates, which serve as the basis of this plan, shall be established by the Company through time study wherein proper allowances are made for unavoidable delays and incentive earnings. These production rates are guaranteed by the Company to remain unchanged except as agreed upon in this contract.

ARTICLE XIV—Full Agreement Clause

This Contract represents complete Collective Bargaining and full agreement by the parties in respect to rates of pay, wages, hours of employment or other conditions of employment which shall prevail during the term hereof and neither party may hereafter negotiate on any other matters during the life of this agreement.

POSITION OF THE UNION

The breach of contract by the Company in failing to assign a group leader to Line 41 not only adversely affects the earnings of the employees on that line but establishes a precedent whereby larger lines and more employees are reduced in earning capacity. The employees on Line 41 are compensated on a group incentive basis; the group leader on a full average plant incentive. It is obvious from a reading of the job description of the group leader that he is an essential element in the ability of the individual employee to maintain the rate. It is no answer for the Company to say that the instructional responsibilities of the group leader can be transferred to a foreman; the latter is responsible for several lines and may frequently be absent while the employees are sitting idle on base wages due to lack of parts and instruction. The group leader, on the other hand, is assigned to one line and is therefore constantly available to maintain the flow of materials and to give needed instruction; his importance to the efficient teamwork of the line as reflected in earnings is clear. Nor is it for new classifications such as "material handlers," whose basis of compensation is unknown to the Union, or instructors, to do the work of group leaders at considerably lesser pay. If these "instructors" or "material handlers" are compensated at a straight hourly rate, they lack the incentive of the group leader who had a direct and immediate interest in high production on the line.

This contract contains no management prerogative clause. During the last negotiation the Company wished to have such a provision added but the Union would not agree. Since the contract does not expressly authorize the Company to eliminate the job classification of group leader and in the absence of a management clause which might be argued as permitting this by implication the Company lacks the contractual right to take the action challenged in this grievance. The Union requests the arbitrator to find that the Company violated the contract and the principles of good collective bargaining and to compensate the group leader for all or part of any earnings lost while foremen, material handlers, instructors, or other persons are performing group leader work while such individuals are on layoff and subject to recall.

POSITION OF THE COMPANY

It is well established in industrial relations and confirmed in numerous published arbitration cases that in the absence of a restriction in the collective agreement management has the inherent right to eliminate jobs, classifications, and to combine duties in interest of production. The only limitation is that the admitted right not be exercised in an arbitrary or discriminatory manner. In this case there is no reference to either job descriptions or group leaders in the body of the contract. The only reference to group leaders is in Exhibit "A" which is for the sole purpose of classifying the employees and to designate the rates of pay for each classification. Such classification and rate of pay simply set forth the rate that must be paid to jobholders in particular jobs and does not mean that there must be an employee or employees in each classification at all times. The incumbent group leader on Line 41 resigned from the Company and was not replaced because it was determined that a group leader for so small a group would not make for an efficient operation. In addition, there were no group leaders available with experience on this line. Since it was anticipated that the line would be moved to another plant, it would have been poor management to spend from eight weeks to three months training a group leader for a nonexistent job. Furthermore, group leaders are used as an adjunct in assisting foremen in the operation of the department. Where the department is so small, as here, such a classification is a surplus one. The foreman is fully capable of taking care of all supervisory duties. There is no instructor on Line 41 and the use of a material handler is proper. There is such a classification listed in Appendix A called Material Handler (Machine Shop). The duties of the material handler here are comparable and therefore it was not deemed necessary to add a new job classification or description to be filed with the others.

The Union's position that the absence of a management prerogative clause prevents the Company from exercising traditional prerogatives is untenable. Management has an inherent right to make all essential decisions designed to make the Company competitive. The elimination of jobs and the combination of job duties is one of them. Limitations on this basic right can be granted only at the bargaining table by the Company. Since this contract contains no such limitations, it follows that the Company's decision in this case must be confirmed and the grievance denied.

QUESTIONS

1. The Union argues here that the signing of an agreement without a management's rights clause after negotiations on the inclusion of such a clause means that management has only those rights explicitly stated in the contract. What influence should an unsuccessful management argument for a management's rights clause in negotiations have on this case?

2. What is the significance of Company motivation in a case of this type? The Company here claims that it couldn't fill the job from present employees and that the job was going to be moved to another plant in the near future. Without these special circumstances, could the Company eliminate the job for such a reason as saving money?

3. What kinds of evidence should the Union and Company supply in the controversy over loss of incentive earnings resulting from the elimination of the group leader job? How would you judge the validity of the evidence that might be supplied?

Case 16

REDUCTION IN MACHINE CREW SIZE

COMPANY: National Container Corporation
            Jacksonville, Florida

UNION: International Brotherhood of Pulp, Sulphite and Paper Mill
               Workers
            Locals 426 and 614

ARBITRATOR: A. B. Marshall

Changes in the size of work crews and methods of work frequently cause grievances. This case involves earnings as well as crew size.

The following discussion of the issue and facts in the case was prepared by A. B. Marshall, the arbitrator.

The issue arises out of the Union's grievance dated March 21, 1957, as amended by the Union's statement to the Company dated March 27, 1957.

The grievance of March 21, 1957, is in the form of a letter to the Company's plant manager and reads as follows:

The Press Department is aggrieved and disturbed over management's discontinuance of a second press helper on No. 6 and No. 3 presses, thus creating a two man crew. This is in violation of the Labor Agreement, and the Union must insist that management adhere to the Labor Agreement, and in this case, restore a three man crew to No. 6 and No. 3 presses. A two man crew creates an overwork load on the operator, and also is breaking management's past policy.

The amendment to the above grievance dated March 27, 1957, reads as follows:

We wish to hereby amend the grievance of March 21st regarding the discontinuance of second press helpers on various machines.

The Press Department employees are aggrieved because of the Company acting on its own, in reducing the crew coverage without consulting the Union, thereby causing several old established procedures to be changed and causing the following inequities to be created without giving proper consideration to the Union.

1. The Company failed to notify the Union or to make any effort towards reaching a mutual agreement concerning any of the changes involved.

2. Management's action in reducing the work force on the presses changes an established policy and created an excessive work load on the press operators and first helpers when working under normal operating conditions.

3. The changes put into effect by management without giving proper notice or consideration to the Union will cause the press operators and first helpers to take a considerable reduction in wages, under the established production bonus plan which is in effect covering the employees in this plant.

4. Because of the company continuing to reduce the work force which this grievance effect.

5. Management's attitude in arguing and aggravating the employees involved on the job beyond reason.

The Union feels that these matters should be resolved in a reasonable manner and mutual agreement between the company and the Union and recommends that this be done by following the established policies under which the plant has been previously operated, thus eliminating excessive work loads and not effecting the present wage structure. All things to be as they were before any changes were made."

The Company pointed out at the oral hearing that it did not understand that the grievance included the Number 1 press. However, the Union stated that its grievance did include the Number 1 press. It was noted by the Company that no mention of the Number 1 press was made in the grievance filed by the Union.

PRINTING PRESSES NOS. 6, 3, AND 1

The Number 6 press was bought secondhand and installed at the Jacksonville plant soon after February 28, 1955. In May, 1955, the Longway Hooper press began to be used for impressions on Falstaff box orders, with a fixed speed machine of 30 impressions per minute.

The Number 3 Longway Hooper press was also bought secondhand and placed into operation on Falstaff box orders soon after being received in the Jacksonville plant on June 15, 1956, and March 31, 1957, the machine speed was increased to 40 impressions per minute. Industrial Engineer McDonald testified that the standards department was not notified until after April 1, 1957, that the speed had been changed, although it is his best information that it was changed very shortly after June 15, 1956. It is estimated that Number 6 and 3 presses are about 30–50 years old.

The Number 1 press, Printer Slotter has been in operation for a number of years. It is used on Falstaff orders only in connection with trimming the body, taking about a quarter inch off of each side. Information furnished by the Company is to the effect that the standard was originally set up for both a two-man crew and a three-man crew. Number 1 is a variable speed machine.

As noted above, Numbers 6 and 3 presses produce boxes for Falstaff beer orders. Three-man crews were used until sometime prior to March 21, 1957, when the Company announced that it would operate with two-man crews. The reason for the change in the number of men on the crew, according to the company, was mostly because it was thought unnecessary to have 100 per cent inspection of the boxes; this meant that two men would be able to handle production from the machines. New standards were set up for both presses, covering both two-man and three-man crews. However, two-man crews are presently operating the presses.

It is understood that the standard originally applied to the Number 6 press in 1955 was applied to the Number 3 press on June 15, 1956, and that even though the speed of Number 3 was increased from 30 to 40 impressions per minute the standard was not changed as long as the three-man crew was functioning. According to the Company, this accounts for the "inflated" earnings during the period prior to March, 1957, on the Number 3 press.

The three-man crew works with an operator, a first helper and a second helper, referred to as an operator, a feeder, and take-off man. The two-man crew consists of an operator and a feeder, the second helper being eliminated; the feeder's work is not affected but the operator takes over some of the work of the second helper, most of the inspection work of the latter job being discontinued.

THE PRODUCTION BONUS AND INCENTIVE SYSTEMS

In a Memorandum of Agreement, dated June 1, 1953, the parties agreed concerning certain provisions regarding an Incentive Production System, several of the most pertinent provisions for the purpose of this arbitration proceeding being as follows:

. . . The plan must provide an earnings opportunity to the individual or incentive group, while working on incentive, of at least 15% above the day or hourly rate for the job.

. . . It is further agreed that the UNION shall be supplied with three (3) copies of all standards and incentives, in addition to the standards and incentives being posted in the appropriate areas. Should an established and accepted standard be changed, the Company will discuss the matter with the UNION and furnish, in writing, three (3) copies of the reasons and basis for such change. . . .

The parties also agreed under date of June 1, 1953, on a Standard Practice for the Administration of Incentive System, several pertinent provisions of this agreement being noted below. Under the caption, "Establishing a Standard," it was provided as follows:

1. The Company shall observe and study a given operation to determine the most efficient method of doing a job.
2. The Company then shall make a time study of the job while in operation under the prescribed method. Such time study shall be on the basis of a reasonably efficient pace (one that an employee could be expected to consistently maintain for an eight hour shift).
3. After a Standard has been placed in effect and given a reasonable trial, not to exceed a 60 day period, and found to be fair and adequate, it shall become a permanent standard. Such standard shall include a credit of no less than an average of 15% as an allowance for personal time, fatigue, hazards and special conditions and minor delays of less than 6 minutes.
4. Standards will be expressed in time and posted at the operating time.

Under the caption, "Changing a Standard," it is provided:

1. A permanent Standard that has proven to be fair and adequate shall not be changed unless there is a bonafide change in method, material, equipment, or conditions that would affect the Standard by as much as 5%.
2. It is recognized that there might be a series of minor changes in a job, which separately are not 5%, but together are 5% or more. Thus, in order to keep the program up to date and fair to all employees, if either of the signatory parties request, an annual review of all Standards will be corrected to reflect the accumulated changes."

Under the caption, "Settlement of Disputes," it is provided:

1. Any question by the Union as to the accuracy of a Standard will be checked immediately by the Standards Department under actual operating condition. The results of the observation will be given the same day if possible.
2. If such report is not satisfactory, the Union shall then be entitled to start a grievance at the level of Superintendent. . . .

Under the caption, "Computing Production Bonus Efficiency and Earnings," it is provided:

1. Standards are based on a normal sixty-minute productive hour. Par efficiency is considred to be a fifty-minute hour. The start-to-earn point under the Production Bonus System shall be a forty-five minute hour; one (1%) per cent for each additional minute. It is understood that no production bonus shall be paid to an employee for an efficiency exceeding an average of ninety-five in one day. . . .

BACKGROUND OF GRIEVANCE

On May, 1957, the Company discontinued its use of a second helper on the Number 3 and Number 6 presses when used to print ends for Falstaff cartons. In addition, the second helper was also discontinued on the Number 1 press when used to trim bodies for Falstaff cartons. Some of the details concerning these presses have been noted above.

New standards providing for both a two-man and a three-man crew were issued on May 1, 1957, as follows:

Three Man Crew—Printing is accomplished on the Longway Hooper using brass printing dies mounted on the steel cylinder with screws. The crew consists of three persons—the operator who switches, loads in and out on skids with shared jack, preloads the feed table, keeps fountains full of ink and makes necessary quality checks and adjustments; the feeder who feeds each sheet from the preloaded stack on to the feed bar holding each sheet against the feed bar to insure squareness; and a take-off man who catches each sheet, inspects, squares it against a right angle back and side stop, counts (last run of body only) and asides handful to skid—30 maximum impressions per minute.

Two Man Crew—The crew consists of two persons; the operator who switches loads in and out on skids with shared jack, preloads the feed table, keeps fountains full of ink, makes necessary quality checks and adjustments, and asides handful to skid; the feeder who feeds each sheet from the preloaded stack on to the feed bar holding each sheet against the feed bar to insure squareness.

The reason given by the Company for the two-man crew, as noted above, is that 100 per cent inspection is no longer necessary for the Falstaff orders.

The above standards take the place of the three-man standard established in the spring of 1956 as a result of Falstaff changing from a two-color to the present three-color carton, which necessitated running the box bodies and ends twice to complete the printing. According to information furnished by the Company, the original standard for the box ends on the machines was for a five-man crew.

The standard for the Number 1 machine was established August 8, 1955, and provided both for a two-man and for a three-man crew so no changes needed to be made. This machine is also concerned with the Falstaff order.

It is contemplated by the Company that a return may have to be made to 100 per cent inspection, therefore the retention of the three-man standard.

It was also noted by the Company that "the operator's duties on a two-man crew are identical with his duties on a three-man crew except that he is required to aside handfuls of the blanks to the skid on the take-off end of the machine on the two-man crew."

The hourly production expected from the Number 6 press has been reduced from 1,455 to 1,310 and the hourly production expected from the Number 3 press has been reduced from 1,820 to 1,622, this being reflected in the establishment of the incentive standards; in addition, according to the Company, there is built into the standards for the two-man crew some time allowance for shutdowns for the operator to fill the ink fountains and adjust the register.

COMPANY'S POSITION

The Company claims that in making the changes to the two-man crews it was exercising its management prerogative to direct the working force and to make changes in methods and product, a principle firmly established in labor-management relations and supported by numerous arbitration decisions: Republic Steel Corporation; Illinois Bell Telephone Company; Youngstown Sheet and Tube Company. The Company insists that the changes made were primarily changes in methods of operation, not changes in working conditions as claimed by the Union, the chief change being the elimination of the second helper. This change is said to have had the same effect as the introduction of technological improvements. "The Company wishes to make it clear that it does not believe it can change working conditions and work practices in complete disregard of the Union's rights under Article IX of the bargaining agreement. The Company does assert, however, that there is a difference between a change in the method of operation, which the Company has admittedly the right to do and which may incidentally affect working conditions, and a change in working conditions as such which would be prohibited under Section IX of the bargaining agreement," such difference being recognized in the following arbitration decision: Goodyear Tire and Rubber Company of Alabama. The Company submits that the changes made to the two-man crews were essentially changes in methods of production that affected working conditions only because of the elimination of some of the inspection work by doing away with the second helper.

Reference is made by the Company to the Union's claim that it was not given proper notice of the intended reduction in the size of the crews. In reply the Company points out that the agreement provides for no such notice, that the Company had the right to make these changes if it wishes to do so. The Company also points out that during the grievance meetings this matter was not discussed at all and that at the oral hearing the Union did not attempt to refute the Company's statement in this respect.

"The Company submits that the Union is in effect objecting to the increased work load on the operator and the alleged loss of wages resulting from the elimination of the second helper rather than the Company's right to make such changes," and in substantiation of this view cites from pages 42 and 43 of the transcript which contains statements of the Union's representative. In this connection the Company notes that the Carroll report shows on the basis of a study that the operator on a two-man crew on the Number 3 machine spent 44.8 per cent of the total operating time waiting for the stack to build up at the take-off end of the machine and that the operator on a two-man crew on the Number 6 machine spent 59.4 per cent of the total operating time of that machine in the same manner. It is pointed out that to accomplish the production of 1,310 blanks an hour on the Number 6 press with a 15 per cent bonus it is only necessary that the operator work 23.4 minutes per hour and the feed 40.8 minutes per hour; to accomplish the expected production of 1,622 blanks per hour on the Number 3 press with a 15 per cent bonus it is only necessary that the feeder work 54.4 minutes per hour and the operator 31.2 minutes per hour. In this connection it is noted by the Company that the work load of the feeder had not been questioned by the Union. There was also testimony by Company witnesses that the work load on the presses is in general less than on other jobs in the plant and in other Owens-Illinois plants.

The Company asserts that it has met the requirements of the contract with respect to the Memorandum of Agreement, dated June 1, 1955, regarding the production bonus and incentive system, parts of which have been summarized above.

It is the Company's position that the Union's consent is not necessary for standards to be changed, that it is only necessary to discuss the changes with the Union and furnish three copies of the reason and basis for the change. The changes were discussed with the Union "on several occasions including four grievance meetings." The jobs have been restudied by the plant engineer and also by Mr. Carroll from the Toledo office. The Company points out that although three copies of the standards were not furnished the Union, this was in accordance with a new procedure whereby the Company keeps a complete list of all standards for the Union which are available to it at all times, a procedure that has not been objected to by the Union.

With reference to the guarantee of incentive earnings it is contended by the Company "that the two-man standards for the No. 1, No. 3 and No. 6 presses do provide an earnings opportunity of at least 15% and that the production efficiencies contained in Company Exhibit No. 4 and in Mr. Carroll's report, Company Exhibit No. 5, prove that such opportunity has been realized." The Company's Exhibit 4 attempts to verify this conclusion. "The average efficiencies on the No. 3 press since the change in standards have been 68.6 for a three-man crew as compared to 68.5 for the two-man crew, without Mr. Connell's efficiency rating, or 65.2 with Mr. Connell's efficiency rating. . . . It should also be noted that the average efficiency for a two-man crew on the No. 6 press from March 1, to June 30, 1957, was higher than the average efficiency of the three-man crew for the same period." The Company explains that the earnings of the Number 3 press were inflated since based on the presses running at a fixed speed of 30 impressions per minute whereas actually this press was running at a fixed speed of 40 impressions per minute.

UNION'S POSITION

The Union bases its case on its allegations that the Company has disturbed present work practices in establishing the two-man crews, that the Company had no right to make the change it did without consultation with and mutual agreement with the Union, that the work load on the presses is too heavy at the present time, that there has been no change in method and no technological change to justify the two-man crews, that the men involved have all suffered financial loss as a result of the change to the two-man crews, and that the Company went about making the changes to the two-man crews without due regard to the Union and the employees and then tried to justify its action by the manipulation of figures.

It is pointed out that the crew coverage of the presses were negotiated with the Company at the same time that the rates were set for the jobs. In setting the rates for the jobs in question various customary factors entered into the picture, very important ones being work conditions and practices and the job content of each job. In this connection the Union cites Section IX of the contract, entitled Work Conditions and Practices:

It is further understood and agreed that all regulations and instructions of the company, work regulations and practices, safety rules, copies of which are attached, which do not conflict with the provisions of the Agreement or with State and Federal Laws, are affirmed and will continue in force and effect during the life of this Agreement or any extension thereof, unless changed by mutual consent of the parties signatory hereto.

We believe that it was not proper for the management to make a change of this sort and of this magnitude during the life of a signed Labor Agreement without the mutual consent of the Union.

The Union contends that there was absolutely little or no reduction in the job content of the three people on the presses. The Company had just as much need for the third helper on the day that they took him off as on the day they put him on. Taking off the second helper affected the job content of the remaining two jobs, and also added to the responsibility of these jobs.

The Union does not argue that the Company has no right to install laborsaving devices that will dissipate the need of a man for there is no question but that when a man is no longer needed on a job the Company has a right to take him off the job. In the present case, if the Company had installed an automatic feeder on the presses, thereby doing away with the need for a human feeder, the Union would not have complained or filed a grievance for the Company would have been within its contractual rights. What the Company actually did was to make use of the "stretch out" system by arbitrarily reducing the crew coverage to two men, expecting the two remaining men to do a job formerly performed by three men.

Attention is called to the testimony of Mr. Connell and Mr. Hand who are regular employees on the presses involved in this case. "Both of these men testified that their earnings have been less since the reduction of the crew." They submitted for the consideration of the Arbitration Board check stubs to establish their conclusions that their earnings had suffered as a result of the change to the two-man crews. Not only have the men on these jobs had their pay reduced, they have to work harder for what they get.

Objection is made to the way the Company went about making the changes, being described as inappropriate and highhanded. The Union did not know that the changes were being contemplated until advised that changes would be made to the two-man crews.

The Union states that it has no faith in the time studies that were made. This is because the facts of the case, as they appear to the Union, are such as to preclude the possibility of being fair when two men do the work formerly performed by three men. The Union concludes that the employees have given the two-man crew experiment an honest effort and that it has not worked out.

QUESTIONS

1. Is this dispute over technological change, or working conditions, or wages, or production standards? Why?
2. The union's concluding statement implies that the two-man crew is "experimental." How might experimental crews be compensated during the shakedown cruise? What are the advantages and disadvantages of each of these methods?
3. What weight should be given to the Union-submitted evidence of income loss?
4. What advantages and disadvantages to management are inherent in the union's suggestion of advanced consultation on this type of change?
5. Write an opinion and an award in this case.

Case 17

A NEW RULE IN "CLOCKING IN" AND "CLOCKING OUT"

COMPANY: McCord Corporation
            Washington, Indiana
UNION: International Association of Machinists
            Local 2041
ARBITRATOR: Daniel E. Lewis

To what extent is the Union's approval required for a new plant rule formulated by management during the term of a collective bargaining agreement?

The following discussion of the issue and facts in this case was prepared by Daniel E. Lewis, the arbitrator.

ISSUE

Did the Company violate the collective bargaining agreement between the parties by requiring that all hourly employees who leave the plant for lunch must clock out and in, said requirement being instituted without discussion with the Union?

SUMMARY STATEMENT OF THE FACTS

This dispute came up for hearing before the arbitrator appointed by the Federal Mediation and Conciliation Service upon the failure of the parties to arrive at a satisfactory settlement of the following grievance dated September 11, 1964:

> Company Posted Rule—And by so doing violated Article I, Article IV. Section 1—of Collective Bargaining now in effect: by changing conditions of employment and hours of employment without bargaining with International Association of Machinists; Local 2041, which is the recognized collective bargaining agent. Company by so doing also violated last paragraph of shop rules, which required that any changes or additions in rules shall be discussed with union committee before being posted in the plant. (We the committee ask that the additions of rules be discontinued.) Union Committee 9/11/64

The parties made numerous attempts to settle the dispute between them in the various steps of the grievance procedure (the written answers to which are not made a part hereof).

Under date of September 14, 1964, the Company posted a notice to all employees from the office of the plant manager, T. J. Grady. The subject of this notice was "Instructions Regarding Leaving and Entering the Plant," said instructions being introduced into evidence and identified as company Exhibit No. 1. There are 12 instructions set out in the notice at issue, only one of which, the instruction designated No. 5, is at issue. Said instruction No. 5 states: "All hourly employees who leave the plant for lunch must clock out and in."

This so called "instruction" was instituted by the Company in order to have a more accurate and better control of the work force, especially during lunch periods, by having employees clock in and out during such periods. At the time the instruction was put into effect, the Company was undergoing a change in its guard system wherein an outside agency was taking over the guard duties originally performed by the Company's own employees. When the Company's own employees were performing guard duties, the guards were able to record on slips of paper the names of employees who went out of the plant and those who came in late in order that proper deductions could be made from wages. It was felt that the installation of an outside agency for the handling of guard duties would require a closer check of employees going out of the plant and coming into the plant during the lunch period. As a result, the Company posted a list of instructions, Company Exhibit 1 (above). The posting of these instructions led to the filing of the subject grievance.

The following language found in the rules accompanying the contract and attached to the contract, together with certain sections of the contract of the collective bargaining agreement itself, require interpretation:

McCord Corporation
Washington, Indiana
Shop Rules

It is understood that the following Shop Rules are not part of the negotiated agreement. (Opening paragraph as to shop rules.)

"Any amendments, additions or revisions of these rules shall be discussed with the Union Committee before being posted in the plant. (Closing paragraph as to shop rules.)

Article VII—Arbitration

(35) Jurisdiction of Arbitrator—The jurisdictional authority of the Arbitrator is defined as and limited to the determination of any grievance which is a controversy between the parties or between the Company and employees covered by this Agreement concerning compliance with any provision of this Agreement and is submitted to him consistent with the provisions of this Agreement.

POSITION OF THE PARTIES

Union's Position

The Union takes the position that inasmuch as a new three-year agreement was negotiated and signed, effective September 1, 1964, and inasmuch as the Company had not mentioned a desire to change or to add to the rules, the Company could not institute what the Union describes as a new rule, set out in Item No. 5 of Company's Exhibit No. 1 (above). For the company to install a new rule as set out in Item No. 5, it would be necessary for it to get the consent of the Union. Putting the new rule or change into effect without consultation with the Union and without the Union's consent was a violation of contract and a violation of the language. Further, in the "shop rules," the Union further pointed out that the change made by Item No. 5 of the notice in dispute was being made at the very time the parties were involved in contract negotiations; yet, no effort was made to acquaint the Union with this fact, nor was there any discussion as to the institution of the proposed new rule. Prior to the time of establishing the new rule, employees were penalized by loss of a certain number of minutes of paying time when arriving a little after the lunch hour. The former penalty will not only be continued but in addition, violation of the punching in late rule will result in penalty layoffs for employees.

Under such circumstances, the Union takes the position that the arbitrator should direct the Company to render the posting of Item No. 5, as set out in Company Exhibit No. 1 (above), of no force and effect. The Union further takes the position that the system for punching in and punching out at the lunch hour should be the same as it was prior to installation of the new rule by the Company, with the resultant elimination of the penalty of layoff for violation of said rule.

Company's Position

The Company takes the position that under the collective bargaining agreement it has the exclusive right to establish rules governing the conduct of its employees, as more particularly set out in Article IV of such agreement. There is nothing in the agreement that requires the Company to share its responsibility for managing and directing the work force with the Union. As a result, the Company can establish "rules of conduct" without securing the Union's consent so long as such rules are not in conflict with provisions of the agreement and are not discriminatory in nature.

The Company, in posting the notice in dispute, did so with the feeling that it was merely giving its employees instructions which would lead to better control of employees leaving the plant and entering the plant on an irregular basis. Thus, the Company takes the position that it did not change a working condition by the requirement set out in Item 5 of Company Exhibit No. 1 (above), nor did it institute a new shop rule.

Even if the arbitrator were to take the position that the instruction at issue is a "shop rule," the Company need not receive Union approval before placing such a rule in effect. Shop rules are not part of the negotiated Agreement, and informing the Union as to the installation of a new shop rule is merely a courtesy, not a contractual requirement. The disputed instruction was merely set up for the purpose of establishing better administrative control. There is nothing to indicate that the Company's action in instituting such a rule will in any way discriminate against an employee because of Union membership.

Inasmuch as the Union has made no showing that Item 5 of Company Exhibit No. 1 (above) is discriminatory in nature and inasmuch as the Company does not in any way violate any provision of the collective bargaining agreement, the Company feels the grievance should be dismissed.

QUESTIONS

1. Are the opening and closing paragraphs of the shop rules contradictory? If so, which paragraph governs? Does the arbitrator have jurisdiction in this case?
2. The Union argues that its consent must be obtained before a new rule may be instituted while the Company argues that a discussion of a new rule with the Union is a mere courtesy which may be overlooked. What are the implications of both interpretations?

Case 18

"BANKING" OF PRODUCTION BY INCENTIVE WORKERS AS BASIS FOR DISCHARGE

COMPANY: Harnischfeger Corporation
Milwaukee, Wisconsin

UNION: United Steelworkers of America
Local 1114

ARBITRATOR: Harold M. Gilden

Can an incentive worker be disciplined for high production which he "banks" and reports in such a way as to stabilize his earnings? What is the impact of such actions on the efficient operation of an enterprise?

Harold M. Gilden, the arbitrator, prepared the following discussion of the issues and facts involved in the case.

ISSUE

Grievance dated April 23, 1964, filed by X——, challenging the propriety of his discharge on April 22, 1964, and requesting reinstatement with full back pay.

NATURE OF CASE

X——, the grievant herein, was hired by the Company as a radial drill press operator on September 9, 1959, and continued to be employed in that classification until April 22, 1964, the date of his discharge.

For April 21, 1964, X—— turned in a work ticket which showed that he had produced 100 pieces of Part No. 15F-427 (order no. 360292) in an elapsed time of six hours. On the following day, April 22, 1964, X——'s work ticket reported that he worked the full eight hours of the shift in running 120 pieces of Part No. 15F-427 (order no. 360292).

It so happened that X——'s immediate supervisor foreman, Frank Wilhelm, sometime during the morning of April 22, 1964, was informed that all 300 pieces of Part No. 15F-427, the total run scheduled to be produced on order no. 360292, were completed. Wilhelm made an on-the-spot inspection of the finished pieces and verified the accuracy of this report. Actually, X—— did not run any pieces of Part No. 15F-427 on April 22, but instead utilized the full eight hours of his shift in working ahead on other jobs that were scheduled to be produced in his department.

On April 22 Wilhelm talked to X——about the apparent discrepancy in the production figures given by X——on his work tickets relating to Part No. 15F-427 and the finished run of 300 pieces already produced and X—— admitted that he had already run all 300 pieces.

Only the week before, around April 14 or 15, Wilhelm had called X——aside and told him that the second-shift radial drill press operators had complained about X——'s "banking" activities and Wilhelm suggested to X——that if X—— was "banking," he should stop it immediately.

After reviewing X——'s employment record with the Company, which revealed four disciplinary suspensions of three days each for various infractions other than banking, a one-day layoff, four written warnings plus the verbal warning given him on "banking," it was decided that he should be discharged and he was terminated on April 22, 1964.

CONTENTIONS

The Union says that special circumstances are present in this case which distinguish it from run-of-the-mill dishonesty situations; that the plant rule relied upon by the Company does not specifically relate to "banking"; that this is the first case in which the rule has been used in this connection; that occasionally employees are directed to rework jobs under circumstances where such performance is absorbed by the employee and not accurately reflected on the work card; that X——had accumulated a bank of 24 standard hours not only to improve his position but, in part, to compensate for the Company's failure to apply the proper rate; that the bank created by X—— simply put him in the same relative position he would have been in had scheduling practices been such as to avoid protracted periods of idle time; that none of the disciplinary penalties assessed against X—— during the approximately five years that X—— had been employed were for "banking," or for any activity reasonably related thereto; that the quality of X——'s work performance was sufficiently high to gain him a merit increase which he held at the time of his discharge; that "banking" had widespread acceptance in the shop and its existence was common knowledge; that X—— had to keep his work cards locked up to prevent employees on other shifts from utilizing his "bank"; that management had no established policy opposed to banking, but in effect winked at the practice and permitted it to exist; that other arbitrators have refused to sustain disciplinary action for employee laxity to which the Company itself was a party; that in resorting to an accepted practice to maintain a favorable earning structure, X——'s actions are readily differentiated from cases involving employee attempts to obtain pay for work not performed; that in discharging X——, the Company departed from a long existing practice of toleration, acquiescence, and even permissive participation in the practice of "banking"; that X—— should not be the first scapegoat of a new policy which the Company desires to put into effect; that "banking" exists at this plant and if it is a problem it should be met head-on across the bargaining table and not resolved indirectly through the discharge of a selected victim; that X—— should be reinstated to employment and that if any punishment is merited, it should be limited to a loss of some back pay.

The Company says that honesty is basic where employees are compensated under an incentive program; that supervisors cannot possibly count every piece produced so the Company must rely on employee truthfulness; that reliance on the integrity of the employee is implicit in the mechanics of any "honor system"; that there is not one scintilla of evidence that the Company was aware of "banking" or that it ever condoned it; that the Company's standard hours program is based on employee honesty and that X—— knew he was performing dishonestly; that current correct reporting of time spent on jobs is the heart of the standard hour program; that if "banking" goes on, the Company doesn't know its costs, can't properly assign the work load and can't properly price its product; that each man cannot possibly be watched every moment and it is only feasible to check employees on a spot basis; that the grievant was specifically warned that "banking" was prohibited; that the nature and extent of X——'s banking practices warrants his discharge; that the record is abundantly clear that for a long time X—— was laying out his own work load and determining the amount of compensation he should receive per work day; that this was not a one-card inadvertent type of falsification but a carefully concealed plan of running this radial drill press for X——'s benefit regardless of the Company's costs, its work schedules and work allocations; that were this practice to be adopted by the majority of employees on standard hours, it would completely annihilate the Company's costs and production setup; that this is a clear case of an employee practicing a fraudulent scheme for a period of years and who continues to engage in it after being warned to stop; that the grievance should be denied.

APPLICABLE CONTRACT PROVISIONS

Section 7. Discharge Cases. In the event any employee is discharged from and after the date hereof and he believes that he had been unjustly dealt with, such discharge shall constitute a case arising under the method of adjusting grievances herein provided. . . . In the event it should be decided under the rules of this agreement that an injustice has been dealt the employee with regard to the discharge, the Company shall reinstate such employee and pay full compensation at not less than the employee's regular rate for the time lost less any outside wages accrued during the period. . . .

Section 8. The Management of the plant and the direction of the working forces and of the affairs of the Company, including the right to hire discipline, or discharge for proper cause, or to transfer from one job to another except as limited by Section 3, and the right to layoff because of lack of work or for other legitimate reasons is vested exclusively in the Company.

PLANT RULES

* * * These are the things which can lead to discipline, up to and including discharge:

*   *   *   *

10. Falsifying records, reports, or applications for employment.

In November, 1963, less than six months before his discharge, X—— was suspended for three days for requesting a down time allowance of 3.2 hours due to no work, when in fact there were jobs waiting to be finished.

QUESTIONS

1. Compare "banking" to "punching another person's time card" and to "theft."
2. From the facts given in the case, is "banking" a widespread practice at this company? If "banking" were a widespread practice and management wanted to stop it, what steps should management take?
3. Why would second-shift employees complain about X——'s "banking"?
4. Assume that "banking" is possible only when production standards are loose. Since management has sole responsibility for establishing production standards, do these loose standards condone the practice of "banking"?

Case 19

RATE CHANGES DUE TO RATE SETTING ERRORS

COMPANY: Orr and Sembower, Inc.
UNION: United Steelworkers of America
ARBITRATOR: Jacob Seidenberg

What constitutes a "clerical error" under an agreement which permits the employer to revise incentive wage rates which contain "clerical errors"?

The following discussion of the issue and facts in this case was prepared by Jacob Seidenberg, the arbitrator.

ISSUE

Whether the Company cut the rates in violation of the "Guarantee of Standard Allowed Time" provision of the 1959 Supplemental Agreement.

FACTS

The Company and the Union, despite objections and protests raised by some employees, instituted by Supplemental Agreement dated May 21, 1959, an individual incentive plan in lieu of an existing production performance bonus with a 50–50 arrangement. The prior plan had been in effect from 1953 until the middle of 1959. The new individual incentive plan was installed in the plant on a departmental basis, one department at a time. Under the plan incentive rates were developed by two methods. One involved the use of time studies, and the other involved the use of standard data developed at other production machine shops. The time Study method involved the use of rate sheets and the standard data method used Standard Data Charts.

Most of the rates in the machine shop were established from standard data charts while the other rates were developed from time studies made in the shops. From January until November, 1960, the time studies were the sole source for the establishment of incentive rates. But in the summer of 1960 the Company determined that faster and more accurate coverage could be obtained from the use of standard data and consequently switched to this method. In November, 1960, the first standard data chart was issued and used to determine the rates in the main gas piping assemblies. Since the incentive plan had been installed in the assembly department in January, 1960, the rates which had been developed prior to November by the use of the time study method, under the terms of the Supplemental Agreement, had to be, and were, maintained.

The incentive rates are developed in the plant by a review of the existing standard data or the rate sheets from a study of the applicable drawings and the present rate structure. This work is performed by a standards setting clerk under proper supervision. This position is considered by the Company to be a training job for time study and data work. Time Study work is considered to be more difficult and more responsible and is paid a higher salary than standards setting work.

The provision of the Supplemental Agreement which is relevant to the resolution of the grievance states, in part, as follows:

Guarantee of Allowed Standard Time
The Company agrees not to revise allowed time for any operations, unless there is a clerical error or unless changes are made that justify a restudy. Such changes may be methods, feeds, speeds, mechanical equipment, tools,

fixtures, materials and designs. Any such change shall not affect an operator's incentive opportunity, provided that the operator maintains substantially the same efficiency and effort on the changed operations as before such changes were affected.

UNION'S POSITION

The Union maintains that under the "Guarantee of Allowed Standard Time" provision the Company has no right to change, unilaterally and without Union concurrence, the rates in question. The Company is undertaking to revise rates which have been in effect for years, rates which the Company knew about and for which it was willing to pay.

If the Company is permitted to change rates at will, then there is no value in having an established rate, no matter how long it has been in effect. All the Company has to do to change a rate is to declare it a mistake. An employee who has become proficient at his job would have to be careful about his output if his rates could be cut at will. In the Company's action giving rise to this grievance, what the Company is calling mistakes are not clerical errors and therefore are not within contract provision.

The Union has not objected in the past to the Company's making legitimate rate changes as long as they were done in accordance with the terms of the contract. This is evidenced by the fact that this grievance is the first one that has gone to arbitration on the issue of rate changing. Other rate changes were done pursuant to the provisions of the agreement and not arbitrarily.

The Union denies the Company allegations that it has only changed rates for four specified reasons and that it has always changed rates for these reasons without Union protest. This is the first time that the Company has changed rates by departing from the contractually established procedures.

In addition the Union wishes to direct attention to Section 5 of the agreement, "Rate Establishment and Adjustment." That contract provision only allows three months within which to challenge a rate, and after that the rate is fixed. The Union disagrees with the Company's contention that Section 5 does not apply to incentive rates. The Union believes that the section applies both to hourly rated and incentive jobs.

The Union also cites an award rendered by the umpire in a Bethlehem Steel case which held that the Company may not correct a longstanding error in the administration of an incentive plan when the agreement provided that rates in effect shall remain in effect unless changed with the consent of the Union.

COMPANY'S POSITION

The Company maintains that it has not improperly changed any rates in violation of the agreement. It has not even changed rates which were improperly set by time study methods. It has classified these improper rates as "red circle" rates and honored them even though it knows full well these rates are incorrect.

The only rates which the Company has corrected are those which are permissible under the Supplemental Agreement, are the result of mistakes made by the employees working in the "standards setting" category, and are of the following nature:

1. Use of a rate sheet when standard data chart should have been used.
2. Use of standard data chart when rate sheet should have been used.
3. Application of data on rate sheet or standard data chart.
4. Arithmetical mistakes.

The Company has consistently made revisions in mistakes resulting from these four types of mistakes. The Company has furnished the Union since August, 1961, with copies of all wage changes made. The figures show the following:

1. Over 60,000 rates have been issued since the individual incentive system was initiated.
2. The Company has made 588 corrections in the 60,000 rates due to mistakes in the four mentioned categories.
3. Of these 588 corrections, 76 were arithmetical errors and 512 were improper establishment of rates from available data.
4. Of the 588 corrections, 376 increased the rates and 212 decreased the rates.

The Company's action in correcting those rates, which have come within the four mentioned categories, are "clerical errors" and are within the terms of the "Guarantee of Standard Time Allowance" provision of the Supplemental Agreement of 1959. The Company's evidence, in the form of the exhibits it introduced, clearly demonstrates that the types of errors which have been corrected in the past without Union objection fall within the four specified kinds of mistakes. As far as the Company knows, all the rate changes involved in this grievance come within the four categories of mistakes cited here.

The Company also denies that Section 5 of the contract has any applicability to this dispute. Preliminarily, the Company wishes to state that this Section was never mentioned at any stage of the grievance procedure. But in any event, the parties executed a supplemental agreement on October 2, 1959, which specifically governs the method for adjusting incentive rates, including the procedure for investigating incentive rate grievances. It is this supplemental agreement, and not the Section 5 of the contract, which governs.

QUESTIONS

1. Are the four categories of mistakes listed by the Company all of the same character?

2. What weight should be given to the Bethlehem Steel case cited by the Union?

3. The written grievance in this case demanded that the Company cease the practice of cutting rates, but contained no request for damages. In the hearing, the union asked for monetary relief for the aggrieved employees. If you were to uphold the Union's argument, what relief would you grant?

Case 20

SHIFT CHANGES OCCASIONED BY DAYLIGHT SAVING TIME

COMPANY: Hanna Nickel Smelting Company
            Riddle, Oregon
UNION: United Steelworkers of America
ARBITRATOR: Paul L. Kleinsorge

What shift time arrangements should be made in an around-the-clock operation when daylight saving time becomes effective?

The following discussion of the issue and facts in this case was prepared by Paul L. Kleinsorge, the arbitrator.

THE CASE

The Hanna Nickel Smelting Company plant at Riddle, Oregon, operates on an around-the-clock basis, with four crews rotating to cover three shifts. The day shift runs from 7 A.M. to 3 P.M.; the swing shift, from 3 P.M. to 11 P.M.; and the graveyard shift, from 11 P.M. to 7 A.M.

At 12:01 A.M. on April 28, 1963, the state of Oregon went on daylight saving time. In anticipation of this change, the Hanna Nickel Smelting Company notified its employees on April 11 that the Company's clocks would be moved ahead one hour at 12:01 A.M. on April 28, and that the shifts would operate on a daylight saving time basis until the state returned to standard time in October.

When the change was made on April 28, one result was that the "A" crew, which was working the 11 P.M. to 7 A.M. shift that night, actually worked only seven hours instead of eight. The Company paid the "A" crew for the seven hours actually worked rather than for eight. The union maintains that under the terms of the collective bargaining agreement, "A" crew is entitled to eight hours' pay. The Company denies this claim.

When the return was made to standard time in October, the Company deliberately set its clocks back one hour at a time when the "A" crew was on the 11 P.M. to 7 A.M. shift. Thus on this occasion "A" crew actually worked nine hours instead of eight, and was paid for nine hours with time and one-half for the ninth hour. Over-all, the "A" crew received one-half hour's pay more than it would have received if there had been no changes in time. The Company maintains that it was within its rights under the terms of the contract to handle the matter in this way.

A second issue involving one hour's overtime pay to "C" crew was withdrawn by the Union at the hearing. The only issue, therefore, concerns the question whether "A" crew is entitled to eight hours' pay rather than the seven actually worked on the shift when daylight saving time was instituted.

THE ARGUMENTS

Union

The Union states that the showup and recall clause of the contract (Article VII, Section 6) provides a minimum guarantee of eight hours' pay. The pertinent parts of this clause are:

Showup or recall time shall be paid as follows: employees who are regularly scheduled or who are notified to report and who do report for work shall be allowed in the event of no work for which they were scheduled or for which they were notified to report, or called out, is available: (a) four (4) hours pay at the standard hourly wage rate of the occupation for which they were scheduled or for which they were notified to report or called out; or (b) for those who actually begin work at least eight (8) hours pay at the rate of the classification in which the work is performed. . . .

The Union argues that since "A" crew was regularly scheduled for work and actually worked seven hours, "A" crew is entitled to eight hours' pay under the "b" part of the showup and recall clause.

Company

The Company denies that the showup and recall clause, when placed in its proper perspective, guarantees eight hours' pay or pre-empts the Company's right to schedule for any given number of hours. The Company states that the showup and recall clause was meant to provide compensation for inconvenience. That is, it is meant to provide compensation to those who report for work and then find after reporting there is no work or not enough work. The Company says that in the present case there was no inconvenience. The crews had been notified in advance what the schedules were to be. Since there was no inconvenience, there is no reason for additional compensation beyond the hours actually worked.

The Company argues that the showup and recall clause does not guarantee a workday or a workweek. The fact that there is a four-hour provision in the clause indicates that the parties to the agreement contemplated something less than eight hours. The Company points out that a guaranteed workday or workweek would be a very stringent requirement, and that such a requirement cannot be implied from the language of the clause. If the parties had meant to impose such guarantees when the contract was drawn, they would have spelled out the guarantees in detail. The Company claims that its prerogative to schedule work specifically is provided in the agreement. Article V states that ". . . the scheduling of work and the control and regulation of the use of all equipment and other property of the Company are the exclusive functions of the Company. . . ." In addition, although the agreement provides that the normal hours of work shall be 8 per day and 40 per week, it does so with the specific proviso that these work periods are for the purpose of computing overtime and "not as a limitation on the scheduling of employees." (Article VII, Section 1) The Company concludes that the idea of a guaranteed workday or workweek is in conflict with these provisions, and, therefore, was never intended.

The Company maintains further that Article VII, Section 6, really denies the Union its request, since the clause clearly states that it is applicable only when *no* work is available. In the present case, work to the extent of seven hours was available for "A" crew, was so scheduled, and was performed by "A" crew. The Company feels that in this circumstance, "A" crew does not qualify for showup time under the "no work" phrase of Article VII, Section 6.

QUESTIONS

1. Did the parties anticipate a daylight savings time problem when they negotiated Article VII, Section 6? Is the intent of Article VII, Section 6, to compensate employees for inconvenience?
2. What is the relevance of the Company's action in scheduling a nine-hour shift for the "A" crew in October to the interpretation of the agreement?
3. What alternatives in terms of shift scheduling were available to the company on April 28?

Case 21

ELIGIBILITY FOR HOLIDAY PAY AND LAYOFFS

COMPANY: Metropolitan Body Company

UNION: United Automobile, Aerospace and Agricultural
             Implement Workers of America
             Local 505

             Connecticut State Board of Mediation and Arbitration:
             Joseph F. Donnelly, Vincent J. Sirabella, and
             George H. Reama.

When does a layoff begin in connection with eligibility for holiday pay which excludes "those on layoff"?

The following discussion of the issue and facts in this case was prepared by Joseph F. Donnelly and Vincent J. Sirabella, two of three arbitrators in this case. George H. Reama dissented.

MATTER FOR ARBITRATION

In a signed stipulation the parties submitted the following question: Were the employees who were laid off on May 29, 1964, entitled to holiday pay for Memorial Day?

CONTRACT CLAUSE INVOLVED

Article VIII, Hours of Work and Holidays

Section 4.

(a) The Plant will close for New Year's Day, Good Friday, Memorial Day, Independence Day, Labor Day, Thanksgiving Day, Christmas Day, and the half day before Christmas and New Years, (it is agreed that the half day before Christmas and the half day before New Years may be redesignated by joint agreement between the Union and the Company three (3) months prior to the holiday to be designated). The Company agrees to pay eight (8) hours pay at the employee's current straight time average hourly rate to all employees except those on Layoff or absent without a reasonable excuse on the work day before or the work day after the holiday. Employees who are absent the day before or the day after the designated holiday due to authenticated injury or illness, but who work at least one (1) day during the week in which the holiday falls shall be eligible for the holiday pay.

(b) When one of the holidays designated herein falls within the employee's scheduled vacation, he will be granted an additional day off with pay to be taken either immediately preceding or immediately following his scheduled vacation.

(c) In the event that one of the above mentioned holidays falls on Saturday or Sunday, the Company agrees that pay for such holidays will be in accordance with the provisions of this section.

(d) With respect to the holidays referred to in the above section hereof, employees who work on such days shall receive pay of double time of their regular rate of pay for the time actually worked in addition to the regular holiday pay for which they may be eligible.

AGREED-ON FACTS

On May 27, 1964, the Company notified 21 employees that they would be laid off on May 29. Saturday, May 30, was a scheduled holiday, which by agreement of the parties was to be observed on Monday, June 1. Claiming that the employees in question were on layoff, the Company did not pay them for the holiday.

UNION POSITION

The union claims that the language of Article VIII, Section 4, obliges an employee to work either the day before or the day after a holiday. The employees in question are entitled to holiday pay because they worked the day before the holiday.

Moreover, holiday pay is part of an employee's total earnings. It is part of his negotiated benefits. He cannot be deprived of this benefit by the unilateral action of the Company in invoking a layoff.

The Union rejects the claim of the Company that the employees were on layoff. They had been notified of a layoff but the layoff did not begin until they began to lose time. This means that they were not on layoff until the following Tuesday and on this basis they have a claim to holiday pay.

COMPANY POSITION

The company states that under the agreement employees must work both the day before the holiday and the day after the holiday unless excused in accord with Article VIII, Section 4. However, it is not on this basis that the employees were denied holiday pay. On May 27, these employees were notified that they would be laid off effective at 3:30 P.M. on May 29. They were so laid off. Clearly under Article VIII, Section 4, they are not entitled to holiday pay.

QUESTIONS

1. Evaluate the Union's claim that the agreement obligates an employee to work only either the day before or the day after a holiday to be eligible for holiday pay.
2. Is holiday pay a negotiated benefit earned by past service or is it an investment by the Company in *future* employee productivity? What is the purpose of the agreement language requiring the employees' presence on the workday immediately preceding and/or immediately following the holiday?
3. For the 21 employees, did the layoff start on May 27 (date of notification), or May 29 (last day worked), or June 2 (first day of lost pay)?

Case 22

TERMINATION OF HEALTH INSURANCE DUE TO ECONOMIC ADVERSITY

COMPANY: Plymouth Citrus Co-op
Plymouth, Florida

UNION: Retail, Wholesale and Department Store Union
Local 1025

ARBITRATOR: A. J. Goodman

Does grave economic adversity caused by severe weather conditions justify the termination of health insurance and the discharge of employees?

The following discussion of the issues and facts in this case was prepared by A. J. Goodman, the arbitrator.

THE ISSUE IS:

"Did the Company have the right under the circumstances to terminate the insurance coverage of certain of the employees?"

The "circumstances" above referred to involve the termination of 40 employees and the cancellation of their insurance. The dispute arose and is arbitrated under the current collective bargaining agreement (Joint Exhibit 1 hereafter referred to as CBA) which was entered into on the 15th day of December, 1962, and is effective to and including December 15, 1964.

THE CASE

On May 30, 1963, at a meeting between representatives of the Union and the Company, Mr. Frank J. Poitras, secretary-manager of Plymouth Citrus Products Co-op, informed the Union that the Company intended to terminate the group insurance program for certain of its employees who would not be recalled when the citrus processing season begins in December.

The next day Mr. Poitras sent the following letter to a list of 40 employees:

May 31, 1963

CERTIFIED MAIL
DEAR MR. P_____:

The full effect on the citrus industry of last winter's freeze is much greater than anyone anticipated. Large numbers of trees were killed outright and many others have had to be pruned back extensively. Here at Plymouth, we are faced with a very substantial loss of fruit for processing for a long time to come.

This loss of fruit means that, for the next two or three seasons at least, there is practically no likelihood that you—and many other employees—will be recalled. We are advising you now so you can make other plans, in light of this unfortunate outlook.

Since it is, for all practical purposes, a certainty your job will not be available, we find it necessary to drop you from coverage in our Group Insurance Program. However, you may exercise your conversion privileges for Group Hospitalization and Group Life Insurance; if you want to do this, we will be pleased to help you in every way possible.

> Sincerely
> PLYMOUTH CITRUS
> PRODUCTS CO-OP
> (sgd) Frank J. Poitras
> FRANK J. POITRAS
> Manager

FJP:ec

At a joint meeting held on June 7, 1963, the Union challenged the action taken by the Company and as the parties could not agree, it was decided to submit the questions to arbitration.

Subsequently on June 20th, 1963, Mr. Poitras sent another letter to the 40 employees as follows:

Plymouth Florida, U.S.A.
June 20, 1963

CERTIFIED MAIL

In our recent letter we advised "there was little, if any likelihood that you—and many other employees—will be recalled to work in our Plant for the next two or three seasons." Since that time, it has become certain there will not be any work here for you and we, therefore, find it necessary to terminate your employment completely.

We have notified our group insurance carriers of your termination and can now give you specific dates regarding these coverages:

A. Termination of Employment
June 17, 1963

B. Termination of Blue Cross &
Blue Shield
June 17, 1963

C. Termination of Accident &
Sickness
Last day worked

D. Termination of Group Insurance
June 17, 1963

E. Termination of Conversion
Privilege Group Life Insurance
and Blue Cross-Blue Shield
Health Insurance
June 16, 1963

We regret the necessity for taking these measures and hope that you will find it possible to make satisfactory arrangements over this trying period.

Sincerely
PLYMOUTH CITRUS
PRODUCTS CO-OP
(sgd) Frank J. Poitras
FRANK J. POITRAS
Manager

Although the entire CBA is before the arbitrator, by stipulation the parties made particular reference to the following provisions:

ARTICLE III
Management Prerogatives

3.1 It is recognized that the conduct of the business operations of the Company, the fixing of its policies and the direction of the working forces are vested in the Company, including the use of its discretion and judgment as to the selection and retention of employees; the determination of the times and days of operations; the regulation of the use of all equipment and other property of the Company and the right to make reasonable rules and regulations for the conduct of the business and the employees while on the job, except as modified by any of the provisions of this Agreement.

ARTICLE X
Seniority

10.1 Seniority for the purposes of this Agreement is defined as the total length of uninterrupted employment with the Company of any employee. Employment interrupted for reasons set forth in paragraph 10.8 of this Article shall cause loss of seniority.

10.5 The principle of seniority shall apply to layoffs, recalls, and promotions, in that the employee with the longest seniority will be given first consideration provided he is qualified to perform the work.

10.8 Employment interrupted for the following reasons shall result in the loss of seniority:
1. Voluntary termination of employment
2. Discharge for just cause
3. Absence from work for a period of three (3) consecutive working days without notifying the Department Foreman and without a valid excuse
4. Continuous layoff in excess of one (1) year.

ARTICLE XI
Group Insurance

11.6 Duration of Coverage
  A. Group Life Insurance of any covered employee shall remain in force as long as the employee remains employed by the Company (including periods of layoff for lack of work, and periods of incapacity or leaves of absence).

Upon termination of employment—Group Life Insurance shall remain in force for the next thirty-one (31) days during which time the employee may convert his group life insurance to individual life insurance. Upon the conclusion of the aforesaid thirty-one (31) day period the employee's life insurance policy under the group plan shall terminate.

  B. Hospitalization and Surgical Insurance of any covered employee and any eligible dependent shall remain in force as long as the employee remains employed by the Company (including periods of layoff for lack of work and periods of incapacity or leaves of absence).

Upon termination of employment with the Company, termination of coverages and conversion privileges are those set forth in the certificate of insurance, a copy of which has been attached hereto and made part of this agreement.

  C. Accident and Sickness Insurance for eligible employees remains in force during all periods of active employment, but not for such periods as the employee may be laid off for lack of work, or is absent because of extended leave of absence for personal reasons other than nonoccupational injury or illness.

Upon termination of employment all coverage immediately ceases.

THE UNION'S POSITION

The Union concedes that the 1962 freeze was the worst the industry ever has experienced, and there is no contention on their part that citrus fruit shipments will not be curtailed to the extent contemplated by management. However, the Union does challenge the action taken by the Company in terminating certain individuals out of seniority, as well as the cancellation of their insurance. The Union points out that while the Company notified 40 employees of their termination, it is a fact that 6 of the 40 who received letters from the Company dated May 31 and June 20, 1963, actually are at work at this time. They maintain further that it is possible, even probable, that by the time December arrives additional people on the list will be recalled.

The Union contends that employees laid off at the end of the 1962–63 processing season are entitled to insurance coverage during their layoff up to one year. Their contention is supported by testimony to the effect that an insurance plan they first proposed to the Company during negotiations provided insurance coverage for laid-off employees for three to six months. The Company in rejecting the proposal had stated that it could provide insurance for a longer period of layoff (one year for Group Life and Hospital and Surgical), at a cost much less than seven cents per hour required under the Union plan. Finally, the Union challenges the right of the Company to select 40 persons whom it does not now intend to recall in December, and terminate their employment under Article X, Paragraph 10.8, as of June 17, 1963.

THE COMPANY'S POSITION

The Company offered testimony to the effect that because of the devastating freeze on December 11, 12, 13, and 14, 1962, citrus trees were either lost entirely or were so severely damaged that it will be years before fruit production reaches the 1961–62 level. This belief is supported by expert advice received from Florida Crop and Livestock Reporting Service, as well as from the Citrus Growers Mutual Association. Company representatives testified that a comprehensive study indicates that during the 1963–64 season, under optimum conditions, Florida citrus fruit growers expect to ship only 43 percent of the quantity they shipped in the 1961–62 season. The Company maintains that it is obvious, therefore, that a number of employees who have been engaged in the citrus industry will have to find other fields of employment if they wish to continue working.

The Company further contends that the anticipated shortage of fruit during the 1963–64 season compels the Company to make drastic changes in its operations both with respect to the number of employees required and as to the manner in which it plans to operate its processing plant. Heretofore the Company operated three eight-hour shifts six and seven days per week. As of this time it anticipates operating two 12-hour shifts three days per week. In making plans for this type of operation it has been necessary, said the Company, to make certain changes in job classifications. These changes, plus the longer 12-hour shifts, make it necessary to eliminate the females and a few males who either are advanced in age or who have physical handicaps and are therefore unable to perform the work which would be required of them.

Company representatives testified that during negotiations the only discussions having to do with continued insurance coverage was for the regular layoff from one season to another, a period of from five to six months.

The Company further holds that Article X, Paragraph 10.8, Section 4, which provides for loss of seniority for "continuous layoff in excess of one year," does not abridge its right to discharge any employee or group of employees for just causes and that among those reasons considered "just cause" would be the curtailment of employment, job disappearance, and changes in job classifications. The Company argues that any other interpretation would bind the Company to its employees under the most unreasonable circumstances, such as destruction of the plant by fire, war, or sabotage; or as in the present situation, the loss of work and jobs through a severe reduction of fruit for processing during the coming season.

In view of all the factors involved, the Company feels that it not only has the contractual right to terminate the 40 employees but also has the right to cancel their insurance. In support of its argument the Company refers to Article III and to Article X, Paragraph 10.8, of the CBA.

QUESTIONS

1. Both parties agree that the employer has been hit by extreme economic adversity beyond his control. What weight should be given this factor?
2. Are job disappearances or changes in job classifications "just causes" for discharge? Are they a basis for permanent layoff? Under the agreement discussed here is there a difference between "discharge" and "termination" as they relate to insurance plans?
3. How would you rule in this case? Why?

Case 23A

THE YEAR-END BONUS

COMPANY: Mid-State Steel, Incorporated
            Nashville, Tennessee
UNION: International Association of Machinists
            District Lodge 155
ARBITRATOR: Engene Russell

Is the employer required to continue the eight-year practice of giving employees a Christmas bonus after the negotiation of his initial collective bargaining agreement?

The year-end bonus is also the subject of Case 23B.

The following discussion of the issue and the facts in this case was prepared by Eugene Russell, the arbitrator.

THE GRIEVANCE IS:

December 30, 1963, X——, warehouseman, Hourly Pay $1.82.

"Nature of Grievance: For the past several years, the Company paid a year-end bonus to all employees who are now part of the bargaining unit, represented by District Lodge 155, International Association of Machinists, AFL-CIO. This year the Company failed to pay the employees their year-end bonus.

"The Union contends that the payment of this year-end bonus is an established past practice and is part of the fringe benefits and wages the employees earned as employees of the Company. The Union further contends that during the recent collective bargaining negotiations this bonus was not negotiated away and therefore the Company is obligated to pay this as a benefit owed the employees.

"Further, the Union contends that this bonus information was withheld from the Union prior to commencing negotiations and all during said negotiations.

"Because of the foregoing the Union requests that all employees of the bargaining unit be paid this bonus due (amount $35 each).

Date Submitted to Immediate Supervisor   12/30/63 X——, Steward"

Company President's answer:

"The Union complaint was discussed in the third step of the Grievance Procedure on January 2, 1964.

"It is the Company's position—as brought forth in the discussion—that the matters alleged in the Union complaint are false, totally without merit and do not constitute a grievance as defined in the Union-Company Agreement.

"The Company, therefore, denies the relief sought."

Union Exhibits 1 and 2

July 18, 1963
Re: Case No. 26-RC-1952
And Negotiations

Mr. P. G. Banker, President
Mid-State Steel, Inc.
401 Driftwood Street
Nashville 10, Tennessee
DEAR MR. BANKER:

As you know, District Lodge 155 of the International Association of Machinists, AFL-CIO, has been certified as bargaining representative for your employees.

Accordingly, I request that we agree to a date for the purpose of commencing negotiations.

Further, I request a copy of the current wage rates, seniority dates and the classification of each employee covered by this certification. In addition to this, I request a list of fringe benefits such as, insurance, holidays, vacations and bonuses.

I would like to commence meeting around August 1st of this year at a time so as to not hamper your production operations as there will be some of your employees on my committee.

Thank you,
G. W. WELLS
Business Representative

July 19, 1963
Mr. G. W. Wells, Business Representative
District Lodge No. 155
International Association of Machinists
1003 First Avenue, South
Nashville, Tennessee
DEAR MR. WELLS:

This will acknowledge your letter of July 18, relative to bargaining negotiations for the employees of our Company which you represent.

Because of the absence of some of our key personnel during the first full week of August, it appears that August 12, at 3:30 P.M. is the earliest convenient time for our initial bargaining session.

If the foregoing date and time is convenient for you, please advise accordingly.

In regard to your request for wage rates, seniority, etc., we are pleased to advise that this information will be furnished to you at the appropriate time during the course of our negotiations.

Very truly yours,
MID-STATE STEEL, INC.
P. G. BANKER
President

COMPANY EXHIBITS 1, 2, AND 3

"A special meeting of the Board of Directors of Mid-State Steel, Inc., Nashville, Tennessee, was called at the principal office of the Company at 401 Driftwood Street on December 20, 1960, at 2 P.M.

All the directors were present, namely, P. G. Banker, G. O. Stanley, and F. F. Swint.

Mr. Banker acted as chairman and Mr. Swint as secretary.

Mr. Banker proposed that Christmas presents be given to warehouse employees in the amount of $25 each. Mr. Stanley approved the motion and Mr. Swint seconded.

* * * *

"A special meeting of the Board of Directors of Mid-State Steel, Inc., Nashville, Tennessee, was called at the principal office of the Company at 401 Driftwood Street on November 29, 1961, at 10:30 A.M.

All the directors were present, namely, P. G. Banker, G. O. Stanley, and F. F. Swint.

Mr. Banker acted as chairman and Mr. Swint as secretary.

Mr. Banker proposed that Christmas presents be given to each of the warehouse employees in the amount of $35. Mr. Swint approved the motion and Mr. Stanley seconded.

* * * *

"A special meeting of the Board of Directors of Mid-State Steel, Inc., Nashville, Tennessee, was called at the principal office of the Corporation at 401 Driftwood Street, on December 12, 1962, at 10 A.M.

All the directors were present, namely, P. G. Banker, Jr., G. O. Stanley, and F. F. Swint.

Mr. Banker acted as chairman and Mr. Swint as secretary.

Mr. Banker proposed that Christmas presents be given to the warehouse employees in the amount of $35 each. Mr. Swint approved the motion and Mr. Stanley seconded.

STIPULATIONS

It was stipulated and agreed that the collective bargaining agreement be filed as Joint Exhibit 1, and the written Grievance and Answer thereto be filed as Joint Exhibit 2.

It was further stipulated and agreed that the Grievance was timely filed and processed.

THE ISSUE

The Company questioned the arbitrability of the Grievance but agreed to present the facts in the case and leave such determination to the arbitrator.

No stipulated issue was agreed to by the parties, but the arbitrator has determined the issue to be as follows:

"Is the Company obligated to pay a Christmas Bonus to the Grievant and members of the Bargaining Unit for the year 1963?"

POSITION OF THE UNION

The Union contends that the facts of this case are simple. That for at least eight years prior to 1963 the Company has paid to its employees, now represented by the Union, a Christmas and/or year-end bonus. However, for the year ended 1963, the Company did not pay said bonus, and at all times since has refused to pay.

It is the position of the Union that the Company is obligated to pay the bonus of $35 to each employee covered under the terms of the bargaining agreement and that the Company is, and was without authority to change its policy in regards to the bonus until such is negotiated through the Union.

The Union urges, as a matter of custom and past practice, and absent contract language to the contrary, coupled with the fact that the Company failed to furnish to it the information requested in Union Exhibit No. 1, the grievance should be sustained.

Mr. P. G. Banker, company president, said on cross examination that he believed the employees had grown to expect the bonus. Surely, this is true and rightfully so, because of the period of eight years' time involved.

The Company admitted that during a period of time some three years ago, under a Teamsters Union agreement, they paid the bonus, and there was not a clause to that effect contained within the written bounds of that agreement. Further, the Company admitted for three years thereafter under Company written rules and regulations, but absent any rule to the effect of a bonus, it nonetheless paid the bonus.

The Union further contends that all benefits and conditions enjoyed by a group of employees at the time of Union certification by the NLRB freezes, so to speak, and remains *status quo* until such time as they are altered, amended, abridged, and/or disposed of through collective bargaining.

The Union insists that the Company knowingly hid the fact of the bonus from the Union during the recent initial negotiations.

POSITION OF THE COMPANY

The Company contends that for a number of years it has given a Christmas present to each of its employees on the last working day before December 25. In each of the last eight years, the Christmas present has been either cash or a check in amounts varying from $15 to $35. Prior to Christmas of 1955, the Christmas gift, when given, was a bottle of whiskey, a turkey, a basket of fruit or something other than money.

In each of the eight years beginning in 1955, the directors of the Company formally adopted a resolution authorizing the giving of Christmas gifts to employees. Only in the years 1960, 1961 and 1962, was the amount of the gift specified. In the five years preceding 1960, the Board of Directors authorized the gifts and directed the officers of the Company to determine the amount. During these eight years, the amount of each employee Christmas gift has varied from $15 to $35 but the gift in each year has not always been in a larger amount than that given in the preceding year. In other words, during this eight-year period, the amount of the gifts has decreased as well as increased.

In each year in which Christmas gifts were given, each employee received the same amount. No formula has ever been used to compute the amount of the gift and the employee's hourly rate of pay or length of service has been irrelevant in determining the amount of his gift. It has always been the practice of the Company to present the gift to the employee on the last working day before Christmas Day and to enclose the check or cash in an envelope containing a Christmas greeting. The Christmas gift was always separate from any pay check which the employee might be receiving at the same time. The Board of Directors of the Company did not authorize any Christmas gift to employees in December of 1963. It is the position of the Company that the Christmas gifts voluntarily given from time to time may be discontinued by the Company unilaterally at any time.

BACKGROUND AND DISCUSSION

The Union was certified as the collective bargaining agent of the Company's employees in the summer of 1963. For three years prior to such time, the Company had negotiated an agreement in each year with a committee of employee representatives and for a number of years before that, the Company had had collective bargaining agreements with a Local of the Teamsters Union.

Following the certification of the Union, negotiations for a contract commenced, culminating in a contract executed on December 5, 1963, effective as of November 30, 1963. Prior to these negotiations, the Union wrote to the Company requesting a list of fringe benefits such as holidays, vacations, and bonuses, to which the Company replied that all information would be furnished during the course of negotiations. During most of the bargaining sessions, X—— and Leroy Harris, employees of the Company, were present. These two men had been employees of the Company for a number of years. During the negotiations, the Union never at any time requested negotiations with respect to the Christmas gifts and the Company negotiated in good faith on any issue raised by the Union. The Company did not submit the question of Christmas gifts to the Union as a subject for bargaining because it had never considered such gifts as constituting bonuses.

In the course of the negotiations, the Union presented a proposed contract which included a provision entitled "Maintenance of Privileges." This provision is as follows: "Any and all privileges enjoyed by the employees prior to the date of this agreement will not be denied to them because of the signing of this agreement, unless the parties, through collective bargaining, mutually agree to changes or have specifically waived any of these privileges." The Company took the position that this proposal was unacceptable because it was too vague. However, the Company representatives told the Union representatives that if they would specify the particular privileges they had in mind, the Company would bargain on any of such privileges. The two employees who were present during most of the bargaining sessions must have known that they had been receiving Christmas gifts for a number of years, but the question of Christmas gifts was never raised. The contract finally executed did not contain the provision quoted above.

QUESTIONS

1. In this case the Company argues that past practice establishes the fact that the Christmas bonus was a unilateral gift. The Union argues that past

practice establishes the fact that the Christmas bonus was a wage supplement. Neither party can cite any contract language to support their position. Which past practice should prevail?

2. In what significant respects does this case differ from the Tonawanda Publishing case (Case 23B)?

3. How would you rule in this case? Why?

Case 23B

THE YEAR-END BONUS

COMPANY: Tonawanda Publishing Company

UNION: Newspaper Guild of Buffalo
             Local 26

ARBITRATOR: Peter Seitz

This case deals with a year-end bonus, the same topic as case 23A. The following discussion of the issue and facts in this case was prepared by Peter Seitz, the arbitrator.

ISSUE

The issue presented for decision is whether the Employer has violated Article VI, Paragraph 7, of the collective bargaining agreement by refusing and failing to pay the Christmas bonus in 1962, and if it has, the appropriate relief to be directed.

Paragraph 7 reads:

7. There shall be no reduction in salaries during the life of this agreement except as may occur in Section 2b and 2c of this article. (The exceptions have no direct relationship to this case.)

BACKGROUND

In the briefest compass, the relevant and significant facts are as follows:

From at least 1947 (and prior to the recognition of the Guild) through 1961, the publisher, each year, made a Christmas payment to employees. Until 1960 the payment was in an amount equal to one-half the gross weekly salary of the recipient excepting that employees who had less than one year of service received a prorated payment. Employees not on the payroll at the time received no Christmas payment. In 1960 and 1961 the Company departed from this procedure and practice to this extent: The Company in those years deducted the appropriate withholding taxes from the moneys paid. Accordingly, there was a reduction in the amounts of the payments on a given salary. Employees were given stubs reflecting the accounting procedures involved somewhat similar to stubs received by employees generally when deductions are made from their paychecks. No complaint was voiced or grievance filed with respect to this variance from past usage.

The money was paid by check handed to each employee by Mrs. Ruth L. Hewitt, general manager of the publisher, a few days before each Christmas, and the giving was accompanied by a handshake and Christmas greetings and an expression of "appreciation for a good job done."

This Christmas payment had been made to all employees in all departments of the Employer excepting the publisher and the assistant publisher. So far as the record reveals, there were no employees on the active payroll at the time of giving who failed to receive a check or who received a check in a lesser amount than would result from the formula referred to above.

None of the several labor agreements entered into by the parties refer to a Christmas bonus or gift. The only discussions between the parties with reference to such a payment took place in 1954—10 years ago. According to my notes taken at the hearing, Mrs. Hewitt testified:

> The Guild wanted inclusion of the bonus as part of the contract. The Company said because it was a gift it should not be part of the contract. The Union felt if the paper should be sold, it needed assurances that the bonus would be paid in the contract year. The Company agreed to include a statement in a supplement to the 1954 contract.

Louis Simon, a Guild witness who was present when the request was made for a writing with respect to the payment, testified:

> Management said this was not necessary—it was not necessary to add language to the contract that was already practice.

Harvey Hough, managing editor, also testified that the Guild representative said the Guild wanted the bonus written into the contract "because Mrs. Hewitt could die or the paper be sold."

Thus, in a document signed by both parties dated September 9, 1954, among other things, it is stated:

> This letter confirms the agreement to pay members of the Editorial department who have been employed by The News for the entire year of 1954 a Christmas gift in the amount of one half week's salary at Christmas 1954, and to those with less than one year's employment a proportionate amount based on length service during 1954.

In 1961 the parties were bargaining with respect to a new agreement. In July, 1962, Mrs. Hewitt, on behalf of the publisher, gave the Guild some data in writing reflecting unfavorable advertising receipts. She testified:

At about the time of the exhibit I spoke to Carl Rothfuse, a member of the Board of Directors and an officer of the Corporation, and discussed the economic problems of the paper with him and said I felt it was necessary to discontinue the bonus. He advised to wait until later. I made a decision around Thanksgiving when I had 11 months [advertising] figures.

The record of testimony is in some confusion as to the dates of events occurring in late November, 1961, and early December. Mrs. Hewitt was of the opinion that the terms of the agreement were finally agreed upon in late November, when she said she made her decision to discontinue the Christmas payment. The weight of the evidence, however, persuades me that negotiations were not completed before December 3, 1961. At any rate, in the 1961 negotiations there was no reference made to the Christmas payment.

Apparently, it took some time to reduce the new agreement to writing for signature. Earle Y. Hannel, one of the two signatories for the Guild, placed his signature on the document, he says, on December 18, 1962. (This is the date written in, apparently in Hannel's handwriting, above the typed names of the signatories). Then, according to his testimony at 7 A.M. the next day, December 19, he saw a notice on the bulletin board. The notice stated that the Christmas bonus would be discontinued because of a decrease in advertising linage in 1962. No copy of the notice is available as an exhibit. Mrs. Hewitt testified that her decision to discontinue the bonus was made in late November, but she posted the notice on December 19 "because this was the period of the year when the bonus was to be paid."

QUESTIONS

1. Should the bonus be considered as a gift or as salary?
2. Did the decline of advertising revenues create a situation which would free the company from the bonus obligation?
3. Did the Company violate the contract?

Case 24

A CHANGE IN SHIFT SCHEDULES

COMPANY: Cannon Electric Company

UNION: United Automobile Workers
             Local 811

ARBITRATOR: Frederic Meyers

This case involves the right of management to unilaterally change shift schedules.

The following discussion of the issue and facts in the case was prepared by Frederic Meyers, the arbitrator.

The parties submitted the following issue to arbitration:

1. Did the Company violate the collective bargaining agreements as alleged in Grievance No. 22616?

2. If so, what is the proper remedy?

Grievance No. 22616, dated April 24, arising in the die cast department and signed by Committeeman Joe Kalin makes the following claim:

> Violation of contract. Improper change of hours of work. (See Bulletin 4/23/62 signed R. D. Murray.) Union requests hours of work for Die Cast Department remain from (7–3:30) (3:30–12) (12–7) per contract and per agreement between Co. and Union. Union requests Co. reinstate these hours immediately in all Dept's where changed. Union requests employees be paid for all money lost.

THE FACTS OF THE CASE

The facts of this matter are quite simple, the issue more complex. Article XVIII, Section 2, of the collective agreement provides and has provided over many years as follows:

> Unless changed by mutual agreement between the Company and the Union, the normal hours of employment shall be as follows:
> Shift No. 1: 8 A.M. to 4:30 P.M., less 30 minutes for meals.
> Shift No. 2: 4:30 P.M. to 1 A.M., less 30 minutes for meals.
> Shift No. 3: 1 A.M. to 8 A.M., less 30 minutes for meals.

However, since approximately 1952 the die cast department had begun and terminated each shift an hour earlier than the schedule described in the above provision of the contract. There is no evidence as to the circumstances under which this arrangement came into being.

On April 23, 1962, the Company posted a bulletin announcing that effective April 30, 1962, shifts in the die cast department were to begin and end one hour later than had been the practice. The new hours, therefore, coincided with those provided in Article XVIII, Section 2.

Posting of the bulletin had been preceded by discussion between the Union and the Company. The parties differ on their construction of these meetings. The Union maintains that their purpose was to reach mutual agreement on the proposed change, and that it was unable to agree. The Company maintains that the purpose was to inform the Union of its intention and to accomplish the transaction with a minimum of friction.

Considerable evidence was introduced as to the purpose of the change. Suffice it here to say that the change was initiated by the Company in good faith and as an exercise of business judgment. In no way was it arbitrary, capricious, or discriminatory.

Likewise, some evidence was introduced as to the attitude of the employees, and allegations are made by the Union as to the inconvenience the change worked. Suffice it also here to say that presumptively the Union is acting in good faith in the interest of and as representative of the employees.

THE POSITION OF THE COMPANY

The Company points first to the Management Prerogatives clause of the collective agreement, and especially to a change in that clause negotiated in the last agreement. That clause provides:

The right to hire, promote, discharge or discipline for just cause, maintain discipline and efficiency of employees, determine the type of products to be manufactured, the schedule of production, the location of plants, the methods, processes and means of manufacturing are examples of management prerogatives. *However, it is understood that the Company retains all of its rights to manage and operate the business except as may be limited by an express provision of this Agreement.*

The underlined sentence was not a part of the preceding agreements, and the Company calls particular attention to the fact that this sentence provides that only *express* and not implied provisions of the agreement limit the exercise of management rights.

The Company further calls attention to the arbitration clause of the contract which contains the usual limitation on the powers of an arbitrator, providing that he "shall have no power to subtract from or alter, change or modify the terms of this agreement. . . ."

The Company proceeds, then, to argue that since no *express* provision of the collective agreement establishes the practice of working hours in the die cast department differing from those provided for in Article XVII cited above, the right to return to those hours is a management prerogative with which the arbitrator cannot interfere. It maintains that the past practice has been a privilege extended to the employees in the die cast department by the Company which the Company has the unilateral right to withdraw.

The Company also points to the fact that this contract contains no clause generally preserving past practices, but only practices with respect to certain specific matters. It infers that since the practice in dispute is not specifically protected, it lies within the domain of unilateral management rights to withdraw.

The Company cites various published arbitration awards in support of its position.

THE POSITION OF THE UNION

The Union argues that management rights with respect to establishing shift schedules are expressly limited by Article XVIII, which establishes normal hours of work. Article XVIII provides that the specific "normal" work schedules provided in Article XVIII may, by the terms of this article, be altered by mutual agreement. This, in fact, was done some 10 years ago. Such a mutual agreement becomes a part of the agreement and cannot be altered except by subsequent mutual agreement, and not by unilateral action.

The Union calls attention to the provision of the Arbitration clause which enables the arbitrator in interpreting or applying the provisions of the agreement to "consider all relevant evidence including but not limited to the past practice of the parties." It argues that since the practice in question has been clear and consistent for ten years, it has become a part of the contract.

The Union points to the fact that if the hours of the die cast department were not the "normal" hours, the employees would have been entitled to certain premium pay. Since they did not receive it, the hours in question must have been the contractual normal schedule.

COMMENTS OF THE ARBITRATOR

The arbitrator must, of course, decide within the limits placed upon him by the contract and the submission agreement, that is, he cannot alter, add to, or subtract from the provisions of the agreement. The Company construes this limitation and the use of the word "express" in the Management Prerogatives clause to mean that since there is no written part of the last negotiated collective contract to sustain the claim of the Union, it must be denied. The Union, on the other hand, argues that the agreement contains more than its written provisions.

QUESTIONS

1. Why would the Company agree to arbitrate this case?
2. How would you rule in this case? Why?

Case 25

COMPANY PRACTICE VS. AGREEMENT LANGUAGE IN RECALL FROM LAYOFF

COMPANY: Seymour Manufacturing Company

UNION: United Automobile, Aircraft and Agricultural Implement Workers of America
Local 1827

ARBITRATOR: Sidney L. Cahn

Does the long continuance of a practice clearly contrary to the wording of the agreement take precedence over the agreement?

The following discussion of the issue and facts in this case was prepared by Sidney L. Cahn, the arbitrator.

THE ISSUE

"Did the Company violate the Collective Bargaining Agreement, Article VIII, Sections 1, 2(a), 2(c), 5, 6, and 15, governing seniority for the purposes of recall when it recalled employees L—— and M—— instead of employees X——, Y——, and Z——? If so what should be the remedy?"

THE FACTS

In June, 1963, the Company laid off a number of its employees predicated upon its shutdown of the rolling mills. Among the employees laid off at that time where the three grievants, X——, Y——, and Z——. X—— was then a roller in the rolling mill with a plant-wide seniority, date of November 7, 1949; Y—— was then a jitney driver in the rolling mill with a plant-wide seniority, date of October 26, 1949; and Z—— was then a pickler in the wire mill with a plant-wide seniority, date of February 14, 1950. Other employees laid off included L—— and M——, fine wire drawers in the wire mill, with plant-wide seniority dates of July 31, 1961, and August 4, 1961, respectively.

In the Spring of 1964 two jobs of fine wire drawer in the wire mill became open, one on April 20 and the other on April 27. The Company recalled L—— and M—— to the jobs. None of the grievants (all of whom had greater plant-wide seniority than L—— or M——, but none of whom had ever worked the jobs in question) were recalled to work until a later date.

The Union filed the instant grievance claiming that plant-wide length of service should have been the sole criterion employed in determining which employees should be first recalled. Under this criterion, concededly all of the grievants would have been entitled to have been recalled prior to either L—— or M——.

OPINION

Article VIII of the parties' collective bargaining agreement dated November 15, 1961, deals with the question of seniority. This article *inter alia* sets forth general policy in Section 1 (i.e., "to provide maximum job security and opportunity based upon—continuous service"); it defines "seniority" as "total length of unbroken service" in (Section 2); it provides for departmental seniority to govern in the case of layoffs from a department (Section 3) with the right of a laid-off employee to exercise plant seniority to replace an employee in another department with less plant seniority (Section 5); and it considers the questions, among others, of recalls to work (Section 6); bidding for open jobs (Section 7); promotions (Section 8); and retention of certain employees by the Company regardless of seniority (Section 15).

Section 6 of this article is the section dealing with the immediate problem before me. This section provides as follows:

> Rehiring in all mills except the Laboratory Department shall be on the basis of plantwide seniority, *governed by the nature of the job to be filled, with due consideration being given to the necessary skill and ability to do* the required work. (emphasis supplied).

This section then goes on to deal with the exception pertaining to the laboratory department, not here relevant.

The grievants in the instant case all had greater plant-wide seniority than both L—— and M——. Although Section 15 of this article gives the Company the right with certain limitations "to retain seven employees, irrespective of seniority, who possess value to the operation of the Company" it is conceded that neither L—— nor M—— were recalled pursuant to this section, and accordingly it need not concern me any further. The sole question, therefore, is whether the above-emphasized language found in Section 6 applies to the instant case and justifies the Company's recall of L—— and M——.

The Union has not attempted to show that at the time L—— and M—— were recalled any of the grievants possessed "the necessary skill and ability to do the required work" as contemplated by the emphasized language. It argues instead that the Company has at least, since 1946, totally disregarded contractual references in this and prior agreements as to skill and ability in recalling employees; that it has been solely governed by length of continuous service in recalling employees whether employees were recalled to jobs previously held or to jobs never held by them; and that by reason of this fact the Company has in effect waived any rights it may have had to rely upon the emphasized language and to question a senior employee's skill and ability in recalling him from layoff.

The testimony introduced was impressive and convincing on this score. It appears without contradiction and in fact was admitted that since at least 1946, until the instant situation, the Company consistently recalled its employees based solely upon plant-wide seniority, and without reference to skill and ability. Only three alleged "exceptions" to this practice were shown.

(*a*) One alleged exception dealt with employees recalled to jobs in the laboratory department; this, however, is clearly made an exception to Section 6 by the express language of that section and accordingly is not a relevant exception to the practice claimed by the Union;

(*b*) Another exception occurred in 1949 when the Company recalled a junior employee to a wire drawer job in preference to a utility man on layoff; this exception resulted in a grievance which was settled to the satisfaction of the Union by calling in additional help;

(c) The third and only relevant exception involved the recall in October, 1963, without objection by the Union, of a junior employee to the job of machinist third class. However, even as to this exception the Union took the position that this was consistent with the practice, claiming that this recall was made pursuant to Section 15 referred to above, and was not made pursuant to Section 6; the Company took issue with this claim and this is the only factual matter in dispute.

Under Article X, Section 5, of the collective bargaining agreement, the arbitrator has no authority to "add to, subtract from or in any way modify" the terms of the parties' collective bargaining agreement.

QUESTIONS

1. The arbitrator here is confronted with a choice between agreement language and the existence of a well-established practice. What factors should he consider in making his choice?
2. How would you rule in this case? Why?

Case 26

PHYSICAL REQUIREMENTS AS A BASIS FOR RECALL FROM LAYOFF

COMPANY: National Lead Company, Doehler-Jarvis Division
Pottstown, Pennsylvania

UNION: United Automobile Workers
Local 1056

ARBITRATOR: Jacob Seidenberg

Can the records of previous physical examinations be used as a basis for disqualifying senior employees from recall to work?

The following discussion of the issue and facts in this case was prepared by Jacob Seidenberg, the arbitrator.

ISSUE

Whether the Company violated the contractual provisions pertaining to recall of laid-off employees.

FACTS

The relevant contract provisions pertaining to the grievance are the following:

Article 58 (Master Agreement)

No new employee shall be hired in any seniority unit while Employees with seniority in such unit are laid off nor shall any new employee be hired while any qualified Employees in any seniority unit are laid off nor shall any Employee be transferred or recalled to take the place of transferred or laid off Employee with greater seniority for a period longer than three (3) working days. Such qualified laid off Employees shall be given an opportunity to work in any seniority unit as new employees, until such time as they are recalled to work in their own seniority unit. . . .

Article 55 (Local Supplement)

PLANT SENIORITY

Plant seniority is accumulative in years, months, and days from the Employee's first day of continuous, unbroken seniority employment with the Company and is used only for rehire to jobs other than the department or division from which laid off.

This means that as Employees are laid off from any division or department, they are chronologically placed on a plant seniority list. Then as additional help is needed in any division or department in compliance with Article 58 of the Master Agreement, qualified Employees are rehired from the plant list to fill such openings.

. . .

When Employees are laid off from any division, they shall designate which future job vacancies they will accept under plant seniority. The Company shall not be held liable for failure to recall to jobs not designated or for which they are not qualified.

The seven grievants, with service dates from December 2, 1942, to January 21, 1943, were on laid-off status from the cleaning department on May 31, 1963, when the Company advertised vacancies in the zinc casting department. The Company ultimately filled the six jobs—five from the plant seniority list with employees who had no prior experience in the casting department, and one with an employee who had formerly worked in the casting department. The grievants had never worked in the casting department. The employees who were named to fill the vacancies had later service dates than the Grievants, which gave rise to the instant grievance.

In accordance with Article 55 of the Supplemental Agreement, the Company maintains two seniority recall lists. One is for production and the other is for skilled workers. Laid-off workers are afforded the opportunity of designating the jobs for which they want to be considered outside their own unit, in the event vacancies occur in these other units. The Union states that most laid-off production workers indicate that they will take any production job available in the plant.

It is unquestioned that it is the established practice (there being no contract provision dealing with the matter) for the Company's medical department to give an examination to all recalled employees who had been laid off for 10 days or more. Apparently, all newly hired employees also receive physical examinations.

The Company did not recall the seven grievants because it determined, without subjecting the grievants to a medical examination, that they were not physically qualified to do the work in the casting department.

The formal job description of each job in the plant contains, where relevant, its physical requirements. But these requirements are not posted when the job is advertised for bidding.

UNION POSITION

The Company was guilty of arbitrary action in passing over the grievants and selecting men of lesser seniority, allegedly for physical reasons, by not giving the grievants a proper medical examination to determine their physical condition to do the work in question. A proper construction of Articles 55 and 58 of the cognizant agreements required the Company to recall the men in accordance with their seniority standing and then to subject them to a medical examination to ascertain their physical abilities or disabilities.

The Union contends that any production department worker is qualified to work in the die casting department. The Company was guilty of a continuing violation of the agreement by passing over senior employees in favor of junior employees for medical reasons, without first subjecting the senior employees to a current medical examination.

COMPANY POSITION

The Company has the contractual right to select qualified employees for existing vacancies. The determination as to whether an employee is competent or qualified for a job is a matter clearly within the prerogative of management.

The Company did not recall any of the grievants because its medical records clearly indicated that these men were not physically able to meet the requirements of the job as set forth in the job description, and therefore no useful purpose would have been served by having the men recalled solely for the purpose of being told that they were not physically qualified for the vacancies in the casting department.

The Company recounted in some detail the physical disabilities of the grievants as stated on the medical records which resulted from prior medical examinations given them when they had been recalled from other layoffs. The Company also stated that it would know, as a result of the medical insurance program in effect in the plant, of any corrective action taken by these men to remove the disabilities contained in the medical records.

The Company acted in good faith and without malice or prejudice toward the grievants. This is evidenced by the fact that when jobs became available in the cleaning department, for which the men were physically qualified, they were recalled to work in accordance with their seniority.

In any event, the Company contends that there were only five jobs in issue because one of the men hired for the casting department (X——) had had prior casting department experience, which placed him in a preferred position as compared to the grievants, who had no prior casting department experience.

QUESTIONS

1. The cited sections of the agreement make no reference to physical examinations and the posted job descriptions made no reference to physical requirements. By what authority does the Company subject returning employees to physical examinations?
2. The Company seeks to support its failure to recall the grievants on medical records from previous physical examinations. Under what conditions would this position be sound?
3. Assume that there was good reason to believe that the grievants in this case could not pass the physical requirements for the jobs in the casting department. Why would the Union grieve?
4. The Company had no program for making regular periodic medical examinations of its employees. Would this fact influence your decision?
5. If you ruled that the Company had violated the agreement, what remedy would you provide for the grievants?
6. Write a fair agreement clause which would establish a clear procedure for determining the physical ability of men on layoff to perform work when vacancies occur.

Case 27

"MARKED DIFFERENCES" IN PERFORMANCE AS A BASIS FOR LAYOFF

COMPANY: McEvoy Company
Houston, Texas

UNION: International Association of Machinists
Lodge 12, District 37

ARBITRATOR: R. H. Morvant

How are "marked differences" in performance measured? What problems arise in applying these marked differences as a criterion in layoffs?

The following discussion of the issue and facts in this case was prepared by R. H. Morvant, the arbitrator.

THE QUESTION

From the contentions of the parties and from the evidence and testimony presented, the following questions developed to be answered by the arbitrator:

1. Did the Company violate the collective bargaining agreement and in particular Article VI of said agreement when they laid off X__ on or about August 21, 1963?
2. If answer to question No. 1 above is affirmative, what remedy is ordered?

THE FACTS

The grievant, X——, was employed by the Company on January 5, 1955, as an engine lathe operator. In August of 1963 the Company found it necessary to lay off a number of employees. On August 12, 1963, Gordon Gibson, general shop superintendent, drafted a list of employees to be laid off based on a list of machines which were to be shut down rather than on the employees' seniority status. When this list was submitted to the shop committee they protested that it was not in accordance with the plant seniority provisions of the labor agreement. The list was withdrawn and a new list submitted by W. C. Uhl, shop superintendent, based upon plant seniority, except that the grievant, X——, was now marked for layoff where in the previous list X—— had not been mentioned. Further, the seniority list of the lathe operators indicates that there were three operators junior to X—— at the time of his layoff.

From the testimony of the Company, which was unrefuted by the Union, it is gathered that while the first list was being discussed by the men in the shop and before it was withdrawn, several junior lathe operators approached the Company requesting that the "marked difference" provision of Article VI be utilized in their behalf in the engine lathe department. Further, it is to be gathered that the Company did use a relative efficiency report of the lathe operators to determine "marked differences" between the operators and thus determined that X—— should be laid off even though he was senior to others in the department.

When the Company submitted the layoff list dated August 21, 1963, to the Union, some of the men on the list chose to bump into their classifications which they had the right to do by virtue of their seniority and Article VI. X——, however, chose not to bump but elected layoff status from which, on August 23, 1963, he filed a grievance protesting his layoff out of line of his seniority.

The grievance was processed through the various steps of the grievance procedure of the collective bargaining agreement without arriving at a settlement satisfactory to the parties; hence, the grievance was processed to arbitration.

The following excerpts from the collective bargaining agreement existing between the parties are pertinent to this case:

Article I—Preamble

"The intent and purpose of the parties hereto is that this agreement will promote, improve and maintain industrial, economic, and harmonious relations between the Union and the Company, and to set forth herein the basic agreement covering the rates of pay, hours of work, and conditions of employment to be observed between the Union and the Company.

The Union agrees to cooperate with the Company to increase productivity. The Union will urge its members to produce more and will work with the Company to eliminate other causes for inefficiency.

Article IV—Management's Rights

The Management of the plant and of the work and direction and classification of the working forces, including the right to hire, suspend, or discharge for proper cause, or transfer, and the right to relieve employees from duty because of lack of work or for any other legitimate reason shall be vested in the Company. This authority will not and cannot be used for the purpose of discrimination.

The Company reserves the right to adopt, establish, submit, revise, and enforce reasonable factory and safety rules. Such rules shall not be used for the purpose of unlawful discrimination or to violate the express provisions of this agreement.

Article VI—Seniority

Section 1. In promotion, demotion, layoff and restoration to service, plant seniority shall prevail unless there is a marked difference in ability. In this connection Management and the Shop Committee shall confer prior to promotion, layoff, or restoration of service, and in the event Management and the Shop Committee are unable to agree, Management shall have the right to make the determination, subject to the grievance procedure provided in the contract.

The "marked difference" between the lathe operators was established by efficiency reports of the employees during the 18-month period between January 1, 1962, and July 1, 1963. The records of the men employed as lathe operators are as follows:

Employee	Seniority Date	Relative Efficiency
Baker	3–24–41	76%
Parker	8–8–49	68%
Storey	8–29–51	71%
Rich	1–5–55	61%
X——	1–5–55	52%
Vaughn	8–18–56	78%
Stewart	12–1–56	75%
Bridwell	1–14–57	77%

The efficiency of an employee is based upon amount of pieces produced times the "job standard" divided by actual time devoted. In other words a "job standard" is previously established by time and motion study. Employee assigned to manufacture these pieces is graded in efficiency by the number of pieces he runs divided by the time devoted and the result compared to the standard. The result is shown in percentages of the previously set standard. The standard, however, does not apply to all of the work assigned to the operator. Hence, as it is possible for an operator to be assigned work not "standardized" or not subject to "standardization," the Company established codes to distinguish the various means of accomplishing the work under the various conditions to be encountered.

1. Code 1—Work performed on the same kind of machine and with the same kind of machine and with the same kind of material under which the standard is set. Presumably ideal as to both machine and material. Standard applies.

2. Code 2—Pieces made with the same material but on a different machine. No standard applies.

3. Code 3—Pieces made on the same machine but with substitute material. No standard applies.

4. Code 4—Pieces made with both material and machine substituted. No standard applies.

5. Rush Work—No standard applies.

6. Rework—Errors in pieces corrected. No standard applies.

7. Repair Work—Used pieces sent in by customer repaired. 100 per cent efficiency credit allowed.

THE ISSUE

The Union contended that for the past 20 years layoffs have been made under the seniority rule in spite of the exceptions offered by the Company. Thus, the Union argued, the basic contractual provisions here involved must mean what the parties have interpreted them to mean in 20 years of contractual relations. In the past, when layoffs were necessary, the Company selected the classification and number of employees to be reduced and submitted the list of names to the Union, the Union argued. Further, the Union stated, such a list was composed of the junior employees in the classification to be reduced. These junior employees from a department forced to reduce manpower were then permitted to bump into lower or parallel classifications where their plant seniority and qualifications permitted such bumping. In such instances, the Union argued, qualifications meant only "if the employee could perform the work," he could bump. In any event, the Union concluded, the circumstances giving rise to the instant grievance is a radical departure from a tried and tested system which has worked best over the years.

Concerning the six examples of departure from strict seniority which the Company cited, the Union argued there is not enough similarity between them and this instant case to prove a precedent of sufficient weight to permit a departure from well-established past practice. Continuing, the Union pointed out that only two of the cases cited were arbitrated, and of the remaining four either no grievance was filed, or the grievance was dropped at the grievant's request after being filed.

After briefly discussing the two arbitration cases which upheld the "marked difference" argument of the Company, the Union stated:

> So, each of the cases litigated reveal that the employee senior in the plant who was attempting to prevail on the strength of his seniority was a mere novice on the job in comparison to the junior employee retained. It is questionable in each case whether or not it could be said that the senior employee was actually qualified to perform the work. In all things said in the case it has never been maintained by the Union that any employee could prevail on seniority alone. An employee could not retain a job on his seniority unless he had substantial qualifications to perform the work in question, and he had to have more than just an orientation period on the work.

Concerning the three cases cited in which no grievance was filed and the one case in which a grievance was filed and later dropped, the Union takes the position that such incidents should not be considered as precedents. Under the agreement the right to file a grievance rests only with the employee affected, the Union argued. Arguing further, the Union stated, "By clear contract language the Union has bargained away its right to file grievances; by practice, it has been the employee who has the right either to drop or pursue a grievance once entered. Hence, an incident which could have been the basis of a grievance, or an incident under which a grievance was filed and dropped prior to final litigation, should not be considered as precedent."

In comparing the six cases cited by the Company to this instant case the Union pointed out that production efficiency was not used in the previous cases as it was in this instant case. Further the Union argued that the efficiency reports were unilaterally established by the Company without the acquiescence or co-operation of the Union. Thus, the Company violated Article VI in that they failed to confer with the Union as to who is to be laid off and how "marked difference" is to be determined.

The Union contends it is their belief that the efficiency reports devised by the Company are not competent to measure "marked difference." In the Union's opinion the standards are inaccurate and the manner in which they are kept bespeaks of haphazardness. The Union also argued that the use of efficiency reports was a departure from past practice in that the grievant survived at least three layoffs during his tenure of employment and that on one such occasion Bridwell, the junior in the department, was laid off but allowed to bump. At that time, the Union argued, it is evident from the Company testimony that the efficiency records were neither known nor used in the layoff.

In conclusion, the Union requested that the grievance of X—— be sustained and that he be reinstated to his former position without loss of pay or other rights or benefits.

COMPANY'S POSITION

The Company argued strongly and repeatedly that Article VI gives them the right to lay off out of line of seniority where there is a "marked difference in ability." In this instant case the Company contends the efficiency difference between X—— and Bridwell ranges between 24 per cent to 37 per cent, thus eliminating any doubt that a "marked difference existed" between the men regardless of their seniority status.

Concerning their past practice, the Company argued that from the evidence and testimony it is clear that the "marked difference" language of the agreement has been used where applicable. In such instances in the past, the Company pointed out, the Union at times grieved or failed to grieve and on two occasions went to arbitration and was denied. Thus, the Company argues, there can be no doubt that the "marked difference" provision has been used in the past and that the evidence does not support the Union's contentions regarding past practice.

Concerning the Union's attack on the Company's efficiency standards, the Company argued that regardless of their attempt to discredit, the fact remains that both X—— and Bridwell were measured against the same yardstick. In discussing their standards the Company pointed out that approximately 50 per cent of a man's work would be performed under Code 1, which is work that is performed by an employee when circumstances are as nearly correct as possible. Using only Code 1 work, the Company made the following comparison between Bridwell and X——. During the 18-month period which was used, X—— performed 1,297 hours of Code 1 work, while Bridwell's total was 1,093 hours. The production efficiency difference between the men in this period was 25 per cent. Using the same period but comparing work involving the same operations, number of parts, etc., the difference between the two men was 23 per cent. The hours involved in this latter comparison were Bridwell 293 and X—— 400. From this comparison the "marked difference" in the production efficiency of the two men is clearly demonstrated, the Company argued.

When questioned by the arbiter as to whether the Company was misusing and misinterpreting the seniority and layoff provision of the agreement, by confusing their right to discipline for inefficiency with their right to layoff out of line of seniority, the Company answered:

The Employer submits that it has not misapplied the provision of this agreement. The express language of the agreement contemplates that the 'marked difference' is applicable to the layoff situation. At no time has the Employer taken the position that X——'s layoff was disciplinary. To the contrary, the layoff was occasioned solely by forces outside the production department. It was inventory control which designated the machines and shifts which were to be discontinued. This was an economic decision which resulted in an economic layoff to a number of men. If this layoff had not come along,

X_____ would probably still be working at McEvoy and his supervisors would probably still be discussing his production efficiency with him on a weekly basis.

In conclusion, the Company submitted that the layoff of X—— was made in full compliance with the labor agreement and that the grievance should therefore be denied.

THE OPINION

From the facts, evidence, and testimony presented in this case one could quite readily reach the hasty conclusion that this case is concerned with simple contract interpretation. But unfortunately such a conclusion would be in error and an oversimplification of a very complex problem. In truth the parties in this case are not apart or in dispute as to the correct interpretation of Article VI. The Company stoutly maintains that contractually they have the right to lay off out of the line of seniority where there is a "marked difference of ability." The Union confirms this interpretation and in point of fact concurs in the Company position when they stated in their post-hearing brief:

* * *In all the things said in this case it has never been maintained by the Union that any employee could prevail on seniority alone. An employee could not retain a job on his seniority unless he had substantial qualifications to perform the work in question, and he had to have more than just an orientation period on the work.

Under these circumstances, it is safe to conclude that both parties agree that seniority alone is not absolute in layoffs where a substantially marked difference of ability exists between employees in a department. In other words, as there is no evident dispute between the parties as to the correct interpretation of the contract, the difference between the parties must lie in other areas.

While there seems to be agreement between the parties as to the correct contract interpretation, conversely there is sharp conflict between the parties as to past practice involving layoff. The Company maintains that it has been their practice to use the "marked difference" provision whenever applicable and thus lay off out of line of seniority. The Company also argues that the Union did not always protest such a procedure, and that in the two cases that went to arbitration the arbiter upheld the Company. The Union, however, strongly argues that production efficiency reports were new and had never been used before in deciding "marked difference" between employees. In this instant case, the Union claims that, by using efficiency reports to determine "marked differences" between employees, the Company violated the contract as well as established past practice.

At this point the dispute between the parties becomes clear, and it best can be described by asking: (1) Is the use of efficiency reports a new method established by the Company to determine marked differences between employees for purposes of layoff; (2) does the use of efficiency reports conflict with past practice to the point that it may not now be used; and (3) are the present efficiency reports used by the Company a good measurement capable of truly determining "marked differences" between employees for purposes of layoff? In the opinion of this arbiter the answers to these questions are the crux of the differences between the parties, and the heart of their dispute.

QUESTIONS

1. Do you agree with Arbitrator Morvant's opinion that this case is not "concerned with simple contract interpretation" but involves the more complex issue of past practice? Why?
2. Referring to the negotiation of Article VI, Section 1, did the Union consciously agree to layoffs based on ability? Would this be a wise decision on the part of the Union? What conditions would make such an agreement necessary from the viewpoint of the Union?
3. From the facts presented in the case, discuss the validity of the Company's "relative efficiency" measure. In general practice, layoffs based on "relative efficiency" are very uncommon. Why?
4. Is an employer forever bound to continuing past practice? Is the only way that an employer can break from past practice to negotiate a new clause specifying exactly what new method he intends to use?
5. How would you rule in this case? Justify your award.

Case 28

DISCHARGE OF A SENIOR EMPLOYEE FOR "FAILURE TO PERFORM WORK AS REQUIRED"

COMPANY: Hawaiian Telephone Company

UNION: International Brotherhood of Electrical Workers
Local 1260

ARBITRATOR: Ted T. Tsukiyama

What obligation does an employer have to an employee 48 years old with 26 years of seniority who appears to be incapable of doing the job she has filled for this long time?

The following discussion of the issue and facts in this case was prepared by Ted T. Tsukiyama, the arbitrator.

ISSUE

Was the Company's action on July 20, 1964, in discharging the grievant on ground of "failure to perform work as required" undertaken with just cause in accordance with the terms of the collective bargaining agreement in effect between the parties?

CONTRACT CLAUSE

Section 6 of the agreement covering discipline applicable in this grievance is quoted in part as follows:

Supervision and Discipline

6.1 The supervision and control of all operations and the direction of all working forces, which shall include, but not be limited to, the right to hire, to establish work schedules, to suspend or discharge for proper cause, to promote or transfer employees, to relieve employees from duty because of lack of work, or for other legitimate reasons, shall be vested exclusively in the Company, except as otherwise covered in this Agreement.

6.2 Proper causes for suspension or discharges shall include, but not be limited to, insubordination, pilferage, use of intoxicants during working hours, incompetence, failure to perform work as required, falsification of reports, violation of the terms of this Agreement, violation of the secrecy of communications, failure to observe safety rules and regulations, failure to observe the Company's House Rules, which shall be conspicuously posted.

BACKGROUND FACTS

Up to the time of her discharge, grievant was employed as a toll operator in the traffic department of the Company. Grievant is 48 years old and had started working with the Company on another island in 1936. After nine years she began working for the Company in its Honolulu office where, after a maternity leave in 1947, she worked up to the date of discharge—a total period of 26 years' employment with the Company. The toll operator's job duties generally involve the placing and maintaining of long-distance calls for customers on the switchboard, servicing such calls to the extent necessary, and registering certain pertinent information concerning each call on an IBM mark sense card to be used by the Company for billing purposes.

About August 5, 1963, it came to the attention of the general traffic manager that the grievant was committing a significant number of "ticket errors" and "irregularities" in the performance of her duties as toll operator. Grievant's work record was reviewed by the manager at that time upon discovery of an erasure on one of her ticket entries, which is considered a serious "irregularity" on the toll board operations. The "irregularities" noted on her record included tardiness, talking at the switchboard, monitoring (listening) of calls, dozing off at the board, failure to give notifications, and low board loads and failure to collect on toll calls. The Company found grievant particularly weak in "ticket errors" which consisted of errors made on the mark sense cards, which were rejected by the IBM machines or which were otherwise not acceptable for billing purposes. Such errors included failure to mark certain capsules (spaces), marking the wrong capsule, or failing to note necessary data on the cards. The chief operator recommended dismissal of grievant but the traffic manager, considering grievant's long seniority with the Company, sent grievant a written reprimand and warning on August 26, 1963 (Company's Exhibit "A"), which listed all of her job weaknesses, required at least average job performance in the future, and exhorted her to do better.

On or about April 19, 1964, grievant failed to collect a $109.75 charge from a coin station call. Another review of her work record subsequent to August, 1963, revealed a high average of ticket errors committed by grievant, which convinced her superiors that the warning had not been effective, and grievant was consequently suspended for two weeks following this incident. The evidence shows that from the August, 1963, warning letter to the suspension in April, 1964, grievant's work record indicated at least seven failures to notify, four late notifications, several failures to collect, poor timing (failure to record correct time on each call), and numerous ticket errors (e.g., 156 errors for December, January, February, 1964). When notified of her suspension, grievant requested her chief operator to be transferred to the auxiliary operators' group in the department, but this was denied on the basis of a department policy prohibiting transfers between the toll and auxiliary work groups. The letter of suspension (Company's Exhibit "B") sent to her on April 23, 1964, listed all of her recent failures and insisted that her future performance (1) must abide by all work rules, (2) must show a 65 per cent improvement in ticket errors, failure to notify, etc., (3) must not fail to collect on pay station calls, and (4) show good attendance and punctuality. Otherwise discipline, including dismissal, would follow.

Although the chief operator again recommended discharge on April 23, 1964, the traffic manager recommended against grievant's dismissal at this point because of her long years of service and because he thought the Company should make further attempt to rehabilitate grievant's work performance. Thus when grievant returned from her suspension, two service assistants were assigned to give special supervision, attention, and training to the grievant on her mark sensing work at the switchboard. During the remainder of the month of May, 1964, grievant received special supervision from Pauline Nakamori up to 1½ hours per day and about six 15–20 minute special training sessions from Irene Iseri until the first part of June, when the special assignments were terminated. Both service assistants testified that grievant showed improvement in her mark sensing work during the limited periods they supervised grievant.

During May, June, and July of 1964, an unexpected heavy load of long-distance traffic calls occurred, resulting in a six-day workweek with considerable overtime for the toll operators group. In the middle of July, 1964, a compilation sheet of operators' ticket errors revealed that grievant had committed 121 ticket errors during the month of June, which called for another review of her record by the traffic manager. The traffic manager and chief operator found that grievant had the highest number of ticket errors among the operators (29.38 error average) for that month and concluded that she had made no improvement in failures to notify, timing, and mark sensing; thus they found no alternative but to dismiss the grievant. Grievant was dismissed on July 20, 1964, on grounds of "failure to perform work as required" under Section 6 of the agreement.

DISCUSSION

There is no evidence in the record that grievant consciously or knowingly or deliberately committed the shortcomings and errors noted in her performance record. There is not even a suggestion of any evidence that she wilfully "laid down" on the job or wantonly committed irregularities and errors to spite the Company or her superiors. The evidence does reveal that grievant often tried to alibi or offer excuses, such as personal or domestic problems, when confronted with her poor performance, that she has a crusty temperament and is probably not easy to work with or over, that she felt the Company should be more tolerant of the job weaknesses of "old-timers" like herself. It is also easily inferable from her statements that she chaffed at finding herself, a veteran of many years' service, taking direction from employees much younger than herself who had ascended into "supervisory" positions over her. On one occasion, she argued with a service assistant about the length of a coffee break and signing out (7/11/64—charged with "unco-operative attitude").

She may have been unfit, unable, or incapable of meeting certain job standards, but this is not to say she was unwilling or refused to do what she was physically and mentally able to perform. There was no instance shown where she balked at carrying out any order or instruction of her superiors or was otherwise guilty of insubordination. When her superiors asked her to try to improve her work, the evidence shows that she did make a genuine and bona fide attempt (albeit the results were not satisfactory to the Company).

WORK RECORD

Grievant regularly committed a high, if not one of the highest, number of mark sense ticket errors compared to the other toll operators. In addition there were at least four failures to collect on toll calls involving sums of $55 and $25.30 besides the 4/19/64 incident, customer complaints for eight failures to give three-minute notification and for four late notifications, and poor timing and overlapping operations, contributing to her ticket and billing errors. She was also tardy to work a dozen times. In view of this type of performance record, I find the Company's action in reprimanding grievant on her 7/18/63 ticket erasure and suspending her for two weeks on her 4/19/64 failure to collect to be fully warranted. And the Company's efforts toward corrective discipline in lieu of discharge on these occasions, as reflected by the traffic manager's recommendation that she be given another chance and more rehabilitation, was most considerate and commendable.

In the 2½-month period following her return from suspension on May 5, 1964, the evidence shows that Grievant had three complaints for failure to notify and one late notification, two failures to collect, 26 ticket errors for April (3 weeks), 42 ticket errors for May (27 days) and 121 ticket errors for June. Bearing in mind the four minimum conditions set forth in the Company's suspension letter of 4/19/64, grievant fell down in two areas (ticket errors and failure to collect) and the promised disciplinary action was forthcoming.

Against this record several counterconsiderations should be weighed. The two service assistants who gave grievant direct and personal supervision testified that grievant's mark sensing and board work was improving during the limited time they were assigned to her. (Note that grievant's ticket error average for May (27 days) while under special training was roughly 70 per cent of her monthly average up to that time). Why, then, should grievant's ticket errors suddenly jump more than 200 per cent over her usual average in the very next month? There is no indication that the Company attempted to look into the reasons for this unusual phenomenon, an astoundingly dramatic and high error level even for this subject. Nothing in the record explains why those working around and over grievant had not been aware that her ticket errors during June had become alarmingly frequent and high, a fact not discovered until two weeks passed in July. It was made clear that neither the traffic manager nor the chief operator interviewed or obtained an evaluation report from the two employees who were specially assigned to help grievant and upgrade her work, which raises another question as to the seriousness or bona fides of the attempted rehabilitation. In explaining why the two service assistants were not consulted, the traffic manager stated they were not supervisory employees and were not in a position to judge "over-all performance" of an operator, but further went on to state that errors were the heavyweight item in over-all job performance—the very item these two employees were instructed to correct and improve. Further, the traffic manager repeatedly emphasized grievant failed to improve in "over-all performance," yet it is clear that it must have been only the 121 ticket errors in June that precipitated her downfall, since other aspects of her performance did not appear noticeably bad in comparison with her prior record. Also, there was no evidence to show how the Company determined that grievant had failed to make a 65 per cent improvement in her performance as laid down in the April 23, 1964, "ultimatum." Finally, consideration must be given to the unexpected peak traffic that hit the Company during this exact period from May to July, which caught it short staffed, required a heavier workweek and overtime schedule for all operators, and which, incidentally, raised the ticket error average for all operators during this period. In short, this exact period when grievant's job was put at stake was a highly abnormal period for all concerned. Suffice it to surmise that grievant probably "got lost in the shuffle" during this rush period and was forgotten until those 121 errors came to light.

QUESTIONS

1. Is there a difference between "incompetence," "failure to perform work as required," and "falsification of records"? Is the grievant guilty of each of these offenses?
2. Evaluate the Company's efforts at constructive discipline as applied to the grievant.
3. What weight should be given to the grievant's "attitude" and long service record in this discharge proceeding?

Case 29

VOLUNTARY OR FORCED RETIREMENT?

COMPANY: Louisville Public Warehouse
             Louisville, Kentucky

UNION: International Brotherhood of Teamsters
             General Drivers, Warehousemen and Helpers, Local 89

ARBITRATOR: Louis C. Kesselman

Is old age a justifiable cause for discharge or forced resignation? This is one of several questions raised by this case.

The following discussion of the issue and facts in this case was prepared by Louis C. Kesselman, the arbitrator.

The issue is "Whether or not the discharge of William Wilding on July 5, 1957 and the alleged forced resignation of Edward Roehr on June 28, 1957, were in accordance with Article V and Article VII, paragraphs (a) and (b) of the existing agreement between the parties?"

CONTRACT PROVISIONS INVOLVED

Article V. Extra Contract Agreements
    The Company shall not ask employees who are members of the Union to enter into any agreement in conflict with this agreement . . .
Article VII. Discharge or Suspension
    (a) The Employer shall not discharge or suspend any employee without just cause, but in respect to discharge must give at least one (1) warning notice of the complaint against such employee to the employee, in writing, with a copy to the Union, except that no warning notice need be given to an employee before he is discharged or suspended for dishonesty, drunkenness,

use of alcoholic beverages while on duty, keeping intoxicating liquor on Company premises, smoking where smoking is not allowed, disobedience of posted Company rules or participation in a strike or slow down, or refusal to perform his usual normal duties as directed by management.

(b) Discharge must be by proper written notice to the employee and the Union. Warning notices shall have no force or effect after nine (9) months from the date thereof. Any employee may request an investigation as to his warning notice, discharge or suspension and such request shall be handled as provided for in Article XIV of this Agreement.

Article VIII. Sickness or Injury

In case of sickness and inability to work, the employee shall receive his former position and seniority upon recovery within six (6) months but only if he is physically fit and able to perform his regular work satisfactorily. In case of injury on the job the six (6) months limit shall not apply.

Article XIII. Classifications and Hourly Rates

Warehouseman $1.95

BACKGROUND

In June, 1957, Edward Roehr, 67-year-old warehouseman employed since October 5, 1937, was told by Company President W. H. Kinnaird that he was not physically able to perform the normal work required of a warehouseman and that his services would have to be terminated. Kinnaird told Roehr that if he would resign without waiting for discharge, he would be given $750 in severance pay. Roehr accepted the offer as of June 28, 1957, and was given a check for $560.12 for terminal pay minus deductions.

A similar conference was held with William Wilding, 64-year-old warehouseman, employed since May 13, 1936. On June 27, 1957, Wilding was sent a letter with a copy to the Union, in which he was told, "In our opinion, your age and physical condition make it impossible for you to do the full work required of a warehouseman." He was offered $1,000 in a lump sum or in installments if he would retire voluntarily by July 5, 1957. If the offer were not accepted by that date, stated the letter, "it will be withdrawn and we will proceed to exercise our legal rights as we see fit." Wilding was discharged on July 5, 1957, when the Company's deadline for voluntary retirement passed. He received no severance pay.

On July 9, 1957, Wilding and Roehr filed grievances protesting their dismissals. Failure of the parties to resolve the grievances satisfactorily resulted in their submission to arbitration in accordance with Article XIV of the agreeent.

UNION'S CONTENTIONS

1. The Company is not justified in discharging Wilding and Roehr for old age under the discharge for "just cause" provision in Article VII (a) of the agreement.

2. The Company failed to give Wilding and Roehr "at least one (1) warning notice of the complaint . . . in writing, with a copy to the

Union" as required by Article VII (a). Roehr received no notice in writing. Wilding received a letter dated June 27, 1957, which was not a warning notice but rather a "proposition and a threat that if he does not accept the Company's proposition, he would be discharged." Roehr's resignation was forced, not voluntary.

3. The Company violated Article V of the agreement and Section 9 of the Labor Relations Act by bargaining with the employees individually in conflict with the agreement.

4. The Company's charge that the two men had worked approximately 18½ years in the bottling house and had not been hired to do warehouse work is ill-founded because bottling house work is comparable to warehouse work. In any case, if their warehouse work had not been satisfactory, the Company should have put them on notice before 18 months had elapsed.

5. Medical certificates bear out the contention that the two men are in excellent physical condition for their ages and "are perfectly capable to continue to perform, as required by management."

6. The Company admits that the two men were willing employees and had never refused to perform any work assigned to them. Therefore, the Company "had no right whatsoever to complain about the quantity or quality of work done by these two men, let alone discharging them for something that they had no right to complain about in the first place."

7. The Company is "asking the arbitrator to permit them to discharge an employee or to make a deal with an employee in the form of severance pay, because of their old age, and the Union's argument is, that this is not grounds for discharge . . . this problem should be decided by contract negotiations in form of severance pay, pension plans, or retirement plans on a collective bargaining basis for all employees. Union offered to negotiate such a plan when the question of retiring Wilding, and Roehr first arose.

8. If the Company is permitted to discharge employees for old age it will make it difficult to negotiate a pension plan with this and other companies signatory to the agreement.

9. Union did not agree to Company's right to retire men but indicated willingness to withdraw objection if the separation pay was equivalent to the proposed Union pension plan and the men involved were willing to go along.

10. Fellow employees did not object to working with Wilding and Roehr.

11. The Company has always taken care of older employees until recently by finding lighter work for them to do.

COMPANY'S CONTENTIONS

1. Wilding was discharged and Roehr resigned not because they had reached a specific retirement age but rather because of their inability to

perform the work. "Inability of an employee to perform the duties for which he was employed is 'just cause' for discharge under the opening clause of Article VII."

2. Management has the sole prerogative to determine whether an employee is physically able to perform his normal duties, so long as Management acts in good faith. No charge of ulterior motive or lack of good faith has been made.

3. The Company's officers and supervisors are unanimous in their judgments that these men were physically unable to do the work required of them as warehousemen.

4. Fellow employees had freely criticized the inability of the two men to do their share of the work in the warehouse.

5. Wilding is unable to operate a fork-lift truck, pull tags off appliances, serve as an efficient checker, or do general warehouse duties without danger to himself. Wilding is unable to raise his arms above his shoulders although the stacking of various commodities requires higher lifting. Roehr is similarly unable to do the work of a warehouseman. At the hearing Roehr refused to say whether he wanted his job back if it involved performing exactly the same type and amount of heavy labor performed by the other warehousemen.

6. Article VIII by requiring re-employment of a sick or injured employee "only if he is physically fit and able to perform his regular work satisfactorily" shows that both parties agreed that inability to do the work is "just cause" for discharge.

7. The medical statements in behalf of Wilding and Roehr were solicited and were not based upon observation of the jobs which the men were expected to do.

8. It is neither feasible nor practical in the Company's operation to put some warehousemen on light work exclusively and leave the heavy work for others. There is no differentiation in the wage classifications for warehousemen performing light duties and those performing heavy work. The Company has had no past practice of putting men suffering from physical disability on lighter work in the warehouse which is the Company's only operation at present.

9. The Company attempted to work out the problem with the Union's Business Agent who refused to discuss the cases of the two men unless the Company would adopt the Union's pension plan. The Union by implication recognized the Company's right to discharge physically unfit employees by stating its willingness to accept $5,000 to $5,400 each for the men, rather than the sum proposed by the Company. In effect, the Company followed the procedure for separating physically unfit older workers suggested by Joe Burrell, Union Vice-President at the time the contract was negotiated.

10. The Company complied with Article VII (a) by providing a warning notice to Wilding and a copy to the Union. Notice did not say

that the employee was doing something wrong and that he had to correct it "because Wilding's physical condition was something which was beyond his power to correct." No warning notice was necessary in the case of Roehr because he voluntarily chose to resign. Roehr was not threatened or coerced to resign; to the contrary, he was happy to resign and receive a gratuity.

11. The Company did not violate Article V by asking employees to enter into any agreement in conflict with the contract. Company did not discuss "rates of pay, wages, and hours of employment or conditions of employment" with the men without Union representatives being present.

QUESTIONS

1. Was Roehr discharged or did he voluntarily resign?
2. Does a belief on the part of the Company that an employee is unable to correct his alleged inability to perform work free the Company of the obligation to warn an employee before discharge?
3. What bearing does the Business Agent's refusal to discuss the Roehr and Wilding cases unless the Company adopted the Union's pension plan have on issue in these cases? Had the employer given $5,000 and $5,400 each for the men, could the Union still argue that the Company had violated the agreement?
4. Did the Company conferences with Wilding and Roehr violate the agreement? Why or why not?
5. Are Wilding and Roehr entitled to light work or special treatment in deference to their age and long service to the Company?
6. Does this situation suggest any principles that might be applied to such matters as work assignments, severance pay, and pension plans? Prepare a check list of collective bargaining issues raised by this case which should be considered in the next union-management negotiations.

Case 30

TESTS AS MEASURES OF ABILITY IN JOB BIDDING

COMPANY: National Seal Company
                  Van Wert, Ohio

UNION: United Rubber Workers of America
                  Local 426

ARBITRATOR: Harry J. Dworkin

Can the employer eliminate a senior employee from consideration for a new job on the basis of test scores? This case involves the interpretation of an agreement on promotion and transfers.

The following discussion of the issue and facts in this case was prepared by Harry J. Dworkin, the arbitrator.

The issue submitted for arbitration and developed during the course of the hearing concerns itself with the application of the contract provisions pertaining to seniority and the qualifications and "job requirements" of employees who bid for a job opening in a particular classification.

The grievant, Frances Brotherwood, bid for the job of packer and machine operator which had been duly posted by management. In accordance with the established procedure, the company gave a test to the job applicants in order to determine whether they met the job requirements with particular reference to aptitude for simple mathematics. On the basis of the results of the examination, the grievant was given a failing score and was adjudged by the company to lack the job requirements insofar as they concerned proficiency in simple mathematics. The grievant, although having greater seniority, was bypassed and the job was given to an applicant who was successful in the examination, even though she had less seniority than the grievant.

The Union thereupon processed a grievance on behalf of Frances Brotherwood, claiming that she was entitled to the job vacancy. The grievance is as follows:

STATEMENT OF GRIEVANCE

I signed a job posting for the job of packer in the packing department on the 2nd shift. The job was given to a employee who has less seniority than I do. The Co. made a mistake in giving the job to the less senior employee. I am asking to be given the job & back pay up to the time the less senior employee was transferred to that job.

P.S. I have done the job several times before the job posting was put up.

(Signed) Frances Brotherwood
Signature of Employee

COMPANY RESPONSE

The company's answer was based on the fact that she failed to attain the minimum requirements necessary to qualify:

Performance on numbers test fell considerably below the minimum requirements necessary to qualify for the job. The position was filled by a person meeting minimum qualifications.

The company further explained its position in a subsequent step of the grievance procedure:

The contract provides that selection of employees to fill this job will be made on the basis of seniority and job requirements.

Because employees performing this job are required to calculate, from the number of shipping cases and seals per case, the seals packed, and are responsible for making the final report of transfer to the shipping department, the requirements of this job include reasonable proficiency at simple arithmetic.

The aggrieved states that she has done this job. It is true that she has done *a part* of this job. But obviously she is not qualified to do *all* the job.

The job was given to the most senior employee who met the minimum job requirements.

In an explanatory letter to the union dated December 21, 1956, the company pointed out that this is the only female job in the plant except department clerks on which written tests are used to determine whether or not the employee meets the job requirements. Since this job involves the computation of seals packed for delivery to the customer, this requirement along with legibility of writing is critical on the job. The math requirements can be determined objectively by tests which have been standardized for industry and such tests have been used for at least the past four years for that purpose.

The test that was used for the purpose of determining mathematical proficiency is prepared by the Industrial Psychology Corporation and its use is explained by the company as follows:

The test used is standardized on a percentile basis. The lowest 1% of scores are in the 1st percentile group and the highest 1% in the 100th percentile group, etc. The minimum acceptable on the job is a score in the 25th percentile group. (Far below average but acceptable as a minimum.) This is consistent with the requirement for successful bidding on the job for at least the past 4 years, and has been required of other employees bidding on this job. Frances' score was in the 8th percentile group. To award her the job when in the past other bidders who came closer to meeting the job requirement were denied the job would not only be hazardous as far as computing seals packed is concerned but would also be discriminatory. There were no grievances filed in the other cases.

As was previously suggested, if Frances believes there were any circumstances at the time she took the test which did not permit her to work on it effectively, we were and are willing for her to take another form of the same test.

The examination paper itself was introduced in evidence and the following portion is indicative of the nature of the test given:

	1	2	3	4	Answer
4 plus 7 plus 3 equals:	12	13	14	15	( )
24 divided by 6 plus 3 equals:	7	8	6	10	( )
5 times 9 plus 4 equals:	45	49	51	54	( )

The job description for the packer and machine operator (female) includes the following duties:

What duties does the incumbent personally perform in the usual course of work?

Duties include operations related to packaging of seals and preparation of cartons and cases. These operations involve packing finished seals in rolls, cartons or envelopes; operating equipment such as multigraph, printing press, box opener, box closer and stapler; and preparing shipping cases for packing.

Must be able to read and interpret Production Orders, count production, make out stock receipts, etc.

Performs other duties as directed.

Specific education requirements: High school graduation or equivalent.

The job of packer and machine operator was created in November, 1954, resulting from an amalgamation of two then existing separate jobs, and since that time the posting of the job indicated a requirement of proficiency in simple arithmetic and "all of the employees have taken the test." The company has consistently utilized the test as a means for determining whether the employee met the job requirements with reference to proficiency in simple mathematics, and the union has consistently opposed the use of the test, and has refused during the course of prior contract negotiations to acknowledge the propriety of the test by way of contract language. However, no prior grievance has been filed by any employee although successful applicants for jobs have been rated in part by the results of the examination.

In accordance with the terms of the current contract, the issue was developed by the parties during the course of the oral hearing, at which time the parties submitted oral testimony and documentary evidence in support of their respective positions. An opportunity was given the parties to file a brief by way of summation, the union indicating that it preferred to submit the case on basis of the evidence adduced, whereas the company has filed a post-hearing brief. In addition, all of the proceedings before the arbitrator were embodied in a transcript of the evidence which has been considered in the preparation of this opinion and award.

PROVISIONS OF CONTRACT

The collective bargaining agreement between the company and the union, effective November 1, 1956, provides as follows with reference to the filling of vacancies:

Section 3. Job Bidding and Shift Preference.
    . . . Selection of employees to fill such jobs shall be made on the basis of seniority and job requirements for all jobs except machine set up classifications. . . .

A trial period is given to employees who have successfully bid for a job opening:

Section 4. General Provisions.
    B. An employee transferred to a job as a result of job bidding will have a reasonable trial period not exceeding thirty (30) calendar days. If he fails to qualify for the job during this period he will return to the job from which he transferred and all other employees affected by the return of this employee will be moved back to their former jobs also.

The contract further contains the customary management prerogative clause:

Article I. Statement of Policy.
    The right to hire, promote, discharge or discipline for just cause and to maintain discipline and efficiency of employees is solely the responsibility of the Company, subject to the terms of this Agreement.

Position of the Union

The Union bases its grievance upon the charge that the Company violated the collective bargaining agreement and the provisions relating to the filling of vacancies, and contends that the grievant had greater seniority than the employee who was assigned to the job. Accordingly, the Union claims that the grievant was bypassed in violation of her rights under the contract.

It is the Union's position that on the basis of seniority, prior job experience, and familiarity with the duties required, the grievant was entitled to the opportunity to bid for the job and that she should have been permitted to fill the job on a trial basis since she, in fact, possessed the job requirements and had the ability to do the work required. The Union points to her background and experience, including the fact that she had performed the job on a temporary basis for a total period of thirty-three (33) days, and that her work generally was satisfactory.

The Union contends that the examination used by the company in determining an employee's aptitude is unjust and beyond the scope of the contract. The Union states that the examination is "an added burden on the part of an employee who bids on a job."

The Union further points out that in the contract negotiations it informed the Company that it would not accept or recognize written tests on job bidding, and that the language in the present contract governing selection of employees to fill job vacancies omits any reference to written examinations and requires that selection be made on the basis of "seniority and job requirements."

In the course of the contract negotiations, the Union represents that the Company had consistently endeavored to phrase the contract in such a manner as to put job requirements ahead of seniority, while the Union has maintained the position that seniority should be the determining factor in job promotion with the ability to meet the job requirements a matter of secondary significance. In any event, written tests were at no time agreed to by the Union as the means for determining whether an employee was possessed of the required aptitude and qualifications.

Furthermore, as evidence that the grievant had the qualifications for the job, the Union established that previously she had been assigned to this classification on a temporary basis and had performed the work satisfactorily and without complaint.

The Union reasons that under Section 3 of the contract seniority is the determining factor in the designation of the applicant for an available position where such applicant has the ability to perform the work and is possessed of the necessary physical qualifications: that in the event there is any question or doubt concerning such applicant's ability or fitness she should be accorded a qualifying trial period of thirty (30) days; that in this instance the grievant was denied the right to qualify for the job as specified in Section 4(B) of Article VIII of the agreement. While the Union acknowledges that the contract language requires that vacancies be filled on the basis of both seniority and job requirements, it points out that the contract language does not include the testing procedure adopted by the Company, and that this is, therefore, an "added burden" not within the scope of the contract.

With reference to the uncontroverted evidence on behalf of the Company that the Company had consistently since November 1, 1956, when the job as presently described came into existence, required that all of the employees who bid on the job vacancies in the classification take the test, and that no prior grievances had been filed in similar situations, the Union representative states as follows:

I might say this, that some of the tests that the company referred to that they had been denied jobs, the Union was aware of some of those. They were protected. Because of individual circumstances or feelings, the employees did not wish to protest and file a grievance and process it on through. We do not consider, because one employee does not consider it important enough to process a grievance—that it does not relinquish the rights of another employee to protest and file a grievance.

The Union asserts that it has never orally or in writing acknowledged the validity or propriety of the tests used by the Company, and that, in fact, it has orally protested their use on a number of occasions. The Union therefore states that although the contract required that when a vacancy occurred in a classification, the employee with the highest seniority was entitled to first preference provided he met the job requirements, this procedure was not followed or adhered to by the Company.

The employee who was awarded the position had less seniority than the grievant, and, in the event there remained any doubt or question as to the ability of the grievant to do the job required, she should have been given a thirty (30) day qualifying trial. Accordingly, the Union states that the Company violated the contract with reference to seniority and requests that the arbitrator rule that she be assigned to the job, together with an award of compensation of any lost wages.

POSITION OF THE COMPANY

The Company contends that the Union's claims are unfounded and that its action with respect to the assignment of an employee to the classification of packer and machine operator was fully justified and warranted by the evidence and was consistent with the terms of the collective bargaining agreement, and in accordance with established past practice. The Company's position is that its action was not the result of any arbitrary, capricious, or discriminatory conduct or bias toward the grievant, and points out that the contract does not provide for filling a vacancy on the basis of seniority alone; that the express language of the contract requires that that the employee's rights to the job in question must be determined on whether the applicant can fulfill the job requirements.

Furthermore, the procedure which was followed in this instance has been consistently adhered to since November 1, 1954, in the filling of approximately eighteen (18) vacancies in which each applicant was required to take a test to determine mathematical proficiency, and that no prior grievance has been filed. The Company vigorously contends that the testing method is the only known means for objectively determining the proficiency of the applicant for the job, and whether she is possessed of the job requirements involved in the job description.

The examination which the grievant failed to pass by the required minimum grade is prepared by the Industrial Psychology Corporation and is a type of test used widely in industry. The test is standardized on a percentile basis and, to determine average proficiency in simple arithmetic, anyone whose score is twenty-five (25) percentile or above meets the requirements and is considered as having demonstrated the minimum mathematical proficiency required. On the basis of the results of the examination, the Company gave the job to the employee who met the minimum posted job requirements in preference to the grievant who claimed the job on the basis of her seniority plus job experience.

Since the time this job was classified, all persons who have made application for existing vacancies have been required to meet the job requirements, one of which being "average proficiency in simple arithmetic." The Company has uniformly insisted that all applicants for these jobs pass a test to establish the necessary knowledge and has consistently refused the job to senior applicants who did not meet the requirements. At least eighteen (18) employees were denied jobs during 1955 and 1956 for failure to pass the same test which was given to the grievant without any formal grievance having been filed. The test itself is reasonable and was properly administered.

The Company points out that it is a standard test, widely used and accepted in industry generally. There is no recognized means for objectively and fairly determining an employee's proficiency in simple arithmetic except through a test in the subject matter. Since the job description and evaluation plan require that the applicant be either a high school graduate or have the equivalent educational background, and since the applicant was not a high school graduate, the test was a reasonable requirement in order to determine whether she had the "equivalent" requirement.

In the interpretation of the contract language pertaining to job bidding, the Company points out that under the express language of the agreement, the job must be given to the senior employee who meets the job requirements "not to some employee who has temporarily worked on the job or who claims to be qualified by ability or who thinks he can learn the job in a reasonable time. *The employee must meet the job requirements."*

Thus, the Company urges that there is an apparent difference between the phrases, "meeting job requirements" and "ability to qualify or perform a job." The successful bidder for a vacancy must *first* meet the job requirements and *then* qualify on the job within a reasonable time. To grant the grievance in this case would have the effect of leaving the Company completely without any objective standard to apply in filling job vacancies and would result in interminable grievances on the part of senior employees whose claims to the vacancies would be based solely upon their length of service in disregard of their lack of ability to meet the requirements of the job.

Furthermore, the Company represents that the practice of requiring the job applicants to submit to a reasonable examination has been followed for almost three years and it would be unfair to both the Company and the employees to upset the established procedure, and would render the contract terms meaningless; this would be tantamount to reading into the contract language limitations that are not therein expressed.

By way of summary of its position, the Company states that the test and the manner in which it is given are both fair and reasonable and is within the inherent right of the Company in light of the pertinent contract language referred to:

This right rests not only upon past practice, but upon the contractual power to fix job requirements and require some proof that they are met. Without objective means of measuring the meeting of job requirement, they are meaningless. A requirement of a certain height is nonsense if the man's height cannot be measured. A job requirement of average proficiency in simple arithmetic is nonsense if the employee's proficiency cannot be measured. There is absolutely no way to measure objectively and impartially the physical or mental attainments of an applicant other than by a test. The Union has not and cannot suggest any alternative.

Accordingly, the Company alleges that it has faithfully followed the clear language of the contract in the awarding of the job; that the test was voluntarily taken by the applicant and was fairly administered; that she failed to demonstrate the minimum requirement of mathematical proficiency; and that, therefore, the job was properly assigned to the employee with less seniority who qualified under the testing procedure. The Company urges that, for the aforesaid reasons, the union's grievance be denied.

QUESTIONS

1. Does the Union's repeated refusal to accept tests or an agreement upgrading the ability criterion in negotiations deny management the right to use non-discriminatory testing methods in determining ability?

2. Does the wording of the agreement clearly define the relative emphasis which will be given to ability and seniority?

3. On what basis did the Company justify its promotion of a junior employee?
4. Under this agreement, who is the final judge of ability? Who determines the criteria for this judgment?
5. The Union argues that the grievant's past temporary placement on the job is substantiation for her ability. The Company later attempted to rebut this argument by introducing evidence of errors in the grievant's work. What is the relevancy of the Union's contention and the Company's rebuttal to the issue in this case?

Case 31

MECHANICAL APTITUDE TESTS FOR FILLING NEW JOBS

COMPANY: Pretty Products, Incorporated

UNION: United Rubber, Cork, Linoleum and Plastic Workers of America
             Local 50

ARBITRATOR: Maurice E. Nichols

Are mechanical aptitude tests the same as a "trial" on a new job? Does a union's past failure to challenge tests commit the union to their use in the future?

The following discussion of the issues and facts in this case was prepared by Maurice E. Nichols, the arbitrator.

BACKGROUND

The Company is a producer of rubber products, many of which are sold to automobile companies and accessories dealers. The business is highly competitive, and frequent model and style changes necessitate changes in and modifications of equipment, tools, and fixtures. The effectiveness of the maintenance department materially influences and controls the productivity of the producing department. For some period of time prior to the events resulting in this dispute the job titled Maintenance Helper had not been filled, although it is listed (with stipulated rates of pay) in the rate schedule attached to and made a part of the collective bargaining agreement.

The Company had experienced an acute shortage of capable maintenance personnel. The department has operated six and seven days per week (most men averaging 55 hours per week), and it was still necessary to contract out some maintenance work. On January 2, 1964, the Company posted a job opening for Maintenance Man B, indicating on the posted notice that tests would be used in determining the successful bidder. The Union grieved (Union Ex. 1), stating:

Grievance No. 10
We feel that the wording used by the Company in the job posting for Maintenance Man-B dated Jan. 2 indicates the Company's intention to violate paragraph 60 and/or provisions or the Union-Company Agreement. It appears as though it may have been designed to discourage prospective bidders. We ask that said job posting be voided and the Maintenance Man-B job be posted and filled in the same manner as any other vacancy, in accordance with the Agreement.

The Union
S/SIMON CHENEY, Pres.
WILLIAM A. NOON

The Company replied:

Management does not believe that the Union ever intended that any part of the Union-Management Agreement should support an unworkable situation. The job posting in question could not possibly be satisfactorily filled by open bidding as requested above. Any employee who thinks he could do the work required by this classification has a perfect right to sign the posting and demonstrate his ability in a practical test. Management has no intention of discouraging any employee who has the ability and skills to fill this job.

S/H. D. ROBSON
Personnel Department 1/3/64

Following further discussion of this dispute and the problem of obtaining maintenance personnel, the Company postponed activation of this posting by submitting the following letter:

January 9, 1964

U.R.C.,. & P.W.A.
LOCAL 50
Coshocton, Ohio

Gentlemen:
This letter is in answer to your grievance #10 dated January 3, 1964, and signed by Simon Cheney and William Noon.
The company will take no action on the job posting which you have objected to and will in the near future present a plan for your consideration on establishing an apprentice program and a method to improve the language in the contract and our over-all maintenance situation.

Yours truly
S/EARL RICHARD
Plant Superintendent

The parties then proceeded to negotiate, attempting to reach a mutually acceptable maintenance apprentice program. They arrived at a program which was accepted by the Union committee but rejected by the Union membership. At this point, the Company issued the following letters—both dated April 9, 1964 (three months after postponement):

Gentlemen:
This is in reference to our letter dated January 9, 1964, pertaining to your grievance #10 dated January 3, 1964, and signed by Simon Cheney and William Noon.

In our letter we stated that we would take no action on the job posting which was posted on January 3, 1964, for Maintenance Man "B" and signed by G. Robinson and Cecil E. Johnson and that we would present a plan for your consideration on our over-all maintenance situation.

Since no agreement has been reached on this situation we are advising you that this job posting is being voided as of this date.

Yours truly,
S/Earl Richard
Plant Superintendent

The second letter (April 9, 1964):

Gentlemen:

Since the Union has seen fit to reject all proposals made by the Company on a very serious situation in our Maintenance department, this letter is to advise you that any and all proposals made by the Company to the Union regarding the Maintenance Program have been withdrawn as of this date.

Yours truly,
Earl Richard
Plant Superintendent

The Company then proceeded to post the following:

DATE   May 25, 1964
OPENING   Maintenance Helpers
BASE RATE $1.96

_____
_____
_____

Passing a mechanical aptitude test will be a necessary qualification.

All things being equal, the one having the most seniority and the necessary qualifications will be accepted.

Eight employees bid on the job. All were given aptitude tests covering three areas: (1) Mechanical Knowledge; (2) Space Relations; (3) Shop Arithmetic. These were standard tests used extensively in measuring mechanical aptitude. Of the eight employees bidding (and subsequently tested), three were selected. The grievant, who had the greatest length of service, was not one of the three. As a result, he filed the grievance:

June 11, 1964

Grievance No. 22

I feel that I should have the job as maintenance helper. Men with less seniority than I were put on the job.

The Company has violated Paragraph 60 of the contract.

S/P. M.

This protest was processed through the steps of the grievance procedure and, not being resolved, is the Issue to be resolved in these proceedings.

CONTENTIONS OF THE UNION

The Union bases its position on the specific language of Paragraph 60:

60. When vacancies occur, or new jobs are created, such vacancies or jobs shall be posted for bids, concurrently in the department and plant wide for forty-eight (48) hours, and senior regular employees (as defined in Paragraph 49) *shall be given the opportunity to trial on such jobs as per classification* (male or female) if the employee so desires. Jobs will be filled in the following manner: (Emphasis added.)

    1. Senior employees within the department.
    2. Senior employees, plant-wide.
    3. After the application of Paragraph 66, new hires.

It is the contention of the Union that the senior bidder on any job is entitled (by the language of this paragraph 60) to a trial period on the job. There are no exceptions. Until and/or unless these provisions of the agreement are changed by negotiations between the parties, they must be complied with. To do otherwise would render seniority useless and of no purpose to secure a better or more satisfactory job.

The Union asks that the grievance be sustained and the grievant made whole for any loss of earnings sustained since the date of the grievance.

CONTENTIONS OF THE COMPANY

The Company disagrees with the Union premise that isolates Paragraph 60 and thereby disregards all other paragraphs having to do with job placement and further contends that the language of the agreement should be interpreted with due consideration given to practice which has been in effect for an appreciable period of time without protest.

The Company submits that it has, for many years past, included tests as a part of the trial for maintenance jobs. Company Exhibit No. 1 (May 15, 1962) was submitted as an example and is shown on the following page.

DATE—MAY 15, 1962
OPENING—DEPARTMENT "Z"
MAINTENANCE MEN—"B"
BASIC RATE—$2.25 PER HOUR

Men must be qualified to weld without instruction, as no supervision will be on the night shifts, qualified to do electrical wiring, steam piping, machine and equipment repairs.
Examinations will be given to applicants after the postings are down.

All things being equal and conditions remaining the same, the person most qualified and having the most seniority will be selected for the job.

The Union had co-operated in giving these tests—assigning observers to be present when tests were given. Those observers were supplied information about the tests and their influence on determination of the successful bidder. There have been two labor agreements (each of three-years' duration) negotiated since the testing program was installed, and at no time has the use of tests been challenged during these negotiations. The Company contends, therefore, that there is an established practice of using tests in selecting maintenance personnel.

The Company points to the fact that no objection was raised when the job of maintenance helper was posted on May 25, 1964. In fact, no protest was filed when the tests were administered to the eight applicants. It was only when the jobs were awarded and the grievant was not included that any dissenting opinion was voiced.

With respect to the influence of test scores on selection, the Company points out that the three selected were not the highest on tests but were the longest service employees among those that achieved *satisfactory scores* on the tests. The grievant was seventh—scoring 21 points out of a total of 109. Six of the eight scored over 50. In checking answers to questions (applicants were not required to write answers), the grievant was the only one of the eight who failed to follow the simple instructions (he checked 2 or 3 of the multiple choice answers to certain questions). Had this been charged against him, his score would have been 17 instead of 21. It is obvious, the Company states, that this applicant could not have performed maintenance work—particularly since it was contemplated that the helper would, as soon as feasible, be upgraded to Maintenance B status, and the agreement (Par. 60 quoted earlier) gives preference to applicants "within the department."

The Company rejects the interpretation of agreement language which recognizes only length of service in determining one's right to a job. It cites:

Par. 53—Which requires previous experience in order to exercise plant-wide bumping privileges.
Par. 59—Senior employees must be qualified operators in order to exercise shift preference.
Par's. 62 & 63—emphasize ability and management judgment.
Par. 64—Seniority plays a minor part in selection of inspectors.
Par's. 75 & 76—benefit certain unfortunate employees, but only if they have proper qualifications and ability.

Thus, the Company submits, the over-all language of the agreement indicates an awareness of the parties which negotiated it of the importance of qualifications for assignment to critical jobs. Maintenance jobs are most critical—particularly under present conditions where the shortage of personnel is so acute. It is unreasonable to presume that the Company ever agreed to terms which would require it knowingly to assign incompetent personnel to such vital work.

The Company cites the strong management rights clause:

Par. 88—The right to hire, promote, discharge, or discipline for just cause and to maintain discipline and efficiency of employees, is recognized as the responsibility of the Company except that the Union members shall not be discriminated against as such. The Union recognizes that the Company has the exclusive right to manage plant and direct its affairs and working forces, so long as it does not conflict with this Agreement. . . ."

Since nothing in the agreement prohibits the use of tests as part of the "trial" called for in Paragraph 60, it is the contention of the Company that this Paragraph 88, coupled with the clearly established past practice, gives it the unquestioned right to use such tests so long as it does so in a purely nondiscriminatory manner.

The Union withdrew from consideration under these proceedings any question of grievant's qualifications for the work in the maintenance department. It limited the discussion and argument (no witnesses were questioned) to the allegedly "clear and unambiguous" language of Paragraph 60 which requires that *"senior regular employees shall be given the opportunity to trial on such jobs . . . if the employee so desires."* It holds that no consideration may be given to any factor other than seniority when considering bids for job openings.

QUESTIONS

1. Does the Union failure to contest the Company's claim that tests have been used to fill maintenance jobs in the past dilute the clear wording of Paragraph 60?
2. What is a "trial"?
3. Is the issue here limited to Paragraph 60 or should paragraphs 53, 59, 62 & 63, 64, and 75 & 76 be "read into" Paragraph 60? Why?
4. Do you think that the Union's decision to argue this case solely on Paragraph 60 and not to challenge the tests used or to assert the competence of the grievant was in the best interest of the grievant and the Union? Why?

Case 32

"SKILL AND ABILITY" REQUIREMENTS FOR PROMOTION

COMPANY: Emhart Manufacturing Company

UNION: United Automobile Workers
             Local 462

ARBITRATOR: Burton B. Turkus

Is an employee's record of absenteeism evidence of lack of "skill and ability" and therefore grounds for disqualification for promotion?

The following discussion of the issue and facts in this case was prepared by Burton B. Turkus, the arbitrator.

ISSUE

"Under the provisions of the contract, is the Company required to promote X—— to the job of Tool Crib Lead Man? If yes, what shall the remedy be?"

RELEVANT CONTRACT PROVISIONS

Article IX, VACANCIES AND PROMOTIONS, in pertinent part, provides:

Section 4. When permanent vacancies exist to which no employee has recall rights, and which offer an opportunity for promotion or advancement to employees, such vacancy will be posted by the Company on the bulletin board for not less than three (3) working days. Employees interested in the vacancy shall make such application for the opening by personally signing the bulletin board notice. Employees who make application will be advised of the outcome by his supervisor. Employees on recall status interested in the vacancy will notify their foreman or the Personnel Department.

Section 5. The Company will fill such vacancies from employees who make application *on the basis of seniority provided such employees have the skill and ability to meet the requirements of the job classification.* (Emphasis added.)

* * *

Section 7. If no qualified employees bid for the vacancy, the Company may select candidates from any source to fill such vacancy.

BACKGROUND OF THE DISPUTE

The job involved is a newly created one—a direct result of the Company's reorganization of the tool room system and function. Prior to reorganization, the only job classification applicable to the tool room was "Tool Room Attendant" carrying a Labor Grade H 6 classification. After reorganization, the new position of "Tool Crib Lead Man" was created and after negotiation with the Union was assigned Labor Grade No. 10, the highest in the plant.

The function of the tool room is to provide the entire shop with adequate tools. The tool room system prior to reorganization was antiquated—and the service provided had been unsatisfactory and inadequate. There were constant, frequently justified complaints by the Union and employees of delays encountered in locating tools and of the inadequacy (poor working condition) of the tools supplied to the men in the plant. In short, the tool room situation had become a potent source of discussion, irritation, and dissatisfaction.

As a consequence, the Company, based on a study by its industrial engineers, reorganized the tool room system and function. At a substantial cost, changes in location or ordering points were made to bring the tool crib into close proximity to the cutter grinders for efficiency and better liaison. Newly designed cabinets and bins were fabricated and an improved and modernized record keeping and reordering system was installed to expedite the finding of needed tools and to assure that the tools supplied were in proper working condition. To secure adequate management and function of the tool crib as reorganized, the new position and job description of tool crib lead man resulted.

The tool crib lead man, as provided in the job description, is responsible for the effective operation of the tool crib. He is required to have a good working knowledge of machine-shop practice and machine cutting tools and accessory equipment; to assist with the guide tool and cutter grinding operations; and to check tools and cutters for proper grinding. He must maintain, in accordance with established procedures, all inventory records, and all records required for receipt, storage, issuance and transfer of tools, jigs and fixtures. He assigns work to other employees and instructs and checks the quality of work of the other tool crib employees. The tool crib lead man carries out these responsibilities with a minimum of detailed supervision and reports directly to the plant superintendent rather than to the foreman or general foreman.

On October 4, 1963, the Company, in accordance with the provisions of Article IX of the labor agreement of the parties, posted the job of tool crib lead man for bidding. The job description was attached to the posting. Along with several others, grievant, X——, bid for the job. At the time of his bid, X—— had 14 years seniority with the Company, was a tool and cutter grinder (A) on the night shift, and held a red circle rate of Labor Grade 10, the highest labor grade under the contract.

The Company determined that none of the applicants were qualified to meet the requirements of the job of tool crib lead man and on October 9, 1963, assigned the job to another (who had not bid for the job) under the provision of Article IX of the contract.

At this point all other applicants (bidders for the job) then had their names withdrawn and the Union on October 15, 1963, filed a formal grievance in behalf of X——, asserting that the Company had violated the contract by reason of its failure to promote him to the tool crib lead man job for which he was fully qualified. The grievance was processed through the various steps of the grievance procedures and submitted to arbitration under the stipulated issue aforesaid.

THE FACTS

The proof in the instant case was concentrated on the issue of "skill and ability to meet the requirements of the job classification"—the matter of grievant's seniority was not in the area of controversy.

The regularly scheduled work within the plant contemplates 2,000 hours per year. The average number of hours during which employees were absent is 80 hours per year.

In 1961, the grievant was absent for various reasons a total of 192 hours. In 1962, he was absent a total of 674 hours. In 1963, from January to October (October 9, 1963, being the date of the Company's decision not to promote him), he was absent a total of 285 hours.

The preponderant bulk of these absences was due to a variety of illnesses but also included absences for other reasons. In 1961 he was absent and away from work for personal or tardiness reasons a total of 30 hours; in 1962, a total of 122 hours and in 1963, a total of 39 hours.

While amassing this absentee record, which "the Union readily concedes was top-heavy," the grievant during the three-year period preceding his bid for promotion was engaged in a series of outside business activities alien to his regular employment. In 1961 and 1962 he had an orange juice business; in 1960 and 1961 he had a TV repair business; and in 1962 and 1963 he had a gasoline station business (which he sold in March, 1963), admittedly devoting an average of between four to five hours a day thereto.

The grievant's excessive absenteeism and simultaneous devotion to outside business ventures was a matter of serious concern and Company action for a substantial period of time prior to his bid for promotion. In a series of discussions in which he pointed up the impact upon the Company of the unpredictable excessive lost time and the contributory nature of grievant's outside business thereto, the plant manager personally "tried everything that was published on the subject," including two visits to grievant's gasoline station for discussion designed to have grievant improve his attendance record, but to no avail.

Preparatory, then, to ultimate termination if the procedure proved ineffective, the grievant was given an oral warning on October 1, 1962, that his lost time record must be improved. On November 5, 1962, he was given a written warning that "unless your lost time record shows a definite improvement disciplinary action will be taken." On February 1, 1963, the grievant was given another written warning, to wit:

Your excessive absence during the past year has placed a hardship on the company. We have had an off-balanced condition because of your unpredictable excessive lost time. We can no longer tolerate this condition and hereby offer you a six-month leave of absence, or as an alternative, work your scheduled hours for a year, or the company suggests you resign. If none of these suggestions results in correction of this condition, the company must take appropriate action.

At or about the time of that written warning, the plant manager found the grievant at his gasoline station directing his 14-year-old son "how to change a tire." Father and son were the only individuals at the station and grievant's hands as well as his clothes indicated that he had been performing some labor at the very time that he was absent from work on account of sickness.

The job to which the grievant sought to be promoted by his bid constitutes the only tool crib lead man in the plant. The entire shop, moreover, is dependent upon the tool room. Regular attendance on the part of the tool crib lead man, responsible for the effective operation of the tool room, is an essential requirement of the job.

QUESTIONS

1. Is a good attendance record a part of "the skill and ability to meet the requirements of the job classification"?
2. What consideration should be given to the series of warnings given to X——in view of the fact that no formal disciplinary action had been taken against him?
3. How would you rule in this case?

Case 33

CONFLICT OF LOYALTY TO THE COMPANY AND THE UNION

COMPANY: Contra Costa Readymix and Building Materials, Inc.

UNION: International Brotherhood of Teamsters
Local No. 70

ARBITRATOR: Adolph M. Koven

This case involves the dual loyalty of a worker to his employer and to his union.

The following discussion of the issue and facts in this case was prepared by Adolph M. Koven, the arbitrator.

THE ISSUE

Was J— P— discharged for just cause under Article X of the Contract? If not, what is the appropriate remedy under Article X?

Relevant Sections of the Contract

Article X. Union Activity

No employee shall suffer discharge without just cause. In the event of discharge without just cause the employee may be reinstated with payment for time lost. In the event of a dispute, the existence of "just cause" shall be determined as provided in Article IX, "Adjustment of Grievances."

Article IX. Adjustment of Grievances

The Umpire shall have only that limited jurisdiction and authority necessary to interpret, apply, or ascertain compliance with the provisions of this Agreement, insofar as shall be necessary for the determination of grievances appealed to the Umpire. Among those subjects the Umpire shall have neither jurisdiction nor authority to consider or decide shall be those subjects although not limited thereto, involving . . . the assignment of work duties . . . the scheduling of work, and working conditions not otherwise agreed to within the Agreement. The Umpire shall not have jurisdiction or authority to add to, detract from, or alter in any way, the provisions of this Agreement.

ARTICLE XVII. Prior Agreements and/or Practices

All written and/or oral agreements, all past practices, including agreements resulting from grievance settlements not specifically contained or referred to in this Contract shall become null and void as of the effective date of this Agreement.

On December 21, 1961, the grievant was directed to make piers. When asked by the dispatcher to do this work, the grievant replied, "I can't," and stated that the Union had told him he was not to do yard work. After the dispatcher had pointed out the consequences of a refusal, the grievant was directed to get his timecard and report to the general manager. To the general manager, the grievant still insisted, "I can't," when asked to give his reason for refusing to pour piers. The grievant was thereupon discharged.

Two sister locals of the Teamsters, Warehouse Local No. 853, and Auto Truck Drivers Local No. 70, each have contracts with the Company. Though making piers is covered in its contract by Local No. 853, there is no jurisdictional dispute between the two sister locals. Prior to two years ago when Local No. 853 signed its first contract with the Company, Local No. 70 performed yard work. Currently Local 70 also performs similar work in other plants in the industry.

The problem of doing such work was first raised when employees returned to work on December 1, right after their four-month strike ended. On December 4, the dispatcher was approached by two employees who raised the question of making piers and stated they had been instructed by the Union not to do such work. The dispatcher told them they would be well off to follow work orders until the matter was straightened out between the parties. During that day following that discussion, one of these two employees was assigned to make piers and did the work without refusal.

On December 6, two employees refused to set up screens because they had been told not to do this work by their Union. They are still in the employ of the Company despite this refusal. As a result of this incident, the president of the Company directed his management staff to warn the employees that any refusal from then on would result in disciplinary consequences.

Accordingly, on the next day, December 7, the employees were put on notice by both the general manager and the dispatcher, who each contacted different employees. The general manager stated he personally warned the grievant on this day, which the grievant denies.

A major incident next occurred on December 15. Edwards, a Local No. 70 member, when asked to do yard work stated that "I am sorry but I can't" because he could not afford a $50 fine. Edwards was then sent to see the general manager and while discussing his dilemma, the work in the meantime was completed by a Local 853 man, so that the issue of refusing to do the work was never sharply joined. The Company views the difference between the Edwards' incident and the grievant's situation as a matter of lucky circumstances for Edwards and in the difference of attitude of both men. Earlier that day, another Local No. 70 employee had been asked to do yard work and followed the order without refusal.

The next and last incident, of course, occurred on December 21, and involved the grievant's refusal to pour piers and his subsequent discharge.

On the grievant's background and the facts of his discharge, there was considerable testimony. He had been an employee since June, 1955, and was characterized by the Company as an average driver with a fair work history. The grievant described himself as one who had always tried to do a good job. The Company stated that he had never before refused to do work assigned to him and that his discharge was related only to this one event of December 21, and not to any previous history.

The general manager, president of the Company, and dispatcher each testified that on December 7, 14, and 21, respectively, they personally either warned the grievant of the consequences of a refusal or put him on notice that he would have to carry out any order given him by a supervisor. The grievant denies that management ever talked with him until the day of discharge about the problem of not doing the work.

In his testimony, the general manager stated that the grievant refused to disclose his reason to him for refusing to make piers, and it was his feeling that the grievant was daring the Company to do something about his refusal. Yet, he would not characterize the grievant's manner as belligerent and stated that the grievant would not, in his opinion, have refused to do any other work in Local No. 70's jurisdiction if given such an assignment. Perhaps if there had been a long discussion of the problem, as there had been with Edwards, the Company might have relented in its decision to discharge.

According to the grievant, on December 21, when the dispatcher told him he was supposed to do the work and if he had any objections to file a grievance afterward, he replied that if he would do that, he would be "scabbing" on the warehouse Union. When the dispatcher insisted, the grievant stated he wasn't refusing, but he just couldn't make piers. Furthermore when he was called into the general manager's office he wasn't testing the Company, but was just "scared" because he didn't want to get fired.

There have been a considerable number of times when the grievant was instructed by the Union that he should not do Local No. 853 work, and that he would be "scabbing" on the warehouse Union if he did. The reason he did not tell the general manager the basis for his refusal is that he was directed by the Union not to give the reason. He has also been directed by the Union not to file a grievance, first, because he was not supposed to do such work in the first instance, and second, because filing a grievance would be a useless act since the umpire under the contract does not have the authority to decide grievances involving questions of work assignments. Apparently the Company also holds the same view that an arbitrator would not have such authority.

Both parties stated for the record that they have not submitted the issue of deciding work jurisdiction to this arbitrator in the instant case and that he is precluded from making an award which affects the work jurisdiction of the two Unions with whom the Company has collective bargaining agreements.

POSITION OF THE COMPANY

The grievant was discharged for refusing to do work under a proper work order. He had ample warning of the consequences of any refusal, for he was warned in some fashion on December 4, and specifically on December 7, 14, and 21, by the general manager, president of the Company, and dispatcher, respectively.

If it is correct to say that the blame for generating the situation falls upon the Union, then the equities may suggest that the Union has been unfair to the grievant. However, this was a situation where the Company had to act, and if the grievant willingly or unwillingly became the foil of the Union, then it also became the grievant's problem and not the Company's. The Company could do nothing other than what it did do. It had no other alternative.

But the grievant had a choice. He could have done the work, he could have discussed his situation with management, and he could have resorted to the grievance procedure. The grievant had the time from December 4 until December 21, a period of 17 days, to think through his situation. Instead he made a deliberate intentional attack upon the authority of the Company.

The only question before the arbitrator is not whether disciplinary action was proper but only whether discharge was the proper penalty for this industrial offense. Discharge was a proper penalty because the question of work jurisdiction never serves as a ground for mitigation. The grievant cannot look to misunderstanding as a mitigating factor, for he knew exactly where he stood, and instead of taking on the Union and the $50 fine, he chose to take on the Company. He did so at his peril.

The only other possible point in the grievant's favor is the alleged discrimination in favor of Edwards. But the cases differ on the facts. Edwards was never faced with the ultimate order to do the work and so did not have the opportunity to refuse. The grievant, however, was given an order. He refused to carry it out. It was for this refusal that he was discharged.

Since this is the type of offense which warrants discharge and one which has been consistently upheld by arbitrators, the discharge of this grievant should be sustained.

POSITION OF THE UNION

This is a case involving the broad terms of just cause and involves a claim by the Company against the grievant of insubordination where he declines to perform certain work.

No one has claimed that the grievant was defiant or recalcitrant, but rather that his attitude was one of peaceful resistance to an order. The compliance with that order would have subjected him to sanctions from another source. And since his attitude cannot be said to have been malicious, certainly the Company should not have insisted on being so retaliatory and so bent on recrimination as to treat this grievant, an employee of seven years' standing, as if it were dealing with a man who had repeatedly refused to perform work.

A discharge must be examined in the light of the sociological questions involved, because discharge is a punishment. More and more in our modern time, punishment is exacted only where it serves some valuable social or industrial purpose. The Union believes that retaliation, although that might be the momentary instinct which all of us sometimes give in to and which could have been involved in the case, cannot be advanced as a justification for the discharge.

At the time of the discharge, the grievant did not have the full opportunity to consult with someone with a little more expert knowledge on such a complicated question of resolving the dilemma of a choice between loyalties. Subsequent to his discharge he has had time to think it over and has come to a different conclusion. The grievant has now come to a clearer understanding as to what he must now do and that is to follow Company orders as given until the parties resolve their difficulties on the larger issue.

What purpose is served by holding that the grievant cannot go back to work where the only complaint the Company has is that on one day he declined to do work which he now says he will do? It cannot serve any valuable purpose at all. And this is particularly true because there is no damage to the Company resulting from that particular incident on that one day.

Thus, the Union urges that the grievant be reinstated and that he be compensated for time lost, with restoration of seniority and other rights.

QUESTIONS

1. What rights on the part of J—— P——, the Company, and the Union are involved here?

2. Both the Company and the Union reminded the arbitrator that he is *not* authorized to settle the jurisdictional dispute involved in this case. How would the arbitrator's ruling on J—— P——'s discharge influence the outcome of the jurisdictional dispute?

3. Both the Company and the Union admit that J—— P—— is the unfortunate victim of circumstances beyond his control. Is this a fair conclusion or did J—— P—— have control over his own fate?

4. How would you rule in this case? Why?

Case 34

AN ACCIDENT RECORD AS A BASIS FOR DISCHARGE

COMPANY: Our Own Bakeries, Inc.

UNION: Retail, Wholesale and Department Store Union
Local No. 655

ARBITRATOR: Robert S. Thompson

This case involves the discharge of a truck driver for a second serious accident in six months. This case requires not only a definition of just cause but also consideration of the standards of discipline which are appropriate to employees who work without direct supervision and have individual responsibility for very expensive equipment.

The following discussion of the issue and facts in the case was prepared by Robert S. Thompson, the arbitrator.

Our Own Bakeries is a large and well-known wholesale bakery which distributes its products throughout the Upper Peninsula of Michigan and parts of Wisconsin. Robert Carlton, the grievant, was a transport driver, one of six such who drove large tractor-trailer equipment. The route covered by Mr. Carlton was from Marquette to Ironwood, a round distance of about 310 miles. His schedule called for leaving Marquette about 1 A.M. and returning about 11 A.M. He had been employed with the Company about nine years, the last four years as a transport driver. On October 29, 1960, he had an accident which resulted in the total loss of his tractor-trailer and merchandise. The next day, October 30, he was discharged because of a poor driving and accident record.

ACCIDENT RECORD

From testimony at the hearing and various accident reports entered into evidence by the Company, a summary of Mr. Carlton's record is presented below:

October 29, 1960, 5 A.M. heavy fog, poor visibility, vehicle left the road on the left side of highway. Tractor-trailer and merchandise nearly a total loss.

Mr. Carlton had cut on temple and a bruised leg, but walked mile to phone police. Officer did not reach scene until about two and a half hours later. Sales manager, Mr. Roberts, in charge of transport drivers, came out from Marquette. Accident report stated: "It is the opinion of the officer that the driver fell asleep causing him to drive to the left side of the road." Mr. Carlton stated he did not know what happened. Testified that it had taken him from 30–45 minutes to drive 18 miles; that poor visibility made it impossible to follow the center line; also suggested that trailer might have turned over because of imbalance in loading. Estimated damages about $4,100. Not ticketed.

March 22, 1960, 12:45 A.M. Struck private automobile parked or stalled on highway. Impact pushed car into driver who was standing near. Severe blizzard conditions with low visibility. No police report in evidence. Not ticketed. Insurance carrier paid claims in amount of $937.60.

November 6, 1959, 1:30 A.M. Mr. Carlton's trailer was struck from behind by tractor-trailer driven by Mr. Bengry, another transport driver employed by the Company. Heavy snow storm. Grievant was to make left turn from Highway 41 into Highway 95. Snow plow at the intersection and to left of grievant's truck. Grievant stopped when hit. Company alleged that grievant was in conversation with snow plow operator. Grievant claims snow plow was blocking intersection. Snow so thick rear lights probably obscured. Extensive damage to both units. Tractor of other truck was total loss. Not ticketed.

April 17, 1956, 9:10 A.M. Slippery conditions. Grievant started to slow down as a private automobile approached from other direction. Double tracks slipped off right side of pavement; his truck started to skid; touched brake and went into a jackknife to the left side of road. Approaching car hit grievant's truck toward right rear. Driver of car seriously injured and passenger (wife) killed. State trooper who investigated checked these items on report: Vision *not* obscured; excessive speed; snowing; no improper driving by second driver. Not ticketed. Insurance carrier paid in total of $12,969 in claims.

In addition to the accidents listed above, the record of Mr. Carlton on file with Michigan Secretary of State shows the following:

November 21, 1956. Closed without action.
January 21, 1959. Drove left of center line. Improper left turn.
July 13, 1960. Driving 80 miles in 65 mph zone.

Before his employment by the Company, when 17 years old, Mr. Carlton was involved in a fatal accident. This was in 1945. In a suit for $25,000 damages the judge directed a verdict in favor of the defendant, Mr. Carlton.

Complete data as to the accident records of the other transport drivers was not available. Ray Trevillion, driver with highest seniority, has had one accident in the last five or six years (due to falling asleep). John Stone, sales route driver for four years, and transport driver for last six months, has had two nonticketed accidents in that period.

PUBLISHED AWARDS

An examination of a number of published arbitration awards (several cited by Mr. Kirkwood plus others) turns up little of assistance in the instant matter. In contrast to the law, precedent is generally considered to have little weight in arbitration. The situation in each arbitration tends to be unique, and part of the usefulness and vitality of arbitration inheres in its rejection of legalisms. However, published awards are sometimes helpful in being suggestive. With respect to discharge of truck and bus drivers for highway accidents, the decisions show wide diversity.

In Hudson County Bus Owners Association, 3 LA 786, the discharge of a bus driver was upheld on the ground of a bad record of minor accidents and one serious accident; in Schreiber Trucking Company, 5 LA 430, a discharge following a third accident was sustained, mainly on the basis that the "driver habitually drove at excessive speed"; in Ward Baking Co., 8 LA 837, discharge of a driver-salesman was affirmed after his sixth accident within three years (average rate of other company drivers within same three-year period was one accident); in Chestnut Farms, Chevy Chase Dairy, 8 LA 897, a driver with five accidents within a period of less than a year was held to be properly discharged. In Kroger Co., 24 LA 48, a seventh accident within five years, with the last four of the seven occurring within a three-month period, plus a warning that the next accident would bring discharge, was considered to justify discharge.

On the other hand, discharges were voided and reinstatements directed in the following: In Boston & Maine Transportation Co., 5 LA 3, a driver involved in an accident resulting in several deaths was reinstated even though there was evidence of violation of safety rules; in Mason & Dixon Lines, 9 LA 775, a trailer truck driver who lost control and collided with a gasoline truck causing a loss of $30,000 was reinstated even though he had failed to take action which might have kept his truck on the road; in Safe Bus Co., 21 LA 456, a bus driver who had had two accidents within six months and who was at fault in the second was reinstated even though the damages exceeded $1,000; in Pacific Greyhound Lines, 30 LA 830, reinstatement without back pay was ordered of a driver responsible for a serious accident in which his bus struck a truck in the rear on a highway.

.   .   .

This arbitration is based upon a contractual agreement between the parties. Article VII acknowledges the power to discharge, but it also requires that "this power be exercised with justice with regard for the reasonable rights of the Employees."

QUESTIONS

1. Do the cited cases suggest standards for an award in this dispute?
2. In assessing Carlton's accident record, what weight should be given to negligence, extent of damage resulting, driving conditions, the obligation to meet a delivery schedule, the elapsed time between accidents?
3. How would you rule in this case? Why?

Case 35

DISCIPLINE FOR UNEMPLOYMENT COMPENSATION FRAUD

COMPANY: Ford Motor Company

UNION: United Automobile Workers

ARBITRATOR: Harry H. Platt

The Ford Motor Company paid its first Supplemental Unemployment Benefits in 1956 under an agreement negotiated in 1955. This case is a general union grievance against a new rule which the Company sought to implement.

The following discussion of the issue and facts in the case was prepared by Harry H. Platt, Ford-UAW umpire.

The Union in this case is questioning the reasonableness of a recent Company rule which would subject employees to discipline for fraudulently obtaining unemployment compensation benefits.

BACKGROUND OF DISPUTE

Apparently this is not a new problem for the Company. Its figures show that at the Rouge, for the five-year period from 1952 through 1956, roughly 1 per cent of all new and renewed compensation claims were fraudulent. Other investigations by the Company indicate that the Rouge experience is typical and that some employee fraud in connection with compensation claims exists in other plants as well.

Although the unemployment compensation laws are by no means uniform in the several states where Ford plants operate, certain general considerations seem to be present in most of the laws. The fund from which compensation payments are made is usually created and maintained by employer contributions alone (in New Jersey, however, contributions are also made by employees). Each employer has an experience record or rating account which determines his contribution rate. The poorer the experience record, the higher the contribution rate. Since excessive or unjustified payment of compensation benefits, left uncorrected, adversely affects the employer's experience record, it also increases his contribution to the fund. Whether or not the improper payment was a consequence of employee fraud is a question for the State Commission to decide. It may make its own investigation and hold a hearing before reaching a decision. If an employee is found to have committed fraud the compensation laws provide for such penalties as restitution of improper payments, cancellation of accrued credits, forfeiture of future benefits, and criminal action (misdemeanor) involving fine or imprisonment or both. One or more of these penalties may be invoked by the Commission.

The Company constantly seeks to improve its experience record and thereby decrease its costs. One way of achieving this objective is to discover and correct improper payments. This is done by checking the Commission's reports of benefits paid against the Company's own records. If discrepancies or mistakes are found, the improper payments are protested and the Commission is asked to credit the Company's experience record. This involves considerable administrative work by the Company as well as occasional appearances before the Commission. However, these procedures simply serve to uncover fraud after it has been committed; they do not strike at the root of the problem—the fraudulent claim itself. In order to discourage and minimize such claims, the Company decided to institute a rule against fraud in obtaining unemployment compensation benefits. On October 1, 1956, the Union was notified that the rule would be effective as of November 1. Notices were posted in each of the Company's plants which read as follows:

NOTICE TO EMPLOYEES

During the past several years, there has been a significant increase in the number of employees who have received Unemployment Compensation benefits fradulently, according to a recent study made by the Company.

While the Company realizes that the great majority of its employees are honest, law-abiding citizens, this dishonest action on the part of a few hurts all of us. As you know, the Company bears the full cost of Unemployment Compensation to its employees. Overpayment of such benefits can result in higher tax rates and higher costs which, in the long run, affect the welfare and security of every Ford man and woman.

To protect both you and the Company from these few dishonest employees, the Company is instituting a rule, effective November 1, 1956, against such fraud in obtaining Unemployment Compensation payments. Violation of this rule will subject employees to disciplinary action up to and including discharge. The Union has been notified of this rule, according to the provisions of the Agreement.

It is not, of course, the intention of the Company to discipline an employee who may be overpaid through error on the part of the state agency or through unintentional misrepresentation or omission of fact due to misunderstanding. The rule is designed only to deter those who obtain Unemployment Compensation payments to which they are not entitled.

PLANT MANAGER

CONTRACT PROVISION

Article IV, Section 5 of the agreement grants the Company the right "to make such reasonable rules and regulations not in conflict with this Agreement, as it may from time to time deem best for the purposes of maintaining order, safety, and/or effective operation of Company plants," reserving to the Union the right to question the reasonableness of such rules or regulation through the grievance procedure. Thus, plainly, the Company is not limited to making rules and regulations for the preservation of good order or safety. Its authority extends to making such rules as may be necessary to maintain effective operation of its plants. And no doubt a rule designed to protect the Company and its employees from the consequences of fraud, cheating, imposition, and impairment of the unemployment compensation fund by persons who are in fact not unemployed has a real and substantial relation to the effective operation of its plants. In this posture of the case, the only question which remains to be decided is whether the rule under consideration is unreasonable or whether it invades any employee right under the agreement.

UNION POSITION

The Union attacks the rule on several fronts. It asserts that a claimant for unemployment compensation, because he is unemployed, cannot be considered a Company employee subject to its rules. It contends also that inasmuch as the fraudulent receipt of unemployment compensation is remediable under the state unemployment compensation laws, adding an industrial discipline penalty would violate the principle that a person should not be placed in double jeopardy for the same offense. And finally, it states, the rule is in conflict with the agreement because the Company, in negotiating the Supplemental Benefit Plan in 1955, proposed that both discipline and forfeiture of credit units should be the penalty for willful misrepresentation of material facts in connection with an application for benefits under the Plan, but because of Union opposition to the proposal the Plan provides only for forfeiture of credit units as a penalty.

QUESTIONS

1. The *timing* of this new rule possibly posed a special challenge to the Union. Why?
2. Is the Union's protest of this rule an attempt to protect dishonesty? Why or why not?
3. Discuss the validity of each of the Union's claims.
4. If you decided this case in favor of the Company, what effect would your ruling have on the disciplinary measures taken against individual employees filing fraudulent unemployment compensation claims?

Case 36A

FALSIFICATION OF MEDICAL HISTORY
AS A BASIS FOR DISCHARGE

COMPANY: Caterpillar Tractor Company

UNION: Allied Industrial Workers
              Amalgamated Local 806

ARBITRATOR: George H. Young

This case involves the issue of falsification of medical records in an application for employment. The same issue is involved in Case 36B.

The following discussion of the issue and facts in the case was prepared by George A. Young, the arbitrator.

FACTS

The material facts are not in dispute. C—— F——, the grievant, was hired by the Company as a turret lathe operator on February 3, 1960. He was discharged on June 24, 1960. The grounds for the discharge are set forth in a letter of June 24, 1960, from R. H. Hennerichs, the employment supervisor, to the grievant which reads as follows:

Mr. C—— F——
——North——Street
Milwaukee, Wisconsin

Dear C——:
This letter is to inform you that you are discharged from employment at this plant effective today. The reason for your discharge is falsification of your application for employment and your medical record questionnaire.

Your specific false responses on these two documents are as follows: On the application for employment when asked "Have you ever had trouble with the following?—'Back' "—you indicated a "No" response. Your signature appears on this section of the form titled "Physical Condition." Your signature also appears on the application form immediately after the paragraph which begins with this sentence: "I understand that any false statements made by me on this application may prevent my employment or may be cause for dismissal if hired." We are exercising this cause for dismissal.

In addition, during your pre-employment physical examination, you completed a Medical Record questionnaire. On the Personal Medical History section you were asked "Have you had or do you now have the following—'Back trouble.' " Your response was "No." Your signature appears at the end of this questionnaire after the statement, "I certify that the above information is true and correctly recorded. I understand that any misleading or incorrect statements will be cause for immediate dismissal, in the event of employment."

There have been two separate occurrences this week that prove your above responses were false. The first was during your telephone call to me Tuesday morning, June 21. You told me that you were "placing yourself under the care of Dr. Regan, a spine specialist, a family doctor who had treated you before for back trouble." Also, a medical certificate, dated October 12, 1959, from Dr. Samuel Graziano, attached to your Prudential life insurance policy, states two occurrences of prior back medical history (1) a sprained back in April 1957 and (2) a pilonidal cyst at base of the spine that ruptured in 1957. Both of these instances are within the last three years, the recent past.

Please come into the plant to check out as soon as you can. Then your tools and pay due and our issued property and separation records can be completed.

Very truly yours,
R. H. HENNERICHS
Employment Supervisor

The grievant applied for the job in response to a newspaper ad. He testified that he filled out the application forms somewhat hurriedly in the hope that by completing them as quickly as possible, he might gain some priority over other applicants for the job who were present. He was interviewed, given a pre-employment physical examination, and hired.

JOB ACCIDENT

On June 6, 1960, the grievant was attempting to tighten a chuck on the turret lathe which he was operating. He was pulling on a T wrench when the wrench slipped out of the socket causing him to spin around and strike his back against the machine. He suffered some pain, but completed his shift. The grievant attempted to continue work for some days following the accident, but the pain increased in intensity to the point where his wife called the physician for the Company, Dr. Sabljak, who arranged for the grievant's hospitalization at St. Luke's Hospital and called in an orthopedic surgeon for consultation. Both Dr. Sabljak and his consultant diagnosed the grievant's trouble as a disc condition in his spine and concluded to treat it conservatively with traction. This grievant remained in the hospital until June 20, 1960, but his condition did not improve. He was discharged from the hospital on June 20, 1960, for reasons which were never clearly specified. Thereafter, on June 21, 1960, the grievant called Mr. Hennerichs stating that he was no better and wanted to see Dr. Regan, another orthopedic surgeon who had treated the grievant for a back sprain some three years before. Dr. Regan concluded that the indicated treatment was to operate to remove the injured disc and did so.

On June 20, 1960, the grievant gave a statement regarding his accident of June 6, 1960, to an investigator for the insurance company carrying the workmen's compensation insurance for the Company. The grievant's written statement to the insurance claims investigator recites: "I never had any serious injury or other trouble involving my back prior to this in my lifetime. In fact, I passed a physical examination on October 12,

1959, by Dr. Samuel A. Graziano here in Milwaukee for a $5,000 life policy with Prudential."

The grievant showed the policy to the claims investigator who found attached to it the examining physician's report which disclosed that the grievant had indicated he had been treated for some back trouble in 1957 and also consulted his family doctor about a cyst at the base of his spine. The Company, on learning of this, discharged the grievant through Mr. Hennerichs' letter of June 24, 1960.

The grievant's testimony regarding the 1957 back sprain is that he tripped and stumbled while engaged in a bowling game. He completed the game but his back ached for the next day or two and he consulted his family doctor who told him that he did not treat back cases and arranged an appointment for him with Dr. Regan. Dr. Regan told him it was nothing to worry about and taped his back, leaving it taped for a period of from five to seven days. The grievant also testified that his family doctor when consulted about the cyst told him that he might have it removed or it might burst of its own accord without treatment and disappear, which it apparently did. Neither the back sprain nor the cyst disabled the grievant in any way, except for the discomfort naturally involved, or caused him to lose any time from his then employment.

It is undisputed that the grievant did not mention either his prior back sprain or the cyst in his employment application or the medical record questionnaire and it is the failure to provide this information which the Company contends is proper cause for discharge.

ISSUE

The parties stipulated at the hearing that the sole issue to be decided at this time by the Board of Arbitration is whether or not the grievant was discharged for proper cause under Article IX, Section 2, of the agreement.

OPINION AND DECISION

The Union contends that the errors and omissions on the grievant's employment application forms were inadvertent, not intended to mislead the Company, and at most were of such a minor nature as to be immaterial and not proper cause for discharge. The Company asserts with equal vigor that whether made intentionally or through negligence, errors and omissions on application forms which result in the Company's employing a job applicant without having full and complete information on his physical condition and medical history cannot be tolerated, and, in any event, the failure to report the back sprain in 1957 cannot be dismissed as immaterial in this case because the Company physician, Dr. Sabljak, testified that had he known of it, he would not have cleared Mr. F—— for employment.

This arbitrator has read the opinions and decisions rendered by other arbitrators in numerous cases involving discharge for misstatements or omissions on job application forms and the arguments advanced by the parties in this case set forth the general standards or guidelines followed in deciding such cases. Inadvertent and immaterial falsifications or omissions generally have been held not to be proper grounds for discharge. Conversely, falsification or withholding of information that is significant to the hiring process generally has been considered proper cause for discharge. The commonly accepted standard is not difficult to ascertain or to state, but other decisions have not proved helpful in this case because each decision seems to depend upon the peculiar facts involved.

The Company emphasizes in its argument that since the grievant would not have been hired if his prior back sprain had been disclosed (according to the undisputed testimony of Dr. Sabljak), this is practically conclusive. The Company argues it should not be precluded from taking the action that it would have taken if it had known when F—— was hired what it knows now.

QUESTIONS

1. How would you rule in this case?
2. The issue in the Caterpillar case is similar to the issue in the Rexall case. In one of these cases, the arbitrator upheld discharge and in the other case, the arbitrator refused to uphold the discharge. To what extent are the facts and circumstances in the two cases different?
3. In the absence of a specific medical records clause in a collective bargaining agreement, how can management protect its right to discharge an employee for falsification of medical records?
4. Why would the union defend an employee who had falsified his application for employment?

Case 36B

FALSIFICATION OF MEDICAL HISTORY AS A BASIS FOR DISCHARGE

COMPANY: Rexall Drug Company
             Columbus, Ohio

UNION: Retail, Wholesale, and Department Store Union
             Local 379

ARBITRATOR: Harry J. Dworkin

This case involves the issue of falsification of medical records in an application for employment, the same issue is involved in Case 36A.

The following discussion of the issue and facts in the case was prepared by Harry J. Dworkin, the arbitrator.

THE ISSUE

The grievant was hired on July 30, 1957. She was in the employ of the Company for approximately five years, classified as an inventory clerk in the warehouse. On January 17, 1962, she was discharged on four counts of alleged employee misconduct: (1) willful falsification of her application for employment form and physical examination record in failing to disclose prior injuries and disabilities, (2) chronic absenteeism, (3) unco-operative attitude in failing to properly carry out her assigned duties and instructions of supervision, and (4) false filing of claim for nonindustrial sick benefits.

The evidence established that on July 2, 1957 the grievant completed her application for employment, and was thereafter hired on July 30, 1957. One part of the application signed by the grievant included the following question: "Have you ever received compensation for injury? When?" These questions were left unanswered. Another portion of the application, entitled "Physical Examination Record," required answers as to whether the applicant had ever been treated for any of 38 listed conditions, including "backache" and "back injury." The grievant signed the applicaton leaving all of the spaces opposite the columns of physical conditions unanswered. The form required a checkmark in the event the applicant had ever had any of the enumerated conditions, or received treatment for such.

The record evidence submitted to the hearing established that in 1953 the grievant had sustained an industrial injury to her back while employed at Albers Supermarket. This prior employment, as well as the injury, came to light when she filed an application with the Bureau of Workman's Compensation of Ohio for a back injury sustained on June 25, 1958, while in the employ of Rexall. The June 25 injury resulted when a forklift truck struck a pallet on which she was seated, throwing her to the cement floor and injuring her back. Her supporting affidavit was filed on January 11, 1960, approximately 18 months after the accident. She claimed that the pain radiated from her lower back into her left leg.

A record of the emergency room of Mt. Carmel Hospital also established that on May 16, 1956, the grievant had been involved in an auto accident while leaving the Westinghouse plant, where she was then employed. The diagnosis was "possible back injury." A claim was asserted against the driver of the automobile, which was later settled through the assistance of her attorney.

On March 10, 1959, while employed by Rexall, the grievant was confined in St. Anthony's Hospital with an admission diagnosis of "low back pains." The personal history related that approximately five years earlier, she had developed a pain in her back which was recurrent, "sharp and of constant severity," and that for the past two years she had "a continued ache in her entire back area—it would vary in intensity but was always present," with occasional sharp pains in the upper back which radiated the inguinal area.

On January 5, 1954, the grievant was admitted to White Cross Hospital with a diagnosis of "herniated nuclear pulposis," and complaints of "back-ache." This history as given by the patient disclosed that while lifting a case of canned beans, she felt a sharp pain in her back. This occurred while employed at Albers. She had experienced frequent attacks of pain in her back, "two to three times a week." Her treatment consisted of traction to both legs.

The information as regards the grievant's prior back injury, and her previous employment with Albers, was disclosed when the grievant processed her application for additional compensation, relating to her injury on June 25, 1958, while employed by Rexall. A Company representative attended the hearing during which her prior back injury was discussed with the hearing officer. In her application the grievant stated that the disability resulting from the Rexall injury consisted of "pain all over my back and my left leg." The affidavit of her attending physician, dated January 14, 1960, disclosed that he first treated the claimant on approximately May 16, 1956, because of a "compression fracture T 10," which injury she sustained in the auto accident while employed at Westinghouse. Her physician fitted her with a Taylor brace as part of his treatment.

DISABILITY AWARD

As a result of the Rexall accident, she was awarded permanent partial disability of 10 per cent. The award was apparently on the basis that the Rexall accident aggravated her pre-existing back disability. The records revealed that she had been awarded permanent partial disability to the extent of 40 per cent of 1956 resulting from the Albers accident in 1954, and a 10 per cent increase in disability due to the Rexall occurrence, making a total over-all disability of 50 per cent. The medical department recommended the additional 10 per cent disability on the basis that her Rexall accident "aggravated her pre-existing back disability."

Other record evidence related to the grievant's application for surgical and hospital benefits under a plan maintained by the Company with the John Hancock Life Insurance Company. Under this plan employees are entitled to make application for benefits for sick leave compensation and medical expense when due to nonindustrial sickness or accidental injury. The claimant filed an application for benefits for the period March 10 to April 27, 1959, in which she stated that her disability was not due to injury. She was paid $153.45 for medical benefits, and $520 in sick leave compensation or a total of $673.45. The claim for sick leave benefits included charges incurred at St. Anthony's Hospital and medical fees for treatment of her back injury on June 19, 1958, while working at Rexall. In support of her claim for sick leave benefits, the grievant wrote to the Company on April 16, 1959, that "my back sprain wasn't due to an accident. I don't know what caused it, and the doctor doesn't either." This letter was written during the pendency of the grievant's claim for workmen's compensation. At least one of her physicians whose charges were included in the nonindustrial claim for medical payment was also compensated by the Commission, as evidenced by his fee statement submitted to the Bureau for treatment of her back on April 2, 1959. The Company claims that the grievant deliberately made application under the medical plan for a nonindustrial condition, and collected on her claim, knowing that her back condition for which she was disabled was caused in part by her 1958 accident at Rexall, as evidenced by her claim for workmen's compensation, and the proof on file in connection with her claim.

In addition to the foregoing, the Company asserted that termination was justified on the basis of her chronic absentee record. The grievant's supervisor testified that she had the poorest attendance record in the Columbus operation; that since her employment, she had been absent 223 full days and 28 half days out of a possible 700 workdays; that if the two 13-week sick leave absences were to be disregarded, the grievant lost 93 full days and 28 half days out of a possible 570 workdays. The record further indicated that out of 41 scheduled workweeks, the grievant had missed work in 21 separate weeks, and that she had been warned that her attendance record had to show substantial improvement.

Finally, the Company represented that the grievant manifested an unco-operative work attitude and failed to carry out the instructions of management. Specifically, the Company claimed that the grievant did not adhere to the order-filling procedure with reference to the selection of stock, which was required to be on a first-in first-out basis. The Company states that the grievant disregarded instructions in filling orders, and that on the basis of her unsatisfactory work attitude, together with the other acts of employee misconduct, termination was justified.

PERTINENT PROVISIONS OF CONTRACT

The Union claims that the discharge was unjust and that the Company's action was discriminatory in violation of Article III, Section 1 of the labor agreement:

The Union agrees that its members will individually and collectively perform loyal and efficient work in service and that they will use their influence and best efforts to protect the property of the Company and its interests and that they will cooperate with the Company and the employees of all departments in promoting efficient operations and advancing the welfare of the Company and services at all times. The Union further agrees that its members will cooperate with and assist the Company in simplifying and improving job methods and performance. The Company agrees that it will cooperate with the Union in a mutual effort to promote harmony and efficiency among all the Company's employees. The Company further agrees that it will not discriminate against Union Members in any way whatsoever.

Article II, Section 7, makes reference to the Company booklet furnished to all employees, entitled "Welcome to Rexall":

GETTING HIRED. It is Rexall policy to hire only the men and women best able to perform the work on the jobs available. Therefore, you are hired *only after a careful review of your work history* and qualifications and after you have been interviewed by your prospective supervisor. (Emphasis added.)

The Company relies upon Article III, quoted above, directing attention to the contractual obligations of employees to perform loyal and efficient work, and to co-operate in promoting efficient operation. The Company also relies on Article XV, Management Rights:

The direction of working forces, including but not limited to the right to plan and control operations, hire, promote, determine ability, suspend or discharge for proper cause, to enforce established rules of conduct, to relieve employees from duty because of lack of work, or for other legitimate reasons, and to introduce new and improved methods or facilities of operation is hereby vested exclusively in the management of the Company; and it is the *responsibility and the right of the Company to maintain discipline and efficiency*, but the Company shall be the sole judge of the quality of work required and shall have that freedom of action necessary to discharge its responsibilities for the successful operation of the Company, and all other functions of management not expressly limited by this Agreement, provided nothing contained herein shall be used for the purpose of discriminating against any employees. Rights not expressly waived by this Agreement shall be retained by the Company. The listing of specified rights in this Agreement is not intended to be nor shall be considered restrictive of, or a waiver of any rights of the Company not listed herein whether or not such rights have been exercised by the Company in the past. (Emphasis added.)

POSITION OF UNION

The Union maintains that a reasonable appraisal of all of the evidence and background giving rise to this grievance fails to establish the existence of just cause, and that the discharge was unwarranted. The Union maintains that the Company acted in a discriminatory manner in terminating the grievant's employment, in disregard of the express prohibition of the labor agreement. The Union feels that the Company was motivated in this case by ulterior considerations and that its decision to discharge the grievant was prompted by the fact that she had filed a claim for workmen's compensation, which after being denied twice, was allowed on appeal. The Union claims that the Company was apprised of her 1954 injury during the initial hearing with reference to her claim, the first hearing being on February 16, 1960, and that she was allowed to continue on her job without any action being taken until the Commission ruled in favor of the claimant early in January, 1962. Accordingly, the Union reasons that the claim that the grievant had falsified her work record was advanced only after she had prevailed with reference to her Rexall accident; that if the reasons advanced by the Company had in fact been the true basis for her discharge, the Company would have taken action after it became aware of her prior accident, in February, 1960.

As regards the failure to disclose her prior back injury, the grievant stated at the hearing that she was not specifically questioned concerning this, and that she did not read all of the employment application, and therefore was not fully aware of its contents. The grievant acknowledged that she had completed other applications including those relating to her employment at Westinghouse, General Motors, and Sylvania Electric, all of which information was omitted in her Rexall application. She acknowledged that she had an auto accident in 1956 while leaving the Westinghouse plant, that she was off work due to her disability, and that she was required to wear a back brace for approximately one month.

The Union maintains that the Company was neglectful of its own responsibility in failing to make a careful review of her work history and qualifications in accordance with the policy expressed in "Welcome to Rexall." Under all of the circumstances, the Union reasons that the omission on the grievant's application form was not of sufficient and serious import to warrant termination of employment, particularly where the Company became aware of the omission sometime prior to her termination. Similarly, the Union claims that the omissions in the grievant's applications were not of major significance, that the Company's decision to terminate her employment resulted from the fact that management was irked when her appeal was allowed for compensation resulting from her Rexall accident, and that her five-year employment record precludes her discharge. In view of the circumstances, the Union urges that the arbitrator rule that the Company has failed to support its position, that her discharge was discriminatory and in violation of the labor agreement.

POSITION OF COMPANY

The Company denies that its decision to discharge the grievant was motivated by a discriminatory attitude, or that her discharge was in any way related to the fact that she prevailed in her workmen's compensation claim. The Company's grounds for the discharge are predicated upon the evidence relating to the five counts of employee misconduct, and particularly that she deliberately withheld information as regards her prior injuries, accidents, and places of employment, when completing her application. The company states that the required information was of major importance in order to enable management to determine whether the applicant is eligible for employment in the type of work which was available. Particularly, the Company points to the fact that she had been declared to be 40 per cent disabled on a permanent partial basis as a result of her back injury while employed at Albers, and that she withheld the name of this employer, as well as others.

The Company claims that it was not aware of the "deliberate falsifications" of her employment application until some time in 1960, and was not aware of the "degree of deception" until 1962. The Company stated that it would have been improper to have acted prior to the final notice by the Industrial Commission as regards her 50 per cent back disability, which included 10 per cent aggravation due to the industrial accident at Rexall in 1958. The Company reasons that a decision prior to the final ruling by the Commission would have been premature and that it withheld final action until management had "complete proof of the falsification of (the) employment application."

The Company reasons that the deliberate withholding of pertinent information on the employment application, the failure to complete the physical examination record, the false claims for medical benefits and sick leave benefits under the insurance plan, together with her poor work attitude and job performance, and her chronic absenteeism, cumulatively presented a case which precluded her continued employment with the Company. For the foregoing reasons, the Company maintains that just cause has been amply established, and that the discharge should be upheld.

OPINION OF ARBITRATOR

The principal issue before the arbitrator is whether the grievant's discharge was for just cause, and consistent with the facts disclosed by the evidence, and the terms of the labor agreement.

QUESTIONS

1. How would you rule in this case?
2. The issue in the Rexall case is similar to the issue in the Caterpillar case. In one of these cases, the arbitrator upheld discharge and in the other case, the arbitrator refused to uphold the discharge. To what extent are the facts and circumstances in the two cases different?
3. What is the significance of the fact that this report is silent on whether the Physical Examination Record contained a statement that falsification of this report was a grounds for discharge?
4. What is the significance of the fact that the Union did not argue that the grievant had overlooked the back injury question on the Physical Examination Record?

Case 37

SLEEPING ON THE JOB AS A BASIS FOR DISCHARGE

COMPANY: Rockwell-Standard Corporation, Transmission and Axle
            Division
            Kenton, Ohio

UNION: Allied Industrial Workers
            Local 109

ARBITRATOR: Edwin R. Teple

*Under what conditions is sleeping on the job grounds for discharge?
The following discussion of the issue and facts in this case was
prepared by Edwin R. Teple, the arbitrator.*

THE ISSUE

The only question in this case is whether the Company's action discharging the grievant, E—— C——, for sleeping on the job was for just cause as required by the terms of Article IV, Section 1, of the collective bargaining agreement between these parties.

THE CIRCUMSTANCES

The grievant had been employed by the Company for a period of 13½ years, first as a machine operator for about 1½ years and 12 years as an inspector. His work record was without blemish, the grievant having had no warnings or prior penalties of any kind. On August 17, 1962, however, he was found sleeping on the job and was discharged immediately. Thereafter, under date of August 20, 1962, the following grievance report was filed by the Union Committee.

We the bargaining committee believe the penalty imposed on Mr. E—— C—— to be much too strong. We are requesting the plant mgr. to reconsider and restore Mr. C——to working status. On the basis of his 13 years of service with no previous record of disciplinary action of a serious nature.

The parties stipulated that the grievant was found asleep at approximately 5:30 A.M. on the third shift (11:30 P.M. to 7:30 A.M.) on the day in question. It was also agreed that he was found in a position back in the stock room which amounted to concealment.

According to the grievant, he had his lunch at the usual time between 3:30 and 4 A.M., and then went back to work and made his rounds. He testified that he saw the foreman at approximately 5:10 A.M. over in heat treat, but the foreman did not see the grievant at that time. The grievant testified that he went out to the stockroom at about 5:20 A.M.

The foreman testified that he had heard that the grievant had been doing some sleeping. Several "boys," according to the Company witness, had noticed grievant was away "an awful lot." According to the foreman, a guard had told him that he found the grievant asleep on one previous occasion, but the guard did not testify and apparently no official action was taken. On the night in question, the foreman testified, he needed the grievant in the department, and began looking for him sometime after lunch—he didn't know just what time it was when he started looking. He also said that some of the men started kidding him about hunting for someone sleeping. He finally found an opening back in the stock room and when he crawled up in there he found the grievant.

The testimony of the Union witnesses was concerned largely with the Company's disciplinary policy when other workmen had been found sleeping. According to them, sleeping on the midnight shift was not uncommon, although it developed on cross-examination that most of this occurred during the lunch period. In the case of a cutter-grinder who was found sleeping on the job, it was said, the employee was sent home for the balance of the shift and was given a three-day suspension. This was the most severe penalty previously imposed for this infraction that the Union witnesses could recall.

The Company witnesses testified that sleeping definitely was not condoned and was considered a serious infraction. It was admitted, however, that there was no posted rule on the subject and no prescribed penalty.

In the case of the cutter-grinder, his foreman testified that when he found the employee he was already up but he had a pillow and it clearly appeared that he had been sleeping. On the basis of the circumstantial evidence, he was given an "abnormal" for sleeping. In the Company's vernacular, an "abnormal" is a written warning or other penalty for some infraction which the Company feels should warrant discipline. As this witness recalled, he was given a week off without pay.

The same foreman testified that he had issued "abnormals" to another employee for sleeping. He did not know, however, if the employee's eventual discharge was for this or some other reason. This particular employee was issued two abnormal reports for too much time off in 1951. In 1953 he was discharged for his third abnormal, which was issued when he was found sleeping.

Another employee, working in quality control, was discharged early in 1959 for failure to report for work. This man was subsequently reinstated under a special agreement between the parties and placed on probation for two years, subject to immediate discharge for any major violation of factory rules or practices. Thereafter, he was discharged in October, 1960, for sleeping on the job.

The grievant admitted that he could have asked for a pass-out to go home if he got sleepy on the job. On the date of the incident in question, he testified that he had a headache and his back had been bothering him. He said he had been working in the drum department and had been doing quite a bit of heavy lifting. However, he lives 15 miles from the plant and was riding with someone else on August 17 so did not consider requesting a pass-out.

COMPANY'S POSITION

The Company takes the position that just cause has been admitted by the Union and that the grievance amounts merely to a plea for clemency. According to the Company, it is a generally accepted rule that once just cause has been established the arbitrator should not substitute his judgment for that of management. Arbitrators have universally held, the Company maintains, that discharge is an appropriate penalty for sleeping on the job.

UNION'S POSITION

The Union contends that in previous cases of discharge at this plant the employees had poor work records of one kind or another. The Union also claims that in these other cases the employees were put back to work pursuant to special agreements between the Company and the Union. In contrast, the Union points out, the grievant had a good prior work record. The Company had no fixed rule, it is said, for the penalty to be imposed for sleeping on the job.

The Union contends that in this case it is simply seeking equal justice for the grievant and on this basis requests reinstatement of the grievant with loss of wages and seniority for one year.

QUESTIONS

1. Sleeping on the job is a serious offense. However, arbitration awards have been widely divided on: (a) proof of sleeping, (b) the consequences and causes of sleeping, and (c) proper penalties. In this case, what were the consequences of E—— C——'s sleeping? What is the significance of the fact that E—— C—— was asleep in a concealed place?
2. What weight should be given to the fact that E—— C——'s 13½ year employment record is without blemish?
3. What is the disciplinary policy of Rockwell-Standard in regard to sleeping on the job?
4. How would you rule in this case?

Case 38

CREATING A DISTURBANCE AS A BASIS FOR DISCHARGE

COMPANY: F. H. Lawson Company
            Cincinnati, Ohio

UNION: International Association of Machinists
            District 34, Local Lodge 1089

ARBITRATOR: Samuel S. Kates

When two employees are engaged in a fight, or "horseplay," should the disciplinary penalty be the same for both?

The following discussion of the issue and facts in this case was prepared by Samuel S. Kates, the arbitrator.

ISSUE

As stipulated by the parties at the arbitration hearing, the issue to be determined is whether the grievant under Grievance No. 278 was discharged for just cause on October 5, 1964, and if not, what remedy should be awarded.

The grievant was hired in November, 1959, and was discharged October 5, 1964. The Company's termination sheet states that he was "dismissed" for "creating a disturbance." A second man (hereinafter called Jerry) who was dismissed at the same time as the grievant in connection with the same incident is shown in the latter's termination sheet as having been dismissed for "fighting."

Each of these dismissed employees filed grievances in connection with such dismissal, but Jerry's grievance was not carried to arbitration and his dismissal now stands unchallenged. The grievant's challenge to his dismissal for "creating a disturbance" is the one involved in the present arbitration.

The incident directly resulting in both dismissals and the events leading to it are shown by the evidence to have been substantially as follows:

Several weeks before October 5, 1964, the grievant borrowed from Jerry a pair of tinsnips owned by Jerry, worth about $6 when new, for use in connection with the grievant's work in the plant. That same day they were missed by the grievant after he had been away from his work station for a short time. He promised Jerry that he would get him another pair.

The grievant, who had a second job in an automobile service station immediately after ending each day's work for the Company, found it inconvenient to shop for another pair of tinsnips. When urged by Jerry to buy them, the grievant became annoyed, told Jerry he was "getting too smart," and raised a doubt as to whether he would actually replace the tinsnips. Jerry reported this to his own supervisor. That supervisor reported it to the grievant's supervisor, who talked with the grievant about it. Thereafter, the grievant's supervisor reported the matter to the personnel director, after additional time had passed without replacement of the tinsnips.

The personnel director talked with the grievant about this, who asked whether he was being ordered by the Company to replace the tinsnips. The personnel director told the grievant that he was not being ordered to replace the tinsnips, but that the matter ought to be resolved. In the meantime, in an atmosphere of oral horseplay, apparently continuously prevalent in the area where the grievant was working, others in the area were teasing both Jerry and the grievant about the matter, seeking to arouse each against the other.

In any event, the grievant did buy another pair of tinsnips during the week end preceding October 5, and brought them to the plant on the 5th. That same morning the grievant sent word to Jerry through another employee that he had brought the replacement tinsnips to the plant and would give them to Jerry after the end of the shift at 3:30 that day.

At about 2 o'clock, Jerry was returning from the washroom near the grievant's work station. The grievant called him over, and in effect said that he had bought a pair of tinsnips but because Jerry had been "too smart" he wasn't sure he would give them to him. This, coupled with teasing remarks and laughter by others working nearby, resulted in heated words between Jerry and the grievant. Without adequate provocation, Jerry struck the grievant with his fist. The grievant thereupon reached for the tinsnips. Jerry pulled a knife from his pocket, opened it, and through the threat of the knife forced the grievant to drop the tinsnips. Jerry turned to leave. The grievant reached to pick up the tinsnips. Others nearby shouted to Jerry that the grievant was reaching for the tinsnips. Jerry promptly turned and kicked the grievant while he was reaching for the tinsnips. Jerry then left.

The evidence did not show that the grievant at any time struck Jerry, or that he did more than undertake to defend himself.

The grievant promptly reported the incident to the Company's executive vice-president. Both men were dismissed shortly thereafter on the same day.

The next day, the Company's senior vice-president of manufacturing made an investigation of the matter. On the basis of this investigation he affirmed the discharges. In this investigation he learned of incidents involving the grievant of which he had no prior knowledge, but most of which had been known to his subordinates in supervision, as mentioned below.

The grievant's personnel file disclosed only three writings involving any alleged previous breaches of duty by the grievant, one in December, 1961, asking the grievant to "please be more careful" about ringing out his time card; the second in September, 1962, warning the grievant of his "slipshod method of ringing in and out" and indicating that he would "on the next occasion be reprimanded, plus a layoff of two or three days to jog your memory," and the third showing that the grievant had been transferred from his towmotor job in June, 1963, because of carelessness and property damage. No disciplinary suspension was ever imposed against the grievant.

The evidence indicates that previously, in the course of the grievant's employment, he had at various times been guilty of idling and spending excessive working time in talking with other employees, but apparently no special point of this was made to him by management at any of these times; he had said to a certain supervisor of another department who had criticized him, "You can't talk that way to me," and had been called to the office about it but nothing was done there beyond a general discussion; he had at times argued with other employees—but oral spats among employees in this plant were not uncommon and no special point of this was made by management; he had boasted of his fighting abilities—but there was no evidence of any actual fighting by him in the plant or relating to his work (except the shaking incident mentioned below); he would at times playfully punch others in the plant on the arm or shoulder, but no special point of this was made to him by management; at times he was such a good worker that he was complimented by supervision, while at other times his work was not good; he was absent for illness, but the frequency of these absences or how they compared with the absences of other employees was not shown.

Within a couple of months before the October 5 discharge, the grievant had told a woman employee to kiss his a——when she upbraided him for not bringing her enough material of the proper kind. She also saw him shaking an older man who had inadvertently removed the grievant's coffee from a truck which such older man had to move. These incidents were reported to management by this woman, but nothing was said to the grievant by management about them, and no reprimand or warning was given him and no discipline was imposed.

There was also some secondary hearsay testimony about the grievant having pushed a truck out of his way in anger and bumping another employee. This was apparently not known to management until after the grievant's discharge.

Evidence was also presented, which was received conditionally, over objection, that the grievant had been court-martialed while in the military service some years before for being absent from duty without leave

(AWOL); that in the summer of 1963 he had been convicted of assault and battery in connection with an altercation originating outside a barroom after working hours, and that he had been sentenced to pay court costs and to serve five days, with the days suspended; that he had a military service-connected disability involving a back ailment and a related nervous condition for which he had been awarded a 10 per cent disability allowance by the government; that his wife, in connection with her own nervous breakdown, had had the grievant committed to a hospital for examination for 30 days for an alleged nervous condition, although he was released within 11 days. The Company did nothing by way of complaint, reprimand, warning, or attempted discipline about these matters.

The Company sought to show certain other occurrences outside the plant involving the grievant, which I held and still hold to be irrelevant to the present case.

The Company sought to suggest, at least by inference, that the grievant was subject to a persecution complex and to delusions of being spied upon, but in my opinion the evidence failed to support these suggestions. The evidence showed that the grievant had been examined by VA doctors in January, 1964, without any finding of mental, emotional, or physical disability, and that after his dismissal from his job the grievant sought another examination because of comments as to his emotional state made by a Company official, but was unable to have it made before the date of the arbitration hearing.

The grievant had been a Union official before his discharge but was so no longer at that time.

A company booklet pertaining to employee conduct was received in evidence. This booklet refers to the Company's more than 140 years of continuous existence, and specifies close to 50 different offenses for which warning or punishment might be expected. In one place the booklet states as follows:

Listed here are the actions or types of conduct which we consider undesirable and for which the employee will be dismissed without warning. In general, these cover practices involving—dishonesty, insubordination, destructiveness, carelessness, creating a disturbance, or contributing to improper working atmosphere.

Then follow a list of 23 offenses which are included within the above-quoted general statement, including among these specific offenses: "Fighting or wrestling in the plant."

There is no evidence to show whether the Union had or had not agreed to the enforceability of these rules of conduct and the indicated penalties as written.

The booklet goes on to state that:

Certain other objectionable actions or tendencies will result in a verbal or written warning for the first offense, a reprimand including restriction of privileges and/or layoff for a second offense, and dismissal without further warning for any additional violation.

Among these "other objectionable actions or tendencies" are "tardiness, poor attendance, horseplay . . . carelessness . . . inefficiency, inability to do the work . . . violating any established procedure."

Except for very serious first offenses in themselves warranting dismissal the Company has subscribed to the principle of progressive corrective discipline.

QUESTIONS

1. What weight should be given to the company booklet in view of the fact that there were no negotiated rules?
2. The arbitrator received conditionally, over objection, evidence on the grievant's court-martial, marital relationship, and off-duty personal conduct. What weight should be given to such evidence in a ruling?
3. What is progressive corrective discipline? Does the Company practice of this principle have an influence on this case?
4. Fighting on the job is considered to be a most grave offense. Was the grievant guilty of this or of provoking this "fight"?

Case 39

AUTHORITY OF UNION COMMITTEE TO MAKE FINAL DISPOSITION OF A GRIEVANCE

COMPANY: Marathon Millwork Corporation

UNION: Midwestern Millmen District Council
Local Union 1451

ARBITRATOR: Robert J. Mueller

This case involves the right of a grievance committee to make a final disposition of a grievance and the right of a grievant to due process.

The following discussion of the issue and facts involved in the case was prepared by Robert J. Mueller, the arbitrator.

The Marathon Millwork Corporation is engaged in the business of manufacturing wood and building products in Wausau, Wisconsin. During the course of its business, an employee, who also happened to be the president of the Local Union, was discharged from his employment. Pursuant to the provisions of the collective bargaining agreement existing between them, the employee submitted a grievance to the Employer disputing his discharge. No satisfactory adjustment was made in step one, and the grievance was then submitted to the shop committee composed of the vice-president of the Union and three stewards. A meeting was held between said shop committee and the Employer, at which time the shop committee signed the following document:

Oct. 22, 1960

As members of the Union Shop Committee, we as individual members unanimously agreed that the Company was justified in its action by discharging Leonard Habeck on October 10, 1960.

Marvin Roepke
Theodore J. Blue
Laurence Van Densen
Courtney Hoyt

Upon being advised of this action, the grievant took up the matter with the business representative of the Union, Mr. Robert Warosh. Warosh contacted the Employer and attempted to resolve the matter and upon being unable to do so, requested the Wisconsin Employment Relations Board to appoint an arbitrator to determine the dispute, the Employer concurring therein. On November 8, 1960, the Board appointed the undersigned as arbitrator. A hearing was held in Wausau, Wisconsin, on December 8, 1960, wherein the parties, including the grievant, were given full opportunity to offer oral and written evidence, and to make such arguments as they deemed pertinent.

EMPLOYER'S POSITION

At the outset of the hearing, the Employer contended that the only issue before the arbitrator was the question of the procedural finality of the settlement between the shop committee and the Employer. The Employer asserted that the merits of the discharge were not arbitrable on the basis that the grievance had been disposed of in a final and binding manner pursuant to the second step of the contract.

UNION'S POSITION

The Union contended that the grievant was deprived of his rights of due process inasmuch as he was not present at the final disposition of his case, nor was he consulted by the shop committee at any time during the meeting of step two and the rendering of the decision.

ISSUE

Does the agreed settlement between the Employer and the Union shop committee, which was executed in writing, constitute a final disposition of the grievance of Lenard Habeck?

PERTINENT CONTRACT PROVISIONS

Article XII—Grievances
A. The Union may as it desires select one (1) Shop Steward and a Shop Committee from its members working in the Plant. There is, however, to be no

Union activity of any kind on Company time or on Company property except that a representative of the Union shall be privileged to confer with the steward in the office during working hours at reasonable times, but must first apply to the office. There shall be no responsibility on the part of the Company to compensate the steward or shop committee for conferences or meetings unless such conferences or meetings are requested by the Company.

B. Both the Company and the Union shall have the right to submit grievances which shall be submitted to the other party in writing within one (1) week after the cause of the grievance first arose. If no satisfactory adjustment is made within (1) working day, the Shop Committee shall take up the matter with the Company and if no adjustment is made within one (1) working day, a Union Representative shall take up the matter with the Company within two (2) working days thereafter. Should such representative and Company still be unable to agree, the matter may be referred to Arbitration in the following manner.

DISCUSSION

The Union contends that Habeck was deprived of his due process when he was not present at the disposition of his grievance. The Employer on the other hand asserts that he was afforded due process in accordance with the terms of the collective bargaining agreement.

QUESTIONS

1. Under what authority did Mr. Warosh intervene?
2. Why did the employer agree to arbitration on this case?

Case 40

JOB CHANGES AND SUPERSENIORITY FOR STEWARDS

COMPANY: Duro Company
             Dayton, Ohio

UNION: United Automobile Workers
             Local Union No. 888

ARBITRATOR: Walter G. Seinsheimer

This case involves the impact of a substantial change in business on superseniority for stewards.

The following discussion of the issue and facts in the case was prepared by Walter G. Seinsheimer, the arbitrator.

The grievance is:

Failure on the Company's behalf to recognize Committeeman's top seniority rights as stated in the Agreement.[1]

[1] It was indicated on the grievance form that "This is a Policy Grievance."

Remedy requested was:

Give the Committeeman top seniority rights due him, and also pay Committeeman all money lost while waiting for these rights to be established.

Foreman's answer:

The Company laid off according to the Seniority provisions of Article VII. Regular members of the shop committee head the seniority list in their own department and areas. The departments with which these two committeemen are concerned are being discontinued, as explained to the committee and the International Representative, in our meeting of 1/12/62.

PERTINENT CONTRACT PROVISIONS

The Union claimed in the grievance that Article VII, Section 2, and Article IV, Secion 1, had been violated; these, and others cited during the hearing, are as follows:

Article VII, Section 2:
Regular members of the Shop Committee shall head the seniority lists in their own department and areas as provided in the Representation Section of this Agreement during their term of office and shall revert to their regular places on the seniority lists at the end of their services in such capacity.
Article VII, Section 4: Lay-off and Rehire Procedures:
For extended periods of lay-off the work force will be reduced according to the following procedure:
(a) For the purpose of applying this procedure the work force has been divided into Job Classification Groups according to the Flow Chart, Appendix B.
(b) When a lay-off is scheduled the Chairman of the Shop Committee will be advised so that the seniority list can be examined and the rights of any employees affected can be explained.
(c) When there are employees in the Job Classification Group affected who will remain after the lay-off and who are capable of performing the jobs which remain, the employees with the least seniority will be laid off first from that Job Classification Group. When an employee or employees are displaced from a Job Classification Group by reason of seniority, they will move into the next Job Classification Group according to the Flow Chart. They will be assigned jobs in that Job Classification Group, which they are qualified to perform, if such jobs are held by employees of lesser seniority. When these changes are made, the employee or employees with the least seniority will move into the next Job Classification Group according to the Flow Chart, where the same procedure will be followed. Capable of performing the job shall mean, for the purpose of this Article, that the employee possesses the physical and mental ability to perform the job in a workmanlike manner. If there is a disagreement as to whether an employee is capable of performing the job, the matter will be discussed between the Company and the Shop Committee. Factors to be considered will include the nature of the work to be done, whether or not the particular employee has had satisfactory experience on that job or a similar job and whether or not any special skills or knowledge not readily acquired are necessary for proper performance of the job. If the Company and the Shop Committee agree, the affected employee may be given

a trial period on the job. If the matter cannot be satisfactorily settled in this manner it may be submitted through the grievance procedure.

(d) An employee displaced from Group 5 will be allowed to exercise his seniority in any other Job Classification Group (except Groups 1 and 2) displacing an employee in that Job Classification Group with lesser seniority provided he is capable of performing the job and has demonstrated that capability either of The Duro Co. or with some other company. An employee will not be allowed to exercise his seniority from any Job Classification Group into Groups 1 or 2 unless he has had prior satisfactory experience on that job with the Company.

Article VII, Section 8:

The Chairmen of the Shop Committee will be given notice of all lay-offs at or before the time such notice is given to the employee, so that the Chairman of the Shop Committee will be able to check the seniority lists as to the employee affected.

Article VII, Section 9:

When deemed by it necessary, the Company shall have the right to retain or recall any employee, irrespective of seniority, who by reason of special knowledge, training or skill, has special value to the Company. The Company agrees not to abuse this right, and further agrees to explain fully to the Shop Committee the reasons for exercising this right.

Article IV, Union Representation:

Section 1. The employees of the bargaining unit shall be represented by Shop Committee of not more than 3 regular members, to be elected in any manner determined by the Union. All members of the Shop Committee must be employed by the Company. The Union shall elect three alternate members to the Shop Committee but only when a regular member of the Shop Committee is not at work shall his alternate be recognized by the Company. The Union will give written notice to the Company showing the names and terms of office of the three regular members of the Shop Committee, and also the three alternate members.

Section 2. The Company agrees to recognize all committeemen designated by the Union, for the purpose of discussing and adjusting grievances. The Union will notify the Company in writing of any changes made in the committeemen.

Section 3. For the purposes of the grievance procedure hereinafter provided, the bargaining unit will be divided into three areas as follows:

AREA I. Machine Shop, Tool Room, and Sub Assembly.

AREA II. Assembly Department, Shipping Department, Stock and Material Handling, and Service Department.

AREA III. Tank Shop, Inspection, Janitors and Maintenance.

The Union will designate and furnish the Company in writing the name of one regular member and one alternate member of the Shop Committee to represent the Union as to each of the three areas. The Union shall also designate one of the members of the Shop Committee to act as Chairman.

Section 4. The Company shall negotiate with the Shop Committee as representatives of the Bargaining Unit, and will discuss and attempt to adjust all grievances with this Committee.

BACKGROUND AND POSITION OF THE PARTIES

The situation arose out of the fact that the Company substantially reduced its scope and volume of operations. Late in the year of 1961 the

Company disposed of its domestic water pump, tank and hot dip galvanizing operations and moved from a three-story building with 90,000 square feet to a one-floor building with slightly over 13,000 square feet. It reduced its work force from 60 to 65 employees, to 6 employees.

The Company retained the water softening and filtering end of the business on an assembly basis, as it eliminated its tank shop and all machining operations.

Prior to the contraction, the operations were divided up as indicated in Section 3 of Article IV above, with:

AREA I. Including the Machine Shop, Tool Room, and Sub Assembly.
AREA II. Assembly Department, Shipping Department, Stock and Material Handling, and Service Department.
AREA III. Tank Shop, Inspection, Janitors and Maintenance.

As provided in this section, a committeeman was assigned to represent the Union in each of these three areas.

According to the Company, all the former operations were discontinued except for assembly of water softening and filtering equipment, plus certain other auxiliary operations, such as final inspection, clean up, and maintenance. This last was mostly involved with the moving from the large building to the smaller, and according to management, would probably also be eliminated in the very near future.

Since the biggest bulk of the work fell in the assembly category, the Company decided that the top seniority of Dewey Watkin, committeeman for Area II, should be recognized, and he was retained. Further, the Company reasoned that the contract Article VII, Section 2, provides that a committeeman head the list only in his own department, and since these other departments to all intent and purpose were eliminated, jobs as well as physical area, then no superseniority could be considered for Roll and Bilbey, who were committeemen for Areas I and III.

The Company maintained that the reason for superseniority for committeemen "was to insure that so long as there were employees in the particular departments and areas, there would be a committeeman available to represent them." With the elimination of the departments as well as jobs, and the reduction of large areas on multiple floors to a simple one-floor setup with six persons, the reasons for the superseniority for more than one committeeman no longer existed. Furthermore, it was pointed out that it "would be an injustice to two other employees with much greater seniority who would have to be displaced."

Believing that it had handled the matter in the proper way with a reasonable interpretation of the literal language of the contract, and consistent with the whole seniority principle, the Company concluded its arguments by pointing out that when the parties signed the contract earlier in the year there was no contemplation of the tremendous change, and that the agreement was made for an entirely different setup than what is now in existence; that the employees when they ratified the contract with superseniority for their committeemen did not intend to abandon "their seniority status to provide jobs for committeemen, when there was no useful purpose to be served."

The Union maintained that some work that had been done in all three areas was still being performed, such as subassembly from Area I and inspection, which was included in Area III. This, added to the fact that the contract makes no mention of plant size or number of persons to be represented by committeemen, indicates all three committeemen should have been retained.

It was pointed out that the parties in this situation were not dealing with "what is morally right, only with what the Contract says."

The Union stated that it understood there were mitigating circumstances that caused management to do what it did; it also pointed out that the Company could have discussed the matter with the representatives and that probably an agreement could have been reached that would have alleviated the situation. However, it was claimed that the Company did not see fit to do this, and the Union feels duty bound to insist that management abide by the contract, even though the Union finds it distasteful to displace persons with much longer service than the committeemen.

During the hearing the parties indicated that they were negotiating a new contract and in its post-hearing brief the Union called attention to the changes in the representation section of the agreement, a copy of which was sent to me. It was also pointed out by the Union that during the hearing they indicated they "would have been agreeable to modifying the Representation Section of the Agreement when Management reduced the employment, but Management indicated no desire to do so and simply stated that under the terms of the Agreement they were right, and that the Union should pursue the issue to arbitration."

The Union concluded its arguments by stating that the representation section of the old contract clearly calls for superseniority for committeemen, and that there is no alternative but for it to demand that the two committeemen be returned to work and be reimbursed for all time lost.

QUESTIONS

1. What is the purpose of superseniority for stewards? Does superseniority for stewards attach to the person of the steward or to the job of the steward?
2. What intraunion problems develop as a result of this case going to arbitration?
3. If the union finds it "distasteful to displace persons with much longer service than the committeemen," why did the Union take this case to arbitration?
4. How would you rule in this case? Why?

Case 41

PAYMENT FOR STEWARDS' TIME ON GRIEVANCE PROCESSING

COMPANY: Goss Company, A Division of Miehle-Goss-Dexter, Inc.

UNION: International Association of Machinists
              District 8

ARBITRATOR: William H. Pedrick

Did the employer have a right to unilaterally promulgate a rule specifying the maximum amount of time union officers would be compensated for in handling grievances?

The following discussion of the issue and facts in the case was prepared by Willard H. Pedrick, the arbitrator.

ISSUE

Did the Company have authority under the contract to issue a rule limiting the amount of grievance time for shop chairman, co-chairmen, and committeemen to be paid for by the Company?

EXTRACTS FROM THE RULE IN QUESTION

GRIEVANCE TIME FOR GOSS EMPLOYEES REPRESENTING
THE INTERNATIONAL ASSOCIATION OF MACHINISTS,
DISTRICT #8—EFFECTIVE JULY 13, 1964

The following rule defines the maximum amount of grievance time for which the shop Chairman, Co-Chairmen and Committeemen will receive their regular hourly rate of pay from the Goss Company. No payment shall be made by the Goss Company for any grievance time charged by the shop Chairman, Co-Chairmen or Committeemen beyond the limits of this rule.

This rule is instituted to define the limits to which the Goss Company will allow payment for grievance time, and is not to be construed as a rule that sets a limit on the amount of time that the shop Chairman, Co-Chairmen or Committeemen may spend on grievance activity.

For purposes of this rule, grievance time is defined as the time required to investigate and process grievances or other matters arising under the contract and applies only to the time spent in the Goss plant during the regular shift of the shop Chairman, Co-Chairman or Committeeman charging such time.

The shop Chairman will be allowed a maximum of forty (40) hours of paid grievance time per each four week period.

The shop Co-Chairmen will each be allowed a maximum of twenty-four (24) hours of paid grievance time per each four week period.

* * * * *

The shop Committeemen will each be allowed a maximum of four (4) hours of paid grievance time per each four week period.

Prior to engaging in any grievance activity or any other activity arising under the contract during working hours of their shift, union representatives must notify their foreman and must also notify the foreman of the department to be visited in accordance with the terms of the contract.

The Pertinent Provisions of the Contract:

Article 1—Recognition:

Section D—There shall be no discrimination against any employee because of his acting as an officer or committeeman or any other lawful and proper activities in the interest of the Union.

Article II—Management

Section A—The Management of the plant, and the direction of the working force, including the right to continue and to adopt such rules and regulations and institute such methods as the Company may from time to time deem necessary and proper to carry on its business . . . is vested solely in the Company, provided that any action taken hereunder shall not conflict with any of the express terms of the Agreement.

Article X—Grievances

Section D—No shop Chairman or Committeeman shall leave his job or department for the purpose of handling grievances or for any other purpose under this Agreement without first notifying his foreman. Should the Foreman be unavailable, the Chairman or the Committeeman shall leave a note at the Foreman's desk establishing the location of this visit. Such Shop Chairman or Committeeman also shall notify the Foreman of the Department to be visited by him that the purpose of his visit is to discuss with an employee in said department a matter arising under this Agreement.

Section A—Should any employee or employees believe the Company has violated any of the provisions of this Agreement, he may initiate a grievance which shall be processed in the following order:

1. Between the aggrieved employee or employees together with the Department Committeeman and the Foreman of the department or departments involved; if not settled, then,
2. Between the Shop Committee Chairman, Department Committeeman and the Shop Superintendent; if not settled, then,
3. Between the Shop Committee Chairman, Co-Chairman and the Personnel Director.

SUMMARY STATEMENT OF FACTS

For a very long time, said by the Union to be as long as 50 years, the Company has paid employees without deduction for time spent by the employees as Union representatives in adjusting grievances. The Company agrees that it has for a very long period paid for such "grievance time." Against the background of this settled practice the present contract confirms this practice in its provision in Article X governing the procedure to be followed when a shop chairman or committeeman leaves his duty post "for the purpose of handling grievances" or other "matters arising under this Agreement."

Over a period of several years the Company has kept records, not challenged as to accuracy, on the average hours per week spent on "labor relations time" by shop chairman, co-chairmen and committeemen. These records indicate that whereas an average of 15 to 30 hours per week was charged as "labor relations time" in the period 1959 to 1962 inclusive, in the years 1963 and 1964 the figure jumped to 52 and 79 hours per week respectively. The Company undertook to deal with the matter by the rule in question issued under an effective date of July 13, 1964. Under the prescribed rule the Company announced that it would continue to pay for "grievance time" only within the limits of 10 hours per week for shop chairman, 6 hours per week for co-chairman and 1 hour per week for shop committeemen. Depending on the number of co-chairmen and shop committeemen this time allowance is in line with the 1959–62 experience.

The Company has made no charge of malingering on the part of the chairman and committeemen and apart from the very substantial increase in the over-all amount of time spent on labor relations matters the Company has not charged that any particular amount of time expended was unwarranted. It is fair to say that the Company attitude is one of skepticism as to whether the grievance work really required the expenditure of time in fact charged to that activity.

There has been a modest increase in the number of employees in the plant with 918 in 1958, a drop to 786 and 880 in 1959 and 1960 respectively, with increases since that date bringing the number to 1,072 for 1964. There is some evidence that in the past two years the Company has been endeavoring to regularize its procedures with employees, or as it is sometimes said, "To go by the book," with the generation of some friction in the process.

Prior to the issuance of the rule of July 13, 1964, the Company did not consult with the Union and in fact the rule was issued unilaterally by the Company on its own authority.

Since the promulgation of the rule of July 13, 1964, there has been no instance of an employee's actually suffering a wage deduction on account of time spent on grievance matters beyond that specified by the rule.

THE UNION'S CONTENTIONS

The Union contends that the Company has no authority unilaterally to prescribe a limit for the "labor relations time" to be paid for by the Company in the face of an established practice of many years' duration of paying for all "labor relations time."

THE COMPANY'S CONTENTIONS

The Company contends that it has authority to correct abuses in expenditure of excessive time on labor relations matters by employees serving as chairman and co-chairman. The Company further contends that the established practice of payment for "labor relations time" relates to a period during which the amounts of such time were reasonable and that the rule issued by the Company really returns to the settled practice. The Company's position is that the rule in question was within the authority of the Company as a reasonable measure intended to restore the former practice and accordingly was not a matter requiring negotiation or evidencing any anti-Union discrimination.

QUESTIONS

1. "Labor relations time" can be an expensive item. How could the Company bring it under control?
2. What is the significance of past practice in this case?
3. How would you rule in this case? Why?

Case 42

UNION REPRESENTATION DURING OVERTIME WORK

COMPANY: Lionel Pacific, Inc.

UNION: International Association of Machinists
              Aeronautical Lodge 720

ARBITRATOR: Thomas T. Roberts

Under a clause providing for union representation during overtime work, what is the responsibility of the Union to assure that a committeeman is available for such work?

The following discussion of the issue and facts in this case was prepared by Thomas T. Roberts, the arbitrator.

ISSUES

A hearing in this matter was conducted on October 15, 1964, in the offices of the Company located at Gardena, California. At the time of the hearing, the parties orally stipulated to the following statement of the issues herein submitted:

1. Did the Company violate Article XV, Section 5 of the existing Company-Union agreement on August 26, 1964?
2. If so, what is the appropriate remedy, if any?

STATEMENT OF FACTS

This grievance arose under, and is controlled by, the agreement between the parties effective from November 11, 1963, through November 10, 1964.

The Company is engaged primarily as a subcontractor to the aerospace industry. The Union is the exclusive collective bargaining representative for production, maintenance, shipping and receiving employees, and truck drivers at its Gardena, California, facility.

The instant dispute involves two hours of overtime worked beyond the 3:30 P.M. termination of the day shift on August 26, 1964. It was originally agreed that three employees were then designated as "chairmen" for the purpose of in-plant Union representation and that none worked beyond the end of the shift, so that no such representation was available during the period from 3:30 P.M. to 5:30 P.M. Later, the Company asserted, one of the employees who did work overtime was also a duly appointed chairman.

At approximately 2:10 P.M. on the day in question, Mr. John Wilson, a chairman, was asked if the job to which he was then assigned could be finished that day on an overtime basis. He replied that it could. Sometime later in the afternoon, a decision was made to retain 19 bargaining unit employees to work a total of two hours beyond the end of the shift.

At 3:25 P.M., Mr. Wilson was asked to work the indicated overtime. He declined because of prior personal commitments. No effort was then made to contact the remaining chairmen in order to offer them an opportunity to work the overtime.

On August 28, 1964, a grievance was filed by the Union on behalf of X——, one of the chairmen on the day shift, which alleges that the Company violated the agreement by not arranging for the presence of a chairman during the overtime hours worked on August 26, 1964. The grievance (which asks that X—— be paid as though he had so worked) was denied by the Company and the matter has ultimately come to arbitration.

CONTROLLING CONTRACT PROVISIONS

ARTICLE XV
Overtime

5. In the event scheduled overtime requires ten (10) employees or more, a Chairman or Chairmen will be part of the overtime work force.

POSITION OF THE UNION

It is the position of the Union that the failure of the Company to solicit all three chairmen for the overtime work in question was a violation of the agreement between the parties.

The Union argues Article XV, Section 5, requires the Company to arrange for the presence of a chairman when 10 or more employees work overtime and that obligation is excused only in a situation where all of the duly appointed chairmen decline such work.

In conclusion, the Union asks that the grievant, Chairman X——, be awarded two hours of overtime wages to compensate for his not having been asked to so work on August 26, 1964.

POSITION OF THE COMPANY

It is the position of the Company that it fully complied with its commitment under Article XV, Section 5, when Chairman Wilson was offered and declined the opportunity to work overtime.

The Company states that after the processing of the instant grievance, but prior to arbitration, it discovered that Roger Spradlin worked the overtime here in dispute and, further, that he was a duly appointed chairman on August 26, 1964.

The Company argues that it was the responsibility of Mr. Wilson, as a chairman, to work the overtime when he was asked to do so and the Union is therefore estopped from requesting that the grievant be paid for hours not worked.

Finally, the Company contends that when Mr. Wilson, at 3:25 P.M., was asked and declined to work overtime, sufficient time did not remain before the end of the shift to seek out the remaining chairmen in order to ascertain whether or not they would be available for such work.

Under the agreement, "all overtime is understood to be on a voluntary basis."

QUESTIONS

1. To what extent is the Union responsible for providing a chairman to work overtime under Article XV, Section 5?
2. Did the presence of Roger Spradlin on August 26 overtime fulfill the obligation of the agreement?
3. How much time did the Company have to arrange for the presence of a chairman? Did it use this time wisely? If all chairmen had refused overtime could the Company schedule overtime on August 26?

Case 43

POWERS OF THE ARBITRATOR

This case is based on a Bureau of Labor Statistics survey[1] *of arbitration procedures in labor agreements covering over 1,000 workers effective in 1961–62. Three topics will be discussed in this case? (1) the prevalence*

[1] U.S. Department of Labor, Bureau of Labor Statistics, *Major Collective Bargaining Agreements: Arbitration Procedures*, Bulletin No. 1425-6 (June, 1966).

of grievance arbitration, (2) methods of limiting the arbitrator's power, and (3) how strikes may occur under agreements providing for arbitration.

THE PREVALENCE OF GRIEVANCE ARBITRATION

American collective bargaining agreements covering 1,000 or more workers each and effective in 1961–62 made very heavy use of grievance arbitration. Provision for arbitration of some or all grievance disputes was incorporated in 94 per cent of the agreements analyzed and these agreements covered 96 per cent of the workers considered. The use of grievance arbitration shows a steady increase in popularity; in 1944, 1949, and 1952 Bureau of Labor Statistics studies, arbitration provisions were found in 73, 83, and 89 per cent of the agreements respectively.[2]

LIMITS ON THE POWER OF THE ARBITRATOR

The jurisdiction of the arbitrator in grievance disputes is typically defined in two basic ways: (1) in regard to disputes which are arbitrable and (2) in relation to the scope of his decisions.

In regard to the arbitrability of specific grievances, three alternatives are available to the parties: (1) to limit arbitrable grievances to the interpretation of the written agreement between them, (2) to make all disputes and differences subject to arbitration, and (3) to limit arbitration to the written agreement *and* to exclude certain issues covered by the agreement from arbitration. The issues most commonly excluded from arbitration but covered by the agreement are:

> Wage adjustments (individual and general).
> Administration of supplementary benefits.
> Production standards and plant administration.

The reasons for such exclusions usually were not indicated by the agreement and, although they may have been fully understood by the parties, they are not always clear to outsiders reading the agreements. Some exclusions undoubtedly were intended to preserve certain management prerogatives, others to preserve union prerogatives. Some were necessary because the parties had agreed upon other methods of handling certain problems, and possibly were motivated by a mutual desire not to overburden the arbitration machinery with trivialities. It seems reasonable to assume, however, that underlying many exclusions was a strongly held belief of one or both parties that the issue in question was too important or too subtle to be entrusted to a decision of a third party.

The scope of the decisions of an arbitrator very commonly is limited by either an explicit or implicit statement that:

[2] *Ibid.,* p. 5.

The arbitrator shall have no authority to add to, subtract from, modify, or amend any provisions of this agreement.

HOW STRIKES MAY OCCUR WITHOUT VIOLATING AGREEMENTS

Despite the widespread prevalence of grievance and arbitration procedures and no-strike–lockout pledges, a strike not constituting a violation of the letter of the agreement is possible in about half of all major agreements studied by the Bureau of Labor Statistics. Figure 43–1 shows how these strikes are possible.

FIGURE 43–1

HOW STRIKES MAY OCCUR DURING THE TERM OF AGREEMENTS WITHOUT VIOLATING THE AGREEMENTS

(1,717 major agreements)

Strikes banned	Strikes possible
Absolute ban on strikes (757)	
Not all possible disputes subject to grievance and/or arbitration (594)	
No arbitration (9)	
All disputes subject to arbitration (154)	
Limited ban on strikes (780)	
All disputes subject to arbitration (64)	Strikes banned over disputes subject to arbitration but not all possible disputes subject to grievance and/or arbitration (285)
	Arbitration provided but strike ban waived if agreement violated (331)
	Arbitration required mutual consent (35)
	No arbitration (62)
	Other (3)
No ban on strikes (180)	
All disputes subject to arbitration (25)	Arbitration provided but not all possible disputes subject to grievance and/or arbitration (118)
	No arbitration (37)
Total agreements.........(846)................................(871)	

SOURCE: U.S. Department of Labor, Bureau of Labor Statistics, *Major Collective Bargaining Agreements: Arbitration Procedures*, Bulletin no. 1425-6, Washington, D.C.: June 1966, p. 91.

Appendix

Major Statutory Laws on Collective Bargaining

Norris–La Guardia Act
Taft-Hartley Act as Amended
Landrum-Griffin Act as Amended

APPENDIX

The major federal laws on collective bargaining in effect at the close of 1966 were the Railway Labor Act of 1926 as amended; the Norris–La Guardia Act of 1932; the Labor-Management Relations Act of 1947 (Taft-Hartley Act) as amended by Public Law 86–257, 1959 (Landrum-Griffin Act); and the Labor-Management Reporting and Disclosure Act of 1959 (Landrum-Griffin Act) as amended. The Railway Labor Act of 1926 will not be covered in this appendix because of its limited application.

This appendix is designed as a ready reference to the *major* elements of national labor relations law. This appendix excludes the rich interpretations of the statutes cited which have been developed by the National Labor Relations Board and the courts.

THE NORRIS–LA GUARDIA ANTI-INJUNCTION ACT OF MARCH 23, 1932

This law was passed for the purpose of eliminating certain abuses of the injunction in labor disputes. It severely restricts the authority of federal courts to issue injunctions in labor disputes. The full text of the original law is reproduced below. The Norris–La Guardia Act was amended by the Labor Management Relations Act of 1947 (the Taft-Hartley law).

NORRIS–LA GUARDIA ANTI-INJUNCTION ACT
OF MARCH 23, 1932

(PUBLIC—No. 65—72D CONGRESS)
(H.R. 5315)

AN ACT

To amend the Judicial Code and to define and limit the jurisdiction of courts sitting in equity, and for other purposes.

Be it enacted by the Senate and House of Representatives of the United States of America in Congress assembled, that no court of the United States, as herein defined shall have jurisdiction to issue any restraining order or temporary or permanent injunction in a case involving or growing out of a labor dispute, except in a strict conformity with the provisions of this Act; nor shall any such restraining order or temporary or permanent injunction be issued contrary to the public policy declared in this Act.

Sec. 2. In the interpretation of this Act and in determining the jurisdiction and authority of the courts of the United States, as such jurisdiction and authority are herein defined and limited, the public policy of the United States is hereby declared as follows:

Whereas under prevailing economic conditions, developed with the aid of governmental authority for owners of property to organize in the corporate and other form of ownership association, the individual unorganized worker is commonly helpless to exercise actual liberty of contract and to protect his freedom of labor, and thereby to obtain acceptable terms and conditions of employment, therefore, though he should be free to decline to associate with his fellows, it is necessary that he have full freedom of association, self-organization, and designation of representatives of his own choosing, to negotiate the terms and conditions of his employment, and that he shall be free from the interference, restraint, or coercion of employers of labor, or their agents, in the designation of such representatives or in self-organization or in other concerted activities for the purpose of collective bargaining or other mutual aid or protection; therefore, the following definitions of, and limitations upon, the jurisdiction and authority of the courts of the United States are hereby enacted.

SEC. 3. Any undertaking or promise, such as is described in this section, or any other undertaking or promise in conflict with the public policy declared in section 2 of this Act, is hereby declared to be contrary to the public policy of the United States, shall not be enforceable in any court of the United States and shall not afford any basis for the granting of legal or equitable relief by any such court, including specifically the following:

Every undertaking or promise hereafter made, whether written or oral, express or implied, constituting or contained in any contract or agreement of hiring or employment between any individual, firm, company, association, or corporation, and any employee or prospective employee of the same, whereby

(a) Either party to such contract or agreement undertakes or promises not to join, become, or remain a member of any labor organization or of any employer organization; or

(b) Either party to such contract or agreement undertakes or promises that he will withdraw from an employment relation in the event that he joins, becomes, or remains a member of any labor organization or of any employer organization.

SEC. 4. No court of the United States shall have jurisdiction to issue any restraining order or temporary or permanent injunction in any case involving or growing out of any labor dispute to prohibit any person or persons participating or interested in such dispute (as these terms are herein defined) from doing, whether singly or in concert, any of the following acts:

(a) Ceasing or refusing to perform any work or to remain in any relation of employment;

(b) Becoming or remaining a member of any labor organization or of any employer organization, regardless of any such undertaking or promise as is described in section 3 of this Act;

(c) Paying or giving to, or withholding from, any person participating or interested in such labor dispute, any strike or unemployment benefits or insurance, or other moneys or things of value;

(d) By all lawful means aiding any person participating or interested in any labor dispute who is being proceeded against in, or is prosecuting, any action or suit in any court of the United States or of any State;

(e) Giving publicity to the existence of, or the facts involved in, any labor dispute, whether by advertising, speaking, patrolling, or by any other method not involving fraud or violence;

(f) Assembling peaceably to act or to organize to act in promotion of their interests in a labor dispute;

(g) Advising or notifying any person of an intention to do any of the acts heretofore specified;

(h) Agreeing with other persons to do or not to do any of the acts heretofore specified; and

(i) Advising, urging, or otherwise causing or inducing without fraud or violence the acts heretofore specified, regardless of any such undertaking or promise as is described in section 3 of this Act.

SEC. 5. No court of the United States shall have jurisdiction to issue a restraining order or temporary or permanent injunction upon the ground that any of the persons participating or interested in a labor dispute constitute or are engaged in an unlawful combination or conspiracy because of the doing in concert of the acts enumerated in section 4 of this Act.

SEC. 6. No officer or member of any association or organization, and no association or organization participating or interested in a labor dispute, shall be held responsible or liable in any court of the United States for the unlawful acts of individual officers, members, or agents, except upon clear proof of actual participation in, or actual authorization of, such acts, or of ratification of such acts after actual knowledge thereof.

SEC. 7. No court of the United States shall have jurisdiction to issue a temporary or permanent injunction in any case involving or growing out of a labor dispute as herein defined, except after hearing the testimony of witnesses in open court (with opportunity for cross-examination) in support of the allegations of a complaint made under oath, and testimony in opposition thereto, if offered, and except after findings of fact by the court, to the effect—

(a) That unlawful acts have been threatened and will be committed unless restrained or have been committed and will be continued unless restrained, but no injunction or temporary restraining order shall be issued on account of any threat or unlawful act excepting against the person or persons, association, or organization making the threat or committing the unlawful act or actually authorizing or ratifying the same after actual knowledge thereof;

(b) That substantial and irreparable injury to complainant's property will follow;

(c) That as to each item of relief granted greater injury will be inflicted upon complainant by the denial of relief than will be inflicted upon defendants by the granting of relief;

(d) That complainant has no adequate remedy at law; and

(e) That the public officers charged with the duty to protect complainant's property are unable or unwilling to furnish adequate protection.

Such hearing shall be held after due and personal notice thereof has been given, in such manner as the court shall direct, to all known persons against whom relief is sought, and also to the chief of those public officials of the county and city within which the unlawful acts have been threatened or committed charged with the duty to protect complainant's property: *Provided, however,* That if a complainant shall also allege that, unless a temporary restraining order shall be issued without notice, a substantial and irreparable injury to complainant's property will be unavoidable, such a temporary restraining order may be issued upon testimony under oath, sufficient, if sustained, to justify the court in issuing a temporary injunction upon a hearing after notice. Such a temporary restraining order shall be effective for no longer than five days and shall become void at the expiration of said five days. No temporary restraining order or temporary injunction shall be issued except on condition that complainant shall first file an undertaking with adequate security in an amount to be fixed by the court sufficient to recompense those enjoined for any loss, expense, or damage caused by the improvident or erroneous issuance of such order or injunction, including all reasonable costs (together with a reasonable attorney's fee) and expense of defense against the order or against the granting of any injunctive relief sought in the same proceeding and subsequently denied by the court.

The undertaking herein mentioned shall be understood to signify an agreement entered into by the complainant and the surety upon which a decree may be rendered in the same suit or proceeding against said complainant and surety, upon a hearing to assess damages of which hearing complainant and surety shall have reasonable notice, the said complainant and surety submitting themselves to the jurisdiction of the court for that purpose. But nothing herein contained shall deprive any party having a claim or cause of action under or upon such undertaking from electing to pursue his ordinary remedy by suit at law or in equity.

SEC. 8. No restraining order or injunctive relief shall be granted to any complainant who has failed to comply with any obligation imposed by law which is involved in the labor dispute in question, or who has failed to make every reasonable effort to settle such dispute either by negotiation or with the aid of any available governmental machinery of mediation or voluntary arbitration.

SEC. 9. No restraining order or temporary or permanent injunction shall be granted in a case involving or growing out of a labor dispute, except on the basis of findings of fact made and filed by the court in the record of the case prior to the issuance of such restraining order or injunction; and every restraining order or injunction granted in a case involving or growing out of a labor dispute shall include only a prohibition of such specific act or acts as may be expressly complained of in the bill of complaint or petition filed in such case and as shall be expressly included in said findings of fact made and filed by the court as provided herein.

SEC. 10. Whenever any court of the United States shall issue or deny any temporary injunction in a case involving or growing out of a labor dispute, the court shall, upon the request of any party to the proceedings and on his filing the usual bond for costs, forthwith certify as in ordinary cases the record of the case to the circuit court of appeals for its review. Upon the filing of such record in the circuit court of appeals, the appeal shall be heard and the temporary injunctive order affirmed, modified, or set aside with the greatest possible expedition, giving the proceedings precedence over all other matters except older matters of the same character.

SEC. 11. In all cases arising under this Act in which a person shall be charged with contempt in a court of the United States (as herein defined), the accused shall enjoy the right to a speedy and public trial by an impartial jury of the State and district wherein the contempt shall have been committed: Provided, That this right shall not apply to contempts committed in the presence of the court or so near thereto as to interfere directly with the administration of justice or to apply to the misbehavior, misconduct, or disobedience of any officer of the court in respect to the writs, orders, or process of the court.

SEC. 12. The defendant in any proceeding for contempt of court may file with the court a demand for the retirement of the judge sitting in the proceeding, if the contempt arises from an attack upon the character or conduct of such judge and if the attack occurred elsewhere than in the presence of the court or so near thereto as to interfere directly with the administration of justice. Upon the filing of any such demand the judge shall thereupon proceed no further, but another judge shall be designated in the same manner as is provided by law. The demand shall be filed prior to the hearing in the contempt proceeding.

SEC. 13. When used in this Act, and for the purposes of this Act—

(a) A case shall be held to involve or to grow out of a labor dispute when the case involves persons who are engaged in the same industry, trade, craft, or occupation; or have direct or indirect interests therein; or who are employees of the same employer; or who are members of the same or an affiliated organization of employers or employees; whether such dispute is (1) between one or more employers or associations of employers and one or more employees or associations of employees; (2) between one or more employers or associations of employers and one or more employers or associations of employers; or (3) between one or more employees or associations of employees and one or more employees or associations of employees; or when the case involves any conflicting or competing interests in a "labor dispute" (as hereinafter defined) of "persons participating or interested" (as hereinafter defined).

(b) A person or association shall be held to be a person participating or interested in a labor dispute if relief is sought against him or it, and if he or it is engaged in the same industry, trade, craft, or occupation in which such dispute occurs, or has a direct or indirect interest therein, or is a member, officer, or agent of any association composed in whole or in part of employers or employees engaged in such industry, trade, craft, or occupation.

(c) The term "labor dispute" includes any controversy concerning terms or conditions of employment, or concerning the association or representation of persons in negotiating, fixing, maintaining, changing, or seeking to arrange terms or conditions of employment, regardless of whether or not the disputants stand in the proximate relation of employer and employee.

(d) The term "court of the United States" means any court of the United States whose jurisdiction has been or may be conferred or defined or limited by Act of Congress, including the courts of the District of Columbia.

SEC. 14. If any provision of this Act or the application thereof to any person or circumstance is held unconstitutional or otherwise invalid, the remaining provisions of the Act and the application of such provisions to other persons or circumstances shall not be affected thereby.

SEC. 15. All Acts and parts of Acts in conflict with the provisions of this Act are hereby repealed.

Approved, March 23, 1932.

The National Labor Relations Act of 1935 (Wagner Act)

From 1935 to 1947, the Wagner Act was the major federal law regulating collective bargaining. This law provided for the establishment of the National Labor Relations Board to certify employee representatives for collective bargaining and to prevent five "unfair labor practices" *by management*. These management unfair labor practices were essentially unchanged by the Labor Management Relations Act of 1947.

THE LABOR MANAGEMENT RELATIONS ACT OF 1947 (TAFT-HARTLEY LAW AS AMENDED)

Title I of the Labor Management Relations Act was entitled Amendments to the National Labor Relations Act. The major change was the addition of Section 8(b), unfair labor practices by labor organizations. The Taft-Hartley law also made major procedural changes in National

Labor Relations Board operations and added four entirely new titles to collective bargaining law. The Taft-Hartley law has been amended by Public Law 189, 82d Congress, and the Landrum-Griffin law (the Labor Management Reporting and Disclosure Law of 1959). The Taft-Hartley law and its amendments are shown in the text below:

TEXT OF LABOR MANAGEMENT RELATIONS ACT, 1947, AS AMENDED BY PUBLIC LAW 86–257, 1959*

[PUBLIC LAW 101—80TH CONGRESS]

AN ACT

To amend the National Labor Relations Act, to provide additional facilities for the mediation of labor disputes affecting commerce, to equalize legal responsibilities of labor organizations and employers, and for other purposes.

Be it enacted by the Senate and House of Representatives of the United States of America in Congress assembled,

SHORT TITLE AND DECLARATION OF POLICY

SECTION 1. (a) This Act may be cited as the "Labor Management Relations Act, 1947."

(b) Industrial strife which interferes with the normal flow of commerce and with the full production of articles and commodities for commerce, can be avoided or substantially minimized if employers, employees, and labor organizations each recognize under law one another's legitimate rights in their relations with each other, and above all recognize under law that neither party has any right in its relations with any other to engage in acts or practices which jeopardize the public health, safety, or interest.

It is the purpose and policy of this Act, in order to promote the full flow of commerce, to prescribe the legitimate rights of both employees and employers in their relations affecting commerce, to provide orderly and peaceful procedures for preventing the interference by either with the legitimate rights of the other, to protect the rights of individual employees in their relations with labor organizations whose activities affect commerce, to define and proscribe practices on the part of labor and management which affect commerce and are inimical to the general welfare, and to protect the rights of the public in connection with labor disputes affecting commerce.

TITLE I—AMENDMENT OF NATIONAL LABOR RELATIONS ACT

SEC. 101. The National Labor Relations Act is hereby amended to read as follows:

FINDINGS AND POLICIES

SECTION 1. The denial by some employers of the right of employees to organize and the refusal by some employers to accept the procedure of

---

* Section 201(d) and (e) of the Labor-Management Reporting and Disclosure Act of 1959 which repealed Section 9(f), (g), and (h) of the Labor Management Relations Act, 1947, and Section 505 amending Section 302(a), (b), and (c) of the Labor Management Relations Act, 1947, took effect upon enactment of Public Law 86–257, September 14, 1959. As to the other amendments of the Labor Management Relations Act, 1947, Section 707 of the Labor-Management Reporting and Disclosure Act provides:

The amendents made by this title shall take effect sixty days after the date of the enactment of this Act and no provision of this title shall be deemed to make collective bargaining lead to strikes and other forms of industrial strife or unrest, which have the intent or the necessary effect of burdening or obstructing commerce by (a) impairing the efficiency, safety, or operation of the instrumentalities of commerce; (b) occurring in the current of commerce; (c) materially affecting, restraining, or controlling the flow of raw materials or manufactured or processed goods from or into the channels of commerce, or the prices of such materials or goods in commerce; or (d) causing diminution of employment and wages in such volume as substantially to impair or disrupt the market for goods flowing from or into the channels of commerce.

The inequality of bargaining power between employees who do not possess full freedom of association or actual liberty of contract, and employers who are organized in the corporate or other forms of ownership association substantially burdens and affects the flow of commerce, and tends to aggravate recurrent business depressions, by depressing wage rates and the purchasing power of wage earners in industry and by preventing the stabilization of competitive wage rates and working conditions within and between industries.

Experience has proved that protection by law of the right of employees to organize and bargain collectively safeguards commerce from injury, impairment, or interruption, and promotes the flow of commerce by removing certain recognized sources of industrial strife and unrest, by encouraging practices fundamental to the friendly adjustment of industrial disputes arising out of differences as to wages, hours, or other working conditions, and by restoring equality of bargaining power between employers and employees.

Experience has further demonstrated that certain practices by some labor organizations, their officers, and members have the intent or the necessary effect of burdening or obstructing commerce by preventing the free flow of goods in such commerce through strikes and other forms of industrial unrest or through concerted activities which impair the interest of the public in the free flow of such commerce. The elimination of such practices is a necessary condition to the assurance of the rights herein guaranteed.

It is hereby declared to be the policy of the United States to eliminate the causes of certain substantial obstructions to the free flow of commerce and to mitigate and eliminate these obstructions when they have occurred by encouraging the practice and procedure of collective bargaining and by protecting the exercise by workers of full freedom of association, self-organization, and designation of representatives of their own choosing, for the purpose of negotiating the terms and conditions of their employment or other mutual aid or protection.

DEFINITIONS

SEC. 2. When used in this Act—

(1) The term "person" includes one or more individuals, labor organizations, partnerships, associations, corporations, legal representatives, trustees, trustees in bankruptcy, or receivers.

(2) The term "employer" includes any person acting as an agent of an employer, directly or indirectly, but shall not include the United States or any wholly owned Government corporation, or any Federal Reserve Bank, or any State or political subdivision thereof, or any corporation or association operating a hospital, if no part of the net earnings inures to the benefit of any private shareholder or individual, or any person subject to the Railway Labor Act, as amended from time to time, or any labor organization (other than when acting as an employer), or anyone acting in the capacity of officer or agent of such labor organization.

---

an unfair labor practice, any act which is performed prior to such effective date which did not constitute an unfair labor practice prior thereto.

(3) The term "employee" shall include any employee, and shall not be limited to the employees of a particular employer, unless the Act explicitly states otherwise, and shall include any individual whose work has ceased as a consequence of, or in connection with, any current labor dispute or because of any unfair labor practice, and who has not obtained any other regular and substantially equivalent employment, but shall not include any individual employed as an agricultural laborer, or in the domestic service of any family or person at his home, or any individual employed by his parent or spouse, or any individual having the status of an independent contractor, or any individual employed as a supervisor, or any individual employed by an employer subject to the Railway Labor Act, as amended from time to time, or by any other person who is not an employer as herein defined.

(4) The term "representatives" includes any individual or labor organization.

(5) The term "labor organization" means any organization of any kind, or any agency or employee representation committee or plan, in which employees participate and which exists for the purpose, in whole or in part, of dealing with employers concerning grievances, labor disputes, wages, rates of pay, hours of employment, or conditions of work.

(6) The term "commerce" means trade, traffic, commerce, transportation, or communication among the several States, or between the District of Columbia or any Territory of the United States and any State or other Territory, or between any foreign country and any State, Territory, or the District of Columbia, or within the District of Columbia or any Territory, or between points in the same State but through any other State or any Territory or the District of Columbia or any foreign country.

(7) The term "affecting commerce" means in commerce, or burdening or obstructing commerce or the free flow of commerce, or having led or tending to lead to a labor dispute burdening or obstructing commerce or the free flow of commerce.

(8) The term "unfair labor practice" means any unfair labor practice listed in section 8.

(9) The term "labor dispute" includes any controversy concerning terms, tenure or conditions of employment, or concerning the association or representation of persons in negotiating, fixing, maintaining, changing, or seeking to arrange terms or conditions of employment, regardless of whether the disputants stand in the proximate relation of employer and employee.

(10) The term "National Labor Relations Board" means the National Labor Relations Board provided for in section 3 of this Act.

(11) The term "supervisor" means any individual having authority, in the interest of the employer, to hire, transfer, suspend, lay off, recall, promote, discharge, assign, reward, or discipline other employees, or responsibly to direct them, or to adjust their grievances, or effectively to recommend such action, if in connection with the foregoing the exercise of such authority is not of a merely routine or clerical nature, but requires the use of independent judgment.

(12) The term "professional employee" means—

(a) any employee engaged in work (i) predominantly intellectual and varied in character as opposed to routine mental, manual, mechanical, or physical work; (ii) involving the consistent exercise of discretion and judgment in its performance; (iii) of such a character that the output produced or the result accomplished cannot be standardized in relation to a given period of time; (iv) requiring knowledge of an advanced type in a field of science or learning customarily acquired by a prolonged course of specialized intellectual instruction and study in an institution of higher learning or a hospital, as distinguished from a general academic education or from an apprenticeship or from training in the performance of routine mental, manual, or physical processes; or

(b) any employee, who (i) has completed the courses of specialized intellectual instruction and study described in clause (iv) of paragraph (a), and (ii) is performing related work under the supervision of a professional person to qualify himself to become a professional employee as defined in paragraph (a).

(13) In determining whether any person is acting as an "agent" of another person so as to make such other person responsible for his acts, the question of whether the specific acts performed were actually authorized or subsequently ratified shall not be controlling.

NATIONAL LABOR RELATIONS BOARD

SEC. 3. (a) The National Labor Relations Board (hereinafter called the "Board") created by this Act prior to its amendment by the Labor Management Relations Act, 1947, is hereby continued as an agency of the United States, except that the Board shall consist of five instead of three members, appointed by the President by and with the advice and consent of the Senate. Of the two additional members so provided for, one shall be appointed for a term of five years and the other for a term of two years. Their successors, and the successors of the other members, shall be appointed for terms of five years each, excepting that any individual chosen to fill a vacancy shall be appointed only for the unexpired term of the member whom he shall succeed. The President shall designate one member to serve as Chairman of the Board. Any member of the Board may be removed by the President, upon notice and hearing, for neglect of duty or malfeasance in office, but for no other cause.

(b) The Board is authorized to delegate to any group of three or more members any or all of the powers which it may itself exercise. The Board is also authorized to delegate to its regional directors its powers under section 9 to determine the unit appropriate for the purpose of collective bargaining, to investigate and provide for hearings, and determine whether a question of representation exists, and to direct an election or take a secret ballot under subsection (c) or (e) of section 9 and certify the results thereof, except that upon the filing of a request therefor with the Board by any interested person, the Board may review any action of a regional director delegated to him under this paragraph, but such a review shall not, unless specifically ordered by the Board, operate as a stay of any action taken by the regional director. A vacancy in the Board shall not impair the right of the remaining members to exercise all of the powers of the Board, and three members of the Board shall, at all times, constitute a quorum of the Board, except that two members shall constitute a quorum of any group designated pursuant to the first sentence hereof. The Board shall have an official seal which shall be judicially noticed.

(c) The Board shall at the close of each fiscal year make a report in writing to Congress and to the President stating in detail the cases it has heard, the decisions it has rendered, the names, salaries, and duties of all employees and officers in the employ or under the supervision of the Board, and an account of all moneys it has disbursed.

(d) There shall be a General Counsel of the Board who shall be appointed by the President, by and with the advice and consent of the Senate, for a term of four years. The General Counsel of the Board shall exercise general supervision over all attorneys employed by the Board (other than trial examiners and legal assistants to Board members) and over the officers and employees in the regional offices. He shall have final authority, on behalf of the Board, in respect of the investigation of charges and issuance of complaints under section

10, and in respect of the prosecution of such complaints before the Board, and shall have such other duties as the Board may prescribe or as may be provided by law. In case of a vacancy in the office of the General Counsel the President is authorized to designate the officer or employee who shall act as General Counsel during such vacancy, but no person or persons so designated shall so act (1) for more than forty days when the Congress is in session unless a nomination to fill such vacancy shall have been submitted to the Senate, or (2) after the adjournment *sine die* of the session of the Senate in which such nomination was submitted.

SEC. 4. (a) Each member of the Board and the General Counsel of the Board shall receive a salary of $12,000* a year, shall be eligible for reappointment, and shall not engage in any other business, vocation, or employment. The Board shall appoint an executive secretary, and such attorneys, examiners, and regional directors, and such other employees as it may from time to time find necessary for the proper performance of its duties. The Board may not employ any attorneys for the purpose of reviewing transcripts of hearings or preparing drafts of opinions except that any attorney employed for assignment as a legal assistant to any Board member may for such Board member review such transcripts and prepare such drafts. No trial examiner's report shall be reviewed, either before or after its publication, by any person other than a member of the Board or his legal assistant, and no trial examiner shall advise or consult with the Board with respect to exceptions taken to his findings, rulings, or recommendations. The Board may establish or utilize such regional, local, or other agencies, and utilize such voluntary and uncompensated services, as may from time to time be needed. Attorneys appointed under this section may, at the direction of the Board, appear for and represent the Board in any case in court. Nothing in this Act shall be construed to authorize the Board to appoint individuals for the purpose of conciliation or mediation, or for economic analysis.

(b) All of the expenses of the Board, including all necessary traveling and subsistence expenses outside the District of Columbia incurred by the members or employees of the Board under its orders, shall be allowed and paid on the presentation of itemized vouchers therefor approved by the Board or by any individual it designates for that purpose.

SEC. 5. The principal office of the Board shall be in the District of Columbia, but it may meet and exercise any or all of its powers at any other place. The Board may, by one or more of its members or by such agents or agencies as it may designate, prosecute any inquiry necessary to its functions in any part of the United States. A member who participates in such an inquiry shall not be disqualified from subsequently participating in a decision of the Board in the same case.

SEC. 6. The Board shall have authority from time to time to make, amend, and rescind, in the manner prescribed by the Administrative Procedure Act, such rules and regulations as may be necessary to carry out the provisions of this Act.

RIGHTS OF EMPLOYEES

SEC. 7. Employees shall have the right to self-organization, to form, join, or assist labor organizations, to bargain collectively through representatives of their own choosing, and to engage in other concerted activities for the purpose

* Pursuant to Public Law 88–426, 88th Congress, 2d Session, Title III, approved August 14, 1964, the salary of the Chairman of the Board shall be $28,500 per year and the salaries of the General Counsel and each Board member shall be $27,000 per year.

of collective bargaining or other mutual aid or protection, and shall also have the right to refrain from any or all of such activities except to the extent that such right may be affected by an agreement requiring membership in a labor organization as a condition of employment as authorized in section 8(a) (3).

UNFAIR LABOR PRACTICES

Sec. 8. (a) It shall be an unfair labor practice for an employer—

(1) to interfere with, restrain, or coerce employees in the exercise of the rights guaranteed in section 7;

(2) to dominate or interfere with the formation or administration of any labor organization or contribute financial or other support to it: *Provided,* That subject to rules and regulations made and published by the Board pursuant to section 6, an employer shall not be prohibited from permitting employees to confer with him during working hours without loss of time or pay;

(3) by discrimination in regard to hire or tenure of employment or any term or condition of employment to encourage or discourage membership in any labor organization: *Provided,* That nothing in this Act, or in any other statute of the United States, shall preclude an employer from making an agreement with a labor organization (not established, maintained, or assisted by any action defined in section 8(a) of this Act as an unfair labor practice) to require as a condition of employment membership therein on or after the thirtieth day following the beginning of such employment or the effective date of such agreement, whichever is the later, (i) if such labor organization is the representative of the employees as provided in section 9(a), in the appropriate collective-bargaining unit covered by such agreement when made, and (ii) unless following an election held as provided in section 9(e) within one year preceding the effective date of such agreement, the Board shall have certified that at least a majority of the employees eligible to vote in such election have voted to rescind the authority of such labor organization to make such an agreement: *Provided further,* That no employer shall justify any discrimination against an employee for nonmembership in a labor organization (A) if he has reasonable grounds for believing that such membership was not available to the employee on the same terms and conditions generally applicable to other members, or (B) if he has reasonable grounds for believing that membership was denied or terminated for reasons other than the failure of the employee to tender the periodic dues and the initiation fees uniformly required as a condition of acquiring or retaining membership;

(4) to discharge or otherwise discriminate against an employee because he has filed charges or given testimony under this Act;

(5) to refuse to bargain collectively with the representatives of his employees, subject to the provisions of section 9(a).

(b) It shall be an unfair labor practice for a labor organization or its agents—

(1) to restrain or coerce (A) employees in the exercise of the rights guaranteed in section 7: *Provided,* That this paragraph shall not impair the right of a labor organization to prescribe its own rules with respect to the acquisition or retention of membership therein; or (B) an employer in the selection of his representatives for the purposes of collective bargaining or the adjustment of grievances;

(2) to cause or attempt to cause an employer to discriminate against an employee in violation of subsection (a)(3) or to discriminate

against an employee with respect to whom membership in such organization has been denied or terminated on some ground other than his failure to tender the periodic dues and the initiation fees uniformly required as a condition of acquiring or retaining membership;

(3) to refuse to bargain collectively with an employer, provided it is the representative of his employees subject to the provisions of section 9(a);

(4) (i) to engage in, or to induce or encourage any individual employed by any person engaged in commerce or in an industry affecting commerce to engage in, a strike or a refusal in the course of his employment to use, manufacture, process, transport, or otherwise handle or work on any goods, articles, materials, or commodities or to perform any services; or (ii) to threaten, coerce, or restrain any person engaged in commerce or in an industry affecting commerce, where in either case an object thereof is:

(A) forcing or requiring any employer or self-employed person to join any labor or employer organization or to enter into an agreement which is prohibited by section 8(e);

(B) forcing or requiring any person to cease using, selling, handling, transporting, or otherwise dealing in the products of any other producer, processor, or manufacturer, or to cease doing business with any other person, or forcing or requiring any other employer to recognize or bargain with a labor organization as the representative of his employees unless such labor organization has been certified as the representative of such employees under the provisions of section 9: *Provided,* That nothing contained in this clause (B) shall be construed to make unlawful, where not otherwise unlawful, any primary strike or primary picketing;

(C) forcing or requiring any employer to recognize or bargain with a particular labor organization as the representative of his employees if another labor organization has been certified as the representative of such employees under the provisions of section 9;

(D) forcing or requiring any employer to assign particular work to employees in a particular labor organization or in a particular trade, craft, or class rather than to employees in another labor organization or in another trade, craft, or class, unless such employer is failing to conform to an order or certification of the Board determining the bargaining representative for employees performing such work:

Provided, That nothing contained in this subsection (b) shall be construed to make unlawful a refusal by any person to enter upon the premises of any employer (other than his own employer), if the employees of such employer are engaged in a strike ratified or approved by a representative of such employees whom such employer is required to recognize under this Act: *Provided further,* That for the purposes of this paragraph (4) only, nothing contained in such paragraph shall be construed to prohibit publicity, other than picketing, for the purpose of truthfully advising the public, including consumers and members of a labor organization, that a product or products are produced by an employer with whom the labor organization has a primary dispute and are distributed by another employer, as long as such publicity does not have an effect of inducing any individual employed by any person other than the primary employer in the course of his employment to refuse to pick up, deliver, or transport any goods, or not to perform any services, at the establishment of the employer engaged in such distribution;

(5) to require of employees covered by an agreement authorized under subsection (a)(3) the payment, as a condition precedent to becoming a member of such organization, of a fee in an amount which the Board finds excessive or discriminatory under all the circumstances. In making such a finding, the Board shall consider, among other relevant factors, the practices and customs of labor organizations in the particular industry, and the wages currently paid to the employees affected;

(6) to cause or attempt to cause an employer to pay or deliver or agree to pay or deliver any money or other thing of value, in the nature of an exaction, for services which are not performed or not to be performed; and

(7) to picket or cause to be picketed, or threaten to picket or cause to be picketed, any employer where an object thereof is forcing or requiring an employer to recognize or bargain with a labor organization as the representative of his employees, or forcing or requiring the employees of an employer to accept or select such labor organization as their collective bargaining representative, unless such labor organization is currently certified as the representative of such employees:

(A) where the employer has lawfully recognized in accordance with this Act any other labor organization and a question concerning representation may not appropriately be raised under section 9(c) of this Act,

(B) where within the preceding twelve months a valid election under section 9(c) of this Act has been conducted, or

(C) where such picketing has been conducted without a petition under section 9(c) being filed within a reasonable period of time not to exceed thirty days from the commencement of such picketing: *Provided,* That when such a petition has been filed the Board shall forthwith, without regard to the provisions of section 9(c)(1) or the absence of a showing of a substantial interest on the part of the labor organization, direct an election in such unit as the Board finds to be appropriate and shall certify the results thereof: *Provided further,* That nothing in this subparagraph (C) shall be construed to prohibit any picketing or other publicity for the purpose of truthfully advising the public (including consumers) that an employer does not employ members of, or have a contract with, a labor organization, unless an effect of such picketing is to induce any individual employed by any other person in the course of his employment, not to pick up, deliver or transport any goods or not to perform any services.

Nothing in this paragraph (7) shall be construed to permit any act which would otherwise be an unfair labor practice under this section 8(b).

(c) The expressing of any views, argument, or opinion, or the dissemination thereof, whether in written, printed, graphic, or visual form, shall not constitute or be evidence of an unfair labor practice under any of the provisions of this Act, if such expression contains no threat of reprisal or force or promise of benefit.

(d) For the purposes of this section, to bargain collectively is the performance of the mutual obligation of the employer and the representative of the employees to meet at reasonable times and confer in good faith with respect to wages, hours, and other terms and conditions of employment, or the negotiation of an agreement, or any question arising thereunder, and the execution of a written contract incorporating any agreement reached if requested by either party, but such obligation does not compel either party to agree to a proposal or require the making of a concession: *Provided,* That where there is in effect a collective-bargaining contract covering employees in an industry affecting commerce, the duty to bargain collectively shall also mean that no party to such contract shall terminate or modify such contract, unless the party desiring such termination or modification—

(1) serves a written notice upon the other party to the contract of the proposed termination or modification sixty days prior to the expiration date thereof, or in the event such contract contains no expiration date, sixty days prior to the time it is proposed to make such termination or modification;

(2) offers to meet and confer with the other party for the purpose of negotiating a new contract or a contract containing the proposed modifications;

(3) notifies the Federal Mediation and Conciliation Service within thirty days after such notice of the existence of a dispute, and simultaneously therewith notifies any State or Territorial agency established to mediate and conciliate disputes within the State or Territory where the dispute occurred, provided no agreement has been reached by that time; and

(4) continues in full force and effect, without resorting to strike or lockout, all the terms and conditions of the existing contract for a period of sixty days after such notice is given or until the expiration date of such contract, whichever occurs later:

The duties imposed upon employers, employees, and labor organizations by paragraphs (2), (3), and (4) shall become inapplicable upon an intervening certification of the Board, under which the labor organization or individual, which is a party to the contract, has been superseded as or ceased to be the representative of the employees subject to the provisions of section 9(a), and the duties so imposed shall not be construed as requiring either party to discuss or agree to any modification of the terms and conditions contained in a contract for a fixed period, if such modification is to become effective before such terms and conditions can be reopened under the provisions of the contract. Any employee who engages in a strike within the sixty-day period specified in this subsection shall lose his status as an employee of the employer engaged in the particular labor dispute, for the purposes of sections 8, 9, and 10 of this Act, as amended, but such loss of status for such employee shall terminate if and when he is reemployed by such employer.

(e) It shall be an unfair labor practice for any labor organization and any employer to enter into any contract or agreement, express or implied, whereby such employer ceases or refrains or agrees to cease or refrain from handling, using, selling, transporting or otherwise dealing in any of the products of any other employer, or to cease doing business with any other person, and any contract or agreement entered into heretofore or hereafter containing such an agreement shall be to such extent unenforceable and void: *Provided,* That nothing in this subsection (e) shall apply to an agreement between a labor organization and an employer in the construction industry relating to the contracting or subcontracting of work to be done at the site of the construction, alteration, painting, or repair of a building, structure, or other work: *Provided further,* That for the purposes of this subsection (e) and section 8(b)(4)(B) the terms "any employer," "any person engaged in commerce or in industry affecting commerce," and "any person" when used in relation to the terms "any other producer, processor, or manufacturer," "any other employer," or "any other person" shall not include persons in the relation of a jobber, manufacturer, contractor, or subcontractor working on the goods or premises of the jobber or manufacturer or performing parts of an integrated process of production in the apparel and clothing industry: *Provided further,* That nothing in this Act shall prohibit the enforcement of any agreement which is within the foregoing exception.

(f) It shall not be an unfair labor practice under subsections (a) and (b) of this section for an employer engaged primarily in the building and construction industry to make an agreement covering employees engaged (or who, upon their employment, will be engaged) in the building and construction industry with a labor organization of which building and construction employees are members (not established, maintained, or assisted by any action defined in section 8(a) of this Act as an unfair labor practice) because (1) the majority status of such labor organization has not been established under the provisions of section 9 of this Act prior to the making of such agreement, or (2) such agreement requires as a condition of employment, membership in such labor organization after the seventh day following the beginning of such employment or the effective date of the agreement, whichever is later, or (3) such agreement requires the employer to notify such labor organization of opportunities for employment with such employer, or gives such labor organization an opportunity to refer qualified applicants for such employment, or (4) such agreement specifies minimum training or experience qualifications for employment or provides for priority in opportunities for employment based upon length of service with such employer, in the industry or in the particular geographical area: *Provided,* That nothing in this subsection shall set aside the final proviso to section 8(a)(3) of this Act: *Provided further,* That any agreement which would be invalid, but for clause (1) of this subsection, shall not be a bar to a petition filed pursuant to section 9(c) or 9(e).*

REPRESENTATIVES AND ELECTIONS

SEC. 9. (a) Representatives designated or selected for the purposes of collective bargaining by the majority of the employees in a unit appropriate for such purposes, shall be the exclusive representatives of all the employees in such unit for the purposes of collective bargaining in respect to rates of pay, wages, hours of employment, or other conditions of employment: *Provided,* That any individual employee or a group of employees shall have the right at any time to present grievances to their employer and to have such grievances adjusted, without the intervention of the bargaining representative, as long as the adjustment is not inconsistent with the terms of a collective-bargaining contract or agreement then in effect: *Provided further,* That the bargaining representative has been given opportunity to be present at such adjustment.

(b) The Board shall decide in each case whether, in order to assure to employees the fullest freedom in exercising the rights guaranteed by this Act, the unit appropriate for the purposes of collective bargaining shall be the employer unit, craft unit, plant unit, or subdivision thereof: *Provided,* That the Board shall not (1) decide that any unit is appropriate for such purposes if

---

* Section 8(f) is inserted in the Act by subsection (a) of Section 705 of Public Law 86–257. Section 705(b) provides:

> Nothing contained in the amendment made by subsection (a) shall be construed as authorizing the execution or application of agreements requiring membership in a labor organization as a condition of employment in any State or Territory in which such execution or application is prohibited by State or Territorial law.

such unit includes both professional employees and employees who are not professional employees unless a majority of such professional employees vote for inclusion in such unit; or (2) decide that any craft unit is inappropriate for such purposes on the ground that a different unit has been established by a prior Board determination, unless a majority of the employees in the proposed craft unit vote against separate representations or (3) decide that any unit is appropriate for such purposes if it includes, together with other employees, any individual employed as a guard to enforce against employees and other persons rules to protect property of the employer or to protect the safety of persons on the employer's premises; but no labor organization shall be certified as the representative of employees in a bargaining unit of guards if such organization admits to membership, or is affiliated directly or indirectly with an organization which admits to membership, employees other than guards.

(c)(1) Wherever a petition shall have been filed, in accordance with such regulations as may be prescribed by the Board—

> (A) by an employee or group of employees or any individual or labor organization acting in their behalf alleging that a substantial number of employees (i) wish to be represented for collective bargaining and that their employer declines to recognize their representative as the representative defined in section 9(a), or (ii) assert that the individual or labor organization, which has been certified or is being currently recognized by their employer as the bargaining representative, is no longer a representative as defined in section 9(a); or
>
> (B) by an employer, alleging that one or more individuals or labor organizations have presented to him a claim to be recognized as the representative defined in section 9(a);

the Board shall investigate such petition and if it has reasonable cause to believe that a question of representation affecting commerce exists shall provide for an appropriate hearing upon due notice. Such hearing may be conducted by an officer or employee of the regional office, who shall not make any recommendations with respect thereto. If the Board finds upon the record of such hearing that such a question of representation exists, it shall direct an election by secret ballot and shall certify the results thereof.

(2) In determining whether or not a question of representation affecting commerce exists, the same regulations and rules of decision shall apply irrespective of the identity of the persons filing the petition or the kind of relief sought and in no case shall the Board deny a labor organization a place on the ballot by reason of an order with respect to such labor organization or its predecessor not issued in conformity with section 10(c).

(3) No election shall be directed in any bargaining unit or any subdivision within which, in the preceding twelve-month period, a valid election shall have been held. Employees engaged in an economic strike who are not entitled to reinstatement shall be eligible to vote under such regulations as the Board shall find are consistent with the purposes and provisions of this Act in any election conducted within twelve months after the commencement of the strike. In any election where none of the choices on the ballot receives a majority, a run-off shall be conducted, the ballot providing for a selection between the two choices receiving the largest and second largest number of valid votes cast in the election.

(4) Nothing in this section shall be construed to prohibit the waiving of hearings by stipulation for the purpose of a consent election in conformity with regulations and rules of decision of the Board.

(5) In determining whether a unit is appropriate for the purposes specified in subsection (b) the extent to which the employees have organized shall not be controlling.

(d) Whenever an order of the Board made pursuant to section 10(c) is based in whole or in part upon facts certified following an investigation pursuant to subsection (c) of this section and there is a petition for the enforcement or review of such order, such certification and the record of such investigation shall be included in the transcript of the entire record required to be filed under section 10(e) or 10(f), and thereupon the decree of the court enforcing, modifying, or setting aside in whole or in part the order of the Board shall be made and entered upon the pleadings, testimony, and proceedings set forth in such transcript.

(e)(1) Upon the filing with the Board, by 30 per centum or more of the employees in a bargaining unit covered by an agreement between their employer and a labor organization made pursuant to section 8(a)(3), of a petition alleging they desire that such authority be rescinded, the Board shall take a secret ballot of the employees in such unit and certify the results thereof to such labor organization and to the employer.

(2) No election shall be conducted pursuant to this subsection in any bargaining unit or any subdivision within which, in the preceding twelve-month period, a valid election shall have been held.

PREVENTION OF UNFAIR LABOR PRACTICES

Sec. 10. (a) The Board is empowered, as hereinafter provided, to prevent any person from engaging in any unfair labor practice (listed in section 8) affecting commerce. This power shall not be affected by any other means of adjustment or prevention that has been or may be established by agreement, law, or otherwise: *Provided,* That the Board is empowered by agreement with any agency of any State or Territory to cede to such agency jurisdiction over any cases in any industry (other than mining, manufacturing, communications, and transportation except where predominantly local in character) even though such cases may involve labor disputes affecting commerce, unless the provision of the State or Territorial statute applicable to the determination of such cases by such agency is inconsistent with the corresponding provision of this Act or has received a construction inconsistent therewith.

(b) Whenever it is charged that any person has engaged in or is engaging in any such unfair labor practice, the Board, or any agent or agency designated by the Board for such purposes, shall have power to issue and cause to be served upon such person a complaint stating the charges in that respect, and containing a notice of hearing before the Board or a member thereof, or before a designated agent or agency, at a place therein fixed, not less than five days after the serving of said complaint: *Provided,* That no complaint shall issue based upon any unfair labor practice occurring more than six months prior to the filing of the charge with the Board and the service of a copy thereof upon the person against whom such charge is made, unless the person aggrieved thereby was prevented from filing such charge by reason of service in the armed forces, in which event the six-month period shall be computed from the day of his discharge. Any such complaint may be amended by the member, agent, or agency conducting the hearing or the Board in its discretion at any time prior to the issuance of an order based thereon. The person so complained of shall have the right to file an answer to the original or amended complaint and to appear in person or otherwise and give testimony at the place and time fixed in the complaint. In the discretion of the member, agent, or agency conducting the hearing or the Board, any other person may be allowed to intervene in the said proceeding and to present testimony. Any such proceeding shall, so far as practicable, be conducted in accordance with the rules of evidence applicable in the district courts of the United States under the rules of civil procedure for the district courts of the United States, adopted by the Supreme Court of the United States pursuant to the Act of June 19, 1934 (U.S.C., title 28, secs. 723-B, 723-C).

(c) The testimony taken by such member, agent, or agency or the Board shall be reduced to writing and filed with the Board. Thereafter, in its discretion, the Board upon notice may take further testimony or hear argument. If upon the preponderance of the testimony taken the Board shall be of the opinion that any person named in the complaint has engaged in or is engaging in any such unfair labor practice, then the Board shall state its findings of fact and shall issue and cause to be served on such person an order requiring such person to cease and desist from such unfair labor practice, and to take such affirmative action including reinstatement of employees with or without back pay, as will effectuate the policies of this Act: *Provided,* That where an order directs reinstatement of an employee, back pay may be required of the employer or labor organization, as the case may be, responsible for the discrimination suffered by him: *And provided further,* That in determining whether a complaint shall issue alleging a violation of section 8(a)(1) or section 8(a)(2), and in deciding such cases, the same regulations and rules of decision shall apply irrespective of whether or not the labor organization affected is affiliated with a labor organization national or international in scope. Such order may further require such person to make reports from time to time showing the extent to which it has complied with the order. If upon the preponderance of the testimony taken the Board shall not be of the opinion that the person named in the complaint has engaged in or is engaging in any such unfair labor practice, then the Board shall state its findings of fact and shall issue an order dismissing the said complaint. No order of the Board shall require the reinstatement of any individual as an employee who has been suspended or discharged, or the payment to him of any back pay, if such individual was suspended or discharged for cause. In case the evidence is presented before a member of the Board, or before an examiner or examiners thereof, such member, or such examiner or examiners, as the case may be, shall issue and cause to be served on the parties to the proceeding a proposed report, together with a recommended order, which shall be filed with the Board, and if no exceptions are filed within twenty days after service thereof upon such parties, or within such further period as the Board may authorize, such recommended order shall become the order of the Board and become effective as therein prescribed.

(d) Until the record in a case shall have been filed in a court, as hereinafter provided, the Board may at any time, upon reasonable notice and in such manner as it shall deem proper, modify or set aside, in whole or in part, any finding or order made or issued by it.

(e) The Board shall have power to petition any court of appeals of the United States, or if all the courts of appeals to which application may be made are in vacation, any district court of the United States, within any circuit or district, respectively, wherein the unfair labor practice in question occurred or wherein such person resides or transacts business, for the enforcement of such order and for appropriate temporary relief or restraining order, and shall file in the court the record in the proceedings, as provided in section 2112 of title 28, United States Code. Upon the filing of such petition, the court shall cause notice thereof to be served upon such person, and thereupon shall have jurisdiction of the proceeding and of the question determined therein, and shall have power to grant such temporary relief or restraining order as it deems just and proper, and to make and enter a decree enforcing, modifying, and enforcing as so modified, or setting aside in whole or in part the order of the Board. No objection that has not been urged before the Board, its member, agent, or agency, shall be considered by the court, unless the failure or neglect to urge such objection shall be excused because of extraordinary circumstances. The findings of the Board with respect to questions of fact if supported by substantial evidence on the record considered as a whole shall be conclusive. If either party shall apply to the court for leave to adduce additional evidence and shall show to the satisfaction of the court that such additional evidence is material and that there were reasonable grounds for the failure to adduce such evidence in the hearing before the Board, its member, agent, or agency, the court may order such additional evidence to be taken before the Board, its member, agent, or agency, and to be made a part of the record. The Board may modify its findings as to the facts, or make new findings, by reason of additional evidence so taken and filed, and it shall file such modified or new findings, which findings with respect to questions of fact if supported by substantial evidence on the record considered as a whole shall be conclusive, and shall file its recommendations, if any, for the modification or setting aside of its original order. Upon the filing of the record with it the jurisdiction of the court shall be exclusive and its judgment and decree shall be final, except that the same shall be subject to review by the appropriate United States court of appeals if application was made to the district court as hereinabove provided, and by the Supreme Court of the United States upon writ of certiorari or certification as provided in section 1254 of title 28.

(f) Any person aggrieved by a final order of the Board granting or denying in whole or in part the relief sought may obtain a review of such order in any circuit court of appeals of the United States in the circuit wherein the unfair labor practice in question was alleged to have been engaged in or wherein such person resides or transacts business, or in the United States Court of Appeals for the District of Columbia, by filing in such court a written petition praying that the order of the Board be modified or set aside. A copy of such petition shall be forthwith transmitted by the clerk of the court to the Board, and thereupon the aggrieved party shall file in the court the record in the proceeding, certified by the Board, as provided in section 2112 of title 28, United States Code. Upon the filing of such petition, the court shall proceed in the same manner as in the case of an application by the Board under subsection (e) of this section, and shall have the same jurisdiction to grant to the Board such temporary relief or restraining order as it deems just and proper, and in like manner to make and enter a decree enforcing, modifying, and enforcing as so modified, or setting aside in whole or in part the order of the Board; the findings of the Board with respect to questions of fact if supported by substantial evidence on the record considered as a whole shall in like manner be conclusive.

(g) The commencement of proceedings under subsection (e) or (f) of this section shall not, unless specifically ordered by the court, operate as a stay of the Board's order.

(h) When granting appropriate temporary relief or a restraining order, or making and entering a decree enforcing, modifying, and enforcing as so modified, or setting aside in whole or in part an order of the Board, as provided in this section, the jurisdiction of courts sitting in equity shall not be limited by the Act entitled "An Act to amend the Judicial Code and to define and limit the jurisdiction of courts sitting in equity, and for other purposes," approved March 23, 1932 (U.S.C., Supp. VII, title 29, secs. 101–115).

(i) Petitions filed under this Act shall be heard expeditiously, and if possible within ten days after they have been docketed.

(j) The Board shall have power, upon issuance of a complaint as provided in subsection (b) charging that any person has engaged in or is engaging in an unfair labor practice, to petition any district court of the United States (including the District Court of the United States for the District of Columbia), within any district wherein the unfair labor practice in question is alleged to have occurred or wherein such person resides or transacts business, for appropriate temporary relief or restraining order. Upon the filing of any such petition the court shall cause notice thereof to be served upon such person, and thereupon shall have jurisdiction to grant to the Board such temporary relief or restraining order as it deems just and proper.

(k) Whenever it is charged that any person has engaged in an unfair labor practice within the meaning of paragraph (4)(D) of section 8(b), the Board is empowered and directed to hear and determine the dispute out of which such unfair labor practice shall have arisen, unless, within ten days after notice that such charge has been filed, the parties to such dispute submit to the Board satisfactory evidence that they have adjusted, or agreed upon methods for the voluntary adjustment of, the dispute. Upon compliance by the parties to the dispute with the decision of the Board or upon such voluntary adjustment of the dispute, such charge shall be dismissed.

(l) Whenever it is charged that any person has engaged in an unfair labor practice within the meaning of paragraph (4) (A), (B), or (C) of section 8(b), or section 8(e) or section 8(b)(7), the preliminary investigation of such charge shall be made forthwith and given priority over all other cases except cases of like character in the office where it is filed or to which it is referred. If, after such investigation, the officer or regional attorney to whom the matter may be referred has reasonable cause to believe such charge is true and that a complaint should issue, he shall, on behalf of the Board, petition any district court of the United States (including the District Court of the United States for the District of Columbia) within any district where the unfair labor practice in question has occurred, is alleged to have occurred, or wherein such person resides or transacts business, for appropriate injunctive relief pending the final adjudication of the Board with respect to such matter. Upon the filing of any such petition the district court shall have jurisdiction to grant such injunctive relief or temporary restraining order as it deems just and proper, notwithstanding any other provision of law: *Provided further,* That no temporary restraining order shall be issued without notice unless a petition alleges that substantial and irreparable injury to the charging party will be unavoidable and such temporary restraining order shall be effective for no longer than five days and will become void at the expiration of such period: *Provided further,* That such officer or regional attorney shall not apply for any restraining order under section 8(b)(7) if a charge against the employer under section 8(a)(2) has been filed and after the preliminary investigation, he has reasonable cause to believe that such charge is true and that a complaint should issue. Upon filing of any such petition the courts shall cause notice thereof to be served upon any person involved in the charge and such person, including the charging party, shall be given an opportunity to appear by counsel and present any relevant testimony: *Provided further,* That for the purposes of this subsection district courts shall be deemed to have jurisdiction of a labor organization (1) in the district in which such organization maintains its principal office, or (2) in any district in which its duly authorized officers or agents are engaged in promoting or protecting the interests of employee members. The service of legal process upon such officer or agent shall constitute service upon the labor organization and make such organizations a party to the suit. In situations where such relief is appropriate the procedure specified herein shall apply to charges with respect to section 8(b)(4)(D).

(m) Whenever it is charged that any person has engaged in an unfair labor practice within the meaning of subsection (a)(3) or (b)(2) of section 8, such charge shall be given priority over all other cases except cases of like character in the office where it is filed or to which it is referred and cases given priority under subsection (1).

INVESTIGATORY POWERS

Sec. 11. For the purpose of all hearings and investigations, which, in the opinion of the Board, are necessary and proper for the exercise of the powers vested in it by section 9 and section 10—

(1) The Board, or its duly authorized agents or agencies, shall at all reasonable times have access to, for the purpose of examination, and the right to copy any evidence of any person being investigated or proceeded against that relates to any matter under investigation or in question. The Board, or any member thereof, shall upon application of any party to such proceedings, forthwith issue to such party subpenas requiring the attendance and testimony of witnesses or the production of any evidence in such proceeding or investigation requested in such application. Within five days after the service of a subpena on any person requiring the production of any evidence in his possession or under his control, such person may petition the Board to revoke, and the Board shall revoke, such subpena if in its opinion the evidence whose production is required does not relate to any matter under investigation, or any matter in question in such proceedings, or if in its opinion such subpena does not describe with sufficient particularity the evidence whose production is required. Any member of the Board, or any agent or agency designated by the Board for such purposes, may administer oaths and affirmations, examine witnesses, and receive evidence. Such attendance of witnesses and the production of such evidence may be required from any place in the United States or any Territory or possession thereof, at any designated place of hearing.

(2) In case of contumacy or refusal to obey a subpena issued to any person, any district court of the United States or the United States courts of any Territory or possession, or the District Court of the United States for the District of Columbia, within the jurisdiction of which the inquiry is carried on or within the jurisdiction of which said person guilty of contumacy or refusal to obey is found or resides or transacts business, upon application by the Board shall have jurisdiction to issue to such person an order requiring such person to appear before the Board, its member, agent, or agency, there to produce evidence if so ordered, or there to give testimony touching the matter under investigation or in question; and any failure to obey such order of the court may be punished by said court as a contempt thereof.

(3) No person shall be excused from attending and testifying or from producing books, records, correspondence, documents, or other evidence in obedience to the subpena of the Board, on the ground that the testimony or evidence required of him may tend to incriminate him or subject him to a penalty or forfeiture; but no individual shall be prosecuted or subjected to any penalty or forfeiture for or on account of any transaction, matter, or thing

concerning which he is compelled, after having claimed his privilege against self-incrimination, to testify or produce evidence, except that such individual so testifying shall not be exempt from prosecution and punishment for perjury committed in so testifying.

(4) Complaints, orders, and other process and papers of the Board, its member, agent, or agency, may be served either personally or by registered mail or by telegraph or by leaving a copy thereof at the principal office or place of business of the person required to be served. The verified return by the individual so serving the same setting forth the manner of such service shall be proof of the same, and the return post office receipt or telegraph receipt therefor when registered and mailed or telegraphed as aforesaid shall be proof of service of the same. Witnesses summoned before the Board, its member, agent, or agency, shall be paid the same fees and mileage that are paid witnesses in the courts of the United States, and witnesses whose depositions are taken and the persons taking the same shall severally be entitled to the same fees as are paid for like services in the courts of the United States.

(5) All process of any court to which application may be made under this Act may be served in the judicial district wherein the defendant or other person required to be served resides or may be found.

(6) The several departments and agencies of the Government, when directed by the President, shall furnish the Board, upon its request, all records, papers, and information in their possession relating to any matter before the Board.

Sec. 12. Any person who shall willfully resist, prevent, impede, or interfere with any member of the Board or any of its agents or agencies in the performance of duties pursuant to this Act shall be punished by a fine of not more than $5,000 or by imprisonment for not more than one year, or both.

LIMITATIONS

Sec. 13. Nothing in this Act, except as specifically provided for herein, shall be construed so as either to interfere with or impede or diminish in any way the right to strike, or to affect the limitations or qualifications on that right.

Sec. 14. (a) Nothing herein shall prohibit any individual employed as a supervisor from becoming or remaining a member of a labor organization, but no employer subject to this Act shall be compelled to deem individuals defined herein as supervisors as employees for the purpose of any law, either national or local, relating to collective bargaining.

(b) Nothing in this Act shall be construed as authorizing the execution or application of agreements requiring membership in a labor organization as a condition of employment in any State or Territory in which such execution or application is prohibited by State or Territorial law.

(c)(1) The Board, in its discretion, may, by rule of decision or by published rules adopted pursuant to the Administrative Procedure Act, decline to assert jurisdiction over any labor dispute involving any class or category of employees, where, in the opinion of the Board, the effect of such labor dispute on commerce is not sufficiently substantial to warrant the exercise of its jurisdiction: *Provided,* That the Board shall not decline to assert jurisdiction over any labor dispute over which it would assert jurisdiction under the standards prevailing upon August 1, 1959.

(2) Nothing in this Act shall be deemed to prevent or bar any agency or the courts of any State or Territory (including the Commonwealth of Puerto Rico, Guam, and the Virgin Islands), from assuming and asserting jurisdiction over labor disputes over which the Board declines, pursuant to paragraph (1) of this subsection, to assert jurisdiction.

Sec. 15. Wherever the application of the provisions of section 272 of chapter 10 of the Act entitled "An Act to establish a uniform system of bankruptcy throughout the United States," approved July 1, 1898, and Acts amendatory thereof and supplementary thereto (U.S.C., title 11, sec. 672), conflicts with the application of the provisions of this Act, this Act shall prevail: *Provided*, That in any situation where the provisions of this Act cannot be validly enforced, the provisions of such other Acts shall remain in full force and effect.

Sec. 16. If any provision of this Act, or the application of such provision to any person or circumstances, shall be held invalid, the remainder of this Act, or the application of such provision to persons or circumstances other than those as to which it is held invalid, shall not be affected thereby.

Sec. 17. This Act may be cited as the "National Labor Relations Act."

Sec. 18. No petition entertained, no investigation made, no election held, and no certification issued by the National Labor Relations Board, under any of the provisions of section 9 of the National Labor Relations Act, as amended, shall be invalid by reason of the failure of the Congress of Industrial Organizations to have complied with the requirements of section 9(f), (g), or (h) of the aforesaid Act prior to December 22, 1949, or by reason of the failure of the American Federation of Labor to have complied with the provisions of section 9(f), (g), or (h) of the aforesaid Act prior to November 7, 1947: *Provided*, That no liability shall be imposed under any provision of this Act upon any person for failure to honor any election or certificate referred to above, prior to the effective date of this amendment: *Provided, however*, That this proviso shall not have the effect of setting aside or in any way affecting judgments or decrees heretofore entered under section 10(e) or (f) and which have become final.

EFFECTIVE DATE OF CERTAIN CHANGES*

Sec. 102. No provision of this title shall be deemed to make an unfair labor practice any act which was performed prior to the date of the enactment of this Act which did not constitute an unfair labor practice prior thereto, and the provisions of section 8(a)(3) and section 8(b)(2) of the National Labor Relations Act as amended by this title shall not make an unfair labor practice the performance of any obligation under a collective-bargaining agreement entered into prior to the date of the enactment of this Act, or (in the case of an agreement for a period of not more than one year) entered into on or after such date of enactment, but prior to the effective date of this title, if the performance of such obligation would not have constituted an unfair labor practice under section 8(3) of the National Labor Relations Act prior to the effective date of this title, unless such agreement was renewed or extended subsequent thereto.

Sec. 103. No provisions of this title shall affect any certification of representatives or any determination as to the appropriate collective-bargaining unit, which was made under section 9 of the National Labor Relations Act prior to the effective date of this title until one year after the date of such certification or if, in respect of any such certification, a collective-bargaining contract was entered into prior to the effective date of this title, until the end of the contract period or until one year after such date, whichever first occurs.

Sec. 104. The amendments made by this title shall take effect sixty days after the date of the enactment of this Act, except that the authority of the

* The effective date referred to in Sections 102, 103, and 104 is August 22, 1947. For effective dates of 1959 amendments, see footnote on first page of this text.

President to appoint certain officers conferred upon him by section 3 of the National Labor Relations Act as amended by this title may be exercised forthwith.

TITLE II—
CONCILIATION OF LABOR DISPUTES IN INDUSTRIES AFFECTING COMMERCE; NATIONAL EMERGENCIES

SEC. 201. That it is the policy of the United States that—

(a) sound and stable industrial peace and the advancement of the general welfare, health, and safety of the Nation and of the best interest of employers and employees can most satisfactorily be secured by the settlement of issues between employers and employees through the processes of conference and collective bargaining between employers and the representatives of their employees;

(b) the settlement of issues between employers and employees through collective bargaining may be advanced by making available full and adequate governmental facilities for conciliation, mediation, and voluntary arbitration to aid and encourage employers and the representatives of their employees to reach and maintain agreements concerning rates of pay, hours, and working conditions, and to make all reasonable efforts to settle their differences by mutual agreement reached through conferences and collective bargaining or by such methods as may be provided for in any applicable agreement for the settlement of disputes; and

(c) certain controversies which arise between parties to collective-bargaining agreements may be avoided or minimized by making available full and adequate governmental facilities for furnishing assistance to employers and the representatives of their employees in formulating for inclusion within such agreements provision for adequate notice of any proposed changes in the terms of such agreements, for the final adjustment of grievances or questions regarding the application or interpretation of such agreements, and other provisions designed to prevent the subsequent arising of such controversies.

SEC. 202. (a) There is hereby created an independent agency to be known as the Federal Mediation and Conciliation Service (herein referred to as the "service," except that for sixty days after the date of the enactment of this Act such term shall refer to the Conciliation Service of the Department of Labor). The Service shall be under the direction of a Federal Mediation and Conciliation Director (hereinafter referred to as the "Director"), who shall be appointed by the President by and with the advice and consent of the Senate. The Director shall receive compensation at the rate of $12,000* per annum. The Director shall not engage in any other business, vocation, or employment.

(b) The Director is authorized, subject to the civil-service laws, to appoint such clerical and other personnel as may be necessary for the execution of the functions of the Service, and shall fix their compensation in accordance with the Classification Act of 1923, as amended, and may, without regard to the provisions of the civil-service laws and the Classification Act of 1923, as amended, appoint and fix the compensation of such conciliators and mediators as may be necessary to carry out the functions of the Service. The Director is authorized to make such expenditures for supplies, facilities, and services as he deems necessary. Such expenditures shall be allowed and paid upon presenta-

* Pursuant to Public Law 88–426, 88th Congress, 2d Session, Title III, approved August 14, 1964, the salary of the Director shall be $27,000 per year.

tion of itemized vouchers therefor approved by the Director or by any employee designated by him for that purpose.

(c) The principal office of the Service shall be in the District of Columbia, but the Director may establish regional offices convenient to localities in which labor controversies are likely to arise. The Director may by order, subject to revocation at any time, delegate any authority and discretion conferred upon him by this Act to any regional director, or other officer or employee of the Service. The Director may establish suitable procedures for cooperation with State and local mediation agencies. The Director shall make an annual report in writing to Congress at the end of the fiscal year.

(d) All mediation and conciliation functions of the Secretary of Labor or the United States Conciliation Service under section 8 of the Act entitled "An Act to create a Department of Labor," approved March 4, 1913 (U.S.C., title 29, sec. 51), and all functions of the United States Conciliation Service under any other law are hereby transferred to the Federal Mediation and Conciliation Service, together with the personnel and records of the United States Conciliation Service. Such transfer shall take effect upon the sixtieth day after the date of enactment of this Act. Such transfer shall not affect any proceedings pending before the United States Conciliation Service or any certification, order, rule, or regulation theretofore made by it or by the Secretary of Labor. The Director and the Service shall not be subject in any way to the jurisdiction or authority of the Secretary of labor or any official or division of the Department of Labor.

FUNCTIONS OF THE SERVICE

SEC. 203. (a) It shall be the duty of the Service, in order to prevent or minimize interruptions of the free flow of commerce growing out of labor disputes, to assist parties to labor disputes in industries affecting commerce to settle such disputes through conciliation and mediation.

(b) The Service may proffer its services in any labor dispute in any industry affecting commerce, either upon its own motion or upon the request of one or more of the parties to the dispute, whenever in its judgment such dispute threatens to cause a substantial interruption of commerce. The Director and the Service are directed to avoid attempting to mediate disputes which would have only a minor effect on interstate commerce if State or other conciliation services are available to the parties. Whenever the Service does proffer its services in any dispute, it shall be the duty of the Service promptly to put itself in communication with the parties and to use its best efforts, by mediation and conciliation, to bring them to agreement.

(c) If the Director is not able to bring the parties to agreement by conciliation within a reasonable time, he shall seek to induce the parties voluntarily to seek other means of settling the dispute without resort to strike, lockout, or other coercion, including submission to the employees in the bargaining unit of the employer's last offer of settlement for approval or rejection in a secret ballot. The failure or refusal of either party to agree to any procedure suggested by the Director shall not be deemed a violation of any duty or obligation imposed by this Act.

(d) Final adjustment by a method agreed upon by the parties is hereby declared to be the desirable method for settlement of grievance disputes arising over the application or interpretation of an existing collective-bargaining agreement. The Service is directed to make its conciliation and mediation services available in the settlement of such grievance disputes only as a last resort and in exceptional cases.

SEC. 204. (a) In order to prevent or minimize interruptions of the free flow of commerce growing out of labor disputes, employers and employees and their representatives, in any industry affecting commerce, shall—

(1) exert every reasonable effort to make and maintain agreements concerning rates of pay, hours, and working conditions, including provision for adequate notice of any proposed change in the terms of such agreements;

(2) whenever a dispute arises over the terms or application of a collective-bargaining agreement and a conference is requested by a party or prospective party thereto, arrange promptly for such a conference to be held and endeavor in such conference to settle such dispute expeditiously; and

(3) in case such dispute is not settled by conference, participate fully and promptly in such meetings as may be undertaken by the Service under this Act for the purpose of aiding in a settlement of the dispute.

Sec. 205. (a) There is hereby created a National Labor-Management Panel which shall be composed of twelve members appointed by the President, six of whom shall be selected from among persons outstanding in the field of management and six of whom shall be selected from among persons outstanding in the field of labor. Each member shall hold office for a term of three years, except that any member appointed to fill a vacancy occurring prior to the expiration of the term for which his predecessor was appointed shall be appointed for the remainder of such term, and the terms of office of the members first taking office shall expire, as designated by the President at the time of appointment, four at the end of the first year, four at the end of the second year, and four at the end of the third year after the date of appointment. Members of the panel, when serving on business of the panel, shall be paid compensation at the rate of $25 per day, and shall also be entitled to receive an allowance for actual and necessary travel and subsistence expenses while so serving away from their places of residence.

(b) It shall be the duty of the panel, at the request of the Director, to advise in the avoidance of industrial controversies and the manner in which mediation and voluntary adjustment shall be administered, particularly with reference to controversies affecting the general welfare of the country.

NATIONAL EMERGENCIES

Sec. 206. Whenever in the opinion of the President of the United States, a threatened or actual strike or lock-out affecting an entire industry or a substantial part thereof engaged in trade, commerce, transportation, transmission, or communication among the several States or with foreign nations, or engaged in the production of goods for commerce, will, if permitted to occur or to continue, imperil the national health or safety, he may appoint a board of inquiry to inquire into the issues involved in the dispute and to make a written report to him within such time as he shall prescribe. Such report shall include a statement of the facts with respect to the dispute, including each party's statement of its position but shall not contain any recommendations. The President shall file a copy of such report with the Service and shall make its contents available to the public.

Sec. 207. (a) A board of inquiry shall be composed of a chairman and such other members as the President shall determine, and shall have power to sit and act in any place within the United States and to conduct such hearings either in public or in private, as it may deem necessary or proper, to ascertain the facts with respect to the causes and circumstances of the dispute.

(b) Members of a board of inquiry shall receive compensation at the rate of $50 for each day actually spent by them in the work of the board, together with necessary travel and subsistence expenses.

(c) For the purpose of any hearing or inquiry conducted by any board appointed under this title, the provisions of sections 9 and 10 (relating to the attendance of witnesses and the production of books, papers, and documents) of the Federal Trade Commission Act of September 16, 1914, as amended (U.S.C. 19, title 15, secs. 49 and 50, as amended), are hereby made applicable to the powers and duties of such board.

SEC. 208. (a) Upon receiving a report from a board of inquiry the President may direct the Attorney General to petition any district court of the United States having jurisdiction of the parties to enjoin such strike or lock-out or the continuing thereof, and if the court finds that such threatened or actual strike or lock-out—

(i) affects an entire industry or a substantial part thereof engaged in trade, commerce, transportation, transmission, or communication among the several States or with foreign nations, or engaged in the production of goods for commerce; and

(ii) if permitted to occur or to continue, will imperil the national health or safety, it shall have jurisdiction to enjoin any such strike or lock-out, or the continuing thereof, and to make such other orders as may be appropriate.

(b) In any case, the provisions of the Act of March 23, 1932, entitled "An Act to amend the Judicial Code and to define and limit the jurisdiction of courts sitting in equity, and for other purposes," shall not be applicable.

(c) The order or orders of the court shall be subject to review by the appropriate circuit court of appeals and by the Supreme Court upon writ of certiorari or certification as provided in sections 239 and 240 of the Judicial Code, as amended (U.S.C., title 29, secs. 346 and 347).

SEC. 209. (a) Whenever a district court has issued an order under section 208 enjoining acts or practices which imperil or threaten to imperil the national health or safety, it shall be the duty of the parties to the labor dispute giving rise to such order to make every effort to adjust and settle their differences, with the assistance of the Service created by this Act. Neither party shall be under any duty to accept, in whole or in part, any proposal of settlement made by the Service.

(b) Upon the issuance of such order, the President shall reconvene the board of inquiry which has previously reported with respect to the dispute. At the end of a sixty-day period (unless the dispute has been settled by that time), the board of inquiry shall report to the President the current position of the parties and the efforts which have been made for settlement, and shall include a statement by each party of its position and a statement of the employer's last offer of settlement. The President shall make such report available to the public. The National Labor Relations Board, within the succeeding fifteen days, shall take a secret ballot of the employees of each employer involved in the dispute on the question of whether they wish to accept the final offer of settlement made by their employer as stated by him and shall certify the results thereof to the Attorney General within five days thereafter.

SEC. 210. Upon the certification of the results of such ballot or upon a settlement being reached, whichever happens sooner, the Attorney General shall move the court to discharge the injunction, which motion shall then be granted and the injunction discharged. When such motion is granted, the

President shall submit to the Congress a full and comprehensive report of the proceedings, including the findings of the board of inquiry and the ballot taken by the National Labor Relations Board, together with such recommendations as he may see fit to make for consideration and appropriate action.

COMPILATION OF COLLECTIVE-BARGAINING AGREEMENTS, ETC.

SEC. 211. (a) For the guidance and information of interested representatives of employers, employees, and the general public, the Bureau of Labor Statistics of the Department of Labor shall maintain a file of copies of all available collective-bargaining agreements and other available agreements and actions thereunder settling or adjusting labor disputes. Such file shall be open to inspection under appropriate conditions prescribed by the Secretary of Labor, except that no specific information submitted in confidence shall be disclosed.

(b) The Bureau of Labor Statistics in the Department of Labor is authorized to furnish upon request of the Service, or employers, employees, or their representatives, all available data and factual information which may aid in the settlement of any labor dispute, except that no specific information submitted in confidence shall be disclosed.

EXEMPTION OF RAILWAY LABOR ACT

SEC. 212. The provisions of this title shall not be applicable with respect to any matter which is subject to the provisions of the Railway Labor Act, as amended from time to time.

TITLE III

SUITS BY AND AGAINST LABOR ORGANIZATIONS

SEC. 301. (a) Suits for violation of contracts between an employer and a labor organization representing employees in an industry affecting commerce as defined in this Act, or between any such labor organizations, may be brought in any district court of the United States having jurisdiction of the parties, without respect to the amount in controversy or without regard to the citizenship of the parties.

(b) Any labor organization which represents employees in an industry affecting commerce as defined in this Act and any employer whose activities affect commerce as defined in this Act shall be bound by the acts of its agents. Any such labor organization may sue or be sued as an entity and in behalf of the employees whom it represents in the courts of the United States. Any money judgment against a labor organization in a district court of the United States shall be enforceable only against the organization as an entity and against its assets, and shall not be enforceable against any individual member or his assets.

(c) For the purposes of actions and proceedings by or against labor organizations in the district courts of the United States, district courts shall be deemed to have jurisdiction of a labor organization (1) in the district in which such organization maintains its principal offices, or (2) in any district in which its duly authorized officers or agents are engaged in representing or acting for employee members.

(d) The service of summons, subpena, or other legal process of any court of the United States upon an officer or agent of a labor organization, in his capacity as such, shall constitute service upon the labor organization.

(e) For the purposes of this section, in determining whether any person is acting as an "agent" of another person so as to make such other person responsible for his acts, the question of whether the specific acts performed were actually authorized or subsequently ratified shall not be controlling.

RESTRICTIONS ON PAYMENTS TO EMPLOYEE REPRESENTATIVES

SEC. 302. (a) It shall be unlawful for any employer or association of employers or any person who acts as a labor relations expert, adviser, or consultant to an employer or who acts in the interest of an employer to pay, lend, or deliver, or agree to pay, lend, or deliver, any money or other thing of value—

(1) to any representative of any of his employees who are employed in an industry affecting commerce; or

(2) to any labor organization, or any officer or employee thereof, which represents, seeks to represent, or would admit to membership, any of the employees of such employer who are employed in an industry affecting commerce; or

(3) to any employee or group or committee of employees of such employer employed in an industry affecting commerce in excess of their normal compensation for the purpose of causing such employee or group or committee directly or indirectly to influence any other employees in the exercise of the right to organize and bargain collectively through representatives of their own choosing; or

(4) to any officer or employee of a labor organization engaged in an industry affecting commerce with intent to influence him in respect to any of his actions, decisions, or duties as a representative of employees or as such officer or employee of such labor organization.

(b)(1) It shall be unlawful for any person to request, demand, receive, or accept, or agree to receive or accept, any payment, loan, or delivery of any money or other thing of value prohibited by subsection (a).

(2) It shall be unlawful for any labor organization, or for any person acting as an officer, agent, representative, or employee of such labor organization, to demand or accept from the operator of any motor vehicle (as defined in part II of the Interstate Commerce Act) employed in the transportation of property in commerce, or the employer of any such operator, any money or other thing of value payable to such organization or to an officer, agent, representative or employee thereof as a fee or charge for the unloading, or the connection with the unloading, of the cargo of such vehicle: *Provided*, That nothing in this paragraph shall be construed to make unlawful any payment by an employer to any of his employees as compensation for their services as employees.

(c) The provisions of this section shall not be applicable (1) in respect to any money or other thing of value payable by an employer to any of his employees whose established duties include acting openly for such employer in matters of labor relations or personnel administration or to any representative of his employees, or to any officer or employee of a labor organization, who is also an employee or former employee of such employer, as compensation for, or by reason of, his service as an employee of such employer; (2) with respect to the payment or delivery of any money or other thing of value in satisfaction of a judgment of any court or a decision or award of an arbitrator or impartial chairman or in compromise, adjustment, settlement, or release of any claim, complaint, grievance, or dispute in the absence of fraud or duress; (3) with respect to the sale or purchase of an article or commodity at the prevailing market price in the regular course of business; (4) with respect to money deducted from the wages of employees in payment of membership dues in a labor organization: *Provided*, That the employer has received from each employee, on whose account such deductions are made, a written assignment which shall not be irrevocable for a period of more than one year, or beyond the termination date of the applicable collective agreement, whichever occurs sooner; (5) with respect to money or other thing of value paid to a trust fund established by such representative, for the sole and exclusive benefit of the employees of such employer, and their families and dependents (or of such employees, families, and dependents jointly with the employees of other employers making similar payments, and their families and dependents): *Provided*, That (A) such payments are held in trust for the purpose of paying, either from principal or income or both, for the benefit of employees, their families and dependents, for medical or hospital care, pensions on retirement or death of employees, compensation for injuries or illness resulting from occupational activity or insurance to provide any of the foregoing, or unemployment benefits or life insurance, disability and sickness insurance, or accident insurance; (B) the detailed basis on which such payments are to be made is specified in a written agreement with the employer, and employees and employers are equally represented in the administration of such fund, together with such neutral persons as the representatives of the employers and the representatives of employees may agree upon and in the event the employer and employee groups deadlock on the administration of such fund and there are no neutral persons empowered to break such deadlock, such agreement provides that the two groups shall agree on an impartial umpire to decide such dispute, or in event of their failure to agree within a reasonable length of time, an impartial umpire to decide such dispute shall, on petition of either group, be appointed by the district court of the United States for the district where the trust fund has its principal office, and shall also contain provisions for an annual audit of the trust fund, a statement of the results of which shall be available for inspection by interested persons at the principal office of the trust fund and at such other places as may be designated in such written agreement; and (C) such payments as are intended to be used for the purpose of providing pension or annuities for employees are made to a separate trust which provides that the funds held therein cannot be used for any purpose other than paying such pensions or annuities; or (6) with respect to money or other thing of value paid by any employer to a trust fund established by such representative for the purpose of pooled vacation, holiday, severance or similar benefits, or defraying costs of apprenticeship or other training program: *Provided*, That the requirements of clause (B) of the proviso to clause (5) of this subsection shall apply to such trust funds.

(d) Any person who willfully violates any of the provisions of this section shall, upon conviction thereof, be guilty of a misdemeanor and be subject to a fine of not more than $10,000 or to imprisonment for not more than one year, or both.

(e) The district courts of the United States and the United States courts of the Territories and possessions shall have jurisdiction, for cause shown, and subject to the provisions of section 17 (relating to notice to opposite party) of the Act entitled "An Act to supplement existing laws against unlawful restraints and monopolies, and for other purposes," approved October 15, 1914, as amended (U.S.C., title 28, sec. 381), to restrain violations of this section, without regard to the provisions of sections 6 and 20 of such Act of October 15, 1914, as amended (U.S.C., title 15, sec. 17, and title 29, sec. 52), and the provisions of the Act entitled "An Act to amend the Judicial Code and to define and limit the jurisdiction of courts sitting in equity, and for other purposes," approved March 23, 1932 (U.S.C., title 29, secs. 101–115).

(f) This section shall not apply to any contract in force on the date of enactment of this Act, until the expiration of such contract, or until July 1, 1948, whichever first occurs.

(g) Compliance with the restrictions contained in subsection (c)(5)(B) upon contributions to trust funds, otherwise lawful, shall not be applicable to contributions to such trust funds established by collective agreement prior to January 1, 1946, nor shall subsection (c)(5)(A) be construed as prohibiting contributions to such trust funds if prior to January 1, 1947, such funds contained provisions for pooled vacation benefits.

BOYCOTTS AND OTHER UNLAWFUL COMBINATIONS

SEC. 303. (a) It shall be unlawful, for the purpose of this section only, in an industry or activity affecting commerce, for any labor organization to engage in any activity or conduct defined as an unfair labor practice in section 8(b)(4) of the National Labor Relations Act, as amended.

(b) Whoever shall be injured in his business or property by reason of any violation of subsection (a) may sue therefore in any district court of the United States subject to the limitations and provisions of section 301 hereof without respect to the amount in controversy, or in any other court having jurisdiction of the parties, and shall recover the damages by him sustained and the cost of the suit.

RESTRICTION ON POLITICAL CONTRIBUTIONS

SEC. 304. Section 313 of the Federal Corrupt Practices Act, 1925 (U.S.C., 1940 edition, title 2, sec. 251; Supp. V, title 50, App., sec. 1509), as amended, is amended to read as follows:

SEC. 313. It is unlawful for any national bank, or any corporation organized by authority of any law of Congress to make a contribution or expenditure in connection with any election to any political office, or in connection with any primary election or political convention or caucus held to select candidates for any political office, or for any corporation whatever, or any labor organization to make a contribution or expenditure in connection with any election at which Presidential and Vice Presidential electors or a Senator or Representative in, or a Delegate or Resident Commissioner to Congress are to be voted for, or in connection with any primary election or political convention or caucus held to select candidates for any of the foregoing offices, or for any candidate, political committee, or other person to accept or receive any contribution prohibited by this section. Every corporation or labor organization which makes any contribution or expenditure in violation of this section shall be fined not more than $5,000; and every officer or director of any corporation, or officer of any labor organization, who consents to any contribution or expenditure by the corporation or labor organization, as the case may be, in violation of this section shall be fined not more than $1,000 or imprisoned for not more than one year, or both. For the purposes of this section "labor organization" means any organization of any kind, or any agency or employee representation committee or plan, in which employees participate and which exists for the purpose, in whole or in part, of dealing with employers concerning grievances, labor disputes, wages, rates of pay, hours of employment, or conditions of work.

TITLE IV

CREATION OF JOINT COMMITTEE TO STUDY AND REPORT ON BASIC PROBLEMS AFFECTING FRIENDLY LABOR RELATIONS AND PRODUCTIVITY

* * * * * * *

TITLE V

DEFINITIONS

SEC. 501. When used in this Act—

(1) The term "industry affecting commerce" means any industry or activity in commerce or in which a labor dispute would burden or obstruct commerce or tend to burden or obstruct commerce or the free flow of commerce.

(2) The term "strike" includes any strike or other concerted stoppage of work by employees (including a stoppage by reason of the expiration of a collective-bargaining agreement) and any concerted slow-down or other concerted interruption of operations by employees.

(3) The terms "commerce," "labor disputes," "employer," "employee," "labor organization," "representative," "person," and "supervisor" shall have the same meaning as when used in the National Labor Relations Act as amended by this Act.

SAVING PROVISION

SEC. 502. Nothing in this Act shall be construed to require an individual employee to render labor or service without his consent, nor shall anything in this Act be construed to make the quitting of his labor by an individual employee an illegal act; nor shall any court issue any process to compel the performance by an individual employee of such labor or service, without his consent; nor shall the quitting of labor by an employee or employees in good faith because of abnormally dangerous conditions for work at the place of employment of such employee or employees be deemed a strike under this Act.

SEPARABILITY

SEC. 503. If any provision of this Act, or the application of such provision to any person or circumstance, shall be held invalid, the remainder of this Act, or the application of such provision to persons or circumstances other than those as to which it is held invalid, shall not be affected thereby.

THE LANDRUM-GRIFFIN ACT OF 1959 AS AMENDED

Popularly known as the "union reform law," the Landrum-Griffin Act contains seven titles, the first six regulating the internal affairs of unions and employers and the seventh amending the Taft-Hartley Act. Landrum-Griffin Title VII amendments to the Taft-Hartley Act are shown in that act above. What follows is the first six titles of the Landrum-Griffin Act.

LABOR-MANAGEMENT REPORTING AND DISCLOSURE ACT OF 1959, AS AMENDED[1]

[Revised text showing in bold face new or amended language provided by Public Law 89—216, as enacted September 29, 1965, 79 Stat. 888]

AN ACT

To provide for the reporting and disclosure of certain financial transactions and administrative practices of labor organizations and employers, to prevent

[1] Public Law 257, 86th Congress (73 Stat. 519–546), as amended by Public Law 216, 89th Congress (79 Stat. 888). This revised text has been prepared by the U.S. Department of Labor.

abuses in the administration of trusteeships by labor organizations, to provide standards with respect to the election of officers of labor organizations, and for other purposes.

Be it enacted by the Senate and House of Representatives of the United States of America in Congress assembled, That this Act may be cited as the "Labor-Management Reporting and Disclosure Act of 1959."

Declaration of Findings, Purposes, and Policy
(29 U.S.C. 401)

SEC. 2. (a) The Congress finds that, in the public interest, it continues to be the responsibility of the Federal Government to protect employees' rights to organize, choose their own representatives, bargain collectively, and otherwise engage in concerted activities for their mutual aid or protection; that the relations between employers and labor organizations and the millions of workers they represent have a substantial impact on the commerce of the Nation; and that in order to accomplish the objective of a free flow of commerce it is essential that labor organizations, employers, and their officials adhere to the highest standards of responsibility and ethical conduct in administering the affairs of their organizations, particularly as they affect labor-management relations.

(b) The Congress further finds, from recent investigations in the labor and management fields, that there have been a number of instances of breach of trust, corruption, disregard of the rights of individual employees, and other failures to observe high standards of responsibility and ethical conduct which require further and supplementary legislation that will afford necessary protection of the rights and interests of employees and the public generally as they relate to the activities of labor organizations, employers, labor relations consultants, and their officers and representatives.

(c) The Congress, therefore, further finds and declares that the enactment of this Act is necessary to eliminate or prevent improper practices on the part of labor organizations, employers, labor relations consultants, and their officers and representatives which distort and defeat the policies of the Labor Management Relations Act, 1947, as amended, and the Railway Labor Act, as amended, and have the tendency or necessary effect of burdening or obstructing commerce by (1) impairing the efficiency, safety, or operation of the instrumentalities of commerce; (2) occurring in the current of commerce; (3) materially affecting, restraining, or controlling the flow of raw materials or manufactured or processed goods into or from the channels of commerce, or the prices of such materials or goods in commerce; or (4) causing diminution of employment and wages in such volume as substantially to impair or disrupt the market for goods flowing into or from the channels of commerce.

Definitions
(29 U.S.C. 402)

SEC. 3. For the purposes of titles I, II, III, IV, V (except section 505), and VI of this Act—

(a) "Commerce" means trade, traffic, commerce, transportation, transmission, or communication among the several States or between any State and any place outside thereof.

(b) "State" includes any State of the United States, the District of Columbia, Puerto Rico, the Virgin Islands, American Samoa, Guam, Wake Island, the Canal Zone, and Outer Continental Shelf lands defined in the Outer Continental Shelf Lands Act (43 U.S.C. 1331–1343).

(c) "Industry affecting commerce" means any activity, business, or industry in commerce or in which a labor dispute would hinder or obstruct commerce or the free flow of commerce and includes any activity or industry "affecting commerce" within the meaning of the Labor Management Relations Act, 1947, as amended, or the Railway Labor Act, as amended.

(d) "Person" includes one or more individuals, labor organizations, partnerships, associations, corporations, legal representatives, mutual companies, joint-stock companies, trusts, unincorporated organizations, trustees, trustees in bankruptcy, or receivers.

(e) "Employer" means any employer or any group or association of employers engaged in an industry affecting commerce (1) which is, with respect to employees engaged in an industry affecting commerce, an employer within the meaning of any law of the United States relating to the employment of any employees or (2) which may deal with any labor organization concerning grievances, labor disputes, wages, rates of pay, hours of employment, or conditions of work, and includes any person acting directly or indirectly as an employer or as an agent of an employer in relation to an employee but does not include the United States or any corporation wholly owned by the Government of the United States or any State or political subdivision thereof.

(f) "Employee" means any individual employed by an employer, and includes any individual whose work has ceased as a consequence of, or in connection with, any current labor dispute or because of any unfair labor practice or because of exclusion or expulsion from a labor organization in any manner or for any reason inconsistent with the requirements of this Act.

(g) "Labor dispute" includes any controversy concerning terms, tenure, or conditions of employment, or concerning the association or representation of persons in negotiating, fixing, maintaining, changing, or seeking to arrange terms or conditions of employment, regardless of whether the disputants stand in the proximate relation of employer and employee.

(h) "Trusteeship" means any receivership, trusteeship, or other method of supervision or control whereby a labor organization suspends the autonomy otherwise available to a subordinate body under its constitution or bylaws.

(i) "Labor organization" means a labor organization engaged in an industry affecting commerce and includes any organization of any kind, any agency, or employee representation committee, group, association, or plan so engaged in which employees participate and which exists for the purpose, in whole or in part, of dealing with employers concerning grievances, labor disputes, wages, rates of pay, hours, or other terms or conditions of employment, and any conference, general committee, joint or system board, or joint council so engaged which is subordinate to a national or international labor organization, other than a State or local central body.

(j) A labor organization shall be deemed to be engaged in an industry affecting commerce if it—

(1) is the certified representative of employees under the provisions of the National Labor Relations Act, as amended, or the Railway Labor Act, as amended; or

(2) although not certified, is a national or international labor organization or a local labor organization recognized or acting as the representative of employees or an employer or employers engaged in an industry affecting commerce; or

(3) has chartered a local labor organization or subsidiary body which is representing or actively seeking to represent employees of employers within the meaning of paragraph (1) or (2); or

(4) has been chartered by a labor organization representing or actively seeking to represent employees within the meaning of paragraph (1) or (2) as the local or subordinate body through which such employees may enjoy membership or become affiliated with such labor organization; or

(5) is a conference, general committee, joint or system board, or joint council, subordinate to a national or international labor organization, which includes a labor organization engaged in an industry affecting commerce within the meaning of any of the preceding paragraphs of this subsection, other than a State or local central body.

(k) "Secret ballot" means the expression by ballot, voting machine, or otherwise, but in no event by proxy, of a choice with respect to any election or vote taken upon any matter, which is cast in such a manner that the person expressing such choice cannot be identified with the choice expressed.

(1) "Trust in which a labor organization is interested" means a trust or other fund or organization (1) which was created or established by a labor organization, or one or more of the trustees or one or more members of the governing body of which is selected or appointed by a labor organization, and (2) a primary purpose of which is to provide benefits for the members of such labor organization or their beneficiaries.

(m) "Labor relations consultant" means any person who, for compensation, advises or represents an employer, employer organization, or labor organization concerning employee organizing, concerted activities, or collective bargaining activities.

(n) "Officer" means any constitutional officer, any person authorized to perform the functions of president, vice president, secretary, treasurer, or other executive functions of a labor organization, and any member of its executive board or similar governing body.

(o) "Member" or "member in good standing," when used in reference to a labor organization, includes any person who has fulfilled the requirements for membership in such organization, and who neither has voluntarily withdrawn from membership nor has been expelled or suspended from membership after appropriate proceedings consistent with lawful provisions of the constitution and bylaws of such organization.

(p) "Secretary" means the Secretary of Labor.

(q) "Officer, agent, shop steward, or other representative," when used with respect to a labor organization, includes elected officials and key administrative personnel, whether elected or appointed (such as business agents, heads of departments or major units, and organizers who exercise substantial independent authority), but does not include salaried nonsupervisory professional staff, stenographic, and service personnel.

(r) "District court of the United States" means a United States district court and a United States court of any place subject to the jurisdiction of the United States.

TITLE 1—BILL OF RIGHTS OF MEMBERS OF LABOR ORGANIZATIONS

Bill of Rights
(29 U.S.C. 411)

SEC. 101. (a)(1) EQUAL RIGHTS.—Every member of a labor organization shall have equal rights and privileges within such organization to nominate candidates, to vote in elections or referendums of the labor organization, to attend membership meetings and to participate in the deliberations and voting upon the business of such meetings, subject to reasonable rules and regulations in such organization's constitution and bylaws.

(2) FREEDOM OF SPEECH AND ASSEMBLY.—Every member of any labor organization shall have the right to meet and assemble freely with other members; and to express any views, arguments, or opinions; and to express at meetings of the labor organization his views, upon candidates in an election of the labor organization or upon any business properly before the meeting, subject to the organization's established and reasonable rules pertaining to the conduct of meetings: *Provided*, That nothing herein shall be construed to impair the right of a labor organization to adopt and enforce reasonable rules as to the responsibility of every member toward the organization as an institution and to his refraining from conduct that would interfere with its performance of its legal or contractual obligations.

(3) DUES, INITIATION FEES, AND ASSESSMENTS.—Except in the case of a federation of national or international labor organizations, the rates of dues and initiation fees payable by members of any labor organization in effect on the date of enactment of this Act shall not be increased, and no general or special assessment shall be levied upon such members, except—

(A) in the case of a local organization, (i) by majority vote by secret ballot of the members in good standing voting at a general or special membership meeting, after reasonable notice of the intention to vote upon such question, or (ii) by majority vote of the members in good standing voting in a membership referendum conducted by secret ballot; or

(B) in the case of a labor organization, other than a local labor organization or a federation of national or international labor organizations, (i) by majority vote of the delegates voting at a regular convention, or at a special convention of such labor organization held upon not less than thirty days' written notice to the principal office of each local or constituent labor organization entitled to such notice, or (ii) by majority vote of the members in good standing of such labor organization voting in a membership referendum conducted by secret ballot, or (iii) by majority vote of the members of the executive board or similar governing body of such labor organization, pursuant to express authority contained in the constitution and bylaws of such labor organization: *Provided*, That such action on the part of the executive board or similar governing body shall be effective only until the next regular convention of such labor organization.

(4) PROTECTION OF THE RIGHT TO SUE.—No labor organization shall limit the right of any member thereof to institute an action in any court, or in a proceeding before any administrative agency, irrespective of whether or not the labor organization or its officers are named as defendants or respondents in such action or proceeding, or the right of any member of a labor organization to appear as a witness in any judicial, administrative, or legislative proceeding, or to petition any legislature or to communicate with any legislator: *Provided*, That any such member may be required to exhaust reasonable hearing procedures (but not to exceed a four-month lapse of time) within such organization, before instituting legal or administrative proceedings against such organizations or any officer thereof: *And provided further*, That no interested employer or employer association shall directly or indirectly finance, encourage, or participate in, except as a party, any such action, proceeding, appearance, or petition.

(5) SAFEGUARDS AGAINST IMPROPER DISCIPLINARY ACTION.—No member of any labor organization may be fined, suspended, expelled, or otherwise disciplined except for nonpayment of dues by such organization or by any officer thereof unless such member has been (A) served with written specific

charges; (B) given a reasonable time to prepare his defense; (C) afforded a full and fair hearing.

(b) Any provision of the constitution and bylaws of any labor organization which is inconsistent with the provisions of this section shall be of no force or effect.

Civil Enforcement
(29 U.S.C. 412)

SEC. 102. Any person whose rights secured by the provisions of this title have been infringed by any violation of this title may bring a civil action in a district court of the United States for such relief (including injunctions) as may be appropriate. Any such action against a labor organization shall be brought in the district court of the United States for the district where the alleged violation occurred, or where the principal office of such labor organization is located.

Retention of Existing Rights
(29 U.S.C. 413)

SEC. 103. Nothing contained in this title shall limit the rights and remedies of any member of a labor organization under any State or Federal law before any court or other tribunal, or under the constitution and bylaws of any labor organization.

Right to Copies of Collective Bargaining Agreements
(29 U.S.C. 414)

SEC. 104. It shall be the duty of the secretary or corresponding principal officer of each labor organization, in the case of a local labor organization, to forward a copy of each collective bargaining agreement made by such labor organization with any employer to any employee who requests such a copy and whose rights as such employee are directly affected by such agreement, and in the case of a labor organization other than a local labor organization, to forward a copy of any such agreement to each constituent unit which has members directly affected by such agreement; and such officer shall maintain at the principal office of the labor organization of which he is an officer copies of any such agreement made or received by such labor organization, which copies shall be available for inspection by any member or by any employee whose rights are affected by such agreement. The provisions of section 210 shall be applicable in the enforcement of this section.

Information as to Act
(29 U.S.C. 415)

SEC. 105. Every labor organization shall inform its members concerning the provisions of this Act.

TITLE II—REPORTING BY LABOR ORGANIZATIONS, OFFICERS AND EMPLOYEES OF LABOR ORGANIZATIONS, AND EMPLOYERS

Report of Labor Organizations
(29 U.S.C. 431)

SEC. 201. (a) Every labor organization shall adopt a constitution and bylaws and shall file a copy thereof with the Secretary, together with a report, signed by its president and secretary or corresponding principal officers, containing the following information—

(1) the name of the labor organization, its mailing address, and any other address at which it maintains its principal office or at which it keeps the records referred to in this title;

(2) the name and title of each of its officers;

(3) the initiation fee or fees required from a new or transferred member and fees for work permits required by the reporting labor organization;

(4) the regular dues or fees of other periodic payments required to remain a member of the reporting labor organization; and

(5) detailed statements, or references to specific provisions of documents filed under this subsection which contain such statements, showing the provisions made and procedures followed with respect to each of the following: (A) qualifications for or restrictions on membership, (B) levying of assessments, (C) participation in insurance or other benefit plans, (D) authorization for disbursement of funds of the labor organization, (E) audit of financial transactions of the labor organization, (F) the calling of regular and special meetings, (G) the selection of officers and stewards and of any representatives to other bodies composed of labor organizations' representatives, with a specific statement of the manner in which each officer was elected, appointed, or otherwise selected, (H) discipline or removal of officers or agents for breaches of their trust, (I) imposition of fines, suspensions, and expulsions of members, including the grounds for such action and any provision made for notice, hearing, judgment on the evidence, and appeal procedures, (J) authorization for bargaining demands, (K) ratification of contract terms, (L) authorization for strikes, and (M) issuance of work permits. Any change in the information required by this subsection shall be reported to the Secretary at the time the reporting labor organization files with the Secretary the annual financial report required by subsection (b).

(b) Every labor organization shall file annually with the Secretary a financial report signed by its president and treasurer or corresponding principal officers containing the following information in such detail as may be necessary accurately to disclose its financial condition and operations for its preceding fiscal year—

(1) assets and liabilities at the beginning and end of the fiscal year;

(2) receipts of any kind and the sources thereof;

(3) salary, allowances, and other direct or indirect disbursements (including reimbursed expenses) to each officer and also to each employee who, during such fiscal year, received more than $10,000 in the aggregate from such labor organization and any other labor organization affiliated with it or with which it is affiliated, or which is affiliated with the same national or international labor organization;

(4) direct and indirect loans made to any officer, employee, or member, which aggregated more than $250 during the fiscal year, together with a statement of the purpose, security, if any, and arrangements for repayment;

(5) direct and indirect loans to any business enterprise, together with a statement of the purpose, security, if any, and arrangements for repayment; and

(6) other disbursements made by it including the purposes thereof; all in such categories as the Secretary may prescribe.

(c) Every labor organization required to submit a report under this title shall make available the information required to be contained in such report to all of its members, and every such labor organization and its officers shall be under a duty enforceable at the suit of any member of such organization in any State court of competent jurisdiction or in the district court of the United States for the district in which such labor organization maintains its principal office, to permit such member for just cause to examine any books, records, and accounts necessary to verify such report. The court in such action may, in its discretion, in addition to any judgment awarded to the plaintiff or plaintiffs, allow a reasonable attorney's fee to be paid by the defendant, and costs of the action.

(d) Subsections (f), (g), and (h) of section 9 of the National Labor Relations Act, as amended, are hereby repealed.

(e) Clause (i) of section 8(a) (3) of the National Labor Relations Act, as amended, is amended by striking out the following: "and has at the time the agreement was made or within the preceding twelve months received from the Board a notice of compliance with sections 9 (f), (g), (h)."

Report of Officers and Employees of Labor Organizations
(29 U.S.C. 432)

SEC. 202. (a) Every officer of a labor organization and every employee of a labor organization (other than an employee performing exclusively clerical or custodial services) shall file with the Secretary a signed report listing and describing for his preceding fiscal year—

(1) any stock, bond, security, or other interest, legal or equitable, which he or his spouse or minor child directly or indirectly held in, and any income or any other benefit with monetary value (including reimbursed expenses) which he or his spouse or minor child derived directly or indirectly from, an employer whose employees such labor organization represents or is actively seeking to represent, except payments and other benefits received as a bona fide employee of such employer;

(2) any transaction in which he or his spouse or minor child engaged, directly or indirectly, involving any stock, bond, security, or loan to or from other legal or equitable interest in the business of an employer whose employees such labor organization represents or is actively seeking to represent;

(3) any stock, bond, security, or other interest, legal or equitable, which he or his spouse or minor child directly or indirectly held in, and any income or any other benefit with monetary value (including reimbursed expenses) which he or his spouse or minor child directly or indirectly derived from, any business a substantial part of which consists of buying from, selling or leasing to, or otherwise dealing with, the business of an employer whose employees such labor organization represents or is actively seeking to represent;

(4) any stock, bond, security, or other interest, legal or equitable, which he or his spouse or minor child directly or indirectly held in, and any income or any other benefit with monetary value (including reimbursed expenses) which he or his spouse or minor child directly or indirectly derived from, a business any part of which consists of buying from, or selling or leasing directly or indirectly to, or otherwise dealing with such labor organization;

(5) any direct or indirect business transaction or arrangement between him or his spouse or minor child and any employer whose employees his organization represents or is actively seeking to represent, except work performed and payments and benefits received as a bona fide employee of such employer and except purchases and sales of goods or services in the

regular course of business at prices generally available to any employee of such employer; and

(6) any payment of money or other thing of value (including reimbursed expenses) which he or his spouse or minor child received directly or indirectly from any employer or any person who acts as a labor relations consultant to an employer, except payments of the kinds referred to in section 302(c) of the Labor Management Relations Act, 1947, as amended.

(b) The provisions of paragraphs (1), (2), (3), (4), and (5) of subsection (a) shall not be construed to require any such officer or employee to report his bona fide investments in securities traded on a securities exchange registered as a national securities exchange under the Securities Exchange Act of 1934, in shares in an investment company registered under the Investment Company Act of 1940, or in securities of a public utility holding company registered under the Public Utility Holding Company Act of 1935, or to report any income derived therefrom.

(c) Nothing contained in this section shall be construed to require any officer or employee of a labor organization to file a report under subsection (a) unless he or his spouse or minor child holds or has held an interest, has received income or any other benefit with monetary value or a loan, or has engaged in a transaction described therein.

Report of Employers
(29 U.S.C. 433)

SEC. 203. (a) Every employer who in any fiscal year made—

(1) any payment or loan, direct or indirect, of money or other thing of value (including reimbursed expenses), or any promise or agreement therefor, to any labor organization or officer, agent, shop steward, or other representative of a labor organization, or employee of any labor organization, except (A) payments or loans made by any national or State bank, credit union, insurance company, savings and loan association or other credit institution and (B) payments of the kind referred to in section 302(c) of the Labor Management Relations Act, 1947, as amended;

(2) any payment (including reimbursed expenses) to any of his employees, or any group or committee of such employees, for the purpose of causing such employee or group or committee of employees to persuade other employees to exercise or not to exercise, or as to the manner of exercising, the right to organize and bargain collectively through representatives of their own choosing unless such payments were contemporaneously or previously disclosed to such other employees;

(3) any expenditure, during the fiscal year, where an object thereof, directly or indirectly, is to interfere with, restrain, or coerce employees in the exercise of the right to organize and bargain collectively through representatives of their own choosing, or is to obtain information concerning the activities of employees or a labor organization in connection with a labor dispute involving such employer, except for use solely in conjunction with an administrative or arbitral proceeding or a criminal or civil judicial proceeding;

(4) any agreement or arrangement with a labor relations consultant or other independent contractor or organization pursuant to which such person undertakes activities where an object thereof, directly or indirectly, is to persuade employees to exercise or not to exercise, or persuade employees as to the manner of exercising, the right to organize and bargain collectively through representatives of their own choosing, or undertakes to supply such employer with information concerning the activities of employees or a labor organization in connection with a labor dispute involving such employer,

except information for use solely in conjunction with an administrative or arbitral proceeding or a criminal or civil judicial proceeding; or

(5) any payment (including reimbursed expenses) pursuant to an agreement or arrangement described in subdivision (4);

shall file with the Secretary a report, in a form prescribed by him, signed by its president and treasurer or corresponding principal officers showing in detail the date and amount of each such payment, loan, promise, agreement, or arrangement and the name, address, and position, if any, in any firm or labor organization of the person to whom it was made and a full explanation of the circumstances of all such payments, including the terms of any agreement or understanding pursuant to which they were made.

(b) Every person who pursuant to any agreement or arrangement with an employer undertakes activities where an object thereof is, directly or indirectly—

(1) to persuade employees to exercise or not to exercise, or persuade employees as to the manner of exercising, the right to organize and bargain collectively through representatives of their own choosing; or

(2) to supply an employer with information concerning the activities of employees or a labor organization in connection with a labor dispute involving such employer, except information for use solely in conjunction with an administrative or arbitral proceeding or a criminal or civil judicial proceeding;

shall file within thirty days after entering into such agreement or arrangement a report with the Secretary, signed by its president and treasurer or corresponding principal officers, containing the name under which such person is engaged in doing business and the address of its principal office, and a detailed statement of the terms and conditions of such agreement or arrangement. Every such person shall file annually, with respect to each fiscal year during which payments were made as a result of such an agreement or arrangement, a report with the Secretary, signed by its president and treasurer or corresponding principal officers, containing a statement (A) of its receipts of any kind from employers on account of labor relations advice or services, designating the sources thereof, and (B) of its disbursements of any kind, in connection with such services and the purposes thereof. In each such case such information shall be set forth in such categories as the Secretary may prescribe.

(c) Nothing in this section shall be construed to require any employer or other person to file a report covering the services of such person by reason of his giving or agreeing to give advice to such employer or representing or agreeing to represent such employer before any court, administrative agency, or tribunal of arbitration or engaging or agreeing to engage in collective bargaining on behalf of such employer with respect to wages, hours, or other terms or conditions of employment or the negotiation of an agreement or any question arising thereunder.

(d) Nothing contained in this section shall be construed to require an employer to file a report under subsection (a) unless he has made an expenditure, payment, loan, agreement, or arrangement of the kind described therein. Nothing contained in this section shall be construed to require any other person to file a report under subsection (b) unless he was a party to an agreement or arrangement of the kind described therein.

(e) Nothing contained in this section shall be construed to require any regular officer, supervisor, or employee of an employer to file a report in connection with services rendered to such employer nor shall any employer be required to file a report covering expenditures made to any regular officer, supervisor, or employee of an employer as compensation for service as a regular officer, supervisor, or employee of such employer.

(f) Nothing contained in this section shall be construed as an amendment to, or modification of the rights protected by, section 8(c) of the National Labor Relations Act, as amended.

(g) The term "interfere with, restrain, or coerce" as used in this section means interference, restraint, and coercion which, if done with respect to the exercise of rights guaranteed in section 7 of the National Labor Relations Act, as amended, would, under section 8(a) of such Act, constitute an unfair labor practice.

Attorney-Client Communications Exempted
(29 U.S.C. 434)

SEC. 204. Nothing contained in this Act shall be construed to require an attorney who is a member in good standing of the bar of any State, to include in any report required to be filed pursuant to the provisions of this Act any information which was lawfully communicated to such attorney by any of his clients in the course of a legitimate attorney-client relationship.

Reports Made Public Information
(29 U.S.C. 435)

SEC. 205. (a)[2] The contents of the reports and documents filed with the Secretary pursuant to sections 201, 202, **203, and 211** shall be public information, and the Secretary may publish any information and data which he obtains pursuant to the provisions of this title. The Secretary may use the information and data for statistical and research purposes, and compile and publish such studies, analyses, reports, and surveys based thereon as he may deem appropriate.

(b)[3] The Secretary shall by regulation make reasonable provision for the inspection and examination, on the request of any person, of the information and data contained in any report or other document filed with him pursuant to section 201, 202, **203, or 211.**

(c)[4] The Secretary shall by regulation provide for the furnishing by the Department of Labor of copies of reports or other documents filed with the Secretary pursuant to this title, upon payment of a charge based upon the cost of the service. The Secretary shall make available without payment of a charge, or require any person to furnish, to such State agency as is designated by law or by the Governor of the State in which such person has his principal place of business or headquarters, upon request of the Governor of such State, copies of any reports and documents filed by such person with the Secretary pursuant to

[2] Prior to amendment by section 2(a) of Public Law 89–216, the first sentence of section 205(a) read as follows: "Sec. 205. (a) The contents of the reports and documents filed with the Secretary pursuant to sections 201, 202, and 203 shall be public information, and the Secretary may publish any information and data which he obtains pursuant to the provisions of this title."

[3] Prior to amendment by section 2(b) of Public Law 89–216, section 205(b) read as follows: "(b) The Secretary shall by regulation make reasonable provision for the inspection and examination, on the request of any person, of the information and data contained in any report or other document filed with him pursuant to section 201, 202, or 203."

[4] Prior to amendment by section 2(c) of Public Law 89–216, the second sentence of section 205(c) read as follows: "The Secretary shall make available without payment of a charge, or require any person to furnish, to such State agency as is designated by law or by the Governor of the State in which such person has his principal place of business or headquarters, upon request of the Governor of such State, copies of any reports and documents filed by such person with the Secretary pursuant to section 201, 202, or 203, or of information and data contained therein."

section 201, 202, **203, or 211,** or of information and data contained therein. No person shall be required by reason of any law of any State to furnish to any officer or agency of such State any information included in a report filed by such person with the Secretary pursuant to the provisions of this title, if a copy of such report, or of the portion thereof containing such information, is furnished to such officer or agency. All moneys received in payment of such charges fixed by the Secretary pursuant to this subsection shall be deposited in the general fund of the Treasury.

Retention of Records
(29 U.S.C. 436)

SEC. 206. Every person required to file any report under this title shall maintain records on the matters required to be reported which will provide in sufficient detail the necessary basic information and data from which the documents filed with the Secretary may be verified, explained or clarified, and checked for accuracy and completeness, and shall include vouchers, work-sheets, receipts, and applicable resolutions, and shall keep such records available for examination for a period of not less than five years after the filing of the documents based on the information which they contain.

Effective Date
(29 U.S.C. 437)

SEC. 207. (a) Each labor organization shall file the initial report required under section 201(a) within ninety days after the date on which it first becomes subject to this Act.

(b)[5] Each person required to file a report under section 201(b), 202, 203(a), **the second sentence of section 203(b), or section 211** shall file such report within ninety days after the end of each of its fiscal years; except that where such person is subject to section 201(b), 202, 203(a), **the second sentence of section 203(b), or section 211,** as the case may be, for only a portion of such a fiscal year (because the date of enactment of this Act occurs during such person's fiscal year or such person becomes subject to this Act during its fiscal year) such person may consider that portion as the entire fiscal year in making such report.

Rules and Regulations
(29 U.S.C. 438)

SEC. 208. The Secretary shall have authority to issue, amend, and rescind rules and regulations prescribing the form and publication of reports required to be filed under this title and such other reasonable rules and regulations (including rules prescribing reports concerning trusts in which a labor organization is interested) as he may find necessary to prevent the circumvention or evasion of such reporting requirements. In exercising his power under this section the Secretary shall prescribe by general rule simplified reports for labor organizations or employers for whom he finds that by virtue of their size a detailed report would be unduly burdensome, but the Secretary may revoke

---

[5] Prior to amendment by section 2(d) of Public Law 89–216, section 207(b) read as follows: "(b) Each person required to file a report under section 201(b), 202, 203(a), or the second sentence of 203(b) shall file such report within ninety days after the end of each of its fiscal years; except that where such person is subject to section 201(b), 202, 203(a), or the second sentence of 203(b), as the case may be, for only a portion of such a fiscal year (because the date of enactment of this Act occurs during such person's fiscal year or such person becomes subject to this Act during its fiscal year) such person may consider that portion as the entire fiscal year in making such report."

such provision for simplified forms of any labor organization or employer if he determines, after such investigation as he deems proper and due notice and opportunity for a hearing, that the purposes of this section would be served thereby.

Criminal Provisions
(29 U.S.C. 439)

SEC. 209. (a) Any person who willfully violates this title shall be fined not more than $10,000 or imprisoned for not more than one year, or both.

(b) Any person who makes a false statement or representation of a material fact, knowing it to be false, or who knowingly fails to disclose a material fact, in any document, report, or other information required under the provisions of this title shall be fined not more than $10,000 or imprisoned for not more than one year, or both.

(c) Any person who willfully makes a false entry in or willfully conceals, withholds, or destroys any books, records, reports, or statements required to be kept by any provision of this title shall be fined not more than $10,000 or imprisoned for not more than one year, or both.

(d) Each individual required to sign reports under sections 201 and 203 shall be personally responsible for the filing of such reports and for any statement contained therein which he knows to be false.

Civil Enforcement
(29 U.S.C. 440)

SEC. 210. Whenever it shall appear that any person has violated or is about to violate any of the provisions of this title, the Secretary may bring a civil action for such relief (including injunctions) as may be appropriate. Any such action may be brought in the district court of the United States where the violation occurred or, at the option of the parties, in the United States District Court for the District of Columbia.

Surety Company Reports[6]
(29 U.S.C. 441)

Sec. 211. Each surety company which issues any bond required by this Act or the Welfare and Pension Plans Disclosure Act shall file annually with the Secretary, with respect to each fiscal year during which any such bond was in force, a report, in such form and detail as he may prescribe by regulation, filed by the president and treasurer or corresponding principal officers of the surety company, describing its bond experience under each such Act, including information as to the premiums received, total claims paid, amounts recovered by way of subrogation, administrative and legal expenses and such related data and information as the Secretary shall determine to be necessary in the public interest and to carry out the policy of the Act. Notwithstanding the foregoing, if the Secretary finds that any such specific information cannot be practicably ascertained or would be uninformative, the Secretary may modify or waive the requirement for such information.

TITLE III—TRUSTEESHIPS

Reports
(29 U.S.C. 461)

SEC. 301. (a) Every labor organization which has or assumes trusteeship over any subordinate labor organization shall file with the Secretary within

---

[6] Section 211 was added by section 3 of Public Law 89–216 (79 Stat. 888).

thirty days after the date of the enactment of this Act or the imposition of any such trusteeship, and semiannually thereafter, a report, signed by its president and treasurer or corresponding principal officers, as well as by the trustees of such subordinate labor organization, containing the following information: (1) the name and address of the subordinate organization; (2) the date of establishing the trusteeship; (3) a detailed statement of the reason or reasons for establishing or continuing the trusteeship; and (4) the nature and extent of participation by the membership of the subordinate organization in the selection of delegates to represent such organization in regular or special conventions or other policy-determining bodies and in the election of officers of the labor organization which has assumed trusteeship over such subordinate organization. The initial report shall also include a full and complete account of the financial condition of such subordinate organization as of the time trusteeship was assumed over it. During the continuance of a trusteeship the labor organization which has assumed trusteeship over a subordinate labor organization shall file on behalf of the subordinate labor organization the annual financial report required by section 201(b) signed by the president and treasurer or corresponding principal officers of the labor organization which has assumed such trusteeship and the trustees of the subordinate labor organization.

(b) The provisions of section 201(c), 205, 206, 208, and 210 shall be applicable to reports filed under this title.

(c) Any person who willfully violates this section shall be fined not more than $10,000 or imprisoned for not more than one year, or both.

(d) Any person who makes a false statement or representation of a material fact, knowing it to be false, or who knowingly fails to disclose a material fact, in any report required under the provisions of this section or willfully makes any false entry in or willfully withholds, conceals, or destroys any documents, books, records, reports, or statements upon which such report is based, shall be fined not more than $10,000 or imprisoned for not more than one year, or both.

(e) Each individual required to sign a report under this section shall be personally responsible for the filing of such report and for any statement contained therein which he knows to be false.

Purposes for Which a Trusteeship May Be Established
(29 U.S.C. 462)

Sec. 302. Trusteeships shall be established and administered by a labor organization over a subordinate body only in accordance with the constitution and bylaws of the organization which has assumed trusteeship over the subordinate body and for the purpose of correcting corruption or financial malpractice, assuring the performance of collective bargaining agreements or other duties of a bargaining representative, restoring democratic procedures, or otherwise carrying out the legitimate objects of such labor organization.

Unlawful Acts Relating to Labor Organization Under Trusteeship
(29 U.S.C. 463)

Sec. 303. (a) During any period when a subordinate body of a labor organization is in trusteeship, it shall be unlawful (1) to count the vote of delegates from such body in any convention or election of officers of the labor organization unless the delegates have been chosen by secret ballot in an election in which all the members in good standing of such subordinate body were eligible to participate or (2) to transfer to such organization any current receipts or other funds of the subordinate body except the normal per capita tax and assessments payable by subordinate bodies not in trusteeship: *Provided,*

That nothing herein contained shall prevent the distribution of the assets of a labor organization in accordance with its constitution and bylaws upon the bona fide dissolution thereof.

(b) Any person who willfully violates this section shall be fined not more than $10,000 or imprisoned for not more than one year, or both.

Enforcement
(29 U.S.C. 464)

SEC. 304. (a) Upon the written complaint of any member or subordinate body of a labor organization alleging that such organization has violated the provisions of this title (except section 301) the Secretary shall investigate the complaint and if the Secretary finds probable cause to believe that such violation has occurred and has not been remedied he shall, without disclosing the identity of the complainant, bring a civil action in any district court of the United States having jurisdiction of the labor organization for such relief (including injunctions) as may be appropriate. Any member or subordinate body of a labor organization affected by any violation of this title (except section 301) may bring a civil action in any district court of the United States having jurisdiction of the labor organization for such relief (including injunctions) as may be appropriate.

(b) For the purpose of actions under this section, district courts of the United States shall be deemed to have jurisdiction of a labor organization (1) in the district in which the principal office of such labor organization is located, or (2) in any district in which its duly authorized officers or agents are engaged in conducting the affairs of the trusteeship.

(c) In any proceeding pursuant to this section a trusteeship established by a labor organization in conformity with the procedural requirements of its constitution and bylaws and authorized or ratified after a fair hearing either before the executive board or before such other body as may be provided in accordance with its constitution or bylaws shall be presumed valid for a period of eighteen months from the date of its establishment and shall not be subject to attack during such period except upon clear and convincing proof that the trusteeship was not established or maintained in good faith for a purpose allowable under section 302. After the expiration of eighteen months the trusteeship shall be presumed invalid in any such proceeding and its discontinuance shall be decreed unless the labor organization shall show by clear and convincing proof that the continuation of the trusteeship is necessary for a purpose allowable under section 302. In the latter event the court may dismiss the complaint or retain jurisdiction of the cause on such conditions and for such period as it deems appropriate.

Report to Congress
(29 U.S.C. 465)

SEC. 305. The Secretary shall submit to the Congress at the expiration of three years from the date of enactment of this Act a report upon the operation of this title.

Complaint by Secretary
(29 U.S.C. 466)

SEC. 306. The rights and remedies provided by this title shall be in addition to any and all other rights and remedies at law or in equity: *Provided*, That upon the filing of a complaint by the Secretary the jurisdiction of the district court over such trusteeship shall be exclusive and the final judgment shall be res judicata.

TITLE IV—ELECTIONS

Terms of Office; Election Procedures
(29 U.S.C. 481)

SEC. 401. (a) Every national or international labor organization, except a federation of national or international labor organizations, shall elect its officers not less often than once every five years either by secret ballot among the members in good standing or at a convention of delegates chosen by secret ballot.

(b) Every local labor organization shall elect its officers not less often than once every three years by secret ballot among the members in good standing.

(c) Every national or international labor organization, except a federation of national or international labor organizations, and every local labor organization, and its officers, shall be under a duty, enforceable at the suit of any bona fide candidate for office in such labor organization in the district court of the United States in which such labor organization maintains its principal office, to comply with all reasonable requests of any candidate to distribute by mail or otherwise at the candidate's expense campaign literature in aid of such person's candidacy to all members in good standing of such labor organization and to refrain from discrimination in favor of or against any candidate with respect to the use of lists of members, and whenever such labor organizations or its officers authorize the distribution by mail or otherwise to members of campaign literature on behalf of any candidate or of the labor organization itself with reference to such election, similar distribution at the request of any other bona fide candidate shall be made by such labor organization and its officers, with equal treatment as to the expense of such distribution. Every bona fide candidate shall have the right, once within 30 days prior to an election of a labor organization in which he is a candidate, to inspect a list containing the names and last known addresses of all members of the labor organization who are subject to a collective bargaining agreement requiring membership therein as a condition of employment, which list shall be maintained and kept at the principal office of such labor organization by a designated official thereof. Adequate safeguards to insure a fair election shall be provided, including the right of any candidate to have an observer at the polls and at the counting of the ballots.

(d) Officers of intermediate bodies, such as general committees, system boards, joint boards, or joint councils, shall be elected not less often than once every four years by secret ballot among the members in good standing or by labor organization officers representative of such members who have been elected by secret ballot.

(e) In any election required by this section which is to be held by secret ballot a reasonable opportunity shall be given for the nomination of candidates and every member in good standing shall be eligible to be a candidate and to hold office (subject to section 504 and to reasonable qualifications uniformly imposed) and shall have the right to vote for or otherwise support the candidate or candidates of his choice, without being subject to penalty, discipline, or improper interference or reprisal of any kind by such organization or any member thereof. Not less than fifteen days prior to the election notice thereof shall be mailed to each member at his last known home address. Each member in good standing shall be entitled to one vote. No member whose dues have been withheld by his employer for payment to such organization pursuant to his voluntary authorization provided for in a collective bargaining agreement shall be declared ineligible to vote or be a candidate for office in such organization by reason of alleged delay or default in the payment of dues. The votes cast by members of each local labor organization shall be counted, and the results published, separately. The election officials designated in the constitution and bylaws or the secretary, if no other official is designated, shall preserve for one year the ballots and all other records pertaining to the election. The election shall be conducted in accordance with the constitution and bylaws of such organization insofar as they are not inconsistent with the provisions of this title.

(f) When officers are chosen by a convention of delegates elected by secret ballot, the convention shall be conducted in accordance with the constitution and bylaws of the labor organization insofar as they are not inconsistent with the provisions of this title. The officials designated in the constitution and bylaws or the secretary, if no other is designated, shall preserve for one year the credentials of the delegates and all minutes and other records of the convention pertaining to the election of officers.

(g) No moneys received by any labor organization by way of dues, assessment, or similar levy, and no moneys of an employer shall be contributed or applied to promote the candidacy of any person in an election subject to the provisions of this title. Such moneys of a labor organization may be utilized for notices, factual statements of issues not involving candidates, and other expenses necessary for the holding of an election.

(h) If the Secretary, upon application of any member of a local labor organization, finds after hearing in accordance with the Administrative Procedure Act that the constitution and bylaws of such labor organization do not provide an adequate procedure for the removal of an elected officer guilty of serious misconduct, such officer may be removed, for cause shown and after notice and hearing, by the members in good standing voting in a secret ballot conducted by the officers of such labor organization in accordance with its constitution and bylaws insofar as they are not inconsistent with the provisions of this title.

(i) The Secretary shall promulgate rules and regulations prescribing mimimum standards and procedures for determining the adequacy of the removal procedures to which reference is made in subsection (h).

Enforcement
(29 U.S.C. 482)

Sec. 402. (a) A member of a labor organization—

(1) who has exhausted the remedies available under the constitution and bylaws of such organization and of any parent body, or

(2) who has invoked such available remedies without obtaining a final decision within three calendar months after their invocation,

may file a complaint with the Secretary within one calendar month thereafter alleging the violation of any provision of section 401 (including violation of the constitution and bylaws of the labor organization pertaining to the election and removal of officers). The challenged election shall be presumed valid pending a final decision theron (as hereinafter provided) and in the interim the affairs of the organization shall be conducted by the officers elected or in such other manner as its constitution and bylaws may provide.

(b) The Secretary shall investigate such complaint and, if he finds probable cause to believe that a violation of this title has occurred and has not been remedied, he shall, within sixty days after the filing of such complaint, bring a civil action against the labor organization as an entity in the district court of the the United States in which such labor organization maintains its principal office to set aside the invalid election, if any, and to direct the conduct of an election or hearing and vote upon the removal of officers under the supervision of the Secretary and in accordance with the provisions of this title and such rules and regulations as the Secretary may prescribe. The court shall have power to take such action as it deems proper to preserve the assets of the labor organization.

(c) If, upon a preponderance of the evidence after a trial upon the merits, the court finds—

(1) that an election has not been held within the time prescribed by section 401, or

(2) that the violation of section 401 may have affected the outcome of an election,

the court shall declare the election, if any, to be void and direct the conduct of a new election under supervision of the Secretary and, so far as lawful and practicable, in conformity with the constitution and bylaws of the labor organization. The Secretary shall promptly certify to the court the names of the persons elected, and the court shall thereupon enter a decree declaring such persons to be the officers of the labor organization. If the proceeding is for the removal of officers pursuant to subsection (h) of section 401, the Secretary shall certify the results of the vote and the court shall enter a decree declaring whether such persons have been removed as officers of the labor organization.

(d) An order directing an election, dismissing a complaint, or designating elected officers of a labor organization shall be appealable in the same manner as the final judgment in a civil action, but an order directing an election shall not be stayed pending appeal.

Application of Other Laws
(29 U.S.C. 483)

SEC. 403. No labor organization shall be required by law to conduct elections of officers with greater frequency or in a different form or manner than is required by its own constitution or bylaws, except as otherwise provided by this title. Existing rights and remedies to enforce the constitution and bylaws of a labor organization with respect to elections prior to the conduct thereof shall not be affected by the provisions of this title. The remedy provided by this title for challenging an election already conducted shall be exclusive.

Effective Date
(29 U.S.C. 484)

SEC. 404. The provisions of this title shall become applicable—

(1) ninety days after the date of enactment of this Act in the case of a labor organization whose constitution and bylaws can lawfully be modified or amended by action of its constitutional officers or governing body, or

(2) where such modification can only be made by a constitutional convention of the labor organization, not later than the next constitutional convention of such labor organization after the date of enactment of this Act, or one year after such date, whichever is sooner. If no such convention is held within such one-year period, the executive board or similar governing body empowered to act for such labor organization between conventions is empowered to make such interim constitutional changes as are necessary to carry out the provisions of this title.

TITLE V—SAFEGUARDS FOR LABOR ORGANIZATIONS

Fiduciary Responsibility of Officers of Labor Organizations
(29 U.S.C. 501)

SEC. 501. (a) The officers, agents, shop stewards, and other representatives of a labor organization occupy positions of trust in relation to such organization and its members as a group. It is, therefore, the duty of each such person, taking into account the special problems and functions of a labor organization, to hold its money and property solely for the benefit of the organization and its members and to manage, invest, and expend the same in accordance with its constitution and bylaws and any resolutions of the governing bodies adopted thereunder, to refrain from dealing with such organization as an adverse party or in behalf of an adverse party in any matter connected with his duties and from holding or acquiring any pecuniary or personal interest which conflicts with the interests of such organization, and to account to the organization for any profit received by him in whatever capacity in connection with transactions conducted by him or under his direction on behalf of the organization. A general exculpatory provision in the constitution and bylaws of such a labor organization or a general exculpatory resolution of a governing body purporting to relieve any such person of liability for breach of the duties declared by this section shall be void as against public policy.

(b) When any officer, agent, shop steward, or representative of any labor organization is alleged to have violated the duties declared in subsection (a) and the labor organization or its governing board or officers refuse or fail to sue or recover damages or secure an accounting or other appropriate relief within a reasonable time after being requested to do so by any member of the labor organization, such member may sue such officer, agent, shop steward, or representative in any district court of the United States or in any State court of competent jurisdiction to recover damages or secure an accounting or other appropriate relief for the benefit of the labor organization. No such proceeding shall be brought except upon leave of the court obtained upon verified application and for good cause shown which application may be made ex parte. The trial judge may allot a reasonable part of the recovery in any action under this subsection to pay the fees of counsel prosecuting the suit at the instance of the member of the labor organization and to compensate such member for any expenses necessarily paid or incurred by him in connection with the litigation.

(c) Any person who embezzles, steals, or unlawfully and willfully abstracts or converts to his own use, or the use of another, any of the moneys, funds, securities, property, or other assets of a labor organization of which he is an officer, or by which he is employed, directly or indirectly, shall be fined not more than $10,000 or imprisoned for not more than five years, or both.

Bonding
(29 U.S.C. 502)

SEC. 502. (a)[7] Every officer, agent, shop steward, or other representative or employee of any labor organization (other than a labor organization whose

---

[7] Prior to amendment by section 1 of Public Law 89–216, the first sentence of section 502(a) read as follows: "Sec. 502.(a) Every officer, agent, shop steward, or other representative or employee of any labor organization (other than a labor organization whose property and annual financial receipts do not exceed $5,000 in value), or of a trust in which a labor organization is interested, who handles funds or other property thereof shall be bonded for the faithful discharge of his duties." Section 1 of Public Law 89–216 also added the proviso at the end of section 502(a).

property and annual financial receipts do not exceed $5,000 in value), or of a trust in which a labor organization is interested, who handles funds or other property thereof shall be bonded **to provide protection against loss by reason of acts of fraud or dishonesty on his part directly or through connivance with others.** The bond of each such person shall be fixed at the beginning of the organization's fiscal year and shall be in an amount not less than 10 per centum of the funds handled by him and his predecessor or predecessors, if any, during the preceding fiscal year, but in no case more than $500,000. If the labor organization or the trust in which a labor organization is interested does not have a preceding fiscal year, the amount of the bond shall be, in the case of a local labor organization, not less than $1,000, and in the case of any other labor organization or of a trust in which a labor organization is interested, not less than $10,000. Such bonds shall be individual or schedule in form, and shall have a corporate surety company as surety thereon. Any person who is not covered by such bonds shall not be permitted to receive, handle, disburse, or otherwise exercise custody or control of the funds or other property of a labor organization or of a trust in which a labor organization is interested. No such bond shall be placed through an agent or broker or with a surety company in which any labor organization or any officer, agent, shop steward, or other representative of a labor organization has any direct or indirect interest. Such surety company shall be a corporate surety which holds a grant of authority from the Secretary of the Treasury under the Act of July 30, 1947 (6 U.S.C. 6–13), as an acceptable surety on Federal bonds: *Provided,* **That when in the opinion of the Secretary a labor organization has made other bonding arrangements which would provide the protection required by this section at comparable cost or less, he may exempt such labor organization from placing a bond through a surety company holding such grant of authority.**

(b) Any person who willfully violates this section shall be fined not more than $10,000 or imprisoned for not more than one year, or both.

Making of Loans; Payment of Fines
(29 U.S.C. 503)

SEC. 503. (a) No labor organization shall make directly or indirectly any loan or loans to any officer or employee of such organization which results in a total indebtedness on the part of such officer or employee to the labor organization in excess of $2,000.

(b) No labor organization or employer shall directly or indirectly pay the fine of any officer or employee convicted of any willful violation of this Act.

(c) Any person who willfully violates this section shall be fined not more than $5,000 or imprisoned for not more than one year, or both.

Prohibition Against Certain Persons Holding Office
(29 U.S.C. 504)

SEC. 504. (a) No person who is or has been a member of the Communist Party[8] or who has been convicted of, or served any part of a prison term resulting from his conviction of, robbery, bribery, extortion, embezzlement, grand larceny, burglary, arson, violation of narcotics laws, murder, rape,

---

[8] The U.S. Supreme Court, on June 7, 1965, held unconstitutional as a bill of attainder the section 504 provision which imposes criminal sanctions on Communist party members for holding union office (*U.S.* v. *Brown,* 381 U.S. 437, 85 S. Ct. 1707).

assault with intent to kill, assault which inflicts grievous bodily injury, or a violation of title II or III of this Act, or conspiracy to commit any such crimes shall serve—

(1) as an officer, director, trustee, member of any executive board or similar governing body, business agent, manager, organizer, or other employee (other than as an employee performing exclusively clerical or custodial duties) or any labor organization, or

(2) as a labor relations consultant to a person engaged in an industry or activity affecting commerce, or as an officer, director, agent, or employee (other than as an employee performing exclusively clerical or custodial duties) of any group or association of employers dealing with any labor organization,

during or for five years after the termination of his membership in the Communist Party, or for five years after such conviction or after the end of such imprisonment, unless prior to the end of such five-year period, in the case of a person so convicted or imprisoned, (A) his citizenship rights, having been revoked as a results of such conviction, have been fully restored, or (B) the Board of Parole of the United States Department of Justice determines that such person's service in any capacity referred to in clause (1) or (2) would not be contrary to the purposes of this Act. Prior to making any such determination the Board shall hold an administrative hearing and shall give notice of such proceeding by certified mail to the State, county, and Federal prosecuting officials in the jurisdiction or jurisdictions in which such person was convicted. The Board's determination in any such proceeding shall be final. No labor organization or officer thereof shall knowingly permit any person to assume or hold any office or paid position in violation of this subsection.

(b) Any person who willfully violates this section shall be fined not more than $10,000 or imprisoned for not more than one year, or both.

(c) For the purposes of this section, any person shall be deemed to have been "convicted" and under the disability of "conviction" from the date of the judgment of the trial court or the date of the final sustaining of such judgment on appeal, whichever is the later event, regardless of whether such conviction occurred before or after the date of enactment of this Act.

Amendment to Section 302, Labor Management Relations Act, 1947

SEC. 505. Subsections (a), (b), and (c) of section 302 of the Labor Management Relations Act, 1947, as amended, are amended to read as follows:

"SEC. 302. (a) It shall be unlawful for any employer or association of employers or any person who acts as a labor relations expert, adviser, or consultant to an employer or who acts in the interest of an employer to pay, lend, or deliver, or agree to pay, lend, or deliver, any money or other thing of value—

"(1) to any representative of any of his employees who are employed in an industry affecting commerce; or

"(2) to any labor organization, or any officer or employee thereof, which represents, seeks to represent, or would admit to membership, any of the employees of such employer who are employed in an industry affecting commerce; or

"(3) to any employee or group or committee of employees of such employer employed in an industry affecting commerce in excess of their normal compensation for the purpose of causing such employee or group or committee directly or indirectly to influence any other employees in the exercise of the right to organize and bargain collectively through representatives of their own choosing; or

"(4) to any officer or employee of a labor organization engaged in an industry affecting commerce with intent to influence him in respect to any of his actions, decisions, or duties as a representative of employees or as such officer or employee of such labor organization.

"(b)(1) It shall be unlawful for any person to request, demand, receive, or accept, or agree to receive or accept, any payment, loan, or delivery of any money or other thing of value prohibited by subsection (a).

"(2) It shall be unlawful for any labor organization, or for any person acting as an officer, agent, representative, or employee of such labor organization, to demand or accept from the operator of any motor vehicle (as defined in part II of the Interstate Commerce Act) employed in the transportation of property in commerce, or the employer of any such operator, any money or other thing of value payable to such organization or to an officer, agent, representative or employee thereof as a fee or charge for the unloading; or in connection with the unloading, of the cargo of such vehicle: *Provided*, That nothing in this paragraph shall be construed to make unlawful any payment by an employer to any of his employees as compensation for their services as employees.

"(c) The provisions of this section shall not be applicable (1) in respect to any money or other thing of value payable by an employer to any of his employees whose established duties include acting openly for such employer in matters of labor relations or personnel administration or to any representative of his employees, or to any officer or employee of a labor organization, who is also an employee or former employee of such employer, as compensation for, or by reason of, his service as an employee of such employer; (2) with respect to the payment or delivery of any money or other thing of value in satisfaction of a judgment of any court or a decision or award of an arbitrator or impartial chairman or in compromise, adjustment, settlement, or release of any claim, complaint, grievance, or dispute in the absence of fraud or duress; (3) with respect to the sale or purchase of an article or commodity at the prevailing market price in the regular course of business; (4) with respect to money deducted from the wages of employees in payment of membership dues in a labor organization: *Provided*, That the employer has received from each employee, on whose account such deductions are made, a written assignment which shall not be irrevocable for a period of more than one year, or beyond the termination date of the applicable collective agreement, whichever occurs sooner; (5) with respect to money or other thing of value paid to a trust fund established by such representative, for the sole and exclusive benefit of the employees of such employer, and their families and dependents (or of such employees, families, and dependents jointly with the employees of other employers making similar payments, and their families and dependents): *Provided*, That (A) such payments are held in trust for the purpose of paying, either from principal or income or both, for the benefit of employees, their families and dependents, for medical or hospital care, pensions on retirement or death of employees, compensation for injuries or illness resulting from occupational activity or insurance to provide any of the foregoing, or unemployment benefits or life insurance, disability and sickness insurance, or accident insurance; (B) the detailed basis on which such payments are to be made is specified in a written agreement with the employer, and employees and employers are equally represented in the administration of such fund together with such neutral persons as the representatives of the employers and the representatives of employees may agree upon and in the event of the employer and employee groups deadlock on the administration of such fund and there are no neutral persons empowered to break such deadlock, such agreement provides that the two groups shall agree on an impartial umpire to decide such dispute, or in event of their failure to agree within a reasonable length of time, an impartial umpire to decide such dispute shall, on petition of either group, be appointed by the district court of the United States for the district where the trust fund has its principal office, and shall also contain provisions for an annual audit of the trust fund, a statement of the results of which shall be available for inspection by interested persons at the principal office of the trust fund and at such other places as may be designated in such written agreement; and (C) such payments as are intended to be used for the purpose of providing pensions or annuities for employees are made to a separate trust which provides that the funds held therein cannot be used for any purpose other than paying such pensions or annuities; or (6) with respect to money or other thing of value paid by any employer to a trust fund established by such representative for the purpose of pooled vacation, holiday, severance or similar benefits, or defraying costs of apprenticeship or other training programs: *Provided,* That the requirements of clause (B) of the proviso to clause (5) of this subsection shall apply to such trust funds."

TITLE VI—MISCELLANEOUS PROVISIONS

Investigations
(29 U.S.C. 521)

Sec. 601. (a) The Secretary shall have power when he believes it necessary in order to determine whether any person has violated or is about to violate any provision of this Act (except title I or amendments made by this Act to other statutes) to make an investigation and in connection therewith he may enter such places and inspect such records and accounts and question such persons as he may deem necessary to enable him to determine the facts relative thereto. The Secretary may report to interested persons or officials concerning the facts required to be shown in any report required by this Act and concerning the reasons for failure or refusal to file such a report or any other matter which he deems to be appropriate as a result of such an investigation.

(b) For the purpose of any investigation provided for in this Act, the provisions of sections 9 and 10 (relating to the attendance of witnesses and the production of books, papers, and documents) of the Federal Trade Commission Act of September 16, 1914, as amended (15 U.S.C. 49, 50), are hereby made applicable to the jurisdiction, powers, and duties of the Secretary or any officers designated by him.

Extortionate Picketing
(29 U.S.C. 522)

Sec. 602. (a) It shall be unlawful to carry on picketing on or about the premises of any employer for the purpose of, or as part of any conspiracy or in furtherance of any plan or purpose for, the personal profit or enrichment of any individual (except a bona fide increase in wages or other employee benefits) by taking or obtaining any money or other thing of value from such employer against his will or with his consent.

(b) Any person who willfully violates this section shall be fined not more than $10,000 or imprisoned not more than twenty years, or both.

Retention of Rights Under Other Federal and State Laws
    (29 U.S.C. 523)

SEC. 603. (a) Except as explicitly provided to the contrary, nothing in this Act shall reduce or limit the responsibilities of any labor organization or any officer, agent, shop steward, or other representative of a labor organization, or of any trust in which a labor organization is interested, under any other Federal law or under the laws of any State, and, except as explicitly provided to the contrary, nothing in this Act shall take away any right or bar any remedy to which members of a labor organization are entitled under such other Federal law or law of any State.

(b) Nothing contained in titles I, II, III, IV, V, or VI of this Act shall be construed to supersede or impair or otherwise affect the provisions of the Railway Labor Act, as amended, or any of the obligations, rights, benefits, privileges, or immunities of any carrier, employee, organization, representative, or person subject thereto; nor shall anything contained in said titles (except section 505) of this Act be construed to confer any rights, privileges, immunities, or defenses upon employers, or to impair or otherwise affect the rights of any person under the National Labor Relations Act, as amended.

Effect on State Laws
    (29 U.S.C. 524)

SEC. 604. Nothing in this Act shall be construed to impair or diminish the authority of any State to enact and enforce general criminal laws with respect to robbery, bribery, extortion, embezzlement, grand larceny, burglary, arson, violation of narcotics laws, murder, rape, assault with intent to kill, or assault which inflicts grievous bodily injury, or conspiracy to commit any of such crimes.

Service of Process
    (29 U.S.C. 525)

SEC. 605. For the purposes of this Act, service of summons, subpena, or other legal process of a court of the United States upon an officer or agent of a labor organization in his capacity as such shall constitute service upon the labor organization.

Administrative Procedure Act
    (29 U.S.C. 526)

SEC. 606. The provisions of the Administrative Procedure Act shall be applicable to the issuance, amendment, or rescission of any rules or regulations, or any adjudication, authorized or required pursuant to the provisions of this Act.

Other Agencies and Departments
    (29 U.S.C. 527)

SEC. 607. In order to avoid unnecessary expense and duplication of functions among Government agencies, the Secretary may make such arrangements or agreements for cooperation or mutual assistance in the performance of his functions under this Act and the functions of any such agency as he may find to be practicable and consistent with law. The Secretary may utilize the facilities or services of any department, agency, or establishment of the United States or of any State or political subdivision of a State, including the services of any of its employees, with the lawful consent of such department, agency, or establishment; and each department, agency, or establishment of the United

States is authorized and directed to cooperate with the Secretary and, to the extent permitted by law, to provide such information and facilities as he may request for his assistance in the performance of his functions under this Act. The Attorney General or his representative shall receive from the Secretary for appropriate action such evidence developed in the performance of his functions under this Act as may be found to warrant consideration for criminal prosecution under the provisions of this Act or other Federal law.

Criminal Contempt
(29 U.S.C. 528)

SEC. 608. No person shall be punished for any criminal contempt allegedly committed outside the immediate presence of the court in connection with any civil action prosecuted by the Secretary or any other person in any court of the United States under the provisions of this Act unless the facts constituting such criminal contempt are established by the verdict of the jury in a proceeding in the district court of the United States, which jury shall be chosen and empaneled in the manner prescribed by the law governing trial juries in criminal prosecutions in the district courts of the United States.

Prohibition on Certain Discipline by Labor Organization
(29 U.S.C. 529)

SEC. 609. It shall be unlawful for any labor organization, or any officer, agent, shop steward, or other representative of a labor organization, or any employee thereof to fine, suspend, expel, or otherwise discipline any of its members for exercising any right to which he is entitled under the provisions of this Act. The provisions of section 102 shall be applicable in the enforcement of this section.

Deprivation of Rights Under Act by Violence
(29 U.S.C. 530)

SEC. 610. It shall be unlawful for any person through the use of force or violence, or threat of the use of force or violence, to restrain, coerce, or intimidate, or attempt to restrain, coerce, or intimidate any member of a labor organization for the purpose of interfering with or preventing the exercise of any right to which he is entitled under the provisions of this Act. Any person who willfully violates this section shall be fined not more than $1,000 or imprisoned for not more than one year, or both.

Separability Provisions
(29 U.S.C. 531)

SEC. 611. If any provision of this Act, or the application of such provision to any person or circumstances, shall be held invalid, the remainder of this Act or the application of such provision to persons or circumstances other than those as to which it is held invalid, shall not be affected thereby.

TITLE VII—AMENDMENTS TO THE LABOR MANAGEMENT RELATIONS ACT, 1947, AS AMENDED

(The Title VII amendments to the Labor Management Relations Act, 1947, as amended, have been incorporated into the text of the latter act as presented above.)

Indexes

INDEX OF AUTHORITIES CITED

INDEX

797